PELICAN BOOK

THE SPANISH CIV

Hugh Thomas was born in 1931 and educated at Sherborne, Dorset and Queens' College, Cambridge. He was Professor of History at the University of Reading from 1966 to 1976. Since 1979 he has been Chairman of the Centre for Policy Studies. In 1981 he was created a Life Peer. *The Spanish Civil War*, which gained the Somerset Maugham Prize, was published in 1961. His other main study of a Hispanic revolutionary experience, *Cuba or the Pursuit of Freedom*, was published in 1971. He has written several novels, such as *The World's Game* and *Havannah*, and a study of the Suez crisis of 1956, *The Suez Affair*, which was published in the Pelican series. His other books include *Europe: The Radical Challenge*, *Goya and The Third of May, 1808*, a biography of John Strachey, and *An Unfinished History of the World*, which gained the Arts Council's prize for history in 1980 in its National Book Awards and has been published in a revised edition in 1982. His latest book is *Armed Truce*, a history of the origins of the cold war.

PENGUIN BOOKS

THE SPANISH CIVIL WAR

HUGH THOMAS

The Spanish Civil War

THIRD EDITION

REVISED AND ENLARGED

PENGUIN BOOKS

IN ASSOCIATION WITH HAMISH HAMILTON

PENGUIN BOOKS

Published by the Penguin Group
27 Wrights Lane, London W8 5TZ, England
Viking Penguin Inc., 40 West 23rd Street, New York, New York 10010, USA
Penguin Books Australia Ltd, Ringwood, Victoria, Australia
Penguin Books Canada Ltd, 2801 John Street, Markham, Ontario, Canada L3R 1B4
Penguin Books (NZ) Ltd, 182–190 Wairau Road, Auckland 10, New Zealand

Penguin Books Ltd, Registered Offices: Harmondsworth, Middlesex, England

First published by Eyre & Spottiswoode Ltd 1961
Revised edition published in Penguin Books 1965
Reissued in Pelican Books 1968
Reprinted 1971, 1974
Third edition, revised and enlarged, published simultaneously with Hamish Hamilton 1977
Reprinted 1979, 1982, 1984
Reprinted with a new Preface 1986
Reprinted 1988

Made and printed in Great Britain by
Hazell Watson & Viney Limited
Member of BPCC plc
Aylesbury Bucks
Set in Monotype Times

Contents

List of Maps vi
Acknowledgements viii
Author's Notes ix
Some Groups and Political Parties, with abbreviations x
Abbreviations used in the Notes xi
Preface xiii
Preface to the 1986 Reprint xix

Book One: The Origins of the War 1
Book Two: Rising and Revolution 197
Book Three: World War in Miniature 465
Book Four: The War of Two Counter Revolutions 675
Conclusion 918

Appendix One: The Spanish Bourbons and the Carlist Claim 961
Appendix Two: The Economics of Spain 962
Appendix Three: The International Brigades 968
Appendix Four: Exchange Rates to the £ 970
Appendix Five: The Life and Death of the Peseta on the Tangier Exchange 971
Appendix Six: Catalan Industrial Production 1936–8 973
Appendix Seven: An Estimate of Foreign Intervention in the Spanish Civil War 974
Appendix Eight: Guernica 986

Bibliographical Note 992
Select Bibliography 1009
Index 1042

List of Maps

1. The physical features of Spain 12
2. Regions and provinces of Spain 15
3. Spanish Morocco 18
4. The revolution in Asturias, 1934 137
5. Madrid during the Second Republic 150
6. Spanish military arrangements, 1936 176
7. Captain Bebb's flight, July 1936 213
8. Barcelona, July 1936 234
9. Division of Spain at the end of July 1936 256
10. The fighting in the Guadarramas, July–August 1936 314
11. The Catalan invasion of Aragon, July–August 1936 317
12. The advance of the Army of Africa, August–October 1936 372
13. The campaign in Guipúzcoa, August–September 1936 378
14. The invasion of Majorca, August 1936 382
15. Division of Spain, August 1936 402
16. The advance on Madrid, September–November 1936 433
17. The battle of Madrid, November 1936 474
18. The battles of Boadilla and the Corunna Road, December 1936 489
19. The fighting for Málaga, February 1937 584
20. The battle of the Jarama, February 1937 590
21. The battle of Guadalajara, March 1937 598
22. The battles around Madrid, November 1936–March 1937 605
23. Division of Spain, March 1937 610
24. The campaign in Vizcaya, March–June 1937 613
25. Naval Non-Intervention Patrol 684
26. The battle of Brunete, July 1937 712

27. The Santander campaign, August 1937 719
28. The Aragon offensive, August–October 1937 727
29. The Asturias campaign, September–October 1937 730
30. Division of Spain, October 1937 732
31. The battle of Teruel, December 1937–February 1938 790
32. The campaigns in Aragon and the Levante, March–July 1938 799
33. Division of Spain, July 1938 833
34. The battle of the Ebro, July–November 1938 839
35. The campaign in Catalonia, December 1938–January 1939 870
36. Division of Spain, February 1939 885

All maps were drawn from roughs by Douglas London

Acknowledgements

I should like to thank the large number of people who have written to me about one matter or another arising from the civil war since this book was first published. Both they and the many to whom I have spoken since that time are too numerous to mention by name, but I am grateful to them. I am also grateful to a number of friends who have helped or advised me over one part or another of the book; in particular, to Mr Paul Preston, for suggestions about the revision of the chapters dealing with the republic, and other help; to Vice Admiral Sir Peter Gretton, for advice on the naval side of the war; to Mr Norman Cooper, for help in the chapters dealing with the nationalist economy; to Mrs Jill Edwards, for her work on non-intervention and the British government's role; to Dr Michael Alpert; and to Mr Norman Jones, for his suggestions on Catalonia. I am also very grateful to Mr Ronald Fraser, who kindly read the proofs.

Acknowledgements are due to the late Mr W. H. Auden and Messrs Faber & Faber for permission to quote from his poem 'Spain'; to Mr Edgell Rickword for permission to quote from his poem 'To the Wife of a Non-Intervention Statesman'; to Mr A. L. Lloyd for his translation of a poem by Miguel Hernández; to Librairie Gallimard for permission to quote from Claudel's *Aux Martyrs Espagnols*; to the late Mr C. Day-Lewis and the Bodley Head for permission to quote from his poem 'Nabarra'.

Author's Notes

1. *Spanish place names:* The following Spanish names have been anglicized:

Andalucía – Andalusia	Mallorca – Majorca
Aragón – Aragon	Menorca – Minorca
Castilla – Castile	Navarra – Navarre
Cataluña – Catalonia	Sevilla – Seville
La Coruña – Corunna	Zaragoza – Saragossa
Extremadura – Estremadura	Duero – Douro
	Tajo – Tagus

2. Catalan names are usually given in Spanish.

3. *References in footnotes:* The first time a book is mentioned, the title and place and date of publication are given, following the full name of the author; subsequently, the name only of the author is given. Where a second (or third) book by the same author is mentioned, further references to both that book and the author's first-mentioned book are given with a short title.

4. Names of political parties have mostly been translated, e.g. 'Left Republican' for Izquierda Republicana; but some have been left in their original form, e.g. Esquerra, Falange. Spanish titles of nobility have usually been left in the original, e.g. Conde de Rodezno, though where the person concerned was well known in England in his own right, he has been left anglicized (e.g. Duke of Alba, not Duque de Alba). Other European titles have usually been anglicized (e.g. Count Ciano). Other names have been left as is usual in English historical works, e.g. Don Carlos, but Charles V.

5. In the civil war, the names of the contending parties have been usually called the nationalists and the republicans.

6. I have usually translated the Spanish ranks '*Teniente Coronel*' and '*Coronel*' as simply Colonel: this abbreviation is normal in English, less permissible in Spanish. I hope the lieutenant-colonels whom I have prematurely promoted will overlook this.

Some Groups and Political Parties

with their abbreviations and approximate English equivalents

CEDA (Confederación Española de Derechas Autónomas) – Catholic Party

CNT (Confederación Nacional de Trabajo) – Anarcho-Syndicalist Trades Union

FAI (Federación Anarquista Ibérica) – Anarchist Doctrinal Vanguard

FIJL (Federación Ibérica de Juventudes Libertarias) – Anarchist Youth

JAP (Juventud de Acción Popular) – Catholic Action Youth Movement

JCI (Juventud Comunista Ibérica) – POUM (see below) Youth

JONS (Juntas de Ofensiva Nacional-Sindicalista) – Fascists

JSU (Juventudes Socialistas Unificadas) – United Youth Movement

POUM (Partido Obrero de Unificación Marxista) – Revolutionary (i.e. anti-Stalinist) Communists

PSUC (Partido Socialista Unificado de Cataluña) – United Catalan Socialist Party – a pseudonym for the communists in Catalonia

UGT (Unión General de Trabajadores) – Socialist Trade Union

UME (Unión Militar Española) – Right-wing officers' group

UMRA (Unión Militar Republicana Antifascista) – Republican officers' group

Abbreviations used in the Notes

CAB British cabinet minutes (unpublished, in the Public Record Office) – with the appropriate reference thereafter

FD French foreign policy documents 2e Série 1936–9 tome III onwards

FO Foreign Office, alluding to unpublished papers in the Public Record Office

GD German foreign policy documents Series D vol. 3 unless otherwise stated

NIC Non-Intervention Committee documents

NIS Non-Intervention Sub-committee documents

USD United States foreign policy volumes 1936–9

Preface

THIS book was first published in April 1961. It was the month of the Cuban exiles' ill-fated expedition to the Bay of Pigs and of the rising of the four famous generals against De Gaulle, and three months before Harold Macmillan's application for Britain to join the European Community. At that time, no general historical study of the Spanish Civil War had then been written, if one excepts the much earlier books by Salvador de Madariaga (the second half of his *Spain*, published in 1946) and by Julián Zugazagoitia (*Historia de la guerra de España*, published in 1940). The idea of writing a general history of the war had admittedly come to several people besides myself: another general history, *La Révolution et la guerre d'Espagne*, by two Frenchmen, Pierre Broué and Émile Témime, was published almost at the same time as mine, and the American historian Gabriel Jackson was working on the theme (though his *The Spanish Republic and the Civil War* was published only in 1965). Already, too, one or two monographs had been, or were being, prepared: these included Professor Cattell's two books on communism and Russian policy (1955 and 1957), Robert Colodny's book on the siege of Madrid (1958) and Burnett Bolloten's somewhat inquisitorial study of communist behaviour, *The Grand Camouflage*, published at the same time as my book. Thus a history of the Spanish Civil War was 'needed', as publishers put it. Passions seemed somewhat to have cooled among those who fought, or had sympathized, with one side or the other. At the same time, too, much material bearing on the Spanish Civil War either had become available or could be found. Little of this had really been used to good effect.

As for Spain itself, the civil war seemed both historically and politically dead. It requires now an effort of the imagination to remember the intellectual mood in Spain in 1958 or 1959. The recent past was as forbidden a subject as the immediate future. To probe too deep risked silence or enmity. Almost nobody in Spain was writing works on very modern history which could be in any way regarded as seriously historical.[1] Not only the war but the republic was taboo. It was as if a heavy curtain had been drawn over the events since the exile of the King in 1931 – no less impenetrable because the heaviness was that of dust as much as of iron. The then government of Spain did use the recent past, it is true, but as a part of its current policies: to impress, to justify, even to terrify. There used to be sold, I remember, at the kiosk in the Plaza de Cibeles, a series of pamphlets written about one incident or other of the civil war: *Temas Españoles*. These pamphlets, sold at two pesetas, told how, after frightful slaughter, General Franco and his colleagues had saved Spain, in a 'crusade of liberation' from communism, atheism and freemasonry.

This propaganda had gone home. But surely some kind of knowledge of, or truthful recovery of, the past was desirable if the future were to be faced with confidence? Perhaps a historical study might play some part in this if executed calmly? So in my book I sought to avoid polemics, to state the facts so far as I could, with such serenity as I could muster, and, so far as possible, avoiding recriminations. Of course, I thought representative government superior to the rule of reactionary, or revolutionary, authoritarianism, but since one version or other of the latter played a decisive part in the civil war and representative government vanished, I could not be accused of being too biased. I allowed myself a few indulgences, it is true, for which I was criticized – for example, the role of the International Brigades, particularly the British contingent, was given too much attention. I suppose that I thought I was writing primarily for an English audience.

That turned out, as it happened, not to be true, since the book was more widely distributed in the USA, France, Italy and Spain itself than it was in England. The Spanish reception was particularly interesting. Before the book was published in England, I was approached by a group of Spaniards in Paris who were anxious to start a new publishing house. Could they publish my book? I realized that, in 1961, there was no chance of the book being published in Spain. So Ruedo Ibérico published it in late 1961 and, between then and early 1962, they smuggled many copies across the border. Thereafter, things were more difficult, since the Spanish ministry of infor-

1. An exception might be Diego Sevilla Andrés, author of a history of the politics of the republican zone in the war.

mation and tourism (which was responsible for censorship) fell into the capable hands of Manuel Fraga Iribarne. Previously, the ministry had not only been intolerant but incompetent. So, though almost everything politically interesting was condemned, almost everything got through, in one way or another. Señor Fraga was more liberal. But what he did ban, he resolved to keep out; and it was still too early for a historical study of the civil war, written by an Englishman, to be distributed in Spain. Hence Ruedo Ibérico had more difficulty in selling the book after Señor Fraga came to power. But their sales continued and, at any time in the 1960s, one could buy *The Spanish Civil War* in Spain if one went to the right bookshop, under the counter.

In the time of Fraga, nevertheless, the intellectual life of Spain quickened. The influx of a formidable number of tourists and the emigration of so many Spaniards to work in northern Europe perhaps made that inevitable. Time helped. So did prosperity, which has made many in Spain forget, or forgive, the past. Moreover, in the ensuing ten years, many died who had played a major part in the civil war, while some came to maturity who had played none. At all events, during the 1960s and early 1970s, the republic and the civil war came to be written about in Spain with attention to truth and with intellectual rigour. Some writers deliberately supported by the régime even made scholarly contributions (for example, the volumes of Colonels Martínez Bande and Salas Larrazábal, whose works on the military side of the war cannot be neglected, even if few would agree with all their conclusions), and, in the early 1970s, there have been so many books published about the civil war and its origins that it is almost as if the study of the recent past were a substitute for an active political life. Polemics continue, but there is no doubt that they are of a different character from those of the past. There are many points of view. Much interesting work has also, of course, been done outside Spain on modern Spanish history (by, for example, Raymond Carr, Edward Malefakis, Richard Robinson, Stanley Payne and Herbert Southworth, to name only a few, dissimilar persons). Nevertheless, it would be foolish for anyone in 1976 to be under any illusions as to where the best work is now being done on the history of modern Spain: that is, in Spain itself. Certain inhibitions survive, it is true: but such studies as those of Angel Viñas, José María Bricall or

Alberto Balcells, to name only three new historians, show how much can now be done. There have also been published important memoirs, such as those of José María Gil Robles. Without doubt, the curtain on the past that seemed so stifling when I was first in Spain in the 1950s has been drawn back. The death of General Franco in 1975 made this even more evident.

Hence a new edition of my book was overdue. I had followed the controversies and tides of polemic which had washed over the subject. I made some changes in the Penguin and Pelican editions of the book, but in those I made no serious reconsideration of the balance of the undertaking. With so much new work now done, I had to choose between allowing my book to become itself a memory in the history of the literature of the war, and bringing it up to date, by more research as by taking into account the new material. I resolved on the latter course. I delayed as long as I could, not finding it at first easy to take up again the old controversies – a revolutionary army or a regular one, the responsibility for the war, the significance of intervention – upon which I had delivered fairly firm judgements in 1961. But, in addition to corrections of fact, or of interpretation, I had in the end to recast certain chapters and even rewrite others. The result is undoubtedly a new book, though I have tried to keep the form of the old one as much as possible. Indeed, I felt a certain obligation to my old readers to keep the structure much as I had it in the late 1950s though, had I started completely afresh now, I might have had a different approach to that also.

I am aware that, if this book in its new form is read, people will point out alterations which prove that the author too has changed – moved to the Right, as he has got older, for example, or moved to the Left, so as to keep up with the young. It may be that my angle of vision has altered: I am not aware of it. I have been harder, it is true, on the socialist youth in dealing with the months before the war than I was in 1961, and probably rather harsher on the victors' lack of magnanimity after the war. I now think that the anarchists' ideas for the regeneration of society were more original, provided they were put into effect in a mixed society, than I thought in 1960. I am also more conscious in 1976 than I was in 1960 of the difficulties facing political personages and of the more narrow margins within which they have to move. In the main, however, my judgements on personalities survive. But I think I am now fairer to Manuel Azaña than I was, partly because of self-revelations from his published diary. Perhaps I am more, rather than less, critical of General Franco. I also hope the reader will find that the economic and social side of the war has been treated better and I believe that the impact of certain classes of weapons is considered more adequately than it was.

There is also the question of perspective. In 1960, it was still just possible to look on the military régime directed by Franco as an aberrant one, and to feel that representative government, such as that practised between 1931 and 1936[1] and before 1923 with less honesty but greater success, was the 'norm' of modern Spanish life, as well as the ideal. Now, however, whatever may be the ideal, if one looks back on the last fifty years of Spanish life, the five years of the republic seem a break with the general tendency towards authoritarian rule which began in the crisis of 1917, seemed confirmed by General Primo de Rivera's *coup d'état* in 1923, and was reconfirmed in no uncertain way by the rising of July 1936, and by General Franco's *coups d'état* of October 1936 and April 1937. The tendency continued towards autocracy as Spain gradually recovered from her long decline – a recovery which began in 1898, a moment when her fortunes seemed at their nadir.

I am under no illusion that the last words of this book will be the last word on the Spanish Civil War. History necessitates continual reconsideration. Sometimes a foreigner seems the worst person to write of another country's history, sometimes the best. The issues involved in the Spanish war, however, transcend Spain and embrace Europe, just as much as the conflict did at the time. Indeed, since the matters considered concern the achievement and collapse of representative government, the rise and triumph of authoritarianism on both Right and Left, the clash of enthusiasms which turn into brutalities, the impact of technology on a still backward country, and the relation between civil war and international crises, there is no need to think that the significance of the Spanish Civil War is confined to Europe. Nor indeed to the 1930s. Here again is one salutary difference between the present and the time when I wrote my first edition. Then, at the beginning of the Kennedy era, the world seemed bathed in a sunny optimism, easy now to remember as a second

1. Or merely 1931 to 1934? When does the civil war begin?

belle époque, impossible to revive. There then seemed no reason to suppose that the world's economic growth would not continue forever, with increasingly enlightened advanced countries paying more and more attention to the needs of the poorer ones. The cold war seemed at an end. The Spanish war appeared to be an event in a remote, black past, buried before the Second World War. Today, the issues which led to the worst civil war in Europe for several centuries seem only too close in many countries – and not just 'Latin' ones. The ring of the words of people as various as Manuel Azaña and Antonio Maura seems uncomfortably relevant; and, indeed, the words of the first named, which still in 1976 as in 1961 conclude this book, seem an appropriate exhortation not only to Spaniards but to mankind. But perhaps too this mood will seem, a decade hence, peculiarly characteristic of a by then forgotten time of troubles!

March, 1976

H. T.

Preface to the 1986 Reprint

This work was first published in 1961 and later that year and the next in several foreign languages, including Spanish. The Spanish edition was, however, not published in Madrid because it was banned there by the censors in the Ministry of Information: so it was produced (as its first book, I think) by a Spanish émigré publishing house in Paris and subsequently smuggled into Spain. Revised editions followed in English. The fully revised edition of 1976 was pubished in English and Spanish. By that time General Franco had died and the new government led by Adolfo Suárez, on the designation of King Juan Carlos, was in process of abolishing the censorship. Thereafter, the book sold in many editions in Spain; there was even an illustrated version sold as a partwork in kiosks at railway stations or street corners.

I think that the censorship in Spain in the 1960s helped the sales of the book in the 1970s. By the time of Franco's death, the appetite for all books previously banned was voracious, especially when they treated of such sensitive questions as the very civil war which had brought Franco to power. However, the success of all these publications – not just mine but that of other historians, Spanish as well as English, French as well as American – played quite a part in the success also of the transition to democracy after Franco. The recovery of knowledge of why the previous democracy in Spain went wrong in the 1930s was a real help in the 1970s. The recollection in tranquillity of just how horrible a failure the civil war had been helped those concerned to make a new Spain to avoid destructive rhetoric. By suggesting that the responsibility for the conflict was not easily decided, and the guilt for the most odious actions fairly widely spread, vengeance was avoided – a fact not wholly to be expected when it is recalled how many people who had played a part in the civil war were, and are, still alive. 'Poetry,' said Shelley, 'is capable of saving us.' Cannot the same claim be made for history?

Perceptions of the Spanish war differ from one period of ten years to the next. It now appears to have been Spain's particular contribution to the continent-wide breakdown which occurred between 1914 and 1945: not a specifically Spanish descent into barbarism and certainly not a charcteristic one. In past centuries no one thought that nations engaged in war could last when they ran out of money. The events of 1914 showed that to be false. No one supposed in the last century that civil wars would go on if the two sides ran out of arms: in Spain it was shown, as many other such conflicts since then have shown, that other more well-provided countries can furnish the war *materièl* to enable the fighting to go on indefinitely. A lot of people were killed in Spain: but since my first edition questioned, I believe for the first time, in a historical work, the reliability of the estimate of 'a million dead', and suggested that 500,000 might be a maximum, the estimates for casualties have dropped and dropped. Now it would be perfectly admissible to argue that Spain lost fewer people dead in acts of violence than any other major European nation in this century.

That is an important reflection.Spain, little understood and often privately disliked by patronizing northern peoples ('an old Spanish custom' in London's Fleet Street means, I believe, the habit of being paid for work that is not done), is frequently held to be a more violent nation than it actually is. Isolated by good fortune and by geography from the so-called 'world's game' of European and great power rivalry since 1815, 'it has more lessons to offer other peoples than it has to learn: above all, it has grasped more successfully than other nations the art of combining progress with the persistence of tradition. Its recent achievement of delegating authority to autonomous regions is not universally popular in Spain because the central government continues as expensive as before. But I suspect it is the way that all advanced countries should go if they continue to wish half their economy to be managed by the State. These are grand issues. No doubt their chronicling in future works of history will exert an influence in the future if people are to go on living as happily in Europe as, despite everything, most of us are now.

HUGH THOMAS
Sanlúcar de Barrameda, Cádiz
29 September, 1985

BOOK ONE

THE ORIGINS OF THE WAR

'Every Spaniard's ideal is to carry a statutory letter with a single provision, brief but imperious: "This Spaniard is entitled to do whatever he feels like doing".'

ANGEL GANIVET

[illegible] his ideas to carry
a statutory letter with [illegible]
provision, [illegible]
[illegible]

cont[illegible]
ven [illegible]
the [illegible]
as t[illegible]
nce [illegible]

1

PROLOGUE

The Cortes on 16 June 1936 – the government of Casares Quiroga – Gil Robles speaks – the threats to democratic life – La Pasionaria – Calvo Sotelo's dispute with the Prime Minister

---

THE Cortes, the parliament of Spain, stands half-way up the hill leading from the Prado to the Puerta del Sol.[1] Bronze lions cast from guns captured in the Moroccan Wars guard its doors. At the summit of its Corinthian columns, Justice hopefully embraces Labour on a granite pediment. Today, the gilded corridors and saloons of the Cortes are used only occasionally, when a few honorific dignitaries give formal assent to decrees issued by the Head of State. On 16 June 1936, however, this classical building was the centre of all Spain.

Over five years had then passed since King Alfonso XIII had abandoned the Spanish throne – to avoid, as he put it (perhaps exaggerating his own importance in the minds of his people), the disaster of a civil war. These had been five years of parliamentary activity. Before the King left, there had been eight years, from 1923 till 1931, when, most of the time under the amiable military dictator General Primo de Rivera, the Cortes had been as deserted as it is today. Now, in June 1936, parliamentary life in Spain seemed likely to be destroyed.

An anxious group of middle-aged, middle-class liberals were gathered on the blue government bench at the front of the semi-circular debating chamber. Honest and intelligent men, they and their followers hated violence. They admired the pleasing, democratic ways of Britain, France and America. In both this hatred and this admiration, they were, however, unusual among Spaniards of their time, solitary even among the four hundred other deputies sitting or standing around and above them, as best they could, in the crowded

1. The animated central square of Madrid where many revolutions have begun.

debating chamber.[1] Yet the men of this government had a fanaticism of their own hardly typical of the practical-minded countries which they desired to reproduce in Spain.

Observe, for example, the Prime Minister, Santiago Casares Quiroga.[2] A rich man from Galicia in the north-west of Spain, he had spent much of his life calling for home rule for his own poor province, although the only advantage the *gallegos*[3] could have gained from this would have been a better rail service.[4] Although Casares seemed to act according to liberal, Wilsonian principles formulated beyond the Pyrenees, no one could have been more Spanish. He was a passionate liberal when the rise of organized labour caused liberalism to seem almost as anachronistic as the liberals' foe of feudalism. Yet since there had not been in Spain a successful middle-class revolution on the model of that in France in 1789, one can hardly blame Casares and his friends for their attitude. In the early years of the republic, in 1931 and 1932, the eyes of Casares Quiroga (then minister of the interior) had appeared, to both friends and enemies, to burn in his small head like those of St Just. Now they were marked by a strange, ironic optimism, only explicable as a symptom of the tuberculosis from which he was already suffering.

The nature of the crisis in Spain was described on 16 June 1936 by Gil Robles, the sleek, fat and almost bald, but still young, leader of the Spanish catholic party, the CEDA.[5] His party was conservative, and catholic, and it included those who wanted to restore a

1. The Cortes of the Second Republic had 473 members.

2. A Spaniard's full name consists of his christian name (or names), his father's surname (also his own), and his mother's surname, placed in that order. Spaniards sometimes call themselves by all these names. They often drop their last name (that of their mother) and refer to themselves by their father's name – with, of course, their christian names. But wherever their father's name is commonplace, it is often not used alone, and the mother's is sometimes used in its place. Thus, for García Lorca, no one would say 'García', and today he is referred to as 'Lorca'. The miners' leader in Asturias, González Peña, might be referred to as Peña where the context was clear, but never as González. Other Spaniards might use their mother's name because it seems more mellifluous; or more grand.

3. Natives of Galicia.

4. That was necessary. It is a commentary on Spain rather than on Galicia that autonomy seemed the best way to achieve it.

5. Confederación Española de Derechas Autónomas (Spanish Confederation of autonomous movements of the Right). For the CEDA see below, p. 108.

monarchy, as well as those who desired a christian democratic republic. Some in the CEDA, particularly in the youth movement (JAP),[1] were almost fascists; and some admired Dollfuss's corporate state. Gil Robles was eloquent and able, but hesitant and devious. He was as hated by monarchists and fascists as he was by socialists. Yet he had created the first middle-class Spanish mass party. Now he recalled that the government had had, since the elections in February, exceptional powers, including press censorship and the suspension of constitutional guarantees. Nevertheless, during those four months, 160 churches, he said, had been burned to the ground, there had been 269 mainly political murders, and 1,287 assaults of varying seriousness. Sixty-nine political centres had been wrecked, there had been 113 general strikes and 228 partial strikes, while 10 newspaper offices had been sacked. 'Let us not deceive ourselves!' concluded Gil Robles. 'A country can live under a monarchy or a republic, with a parliamentary or a presidential system, under communism or fascism! But it cannot live in anarchy. Now, alas, Spain is in anarchy. And we are today present at the funeral service of democracy!' Angry cries broke out from all over the chamber, some in agreement, some in dissent.[2]

The conditions of the country and the régime were as grave as Gil Robles suggested, even if the figures seemed suspiciously precise, and even if some of the disorder caused was the work of the Right: the building of *El Ideal*, a right-wing newspaper in Granada, had been apparently burned by young men of the right, and there was other provocation.[3] In addition to the violence, men at both extremes of the political spectrum were being drilled for fighting, as military formations. 'All out on Sunday' was an instruction by a score of political leaders. Neither Casares Quiroga nor Gil Robles, representing groups which had been prominent in the history of the Second Republic,[4] could any longer control events. Both, indeed, were sustained in the Cortes by the votes of deputies whose aims were different from their

1. Juventud de Acción Popular (Popular Action youth movement).

2. *Diario de Sesiones de las Cortes Españolas*, 16 June 1936. See Gil Robles's memoirs, *No fue posible la paz* (Barcelona, 1968).

3 Ian Gibson, *The Death of Lorca* (London, 1973), p 14.

4. Casares Quiroga was a member of the Republican Left party, which had absorbed the Galician autonomists.

own. The elections of the preceding February had been contested by two alliances: the Popular Front, and the National Front. Besides the liberals like Casares, the former had consisted of the large socialist party, the small communist party, and other working-class groups. Behind the socialist party there was the powerful socialist trade union, the UGT (Unión General de Trabajadores),[1] one of the best organized workers' movements in Europe. The National Front consisted not only of the CEDA, but also of monarchists, agrarians, representing the large landowners of the south and centre, and some other right-wing parties. It was the political front for all the forces of old Spain, the army, as well as of the church and the bourgeoisie.

The Popular Front had gained the day in February 1936 though, by the Spanish electoral law, their majority of seats in the Cortes was greater than their total of votes cast would have entitled them under a strict system of proportional representation. Not all the parties which had shared in the electoral alliance took part in the government. Indeed the government was composed of liberal republicans,[2] while it depended for its majority upon the working-class groups. This is never a recipe for strong government. It was peculiarly unhappy in Spain in 1936, when the working-class parties were already in a perpetual state of revolutionary effervescence; and, apart from those groups who cooperated with the democratic system so far as to contest seats in the Cortes, there remained, outside, the great army of nearly two million anarchist workers, chiefly in Andalusia or Barcelona, organized in the CNT (Confederación Nacional de Trabajo),[3] and directed by a secret society, the FAI (Federación Anarquista Ibérica).[4] This huge, self-absorbed and passionate movement, already throbbing like a great city at war, despised the progressive government of Casares Quiroga as much as it had in the past hated the governments of the Right. Then there was the army. Who

1. General Union of Workers. Miguel Maura (*El Sol*, 18 June 1936) estimated this union to number 1,447,000 workers, on the basis of the director-general of security's estimate.

2. The two 'pure' republican parties, the Republican Left and the Republican Union, had been joined by representatives of the autonomy parties of Galicia and Catalonia.

3. National Confederation of Labour. Miguel Maura (*El Sol*, 18 June 1936) gave a figure of 1,577,000 for the CNT. Probably an underestimate.

4. Iberian Anarchist Federation.

in that early summer in Madrid had not heard rumours of plots by leading generals, to establish 'order' or a military dictatorship? Indeed, after Gil Robles had finished speaking in the Cortes, a socialist deputy declared that the churches were being burned by *agents provocateurs* to justify just such a military rebellion.

The socialists were divided. Some were reformists. Some were intellectual fabians. A few were revolutionaries. Some were dazzled by the flattery of communists, some aghast at the recent rise of communist influence. But all could agree with the accusations levelled at the Right by their spokesman.

When their cheering had died down, the monarchist leader, Calvo Sotelo, proudly rose. Like Casares Quiroga, he was a native of Galicia; but also, like Casares, he lacked the dispassion for which that green region is celebrated. Had he gipsy blood? Was he as strong a man as his handsome face suggested? A Spanish Roosevelt, or a cleverer, Spanish Mussolini? All people knew for certain was that he was violent, eloquent, and able. On leaving the University of Saragossa in 1915 he had been named private secretary to Maura,[1] the high-minded conservative Prime Minister of Alfonso XIII. Shortly afterwards, Maura made him civil governor[2] of Valencia at twenty-five. General Primo de Rivera gave him the ministry of finance at thirty-two. Prudently spending the first years of the republic in Paris to escape condemnation for the financial mistakes of the dictatorship, he returned to Spain only when the republic had begun to founder. Elected to the Cortes as a monarchist, he believed above all in his own star. The eclipse of Gil Robles had been his gain. Already experienced and at the height of his powers, he spoke as if he thought the future of Spain were in his hands.[3]

1. He had gone into an election with the simple programme, '*¡Nosotros somos nosotros!*' ('We are us!'). Perhaps appropriately, in that statesman's last years, his opponents used the even simpler slogan, '*¡Maura no!*'

2. The forty-nine provinces of Spain were administered by civil governors established in the provincial 'capitals'. These were political appointments, under the ministry of the interior. The authority of the civil governor was shared by the commander of the garrison of the city in question, who was styled the military governor, appointed by the minister of war.

3. The best study of Calvo Sotelo is that contained in Richard Robinson, *The Origins of Franco's Spain* (Newton Abbot, 1970), p. 215f. See also Aurelio Joaniquet, *Calvo Sotelo, una vida fecunda* (Santander, 1939).

The disorder in Spain, he said, in a speech punctuated by interruptions, was the result of the democratic constitution of 1931. No viable state, he believed, could be built upon that constitution.

Against this sterile state [he went on] I am proposing the integrated state, which will bring economic justice, and which will say with due authority: 'no more strikes, no more lock-outs, no more usury, no more capitalist abuses, no more starvation wages, no more political salaries gained by a happy accident,[1] no more anarchic liberty, no more criminal conspiracies against full production'. The national production will be for the benefit of all classes, all parties, all interests. This state many may call fascist; if this be indeed the fascist state, then I, who believe in it, proudly declare myself a fascist!

When the ensuing storm of derision and applause had died down, he went on:

When I hear talk of the danger from monarchist generals, I smile a little, for I do not believe (and you will grant me a certain [he paused] *moral* authority for this assertion), that there is, in the Spanish army, a single soldier disposed to rise on behalf of a monarchy and against the republic. If there were such a person, he would be mad – I speak with all sincerity, mad indeed, as would be any soldier who, before eternity, would not be ready to rise on behalf of Spain, and against anarchy – if *that* should be necessary.

Calvo Sotelo had in fact already secretly committed himself to support a military rising if it should come.[2] The Speaker of the Cortes, the swarthy Diego Martínez Barrio, requested Calvo Sotelo not to make such announcements, since his intentions could be misunderstood. The Speaker was an experienced politician of obscure birth from Seville, who had been once briefly Prime Minister. Now he was leader of the Republican Union party. Open, sympathetic, but vain, he had hitherto successfully represented in his political life the idea of compromise. This was so rare in Spanish affairs that his enemies attributed his rise to his occult power as a freemason of the thirty-third grade.

With deliberation, the Prime Minister answered Calvo Sotelo:

1. All ministers of the republic were entitled to a pension.
2. See below, p. 184.

After Your Excellency's[1] words, the responsibility for whatever happens will be yours. You come here today with two aims only: to condemn parliament as impotent, and to inflame the army, trying to detach units from their loyalty to the republic. But I give my assurance. Parliament *will* work. The army *will* do its duty.

The most famous Spanish communist, Dolores Ibarruri, known as 'La Pasionaria' (the passion flower), spoke next. Always dressed in black, with a grave but fanatical face which caused the masses who listened to her speeches to suppose her a revolutionary saint, she was now forty. Years before, as a girl, she had been a devout catholic. In those days she had wandered from village to village in the Basque provinces, selling (according to one account) sardines from a great tray which she bore on her head.[2] But Dolores la Sardinera married a miner from Asturias, one of the obscure founders of the socialist party in northern Spain. Personal tragedies accumulated – three of her daughters died in infancy – against a harsh background of struggle.[3] She transferred her devotion from the Virgin of Begoña to the prophet of the British Museum Reading Room. The Right spread rumours that she had once cut a priest's throat with her own teeth. She was to become a great orator, and was already an artist in words and timing. But her personality was less strong than it publicly appeared and her enemies on the Trotskyite Left explained the success of her oratory as attributable to secret Svengalis sent from Moscow. She was nevertheless a simple, direct, and powerful woman who had been to prison many times – thrice under the republic – and twice to Moscow too. In the Cortes, she stood out as the only striking leader in the small if growing Spanish communist party. There were only seventeen communist deputies, all 'unknown and ignorant' in the view of Indalecio Prieto, a socialist moderate, and, outside, the party had 130,000 members at most.[4]

More important, La Pasionaria also represented the idea of revolutionary womanhood, a strong force in a country which had given

1. Literally, 'Lordship' (*Su Señoria*) was the address used in the Cortes.

2. 'El Campesino' (Valentín González), *Comunista en España y anti-Stalinista en la URSS* (Mexico, 1952), p. 110.

3. Dolores Ibarruri, *El único camino* (Paris, 1962), p. 102. She had been a member of the central committee of the party since 1930.

4. The same report quoted by Maura and mentioned above gave the communists 133,000. For Prieto's comment, see *De mi vida* (Mexico, 1965), vol. II, p. 146.

the Virgin a special place in religion. As long ago as 1909, women in Barcelona had been the most eloquent, daring and violent among strikers, church-burners and looters of nunneries.[1]

When La Pasionaria spoke in the Cortes on 16 June, she dismissed the fascists of Spain as gangsters. But was there not a 'fascist international', directed from Berlin and Rome, which had already designated a day of reckoning in Spain?

A Catalan businessman, Juan Ventosa, next expressed his alarm at the apparent optimism of the Prime Minister. Ventosa, twice finance minister under the King, had been in politics for many years and was the political lieutenant of Francisco Cambó, the greatest financier of Barcelona and one of the richest men in Spain. It was said that Cambó's wealth had already been transferred abroad. The question was, was it wiser, from the point of view of the flight of capital, to seem hopeful or concerned? The government could never decide. Joaquín Maurín, leader of the rebel communist party known as the POUM,[2] announced next that there existed already a pre-fascist situation in the country. Then Calvo Sotelo rose once more to answer the Prime Minister:

My shoulders are broad [he said]. I do not shun, indeed I accept with pleasure, the responsibility for what I do . . . I recall the answer given by St Dominic of Silos[3] to a Spanish king: 'Sire, my life you may take from me, but more you cannot take'. Is it not, indeed, better to perish gloriously, than to live in contempt? But I, in turn, bid the Prime Minister to reckon up his responsibilities; if not before God, since he is an atheist, at least before his conscience, inasmuch as he is a man of honour.

He spoke then of the roles of Kerensky and Karolyi in delivering Russia and Hungary over to communist revolution:

1. For 1909, see below, p. 18. Barcelona took a long time to forget the radical fishwife Carmen Alauch; the prostitute María Llopis; the radical madame, 'La Bilbaina'; Rosa Estelrich, 'La Valenciana'; Mercedes Monje; Trinidad de la Torre; Enriqueta Sabater; and all the other '*Damas Radicales*', or '*Damas Rojas*', who, wearing white bows as uniform, had helped to organize the pacifist strikes and church burnings of 1909.

2. Partido Obrero de Unificación Marxista (Workers' party of Marxist unity). See below, p. 119.

3. A local saint from near Burgos. Calvo Sotelo should really have spoken of St Dominic de Guzmán.

My honourable friend will not be a Kerensky, since he is not unconscious of what he is doing. He possesses full knowledge of what he conceals, and of what he thinks. God grant that he will never be compared with Karolyi, the conscious betrayer of a thousand-year civilization!

Calvo Sotelo sat down. As he did so, shouts and applause rang through the chamber.

The reverberations of this debate, with its threats and warnings, echoed all over Spain. They found their way to the President, Manuel Azaña, the embodiment of the republic, gloomily watching the collapse of his hopes from the rich loneliness of the National Palace.[1] They found their way to those generals who for so long had been employing their ample leisure with tactical schemes for a military rising against the government. They reached, too, José Antonio Primo de Rivera, son of the old dictator and leader of the Spanish fascists, the Falange, in his prison in the port of Alicante, whither he had been vainly sent on a trivial charge, virtually as a hostage for the good behaviour of his followers. They reached to that other group of Spaniards whose aspirations lay outside the Cortes, the anarchists. They found their way to most of the 24½ million people who then formed the population of Spain. The questions in every mind as the summer mounted, as the bull-fight season attained its meridian, were: 'How long will this go on?' 'Will there be a revolution?' and 'Could it be war?' For while there had been no civil wars in most of Europe since the seventeenth century, Spain, the one major European country to have kept out of the Great War, had fallen back into conflict within her national frontiers three times in the nineteenth century.

1. Previously (and later) the Royal Palace.

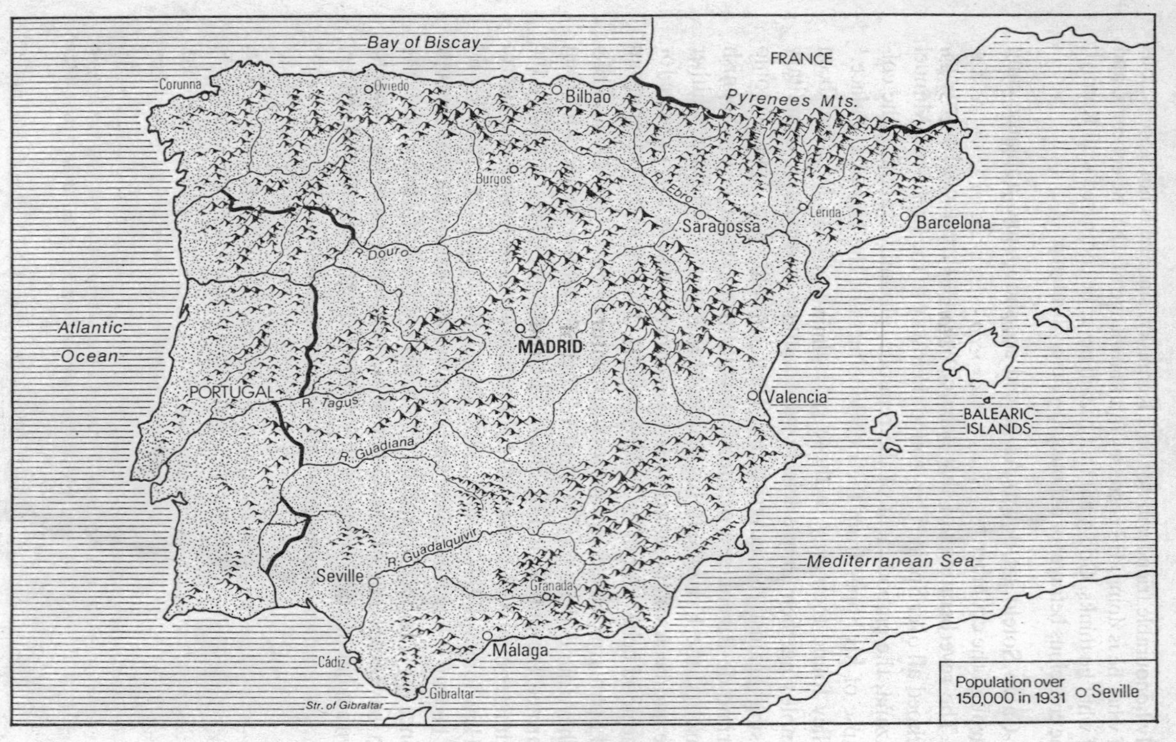

1. The physical features of Spain

2

The collapse of the absolute monarchy – the restoration and regency – the 'Tragic Week' of Barcelona – Morocco – breakdown of the parliamentary régime – Primo de Rivera's dictatorship – his fall – end of the monarchy

THIS debate in the Cortes was the culmination of the several passionate quarrels as to how Spain should be governed which had continued since 1808. In that year, the enfeebled monarchy made an abject surrender before Napoleon. The British under the Duke of Wellington helped the Spanish people to drive out the French in the ensuing War of Independence.[1] The Bourbons were brought back in the loathsome person of Ferdinand VII. But the monarchy was no longer sacrosanct. For almost three centuries before 1808, Spain had been the most peaceful and untroubled of European countries; from then on, it would be among the most turbulent of them.

The political history of the succeeding half-century was marked by a struggle over the constitution. The contestants were the church and the army, the two Spanish institutions which had survived with credit from the War of Independence, the former being conservative, the latter being honeycombed with free-thinking masonic lodges. Throughout, this quarrel was almost war.[2] In 1820, liberal officers forced a constitution upon King Ferdinand who, in 1823, brought in a French army, the 'hundred thousand sons of St Louis', to do away with it. In 1834, the quarrel turned into the First Carlist War, when the church, and the advocates of regional rights in the north, rallied to the cause of Don Carlos, the brother of the dead Ferdinand. Don Carlos claimed the throne in the place of his infant niece, Isa-

1. There is no reason to doubt that the rising against Murat and Joseph Bonaparte was popular and national. Fichte, in his *Addresses to the German People*, praised this example of 'a people in arms' and adjured the Germans to follow the Spaniards' example. They did.

2. At the start of this agitated half-century, the Spanish colonies in central and southern America revolted and, in the name of liberalism, became independent.

bella II, Ferdinand's daughter. Isabella was championed by the liberals and the army, both representing the claims of Castile to dominate the Peninsula. This war of religion and of secession ended in 1839, when the liberals won, but peace took the form of a compromise between the armies of both sides. Carlist officers, for instance, were permitted to join the regular Spanish army. Partly as a result (and partly because the confiscation of the church's lands in 1837[1] reduced the influence of that institution), the quarrel between liberals and clerical conservatives took the form thereafter of a succession of *coups d'état* (*pronunciamientos*) by one general after another.

This curious era ended in 1868, when Queen Isabella, a nymphomaniac, was herself expelled by the greatest of Spain's liberal generals, Prim. If the occasion of her departure was her excessive reliance on Father Claret, her confessor, the real cause was a revolt against the style of government over which Isabella and her 'Court of Miracles' had vaguely presided. The succeeding seven years were confused. A brother of the King of Italy, the Duke of Aosta, was brought in as King Amadeo I. This attempt at bourgeois monarchy could not contain the violence rearoused between liberals and conservatives, newly in arms. Amadeo abdicated. The First Spanish Republic was proclaimed. This republic was at first intended as a federal one, in which the provinces would have substantial rights. But the intellectuals who planned this were powerless to ensure the survival of central authority of any kind. In the north, the Carlists rose again under a grandson of the Old Pretender, and were generally supported by the church throughout the Peninsula. In the south and south-east, many of the coastal towns proclaimed themselves independent cantons. Once again, the army eventually took power. While restoring order, the generals decided that there was no alternative save to bring back Queen Isabella's son, then a cadet at Sandhurst, as King Alfonso XII.

A constitution was promulgated in 1876. Thanks to favourable European conditions of trade, Spain was prosperous in the 1880s. Universal male franchise was nominally introduced. But the results of the elections were always defrauded by an informal pact, the *turno pacífico*, between the two main parties, carried out by the agency of the minister of the interior and local political bigwigs, the *caciques*. The people of Spain came to look upon the parliamentary system, a

1. The church was compensated in cash and in wages. See below, p. 51.

2. Regions and provinces of Spain

Last to hold out against Franco

deliberate imitation of English practice, as a means of excluding them from politics. Alfonso XII, meanwhile, died in 1885, at the age of twenty-eight, leaving a posthumous son, Alfonso XIII, for whom his mother, María Cristina, ruled as Regent till 1902.[1]

The 'pious fraud' of the constitution was one reason for the spread of revolutionary ideas throughout the working class. By the time of the First World War, there existed in Spain two general trade unions. The first, the CNT (Confederación Nacional de Trabajo),[2] was inspired by the anarchist ideas of Bakunin; the second, the UGT (Unión General de Trabajadores),[3] was Marxist, though more reformist than revolutionary. The socialists of the UGT collaborated with the political system so far as to seek election to the Cortes and, in the cities, where the *caciques*' manipulation of votes became increasingly difficult, succeeded in gaining election. But the anarchists saw the constitution as unclean; and the violence, murders, and lightning strikes undertaken intermittently by the anarchist militants kept the governments in turmoil. Both these working-class movements desired to regenerate Spain through education, superior public morality, pacifism and anti-clericalism, as much as through politics.

Two other problems, however, caused the collapse of the constitution established at the restoration. The first was that of Catalonia. Many Catalans aspired to a recognition of their separate character from the rest of Spain. Catalonia had continued, after Spanish unification, to live as a region of its own and to look to its own capital of Barcelona, never to Madrid. The 'Catalan question' became acute because of the industrial development of that capital during the nineteenth century. Irritation with the incompetence of the government at Madrid led the new rich of Barcelona at the end of the century to Catalan nationalism. This, together with the anarchist faith of the workers, the high rates of illiteracy and the demagogic atmosphere inculcated by a centralist, opportunist, but wild party, the Radicals,[4] made Barcelona (growing fast in population) at the turn of the cen-

1. It was during this period that all the main actors of the civil war between 1936 and 1939 were born. An old man of seventy in 1936 would have remembered the Carlist Wars of the seventies from his childhood. One of eighty might have taken part.

2. National Confederation of Labour. See below, p. 60.

3. General Union of Workers. See below, p. 39.

4. See below, p.34.

tury the most turbulent city in Europe: the 'city of bombs'. The great strike in Barcelona in 1902 and that in Bilbao in 1903 were major battles in which the nerves of all were fully extended. The ornate architecture favoured by the prosperous bourgeoisie was the lavish backcloth to a mounting series of anarchist crimes. 'In Barcelona, a revolution does not have to be prepared,' wrote the civil governor, Angel Ossorio y Gallardo, 'since it is always prepared.'[1] Meantime, Catalan aspirations began to be echoed in the more tranquil Basque provinces, where a similarly self-sufficient bourgeoisie was becoming rich from iron, banking and commerce.

The third crisis of the régime derived from the colonial wars in, first, Cuba, then Morocco. The Cuban War of 1895 turned into the Spanish American one of 1898; all was lost, save honour. The defeat inflamed the Catalan problem, since Cuba had been the best market for Catalan textiles. The loss of Cuba was also of psychological concern since many Catalan fortunes had been based on Cuban commerce.[2] In addition, the loss of the last vestige of empire caused a national crisis. It gave force to old causes of discontent, fired new ones. The year of defeat, 1898, was thus a turning-point: Spaniards were forced to think of themselves as a poor European country with few resources.

Morocco, however, offered a new chance of empire. But it caused new upheavals too. Spain had held the two northern Moroccan ports of Melilla and Ceuta for several hundred years. She had tried to extend her rule there in the 1860s, and there had been further fighting, near Melilla, in the 1890s. Spain was understandably reluctant to allow any other European power to establish herself on the north coast of Africa facing her. In 1904, as part of the *Entente Cordiale* between Britain and France, France and Spain divided Morocco into zones of influence, Spain taking the smaller, northern part. Morocco was then backward, lawless and ripe for European interest, if not investment, though the tribes of both zones had a formal loyalty to

1. Angel Ossorio y Gallardo, *Julio de 1909, declaración de un testigo* (Madrid, 1910), p. 13. Catalonia is discussed on p. 43. Cf. Joaquín Romero Maura, *La rosa de fuego* (Barcelona, 1974).

2. See Raymond Carr, *Spain 1808–1939* (Oxford, 1966), p. 397; and R. J. Harrison, 'Catalan Business and the Loss of Cuba 1898–1914', *Economic History Review*, XXVII, no. 3, August 1974.

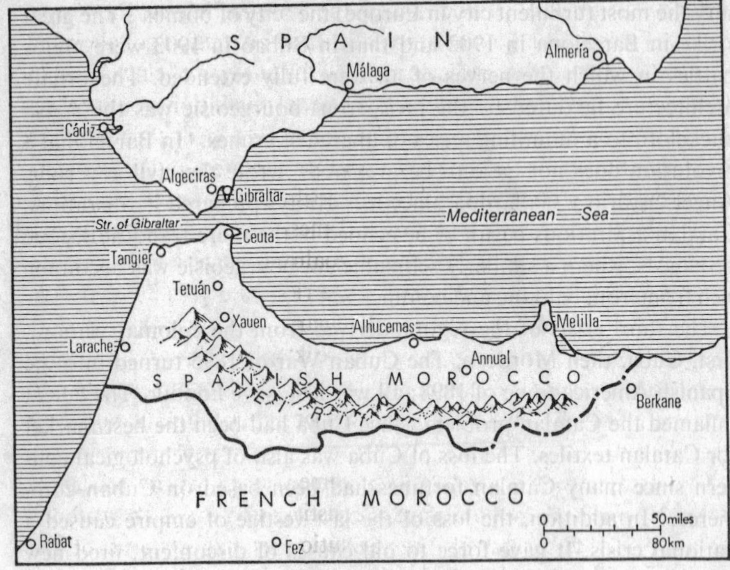

3. Spanish Morocco

a sultan at Fez. The ill-informed Spanish populace was probably as critical of these high-handed arrangements as was the indolent sultan; neither was consulted. Economic interest, however, followed the flag: the iron mines of Morocco were rich. A gradual extension of Spanish commerce followed, partly the reflection of similar French action (had Spain shown no interest, France would have absorbed the whole of Morocco). A Spanish colonization company was founded, and bought land in the wake of slowly advancing troops. But then the advances stopped; Moroccan tribesmen closed ranks; a series of set-backs forced the army to call for reinforcements; in 1909, there were serious defeats; by September of that year, the Spanish army was 40,000 strong in Morocco. But it was by then committed to an imperial adventure whose only end could be the conquest of north Morocco at a cost which the country could not afford.

Already there were, in 1909, horrible repercussions at home when Antonio Maura's government called up 850 reservists, some from Catalonia, all from north-east Spain. When the men went reluctantly to their ships in the harbour at Barcelona, a general strike was called in protest. A week of rioting ensued, the *Semana Trágica*, the Tragic Week, of Barcelona. Radicals, socialists and anarchists collaborated in organizing the strike, radicals inspired the burning of churches that followed. Many people hoped that a national revolution would ensue. But, bereft of real political direction, the rioters spent themselves in pointless destruction. While radical leaders hesitated, radical women, clerks, criminals, boys and prostitutes terrified nuns out of nunneries, burned their possessions, killed their domestic animals and chickens, and disinterred bodies. A handsome coalman danced with one disinterred corpse outside the house of the rich Marqués de Comillas, 'delighted to be of use as a revolutionary'. Eventually, the army resumed control; some 120 people were killed,[1] though only three clergy among them; the rioters had wanted to destroy 'property and illusions', not life. About fifty churches or other religious buildings were burned.

This disaster was a shock which seemed to show how violent a nation lay underneath the surface of constitutional rule. The authorities were less disturbed by the revolutionary expectations of the radicals or the anarchists than by the apparently meaningless destruction caused by the populace once their blood was up. The Tragic Week was a setback to the idea that a parliamentary democracy might gradually be established: if the masses were as they showed themselves in 1909, the political class of the day thought, real democracy would result in ruin. Henceforward, politicians avoided general elections if they could and tried to arrange coalitions out of groups of parliamentarians already in the legislature. The international demonstrations of outrage against the execution of the anarchist schoolmaster, Ferrer, accused of being the prime organizer of the riots,[2] also had a contra-productive effect: the upper classes saw in these protests the hypocritical, as well as hysterical and ill-informed, reactions of a mysterious coalition of international busybodies and freemasons to become sadly famous as 'anti-Spain'.

1. Joan Ullman, *The Tragic Week* (Cambridge, Mass., 1968), p. 288f. The 'aimlessness' of these riots has been exaggerated and so has the anarchist part: more important were the radicals. Still, no doubt the civil governor, Ossorio y Gallardo, was right when he said, 'On each street they shouted different things and fought for different purposes' (*Julio de 1909*, Madrid, 1910, p. 54). Five men were executed after subsequent trials, one of them the coalman.

2. See below for Ferrer, p. 64.

The Prime Minister, Maura, who was as a result of international complaints dismissed by the King and abandoned by many influential conservatives, believed that this 'surrender in the Cortes' after the 'victory in the streets' doomed the régime, since it had been seen to have given way to disorder, propaganda and malice. Thereafter the conservative party, which had held together since the 1870s, followed the liberals into disintegration. Maura moved into the wings of politics as the focus of a movement of young men angry with parliamentarianism, anxious for regeneration, but unable to gain a majority for a government. In *Maurismo* there were to be seen the springs of fascism – evident in other countries before 1914 as well (with Déroulède and Maurras in France, D'Annunzio in Italy, and even the Ulster volunteers). Maura promised a 'revolution from above'. The malicious said that he merely desired a 'revolution without a revolution'.

The Moroccan wars continued, though unsuccessfully. Tangier, north Morocco's best port, was excluded from the Spanish protectorate in 1912, as an international city, and the tribes refused to accept the Spanish 'civilizing' presence. Men, money, food and emotion continued to be poured into the country by a Spain that could only afford the first. The tribes had never been subject to the sultan; only Spain gave them a unity. In seeking an empire, Spain thus helped to inspire modern Moroccan nationalism.

The three main problems in modern Spain (working-class unrest, the regional question, and the colonial wars) upset the restoration settlement in the end. Perhaps anyway that political edifice was too fragile to be able to outlive for long the gifted conservative historian, Cánovas, who was its main architect, and Sagasta, the 'old shepherd', his liberal opponent. Personalities count in modern politics as much as they did in the epoch of kings. Cánovas was assassinated, Sagasta died. Maura failed as a potential successor to Cánovas as much through the strength of his personality as through the weakness of his programme. Sagasta's ultimate successor, José Canalejas, was, it was true, a journalist, orator and reformer of the first order. His government between 1910 and 1912 seemed a time of battle against the clerical control of education and the freedom of the orders to organize schools without state inspection. In fact, Canalejas revised the system of taxation to benefit the poor, temporarily solved the

Catalan question by the grant of *Mancomunidad* (limited self-government), and reached a compromise with the church in the *Ley de Candado* (Law of the Padlock) which limited the growth of religious orders, unless they had government permission. Canalejas also abolished the system whereby the rich could buy themselves out of military service. Well might an English historian celebrate him as 'the only liberal who got things done'.[1] He was assassinated by an anarchist in 1912. His successors as liberal leaders (the Conde de Romanones, García Prieto, Santiago Alba) had neither Canalejas's energy nor his gifts.

*

The First World War brought the problems of restoration Spain to a climax. The conflict benefited all neutral nations, and in Spain it created much wealth, contrasting with much surviving poverty. Basque ships, Catalan textiles, Asturian coal, zinc and copper, all gained high prices. The consequent inflation was felt most by the working class, though wages went up and, in some jobs, outstripped prices. Huge numbers of workers were, as it were, sucked up to Barcelona on the train from Murcia and Almería which became known as the *transmiseriano*. The atmosphere was confused by sterile arguments as to which side Spain should support in the war. (The Left were mostly pro-Ally, the Right mostly pro-German; so that the King could say that only he and 'the rabble' hoped that Britain would win.) Meantime, the government of the Conde de Romanones (who personally preferred the Allies) was turning a blind eye to the activities of terrorists financed by German agents who attacked pro-Allied industrialists. Romanones eventually himself resigned on the issue of whether German submarines should be allowed to use Spanish bases to refit in the battle of the Atlantic.

The army now re-entered politics. The situation had been complicated by the growth of so-called *juntas de defensa*, professional associations of junior infantry officers protesting against the low pay which, like that of the agricultural workers, had not kept pace with inflation. The *juntas* also disliked promotion by 'combat merits' (*méritos de guerra*) or royal favouritism which was enjoyed by the officers fighting in Morocco. The *juntas* were founded in Barcelona

1. Carr, p. 495.

and spread all over Spain. In May 1917, their leader, Colonel Benito Márquez, a foolish, deaf officer, was arrested for insubordination, with some colleagues. Other *junteros* asked to be arrested too. The King ensured the release of all of them and the government fell. All politicians were shocked at this new surrender. But the press liked the *juntas* and gave unwise publicity to the notion that they might take the first step in a nation-wide movement of regeneration. Cambó, the financier who was leader of the Catalan bourgeois movement, the Lliga Regionalista (founded in 1901), thought so too.

Meantime, in the south of Spain, the intoxicating news of the Russian Revolution inspired widespread unrest including strikes, occupations of land and intimidation of rural guards, these actions being mostly inspired by anarchists; while, in Barcelona, the anarchist unions believed that the crisis offered them a supreme opportunity.

In the face of this multi-sided challenge, a new government, headed by a conventional conservative, Eduardo Dato, suspended constitutional guarantees and closed the Cortes. The more progressive politicians, outraged, responded by convening an alternative 'Assembly' of Catalan nationalists which met in Barcelona to 'renovate' the Spanish constitution. The government declared this seditious, and introduced censorship. The 'Assembly' movement might have gone far had it not been for reckless action by the Left. The socialists, caught up in the mood of the moment, had, in 1916, deserted their cautious reformism, and prepared a general strike aiming at revolution: their programme provided for the end of the monarchy; a seven-hour working day; the abolition of the army and its substitution by a militia; separation of church and state; nationalization of land; the closure of monasteries and nunneries; and, important in 1917, no declaration of war unless there were a plebiscite.[1]

Dato took a firm stand. He first defined a railway strike as a threat to the state and treated it accordingly (the government had encouraged the railway companies to take a hard line). Playing on the knowledge that the *junteros* also really opposed any alteration of the social order, and that the Catalan progressive bourgeoisie, however truculent, desired anything rather than revolution, the government met the general strike with the army.

1. For the events of this year and the following crisis, see Gerald Meaker's *The Revolutionary Left in Spain, 1914–1923* (Stanford, 1974), p. 153f.

The socialists thought that for once they had made a satisfactory alliance with the anarchists, as with some politicians of the Centre, the reformist republicans. But their tactics had not been well coordinated, and the strike failed. The army directed the subsequent repression, the *junteros* being deaf to the appeals of socialists. Seventy people were killed (mostly in Barcelona, fighting to keep, or to prevent, the trams running), and the Catalan Lliga, shaken by the revolution for which they had been partly responsible, agreed to participate in a coalition government, led by Maura, which bought off the *junteros* with promotions. The unofficial parliamentary assembly did meet again, in Madrid, but the mood was cautious: it called for a constituent Cortes to rewrite the constitution and was not heard of again. Cambó was now in the government as minister of development. It was his great opportunity and he showed himself as able a planner as he had been a money-maker. But the government did not last. Nor did any other. For nearly five years, a series of conservative governments failed even to resolve quarrels in the conservative party. They were unable to deal with the consequences of a post-war economic recession accompanied by continuing disasters in Morocco and working-class violence in both Andalusia and Barcelona. The wonder is not that the constitution was overthrown in the end, but that it lasted as long as it did in a country where military intervention had occurred so often during the preceding century. Perhaps it did not last really after 1917: a democracy can hardly exist if several provinces are only kept from revolution by the brutality of the civil guard,[1] and the largest industrial city from civil war by counter-terrorism sponsored by industrialists, and winked at by the police.

No doubt the world economic situation was partly to blame. During the war, Spanish employers had expanded their enterprises, but had now to contract. They would fight labour now, since there was a glut of workers; in the war, there had been a shortage. But in the clash of labour and capital, between 1917 and 1923, a class war was to be seen which often came close to outright conflict, and over issues other than economic: employers believed themselves threatened by bankruptcy if not revolution, the anarchists believed that they were on the brink of the millennium. Since, whatever the views of the

1. See below, p. 77.

central government, the local military authorities usually agreed with the employers, and often arrested strikers, the character of the conflict became more and more violent. The rule of General Martínez Anido (previously known as a sanguinary governor in Melilla) as civil governor of Barcelona from 1920 to 1922 was notoriously ruthless: a type of repression not seen in Spain for generations. He gave support to the *sindicatos libres*, free syndicates, which seemed more and more an employers' union of strike breakers, though they had some respectable backing from catholic social reformers. Gunmen infiltrated them and terrorism flourished among the anarchists. In other parts of Spain there were similar tragic events: in Andalusia, anarchist committees seized municipal governments, landowners left, increased wages were won; but, in the end, the army overcame the strikers. In Madrid, where there were also severe strikes in 1921, socialists and anarchists fought each other, each regarding the others as traitors.

In the end, the anarchists ruined their chances of revolution, such as these were, by internal disputes. Many leaders were murdered. So, too, was the conservative Prime Minister, Dato. By 1923, the CNT was exhausted. So was Spain. Violent reactions had been shown to be increasing on every side in public life, and enmities had been made which would never be forgotten. Not for the last time, the anarchists helped to wreck a system which, for all its faults, was susceptible of peaceful change, and whose successor was one much less to their liking.

The Moroccan wars continued to tie down the Spanish army. After some minor victories a slow campaign against the Riffian tribes, led by the brilliant Abd-el-Krim and his brother, culminated in the defeat at Annual in 1921. There, General Fernández Silvestre, a romantic, popular, but imprudent officer, a friend of the King's, was overwhelmed, with all his staff. The army in east Morocco panicked, one Spanish fort after another fell, and the Riffians reached the outskirts of Melilla. At least 15,000 Spanish citizens and soldiers were killed.[1] The disaster was shocking: even more so, the inquiry, directed by General Picasso, which revealed a state of unpreparedness and cor-

1. David Woolman, *Rebels in the Rif* (London, 1969), p. 96. For a description of the panic, see Arturo Barea, *The Forging of a Rebel* (New York, 1946), p. 304f.

ruption difficult to imagine, impossible to overlook. Abd-el-Krim's rebellion and the virtual achievement of a Riffian state (despite the 150,000 Spanish troops now seeking his defeat) proved that, while the French under the great Lyautey had achieved much in Morocco, the Spaniards had done little in their zone. Furthermore, the King was believed to have given General Silvestre encouragement, by telegram, for his rashness.[1]

All this, and the 'responsibility' for the disaster, was expected to come into the open in the autumn of 1923. The Cortes adjourned for the summer. It never met again in the same way. By 1923, the constitutional monarchy seemed bruised to death, even though one threat, that of the *junteros*, had been removed by their dissolution a year before. Partly because of the local power of the *caciques*, the political parties of the restoration had failed to develop much beyond *tertulias*, semi-social gatherings which met in cafés around a single figure. Some of the politicians, such as those in the Republican Reformist party, were democrats. But public opinion had no love for this Cortes. The politicians, for their part, knew that the army would not resist a popular general. There was thus no will to oppose an ultimatum, presented in the nineteenth-century style, by the chosen leader of a group of important generals, General Miguel Primo de Rivera, captain-general of Catalonia:

We have reason on our side and, therefore, force, though so far we have used force with moderation. If an attempt is made to trick us into a compromise which our conscience considers dishonourable, we shall demand greater penalties, and impose them with greater severity. Neither I, nor the garrisons of Aragon, from whom I have just received a telegram in support, will agree to anything but a military dictatorship. If the politicians make an attempt to defend themselves, we shall do the same, relying on the help of the people, whose reserves of energy are great. Today we are resolved on moderation, but, on the other hand, we shall not shrink from bloodshed.

1. The 'telegram', never found, was believed to have said: 'Olé, boys! I'm waiting for the 25th!' (*'Olé, los hombres! El 25 te espero!'*) Rightly or wrongly, the King was never forgiven. V. S. Pritchett, travelling in Spain in the 1920s, found that, whenever he asked whether the monarchy might survive, people said, 'He should not have sent that telegram!'

The dictatorship of General Primo de Rivera followed. King Alfonso acquiesced, knowing what was planned beforehand.[1] He was exasperated with politicians and liked soldiers. This new system lasted until January 1930. 'My Mussolini', was how King Alfonso presented Primo to King Victor Emmanuel of Italy. But the general was no fascist. He was already fifty-three in 1923, white-haired, though tough. He possessed neither a mass-following, nor an expansionist foreign policy. He would have given up Morocco if he could have done so. The movement which he tried to create, the Patriotic Union,[2] an association of 'all men of good will', never gathered weight. Although he used officers to run the municipal governments for three years, imprisoned or exiled those who opposed him, and banned political parties, there were no political executions during his six and a half years of power.[3] His *pronunciamiento* was even welcomed at first by intellectuals such as José Ortega y Gasset, who thought that an 'iron surgeon' was needed for Spain's illnesses. So did both *junteros* and officers serving in Morocco, agreeing for once. The minister of the interior and the director general of security (always an important official in Spain) were, however, Generals Martínez Anido and Arleguí, the ruthless rulers of Barcelona between 1920 and 1922. These officers kept political parties out of sight. Meantime, an ambitious programme of public works (new dams, railways, rural electrification, and roads) gave the dictatorship the appearance of prosperity. The terms of trade improved, as everywhere in the late 1920s, and both production and commerce increased 300 per cent.[4] The socialists agreed to collaborate and the UGT, unlike their anarchist rivals, bid fair to become a kind of official trade union such as was found in Sweden. The financial policy of the young Calvo Sotelo gained for Primo the support of Spanish capital, and banks for the first time interested themselves in development through credit. (Maura's influence was indirectly considerable on this régime to

1. From the document made public by the Conde de Romanones in the Cortes during King Alfonso's 'trial' in December 1931.

2. Unión Patriótica (UP).

3. Three anarchists were, however, killed in a skirmish at Vera de Bidasoa on the French frontier on 6–7 November 1924, having been provoked by the civil guard.

4. Ramón Tamames, *Estructura económica de España* (Madrid, 1969), p. 203.

which he gave no formal backing.)[1] It was an era of wonderful schemes, in Spain as elsewhere: a great waterway project was begun in the Ebro and Douro valleys; and there was a famous industrial exhibition in Barcelona. Huge stadia were built, preparing the way for the rise of football and the decline of bullfighting. Production was successful in light industry. Above all, the dictator miraculously brought to a successful conclusion the running sore of the Moroccan War, although Abd-el-Krim had really beaten the Spaniards when the French were drawn into the conflict. Abd-el-Krim went into captivity in Réunion Island, and it seemed – and seeming was what mattered – that Spain had won a military victory, for the first time in many generations.[2]

Yet the dictatorship can only be measured by the personality of Primo de Rivera himself. He was patriotic, magnanimous, sympathetic, and tolerant, while both his physical and his moral courage, in Cuba, the Philippines and Morocco, were well-attested. Once he entered a theatre and began to smoke, while notices everywhere proclaimed that smoking was forbidden; on being informed of this, he rose and announced, cigar in hand, 'Tonight, everyone may smoke!' A widower, he would work hard for months on end and then disappear for a lost weekend of dancing, drinking, and lovemaking with gipsies. He would be observed almost alone in the streets of Madrid, swathed in an opera cloak, making his way from one café to another, and, on returning home, would issue a garrulous and sometimes intoxicated communiqué, full of unexpected metaphors and embarrassing confidences, which he might have to cancel in the morning. He desired to run Spain as an enlightened despot, at a time, however, when despotism could only last if it were brutal.

Primo de Rivera fell in the end partly because he persecuted, but did not crush, the liberal and professional middle class; for example, the affair of La Caoba (the mahogany girl) scandalized many. La Caoba was an Andalusian courtesan who, when implicated in a drug case, appealed to Primo de Rivera. The dictator ordered the judge to

1. He died in 1925.

2. Abd-el-Krim died in Morocco, whither he had just returned, in 1963. An obituary note in *African Revolution* (May 1963) spoke of him as 'Our Master' who first showed 'men of colour that imperialism was not invincible'. (The writer forgot Toussaint.)

release her. The judge refused and was supported in this by the president of the Supreme Court. Primo transferred the first, and sacked the latter. Those who protested, such as Unamuno, the philosopher, poet, journalist and professor of Greek, were sent to confinement on the hot Canary island of Fuerteventura. This action was unfortunately symptomatic of Primo's attitude to the rules of law, which he made and broke with impunity. The practice subverted more than his system; it prepared the way for a reckless attitude to law in the late 1930s on the part of the Spanish Right which would have been unheard of in the nineteenth century.

Primo also offended the army, and even the King, by changes which affected the always delicate matter of promotions in the corps of artillery. When the artillery officers tried to protest, Primo closed down the corps and released the men from their oaths of obedience to their officers. Similarly, orthodox bankers were alarmed by Calvo Sotelo's plans for income tax, and, even more, by the Extraordinary Budget, whose aim was to finance public works from loans, the interest upon which would be met out of revenue. Nobody, save the immediate beneficiaries, liked the monopolies for telephones (granted to the American International Telegraph and Telephone Company), the sale of petrol (granted to CAMPSA,[1] a group of banks), or tobacco in Morocco (sold to the Majorcan millionaire, Juan March), especially when the consequence of the petrol monopoly was to make the country dependent on Russian oil.

Primo's consultative and nominated National Assembly drafted a new constitution, in which the elected and the corporative element were combined. The first disturbed the Right, the second was rejected by liberals and the Left. Nor did the King like a system which envisaged him sharing his powers of dismissal with a Spanish copy of Mussolini's Grand Fascist Council. So this scheme did not point the way to a return to 'normality', such as the dictator expected. When he abolished press censorship, he received a hail of criticism. The students opposed him bitterly. There were two unsuccessful *pronunciamientos* against him, in Valencia and Andalusia, the one led by a seventy-year-old conservative politician, Sánchez Guerra, the other by the ambitious young General Goded, who had been chief of staff to the victorious field commander General Sanjurjo, in the Moroccan

1. Compañía Arrendataria del Monopolio de Petróleo, Sociedad Anónima.

campaign. The era of *pronunciamientos* seemed to have begun again. The peseta fell, while the slump of 1929 caused the collapse of several of those grandiose financial schemes which Calvo Sotelo had introduced. The coming of cinemas and the radio, and the extension of the use of the telephone and the motor-car raised popular expectations, particularly the cinemas, of which there were more in Spain by 1930 than in France. In the end, desirous of reassurance, Primo took the curious step of addressing a telegram to all the captains-general of Spain, asking them to find out if the senior officers still supported him. They wrote back mentioning their loyalty to the monarch; few mentioned the dictator. The King told Primo that he was Prime Minister not by virtue of the army's support, but by the King's command. Alfonso anyway now thought that he might be the saviour of Spain himself and made it plain that he hoped that Primo would retire. He did so. 'And now,' the dictator remarked, in the last of his famous communiqués, 'and now for a little rest, after 2,326 days of continuous uneasiness, responsibility, and labour.'[1] He left Spain, and died a few months later in the Hotel Pont Royal, in Paris, alone and unhappy. He was only sixty.

He left behind him no basis for a régime. For a while, the King attempted to govern as Primo had governed, through a directory of ministers, led by General Berenguer, who had been an able and honest high commissioner in Morocco, but was no politician. It would anyway have tried the most skilful statesman to lead Spain back to the constitution of 1876, as the King desired. Berenguer himself said that he assumed power when Spain was like 'a bottle of champagne, about to blow out its cork'.[2] Republican sentiments spread through the country. Many army officers, as well as the remains of Primo's Patriotic Union, thought that the King had behaved dishonourably in accepting the dictator's resignation. Others were now unrepentant republicans. The church was equivocal, with some of its most influential figures concerned (following the still Wilsonian mood of Pope Pius XI) to establish a democratic system if at all possible. Other churchmen were more opportunistic. Neither bourgeoisie nor lower classes had anything to hope for from a continuance

1. Communiqué printed in Miguel Maura, *Asi cayó Alfonso XIII...* (Mexico, 1962), pp. 34–5.

2. Emilio Mola, *Obras completas* (Valladolid, 1940), p. 231.

of the monarchy. The King, however, was not prepared to establish a royal dictatorship of the Balkan type, and General Berenguer dilly-dallied before calling for elections. In the summer of 1930, a pact was signed at the summer watering-place of San Sebastián between several republican politicians and intellectuals, the socialists, and the advocates of Catalan nationalism. The former conceded autonomy for the Catalans who, in return, agreed to support the republican plots, such as they were. In Madrid, three eminent intellectuals, Dr Gregorio Marañón, Ortega y Gasset and the novelist Ramón Pérez de Ayala, formed themselves into a 'movement for the service of the republic'. Ortega (whose earlier, well-phrased criticisms of parliament had helped Primo) wrote a famous article announcing, 'Spaniards! Your state is no more! Reconstitute it! '*¡Delenda est monarquía!*'.[1] More importantly, numerous discontented officers supported the rebels, and even the anarchists, submerged but alive, gave weary sympathy to the bourgeois opponents of the King. In December, a *pronunciamiento* was prepared. The plotters issued the following statement:

> A passionate demand for Justice surges upwards from the bowels of the Nation. Placing their hopes in a Republic, the people are already in the streets. We would have wished to communicate the people's desires through the due process of Law. But this path has been barred to us. When we have demanded Justice, we have been denied Liberty. When we have demanded Liberty, we have been offered a rump parliament like those of the past, based on fraudulent elections, convoked by a dictatorship, the instrument of a King who has already broken the Constitution. We do not covet the culminating drama of a revolution. But the misery of the people of Spain moves us greatly. Revolution will always be a crime or an act of insanity when Law and Justice exist. But it is always just when Tyranny prevails.

These republicans were men who not only opposed the idea that a single man, even if a Bourbon, could dismiss and appoint a prime minister, but who also saw in the idea of the abolition of the monarchy a step towards the modernization of Spain.

The sequel was swift. First, the garrison at Jaca, in Aragon, in the foothills of the Pyrenees, led by two zealous young officers, Captain Fermín Galán and Lieutenant García Hernández, rose against the monarchy before the conspirators in the rest of Spain gave the word.

1. *El Sol*, 15 November 1930.

Captured while marching their men in the direction of Saragossa, the two officers were shot for rebellion. The indignation at the executions was great. Elsewhere, the movement failed. A young captain in the air force, Ramón Franco (a national hero because of his flight in the *Non Plus Ultra* across the south Atlantic to Buenos Aires for the first time), set out to bomb the Royal Palace, hesitated, and dropped pamphlets instead; he then fled to Portugal. The signatories of the Pact of San Sebastián were arrested. When they were tried, they defended themselves by saying that the King had broken the constitution in accepting Primo de Rivera as dictator. From their much visited cells, the republicans' reputation grew. Several small parties were founded to raise enthusiasm for the monarchy: they failed to do so. Primo de Rivera's Patriotic Union became converted as the Monarchical Union, but defended the memory of the dictator, not the future of the King. General Berenguer offered elections. The idea was refused as insincere and the general, ill, resigned thankfully. After unsuccessful negotiations with politicians, the King named as Prime Minister another officer, Admiral Aznar, who was unknown and inexperienced. He and the King decided to test opinion by holding municipal, not general, elections in April. In the interim, student riots of a violent kind forced the civil guard on to the defensive.

These elections were held in an exuberant atmosphere, and assumed the character of a plebiscite. Huge meetings were addressed all over the country by would-be politicians of every sort. When the final results of the poll on 12 April began to come in, it was obvious that, in all the large towns of Spain, the candidates who supported the monarchy had been defeated. The size of the republicans' vote in Madrid and Barcelona (then with populations of 950,000 and 1 million respectively)[1] was enormous. In the country, the monarchy gained enough seats to secure for its friends a majority in the nation as a whole. But it was realized that, there, the *caciques* were powerful enough to prevent a fair vote.[2] In several places, a republic was pro-

1. Populations of other big cities in Spain in 1931 were: Valencia, 320,000; Seville, 229,000; Saragossa, 175,000; Málaga, 190,000; and Bilbao, 160,000.

2. The final figures were never published and were probably never counted. On the evening of 14 April, 29,953 monarchists had been elected, and 8,855 members of republican parties. Some 40,000 councillors remained to be elected. 29,804 councillors had already been elected on 5 April, in places where these candidates

claimed – the first being Eibar, in the Basque provinces. By the evening of 14 April, crowds were gathering in the streets of Madrid. The cabinet, aghast and intimidated, advised the King to accept the republican leaders' advice to leave the capital 'before sunset', to prevent bloodshed. Only one minister, Juan de la Cierva (the minister of the interior at the time of the 'Tragic Week' in 1909), wanted to resist. If the King had done so, he might have triumphed in Madrid, but he would have found the provincial capitals disposed to fight. A civil war might there and then have followed. After some hesitation, Alfonso, therefore, issued a dignified announcement:

> Sunday's elections have shown me that I no longer enjoy the love of my people. I could very easily find means to support my royal powers against all comers, but I am determined to have nothing to do with setting one of my countrymen against another in a fratricidal civil war. Thus, until the nation speaks, I shall deliberately suspend the use of my royal prerogatives.

With these grave and cryptic words, the King drove away from Madrid to the coast, and to exile.

The experiment of constitutional monarchy tried between 1874 and 1923 failed because it was a defensive political arrangement brought into effect in reaction to the revolutionary confusion of 1868–74. Its statesmen could, to begin with, play on the desire for survival (*ansia de vivir*), which affects even the poor, after an upheaval. The turbulence revived and Primo de Rivera could for a time count again on that conservative mood. He believed too that only an authoritarian system could preside over Spain's modernization. The succeeding years, more particularly after the flight of the King, were again tumultuous, despite their orderly beginning. Thus many came to believe that Primo de Rivera's work could be continued, in a more well-regulated manner; while others also sought authority, since they feared the future. For the time being, however, the destiny of Spain was in the hands of those who welcomed change and the opportunities it offered.

---

were unopposed. The overwhelming majority were monarchists – 8 to 1, according to Ben-Ami, whose account is the best (see S. Ben-Ami, *The Origins of the Second Republic*, Oxford thesis, 1974).

3

The coming of the Second Republic – Alcalá Zamora – the radicals – the republicans – Azaña – the Free Institute of Education – the Spanish socialists – the Catalan question – Cardinal Segura

'THIS young and eager Spain has at last arrived at its majority,' exclaimed the republicans rapturously in 1931: a strange comment on one of the oldest nation states and one which had already seen the failure of many attempts at regeneration. The republic was another such attempt. At first, it promised well. After all, the monarchy had been overthrown without bloodshed. A new government took over the ministries in Madrid with ease. The first Prime Minister of the republic was Niceto Alcalá Zamora, a barrister from Andalusia, with the flowery style of eloquence typical of that region. Warm-hearted, honest, erudite and confident, Alcalá Zamora was also vain and meddlesome, and, while in Madrid he appeared to love liberty more than life, he seemed the embodiment of the old-time political boss in Priego, his remote home town in the south. Once a minister of the King before Primo de Rivera's dictatorship, chairman of the revolutionary committee set up at San Sebastián, he and others of his cabinet were mobbed by cheering crowds as they drove slowly through Madrid towards the ministry of the interior. Both Don[1] Niceto and Miguel Maura,[2] who became minister of the interior and was, therefore, immediately responsible for the maintenance of order

1. 'Don' is somewhat like 'Esquire', though it is more democratic. It is rarely used in reference to anyone under forty, and it is employed in speech. It is a term of respect for any established person and may be used for a king ('Don Alfonso'), or a baker.

2. A son of Antonio Maura, and brother of the Duque de Maura, who had been a member of the King's last cabinet until 14 April. Miguel was regarded as the black sheep of this remarkable jewish-catholic family until his niece, Constancia de la Mora y Maura, married the republican air chief Hidalgo de Cisneros, and became a communist. See his story of the change of régime, *Así cayó Alfonso XIII . . .* (Mexico, 1962). A favourable impression of Alcalá Zamora is on p. 212f. Alcalá Zamora wrote memoirs, as yet (1976) unpublished.

in the country, were catholics. They could thus be regarded as expressing the acceptance by at least a party within the church of the end of monarchy. Was it not rumoured, after all, that 'the village priests had voted for the republic' in the famous municipal elections? (But the mayor of one small town had telegraphed the ministry of the interior: 'We have declared for the republic. What shall we do with the priest?')

The other members of the first cabinet of the republic were anti-clerical if not atheist. There were two members of the radical party, which had risen to notoriety in Barcelona in the early years of the century: first, Alejandro Lerroux, son of an Andalusian cavalry vet, the radicals' founder and, in the nineties, known as 'the Emperor of the Paralelo' (the roughest district of Barcelona), was, at sixty-seven, foreign minister of the republic. Age had cooled the passions of this corrupt demagogue. Willing to take a bribe from almost any government or offer one to almost any potential backer, enriched by business, he was no longer the man who had called on his followers in 1905 from the slums of Barcelona to rise against their employers and the church: 'Young barbarians of today! Enter and sack the decadent civilization of this unhappy country! Destroy its temples, finish off its gods, tear the veil from its novices and raise them up to be mothers! Fight, kill, and die!'[1] Lerroux was now an experienced orator, journalist and politician, sympathetic, even affectionate, to his friends, tactful, ever seeking a compromise – if only because he was anxious to be off to the theatre or a banquet. His party had split: many of those who had been radicals in 1910 had become socialists or anarchists. Lerroux was no longer a revolutionary, the radicals were not radical, and few remembered even the days when it was said that 'a Lerrouxista without his gun is like a catholic without his rosary'. His inclusion in the cabinet, with his moderate lieutenant, Diego Martínez Barrio, an arch-freemason from Seville,[2] however, caused some anxiety among the Spanish hierarchy which was none the less real for being unnecessary. A few years later, a catholic

1. *La Rebeldía* of 1 September 1906, quoted *Historia de la cruzada española* (ed. Joaquín Arrarás) (Madrid, 1940–43), vol. I, p. 44. (Henceforth referred to as *Cruzada*; references are to the folios rather than the volumes.) 'Young barbarians' was the nickname of the radical youth movement.

2. Speaker of the Cortes in 1936. See above, p. 8.

deputy summed up the radical party as being like the voyage of a ship: 'people of all ages and conditions, of the most diverse ideologies, brought together merely to travel'.[1]

There were, however, a more formidable group of anti-clerical politicians than these radicals, in the first ministry of the Second Republic. These were those middle-class or professional men who, representing thousands like them, were the heirs of the nineteenth-century liberal reformers of Spain. They were the men of the constitution of Cádiz of 1812, who had sought for a hundred years to limit the power of the religious orders, the great estates, and other restraints on mercantile freedom. They were men whose intellectual outlook had been either directly or indirectly formed by the Institución Libre de Enseñanza (Free Institute of Education), founded under the restoration as a free, and free-thinking, university, then as an enlightened school, by a group of university professors, who had refused to take an oath of loyalty to 'church, crown, and dynasty' and were, therefore, deprived of their teaching posts.[2] The state of mind inculcated by the Free Institute derived partly from admiration of English toleration, partly from the idealistic pantheism of the German philosopher Karl Krause, whose lectures the first leader of the dissident professors, Sanz del Río, had attended in Berlin. The Institute was at first anti-political. But there has not yet been a period in Spanish history when the advocacy of free thought has been a politically neutral act. Reluctantly, therefore, through their love of intellectual truth, these intellectuals, led by Sanz del Río's successor and disciple, Francisco Giner de los Ríos, were drawn into political attitudes. The Institute was also partly responsible for that renaissance of Spanish culture which followed the loss of the last American colonies in the Spanish American War of 1898 and whose prime mover was distress at Spanish backwardness, complacency and procrastination.[3] Later, the spirit of the Institute moved those who were the most formidable intellectual opponents of the dictatorship of

1. Jesús Pabón, *Palabras en la oposición* (Seville, 1935), p. 196.

2. See Vicente Cacho Viu, *La Institución Libre de Enseñanza* (Madrid, 1962).

3. This was the celebrated 'Generation of '98', associated loosely with the professor of Greek, Miguel de Unamuno; the social analyst, Ortega y Gasset; the social historian, Joaquín Costa; the essayist, Angel Ganivet; the poet of Castile, Antonio Machado; the eccentric Galician poet, Valle Inclán; the unpredictable publicist, Ramiro de Maeztu; the novelist, Pío Baroja; the essayist, Azorín; the

General Primo de Rivera. Their hope was that the personal contact between teacher and taught would become the model for the university and other 'institutes', since the existing establishment, and its college the 'Residencia' in Madrid (with its *junta* of further studies, designed to help Spanish students go abroad), could do no more than influence the middle-class leaders of the future.

These republicans were represented in the new cabinet of 1931 by several men. There was the minister of justice, Fernando de los Ríos, a nephew of Francisco Giner de los Ríos, himself professor at the University of Granada, theoretically a socialist but, with his flowing and beautiful Castilian speech, above all a humanist and too individual and gentle to be a reliable Marxist. There was the minister of marine, Casares Quiroga, the Galician lawyer who was to be Prime Minister at the start of the civil war.[1] There was the jacobin from Asturias, Alvaro de Albornoz, who, with the experienced Catalan republican, Marcelino Domingo, were leaders of what they called the Republican Radical Socialist party, modelled on the French party of Clemenceau and Ferry. They were ministers of 'development' and of education, respectively. There was, too, the new minister of war, Manuel Azaña, who, though not himself an old pupil of the Free Institute, reflects its effect.

Had he lived in a less turbulent country, Azaña might have given his life to literature. As it was, his brilliant translations from George Borrow, G. K. Chesterton, and Voltaire, an autobiographical novel about his schooldays, and a number of critical and polemical works are all that he left behind – save for a collection of speeches and a remarkable diary.[2] For he was drawn into politics by the conditions of his country. He regarded 'politics as an art, with the people as the palette'.[3] Azaña was born in 1880, in a house between two convents in Alcalá de Henares, the crumbling cathedral city twenty miles from Madrid, the birthplace of Cervantes. He came from a family known in Alcalá for public service and liberal politics. His mother died when

playwright, Benavente; and, perhaps, the painter Zuloaga; who were the leading intellectuals in Spanish universities about the year 1898. See Aldo Garosci, *Gli intellettuali e la guerra di Spagna* (Turin, 1959), p. 7. Carr (p. 525f.) is sceptical.

1. See above, p. 4.

2. Remarkable, since no other Spanish politician since 1810 has kept a diary.

3. A remark in *La velada en Benicarló*.

he was nine. Azaña lost his religious faith at the Augustinian college at the monastery of El Escorial against whose formal education he rebelled. He then took a law degree, and studied in Paris. He passed into the civil service, becoming chief clerk at the registration office (the Spanish equivalent of Somerset House). Living alone either at Alcalá or in Madrid, carrying on literary work, translating here, reviewing there, Azaña seemed representative of many other middle-class intellectuals of the period – and not only in Spain. Several things, however, marked out Azaña from others. First, he was ugly. His consequent self-consciousness led him to keep very much to himself, to subject himself to constant self-analysis in his writings and even in his speeches, to shun society (especially that of women), even to be scorned by his fellow-intellectuals – and, in consequence, to lay up within himself intellectual reserves which were to bring him to the leadership of Spain and which help to explain his bitter tongue and his lonely arrogance, shown in times both of victory and of defeat. Unamuno said that Azaña was capable of starting a revolution to ensure that his books would be read. Fastidious and sensitive to a degree, he was accused of being a homosexual, though there was no evidence for that. He did eventually marry, in 1929, at forty-nine, the much younger sister of Cipriano Rivas Cherif, his one-time collaborator on his literary magazine. He was also eloquent. He showed this first in many speeches at the Ateneo, the club in Madrid which had been the centre of progressive activity in Spain since the early nineteenth century. As a result, Azaña became connected with, and respected by, other republican leaders. His speeches were cold and monotonous, but fascinating and well constructed. He became editor of a political journal, *España*, the Ateneo's president, and then founded Republican Action, a republican party of his own. Azaña became minister of war in 1931, since no one else among the unmilitarily-minded liberals had troubled to inform themselves about the army. Immediately, Azaña sought in his speeches and conduct to imbue the new republic with a dignity which only time could really have given it, but which it needed immediately to be able to survive at all.

An admirer of Cromwell, Azaña knew no economics. He cultivated a superhuman detachment and an intellectual purity which led him to overlook some of the existing facts of Spanish life. Utterly unselfseeking, the enemies who quickly gathered were forced to personal insult in order to attack him. Yet at times thousands were to regard him as the 'strong man of the republic'. Adored by those who knew him well, he often seemed bitter, scornful and narrow-minded to his opponents. He chose men badly. He believed the republic should be radical or cease to exist. Always lucid, master of every subject on which he spoke, vacillating at critical moments, ironic in the face of disaster, given to bouts of dictatorial intransigence and of optimism tempered by despair, he was something of a physical coward though he took pains to conceal that fact. Azaña was the ablest and most cultivated of the republic's politicians. Unfortunately, the two strongest political drives in his mind were negative hostility to the church and to the power of the army.[1] He lacked a mass party and, therefore, had to choose in the first years of the republic whether to ally with Lerroux's radicals or with the socialists. He chose the latter.

Azaña, Domingo, and Albornoz stood for a republicanism which had grown vigorously in the last years of the dictatorship: 450 republican clubs, with a membership of nearly 100,000, had Azaña's views and outlook. Azaña inherited also many old liberals, who had played such an important part in the politics of the restoration. But this following was Azaña's only on sufferance: the anti-clerical petty bourgeoisie, artisans, teachers, doctors, civil servants, who voted for Azaña in 1931 could be, and were, tempted away both by more radical and more conservative leaders.[2] Azaña was certainly a statesman; but like other Spanish politicians of distinction, he found it hard to hold an elusive following. Nor was he an innovator; many of his policies had antecedents in the programmes of the liberals of Canalejas's time or in the ideas of the reformist republicans to which Azaña had himself for a time belonged. The 'republicans' were individuals, not party men: hence many of their difficulties.

In addition to Fernando de los Ríos, there were also two socialists in the first cabinet of the republic. These were Indalecio Prieto and Francisco Largo Caballero, the secretary general of the socialist

1. See his diaries in vols. III and IV of his *Obras completas* (Mexico, 1966–8).

2. Joaquín Maurín (*Revolución y contrarevolución en España*, Paris, 1966) argued that those who voted for Azaña in 1931 would, if they were young enough, form the support for the communist party in its 'bourgeois' incarnation between 1936 and 1939 (if old enough they would have voted for the liberals in 1910).

general trade union, the UGT.[1] The socialist party had some 20,000 members and the union a little less than 300,000.[2] Founded in 1879 by those Spaniards who supported Marx in his quarrel against the anarchists,[3] the growth of both party and union had, until just before the First World War, been slow. Neither could gain much foothold in industrial Barcelona, where the anarchists became so powerful. Hence the socialists found their members among the typographers and building workers of Madrid, among the coal miners of Asturias, and in the industrial areas growing up around Bilbao, particularly among unskilled non-Basque immigrants from Castile or Galicia, who, indeed, caused the first serious strikes in Spain, in the 1890s.

In 1908 the UGT, a small, rather ascetic, union organized on the English model with paid officials and carefully gathered strike funds, still had only about 40,000 members. The party numbered 6,000. Three new developments began to stimulate membership. The first, copied from the radical party, was the idea of the *casas del pueblo*, socialist club houses, in which were to be found the committee-rooms of the local trade-union branch, a free lending library, and a café. The barracks of the civil guard, the church, and the town hall were now accompanied in most of the cities and whitewashed *pueblos* of Spain by a fourth building, also, like them, the expression of a centralizing idea, but one combining Marxist thought with education. The second development was a tactical alliance with middle-class republicans, which gave the socialists a seat in the Cortes and hence brought the leaders into parliamentary politics. The third was the war of 1914–18, which brought prosperity to Spain, greater political consciousness, and greater interest in the affairs of the rest of Europe. Immigrants into the cities from the country were easily persuaded into socialism, particularly when the socialists supported workers in their struggle to avoid being called up to fight in Morocco. The socialists were consistently against Germany in the Great War, and were in touch with Cambó and others in their regeneratory schemes in 1917 with, as has been seen, temporarily bad results for them.[4] The socialists from that time on included many middle-class intellectuals

1. See above, p. 6.

2. 277,011 in 1930. The real figure may have been larger since this gives members who paid membership fees.

3. See below, p. 60.   4. See above, p. 22.

as well as workers. The UGT had by 1920 200,000 members. That year, the socialist party was first tempted by, and then broke with, the Russian bolsheviks.[1] A few socialists left to found, with certain discontented anarchists, the Spanish communist party, which remained, however, for a long time, insignificant.[2]

In 1925, the venerable, single-minded, patient and incorruptible father of the Spanish socialists, Pablo Iglesias, died. As a young printer, he had helped to achieve the break with Bakunin in 1872 and ever since had shrewdly and honourably led the party through innumerable vicissitudes. His successor, in the party and the UGT, was his chief lieutenant, Francisco Largo Caballero, a plasterer who had spent his life as a union official and as a conscientious member of the Madrid Municipal Council, successfully setting up sickness insurance schemes and libraries, arranging courses of lectures and negotiating with employers.[3] Aged sixty-two in 1931, Largo Caballero had taken part in Madrid's first strike of building workers, in 1890, and was a man without liking, or talent, for parliaments. He was no speaker. He believed in committees, not theories. He had given no encouragement to any who had wanted to strike when Primo de Rivera 'pronounced'. He had agreed to collaborate (even if briefly) with the dictatorship of Primo de Rivera as 'councillor of state'. The explanation for that was to be found in the socialists' contempt for the constitutional monarchy and in Largo's morbid fear of losing ground to his rivals in the working class, the anarchists, who, though disorganized, were still more numerous than the socialists. The UGT had, for a long time, been almost respected by the bourgeoisie for its discipline, its effective 'machine', with its myriad committees, its practical, even reasonable, behaviour in strikes (in contrast with the anarchists), and its centralist flavour. It was not surprising that Largo

1. At first, the socialists were in favour of affiliation to the Comintern. Before committing themselves, they dispatched Fernando de los Ríos to Russia as a *rapporteur*. 'But where is liberty?' asked that bearded individualist from Andalusia. 'Liberty,' replied Lenin, 'what for?' ('*La liberté? Pour quoi faire?*')

2. See below, p. 116.

3. See Francisco Largo Caballero, *Mis recuerdos, cartas a un amigo* (Mexico, 1954). In 1905, Iglesias and Largo Caballero had succeeded in being elected to the Madrid Municipal Council for the first time by emulating the electoral frauds perfected by their opponents. Iglesias entered the Cortes in 1910, and Largo Caballero, and several other socialists, followed in 1917.

Caballero should become the first minister of labour under the republic. The arbitration committees of employers, unions, and a governmental casting vote, which he had set up under Primo to resolve wage disputes, were the predecessors of a similar system which he introduced in 1931. Largo Caballero owed his popularity to the fact that thousands of Spanish workers saw in him a reflection of their own struggles; he was the man *par excellence* of the *casas del pueblo*, who had risen through his own fortitude, dour persistence and honesty, as well as a resolve to avoid intemperate revolutionary action.

Indalecio Prieto, his colleague in the republican cabinet – he was minister of finance – was a very different sort of socialist. Born in Oviedo, he removed as a child with his widowed mother to Bilbao, where he worked as a newsboy. His quick brain attracted the attention of a Basque millionaire, Horacio Echevarrieta, who made him first his *homme de confiance* and, later, editor of his newspaper, *El Liberal de Bilbao*. In 1918, Prieto was elected as a socialist to the Cortes where his easy eloquence attracted attention – and the jealousy of Largo Caballero. Thereafter, the antagonism between the two marked the Spanish socialist party, being itself the reflection of a genuine division of attitudes as to what sort of party it should be. Prieto had become prosperous. Bald, with a double chin and small eyes, his head set on a diabetic body of gigantic dimensions, he seemed, and behaved, more as an enlightened member of the upper classes than as a labour leader. 'The first quality of Prieto is his great heart,' wrote Miguel Maura of him. 'I have known few, tremendously few, people more self-sacrificing, more compassionate, more disinterested than Prieto.' He was mercurial, but surprisingly dedicated to party discipline. As a successful parliamentarian, he had opposed the socialist collaboration in the government of Primo de Rivera, and it had been he who had persuaded the socialists to join the conspiracy against the monarchy of 1930. Aged forty-eight in 1931, Prieto was popular with the middle class.[1] But, among workers, the sterner figure of Largo Caballero always commanded more affection.

The president of both the UGT and the party until 1931 was Julián Besteiro, the third most influential Spanish socialist, professor of philosophy and, though theoretically a Marxist, in party politics a

1. See Maura, p. 216.

moderate. But he was against the idea of the socialists serving in the government. As a result, he soon resigned from the presidency of both party and union. Besteiro was humane, friendly, wise, learned, but reserved; no one '*tutoyered*' him.[1]

The Spanish working class in the 1930s comprised 8 million, out of a population of 24 million. About 4½ million (54.5 per cent) worked on the land; and the socialists, as yet, had little following among them, though they soon would. The socialists had also still little following in Catalonia, where nearly three-quarters of Spanish industry was concentrated. But if they had in consequence few members in Spain's largest industries – the 300,000 who worked in the clothes manufacturing and the textile industries – they had considerable backing among the 270,000 builders, the 200,000 who worked in food industries, the 100,000 miners, and the 120,000 metallurgical workers. They also had strength among the 60,000 transport workers, and among the half million or so artisans.

The last member of the republican cabinet of 1931 was a Catalan classical historian, Nicolau d'Olwer, who became minister of 'the national economy'. Though he had been active in Catalan politics in the 1920s, he was less of a professional politician than anyone in the cabinet; his inclusion in it was intended to please the Catalan nationalists. As an economist, it was said of him, he was 'a great hellenist'.

Five of the members of this government had one attribute in common: they were freemasons and, therefore, suspected by their conservative enemies of anti-Spanish loyalties.[2]

In the nineteenth century, most Spanish liberals had been members of one or other of the masonic lodges which, though introduced into Spain in the eighteenth century, spread during the Napoleonic Wars. In the twentieth century, progressive persons seem, in Spain and elsewhere on the continent, to have felt obliged to join a lodge largely as a gesture. Although they subscribed to the French revolutionary principles of liberty, equality and fraternity on their induction masons, however, formed a secret society without any real policy.

1. Gil Robles, p. 448.

2. Joaquín Arrarás, *Historia de la segunda república española* (Madrid, 1956–64), vol. I, p. 53. The five were de los Ríos, Martínez Barrio, Alvaro de Albornoz, Casares Quiroga, and Marcelino Domingo. Azaña became a mason early in 1932.

Yet though without overt political purposes, Spanish masonry was anti-religious as well as anti-clerical.[1] Since to disbelieve in God in Spain was an act with political consequences, churchmen and the Right believed masonry to be a devilish international plot, organized in the City of London, yet designed to establish atheistic communism. To the Jesuits, masonry seemed especially vile since its secret ways appeared a profane parody of their own order.[2] Such hostility, of course, would be likely to increase the secretiveness of the masons. But the freemasons of Spain did not, even so, have any political front. The French masons may have financed anti-clericalism in other countries and the Spanish lodges were useful meeting-places for plotting against Primo de Rivera. But later, there were divisions within them. Some generals, such as Goded, Queipo de Llano, and Cabanellas, belonged to a military lodge, many of whose members were fervent republicans. The relation of masonry to Marxism was also hotly debated. Men of the Free Institute were rarely freemasons. The freemasons cannot, therefore, be regarded as of determining importance in the 1930s, though some politicians, such as Martínez Barrio, did owe much of their influence to their rank in the masonic order.[3]

*

The problem of Catalonia was the first with which the new republic had to deal. The four provinces of Catalonia had enjoyed a medieval past of prosperous independence and commercial pre-eminence upon

1. It seems that there was a breach between English and continental masons in the 1880s, when the continental brothers decided that they could no longer stomach any reference to God, even under the name of the 'Supreme Architect', in the statutes of their order.

2. Since many distinguished people became masons who could not be accused of being secret communists, the clerical publicists were obliged to distinguish between those who were blind instruments in the hands of 'the terrible brother', and those who knew his dark purposes.

3. There is a useful account of Spanish freemasonry in *La Révolution espagnole vue par une républicaine* (Paris, 1937), by a woman deputy of the radical party, Clara Campoamor. See also Gabriel Jackson, *The Spanish Republic and the Civil War 1931–1939* (Princeton, 1965), p. 510. The catholic deputy, Gil Robles (p. 94), gives an enumeration of Spanish masons which must presumably reflect what he and the church thought were the right numbers: of the total of a little over 11,600, 3,660 were natives of Cádiz, suggesting the importance of that port in the eighteenth or nineteenth century, more than the twentieth.

which it was easy for romantics to dwell. Industrialization and the spread of literacy in the nineteenth century, as has been seen, created a desire for home rule which, when thwarted, turned into a nationalist movement. Richer than any other part of the Peninsula, with a modern class structure and a Mediterranean culture, Catalonia might have been prosperous within a Spanish federal state. It was certain to be rebellious within the centralized, unimaginative Bourbon structure. Hostility to free trade and desire for protection, played a part in the rise of Catalan nationalism. Catalans also believed themselves a 'vital member' attached to the 'dying body' of Castile.

Catalanism, however, owed its strength to a combination of this economic interpretation with a literary renaissance expressed by the Floral Games which had begun in 1859, the poetic competitions in Catalan, as well as by the works of several poets, headed by the romantic priest Verdaguer. In the early years of the twentieth century, Catalonia's economic importance was increased by the development of hydro-electric power in the eastern Pyrenees. Power was brought to Madrid and Valencia from Catalonia, while the electricity supply itself was concentrated in the large North American financed and owned 'La Canadiense' (the Barcelona Traction Company). Meantime, the Bible was translated into Catalan by the monks of the Benedictine monastery of Montserrat, a flood of original and translated literature poured from Catalan presses, a vast dictionary was compiled, and many newspapers were founded. Catalan was more widely spoken than ever, and became the customary language of town councils. Excursions to rediscover inland Catalonia, the cult of the national dance (the 'Sardana'), the creation of popular choirs, even the adoption of a national deity (Mare de Déu de Montserrat) were the cultural manifestations of a strong political nationalism which, despite setbacks, still held the loyalty in 1931 of most of the Catalan middle class. The church gave some backing for the Catalan movement, largely for the negative reason that Catalanism was anti-liberal in the sense that all regional movements had once been so. But the federalism into which Catalanism might easily fit was nevertheless more Left than Right.

There were a multitude of political parties in Catalonia, each dominated by people who, to a lesser or greater degree, rejected the authority of the Castilian unitary state. No party, admittedly, had

had much of a history under Primo de Rivera, either in Catalonia or elsewhere. Even the centres of the once promising party of the Catalan bourgeoisie, the Lliga Regionalista, had been closed. But the triumph of the anti-monarchists in the municipal elections of April 1931 was even greater at Barcelona than elsewhere. To be precise, furthermore, the victory there had been gained by the Esquerra, a new party whose name was the Catalan word for 'left'. Its leader was an elderly, honourable, romantic colonel, Francisco Maciá, 'el avi' (the grandfather), who had spent the years of Primo's dictatorship plotting in France, Latin America and even Moscow. The leader apart, the Esquerra was a party of intellectuals, small businessmen and of the lower middle class of Barcelona.[1] By 1930, the Catalan industrialists had been frightened by the actions of the anarchists in their factories between 1917 and 1923, and by the failure of so many brave enterprises, into alliance with the Spanish orthodox Right. The Catalan upper class had once hoped to regenerate Spain through the revival of Catalonia. Their leader, Cambó, had fought the old local *caciques* at the beginning of the century.[2] But now he fought the Left and radicals. The Catalan movement had, on several occasions, united both Left and Right in the nationalist cause (notably in the alliance of Solidaridad Catalana in 1906) but the chance of a revival of that common front was now remote.

In 1913, the provincial councils of the four Catalan provinces had

1. The Esquerra Republicana de Catalunya, to give it its full name, was a combination of an old, mainly lower-middle-class radical party, the Partit Republica Catalanista (PRC); Estat Catalá, a group of separatists, headed by Maciá; and a group of Catalan socialists formed around the journal, *L'Opinió*. Other Catalan parties active in 1931 included Acció Catalá (deriving from a Lliga youth split in 1922), which did badly in the elections. The Lliga and radicals came a bad second and third to the Esquerra, which had included, in its manifesto, the phrase 'the socialisation of wealth for the benefit of the community', thereby attracting some of the revolutionary Left. Maciá, the best-known man on the Catalan Left, had been dismissed from the army in 1906 for attacking the Law of Jurisdictions (see below, p. 92).

2. Tomás Pamiés, in his *Testamento de Praga* (Barcelona, 1970) recalls (p. 53) that he first heard the word 'revolution' in the speeches of a group of strangers who had come to Balaguer (Lérida) in 1908: one speaker was Cambó. Pamiés joined the 'revolutionaries' and became subsequently an anarchist, then a communist and, after twenty-five years' exile, died as municipal gardener in Prague in 1968.

been merged, under Canalejas's law, for some of their functions, into a precursor of autonomy, the *Mancomunidad*, which had not affected Spanish sovereignty. It had been abolished by Primo. Would it now be restored? Or would the Esquerra go further? Manuel Carrasco Formiguera, a Catalan lawyer, called on Catalonia 'to declare war on Spain'. When the elected councillors in 1931 came out onto a balcony in the Plaza San Jaime, there were heard not only the 'Marseillaise' and 'Els Segadors', the Catalan national anthem, but also cries for an independent Catalan republic. Luis Companys, Maciá's lieutenant, a young lawyer (who had gained a reputation in the early 1920s for defending anarchists for nugatory fees) proclaimed the republic as 'the Catalan republic'; and Maciá spoke of 'the Catalan state and republic' from the same balcony an hour later. So Nicolau d'Olwer and Marcelino Domingo (both by birth Catalans) with Fernando de los Ríos made a hasty visit to Barcelona to persuade Maciá to await the passage of a Catalan statue of home rule by the new Cortes (which would shortly be elected). Maciá agreed, although Barcelona was in his hands. No doubt he was wise to be patient, since Barcelona was far from having only Catalan inhabitants: over a third of the city's population had been born outside Catalonia. Their political views could not be guessed.[1]

The honeymoon of the new republic lasted a month. During this time, the republic was caricatured in the press as *la niña bonita*, the pretty girl, in the style of the happy Marianne north of the Pyrenees; she had first appeared as representing the constitution of Cádiz in 1812. The government made plans for an election in June for a provisional Cortes. That would approve a constitution. Meanwhile, the royal flag of red and gold was changed for a tricolour in red, yellow and purple, the royal national anthem was altered from the 'Royal March' to the 'Hymn of Riego' (the constitutionalists' song in 1820), and many streets were rechristened with republican names. Companys, who became the first republican civil governor of Barcelona, destroyed police records of anarchists and common criminals alike. The government published plans for thousands of new primary schools and, on 6 May, decreed that henceforth religious instruction was no longer obligatory in state schools: it would be 'available' to

1. Alberto Balcells, *Crisis económica y agitación social en Cataluña (1930–1936)* (Barcelona, 1971), p. 18.

those whose parents requested it. The change was a startling one in Spain.

The enemies of the republic were, nevertheless, gathering. The anarchists took advantage of Maciá's benevolent attitude to them and of the lurch of the country away from authoritarianism to settle some old scores in Barcelona, despite their national leadership's declaration that they were against a return to terrorism. The republic carried out, meantime, no purge of either the national or the local administration, nor of the police, the teachers and government agencies. The judiciary remained the same. So, of course, did the army. This combination of inexperienced, reformist politicians and a conservative governmental structure left many difficulties ahead.

Then, though the great depression had been less severe in Spain than in the more advanced industrial countries, it did present great difficulties all the same, particularly in the mining areas. During the course of 1931, the effect of the depression would begin to be felt in Catalonia. Meantime, the return of many workers from abroad, particularly from the Americas, would exacerbate unemployment in the poorer regions, such as Galicia and Andalusia. In the country, unemployment would always be twice as severe as, if less noticed than, in the towns. Yet at this time Spain had no unemployment relief, and her social services generally were rudimentary in comparison with what existed in northern Europe.[1] Finally, the first shot in a contest between church and state which was to continue until the civil war was the grave but violent pastoral letter of Cardinal Segura, archbishop of Toledo and primate of the Spanish Church, made public at the beginning of May. This determined prelate combined intelligence with obstinacy. A bishop at thirty-five, he had been translated from his wild Estremaduran diocese by the special intervention of the King. He was a scholar who boasted of three doctorates, and, when he undertook social work once a year, he worked as hard as a parish priest. In 1931, he was still under fifty, and at the height of his powers. His pastoral letter began with a eulogy of Alfonso XIII and ended with these threatening words:

If we remain 'quiet and idle', if we allow ourselves to give way to 'apathy and timidity'; if we leave open the way to those who are attempting to

1. The general economic history of the republic is discussed on p. 186, below. See Balcells, p. 10.

destroy religion, or if we expect the benevolence of our enemies to secure the triumph of our ideals, we shall have no right to lament when bitter reality shows us that we had victory in our hands, yet knew not how to fight like intrepid warriors prepared to succumb gloriously.[1]

1. *El Sol*, 7 May 1931. 'Quiet and idle', and 'apathy and timidity' were phrases used in an encyclical of Leo XIII. Segura hated fascism and was a friend of England in the Second World War.

4

The church in Spain in 1931 – its role in Spanish history – the church and education – relations with the Vatican – El Debate

THE church in Spain in the 1930s included about 20,000 monks, 60,000 nuns, and 35,000 priests. There were nearly 5,000 religious communities, of which about 1,000 were male, the rest female.[1] Two-thirds of the Spaniards in the 1930s were, however, not practising catholics – that is, though they might use churches for baptisms, weddings, and funerals, they never confessed or went to mass. According to a Jesuit, Father Francisco Peiró, only 5 per cent of the rural population of New Castile carried out their Easter duties in 1931. In some villages of Andalusia, only 1 per cent of men attended church.[2] In some villages, the priest said mass alone. In the rich parish of San Ramón, in Madrid's suburb of Vallecas, 90 per cent of those educated in religious schools did not confess or attend mass after leaving school.[3] Though figures in the country were very different, those quoted give statistical support to the unwise remark of Manuel Azaña that Spain had 'ceased to be catholic'.[4]

Azaña meant that Spain was no longer totally catholic, as she had seemed, for instance, in the golden sixteenth century. At that time, the church alone had united the provinces. The Spanish Inquisition, instituted as the tribunal of religious orthodoxy, was the only legal

1. *Anuario Estadístico de España*, 1931, pp. 664–5. See José M. Sánchez, *Reform and Reaction* (Chapel Hill, 1964).

2. Spanish women are much more religious than men, one more sign of the dominant feminine position in the church expressed by the part allotted in Spain to the Virgin Mary, so extreme as to verge on mariolatry.

3. Quoted Gerald Brenan, *The Spanish Labyrinth* (Cambridge, 1943), p. 53.

4. Speech of 13 October 1931 in *Obras completas*, vol. III, p. 51. Azaña's diary for that day, though it notes the approval with which the speech was received, did not indicate that he was aware of having said anything likely to be used against him. See vol. IV, p. 177: 'the speech went very well, like a dream, and I was measuring the effect of it, word by word . . . Lerroux . . . covered me with eulogies'. If Azaña had said that Spain had ceased to be clerical, he would have been more accurate.

body to be respected throughout the land. Financed by the wealth brought by the American colonies, the Habsburg kings had sought to realize a catholic cultural and political unity in Europe never achieved even at the height of the middle ages. The powerful Spanish armies had been used in a new attempted *Reconquista* – that of Europe from the protestants and of the Mediterranean from the Turks. The Spanish king had proudly buckled on the temporal sword of the counter-reformation, while the Society of Jesus, founded by the Basque Ignatius and always retaining Spanish characteristics, became its theological leaders.

The golden century of Spain, therefore, when that country joined forever the ranks of those which have been once, however briefly, the greatest on earth, marked also the apogee of the Spanish church. While the church was the link binding the nation together geographically, it also did so socially. Spanish theologians were freed by the absence of a reformation from the arguments about forms of service which wearied the north of Europe. They, therefore, could discuss, in almost modern terms, the relations between citizen and society, and even argue as to the desirability of a more equal distribution of land. Great nations decline, however, for the same reasons which earlier raised them above others. The bastard-medieval aspirations of the Habsburgs exhausted the treasury. The Spanish church's hostility to commerce, in addition to the ease with which gold and silver could be imported from America, extinguished the economic vitality of Spain. The tension between christians and newly converted jews (*conversos*) gave the intellectual controversies of this period an almost racist flavour; the 'golden century' turned leaden long before it was over. Cervantes, writing when the economic consequences of the furious Spanish pursuit of grandeur were being already felt, made Don Quixote, the greatest character in Spanish literature, the archetype of the knight errant in search of vain glory; and the quixotic maintenance of a medieval set of judgements in the new world of post-renaissance Europe swiftly became the mark of the country which had been the first to reveal the real New World beyond the Atlantic. The ideas of social justice preached by the theologians reinforced a pre-commercial outlook as much reminiscent of scholasticism as anticipatory of socialism. The intellectual decline of the church continued, so that learned men in the greatest university of

Spain, at Salamanca, were solemnly discussing, in the eighteenth century, what language the angels spoke and whether the sky was made of wine-like fluid or bell metal.[1] During these years, there was hardly a single protestant in Spain, and hardly a single critic of the church's hold over the mind of the nation. Spain possessed, until the eighteenth century, the largest empire in the world. But Spanish culture became, like the customs of the court, over-formal, and declined after the death of Velázquez in 1660. The free institutions of the provinces, once the most living of Spanish things, decayed under the dead hand of the bureaucracy of the Habsburgs and their Bourbon descendants.

In the eighteenth century, the ideas of the French *philosophes* began to be popular at the court of the Spanish Bourbons. But, after the collapse of the Bourbons in the Napoleonic Wars, the church, gaining popularity from its opposition to Napoleon, became the centre of resistance to liberal ideas. Its most violent protagonists grouped themselves into the Society of the Exterminating Angel. The First Carlist War followed. During this era, the low level of clerical intellect persisted.

The liberals' greatest success was to disentail the church lands in 1837. Though the church received compensation, it was in cash. The land could not be repurchased from the middle-class speculators who had bought it up. Henceforth, though the church maintained an implacable opposition to liberal ideas, its hold over the working class was reduced.[2]

The development of the Free Institute of Education in the late nineteenth century, coincided with, or was inspired by, a revival of the church. The losing battle which Rome had fought in France, Germany, and Italy in the last quarter of the nineteenth century

1. Antonio Ballesteros, *Historia de España*, vol. VI (Barcelona, 1919–36), p. 288, qu. Brenan, p. 117.

2. By the Concordat of 1851, still in operation in 1931, the church accepted disentailment, agreed to the sale of church lands (provided the profits were invested in state bonds and distributed to the clergy) and accepted the state's nomination of bishops. In return, the church's right to acquire any kind of property was accepted, catholicism was reaffirmed as 'the only religion' in Spain, the church was given the right to direct the conscience of state schools, the state paid to keep up church buildings and, above all, churchmen received stipends from the state, virtually as civil servants, ranging from 160,000 reales for archbishops, to 2,200 for rural priests.

caused the elaboration of a policy to keep at least one country – Spain – 'safe from liberal atheism'. Thousands of Spanish clergy returned from Cuba or the Philippines. The orders multiplied. Many French and, later, Portuguese priests came too. A burst of religious building followed, with the consolidation of the church's wealth in capital. The Jesuits and Marianist fathers were, rightly, believed to hold vast fiefs in all sorts of concerns, from antique-furnishing businesses to, later, dance-halls and cinemas. The interpretation put by the orders upon the modernizing encyclicals of Popes Leo XIII and Pius XI was, indeed, that they permitted the clerical accumulation of clerical capital. A prominent Catalan businessman made a famous calculation in 1912 that the orders controlled a third of the capital in the country. In a popular catechism published in 1927, the question 'What kind of sin is committed by one who votes for a liberal candidate?' elicited the answer, 'Generally a mortal sin'. But the answer to 'Is it a sin for a catholic to read a liberal newspaper?' was, 'He may read the Stock Exchange News'.[1] Yet the new catholicism was not a cynical movement. Though it favoured the status quo and the better off, it was charitable, evangelical, educational: above all, educational. Certain orders, especially the Jesuits and the Augustinians, had excellent, if conventional, secondary schools (such as that at El Escorial, where Azaña was educated).

Between 1909 and 1917, the main political argument in Spain had been that over the church's role in secondary and higher education. The state claimed to provide primary education free to all and, in every provincial capital, there was a state secondary school often poor in quality. But the schoolmasters were mainly catholics, and children spent much time saying the rosary. (Schools were too few – in 1930 in Madrid alone there were 80,000 children who did not go to school.) Through its authority in the state schools as well as those run by orders, the church was able to maintain its influence over the young. The liberals' attempt to change this had won some concessions but, in the end, failed. As in France at the turn of the century, the position of the church in both the education and hence the general culture of the country was becoming a matter of obsession for those who rejected it. Workers came to think of the orders' mis-

1. *Nuevo Ripaldo enriquecido con varios apéndices* (14th ed., Madrid, 1927), p. 117.

sions in working-class suburbs as the most pernicious of evils, particularly if they had a state subsidy and even more if, under the guise of education, they seemed to peddle a false ethic to the ignorant. Intellectuals such as Manuel Azaña or the young film maker, Luis Buñuel, could not forget the church, even if they rejected religion.

As for the church, when Cardinal Segura made his attack on the republic in May 1931, he did not speak for all his flock. The political feelings of the Spanish church were too contradictory to be summed up in one strong letter. Many members of the hierarchy and the orders might be as monarchist as the primate, through fear of what might come rather than from loyalty to what had passed away. But the group of intellectual catholics who wrote for the Madrid newspaper *El Debate* favoured a more liberal catholicism which might perhaps capture the urban proletariat for the church or make some concessions towards democracy. Cardinal Segura had denounced *El Debate* as a 'liberal rag'. A controversy broke out between *El Debate* and the monarchist *ABC* during the first weeks of the republic over the 'accidentalist' interpretation which the first gave to the republic: namely, that, while the church was eternal, forms of government were temporal. *ABC* regarded this attitude as cowardly.

Thus no clear statement can be made of the political attitude of the church as such. It was true, certainly, that, since the confiscation of ecclesiastical lands during the previous century, the orders and the hierarchy had been capitalists. But many individual monks and most priests (except for those in fashionable quarters of large cities) received as small a wage as their parishioners.[1] The hierarchy was rightly regarded as the ally of the upper classes. But the village priest, and even the priest in a poor part of a big town, was often looked upon as a comparatively amiable counsellor, one who could, sometimes with success, intervene with the authorities on behalf of the oppressed.[2] The Spanish working class, however, were maddened when a priest openly showed himself hypocritical, by flagrantly contradicting Christ's teaching on poverty, or showing himself a respecter of well-born persons. Then no fate would be considered too unpleasant for him, and his church would be in danger of fire. (Asked

1. This, of course, helped to maintain their low intellectual level.

2. This was especially the case in the Basque provinces of the north of Spain. See below, p. 86.

for the keys of his church by anarchist incendiarists during the events of 1909, the priest of Palomós replied: 'Certainly, let's burn the church, but let's also burn the factory. Both of us will thus lose our daily bread. Let's begin with the factory.' The priest started off down the hill, but neither edifice was burned.)[1] During the riots of 1909, the working class of Barcelona showed complete ignorance of, as well as interest in, what transpired in nunneries. Some of these mysterious buildings were supposed to harbour the bodies of martyred girls, as well as stocks and shares. But the corpse exposed in the school of the sisters of the Immaculate Conception in Puerto Seco turned out to be that of the embalmed Leonor of Aragon who died before 1450. It was also widely supposed that nuns must be rich if they were able to live such a contemplative life. Every nunnery was thus held to be a 'conspiracy against democracy'.

It was always rare, even in moments of revolution, for villagers to kill their own priest or to burn his church, unless he was known as a friend of the bourgeoisie. In these circumstances, even then, the act would often be left to people who might come in from other *pueblos*. It was certainly uncommon for Spaniards to destroy the effigy of a local Virgin or a local church. The archbishop of Valladolid once remarked that 'these people would be ready to die for their local Virgin, but would burn that of their neighbours at the slightest provocation'.[2] Still, in the Tragic Week of 1909, workers carried away with hatred of religion had beheaded and quartered religious images, prised open tombs, sought above all to destroy. The secretive orders continued to be held responsible for every cataclysm; a belief which suited, and was stimulated by, anarchists and republican anti-clericals alike.

The Spanish church in the twentieth century embarrassed the Vatican. The public demonstrations of fanaticism and superstition were far from showing a true religious spirit.[3] Pope Pius XI was in 1931 at least as liberal as the Madrid writers on *El Debate*. His secretary of state, Eugenio Pacelli, was already toying with those ideas for christian democratic parties which he brought to more suc-

1. José Brissa, *La revolución de julio en Barcelona* (Barcelona, 1910), p. 185, qu. Ullman, p. 324.

2. Recollection of Father Alberto Onaindía.

3. Azaña's comment, in his *Causas de la guerra de España* (*Obras*, vol. III, p. 464).

cessful fruition when Pope (as Pius XII) after the Second World War. When, on 22 May 1931, the government issued a decree proclaiming religious freedom, Cardinal Segura travelled to Rome, where Pope Pius suggested to him that the tactful caution of the nuncio, Monsignor Tedeschini, was the best policy for the church in Spain. But Segura made a public attack from Rome on the government. His reputation was not enhanced when, a month later, he returned secretly across the Pyrenees, without passing a customs post. He reached Guadalajara before being apprehended. The government then escorted him from the country, under guard. (It had become known that Segura had been interested in selling ecclesiastical treasures to help the church to build up a fund with which to fight the republic.) The cardinal did not return to Spain until after the start of the civil war. After some delicate diplomacy, Monsignor Gomá, a scholar who had been bishop of Tarazona, was named to succeed him as primate and archbishop of Toledo.[1]

Herrera and his friends on the newspaper *El Debate*, meantime, launched a constitutional catholic movement, National Action (Acción Nacional), in late April 1931, whose purpose was an electoral organization to bring together 'the elements of order'. But some of the members of this supposedly 'liberal' party, such as Antonio Goicoechea and the Conde de Vallellano, were almost authoritarian monarchists. The poet José María Pemán, the 'man of ideas' in Primo's Patriotic Union, also a member, was a romantic in love with the past.[2] It seemed an unpromising beginning to Spain's first con-

1. The Vatican soon quarrelled with the republic by refusing to accept the ambassador, Luis de Zulueta, whom the government had named for the Holy See. Cardinals Gomá and Segura met on 23 July 1934 in France and had a curious discussion, in which they agreed Pope Pius XI was a man 'without affection, cold and calculating', who had too much sympathy for Catalonia and was being misled by Angel Herrera and Cardinal Vidal y Barraquer, the archbishop of Tarragona. (Juan de Iturralde, *El catolicismo y la cruzada de Franco*, Bayonne, France, 1955, vol. I, p. 265.) For speculation that Angel Herrera and Monsignor Tedeschini, the papal nuncio, encouraged the expulsion of Segura, see Iturralde, vol. I, p. 344f. Tedeschini was liberal-minded, and, when he first came to Spain in 1921, had helped to create a still-born Spanish version of the Italian Partito Popolare. See Javier Tusell, *Historia de la democracia cristiana en España* (Madrid, 1974), vol. I, p. 104f.

2. It is evident that, at a local level, National Action represented a drawing together of local landowning or industrial interests. National Action soon had to

servative party with a mass movement; yet such it eventually became, playing on the fears of those who were outraged by the growing anti-clericalism of the government and its friends.

Anti-clericalism was understandable in Spain in the 1930s, and the liberals who were moved by the cause of removing the stranglehold of catholicism over education and culture were acting within a great nineteenth-century tradition. But the real cultural problem in Spain was lack of education. Nearly twenty Spanish provinces, for example, had an illiteracy rate of 50 per cent or over and only two provinces (Barcelona and the Basque province of Alava) had one less than 25 per cent. Madrid had 26 per cent. It would have been wiser, and more long-sighted, if the republic had concentrated on the creation of new schools, rather than attacking orders which maintained good if exclusive ones already, however much Azaña had been distressed by Father Montes at the Augustinian school. Further, like it or not, the church in Spain did incorporate a long tradition in Spanish life; indeed, it had created the pattern of that life. It was easy, therefore, to represent anti-clericalism as being an element of 'anti-Spain': which many did.

---

change its name to Popular Action, when the government pettily insisted that the word 'National' was not to be used for other than government enterprises.

5

The riots of May 1931 – the burning of the churches – the monarchists' plots – character of Spanish anarchism

On Sunday 10 May 1931, within a few days of the publication of Cardinal Segura's pastoral letter, a group of army officers and aristocrats believed to be specially loyal to King Alfonso were observed gathering at a house in the Calle Alcalá, one of the main streets of Madrid. Nominally, they were merely founding the Independent Monarchist Club 'to serve as a link between the elements wishing to work for the substantive ideals of monarchy'. It was a right-wing, monarchist response to the 'liberal' catholics' National Action. But the 'Royal March' was played on a gramophone. A crowd gathered. Two monarchists (one of them was the Marqués Luca de Tena, editor of *ABC*, the monarchist daily newspaper) who arrived late, were delighted by the number of people in the street, and shouted '*¡Viva la Monarquía!*' Their taxi-driver replied by crying '*¡Viva la República!*' The monarchists protested to the driver, and a rumour immediately spread that they had killed him. The crowd became infuriated, and set fire to several motor-cars of the monarchists attending the meeting inside. In a moment, the number of people in the street seemed to increase one hundredfold. The republic's honeymoon was over. An angry crowd set out for the offices of *ABC*, which they proceeded to burn. The minister of the interior, Miguel Maura, threatened to resign unless he was able to call out the civil guard,[1] but the government understandably hesitated. Azaña said that all the convents of Madrid were not worth one republican life. The crowds eventually dispersed. But the next day, the riots took on a new lease

1. See below, p. 77. Maura's account is the best (p. 241f.) Cf. also Azaña, vol. IV, p. 303. He places some blame on the liberal monarchist general, Carlos Blanco, who surprisingly was the government's new director-general of security. For the monarchist side of the story, see Juan Ignacio Luca de Tena, *Mis amigos muertos* (Barcelona, 1971), p. 97f. The monarchists were besieged in the club from 12.30 till 5 p.m.

of life. The Jesuit church in the Calle de la Flor, in the centre of Madrid, was burned to the ground. On its charred walls the words 'The Justice of the People on Thieves' were chalked up.[1] Several other churches and convents in Madrid were also burned during the day.[2] Within a few days the fires had spread to Andalusia, especially to Málaga. Maura got permission to use the army instead of the hated civil guard, and martial law was proclaimed. There was widespread alarm all over Spain. No one died, though several monks escaped only just in time. Even so, the republic had clearly stained its record. Some hundred churches had been damaged throughout Spain. The government publicly blamed the monarchists for provoking the riot, and suspended not only *A B C* but also *El Debate*.

Some of those gathered in the house in the Calle Alcalá would no doubt have liked an insurrection against the republic. They did not have, for this, the approval of King Alfonso (then in Paris), who had encouraged his friends (including army officers) to serve the republic.[3] Some days before, he had given a dignified interview to *A B C*, in which he had said: 'Monarchists who wish to follow my advice will not only refrain from placing obstacles in the government's path, but will support it in all patriotic policies. High above the formal idea of the republic or the monarchy stands Spain.'[4] Though, no doubt, he saw this method as the best means of being able to return to the Spanish throne, Don Alfonso obviously did not wish to make matters impossible for the new government. As a result, the vast majority of the officers of the army, air force and navy took an oath to the new régime.[5] But some had no intention of working with the repub-

1. Lawrence Fernsworth, *Spain's Struggle for Freedom* (Boston, 1957), p. 131.

2. All religious houses in Spain, whether lived in by monks or nuns, are known as '*conventos*'. Among the fires was one in the archives of the Colegio de Santo Tomás de Villanueva in Valencia, a seminary in which Earl Hamilton, the historian of price rises in the sixteenth century, was then at work. The burnings in Málaga seem partly to have been due to the incompetence of the civil governor, Antonio Jaén, a friend of Alcalá Zamora's, and to the negligence of the military governor, General Gómez Caminero.

3. Juan Antonio Ansaldo, *¿Para qué . . . ?* (Buenos Aires, 1951), p. 15.

4. *A B C*, 5 May 1931.

5. See below, p. 92. On 25 April, Azaña had issued a decree allowing all officers who wished to do so to retire on full pay. This over-zealously fair act merely created a number of unemployed officers with means and time to plot against the new régime.

lic.[1] The leading spirits among these potential plotters were Generals Orgaz, Cavalcanti, and Ponte. Others active were the Marqués de Quintanar, busy looking for money; Ramiro de Maeztu, once a member of the Generation of 1898, who had since then been attracted by anarchism, been also an ambassador, a journalist, and was now almost a fascist; the Carlist intellectual, Víctor Pradera; and young monarchists, such as Sáinz Rodríguez, enormously fat ('a latifundium of flesh', as he was once described), erudite, and bohemian. These conspirators soon decided to form a new and legal monarchist party; they would found, under the inspiration of *Action Française* in France, a review *Acción Española* (not to be confused with the party known as Acción Nacional) under Ramiro de Maeztu's editorship, which would publicly argue in favour of an insurrection against the republic (the editorial office would also form a centre of studies to 'collect texts on the question of the legality of an insurrection'); and they would found an organization to create 'the ambience of revolution' in the army.[2] Other right-wing political groups were soon in being: Acción Castellana; a Valencian regional Right movement headed by an ex-Carlist journalist, Luis Lucía; and an agrarian party of Castilian landowners. The old Carlist movement was also busy.[3] Other monarchists discussed how they could disrupt the government's economic policy by encouraging the flight of capital. These Spanish monarchists of the 1930s were influential, rich, more authoritarian than the King whose cause they nominally supported, and certainly showed much more imagination in their efforts to overthrow the republic than they had in trying to defend the King.[4]

As for those who protested against them that Sunday morning in 1931, some were simply citizens of Madrid walking down the main street of the capital: a frequent custom on Sunday morning. But the careful church-burnings (and the burning of the headquarters of *ABC*) were probably the work of anarchists.[5]

1. None of these early plotters against the republic seems to have taken the required oath to serve and defend it.

2. The plots against the republic now have an ample literature. See Paul Preston, *The Journal of Contemporary History*, vol. VII, 3/4 (July–October 1972).

3. See below, p. 96.

4. Some were, like Goicoechea, 'young *Mauristas*' in 1913.

5. But see Maura, p. 246 and p. 254 for a report that some of Azaña's younger admirers in the Ateneo had been planning to burn the *conventos* as a protest

The aspirations of the Spanish anarchists in 1931 had been modified, though not changed, since the arrival in Spain of Bakunin's first emissary in 1868. Before that time, the whole body of revolutionary socialist ideas had had few Spanish adherents. A few intellectuals of the artisan class had been attracted by federalism: Proudhon was translated into Spanish by Pi y Margall, one of the leaders (and for a time Prime Minister) of the First Republic. In 1868, there arrived in Madrid Giuseppe Fanelli, an Italian deputy, once a companion-in-arms of Garibaldi, now a passionate admirer of Bakunin, still the leading figure in the International. Although Fanelli spoke no Spanish, and though only one among his audience of ten (mainly printers) understood French, his ideas had an extraordinary effect.[1] Fanelli brought Spanish workers into contact with Europe and suggested the necessity for organization. Two Spaniards later visited Bakunin in Basle. By 1873, there were 50,000 'Bakuninists' in Spain, at first known as 'internationals' and, later, by the more accurate name of anarchists. To these, a new truth seemed to have been proclaimed. The state, being based upon ideas of obedience and authority, was evil. In its place, there should be self-governing communes – municipalities, professions, or other societies – which would make voluntary pacts with each other. All collaboration with parliaments, governments and organized religion was to be condemned. Criminals would be punished by the censure of public opinion. Bakunin was influenced, like Tolstoy, in forming such views, by a nostalgia for the Russian village life which he had himself known in childhood. The Spaniards, among whom his ideas so fruitfully spread, can also be represented as hankering for a similar simplicity of the days before the grasping modern state, of the medieval village societies and provincial autonomous units which had flourished in Spain as in the rest of Europe. Money in much of Spain was then still an innovation.

---

against the government's slowness in dealing with the church. The leader of these hooligans was Pablo Rada, a radical mechanic, who had flown with Ramón Franco across the south Atlantic on his first flight. (In the course of the civil war, Rada once again flew from the republic across the Atlantic, with substantial quantities of money.)

1. There had been a few isolated anarchists in Spain before 1868, none with a following. The account of Fanelli's talk to twenty-one young Madrid printers by Anselmo Lorenzo, *El proletariado militante* (Barcelona, 1901–23), vol. I, p. 123, is deservedly famous.

Anarchism was thus more a protest against industrialization than a method of organizing it to the public advantage. The church, which was to suffer so much in consequence, may have helped to prepare the way; its hostility to the competitive instinct, particularly of its Spanish practitioners, made the ideas of Fanelli seem merely an honest continuation of the old faith; perhaps even the real reformation which had never come. This was a time when landlords (especially the new ones who had taken over church lands) recognized fewer and fewer obligations towards peasants, who became increasingly a landless proletariat without rights.[1]

The disputes between Marx and Bakunin in the International divided its branch in Spain. The mass of the Spanish movement, the anarchists, continued, almost alone in Europe, to follow Bakunin. A minority, the socialists, formed a party of their own, following Marx. The first anarchist initiates – printers, schoolmasters, and students – began a deliberate policy of education, directed mainly at the Andalusian labourers. Revolutionary militants moved about from village to village, living like wandering friars. They organized night schools, where peasants learned to read, to become teetotal, vegetarian, to be faithful to their wives, and perhaps to discuss the moral evil of tobacco or coffee. Though the weak government banned the internationals in 1872, anarchists took the lead among the cantonalist revolutionaries of those years. In a great strike that year at Alcoy (Alicante), the anarchists transformed the local council into a committee of public safety, killed the mayor and the civil guard, and carried the heads of the latter around the town in triumph – a hint of the many troubles that were to follow.

The restoration in 1874 brought repression and the movement went underground. Numbers shrank, quarrels ensued, as bitter as they can only be when they are in the void, old militants were calumniated and betrayed. Several non-political trade unions were founded free of anarchist influences. Still, some middle-class radicals, such as the heroic Fermín Salvochea from Cádiz, became anarchists. Preaching freedom, such men were self-disciplined. Opponents of conventional marriage (as well as of the abolition of middle- and upper-class moral standards), they lived like saints. Their followers strove to emulate

1. The theory of anarchism as compensation for desertion by the church gets its best expression in Brenan, p. 131f.

them, often attempting to hasten the millennium by some violent, spontaneous act which would be repressed with a ruthlessness which itself bred further violence. Throughout the south of Spain, however, during the eighties, nineties, and the first ten years of the twentieth century, anarchism continued to spread as if it were a religion, hampered by persecution or famine, but never conquered, with more and more agricultural workers coming to believe that one day, perhaps after the very next seizure of land, the fabric of the old Spain, with the priest and the landlord, would fall away, ushering in the world of love, and the redistribution of large estates. Those who would have been bandits in the 1840s became anarchists in the 1880s. Andalusia, for so long neglected by the upper class, had its revenge by advocating a creed whose day of triumph would mean the physical destruction of that upper class and its friends and servants. Many peasants learned to read under anarchist instruction, and they were likely to believe implicitly much of what they read in the ill-printed tracts by Bakunin and Proudhon. When they found that Bakunin had said that the new world would be won only after the last king had been strangled in the guts of the last priest, they would be inclined to wish to test whether that was so. With a pistol and an encyclopedia, could not everything be achieved? This millenarian mood, conceived in clandestinity, survived long into the time of freedom of association.

The landowners and the civil guard continued in a semi-permanent state of panic at the threat apparently presented to them in revolutionary Andalusia, and began to act as if they too lived as far from practicality as their enemies, whom they credited with a degree of organization removed from the truth. The most famous incident was the conspiracy of *la Mano Negra* (the Black Hand) in 1883, which the civil guard claimed to have staunched, after a number of crop burnings and shootings of rural guards, and just before the whole upper class of Andalusia were to be massacred. Though there was no such plan, fourteen militants were garrotted in the main square of Cádiz, as a result, after a perfunctory trial. This temporarily put an end to anarchist activity in Andalusia, though most villages had still their *obrero consciente*, the worker who kept the anarchist conscience.[1]

1. Edward Malefakis, *Agrarian Reform and Peasant Revolution in Spain* (New Haven, 1970), p. 137; José Díaz del Moral, *Historia de las agitaciones campesinas andaluzas: Córdoba* (Madrid, 1929), p. 226.

Nine years later, 4,000 peasants armed with sickles marched into Jerez, shouting '*¡Viva la Anarquía!*', and killed a number of mercenary shopkeepers. The rising was put down with cavalry, four men were executed and many condemned, even one (Salvochea) who was in prison at the time of the great march.

'The Idea' (as anarchism was known to its followers) also reached Barcelona, partly perhaps as a result of the immigration of Andalusian workers to the textile factories, though most of the increase in the size of Barcelona was due to people coming in from the Catalan countryside. Catalan anarchists numbered 13,000 by 1880, Andalusia having about 30,000. But membership was shifting and it seemed sometimes that the textile workers of Barcelona might be won for socialism. Catalan anarchism furthermore was always a more organized affair than that of Andalusia; from the start, the workers realized that planning was necessary to defeat both rival unions (based on cooperative ideas) and the industrialists. On the other hand, the impoverished landless labourers of the south were dominated by the dream of running their own village without the brutality of the landlord's agent and the civil guards, the mercenary slyness of the village shopkeeper and the patronizing interference of the priest. Disputes between these two schools in the libertarian movement rumbled on at innumerable congresses in the 1890s, with the former denouncing the latter as criminals, the latter describing the collectivists as only interested in a higher standard of living. But, even in Barcelona, terrorism caught the imagination of the unskilled and often illiterate workers who had recently come into the city from the country, and even the most high-minded were unable to deny the value of the 'propaganda of the deed', as the Italian anarchist, Malatesta, put it: some sudden outrageous act which would throw the bourgeoisie into panic. There was a famous attempt on the captain-general, Martínez Campos, in 1893; his would-be assassin was executed; and a friend of his in revenge threw a bomb into the Liceo Theatre, Barcelona, killing twenty-one. The assassin, as well as several innocent people, were executed in reprisal. There was another bomb attack on a Corpus Christi day procession, killing ten. Anarchist responsibility was never proved, but five anarchists were executed, and others herded into Montjuich castle, where several died of neglect. An international scandal followed, and the Prime Minister,

Cánovas, was murdered in turn by an Italian anarchist. By then, though friendships existed between Spanish anarchists and their comrades beyond the Pyrenees (including the Russians), the movement now seemed indigenously Spanish, chiefly through its absorption of the lower-middle-class federalism of Pi y Margall, which underlay much Spanish political speculation (as late as 1937, a leading anarchist intellectual, Federica Montseny, declared herself closer to Pi than to Bakunin).[1]

In the early years of the twentieth century, a number of rationalist schools were started in Barcelona aiming to give a more sophisticated version of anarchism, the most celebrated being the Escuela Moderna at Barcelona run by Francisco Ferrer, a mason, agitator, conspirator, gambler on the stock exchange, philanderer and optimist.[2] These schools were radical educational experiments, in the tradition of Tolstoy, which, in the catholic atmosphere of Spain, were bound to cause scandal: Ferrer, for instance, deliberately flouted convention by taking his pupils for a picnic on Good Friday. It was scarcely an accident that the would-be murderer of the King and Queen at their wedding in 1906 was Mateo Morral, employed by Ferrer in his publishing firm in Barcelona. Ferrer himself, on the other hand, almost certainly had little to do with the preparation of the Tragic Week in Barcelona, though he was tried and shot for being 'the chief planner' of it, on the mendacious evidence of a few radicals anxious to destroy him. (He was in truth executed because he had long advocated a revolution, even if he had not organized one.) Ferrer's death gave the anarchists an internationally-known martyr and damaged the radicals, who had made inroads into the anarchists' strength among Catalan workers.[3] The government assumed that the anarchist labour federation in Barcelona had been the instrument through which

1. José Peirats, *La CNT en la revolución española* (Toulouse, 1951–3), vol. I, p. 72.

2. Ullman, p. 94f.; see also Sol Ferrer, *Francisco Ferrer* (Paris, 1962).

3. The role of Ferrer in 1909 was never cleared up; did he give money to hire incendiarists, did he try and finance continued fighting while he bought state bonds which were bound to go up if the revolution failed? See Ullman, p. 306f. Some alleged that the whole rebellion was a 'stock market manoeuvre'. Ferrer was arrested since, already in hiding and believed to be in France, he signed a note renewing an overdraft.

Ferrer had worked, helped by the French workers, not to speak of international freemasonry; anarchists were persecuted; and the workers turned more and more towards them in consequence, and away from political programmes, such as those of the radicals. Thereafter, too, moderate labour leaders lost ground to more violent ones, ready to look romantically on the Tragic Week as a Spanish version of the Commune de Paris, an 'epic', if possible, to be re-enacted.

The Tragic Week led too to the formation in 1910 of the first nationwide workers' federation, the Confederación Nacional de Trabajo, CNT,[1] which was from the start dominated by anarchists. Inaugurated in 1911, the CNT's leaders combined the ideas of the survivors of Bakunin's generation with those of Prince Kropotkin, Malatesta and Ferrer, and were also influenced (as Ferrer had been) by ideas from France, the articulate leaders of whose working class were in the full flood of enthusiasm for 'syndicalism' and the idea of economic warfare to the death. No doubt the members of the CNT were still in a minority even among organized workers in Barcelona. But their verve and violence commanded attention. Their tactics included sabotage, riots and anti-parliamentarianism, above all, the revolutionary general strike, carefully planned and ruthlessly carried out, which became the central hope of Spanish workers as the means of achieving the goal of 'libertarian communism'. Since it was supposed that the properly timed strike would be immediately effective, there was no strike fund, nor could many anarchist workers have afforded to contribute to one. Nor, until 1936, was there more than one paid official of the union. At meetings, there were no agendas, and there were no headquarters, apart from the editorial offices of the newspapers or the printers.

The World War intensified all Spanish labour's interest in Europe. The Russian Revolution raised this preoccupation to the highest excitement. German agents were active in Catalonia, bribing both gangsters and corrupt anarchists to attack pro-Allied businessmen, also securing the services of the corrupt chief of the political section

1. National Confederation of Labour. This was the successor to *Solidaridad Obrera*, founded in 1907, which had been a coalition of Catalan workers' movements, dominated by, but not exclusively composed of, anarchists. The socialists withdrew when this movement became a national one.

of the Barcelona police. The interminable governmental crises of the monarchy suggested to anarchist leaders that their hour was near. Membership of the CNT apparently reached 700,000 by 1918, while over 200 anarchist newspapers and periodicals flourished – Barcelona alone listing 29 publications between 1900 and 1923.[1]

The power attained by the CNT over the Spanish working class in Barcelona and Andalusia by the end of the World War presented a problem of its own, since it bred dissension between the purists, who would accept nothing less than a complete social revolution, and the more moderate wing which, while retaining the same goals for the future, nevertheless believed that some short-term alleviation of bad conditions was a worthwhile goal, along with a modicum of strategy, a few allies and a little knowledge of the international scene. The moderates were led by the 'Noi del Sucre' (the sugar boy), the nickname of Salvador Seguí, a sugar worker of oratorical gifts, who was an enemy of indiscriminate terrorism. The attempts of the government to crush the whole movement, and the anarchists' determination to preserve the advantages they had won from the industrialists during the World War, led (as has earlier been seen) to a five-year period of gang warfare in Barcelona, between CNT militants and *pistoleros* hired by the employers. The struggle was begun in 1919 by a strike in the Barcelona electricity plant, La Canadiense. The government accepted an eight-hour day. But a combative management locked out the workers. A general strike followed, peaceful in intent, converted or provoked into violence. Seguí did his best to refound the anarchist movement on realistic principles. He even preached patience. But before long, most of the leading Barcelona anarchists, including Seguí and his lawyer Layret, were murdered, either by *pistoleros* in the street or while 'trying to escape' from confinement, the so-called *Ley de Fugas* (Law of Escapes).[2] The civil governor,

1. Díaz del Moral, pp. 575–7. The FNAE (Federación Nacional de Agricultores de España), an agricultural counterpart to the CNT, was founded in 1913 and merged with the CNT in 1918.

2. Peirats, vol. I, p. 9, gives an 'incomplete' list of anarchist leaders killed in this period; the list numbers 106. A description of the government's backing of the anti-anarchist *pistoleros* and the amount they received per killing was published in *Tiempos nuevos* (Paris) in 1925. It is reprinted in Peirats, vol. I, pp. 10–13. Far the best account of this period is given by Meaker, in the book previously cited.

General Martínez Anido, fought the anarchists with every weapon he could find, including not only the rival, government-favoured union, the Sindicato Libre, but a special constabulary, the Somaten (a revival of a similarly named force of Catalan irregulars who had fought Napoleon). Violence and murder became day-to-day occurrences, political crimes accompanied by gangsterism, deaths of police, ordinary workers, and passers-by. Altogether some 1,000 people died for 'political' reasons in Barcelona between 1917 and 1923.

The Russian Revolution, meantime, presented a temptation to the anarchist movement. Enthusiasm was greatest in Andalusia, where the years 1918–21 were thought of as the 'bolshevik triennium'.[1] In 1920, the national congress of the CNT sent Seguí's chief rival, Angel Pestaña, to Moscow to report on the Russian Revolution. Like the socialist delegation, he was unfavourably impressed, especially by the persecution of the Russian anarchists and the crushing of the opposition generally. Pestaña therefore spoke in Moscow against the Twenty-one Conditions named as necessary for joining the Third Communist International (Comintern). He could not, however, make his report when he got back to Spain, since he was arrested on arrival and spent the next months in prison. In 1921, another invitation to Moscow resulted in the loss for the movement of its new secretary-general Andrés Nin, and some other intellectuals, who joined the communists: but this had no effect on the mass of the movement.[2] Pestaña was soon out of gaol and, with the only one of Nin's group to remain an anarchist, Gaston Leval, pointed out how quickly Lenin had organized a police and a censorship. The anti-communist faction triumphed, and the anarchists, instead of affiliating with Moscow, joined the new, small anarchist International, the International Working Men's Association, AIT, with its headquarters in Berlin.[3]

The dictatorship of Primo de Rivera saw the eclipse of militant anarchist activity, most of the leaders being either dead, in exile, or in gaol: anarchist newspapers were banned, though not all their

1. The character of these years has been touched on on p. 23 above.

2. Nin is further discussed on p. 120 below.

3. See below, p. 117. 'The Russian Revolution', said a famous old anarchist, Eleuterio Quintanilla, 'does not express our ideals. It is a revolution of socialist character. Its direction and orientation do not respond to the needs of the workers, but of political parties.'

periodicals. Some rationalist schools were allowed to stay open. The more violent anarchist leaders, including a famous gang named *Los Solidarios*, gathered in France and directed forays across the border. Among these men a number of legendary anarchist warriors appeared: notably two inseparable men of violence, Buenaventura Durruti and Francisco Ascaso. Durruti was a railway worker from León, Ascaso was a baker and a waiter. Their most notorious crimes were the murder of the archbishop of Saragossa in 1923, the attempt on King Alfonso (in Paris) in 1924, and the celebrated assault on the bank of Spain at Gijón. They fled from Spain, wandered through South America, and set up an anarchist bookshop in Paris. Four countries, Ilya Ehrenburg later approvingly remarked, had condemned Durruti to death.[1] These men and their companions were not, of course, common criminals. They were dreamers with a violent mission, characters whom Dostoyevsky would have been proud to have created. For some, Durruti was a 'thug', 'killer', or 'hooligan'; for others he was the 'indomitable hero', with a fine 'imperious head eclipsing all others, who laughed like a child and wept before the human tragedy'.[2] Most of the *solidarios* believed that some alliance was necessary with other enemies of the dictatorship, and several of them, in exile, despite their advocacy of revolutionary violence, prepared to contemplate a long time of preparation before a real general strike. They also made plans for a revolutionary anarchist army in the style of Nestor Makhno, the Ukrainian, whom they knew.

In July 1927, at a secret meeting at Valencia, the leading militant anarchists left in Spain meantime formed a new society, the Federación Anarquista Ibérica (FAI), designed to resist revisionism. This became, in the next few years, a revolutionary élite dedicated to lead the masses towards realization of the right revolutionary moment. The FAI was not a centralized organization but instead a number of separate groups acting without cohesion: hence its weakness in crisis.

At the end of the dictatorship, and with the coming of the republic, this powerful, secret group – its organization and numbers were un-

1. Ilya Ehrenburg, *Ils ne passeront pas* (Paris, 1937), p. 13.

2. See Ricardo Sanz, *E' sindicalismo y la política: los 'solidarios' y 'nosotros'* (Toulouse, 1966); J. Romero Maura, 'The Spanish Case' in David Apter and James Joll, *Anarchism Today* (London, 1971); Juan Llarch, *La muerte de Durruti* (Barcelona, 1973).

known[1] – came more and more into dispute with the reformist group, now led by Pestaña, who desired to establish a syndicalist *political* party which would have had much the same relation to the CNT as the socialist party did to the UGT. Another moderate leader was Juan Peiró, a glass-maker, who defined anarchism as 'tolerance, nobility and anti-dogmatism, as well as the exemplary value of forming cooperatives of production and consumption'. The republic brought the movement face-to-face with a dilemma: one single document admitted that the republic's constituent Cortes[2] was 'the consequence of a revolutionary act, in which, directly or indirectly, we have intervened', and also proclaimed that 'we face the constituent Cortes in the same fashion as we face all power which oppresses us. We are in open war against the state.'[3] The *solidarios*, on their return from exile, naturally attached themselves to the FAI. They were younger than old CNT leaders, such as Pestaña, and profited from the mood of impatience among the youth of Spain to press forward towards the uncompromising.

The anarchist movement had a clever tactical leader in the 1930s in Juan García Oliver. To Cyril Connolly, the English critic, he described his aim as 'to eliminate the beast in man'.[4] But he had himself spent years in prison for crimes of violence.

The CNT was in 1931 divided on grounds of doctrine, geography and age. The workers of the cities, above all of Barcelona, can be regarded as syndicalists, and were still groping for that 'vertical' order of society first suggested by French trade unionists in the late nineteenth century. Their plan continued to be that the workers in one factory should delegate members to a 'syndicate', which would negotiate with other syndicates all questions of lodging, food, and entertainment. The rural anarchists, notably in Andalusia, still represented an idealization of their own *pueblo*, whose inhabitants would cooperate to form their own self-sufficient government. (The significance of the latter ideal is suggested by the second meaning of the word *pueblo*, which can be translated 'people', as opposed to the upper or middle classes. The inference was that the latter were

1. Peirats, vol. II, p. 347, says the FAI was 30,000 strong in 1936.
2. See below, p. 72. 3. Peirats, vol. I, pp. 42, 43.
4. Cyril Connolly, *The Condemned Playground* (London, 1945), p. 195. See his remarkable speech as minister of justice in January 1937, p. 538.

foreigners in their own town.) The practical consequence was that there was, in any given *pueblo*, still at least one anarchist who maintained the CNT connection, who kept a black and red anarchist flag ready in an emergency to fix on the headquarters of the civil guard, living as the conscience of the place, and who could, given the opportunity for action, count on the support of many others – a fact which makes all estimates of number illusory. Probably over a million and a half Spanish workers were anarchist in outlook in the thirties; but the 'militants' numbered no more than 200,000.[1]

Most anarchists believed that the CNT was not only a revolutionary organization, but the outline for a future ideal society as well. It was supposed that, after the revolution, the different *pueblos* would be linked together, for exchange of goods, to their neighbours in a regional federation of towns and villages, while the federations themselves would collaborate with other federations exchanging statistics and surplus produce. Similar federations would be formed in towns, linking factories together with suppliers or importers of raw materials. Anarchist intellectuals would justify their views by saying that there was no hope of justice in any society unless it was first achieved among small groups of men. Many anarchists hated even the idea of property. Thus the anarchist youth, the Federación Ibérica de Juventudes Libertarias (FIJL), declared themselves against property since it was:

> an inhuman injustice that a man should keep for himself wealth produced by others or even a part of the earth . . . which is as sacred to humanity as life is for the individual; because it has its origin in a violent and criminal exploitation of the stronger against the weaker, creating the odious existence of parasites . . . living on the work of others; because it creates capitalism and the law of salaries which condemns man to a permanent economic slavery and to economic disequilibrium; because it is the cause of prostitution, the most infamous and degrading outrage that society inflicts on the human conscience, condemning woman to make the object of commerce an act which is both the purest and the most spiritual known to humans. We are . . . against the state because it restrains the free un-

1. Brenan, p. 140. The anarchists claimed 600,000 members in June 1931, 250,000 in Catalonia (*Solidaridad Obrera*, 12 June 1931). Balcells says the CNT had 58 per cent of the workers in Barcelona, and between 30 and 35 per cent of the workers in Catalonia.

folding and normal development of ethical, philosophical, and scientific activities of people and because it is the foundation of the principles of authority and property through the armed forces, police and judiciary . . .[1]

Despite all these views, however, there was no suggestion that children should be brought up in common, and free love was despised.

It was natural that the anarchists should be suspicious of Largo Caballero's labour exchanges and arbitration committees which, under Primo de Rivera as under the republic, they believed threatened their *raison d'être*. That lack of interest in a promising programme of social legislation shows how the movement, though its members were often courageous and imaginative, was too easily able to forget that there were others in Spain, including both socialists and capitalists, who had points of view worthy of being heard. Anarchists often had indeed only 'the Idea' of libertarian revolution to sustain them. They forgot that the men of 'the Idea' were never a majority of the working class.

Some unions did exist in Spain which were neither socialist nor anarchist, whose members were both catholics and hostile to militant atheism and revolutionary talk. The National Catholic Agrarian Confederation even claimed a following of 600,000 peasant families in 1919. That body, however, confined its activities to Castile and Navarre and concentrated less on ideology than on such practical matters as marketing manure and the purchase of seed. Some attempts in the past had also been made at comprehensive social legislation. There was, for example, a Workers' Compensation Act of 1909, an eight-hour day was introduced in 1918, and social insurance had been brought in during the 1920s. The difficulty was not only anarchist reluctance to cooperate but the state's incapacity to ensure that laws were enforced. Similarly, the cooperatives which were introduced in some Catalan or Castilian fishing and agricultural communities were eccentric exceptions to the growing disharmony in social affairs.[2]

1. Peirats, vol. II, p. 122. 2. Carr, p. 463.

6

Anarchist strikes – the republican constitution – Castilblanco – the Agrarian Law – condition of Spanish agriculture

THE events of May 1931 gave to the new republican government a warning of the threats which seemed likely to beset it from both Left and Right. But the ministers knew nothing of the details of the monarchists' plans: rumours, of course, there were, and verbal menaces. Nor did they take the anarchists as seriously as they should have done. They attributed the church burnings to the provocation of the monarchists. On 28 June, an election was held which suggested that the majority of the people were behind the régime. This election, for a constituent Cortes, was held on the understanding that one member would represent about 50,000 male votes. Deputies were chosen for provincial, not local, electoral districts, so as to try and avoid the local *caciques*' power. (Towns over 100,000 were separate constituencies.) They were the fairest elections that had been held in Spain. As a result, there were elected 117 socialists (a true reflection of the growth in socialist numbers during the weeks since April); 59 radical socialists and 27 members of Azaña's Republican Action party; 89 radicals, following Lerroux; and 27 right republicans, following Alcalá Zamora. In addition, there were elected 33 members of the Catalan Esquerra and 16 Galician nationalists. All these could be expected to vote generally with the government.[1] Against these, the non-republican Right could muster only 57 members, despite evidence that the old *caciques* were still often strong enough to exercise an improper influence. The monarchist party seemed 'nothing but an incitement to riots'.[2] Many agricultural workers who might have been expected to be indifferent to the republic had been won to

1. Women could be candidates but were not to be voters till 1933. The second round of the elections were on 12 July.

2. *El Imparcial*, qu. Ben-Ami, p. 286. Republicans assumed predominance in many rural town halls by substituting their own also questionable brand of electoral management in place of monarchist *caciquismo*.

it by the new land legislation.[1] The catholics' National Action won only six seats. The Right had been taken by surprise by the fall of the monarchy, the old leaders could not agree with each other as to what policy to follow, and such new right-wing leaders as were already in the wings of Spanish politics had as yet no following. Had it not been for the government's minor anti-clerical decrees during the early summer, opposition might not have got under way for some years. But these included such things as a ban on showing images of saints in schoolrooms, on the ground that the kissing of such things was insanitary; and the minister of education was allowed to confiscate artistic objects from churches if there were danger of their deterioration. These pinpricks wounded, but did not injure. Meantime, the new constituent Assembly was in many ways a gathering of individuals, more than of parties. Only the socialists were an organized movement. The other republican groups were groups of friends. There were numerous essentially independent members such as Ortega, Unamuno and Dr Marañón, the 'founders' of the republic.

The government's confidence was, however, reduced by a series of strikes organized by the anarchists in July and August. In a building workers' strike in Barcelona, strikers, besieged in a house in the Calle de Mercaders, said they would not give in except to regular soldiers. A unit arrived and the men surrendered; they were shortly machine-gunned by the forces of order.[2] Three deaths occurred during a general strike in San Sebastián. The government even called on the army, including artillery, to crush a general strike in Seville, arising from a telephone strike. No less than thirty anarchists, including some gunmen, were killed and two hundred wounded. If they had reacted too slowly to the burning of the *conventos*, the government had now reacted too strongly. Animosity between the anarchists and socialists was, however, stilled that summer by the anarchists' own dissensions. The opponents of the FAI's aspirations to élite leadership published in August a manifesto, signed by thirty leading anarchists (thereafter known as the *treintistas*). The FAI were guilty, they said,

of developing an over-simplified concept of revolution . . . which would hand us over to republican fascism . . . The revolution does not trust ex-

1. Discussed on p. 83 below. 2. Peirats, vol. I, p. 49.

clusively in the audacity of a more or less courageous minority, but instead it seeks to be a movement of the whole working class marching towards its final liberation, which alone will decide the character and precise moment for the revolution.[1]

The FAI were strong enough to resist this criticism and even succeeded in expelling the *treintistas* from the CNT. This victory was one of youth against middle-age: most *FAIistas* were in their twenties or thirties, most *treintistas* older. The movement was, however, weakened as a whole since some of the local federations followed those of their leaders who had signed the manifesto. Some of the *treintistas* never rejoined the movement; Angel Pestaña, for example, formed a small splinter party which never gathered any momentum. Others, such as Roldán Cortada in Barcelona, became communists. Meantime, in the countryside, a sharp clash between newly militant, and organized, young agricultural workers and the representatives of old Spain seemed inevitable, particularly in the south, where there was no liberal middle class as there was in the cities.[2]

By the autumn of 1931, a committee of the Cortes had, meantime, prepared a draft constitution. Here the government (or, rather, the drafters) blundered. It would have been too much to hope that the new régime could refrain from preparing a written constitution. But it was a grave mistake to make the constitution of the republic a controversial political document, full of emotive phraseology. The liberals of 1931 were repeating the mistake of their nineteenth-century predecessors. They identified the new régime with their own political views. Thus the draft constitution began by announcing 'Spain is a democratic republic of workers of all classes, organized in a régime of liberty and justice'. Government 'emanated from the people' and all citizens were equal. The country would renounce war as an instrument of national policy. No titles of nobility would be recognized. Both sexes would vote at twenty-three. There would be only one chamber. Property would be 'the object of expropriation for social utility'. Some of these clauses might be invoked to justify socialism; others could be regarded as giving safeguards against it. Then, since

1. Peirats, vol. I, pp. 55–7; Cesar Lorenzo, *Les Anarchistes espagnoles et le pouvoir* (Paris, 1969), p. 69. See too Abel Paz, *Durruti: le peuple en armes* (Paris, 1972).

2. Cf. Jackson, p. 30.

the men of the republic feared a meddlesome Head of State, such as King Alfonso had been, the powers of the President were limited by a six-year term, and ineligibility for immediate re-election. The President would, however, nominate the Prime Minister. The acts of the President would only be valid if signed by a cabinet minister, but the President could veto laws which he did not like. He could be removed nevertheless if he were to dissolve the Cortes twice.

The religious clauses brought most fury. Article 26 separated church and state. The payment by the state to priests was to stop in two years, though these salaries had been part of the compensation which the church had been paid after the confiscation of their lands in 1837. All religious orders had to register with the ministry of justice. If they were judged a danger to the state, they would be dissolved.[1] They would have to pay ordinary taxes. Orders which required a vow beyond the three normal canonical vows would anyway be dissolved. This was merely another way of dissolving the Jesuits, from whom (above a certain rank) a special oath of loyalty to the Pope is customarily exacted. No order was to be permitted to hold more property than it required for its own subsistence, nor was any order to be allowed to indulge in commerce. All orders were to submit their annual accounts to the state. All education, meanwhile, was to be inspired 'by ideals of human solidarity'. Religious education, that is, was to end. Every 'public manifestation of religion' – including the Holy Week, Epiphany and even carnival processions – would have to be officially approved; while divorce was to be granted as a result of mutual disagreement between the parties, or on the petition of either party, if just cause could be shown. Civil marriages were to be the only legal ones.

The inclusion of such sweeping anti-clerical clauses in the constitution of the republic was ambitious, but foolish, whatever the merits of the case might be. It might have been that the application of such conditions would ultimately have made for a juster Spain. Nevertheless, it would have been wiser to have delayed before the presentation of total disestablishment. It would have been wiser too to have delayed dissolution until the place of the Augustinian and Jesuit schools could have been taken by lay establishments of comparable

1. An earlier draft of the constitution had provided for the dissolution of all orders.

quality. For, with all their shortcomings, these orders had created the best secondary schools in the country – for those who could pay. Even liberal newspapers denounced these measures. Yet Azaña thundered in the Cortes: 'Do not tell me that this is contrary to freedom. It is a matter of public health.' Unfortunately, Spanish liberalism had come to look on the church as a scapegoat for all Spain's ills; but no such simple explanation was, in fact, honest. Furthermore, these ideas were far from innovations: the Jesuits had been expelled before, and compulsory religious education had been dropped in 1913, to be restored by Primo de Rivera. The difficulty was that Spanish catholics were forced into having to oppose the constitution of the republic if they wished to criticize its educational policy.[1]

The debates in the Cortes on these clerical clauses brought the first of many governmental crises in the Second Republic. Alcalá Zamora, the Prime Minister, and Miguel Maura, the minister of the interior, both catholic 'progressives', resigned in October. In both resignations, personal relations as well as principles were involved. The Speaker of the Cortes, the serene Besteiro, assumed the temporary rank of President of Spain and called on Azaña to form another government. Since Azaña had assumed the leadership of the government parties in the Cortes on both military and religious matters, he was the obvious choice: he was the one success of the new régime. But his promotion outraged the radical Lerroux, who regarded himself as representing the senior conscience of republicanism and who soon passed, with his ninety followers, into opposition.[2] Thereafter, the government was more strictly anti-clerical, being a coalition of republicans of Azaña's way of thinking, and of socialists. Alcalá Zamora admittedly became the first President of the republic. So it could not have been said that the catholics were wholly excluded from the régime. The departure of Alcalá Zamora and Maura from the government signified their failure to expand their following into a broadly based party; that role would be filled by the as yet tiny National Action movement, whose right-wing character was undoubted, if its republicanism was suspect. For a time, many middle-class and right-wing voters placed their hopes, and votes, with

1. See Marcelino Domingo, *La experiencia del poder* (Madrid, 1934). For a summary of attitudes by the Right, see Robinson, p. 59f.

2. For an intimate picture of this crisis, see Azaña, vol. IV, p. 172f.

Lerroux, who was flattered to find himself spoken of as a 'great man of government' or 'the Spanish Tardieu'.

The constitution became law at the end of 1931. It remained for the government to introduce the legislation which would enact all its clauses. The ministers busied themselves first with a law 'for the defence of the republic'. The constitution provided for the suspension of all guarantees of freedom for thirty days, in the case of an emergency. The new law empowered the minister of the interior to suspend public meetings. A modest income tax was introduced for the first time in Spain. These things were vigorously fought by the few right-wing deputies. Then, on the last day of 1931, a terrible incident occurred which caught the attention of the whole country.

In the wild and empty region of Estremadura, near the monastery of Guadalupe, there stood a small *pueblo* of nine hundred inhabitants named Castilblanco. The conditions here were much as they were elsewhere in the region. There was no special shortage of food. Violence was previously unknown. The local socialists desired to demonstrate, along with others in other *pueblos*, against the unpopular civil governor of Badajoz. Permission to do so was refused. They determined to go ahead. The civil guard then came to the defence of the authorities.

The civil guard ('*la Benemérita*', the 'well deserving', as it was known by the middle class) numbered about 30,000. It had been established in 1844 to keep order in the countryside, then agitated by bandits using guerrilla methods successfully employed against the armies of Napoleon. The civil guard was organized as part of the army, being led by a general and serving officers. Many of the rank and file were ex-regular soldiers and non-commissioned officers. With their green uniforms, three-cornered hats, their Mauser rifles, and gaunt barracks, this police force was regarded as if it were an army of occupation. Members of the civil guard never served in the part of Spain from whence they came. They were not encouraged to be friendly with anyone in the village in which they were quartered. They had a reputation for ruthlessness. 'When one joins the civil guard,' wrote the novelist, Ramón Sender, 'one declares civil war.'[1] The personnel during the republic, being the same as during the monarchy, were as brutal in the 1930s as they had been in the 1920s.

1. Ramón Sender, *Seven Red Sundays* (London, 1936), p. 171.

In Castilblanco in 1931, the civil guard were as unpopular as elsewhere in Spain. Their fate was terrible. When they tried to prevent the holding of the socialist meeting, the village fell upon them. Four were killed. Their eyes were gouged out. Their bodies were mutilated. On one of the bodies thirty-seven knife wounds were afterwards discovered; and, as in the town of Fuenteovejuna in Lope de Vega's play of that name, there was no possibility of bringing the killers to trial. The village, no single person, was responsible.[1] This tragedy was followed by several comparable, but less dramatic, events in other *pueblos*. In Arnedo (Logroño) the civil guards wreaked vengeance and killed seven peaceful demonstrators. The civil guard were everywhere on the offensive after Castilblanco. But in Sallent, in the Llobregat valley near Barcelona, the CNT took over the town, raised a red flag on the town hall, abolished private property and money, and declared themselves an independent society. The government took five days to recapture the town. Many anarchists from all over Spain were deported as a result. Among them were the *solidarios*, Durruti and Francisco Ascaso. The latter wrote from his prison ship: 'Poor bourgeoisie which has to have recourse to such action to survive. But of course they are at war with us, and it is natural that they defend themselves by martyrizing, murdering, and exiling us.'[2] This punishment did not prevent the FAI, worried at the growth of numbers in the socialist agricultural workers' union, from virtually declaring war on the republic and the rural bourgeoisie for the rest of 1932. It was a terrifying time for the landlord's agent and his friends.

The frequency of these explosions encouraged the government to broach a discussion of those fundamental social problems which lay at the heart of Spanish working-class unrest, particularly the problem of Spanish agriculture.

*

Spain was a dry land with bad soil. Its natural aridity had been increased by deforestation and the grazing of the famous flocks of sheep which, for centuries, had roamed central Spain. Forests had been destroyed by donkeys, goats, the demands of building (houses and

1. Six people were afterwards condemned to life imprisonment. See Luis Jiménez Asúa, *Castilblanco* (Madrid, 1933).

2. Peirats, vol. I, p. 51.

ships) and peasant prejudice against trees. The lack of fodder prevented animals from being used as much as elsewhere in Europe; while agricultural machinery scarcely existed in 1930. Rainfall was low except in the north-west, and the unpredictability of such rain as there was made farming even more hazardous. The 'golden fringe' of the Mediterranean, and a few favoured valleys and irrigated plains, produced much of the available food. The social contrast between these prosperous regions and the poor, windy deserts of the centre was striking. Many farmers slaved away all their lives on sterile soils. Water and fuel preoccupied farmers far more of the time than they did in northern Europe. Yield was lower too: for example, the acreage in vineyards was the same as in France but it produced only about two-thirds of what France did.[1] Long distances between villages and fields, bad transport, bad roads, shortage of manure and ignorance of modern agricultural possibilities all kept low the incomes of those who worked on the land. Though distribution of food had been improved because of the railway and road programmes of Primo de Rivera, it still took too long to take perishable goods from the rich Valencian irrigated land or the Guadalquivir valley to mountain villages or to Madrid: hence the limited food available.

Spanish agriculture had been, for several generations, the object of debate, as was understandable since it was still by far the main source of wealth in the country. It accounted for about two-fifths of the Spanish national income in the 1930s though most labourers' wages did not give them enough to buy their food. Still, well over half the population lived from the land. Agrarian reform had been discussed in the eighteenth century but, along with many other good ideas suggested by the enlightened ministers of King Charles III, little had come of it. In the nineteenth century, the church lands had been confiscated and resold, and there were other well-intentioned acts designed to remove feudalism from the land. But this legislation had done nothing to change the structure of Spanish agriculture; what was done was to the disadvantage of the poor. Agricultural reform began to be discussed at the end of the nineteenth century, and the economist Joaquín Costa, a member of the famous Generation of '98, had argued that irrigation, internal colonization and a collective

1. René Dumont, *Types of Rural Economy* (London, 1957), p. 218; see, too, Carr, p. 417f.

approach, might work wonders. With much unrest on the land, that seemed to be desirable, but, apart from the setting up of a few technical schools, little was done. Yet the subject was extensively discussed and several laws for, at least, the improvement of agriculture were introduced, and usually cut to pieces in the Cortes.[1]

In the 1930s, the land was characterized by three main problems: first, the problems of the tiny farms, or *minifundia*, which could not give their owners an adequate living, and which were often much split up. These farms were found specially in rainy Galicia, but were also to be found elsewhere in northern Spain: while Soria, in Castile, had some of the most extreme examples. Second, there were also many large estates, *latifundia*, often owned by absentees, farmed negligently, and sometimes giving the owners or their representatives a dominant economic position in the locality. The characteristic land of *latifundia* was western Andalusia and Estremadura, beautiful and mountainous if rough and stony. Third, there were problems arising from different sorts of tenancies. Most of Castile, for example, was an area of poor tenant farmers insecure from a variety of mainly legal reasons. In other regions, such as the Basque country, the Levante, and the Cantabrian coast, farms were often prosperous, being usually well irrigated; they presented no social problem, since they employed only a few people apart from the family of the farmer.

The problem of the *latifundia* seemed the most severe one in Spain. Accurate statistics on this matter are difficult to find. Though the church since the nineteenth century had ceased to be a large proprietor, the nobility continued to be: noble property constituted a quarter of land in Toledo, an eighth in Cáceres, while perhaps 6 per cent of cultivated land as a whole was in the hands of families of title. Old families, such as the Duques de Medinaceli, Peñaranda, Villa Hermosa, or Alba, all owned estates of more than 75,000 acres. Nevertheless, most great estates belonged to the bourgeoisie, rather than to the nobility. It is difficult, because of the duplication of holdings and the combination of families, to know quite how important the *latifunda* were in the economy, but over half of cultivable Spain was owned by people whose total holdings exceeded the, by Spanish standards, quite large farm of 250 acres. On these estates, the culti-

1. Pre-republican agrarian reform is usefully summarized in Appendix E to Malefakis, pp. 427–38.

vation of traditional crops (particularly olives and wine) was usually pursued, and promising new ones (cotton, rice, wheat) often neglected, for lack of capital investment. Fertilizers, irrigation and mechanization were also all ignored and much land (though little fertile land, probably) left uncultivated. Many such estates, it is true, were rented out at high prices. But all who worked on these farms lived in the large white dormitory towns of the south and west, and were hired, or not, as the case might be, by the proprietor's agent at dawn and paid an insignificant wage (3.50 pesetas a day, say) except at harvest.[1] Labour was almost twice as great as demand. The annually increasing population could be absorbed by new industry neither in Madrid nor in Catalonia – nor by emigration to America (that possibility ceased after 1930). Unemployment was, therefore, rife: the average year's work in Andalusia was between 180 to 250 days a year, often 130. Wages during the harvest were close to the average in towns, but local workers then found themselves in competition with migrant, or even Portuguese, workers. There was always new labour to be brought in, and the only strikes which could begin to have any real effect were those mounted during the harvest, and many conscientious workers would shrink from anything so destructive.

The landless labourers of the Spanish south were, however, the most potentially revolutionary group in the country. Their conditions had worsened in the hundred years since the disentailment of the church's lands. A hundred small alleviations available in the old inefficient 'feudal' system had vanished with modern capitalist farming – from the possibility of gleaning, to the availability of common lands for grazing and the collection of firewood. Few landless labourers even had gardens. Thus peasants responded to the appeal of anarchism, and most Andalusian and Estremaduran agricultural workers were either entirely or partially anarchists by, say, 1920. Between 1903 and 1906, and between 1917 and 1920 (the 'bolshevik three years'), there had been innumerable strikes, attempts at intimidation, acts of violence and, in consequence, a worsening of relations on the land. The socialists were beginning to make headway in these areas too. The labourers concerned had no tenure and, being underemployed if not unemployed, were easily accessible to revolutionary

1. Balcells estimates the average agricultural wage at 2.80 pesetas a day, and the harvest wage at 5.50 pesetas. Average working reached 250 days.

propaganda: and once it became known that so-and-so was an anarchist, his chances of getting back to a job were correspondingly less.

There were also problems for the small owners. Most of those whose estates seemed to be tiny – over three-quarters of smallholdings (that is, those under 25 acres) were under one and a quarter acres – were really gardeners growing potatoes who had some other jobs as fishermen, migrant workers or day labourers. In the 1930s, pressure on these farmers was the greater because the old outlet of emigration to the Americas, particularly important in Galicia, had stopped. As for tenant farmers proper, few had their tenure fixed by a written agreement and, if they did, it was for a short time. Tenants could not pass on their farms as of right to their sons; and, if the estate were sold, or the owner died, the new proprietor could renounce existing leases. Many tenant farmers were in heavy debt to local moneylenders. Then there was the problem of the '*rabassaires*' of Catalonia (from *rabassa morte*, dead vine, in Catalan). These were farmers who had grown vines on the edge of certain large estates, and held them until the vine was dead: in the past, usually fifty or sixty years. The wine disease of phylloxera in the late nineteenth century caused new vines to be planted, with shorter lives, of twenty-five years. The *rabassaires* were now trying to secure ownership of the land concerned. During the republic, their position would become more and more radical. Apart from them, few sharecroppers, tenant farmers, or private farmers joined any of the revolutionary parties. All were conscious of their status, which they regarded as above that of a mere worker.

The socialists had been interesting themselves in agricultural questions since the early 1920s. An 'agricultural secretariat' in the UGT had been founded in 1927. Their plans included a general agrarian reform, comparable to the reforms of Mexico, or of east Europe after 1919, to be passed by the Cortes after due consultation of experts and analyses on the spot. Their short-term plans were those introduced as decrees by Largo Caballero as minister of labour, in May 1931. Henceforth, tenant farmers could only be evicted if they had not paid rent or had not cultivated land. Tenants who gave up their leases were to be paid by the landlords for improvements, if any. Tenants could get their rents reduced in the event of a bad harvest, or if the rent exceeded the income of the farm. Collective approaches, from groups of farmers, were to be favoured in applications for leases (the socialists in the government desired to encourage collectivization, though not to force it on the unwilling). An eight-hour day would be normal, permitting overtime pay for extra work. Mixed arbitration boards, or 'juries', of landowner and peasant would decide wage disputes: a chairman would either be elected or, if there were no agreement, he would be appointed by the (for the moment, socialist) minister of labour. The law of *Términos municipales*, municipal boundaries, meant that employers had to offer jobs to people of the town concerned before making offers to outsiders; and a law entitled *Laboreo forzoso*, obligatory labour, obliged landowners to farm their estates in the 'traditional' manner of the region – that is, they could not turn over to something new in order to thwart, or out-manoeuvre, their labourers, so as to keep wages down.

Of these, the law of *Términos municipales* had a decisive effect in removing the proprietor's freedom of action to hire whom he wanted and to go outside the village in order to defeat a local strike. But the decree adversely affected migrant workers. Its effect was to prevent a further drift of labour to the cities and did nothing to encourage the investment in the land which alone could have created more jobs there.[1] Nevertheless, agricultural workers were impressed. No matter that their expectations were extravagantly aroused so as to hope that the eventual agrarian reform would give real power to the poor. No matter that the decrees on leases overworked the courts. Agricultural workers began to join the agricultural section of the UGT, the FNTT (Federación Nacional de Trabajadores de la Tierra), in such vast numbers that, by 1932, there were some 450,000 socialist, mostly landless, farm workers, now outnumbering the anarchists on the land for the first time. Furthermore, these workers constituted half the total number of members of the UGT, whose character, therefore, was changing: instead of a city-based union of the traditional proletariat, practical and disciplined, in the next year or two it became partly, at least, millenarian and irregular, in expectation and style. Meantime, the new decrees had another effect, by paving the way for higher wages: earnings doubled between 1931 and 1933, in consequence of Largo's mixed arbitration boards' decisions.

Work began too on an agrarian reform proper. The first plan,

1. Carr, p. 419.

which had the advantages of simplicity, efficacy and political practicability, sought to resettle 60–75,000 landless labourers a year on land 'temporarily' sequestered from the largest proprietors, the whole to be paid for by a surtax on all large landowners. This scheme was too modest for the socialist party, and too extreme for the radicals. Alcalá Zamora introduced a scheme of his own, as did a Cortes committee on agriculture. All these plans were rejected. Finally, in March 1932, Marcelino Domingo, Azaña's well-intentioned but ignorant new minister of agriculture, put forward a plan of great complexity. About half the surface of Spain was technically to be regarded as expropriatable, even if only a small amount was to be taken over to begin with. Peasants were to be settled either as individual farmers, or as members of a collective, according to the vote of the municipality concerned. All land taken over would be compensated for, except for the lands of grandees or others who had established their estates in the nineteenth century by foreclosing as private farms what had formally been theirs merely to administer under feudal arrangements abolished in 1811. Landless workers were to be at the head of the list of those who desired to go as settlers on new land, but private farmers could also apply. Settlers could not sell, mortgage or lease the land that they obtained: the state would be the new proprietor. An Institute of Agrarian Reform was set up to administer these arrangements, and to inspire technical education, investment and irrigation.

The land to be taken over was, first, land owned by a single person in a single municipality above a certain maximum, that maximum to vary according to crop (grain, 730 acres; uncultivated land, 1,600 acres; vineyards, 360 acres). Second, land near the municipality was expropriatable if it were not cultivated, and if the owner also had more than 1,000 pesetas' worth of land in that same township. 'Feudal' lands (with signorial jurisdiction), badly cultivated lands, lands that could be irrigated and were not, and continuously leased lands could also be expropriated. Only the lands of grandees of Spain – the highest rank of nobility – were affected on a national, not a municipal, basis, in the sense that these noblemen were limited to a maximum holding regardless of where it was.

All these provisions were hedged in by qualifications, so that, in the end, except for grandees, the properties of great landowners were not affected much if they were widely spread. Why, it was demanded, understandably, should grandees be treated in one way and *nouveaux riches* in another? Forest and pasture were also exempted. The laws worried small farmers without transforming the basis of agriculture in Spain. Largo Caballero might well say that the law was 'an aspirin to cure an appendicitis'. It was, however, a start and, if it had been carried through fairly, with some modifications and improvements after experience, it might have had a striking effect, particularly if the plan to increase substantially the irrigated land had been put into effect at the same time.[1] But the reform was not properly introduced at all.

First, the agrarian politicians, led by the Carlist, José María Lamamié de Clairac, attacked the law day after day in the Cortes, with great perseverance. Second, the republicans, including Azaña and even the minister, Marcelino Domingo, neglected to attend many of the debates on the agrarian law. Their first concerns were the church, the Catalan question, a free press, and a good educational system. Their knowledge of economic matters was as modest as their interest. Hence the law, though finally passed, was changed during its discussion, and many doubts were raised about it, these being shared by several of its sponsors. The debates alternated in the summer of 1932 with those on the statute of Catalan autonomy. When the Agrarian Law was finally passed, there was no urgency to put it into effect. The minister seemed still to regret his time at the ministry of education. Yet great hopes had been aroused among agricultural workers. These expectations would soon turn sour when thwarted. Agrarian reform had become in Spain, as elsewhere, a myth. Like the phrase 'general strike', or the words 'liberty' or 'revolution', it seemed a programme in itself, regardless of the fact that big and small farms have as different problems as wet and dry regions. Something could be done to alleviate the misery of agricultural life in Spain by legislation and investment but since water control, drainage, irrigation, and the provision of chemical fertilizers are all dependent upon investment and industry, the only real solution to the agrarian problem was to find a way to reduce the population on the land by encouraging industry.

1. Spain had about 4 million acres under irrigation and the republic planned another 2.5 million.

7

The Catalan statute – the Basques – the army – new plots – General Sanjurjo's rising

A PLEBISCITE had been held in Catalonia. This had given 592,961 votes for home rule, and only 3,276 votes against. In no free elections anywhere, perhaps, has so overwhelming a vote been given. By the summer of 1932, a Catalan statute had become law. The four provincial councils would be reorganized as a Catalan government, with the name of *Generalidad*, the ancient name for the medieval governorship-general of Catalonia. Catalan and Spanish would both be official languages. Catalonia, like Ulster, would continue to send deputies to the central parliament, as well as to the new local chamber in Barcelona. Socialists, radicals and Castilian intellectuals such as Unamuno collaborated with the Right in their attack on the statute. The *Generalidad* had, however, no powers at all in respect of foreign affairs, defence and frontier control; and only acted as the 'agent' of the central government in respect of public order, justice, education, communications and public works. The Catalan parliament could only initiate legislation in respect of local administration, health, poor relief and civil law. Any conflict of interest was to be resolved by a Tribunal of Constitutional Guarantees. But, even so, it was a great moment when Colonel Maciá appeared with Azaña on a balcony in the Plaza de San Jaime in Barcelona to receive the cheers of the crowds, who had waited for so long for the satisfaction of their desires. 'I have every confidence', said Maciá, 'in the goodwill with which you will receive this statute. But it is not the statute for which we voted.' Thus began the short, tragic history of the Catalan republic.

Meantime, another bid for home rule was being made by the Basques.

The Basques were a race of about 600,000 people who had lived from the earliest times around the western end of the Pyrenees. Of these, about 450,000 lived in Spain, the rest in France.[1] The origin of this people is unknown. Those anxious to belittle the differences between Basques and Spaniards have identified the traditional Basque dance, the 'Espata Danza', with the 'Tripidium' of the Iberians, observed by Strabo. They have, therefore, argued, persuasively though not conclusively, that the Basques are Iberians who have preserved, in their remote valleys, their identity. The Basque language is close to what is known of Iberian. It is a primitive one, without much of a literature. The only certainty about Basque history is the existence of an individual society in the mountainous Spanish provinces of Guipúzcoa, Vizcaya, Alava, and Navarre[2] (and, to a lesser extent, among the Basques in France) since before records began.

The main characteristics of this society have been, from time immemorial, religious devotion, political isolation, and agricultural self-sufficiency. Since the church here remained close to the land, the churches stayed the centres of civic life. Local councils customarily still met in verandahs on the side of these squat buildings. The Basque priests claimed that, in 1936, almost all the agricultural population of Guipúzcoa, Alava, and Vizcaya and over half of those in industrial areas (among those who were Basques by blood)[3] were practising Christians.[4]

Politically, from the early middle ages at least, assemblies composed of representatives of all men over twenty-one would meet every two years under an oak tree at Guernica, in Vizcaya. There, the monarch, or his representative, would swear to respect Basque rights. An executive council would then be elected by lot to rule for the next two years. Both the oak tree and the city of Guernica acquired a sanctity for the Basques, suggesting a transference to political life of an ancient worship of the oak. These enlightened customs were well developed even before the arrival of the Moors, by whom the Basques

1. The population of the three Basque provinces was 891,710 in 1930; with Navarre, the total reached 1,237,593. By no means all those who lived in the provinces were Basque.

2. Navarre is chiefly inhabited by Basques. But, for reasons which will become clear (see below, p. 96), their political history has taken a different course.

3. The figure sank to 15 per cent among non-Basques living in Basque cities.

4. *Le Clergé Basque* (Paris, 1938), p. 15. Men and women sat separately, as in Ireland and in synagogues.

were never conquered. Yet the Basques had never been independent.[1] Much of Castile was, indeed, colonized by Basque settlers, when it was reconquered from the Moors. The first movement to assert themselves undertaken by the Basques was in the early nineteenth century when, due to their Roman catholicism, as well as to the strength of their local feeling, they formed the heart of the armies of the Carlists in their war against the liberals. As a result, in 1876, their local rights were abolished.

The anger caused by this was, in the late nineteenth century, affected by industrialization. The Basques had long been known for ship-building, because of the numbers of oak trees in Vizcaya. The Basque anchor was a famous export in the eighteenth century. In the late nineteenth century, Bilbao became a large industrial town, due to the easily shipped iron-ore deposits around it. By the twentieth century, 45 per cent of the merchant fleet of Spain came from the Basque provinces, as did nearly all Spain's iron. The Spanish steel industry was also established in the Basque country, and, in the 1930s, Vizcaya produced three-quarters of the steel and half the iron of Spain. (But the heyday of Basque iron ore was over: production in 1929 was half what it had been in 1913.)[2] About a third of total Spanish investment was Basque. A comfortable but progressive middle-class security was expressed by great Basque banks. These broke beyond the bonds of the family firm and came to occupy a dominant place in Spanish banking. The bankers remained understandably centralists, through social and economic interest, but the rest of the Basque middle class, like the Catalans, added their sober weight to that of the romantics who, led by Sabino de Arana (son of a Carlist and a man who became a Basque nationalist in Catalonia), began in the 1890s, to demand the revival, or re-invigoration, of those local rights abolished, after all, such a short time before.

At the beginning of the 1930s, the catholicism of the nationalist movement meant that it could not agree with the republican parties. The Basque party was indeed almost racial in its discouragement of marriage to non-Basques and talk of expelling Castilians. The Basque church strongly backed the nationalist movement and hoped that a

1. Except for those who lived in Navarre, who were ruled by the semi-independent monarchs of that little kingdom until the sixteenth century.

2. Carr, p. 435.

day would come when Basques would cease to learn Castilian, 'the language of liberalism'. Thus it was no surprise when the Basque deputies walked out during the discussion of the clerical clauses of the constitution. The Basques seemed so far to the Right in 1931 that their leader, José Antonio Aguirre, was approached in that year by the inveterate monarchist plotter, General Orgaz, to join a military plot against the republic. 'If you put at my disposal the 5,000 young Basque nationalists who the other day paraded at Deva, I would rapidly make myself master of Spain,' said the general. A few days later, Aguirre was approached by an envoy from King Alfonso who said: 'The King desires to make up for the wrongs suffered by the Basques. The means of restoring your *fueros* (ancient laws) are being studied.' Aguirre, a young lawyer who owed much of his political success to his good looks and to his prowess as a football player at the Bilbao athletic club, rejected both proposals, and, thereafter, monarchists reserved an especial bitterness for the Basque nationalist party.[1] A Basque statute was soon brought forward which would have given the Basques the same degree of autonomy as that enjoyed by the Catalans. (They already had achieved the *Concierto Económico*, a separate arrangement for taxation with the government, and some other items of administrative autonomy.)

In June 1932, delegates from the four provinces met in Pamplona. Those from Navarre rejected the statute, by the narrow margin of 123 to 109. Carlism had always been strong in Navarre and, though Basques and Carlists had seen eye-to-eye in the nineteenth century – indeed, Carlism had had many Basque followers – the two movements differed on the question of where sovereignty should lie in future: in Bilbao, or in Madrid. Henceforward, Navarre's ways diverged from those of the Basques. The delegates from the other three provinces meantime approved the statute by a large majority. This endorsement was subsequently confirmed in a plebiscite of the three

1. The PNV (Partido Nacionalista Vasco) was founded by Arana in 1894. For Orgaz's approach, see José Antonio Aguirre, *De Guernica a Nueva York pasando por Berlín* (Buenos Aires, 1943), pp. 342–3. Orgaz later denied this version of the interview, saying that the request for an alliance was made by Aguirre, who desired officers to train his youth movement (*Mendigoixales*) for a rising. It is possible that monarchist politicians arranged the interview in a way as to leave both under the impression that the other had taken the initiative. (See Iturralde, vol. I, pp. 36–7.)

provinces.[1] For, by this time, all classes in the Basque provinces[2] (many of whom were immigrants from Asturias, Andalusia, or Galicia), backed the demand for limited home rule, if not independence. A large majority, indeed, gave their support to the ancient Basque slogan, 'For God and our old laws'.

Culture played less of a part in the Basque revival than it did among the Catalans. There was no opera house in Bilbao, no Basque equivalent to Catalan artists such as Sert or Gaudí. Their movement gathered momentum through the anti-clericalism of the republic. Unlike the nationalists of Barcelona, the Basques' best markets were outside Spain. They half-believed that they could live by themselves on their wood and iron. It is easy to understand, therefore, why they felt that they had had enough of Spain. It is an ironic tragedy that this distaste for the Spanish connection drew them into the civil war and destroyed them. Equally ironic, the middle-class Basque leaders were mostly Castilian speakers and in some cases spoke the Basque tongue with difficulty.[3]

The growing success of the two separatist parties in Catalonia and the Basque provinces had repercussions elsewhere. A separatist movement in Galicia had been begun during the dictatorship of Primo de Rivera. A statute for Galician autonomy was being planned by Casares Quiroga, minister of the interior in Azaña's government. There were similar stirrings among the Valencians, and even among the Castilians. It did indeed seem to some that Spain might be geographically disintegrating. This was yet one more cause of fear, and a disposition to sanction force, among those who believed that they might lose from such apparent dismemberment.

*

1. Out of a total electorate of 489,887 in the three provinces, 411,756 voted in favour of the statute, 14,196 voted against, and 63,935 abstained. See Martin Blinkhorn, 'The Basque Ulster', *Historical Journal* XVII, no. 3 (1974), pp. 595–613.

2. The working classes in Bilbao were neither so catholic nor so separatist as the bourgeoisie. Their adoption of the centralizing ideas of the socialist UGT, one of whose chief centres was Bilbao, was also to be a cause of fights.

3. The Basque nationalist movement can be followed in M. García Venero, *Historia del nacionalismo vasco* (Madrid, 1945); Aguirre's memoirs; Salvador de Madariaga, *Spain* (London, 1946), pp. 227–35 (hostile); Brenan, pp. 278–80; and Stanley Payne's *Basque Nationalism* (Reno, 1975).

The church and many of the middle class had been estranged from the republic by the religious clauses in the constitution. The landowners had been angered by the Agrarian Law. It was the army who were most offended by the Catalan statute and the developments in the direction of a federal Spanish state.

The days were past when a Frenchman such as Brantôme could feel pride in the human race when he saw the Spaniards riding to their wars in Flanders, 'like princes in their arrogant and insolent grace'. Indeed, in recent times, the Spanish army had shown few suspicions even of competence. Wellington thought the Spaniards fighting by his side brave but ill-disciplined. English observers of the Carlist Wars had noted the same. The First Carlist War was concluded not by a victory in the field, but by a treaty (at Vergara, the word being henceforth a synonym for a humiliating compromise), enabling Carlist officers to join the regular army at full pay. That arrangement had begun an era of preponderance of officers to men in the Spanish army. In the last years of the monarchy, there were 17,000 officers (including 195 generals) for about 150,000 men[1] – a proportion of one officer for every nine men.[2] This excessive size had been the main reason why, in Morocco, the army had been unable to afford good hospitals, tanks or modern manoeuvres.

It was a commonplace to say that this large force was maintained not to fight Spain's enemies abroad, but to enforce order at home. Ever since the Napoleonic Wars, the officers of the Spanish army had been accustomed to a political life. There had been innumerable *pronunciamientos*, successful or unsuccessful, between 1814 and 1868. Between 1868 and 1875, the army, ragged, ill-equipped and ill-disciplined though it was, had deposed the monarch, brought in another prince from Italy, established a republic, restored order, and, finally, recreated the monarchy. Generals had not intervened openly in politics between 1875 and 1923, but they had been consulted, and favoured by both Kings Alfonso XII and XIII, who, as commanders-in-chief, had a special relation with the army. The insults 'made against her honour' by a Catalan newspaper in 1905 secured the

1. *Anuario* 1931; Ramón Salas Larrazábal, *Historia del ejército popular de la república* (Madrid, 1974), vol. I, p. 11.

2. Nineteenth-century figures were more absurd. In 1898 there was one general for every hundred men.

amazing concession, in the Law of Jurisdictions, by a government under duress, that attacks on the army should be tried by military law.[1] In 1917, the army had crushed the general strike, though itself partly at that time restless. From 1923 until 1930, General Primo de Rivera had maintained a military dictatorship, and he had only left office when he had received notice (from fellow generals) that the garrisons were against him. Meantime, the Moroccan Wars had, from 1909 until 1927, given many opportunities for illusions of grandeur, as well as of misery. It was inconceivable that the army should for long remain out of the limelight in the republic.

Azaña, when minister of war, determined to reduce the power of this overmighty institution. With his usual fatal facility for creating a phrase which would be remembered, he announced that he would 'triturate' the enemies of the republic.[2] He attempted to do this by abolishing the Law of Jurisdictions. He also abolished the Supreme Council of the army (and the navy), bringing the services under the ordinary courts. He did away with the vice-regal rank of captain-general. As has been seen, he gave all officers a choice between swearing loyalty to the republic and retiring on full pay. Azaña also made various dismissals intended to make the army a more efficient, if smaller, force. But others of his measures – the annulment of promotions won by gallantry in the field – were bound to make Azaña unpopular. His language was often excessive, his actions high-handed, his advisers taken from an unpopular 'black cabinet', of liberal officers, such as General Ruiz Fornells and Colonel Hernández Sarabia. The army were also bitter at such interference in their ceremonial, or symbolic, life as the abolition of the Oath to the Flag. True, when the chief of staff of the army, General Goded, the highly political general who had helped in Primo de Rivera's *pronunciamiento*, and then had risen against him, arrested a republican colonel, Julio Mangada, for crying '*¡Viva la República!*', after he had himself cried '*¡Viva España!*' at a mess dinner, Azaña supported Goded, and

1. See the illuminating study by Joaquín Romero Maura, *The Cu-Cut Incident: Catalonia and the Spanish Army, 1905* (Reading, 1976).

2. The word was used in a speech at Valencia, and the passage quoted in Maura, p. 227. A hostile account of Azaña's reforms can be seen in the book of one of the republic's greatest enemies, in the end, General Mola, *El pasado, Azaña y el porvenir*, in Emilio Mola, *Obras completas* (Valladolid, 1940).

imprisoned Mangada for insubordination. (Mangada had also thrown his jacket to the ground and stamped on it.) Afterwards, however, Goded was replaced by a less ambitious officer, General Masquelet.[1] There were other such incidents.

Throughout the republic, the Spanish officers numbered 10,000. These were supposed to command 150,000 men who, except for the Foreign Legion and the native Moorish troops (these being known as 'the Army of Africa'), were conscripts doing their national service.[2] The period of conscription was for a year, but it rarely reached nine months: the 150,000 was a nominal figure. This army was spread in garrisons established in the capitals of the provinces. Azaña's reforms did not, however, succeed in cutting the military budget, training was not improved, and preparation for combat neglected.

Most of the leading officers of the army had fought in the wars in Morocco, to whose brutal atmosphere of comradeship under fire many looked back nostalgically. As the years passed, they forgot the blood and remembered the glory. Though many of their comrades had been killed in Morocco, there had been opportunities for swift promotion and unfettered military rule. Many believed, wrongly, that political incompetence at Madrid had caused them to fight that war on a shoestring, without adequate arms or supplies. After Primo de Rivera, with the aid of the French, had defeated the Riffians, the officers who had made their name in those campaigns, the *africanistas*, looked with scorn on those of their colleagues (*peninsulares*) who had not volunteered for the imperial adventure. The Moroccan War had so often been so near to failure, the events of 1921 in particular had been so terrible, that the ultimate victory gave the veterans a special pride. Since the King had been an enthusiastic influence in favour of the protectorate, it was natural that many of these officers should be monarchist. These men could scarcely be described as old-fashioned, for they, unlike their nineteenth-century predecessors, had been conquering territory, not withdrawing from it. The *africanistas* were an offensive élite, romantically moved by having 'written a glorious page' in history, by riding in triumph to sacred Xauen.

1. Goded became inspector general of the army. See Azaña, vol. IV, pp. 414–18.

2. In 1932, officers were to be nominally 7,660 and 1,756 in Africa; other ranks, 105,367, and 41,774 in Africa, including 9,080 Moorish troops (*Anuario*, 1932).

Many of them had had a desire to improve, in a paternal way, no doubt, the lot of the sixty-six tribes of Spanish Morocco: Silvestre, the general who lost at Annual in 1921, had exclaimed in horror when he saw the prisons in Larache: 'This is horrible, inhuman: I will not stand it in a country which is under our protection'.[1] The French General Beaufre, across the hills, wrote 'We fought these colonial wars with a clear conscience, sure that we were bringing with us civilization and progress, certain that we would help these people to emerge from their backward state'.[2] Such were officers' memories; a sergeant recalled: 'For the first twenty-five years of this century, Morocco was a battlefield, a brothel and an immense tavern'.[3]

The 'epic' of Morocco plays an important part in the story of the collapse of the republic, for Generals Sanjurjo, Goded, Franco, Millán Astray, Queipo de Llano and Mola, to name the best-known knights of Africa, as well as some junior officers, such as Colonels Varela and Yagüe, looked on Spain itself as a Moroccan problem of a new kind: infested by rebellious tribes masquerading as political parties and demanding an iron, if fatherly, hand. The *africanistas*, though they might have home-postings by now, also recalled with affection the two forces which had helped them to win. These were the tough and ruthless Foreign Legion, composed, despite its name, mainly of Spaniards, with some Portuguese, French, and Germans, which had been founded in 1920 by General Millán Astray as a shock force; and the Moorish *Regulares*, created by General Berenguer, Primo de Rivera's eventual successor, who were native troops raised from 1911 onwards as half-soldiers, half-policemen, under Spanish officers, to keep down banditry.

Many Spanish army officers saw, in their own traditions, a certain idea of a timeless, supremely Castilian Spain, without politics, creating order and banishing all things non-Spanish (by which they understood separatism, socialism, freemasonry, communism and anarchism). They could persuade themselves that their oath, as officers, to 'maintain the independence of the country and defend it

1. Rosita Forbes, *The Sultan of the Mountains* (New York, 1924), p. 72.

2. General André Beaufre, *The Fall of France, 1940* (London, 1965), p. 30.

3. Barea, p. 251. Serving as a sergeant in Morocco, Barea was scornful of pretensions: 'Civilize the Moroccans? . . . we? We from Castile . . . who cannot read or write. Who is going to civilize us? Our village has no school . . .'

from enemies within and without'[1] took precedence over their oath of loyalty to the republic. The average Spanish officer was by middle life dissatisfied, irritable, and right-wing. In Spain, as elsewhere, the young officer, when still supported by family money, was generally happy. He was happy too while his uniforms and handsome figure could still dazzle the marriageable girls of his family's acquaintance. There followed a short engagement, promotion to captain, marriage. There were mounting expenses, appearances had to be kept up, yet pay remained low. The military zeal of youth departed. The high-spirited lion of the ballroom became an embittered employee of the state: really little more than a policeman in a provincial town. His wife was worn by the exigencies of incessant economizing. She pointed enviously at her husband's once-scorned civilian contemporaries. These experiences might be part of the lot of officers in all countries. In Spain, there seemed a way out. The officer could dream of a *pronunciamiento*, which would place him in a position superior to his clever liberal and commercial friends.[2] Such action was fully in the tradition of Spanish politics and was not an entirely right-wing one either. Yet few officers 'rose' or 'pronounced' out of ambition in Spain, at least in the twentieth century; the would-be rebels were usually dedicated men, according to their lights, whose political restlessness was encouraged by the psychological willingness of their comrades to countenance rebellion on historical grounds.

The Spanish army was, nevertheless, more politically divided than any other in Europe, though the establishment of military academies, during the era of the restoration, had caused the majority of officers to be more often conservative than liberal, as well as creating something of a caste spirit. The divisions within the Spanish middle class were, however, seen in the army as well as in other professional groups. In 1931, a small minority of officers were radical; a larger minority had strong right-wing views; another minority again were loyal to the new republic without other political commitment; the remainder, perhaps half the total, were apolitical and opportunistic, if by education inclined to conservatism and to suspicion of civilians.

1. Article 2 of the Constitutive Law of the army.

2. Antonio Ruiz Vilaplana, *Burgos Justice* (New York, 1938), pp. 207–8. The officers now reaching the opportunities for high rank in the army had been at the Infantry Academy at Toledo at about the time of the Spanish American War.

In 1932, passions were aroused among many officers by the passage of the Catalan statute. It was not only that the creation of a Catalan state seemed to threaten the integrity of the Spain which the officers had sworn to defend. Catalan home rule seemed a deliberate affront to the army itself, which between 1917 and 1923 had spent so much time maintaining Barcelona in a condition of martial law. Had not General Primo de Rivera been harder on Catalan nationalists than on any other of his critics? Further, most officers were Castilian or Andalusian in origin: very few Catalans entered the army.

*

At the same time, other anti-republican schemes were prospering. The meetings which had begun in the Calle Alcalá in May 1931 were continuing, with an ever-widening group of participants. At the end of 1931, King Alfonso in exile abandoned his discouragement of his would-be insurrectionary followers. This followed his own condemnation in the Cortes to exile for life, and the confiscation of his property *in absentia*. A pact was now signed between his party, the orthodox monarchists, and the followers of his distant Carlist cousin. The 'Alfonsists' had now few constitutional prejudices to dispute with the Carlists, who now called themselves 'traditionalists'. So in September 1931, the two groups formally agreed to cooperate. Some future Cortes *fainéant* would no doubt decide who would be absolute king.

The Carlist movement in 1931, for it was no mere political party, had maintained its identity, though little more, since its last defeat in 1876. Like many apparently lost causes, it had split and its members had attacked each other with increasing venom as their numbers dwindled, though Carlist youths had been known to try and break up elections in Catalonia in the 1910s. The Carlist claimant, Don Jaime, was happy to make concessions to ex-King Alfonso, in return for a quiet life. He was a bachelor and his only male heir was his octogenarian uncle, Alfonso Carlos.[1] Alfonso Carlos, though married, had no children. Who knew what would happen to Carlism after these two princes had died? The idea of a monarchy with power exercised by a council of notables, a corporatively elected Cortes, and regional devolution, might survive, under more promising circum-

1. See Jaime del Burgo, *Conspiración y guerra civil* (Madrid, 1970), p. 270f.

stances, now that the Carlists' other cause, that of catholic dominance in the spheres of education and culture, was being challenged so vigorously by republicans. The coming of the republic, indeed, revived Carlism at its grass roots in Navarre, to a lesser extent in Castile, Valencia and Catalonia, in a way which surprised its claimant and its old leaders. The various strands of the movement came together again; the Carlist writer, Víctor Pradera, founded a new journal, a daily newspaper *El Siglo Futuro* flourished in Madrid and, while Don Jaime made friends in Paris with Don Alfonso, young middle-class Carlists began to appear in places, such as Seville, where the cause had never flourished before. Money and members were alike found by an Andalusian lawyer, Manuel Fal Conde, who, for the first time, brought organization to Andalusian Carlism. His recruits were usually young, sometimes working-class and, since there were few family links with Carlists of the 1870s, there was greater emphasis on planning. When Don Jaime died in late 1931, his successor as claimant, Alfonso Carlos, broke off relations with the Alfonsine monarchists. The Carlists were, indeed, happier denouncing the errors of the constitutional monarchy than collaborating with it. Some Carlists, such as the Conde de Rodezno, Carlist secretary-general from 1932 onwards, a Navarrese aristocrat, hoped still to capture all monarchists for Carlist views. But the Navarrese youth movement wanted an end to gentlemanly plots in grand hotels; they wanted action, and not to stay forever, as one of them strangely put it, 'hard-hearted ombre players, assiduous frequenters of cafés'.[1] As in the nineteenth century, the Carlists' greatest strength remained in the north, especially in Navarre. Though technically a Basque province, and though Basque was spoken in many Navarrese villages, the political accidents of the past, and the economic developments of the present, caused Navarre to follow the Carlist, rather than the Basque nationalist, path. For the Navarrese were a contented group of peasant proprietors nestling in the foothills of the Pyrenees. The reason for their majority against the Basque statute was that Navarre had no bourgeoisie anxious to be free to carry on a western, commercial life. Navarre was zealously catholic, with nothing to cause its priests to modernize christian doctrine. A journey to Navarre was still an expedition in the middle ages. Needless to say, the clerical

1. Luis Redondo and Juan de Zavala, *El requeté* (Barcelona, 1957), p. 250.

reforms of the republic caused peculiar resentment in Navarre, and would have been enough by themselves to rekindle the old spirit in those Pyrenean valleys – and elsewhere, for, by mid-1932, there were few large towns which did not have a Carlist branch, usually directed by some polite and aristocratic man of violence.

The political ideas of the Carlists were primitive. Some years later, a group of politicians were discussing the idea of a return of the monarch in the presence of the Conde de Rodezno, who then led the traditionalist party in the Cortes. One of the politicians turned to Rodezno and asked who would be Prime Minister if the King should come back. 'You or one of these gentlemen, it is a matter of secretaries.' 'But what would you do?' 'I!' exclaimed the count. 'I should stay with the King and we should talk of the chase.'[1] The *politique* of the chase was, indeed, the essence of the Carlist view of society. The orthodox monarchists, the Alfonsists, were rich landlords or financiers. The Carlists were to be found among poorer aristocrats, peasants, artisans, and shopkeepers, particularly in regions less favoured by the central government.

There was nothing fraudulent about the Carlists' religious, semi-mystical hostility towards the modern world (especially liberalism and the French Revolution) and their fervent loyalty towards *Dios*, *Patria*, and *Rey*. Yet, while the anarchists thought that a pistol and an encyclopedia would give them a new world, the Carlists put similar faith in a machine-gun and a missal. Others, it is true, were seeking to give the new Carlism a more intellectual colour. Thus Víctor Pradera wrote *El estado nuevo*, an attempt at a new utopia which introduced a strong element of corporativism, save that the author was forced to admit that, in the end, 'the new state' was nothing more than the old one of Ferdinand and Isabella.[2]

The conspiracies against the republic which had begun so soon after the republic had been born came to a premature head in the *pronunciamiento* of General José Sanjurjo, in August 1932. This officer was then the most famous soldier in Spain. It was he, 'the Lion of the Rif', who, as military governor of Melilla and in charge of the successful landing at Alhucemas Bay, had brought back victory to Spain in 1927. Subsequently, he had been a competent high com-

1. Ramón Serrano Súñer, *Entre Hendaya y Gibraltar* (Madrid, 1947), p. 59.
2. Víctor Pradera, *El estado nuevo* (Pamplona, 1934), p. 271.

missioner in Morocco. He was a brave, hard-drinking philanderer, whose sensuous face indicated a mixture of indolence and strength. In 1931, he, as commander of the civil guard, had told the King that he could not count on the corps to support the monarchy. In 1932, when he, had been transferred, to his annoyance, to the less important post of commander of the carabineers (customs guards), he was easily persuaded by his monarchist and military friends that it was his duty to rise against the republic. 'You alone, my general, can save Spain,' they told him.[1] He had doubts about the matter and hardly gave adequate attention to the plot's organization. Apparently, he had been appalled by the village tragedies the previous winter. He had visited Castilblanco soon after the events themselves, and had heard eye-witnesses describe how the women of the village had danced round the corpses of the civil guard. Several Carlist leaders, including Rodezno and Fal Conde, were involved in this plot. A number of aristocratic officers, however, formed the backbone of the conspiracy – including most of those who had been meeting intermittently since May 1931.[2] The rising was partly a bid for the restoration of the monarchy, partly an attempt to overthrow the 'anti-clerical dictatorship of Azaña'. Alfonsists, such as the Conde de Vallellano, Pedro Sáinz Rodríguez and Antonio Goicoechea, Generals Goded and Ponte, were also implicated, while General Emilio Barrera, who, after having been the general who had put down the Andalusian anarchists in 1917–18, had been Primo de Rivera's 'viceroy' in Catalonia, was the chief, if incompetent, coordinator of the plot.[3] The plan envisaged the capture of the main governmental buildings by prominent officers in about a dozen cities. In his manifesto, at Seville, Sanjurjo made use of precisely those words which had been employed by the makers of the republic two years before: 'A passionate demand for justice

1. *Cruzada*, vol. IV, p. 489. Sanjurjo had Carlist connections, since his father had been a brigadier in Don Carlos's army and his mother's brother had been Don Carlos's secretary. He himself had been born in Pamplona in 1872, at the beginning of the Second Carlist War.

2. A large number of these plotters were either young officers who had only taken their oath of loyalty to the monarch in the years immediately before his departure, or were old generals who had served the monarchy for a long time.

3. Lerroux no doubt knew of the conspiracy. He was a friend of Sanjurjo and probably expected to be Prime Minister if the conspiracy was successful. See Azaña, vol. IV, p. 850, for a discussion.

surges upwards from the bowels of the people, and we are moved to satisfy it . . .'[1] Before the rising occurred, a young monarchist airman, Major Ansaldo, was dispatched to try and gain the support of the Italian régime. Ansaldo saw Marshal Balbo; promises of diplomatic help in the event of victory were forthcoming.[2] Inside Spain, a fledgling fascist group, the so-called nationalist party, of Burgos, led by a fanatical lawyer of little importance, Dr Albiñaña, also gave support.

The affair was a fiasco. Azaña and the government knew – apparently through the treachery of a prostitute – what was afoot. Indeed, the matter had been talked about in the cafés for weeks. One of the conspirators, José Félix de Lequerica, a one-time 'Maurista', and newspaper proprietor, was asked by the judge who tried him how he knew the date fixed for the insurrection. 'From my concierge,' was the reply. 'For weeks he has been saying that the date was being postponed. At last, yesterday, he declared solemnly: "It is tonight, Don José Félix." ' General Sanjurjo was briefly triumphant at Seville, but in Madrid everything went wrong. Most of the would-be rebels were captured, after a scuffle in the Plaza de la Cibeles. Azaña nonchalantly watched the battle, a cigarette at his lips, from the balcony of the ministry of war.[3]

In Seville, both communists and anarchists declared a general strike, and several upper-class clubs were burned.[4] Sanjurjo was persuaded to flee to Portugal. Apprehended at Ayamonte, he was brought back to be tried with 150 others, mostly officers and including two scions of the House of Bourbon.[5] The first rising against the republic thus ended in the discomfiture of its opponents. It also resulted in the seizure, without compensation, of the lands of the conspirators; and, illogically also, the immoderate confiscation of the lands of grandees of Spain, if those were above the limits laid down for expropriation under the Agrarian Reform Law. Those lands too would not be paid for. In the heat of the moment, the government,

1. Arrarás, *Historia*, vol. I, p. 464n.

2. Ansaldo, pp. 18–20.

3. See the '*Memorias íntimas*' *de Azaña*, ed. Arrarás (Madrid, 1939), p. 183f.

4. Peirats, vol. I, p. 52.

5. Four of these prisoners – the Duque de Sevilla, and Majors Martín Alonso, Serrador, and Tella – distinguished themselves as nationalist commanders in the civil war.

and then the Cortes, made a special exception in its agrarian policy which could scarcely be justified even by rough justice: who of the grandees had actually supported Sanjurjo? Only two, out of 262.[1]

1. This debate marked, in fact, the final passage of the Agrarian Reform Law (9 September 1932). It might not have passed had not the Sanjurjo rising given the impetus needed.

8

Casas Viejas – decline of Azaña's government – the elections of November 1933 – Gil Robles and the CEDA – José Antonio Primo de Rivera and the origins of the Falange – the beginnings of Spanish communism

---

AZAÑA and his government weathered the rest of the year 1932 without much difficulty. For much of the time, the right-wing papers *ABC*, *El Debate*, and *Informaciones* were suspended. There were an ominously large number of preventive arrests of right-wing politicians and officers, not all of whom were brought to trial. A purge of the civil service was discussed to remove those 'incompatible with the régime'. The autumn session of the Cortes was occupied with the passage of the Law of Congregations, which enacted the religious clauses of the constitution. Many Jesuits had already left Spain, but a great deal of work was still needed to discover which schools they really owned and what other undertakings they had: the Society were masters of camouflaging ownership. Laws were prepared naming the dates for the end of all clerical salaries by November 1933,[1] the end of religious teaching and the beginning of the other restrictions on the orders: ecclesiastical primary schools were to close on 31 December 1933, and secondary schools and colleges or institutes of higher education three months before. This would mean that, in a country where there were already too few schools, another 350,000 children would have to be educated. Herculean efforts were, however, already being made by Fernando de los Ríos, now minister of education, and Rudolfo Llopis, the director of primary education, to realize this part of the republic's ideals. Seven thousand schools were built and the

1. In 1931, the clerical budget had been 66 million pesetas. Bishops' salaries had been suspended in April 1931. Stipends for 1932 were cut to 29.5 million pesetas and the total clerical budget was to be 5 million pesetas. The Church was thus faced with the serious problem of supporting 35,000 priests, of whom 7,000 were over fifty.

annual income of teachers raised to 3,000 pesetas.[1] Travelling schools were sent into remote provinces. By the end of 1932, 70,000 children were being educated in secondary schools in place of the 20,000 three years before. Thereafter, the pace of school building slowed, due to doubts raised about the capacity of some new teachers and the desire of successive governments to balance the budget.[2]

The nation was also engaged by the trial of the Majorcan millionaire Juan March, probably the richest man in Spain from his monopoly for distributing tobacco in Morocco, granted by Primo de Rivera. March was convicted of fraud; but he later bribed his way to a sensational escape from Alcalá prison and, thereafter, apparently used his considerable wealth (valued at £20 million sterling) to try and sabotage the currency of the republic, which, nevertheless, maintained itself in these years at more or less the same rate: about 55 pesetas to the pound.[3]

The uneasy peace of the winter was, however, broken by a new series of agrarian revolts – one of them in Castellar de Santiago (Cuidad Real), where right-wing farmers killed the local socialist trade unionist leader in appalling circumstances; and then, in January 1933, by an almost mortal thrust from the Left. On 8 January, there were some anarchist outbursts in Catalonia. These were inspired by the FAI, particularly by the new anarchist leader García Oliver. Libertarian communism was proclaimed at Sardanola-Ripollet. There were sporadic risings throughout the Levante and Andalusia. The best-known anarchist rising, however, occurred at Casas Viejas in the province of Cádiz. Though the mayor gave in, the civil guard did not, and telephoned for help from nearby Medina Sidonia. The anarchists were briefly masters of the village. The black and red flag waved in the wind. Nobody, however, appears to have been killed, though there were many upper-class families in the town. The priest survived. It is possible that some anarchists believed that the great revolution had been everywhere triumphant. Reinforcements shortly

1. About £70. 2. See Jackson, pp. 60–65, for a good summary.

3. See Manuel Benavides, *El último pirata del Mediterráneo* (Madrid, 1933). The life of March would repay a careful study, were documents available. March invested his fortune in transport. He had once been sympathetic to the idea of a republic.

arrived in the shape of a detachment of the *guardia de asalto* (assault guards). This corps, more efficient and modern than the older civil guard, had been founded after the May riots in 1931 as a new special constabulary for the defence of the republic. Led by Colonel Agustín Muñoz Grandes, an able commander known for his evacuation in 1924 of Spanish troops from Gomara in Morocco, who created the new body out of nothing in three months, the assault guards were made up of officers and men supposed to be loyal to the new régime.[1] They drove out the anarchists, some of whom established themselves on a small hill outside. Meantime, a unit of the civil guard and assault guards embarked on a house-to-house search for arms. One veteran old anarchist, nicknamed 'Seisdedos' (literally, six fingers), refused to open his door. A siege began. Seisdedos, with his daughter-in-law, Josefa, acting as gun-loader, and accompanied by five others, refused to surrender. Two assault guards were shot. Machine-guns were brought up. But the firing continued. Night fell. Seisdedos held his fire. One of Seisdedos's daughters, Libertaria, and a boy escaped from the house. The next morning the forces of the government, furious at being for so long kept at bay, placed petrol round the house and set it ablaze, killing those within. Afterwards, some fourteen prisoners were shot, and the captain of the assault guards concerned, Captain Rojas, told the press that he had had orders to take no prisoners and to shoot these men 'in the guts'.[2] Though Azaña and Casares Quiroga, minister of the interior, had plainly never given such an instruction, they never recovered from the consequences of this outrage. They were accused by the Right, with a certain hypocrisy, of 'murdering the people'. The radical Martínez Barrio, de-

1. Maura, pp. 274–5.

2. See Eric Hobsbawm, *Primitive Rebels* (Manchester, 1959), p. 123; José Plá, *Historia de la segunda república española* (Barcelona, 1940), vol. II, p. 188f; Peirats, vol. I, pp. 55–8. Rojas was tried and sentenced to twenty-one years' imprisonment. He did not serve this. See also Jackson, p. 513f. Rojas, in an interview with Azaña, said that 'we were hard, cruel if you like. Anyone who ran and did not raise his hands on our orders was shot. We fired at anyone who looked out of the windows. When they had shot at us from the chimney stacks, we replied with machine-guns.' (Azaña, vol. IV, p. 452.) Libertaria was murdered in 1936 on the road to Medina Sidonia, by a gang of falangists. (Antonio Téllez, *La guerilla urbana en España*, Paris, 1972, p. 7.)

nounced the government for creating a régime of 'blood, mud, and tears'. Ortega y Gasset openly proclaimed that the republic had disappointed him. 'It was not for this', he said, 'that we worked in the days of the monarchy.' Azaña's majority sank in the Cortes to a low figure.

In April 1933, municipal elections were held in those areas which had returned monarchists in 1931, and which had been as a result deprived of representation. As in 1931, these elections were as important as national ones. For one thing, they were fought much harder than any other had been in Spain before. In hundreds of *pueblos*, the great issue was religion, as much as the class war, even though the two matters were often combined. The initiative in the struggle in many places had been taken by the Left, who in 1931 had found themselves in local control for the first time in history. Acting sometimes in anticipation of the government, local councils had often abolished certain processions during fiestas. Municipal bands had sometimes been forbidden to enter the church. Where processions had been allowed, young socialists had proudly said that they would throw those accompanying the floats or carriages, into the local river. One priest in Andalusia had also been fined by a socialist magistrate for saying mass in his church whose roof had been destroyed by lightning: he had been charged with making a public display of religion. Another priest was fined as a monarchist for alluding to the Kingship of God in the festival of Christ the King. In one parish, the tolling of bells was taxed, in another the wearing of crucifixes forbidden. Churches were also robbed, and sometimes burned, and nobody seemed to make any attempt to apprehend the malefactors. In a church in a village in Aragon, the 'Leftists' soaped the doorway, and watched the faithful slide about with ribald laughter. In many places, the names of famous saints or churchmen were removed from streets and squares.

Then, slowly, a counter-revolution began. Old Spain began to protect the images of the Virgins in processions with armed men, who also stood on the street corners where she might pass. The faithful also now felt under an obligation to make all religious processions more solemn. Catholic Action began to be organized as a right-wing party designed to maintain the 'slow traditional ways of doing things' as opposed to 'direct progressive and violent ideas and actions'.[1]

In the municipal elections of 1933, the government parties returned 5,000 councillors, the Right 4,900, and the Centre opposition, led by Lerroux and his radicals, 4,200. It dawned on both Left republicans and socialists that, even in a democracy, they might lose power. The Right also won victories in the Cortes, particularly over the Rural Lease Bill, because the Left republicans did not attend the debate. Liberal papers turned against Azaña. In September, elections among municipal officials to elect judges for the Supreme Court gave a substantial majority to candidates opposed to the government. The opposition in the Cortes was vociferous and threatened passive disobedience if the bill forbidding the religious orders to teach were to become law. Exhausted and dispirited, Azaña sought first to reshuffle his cabinet and then, when the President made difficulties, resigned. He did so before the church schools were actually closed, and so they were given a further lease of life. After an unsuccessful attempt by Lerroux to form an administration, his lieutenant, Martínez Barrio, formed a caretaker government, and called for general elections on 19 November.

Azaña and his friends went to the polls in defence of their achievements: there had been important laws on leases, arbitration, education, religious orders, agriculture, the army, and Catalan home rule. There had been a new and advanced divorce law, as well as a law legalizing civil marriage, laws on rights for women, and a more fair system of recruitment for the civil service. There had been a new penal code. In one of the most touching experiments, republican students had, under the inspiration of the aged art critic, Manuel Cossío, and the leadership of Luis Santullano, carried out travelling cultural missions into the remotest parts of Spain, bringing poor peasants to free performances of Lope de Vega or readings of Lorca's poems. But even so, many were disappointed with the republic: the Agrarian Reform Institute had as yet only installed 4,600 families.[2] An expropriation commission was still working its way slowly

1. See for this Sánchez, p. 50, and in particular the excellent study by Carmelo Lisón Tolosana, *Belmonte de los Caballeros* (Oxford, 1966), from whose work on an Aragonese *pueblo* some of these instances derive.

2. Malefakis, p. 280.

through the legal problems caused by the dissolution of the Jesuits; it was making poor progress. Like so many others before and since, Azaña had frightened the middle class, without satisfying the workers. His minister of agriculture, Marcelino Domingo, lost votes because of his mismanagement of wheat imports. Above all, political emotions had been everywhere aroused. But the extent of Azaña's defeat was unexpected.

The Left lost in 1933 because, first, in a system favouring coalitions, they were disunited – the socialists gained 1,722,000 votes and won only 60 seats while the radicals with 700,000 votes won 104 seats. But the socialists had refused to collaborate with a 'bourgeois democracy' any more. Secondly, the lavish propaganda of the Right successfully misrepresented the positive work of the republic. There were clearly also some electoral frauds, efforts to intimidate and threats, on both sides. Finally, the introduction of votes for women for the first time in Spain, as usual, profited the Right. Altogether, the parties which had supported the late government gained only 99 seats, of which Azaña's party, Republican Action, gained only 8.

As for the Centre, the radicals won 104 seats and the Lliga, the Catalan businessmen's party, 24. The Right, on the other hand, won 207 seats. Of these 35 were won by an uneasy alliance between Carlists and orthodox monarchists: by now the latter had been organized under the misleading name, Renovación Española, led by Antonio Goicoechea, an ageing dandy who had been the 'young Maurista' leader in 1913, a conservative minister of the interior in 1919, and first president of National Action in 1931. Excluded from that, he had been a conspirator, and imprisoned in consequence, in 1932. In late 1932, he had broken with Popular Action (Acción Popular) as National Action had by then become, and founded a movement of those catholic, right-wing people who could not accept the 'accidentalism' of the catholic party. There were also 29 'agrarians', representing the interests of the Castilian growers of wheat and olives. But the largest group on the Right, and indeed in the entire Cortes, with 117 seats, was the new catholic party, the CEDA (Confederación Española de Derechas Autónomas).[1] The

1. See Robinson, p. 113f. and Gil Robles's *No fue posible la paz*. Gil Robles claimed that the CEDA had 730,000 members in 1933; if true, that would have made it Spain's largest political party ever. This large membership, with some

core of the CEDA was Popular Action. The driving force was Angel Herrera, editor of *El Debate*, one of whose aims (like, no doubt, both Pius XI and his secretary of state, Eugenio Pacelli) was to create a christian democratic party in Spain on the model of those more successful after 1945 in Germany, Italy, and France. But the anti-clerical character of the constitution meant that the members of the CEDA did not accept the régime as it was then organized. The minor measures of anti-clericalism (such as the secularization of cemeteries, the insistence on civil funeral services unless the deceased had specifically requested catholic burial in his will, and the cancellation of church parades in the army) caused as much fury as the more drastic laws. The CEDA, founded formally in March 1933, as an amalgamation of the many small right-wing catholic groups which had grown up since 1931, was an alliance, from many points of view. According to one of its most enlightened members, Manuel Giménez Fernández, some thirty of the CEDA's deputies were social christians; another thirty monarchists, or conservatives; and the remaining sixty, opportunists.[1] The leaders did not wish to offend those rich men on the Right upon whom they relied for funds. José María Gil Robles, the eloquent young barrister who became the leader of the CEDA, had been the parliamentary leader of National, and Popular, Action in 1931 and 1932, and had made his name, still in his early thirties, in the debates on the clerical clauses of the constitution. He had been one of Angel Herrera's main leader writers on *El Debate* and was a lawyer for the Jesuits. He continued to explain his position under the name of 'accidentalism': it was 'accidental' whether Spain had a monarchy or a republic, but it was 'essential' that the law should not conflict with the church.[2] Hence, he had excluded from the CEDA such active monarchists as Goicoechea. Nevertheless, Gil Robles was really a monarchist and he met with, negotiated with and, when necessary, defended monarchist plotters. Yet he also permitted his followers – smallholders in Castile, the urban middle class (except in Catalonia and the Basque country), some landowners – to greet

---

'high finance' support too, enabled the CEDA to spend unprecedented sums in the campaign. The socialist party had still only some 75,000 members, with over a million members of the UGT (Robinson, p. 328).

1. In Sergio Vilar, *La oposición a la dictadura 1931–1969* (Paris, 1969), p. 516.
2. Gil Robles, p. 80.

him at large meetings as *Jefe*, Leader, as if he were indeed a *Duce*, or even a *Führer*. He had visited Germany in 1933 to study nazi propaganda, had been present at the Nuremberg rally and brought back to Spain some nazi ideas for political campaigning – the use of radio, the dropping of pamphlets from aeroplanes, the well-organized psychological preparation of crowds at great meetings for wildly intoxicating speeches. Gil Robles was an accomplished parliamentarian, who, nevertheless, disliked parliament and thought that it might soon be seen to have had its day. His representatives visited the King in Paris, but some of his speeches in 1933 showed sympathy with nazism, as well as with Dr Dollfuss's catholic state in Austria. His vagueness about his ultimate aims, and his reluctance to affirm loyalty to the republic, could only be provocative in the circumstances of the early 1930s, when tales of comparable behaviour elsewhere leading to fascism were frequent. His youth movement, the JAP (Juventud de Acción Popular), was a hectic and impatient group of *señoritos*, who openly boasted of their anti-parliamentarianism: 'the common good cannot be integrated by means of an assembly elected by an inorganic universal suffrage', they would tell their followers in their journal on 8 December 1934. *JAPistas* were a powerful force pressing Gil Robles towards counter-revolution. A dangerous situation was thus developing in Spain in the winter of 1933–4, since the great Spanish socialist party, with all the weight of its prestige and its disciplined trade union, was also heading away from constitutionalism.

This change in the socialist party derived primarily from disillusion at the way that the Right had successfully used the constitution to block reform. The socialists were also distressed at the way that the constitution which they had helped to write had turned out to be so bad a friend to them at the polls. As expected, Largo Caballero had not been a very successful parliamentarian (unlike Prieto). The influx of peasants of the south into the FNTT, the socialist agrarian federation, also played a major part. These new socialist recruits were closer to anarchism than they were to orthodox Marxism. They were certainly different from the disciplined factory and building workers of Bilbao and Madrid. Largo Caballero was speaking in language that they relished when he said that 'If legality is no use to us, if it hinders our advance, then we shall bypass bourgeois democracy and proceed to the revolutionary conquest of power'. Furthermore, the violence of the anarchists in recent months persuaded Largo that he had to try and match them and win more of the Spanish working class for socialism. This, he believed, could only be done by breaking publicly with the republican, middle-class parties, with whom the socialists had collaborated in the government, and by setting out to be the most extreme of all the Spanish proletarian parties. Actually, his conclusion was wrong, since the internal disputes, and probably the violence also, were causing people to abandon anarchism, which certainly had many fewer followers in Barcelona in 1933 than it had had in 1931. Largo also listened to the arguments of his new intellectual advisers, the journalists Luis Araquistain and Julio Alvarez del Vayo, that collaboration with the bourgeois was bound to be a mistake.[1] Meantime, many younger socialists were anxious for the revolution, and for action: 'we greatly enjoyed bomb stories' recalled the socialist youth leader.[2]

Among the many deputies in the Cortes, meantime, elected in 1934 on behalf of small parties, there were two who were the single representatives of their parties. These were José Antonio Primo de Rivera, the barrister son of the old dictator, who proclaimed himself a fascist; and Cayetano Bolívar, who had been returned as communist deputy for Málaga.[3]

Spanish fascism had been initiated, while Primo de Rivera was still dictator, by Ernesto Giménez Caballero.[4] Beginning life, like most European fascists, as a socialist, this excitable would-be D'Annunzio of Spain had come to admire Mussolini through the influence of

1. Araquistain had observed the nazi success as ambassador in Berlin. Madariaga sees these two brothers-in-law of middle-class extraction as the *éminences grises* who drove Largo Caballero, the solid, Fabian socialist, to revolution. There is something in this theory, and certainly their replacement of the much more experienced, and disillusioned, Antonio Fabra Rivas as chief adviser to Largo Caballero assisted in the swing to the Left.

2. Santiago Carrillo, *Demain Espagne* (Paris, 1974), p. 31.

3. In fact Bolívar owed his election to a local Málaga 'popular front', formed by communists, socialists, and republicans (Enrique Matorras, *El comunismo en España*, Madrid, 1935, p. 170).

4. See Stanley G. Payne, *Falange, a Study of Spanish Fascism* (Stanford, 1961). Some of Payne's arguments are challenged by Herbert R. Southworth, *Anti-Falange* (Paris, 1967); see also Maximiniano García Venero, *Falange en la guerra de España; la unificación y Hedilla* (Paris, 1967).

Curzio Malaparte, whom he had known in Italy in 1928. Returning to Spain, he propagated a theory of militant 'latinity'. This attacked everything which had caused the decline of the Mediterranean countries. Germany was viewed at this time by Giménez Caballero with particular hatred, though, for a while, he surprisingly regarded Russia as an ally of the Mediterranean. But Rome was the centre of Giménez Caballero's world, being the capital of religion, as well as of fascism. He revised these views after Hitler's assumption of power in Germany in 1933. Even before that, the nazis had their admirers in Spain. In March 1931, a poor ex-student of the University of Madrid, Ramiro Ledesma Ramos, son of a schoolmaster in Zamora, founded a magazine, *La Conquista del Estado* (*The Conquest of the State*). In this he had proclaimed a policy resembling that of the nazis. Ledesma carried his admiration of Hitler to the extent of copying his quiff. He was otherwise a man of puritan intolerance. In *La Conquista del Estado*, he announced that he did not seek votes, but 'the *politique* of military feeling, of responsibility, and of struggle'. The cadres of the movement were to be 'military-type teams without hypocrisy before the rifle's barrel'.[1] One man was immediately drawn to this steely programme. This was Onésimo Redondo, who, like Giménez Caballero and Ledesma, was of the middle class, and had studied law at Salamanca. He became a lecturer in Spanish at the University of Mannheim, where he admired 'the imperturbable ranks of the nazis'.[2] Returning to his native Valladolid in 1931, he briefly worked as organizer of a syndicate of sugar-beet growers, and later founded his own weekly, *Libertad*, which argued the need for the 'disciplined reaffirmation of the spirit of old Castile'. In September, Redondo and Ledesma drew together, though the former was a catholic and conservative, the latter a lower-middle-class radical. In October, they announced the formation of a movement portentously named Juntas de Ofensiva Nacional-Sindicalista (known as the JONS). The programme was contained in the 'sixteen points' of Valladolid of 1931. These included a denunciation of separatism and of class war, the approval of Spanish expansion to Gibraltar, Tangier, French Morocco, and Algeria, and 'the implacable examination of foreign

1. *Cruzada*, III, p. 423. Ledesma received subsidies from both monarchists and bankers.

2. *Cruzada*, *loc. cit.*

influences in Spain'.[1] Like comparable programmes elsewhere, the document included penalties for those 'who speculated with the misery and ignorance of the people', and demanded the control (the 'disciplining') of profits. Ledesma and Onésimo Redondo gave a place to the roman catholic religion, which they described as embodying the 'racial' tradition of the Spaniards. Catholicism seems to have meant the same to Redondo as Aryan blood did to Hitler. But they criticized the church in Spain of the time. They regarded the CEDA, for instance, as the committed ally of 'reaction', even though from the beginning the falangists spoke in almost the same style as did the leaders of the CEDA youth: thus the JAP's leader, José María Valiente, wanted to 'forge new men, a new authentic youth, happy, optimistic, in short Spanish, and not like that other youth, sad and sour, stuffed with Russian novels, the fitting offspring of the anarchic Generation of '98'.[2] Nor was there much difference between the Falange and the monarchists: 'What is my position? That of a traditionalist? That of a fascist? A bit of each, why deny it?' Such were the comments of the monarchist, Goicoechea.[3]

For the rest of 1931, and all 1932, the activity of the JONS was slight. Lack of funds hampered them and the middle class of Spain was still far from desperation. Redondo took a minor part in Sanjurjo's rising of 1932, though Ledesma despised the officers as reactionaries. Meantime, a more reckless group of richer young men gathered around José Antonio Primo de Rivera.[4]

José Antonio was a tall, handsome lawyer, then in his early thirties, unmarried (with an unhappy romance to forget), and filled with a desire to please. His enemies admitted his charm. He 'carried a dream in his head . . . dangerous for him and for our people, but a dream nevertheless'.[5] His writings leave the impression of a talented undergraduate who has read, but not digested, an overlong course of politi-

1. *Cruzada*, III, pp. 424–5.

2. *El Debate*, 28 June 1932, qu. Robinson, p. 77.

3. Robinson, p. 130.

4. Giménez Caballero in 1932 offered the supreme command of the fascists to Prieto (*El Socialista*, 19 May 1949). There are several lives of José Antonio, of which the most interesting is the *Biografía apasionada* of Felipe Ximénez de Sandoval (Barcelona, 1941). See my *Selected Writings of José Antonio Primo de Rivera* (London, 1972). The views of Gil Robles, with whom José Antonio was friendly, can be seen in *No fue posible la paz*, p. 436f.

5. José Antonio Balbontín, *La España de mi experiencia* (Mexico, 1952), p. 306.

cal theory. He had begun his career as a monarchist, though he was disgusted at many monarchists' treachery (as he termed it) to his father. He remained a catholic. For the paper *El Fascio* (of which only one issue ever appeared), he wrote, in March 1933: 'The country is a historical totality . . . superior to each of us and to our groups. The state is founded on two principles – service to the united nation and the cooperation of classes.'[1] A year later, he announced:

Fascism is a European inquietude. It is a way of knowing everything – history, the state, the achievement of the proletarianization of public life, a new way of knowing the phenomena of our epoch. Fascism has already triumphed in some countries and in some, as in Germany, by the most irreproachably democratic means.[2]

José Antonio was always ready to fight anyone who criticized his father, and his career was in some ways simply an attempt to vindicate the old dictator. From his father, he inherited a contempt for political parties, a belief, instinctive in the father, rationalized in the son, in 'intuition' – the triumph of experience over intellect. José Antonio's point of view was paternalist. The liberal state, he said, has meant 'economic servitude, because it says to the workers with tragic sarcasm: "You are free to work as you wish: no one can force you to accept such and such a condition of work. But as it is we who are the rich, we offer you the conditions we like; if you do not accept them, you will die of hunger in the middle of liberal liberty." '[3] In his charm, aristocratic disdain for money, willingness to take risks, José Antonio was a characteristic *señorito* or playboy from Andalusia, whence his family came. But he had a social conscience which was untypical of that milieu and he had a filial piety similarly uncharacteristic. José Antonio's favourite poem was Kipling's 'If'. He would read sections of this, in Spanish, to his followers, before Sunday parades or possible street fights. He launched his own party, the Falange Española, in October 1933, though he was uncertain about his own potential as a leader: 'The attitude of doubt and the sense of irony which never leaves those of us who have some degree

1. *Cruzada*, vol. I, p. 594.
2. *ibid*, II, p. 21.
3. José Antonio's speech of 29 October 1933 (*Obras completas*, Madrid, 1942, pp. 17–28).

of intellectual curiosity' he wrote 'incapacitates us for shouting the robust, unflinching cries required of leaders of the masses'.[1] 'How I suffer seeing the arms raised high saluting me', he told Ximénez de Sandoval.

Two days after a *JONSista* of Madrid, Matías Montero, had been killed while selling the Falange newspaper, *FE*, by a member of the FUE (the Federación Universitaria Escolar, the main students' union, then controlled by left-wing students and founded in 1927),[2] José Antonio and Ledesma Ramos negotiated the amalgamation of the Falange and the JONS. The latter had had some success in 1933: a student group was formed, the Sindicato Español Universitario (SEU), incorporating 400 students, and about a hundred other 'militants' were organized to fight in the streets, in groups of four.[3] The new united party (which came into being on 11 February 1934) adopted the JONS's symbol of the yoke and arrows but, of the triumvirate in control, two – José Antonio and Ruiz de Alda – came from the Falange and only Ledesma from the JONS. The slogans of the party came from Ledesma: '*¡Arriba!*'; '*¡España, Una, Grande, Libre!*'; and '*Por la Patria, el Pan y la Justicia*'. But José Antonio overshadowed his companions, through his social prestige, his dignity as a deputy – he had been elected by conservative interests in Cádiz – and by his attractive personality. In the spring of 1934, he visited Germany – but he did not see Hitler, and returned to Spain critical of the nazis. Six months before he had been more pleased by Mussolini,[4] while he had himself made 'a deep impression' on Sir Oswald Mosley in England.[5]

1. Letter of 2 April 1933 to Julián Pemartín, quoted in Sancho Dávila and Julián Pemartín, *Hacia la historia de la Falange* (Jerez, 1938), vol. I, p. 24.

2. The opponents of the Falange fired the first shot in a series of engagements – the first falangist killed being a *JONSista* in November 1933 But the Falange had invited this, since, amongst their principles, had been anticipation of force.

3. See Payne, *Falange*, p. 45, and references therein. Ledesma thought that unification with the Falange would give him a bigger platform; José Antonio thought the JONS would help him against the more bourgeois elements of the Falange. Only one member of the JONS seems to have resigned rather than unite with José Antonio – Santiago Montero Díaz, of the university of Santiago, an ex-communist.

4. See his strange article on the subject on his return, in *Obras*, p. 522f.

5. Sir Oswald Mosley, *My Life* (London, 1968), p. 421.

On 14 March 1934, the first national meeting of the Falange and JONS was held at Valladolid. A vigorous but still 'poetic' speech was made by José Antonio, a brawl occurred with some socialists outside, and the movement was off to a good start. Retired officers busied themselves with military training. The leaders continued to speak in bellicose language, though it was not till mid-1934 that José Antonio accepted the full implications of his own words. Even then, he was always a reluctant supporter of terrorism.[1] A decisive event was the beating to death of a young falangist in the Casa del Campo outside Madrid and the subsequent murder of a socialist girl, Juanita Rico, who had desecrated his corpse, by a young falangista diplomat, Alfonso Merry del Val. The falangists saw themselves as an heroic élite of young men, whose mission was to release Spain from the poison of Marxism, as from what they took to be the second-rate, dull, provincialism of orthodox liberal values.

The majority of the members of the Falange were young. Ledesma thought that no one over forty-five should be allowed to be a member, and, indeed, the national syndical state set out to be that of the under-forties. A large minority were dissatisfied sons of the rich, anxious for the climate, at least, of violence. There were a few dissatisfied ex-socialists and ex-communists. Others were survivors of the old dictator's Patriotic Union. Many were frustrated members of the middle class, like Ledesma himself, anxious for a more heroic society than they could afford. Most came from the centre of Spain, though Seville was a source of recruits. In Madrid, there was a hard core of Falange taxi-drivers – perhaps because they had seen the middle class at its worst. Students probably composed the largest single group.[2] Funds came from business and from the monarchists, always willing to have their finger in a new rightist movement, but the party was short of money. Some of the 'ideology' was Carlist in phraseology,

1. Payne, pp. 53–5. This disinclination to countenance violence was a bone of dispute between José Antonio and his more militant followers throughout 1934.

2. Payne gives the official February 1936 breakdown of the origins of the Madrid JONS as:

Labourers and service employees	431	Women	63
White-collar employees	315	Students (excluding those at university)	38
Skilled workers	114	Small businessmen	19
Professional men	166	Officers and aviators	17

and so it was scarcely accidental that one of the army officers who told young falangists elementary facts about handling weapons was the retired Colonel Ricardo Rada, who had the same task with the Carlists at a later date.

*

At the other side of the political battle, the party of Cayetano Bolívar, the communist deputy for Málaga, probably numbered in 1933 about 25,000.[1] Its origins were to be sought among the pro-bolshevik sections of both socialist and anarchist movements at the time of the Russian Revolution. In April 1920, a majority of the executive committee of the socialist youth movement had declared themselves in support of the Soviet Union, and, after a while, formed themselves into the first Spanish communist party, the Partido Comunista Español. Though they were denounced by their own rank and file, in June of the same year a majority of the socialist party proper had pronounced their support of entry into the Comintern, the vote being 8,270 to 5,016, 1,615 abstaining. The socialist trade union, meantime, the UGT, kept to its non-communist position, affiliating to the (Social Democrat) Labour and Socialist International.[2] The second congress of the Comintern was duly held in Moscow. There were no socialist delegates, however, the only Spanish representative there being Angel Pestaña, director of the anarchist paper *Solidaridad Obrera*, who had been dispatched to Russia to make the same inquiry for the anarchists which de los Ríos and Anguiano were to make on behalf of the socialists. Pestaña was critical.[3] The socialists reached Russia shortly after Pestaña returned. They were accompanied by Julio Alvarez del Vayo, then a foreign correspondent accredited to Germany. De los Ríos was hostile, and proposed the annulment of the provisional entry into the Comintern; Anguiano supported entry, with conditions. An extraordinary conference of the socialist party was summoned for April to consider the whole question anew.[4]

1. Communist membership was given as 'nearly 25,000' in an article by 'A. Brons' in *Communist International*, 15 December 1933.

2. Meaker is far the best analyst of these developments.

3. See above, p. 67.

4. See Fernando de los Ríos, *Mi viaje a la Rusia Soviética* (2nd ed., Madrid, 1970).

Several weeks of argument followed, in a highly-charged political atmosphere (Dato, the Premier, was shot by the anarchists on 8 March). Pablo Iglesias, now old, conducted a vigorous campaign against the Comintern, and that tipped the balance; one old comrade from the eighties, García Quejido, took the other view. After long debates, the party finally voted by 8,808 to 6,025 against joining the Third International.[1] The leaders of the *terceristas* (i.e. advocates of joining) broke away to form a second Spanish communist party, the Partido Comunista Obrero de España:[2] they included the young Dolores Ibarruri, 'La Pasionaria'.

A further invitation to Moscow followed: this time to the first congress of the communist federation of trade unions, which became known as the 'Profintern' – in effect, the trade-union section of the Comintern. The two small Spanish communist parties were asked to send a joint delegation, as was the CNT. The latter sent their new secretary-general, Andrés Nin, a young ex-socialist journalist; Joaquín Maurín, a schoolmaster from Lérida; Hilario Arlandis, a sculptor from Valencia; and Gaston Leval, a French anarchist.[3] Nin, a brilliant linguist, admired the Russian Revolution so much that he stayed in Moscow, while Maurín and Arlandis returned to Spain to try and persuade their anarchist friends to support Lenin. Leval alone remained an anarchist, being sceptical of what he saw. The two small Spanish communist parties of socialist ancestry, meantime, were merged with the help of various Comintern delegates – the first of many international communists who appeared in Spain between that date and 1939 to give guidance and, on occasion, punishment to the Spanish communist party.[4] These first delegates included Roy, the Indian communist, the famous revolutionary 'Borodin', Antonio Graziadei, an Italian intellectual communist, and Jules Humbert-Droz, one of the founders of the Swiss communist party. Iglesias commiserated with Roy as a 'victim of a new fanaticism' when

1. Comín Colomer, *Historia*, vol. II, pp. 296–323.

2. Comín Colomer, *op. cit.*, pp. 345–59; Julián Zugazagoitia, *Historia de la guerra en España* (Buenos Aires, 1940), p. 40.

3. Memorandum from Maurín, 10 September 1963. A fifth delegate was an ex-socialist carpenter, Jesús Ibáñez. See Meaker, pp. 422–3.

4. The affairs of Spain were, with those of Portugal, Mexico and South America, looked after by the sixth 'national secretariat' within the Comintern secretariat (ECCI). The whole secretariat included 400 in 1924, but it is anyone's

rejecting his arguments.[1] In 1922, there were perhaps 5,000 members.[2] Maurín and Arlandis associated themselves with the party, their base being in Barcelona. Nearly all the leaders were arrested after Primo de Rivera's *pronunciamiento* in 1923. Others came forward: Oscar Pérez Solís, a mercurial ex-artillery officer, who had been a socialist and at first bitterly resisted the idea of joining with the communists;[3] José Bullejos, a post-office clerk in Bilbao, and his brother-in-law Gabriel León Trilla, a student son of a colonel: all shadowy, semi-conspirators rather than political leaders, acting in the wings of the main Spanish labour movements. All of them usually left Spain when they left gaol.

Of these early communists, Julián Gorkin (born Julián Gómez), in both his origin and his later career, was characteristic.[4] Son of an illiterate carpenter who was a strong republican, Gorkin joined the socialist youth of Valencia but was bowled over by the news of the Russian Revolution. He became a communist in 1921, and founded the party in Valencia when still scarcely out of his teens. He went to France, was expelled by the French police and went 'underground', as a full-time employee of the Comintern, editing a Paris communist paper, and acting as the Comintern's representative among Spanish exiles in those years. Gorkin abandoned the communist party partly because he discovered that he was being spied upon in Moscow by a

---

guess how many there were in the 1930s. See E. H. Carr, *Socialism in One Country*, vol. III, part II (London, 1964), p. 909.

1. M. N. Roy, *Memoirs* (Bombay, 1964), p. 234.

2. The first central committee members were César R. González (ex-socialist), secretary-general; Ramón Lamoneda (ex-socialist, who later returned to the socialists), labour secretary; Juan Andrade (sometime a radical, then a socialist and a future leader of POUM), director of the new communist periodical *La Antorcha*; Evaristo Gil (ex-socialist), Joaquín Ramos, José Baena, Luis Portela (from the socialist youth), and Antonio García Quejido, the best-known Spanish socialist after Iglesias, one of the printers who had founded the socialist party in the 1870s. García Quejido, Lamoneda and Anguiano soon returned to the socialists. Andrade, known for his 'hard, cruel pen', once wrote to a correspondent in Holland, touchingly, to ask if he could not send him a Dutch *compañera*: 'I would enjoy talking with women who are not like the Spaniards, that is very beautiful and very ignorant'.

3. Cf. the interesting study by Meaker.

4. See Julián Gorkin, 'My Experiences of Stalinism', in *The Review*, no. 2, published by the Imre Nagy Institute for Political Research, October 1959.

girl from Tiflis in the pay of the Russian secret political police, the GPU; partly, because the Comintern, through its then chief representative in Paris, the Lithuanian August Guralsky (born Abraham Heifetz, but also alias 'Kleine'), instructed him to plan the murder of General Primo de Rivera – though the mission was abandoned; and partly because Gorkin sided with Trotsky against Stalin in the late 1920s. He broke with the party in 1929 (and afterwards reappeared, along with many others of these early Spanish communists, as a leader of the new anti-Stalinist Marxist party, the POUM).[1]

In 1927, a small new access of strength came from the adhesion of most of the leaders of the Seville anarchists, especially among the port workers, metal workers, and bakers. This gave the party some influence in that city. At the Vizcaya conference of the party in 1928, there was dispute as to whether or not to take part in Primo de Rivera's proposed National Assembly; a Comintern representative, a veteran Polish communist, Henryk Walecki,[2] argued in favour of collaboration but, most unusually, was overruled. A campaign of agitation began against the Assembly. There were, once again, some arrests. New difficulties arose over the question of the policy to be followed towards the Pact of San Sebastián and the municipal elections of 1931. Once again a programme of isolation from all other parties was decided upon, the 'social fascists' (that is, the socialists) and the 'sterile' anarchists being regarded as, if anything, more pernicious than the more obviously bourgeois groups. The only occasion, in fact, during the dictatorship of Primo de Rivera when there was collaboration between the communists and the other political opposition movements in Spain occurred when, in 1925, the Catalan nationalists and the anarchists tried unsuccessfully to make common cause with the communists over a possible Catalan rising.

1. Conversation with Julián Gorkin. For the POUM, see below, p. 303. See also Victor Serge, *Memoirs of a Revolutionary* (London, 1963), p. 158; Gunther Nollau, *International Communism and World Revolution* (London, 1961), p. 69.

2. 'Walecki' was characteristic of a generation of communist international conspirators who play a part in Spain's history. Born Maximilian Horwitz in Warsaw in 1877 of a middle-class family, he was twice sent to Siberia before 1914, was present at Zimmerwald, at the Milan congress of the Italian party in 1921, at the Marseilles conference of the French party that same year, known as 'Brooks' in the USA – where had he not been in the Revolution's cause? He died in gaol in Moscow in 1937.

Colonel Maciá went to Moscow with the then secretary-general, José Bullejos, but the absence of urgency on the Russian side maddened 'el avi', while the Russians could not believe that a man as old as Maciá could achieve anything. Nothing came of the negotiations.[1]

The republic in 1931 thus found the communist party in poor morale after ten sterile years of controversy. The party did not exist in Barcelona, and there were only fourteen members in Bilbao. The highest estimate for membership at that time is 3,000, the lowest (by the Comintern itself) 120.[2] Andrés Nin returned from Russia after nearly ten years, but he had broken with communism over Stalin's persecution of Trotsky. He founded a small new group of his own, Izquierda Comunista. His old ex-anarchist comrade Maurín (who had never seen eye-to-eye with the central leadership) was also ready to break with the communists. He too formed a Marxist, anti-Stalinist splinter group, the Workers' and Peasants' party, (Bloque Obrero y Campesino) BOC. Both Nin and Maurín were regarded as Trotskyist, and, in a rough sense, they were, in that they were Marxists who disliked Stalin. But Trotsky criticized them from his exile in Norway. Their following remained small, but for the time being they prevented the communist party from finding members in Catalonia.[3]

The party began its life in the open in outright opposition to the republic, in accordance with instructions received through a large new Comintern delegation headed by Jules Humbert-Droz (a Swiss who had been for some years chief of the 'Latin' secretariat in the Comintern secretariat), and including 'Pierre', a Caucasian, another Swiss, Edgar Woog, alias Stirner, and a Frenchman, Octave Rabaté. Jacques Duclos was also there. In May 1931, Bullejos went to Moscow, to receive confirmation that the instructions were to 'Prolong the crisis by all possible means, to try and prevent the firm establish-

1. See Jules Humbert-Droz, *Mémoires* (Neuchâtel, 1969), vol. I, p. 212; José Bullejos, *Europa entre dos guerras* (Mexico, 1944) pp. 111–12.

2. Bullejos gave 3,000 (p. 135); *Communist International*, of 15 March 1934, 120. The seventh congress of the Comintern said there were 800 members in 1931. Matorras, p. 84, gave 1,500 as the figure. Underground parties did not collect membership dues and figures are therefore bound to vary.

3. The best accounts of the Izquierda Comunista during the republic are to be found in Grandizo Munis, *Jalones de derrota* (Mexico, 1948), and Andrés Nin, *Los problemas de la revolución española* (Paris, 1971), ed. Andrade. I had also the benefit of talks and correspondence with Joaquín Maurín in 1963.

ment of the republican régime, to frustrate the possibilities of effective social revolution, and, where possible, create soviets'. Humbert-Droz wrote from Madrid to his wife that he and Stirner wrote most of the articles in the communist press and that they all had very little to do: Stirner did a lot of sight-seeing, while Rabaté rose at noon, read the newspapers on the terrace of a café, had an aperitif, lunched well, returned to the café for coffee, and passed the rest of the day in a cinema or in bars. 'Our party', he added, 'sleeps with the deep and innocent dreams of childhood.'[1] That seemed also to be the case when another committee of investigation arrived from Moscow, headed by Walter Stoecker, a German.

The succeeding months were ones of dispute but no success, and the secretary-general, José Bullejos, later said that, throughout, there was enmity between the party leaders and the Comintern delegates, who arrogated to themselves all decisions. The party achieved 190,000 votes in the elections for the constituent Cortes in June 1931, but no deputy. Sanjurjo's rising inspired a manifesto by those members of the secretariat who happened to be in Madrid – Bullejos, Astigarrabía (from the Basque provinces), and Etelvino Vega – which launched the slogan 'Defence of the republic'. Subsequently, the Comintern representatives, on instructions from Moscow, repeated that the principal enemy was the 'butcher government' of Largo Caballero and Azaña, not the monarchists and their allies. Bullejos and the other Spanish leaders disagreed.[2] They left shortly afterwards to discuss this matter in Moscow. All these leaders were eventually expelled from the party and only got back to Spain after five months' enforced stay in Russia.[3] The new directorate of the party were all young (La Pasionaria, the oldest, was thirty-seven in 1933), and all owed their position to their uncritical support of the Moscow delegations in Spain. The new secretary-general, José Díaz, an ex-baker from Seville, and an ex-anarchist, was an honest and hard-working man of limited imagination; he was to be the director-general of the Spanish revolution, a man who always (however reluctantly) followed instruc-

1. Humbert-Droz, vol. II, p. 405f. 2. Bullejos, p. 140.

3. Matorras, pp. 136–7; Bullejos, pp. 134–43, 164–5. Of those expelled, Trilla and Vega later returned to the fold. Trilla was murdered in 1945 in uncertain circumstances. Vega became an army corps commander in the civil war and was shot by Francoist forces in 1939.

tions from Moscow.[1] Vicente Uribe, a metal worker, half-Castilian, half-Basque, who had been to Moscow, was the party theoretician and editor of *Mundo Obrero*. Antonio Mije, talkative, something of a demagogue, alive and feminine in appearance, the 'union secretary', came from Andalusia and was also an ex-anarchist. Jesús Hernández was the party's propagandist, an agitator *par excellence*, a fluent speaker who had been tirelessly active in street-fighting since his early teens when he had been known for an unsuccessful attempt on Prieto's life.

Throughout 1932 and 1933, the party, like the Falange, remained small and insignificant, its chief watchword being antagonism towards the anarchists and socialists. The only important step forward was the formation of a Catalan communist party, an admission that no Madrid-based party could hope to gather support in Catalonia.[2] Attempts to establish a separate, Moscow-orientated, general union failed. But the communists did have, from late 1933, a para-military organization, the MAOC (Milicias Antifascistas Obreras y Campesinas), led by an ex-non-commissioned officer in Morocco, Juan Modesto.[3]

Until 1934, the communists kept themselves to themselves. In the elections of 1933, they won 200,000 votes. They commented: 'The tremendous losses of the socialist party would have been even greater . . . had not the social fascist leaders, in particular Caballero and Co., undertaken new manoeuvres to deceive the working masses and keep them from crossing to our party by left demagogy.' The party argued that Lerroux's government was indistinguishable from Azaña's, and that 'the entire and inescapable responsibility . . . rests on the socialist party . . . the chief pillar of the bourgeois-junker counter revolution'.[4]

The communists were regarded with more alarm than their numbers would have suggested as necessary. This was partly because of the quantity of communist propaganda and partly, of course, because

1. Yet he emerges as the hero of the book by the renegade Jesús Hernández, *La Grande trahison* (Paris, 1953), since, during the civil war, he evidently found many instructions too much for him.

2. The Partit Comunista de Catalunya (Matorras, p. 149).

3. Workers' and Peasants' Antifascist Militias. See Juan Modesto, *Soy del quinto regimiento* (Paris, 1969), p. 14.

4. *Rundschau*, 30 November 1933; and 22 November 1930.

of the party's relations with the Soviet Union. But it was also partly because most members of the Spanish bourgeoisie did not distinguish carefully between one or other of the proletarian parties. The anarchists, after all, said that they were trying to achieve 'libertarian communism', and colonels in Burgos, like sherry exporters in the south, had no sensitivity for the nuances of revolutionary ideology.

The Comintern representative in Spain in the middle and late 1930s was an Argentinian of Italian origin, Vittorio Codovilla (known in Spain as 'Medina'). He had spent his life hitherto organizing communist parties in South America. He was a very fat man, bourgeois in manner and tastes. Jacques Doriot, when still the bright hope of the French communist party in the early twenties, remarked *à propos* of Codovilla's enormous appetite: 'Louis XIII liked having around him men who ate a lot. Codovilla will do well under Stalin.'[1] Later, a Bulgarian, 'Stepanov', came to assist Codovilla.[2] Given the youth and inexperience of the Spanish communists, the importance of these two foreigners in the party's deliberations was critical. It was Codovilla, for instance, who assured José Antonio Balbontín, a deputy who joined the party for a short time in the winter of 1933–4, that the communists would never make common cause with the socialists and republicans against 'monarcho-clerical reaction'.[3] That was in March 1934. Yet, from the summer of 1934 onwards, the policy of the Comintern was indeed to establish a 'Popular Front' of all democratic parties, working-class and bourgeois alike, to resist 'fascism'. From then onwards, therefore, all communist parties, including the Spanish one, spoke of the need to preserve 'parliamentary bourgeois democracy', until it could be replaced by 'proletarian democracy'.

At this time, with the shadows of war and fascism alike growing, the Soviet Union had a good reputation in Spain as elsewhere among Left and progressive people. The great Russian experiment indeed did not yet seem to have betrayed its ideals. Thanks to a successful

1. Julián Gorkin, *Caníbales políticos* (Mexico, 1941), p. 25. Manuel Tagüeña, *Testimonio de dos guerras* (Mexico, 1973), p. 356, gives a favourable picture.

2. Stepanov's real name was S. Mineff and during his career in the Comintern he was also known as Lebedev, Dr Chavaroche and Lorenzo Vanini. He was one of the most experienced professional revolutionaries.

3. Balbontín, p. 123.

programme of propaganda and unprecedented secrecy, the facts of agricultural collectivization were not known, and the persecution of Trotsky not understood. The communist party were to claim that they were responsible for the pact of the Popular Front which fought the Spanish general elections of February 1936. But it required little prompting for the socialists to adopt the salute with the clenched fist and bent arm (originated by the German communists), the red flag, the revolutionary phraseology, the calls to unite in the face of international fascism demanded throughout the world by communist parties. 'Anti-fascism' and 'the Popular Front' were becoming powerful myths, almost irresistible to those who both loved peace and liberty and were impatient with old parties.[1] Equally important on the Right were the myths of empire and national regeneration. The appearance in the Cortes elected in 1933 of a fascist and a communist was a portent and a warning.

1. Probably more important than any secret agent in Spain for the spread of Communist ideas were the tales told by Spanish workers who, after Asturias (see below, p. 143), went to work on the Moscow underground. They thought this a miracle of engineering.

9

Lerroux in power – the great strike of Saragossa – the monarchists at Rome – the Samper government – the Ley de Cultivos *– the Basque councillors – the CEDA enters the government – the October revolution in Madrid, Barcelona, and Asturias – the character of Franco*

THE history of Spain during the two and a half years after the general elections of November 1933 was marked by disintegration. From time to time, individuals would attempt vainly to halt the terrible and, as it transpired, irreversible process. They lacked the energy, luck, self-confidence and perhaps the magnanimity necessary for success.

The government after the elections was a coalition of the Centre, led by radicals. Lerroux became, to his satisfaction, Prime Minister. Gil Robles and the CEDA undertook to support him in the Cortes, but did not join the administration itself. This catholic party stood – ominously, as it seemed – in the wings, waiting for the moment when Gil Robles should give the word to take over power. The transformation, meanwhile, of Lerroux, the anti-clerical, into an ally of the catholic party was too much for his lieutenant, Martínez Barrio, who, after a short period as minister of the interior, passed into opposition at the head of his own group, renamed the Republican Union party.[1] Actually, Lerroux had voted for the previous government's anti-clerical legislation with reluctance. He was already a man of the Right, more than of the Centre. His minister of public works was Rafael Guerra del Río, an intemperate leader of 'Young Barbarians' in 1909; he now seemed a mere machine politician. One added source of confusion was the purely personal matter of the distrust felt for both Lerroux and Gil Robles by President Alcalá Zamora, who intrigued against the former, and tried to avoid calling the latter to form a government. Alcalá distrusted Lerroux for his corruption, and

1. President Alcalá Zamora tried to persuade him not to leave, saying that the radicals were 'the base of the republic'. But Martínez Barrio feared that Lerroux would compromise him in some dishonourable action if he stayed. See his version in Azaña, vol. IV, p. 718.

Gil Robles as a secret monarchist. In the circumstances, he preferred Lerroux and, in fact, never called Gil Robles: a weakening of the democratic process, since the catholic leader was as prepared to work in a bourgeois democracy as much as the socialists were.

Lerroux's first difficulties derived from a series of anarchist challenges. They attacked isolated civil guard posts and derailed the Barcelona–Seville express, killing nineteen people. In Madrid, there was a long telephone strike. In both Valencia and Saragossa there were general strikes lasting for weeks. The great general strike at Saragossa, designed, to begin with, to free prisoners taken by the government the previous year, lasted indeed for fifty-seven days. The CNT never issued strike pay, but the workers' resilience astonished the rest of the country. The anarchist leaders, as usual, for a time believed that they were in the anteroom of the millennium; and some of their *pistolero* friends heightened the drama by sporadic shooting. The strikers decided at one point to send their wives and children away to Barcelona by rail. The civil guard fired on the train, and prevented it from reaching its destination. The evacuees later went by caravan. This unrest was partly the consequence of a new and 'suicidal egoism' of employers who celebrated, throughout Spain, the Right's victory at the polls by attempting to lower wages, raise rents, and enforce evictions.[1] On 8 December, a revolutionary committee, led by Buenaventura Durruti, Cipriano Mera, and Dr Isaac Puente was installed at Saragossa. This fought for several days against the civil police, reinforced by the army, backed by tanks. Durruti became a national legend. In numerous places in Aragon and Catalonia, 'libertarian communism' was briefly established. Violence occurred in many places, causing 87 dead, many wounded, and 700 imprisoned.[2] It was hard to accept that the country was at peace. Not surprisingly, militancy spread more and more through the UGT, especially its largest, but least well led, section, the agrarian FNTT. Their members were hit by falling wages, themselves the consequence

1. The phrase 'suicidal egoism' was used by Gil Robles to describe these actions of his followers, in an interview in *El Debate*, 8 March 1936.

2. Places briefly in anarchist hands included: Barbastro, Alcalá de Gurrea (Huesca), Alcampel (Huesca), Albalate de Cinca (Huesca), Villanueva de Sigena (Huesca), Valderroboll (Guadalajara), Beceite (Teruel), Alcorisa (Teruel), Mas de las Matas (Teruel) and Calanda (Teruel).

of right-wing chairmen having been appointed by the radical minister of labour, José Estadella, to Largo's arbitration boards. The recovery of the agrarian oligarchy was everywhere complemented by a more radical attitude on the part of the workers, supported by a more embittered Largo Caballero. Prieto, a moderate socialist, if ever there was one, did not discourage this, to his everlasting regret. Besteiro did: he criticized the 'anti-governmentalism' in 1934 of his colleagues as much as he had done their 'pro-governmentalism' in 1931, to no avail.

In the new year of 1934, the government introduced a series of measures designed to halt the reforms of their predecessors. The substitution of lay for religious schools was indefinitely postponed. The Jesuits were shortly to be found teaching again.[1] By a clever debating speech, Gil Robles secured that priests would be treated as if they were civil servants on pensions and they began to be paid two-thirds of their salary of 1931. Though the Agrarian Law remained on the statute book, its application was in many places tacitly abandoned. An amnesty was eventually also granted to political prisoners – including General Sanjurjo and all those imprisoned at the time of the rising in 1932. This clemency merely stimulated old plotters to new schemes.

By this time, many small *pueblos* seemed to have been utterly cut into two by politics. In places which still had socialist or left-wing councils, efforts were being made to impose a quite new cultural order, the exact reverse of its predecessor in that religious ideas had given way to atheism, not just agnosticism; religious festivals were giving way to festivals of the revolutionary tradition – The First of May, the anniversary of the Russian Revolution or the death of Galán and García Hernández. Women, whom old Spain had traditionally kept at home behind high windows, came out into the streets wearing party colours, 'forming groups like men, singing, shouting and dancing in great gangs to celebrate the name of Liberty'.[2] The battles took place now over working conditions as well as over the church. For example, in one village in Aragon, a café had been made into a compulsory labour exchange. Everyone had to seek and obtain work through the officials in the café. Nobody liked

1. Though the decree formally banishing them continued to be law.
2. Lisón Tolosana, p. 46.

that and the men of the Right disobeyed, as did all workers who had any old arrangement to work for a particular farmer. The Left called a general strike: the men of the Right went on working, and were picketed. Fighting began and a death occurred. Threats, taunts, and demonstrations then became part and parcel of the life in the village. Everyone began to join one group or another. The uncommitted sought ideologies, while the leaders schemed to make politics out of all entertainments.

People on the Right assumed automatically that Azaña's, and the socialists', defeat meant a victory for old Spain. But was Lerroux's a government of 'provocation' or simply of reaction? Certainly, whether the government liked it or not, all over Spain the old masters of the economy used what they believed to be their opportunity to restore their position; and, as certainly, the socialist party responded by despairing of, even denouncing, the republic. In a speech in his constituency of Granada, even Fernando de los Ríos said as much. From that time on, *El Socialista* regularly argued that the republic was as bad as the monarchy had been and that, in this bourgeois republic, there was no place for the proletariat. Azaña tried to point out to the socialists the danger of this attitude. If the socialists really tried to bring 'the revolution', he said, they would fail. De los Ríos, to whom he spoke, said that 'the masses dominated the leaders'. Azaña replied, 'the feelings of the masses can be changed'. He pointed out that, to prepare an insurrection, as the socialists seemed to be doing, was to invite the army to re-enter politics: 'The army would be delighted to launch a repression against the workers'. De los Ríos passed on Azaña's remarks to Largo who, however, brushed them aside and, three weeks later, the extremist 'Caballerista' view triumphed in the national committee of the Spanish socialist party resulting in the resignation of moderates such as Besteiro, Saborit and Trifón Gómez. A 'pre-revolutionary' commission was then formed, and, on 31 January, Largo told the Madrid socialist party that he desired to reaffirm his belief in the necessity of preparing a proletarian rising.[1] It was a fatal error of judgement.

From that time onwards, the socialists began to arrange military

1. See Azaña, vol. IV, p. 652 for the conversation with de los Ríos, and Marichal's comments in Azaña's *Obras completas*, vol. III, pp. xiv–xv.

training for their youth, and thus joined the insurrectionary Right, as well as the minuscule groups on the edges of Spanish politics such as the Falange and the communists, in the character of their challenge to the bourgeois republic.

The Carlists had been active thus for months. In Navarre, their red berets (*boinas rojas*) were weekly seen in the market-places. A dashing colonel, Enrique Varela, who had twice won Spain's highest medal for gallantry in Morocco, was procured to train these new *requetés* – as the levies had been named in the Carlist Wars, from a line of the marching song of their most ferocious battalion. Varela (whom the Carlist leaders Fal Conde and Rodezno had met in gaol after the 1932 rising) travelled about the Pyrenean villages dressed as a priest, known as '*Tío Pepe*' (Uncle Pepe), acting as a missionary of war. When promoted a general, he was replaced by Colonel Rada.[1] The Carlist communion claimed no less than 700,000 members in 540 sections in early 1934 and, though that surely was a gross exaggeration, there is no doubt that the movement was growing fast, as a result of the quickening political awareness of the catholic petty bourgeoisie in western Andalusia, Navarre, Valencia and parts of Catalonia.[2]

On 31 March 1934, Antonio Goicoechea, the monarchist leader in the Cortes, together with two Carlists (Rafael Olazábal and Antonio Lizarza) and General Barrera (the unsuccessful coordinator of 1932, who had escaped), visited Mussolini. The Spaniards gave an impression of disaccord as to the aim of their plots. Mussolini, however, brushed this aside by saying that all that was necessary was that the movement should be 'monarchist and of a corporative and representative' character. He promised 1½ million pesetas, 20,000 rifles, 200 machine-guns, and 20,000 grenades to the Spanish rebels, and agreed to send more when the rising started. The money was paid the next

1. José María Pemán, *Un soldado en la historia* (Cádiz, 1954), pp. 134–5. Neither Rada nor Varela had Carlist connections. Both were Andalusians. Varela was the son of a sergeant-major and had from the earliest age been a man of overpowering ambition. His bravery in Morocco was a byword. See Antonio Lizarza, *Memorias de la conspiración* (Pamplona, 1954), p. 33. His description of events is borne out by Felipe Bertrán Güell, *Preparación y desarrollo del alzamiento nacional* (Valladolid, 1939).

2. See Martin Blinkhorn, *Journal of Contemporary History*, vol. VII, nos. 3 and 4, 'Carlism and the Spanish Crisis of 1934'.

day.[1] Thereafter, the *requetés* developed fast, committees being formed to deal with, for example, recruitment of officers, propaganda, arms purchase, and strategy.[2] There had been several previous tentative expeditions by monarchist or other plotters to Italy; and now, with the arrival there of ex-King Alfonso, Rome became a new focus of conspiracy against the republic. On the other hand, with the appointment of the energetic Fal Conde as 'royal secretary-general' of the Carlists in May 1934, that movement differentiated itself more and more sharply from the orthodox monarchists, of whom they spoke as the 'riff-raff of the Alfonsine monarchy which has adopted the name of Renovación Española, as if we did not know that the "renovation" with which they entice us is the return of a régime of iniquity'. Rodezno, Fal Conde's predecessor, nevertheless remained influential as the movement's leader in the Cortes, and continued to believe in a broader movement.[3]

Four days after the meeting in Rome, Lerroux resigned in protest against the vacillation of the President, Alcalá Zamora, in giving his signature to the law pardoning Sanjurjo and the plotters of 1932. The new Prime Minister, an indolent Valencian lawyer, Ricardo Samper, was also a radical. He owed his promotion to the fact that he was a friend of President Alcalá Zamora, who instinctively preferred a weak Prime Minister, in order to justify his own interference. Samper did little save try and maintain his majority, though, to be fair, settlements continued under the agrarian law all 1934 until October. His minister of the interior, however, Salazar Alonso, smelled revolution everywhere and removed, as was within his legal power, many town councils on the excuse that they did 'not inspire confidence in matters of public order'. In fact, he sought, by changing such councils, if they were socialist, to get rid of many FNTT members' last political friends in their villages. This was certainly a provocative action, reminiscent of the anti-socialist measures taken by fascist régimes in

1. Lizarza, pp. 23–5. News of this meeting was first revealed when certain documents were captured in Goicoechea's house during the civil war. Goicoechea himself admitted the events in 1937. See *Manchester Guardian*, 4 December 1937, for Goicoechea's admission. A photocopy of the agreement in Goicoechea's hand is frontispiece to José Luis Alcofar Nassaes, *CTV* (Barcelona, 1972).

2. Carlist Archives. From this time onwards Alfonso Carlos's nephew, Xavier de Bourbon-Parme, acted in conjunction with Fal Conde as 'national delegate'.

3. Qu. Robinson, p. 176.

other parts of Europe. Combined with evictions, the revived use of migrant labour and dismissals on political grounds, this action made the countryside most tense in early 1934, when wages were falling and hunger on the increase. Gil Robles's speeches only fanned the flames as young men of the Right began to see that the pendulum of politics was now swinging against ideas of compromise: 'leaders are always right! (*¡los jefes no se equivocan!*)', cried the young *CEDAistas* at a great rally at the Escorial in April.[1] There followed, at the beginning of June, a well-organized peasant strike in the south, during the harvest, by the socialist FNTT. This was fired by the repeal of the Municipal Boundaries Act which had given local *casas del pueblo* the control of labour. The FNTT had gained acceptance of their demands on wage rates and of their proposal for guarantees that all available labour be employed. But they struck over the demand that harvest wages should be paid for the rest of the year. The anarchist leaders agreed to support this, but many socialist moderates did not. Salazar Alonso, the minister of the interior, believing that he had a revolutionary general strike on his hands, sent in the civil guard, imposed press censorship in the south and made many, though short-term, arrests, of socialist leaders, including mayors and even deputies. The strike collapsed, the harvest was brought in with police protection, while the UGT and the moderate leaders were accused of letting down the FNTT by inaction.[2] Next, also in June, a serious situation arose in Catalonia.

The Catalan government, the *Generalidad* (which had made little impact on either the national or the international scene since the passage of the Catalan statute), had passed a law, the *Ley de Cultivos*, which enabled tenant farmers with vines (the *rabassaires*), in the region, to secure a freehold of their farms if they had had them for fifteen years.[3] The proprietors complained to the supreme legal body of the republic, the Tribunal of Constitutional Guarantees, which, by a small majority, rejected the *Ley de Cultivos* on the grounds that the *Generalidad* could not pronounce on such a matter. But Luis Com-

1. The socialist youth tried to prevent trainloads of CEDA supporters from arriving at the Escorial by bending the railway lines. See Santiago Carrillo, *Demain Espagne* (Paris, 1974), p. 42.

2. See for this Paul Preston, *European Studies Review*, vol. I, no. 2.

3. See above, p. 82, for the origins of this problem.

panys, who, on Colonel Maciá's death, in December 1933, had become president of the *Generalidad*, ratified the law of his own accord. In taking this step, which constituted a challenge to the government in Madrid, Companys was egged on by his new right-wing counsellor for the interior, José Dencás. Dencás, a doctor, was a leader of an extreme separatist group, Estat Catalá, founded by Maciá in 1922, now the main faction of militant Catalan youth. They wanted outright independence. They had a green-shirted militia, the *escamots*, headed by a reckless terrorist, Miguel Badía, who had spent most of his youth in gaol for an attempt on the life of Alfonso XIII. For a short time in 1934, Companys nevertheless had Badía as police chief. Even without this complication, the predicament of a left-of-centre Catalan government with a right-of-centre one in Madrid was certain to cause difficulties before long. Azaña had spoken in words of caution to Companys as he had earlier done to de los Ríos. Companys had seemed to appreciate the dangers at first but afterwards had been carried away by what he thought the 'masses' desired.

The serious constitutional dispute thereby engendered was still simmering when the question of the separatist aspirations of the Basques also came to the fore. The Basques' financial relations with the central government in Madrid had been dictated by the *concierto económico* of 1876. This gave the Basques an autonomous fiscal system, by which they taxed themselves and paid a single sum to the state. The municipal councils of the Basque provinces believed that certain laws introduced by Samper's government threatened the *concierto*, and decided to hold municipal elections in the three provinces of Vizcaya, Guipúzcoa, and Alava, wherein the elected representatives would declare themselves publicly on the question of the *concierto*. The government forbade the elections. When, despite this prohibition, the elections were nevertheless held, the new councillors were arrested. A series of wild demonstrations in favour of Basque home rule followed throughout the three provinces. The Basque nationalist party, catholic and bourgeois as they were almost to a man, began to embark upon an alliance with the socialists and the Left that was as bizarre as it was fateful. They were disillusioned with the CEDA and sought new sponsors.

While both separatist problems in Spain had become simultaneously acute, the nation was shocked by the rumour that several cases of arms had been landed in Asturias for the benefit of the socialists by the usually 'moderate' Prieto, on the steamer *Turquesa.*[1] The government proclaimed a state of alarm; Gil Robles, in a great meeting of his youth movement (JAP), held at Covadonga, the sanctuary in Asturias commemorating the point where the Visigoth King Pelayo began the *Reconquista* of Spain from the Moors, announced: 'We will no longer suffer this state of affairs to continue'. The CNT and UGT, acting together, for the first time for many years, proclaimed a general strike in Asturias, so making it difficult for the CEDA delegates to this meeting to return home to Madrid. A week later, Gil Robles declared that, when the Cortes met in October after the summer, he and his party would no longer support the government of Samper. The implication was that he would himself take over power. At this, the UGT issued a statement denouncing Gil Robles, 'the lay Jesuit'. If the CEDA should enter the government without declaring support for the republic, the UGT 'would not answer for their future action'. The inference was that the UGT would regard the entry of the CEDA into the government as the first step towards the establishment of a fascist state in Spain. Largo Caballero then sought to form an *alianza obrera*, a workers' alliance, which he hoped would bring together socialists, communists and anarchists; he outmanoeuvred Prieto and other reformists. Prieto told Besteiro that he would have liked to strangle Largo; Besteiro sensibly replied that it would be 'better to resist him'.[2] But Prieto, de los Ríos and all the moderate leaders, were nevertheless soon swept along by a wave of optimistic militancy in which the youth movement played the main part.

1. These were arms bought from certain Portuguese revolutionaries in Galicia by the socialist deputy, Amador Fernández. The steamer left Cádiz with the destination 'Jibouti' pasted on the cases but was later diverted to the Asturias. See an article of Prieto's in *España Republicana* of Buenos Aires, reprinted in his *Convulsiones de España*, vol. I, p. 109. Afterwards, Prieto fled to France, where he stayed till late 1935. It was not an honourable exile, and he was not allowed to forget it. (He had done the same in 1917 and 1930.)

2. Azaña, vol. IV, p. 904. The socialist journal *Leviatán*, edited by Araquistain, attacked Azaña for his moderation: 'either one renounces the revolution, friend Azaña, and gives oneself up to literature, or one renounces the law, and then law-abiding poets have no function' (qu. Azaña, vol. III, p. xxi).

Gil Robles's reluctance to declare his adhesion to the republic derived from a fear of losing many right-wing supporters if he did so, since he would seem to be accepting the still unrevised anti-clerical clauses of the constitution; he needed the monarchists' financial help and also, perhaps, he had a genuine abhorrence of the republic. But this was the late summer of 1934. The Spanish socialists of the UGT had seen how the German and Austrian socialists had been overwhelmed by Hitler and Dollfuss respectively during the last eighteen months. Where lay the difference between Dollfuss and Gil Robles? Gil Robles did nothing to make it clear.

The time for the reassembly of the Cortes drew near. The atmosphere was worsened by several political murders. On 4 October, Gil Robles withdrew the support of the CEDA from Samper's government, which resigned. Alcalá Zamora still did not ask Gil Robles to form a government. Instead, Lerroux was again entrusted with this task. He included three members of the CEDA in his cabinet, though not Gil Robles himself. Alcalá Zamora still suspected him. Lerroux also had no intention, if he could help it, of letting in a young rival for leadership of Spain's middle class.[1] On the other hand, the President shrank from new elections such as the socialists had expected. Further, he had wanted only one CEDA minister. Gil Robles was strong enough to insist on three.

The reaction was swift and violent. Azaña's Republican Left party,[2] Martínez Barrio and even Miguel Maura denounced the President's action in handing over the republic to its enemies. In Madrid, the UGT proclaimed a general strike, and certain socialist

1. The CEDA's three ministers were: Giménez Fernández (agriculture); Anguera de Sojo (labour); and Aizpún (justice). Salazar Alonso was dropped. Of these, Aizpún was the founder and organizer of the CEDA in Navarre; Anguera de Sojo had once been a Catalan nationalist, but had seemed to have betrayed his colleagues in 1931 as civil governor of Barcelona; and Giménez Fernández was an enlightened scholar, and would be the most socially responsible minister of agriculture under the republic. Anguera had been public prosecutor and as such had been responsible for many confiscations of *El Socialista.* Aizpún was close to the Carlists. Gil Robles's comments are interesting (p. 138), and Azaña (vol. IV, p. 515) regards Anguera as *au fond* a loyal republican. By and large, the Left's hostility to these three men as individuals was not justified.

2. Azaña's old Republican Action party, together with Domingo's Radical Socialists and Casares's Gallegan Autonomy party, had been united, in April 1934, into the Izquierda Republicana (Republican Left).

militants advanced, firing, towards the ministry of the interior in the Puerta del Sol. A few young officers accompanied them. But the CNT did not. *JAPista* youth members ensured essential services.[1] The countryside was inactive, exhausted by the strikes earlier in the year. The *alianza obrera*[2] only extended in Madrid to the socialists and some communists.[3] There was general confusion. Largo Caballero dithered. By the end of the day, the government were masters of the situation, and the socialist leaders had been arrested.

In Barcelona, the entry of the CEDA into the government caused Companys to proclaim 'the Catalan state' as part of a 'federal Spanish republic'. Once again, Companys was stimulated to precipitate action by his counsellor of the interior, Dencás. He was also menaced on the Left by the *rabassaires*, the Catalan vineyard tenants, who threatened physically to take over the land which they held to be theirs under the now-suspended *Ley de Cultivos*. The burden of Companys's appeal to Catalonia was an attack on the fascism of the CEDA, despite the fascist colouring of Dencás's ideas:

> The monarchical and fascist powers which have been for some time attempting to betray the republic have attained their object [announced Companys]. In this solemn hour, in the name of the people and of parliament, the government over which I preside assumes all the functions of power in Catalonia, proclaims the Catalan state of the federal Spanish republic, and, strengthening its relations with those who direct this general protest against fascism, invites them to establish the provisional government of the republic in Catalonia.

This was at once a proclamation of a new relationship between Catalonia and the rest of Spain and also an encouragement to the revolutionaries of Madrid to declare themselves the government, if necessary establishing themselves in Barcelona. A wave of Catalan nationalism, and hostility to all things Castilian, had been sweeping through Catalonia that summer, which Companys, who was weak,

1. Gil Robles, p. 140.

2. The communists agreed to support this in the course of the meeting of their central committee on 11 and 12 September (Branko Lazitch, *Los partidos comunistas de Europa*, Madrid, 1958, p. 338).

3. Largo Caballero officially repulsed the communists when they offered help, according to La Pasionaria (Ibarruri, p. 175). See also discussion in 'Andrés Suárez', *El proceso contra el POUM* (Paris, 1974), p. 38.

found impossible to withstand. Dencás, meantime, would have liked to have declared outright independence.

This Catalan rebellion was, however, crushed nearly as quickly as the general strike had been in Madrid. There was some fighting between Dencás's *escamots* and the *Mozos de Escuadra* (the security force established in Catalonia under the monarchy). Forty people were killed. The anarchists held aloof saying that they would not collaborate with the socialists unless they abandoned their collabora tion with the Esquerra. Dencás promptly arrested Durruti and other anarchist leaders. Companys sent for General Batet, commander of the division quartered in Barcelona, and asked him to transfer his allegiance to the new federal régime. Batet, a Catalan, however, placed himself at the orders of the central government, and declared a state of war. Acting deliberately slowly in order to save life, and allow escapes, he soon arrested Companys and his government – with the exception of Dencás, who escaped down a sewer to freedom, and, ultimately, to Rome. All resistance was quickly overcome in the rest of Barcelona, and Companys broadcast a dignified appeal to his followers to lay down their arms. Companys and his followers were arrested; so, unjustly and illogically, was Azaña, who was in Barcelona for the funeral of his finance minister Jaime Carner.

The 'October revolution' thus failed in Madrid and in Barcelona. There were other outbursts, but, with one exception, these were also crushed. The exception was Asturias.[1] Here the rising – for such it undoubtedly was – was directed by the tough, politically-conscious miners of the region. Their action was politically, rather than economically, inspired. While, elsewhere in Spain, the working-class parties had been divided about the revolution, in Asturias, anarchists, socialists, communists, the Workers' and Peasants' Alliance, the UGT, and the Asturian regional CNT committee, cooperated under the rallying cry UHP! (*¡Uníos, Hermanos Proletarios!*).[2] The ground for this alliance had been prepared by a famous article the previous

1. See *La revolución de octubre en España*, a pamphlet issued by the government in Madrid in 1934; Peirats, vol. I, pp. 83–94; Mrs Leah Manning's *What I Saw in Spain* (London, 1935); Frank Jellinek's account in *The Civil War in Spain* (London, 1938); and Manuel Grossi's vivid diary of events, *La insurrección de Asturias*, written in Cartagena prison in 1935.

2. 'Working-class brothers, unite!' The CNT dockers in Gijón were fervently for the alliance with the socialists, others (e.g. metal-workers in La Felguera) less so.

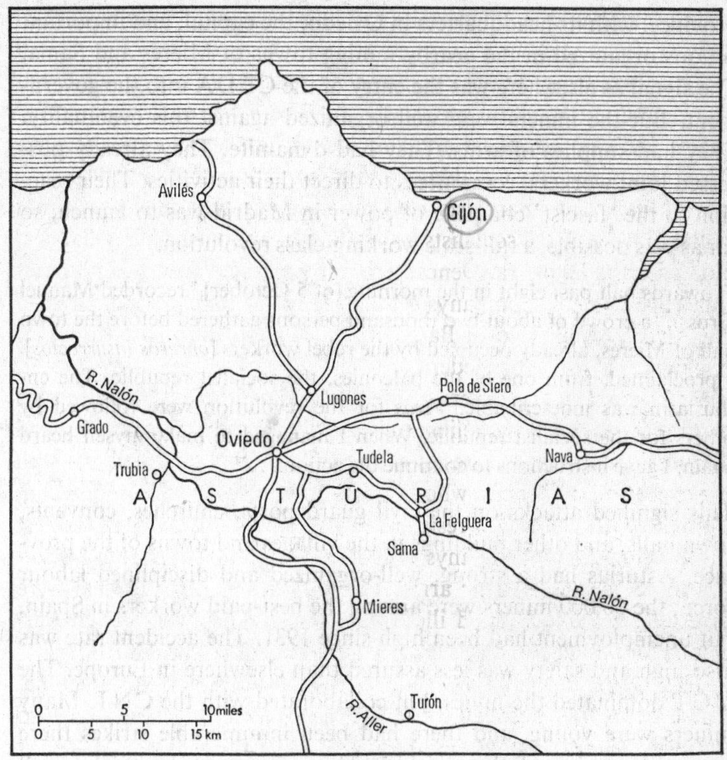

4. The revolution in Asturias, 1934

February by a young leader of the CNT, Valeriano Orobón Fernández, in the journal, *La Tierra*. He had argued that the danger of fascism in Spain was really such that a new working-class alliance was necessary. Only Asturias followed his advice.[1] The FAI had failed to capture the local CNT, and that too helped the alliance. Abroad, the international communist reaction was, for once, swift; on 10 October, the Comintern, that is, its executive committee (the ECCI), announced its proposal, for joint action in support of the Spanish workers' alliance, to the (second) socialist International.[2]

The rising in Asturias was carefully prepared throughout the

1. Qu. Peirats, vol. I, p. 79f.

2. *Rundschau*, iii, 60 (15 November 1934), p. 2680.

province, with its headquarters in Oviedo, the capital, and important actions organized in the nearby mining towns of Mieres and Sama. The signal as elsewhere was the entry of the CEDA into the government. But the miners were well organized against this eventuality. They had supplies of arms. They had dynamite. They already possessed joint workers' committees to direct their activities. Their reaction to the 'fascist' conquest of power in Madrid was to launch, so far as was possible, a full-scale working-class revolution.

> 'Towards half past eight in the morning [of 5 October],' recorded Manuel Grossi, 'a crowd of about two thousand persons gathered before the town hall of Mieres, already occupied by the rebel workers [*obreros insurrectos*]. I proclaimed, from one of the balconies, the socialist republic. The enthusiasm was indescribable. *Vivas* for the revolution were followed by others for the socialist republic. When I managed to make myself heard again, I gave instructions to continue the action . . .'[1]

This signified attacks on the civil guard posts, churches, convents, town halls, and other buildings in the villages and towns of the province. Asturias had a strong, well-organized and disciplined labour force; the 50,000 miners were among the best-paid workers in Spain, but unemployment had been high since 1931. The accident rate was also high and safety was less assured than elsewhere in Europe. The UGT dominated the mines, but collaborated with the CNT. Many miners were young, and there had been innumerable strikes there since the coming of the republic. The communists were also well established in Asturias (particularly in Mieres) and their leadership competent.

Within three days of the start of the revolution, much of Asturias was in the hands of the miners. Each town or village which had been captured was controlled by a revolutionary committee which made itself responsible for the feeding and the security of the inhabitants. A radio station installed at Turón maintained morale. 'Comrades,' announced the revolutionary committee of Grado, 'we are creating a new society . . . it is not surprising that the world which we are forging costs blood, grief and tears; everything on earth is fecund, soldiers of the Ideal! Put up your rifles! Women, eat little, only what is necessary! Long live the social revolution!'[2] The arms factories at Trubia

1. Grossi, p. 25. 2. Peirats, vol. I, pp. 86–7.

and La Vega (Oviedo) were taken over by a committee of their workers and were made to work night and day. Elsewhere, factories and mines were deserted. Recruitment offices demanded the services of all workers between the ages of eighteen and forty for the 'Red Army'. Thirty thousand workers had been mobilized for battle within ten days.[1] The cooperation between the parties surprised even themselves. Even the anarchists recognized 'the need for temporary dictatorship', though the limitation of this activity to a group of *pueblos* prevented questions of state organization from dividing them from the communists. The communists in some *pueblos* showed themselves keener on establishing their own dictatorship than sending men to the front. But, as a rule, the cry *¡UHP!* was in no way misleading.

While the miners of Asturias had thus successfully established a revolutionary soviet throughout their province, they were also engaged all the time in fighting. This particularly occurred in Oviedo and in Gijón. The 1,500 regular troops based in Asturias and elsewhere on the north coast were too few in number to be able to do more than hold out in their besieged garrison in the centre of Oviedo. In the meantime, there was a certain amount of pillage and unprovoked violence on the part of the revolutionaries. The local committees set out to maintain discipline, and there were instances of workers saving the lives of menaced members of the bourgeoisie. There were a number of outrages. Several churches and convents were burned. The bishop's palace, and much of the university, at Oviedo were destroyed during the attempts to capture the Pelayo barracks, which were held by the civil guard. A few businessmen and about twelve priests were shot, especially in Turón. At Sama, thirty civil guards and assault guards sustained a siege of a day and a half. When they surrendered, some were shot. These atrocities were, no doubt, the consequence of confusion, not design; but they made matters much more difficult for the two hitherto moderate socialist leaders, Ramón González Peña and Belarmino Tomás, who, somewhat to their own surprise, found themselves at the head of this revolution.

1. *La revolución de octubre*, p. 40. Grossi speaks of 50,000 miners being under arms by the end of the revolution. Peirats says the CNT had some 22,000 organized workers in the region (vol. I, p. 83). This figure may be an exaggeration. See discussion in Jackson, p. 153.

The government were now faced by what no one denied was a civil war. Indeed, the committee in control at Mieres were contemplating a march on Madrid. Though they did not, of course, know that, Lerroux and his ministers now took several harsh decisions. First, they sent for Generals Goded and Francisco Franco to act as joint chiefs of staff to direct the suppression of the rebellion.[1] Secondly, they accepted the advice of these two officers when they recommended the dispatch of elements of the *Regulares* and of the Foreign Legion to reduce the miners. Goded, as has been seen, had been chief of staff for some months at the beginning of the republic but had been dismissed by Azaña.

Francisco Franco Bahamonde was forty when he reached his new post under Lerroux. Born in 1892 at the naval base at El Ferrol in Galicia, the son of a dissolute naval paymaster and descendant of naval administrators on both sides of his conventional family, Franco was intended for the sea. But there was no room in the naval Cadet School. The naval disaster in the Spanish American War of 1898 was responsible. Instead, he went, in 1907, to the Infantry Academy at Toledo. He was posted to Morocco in 1912, where he became, in quick succession, the youngest captain, major, colonel and general, gaining the last rank after the victorious end to the war. In 1916, he had been severely wounded in the stomach and returned to Spain for four years' garrison-duty at Oviedo. He was second-in-command of the Foreign Legion at its inception in 1920, commanded it from 1923 to 1927 and, in particular, led the landing-party at Alhucemas Bay (under Sanjurjo) in 1925 which brought victory. He had criticized Primo de Rivera to his face, when the dictator seemed to be trying to prepare the army to abandon Morocco, at a famous dinner in 1924. Indeed, he and some other *africanistas* even planned, in that year, to arrest Primo and his staff out of outrage against the idea of abandonment of the territory. Franco was dedicated to his profession – he never drank, never went out with women, and, at that time (as his pious biographers make haste to interject), never seemed religious. His puritanism may be attributed to the indiscretions of his father, the naval paymaster, who separated from his wife in 1907 and lived with a mistress in Madrid thenceforth until his death in 1942, aged

1. General Masquelet, whom Azaña had appointed chief of staff in 1932, was transferred.

eighty-seven; and to the piety of his mother, who died in 1933 on the first step of a pilgrimage to Rome. Franco's childhood was, no doubt, an unhappy time and his adolescence a time of struggle.

Life at Toledo was brutal. Franco always was known as a cruel disciplinarian. He had a reputation for bravery and for good luck under fire: he rode white horses in battle. The relative efficiency of the Foreign Legion owed much to him. He gained his first experience of fighting revolutions during the general strike of 1917, when he was in Oviedo. He married – after delays, due to campaigning – a girl of good Asturian family, Carmen Polo. Franco was short in height and, even in early middle life, had developed a stomach. His voice had also acquired a high-pitched tone which caused him to give to military commands the note of a prayer. To a British politician, he seemed like 'a doctor with a big family practice and a good bedside manner', into whose 'cotton-wool entanglements' of 'amazing complacency' it was impossible to penetrate.[1] He had a great reputation as 'the brilliant young general', but he refused to declare himself on any side in politics, though he had admired the idea of Maura's 'revolution from above' and liked Primo de Rivera in the end. Even when the republic abolished promotions gained by merit, and so relegated him from near the top of the list of brigadier-generals to the bottom, he had taken the blow without much complaint. When, in 1931, it was published in *ABC* that the new government intended to appoint him high commissioner of Morocco, Franco wrote that he would refuse such a post since to accept would reveal 'a prejudice in favour of the régime recently installed, and a lukewarm loyalty to those who only yesterday epitomized the nation'.[2] He was shy, quiet and patient, but also ruthless, ambitious and determined: 'a less straightforward man I never met', said an American journalist who talked to him in 1936.[3] When monarchist conspirators were asked, 'Is Franco with you?', they were unable to give a clear answer. He had not been associated with General Sanjurjo in the *pronunciamiento* of 1932. But he disliked Azaña's reforms, particularly the closure of the new Military Academy at Saragossa, of which he had been the first commandant and to whose courses he had devoted much care (on the inspiration of

1. Sir Samuel Hoare, *Ambassador on Special Mission* (London, 1946), p. 46.
2. *ABC*, 21 April 1931.
3. John Whitaker, 'Prelude to War', *Foreign Affairs*, October 1942.

Germany, which he had visited in 1928). Republicans knew, from addresses that he had given when at Saragossa, that he was a friend of authoritarian rule. They knew too that he had, for a long time, been interested in politics. As early as 1926, he had been demanding books on political theory to be sent to his headquarters.[1] But the general's brother, Ramón, a noted pilot who had been the first man to fly the south Atlantic, was a republican, even a revolutionary: it had been he who in 1930 had dropped republican pamphlets over the Royal Palace during the abortive republican rising.

The government called not only on General Franco, who knew Asturias well, to direct the battle against the miners, but also upon the Foreign Legion and Moroccan troops, because they plainly doubted whether other troops would be successful. The minister of war, the radical Diego Hidalgo, later explained that he was appalled at the alternative prospect of seeing the young conscripts from the peninsula dying in Asturias because of their inexperience. They would be fighting against past-masters of dynamiting and of the technique of the ambush. 'I decided', he wrote, 'that it was necessary to call on the units which Spain maintains for its defence, whose *métier* is to fight and die in the accomplishment of their duty.'[2] Within a few hours of General Franco's arrival at the ministry of war, units of the Foreign Legion were dispatched under Colonel Yagüe to assist the regular garrisons in the north. Another column under a liberal general, López Ochoa, who had led the military side to the republican conspiracy in 1930, fought its way to reinforce the beleaguered garrison in the centre of Oviedo.

The Foreign Legion and the *Regulares* were successful. Accompanied by aircraft, they swiftly relieved Oviedo. Gijón fell on 10 October. In these towns, the conquerors gave themselves over to a vile repression. After fifteen days of war and revolution, only the communists wanted to fight on in the other towns. González Peña resigned his directorship of the revolution. The Legion captured several of the towns house by house. Colonel Yagüe, in command of the Legion, encouraged the exemplary use of brutality in the repression. In the end, the rebels at Sama finally surrendered. Belarmino

1. Information deriving from Dr Gregorio Marañón.
2. *La revolución de octubre*, p. 41.

Tomás, the socialist leader who had been at the centre of all the fighting, spoke in the following terms to a great crowd of miners gathered in the main square:

Comrades, red soldiers! Here before you, certain that we have fulfilled the mandate with which you have entrusted us, we come to speak of the melancholy plight into which our glorious insurrectionary movement has fallen. We have to describe our peace conversations with the general of the enemy army. We have been defeated only for the time being. All that we can say is that, in the rest of the provinces of Spain, the workers did not do their duty and support us. Because of this failure, the government has been able to conquer the insurrection in Asturias. Furthermore, though we have rifles, machine-guns, and cannons, we have no more ammunition. All we can do, therefore, is to arrange peace. But this does not mean that we abandon the class struggle. Our surrender today is simply a halt on the route, where we make good our mistakes, preparing for our next battle which must end in the final victory of the exploited . . .[1]

There followed a severe retribution under the direction of a brutal major of police, Lisardo Doval, known for his ruthlessness. One of the conditions for the surrender of the miners had been that the Legion and the *Regulares* should be withdrawn from Asturias. This condition was not kept, and had only been authorized by General López Ochoa, and not by the ministry of war. These forces behaved in the conquered territory as if they were a victorious army living off the vanquished. Some 1,500–2,000 persons were believed killed, and nearly 3,000 wounded. Of the dead, about 320 were civil guards, soldiers, assault guards and carabineers. The remainder, it must be presumed, were mostly workers. Certainly many deaths occurred after the end of the fighting, at the time when the Legion were 'driving home' their victory.[2] Several thousand, perhaps as many as 30,000, political prisoners were also made in Spain during October and No-

1. Grossi, p. 218. Peirats, vol. I, p. 85, prints the revolutionary committee's last communiqué.

2. A statement by the ministry of the interior on 3 January 1935 gave a casualty list for all Spain in October 1934 of 1,335 killed and 2,951 wounded; 730 buildings had been destroyed or seriously damaged. Fifty-eight churches had been burned. Oviedo was a ruin, and the cost of the rising was estimated at £1 million. No fewer than 90,000 rifles were captured, together with 33,000 pistols, 10,000 cases of dynamite, 30,000 grenades, and 330,000 cartridges.

vember 1934 (though the number may have been half that).[1] Of these, the majority were in Asturias. The *casas del pueblo* of the region were turned into extra prisons, and those held within were subjected to every kind of indignity, including torture.[2] Many were shot 'trying to escape' (perhaps sometimes genuinely). A journalist, Luis de Sirval, who ventured to point out these terrible things, was arrested and murdered in prison by three officers of the Legion. In Madrid, Generals Franco and Goded were regarded as the saviours of the nation, while the right-wing press gave fearful information about the raping of nuns and gouging out of priests' eyes. Otherwise, censorship on Asturias was complete. In the countryside, landlords celebrated by abandoning any willingness whatever to collaborate with agrarian reform, evictions were carried on apace and those socialists who had avoided imprisonment received short shrift in the pursuit of employment. Further terrible resentments were, therefore, created.

1. Deaths and prisoners are impossible to decide in even approximate terms. The figure of 30,000 prisoners, given so much in the past, cannot be confirmed. Perhaps about 35 priests were killed. The censorship of the time prevented, and prevents, an accurate assessment from being available from the press. Police records, where they exist, have not yet been investigated.

2. For a *vraisemblable* account of the repression of the Legion in Asturias, see the first chapters of José Martín Blázquez, *I Helped to Build an Army* (London, 1939), and Ricardo de la Cierva, *Historia*, vol. I, p. 447. See Ignacio Carral, *Por qué mataron a Luis de Sirval* (Madrid, 1935), and Brenan, p. 218.

10

Consequences of Asturias – Lerroux's attempt at a middle way – straperlo *– the republic in an* impasse *– the elections of 16 February 1936*

AFTER the revolution of October 1934 and the manner in which it had been quelled, it would have required a superhuman effort to avoid the culminating disaster of civil war. But no such effort was forthcoming. Most socialist leaders were in prison. They were accompanied there by leaders of the Catalan government, by Azaña, and by several other left-wing politicians. Also in gaol were many anarchists, even though they had played little part in the rising, save in Asturias. The arrest of Azaña, attributable to panic, was followed by his being held in gaol for some months – an indignity for which there was no justification. In these conditions, the rising in Asturias assumed an epic significance in the minds of the Spanish Left. Some, echoing the last words of Belarmino Tomás in the doomed gathering in Sama, prophesied darkly that October 1934 would be to Spain what 1905 had been to Russia. Largo Caballero, who remained in gaol till December 1935, passed his captivity in reading, for the first time, the works of Marx and Lenin. Now approaching seventy, the imagination of this long respected and moderate socialist leader became dominated by revolutionary visions. Many others found their time in gaol 'a veritable school of revolution'.[1] Meantime, in Paris, Romain Rolland expressed the feeling which the combatants certainly felt about the Asturias rising when he announced that the world had seen nothing so beautiful since the Paris Commune. The brutality of the proscription in Asturias caused people to forget that even Azaña would have had to put down the revolution; and news of the repression came through the reports of a Cortes commission and a British parliamentary delegation. Meantime, Largo's mixed arbitration boards collapsed in many places, the building and metallurgical workers were driven back to a forty-eight-hour week and many were

1. Carrillo, p. 48.

dismissed for having taken part in political strikes before October 1934. Employers cut wages wherever they could. CEDA deputies complained, but their voices were lost. On the other hand, no lands taken over by the Institute of Agrarian Reform were actually given back to their owners. Still, from now on a 'revolutionary mentality of the Right and of the Left' clearly dominated all parties.[1]

Asturias caused a thrill of horror to run through the Spanish middle class. To them it seemed that anything, even a military dictatorship, was preferable to disintegration. Would General Franco take over power now that he was chief of staff? Would Gil Robles and the CEDA make the best of their opportunity? Gil Robles knew that, if the rising had been general all over Spain and not confined to Asturias, the consequences might have been different.[2]

Lerroux was still Prime Minister. In the following months, the old pirate did his best to steer a middle path. Thus, when the monarchists demanded that the Catalan statute should be abolished altogether after Companys's revolution, Lerroux (here supported by the CEDA) secured its suspension only, with the Catalan provinces being administered under a governor-general. His minister of agriculture, the CEDA politician Giménez Fernández, continued to try and distribute land, for a time, and introduced legislation to protect smallholders. He desired, for instance, to settle 10,000 farmers during 1935. He was, however, continually thwarted by the same people, such as Lamamié de Clairac, the Carlist, who had so damaged the first Agrarian Bill in its discussions in the Cortes.

The most difficult question for the government, however, concerned the punishment of the rebels of 1934. For, by February 1935, the military tribunals had named twenty death penalties. Of these, two were carried out.[3] The condemned included Companys; socialist deputies, such as poor Teodomiro Menéndez, who had gone almost mad during his imprisonment because of the sounds of torture which he had heard; Ramón González Peña; Belarmino Tomás; and some

1. Jaime Vicens Vives, *Aproximación a la historia de España* (Barcelona, 1968), p. 179.

2. Gil Robles, p. 141.

3. These were, firstly, on Jesús Argüelles, a criminal miner, who had commanded an execution picket responsible for the death of a civil guard, and secondly, on a sergeant, Vázquez, who had deserted from his unit in Asturias and joined the miners.

officers who had sided with the rebellion either in Madrid or in Catalonia. Meantime, many socialist-led municipal councils continued suspended, because their members belonged to the same party as some of the rebels of 1934. Lerroux, picturing the bitterness which would be caused by the execution of, say, Belarmino Tomás and González Peña (the two socialist deputies for Asturias), not to speak of Companys, favoured the commutation of all further death sentences. The CEDA ministers supported the death penalty. Gil Robles argued for this with energy. Lerroux was supported by the President, Alcalá Zamora, who recalled how General Sanjurjo and his coplotters had been reprieved in 1933. The sentences were commuted. The CEDA ministers resigned. After a prolonged crisis, Lerroux reformed a cabinet in which the CEDA had five representatives, including Gil Robles as minister for war.

Gil Robles appointed Franco as chief of staff, bringing him back from command in Morocco where he had been sent the preceding winter. Thereafter, several right-wing officers were promoted, and others believed to be liberals or socialists lost their jobs. Gil Robles also embarked on negotiations to buy arms from Germany.[1] But there were no more executions. Companys and other leaders convicted of rebellion were sentenced to perpetual imprisonment – a sentence which no one believed would be carried out. Largo Caballero was detained with others without trial for months. Azaña was released, the charges against him having failed to gain a two thirds majority in the Cortes, though it was clear from speeches made by politicians on the Right that many hoped to finish with him and the left republicans once and for all.[2]

1. Arms were to be purchased by the war ministry through a businessman, La Iglesia, only CEDA ministers were involved, and Germany even contemplated making available funds to the CEDA's election campaign. (German Documents on Foreign Policy; series C, vol. IV, no. 303.) Much of Gil Robles's work at the war ministry was serious and public spirited. An efficient and well-equipped army was needed. See his memoirs, p. 232f.

2. The Cortes had to decide whether he should or should not be tried by the courts. The vote against Azaña was nevertheless 189 to 68. The CEDA voted against Azaña, to appease the rich monarchists. He had spent two months in detention in a prison ship off Barcelona. The unjust indignity – he had tried to restrain both the socialists and the Catalans from insurrection – greatly affected him.

The venom with which the two sides of the political spectrum now regarded each other was difficult to assuage. But the men of the Centre – and, in these circumstances, both the President and Prime Minister were so – had a chance to resolve matters. They wasted their opportunity. A revision of some clauses of the constitution was proposed. This might have modified the character of regional autonomy, established a senate, and altered the divorce and marriage laws. An independent, if orthodox, financier, Joaquín Chapaprieta, prepared to introduce a budget – which had not been seen in the republic since 1932. He desired to prune corruption and bureaucratic waste. These measures, admirable in themselves, would have cut government spending on education – including the still inadequate teachers' salaries. But no budget and no constitutional revision were ever agreed.[1] (The budget of 1932, repeated annually, was the republic's only finance act.) Then the minister of agriculture, Giménez Fernández, was dismissed in May 1935, over a proposed alteration of the Agrarian Law: his humane ideas had given him the nickname of 'the white bolshevik' in monarchist circles, and his habit of invoking papal encyclicals to defend his drafts infuriated others. His eclipse spelled the end of any idea that the CEDA might modify, rather than shelve, the Law of Agrarian Reform. Chapaprieta formed a government, in which Lerroux became foreign minister. But the radical party was now ruined by scandal.

A Dutch financial adventurer, Daniel Strauss, had persuaded certain ministers to favour a new type of roulette wheel, the *straperlo*. Strauss promised that, in return for permission to introduce this wheel, he would guarantee profits. When the scandal broke, Lerroux's adopted son was found to be intimately concerned with Strauss. Lerroux himself, whose finances had always been devious, was also implicated, as were Salazar Alonso, ex-minister of the interior and mayor of Madrid; the civil governor of Barcelona; and some others. The radicals resigned, amid execration, and the word *straperlo* passed into the language to signify a public scandal. Meantime, the radical party, which had played so important a part in the life of the republic, even though its policies had meant so little, fell apart, and the alliance which Lerroux had sealed with Gil Robles, and which had effectively

1. Chapaprieta's memoirs shed light on the day-to-day workings of Lerroux's government. (*La paz fue posible: memorias de un político*, Barcelona, 1971.)

governed Spain for a year, collapsed too.[1] Within weeks, the Prime Minister quarrelled with Gil Robles, technically over Chapaprieta's desire to introduce a land tax on large holdings and to increase death duties, to 3½ per cent from 1 per cent; but Gil Robles had really provoked the crisis in order to make his final bid for the premiership.

Yet President Alcalá Zamora, who had interfered continuously in the day-to-day running of administration during the preceding year, was still determined to avoid asking Gil Robles to form a government. While Gil Robles himself in late 1935 seemed to have matured from the experimental, catholic corporativist which he had claimed to be in 1933,[2] some of his followers, particularly the *JAPistas*, seemed impatient to take up arms: they had already taken symbols, as well as language, which resembled fascism. They carried a black cross from which hung the letters Alpha and Omega, set in white, and framed in red, hoping thus to symbolize Pelayo, the first king of the *Reconquista*, and an immaculate white ship in a sea of martyrs' blood. Gil Robles had also a programme of constitutional reform which Alcalá Zamora disliked.[3] Finally, personal relations were bad between Gil Robles and the President. The latter was still jealous of the former, while Gil Robles found the President vain. In consequence, the President tried a rash expedient; he asked one of his friends, Manuel Portela Valladares, a politician from Galicia of the days of the monarchy, to form a caretaker government and prepare for new elections.[4] Portela, a freemason and the indefatigable historian of the Priscillian heresy, had been rediscovered as a politician by Lerroux on a beach in northern Spain in the summer of 1934. As minister of the interior earlier in 1935, he had been Alcalá Zamora's informant as to what was going on in the cabinet. The President now hoped that Portela could reorganize the 'forces of the Centre' to take the place of the defunct radical party. Alas, neither Alcalá nor Portela appreciated that the Centre was a diminishing concept.

Gil Robles was outraged at Alcalá Zamora's action. So was his under-secretary at the ministry of war, General Fanjul, who told him 'If you give me the order, I will this very night move into the streets

1. Another scandal, the so-called Nombela case, further weakened the radicals, the next month.

2. Gil Robles, p. 364.

3. For a summary, see Robinson, p. 207.

4. Miguel Maura had tried and failed to form a government too.

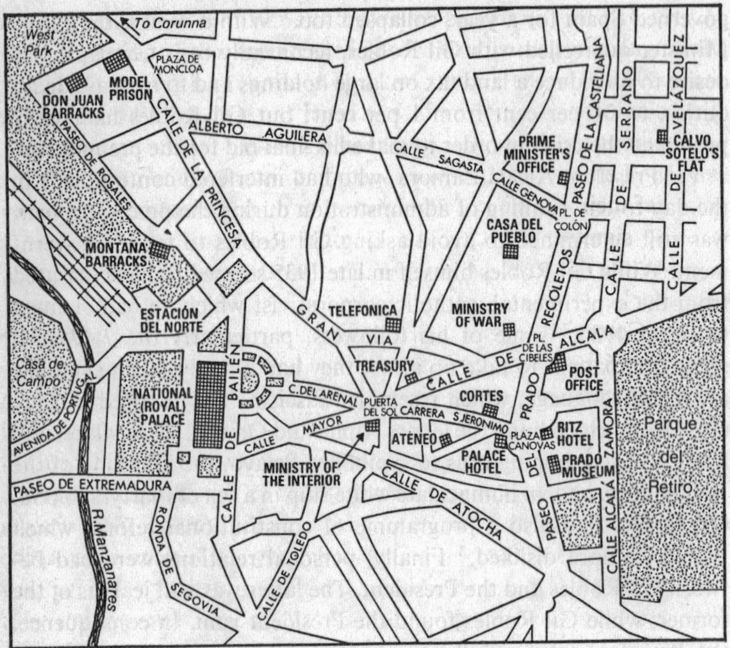

5. Madrid during the Second Republic

of Madrid with the garrison of the capital. General Varela thinks as I do.' Gil Robles's reply was not as explicit as it might have been: 'If the army, grouped around its natural commands, believes that it must temporarily take over power with the object of saving the spirit of the constitution, I will not constitute the least obstacle.' He told Fanjul to consult with the other generals. General Franco, chief of staff, gave his opinion that the army could not be counted upon to carry out a *coup d'état*. So none was embarked upon, despite support for the idea among some officers, falangists and monarchists.[1] Gil Robles left the ministry of war. General Franco wept.[2] Portela formed a caretaker administration of extra-parliamentarians and centre politicians of the second rank. While the Right denounced Gil Robles for cowardice and weakness at abandoning power, the press censorship was relaxed.

1. Gil Robles, pp. 366–7.
2. See Gil Robles, p. 376, for this surprising fact.

Azaña had already begun to restore the fortunes of the Republican Left, with a successful oratorical performance to an audience of perhaps 100,000 in the autumn, outside Madrid, in a field at Comillas: the 'clamorous ovation' which greeted the speech had a resonance throughout the country.[1] Next, the *casas del pueblo* were reopened, and the Left reawoke. Socialists, communists, and the Left made the most of their opportunity: 'October' and 'Asturias' became sacred words, signifying a desperate struggle of heroic revolutionaries against the Foreign Legion – 'the Moors', and the 'butchers of October'.

The Cortes were dissolved on 4 January. The elections were to be held on 16 February. Portela tried to delay the poll by unconstitutional procrastination; he failed. The anyway long electoral campaign which intervened between these dates was, to begin with, dominated by Gil Robles. His photograph as the *Jefe*, with a legend beneath demanding for him 'an absolute majority so that he can give you a great Spain', stared threateningly from the hoardings of the Puerta del Sol. Yet, as the campaign got under way, it became clear to the leaders of the CEDA that their path might not be so easy as they had assumed. They therefore began to arrange common lists with other right-wing parties. The Alfonsine monarchists and Carlists, together with the 'agrarians' and 'independents', stood in alliance in most places with the CEDA in 'the National Front'.

The past year had been an active one for both monarchist parties, with military training for two hundred Carlists at an airfield near Rome disguised as Peruvian officers,[2] and ideological discussion among the monarchists, still veering between 'fascism' and traditionalism. Calvo Sotelo, Primo's minister of finance, had joined Renovación Española but was trying to create an alliance of his own of all authoritarian monarchists: his views had evolved towards fascism during his exile in France, partly from contact with Maurras's Action Française, and he had discussed rebellion with other exiled monarchists. From his writings, and those of Ramiro de Maeztu (editor still of *Acción Española*), Pradera (the Carlist ideologue of 'the new state'), and Sáinz Rodríguez, now the leading Alfonsist

1. Speech in Azaña, vol. III, pp. 269–93. Henry Buckley, *Life and Death of the Spanish Republic* (London, 1940), p. 123, has a good eye-witness description.

2. One among them was Jaime del Burgo.

'theoretician', it certainly seemed as if the ranks of the authoritarian Right were closing.

As for the Falange, José Antonio had been engaged in a long controversy with the old leader of the JONS, Ledesma Ramos. The latter had always regarded José Antonio as a mere *señorito*, and criticized him for his contacts with the church and the upper class.[1] Ledesma started a workers' organization, the CONS (Confederación de Obreros Sindicalistas), which, however, found few followers. José Antonio succeeded in making headway against the Falange extremists who wanted violence, but he had been unsuccessful in creating a policy which his more monarchist financial backers could support as well as Ledesma. In October 1934, José Antonio had been confirmed as leader of the party by only one vote, seventeen to sixteen.[2] Ledesma tried to break the JONS away from the Falange to keep it as a national syndicalist party, even if a minute one: his personal relations with José Antonio had always been bad. When Ledesma wrote some articles denouncing José Antonio as the 'tool of reaction', he was expelled from the Falange. These events, and the financial difficulties of these young Spanish fascists, had prevented their numbers from rising (especially after the rich monarchist Marqués de Eliseda had broken with them) following the Asturias revolution, when one might have expected them to increase their appeal. But they continued to parade in blue shirts on Sundays. In the election cam-

1. José Antonio's relations with the army and other forces of the 'old Spain', which Ledesma denounced, derived partly from financial necessity, partly from his liking for the social connections with which, as the son of the dictator, he had been brought up, but also partly because he had no confidence that his party would grow fast enough to defeat socialism. It was in those words, at least, that he had put it in a curious letter to Franco just before the Asturias rising, on 24 September 1934. In this, he intimated that he would be willing to support a military *coup d'état* to restore the 'lost historical destiny of the country'. Franco did not, apparently, answer the letter. (This information was first published in *Y*, the review of the Sección Femenina of the Falange, in October 1938. It is quoted in full in Ximénez de Sandoval, p. 224, and in his *Obras*, p. 709.)

2. Payne, pp. 66–7. There was also a controversy in the Falange in the autumn of 1934 over the idea that a place in it should be found for Calvo Sotelo: Calvo was making a bid for the leadership of the fascist party in Spain, but José Antonio was not prepared to accept that. In addition, he regarded Calvo Sotelo as a traitor to his father, and as a man who 'had a head only for figures and could not understand poetry'. Ledesma was against Calvo as a reactionary.

paign, the Falange remained outside the right-wing alliance, Gil Robles being unable to agree to the demands for apportionment of seats made by José Antonio. José Antonio's old constituency at Cádiz would have nothing to do with him and the CEDA, like the Carlists, were critical of José Antonio's economic 'corporativism', which they regarded as dangerously socialist. The Falange put up a few candidates, nevertheless, who lambasted the CEDA's 'sterile and stupid biennium in power'. Many of the most energetic falangists were, however, below voting age.[1]

To the Left of this right-wing alliance, there were the various parties of the centre. These included Lerroux and the radicals, the Lliga (the Catalan businessmen), the progressives – followers of Alcalá Zamora – and the specifically named 'Centre party', launched by the Prime Minister, Portela Valladares. Also classed among the centre parties were the Basque nationalist party, which, although since 1934 it had been on bad terms with its natural allies of the CEDA, still hesitated before making a clear alliance with the Left.[2] Portela tried to develop the centre artificially, by appointing his friends to civil governorships, but the stratagem failed.

The Left in the elections of February 1936 was grouped in a Popular Front pact. The name had been proposed by the communist party. The previous July, the seventh congress of the Comintern had been held in Moscow. Dimitrov, the Bulgarian communist, then general secretary of the Comintern (due to his defiant behaviour when accused of setting fire to the Reichstag), had defined the political aims of world communism in the face of the threat to the Soviet Union by the rise of Hitler:

> The formation of a joint People's Front providing for joint action with social democratic parties is a necessity. Cannot we endeavour to unite the communist, social democratic, catholic and other workers? Comrades, you will remember the ancient tale of the capture of Troy. The attacking army

1. The Falange perhaps numbered 5,000 in early 1936 apart from students or schoolboys (Gil Robles, p. 444 fn. 60, reporting Fernández Cuesta): Payne has 10,000, on the evidence of the then treasurer, Mariano García.

2. Or with the Right. A group of Basque deputies were unsuccessfully reprimanded for not joining hands with the CEDA by Monsignor Pizzardo, assistant papal secretary of state. (From a diary of one of those present, qu. Iturralde, vol. I, p. 394.)

was unable to achieve victory until, with the aid of the Trojan Horse, it penetrated to the very heart of the enemy camp. We, revolutionary workers, should not be shy of using the same tactics.[1]

With these words, the international policy of the Popular Front was formally launched. Communist parties were blamed for having in the past treated every bourgeois party as fascist. Now they were adjured to preserve bourgeois, parliamentary democracy until it could be replaced by 'proletarian democracy'. This policy of the Popular Front went further than that of the United Front in the 1920s. Then (as in Eastern Europe, after 1945) communist parties had been instructed to make common cause with other working-class parties only. With the Popular Front, they had to establish relations with middle-class parties also.

It was difficult for the communists to ensure the agreement of Largo Caballero to this alliance: the French communist leader, Duclos, went to Spain specially to persuade him.[2] The persecution after 1934 and the attempt to prosecute Azaña, made for friendship, however short-lived, between the leaders of the Left. Azaña and Prieto really arranged the alliance, the former's prestige having grown greatly during 1935, his own ironic account of his imprisonment in 1934 (*Mi rebelión en Barcelona*) having sold 25,000 copies. (The republican parties had already formed in November a 'Republican Front'.) Azaña and Largo were on bad terms, but the alliance suited them. Nevertheless, Largo Caballero now believed himself a revolutionary socialist and, though he desired a republic without class warfare, thought that for that 'it is necessary for one class to disappear'.[3] The socialist party continued to be divided, both Prieto and Besteiro trying to hold back the majority's renewed swing, under the pressure of the young, towards revolution; or, rather, towards 'bolshevization'. (Prieto returned to Spain from Paris in December 1935, a week after Largo Caballero had been released from gaol.)

The anarchists remained outside the system. Nevertheless, at the

1. Speech of Dimitrov at the seventh meeting of the Comintern on 2 August 1935 (London, 1935), p. 43. The Spanish communists at the meeting were La Pasionaria, José Díaz, Sesé (from Catalonia), Hernández, and Arlandis.

2. Jacques Duclos, *Mémoires 1935–1939* (Paris, 1969), pp. 107–10.

3. *El Socialista*, 28 January 1936, qu. Robinson, p. 246. See De la Cierva, *Historia*, vol. I, p. 579f., for consideration of the origins of the Popular Front.

last minute, they encouraged their members to repeat before the ballot-box the unity expressed in Asturias. This was because one of the main proposals of the Popular Front programme was an amnesty for political prisoners. The right realized the desirability of anarchist abstentions, and in Cádiz, perhaps elsewhere, offered substantial sums to anarchist leaders in return for anti-electoral propaganda.[1]

Other measures in the programme of the Popular Front harked back to Asturias. All unemployed for blatantly political reasons were to be reinstated: a warning to employers who had secured new labour to replace those in prison, or those whom they had sacked after October 1934. An indemnity to the victims of 1934 would be paid by the state. The Catalan statute would be restored. Other regional statutes would be negotiated. The Agrarian Law and other reforms begun in 1933 would be given priority.[2]

The election was fought tempestuously. The government lifted the 'state of alarm' which had existed in many areas since Asturias. The crowds were vast at meetings. Words, but for the moment only words, were violent. 'Vatican fascism', proclaimed one election leaflet, 'offered you work, and brought hunger; it offered you peace, and brought five thousand tombs; it offered you order, and raised a gallows. The Popular Front offers no more, and no less, than it will bring: bread, peace, and liberty!'[3] Bishops explicitly advised catholics to vote against the Popular Front. Largo Caballero declared that, if the Right won, he would 'proceed to declare civil war', and Primo de Rivera that his men would disregard a result 'dangerously contrary to the eternal destinies of Spain'.[4] Lerroux and the radicals concentrated their efforts on destroying the Centre party launched by Portela. Calvo Sotelo appeared for the first time a national figure. His campaign was explicitly anti-republican and anti-democratic. He argued that the constitution was dead, murdered by its own founders. The next Cortes would be a new 'constituent Cortes'.[5] He also told

1. Diego Abad de Santillán, *Por qué perdimos la guerra* (Buenos Aires, 1940), p. 37.

2. Ricardo de la Cierva, *Los documentos de la primavera trágica* (Madrid, 1967), p. 66f.

3. From a leaflet in the possession of the author. The five thousand refers to the number of workers allegedly killed in the repression of Asturias.

4. Qu. Robinson, p. 243 and p. 246.

5. Speech of 13 January 1936 (De la Cierva, *Los documentos*, p. 92).

patriotic Spaniards, in the most vigorous language, that, if they did not vote for the National Front, a red flag would fly over Spain: 'that red flag which is the symbol of the destruction of Spain's past and of her ideals'.

Spain went to the polls on 16 February, the Sunday of the carnival before Lent. 34,000 civil guards and 17,000 assault guards were on duty. There were some disturbances in Granada, where the polling-booth was held up by force, while others stuffed votes into the ballot-urn. But such instances were rare. *The Times* correspondent, Ernest de Caux, reported that voting had been 'generally exemplary'.[1] The results of the first round of the elections, available on 20 February, were, so far as national aggregates are concerned:

4,654,116 (34.3 per cent) for the Popular Front;
4,503,505 (33.2 per cent) for the National Front; and
526,615 (5.4 per cent) for the Centre, including 125,714 Basque nationalists.[2]

The Popular Front had elected 263 deputies, the National Front 133 and the Centre 77. Twenty of these seats (where no one had gained more than 40 per cent of votes cast) remained to be voted for again in a second round of elections, two weeks later. But clearly the Left had a majority of seats, reflecting a definite if slender majority of votes cast.

Since electors voted for alliances and not for individual parties, votes cast for the latter cannot be given. But the main parties gained seats thus: Socialists, 88; Republican Left (that is, Azaña's party), 79; Republican Union (Martínez Barrio), 34; Communists, 14; Esquerra, 22; CEDA, 101; Agrarians, 11; Monarchists (including Calvo Sotelo), 13; Carlists, 15; Portela Valladares's new Centre party, 21; Lliga, 12; Radicals, 9; and Basques, 5. The Falange gained no seats at all.[3] Most of the old leaders were returned, but neither Lerroux nor José Antonio found seats.

1. *The Times*, 17 February 1936. De Caux was exceptionally well-informed.

2. These figures are adapted from those in Javier Tusell, *Las elecciones del Frente Popular* (Madrid, 1971), vol. II, p. 13. My 'adaptation' consists of adding what Tusell describes as 'Popular Front with Centre' and 'Right with Centre' to respectively the Popular Front and the Right.

3. Tusell, pp. 82–3; see also José Venegas, *Las elecciones del Frente Popular*, p. 47. These figures have been interminably disputed but the above appear the most reliable. See, for an analysis, Chapter V of Jean Bécarud's *La Deuxième*

Much juggling was done with these figures afterwards to prove this and that. Such discussions ignored the fact that the electoral system (giving a party which won over 50 per cent of votes 80 per cent of the seats, in a particular province) was purposely arranged to encourage coalitions. Both Right and Left had increased their votes, partly because a few more voted for them in 1936 than in 1933, partly because the centre did badly. *Caciquismo* played a part in country districts, so perhaps the Popular Front's victory was greater there than the figures show; but there was substance to the accusation that the socialists created their own *caciquismo* in some cities. At all events, the Left had won an unexpected victory; and the Right, particularly the CEDA, an unexpected defeat. The eclipse of the Centre was a true reflection of the lack of support for such an artificial neutrality in the country.

There were substantial abstentions: perhaps 28 per cent (in comparison with 32.5 per cent in 1933). Some 9,870,000 voted out of a total electorate of about 13,500,000. Abstentions were mostly in Aragon, Galicia and Andalusia.[1]

It can be argued that the figures suggest that the electorate was moving towards a two-party system;[2] Azaña and Gil Robles were the champions of two well-defined moods, a fact obscured later with the reluctance of several minorities, militarists, anarchists, socialist farmworkers, socialist youth, and fascists, to accept a parliamentary system fairly well established, as can be seen from the realization that 70 per cent voted. This truth, like so many others, was obscured by innumerable propaganda slogans scarcely differentiated from lies: for Lerroux was not 'a Mussolini' (nor was Azaña, though his old friend, Ossorio y Gallardo, once so described him), and the slogan 'Before all for Religion and Spain' was not a fascist device; Azaña was not Kerensky, nor was Largo Caballero Lenin (even if he wanted to be). Neither the parliamentary Right nor the socialists (nor, of course, the army) were exactly constitutional but nor were they firmly unconstitutional: in fact, both, CEDA and socialists, were 'accidentalists',

---

République Espagnole (Paris, 1962). The CEDA's criticisms and explanations are summarized in Gil Robles, p. 509f. Practically no newspaper at the time, nor subsequent writers, have agreed on the figures at these elections.

1. Tusell, *Las elecciones*, p. 13 and p. 24.

2. See Jackson, pp. 523–4.

and the socialists' love affair with democracy lasted only from about 1930 until 1933. Both these parties were bad losers, while the socialists were almost as bad victors. Even in 1933, Largo Caballero had told his followers: 'Today I am convinced that to carry out socialist work within a bourgeois democracy is impossible'.[1] But, as so often, bourgeois democracy often seemed a wonderful, if lost, friend to almost everyone, from the standpoint of a few months on, when two headstrong, totalitarian philosophies, the one deriving from the socialist youth, the Left of the socialist party, the communists and perhaps a section too of the anarchists, and the other deriving from an alliance of fascism, absolute monarchism and catholic youth, clashed in arms.

1. Robinson, p. 138.

11

Franco with Portela Valladares – the prisons opened – Azaña back in power – the Falange's murders – Largo Caballero as 'the Spanish Lenin' – Calvo Sotelo's emergence – Mola at Pamplona – quarrels of the Left – Alcalá Zamora removed – Azaña President – José Antonio joins the conspiracy

---

WHILE the results of the elections were coming in, attempts were made to thwart their consequence. José Antonio offered Portela the services of the Falange and asked for weapons. Then the monarchists asked Gil Robles to carry out a *coup d'état*. He refused but then himself went to Portela, at four in the morning, requested that 'a state of war'[1] be declared immediately and that he be seconded to the government, as 'a minister, secretary, or typist, or whatever you like,' so as to allay the worries of the Right.[2] Portela said that he would think about it, but all that happened was that he telephoned the President to ask him to declare a 'state of alarm'. He did so. Then Franco, chief of staff, urged Portela to declare the 'state of war', having urged his own minister, General Molero, and the director-general of the civil guard, General Pozas, to recommend the same.[3] The 'state of war' would, of course, bring the country under martial law and be in effect a *coup d'état*. Portela, according to Franco, asked why the army did not act on its own initiative. Franco said that,

1. This was the final emergency situation envisaged under the Law of Public Order of 1933. The other two conditions envisaged were a 'state of prevention' and a 'state of alarm'. Under the first, preventive arrests could be made. Under the second, there could be a censorship and the closing of organizations which 'threatened public order'. Spain had had 'a state of alarm' for much of 1935.

2. Gil Robles, pp. 491–2.

3. Dr Marañón had met Franco at dinner at the Spanish Embassy in Paris in January. Franco was returning from the funeral of King George V in London, where he had represented Spain and walked in procession behind the ill-fated Marshal Tukhachevsky, representing Russia. The intellectual physician and the general of the Legion walked along the banks of the Seine, and Franco said that everything would calm down in Spain within a few weeks. (Recollection of Dr Marañón.)

without government support, he would lack the essential help of the civil guard. Portela and the President continued to resist the idea. On the morning of 18 February, Portela tried to hand over power to Azaña, who, however, thought that he should wait until the Cortes met. Portela, anxious to abandon his responsibility, cast around for an alternative course. Franco again tried to dissuade him from handing over power, and Calvo Sotelo also saw the Prime Minister with the same end. In the meantime, the socialists were beginning to talk of a general strike. Portela, exhausted, almost mad, deaf to advice, insisted on resigning.[1] Calvo Sotelo declared that all was lost. The President then asked Azaña to form a government. This was irregular but, in the circumstances of Portela's desire to escape from responsibility, he could scarcely have done otherwise.[2] Portela's civil governors fled with him, so as to create a vacuum needing speedily to be filled.

General Franco, together with Generals Fanjul (lately under-secretary at the war office under Gil Robles), Varela (the ex-trainer of the Carlists), and Emilio Mola, to whom Gil Robles had given the command in Morocco, Orgaz, and Ponte, decided to take no immediate counter-revolutionary step, though both Fanjul and Goded would have liked to have done so.

The enthusiasm, meantime, of supporters of the Popular Front knew no bounds. Crowds massed before the ministry of the interior in Madrid and cried '*!Amnistía!*' (amnesty). In Oviedo, the Popular Front militants anticipated the consequences of the election and opened the prisons, where most of the captives taken after the Asturias revolution were held. Certain common criminals were also released. The first act of Azaña as Prime Minister was to sign an amnesty decree covering political prisoners. The socialist and Catalan leaders of 1934 were freed. Companys and his counsellors left prison, to be hailed again as leaders of their beloved city, amid scenes of enthusiasm such as even Barcelona's leafy avenues had rarely seen. The Tribunal of Constitutional Guarantees then declared illegal the suspension of the Catalan statute: Companys reconstituted his

1. For Portela, see Azaña, vol. IV, p. 718; and for Franco, George Hills, *Franco* (London, 1967), p. 212.

2. This complicated series of events is well disentangled by Robinson (pp. 249–52 and notes). See also Azaña, vol. IV, pp. 563–72.

government as it had been in 1934, except for Dr Dencás, who wisely remained abroad. Azaña too formed his government. It was composed of representatives from his own party, the Republican Left, Martínez Barrio's party, the Republican Union (Martínez Barrio became Speaker of the Cortes), and of Companys's Esquerra. Amos Salvador, an old friend of Azaña's who had financed the literary journal *La Pluma* which Azaña had edited in 1920, became minister of the interior. Familiar faces from 1931–3 included Casares Quiroga at the ministry of public works, Marcelino Domingo at education, and José Giral at the admiralty. General Masquelet, who had been sacked as chief of staff in 1934, became minister of war. If asked, Prieto would have entered the government; but Largo Caballero forbade any such further collaboration.

Azaña approached the prospect of a new period of power in a depressed mood: 'Always I had been afraid that we would come back to power in bad conditions. They could not be worse. Once more we must harvest the wheat when it is still green.'[1] The government had to depend, in order to survive, on the socialists, their allies in the election. Thus the Popular Front survived, feebly. Azaña and his ministers began their new administration with an appeal for calm. They maintained the state of alarm, with press censorship. New civil governors were appointed throughout the country – mainly members of Azaña's own party. Many left-wing, or anyway republican, officers were appointed to the critical positions in the national police forces. Generals Franco and Goded were dispatched to the minor commands in the Canaries and the Balearics respectively. The government also set to work to carry out the provisions of the Popular Front pact. The Institute of Agrarian Reform set to work once more. Other measures attendant on the amnesty decrees were introduced. That meant, however, that employers had to take back men whom they had sacked after the strikes of 1934, and also to indemnify them for lost wages. At the same time, they had either to retain those engaged in their place, or to compensate them. The minister of education returned to the old plans of 1931–2 to substitute state education for that of the religious orders. As a result, the peseta fell, and leading financiers began to remove their wealth – and even themselves[2] – from the country. In Asturias and some other places, owners ceased to run coal mines;

1. Azaña, vol. IV, p. 564. 2. Juan March left on 16 February.

the government took them over, by a kind of provisional nationalization, intending to hand them over to workers' cooperatives in a few months.[1] Meantime, the second round of the elections were duly held, the National Front were in disarray, and the Popular Front were left with a pronounced final victory. The Tribunal for Constitutional Guarantees also found in favour of the Popular Front in numerous disputed election results. The CEDA challenged these judgements, some amendments were made, and four elections were left to be held in May. These constitutional disputes further embittered relations between the victors and the defeated.[2]

But these difficulties were small compared with other threats to law and order in Spain. From the moment of the elections onwards, a trail of violence, murder, and arson spread across the face of the country. This was partly caused by the euphoria of the socialists and anarchists at being released from prison, or at least from the rule of the CEDA and the radicals. It was also the conscious work of the Falange, determined to exacerbate the disorder in Spain and so justify the establishment of a régime of 'order'. Both Calvo Sotelo and Goicoechea blamed their defeat on the CEDA and on the 'foolish appeasement' of 1935. José Antonio Primo de Rivera was himself still ambiguous on the subject of violence. On 21 February, he had circulated a note to local *jefes* (chiefs) throughout Spain: 'The *jefes* will ensure that no one adopts an attitude of hostility towards the new government or of solidarity with the defeated Right . . . Our militants will utterly ignore all blandishments to take part in conspiracies, prospects of *coups d'état* or alliances with forces of order.'[3] For a time after the election, he seems to have coveted an agreement with Prieto. Perhaps Prieto might become leader of a united 'socialist Falange'? But Prieto, though isolated in his own party, refused to negotiate[4] – even if he found, as many did, José Antonio personally sympathetic. Thereafter, José Antonio was unable to restrain his

1. Tamames, p. 226.

2. See Robinson, pp. 256–7. Final figures for the main parties were: Republican Left, 80; Republican Union, 37; Socialists, 90; Communists, 16; Esquerra, 38; Centrists, 14; Radicals, 1 (!); Basque Nationalists, 9; CEDA, 86; Agrarians, 13; Lliga, 13; Monarchists, 11; and Carlists, 8. (Tusell, *Las elecciones*, vol. II, p. 187.)

3. José Antonio, *Obras*, p. 1103.

4. Zugazagoitia, pp. 7–8; Rudolfo Llopis in *Ibérica*, no. 7 (New York, 1957), pp. 4–6.

followers, since they believed that their chance was coming: gunmen were hired, including some ex-legionaries from Morocco,[1] and, after more attacks by the Left, José Antonio began to conclude, reluctantly no doubt, that only a military rising could save Spain. The Falange probably did not possess 25,000 members at the end of February 1936, but this made no difference to their provocatory power.[2] Riding round in motor-cars, armed with machine-guns, the *señoritos* of the Falange did much to increase disorder. 'Paradise', José Antonio had rashly told them, 'is not rest. Paradise is against rest . . . we must hold up our heads in Paradise, as the angels do.' Very well, then, they thought, let us try. Soon, *JA Pistas* and other young rightists began to move over to the Falange in such large numbers that José Antonio began to worry lest his movement lose its identity.[3]

On the Left, the militias and other para-military organizations founded in 1933 or 1934 and banned, with their members gaoled, in 1934, returned also to the streets, against a background of intimidation of employers, violent strikes in the country, and the growth of *une grande peur* of revolution. The militants of the FAI and CNT largely held aloof from these squabbles. They continued to believe that with an encyclopedia and a pistol they would soon be free from every political encumbrance. The decline of the republic filled them with much the same ebullient satisfaction as it did the Falange. Some of the *pistoleros* of the two groups are believed to have worked in common – especially against the socialists, who were wont to refer to the Falange with disgust as the 'FAI-lange'.[4] Meantime, day in, day out, as it seemed, prominent politicians addressed huge meetings in bull rings or public squares, the political preoccupation of the country

1. Payne, p. 99 and references.

2. On the basis of conversations with ex-*jefes provinciales* and other data, Stanley Payne has suggested a figure of 8,700 to be closer for 'the first-line' militants.

3. 15,000 JAPistas had gone over to the Falange by June. See Gil Robles, p. 573.

4. In 1934, José Antonio persuaded some followers of the syndicalist Pestaña, such as Nicolás Alvarez de Sotomayor (an unstable ex-anarchist student), to join the Falange, and there is a tale that José Antonio was sometimes escorted on his journeys to Barcelona by CNT *pistoleros* (José del Castillo and Santiago Alvarez, *Barcelona, objetivo cubierto*, Barcelona, 1958, p. 133). Negotiations as such between the syndicalists and the Falange never got under way.

being expressed in the astonishing numbers who attended such gatherings. The activities of Largo Caballero were particularly inflammatory.

During the weeks after the election of February, Largo Caballero, indeed, had become more intoxicated than ever by the prospect of revolution. Partly he was stimulated by what seemed to him real prospects of power. Partly he was in a hurry. Finally, also, he surrendered to the flattery of his friends in the youth movement. They spoke of him as the 'Spanish Lenin'.[1] This experienced trade union negotiator was entranced by the inappropriate name. While the votes of his party kept the government of Azaña in power, Largo Caballero moved about Spain making declamatory prophecies to wildly cheering crowds that the hour of revolution was near. The real policy of Largo Caballero was no doubt more moderate than he suggested in these apocalyptic orations. When power eventually came to him, in very different circumstances, it is true, Largo showed himself shrewd, practical, humane and unimaginative. But no one could have predicted that. In consequence, from March 1936 onwards, the old quarrel between Largo's wing of the socialist party and those who still looked to Prieto was an open one. Prieto still at this time controlled the socialist party's executive, and the party paper, *El Socialista*. But Largo directed the UGT, the new paper *Claridad*, and led the youth movement and the socialists in Madrid. But despite many good speeches by their leader, the Prietistas were on the defensive. The *Caballeristas* scented victory and expected it to come from the streets. Young socialists used communist phraseology, despised Prieto for his reformism and his discreet flight to France at the time of Asturias, and believed that the future was theirs. The tide of revolutionary 'Caballerismo' ran strongly in early 1936, moving young urban socialists to see in 'the Revolution' the only way to help agrarian workers.[2]

1. According to Stanley Payne, *The Spanish Revolution* (New York, 1970), p. 108, the nickname began to be used by the socialist youth movement for Largo in the summer of 1933.

2. The UGT now numbered 1½ million members. Half were rural workers. Rather more than half the remainder were factory workers or miners. The rest were clerks, 'intellectuals' or shopkeepers. Madariaga, in a famous passage (*Spain*, p. 223), later argued that the quarrel between the two wings of the socialist party made the civil war inevitable.

If the Left were thus both confident and disunited, the Right and what remained of the Centre began, during the spring of 1936, to make common cause. Impelled by a common fear that the rising tide of leftism would overwhelm Spanish society, members of the CEDA, army officers, Carlists, monarchists, the small and the grand bourgeoisie, and even Radical followers of Lerroux, identified the government of Azaña with that of Kerensky before the appearance of the bolsheviks, in the Russia of 1917. Shadows from outside Spain seemed long. Opposition maintained an alliance that victory in the elections would have made impossible. After the Popular Front had taken power, most of those who had been, or voted, Radical in 1931 or 1933 gave tactical support to the right. The CEDA was still the largest single party in the Cortes. But its failure to secure an outright victory suggested to many of its erstwhile voters the failure of that experiment in christian democracy. Gil Robles's place as *Jefe* of the Spanish middle class was taken by the more unscrupulous Calvo Sotelo, who made himself the chief spokesman of the opposition when the Cortes met again. Gil Robles was aware of Azaña's position. He thought that soon the socialists would turn against him. 'I do not believe that the government will allow itself to be overrun, and we are all ready to help it from being so', he told his national council in March. The CEDA's terms for 'cooperation' with the government were announced as: dissolution of all militia forces; a programme of economic reconstruction which the Right could support; and no more campaigns against the catholic schools. Naturally, he and his followers would continue in the Cortes.[1] But then the Cortes did not seem to offer great hope. At least one major constituent group of the CEDA, the Valencian Right (DRV, Derecho Regional Valenciano), openly supported the idea of armed insurrection, under the unstable Luis Lucia, a vice-president of the CEDA.

The anti-republican plot, half-monarchist, half-military, which had its roots so long ago, was once more taking shape. Generals such as Fanjul, Ponte, Orgaz, Goded, Barrera and González Carrasco had been meeting regularly since Gil Robles had left the ministry of war. These officers were, from January 1936, in contact with a right-wing military organization known as the Unión Militar Española, a *junta* of junior officers founded in 1933 to 'maintain a proper patriotism'

1. *El Debate*, 6 March 1936. See Robinson, pp. 253–4.

within the army. The leaders of this group were probably better conspirators than they were soldiers. Their activities had inspired a counter group, Unión Militar Republicana Antifascista, set up in 1934 and organized by a captain, Díaz Tendero, a socialist.[1] The 'exile' of General Franco to the Canaries and of Goded to the Balearics had been intended to banish to harmless places those suspected of treason to the republic: but at the same time, General Mola, previously in command in Morocco, had been transferred to Pamplona, the capital of Navarre, and centre of Carlism.

Before these generals reached their new posts, they held a meeting on 8 March at the house of José Delgado, a catholic businessman.[2] They agreed that they would support a military rising, probably under Sanjurjo, if the President were to give power to Largo Caballero, if the civil guard were to be disbanded, or if anarchy were to overwhelm the country. Generals Varela and Orgaz were, however, anxious for an immediate rising. Mola was more cautious.[3] The

1. The first president of UME was Major Bartolomé Barba, an ex-member of the staff of Azaña, for whom he had developed an obsessive hatred: he had apparently invented the slander that over Casas Viejas in 1933 Azaña ordered the assault guard to shoot the anarchists 'in the guts'. The vice-president was Colonel Rodríguez Tarduchy, a conspirator of 1932. But the UME's national leadership was never important: it was decentralized. The UME had had contact with the Falange and the centrist and monarchist plotters from 1934 onwards. At the beginning, the UME was not really anti-socialist; it had been then an officers' pressure group, later taken over by the Right. Its importance has been exaggerated. UMRA was founded by Colonel Ernesto Carratalá, Major José María Enciso, naval mechanic Rodríguez Sierra and Captain Palacio. None of these were very important, but later two generals joined (Núñez de Prado and Gómez Caminero), and several colonels. Díaz Tendero, an officer who had risen from the ranks and felt frustrated since he could not rise higher than captain (according to the rules), was the nerve of the organization. The communist Modesto says there were over 200 officers in Madrid who belonged to UMRA (Modesto, p. 13). It was actually a merger of the UMR and UMA (Unión Militar Republicana and Unión Militar Antifascista), and perhaps had some links with similar associations founded before 1931.

2. No one agrees who was there, nor precisely what was said. Generals Franco, Orgaz, Villegas, Barrera, Fanjul, Rodríguez del Barrio, Ponte, Saliquet, García de la Herrán, Varela, and González Carrasco, as well as Goded and Mola have all been mentioned as present.

3. B. Félix Maiz, *Alzamiento en España* (Pamplona, 1952), p. 50; José María Iribarren, *Mola* (Saragossa, 1938), p. 44.

generals left behind in Madrid formed themselves into an organizing committee. Franco called on Azaña before he set out for the Canaries, and bluntly warned the Prime Minister against the dangers of communism. Azaña pooh-poohed the idea.[1] On 13 March, Franco met José Antonio at a meeting in the house of Serrano Súñer, his brother-in-law, the CEDA deputy for Saragossa, but nothing was decided.[2] Franco suggested that José Antonio should keep in touch with Colonel Yagüe, of the Foreign Legion. But this seems to have been part of José Antonio's search for a central figure around whom to unite Spain, rather than part of a plot. Meanwhile, the Carlists were busy capturing the mind of General Sanjurjo, who had visited Germany in February – ostensibly to attend the winter Olympic Games. He wanted to assure himself of a source of arms, but the Germans were reluctant to commit themselves; they were still hoping to make a major sale of arms to the Spanish government.[3] After this temporary setback, Sanjurjo became more and more of a Carlist: he was reminded that his father, captain in the army of 'Carlos VII', had died heroically in battle – his remains lying in Navarre. He recalled his grandfather, General Sacanell, also a warrior in the Carlist War. Sanjurjo was all sentiment, and the continuous visits made to him in these months by Carlist chiefs softened his heart. One day, the Carlist leader Fal Conde himself arrived, with his son Pepito dressed as a *requeté*. How the old general wept! He felt himself Carlist through and through.[4] The committee of generals in Madrid were making separate plans, however, under the direction of General

1. This dialogue was oblique. Franco said: 'You are wrong to send me away. At Madrid, I would be of more use to the army and to the peace of Spain.' Azaña answered: 'I do not fear developments. I knew about Sanjurjo's rising, and could have prevented it. I preferred to let it fail.' (*Cruzada*, IX, p. 468.)

2. Joaquín Arrarás, *Franco* (Buenos Aires, 1937), pp. 186–7; Serrano Súñer, p. 8.

3. For a new picture of Sanjurjo's visit, see the meticulous book by Angel Viñas, *La Alemania nazi y el 18 de julio* (Madrid, 1974). But at St Jean de Luz, Prince François-Xavier de Bourbon-Parme, prospective heir of the aged Carlist Pretender, Don Alfonso Carlos, presided over a committee of war. This purchased 6,000 rifles, 150 heavy machine-guns, 300 light machine-guns, 5,000,000 cartridges, and 10,000 hand-grenades. Of these, however, only a few of the machine-guns, bought in Germany, reached Spain before July 1936. The rest were confiscated at Antwerp and the intervention of Prince François-Xavier with his cousin the King of the Belgians could not free them (*Cruzada*, XIII, p. 447).

4. Lizarza, p. 59.

Rodríguez del Barrio. A scheme was put forward for a *coup d'état* on 17 April. Rodríguez del Barrio, Orgaz and Varela would raise Madrid; Villegas, Saragossa; Fanjul, Burgos; Ponte and Saliquet, Valladolid; and González Carrasco, Barcelona. The rising would be 'for Spain', with no specific political goal. After victory only, the generals would consider 'the structure of the régime, symbols etc.'.[1] The planners were in some uncertainty as to whether to advance on Madrid from the provinces, or to concentrate on Madrid and then crush the provinces, perhaps with the help, under both schemes, of Mola, Goded and Franco, in Pamplona, Palma de Mallorca and Las Palmas respectively. Sanjurjo would be titular commander-in-chief.

If the officers were beginning at last to decide what they wanted, the government meanwhile seemed increasingly unable to maintain themselves. Their freedom of action was, furthermore, limited since they needed the votes of the socialists to remain in power. Hence they could close the headquarters of the Falange in Madrid, on 27 February, but could do nothing against the socialist youth. Nor, it is fair to say, did several ministers want to. Azaña might flirt with the idea of some government of the centre, but the Popular Front, of which he was the leader, seemed, both in Madrid and in the provincial capitals, more and more the instrument of the revolutionary socialist Left. Day after day, the tension was maintained by news of a murder here, an attempted lynching there, a church, nunnery, or newspaper office burned down in a provincial capital. On 15 March (when a falangist had placed a bomb in Largo Caballero's house following an attack on Jiménez de Asúa), José Antonio was arrested, nominally on a charge of keeping arms without licence.[2] This left his organization without a leader, and removed a moderating influence. Before his arrest, Azaña apparently sent for José Antonio and suggested that he leave the country. 'I cannot,' answered José Antonio, 'my mother is ill.' 'But your mother died many years ago,' answered Azaña. 'My mother is Spain,' allegedly replied José Antonio, 'I cannot leave her.' Eduardo Aunós, minister of labour under Primo, also proposed that José Antonio should flee the country.

1. Testimony of General González Carrasco in 1946, cited in De la Cierva, *Historia ilustrada*, pp. 225–30.

2. Ximénez de Sandoval, p. 520.

'Certainly not,' answered José Antonio, 'the Falange is not an old-fashioned party of plotters, with its leaders abroad.'

The secretary-general of the party, Raimundo Fernández Cuesta, an old childhood friend and fellow-lawyer of José Antonio, was too weak to provide effective alternative leadership after the leader was in gaol. The Falange henceforth received its orders from José Antonio in the Model Prison, Madrid. But the chain of command was lost.

A week later, the republic received a blow from the Left, in the manner of Casas Viejas. Despite the new impetus given to the agrarian reform, many landless peasants who had voted for the Popular Front considered the pace too slow. The clash came in the *latifundio* regions of Estremadura, politically incandescent since 1931. The tension was exacerbated by the heavy rains of the winter, which had delayed ploughing. Hence, agricultural unemployment was on the increase, while, during the election campaign and immediately afterwards, huge numbers joined the FNTT or the CNT. Early in March, peasants began to move onto one or two large estates, anticipating land reform, but unconnected to the Institute's plans for the villages concerned. The new minister of agriculture, Mariano Ruiz Funes, a professor of law by profession, sensing the mood, tried to hasten the speed of settlement in Estremadura, making use of a 'social utility' clause of the last Land Law of the radical government which had been intended for very different purposes. This concession was not enough. On 25 March, some 60,000 peasants, by pre-arrangement, under the direction of the FNTT of the province, took over some 3,000 farms at five in the morning, cried '*¡Viva La República!*' and started to plough. This settlement, on a single day, of several times the number of farmers who had been established since the passage of the Law of Agrarian Reform, was not gone back upon. Troops were dispatched, but this was no longer 1917; they were withdrawn. Other settlements – numbers are uncertain – in the same region followed, equally unchallenged by the law. The epidemic of occupations ended with the end of the spring ploughing season, but a whole province's economic life had been overturned. In Badajoz, at least, Liberty had come! The land concerned was partly farmed collectively, partly by new peasant proprietors.[1]

1. The only satisfactory account is Malefakis, p. 370.

This occupation was followed or accompanied in other provinces by a crippling series of rural strikes over wages. Many confident labourers would arrive at large farms and demand work with threats. Many landowners left for the cities. So too did such smaller farmers as could afford it. People were even afraid in some villages to go to church, since that seemed an act aligning the church-goer with traditional Spain. Between February and May, there was an enormous wage inflation on the land, particularly in the south. Meantime, regular settlements by the Institute of Agrarian Reform continued: some 70,000 settlers were officially confirmed in March, including those of the great peasant revolt of Badajoz; 20,000 in April; and 5,000 a month between then and July. Perhaps, though, the Institute's figure of 114,000 settlers between February and July was over-modest and that of the minister, Ruiz Funes, more accurate: he said the total was 190,000.[1] One serious incident occurred at Yeste (Murcia), where several peasants were brutally, if accidentally, killed. Alongside these troubles, agriculture itself declined, the harvest being poor, agricultural credit unavailable, and farm managers wondering if it were worthwhile continuing to carry on operations. Terror prevailed in many parts of the countryside in early 1936. This was increased by the FNTT's call to its members to form militias in every village to defend the occupations carried out; actually, militias of sorts existed since 1934, under the guise of athletic associations.[2] Lightning strikes were often called, men came out without warning, with demands for increases in wages or short hours, and obtaining both from landlords or managers too much on the defensive to resist. 'The look of triumph on the faces of the workmen was sometimes very striking' recalled an Englishman in Andalusia.[3]

Youth movements on both sides despised the 'conformism' of party leaders: the socialist youth looked on Prieto as a traitor, and the *JA Pistas* looked on Gil Robles (still under forty) as too old. Several socialist youth leaders visited Moscow in March and returned almost communists.[4] Newsboys in particular fought pitched battles over bales of left- or right-wing newspapers. Youth, on both sides,

1. For discussion, see Malefakis, p. 378.
2. De la Cierva, *Los documentos*, p. 199.
3. Gerald Brenan, *Personal Record* (London, 1974), p. 277.
4. Carrillo, p. 43.

was in the street, and seems to have carried the nation with it, wherever it was going. Motorized squadrons of the JAP drove, like the early fascists in Italy, into working-class districts and shot up their enemies, who replied in kind. All that Azaña could do was to reflect once more that the Spanish working class were 'raw material for an artist'. On 4 April, he gave an interview to Louis Fischer, the American journalist. 'Why don't you purge the army?' asked Fischer. 'Why?' demanded Azaña. 'Because some weeks ago there were tanks in the streets, and you were in the ministry of the interior until two o'clock in the morning. You must have feared a revolt.' 'Café gossip,' answered Azaña. 'I heard it in the Cortes,' returned Fischer. 'Ah, that's one big café,' replied Azaña (many cafés were, in fact, extensions of the Cortes). He added: 'The only Spaniard who is always right is Azaña. If all Spaniards were Azañistas, all would be well.'[1] But to another journalist he admitted, more accurately, '*¡Sol y sombra!* Light and shade! That is Spain.'[2]

In early April a constitutional crisis came, over the presidency. Alcalá Zamora, by the terms of the constitution, could be voted out of his presidential office, since he had dissolved the Cortes twice. The Left proceeded to use the constitution in this way even though they had profited from the last dissolution. The President, the new government found, was 'a furious, inflamed enemy' who seemed to be 'a leader of the anti-republican opposition'. Some thought that Alcalá Zamora might one day stage a virtual *coup d'état* by dissolving parliament and forming an extra-parliamentary government.[3] Largo Caballero and his friends believed that with Alcalá Zamora 'the Bourbon spirit survived in the Palacio de Oriente'.[4] Largo Caballero hoped also to remove Alcalá Zamora from the presidency, and then Azaña effectively from the government, by promoting his presidential candidature.[5] Azaña might, it is true, then ask Prieto to form a government. But the socialist party could veto that idea, and Prieto would probably conform. Thus Azaña and Prieto would both be

1. Louis Fischer, *Men and Politics* (New York, 1941), p. 307. For Fischer, see below, p. 458.

2. Fernsworth, p. 176. Seats in Spanish bull-rings are named either *Sol* or *Sombra*, according as to whether they are shaded or not.

3. Azaña's recollections, in *Obras*, vol. IV, p. 719.

4. Gil Robles, p. 578.

5. See Marichal's conversation with Araquistain on this matter, and Prieto's caustic comments, in Azaña, vol. III, p. xxxii.

'neutralized' and a weak government formed which would be incapable of resisting either Left or Right. The way would then be open to 'revolution'. In the event, Prieto, always nervous lest he might lose his footing in the socialist party, did conform. He was even persuaded to take the lead in the 'impeachment' of the President. When this test came, Alcalá Zamora had indeed no friends. Gil Robles and the CEDA could not vote for him after he had intrigued so long to keep them from power. The monarchists hated him as a traitor to the king. So he left, unregretted, a bitter intriguer hating all his old associates and by them never forgiven.[1]

Azaña did turn out to be the only possible candidate for the presidency for whom the Left would vote. Events seemed to be going the way that Largo Caballero, Araquistain and Alvarez del Vayo hoped. They and their young supporters had now 'absolute faith in their capacity to occupy violently and victoriously the centres of governmental power'.[2] Nevertheless, though violence was certain, victory was less so, and the events of April should have shown that.

On 15 April, a bomb was flung at the presidential tribune during the parade held in the Paseo de la Castellana in honour of the fourth anniversary of the republic. Lieutenant Anastasio de los Reyes, of the civil guard, was shot dead by the assault guards, apparently because he was thought to have had his own revolver trained on Azaña. The funeral of this officer on the 17th occasioned a demonstration. The hearse was accompanied on its way to the East Cemetery by most of the Madrid falangists still at large, all shouting 'Spain! One, Great, and Free!' Enthusiastic members of the socialist youth movement sang the 'International', saluted with their fists, and sprayed the cortège with bullets. At the cemetery itself, a running battle occurred between the falangists and assault guards. About a dozen people were killed during the course of the day – among them Andrés Sáenz de Heredia, a first cousin of José Antonio. The skirmish suggested that civil war had almost begun. The war of rumours was certainly uncontrollable. The Right thus alleged that Bela Kun, the Hungarian communist, who was believed throughout the western world to be a

1. Alcalá Zamora lingered in Spain a month or two and left in early July for South America where he stayed in penurious circumstances till his death in 1949. See Gil Robles's account, pp. 582–95. Martínez Barrio was interim President.

2. Marichal, in Azaña, vol. III, p. xxxiii.

mixture of Robespierre and Lenin, had arrived in Seville, to start a revolution. But it was probably only the journalist Ilya Ehrenburg.

Although conditions seemed promising, the plan for the military rising in April collapsed. All depended on General Rodríguez del Barrio, inspector-general of the army, whose task was to arouse the Madrid garrisons. General Varela was to arrest the minister of war, General Masquelet, and take over the army. But Rodríguez del Barrio was dying of cancer of the stomach. At the last moment, partly because of his health, partly because of cold feet among officers in Barcelona, he postponed the action. General Orgaz waited in vain for the signal in the friendly Italian Embassy. If a rising had occurred in April, it would probably have failed, since neither the Carlists nor the Falange were ready to act. The failure of this attempt led to agreement among the rebellious officers that General Mola in Pamplona should become 'the director' of the whole conspiracy.[1]

Emilio Mola was a courageous, imaginative, devious and literary-minded officer, whose ascetic, spectacle-framed face caused him to seem more a 'papal secretary than a general'.[2] He came from a military family which had been busy in the liberal interest in the nineteenth century. Born in Cuba, active in Morocco with the native troops of the *Regulares* from their formation, gallant at the defence of Dar Akobba, Mola had been director-general of security at the time of the fall of the monarchy, and as such had incurred the special enmity of republican intellectuals: 'Shoot Mola' had been a popular slogan for rioters in 1930–31. As a result, he had been left without employment during Azaña's first government, though his memoirs had been widely read. Before 1936, he had not associated with the plots against the republic. But conspiracy turned out to be peculiarly his *métier*.

His plans were soon made clear. Two branches of the plot, one civil, one military, were to be set up in the main cities of Spain, the Balearic and Canary Isles, and Spanish Morocco. Unlike some, Mola realized that the age of the old-style *pronunciamiento* was past: civilian support was necessary. The aim of the movement, declared Mola, was to establish 'order, peace, and justice'. But it was obvious

1. *Cruzada*, IX, p. 510. Another scheme revolved around an approach to the outgoing President to install a military cabinet.

2. Sefton Delmer, *Trail Sinister* (London, 1961), p. 299.

that the subsequent government envisaged would be tougher, and more lasting than Primo de Rivera's directorate had been: Mola envisaged no mere 'brief parenthesis' in the constitutional life of Spain, as Primo did, in his first *pronunciamiento*. All could take part in the rising (in some ways, the circular read like a company prospectus) 'except those who receive inspiration from abroad, socialists, freemasons, anarchists, communists, etc.'. The provincial representatives were instructed to work out detailed plans for seizing public buildings in their localities, particularly lines of communication, and to prepare a declaration announcing a state of war. General Sanjurjo would fly in from Portugal and become President of a military *junta* 'which will immediately establish the law of the land'. In some places, such as Seville, the Falange was given an important part in the rising, but nowhere were the political aims of that party mentioned. Mola's first plan included the following provision:

> It will be borne in mind that the action, in order to crush, as soon as possible, a strong and well-organized enemy, will have to be very violent. Hence, all directors of political parties, societies, or unions not pledged to the movement will be imprisoned: such people will be administered exemplary punishments, so that movements of rebellion or strikes will be strangled.[1]

The document was signed '*El Director*' – that is, Mola. This conspiracy was organized by a minority of officers relying on the patriotism of others to join in, if the occasion to act were appropriately chosen: not many officers were falangists, and few were even monarchist, though some actual commanders in the critical places in 1936 were the first and more were joining every day. But many retired officers were happy to play a part. Perhaps their wives egged them on: 'You tolerate this? What is the army doing? When will it rise?'[2] During the course of the spring, more and more officers became disturbed at the continuing disorder. In Madrid General Rodríguez del Barrio, meantime, died, as expected. General Varela was imprisoned in Cádiz, and Orgaz exiled to the Canaries. Their activities in April had become known to the government.

1. Qu. Bertrán Güell, p. 123.
2. This was the view of the Lawyer 'Marón' in Azaña's dialogue, *La velada en Benicarló*, *Obras*, vol. III, p. 405.

The Carlists were busy in Lisbon trying to arrange with Sanjurjo the nature of the future Spain after the revolution. Fal Conde wanted the dissolution of all political parties, and a government of three men only – Sanjurjo as President and in control of defence, an education minister, and an 'industrial' minister.[1] During the spring, meantime, negotiations between the conspirators and the Basque nationalists were begun: Mola and the monarchists sought to draw the latter away from their alliance with the Left, and some arms were even made available to them.[2] The canvassing of possible leaders of the rising continued. Through the headquarters of the eight military commands of the Spanish army on the Peninsula, to the smaller commands in the Balearics and the Canaries, to the three mountain brigades and the three general inspectorates, Mola's messengers, sometimes upper-class girls, sometimes officers in civilian dress, travelled patiently and secretly by rail or road: names, dates, tasks were assigned, and re-assigned.

Each of the eight military regions in Spain at that time had on paper one division, and each division had two brigades. Usually, the second brigade was undermanned, because of men being on leave, or because the conscripts had bought themselves out. Hence, the commander of the first brigade in each division was the important officer in the event of a rising. His headquarters were in the same city as that of the regional divisional commander: the other brigade would be in a lesser city, such as indeed was Mola's brigade, in Pamplona (the second, attached to the 6th Division, whose headquarters was at Burgos). Each brigade had two regiments, of which the first was quartered at divisional headquarters: the other three regiments were scattered in other towns, the unit being sometimes only a platoon.

Azaña's government had ensured, as they thought, that all the divisional commanders were republicans; and as it happened, only General Cabanellas in Saragossa, in command of the 5th Division, was party to Mola's plans. The others were hostile. Mola's plan was that those hostile divisions and the other units dependent on them

1. Earlier, the Carlists had wanted a rising by themselves, and Sanjurjo had agreed to head a provisional government of monarchist restoration (with Alfonso Carlos, the Carlist Pretender, as King) if such an isolated rising were to occur.

2. Gil Robles, p. 729.

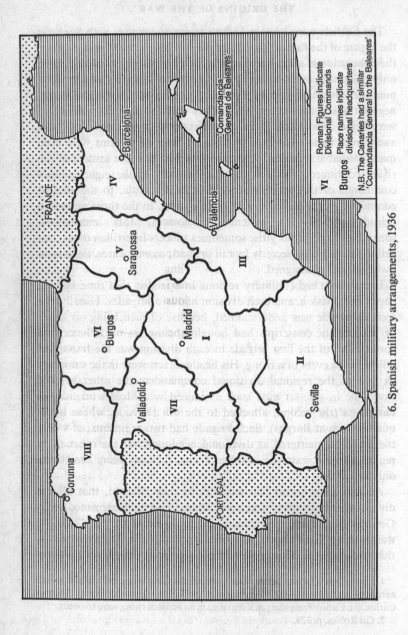

6. Spanish military arrangements, 1936

would be seized by other generals or colonels, either serving in the city concerned, or specially sent there.

Mola's agents went too, of course, to the headquarters of the Army of Africa, where the Foreign Legion and the native troops were ready for action. But Mola's name was not a magic one. Many commanders were reluctant to commit themselves. What was Goded going to do, they asked, and what of Franco? The generals in Madrid, the UME, and the Carlists still seemed to pull in different directions. 'The children normal, the nannies worse,' one of Mola's representatives telegraphed from Andalusia to Pamplona in April, suggesting the unpreparedness of the senior officers and the readiness of younger ones to conspire.[1] What, too, of the Falange? José Antonio in prison still warned 'We will be neither the vanguard, nor the shock troops, nor the invaluable ally of any confused reactionary movement'.[2] Brave words, and they may well have expressed the real views of those old falangists who had been brawling in the streets ever since Ledesma launched *La Conquista del Estado* in 1931. But, by this time, the die was cast. The Falange could obviously not stand aside from a military rising.

On 1 May, the traditional working-class parades were held throughout Spain. They were accompanied by a general strike called for most cities by the CNT. Along the avenues of the great cities, the now virtually bolshevized socialist youth paraded menacingly and confidently, as if part of an embryo Red Army. (*Claridad* on 25 April called on every village to form a militia of a hundred men.) The salute of the clenched fist was given to the sound of the 'International', or to one of the songs composed in the fighting in the Asturias; or perhaps to 'Primero de Mayo' (First of May), or 'The Young Guard'. Large portraits of Largo Caballero, Stalin, and Lenin were carried like banners down the Castellana in Madrid, from whose elegant balconies the bourgeoisie, representing the Spain of Charles

1. 'Las niñas, regular, las encargadas, pésimas' were the actual words of Colonel García Escámez.

2. Francisco Bravo, *Historia de la Falange de las Jons* (Madrid, 1940). Between February and July 1936, the Falange's numbers, like those of the communists, greatly increased, perhaps to as many as 75,000. Apart from Onésimo Redondo's organization at Valladolid (which gained some following also among the workers of Seville), these were young middle-class men or undergraduates not yet established in professions, and more army officers than is sometimes supposed.

V, watched with fascinated horror. Surely this could not go on? Prieto took the opportunity in a major speech in the by-election at Cuenca to point out that 'What no country can endure is the constant blood-letting and public disorder without an immediate revolutionary end'. He argued intelligently that the current excesses merely made things easier for fascism; and he spoke of General Franco as a man of sufficient gifts and youth to lead a military rebellion.[1] But his audiences did not wish to hear caution. Prieto was physically threatened, in a tumultuous meeting at Ecija, by the socialist youth and other *Caballeristas*.[2]

The elections in the disputed provinces (Cuenca and Granada) were in the end decided. In Granada, all thirteen Popular Front candidates won; in Cuenca, three of them, a centrist, a *CEDAista*, and an agrarian were elected: José Antonio's candidature there was disqualified on doubtful grounds, while the proposed candidature of General Franco was withdrawn. In both elections, intimidation by hooligans of the Left may have influenced the result.[3] Four days later, from his prison, José Antonio (who had always liked Sanjurjo) wrote an open letter to the Spanish soldiers, calling upon them to make an end of all the attacks made upon 'the sacred identity of Spain'. 'In the last resort,' he added, 'as Spengler put it, "it has always been a platoon of soldiers who have saved civilization".'[4] Gone were the days when José Antonio would say that serving soldiers were useless, that they were all chicken-hearted, and that the most cowardly was Franco.[5] Even so, the Falange was not yet truly part of the military plot, the details of which they knew nothing.

On 10 May, Azaña was finally elected President in place of Alcalá Zamora, by 238 to 5, in the electoral college assembled in the Retiro Palace. The occasion was marred by a fight in the corridors between Araquistain, still supporting Largo Caballero, and Julián Zugazagoitia, editor of *El Socialista*, which supported Prieto. (The CEDA and right-wing parties had not put forward any candidate, and abstained from voting.) After a few days, Casares Quiroga became

1. De la Cierva, *Los documentos*, p. 235f. The speech is not without ambiguities.
2. Prieto, *Convulsiones*, vol. III, pp. 160–67. He escaped by the back door. Perhaps the incident has been exaggerated.
3. For a right-wing view, see Gil Robles, pp. 558–65.
4. Ximénez de Sandoval, p. 551. 5. Ansaldo, p. 125.

Prime Minister, with a cabinet much like Azaña's.[1] The acid-tongued Casares had a reputation for strength, but it derived from his time as minister of the interior in 1933, and anyway was unjustified: Azaña recalled him at the time of Casas Viejas sitting nervously on the side of his bed, unable to dress himself. Casares was now ill with tuberculosis. Before he was offered the premiership, Azaña approached Prieto, who had had to refuse, since, as expected, his socialist parliamentary group voted against participation in the government (by 49 to 19). The hope of Azaña was for a grand coalition of men of the Centre which, had it been achieved, might have saved the country from war. But he did not press the idea as hard as he might have done, and the project perhaps owes more to the hindsight of historians than to its practical possibilities. Still, Giménez Fernández remained in touch with Prieto on behalf of the CEDA. But these ideas always foundered on the same rock as in early May: the hostility of Largo Caballero, and Largo Caballero's control over his party.

On 21 May, the Madrid socialists agreed on the following aims: 'First, the conquest of power by the working class and by whatever means possible. Secondly, the transformation of individual proprietorship into collective social and common property. In the period

1. The members of this unfortunate administration, apart from Casares (who made himself minister of war), were: Juan Moles, an elderly Catalan nationalist trusted by the CEDA even if he were thought a 'mummy' (*momia*) by Joaquín Maurín, minister of the interior; Enrique Ramos, Azaña's under-secretary and close associate in 1931–3, minister of finance; Augusto Barcia, a prominent freemason, republican lawyer, foreign minister; Mariano Ruiz Funes, professor of law, minister of agriculture; Antonio Velao, director of railways in 1931–3, was minister of public works; Francisco Barnés, a typical product of the Free Institute, was minister of education; José Giral, professor of chemistry, had been one of Azaña's associates since the 1920s, returned to be minister of the navy, a post he had held from 1931–3; Manuel Blasco Garzón, an ex-radical and lawyer who had followed Martínez Barrio into the Republican Union party, minister of justice; Plácido Alvarez Buylla, from a family much associated with the Free Institute, minister of industry; Bernardo Giner de los Ríos, similarly related to the founder of the Free Institute, minister of communications; and Juan Lluhí, a recent Councillor in the *Generalidad*, brought in to be minister of labour. Catalonia had recently been quiet ('the Catalan oasis') despite the murders of Miguel and José Badía, two extreme separatist brothers, and it was thought that Lluhí might thus have a calming effect in Spain generally. The cabinet was intellectually distinguished, and honest, but there were too many lawyers in it and nobody had any experience of industry or even of labour unions.

of transition, the form of government will be the dictatorship of the proletariat.' On 24 May, Largo Caballero made a great speech at Cádiz: 'When the Popular Front breaks up,' he announced, 'as break up it will, the triumph of the proletariat will be certain. We shall then implant the dictatorship of the proletariat, which does not mean the repression of the proletariat, but of the capitalist and bourgeois classes!'[1] Admittedly, Besteiro told a French newspaper that the conditions in Spain were quite different from those in Russia in 1917, and hence the country could not be heading for communism. The communist newspaper *Mundo Obrero* mocked his inadequate Marxism.[2] Though there was now much real violence, the verbal excessiveness on both sides in these months explains much of how matters went from bad to worse. Did Largo hope, by his speeches, to provoke a right-wing military rising whose defeat would lead to his capture of power? It is hard to believe, in fact, that Largo really knew where his rhetoric would lead him. Did the communists?[3] Their leadership was still modest in quality, the 'instructor' from the Comintern, Vittorio Codovilla, no doubt even more insistent than ever on following Moscow's instructions: it must have been a difficult situation for him to find real revolutionary possibilities opening in Spain at the very moment that Stalin desired maximum cooperation with democrats.

In May, the anarchists made their contribution to the debates about the future of Spain at their annual congress at Saragossa. The five-year long controversy between the *treintistas* and the FAI was patched up, the former being re-incorporated into the movement,[4] but the FAI's policy for the piecemeal achievement of 'libertarian communism' by the lightning action of dedicated anarchists in different *pueblos* remained the most favoured tactic. The congress demanded a continuation of these strikes but also suggested new efforts

1. *El Socialista*, 26 May 1936.

2. *Mundo Obrero*, 15 May 1936, quoted De la Cierva, *Los documentos*, p. 456.

3. The stories later circulated and widely believed (by myself among others) that there was a communist plan for a *coup d'état* have been finally laid by Herbert Southworth, in *Le Mythe de la croisade de Franco* (Paris, 1964), p. 170f. The documents were published in fact in *Claridad*, 30 May 1936; Southworth publishes the ironic front page (p. 185). 'How we are going to achieve the revolution by 29 June', ran the headline! A plot of this sort was not, in fact, necessary. The forger may one day come forward.

4. See above, p. 74.

to reach alliance with the UGT, and made demands for both a thirty-six-hour week and one month's holiday with pay and higher wages. On the other hand, there was no sign that anyone realized that there was a danger of fascism; and no agreement, in consequence, on the arming of militias, much less the organization of a revolutionary army, as suggested by Juan García Oliver. Durruti opposed this idea on the ground that a revolutionary army would stifle the revolution.[1] Idealism there was in plenty, but it seemed so purblind in face of likely military moves that the secretary of the CNT, Horacio Prieto, resigned.

One conference document, prepared by the FAI doctor from Rioja, Isaac Puente, author of an influential study, *El comunismo libertario*, well expressed what the anarchists expected:

> At the end of the violent stage of the revolution, the following will be declared abolished: private property; the state; the principle of authority; and, in consequence, the classes which divide men into exploited and exploiters, oppressors and oppressed. Once wealth is socialized, the producers, already free, will be charged with the direct administration of production and consumption. After the setting up in each locality of the free commune [*la comuna libertaria*], we will set the new social mechanism on foot. The producers ... will freely decide the form in which they are to be organized. The *comuna libre* will take over the previous property of the bourgeoisie, such as food, clothes, work implements, raw materials, etc. These ... will pass to the producers so that they can administer them directly for the benefit of the community. The *comunas* will first provide the maximum of commodities for each inhabitant, ensuring assistance to the ill and education to the young ... all able-bodied men will seek to carry out their voluntary duty to the community in relation to their strength and skill. All those functions will have no executive or bureaucratic character. Apart from those with technical functions ... the remainder will carry out their duties as producers, meeting in sessions at the end of the day to discuss the questions of detail which do not require the approval of the communal assemblies ...

The basis of society would be the self-governing communes, though 'the right of autonomy will not exclude the duty of fulfilling agreements of collective convenience'. A group of small villages might be united in one single commune. The associations of industrial

1. Paz, p. 266. This book has a good picture of the congress.

and agricultural producers in each commune would federate nationally, and they would effect exchange of goods. As for the family, the revolution should not operate violently against it on principle. But separate treatment, social and professional, of women would vanish: 'Libertarian communism proclaims free love, without more regulation than the will of the man and woman, guaranteeing to their children the safeguard of the community.' At the same time, through a good sexual education, beginning at school, eugenic selection would be inculcated, so that human beings would henceforward breed conscientiously, in order to produce healthy and beautiful children. (This aspect of the anarchist programme has perhaps been ignored.) The anarchists also had a programme for love:

On the problems of moral idiosyncracy, which love may bring to the society of libertarian communism, the community and the principle of Liberty leave only two roads open . . . absence. For many illnesses, a change of air is recommended. For the illness of love . . . a change of commune is recommended. Religion, that purely subjective manifestation, will be recognized in as much as it stays relegated to the sanctuary of the individual conscience, but in no case will it be permitted as a form of public show, nor a moral and intellectual coercion (all churches thus would be closed).

Illiteracy would be energetically fought. Culture would be restored to 'those who have been dispossessed of it' (by capitalism: the presumption behind the use of the word 'dispossess' clearly being that, in the golden age of the remote past, things were better than they were in 1936). A national federation of education would be installed – its mission being specifically to educate humanity to be free, scientific and egalitarian. In addition:

All questions of rewards and penalties will be excluded . . . The cinema, the radio, the teaching missions . . . will be excellent and effective aids for a rapid intellectual and moral transformation of the existing generations . . . Access to arts and sciences will be free.

There would be no distinction between intellectuals and manual workers, since each would be both.

As evolution is a continuous line, [the programme concluded] even though sometimes not always direct, the individual will always have aspirations . . . to do better than his parents and his contemporaries; all those anxieties of . . . creation – artistic, scientific, literary – will not be at all out of place in the free society which would cultivate them . . . there will be days of general recreation, hours daily for visits to exhibitions, theatres and cinemas.[1]

Communists, socialists and left republicans greeted these aspirations with their usual neglect: the anarchists might be useful to have on the same side as oneself at the barricades, but not at the committee table. But shortly these ideas would be put into practice in thousands of villages and towns.

On 25 May, meantime, General Mola issued a detailed strategic plan.[2] On 27 May, José Antonio entered into correspondence with Mola, a letter being carried to Pamplona by his law clerk, Rafael Garcerán. He did not promise full support as yet, but discussed terms, pledging that 4,000 falangists could help the rising at the start.[3] On 30 May, Sanjurjo gave Mola his blessing to act as coordinator of the conspiracy, on the assumption that he, Sanjurjo, the symbol of victory, would be the head of the new government, and that the Carlists would play a part.[4] On 3 June, Mola had his first discussion with a leading Carlist, José Luis Oriol.[5] That same day, the director-general of security in Madrid, Alonso Mallol, who knew perfectly well what was afoot, drove up to Pamplona to try to catch Mola red-handed; Mola, warned by his friend, Santiago Martín Bagüeñas, the chief of police in the capital, was able to conceal all damaging evidence of conspiracy.[6] Meantime, a senior colonel, Valentín Galarza, 'the technician', took over as chief of staff of the plot, and kept contacts going between the leaders. On 5 June, when José Antonio was transferred from Madrid to Alicante gaol, Mola circulated a political document, describing how the success of the rising would be followed by a 'Directory', comprising a president and four others. All would be officers. They would have the power to issue laws. These would later be ratified by a constituent assembly, elected 'by suffrage in the manner that shall be deemed most appropriate'. The Cortes and con-

1. Qu. Peirats, vol. I, pp. 111–31. 'Does this Paradise have central heating?' a pupil of Federico Urales once asked.

2. Iribarren, p. 57f.

3. *Cruzada*, IX, p. 511. The Garcerán–Mola meeting was on 1 June.

4. Maiz, pp. 103–4; Iribarren, p. 54.

5. *Cruzada*, XIII, p. 447.

6. Jorge Vigón, *General Mola, el conspirador* (Barcelona, 1957), p. 93.

stitution of 1931 would be suspended. Laws not in accord with the 'new organic system' would be abolished, and those people who received 'inspiration from abroad' would be outlawed. But the Carlists did not agree to the programme, despite a six-hour interview between Mola and Fal Conde in the Navarrese monastery of Irache on 16 June.[1] Meantime, ideology even affected the bull-fighting season. At Aranjuez, for example, the two *alguacils* galloped into the ring with clenched fists raised. Uproar followed. Every moveable object – cushions, hats, and bottles – was thrown into the ring in protest. The first fight was delayed three-quarters of an hour while the ring was cleared up.[2] There were brawls, with some deaths, between CNT and UGT in Málaga. A British manager of a lace factory was mysteriously murdered in Barcelona. José Antonio by then apparently had accepted the inevitability of a military rising and of the Falange's part in it. But he did do so less from conviction as from a belief that the Falange would be crushed if it did not side actively with Mola's organization: in the last issue of the banned falangist journal, *No Importa*, he wrote 'Watch the Right. Warning to *madrugadores*: the Falange is not a conservative force.' A little later, he warned against 'thinking that the ills of Spain are due to simple rearrangements of internal order and will vanish when power is handed over to ... charlatans lacking any historical understanding, any authentic education'.[3] Fewer reserves were felt by Calvo Sotelo. Despite the lack of any concession in Mola's programme to the monarchy, he told the general that he only desired to know the hour and the day in order to be one more soldier at the army's orders.[4] Gil Robles was not a part of the conspiracy, but he knew of its existence, and some of the CEDA's funds were later transferred to the use of the plotters.[5] By

1. *Cruzada*, XIII, p. 449. The local mayor told Casares of this meeting. (A. de Lizarra, *Los vascos y la república española*, Buenos Aires, 1944, p. 33.) In addition to Mola's difficulties with the Carlists, he was also not fully at one with the Unión Militar. See the letters in de Castillo and Alvarez, which show that the UME wanted to arraign all the post-1931 ministers for treason.

2. Letter to the author from Desmond Flower.

3. *Obras completas*, pp. 1110–11. '*Madrugadores*' are those who act at dawn, *madrugada*; that is, those who rebel.

4. Maiz, p. 168. Gil Robles says no (p. 730).

5. See Payne, *Politics and the Military in Modern Spain* (Stanford, 1967), p. 330, and Gil Robles, p. 730 and p. 798 fn. 50, where the CEDA leader says he gave

this time, he had convinced himself that the continuing disorder was part of a plan to bring economic collapse as a justification for revolution. His family were already in St Jean de Luz, in France, and he realized that his hour had passed. There is some evidence that he would have liked to have been more a party to the conspiracy than the generals permitted.[1] Not only, however, were his followers leaving him for the Falange; some did so for Calvo Sotelo.

500,000 pesetas from his party's funds in the 'first days of July' to 'help prevent from failing what would inevitably come to pass' – or to help Mola's escape, if necessary.

1. Gil Robles's role in the conspiracy is exhaustively investigated in De la Cierva, *Historia*, vol. I, p. 735f. Apparently he refused to convoke a right-wing rump Cortes in Burgos when asked. For further comments, see Manuel Fal Conde in *ABC*, 2 and 3 May 1968, and Ignacio Luca de Tena, *ABC*, 2, 3, 5, 6 and 9 April 1968. Gil Robles's reply to the latter was in *Ya*, 10 April 1968.

12

The economy under the republic – revolution of the past and the eve of disaster

THE years 1929–32 were the period of world depression; a bad time for a government to take power anywhere. True, had it not been for the depression, Primo de Rivera might not have fallen in Spain. But his successors did not act as if they realized the nature of the economic crisis, though they themselves had been borne to power partly by it. Azaña and his ministers behaved as if they thought they were dealing primarily with constitutional or cultural problems. Even the socialist ministers (between 1931 and 1933, Prieto and Largo Caballero, were ministers of finance and of labour) did not seem to realize the need, in a world financial crisis, of the importance of the direction of the economy. Partly because the ministers were inexperienced, partly because there was doubt about their policies, and partly because no one had money with which to take risks, the Spanish rich and the international financial community were hostile to the republic to begin with. Prieto's arrival at the ministry of finance led, first, to the withdrawal of a loan from J. P. Morgan, negotiated by his immediate predecessor under the King, Juan Ventosa. The church burnings in May 1931 delayed the reopening of negotiations for it. There was a run on the peseta, and substantial export of currency throughout 1931. Prieto later did his best to protect the peseta, negotiating with Russia to buy oil at 18 per cent less than that offered by English and US companies, and insisting on licences for foreign equipment.[1]

Nevertheless, throughout 1931, Prieto, for all the world as if he were an orthodox governor of the Bank of England, concentrated on trying to stabilize the peseta. His even more orthodox successor as minister of finance, Jaime Carner, did the same. They did prevent the international quotation for the peseta from dropping faster than it had before: the consequence was that, while the international value

1. Some discussions in the cabinet about oil supplies are described by Azaña in his diaries.

of the peseta dropped by 25 per cent between 1929 and 1931, it only dropped a little over 10 per cent more by 1932, and remained thereafter stable until 1936. It is arguable that, had it not been for the continuing political uncertainty, the number of strikes, and the threats of revolution from Left and Right, the peseta would have increased its value by 1934. It would seem improbable, at all events, that right-wing or international financial conspiracies can be blamed for the fall of the republic, whatever Juan March might have been doing with his money.[1]

Industry was in these years at a low level for reasons largely out of Spain's control. The figures are dispiriting: taking 1929 as a base of 100, the index of industrial production was below that in 1935; after the elections of 1936, the index fell to 77 in March 1936. The index of share prices was still more gloomy. Again with 1929 as a base, prices had fallen to 63 in 1935.[2] The most depressed side of the Spanish economy were the mines: less coal, than other minerals. Coal production certainly fell, though only moderately, from 7 million tons in 1931, to just under 6 in 1934, rallying to 7 in 1935. Spanish coal could not, however, compete with English prices and, if citrus fruit exports were not to suffer, some English coal had regularly to be imported to balance the trade. On the other hand, the mining of manganese ore dropped to nearly nothing in 1935; production of pyrites, potash and pig iron fell by over a third, between 1930 and 1935; lead, zinc, silver, tungsten and copper by over a half; and iron ore by a quarter. Steel production fell steadily from 1,000,000 tons in 1929 to 580,000 in 1935, not only because of world conditions but because the republic needed less steel than Primo had done: there was no Moroccan war to service, while the republic, like all governments in the 1930s, believed in roads, not railway expansion. Some sectors, however, did well during the republic – electric power, from increased development of hydro-electric plants, increased by nearly half between 1926 and 1936. So did building. In truth, most countries

1. See Appendix I where statistical evidence can be found for most of the arguments in this chapter.

2. The decline in share prices was admittedly accompanied by hoarding, to almost the same extent as investment in equities had fallen: post-office savings stood at 239 million pesetas in 1928 – and at 370 million in 1935. Savings-bank deposits were at 1,608 million pesetas in 1928; they had reached 2,778 million in 1934.

the USA, Britain, France and Germany) had worse problems in the depression than Spain. Thus while Spain's index of industrial production had dropped over 10 per cent, German and US production dropped nearly 50 per cent in 1932.

The most resilient of ministers in the face of these difficulties was Prieto who, when moved from the ministry of finance to that of public works, devoted much time and investment to dams, irrigation schemes and reafforestation, assisting agriculture as well as hydro-electric power. He electrified some railways, began underground central terminals in Barcelona and Madrid, completed Primo's scheme for a Guadarrama train tunnel, and built many roads. It is easy to imagine how large a part schemes of this nature would have played in any government of the centre which he would have directed.

Agricultural figures were much more encouraging. Production of wheat, maize and rice either maintained past levels, or showed an advance. Fish caught off Spanish coasts increased by a third.[1] The area devoted to production of oranges between 1931 and 1935 was nearly half as much again as it was in 1926, while exports of oranges also rose to a record high figure in the years of the republic – reaching (principally to Britain) over 20 per cent of Spanish exports.[2] (The increase was chiefly due to the decline in other exports, such as wine and olive oil.) Nevertheless, as expected, overall export figures in the middle thirties were only about a quarter of the levels obtained in 1930.

Such figures need to be reckoned against the consistent rise in population – nearly 1 per cent a year – so that conditions were worse for a larger population.[3] 100,000 emigrant workers also returned in the 1930s, chiefly from Cuba or South America, and further emigration was impossible.[4]

The economy of Spain was, therefore, marked by mildly declining

1. From 230,646 Tm in 1927 to 340,917 Tm in 1931–4.

2. Figures in Tamames, pp. 86–91. The percentage of Spanish exports represented by oranges was 11.7 per cent in 1926–30, and (for the sake of contemporary comparison), 12.67 per cent in 1959.

3. The population increased from 23.6 million in 1930 to 25.88 million in 1940 – a regular rate of increase of just under one per cent per year, even taking into account the civil war.

4. 39,582, 37,376 and 24,927 in 1931, 1932 and 1933 respectively (Ramón Tamames, *La república, la era de Franco*, Madrid, 1973, p. 58).

industrial production, a severe decline in the mines, static or mildly increasing agricultural production and rising population. Prices remained fairly constant: food was cheap in relation to lodging, as were clothes. But political circumstances naturally dominated the consequences. Between 1931 and 1933, for example, wages rose as a result of Largo Caballero's measures and of a phenomenal wave of strikes with which the employers felt they had no alternative save to settle, for political reasons.[1] The result was layings-off, dismissals, closing of factories – and higher unemployment: indeed, unemployment rose steadily during the republic. Figures are not easy to decide upon; but if, as seems probable, unemployed reached 400,000 after the republic had been in existence for nine months in December 1931, they had probably reached 600,000 by December 1933.[2]

The situation changed somewhat during the *bienio negro*, the two years of radical, centrist, and CEDA government between late 1933 and early 1936. Employers now had no political anxiety about standing up to wage demands. They had the police, the civil guard and the army behind them, and the workers knew it. So, not only did wages not go up, but they clearly were lowered in many places, without any commensurate drop in prices. The working class were under attack; the consequence, as has been seen, was the agricultural strike of early 1934, followed by the revolution and general strike of October 1934. Political feelings were thereafter worsened beyond cure, particularly since so many workers' leaders were imprisoned. But the rate of increase at least in unemployment was lowered. The victory of the Popular Front took the country back to an exacerbated version of the state of affairs prevailing between 1931 and 1933. The stock exchange declined, production fell, and, this time, the crisis affected agriculture. Landlords and employers found themselves not only raising wages, cutting working hours, but, particularly in the country, as has been seen, yielding to demands for labour not only from those sacked between 1933 and 1936, and from those who had been in gaol, but from those who had never had jobs. Even so, unemployment still

1. In 1933, there were well over 1,000 strikes, losing some 14 million work days: such figures are only perhaps meaningful if they are compared with what went before. Thus the number of strikes for the seven years 1929–35 were 96, 402, 734, 681, 1,127, 594 and 164 respectively (Balcells, p. 175).

2. Balcells, p. 53.

rose – in June 1936 reaching a level of 800,000. It can easily be imagined how many of these must have sought to be embraced, if not fed, by one or other of the paramilitary organizations. Indeed, the 'little civil war', as the events between February and July 1936 has been not unfairly described, might be interpreted as having many characteristics of a raid by unemployed *pistoleros*, of both sides of the political spectrum, on the lives and possessions of the salaried.

Given the unstable political situation and the hatreds caused since 1934, the combination of falling production, high wages (obtained by intimidation), the collapse of business confidence, and rising unemployment left the country with only three alternatives: revolution, counter-revolution, or civil war. Gil Robles and Azaña, with their concern for clerical education, now naturally seemed irrelevant. In the first half of 1936, only Calvo Sotelo and Largo Caballero seemed to have any solution to offer: both had collaborated with democratic politics, both had served Primo de Rivera, both now offered authoritarian solutions. The momentum in one direction or the other was difficult for men of the centre to withstand.

*

The twentieth century saw an awakening of the Spanish spirit: the political volatility of the years between 1898 and 1936, and most intensely between 1931 and 1936, was the expression of a vitality which extended through most spheres of national life. The first part of the twentieth century was richer in artistic achievement, for example, than any since the seventeenth century. The most famous names, Picasso, Dali and Miró; García Lorca, Juan Ramón Jiménez, Antonio Machado; Pío Baroja, Buñuel, de Falla, Casals, Unamuno and Ortega – these mark only the peaks of a brilliant period. Spain, in the early twentieth century, was certainly coming out from her long decline. This renaissance was to be seen on the Right as well as on the Left, in education as in art. The harmonious rationalism of the Free Institute of Education was complemented by an already reviving catholicism. Catalan and Basque nationalism were political expressions of both economic and cultural renaissance. The anarchist movement, which continued to grow in numbers until the 1930s, proved that the working classes had also been awakened. The intellectual revival was reflected in a vigorous press: not only every party but every shade of opinion had its own newspaper and often a journal or two as well. Alas, the clash of those, and other, regeneratory hopes could not be contained within the old structures. Thus the midsummer of 1936 saw not only the completion of Lorca's *The House of Bernarda Alba*, but the culmination of a hundred and fifty years of passionate quarrels in Spain.

In 1808, the old monarchy had collapsed and, from 1834, war was waged for five years over the question of a liberal constitution. In 1868, a corrupt monarchy was expelled by the army, and the country dissolved into a conflict which was at once religious and regional, while new working-class organizations were founded by the representatives of Bakunin. In 1898, the Spanish American War brought back the over-large army from the last colonies to unemployed frustration in Spain, surrounded by innumerable reminders of past glory, while a valiant group of middle-class young men sought to prepare the intellectual renaissance of the country by 'placing a padlock on the Cid's tomb'.[1] In 1909, class hatred, exacerbated by both Catalan nationalism and anti-militarism, brought a week of bloody rioting in Barcelona, which vented itself in particular against the church. In 1917, a revolutionary general strike was crushed by an itself half-insurrectionary army, while the military dictatorship of Primo de Rivera, established in 1923 after five years of semi civil war in Barcelona, was the government which gave the country its longest rest from political murders, strikes, and sterile intrigues. The 'liberals', whose protests brought the expulsion of both the dictator, in 1930, and the King, in 1931, proved unable to create a democratic habit powerful enough to satisfy the aspirations of either the working, or the old governing, classes, while the new rulers themselves mortally angered the latter, when not strong enough as well as not radical enough to please the former. In 1932, a section of the Right attempted to overcome their electoral defeat by a *pronunciamiento* in the old style, while, in 1934, a part of the Left, after their own reverse at the polling stations, impelled by their own impatience, as well as by continent-wide fears of fascism, also staged a revolt, which, in Asturias, temporarily established a working-class dictatorship. In February 1936, the two sides which by then had taken shape, and which both referred to themselves by the ominously military word

1. The phrase was the inspiration of the economist, Joaquín Costa. Cf. too Unamuno's 'let us kill Cervantes' which so shocked Lorca.

'front', put their quarrels again to the voters. The narrow victory of the Popular Front over the National Front had brought in a weak if progressive ministry, regarded by its own socialist and communist supporters as the precursor of far-reaching social change. Most of the leading men of Spain in 1936 had lived through a generation of turbulence, and many of them, like Largo Caballero, Calvo Sotelo, Sanjurjo, had played important, if equivocal, roles throughout (Largo had served Primo de Rivera, Sanjurjo had deserted the King). Now the old masters of economic power, led by the army, and supported by the church, that embodiment of Spain's past glory, believed that they were about to be overwhelmed. Opposed to them, were the 'professors' – the enlightened middle class – and most of the labour force of the country, maddened by years of insult, misery, and neglect, intoxicated by the knowledge of the better conditions enjoyed by their class comrades in France and Britain and by the mastery which they supposed that the working class had gained in Russia. The Left were frightened by fascism, the Right by communism. The Right supposed, too, that, unless they proceeded to a counter-revolution, they would be smashed by revolution. The anarchists meanwhile had been in a state of war with society for a generation; and the government's response had been that of a desperate wartime administration, scarcely that of a government at peace. The situation was summed up sharply if haughtily by the French military attaché, Colonel Morell, some months later:

> A parasitical aristocracy, a bourgeoisie little concerned with the public good, a people without leaders. The prestige of the clergy vanished, the system of *caciquismo* enfeebled, the populace has been the prey to agitators and politicians. The bourgeoisie menaced by revolution has, by conviction, or calculation, taken up the cause of rebellion.[1]

Another explanation was that Spain was a conservative country in which an under-exploited economy was kept backward by a stagnant social structure, while a sophisticated political education and the pressure of population made the old system unworkable. There had to be political change if the resources of the country were to be creatively employed. But while radicals were prepared to overthrow the social structure to secure changes, conservatives were prepared

1. *Documents diplomatiques français*, 1932–1939, 2e Série, Tome IV, p. 171.

to use force to shore up the old world. Some of the Left were impatient, the Centre could not hold.

The Second Spanish Republic failed because it came to be rejected by powerful groups both to the Left and to the Right. To the anarchists, the first government of Azaña and the socialists had seemed 'slow and legalistic'.[1] Many socialists agreed with the anarchists on this matter by 1936. But in attempting to solve the most pressing problems which then faced Spain (and whose existence had led to the collapse of previous régimes), the republic estranged many who had at first, with whatever reluctance, contemplated collaboration with it. The five and a quarter years between April 1931 and July 1936 were thus a time when two sides were taking shape in Spain powerful enough to prevent each other from winning immediately, if swords should be drawn. There had been three main quarrels in Spain since the collapse of the monarchy in 1808: that between church and liberals; that between landowners and, later, bourgeoisie, on the one hand, and working class, on the other; and that between those who demanded local rights (notably in Catalonia and in the Basque provinces) and the advocates of central direction by Castile. Each of these three disputes had fed, or been superimposed, onto each other,[2] so that any desire for moderation on the part of one group of contestants was extinguished by a renewed violence on the part of the other.

The problems of Spain were posed also by the question as to whether the democrats, the socialist revolutionaries or the authoritarian Right would be responsible for the modernization and industrialization of the country. The principles of, and hatred for, the French and Russian Revolutions were equally at stake. The desire for renaissance, and the knowledge that Spain was capable of it, was widespread: 'We declare war on black capitalism, exploiter of the poor ... more religion and less Pharisaism; more justice and less liturgy'; thus a founder-member of the CEDA.[3]

The republic was a failure, despite much promising legislation and

1. The phrase occurred in the '*treintista*' manifesto, qu. Peirats, vol. I, p. 45.

2. Though not in the same order as they had been in the past. For example, in the First Carlist War, the liberals were the advocates of control by Castile against the regional claims of the Basques and Catalans, while, in 1936, the heirs of the liberals stood for federation.

3. qu. Robinson, p. 115.

many good schemes begun (such as, for example, the irrigation and resettlement programme of the Badajoz plan, carried through years later under very different political auspices). The determinist might give a simple explanation. A liberal historian is tempted to blame individuals: Azaña, for excessive pride and an occasional frivolity; Gil Robles, for vacillation, rhetoric and lack of candour; both Largo Caballero and Calvo Sotelo for incendiary speeches and disdain for their opponents. Lerroux was indolent and corrupt; Alcalá Zamora meddlesome and vain. Leaving aside lesser figures such as Miguel Maura or Giménez Fernández, Prieto was the outstanding figure who knew what was the right course, even if he was too mercurial to pursue it. In order to keep his standing with the increasingly revolutionary mainstream of the party, even he had to launch himself into impetuous projects, such as the arms smuggling in 1934 or the removal of Alcalá Zamora in 1936. A certain ambiguity and a certain pessimism also characterized him: 'I am a weak man . . . I do not believe that there is anyone so insensate as actually to wish to exercise public power in Spain in these circumstances' he wrote.[1] In 1933, Azaña made a doleful comment that the difficulties of the republic derived less from its explicit enemies than from the men of the régime: their hatreds, ambitions and jealousies.[2] Yet to blame individuals is to forget that politicians are the expression of public moods which are the masses' collective dreams. The republic really fell for the same reasons that upset both the dictatorship and the restoration monarchy: the inability of the politicians then active to resolve the problems of the country within a frame generally acceptable, and, on the other, a willingness, supported by tradition, of some to put matters to the test of force. 'Already there are no pacific solutions', said the falangist bulletin *No Importa*, on 6 June; 'the state must disappear', said *Solaridad Obrera* on 16 April. Spectres caused the war and, afterwards, ghosts dominated the country.

The country was constructed upon quarrels. There were now no habits of organization, compromise, or even articulation respected, or even sought, by all. Insofar as there were traditions common to all Spain, these were of disputes. Spain was indeed invertebrate. As the years went by, all these disputes partook at the same time of half-religious, class, and regional characteristics. The youth of both the

1. Prieto in *El Liberal*, 26 June 1936. 2. Azaña, vol. IV, p. 559.

CEDA and the socialists were intoxicated by absolute visions of exclusive futures, they allowed those to swing against each other, and hence brought down the state. During the republic, the country had been drenched in politics.[1] At the same time, also, many people wanted a 'new Spain' (which might mean a hundred different things) which would be worthy of Spain's great past and, indeed, of the continuing qualities of her people. Such motives moved either superficially or profoundly many of those *señoritos* who sang the falangist hymn '*Cara al Sol*' ('Face to the Sun'):

Face to the sun, wearing the tunic
Which yesterday you embroidered,
Death will find me, if it calls me
And I do not see you again . . .
Arise [*¡Arriba!*] battalions and conquer –
For Spain has begun to awaken.
Spain – United! Spain – Great!
Spain – Free! Spain – Arise![2]

Similar thoughts moved those passionate revolutionaries who sang the anarchist '*Hijos del pueblo*' ('Sons of the People'):

Sons of the people, your chains oppress you
This injustice cannot go on!
If your life is a world of grief,
Instead of being a slave, it is better to die!
Workers,
You shall suffer no longer!
The oppressor
Must succumb!

1. See Raymond Carr, *The Republic and the Civil War in Spain* (London, 1971), p. 14: 'the republic represented a wholesale process of politicization: for five years it incorporated, for good or evil, the mass of Spaniards into political life'. The collapse of the republic might thus be explained by the revolution in communications.

2. '*Cara al Sol*' was written by Agustín de Foxá, Dionisio Ridruejo and José María Alfaro, with José Antonio's help, and first sung in public in February 1936. The martial music was by Juan Tellería. The image of dying face to the sun is a direct copy, presumably conscious, from the poem 'The White Rose' by the Cuban 'apostle' of Liberty, José Martí. The anthem of the catholic youth began: 'Forward, with faith in victory, For the country and for God, To conquer or to die; The laurel of glory awaits us, for History is with us, the future is on our side'.

Arise
Loyal people
At the cry
Of social revolution![1]

The great poet of Castile, Antonio Machado, was hinting the same, when he wrote, in his elegy to the founder of the Free Institute, Francisco Giner de los Ríos:

Vivid, la vida sigue,
Los muertos mueren y las sombras pasan;
Lleva quien deja y vive el que ha vivido.
¡Yunques, sonad! ¡enmudeced, campanas!

Live for life goes on,
The dead die and the ghosts pass;
He who leaves endures; he who has lived lives on!
Anvils, ring out! Church bells, be dumb![2]

1. '*Hijos del Pueblo*', a song in can-can rhythm, despite its words, was selected as the anthem of the anarchist movement at the Second Literary Competition, in the Palacio de Bellas Artes, Barcelona (1890). A better song than any of these was the Carlists' '*Por Dios, Patria, Rey*', composed in the 1830s.

2. Tr. Gerald Brenan, slightly altered.

BOOK TWO

RISING AND REVOLUTION

'The atmosphere of the 19th of July!
One little fact which illustrates
it: at one of my comrades' house
in Barcelona, the control patrol,
after a routine inspection, opened
a bird cage and freed a canary:
it was the day of liberty!'

MANUEL CASANOVA

13

Franco's letter of 23 June – the Carlists – the journey of the Dragon Rapide – the murder of Lieutenant Castillo – the murder of Calvo Sotelo – two funeral services – the Cortes' last meeting

On 23 June, General Francisco Franco wrote from his semi-banishment in the Canaries to the Prime Minister, Casares Quiroga. The letter showed a preoccupation with the divisions within the officer corps, themselves the reflection of the divided nation. Franco protested against the removal of right-wing officers from their commands. These events, said the general, were causing such unrest that he felt bound to warn the Prime Minister (who was also war minister) of the peril 'involved for the discipline of the army'.[1] This letter was a final statement by Franco, 'before history', that he had done his best to secure peace, though he must have known that little could be done at that late hour. The Prime Minister did not, however, reply.

Well on into this summer of 1936 (and despite his activities immediately after the elections) Franco seems to have been vacillating. 'With Franquito or without Franquito,' expostulated Sanjurjo in Lisbon, 'we shall save Spain.'[2] At the end of June, however, all that seemed necessary for a date to be given for the rising was an agreement with the Carlists. For, on 29 June, José Antonio sent orders to local Falange chiefs as to how to conduct themselves; Falange units were to maintain their identity; only one third of any Falange party in a given locality could be placed under military control; reluctant instructions, but instructions, nevertheless.[3]

Yet, on 1 July, Mola had to circulate a document to his co-plotters counselling patience. The army was still far from united, and he had to resort to threats: 'He who is not with us is against us: with *compañeros* who turn out not to be *compañeros*, the triumphant movement will be inexorable'. Franco's vacillations, if they were genuine, were presumably intolerable to him. The Carlists and the

1. *Cruzada*, IX, p. 523. 2. Ansaldo, p. 42.
3. José Antonio, *Obras*, pp. 1113–14.

falangists were so full of demands. The Carlists' obsession was with the colour of the flag under which the rebels should march, the falangists' with problems of authority. Mola even contemplated a withdrawal to Cuba, where he had been born; he thought of suicide, or of killing Fal Conde, but persevered.

In Morocco, the army of Africa began summer manoeuvres. The capital was in the grip of a building strike: the contractors, as well as the anarchist workers, refused to accept arbitration while the UGT did.[1] So much for Largo Caballero's hopes of achieving a workers' alliance. There were also strikes by lift-workers, waiters, and bull-fighters – the two former called by the left of the UGT. (The bull-fighters' strike, however, derived from the success that summer of two Mexican matadors who were fighting *mano a mano*. The press suggested that Mexicans were braver than Spaniards.) The socialists, meantime, were divided, as ever, particularly over the results of new elections which had been forced for the party presidency by the *Caballeristas*. González Peña, the Austrian miners' leader but a friend of Prieto none the less, was elected in a low poll: the *Caballeristas* complained that the *Prietistas* had defrauded the poll, when it turned out that they had excluded all those who had not paid their dues in 1934.[2]

At the end of June, the long expected merger came, between the socialist and communist youth movements, into the JSU (Juventudes Socialistas Unificadas). In this, while the leaders were mostly socialists, such as Santiago Carrillo, the policy was communist. Even among Largo's entourage, this caused alarm. Araquistain, editor of Largo Caballero's newspaper *Claridad*, burst out (illogically, in view of his ardent pro-communist views until then): 'We have lost our youth. What will happen to the Spanish socialist party?'[3] Prieto

1. C. Lorenzo, p. 209 fn. 49. Azaña, vol. III, p. 499, says that in 1937 there was a public meeting to celebrate the anniversary of the building strike, 'among whose merits, in the minds of its panegyrists, was that it precipitated the rising'.

2. González Peña got in by 10,993 to 2,876. A second poll gave him a narrower majority.

3. The remark was made to Henry Buckley, then *The Times* correspondent in Madrid. Araquistain himself, who later became a passionate anti-communist, alleges that he often at this time saw the Comintern agent, Codovilla, arriving to call on Alvarez del Vayo (he lived in a flat above). Santiago Carrillo (*Demain Espagne*, p. 43) confirmed that Codovilla was partly instrumental in making him

could not contain his anger. But Largo Caballero did not seem perturbed. The Madrid socialists were even thinking of a merger of the socialist and communist parties. The socialist youth, like other groups, continued military training, its organizer in this being a famous Italian socialist from Turin, Fernando de Rosa, celebrated for his attempt, in Brussels in 1929, on the life of Prince Umberto of Savoy.[1]

The middle path still had some friends. Miguel Maura, one of the fathers of the republic in 1931, called for 'a national republican dictatorship' to save Spain from anarchy: 'Peaceful citizens', he wrote in *El Sol* in late June, 'now believe the laws are a dead letter.' Neither Prieto nor Maura were to get the chance of a coalition. Too many rumours abounded. Panic spread because of the repetition of an old tale that a group of nuns had poisoned workers' children's chocolates. Murders for political reasons were reported daily. On 2 July, for example, two falangists sitting at a café table in Madrid were killed by shots from a passing motor-car. Later the same day, two men leaving the *casa del pueblo* in Madrid were killed by a gang of men armed with sub-machine-guns. Such minor warfare had continued unchecked since the elections of February. On few of these occasions were the killers apprehended. On 8 July, seventy falangists were arrested in Madrid, and several hundred in the provinces, on a charge of sedition. These included Fernández Cuesta, secretary-general of the Falange. (José Antonio claimed that there were 150,000 falangists in June, of whom nearly 15,000 were ex-JAPistas, and 2,000 were in gaol.) In the ministry of war, meanwhile, loyal republican officers observed conferences among those whom they knew to be enemies of the republic. García Escámez, a subtle and charming Andalusian, who had led part of the Legion in Asturias, and was now Mola's

a communist. He had even visited him in prison in 1935. Carrillo says that he attended meetings of the communist central committee from March 1936 though not yet a communist. Araquistain's political trajectory in the 1930s is hard to follow; at first a strong social democrat, he had become a revolutionary by 1934. After 1936, he was again cautious and thereafter became a right-wing socialist. The July issue of his journal *Leviatán*, however, could not have been more pro-Soviet.

1. Tagüeña, p. 92. De Rosa had been sentenced to five years in Belgium and served two. He went to Spain, took part in the revolution of 1934, was gaoled, and was a hero to the socialist youth.

lieutenant at Pamplona, appeared with news and plans.[1] In the countryside, more and more land was taken over, landowners left their estates, those who stayed were forced to take far more workers than they needed, cattle were killed, the unions encouraged occupations, and the harvest lay neglected. There was much agitation too on the subject of autonomy: representatives of the Aragonese provinces met at Caspe, the mayor of Burgos proposed a statute for Old Castile, while the municipal government of Huelva proposed that that town should withdraw from Andalusia and join an autonomous Estremadura. Upper and middle class Spaniards, on the other hand, left with their families for holidays on the north coast: to remain in Madrid during the summer had become a social stigma. In 1936, it seemed a risk.

On 7 July, Mola wrote to Fal Conde (with the other leading Carlists, in St Jean de Luz) promising to settle the question of the flag after the rising and affirming that he had no relations with any political party. 'You must realize,' he added, 'that everything is being paralysed by your attitude. *Certain things* have so far advanced that it would be impossible now to withdraw. I beg of you for the sake of Spain an urgent reply.'[2] On 7 July, Fal Conde wrote back demanding guarantees that the future régime would be anti-democratic and insisting that the question of the flag be decided immediately. Lamamié de Clairac, the inveterate enemy of the republic's agrarian policy, demanded that there should be no collaboration with Mola without a promise that the monarchy would be restored. Mola, beside himself with anger, refused these conditions. 'The traditionalist movement', he wrote, 'is ruining Spain by its intransigence as surely as is the Popular Front.'[3] The point was, as Mola wrote to the more amenable Conde de Rodezno (who was the Carlist leader in Navarre), that since the garrison of Pamplona was composed of men who could not be relied on for a rebellion, being chiefly Asturians, a handful of Carlists were needed to make them soldiers.[4] On 9 July, General Sanjurjo from Lisbon wrote a conciliatory letter, suggesting that the Carlists

1. Martín Blázquez, p. 72.

2. Carlist Archives, Seville. The 'certain things' were an assurance to the Falange that the rising would occur on 15 July, and the hiring of an aircraft to take Franco to Morocco.

3. Carlist Archives. 4. Lizarza, p. 97.

might use the monarchist flag even if Mola used the republican one: Sanjurjo would guarantee a political régime in accordance with Carlist principles. This solved nothing, but it was about then that Franco in Tenerife finally agreed to join the rebellion, receiving command of all the troops in Morocco – that is, of all the most reliable troops in the Spanish army.[1] 'Do you think Franquito will come?' General Varela asked General Kindelán, a temporarily retired air-force officer of distinction. 'Mola thinks so,' was the reply.[2] It seemed by no means certain. Meanwhile, the streets of Pamplona were prepared for the annual festival of San Fermín. Now, as in other years, young bulls were let loose in the town on their way to the bull-ring and were contested indiscriminately by the young men, watched by women in carnival dress from balconies. Among the men were many who, within a week, would be enrolled among the Carlist forces. Among the spectators could be seen the bespectacled face of Mola, accompanied by the anxious, bearded General Fanjul, the leading plotter from Madrid, and by Colonel León Carrasco, who was to direct the rising of San Sebastián.[3]

In London, Luis Bolín, correspondent of the monarchist daily paper *ABC*, had chartered a Dragon Rapide, from the Olley Airways Company of Croydon, to transport Franco from the Canaries to Morocco, where the plan was that he would seize command of the Army of Africa. A foreign aeroplane was chosen because there were no reliable civil aircraft in Spain. Bolín's instructions from his editor, the Marqués Luca de Tena, a conspirator since 1931, were to go to Las Palmas, but, if no further news reached him by 31 July, he was

1. See Payne, *Politics and the Military*, p. 335 and references. It is possible that Franco only decided to act when, some time between 10 and 13 July, he was told that the others would go ahead even if he did not join them. See e.g. Robinson, p. 288. Others think that Franco and Mola had had a good understanding since late 1935.

2. Robinson, p. 288. Though the Spanish air arm had been incompetent in the Moroccan Wars, Kindelán had had an excellent fighting record there, and enjoys the dubious distinction, it seems, of being among the first ever to use an aircraft for military purposes, against Moroccan tribesmen.

3. Iribarren, p. 70. Maiz records a meeting indicating that some at least of the conspirators thought failure a possibility. 'Whose head will be the first to fall?' Fanjul asked. 'Yours, Joaquín,' replied Lucius Arrieta, a Carlist (Maiz, p. 247). His head fell, though not the first.

to return to England.[1] On 11 July, the English aeroplane left Croydon, piloted by a Captain Bebb, who had no idea of the nature of the enterprise in which he was engaged.[2] Accompanying him were Bolín, a retired major, Hugh Pollard, and two fair-headed young women, one of them Pollard's daughter, the other a friend. These passengers, likewise in ignorance of the purpose of the journey, had been procured by the catholic publisher, Douglas Jerrold, to give the flight the air of an ordinary, rather than an extraordinary, intrigue.[3]

That night in Valencia, the radio station was seized by a nervous group of falangists who announced, mysteriously, that 'the national syndicalist revolution' would soon break out, and vanished before the police arrived. The same day in Madrid, the Prime Minister had been again warned of what was to occur. 'So there is to be a rising?' he inquired with misinterpreted joviality. 'Very well, I, for my part, shall take a *lie-down*!'[4] A little earlier, he had similarly pooh-poohed a report of Carlist activities in Navarre, from Jesús Monzón, communist leader in Pamplona, who came to see him, accompanied by La Pasionaria.[5] But the minister of marine, Giral, was more provident: naval manoeuvres were restricted from being held near Morocco or the Canaries; and loyal telegraph operators were posted at the Madrid naval radio headquarters at Ciudad Lineal and on major ships.[6]

On 12 July, Mola and the Carlists still seemed at odds. But the former managed to secure his ends without really surrendering too much by playing, first, on the enthusiasm for a fight among the Carlist youth in Navarre, who seemed indifferent to the terms of their par-

1. Luca de Tena had been passed the order by General Kindelán, now one of the communication channels of the conspiracy. Bolín's memoirs have now been published as *Spain, the Vital Years* (London, 1967). Juan March paid (Gil Robles, p. 780). For March's help, see also the testimony of Tomás Peire, quoted De la Cierva, *Historia*, vol. II, p. 148.

2. *News Chronicle* (7 November 1936) published an account of these events by the pilot Captain Bebb, with whom I also discussed the matter. Bebb believed that he was being asked to carry a 'Rif chieftain to a revolution'.

3. *Cruzada*, XIII, pp. 62–3. Pollard had had, as Jerrold put it, 'experience of revolutions' (Douglas Jerrold, *Georgian Adventure*, London, 1937, p. 371). Jerrold, chairman of Eyre and Spottiswoode, had been active in putting the case against the republic.

4. Peirats, vol. I, p. 136. '*¿Ellos se levantan? Yo me voy a acostar.*'

5. Ibarruri, p. 244.

6. Evidence of Francisco Giral, Giral's son.

ticipation in the rising, and second on the flexibility of the Conde de Rodezno, who had always desired collaboration with others on the Spanish Right (the Alfonsine monarchists, above all), who hated Fal Conde, and who now, as head of the Carlists on the spot in Pamplona, was able to secure from Prince Xavier de Bourbon-Parme in St Jean de Luz an agreement to support the rising, if one should come before he was able to consult effectively his uncle Alfonso Carlos in Vienna and secure his reply. Naturally, that reply did not arrive quickly, and when it did, battle had already been joined. Mola thus swept, or was swept, into war with the Carlists on his side, with the terms of Carlist participation left vaguer than Fal Conde, Xavier or Alfonso Carlos wanted.[1]

In Morocco, the manoeuvres of the Foreign Legion and *Regulares* ended with a parade taken by Generals Romerales and Gómez Morato, respectively commander of the east zone of Morocco and commander of the Army of Africa. Neither of the two generals, nor the interim high commissioner, Captain Alvarez Buylla, were privy to the plot in which many of the other officers at the parade had leading parts. Gómez Morato was the object of special dislike in orthodox military circles, since he had organized the changes in command ordered by Azaña to secure loyal officers in important positions. The night of the parade, these two generals telegraphed to Madrid that all was well with the Army of Africa. But, at the manoeuvres, the conspirators held last-minute meetings. At a conference of young officers, Colonel Yagüe, a senior commander in the Foreign Legion, had even used the word 'crusade' (afterwards to become conventional usage in nationalist speeches) to describe the movement behind the rising. Yagüe, tough, politically ambitious and frustrated in his career by the republic, was drawn to the Falange. One night, the cry of *CAFE!* – which, to initiates, signified '*¡Camaradas! ¡Arriba Falange Española!*' – was heard at the official banquet at the end of the parade. Alvarez Buylla asked why people were demanding coffee, while the fish was still on the table. He was informed that the cry came from a group of young men, who were, it

1. Payne, *Politics,* p. 337; Blinkhorn, *op. cit.*; see also accounts in Robinson, p. 300; and Burgo, p. 123. François-Xavier de Bourbon-Parme, a remote cousin of the Spanish royal family, had been adopted by Alfonso Carlos as regent and his heir earlier in the year.

was to be feared, a little drunk.[1] The same day, meanwhile, the Dragon Rapide reached Lisbon, where Luis Bolín conferred with Sanjurjo, who assured him that Franco was '*the* man' for a successful rising;[2] afterwards, they left for Casablanca, Cape Yubi, and then, Las Palmas.

That evening at nine o'clock, Lieutenant José Castillo of the assault guards was leaving home, in the Calle Augusto Figueroa, in the centre of Madrid, to begin his duty. Earlier in the year, in April, he had been in command of the assault guards responsible for quelling the riots at the funeral of Lieutenant de los Reyes of the civil guard who had been shot on the fifth anniversary of the start of the republic. Castillo had afterwards been engaged in helping to train the socialist militia. From that time, Castillo had been marked out for revenge by the Falange. In June, he had married; and his bride had received an anonymous letter on her wedding-eve demanding why she was marrying one who would so 'soon be a corpse'. As he left home on 12 July, a hot Sunday of the Madrid summer, Castillo was shot dead by four men with revolvers, who swiftly escaped into the crowded streets.[3]

This was the second socialist officer who had been murdered in recent months – Captain Carlos Faraudo, an engineer also active in helping to train the socialist militia, had been killed by falangists while walking with his wife in Madrid in May. So the news of the death of Castillo caused fury when it reached the assault guard headquarters at Pontejos barracks, next to the ministry of the interior in the Puerta del Sol. The body was laid in the directorate general of security in the ministry. The ex-comrades of the dead Lieutenant were incensed at the government which had allowed this to happen; they demanded measures against the Falange. A group went to complain to the elderly minister of the interior, Juan Moles, and asked him for authorization to arrest certain falangists still at large. He agreed,

1. *Cruzada*, IX, p. 557.

2. Evidence of Luis Bolín, Douglas Jerrold and Captain Bebb.

3. Tagüeña, p. 99. The murderers of Castillo were apparently falangists. One of them seems to have been Angel Alcázar de Velasco, later a prominent if rebellious member of the Falange, who gained the falangist silver medal of valour for his part in this 'victory' (Iturralde, vol. II, p. 107, and private information). Eduardo Alvarez Puga, *Historia de la Falange* (Barcelona, 1972), p. 30, says that the assassins were men of the UME.

demanding the word of honour of the officers that they would only detain those whose names were on the list, and that they would hand over those whom they did arrest to the appropriate authority. They gave their word. Among these men was a captain of the civil guard, Fernando Condés, who had been an intimate friend of Castillo. Condés was broken by Castillo's death. He drove out in an official car without any clear idea where he was heading for, accompanied by several assault guards in civilian dress. The driver took Condés to an address of one falangist; it appeared false. 'Let us go to the house of Gil Robles,' said someone. Condés, still bemused, said nothing. They went to the house of Gil Robles, but he was at Biarritz. Someone suggested that they should go to the house of Calvo Sotelo.

Calvo Sotelo had some premonitions of his danger. On 11 July, La Pasionaria was alleged to have openly threatened his death.[1] One of the two police escorts attached to Calvo Sotelo as a member of the Cortes told Calvo Sotelo's friend, the deputy Joaquín Bau, that his superior officer had been given orders not to prevent any murder of Calvo Sotelo, and that indeed, if the attempt should occur in the country, he was to aid the murderers. The escort had been then changed for one on whom Calvo Sotelo could rely – though the minister of the interior apparently gave no further attention to the matter. It was, it must be said, difficult to know what to believe that summer.

At all events, at about three o'clock in the morning of Monday, 13 July, the *sereno* (nightwatchman) outside the building in which Calvo Sotelo lived in the Calle Velázquez, in a fashionable and modern part of Madrid, allowed Condés, and some of the assault guards to go upstairs to the apartment of their victim. Calvo Sotelo was roused from his bed and persuaded to accompany the intruders to the police headquarters, though his status as a deputy gave him freedom from arrest. Calvo Sotelo saw to his satisfaction the papers of Captain Condés identifying him as a member of the civil guard. One socialist suggested later that Calvo Sotelo believed that he was being taken not to the director general of security, but to Mola, whose code-name in

1. She was supposed to have cried in the Cortes, 'That is your last speech,' as Calvo Sotelo sat down after another violent oration. But there is no record of the remark in *Diario de Sesiones*, nor was it heard by two such reliable witnesses then present as Henry Buckley and Miguel Maura.

the conspiracy was 'the Director'.[1] Anyway, Calvo Sotelo promised to telephone soon to his family, – 'unless', he added, 'these gentlemen are going to blow out my brains'. The car started off fast, no one speaking. After a quarter of a mile, Luis Cuenca, a young Galician socialist sitting beside the politician, shot him in the back of his neck. Neither Condés nor anyone else had apparently expected this *dénouement*. Condés thought first of killing himself, since Calvo Sotelo had given himself up to him. Instead, he drove on to the East Cemetery and handed over the body to the attendant without saying whose it was. Cuenca drove to the office of *El Socialista* and gave Prieto an account of what had happened. The body was identified at noon the next day. Soon afterwards, Cuenca, Condés and others who had been in the car were arrested. They made no attempt to escape. Rumours began; conspiracy was alleged; the name of the Prime Minister was invoked as an accomplice; and accusations have never ceased to multiply.[2]

The middle class in Spain were aghast at this murder of the leader of the parliamentary opposition by members of the regular police, though they might suspect that the victim had been concerned in a conspiracy against the state. It was now natural to assume that the government could not control its own agents, even if it wished to do so. Republicans of the Right or centre, such as Lerroux, or Cambó, or even Gil Robles, thought that, henceforth, they could not contemplate loyalty to a state which could not guarantee their lives.[3] The

1. Juan Simeón Vidarte, *Todos fuimos culpables* (Mexico, 1973), p. 215.

2. The above derives from a personal account by the then lieutenant of the 6th Company of assault guards of Pontejos, Alfredo León-Lupin (Caracas), and from another by the late Manuel Tagüeña, then a socialist student leader and present in the ministry of the interior when Castillo's body arrived. See also Tagüeña's memoirs, pp. 99–100; Zugazagoitia, p. 30; and Prieto, *Convulsiones*, vol. III, p. 133. The possibilities of a premeditated murder cannot be quite excluded, but the government was surely not involved. Other versions identify this Cuenca as Vitoriano Cuenca, a 'bodyguard of the ex-dictator of Cuba, Gerardo Machado'. A very different interpretation of this murder is given by Major Manuel Uribarri (*La quinta columna española*, Havana, 1943, p.171f.) who argued that Condés, a friend of his, deliberately 'executed' Calvo Sotelo in order to rid the republic of a dangerous enemy.

3. After the start of the civil war, Condés and Cuenca were both killed in the Guadarrama. The documents in the ministry of the interior relating to the in-

president of the catholic student association, Joaquín Ruiz Jiménez, who had previously upheld the line of non-violence, decided that St Thomas would have accepted a rebellion as just.[1] The cabinet, meantime, spent 13 July in continuous session. They ordered the closing of monarchist, Carlist, and anarchist headquarters in Madrid. But the members of the two former organizations and many others were busy calling at Calvo Sotelo's home to pay tribute to the dead man. At midnight, Prieto (who declared in that day's issue of *El Socialista* that war would be preferable to this intolerable series of murders) led a delegation of socialists, communists, and the UGT to demand from Casares Quiroga that he should distribute arms to the workers' organizations. Casares refused, acidly adding that, if Prieto continued to come to see him so often, he would be governing Spain himself.[2] Throughout another hot night, Madrid waited. The militiamen of the left-wing parties – those, that is, upon whom the parties would rely if fighting should come, and who had already been provided with the few arms there were in the arsenals of their organizations – kept watch. Members of right-wing parties wondered whose would be the next turn to hear a fatal knock at the door.

Mola at last gave a firm date for the rising: his telegrams read: 'On the 15th last, at 4 a.m., Helen gave birth to a beautiful child.' That meant when interpreted that the rising would begin in Morocco on 18 July at five o'clock in the morning. The garrisons in Spain itself would follow on 19 July. José Antonio had sent a message through his law clerk, Rafael Garcerán, that, if Mola did not act within seventy-two hours, he would himself begin the rebellion with the Falange in Alicante. The plotters accepted now that it would be hard to win in Madrid and, they thought, Seville (though not, apparently, Barcelona). In those places, the garrisons, with the Falange and other militant supporters, were to maintain themselves in their barracks and await relief. Mola, from the north, Goded, from the north-east, and Franco, from the south, would march on the capital. Sanjurjo would fly from Portugal to take command in Burgos. The old campaigners of the Moroccan Wars, headed by 'the Lion of the Rif',

vestigation were seized by a group of militiamen on 25 July and presumably destroyed.

1. Sergio Vilar, p. 636.
2. Zugazagoitia, p. 22.

would thus be at last in command of their own country. At the last minute, Goded changed places with General González Carrasco, another but less prominent *africanista*, to go to Barcelona, on Goded's insistence, since Barcelona was recognized as being more important.[1] Though the conspiracy had been so long discussed, Calvo Sotelo's death really decided the plotters to go ahead; otherwise, they might not have screwed up their courage to the sticking point. Now if they had not acted, they might have been brushed aside by their followers.

The next day, 14 July, there were two funerals in the East Cemetery in Madrid. First, that of Lieutenant Castillo, whose coffin, draped in the red flag, was saluted, with clenched fists, by a crowd of socialists, communists, and assault guards. Then, a few hours later, Calvo Sotelo's body, swathed in Capuchin hood and gown, was lowered into another grave, surrounded by vast crowds saluting with arms outstretched in fascist style. On behalf of all present, Goicoechea, Calvo Sotelo's lieutenant in Renovación Española, took an oath, before God and before Spain, to avenge the murder. The vice-president and permanent secretary of the Cortes who were present were attacked by well-dressed women who shrieked that they wanted nothing to do with parliamentarians. Some shots were fired between falangists and assault guards, and several people were wounded, of

whom four died. These two funerals were the last political meetings in Spain before the civil war.[2]

The atmosphere in Madrid was excited all day. The government suspended the right-wing papers *Ya* and *Época* for publishing sensational accounts of the murder of Calvo Sotelo without submitting their copy first to the censor. The government also prorogued the Cortes, in an attempt to give passions time to cool. The leaders of the right-wing parties protested, and threatened to withdraw from parlia-

1. Iribarren, pp. 63, 91n.; Maiz, *op. cit.* Goded's motives in demanding this change are not quite clear. Iturralde (vol. I, p. 86) alleges that Goded thought Barcelona a suitable place in which to arrange a compromise if the rising should fail. Payne (*Politics*, p. 509) and Prieto, *Palabras al viento* (Mexico, 1942), p. 280, discuss the possibility that Goded had desired to withdraw from the conspiracy when he suspected that Mola might be going to make arrangements with Italy: Goded was a nationalist, not a fascist.

2. For an impression of Madrid in July, see the novel *Vísperas San Camilo 1936*, by Camilo José Cela (Madrid, 1969).

ment altogether. Largo Caballero, returning from a visit to London for a meeting of the Socialist International, left his train near El Escorial at the request of the government and motored to Madrid to avoid the demonstrations which would have attended his arrival at the North Station. But Casares Quiroga assured a parliamentary public works commission in Madrid that there was no truth in a rumour that Mola had been arrested, adding, Mola 'is a general loyal to the republic, and to spread rumours of that sort is to demoralize the régime'.[1] The dispute between UGT and CNT continued, sporadic firing between the two unions being heard in southern suburbs.

On 15 July, the permanent committee of the Cortes (that is, of representatives of all the leading parties in the Cortes in proportion to their numbers) met in Madrid. First, the Conde de Vallellano, for the monarchists, made a formal protest at the death of Calvo Sotelo, and announced that his party would take no further part in parliament, since the country was in anarchy. Within a few hours, he, Goicoechea, and many leading right-wing persons who knew that their lives would be endangered if there were to be fighting in the capital, left for safer cities. Gil Robles, back from Biarritz (with his own life threatened, as it had been for months), paid tribute to the memory of Calvo Sotelo, so lately his rival, whose fate he had so nearly shared. He concluded by announcing that the cabinet had become an administration of blood, mud, and shame. He publicly declared that he had failed to incorporate the CEDA in the democratic process of parliamentary government, and that he washed his hands of parliament. Afterwards, he left again for Biarritz. The Cortes committee, meanwhile, agreed to summon the Cortes for the ensuing Tuesday, 21 July – a request being issued by the party leaders that all deputies should leave firearms in the cloakroom. The forthcoming meeting (which never occurred) was immediately nicknamed the disarmament conference.

The next morning, on 16 July, Mola went to Logroño to meet General Batet, theoretically his superior, and commander of the 6th Division, with its headquarters at Burgos. Batet was known to be loyal to the government, though it had been he who, while in command at Barcelona, had coolly crushed the revolt of 1934 in that city. Mola feared assassination, and the officers who went with him were

1. Lizarra, p. 31.

armed. But Batet merely told Mola that he had heard that certain *pistoleros* were on their way from Barcelona to kill him, and suggested that he should leave Navarre. Mola smiled at the idea. Batet (unaware that his own chief of staff, Colonel Moreno Calderón, was a plotter) also asked Mola for a declaration that he did not intend to rise against the government. 'I give you my word that I shall not launch myself upon an adventure', answered Mola, who later boasted of the adroitness of this remark.[1]

In Madrid, the day passed calmly. The ministry of labour published its award in respect of the building strike, which the employers refused. They nevertheless re-opened their works, pending an appeal. Some UGT workers returned, but the CNT remained out. The government were taking certain steps designed to limit the extent of a rising if one should occur. The destroyer *Churruca* was dispatched from Cartagena to Algeciras, the gunboat *Dato* told to weigh anchor at Ceuta. These measures were to prevent the transport of any units of the Foreign Legion or the *Regulares* to the mainland. But the government was hampered in its precautions by having no knowledge of the loyalty of the commanders of these ships. In fact, they need not have worried: Mola and his friends had made no serious provision for naval commitment to the plot.[2]

In the Canaries, the English captain of the Dragon Rapide was dissimulating, with success, to the authorities at Las Palmas, as to why he had landed without papers at the airport.[3] A message that Bebb had arrived was taken by a diplomat José Antonio Sangróniz to Franco, who prepared to leave Tenerife. Then, General Amadeo Balmes, military governor of Las Palmas, was shot dead at target practice. This mishap (which in the excitable atmosphere was rumoured to be murder, since he had refused to join the plotters) gave Franco, the commander of the army in the whole archipelago, an excuse to go to Las Palmas for the funeral. Otherwise, he had planned to say that he had to make a tour of inspection. The under-secretary

1. Iribarren, p. 89; Maiz, p. 251.

2. The monarchist polemicist, Vegas Latapié, had, however, approached the navy. See Gil Robles, p. 726 fn. 68.

3. Bebb's journey had been full of incident: in Casablanca, he had lost his radio operator, dead drunk in the Casbah; at Cape Yubi there had been a banquet at which Bebb's passengers had celebrated immoderately. Bebb reached Las Palmas on 14 July.

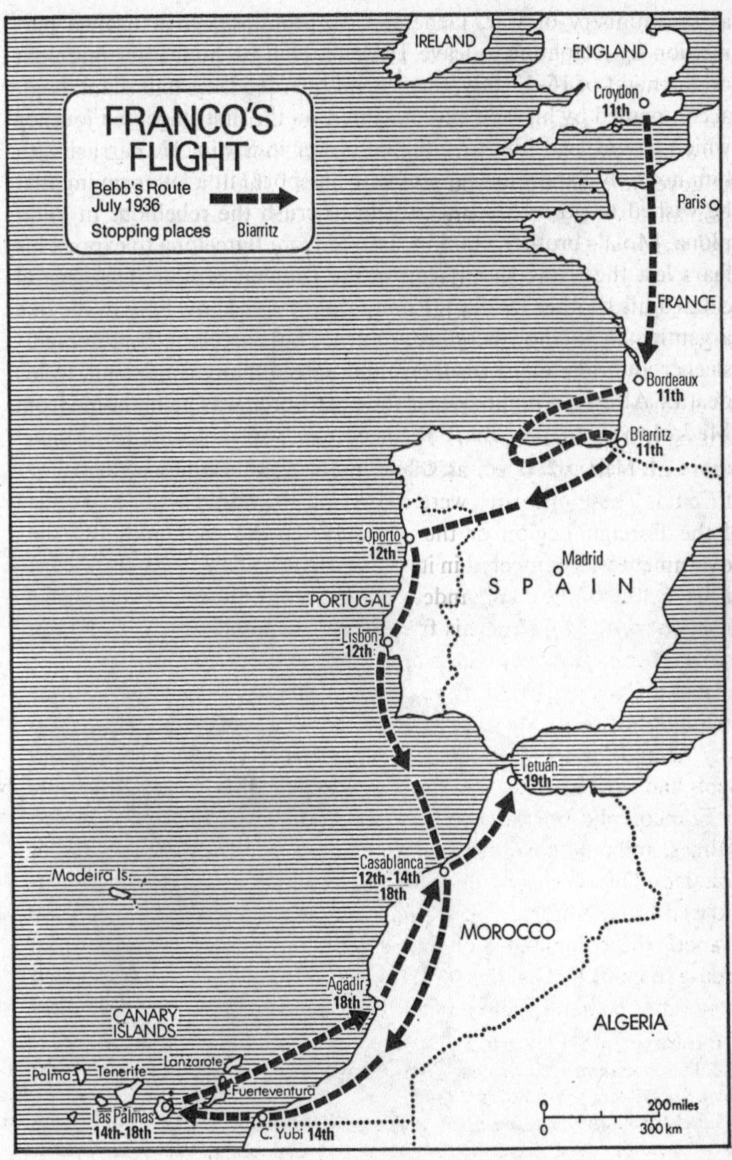
FRANCO'S FLIGHT
Bebb's Route July 1936
Stopping places
Biarritz
IRELAND
ENGLAND
Croydon 11th
Paris
FRANCE
Bordeaux 11th
Biarritz 11th
Oporto 12th
Madrid
SPAIN
PORTUGAL
Lisbon 12th
Tetuán 19th
Casablanca 12th-14th 18th
Madeira Is.
MOROCCO
Agadir 18th
CANARY ISLANDS
ALGERIA
Lanzarote
Palma
Tenerife
Fuerteventura
Las Palmas 14th-18th
C. Yubi 14th
0 200 miles
0 300 km

7. Captain Bebb's flight, July 1936

at the ministry of war, General Cruz Boullosa, gave Franco permission by telephone to leave Tenerife. Half an hour after midnight on the night of 16–17 July, the general boarded the small island boat, accompanied by his wife and daughter, on the first stage of a journey which would lead him to supreme power in Spain. He carried with him not only Sangróniz's diplomatic passport but a letter saying that he wished to go to Madrid to help to crush the rebellion. In Pamplona, Mola's brother, Ramón, arrived from Barcelona to express his fears lest the rising should fail in the Catalan capital. The general calmed his brother (adding 'I don't doubt you know how to die like a gentleman'), who, therefore, returned to Barcelona by the night-sleeper and, like many brothers, and indeed many gentlemen, to his death.[1] Also on a night-sleeper the poet Lorca was going home from Madrid to Granada.[2] Lerroux, meantime, was motoring to Lisbon.[3]

1. Maiz, p. 232. 2. Gibson, p. 51. 3. Lerroux, p. 581.

14

The rising in Morocco – constitutional counter-measures – the risings in Andalusia – Queipo de Llano at Seville – other events of 18 July – Madrid – three governments in a night – Mola's intransigence – the government of Giral

THE rising began at Melilla, the easternmost city of Spanish Morocco, and historically the most important city in Spain's whole Moroccan venture, though Tetuán was the protectorate's capital. In the night of 16–17 July, General Romerales, the local military commander, toured round in search of suspicious activity. At the *casa del pueblo* he joked with socialist leaders: 'The masses at vigil, I see'.[1] He returned home, convinced that all was well. He was the fattest of Spain's four hundred generals, and one of the easiest fooled. The next morning, the officers who were in the plot at Melilla held a meeting in the map department of the headquarters. Colonel Juan Seguí, the leader of both the Falange and the rising in eastern Morocco, told his confederates the exact hour of the rising – five o'clock in the morning of the next day. Arrangements were made for the seizure of public buildings. These plans were revealed to the local leaders of the Falange, one of whom, Alvaro González, was a traitor. He informed the local leader of the Republican Union party, who told the head of the *casa del pueblo*, who told Romerales. When the conspirators returned to the map department after lunch, and when arms had already been distributed, Lieutenant Juan Zaro surrounded the building with troops and police. The lieutenant then confronted his insurrectionary superior officers. 'What brings you here, Lieutenant?' demanded Colonel Dario Gazapo jovially. 'I have to search the building for arms,' answered Zaro. Gazapo telephoned Romerales: 'It is true, my General, that you have given orders to search the map department? There are only maps here.' 'Yes, yes, Gazapo,' replied

1. *Cruzada*, X, p. 17.

Romerales, 'it must be done.'[1] The hour of decision had arrived, prematurely but none the less certainly. Gazapo, an officer who was a member of the Falange,[2] telephoned to a unit of the Foreign Legion to relieve him. Faced with their presence, Zaro vacillated, agreed that his men could not fire on the legionaries, and surrendered. Then Colonel Seguí left for Romerales's office, which he entered with his revolver drawn. Inside, an altercation was going on between those of Romerales's officers who were insisting that the general should resign, and others who wanted to resist. Casares Quiroga, from Madrid, informed by telephone of the sinister meeting in the map department, had ordered Romerales to arrest Seguí and Gazapo. But who would carry out such an order? Romerales was undecided. Then Seguí entered his office and forced the general to surrender at the point of his revolver. The revolutionary officers declared a state of war, occupied all the public buildings of Melilla (including the aerodrome), in the name of General Franco as commander-in-chief in Morocco (despite his continued absence in the Canaries), closed the *casa del pueblo* and left-wing centres, and arrested the leaders of republican or left-wing groups. There was some fighting around the *casa del pueblo* and in the lower-class districts, but the workers were taken by surprise and they had no arms. All those captured who resisted the rebellion were shot, Romerales, the government delegate and the mayor included. By the evening, lists had been obtained of members of trade unions, left-wing parties, and masonic lodges. All such persons were also arrested.[3] Anyone known merely to have voted for the Popular Front in the elections of February was in danger. Melilla was henceforth ruled by martial law. The manner of its insurrection was the model followed throughout the rest of Morocco and Spain.

Colonel Seguí, meantime, telephoned Colonels Eduardo Sáenz de Buruaga and Yagüe, entrusted with the organization of the risings at

1. See Salvador Fernández Alvarez, *Melilla, la primera en el alzamiento* (Melilla, 1939), and Fernández de Castro, *El alzamiento nacional en Melilla* (Melilla, 1940).

2. Maximiniano García Venero, *Falange*, p. 185. According to some, military members of the Falange in July 1936 numbered 30 per cent of the total. This must be an exaggeration.

3 *Documents on German Foreign Policy 1918–45*, Series D, vol. III ('Germany and the Spanish Civil War 1936–9'), p. 9. This volume of the German Foreign Ministry Documents is hereinafter referred to as *GD*.

Tetuán and Ceuta, the other two leading cities of Spanish Morocco. He also telegraphed to Franco (now at Las Palmas for General Balmes's funeral) explaining why the rising at Melilla had had to take place earlier than the hour agreed. Sáenz de Buruaga and Yagüe took action, improvising twelve hours early what had been planned for the 18th.[1] In Madrid, Casares Quiroga sought out General Gómez Morato, the over-all commander in Africa.[2] He found the latter at the Casino in Larache: 'General, what is going on at Melilla?' 'In Melilla? Nothing. Why?' 'Because a garrison has risen.' Gómez Morato left the Casino and flew to Melilla, where he was arrested.[3] At Tetuán, Colonels Asensio, Beigbeder (the ex-military attaché at Berlin, whom the republic had transferred), and Sáenz de Buruaga had by this time also risen. The last-named telephoned the acting high commissioner, Alvarez Buylla, in the Residency there, and, arrogantly referring to him as captain of artillery – in the uniform of which rank he had proudly appeared at the parade at the end of the manoeuvres – demanded his resignation. Alvarez Buylla telephoned Casares Quiroga, who ordered him to hold out at all costs, telling him that the fleet and the air force would relieve him the following day. But the high commissioner was barricaded into his own house, surrounded by a few officers who remained loyal. Outside, Major Antonio Castejón and the 5th *Bandera* of the Foreign Legion[4] were digging trenches in the square. A little later Major de la Puente Bahamonde, a cousin of General Franco, telephoned the high commissioner from Sania Ramel airfield to say that he and his air force squadron would stay loyal to the government. 'Resist, resist', Alvarez Buylla encouraged, as Casares had encouraged him. But, by this time, with night falling, the residency and the airport were the only points in Tetuán not in the hands of the rebel colonels who, like their colleagues at Melilla, had crushed all resistance from the trade unionists and left-wing or

1. Mola's instructions had provided for all units involved in the rising to be 'ready' on the 17th at 5 p.m. ('17 hours on the 17th'), for the rising to begin in Morocco and important staging posts on the Peninsula on the 18th, and in other places (including Pamplona) on the 19th. The news of the rising in Morocco caused confusion among the peninsular plotters: should they keep to the date planned, or also advance their action?

2. See De la Cierva, *Historia ilustrada*, vol. I, p. 252.

3. *Cruzada*, X, p. 44.

4. A *bandera* was a self-contained battalion of 600 men, including maintenance units and mobile artillery.

republican groups. Colonel Beigbeder went to inform the Caliph, Mulay Hassan, and Grand Vizier of Tetuán of what was afoot, and gained their support. Mulay Hassan had been a Spanish puppet since 1925. Soon he would give physical help, in the form of Moroccan volunteers. Beigbeder also took command of the department of native affairs in the city, the civil servants accepting the change from the administration of Alvarez Buylla without a murmur.[1] Beigbeder, an Arabist of distinction, had a great reputation in Morocco, and it was probably due to his skilful use of the telephone and radio, as well as his fluent Arabic, that the rebellion there was consolidated. In Ceuta, at eleven at night, Yagüe, with the second *Bandera* of the Legion, took command of the city more easily, no shots being fired to resist him at all.[2] At Larache, the only other town of importance in Spanish Morocco, on the Atlantic coast, the rising came at two o'clock in the morning on 18 July. Fighting was bitter. Two rebel officers were killed, along with five assault guards, on the other side. But by dawn the town was in the hands of the rebels, and all their enemies arrested, fled or shot.[3] At the same time, Franco, with General Orgaz, who had been dispatched to the Canaries after the failure of the rising in April, made themselves masters of Las Palmas. Franco declared martial law throughout the archipelago. While he was dictating a manifesto, the expected telephone call came from Casares Quiroga. The Prime Minister was told that Franco was visiting garrisons. At a quarter past five in the morning of 18 July, Franco issued his manifesto, making special reference to the exceptional relationship that Spanish officers were supposed to feel towards the country itself, rather than to any particular government, denouncing foreign influences, and promising, in emotive terms, a new order after the victory. No mention was made of the attacks by the republic on the church: the rebellion as yet had not formally become a crusade.[4] The manifesto

1. *Cruzada*, X, pp. 34–40. A left-wing account of the rising in Tetuán was given by Antonio Mata Lloret in *La batalla*, reprinted in *El Sol*, 25 August 1936. Mata, a telegraph officer, alleged that detainees were forced to drink a half-litre of castor oil.

2. *ibid.*, p. 44. 3. *ibid.*, pp. 44–5.

4. Text in Fernando Díaz-Plaja, *La historia de España en sus documentos, el siglo XX: la guerra 1936–1939* (Madrid, 1963), p. 150f. Nor did Franco make any mention of Sanjurjo as the nominal head of the movement. The manifesto was apparently written by the 'auditor of the juridical corps of the army',

ended with a *viva* for the 'honourable Spanish people', after an unexpected reference to fraternity, liberty and equality, 'to be restored in that order of importance'. This manifesto was broadcast on all Canary and Spanish Moroccan radio stations.[1] Then, in the hot dawn of 18 July, the rising began on the mainland.

Casares Quiroga and the government of Spain first attempted to crush the revolt against them by constitutional means. While telephoning Alvarez Buylla and others loyal in Morocco to resist, the Prime Minister ordered several more warships to leave their bases at El Ferrol and Cartagena for Moroccan waters. He remained optimistic, sitting through three hours of a cabinet meeting, without telling his colleagues till the end what he had known before it began.[2] This infuriated both loyal officers and left-wing leaders, who anticipated a rising on the mainland, and who thought that whatever arms the government possessed should be handed over to the unions. But that revolutionary action was refused by Casares, who announced that anyone who gave arms to the workers without his orders would be shot.[3] In consequence, the streets and cafés of Madrid were choked with voluble people, none of them knowing what was happening, and all of them angry, because their lack of arms prevented them being able to take precautions to save themselves if a rising should occur. The demand 'Arms for the People' was lifted high on banners by all the left-wing organizations. In the war ministry, a group of left-wing officers were in control. General Pozas, head of the civil guard, and General Miaja, in command of the 1st Infantry Brigade, based on Madrid, seemed to be loyal, while the commander of the air force, General Núñez de Prado, a strong republican, telephoned to the aerodromes to ensure that the mainly republican airmen were on the alert. Only Melilla, where the aerodrome commander, Captain Bermúdez Reina, had already been shot, failed to answer, though the commander at León was a rebel. Many further changes of command were made in Madrid, while senior officers were dispatched to potentially

---

Lorenzo Martínez Fuset, Franco's legal adviser and a man who played a critical part in the institutionalization of Franco's dictatorship; he accompanied Franco on this journey.

1. *Cruzada*, X, pp. 67–71.
2. Ignacio Hidalgo de Cisneros, *Memorias* (Paris, 1964), vol. II, p. 267.
3. Zugazagoitia, p. 41.

difficult regions. There were some 7,000 men in the Madrid garrisons, and some 6,000 civil guards, assault guards and carabineers. It was essential to try and assure their loyalty.[1] The conspirators in Madrid, meanwhile, held hurried and anxious meetings in their own houses. Their system of communications with Mola was bad and their morale was low.

The first news of the rising given by the government was when Madrid Radio announced that 'No one, absolutely no one, on the Spanish mainland, has taken part in this absurd plot',[2] which would, it was promised, be quickly crushed even in Morocco. While these words were being heard without belief, risings were taking place throughout Andalusia, where there were eight cities which had garrisons of battalion strength or above. There were risings in other towns too, led by either local falangists or the civil guard. Nearly everywhere on 18 July, the civil governors followed the example of the government in Madrid, and refused to cooperate with the working-class organizations who were clamouring for arms. In many cases, this brought the success of the risings and signed the death warrants of the civil governors themselves, along with local working-class leaders. Had the rebels risen in all the provinces in Spain on 18 July, they might have been everywhere triumphant by 22 July. But had the government distributed arms, and ordered the civil governors to do so too, thus using the working class to defend the republic at the earliest opportunity, the rising might have been crushed.[3]

For the republic, the events of 18 July seemed bad enough. From dawn onwards and at various times until mid afternoon, the garrison would rise, and would be supported by the Falange and, in most cases, by the civil guard. In some places, where there was no garrison, the civil guard, Falange, and local right-wing persons would act by themselves. The appointed leader of the rebels would declare a state of war, announcing military law, and this proclamation would be read from the balcony of the town hall in the main square. This

1. R. Salas Larrazábal, vol. I, p. 128. 2. *The Times*, 20 July 1936.

3. The indefatigable German historian of the anarchist movement, Max Nettlau, who arrived shortly in Barcelona, later tried rather unsuccessfully to rationalize this. 'Where a measure of autonomy existed,' he wrote in the CNT–FAI bulletin, on 25 July, 'the people could and did get arms at the right time. Where autonomy did not exist, little or nothing could be done and the enemy thus – and only thus – gained a temporary advantage.'

seizure of power would be resisted by the socialist, communist, and anarchist militias, as best they could, while the civil governor would vacillate in his office and attempt to telephone Madrid. The officers loyal to the republic, and, in most cases, the assault guards, would resist the rising and attempt to rally both the civil government and the working-class organizations. A general strike would be called by both UGT and CNT, and barricades, of paving stones, wood, stone, or sandbags, or of whatever was at hand, would immediately be erected. Fighting would follow, with both sides showing disregard of personal safety.[1]

On 18 July, the risings occurred in Andalusia. In Seville, General Queipo de Llano, commander of the carabineers, carried out an extraordinary *coup de main*. He had come late to the conspiracy, though he was an *africanista*, having been a republican plotter in 1926 and in 1930. He had been promoted by the republic to begin with. But he had expected higher rewards than he had received, and he had been angry at the removal of Alcalá Zamora, whose daughter his own son had married. Like Sanjurjo in 1932, Queipo had no connection with the city previous to the rising, and, indeed, had only arrived there on 17 July, in his Hispano-Suiza (his official motor-car), in which he later boasted that he had earlier carried out '20,000 miles of conspiracy', under pretence of inspecting customs posts. Accompanied by his ADC and three other officers only, he established himself, during the morning of 18 July, in an office in the headquarters that had been abandoned because of the heat. Then he went along the passage to see General Fernández Villa-Abrille, commander of the 2nd Division, that is, of Andalusia. 'I have to tell you,' said Queipo, 'that the time has come to take a decision: either you are with me and my other comrades, or you are with this government which is leading Spain to ruin.' Villa-Abrille was a republican who had conspired with Queipo in 1930; now he and his staff were unable to make up their minds, probably because they were afraid that, as in 1932, the rising would fail, and they would be sent off to a hot colonial gaol. Queipo, therefore, arrested them, and ordered them all to go into the next room. Since there was no key, he ordered a corporal to stand in front of the door and shoot anyone who came out. Next he

1. A recent account, vivid and detailed, is Luis Romero, *Tres días de julio* (Barcelona, 1967).

went, this time accompanied only by his ADC, to the infantry barracks. On arrival, he was surprised to see the troops drawn up under arms on the square. Queipo nevertheless went up to the colonel, whom he had never seen before, and said: 'I shake your hand, my dear Colonel, and congratulate you on your decision to put yourself on the side of your brothers-in-arms in these hours when the fate of our country is being decided'. 'I have decided to support the government', said the colonel. Queipo expressed astonishment, and said, 'Shall we pursue the interview in your office?' Inside, the colonel held to his position, and Queipo withdrew from him the command of the regiment. But no other officer would take his place. Queipo then sent away his ADC to fetch one of the three officers who had been with him from the beginning. He was himself left alone in front of these officers who opposed him. He began to joke with them, and they said that they were afraid of what had happened after Sanjurjo's rising in 1932. Eventually, Queipo found a captain to take over the regiment. He thereupon went to the back of the room and shouted to the other officers at the top of his lungs: 'You are my prisoners'. With docility, they allowed themselves to be shut up. Next, Queipo discovered that there were only 130 men in the regiment. Fifteen falangists, however, appeared, to put themselves at his disposal. This was a small force to capture a great city with a population of a quarter of a million people. Fortunately for Queipo, the commander of the artillery barracks and his officers agreed to support the rising. Heavy guns were brought into the Plaza San Fernando, and the civil government brought into the line of fire behind the Hotel Inglaterra. The shelling of the hotel, in which some assault guards had gathered, began. One shell hit the civil government and the civil governor telephoned Queipo and surrendered, on condition that his life was spared. (It was, though the civil governor, Varela, spent many years in prison.) The civil guard of Seville then rallied to the rising. By the end of the morning, the centre of the city was in Queipo's hands. Meantime, the working-class organizations had tumbled to what was afoot. Radio Seville called for a general strike, and for the peasants of nearby villages to come into the city for arms. But of these there were only a small supply. During the afternoon, the workers built barricades throughout the suburbs. Eleven churches were set ablaze, together with the silk factory belonging to the Marqués Luca de Tena, an important man in the conspiracy. Then Queipo captured the radio station. At eight in the evening, he broadcast the first of what were to become a notorious series of harangues. In a voice seasoned by many years' consumption of sherry, he declared that Spain was saved and that the rabble who resisted the rising would be shot like dogs.[1] But night came with Seville divided in two. Queipo's rousing speech did much to rally Andalusia to the rising: one more technological innovation, the wireless, played a part in war. The possibility of denying on the radio that the rising had been crushed played an essential part in the rebels' partial success, even though most of the large transmission stations – except for Radio Seville – remained in the hands of the government.

Also on 18 July, General Varela (freed from gaol in which he had languished since April) and General López Pinto raised Cádiz, although, as in Seville, victory was not immediate.[2] In Córdoba, Colonel Ciriaco Cascajo, the military governor, battered his civil colleague, Rodríguez de León, a pessimist, into submission by artillery, even though urgent voices on the telephone from the ministry of the interior in Madrid promised relief within hours. Algeciras and Jerez were won for the rebellion without a fight. In Granada, there was a stalemate: General Miguel Campins, the military governor, lectured his officers on the evil of the rising in Morocco. In the streets, supporters of the Popular Front, with the anarchists, carried on day-long demonstrations. The conspirators in the city held their hand, although they listened with enthusiasm to the broadcast of Queipo de Llano. At Jaén, where there was no garrison, the local falangists and *requetés* waited for the signal, but nothing happened, since the colonel in charge of the civil guard, Pablo Iglesias, remained loyal to the republic. Huelva, near the Portuguese frontier, although isolated from the rest of republican Spain by the rising at Seville, stayed in the hands of the Popular Front. General Pozas, from the ministry of the

1. *Canalla*, *canaille*, or rabble, remained Queipo's favourite word throughout the war. Some say that Queipo did not drink. For a study of Queipo de Llano, see Guillermo Cabanellas, *La guerra de los mil dias* (Barcelona, 1973), vol. I, p. 393. For Seville, see also *Cruzada*, XI, pp. 154–202; *ABC de Sevilla*, 18 July 1937; Antonio Bahamonde, *Un año con Queipo de Llano* (Barcelona, 1938), p. 26f.

2. For the rising in Cádiz (described by the Right as *Rusia Chica*, due to the extent of socialist control) see Antonio Garrachón Cuesta's *De Africa a Cádiz y de Cádiz a la España Imperial* (Cádiz, 1938).

interior in Madrid, telephoned an urgent order to the commander of the civil guard to send a column against Queipo in Seville. Major Gregorio de Haro, therefore, set off with a small force of civil guards, but, on arrival at that city, he rallied to Queipo's side.

In Málaga, General Paxtot dithered, and eventually gave up the attempt to declare a state of war when threatened by telephone with bombardment by the fleet. The assault guards remained loyal and fought a company of soldiers which was trying to take the main buildings. The workers attacked the soldiers from the rear. Many soldiers deserted and the people obtained arms from the barracks. The company commander was lynched by the crowd.[1] But this was the last success of the government during the day. In the evening, the last republican resistance in Africa, at Tetuán, came to an end.[2] The fighting in Africa had been bitter and left a mark on the army, as well as on the civilian population. Thus the general in overall charge, Gómez Morato, was in gaol, and the commander in the east, Romerales, shot. (The commander of the western zone, General Capaz, an outstandingly able officer who had conquered Xauen in 1926, disliked the rebellion and so had gone on leave, to Madrid.[3]) In the Foreign Legion, the inspector, Colonel Luis Molina, was dismissed, along with the commander of the first *bandera*, Colonel Blanco Novo, while the commander of the second *bandera*, Yagüe, had taken over general command. Among the five commanders of native troops, three (Colonels Asensio, Barrón and Delgado Serrano) rallied to the rising; the fourth, Colonel Caballero, was shot in Ceuta for refusing to join the rebellion, and the fifth, Colonel Romero Bassart, who had opposed the rising at Larache, fled to French Morocco, and thence to the mainland.[4]

The government in Madrid discovered its defeats by telephone, as

1. Ronald Fraser, *In Hiding, The Life of Manuel Cortes* (London, 1972), p. 131. For an interesting impression of Málaga, see Brenan, *Personal Record*, p. 285.

2. Left-wing resistance continued at Santa Cruz de la Palma till 28 July. Otherwise the Canaries were also conquered for the rising by 20 July. (*Cruzada*, X, p. 76.)

3. Where he would be murdered, for his pains.

4. He was subsequently expelled from the republican army as too revolutionary, and became military adviser to the CNT. See R. Salas Larrazábal, vol. I, p. 88. Gómez Morato was condemned to thirty years' imprisonment for having opposed the rising.

in Morocco; a rebel commander would answer insultingly, crying '*¡Arriba España!*', in place of the civil, or the military, governor. News travelled in this way also to the unions and political parties, who would telephone to their comrades in other towns, and discover enemies in control, say, of the railway station or the post office. André Malraux vividly described these exchanges in his brilliant novel, *L'Espoir*: '*Allô Avila?*' said Madrid. '*Comment ça va chez vous? Ici la gare.*' '*Va te faire voir, salaud! Vive le Christ-Roi!*' '*A bientôt. Salud!*'[1] Throughout the day, Casares continued to act as if he were in command of the country, and as if there were no need for emergency measures. He consulted with generals whom he knew to be loyal to the republic, though they and their officers, particularly those of the radical officers' organization UMRA, were establishing contact with working-class militia leaders. A delegation of taxi-drivers called on the Premier to offer him 3,000 taxis to fight the rebels. The UGT possessed a few rifles, already distributed to the communist–socialist youth, who were now beginning to abandon their jobs, and act permanently as political police in the streets. But those rifles did not seem enough to resist the garrisons of Madrid and their falangist supporters, though as yet there was no sign of any movement in any right-wing quarter. Special editions of *Claridad* and *El Socialista* demanded 'Arms for the People' in banner headlines.[2] 'Arms, arms, arms' was cried all day by masses of young socialists and communists in the streets around the *casa del pueblo*, the ministry of war, and in the Puerta del Sol. But Casares still refused. He dispatched General Núñez de Prado, director of aviation, to Saragossa to attempt to reach a compromise with General Cabanellas, a freemason, in command of the 5th Division there. 'A forthcoming change of ministry will satisfy all the generals' demands and obviate the necessity for a rising', Núñez de Prado told Cabanellas. Nevertheless, he was arrested (and was later shot, together with his ADC).

Back in Madrid, the cabinet sat in continuous, if peripatetic,

1. André Malraux, *L'Espoir* (Paris, 1937), p. 8. Avila did not rise till 19 July. The telephone exchange itself continued to serve both parties impartially – as it did throughout the civil war – a feat of which its American management were justly proud. The role of the telephone in the rising was critical. See the comment by Luis Romero in *Tres dias de julio*.

2. The anarchists in Madrid appeared indifferent to all these events, being still preoccupied by the building strike (Zugazagoitia, p. 57).

session in the ministry of war, in the Royal Palace, and, later still, in the ministry of the interior, in the Puerta del Sol. In the evening, Madrid Radio announced that the rising had everywhere been crushed, even at Seville. This was the first official admission that anything untoward was taking place on the mainland of Spain. The news was followed by a series of decrees dismissing Generals Franco, Cabanellas, Queipo de Llano, and González de Lara from their commands. Thereafter, the wirelesses of the capital played strident music, partly to soothe, partly to exhort, the expectant crowds.[1] From time to time, the loudspeakers would announce: 'People of Spain, keep tuned in! Do not turn your radios off. Rumours are being circulated by traitors. Keep tuned in.'[2] But Casares, with Azaña supporting him, continued to refuse to hand out arms to the masses. Feared as a revolutionary by the Right, the Prime Minister became hated by the Left as a secret reactionary. His nickname, 'Civilón' (civilian), after a famous bull who refused to defend himself, was everywhere repeated scornfully. Liberal Spain was in its death agony. About 5,000 rifles, however, were handed out by Lieutenant-Colonel Rodrigo Gil, chief of the artillery park, a socialist sympathizer, to the UGT.[3] As for the conspirators of Madrid, they continued indecisive.

During 18 July, the government had done what it could to reply to the successful revolution in Morocco. They even dispatched bombers to attack Tetuán and Ceuta. But this caused the Sultan and Grand Vizier to accept more easily the change foisted upon them by Colonel Beigbeder. Nor did the aircraft inflict any military damage. Casares Quiroga also sent three destroyers to Melilla from Cartagena on the morning of 18 July. On their way, the officers heard Franco's broadcast from Las Palmas. They resolved to join the nationalists. On nearing Melilla, they received orders to bombard the town. The captain of the destroyer *Sánchez Barcaíztegui* described the aims of the rising to his men, and then demanded their support for it. He was greeted by a profound silence, which was interrupted by a single cry 'To Cartagena!' This cry was taken up by the whole ship's company.

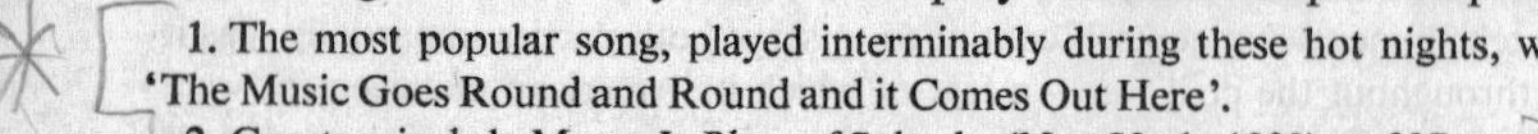

1. The most popular song, played interminably during these hot nights, was 'The Music Goes Round and Round and it Comes Out Here'.

2. Constancia de la Mora, *In Place of Splendor* (New York, 1939), p. 227.

3. Evidence of Margarita Nelken (who accompanied a delegation of the Madrid *casa del pueblo* to Rodrigo Gil) to Burnett Bolloten, *The Grand Camouflage* (London, 1961), p. 29.

The officers were overpowered, and the *Sánchez Barcaíztegui* raised its anchor to break out of the rebel town into the open sea. They bombarded both Melilla and Ceuta before leaving the North African coast. Similar scenes occurred on the *Almirante Valdés*. The ships each formed a committee of their crews to act in place of the officers. The position of the *Churruca*, the third destroyer, remained for a time equivocal.

On nearly all the main ships of the Spanish navy, the officers were busy refusing the orders of the minister of marine, Giral; he dismissed them by telegraph, and gave authority to the chief engineers, giving instructions for the distribution of arms. Hence Giral's reputation as the assassin of the naval officers; but 'he was merely following etiquette in a situation without precedent'.[1] His action did not, however, make the navy efficient as well as loyal. On the contrary, the rebellion and revolution in the fleet enfeebled it.

The constitutional means of opposing the rising thus met with failure. It did so inevitably, since so much of the forces of law and order – the army and the civil guard – were with the rebels, who claimed to represent order themselves, if not law. The only force capable of resisting the rebels was that of the trade unions and left-wing parties. Yet for the government to use that force would mean that it accepted revolution. It is not surprising that Casares shrank from this step. But at the stage that Spanish affairs had reached on the night of 18 July, such a step was also inevitable. Already in the towns where risings had taken place, in Morocco and Andalusia, the opposition to them had been that of the revolutionary parties of the Left. Indeed, in many small towns the rebellion was anticipated by revolution for when the news of the rising in Morocco and Seville reached places with no military garrisons, the reaction of the Left was certainly not to wait until they were attacked.

So now there was to spread over Spain a cloud of violence, in which the quarrels of several generations would find outlet. With communications difficult or non-existent, each town would find itself on its own, acting out its own drama, apparently in a vacuum. There were soon to be not two Spains, but two thousand. The geographical differences within Spain were a prime factor in the social disintegration of the nation. Regional feeling had sown the wind, and now

1. Evidence of Francisco Giral.

reaped the whirlwind. Sovereign power ceased to exist and, in its absence, individuals, as well as towns, acted without constraint, as if they were outside society and history. Within a month, thousands of people[1] would have perished arbitrarily and without trial. Bishops would be murdered and churches profaned. Educated christians would spend their evenings murdering illiterate peasants and professional men of sensitivity. These events inevitably caused such hatreds that, when order was eventually established, it was an order geared solely for the rationalization of hatred known as war.

The terrible prospects ahead were plainly seen by Casares Quiroga, as he feverishly paced his office, recently regilded, in the Paseo de la Castellana. His optimism had proved vain. Exhausted, he decided to resign. The President, Azaña, also had only too clear a vision of the disasters which might lie ahead. He therefore called upon Martínez Barrio, the arch-priest of compromise, to form a government to attempt to treat with the rebels. The men whom he asked to serve as ministers in the middle of the night of 18–19 July were all moderates. They included the middle-of-the-road barrister, Sánchez Román, leader of the small National Republican party, and two of his friends. Sánchez Román had not signed the Popular Front Pact before the February elections; and he represented the best hope for the political compromise which he himself vigorously supported. Martínez Barrio hoped that his name would persuade the rebels to abandon their plans. Instead, it was greeted merely by the crowds which heard it from Madrid Radio in the streets with cries of 'Treason'. Another name, that of Justino de Azcárate as foreign minister, a nephew of the great professor of the Free Institute, was more popular. But Azcárate was in León, not Madrid – and was soon to be a prisoner of the rebels. Thousands of workers pushed their way from the *casa del pueblo* down to the Puerta del Sol. 'Sol, Sol, Sol', cried the crowd as they went and then again: 'Arms, arms, arms'. The attempt at compromise was made. General Miaja, whom Martínez Barrio had named as his minister of war, and who was known as an easy-going republican officer, telephoned Mola at Pamplona. It must have been difficult to get through, since Mola spent most of the night on the telephone, trying to ensure that his rebel officers were going through with his appointed plan. After an exchange of courtesies, Mola

1. See below, pp. 264 and 270, for calculations.

bluntly announced that he was about to rise against the government. Azaña then telephoned to Miguel Maura, then on holiday in La Granja, to ask him to take part in a new coalition. Maura refused and said that it was too late. Largo Caballero anyway would have refused to countenance a government of the centre. He promised that, if such a government were formed, he would 'unleash the social revolution'.[1] A little later, Martínez Barrio telephoned Mola to offer him a post in the government. 'The Popular Front cannot keep order,' answered Mola. 'You have your followers and I have mine. If we were to seal a bargain, we should be betraying our ideals and our men. We should both deserve to be lynched.'[2] After further argument, Mola said, 'What you propose is now impossible. Pamplona is full of Carlists. From my balcony, I can only see red berets. Everyone is ready for the battle. If I tell these men now that I have made an arrangement with you, the first head to roll would be mine. The same would happen to you in Madrid. Neither of us can control our masses.' The telephones were put down and the war began. Mola thus bears great responsibility for the course of events. But then, how could he have drawn back at this stage? If he had, would not the Carlists have brushed him aside? Mola, it seems, realized that there would be a civil war if the *coup* failed; so did General Franco. The vigour with which he spoke was the energy of an intellectual who was now at the eye of a storm which he had himself aroused. A similar telephoned appeal by Martínez Barrio to General Cabanellas at Saragossa also failed.[3]

So, towards dawn at the end of this *nuit blanche* of 18–19 July, new consultations were held between Azaña, Martínez Barrio, and the socialist leaders, Prieto and Largo Caballero. The loudspeakers of Union Radio soon announced that a new government was being

1. Azaña, vol. IV, p. 714; cf. Jackson, p. 243; Maximiniano García Venero, *El General Fanjul* (Madrid, 1967), p. 287, for the programme which Sánchez Román suggested for this government.

2. Bertrán Güell, p. 76; Iribarren, pp. 101–2; Maiz, p. 304. *Diario de Navarra* of 19 July gave news of the conversation. See also the account by Ramón Feced, minister of agriculture in this government, to García Venero, in his *El General Fanjul*, p. 287. Gil Robles (p. 792) says Mola was right not to treat: it was too late.

3. It was said that Cabanellas was finally persuaded to join the rising by a young officer who put a revolver to his head and told him that he had a minute to decide. His son denies this.

formed which would accept 'Fascism's declaration of war upon the Spanish people'. This administration was, however, not new at all. Save that the minister of marine, Professor José Giral, became Prime Minister, General Pozas, the commander of the civil guard, became minister of the interior, and General Castelló, military governor of Badajoz, became minister of war, the cabinet of 19 July was the same as it had been before 18 July. But the socialists, communists, and even anarchists declared themselves behind the ministers, and formally sank their differences.[1] Apparently it was Giral who, while Casares and Martínez Barrio were still reluctant, had insisted that the only solution was to hand over arms to the unions.[2] The new government anyway took the irrevocable step from which Casares, constitutional to the end, had shrunk. The people would be armed! Miaja, commander of the 1st Brigade (and, so briefly, minister of war), was reluctant to carry out this order, but the government insisted.[3] As the sun was rising on 19 July, lorries carrying rifles were driven fast along the streets of Madrid from the ministry of war to the headquarters of the UGT and the CNT, where they were received by the waiting masses (particularly an armed section of the socialist youth with lorries and motor bicycles, known as La Motorizada) with rapturous excitement. But there was a serious problem. 65,000 rifles were handed out, but of these only 5,000 had bolts. The remaining 60,000 bolts were in the Montaña barracks. The ministry of war ordered the colonel in command, Colonel Serra, to hand them over. His refusal to do so marked the beginning of the rising in Madrid.

Similar orders, to distribute what arms there were, were given by telephone to all the civil governments in the provinces, although in

1. Pozas was, surprisingly, an *africanista*, who had led troops to re-occupy Annual in 1925 and with Mola had helped put down the end of the Riffian revolt the following year.

2. Evidence of Francisco Giral.

3. Evidence of Francisco Giral. It appears, however, that one further attempt at compromise was put forward, a few days later, by Sánchez Román, at a cabinet meeting with Prieto and Largo Caballero present. The plan of Sánchez Román was for a general withdrawal to the positions of 19 July, amnesty, disarmament, prohibition of strikes, formation of a national government formed by all the political parties, dissolution of the Cortes, etc. This initiative was not accepted by the new government and probably was impossible. (García Venero, *Historia de las Internacionales*, vol. III, pp. 102–5.)

many cases such orders were too late: for this occurred just when, in the summer dawn of 19 July, the second wave of risings was about to break over Spain. It was at this moment also that Franco at last arrived on African soil, flown by the Dragon Rapide, to be greeted by Colonel Sáenz de Buruaga on the same Sania Ramel airfield at Tetuán where, the previous day, the last republicans, led by Franco's own cousin, Major de la Puente,[1] had been overwhelmed; that the *Churruca* was landing at Cádiz the first unit of the Army of Africa to reach the mainland of Spain, 200 Moorish *Regulares*; and that the crews on the main fleet of warships sailing south to Algeciras were about to rise against their officers. Well might so tough a revolutionary as the communist 'El Campesino' later express his wonderment that a single day could have held so much 'bloodshed and battle'.[2]

1. Fernando de Valdesoto, *Francisco Franco* (Madrid, 1943), p. 123. Franco had left Las Palmas in the Dragon Rapide on the morning of 18 July. Luis Bolín (*Spain, the Vital Years*, p. 48) records a conversation with Franco during the night of 18–19 July in the aeroplane in which the general said, 'It may take longer than most people think but we are certain to win'. The aircraft stopped at Agadir and Casablanca before reaching Tetuán. It is possible that the prudent general delayed his arrival in Morocco till it was certain that his friends had won there. He had placed his wife and daughter on a German passenger boat, *El Wadi*, bound for Le Havre (Luis de Galinsoga, *Centinela de occidente*, Barcelona, 1956, p. 226).

2. El Campesino, p. 5.

15

19 July – battle of Barcelona – Oviedo – the Basque provinces – Saragossa – Pamplona – Valladolid – the rising in Madrid – Toledo and the Alcázar – the end in Barcelona – Corunna and El Ferrol – death of Sanjurjo – a dividing line

---

IN Barcelona, recently quiet, the greatest battle of 19 July was fought. On the previous night, this magnificent city had run wild with rumours. Crowds had massed all the way from the central Plaza de Cataluña down the leafy avenue, the Rambla, with its bars and flowers, to the edge of the harbour at the Plaza Puerta de la Paz where Columbus's statue, on its tall column, surveys the Mediterranean. The agile Companys had found documents proving the rebellious intentions of Captain López Varela, and had sent them to Madrid in the care of the youngest Esquerra deputy in the Cortes, Ramón Casanellas. The general commanding the 4th Division based at Barcelona, Llano de la Encomienda, had warned his officers that, though personally a supporter of the Republican Union party, if circumstances should oblige him to choose between two extreme movements, he would not hesitate to back communism rather than fascism. Among those who heard this were the leaders of the rising planned to begin the next day – including General Fernández Burriel of the cavalry, who was to be in command till General Goded's arrival from Majorca. Their plan was for the 5,000 or so troops in the various barracks on the periphery of the city to join up at the Plaza de Cataluña. They supposed that it would then be an easy task to reduce Barcelona. But the plotters had failed to take adequate account of the lack of enthusiasm for revolt among the civil guard, the assault guards, and the numbers and fighting qualities, in the city at least, of the anarchist workers. In the late evening of 18 July, Companys refused to give 'Arms to the People'. Nevertheless, the CNT took by assault several arms depots including the old prison ship *Uruguay* in the harbour, called for a general strike the next day, and prepared for the struggle. Thus, in one moment, the anarchist leaders passed from the status of hunted criminals to – what? Certainly not defenders of democracy, but 'leaders of the Anti-Fascist Revolutionary Alliance'. Companys received news from Llano de la Encomienda that all was quiet in the garrisons. But the President was unable to sleep. At two in the morning, he and Ventura Gassol, the poet who was his counsellor of culture, walked out into the Rambla, Companys wearing a soft hat pulled low over his eyes, his companion with his customary large-brimmed hat, which gave him the air of a nineteenth-century violinist. The brilliant gaiety of a Saturday night of the Barcelona summer was slowly giving way to something in that city equally traditional: a revolutionary dawn. The crowds suddenly appeared to be less holidaymakers than armed workers and, on the loudspeakers, the dance music was giving way to stirring admonitions to action. At four in the morning, the news was brought to Companys that troops under Major López-Amor had left the Pedralbes barracks in the west of the city and were marching towards the Plaza de Cataluña.

The men in the barracks had been roused early and given a generous portion of brandy, being variously told that they were being sent to crush an anarchist rising or to march round the town in honour of the 'People's Olympiad', a left-wing festival arranged in opposition to the official Olympic Games about to open in Berlin.[1] The People's Olympiad had, of course, now to be cancelled, though some thousands of foreign visitors had already arrived. To puzzle the enemy, the soldiers were instructed to raise their hands in a clenched fist. Careful plans for communication between the rebels, for treatment of prisoners, and for action on reaching their destination were circulated.[2] But the junction between the different columns of rebels was never effected, since each was met by the resistance of the anarchists, the assault guards and the civil guard.[3] The police were also loyal, being headed by Colonel Frederic Escofet who, with Major Pérez Farras, had led the Mozos in 1934 in defence of the *Generalidad*.

1. See Jaume Miravitlles, *Episodis de la guerra civil espanyola* (Barcelona, 1972), p. 35.

2. I have examined photocopies of these orders in a useful memorandum sent to me by Colonel Vicente Guarner.

3. The enthusiasm in Barcelona when a troop of mounted civil guard rode slowly down the Rambla giving the red salute knew no bounds. See Jesús Pérez Salas, *Guerra en España* (Mexico, 1947), pp. 83–100, for further details of republican commands in Barcelona.

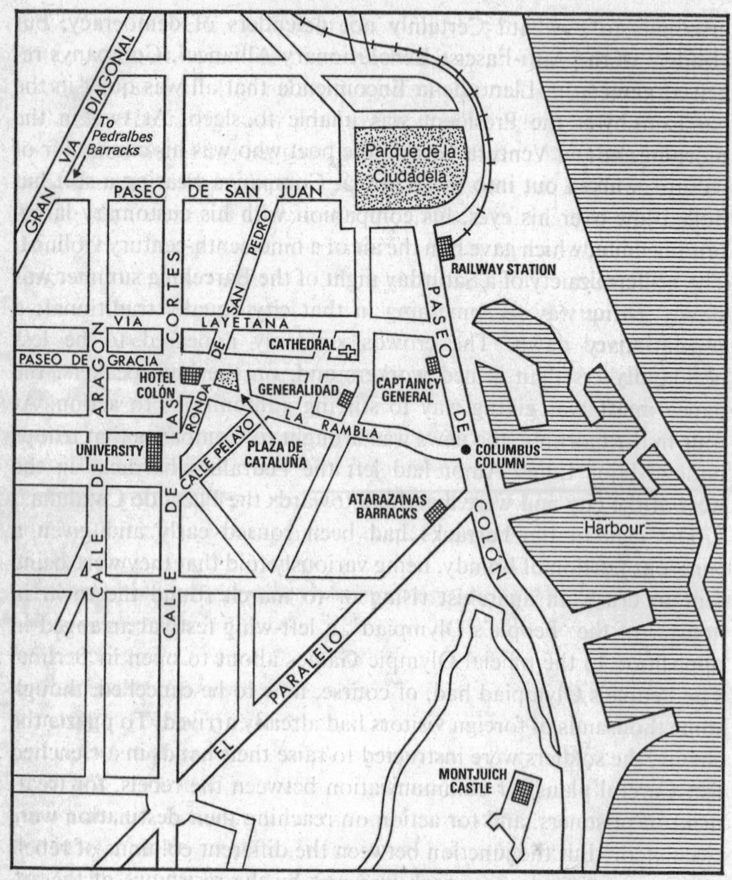

8. Barcelona, July 1936

Some non-commissioned officers had allowed anarchists into the arsenals, and a large force of assault guards had, in a dramatic scene, given their arms to the anarchists who had been beseeching them to do so.[1] An infantry column under Major López-Amor did succeed in reaching the Plaza de Cataluña, and there capturing the telephone

1. Paz, p. 282. A good picture of the fighting in Barcelona from the point of view of the civil guard is in Frederic Escofet's *Al servei de Catalunya i de la república* (Paris, 1973), vol. II.

building by a trick, but they got no further. The officers directing the rebellion were unable to deal with the revolutionary unorthodoxy of their opponents; a second artillery detachment, for example, was overcome by a column of armed workers, who advanced with rifles in the air and, with 'passionate words', begged the rebels not to fire. They then urged the troops to turn their guns on their own officers. Most of the battles of Barcelona were less easy. The secretaries of the Catalan united socialist youth (Francisco Graells) and of the POUM youth (Germinal Vidal), as well as the anarchist secretary in Barcelona (Enrique Obregón), were all killed in the course of the day. Goded arrived by hydroplane from Majorca (which he had secured with hardly a shot fired) in the late morning. He failed either to put enough heart into his men or to ensure the rebellion of the civil guard: General Aranguren, the civil guard commander, continued to affirm that he would only obey the orders of the *Generalidad.* Colonel Jacobo Roldán told Goded that the soldiers were fighting well, but 'God alone knows what will happen when they discover that we are rising against the republic'.[1] As it was, the soldiers were unable to set up their artillery. Fighting continued all day, the Plaza de Cataluña being strewn with dead men and dead horses. The Barcelona aerodrome was kept loyal by its commander, Colonel Díaz Sandino. In the early evening, the old captaincy-general where Goded had set up his headquarters, near the harbour, was stormed. Goded (apparently saved from mob fury by a well-known Barcelona communist, Caridad Mercader, the mother of the future assassin of Trotsky)[2] was captured and induced to broadcast an appeal in dignified, but defeated, tones to his followers to lay down their arms, much as Companys had done in the revolution of 1934: 'Destiny has been adverse, and I have fallen prisoner, so that I release from their obligations towards me all those who have followed me'.[3] Goded spoke thus to restrain his followers in Majorca from sending the aid for which he had earlier begged. The voice of the general was heard all over Spain and gave

1. Francisco Lacruz, *El alzamiento, la revolución y el terror en Barcelona* (Barcelona, 1943), p. 202.

2. *Dépêche de Toulouse*, 26 July, 1936, quoted Pierre Broué and Émile Témime, *La Révolution et la guerre d'Espagne* (Paris, 1961), p. 96.

3. Manuel Goded, *Un 'faccioso' cien por cien* (Saragossa, 1939), p. 58. This volume, by Goded's son, defends the father against the slur that he was becoming a democrat.

heart to the republicans. By the evening, there only held out in Barcelona the Atarazanas barracks near the harbour and the San Andrés barracks with its armoury, some miles outside the city.[1] In these battles, the anarchists and the Catalan security forces (assault guards as well as civil guards) disputed the honours.

Elsewhere on 19 July, the day had been tumultuous. There were many unresolved conflicts. In Asturias, the sappers' regiment of Gijón held out in the Simancas barracks under the military governor, Colonel Antonio Pinilla. In Oviedo, the centre of the revolution of 1934 and, since February 1936, in a perpetual state of revolutionary effervescence, a curious situation had arisen. The city was considered lost for the rising. But Colonel Antonio Aranda, in command of the garrison, who had gained in Morocco the reputation of being one of the cleverest strategists in the army, first posed as 'the sword of the republic' to both the civil governor and the trade unions. He argued that the situation was not serious enough to necessitate the arming of the workers: González Peña, who had led the Asturian rising in 1934, was persuaded, together with Belarmino Tomás, the other socialist leader in the province, to agree with Aranda, whose political affiliations were not known. Four thousand miners, supposing Oviedo securely held, therefore left by train for Madrid. Then, at five in the evening and having spoken with Mola on the telephone, Aranda declared himself with the rebels. He was supported by the assault guards as well as the Falange and civil guard. But the remainder of Asturias was hostile to him and by 20 July he was closely besieged by a new force of miners.[2] It was outrageous to them that Oviedo, the heart of the revolution in 1934, should not rally to the Left in the greater crisis of 1936.

Along the coast, Santander was held for the republic without a fight.[3] In the Basque provinces, the third and southern province of Alava, whose capital is Vitoria, was captured without difficulty for

1. This account of the battle of Barcelona was based on the narratives in *Cruzada*, *The Times*, del Castillo and Alvarez, Pérez Salas, Escofet, Jellinek, Lacruz, Abad de Santillán, *Por qué*, and Franz Borkenau, *The Spanish Cockpit* (London, 1937).

2. Zugazagoitia, p. 33f.; Peirats, vol. I, pp. 148–9.

3. Colonel Pérez García Argüelles refused to join the rebellion. He did nothing. He was condemned to death by the republic but absolved. When Santander fell to Franco in 1937 he was shot (García Venero, *Falange*, p. 157).

the rebels led by General Angel García Benítez, helped by an old friend of Franco's, Colonel Camilo Alonso Vega.[1] But the two other Basque provinces, Vizcaya and Guipúzcoa, were as easily held for the government. In Bilbao there was no rising. The military commander, Colonel Piñeiroa, refused Mola's telephoned demand to support the rising, and the socialist leader Paulino Gómez succeeded in maintaining control. The local officers were dismissed, but not murdered.[2] In San Sebastián, Colonel Carrasco, the military governor, was arrested during the morning. He had been brought only recently into the conspiracy and was not trusted by Mola, though he was a monarchist. Prieto, meanwhile, telephoned incessantly from Madrid to try and make certain that the still far from revolutionary Basque Nationalist Party would continue to support the government. But he need not have worried. By midday, both Bilbao and San Sebastián, together with all the mountainous and fishing villages of the two provinces, had undergone what seemed to be a universal, voluntary mobilization. *Juntas* of defence were set up in both cities, prominent right-wing persons were arrested, their motor-cars requisitioned. The Basque nationalist politicians, led by Manuel de Irujo, were the inspiration of these steps. The military plotters dilly-dallied. At last, a telephone call from Mola encouraged Colonel Vallespín, in the Loyola barracks in San Sebastián, to decisive action. Two cannon in these barracks were pointed at the civil government building, whose entire staff fled, allowing Colonel Carrasco, who was detained there, to escape. This he did, and established himself, with another group of right-wing people, in the María Cristina Hotel. Rebel civil guards also moved into the Gran Casino Club. This was the moment when the handsome summer capital of Spain could have been won for the rising. Everyone was nervous. When a pistol shot was heard over San Sebastián Radio, the announcer had to explain, 'The shot you have just heard was caused by a comrade falling down and loosing off his weapon. There is no victim.'[3] Colonel Vallespín delayed, though Colonel Carrasco declared a state of war. During the night,

1. The population of Alava is partly Basque, partly Navarrese. See above, p. 87. Alonso Vega was a childhood friend of Franco, entered the Legion with him, was taken by him to Saragossa and was later for many years minister of the interior.

2. Iturralde, vol. II, pp. 208–11.

3. *The Times*, 30 July 1936.

a republican column from the nearby arms centre of Eibar began to make for the city.[1] In Galicia, there was no action whatever until 20 July: the conspirators, confused by the premature beginning of the rising in Morocco, held their hands, and the republican representatives their breaths. The naval base at El Ferrol and the two ports of Corunna and Vigo made that region important.

The rebels' main victories on 19 July were in the centre and north of the country. At Burgos, the old capital of Castile, a grave, reserved, conservative city, the rising triumphed without difficulty and with scarcely a shot fired. 'The very stones are nationalist here,' the Condesa de Vallellano remarked proudly to Dr Junod of the Red Cross in August.[2] Colonel Marcelino Gavilán was the moving spirit of the rebels (General Gonzalo González de Lara the military governor having been arrested and taken away to Guadalajara prison the day before). Gavilán arrested the 64-year-old loyal General Batet (commander of the 6th Division), and the equally loyal General Julio Mena, who had been under-secretary for war and had been sent to take over from González de Lara. The wives of the civil guard had earlier prevented the civil governor from giving arms to the people, saying that they would be used to kill their husbands. In this city, there were many prominent right-wing persons, such as Sáinz Rodríguez and Goicoechea, to celebrate the victory, waiting for Sanjurjo, in order to take part in his government.[3] In Saragossa, the troops went out into the streets at dawn, and were in command of the main points of the town before the trade unions could organize any resistance.[4] The powerful forces of the CNT 'wasted too much time talking to the civil governor'.[5] In the rest of Aragon, Huesca and Jaca were as easily gained, though at ancient Barbastro, near

1. *Cruzada*, XXVI, p. 242f.; Lizarra, pp. 20f., 40; Iturralde, vol. II, p. 202f.

2. Marcel Junod, *Warrior without Weapons* (London, 1951), p. 98.

3. *Cruzada*, XII, pp. 401–11; Ruiz Vilaplana, p. 30f.; Iturralde, pp. 31–2. See also Romero, p. 189.

4. *Cruzada*, XV, p. 196f.

5. Peirats, vol. I, p. 149. The failure of the anarchists in Saragossa gave rise to a lively polemic. See Gaston Leval, *L'Espagne libertaire* (Paris, 1971), p. 139f. There was a general strike, but no fighting. This did not prevent a fearful repression. The nerve of the rising there was Colonel Monasterio, who had been one of Gil Robles's aides in 1935.

the Catalan border, the commander of the garrison, Colonel José Villalba, who had apparently said earlier that he would support the rising, decided to support the republicans. (Mola explained, on Burgos Radio later, that Villalba had demanded 100,000 pesetas as a bribe to raise Barbastro for the rebels.)[1] At Teruel, the capital of the southernmost province of Aragon, the leading rebel declared a state of war before seven soldiers only. The civil governor annulled it, but the civil guards and assault guards rallied to the rising. The consequent general strike was not enough to prevent the bloodless success of the rebels.[2]

In Navarre, there was never any doubt about the nationalist victory. Mola declared a state of war at Pamplona with the enthusiastic support of the 6,000 Carlist *requetés* whom he had been promised, and, immediately, the whole province was in his hands. The scenes of religious enthusiasm, combined with warlike zeal, equalled the excitement in Navarre during the nineteenth-century Carlist Wars. In red *boinas*, old men and young poured into Pamplona from nearby villages, all singing the old Carlist song '*Oriamendi*' and demanding arms. No one knew, or cared, that the Pretender, Alfonso Carlos, had forbidden the movement to rise unless they had more explicit political guarantees than Mola had given. Mola had only 1,200 rifles from the Pamplona arsenal to give out but soon another 10,000 were sent up from Saragossa, to complete the Carlists' equipment. Major Rodríguez Medel, the commander in Pamplona of the civil guard, had supported the Popular Front, but he had been murdered by his own men the previous evening.[3] The enthusiasm for war was such that the Pamplona newspaper *Diario de Navarra* came out with the same headlines two days running.[4] Major Martínez de Campos, of the corps of artillery, recalled how lorries, hired by the mayors, began to arrive from the villages far and near. Each lorry, as it circled the main square of Pamplona, received an ovation from the crowds

1. Another theory is that Villalba waited to see on what side Franco was and took the other one.

2. *Cruzada*, VI, p. 237.

3. *Cruzada*, XIII, pp. 460–83.

4. *Diario de Navarra*, 20 and 21 July. It had 'Camino de la Victoria' (Path of Victory) permanently as its subtitle thereafter.

which, at the sound of the bugles, appeared at balconies hung with flags.[1] Mola then prepared to send some of his men south.

At Valladolid, that other cathedral city of the Castilian plain, General Andrés Saliquet, a conservative, moustachioed officer who had offended Azaña, and General Miguel Ponte, an indefatigable monarchist conspirator, unexpectedly appeared in the office of the commander of the division, General Nicolás Molero, a freemason and minister of war with the ill-fated Portela, and demanded his adhesion to their cause. The rebels gave their brother-officer a quarter of an hour to reflect, and retired into an outer room. While the minutes passed, the noise could be heard of the start of street-fighting between falangists and workers. Suddenly, General Molero flung open the door, and cried '*¡Viva la República!*'. One of his aides opened fire. A short fight ensued, two junior officers being killed on either side, but the rebels emerged victorious. Molero was led away, later to be condemned to death for 'rebellion', though he was merely held in prison for many years. In the city, the railway workers fought gallantly all day against their well-armed opponents, who included the civil guard, assault guards, and civilians as well as the falangists. The *casa del pueblo* never surrendered, and was razed to the ground. By evening, however, Valladolid had been conquered. Luis Lavín, the civil governor, who had been appointed by Casares Quiroga to control fascism in the city, found himself deserted by all his staff. He got into his motor-car and attempted to flee to Madrid. He was caught, and brought back a prisoner to his own house, where General Ponte had by then established himself.[2]

Of the other towns of Old Castile, Segovia was won for the rebels without bloodshed, as were Salamanca and Avila, where many falangists, including Onésimo Redondo, were released from prison. Zamora and Palencia were also quickly captured, though the officers, civil guard, and right-wing politicians remained in both cities on tenterhooks for several days, due to the stories of the likely arrival of a train full of miners, who in fact returned to plague Aranda at Oviedo. In León, 2,000 miners did arrive, demanding arms. The

1. Martínez de Campos in St Antony's papers, qu. Carr, p. 652. See also Martínez de Campos's memoir, *Ayer 1931–1953* (Madrid, 1970), ch. II, and del Burgo, p. 13f.

2. For Valladolid, see Iturralde, vol. II, p. 107f.

military governor, General José Bosch, agreed to give them what they wanted on condition that they left the town. In the event, 200 rifles and four machine-guns were handed over. León itself remained unrebellious till the next day, when the miners were well on their way to Madrid.[1] In Estremadura, Cáceres and its province were captured for the rising, but Badajoz, thanks to the loyalty of the garrison under General Luis Castelló (the new minister of war), remained republican. In New Castile and La Mancha, there was only one rebel success – at Albacete, captured by the civil guard. As for Andalusia during 19 July, Queipo de Llano tightened his hand on Seville, but its suburbs remained in working-class hands. In those Andalusian towns, where the rising had been generally successful on 18 July, sporadic fighting continued, the nationalists being greatly assisted in Cádiz and Algeciras by the arrival of units of Moors from the Army of Africa, who had been shipped across the Straits in the destroyer *Churruca*, under the noses of the republican ships, in the dark. The stalemate of Granada persisted all day. Castelló, from the ministry of war, telephoned to General Campins, the military governor, ordering him to equip a column to march on Córdoba. But two senior colonels of the garrison answered that it was doubtful whether the officers would agree to lead such a force. Another colonel, alluding to the general strike then beginning, declared that Granada was already in Marxist hands. Campins suggested that the militias of the Popular Front should undertake the expedition demanded by Madrid. He first went to the artillery barracks and to the assembled officers announced, 'Gentlemen, the military rising has failed. I trust you to remain absolutely loyal to the republic. I have orders from the ministry of war to take over the arms of this garrison.' A silence greeted his words, and that he took for consent. But by midnight the militiamen still remained unequipped.[2]

There was a similar stalemate at Valencia. In mid-morning, all was ready for the rising, with several thousand civilian supporters assured, when bad news came in from Barcelona. General González Carrasco, who had arrived from Madrid to lead the rebels, vacillated, to the fury of Major Barba, the chief organizer of the conspiracy there (he was national chief of the UME). The military governor, General Martínez Monje, who had been trying for some months to play both

1. *Cruzada*, XV, pp. 134–7. 2. *Cruzada*, XI, pp. 275–89.

sides against each other, similarly wavered. The civil governor resigned. The CEDA's leader in the town, the unstable vice-president of the movement, Luis Lucía, who had eddied from regionalism to insurrectionism, condemned the rising, and thus prevented the mass middle-class rally to the rising which so helped it elsewhere.[1] The Valencian workers, led by the anarchist dockers, were massing in the streets. The college of St Thomas of Villanueva and the church of the Two St Johns were pillaged and set on fire. The generals continued to dither, while left-wing officers of the civil guard, led by Captain Manuel Uribarri, began to distribute arms. The matter was thus left unsettled by the time night fell.[2] This uncertainty was reflected down the coast at Alicante, Almería and at Gandia. But there was no doubt about the Popular Front success farther south and throughout all those parts of Andalusia where there had been no rising on 18 July. By nightfall, this poverty-stricken part of Spain was aflame with revolution.

In the Balearics, while Majorca had been secured by Goded for the rebels, the NCOs and troops of the garrison at Minorca prevented the success of the rising there by General José Bosch.[3] By nightfall, that officer had proclaimed a state of war at Port Mahon, but was closely besieged. In Ibiza, the rising triumphed, as in the other small Balearic islands. Discussion of the politics of this archipelago naturally prompts consideration of the whereabouts of the fleet.

On the eventful dawn of 19 July, the cruisers *Libertad* and *Miguel de Cervantes* were sailing south from El Ferrol. They had been dispatched by the government to seek to prevent the Army of Africa from crossing the Straits of Gibraltar. Later, the only seaworthy Spanish battleship, the *Jaime I* (the *España* was under repair at El Ferrol), also left Vigo for the south. Upon all these ships, upon the destroyer *Churruca* which had already landed a cargo of Moors at Cádiz, and upon all the warships at Cartagena, the same revolutionary events occurred as on the three destroyers which had been sent

1. Lucía took refuge from anarchist mobs in a farm, was arrested and kept in gaol as a right-wing deputy. Notwithstanding, after the civil war, he was gaoled by the victorious nationalists and died young in 1942. See tribute by Prieto in *Convulsiones*, vol. II, p. 251. The question whether Lucía's telegram supporting the republic was a fake is explored in del Burgo, p. 207f.

2. Peirats, vol. I, pp. 145–6.

3. Not to be confused with General Carlos Bosch of León.

the day before to Melilla: that is, the men, stimulated by radio messages from the admiralty in Madrid addressed to them and not to their commanders, overwhelmed, imprisoned and in many cases shot those officers who seemed disloyal.[1] The most violent battles occurred on the *Miguel de Cervantes* where the officers, in mid-ocean, resisted the ship's company to the last man. (To the laconic question as to what should be done with the corpses – asked by the committee of the ship's company which took over command – the admiralty replied: 'Lower bodies overboard with respectful solemnity'.)[2] There was, however, little fighting on board the *Jaime I*, whose captain remained in command. So, by the evening of 19 July, an extraordinary fleet, run by self-appointed committees of their crews, was gathered in Gibraltarian waters, so obstructing access by General Franco to southern Spain. The gunboat *Dato*, which remained under the officers' control, did, however, run a second cargo of *Regulares* across the Straits in the evening of 19 July, while part of the 5th *Bandera* of the Legion was flown to Seville by three Breguet aircraft which chanced to be in Morocco.

Confusion continued among the plotters in Madrid. Mola had failed to coordinate there the diverse elements – the army officers around Fanjul, those in the UME, the falangists – who were hostile to the republic. There was doubt whether General Miaja, the Infantry Brigade commander (and very briefly minister of war), was or was not with the rebels. Some said that he was a member of UME, and people remembered that he had been Mola's first captain, in Morocco. At the last minute, there was even ambiguity as to who would lead the rising in Madrid: the politically active Fanjul, or García de la Herrán, the general in charge of the regiment at Carabanchel.[3] Also missing was the 'nerve' of the conspiracy, Colonel Galarza, 'the technician' and coordinator of the plot, who had been arrested. The nominal leader of the rebellion in Madrid, General Villegas, therefore decided that the assignment was too much for him and so General

1. Those officers who were merely imprisoned were mostly shot at Cartagena during August. R. Salas Larrazábal (vol. I, p. 163) puts the figure at 230 out of 675 naval officers on active service, or 34·2 per cent of the total numbers.

2. *El Socialista*, 21 July 1936.

3. The literature is large on what follows; see, in particular, García Venero, *El general Fanjul*, p. 255f., and the same author's *Madrid, julio 1936* (Madrid, 1973), p. 317f.

Fanjul, the deputy who had once been under-secretary for war under Gil Robles, took his place. He arrived at the Montaña barracks in the afternoon. To that large rambling edifice on the west of Madrid, overlooking the valley of the sluggish river Manzanares, and commanded by Colonel Francisco Serra, there also repaired, during the day, officers from other barracks in Madrid, and a number of falangists. General Fanjul gave a lecture on the political aims of the rising, and on its legality. Then the rebels attempted to sally out into the streets of the capital. But by this time a huge crowd, organized by the UGT and CNT, and the political parties, had assembled outside the gates, many of them armed with the UGT's rifles or those 5,000 handed out by the government which did have bolts. The density of the crowd rendered it difficult for the rebels to go out. They, therefore, resorted to firing with machine-guns. The crowd replied; but nothing else happened until the morning. Meantime, that night Dolores Ibarruri, La Pasionaria, made the first of many violent speeches, on the radio, calling on 'workers, peasants, anti-fascists, and patriotic Spaniards' not to permit the victory of 'the hangmen of Asturias': *no pasarán*, they shall not pass, an echo of Verdun, was the watchword, often repeated during the next months.

During the night of 19–20 July, fifty churches in Madrid were set on fire. The working-class parties, led by militia units, of which the MAOC (the communist militia) was the most important, gained effective control of the capital, while loyal republicans consolidated their hold over the ministries, particularly the ministry of war. On 20 July, a crowd even larger than that which had gathered the previous day assembled in the Plaza de España. All shouted 'death to fascism' and 'all to the aid of the republic' with exultant monotony. The lance of Don Quixote, whose statue stands in the centre of the square, was enthusiastically interpreted as pointing to the Montaña barracks.[1] Five hours of bombardment of that fortress followed. Aircraft and three pieces of artillery (drawn by a beer lorry) were included among the weapons of assault. Loudspeakers encouraged counter-rebellion among the soldiers inside the barracks. Inside, Fanjul, though confident, with 2,000 troops and about 500 monarchists and falangists, had no means of concerting measures with the

1. The nationalists later pointed out that Don Quixote's arm, in this statue, is outstretched in fascist salute, and not bent, with a clenched fist.

other garrisons in Madrid. The garrisons could only communicate with each other at this time by signals over the roof-tops. Fanjul nevertheless by this means implored General García de la Herrán, at the suburb of Carabanchel, to send a force to relieve him. But there was no possibility of a relief getting through. With hindsight, it seems that it was a fatal error to retire on the Montaña barracks in this manner; Fanjul hoped to await help there, but he only found disaster. At half past ten, Fanjul and Colonel Serra, the head of the garrison in the barracks, were wounded. The fall of a bomb into the courtyard from a loyal Breguet XIX, from the air base at Getafe, exercised the minds of the rebels. The artillery was also effective. Half an hour later, a white flag appeared at a window of the fortress. The crowd advanced to receive the expected surrender. They were greeted by machine-gun fire. This incident was repeated once more, maddening the attackers. Confusion among the defenders, rather than guile, was probably responsible. Some of the rank and file wanted to yield, and were, therefore, ready to betray their officers. Eventually, a few minutes before noon, the great door of the barracks broke beneath repeated assaults. The crowd burst into the courtyard, where for some moments all was hysteria and bloodshed. A militiaman appeared suddenly at an outside window, and began to throw rifles down to the crowd still in the street. One giant revolutionary conceived it his duty to fling officer after officer, disarmed and yelling, from the highest gallery upon the insensate mass of people in the courtyard beneath. The succeeding massacre beggared description. Several hundred of the defenders, including Serra, were killed. Those who were saved were flung into the Model Prison, many with wounds undressed. General Fanjul was with difficulty carried off to be tried for rebellion. The precious supplies of bolts (and ammunition) were also saved from mass distribution and borne off to the ministry of war by the assault guards, one of whose units in Madrid, led by Major Ricardo Burillo, was wholly loyal (the other two units were less sure).[1]

The successful attackers now marched to the Puerta del Sol. There, however, their victory parade was interrupted by firing from all sides.

1. Burillo, a left-wing aristocrat, puritanical, anti-clerical and romantic, soon became virtually a communist: he told Azaña in 1937 that he had three loyalties: the army, the communist party and the masonic lodge (Azaña, vol. IV, p. 638).

A unit of assault guards cleared the houses surrounding the square, while the people lay on their faces. As for the other garrisons in Madrid, the engineers at El Pardo drove off northward towards Segovia, the officers telling their men that they were on their way to fight General Mola. Among those so tricked was Largo Caballero's son, who was imprisoned for the remainder of the war. In the suburb of Getafe, the air force officers loyal to the government scotched an attempted rising at the air-base there, after one loyal officer at least had been murdered; in that of Carabanchel, the artillery barracks were also captured by loyal officers, together with units of the militias after the colonel, Ernesto Carratalá, one of the founders of the republican officers' group UMRA, had been shot by his staff for attempting to hand out arms to the militia. General García de la Herrán was killed by his own soldiers, for a contrasting reason. One by one the other garrisons fell.[1] The communists, La Pasionaria and Lister, went to infantry barracks No. 1, and, by sheer eloquence, won over the rather reluctant soldiers to the cause of the government.

Immediately afterwards, hastily-armed militia forces, along with elements of the demoralized civil guard and assault guards as well as what remained of the army, were dispatched in taxis, lorries, or requisitioned private motor-cars, southwards towards Toledo and north-east towards Guadalajara. For in both these nearby towns the rising had been temporarily successful. At Toledo, the numerical superiority of General Riquelme's combined regular troops and militia drove back a group of rebels, led by Colonel José Moscardó, the military governor and director of the central school of gymnastics in the army, into the Alcázar, the half-fortress, half-palace, set on a height commanding the city and the river Tagus which had been, since the nineteenth century, the Spanish infantry officers' school. Moscardó resisted attempts by the war office and the government to persuade him to surrender. Eventually, he was barricaded in, with about 1,300 people, of whom 800 were members of the civil guard, 100 officers, 200 falangists or other right-wing militants, and six cadets of the Academy (which was then on its summer vacation). The colonel also took with him 550 women and 50 children, mostly de-

1. The chief sources used in the account of the battles in Madrid were *Cruzada*, XVII, pp. 386–481; Enrique Castro Delgado, *Hombres made in Moscú* (Barcelona, 1965), p. 270f.; *The Times*, 5 August 1936; *El Socialista*, 21–22 July 1936.

pendants of the defenders and other Toledans. Finally, he also took with him Manuel González López, the civil governor, 'with his entire family, and a number of persons (about 100) of left-wing politics as hostages'.[1] The garrison was well supplied with ammunition from the neighbouring arms factory, though food was scarce.

As for the militia making for Guadalajara, both that town and Alcalá de Henares on the way were captured quickly, though the officers at Guadalajara put up a valiant resistance under the leadership of Generals Barrera and González de Lara.[2] In all these battles, new leaders appeared, such as the anarchist chiefs, Cipriano Mera, David Antona, and Teodoro Moro – all builders by trade, street fighters by circumstances; communists such as Enrique Lister, Juan Modesto, and El Campesino; or socialist students, such as Manuel Tagüeña; or old soldiers, whose fighting days were really done, such as the flamboyant *littérateur*, Colonel Mangada, or Colonel Arturo Mena, another loyal officer in his sixties.

Victory over the rising meant, in Madrid and its surroundings as elsewhere, the start of the revolution. Large portraits of Lenin now appeared beside those of Largo Caballero on the hoardings of the Puerta del Sol. Manuel Azaña might still linger, gloomy and aghast, in the Royal Palace; his friends might still hold the portfolios of government; but, in the streets, the 'masses' ruled. The socialist-led UGT was the real executive body in the capital. With the communist–socialist youth as its agents, it maintained such order as existed. Syndicalism had thus come to Madrid as a result of a great anti-syndicalist rising. For the workers, 20 July was a day of triumph. But in the evening, many assassinations were committed by trigger-

1. *The General Cause* (Madrid, 1943), pp. 320–21. The question of whether there were hostages or not in the Alcázar was thus laid to rest by this statement of Moscardó's after the war. See Herbert Southworth, *El mito de la cruzada de Franco* (Paris, 1963, also Fr. edition), p. 54. The Academy was on holiday. Cf. Cecil Eby, *The Siege of the Alcázar* (London, 1966), p. 16, who says all the cadets were on leave, but that six were gathered together by Captain Vela Hidalgo, the Alcázar's cavalry instructor (p. 28). The civil governor went of his free will, being on the Right.

2. They were mostly murdered afterwards. Those who were not killed on the spot were judged and executed. The old conspirator, General Barrera, however, succeeded in escaping, in civilian clothes, and made his way to Burgos. González de Lara had been released from prison by the rebels just before.

happy militiamen. Two republican officers, Colonel Mangada and Major Luis Barceló, also set up summary courts in the Casa de Campo to try officers captured in rebel barracks – men whom, in many cases, they had known, and hated, all their careers. During the evening and the night, the first executions began under this inauspicious authority. Other murders followed in every quarter, the houses of the rich burned, while the clubs, hotels and public buildings became thronged with revolutionaries.

In Barcelona, the rising had also been subdued by the evening of 20 July. The San Andrés barracks, the main armoury of Barcelona, surrendered to the anarchists during the night and made available to them some 30,000 rifles (they had only had 200 the previous day). The Atarazanas barracks next surrendered at half past one, after a prolonged battle, to the anarchists. The anarchist Francisco Ascaso was killed in the assault. Mola's brother, Captain Ramón Mola, had killed himself during the night. Over 500 persons, of whom about 200 were 'anti-fascists', had been killed and 3,000 wounded in the two days' battle.[1] Immediately, President Companys was visited by anarchist leaders, headed by García Oliver, Abad de Santillán, and Durruti. These formidable men of violence sat before Companys with their rifles between their knees, their clothes still dusty from the fight, their hearts heavy at the death of Ascaso.

Companys then spoke as follows:

First of all, I have to admit to you that the CNT and FAI have never been accorded their proper treatment. You have always been harshly persecuted, and I, who was formerly with you,[2] afterwards found myself obliged by political exigencies to oppose you. Today you are masters of the city.

He paused, and then spoke deprecatingly of the part played by his own party in defeating the rising:

If you do not need me [he went on] or do not wish me to remain as President of Catalonia, tell me now, and I shall become one soldier more in the struggle against fascism. If, on the other hand, you believe that, in this position which, only as a dead man, would I have abandoned if the fascists had triumphed, if you believe that I, my party, my name, my

1. CNT–FAI bulletin, 22 July 1936.

2. An allusion to Companys's previous practice as a barrister, when he would often defend anarchists in the courts for nominal fees.

prestige, can be of use, then you can count on me and my loyalty as a man who is convinced that a whole past of shame is dead, and who desires passionately that Catalonia should henceforth stand among the most progressive countries in the world.[1]

Of course, the rebels had risen against the government and the regular security forces had played a great part in defeating them.[2] But the civil guard and assault guards perhaps numbered, like the rebels, only 5,000, and the anarchists had now six times that number of armed men. The loyalty of the security forces was not unquestionable. Companys was thus in a difficult position, but his clever oration posed an acute problem in the minds of the leaders of the anarchists. Should they proceed, as they presumably could in Barcelona at least, to establish 'libertarian communism'; or should they collaborate with the Catalan government? To choose the first might necessitate further fighting with, or at least the suppression of the view of, many republicans, Catalan nationalists, socialists and communists, and risk anarchist lives in other parts of Spain, where the CNT were much weaker. To choose the second was a compromise with the state, forbidden by all their past experience and long-term aims. They chose the second alternative, not without hesitation.[3] The demands of war already threatened the principle of the abolition of government.

But did Companys really have to speak so humbly? Could he not have re-established the authority of both the Catalan and the Spanish state by the effective deployment of the loyal forces of order under Generals Llano de la Encomienda and Aranguren? Or did he hope to profit from the confusion to ensure once and for all, with anarchist help, the separation of Catalonia from Spain? It seems likely that that was his plan. In the meantime, to coordinate anarchist power in the city with the power wielded by the other organizations, a so-called 'Anti-Fascist Militias Committee' of all the parties in Barcelona, was set up, Companys introducing the different groups in the *Generalidad* immediately after the conversation just described. This met nightly, and was composed of three representatives each of the UGT, CNT

1. Juan García Oliver in *De julio a julio* (Barcelona, 1937), p. 193.

2. See the remark of the Catalan politician (subsequently Premier) Juan Casanovas, to Azaña, in Azaña, vol. IV, p. 702.

3. This decision is discussed in C. Lorenzo, p. 102; Abad de Santillán, p. 59; Vernon Richards, *Lessons of the Spanish Revolution* (London, 1953), pp. 33–9.

and Esquerra, two from the FAI, one from the Communists (PSUC),[1] Acción Catalana, the POUM, and the vine-growers (*rabassaires*).[2] This body, dominated at first by its anarchist members, was the real government of Barcelona after the defeat of the rising.[3] Though there were isolated instances of firing at militiamen by concealed rebel sympathizers, the main work thereafter of the committee was to prepare militia forces to march against Saragossa and to organize the revolution in Barcelona. In all this, Companys did not consult the central government and nor did the Anti-Fascist Militias Committee.

In Granada, the stalemate at last came to an end on 20 July. General Pozas telephoned from Madrid to urge upon the civil governor 'desperate and bloody resistance' against the least manifestation of military rising. This was being brewed by Colonels Muñoz and León. General Campins, making unwisely a further visit to the artillery barracks, was denounced as a traitor by one of his own captains. He heard, to his amazement, that the entire officer corps of the garrison, the civil guards, and the assault guards stood with the rebels. Campins turned to leave, to find his way barred. His ADC suggested that the general should sign the declaration of a state of war. This he did, after a visit to the infantry barracks had proved to him that the officers there also were with the rebels. The troops of the garrison of Granada soon received the order to sally out into the streets of the city. But their commander was not General Campins, who was confined to prison, but Colonel Muñoz. The city was then

1. The new Partit Socialist Unificat de Catalunya was composed of four left-wing groups which now drew together under socialist and communist leadership and was dominated by the communists. The four groups were the old Partido Comunista de Cataluña, the Unió Socialista, the Partit Catala Proletari and the Catalan section of the Spanish Socialist party, which controlled the local UGT.

2. The CNT was represented by Juan García Oliver, Durruti and José Asens; the FAI by Aurelio Fernández and Abad de Santillán; the UGT by José del Barrio, Salvador González and Antonio López; the PSUC by José Miret; the POUM by José Rovira; the Esquerra by Jaume Miravitlles, Artemio Ayguadé and Juan Pons; the *rabassaires* by José Torrents Rosell; and Acción Catalana by Tomás Fábregas. These CNT and FAI representatives were interchangeable since the *FAIistas* were members of the CNT and vice versa.

3. The anarchists accepted parity on this committee with the other parties because (according to Abad de Santillán) they wished the same treatment in other areas where they were weak.

occupied. The crowds, being unarmed, dispersed at the arrival of the military before the town hall, and the civil governor and his staff were arrested without resistance. Only one nationalist soldier was killed in this conquest of the centre of the town. By night, only the working-class quarter of El Albaicín, directly beneath the Alhambra, held out. This was not reduced for some days. It was accomplished with innumerable casualties suffered by the working classes.[1]

At Valencia, the stalemate continued for some days still, though the balance was tipped firmly on 20 July towards the republic. The local deputy, Carlos Esplá, together with Mariano Gómez, the local chief magistrate, succeeded in persuading General Martínez Monje, commander of the 3rd Division with headquarters in the city, to remain loyal to the government. For a day or two, this officer was, however, extremely uncertain what to do, even though he had not been approached by the conspirators. Meantime, the garrisons of the city were besieged by thousands of workers. The putative chief conspirator, General González Carrasco, flitting uneasily from refuge to refuge, gave up all for lost, and sought to escape. This he eventually did, by sea, via North Africa, along with Major Barba. His followers in the garrisons remained beleaguered, while eleven churches were set ablaze and the archbishop's palace destroyed.[2] A similar uncertainty was resolved at Alicante, where General García Aldave the military governor, another vacillator, allowed himself also to be persuaded to remain loyal.[3] (In Alicante prison, meanwhile, José Antonio Primo de Rivera and his brother Miguel continued to languish without hope of release.) In Almería, the colonel of carabineers, Crespo Puerta, rose on 20 July and occupied public buildings but was constrained upon to surrender by the arrival of loyal soldiers from Granada and the threat of bombardment by the loyal destroyer, *Lepanto*.

In Seville, the victory of Queipo de Llano was confirmed on 20 July. The capture of the airport, an important one for southern Spain, was a great help to the rebels. A small number of men of the Legion arrived there in a Fokker from Morocco, under Major Castejón. This officer led his men into a final assault on Triana, the working-class

1. *Cruzada*, XI, pp. 281–8. The best brief account is in Gibson, p. 52f.
2. *Cruzada*, XXIII, pp. 460–502; Borkenau, pp. 114–15.
3. *Cruzada*, XXIII, pp. 533–48. The fates of these two generals were different. Martínez Monje remained as military governor, while García Aldave was shot.

district on the other side of the River Guadalquivir. All the districts resisted to the end, with practically no arms. In that named San Julián, the slaughter was horrible. The legionaries forced all the men whom they found there into the streets and killed them with knives. The lower part of Triana was then blasted by cannon.[1]

Also on 20 July, fighting began in Galicia. In Corunna, there were two generals, Enrique Salcedo, the general of the 8th Division, and Rogelio Caridad Pita, the military governor and commander of the 5th Infantry Brigade. The former was fat, cautious, old and lethargic, though he had fought in Morocco and in Cuba. The latter was a vigorous supporter of the Popular Front. The leader of the conspiracy in Corunna was Major Martín Alonso, who had been imprisoned in Villa Cisneros for his part in the rising of 1932, and who had escaped thence in dramatic circumstances. Both generals and the civil authorities hesitated as to whether to arm the trade unions. During the delay, the local CNT held a large meeting of friendship with the UGT, in the bull-ring. A spontaneous orator announced that there were arms hidden in the church of San Pedro de Mezonzo, and a section of the crowd went off to sack that edifice. At last, at midday on 20 July, with the supporters of the Popular Front out in the streets, General Caridad Pita, bringing good news from Barcelona and Madrid, persuaded Salcedo to declare for the government. They arrested Major Martín Alonso. But Colonel Cánovas Lacruz, the commander of the local engineers, nevertheless declared a state of war and sent his men out to take over the town. The workers tried to resist, but they had no arms. The local Falange were quickly armed and, headed by Manuel Hedilla, the leader in Santander who happened to be there, were most helpful to the army. Within a few hours, the rebels had cleared the centre of the town, and had captured the 27-year-old civil governor, Joaquín Pérez Carballo, who, with his wife Juanita, was shot. The two generals were captured by their chiefs of staff, and shot too, some months after, with other officers.[2] The battle continued

1. See the reports of these events by Bertrand de Jouvenel, special correspondent for *Paris-Soir*.

2. Letter, 4 April 1962, of Domingo Quiroga (now in Ecuador). See also García Venero, *Falange* (p. 141f.), for the activities of Hedilla, together with Southworth, *Anti-falange*, p. 109. There were many rumours about the manner of the death of the governor's wife. Pregnant, she had a miscarriage when she heard of her

sporadically for days, the workers being reinforced by a column of tin miners from nearby Noya.[1] Eventually, the fight was decided by the superior weapons of the rebels. The last skirmish here took place in the romantic garden where the grave of Sir John Moore, the Peninsular War hero, is still commemorated.[2] In other places in Galicia, fighting also began: in Vigo, soldiers fell on an unarmed population with brutality, but skirmishing lasted for several days, particularly in the quarter by the port. In the delightful city of Pontevedra, the people of the surrounding villages came in to fight the soldiers as if to a fiesta, with sticks, sickles, knives and clubs – and some dynamite: to no avail. The province fell quickly, with murder more than battle marking the victory.

At the naval base at El Ferrol, a battle between the seamen in the warships and the rebels victorious on land also came to a head on 20 July. Hesitation and division of opinion led to the surrender of the cruiser *Almirante Cervera*. This was followed by the raising of a white flag on the battleship *España*. Thereafter, a number of torpedo boats and coastguard sloops, upon which there had also been revolutions, similarly gave in. Thirty officers had been assassinated, about a similar number of revolutionary seamen were shot. Admiral Antonio Azarola, ex-minister of the navy, and commander of the base, came out in favour of the government, in time only to be arrested. The nationalist capture of this naval shipyard was to be a serious blow to the government in a long war.[3]

In León, the rising occurred at two in the afternoon of 20 July. The civil governor much regretted the absence of the miners who had left for Madrid the previous day. Nevertheless, in great heat, the workers fought with tenacity against the troops who came out under General José Bosch. Nevertheless, the rebels won, as they did in all

husband's execution, tried to commit suicide and was subsequently arrested by falangists who shot her. (A different version appears in Arthur Koestler, *Spanish Testament*, London, 1937, p. 300, and is apparently a genuine, rather than a fabricated, horror story.)

1. Peirats, vol. I, p. 151.

2. *Cruzada*, XIV, pp. 14–28. See also Iturralde, vol. II, pp. 114–15; Jean Flory, *La Galice sous la botte de Franco*, (Paris, 1938); Alfonso Camín, *España a hierro y fuego* (Mexico, 1938), p. 88.

3. For the naval strength of the two parties at the beginning of the war, see below, p. 331.

the province. The only battle of note was fought at Ponferrada, a centre of communications in the region, where certain of the wandering miners who had left Oviedo, thinking it securely in the hands of Aranda, and who had gathered some arms, were massacred in the market-square.[1] At Minorca, the other General Bosch was overwhelmed on 20 July by the combined forces of the Popular Front and of the other ranks in his own garrison. Thus the submarine base of Port Mahon, with most of Spain's submarines, laid down in the course of the First World War, was won for the republic.

One further event of importance occurred on 20 July. Mola had sent to Lisbon a Puss-moth aircraft flown by a young monarchist pilot, Ansaldo, to carry General Sanjurjo, the general-in-chief of the rising, to Burgos. Ansaldo arrived at Sanjurjo's villa to find forty excited people gathered round the 'Lion of the Rif', listening to contradictory news on the wireless, receiving frantic telephone calls, and making incorrect predictions in an *ex cathedra* style. Ansaldo solemnly announced himself 'at the orders of the head of the Spanish state!' All present burst into singing the 'Royal March', many wept with emotion, others cried 'Long live Sanjurjo! Long live Spain!' The Madrid government complained of the use of a Portuguese military airfield by a rebel pilot. The Portuguese authorities, though sympathetic to Sanjurjo, requested Ansaldo to take his plane to a more distant landing-ground. He eventually had to take off from a small field, surrounded by pine-trees, at Marinha. Here, to the pilot's alarm, the general insisted on taking with him a heavy suitcase, which contained full-dress uniform for his use as head of the new Spanish state. It may have been this excessive luggage that made it hard for the aircraft to rise. The propeller struck the treetops and the machine burst into flames. Ansaldo was thrown out with injuries, but his passenger was burned to death – a victim of conformity rather than of sabotage.[2] This casualty left the rising without a head; it was a blow to the Carlists, in particular. Following the murder of Calvo Sotelo, the continuing captivity of José Antonio, and the recent cap-

1. *Cruzada*, XV, pp. 134–47.

2. Ansaldo, p. 51. Sanjurjo rejected the 'splendid bimotor' which Fal Conde sent to Lisbon. For an inquiry into theories of sabotage see José Luis Vila San Juan, *¿Así fue? Enigmas de la guerra civil española* (Barcelona, 1972), p. 31f.

ture of Goded, Franco with Queipo and Mola were left as the outstanding persons on the nationalist side; and, while Mola was coping with the consequences of a far from wholly successful revolution in the north of Spain, and was preparing to fight on three fronts, Franco was already in control of Morocco and of the Army of Africa. As for Queipo, his gifts seemed more those of a propagandist than of a political leader.

By 21 July, a rough line might have been drawn dividing the places where the rising had been generally successful from those where it had mostly failed. Running from half-way up the Portuguese–Spanish frontier in a north-easterly direction, this line would turn to the south-east at the Guadarrama mountains near Madrid, and then to Teruel (about a hundred miles from the Mediterranean in Aragon). It would then run north to the Pyrenees, meeting the Spanish–French frontier about half-way across its length. Except for the long strip of coastline comprising Asturias, Santander, and the two coastal Basque provinces, all to the north and west of this line was nationalist territory (which also comprised Morocco, the Canaries, and the Balearics, except Minorca). To the south and east, save for the main Andalusian cities of Seville, Granada, Córdoba, Cádiz, and Algeciras (all of which, save the last two, were isolated from each other), the territory was principally republican. Within the republican territory, in Toledo, San Sebastián, Valencia, and Gijón, Albacete and Oviedo, certain buildings were held by the rebels. In many generally nationalist towns, skirmishing went on for some days more in working-class suburbs. There were also many places, such as the Sierra de Albarracín, which, lying between rebel Aragon and revolutionary Castile, was as empty of authority as it was of communication and served only as a desert through which secret agents, fugitives, and bandits could pass.

In the Andalusian countryside, the situation was particularly confused. Events in the ancient wool town of Pozoblanco were characteristic. About a hundred and twenty civil guard carried out a successful rising, on 18 July. Then the Left, miners from Linares and some 150 loyal civil guard surrounded the town and starved the civil guard into surrender. The besieged guards with their families were put on a train to Valencia where they were imprisoned in the ship *Legazpi*, where all but twenty-six were subsequently shot. Sixty-four

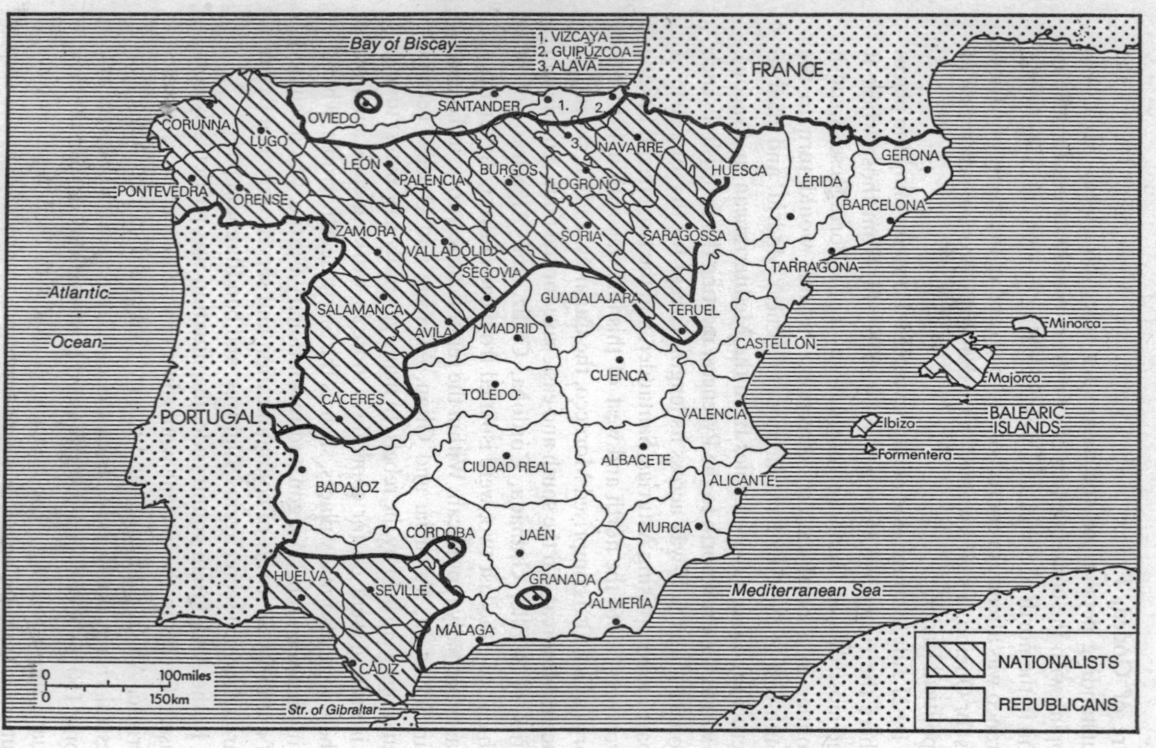

Bay of Biscay
1. VIZCAYA
2. GUIPÚZCOA
3. ALAVA
FRANCE
OVIEDO
SANTANDER
CORUNNA
LUGO
LEÓN
PALENCIA
BURGOS
NAVARRE
LOGROÑO
HUESCA
LÉRIDA
GERONA
BARCELONA
PONTEVEDRA
ORENSE
ZAMORA
VALLADOLID
SORIA
SARAGOSSA
TARRAGONA
SEGOVIA
GUADALAJARA
TERUEL
Atlantic
Ocean
SALAMANCA
AVILA
MADRID
CASTELLÓN
CUENCA
Minorca
Majorca
BALEARIC ISLANDS
Ibiza
Formentera
PORTUGAL
CÁCERES
TOLEDO
VALENCIA
CIUDAD REAL
ALBACETE
ALICANTE
BADAJOZ
CÓRDOBA
JAÉN
MURCIA
GRANADA
ALMERÍA
HUELVA
SEVILLE
MÁLAGA
CÁDIZ
Mediterranean Sea
Str. of Gibraltar
0 100miles
0 150km
NATIONALISTS
REPUBLICANS

9. Division of Spain at the end of July 1936

of the besieged civilians were shot too. Such events were the culmination of innumerable peasant revolts and wild risings of the past.[1] These days saw the culmination, in fact, of a hundred years of class war: violence provoked new brutality, the news of evil in one village causing a new evil in the next. Refugees, for example, would arrive from Queipo de Llano's Seville, in one or other of the villages between there and Córdoba. Their stories would be so terrible that reprisals would be taken on whoever was available. Later in the war, the army might arrive, and the consequent repression would be worse still.[2]

1. I am grateful to Ronald Fraser for correcting an earlier version of this story.

2. As for the few remaining Spanish colonies, events there were delayed, but Guinea, Fernando Po, Ifni, and Villa Cisneros all eventually declared for the nationalists – though Guinea declared first for the government. See Cabanellas, vol. I, pp. 512–14.

16

Nationalist Spain – the persecution – death of García Lorca – the revolution – massacre of the priests – numbers calculated – a search for responsibilities and explanations

BEHIND this dividing-line, there were a hundred Spains, but two worlds. Rebel Spain was the reverse of rebellious. Foreign commentators called it 'white Spain', 'insurgent Spain' or 'fascist Spain', sometimes even, soon 'christian Spain'; but the best word is the more neutral one, 'nationalist' – they called themselves more often the 'nationals' and spoke of the rising as 'the movement'. It seemed to be more a military than a fascist society, partly because the Falange appeared military, uniformed, armed and belligerent. 'Those who don't wear uniforms should wear skirts' was an incessant jibe. Martial law gradually took over the whole field of justice. Administrative and judicial officers were 'investigated', to prove their security in the new conditions. A judge had to be a man of right-wing sympathies and pliant to the military will. All political parties which had supported the Popular Front were banned. Political life ceased. Even the old right-wing and Centre parties, including the CEDA, vanished. The only active political groups were the Falange and the Carlists, and these were 'movements' rather than parties. The *casas del pueblo* and left-wing newspaper offices were closed down. Strikes were made punishable by death. Private rail and road movement was banned. Throughout nationalist Spain, freemasons, members of Popular Front parties, members of trade unions, and, in some areas, everyone who had even voted for the Popular Front in the elections of February, were arrested and many shot. 'That's Red Aranda,' the monarchist Conde de Vallellano remarked to Dr Junod, the astonished Swiss Red Cross representative, while driving past that town on the main Madrid–Paris railway line in August, 'I am afraid we had to put the whole town in prison and execute very many people.'[1] The

1. Junod, p. 89.

remark raises an unavoidable subject: the nature and the extent of the repression.

The number of executions varied from district to district, according to the whim of the local commander or authorities. Civil and military governors and officials of the civil government, if they had been appointed by the Popular Front government, were often shot. So were those who sought to maintain the general strike declared at the time of the rising. Well-known people, such as generals or civil governors, were usually given a semblance of trial by a court-martial perhaps lasting for two or three minutes. Most ordinary people, strikers, trade unionists, anarchists, were not. If the army did a lot of shooting so too did armed gangs of falangists or Carlists. The CEDA's minister of agriculture, Giménez Fernández, narrowly escaped being shot by 'some *señoritos* from Jerez' who arrived at his house in Chipiona. His wife lost her reason. His son who was present thought that he would have been shot if the *señoritos* had not been so drunk.[1] The wives, sisters or daughters of men executed occasionally shared their fate. These atrocities had a special purpose. Though the rebels were determined and often well armed, they were few in number. In places such as Seville or Granada, the large working-class population had to be terrified into acquiescence of the new order before the nationalist commanders could sleep peaceably in their beds. Hence, not only did the rebels act with ruthlessness towards their enemies, but they had also to act openly, and expose the bodies of those whom they killed to public gaze. All that the church officially insisted upon was that those to be killed after trial of any sort should have the opportunity for confession.[2] 'Only ten per cent of these dear children refused the last sacraments before being dispatched by our good offices,' recorded the Venerable Brother at Majorca. Mourning, however, was

1. Recollection in Sergio Vilar, p. 637.

2. There is a description of Queipo's shootings in Seville by Antonio Bahamonde, who worked for months for him as *delegado de propaganda*: see Antonio Bahamonde, *Un año con Queipo*. Bahamonde later escaped. Allowing for an element of propaganda, it is nevertheless a fearful indictment. There is also Flory, *La Galice sous la botte de Franco*, and for Burgos, Antonio Ruiz Vilaplana, *Burgos Justice*. Some of the details in these books may be wrong but they give overall a regrettably truthful picture of the *auto-da-fé* atmosphere of those days.

generally prohibited even to relations of those who had thus made a good death.[1] These shootings went on for months.

The repression was an act of policy, decided upon by a group of desperate men who knew that their original plans had gone awry. But Mola's directives since April had prepared for this eventuality. At a meeting of mayors of the district near Pamplona, on 19 July, Mola repeated the tenor of those explicit, harsh instructions: 'It is necessary to spread an atmosphere of terror. We have to create the impression of mastery . . . Anyone who is overtly or secretly a supporter of the Popular Front must be shot.'[2] This occurred even in Navarre where the rising triumphed with hardly a fight. If the proscription were decided on at the top, it is evident that there was no difficulty whatever in finding officers and soldiers, police, falangists or Carlists, to arrest, try hastily and execute. Why was that? It is scarcely enough to say that the moment was a passionate one. Nor can these atrocities be explained by the knowledge, which soon began to arrive, many times exaggerated, of comparable events in that part of Spain where the rising had not triumphed. There is no easy explanation. The spirit of the Right was enraged and fearful, and many people's blood was up. The new military authorities in nationalist Spain also found it almost as hard to control 'spontaneous' actions as the government did. Thus many were killed without the approval, or authority, of the army.

Day after day, from the time of the success of the rising, the arrests continued. Who knew with what crime those taken would be charged, or whether they would ever come back? The French catholic writer, Georges Bernanos, who was at the time in Majorca, described how men were arrested by the nationalist armed gangs

> every day from lost villages, at the time when they came in from the fields. They set off on their last journey, with their arms still full of the day's toil,

1. Georges Bernanos, *Les Grands cimetières sous la lune* (Paris, 1938,). p. 68. The real terror in Majorca did not begin till after the republican attack on the island in August–September. See below, p. 381. The chief almoner of the prisons of nationalist Spain, Father Martin Torrent, later added a new theological point by saying: 'Happy is the condemned man, for he is the only one who knows when he must die. He has thus the best chance of putting his soul in order before he dies.' (Fr Martin Torrent, *¿ Qué me dice usted de los presos ?*, Alcalá, 1942, p. 68).

2. Iturralde, vol. II, pp. 88–9. On this see also De la Cierva, in Carr, *The Republic and the Civil War*, p. 202.

leaving soup untouched on the table, and a woman, breathless, a minute too late at the garden wall, with a little bunch of belongings hastily twisted into a bright new napkin: *Adios: Recuerdos.*[1]

In most cases, however, arrests were made at night, and the consequent shooting also done in the dark. Sometimes the executions would be single, sometimes collective. Sometimes, plainly, prisoners would be tortured before being killed. Sometimes, the official in charge, out of compassion, would arrange for a supply of wine to be at hand, so that the doomed might steep their despair in the wisdom of intoxication. The next morning, the bodies would be found. Often these would be of distinguished members of the parties of the Left, or of officers loyal to the republic. But no one would dare to identify these corpses. For example, the corpse of a loyal colonel of cavalry (Rubio Saracibar), and other well-known citizens of Valladolid were condemned to rest for ever beneath a tomb marked 'Seven unidentified bodies. Found on the hill near the 102 kilometre stone on the road to Valladolid.'[2] An eye-witness living near by says that a 'dawn patrol' of falangists shot forty persons daily at the beginning of the war: Onésimo Redondo, the founder of the JONS of Castile, recently released from gaol, gave himself over to this work of purging. Prisoners were taken in that city from the prisons in lorries to a certain point outside the city where they were shot – so regularly that a stall selling *churros* was set up to cater for the spectators who would drive up to watch.[3] A Capuchin priest recalled how he was sent for at midnight to hear mass confessions in an open grave from a crowd of condemned men, near Estella (Navarre), afterwards all being shot.[4] One day the body of a *requeté* named Castiella was being buried at Tafalla (twenty miles south of Pamplona). He was a casualty of the

1. Bernanos, pp. 72–3. Bernanos was staying at this time in the house of the falangist family of de Zayas. After the outbreak of the civil war, the Marqués (then head of the Falange in Majorca) and his brother discussed what to do with Bernanos. They decided not to shoot him and he later left. The de Zayas brothers never read *Les Grands cimetières*, and the son of the Marqués afterwards married a daughter of Bernanos (evidence of Carlos de Zayas).

2. Ruiz Vilaplana, p. 65.

3. Descriptions of the events in Valladolid can be seen in Iturralde, vol. II, pp. 107–20. These derive from falangists who took part in them and were later imprisoned in the Hedilla affair (see below, p. 636).

4. Testimony reported Iturralde, vol. II, p. 74.

battlefield. An indignant public demanded that the fifty prisoners in the town prison should be killed in reprisal. The mayor remonstrated that not all those inside deserved to be killed. The public insisted, and the mayor referred the question to the Carlist *junta de guerra* in Pamplona. The *junta* said no: but the public broke into the prison just the same, and hauled out all within, carried them by bus fifteen miles to Monreal, and there in the solitude of the night shot them, including a number of bewildered women.[1]

After a while (at least in the north), the exposure of corpses to the public gaze was suspended, at the request of General Mola. He declared himself inconvenienced by the bodies on the roadside. Henceforward, the executions occurred discreetly in the orchards of a remote monastery or among the boulders on some desolate hillside, while in many places, the executions would be conveniently in the cemetery itself.

Many details of these days remain obscure. Stories were invented for propaganda purposes, sometimes by republican Spaniards, sometimes abroad. Arthur Koestler, then working with the propaganda department of the Comintern in Paris, described how distortions were deliberately written into his book, *L'Espagne ensanglantée*, by his superior, the Czech impresario of propaganda, Otto Katz.[2] But some of the most damning allegations of atrocities were prepared by the respectable council of lawyers in Madrid. Horrible stories echo down the years; how a schoolmaster of Huesca was beaten almost to death by falangists to make him confess knowledge of 'revolutionary plots'; to try and commit suicide, he opened a vein with his teeth.[3] In Navarre, and Alava, Basque nationalists were shot without confessors. One man was apparently told by certain *requetés* to extend his arms in the form of a cross and to cry '*Viva* Christ the King!' while his limbs were amputated. His wife, forced to watch, went mad as he was finally bayoneted to death.[4] A few priests who attempted to intervene

1. *ibid.*, p. 93. Other reports of murders in Navarre can be found in *No me avergoncé del Evangelio* by Marino Ayerra (Buenos Aires, 1958) and *Siete meses y siete dias en la España de Franco* by Father Ignacio de Azpiazu (Caracas, 1964).

2. Arthur Koestler, *The Invisible Writing* (London, 1954), pp. 333–5. See below, p. 341.

3. Fernsworth, p. 205.

4. Azpiazu, p. 115.

were shot also.[1] Whether or no these particular atrocities occurred quite as has been alleged, there need be no doubt that many such events did happen up and down nationalist Spain. They even happened in large numbers in places such as Córdoba and Granada, where the rebellion had been almost immediately successful.[2]

As for the authors of these atrocities, most of them were members of the army or the old parties of the right, or merely civil servants or officers of the civil guard. Of course, the falangists shot a lot of people, but they were not in positions of command and if they sometimes were in execution squads, there were also some who, like the Falange's interim national leader Hedilla, tried (in some individual cases successfully) to stem the tide by protest or the use of influence.[3] The bishop of Pamplona, Marcelino Olaechea, called for an end to blood-letting in Navarre, and there were places where executions were carried out by 'uncontrollables' against the express orders of the authorities. Many large cities, however, had blood-thirsty, even sadistic, police chiefs or military governors who effectively prevented protest: Colonel Díaz Criado in Seville, Major Doval (already well-known from Asturias) in Salamanca, Major Ibañez in Córdoba, Captain Rojas and Colonel Valdés Guzmán in Granada, the ex-republican Joaquín del Moral in Burgos: their names live in history as master-butchers of their own people. Jesús Muro, the falangist leader in Saragossa, the Falange in Andalusia, and Andrés and Onésimo Redondo, in Valladolid, also had much to answer for.

The leaders did not react warmly to pleas for compassion. Mola, when approached to exchange prisoners on one side for those on the other, by the Red Cross representative, Dr Junod, replied: 'How can you expect us to exchange a Spanish gentleman for a Red dog? If I let the prisoners go, my own people would regard me as a traitor . . . You have arrived too late, Monsieur, these dogs have already destroyed the most glorious spiritual values of our country.'[4] Fear of

1. Names given are: the priest of Carmona (Andalusia); and the Franciscans Father Revilla and Father Antonio Bombín killed in Burgos and Rioja respectively. (Iturralde, vol. II, pp. 427–8; see also Bahamonde.)

2. See Gibson, p. 68f., for the best analysis.

3. See García Venero, *Falange*, pp. 234–5, 242, 365; for Hedilla, see p. 516.

4. Junod, p. 98. Junod did, however, wonderful work, even exchanging, only days after this, the socialist mayor of Bilbao, Ercoreca, for Esteban Bilbao, a Carlist deputy.

being thought a traitor was, it is true, an obsession with Mola, but the statement reflected the reality of what most rebels, now that they had burned their boats, believed, their conviction that their opponents were worthless being daily reinforced by the news coming to them from the cities where the rising had been defeated.

It will always, probably, be difficult to know the number of those killed by the rebels or their supporters in these early days of the war. Records were not kept unless there were courts-martial. It was simply part of the process of cleaning up, the *limpieza*, ridding Spain of noxious freemasonry, Marxism, and jewry, a trilogy still menacing to the Spanish Right even though its first leg, so to speak, was relatively harmless and its third had been destroyed in the sixteenth century. Still, a patient examination of mortuary statistics for the whole of Spain may one day tell much, though perhaps not all, of the truth.

Figures have already been given, though often as matters of propaganda rather than based on evidence. They may have been exaggerated without desire to deceive, because the recollection by, say, a survivor from a prison in which there were innumerable nocturnal executions, can easily be magnified by imagination. The best independent study commanding conviction is that done for Granada. 2,137 are listed in the interment records and the cemetery of that city as being shot in Granada between 26 July 1936 and 1 March 1939.[1] The greatest number in a single month was August 1936: 572 were killed. The historian may well suppose, therefore, that the likely numbers shot in Granada and its immediate surroundings were about 4,000 and perhaps for the whole province about double that number.[2]

Probably what happened in Granada was characteristic of national-

1. The study is by Ian Gibson, p. 77 and pp. 167–9. The cause of death is described as 'detonation of firearm' and then 'order of military tribunal'.

2. The dead in Granada included the poet Lorca, the editor of the left-wing *El Defensor de Granada* (Constantino Ruíz Carnero), the professor of paediatrics in Granada University (Rafael García Duarte), the engineer of the road to the top of the Sierra Nevada (Juan José de Santa Cruz), the rector of the university (Salvador Vila), the professor of political law (Joaquín García Labella), the professor of pharmacy (Jesús Yoldi), the professor of history (José Palanco Romero), the best-known doctor in the city (Saturnino Reyes), the mayor (Manuel Fernández Montesinos), and 23 councillors, some socialist, some left republican. Of course, most of the 2,137 victims were ordinary people not easily recognizable by name.

ist Spain generally, both at the moment of the rising and afterwards. Granada had, it is true, a high level of political consciousness, and right-wing bitterness was great, because of the by-elections in June, when the Right believed that they had been thwarted. Nevertheless, the hatreds in Granada existed in Seville, Córdoba, Valladolid, Saragossa, Pamplona and in Corunna too, to name only a few of the capital cities won for the rising. For each of these places substantial figures have been suggested for the dead behind the lines: Navarre 7,000[1] to 8,000[2], Seville 9,000[3], Valladolid 9,000[4], Saragossa 2,000[5], the Balearics 3,000[6]; and even more appalling numbers have been hazarded.[7] In Corunna, 300 were said to have been shot in July and August and in even so small a place as Villagarcía de Arrosa (Pontevedra) 100 were shot.[8] The numbers for all Spain must have been in the tens of thousands: possibly 50,000 for the first six months of the war, and perhaps half that again for the subsequent months, taking into account such repression as was carried out in places conquered by the rebels.[9]

1. Madrid Council of Lawyers' Report (in *Franco's Rule*, published by United Editorial, London, 1938, p. 223f.).

2. Estimate of the ex-president of the Adoración Nocturna in Pamplona, Eusebio Garicano, made to the bishop of Vitoria (Iturralde, vol. II, p. 228: but see comment in del Burgo, p. 88).

3. Madrid Council of Lawyers, *op. cit.*, p. 225.

4. Figure quoted by a 'catholic deputy' and by the head of the British College in Valladolid, to the late Bernard Malley. Iturralde, however, suggests 'over 1,600' (vol. II, p. 109).

5. Madrid Council of Lawyers, *op. cit.*, p. 229. 6. Bernanos, p. 221.

7. E.g. Bahamonde said 150,000 had been executed in Andalusia between 1936 and 1938. Gibson quotes an acquaintance with access to the Granada Audiencia, who suggests 25,000 victims in Granada (p. 167); Jackson (p. 535) has an unnamed but apparently well-informed source who suggests 26,000 for Granada, 32,000 for Córdoba and 47,000 for Seville.

8. Letter of Domingo Quiroga. For the repression in Tuy, see *Historia y vida*, February 1975.

9. 50,000 was the estimate made in the course of the war by the Madrid Council of Lawyers. Though made at the time, their report seems to be seriously compiled. In the earlier editions of this book, I gave a figure of 40,000 for all nationalist executions. Most people criticized it as too low: e.g. Jackson (*loc. cit.*) who suggests 200,000 for the whole war, and Gibson (p. 167), following him. Cabanellas avoids a figure (vol. II, p. 866); Payne, *Politics* (p. 415), also eschews judgement and maintains this *pudeur* in *The Spanish Revolution*, p. 225. Jesús Salas (*La guerra de España desde el aire*, Barcelona, 1969), p. 491, speaks of the

Among those executed were many officers loyal to the republic. These included six generals and an admiral: Núñez de Prado, director-general of aviation; Batet, general of the 6th Division in Burgos; Generals Salcedo and Caridad Pita, the two generals in Corunna; Romerales, in Melilla; Campins, of Granada; and Admiral Azarola, commander of the arsenal at El Ferrol.[1] Among others killed were nearly all the deputies of the Popular Front captured in nationalist territory save Joaquín Maurín, who miraculously managed to conceal his identity for some months, until the worst was over.[2] Thirty-four Popular Front members of the Cortes were shot in 1936,[3] including a quarter (25) of all socialist deputies. Others killed included Arturo Menéndez, the director of security at the time of Casas Viejas, taken off the train at Calatayud between Saragossa and Madrid; the former rector of the University of Oviedo, Leopoldo Alas Argüelles; the penalist, Luis Rufilanches; and the anarchist author of the Saragossa programme, Isaac Puente. But a few isolated instances mean little against the background of the wave of executions which began in July 1936 and continued, if the truth be known, until 1941 or 1942. A large number of doctors, school-masters and civil governors in the towns captured were among the victims. In Teruel, for example, the left republican headmaster of the local secondary school, Joaquín de Andrés, was shot by a picket of ex-pupils.[4]

The most unforgettable of these deaths was that of Federico García Lorca, the greatest Spanish poet of the time. Though never a member of a political party, his brother-in-law was Fernández Montesinos, the socialist mayor of Granada, whose death has just been noted, and Lorca was naturally connected with the whole of the literary Left in Spain. After the victory of the rising in Granada, his home-town (to which he was paying a visit), Lorca took refuge in the house of the Rosales family, friends of his for years, despite their membership of the Falange (José Antonio was also a friend of his). Despite this

---

40,000 I named as 'probably exaggerated'. De la Cierva (in Carr, *The Republic*, p. 202) believes the repression was equivalent on both sides, *ipso facto*, though 'we cannot even begin to guess the figures'. Few others have committed themselves.

1. Many other officers were gaoled, sometimes for long periods, e.g. Generals Gómez Morato, Molero, Mena, Villa-Abrille, and López Viota.

2. Evidence of Joaquín Maurín, New York, 1962.

3. See list in *Franco's Rule*, pp. 209–11.

4. Azaña, vol. IV, p. 685.

protection, he was discovered and shot. The exact responsibility for his death is a matter of doubt. His arrest was the responsibility of the ex-CEDA deputy for Granada, Ramón Ruiz Alonso, but the decision to shoot him was taken by the then almost mad new civil governor of Granada, José Valdés Guzmán, chief of the local falangist militia, as well as a colonel in the garrison. Lorca's execution probably did not happen till the middle of August, about the 18th. His body certainly now rests in an unidentified grave in a remote part of the province of Granada.[1]

The legal justification for all these summary executions was the state of war which had been proclaimed on the day of the rising. The government of the republic were assumed to be the rebels, and the nationalists the legitimate power. In the beginning, no form of trial at all was used. A man shot was deemed a man judged. A series of emergency military tribunals were, however, shortly set up, composed of retired officers and conscripted lawyers. The former acquired legal status and the latter military, so both were pleased.[2] The paradoxical legal position 'troubled all who were not blindly sectarian'.[3] But the blood had gone to people's heads, and remained there a long time. A general who would have hesitated a week in 1935 over a single death sentence, in August 1936 was thoughtlessly approving twenty a day. The rebel commanders, from Mola to the youngest fascist in Valladolid, were henceforward linked by a blood bond which was one reason why they would never give in, or contemplate a compromise. The shootings went on, of prisoners caught in the battles of the summer – either in a ditch, or in the courtyards of prisons, or at crossroads. Probably more people were being shot in August and September than in July. Over this bloodbath, the rebels rode calmly towards power. Some were made the more insensitive to brutality by their need to approve the death of old friends or relations: Franco, for instance, approved the death sentence on his first cousin Major de la Puente, on arriving in Tetuán. Others were made more deter-

1. The most complete inquiry into Lorca's death is in Ian Gibson's *The Death of Lorca* (London, 1973). See also Brenan, *The Face of Spain* (London, 1950), pp. 127–47, and Marcelle Auclair, *Enfance et mort de García Lorca* (Paris, 1968). For ten years, no one alluded to Lorca in nationalist Spain. Then the Falange began to place the blame for his execution on the catholics.

2. Ruiz Vilaplana, p. 159. 3. Ansaldo, p. 83.

mined by deaths of comrades, brothers or sons in the republic. Some of the gang leaders were merely youths who enjoyed killing. Some no doubt believed that they had a duty to extirpate the unclean heresies of liberalism, socialism, communism, anarchism and freemasonry; and the longer the war lasted, the more evil those things seemed.

*

Revolution, meantime, was sweeping through the towns where the nationalist rising had either been defeated or where it had not occurred. Committees of control were everywhere formed, nominally proportionate to the parties of the Popular Front, together with the anarchists. They reflected in fact the political strengths in the place concerned.[1] Everywhere municipal councils vanished, often by force and bloodshed. Police and civil guard, even in places where these forces had been loyal to the republic, in the first days of the rebellion, often also disappeared. Sometimes mayors, if left-wing, would become presidents of revolutionary committees, and sometimes the police would reappear as security officials. The committees would seek then to change the society of the town, and its surroundings, in accordance with the views of the strongest party. The first steps, common to all republican Spain, would be the proscription of right-wing parties, along with the requisition of hotels, right-wing newspaper-offices, factories, and houses of the rich. In the latter, the revolutionary parties and unions would find sumptuous new headquarters. Roads would be guarded by patrols of militiamen. Committees would be set up to deal with all departments of life. Republican Spain, as the country had been in the Napoleonic wars or at the end of the First Republic, seemed to constitute less a single state than an agglomeration of republics.

The revolution began, as the counter-revolution did, with a wave of assassination, destruction, and spoliation. Militia units from the political parties and unions formed themselves into gangs with names resembling those of football teams. There were, for instance, the 'Lynxes of the Republic', the 'Red Lions', the 'Furies', 'Spartacus', and 'Strength and Liberty'. Other gangs took the name of political

1. These committees were formed everywhere save in Madrid, where the government of Giral was nominally in control, though power had passed to the UGT and Largo Caballero (see below, p. 290).

leaders of the Left, in Spain and abroad. Their passions were directed first against the church. Throughout republican Spain, but particularly in Andalusia, Aragon, Madrid and Catalonia, churches and convents were indiscriminately burned and despoiled. Practically nowhere had the church taken part in the rising. Nearly all the stories of firing by rebels from church towers were also untrue,[1] though perhaps, sometimes, priests had permitted monarchists to store arms in their quiet vestries. The church was attacked because of the way that religion had become the critical question of politics since 1931, because of the widespread subordination of priests to the upper classes, and because of the provocative wealth of many churches and the old suspicion about the secretiveness of orders and nunneries. There was some 'provocation' after the Rising, though that might be expected. For instance, the CNT–FAI information bulletin in Barcelona reported on 25 July: 'In San Pablo Hospital on Saturday, a priest entered into a heated argument with a doctor, pulled out a revolver and discharged his whole magazine, not at the doctor, but at the wounded around him. Bystanders were so infuriated that they picked out four of the most priestly and fascist of the brethren and shot them out of hand.' Destruction, rather than loot, was the aim. Federica Montseny, the anarchist, was proudly handed a burned thousand-peseta note.[2] An anarchist in Madrid was heard to upbraid a boy for stealing a chair, rather than breaking it.[3] Certain churches and convents in central positions in Madrid, it is true, were saved from attack by the government. But in Barcelona, only the cathedral and the monastery of Pedralbes were protected. The greatest works of art, however, were preserved, the *Generalidad* mobilizing its guardians to save art collections and libraries. Although many minor treasures were lost, the only disastrous act of vandalism was the burning of ten thousand volumes of the library of the cathedral of Cuenca, including the celebrated *Catecismo de Indias*. Goya's alleged earliest known paintings on the wooden door of a reliquary cabinet in the

1. The Carmelite church in the Calle Lauria in Barcelona had, however, been a rebel stronghold.

2. *De julio a julio*, p. 22.

3. Buckley, p. 123. Protestant churches were not attacked, and remained open. There were, however, only about 6,000 Protestant communicants in all Spain at this time (Arnold Toynbee, *Survey of International Affairs 1937*, *The International Repercussions of the War in Spain*, London, 1938, vol. I, p. 286n.).

parish church of Fuendetodos, his birthplace, were also destroyed. In Vich, the fire which destroyed the cathedral was prevented from spreading to the museum and the bishop's palace. The cathedrals of Gerona and Tarragona, and also the monasteries of Montserrat, Poblet, and Santa Creus, remained intact. Burning of churches was usually watched with unconcern, rather than with excitement. But the breaking of images and of sacred objects, or the wearing by militiamen of ecclesiastical robes, was often greeted with laughter. Thereafter the churches, whether gutted or still usable as a store or refuge, were as firmly closed in republican Spain as were right-wing political party offices.[1]

These attacks were accompanied by a colossal onslaught on the lives of members of the church and of the bourgeoisie. The nationalists after the war have named a figure of about 55,000 for all lay persons reputed murdered or executed in republican Spain during the war.[2] This calculation, large as it is, compares favourably with accusations of three or four hundred thousand made during the course of the war.[3] 6,832 are believed to have been religious persons: 12 bishops, 283 nuns, 4,184 priests, and 2,365 monks.[4] The figure for murdered

1. Convents were emptied of all their denizens. To some, of course, this was an act of freedom.

2. The figure is given as 54,594 in the National Sanctuary at Valladolid. Compare this figure with that in *The General Cause*, p. 402 (85,940). Gabriel Jackson suggests 17,000 killed in the first three months of the civil war, and only a few thousand later (*op. cit.* p. 533). Having looked at the lists in the villages in Andalusia (and reprinted in, for example, the first to the fifth '*Avances*' of the *Informe Oficial sobre los Asesinatos* etc. published 1936–7), I think that he is over-optimistic. It was not only civil guards, priests or businessmen who were killed, but innumerable anti-socialist workers, shopkeepers, clerks, etc. (nor were all civil guards against the republic). Some women (say 4,000) were killed, and probably several hundred children. Jesús Salas in a recent article guesses 65,000 to 70,000.

3. Diego Abad de Santillán (*La revolución y la guerra en España*, Buenos Aires, 1937, p. 176) speaks of a possible 5,000 killed in Catalonia.

4. These were bishops of Jaén, Lérida, Segorbe, Cuenca, Barcelona, Almería, Guadix, Ciudad Real, and Tarragona (suffragan bishop), the apostolic administrator of Barbastro who was titular bishop of Epirus, and the apostolic administrator of Orihuela, who ranked as a bishop. The bishop of Teruel was murdered in Catalonia in 1939. These figures derive from Father Antonio Montero's monumental study *La persecución religiosa en España 1936–9* (Madrid, 1961), p. 762. The figures suggest that about 12 per cent of the Spanish monks,

priests can thus be compared well with Paul Claudel's glorification in his poem '*Aux Martyrs Espagnols*':[1]

On nous met le ciel et l'enfer dans la main et nous avons
 quarante secondes pour choisir.
Quarante secondes, c'est trop! Sœur Espagne, sainte
 Espagne, tu as choisi!
Onze évêques, seize mille prêtres massacrés et pas une
 apostasie!
Ah! Puisse-je comme toi un jour à voix haute témoigner
 dans la splendeur de midi!

But such a comparison is invidious: the figures, like those of the nationalist fury, are overwhelming. Many of these crimes were accompanied by a frivolous, sadistic cruelty. The parish priest of Torrijos, Liberio González Nonvela, for example, apparently told the militiamen who took him prisoner, 'I want to suffer for Christ'. 'Oh do you,' they answered, 'then you shall die as Christ did.' They stripped him and scourged him mercilessly. Next, they fastened a beam of wood on their victim's back, gave him vinegar to drink, and crowned him with thorns. 'Blaspheme and we will forgive you', said the leader of the militia. 'It is I who forgive and bless you', replied the priest. The militiamen discussed how they should kill him. Some wished to nail him to a cross, but in the end they shot him. His last request was to die facing his tormentors so that he might die blessing them.[2] The bishop of Jaén was killed with his sister by a militia-woman nicknamed 'La Pecosa' (The Freckled One) before a crowd of two thousand tumultuous people near Madrid in a piece of swampy ground known as 'Uncle Raymond's pool'. The bishops of Guadix and Almería were forced to wash the deck of the prison ship *Astoy Mendi* before being murdered near Málaga. The bishop of Ciudad Real was murdered while at work on a history of Toledo.

---

13 per cent of the priests, and 20 per cent of the bishops perished. 283 nuns out of 60,000 is a small percentage.

1. This poem was written as a prefatory note to Juan Estelrich's propaganda book (*La Persécution réligieuse en Espagne*, Paris, 1937) on the murders in the church.

2. Manuel Sánchez del Arco, *El sur de España en la reconquista de Madrid* (Seville, 1937), pp. 66–7; Luis Carreras, *The Glory of Martyred Spain* (London, 1939), p. 104.

After he was shot, his card index of 1,200 cards was destroyed. A nun was killed because she refused the proposition of marriage offered to her by one of the militiamen who stormed her convent of Nuestra Señora del Amparo in Madrid. The 'Blood Committee' of El Pardo, just outside Madrid, became gradually intoxicated on communion wine while its members tried the parish priest. One of the militiamen shaved himself after using the chalice as a washing bowl. There were isolated instances of the violation of nuns, before their execution.[1] The corpse of a Jesuit was laid in the Calle María de Molina, Madrid, with the placard 'I am a Jesuit' fastened about his neck. In Cervera (Lérida), rosary beads were forced into monks' ears till their ear-drums were perforated. An exhibition of the exhumed bodies of nineteen Salesian nuns attracted great crowds in Barcelona. Antonio Díaz del Moral of Ciempozuelos (near Madrid) was taken to a corral filled with fighting bulls, where he was gored to unconsciousness. Afterwards, one of his ears was cut off, in imitation of the amputation of the ear of a bull in honour of a matador, following a successful *faena*. Ears of priests were often passed round. Certain persons were burned, and others buried, alive – the latter after being forced to dig their own graves. At Alcázar de San Juan a young man, distinguished for his piety, had his eyes dug out. In that province, Ciudad Real, the crimes were indeed atrocious. A crucifix was forced down the mouth of a mother of two Jesuits. Eight hundred persons were thrown down a mine shaft. Often, the moment of death would be greeted with applause, as if it were the moment of truth in a *corrida*. Then there would be shouts of 'Liberty! Down with fascism'. More than one priest went mad at these events. One Barcelona parish priest wandered crazy for days before being asked for his union card. 'What need have I of cards, I am the priest of St Just', he unwisely remarked.[2] The onslaught on the church in Catalonia and Aragon astonished many of those who lived there. Few suspected that anti-clericalism was so strong. No churches, after all, had burned there in 1931.

1. Assaults on women were rare in Popular Front Spain. Sánchez del Arco, a journalist of *ABC de Sevilla* with the advancing nationalist armies in southern Spain, notes that none had occurred at all in the villages which he visited (Sánchez del Arco, p. 55).

2. Juan Estelrich, *La Persécution réligieuse*, p. 96.

Throughout the country, nobody said '*adiós*' any more, but always '*salud*'. A man named Fernández de Dios even wrote to the minister of justice asking if he could change his surname to Bakunin, 'for he did not want to have anything to do with God'.[1] 'Do you still believe in this God who never speaks and who does not defend himself even when his images and temples are burned? Admit that God does not exist and that you priests are all so many hypocrites who deceive the people:'[2] such questions were put in countless towns and villages of republican Spain. At no time in the history of Europe, or even perhaps of the world, has so passionate a hatred of religion and all its works been shown. Yet one priest who, while 1,215 monks, nuns, and priests died in the province of Barcelona, managed to escape to France through the help of President Companys, was generous enough to admit that 'the reds have destroyed our churches, but we first had destroyed the church'.[3]

Priests who were not killed or who did not flee abroad were simply regarded as men who had chosen a certain *métier*, and were treated in no way different from a dentist, say, or a lawyer – save that they were not allowed to practise or wear the uniform of the cassock. If they had disgraced the *métier*, and had, say, in the past, never worn a clean collar for the funeral of a poor man, but always had done so for a rich man, they would probably be killed.[4] There were some exceptions to the onslaught; for example, the bishop of Minorca remained in his palace till the war ended, and the vicar-general of Tarragona exercised his ministry in prison throughout the war.[5]

Of course, in numbers, the onslaught against laymen was more violent than it was against churchmen. All who could conceivably be

1. The under-secretary of the ministry wrote back saying, 'It would seem advisable to abbreviate the long and complicated procedure where the necessity for the change of name appears justified by its notoriety' (*General Cause*, pp. 196–7). The 'atrocities' have an enormous literature in nationalist Spain, nearly every province being meticulously covered.

2. Estelrich, p. 115.

3. Madariaga, p. 377.

4. I have benefited in the rewriting of this paragraph from discussion with Professor Bosch Gimpera. The same was true of doctors. Doctors known to be devoted to their poor patients were left at liberty.

5. Broué and Témime cite *ABC* of 4 September, which indicates a priest married at Alicante; another entered the communist party. But other instances are rare.

suspected of sympathy for the nationalist rising were in danger. As among the nationalists, the irrational circumstances of a civil war made it impossible to lay down what was or what was not treason. The worthy died, the unworthy often lived. In East Andalusia, lorries manned by the CNT drove into villages and ordered mayors to hand over their fascists. The mayors had often to say that they had all fled but the terrorists would often hear from informers which of the better off people were still there, arrest them and shoot them in a nearby ravine. In many cases, the dead were peasant farmers, denounced by those who owed them money. Support for the CEDA or membership of the old Catalan constabulary in the time of Martínez Anido, the Somaten, was enough to be shot in Sitges (Barcelona).[1] To have been a member of the Falange was almost everywhere fatal, even though many escaped through the neglect or the repentance of their captors. Some of those killed may have deserved their fate: among the summarily executed were *pistoleros* such as Ramón Sales in Barcelona, and Inocencio Faced in Alicante, widely believed to be the murderers of the anarchist leaders Seguí, Boal, Layret, and others between 1919 and 1923.[2] In country districts, revolution itself often consisted primarily of the murder of the upper classes or the bourgeoisie. Thus the description, in Ernest Hemingway's novel *For Whom the Bell Tolls*, of how the inhabitants of a small *pueblo* first beat the male members of the middle class and then flung them over a cliff, is near to the reality of what happened in the famous Andalusian town of Ronda (though the work was the responsibility of a gang from Málaga). There, 512 were murdered in the first month of war.[3] In Guadix, a group of young terrorists, more or less anarchist in outlook, took over the town and killed recklessly for five months.[4]

In the larger towns, where the potential enemy was more numerous, more sophisticated procedures were followed. The left-wing political parties set up investigation bodies which were proud to call themselves, on the Russian model, by the name of *checa*. There were several dozen of these in Madrid alone. A positive maze of different groups, each with power of life and death, each responsible to one

1. Simone Weil's letter to Bernanos, *op. cit.* 2. Peirats, vol. I, p. 182.
3. Pemán, *Un soldado en la historia*, p. 300; letter from Gerald Brenan, 22 June 1961.
4. Gerald Brenan, *South from Granada* (London, 1957), p. 169.

party or department of state or even individual, characterized these first days of the civil war in the republican cities. The different *checas* would sometimes consult with each other before taking their victim 'for a ride' (*dar un paseo*). The language derived from Hollywood; a reflection of the large number of cinemas built in Primo's day. But that formality was not always followed. The cross-examination of suspects was often carried out amid insults and threats. Sometimes, the chief of the *checa* would show a card from a distance to suggest to the accused that it was his own membership card of a party hostile to the Popular Front. Sentences of death by these 'courts' were indicated on the appropriate documents by the letter 'L' for liberty, but with a full stop added. This was an instruction for the immediate execution of the prisoner. That task would be undertaken by special brigades often composed of ex-criminals.

Perhaps the most feared *checa* in Madrid was that known as 'the dawn patrol', from the hour at which it carried out its activities. But there was little to choose between this gang and 'the brigade of criminal investigation' led by an ex-printer, and ex-communist youth leader, Agapito García Atadell,[1] who, apparently with the blessing of the authorities, set up his 'anti-fascist *checa*' in a palace in the Castellana. Both these bodies drew on the archives of the ministry of the interior to help them in their task of tracking members of right-wing parties. (The Falange had destroyed their own list of members; but the Carlists and UME had not.)[2]

In the vast majority of cases, these murders were of the rank and file of the Right. Often members of the working class would be killed by their own acquaintances for hypocrisy, for having kow-towed too often to their social superiors, even simply for untruthfulness. In Altea, near Alicante, for example, a café proprietor was killed with a hatchet by an anarchist for having overcharged for stamps and for the glass of wine that buyers of stamps were forced to take while

1. García Atadell organized the communist youth in the late twenties. He later escaped from the republic with a quantity of loot, but was captured by the nationalists when the Argentinian ship, the *Primero de Mayo*, carrying him to South America, stopped at Santa Cruz de la Palma. Arthur Koestler met him in Seville prison in early 1937. He was garrotted soon after. He became a catholic in gaol. See José Ignacio Escobar, *Asi empezó ...* (Madrid, 1974), and' Arthur Koestler, *The Invisible Writing*, p. 347.

2. Iturralde, p. 124.

waiting.[1] Most of the political leaders of the Right, together with generals and others who had taken part in the rising, were imprisoned. Some of them, such as General López Ochoa, were dragged out of confinement or even hospital to be killed. Others, such as those sent to the Model Prison in Madrid, were treated well for the time being. Four Germans, all members of the nazi party, were shot in Barcelona on 24 July after the looting of the local headquarters of the German labour front.

In the chaos, there were many settlements of personal scores. In his imaginary dialogue written in 1937, *La velada en Benicarló*, Azaña makes a doctor threatened with death and imprisoned simply on the denunciation of a man on whom he had operated unsuccessfully.[2] A convict released from the common prison broke into the apartment of a judge who had condemned him some months before, killed him in the presence of his family, and escaped with the family silver tied up in a sheet.[3] There were also many mistakes: the great cellist Casals had, for some time, his name on the death list at the Barcelona suburb of Vendrell.[4]

Throughout this troubled time, the heads of such men as the President of the republic, Azaña (whose bedroom-window in the National Palace faced the Casa de Campo, where so many killings occurred), did not rest easily at night. Though they could not control the killings, they were, as the government, responsible for them. Since they did not resign, they could hardly expect to escape blame. Some socialists and even Left republicans, as well as communists and anarchists, appear to have inspired many arrests and 'investigations', the need for which could have been only remotely concerned with winning the war. Several of the organizers of these *checas* also went on to positions of responsibility in the republic's police once order

1. In small Spanish villages the purchase of a stamp was a complicated matter. Individual stamps were wrapped up in tissue paper, and folded neatly. The Altea incident was told me by one who lived in Altea. The anarchist was himself later killed by a communist.

2. Azaña, vol. III, p. 393.

3. Madariaga, p. 378.

4. H. L. Kirk, *Pablo Casals* (New York, 1974), p. 401. The anarchists of the suburb in which Casals lived made several visits to his house in search of a friend of Casals, on the Right in politics, who was hiding there.

was restored.[1] Yet many others, motivated by personal feelings rather than politics, went out of their way to intervene on behalf of likely victims of violence. Companys saved the cardinal archbishop of Tarragona when anarchist militiamen had arrested him in the monastery of Poblet, while the bishop of Gerona and many priests and members of the Catalan Lliga were saved by Ventura Gassol (the Catalan councillor for culture). Azaña saved some monks at his old school in the Augustinian monastery at El Escorial. La Pasionaria saved many nuns in Madrid from the FAI. Galarza, though weak as a minister of the interior, saved the president of the catholics' student association, Joaquín Ruiz Jiménez.[2] Juan Negrín, a socialist deputy and professor of physiology, saved many in Madrid. The anarchist leadership also criticized the violence, and tried to stem it within a few days. From 25 July, the CNT and FAI launched a series of protests against illegal violence. On 30 July, Federica Montseny, the anarchist leader, wrote sorrowfully:

> We have confirmed something we only knew in theory, namely that revolution, in which uncontrolled and uncontrollable forces operate imperiously, is blind and destructive, grandiose and cruel ... How much is wrecked in the heat of the struggle and in the blind fury of the storm ... Men are as we have always known them, neither better nor worse ... from the hearts of rogues there springs a latent honesty, from the depths of honest men there emerges a brutish appetite – a thirst for extermination, a desire for blood.[3]

Even more strongly, Juan Peiró, a long-standing member of the CNT, made an eloquent and candid attack on those who

> have killed for the sheer sake of killing, because they could kill with impunity ... many who have been killed were shot because of personal vengeance ... A people in rebellion have been infiltrated by amoral

1. For example, Julio de Mora who headed a *checa* in the palace of the Conde de Eleta and became head of the special department of information (DEDIDE) with the rank of colonel; or Angel Pedrero, who was García Atadell's assistant and successor, and who became later head of the SIM (Servicio de Información Militar) in Madrid in 1937.

2. See Sergio Vilar, p. 450. Galarza became minister of the interior in September. See below, p. 406.

3. Federica Montseny in *La Revista Blanca*, 30 July, qu. Bolloten, p. 41.

elements who rob and murder by profession . . . Many of those who carry out expropriations have had no other interest than to seize other people's money and goods for themselves.[1]

No one admittedly shielded the Catalan commissioner of public order, Frederic Escofet, dismissed because he helped some religious relations escape to France.[2] Still, a number of Popular Front committees were castigated by the government for crimes committed: and one captain of militias, Luis Bonilla, and the anarchist leaders at Valdiviedra and Molins de Llobregat, were later executed for crimes. So was José Olmeda Medina, who had stolen corpses from the church of Carmen in Madrid. The anarchist (Castilian) paper, *Campo Libre*, remarked in August 1937: 'The criminal instincts of uncontrolled elements (in the village of Cabañas de Yepes, Toledo) . . . believed the revolution was a matter of sacking and hooliganism, and, in the first days of the movement [the anarchists used the same word as the nationalists to denote the revolution of July], dealt cravenly with those who had no fault other than being unhappy.' Considerable responsibility must lie, admittedly, with the impotent minister of the interior, General Pozas, the aghast director-general of security, Alonso Mallol, and the incompetent minister of justice, Manuel Blasco Garzón. The agencies over which these gentlemen presided took refuge in denials that crimes had been committed, attributions that those that were killed had been murdered by fascists, and silent endorsement of some of the actions concerned by their subsequent promotion of those directly responsible.

Who were the killers? Doubtless many more than has been realized were criminals, released unexpectedly from gaol, many were reckless. poor boys without conscience and without ideology, most were probably adolescents, many were butchers of the type spawned by all revolutions – for example, the ex-sacristan who was active killing priests in 1936, who afterwards denounced his fellow murderers and busied himself killing republicans in 1939.[3] But the socialist–communist youth played a big part, perhaps as big a part as the anarchists. In Santander, for example, a falangist who enrolled secretly in the

1. Juan Peiró in *Perull a la reraguarda* (Mataró, 1936), p. 91.
2. Payne, *The Spanish Revolution*, p. 226. Escofet saved many.
3. He was shot in Ocaña gaol in 1939. See Sergio Vilar, p. 227.

CNT, testified later that the executions there were carried out by the socialist–communist youth, 'provided with anarchist colours and badges to cause the blame to fall on the CNT and FAI'.[1] On the other hand, the same falangist admitted that he and a few other friends of like views were themselves responsible in Santander for a lot of the 'red' shooting.[2] In Andalusia, the murder gangs usually came from outside the villages where the killings occurred. These gangs would arrive in lorries, armed with sub-machine-guns, and 'force the villages to hand over their reactionaries'.[3] In Jaén, the anarchists stopped the indiscriminate killing, and often the gangs concerned were people of no real political beliefs.[4] Equally often, however, the anarchists killed as if they were mystics, resolved to crush for ever the material things of this world, all the outward signs of a corrupt and hypocritical bourgeois past. When they cried 'Long live liberty' and 'Down with fascism', while some unjust steward was dying, they voiced deep passions of fearful sincerity. Many of those captured in Barcelona were taken thirty miles down the coast to be shot overlooking the superb Bay of Sitges. Those about to die would pass their last moments on earth looking out to sea in the marvellous Mediterranean dawn. 'See how beautiful life could have been,' their assassins seemed to be saying, 'if only you had not been a bourgeois, and had got up early and had seen the dawn more often – as workers do.'

*

Though there was much wanton killing in rebel Spain, the idea of the *limpieza*, the 'cleaning up' of the country from the evils which had overtaken it, was a disciplined policy of the new authorities and a part of their programme of regeneration. In republican Spain, most of the killing was the consequence of anarchy, the outcome of a national breakdown, and not the work of the state; even though some political parties in some cities abetted the enormities, and even

1. Maximiniano García Venero, *Falange*, p. 159; see also Jackson, p. 308.

2. This individual, José Antonio Baruela, later enrolled in the republican air force, killed many militiamen by bombing them before being found out and killed in Santander. Others like him escaped across the lines.

3. Letter from Gerald Brenan, 22 June 1961.

4. Letter from Melchor Ferrer, 7 August 1961.

though some of those responsible ultimately rose to positions of authority. Air raids also caused hatred and were responsible for many deaths, as reprisals. Equally, the voice of Queipo de Llano caused much fear and resulted in the death of many of his own partisans in republican territory. On both sides most of the killing was done by people under twenty-four years old.

The atrocities behind the 'Republican' and the 'Nationalist' lines at the beginning of the civil war were part of the same phenomenon whereby, in the years since 1931, Spanish politics had become sharpened to exclude compromise; this political extremism had fallen into violence, illegality and intolerance before July 1936. The manner in which the military rebellion was carried out, and in which the government replied to it in the first hours, caused a breakdown of restraint such as had not been seen in Europe since the Thirty Years War. On one side, schoolmasters were shot and *casas del pueblo* burned down; on the other, priests and churches. The psychological consequence of this breakdown was to cause each party in the dispute to become dominated by hatred and fear: 'Hatred distilled during years in the hearts of the dispossessed, hatred by the proud, little disposed to accept the "insolence" of the poor, hatred of counterposed ideologies, a kind of *odium theologicum* with which one sought to justify intolerance and fanaticism. One part of the country hated the other and feared it.'[1] Hence there were no opportunities for truces of compromise, and, apart from pessimists (such as Azaña) and a few neutrals (such as Madariaga), no understanding for the attitude of the enemy. There were innumerable instances of heroism, as well as of brutality. The two seem juxtaposed. Perhaps the case of General Batet, commander of the 6th Division at Burgos, is of special significance: he had arrested Companys for rebellion in 1934, and he himself was arrested, for refusing to rebel in 1936, by his own troops. He was then sixty-four and was shot, after seven months' imprisonment in 1937, with his equally innocent ADC. Queipo de Llano and Cabanellas vainly begged Franco for a pardon. Batet addressed the execution squadron thus: 'Soldiers, carry out your duty without allowing it to cause remorse tomorrow. As an act of discipline, you must fire, obeying the voice of the high command.

1. Azaña, *La revolución abortada*, in *Obras*, vol. III, p. 500.

Do it with all your heart. So your general asks you because you commit no crime in carrying out your superiors' orders.'[1] Batet 'knew how to die' like a Spaniard. Many did.

1. Quoted Cabanellas, vol. II, p. 873. Another case is that of General García Aldave, military governor of Alicante, executed also for being neutral, though this time by a left-wing execution picket.

17

The character of nationalist Spain

THE leadership of the nationalists was vested from 24 July onwards in a *junta* established at Burgos under the presidency of the bearded General Cabanellas, the commander at Saragossa. He was allotted this post by Mola to pacify, rather than to dignify, him. He was the senior general concerned, the only serving divisional general who joined the rebellion: Mola was technically a mere brigadier. Mola consulted the monarchists, Goicoechea and the Conde de Vallellano, before setting up the *junta* of Burgos, but not Franco,[1] nor the Carlist leadership, nor the falangists. Mola desired civilians to join, but no names were suggested which commanded general acceptance. Goicoechea urged Mola at all costs to form a *junta*: 'Even though it is a *junta* of colonels, form a *junta* immediately, my General'.[2] The *junta* was composed at first of the leaders of the rising on the Peninsula alone – Generals Mola, Saliquet, Ponte, and Dávila, together with Dávila's two aides, Colonels Montaner and Moreno Calderón. Franco became a member in early August. On the mainland, Franco remained for some time a myth. He was spoken of incessantly, but no one seemed to know where he was.[3] At the beginning of the rising, the nationalist communiqués were very confident. Franco was said to have already crossed to the mainland. Mola was announced at the gates of Madrid. But then the news became vague. People said that Franco was organizing to such a pitch of perfection that defeat would be impossible.[4] Mola, in fact, only established contact with Franco by dispatching to Morocco an emissary by air, Captain Angel Salas Larrazábal, on 21 July.[5]

1. Ruiz Vilaplana, p. 225.
2. Gil Robles, p. 729 fn. 74.
3. Ruiz Vilaplana, p. 45.
4. Lawrence Dundas, *Behind the Spanish Mask* (London, 1943), p. 56.
5. J. Salas, p. 73. No one knew what was going on. See Rafael Abella, *La vida cotidiana durante la guerra civil, I, La España nacional* (Barcelona, 1973), p. 27f., for photographs of newspapers announcing Azaña's arrest in Santander, the fall of Madrid, etc., in the first week of the war.

Mola inaugurated the *junta*. Amid the ringing of all the bells of Burgos in a deafening saraband, the foxy general shouted hoarsely from a balcony in the main square:

Spaniards! Citizens of Burgos! The government which was the wretched bastard of liberal and socialist concubinage is dead, killed by our valiant army. Spain, the true Spain, has laid the dragon low, and now it lies, writhing on its belly and biting the dust. I am now going to take up my position at the head of the troops and it will not be long before two banners – the sacred emblem of the cross, and our own glorious flag – are waving together in Madrid.[1]

The *junta* then held its first meeting, recognized the existence of two armies in rebel Spain, one of the north under Mola, one of the south under Franco (Morocco included), and adjourned to an inconspicuous table in the café of the Casino. Cabanellas and the two colonels thereafter formed a secretariat to give such administrative directions to nationalist Spain as were necessary. The business of government was made difficult by the absence both of civil servants and of all records. But the want of the former was made up for by the voluntary service of members of the middle class. A simple adherence to the well-tried rules of martial law compensated for the lack of records. Further, most judges, solicitors, and police simply carried on in rebel Spain under the rebel *junta* without change of routine, going back, if necessary, on all concessions to change made during the republic. In truth, Cabanellas and his *junta* were as much *rois fainéants* as were Giral, Azaña, and Companys. Mola really ruled north Spain from El Ferrol to Saragossa and from the Pyrenees to Avila. Franco controlled Morocco and the Canaries. Queipo de Llano ruled nationalist Andalusia. His nightly broadcasts, full of inconsequent ribaldries, of threats to kill the families of the 'reds' on the republican fleet, of boasts of the terrible sexual powers of the *Regulares*, and promises to kill 'ten Marxist *canaille*' for every rebel dead, made him famous throughout Spain. He gathered around him a coterie of falangists, Sevillian Carlists, bull-breeders and sherry producers, together with the bull-fighter 'El Algabeño', who became his ADC. In the north, Mola spoke occasionally on Navarre Radio, Castile Radio, or Saragossa Radio, reserving his special hatred for

1. Ruiz Vilaplana, p. 219.

Azaña, 'a monster who seems more the absurd invention of a doubly insane Frankenstein than the fruit of the love of woman. Azaña must be caged up so that special brain specialists can study perhaps the most interesting case of mental degeneration in history.'[1] The general strikes declared by all the workers' organizations had usually been broken by shooting the strike leaders and the UGT and CNT chiefs, as happened in Saragossa.[2] The republic's agrarian reform was allowed to stand if it had been carried out before February 1936; but everything done by the Popular Front was abolished, except in Estremadura where some *yunteros* who had received some grants in the spring of 1936 were permitted to hold on to their land for another year or two, eventually giving it back, however.[3]

Beneath the military government, the Falange was disorganized. José Antonio, Ledesma, Ruiz de Alda and most other known leaders were far away in republican gaols. Redondo was killed in the first days of the war in an ambush near the Guadarramas. The local leaders who survived, usually coming out of the confinement where they had passed the last weeks of the republic's life, had little national standing. For the next month, their old members acted more as a political police than a political party. Some members of the Falange, it is true, organized columns of volunteers, but they were undisciplined, more so than the Carlists, and they found themselves engaged in bureaucratic organization, looking after hospitals, carrying out arrests and executions, as well as fighting: they had little time for securing formal political places in the new order, alongside the generals.[4] Some falangists roamed the countryside with gangs of followers, shooting people of whom they disapproved, afterwards volunteering for one of the more established columns. These actions were deplored, more than is sometimes realized, but they were pardoned too. A German representative, Eberhard Messerschmidt, who travelled in nationalist Spain in August, complained that the Falange had no real aims or ideas. They seemed 'merely young people for whom it is good sport to play with firearms and round up communists and socialists'.[5] Patrols of falangists certainly prowled the streets of

1. *Diario de Navarra*, 16 August 1936.
2. Broué and Témime, pp. 90–91.
3. Malefakis, p. 386 fn. 76. Even the 1932–6 laws were eventually undone, in 1941.
4. García Venero, *Falange*, pp. 172–3.
5. *GD*, p. 88. See below, p. 418.

nationalist Spain giving the fascist salute with outstretched arm, stopping suspicious persons, demanding papers, and shouting '*¡Arriba España!*' at every opportunity. But after a while the mood changed. All the old political parties were discredited. The Carlists appealed only to the ultra-conservative. Many young *JAPistas* had played a part in the fighting on 18 July and now happily exchanged their green shirts for blue ones, joining the Falange in great numbers. Although invited by Mola to return to Spain, Gil Robles delegated his responsibilities to a *junta de mando de las milicias* and withdrew from politics. He 'authorized' his followers to join up in the army, as regular recruits and told them to avoid the forces of repression. On the whole they followed his instructions; but they had anticipated them too. He stayed in Portugal.[1] Lerroux, who escaped from Madrid in time, declared his backing for the rising, but withdrew too from active politics. The mass of the non-military middle class began to see the Falange as their way of identifying themselves with the 'Crusade'. These recruits soon greatly, then overwhelmingly, outnumbered the old survivors. Almost none of them knew anything of ideology. They knew the Falange was against the 'reds'; what else mattered? Thus, 2,000 people signed on for the Falange in Seville in twenty-four hours in July.[2]

In Seville, Queipo's dashing portrait was plastered up all over the city. Elsewhere, after a few days, photographs of Franco were seen everywhere. Shops sold patriotic emblems. Falange posters covered entire façades of buildings. 'The Falange calls you,' these cried, 'now or never. There is no middle course. With us or against us?' Carlist posters were also large, not only in Navarre. 'Our flag is the only flag,' they announced, 'the flag of Spain! Always the same!' The question of which flag the rebels should use was undecided. It seemed still the most important political issue. In Burgos, when Mola had arrived on 21 July, the flags on the balconies were all the red and gold ones of the monarchy: an effect achieved by Eugenio Vegas Latapié. When Mola left, however, he insisted that they were all taken away.[3]

The working class in nationalist Spain were cowed, and with reason. In a decree of 23 July, for example, Queipo included passive

1. He visited Spain and saw Mola in August.

2. Payne, *Falange*, p. 121n.

3. Gil Robles, p. 734 fn. 79.

resistance as a serious offence. Many who had previously been attached to some working-class party rallied to put on the *salvavida*, as Queipo called the blue shirt of the Falange, to secure protection. In several cases, such secret political malingerers were discovered and later punished, sometimes by death.[1] Others were sent to the front with shock battalions.

The nationalists needed, for the establishment of the new society, the support of the church. Except for the Basque church, this they obtained. Franco began to speak of God and the church in the same reverent tone which he had until then reserved for regiments and barracks.[2] Nevertheless, just as there were some priests and monks who supported the republic even though so many of their brothers were being killed, so there were churchmen who felt qualms at the cold-blooded murders in nationalist Spain committed in the name of Christ. For example, two fathers of the Heart of Mary in Seville complained to Queipo de Llano at the execution of so many innocent persons. The priest of the Andalusian village of Carmona was deprived of his living by the Falange for protesting at their executions.[3] There were also the two Franciscans shot in Burgos and Rioja.[4] When, later, Mola's forces entered Oyarzún (Guipúzcoa), an assistant priest, Eustaquio de Uriarte, was forced to write '*Viva España*' a thousand times to make up for a supposed previous lukewarm attitude towards the rising.[5]

Among the hierarchy, only the archbishop of Tarragona, Dr Vidal y Barraquer, and (to a lesser extent) Dr Mateo Múgica, the bishop of Vitoria (whose diocese was the southernmost Basque province), were reluctant to give full support to the 'movement'. Vidal y Barraquer escaped abroad from revolutionary Catalonia. The bishop of Vitoria supported the rising at the beginning but changed his mind, because of the shootings in Navarre. Eventually, he was to leave Spain altogether, officially in order to protect his life against attacks by falangists, really because he was unacceptable in nationalist terri-

1. Bahamonde, pp. 20–21.
2. See Iturralde, vol. II, pp. 55–70.
3. Bahamonde says he was shot. I find no confirmation of this. There were 700 executions in Carmona, according to *O Seculo*, the Portuguese newspaper, in August.
4. See above, p. 263, fn. 1.
5. Iturralde, p. 71.

tory.[1] The primate, Cardinal Gomá, archbishop of Toledo, was slow to give his full support to the movement, although the start of the war found him in Pamplona; it was not till the relief of Toledo (at the end of September) that he was fully forthcoming.[2] Monsignor Marcelino Olaechea, bishop of Pamplona, in a generous speech, did exclaim, at a ceremony in the city on 25 August, 'Enough blood, my children, enough bloody punishments, the blood flowing on the battle-fields is enough in itself!'[3] He also refused, on one occasion, to bless a column of falangists setting out for the front, on the grounds that they were going forth to kill their brother workers.[4] Meantime, the falangists began, as a party, to show a religious concern which had not marked their policy before. Falangists began automatically to attend mass, confession, and to take communion. Propagandists began to represent the ideal falangist as half-monk and half-warrior. The ideal female falangist was described as a combination of St Teresa and Isabella the Catholic.[5] Bishops, canons, and priests, meantime, daily implored the protection of the Virgin for the nationalist troops, begging her to arrange for their swift entry into Madrid.[6] Nationalist Spain seemed indeed to become one immense church, full of fantastic images and passions, battered flags, relics and middle-class communicants. Some priests actually fought with the nationalist forces. The priest of Zafra (Estremadura) was known

1. Iturralde, vol. II, p. 279. Dr Múgica was a monarchist and a conservative who had been almost as much a *bête noire* of the republic as was Cardinal Segura. In the first weeks of the war he supported the rising. He left Vitoria on 14 October. Before this, he had been put on a black list to be killed by a group of falangists, who were probably backed by the local nationalist authorities. See his memoir, *Imperativos de mi conciencia* (Buenos Aires, no date) and the criticisms of it in del Burgo, pp. 88–9.

2. Iturralde, vol. II, pp. 261–5.

3. The text is in Iturralde, vol. II, pp. 454–6. At the same moment, ten miles away on the slopes of the Pyrenees, fifty-six men were being shot, being confessed in groups of seven – except the last seven: '*Coño*,' said the chief of the Falange squadron charged with the execution, 'let them be killed without confession; I have not yet dined' (*op. cit.*, vol. I, p. 74).

4. *op. cit.*, vol. II, p. 299. Monsignor Olaechea admitted that he was 'not of the stuff of martyrs' and gave general support to the 'Crusade'.

5. Dundas, p. 48.

6. See almost any newspaper published in nationalist Spain in late July or August – especially those covering the Feast of St James (25 July) and the Assumption (15 August).

for brutality.[1] Other priests, such as the fanatical Father Fermín Yzurdiaga, from Pamplona, a member of the Falange since 1934, came into their own. Yzurdiaga was, for a time, chief of the propaganda department at nationalist headquarters.

The rebels needed money as much as they needed the church. Their leaders appealed for it on the radio, in public speeches, and in newspapers. Juan March had made credit available, through his foreign interests, and that helped with arms purchases abroad,[2] but much more was needed. Jewellery, precious stones, big and small donations of money and of goods poured into nationalist headquarters. The constant need for more explains the headiness of the speeches and propaganda: one might give to the Cid, to the memory of Ferdinand and Isabella, to the Virgin of the Pillar, even if one might be reluctant to help General Cabanellas or General Mola. Thus to Pamplona there came twenty thousand bottles of marmalade, a thousand woollen capes, thousands of boots, helmets, motor-cars, and lorries by the hundred, and one by one.[3] Middle-class backing for the *Movimiento salvador* was unquestionable. The cities of nationalist Spain reawoke, with the coming of war, after a sleep of centuries: bands, drums, flags, meetings, broadcast speeches sustained the rebels, as if the war were a continuous fiesta, in which the *Marxistas*, not the bulls, would be 'exterminated'. Loudspeakers played bloodthirsty songs such as '*El Novio de la Muerte*' or '*Los Voluntarios*'. Meantime, the local military governors had the power to requisition buses, taxis, private cars and even private houses. Most public buildings were taken over, including all headquarters of left-wing parties. In some places, contributions to the 'movement' were forced, in others bank accounts investigated. Wages and prices were controlled, usually at the level of February 1936 (far more favourable to employers than July), and one of Queipo's first decrees was to increase the working week in the copper mines of Río Tinto to forty-eight hours. Subscription lists were opened for contributions to the war. Queipo de Llano also ensured continuity of wine, olive and fruit exports, thereby pleasing the important Anglo-Andalusian community, and established good relations with Portuguese business too. There were less severe regulations in the zone of Mola than in that of Queipo but it was in the north that, in August, a special series of

1. Bahamonde, p. 77. 2. See below, p. 352. 3. Del Burgo, p. 34.

committees (Comisiones Provinciales de Clasificación) were set up to investigate the economic situation, this being later made into a public state body (the Comisión de Industria y Comercio). Such was the character of the new Spain in the first days of what was variously known as the Blue Age (*Era Azul*) after the falangist colours, and the Year I of the Movement.

18

The revolution in republican Spain

AFTER the end of the first wild rapture of victory over the rising, Madrid became bellicose as well as revolutionary. The streets were full of militiamen in blue *monos* – the boiler-suit which became a kind of uniform in the republican armies on the Madrid front. Rifles were carried (wasted, rather) as symbols of revolution. Many found this invigorating; Azaña did not. He saw this combination of 'frivolity and heroism, true battles and inoffensive parades' as 'menacing'. 'The population showed off a new uniform of negligence, dirt and rags;' he added 'the race seemed darker, because the young warriors let their beard grow, almost always a black beard, and the faces became dark too in the sun.'[1] Middle-class people threw off hats, ties, collars in an effort to appear proletarian in a city where, in the past, it had been an offence to walk about without a tie or jacket. Hundreds of working-class girls were seen in the streets collecting money, in particular for the Comintern's International Red Help. All the time, optimistic loudspeakers announced victories on all fronts; 'heroic' colonels and 'unconquered' commanders briefly made their bows in the republican press, then vanished into oblivion. Cafés, cinemas, and theatres were full; there were a few bull-fights, *alguacils* saluting with clenched fist, matadors wearing berets in place of three-cornered hats.[2]

The UGT really captured authority in Madrid, being responsible for food supply and essential services. The civil servants were in many cases unhappy about the cause for which they found themselves working, and lessened daily in importance, just as, indeed, Giral's government did itself. There were purges in the civil service, but many

1. Actually 'Lluch', in *La velada en Benicarló*, Azaña's socratic dialogue written in the course of the war: see *Obras*, vol. III, p. 394, and his article *La revolución abortada*, in vol. III, p. 500.

2. Mikhail Koltsov, *Diario de la guerra de España* (Paris, 1963), p. 51.

persons potentially disloyal remained. The UGT worked in comparative harmony with the CNT, its old enemy, though the building strike, the cause of their most recent enmity, was not settled until early August, and though there were some violent incidents: a young communist, Barzona, was murdered by the CNT in July.[1] A popular poster, however, showed two dead CNT and UGT militiamen with their blood mingling in a pool beneath. Yet the CNT, much expanded anyway in Madrid in early 1936, had many new recruits in these first days of the revolution: their daily press, such as *Castilla Libre*, *CNT*, and *Frente Libertario*, increased enormously.[2]

Behind the UGT, there loomed the communist party. The propaganda and tactical political skill of its leaders were the chief reason for communist successes, though the hostility between Largo Caballero's and Prieto's wings of the socialist party played a part.[3] Communist propaganda, directed by Jesús Hernández and Antonio Mije, concentrated on two themes – a moderate, non-revolutionary social policy, and the identification of the present resistance to the rising with the resistance of the Spanish people in 1808 to Napoleon. The communist newspaper, *Mundo Obrero*, spoke of the battle as exclusively motivated by the desire to defend the democratic republic. Quite different was *Claridad*, the socialist paper, which, about the same time, announced that 'the people were no longer fighting for the Spain of 16 July'.[4] The united socialist–communist youth led by Santiago Carrillo was, however, by now communized.[5] The divisions of the socialists and the intellectual difficulties facing the anarchists (they could not collectivize the state), opened the way to the increasing communist influence in the capital.

The revolution over which the UGT presided did not at first appear very far-reaching. There was expropriation (only) of those concerns or mansions whose owners were known to have sided with the nationalists. This meant, however, the forcing open of thousands

1. Tagüeña, p. 122.

2. Circulation of these three was 40,000, 40,000 and 35,000 a day in 1936.

3. The communists gained greatly in prestige also from their efficient organization of their so-called Fifth Regiment. See below, p. 322.

4. *Mundo Obrero*, 9 August; *Claridad*, 22 August; both quoted Payne, *Spanish Revolution*, p. 232.

5. See Ibarruri, p. 283.

of bank accounts and innumerable confiscations of residences, jewels, and articles of private wealth.[1]

The socialist–communist youth established itself in the Gran Peña, the well-known conservative club in the Gran Vía, the Ritz Hotel became a military hospital, the Palace Hotel a home for derelict children. Right-wing newspaper-offices were taken over by their left-wing rivals.[2] All industry connected with the supply of war material was also requisitioned, nominally by the ministry of war, in fact by committees of workers. Managers of other firms later asked for the formation of such committees, to share their responsibilities, and so perhaps avoid a worse fate. But, by August, only a third of the industry in Madrid was, even in this way, controlled by the state. Banks were not requisitioned, though they functioned under the supervision of the ministry of finance. There was a moratorium on debts, and a limitation on withdrawals from current accounts, but banking otherwise continued normally. The only other financial policy was a reduction by 50 per cent of all rents.[3] Apart from the nightly assassinations, and the consequent bodies lying in the Casa de Campo, the most obvious outward signs of revolution in Madrid were the collective restaurants organized by the trade unions. To these, was distributed the food which the unions seized on its arrival from the agricultural areas of the Levante. At these restaurants, a cheap but lavish dish of rice and potatoes, boiled with meat, was served in unlimited quantities.[4] There was little bread, a reflection of the rebels' capture of the wheat-growing plains of north Castile. At such collective restaurants, and increasingly in stores and other shops, vouchers issued by the unions were exchanged for a meal or an article. After a while, wages in Madrid began increasingly to be paid by these pieces of paper. Money began to die out, and traders only bought what they were certain to sell. This economic chaos was eventually ended by the Madrid municipality, which controlled the issue of vouchers, and supplied the families of militiamen in the Republic's defence forces,

1. According to *The General Cause*, p. 390, the confiscation of money and securities amounted (in all Spain throughout the war) to 330 million pesetas (£8 million) and of gold and jewels to 100 million pesetas (£2½ million).

2. The monarchist *A B C* was run as *A B C de Madrid* for the Republican Union, the Carlist *Siglo Futuro* was captured by the CNT, and so on.

3. *The Times*, 21 July 1936.

4. Barea, p. 124.

the unemployed, and the beggars of Madrid with the means for food. But many merchants lost money by accepting such promissory notes for which the equivalent in cash was never paid. Militiamen began to be paid 10 pesetas a day (raised in some cases from the factories in which they had been employed, in others paid by the government or the unions),[1] a sum which was paid to their dependants in the event of their deaths. Three times what soldiers received before the war, this payment made them the richest privates in Europe. It also damaged the economy. Meantime, large numbers of refugees thronged the foreign embassies in Madrid, particularly the Latin-American ones, and these diplomatic missions, in many cases, took houses to lodge their guests: sometimes, even, those who took refuge invented embassies for themselves. For example, a rich engineer, Alfonso Peña Boeuf, established an embassy of Paraguay, with three buildings holding three hundred persons, where there was none before.[2]

The towns and countryside of New Castile, republican Estremadura, and La Mancha were, like the capital, dominated by the UGT and by the socialist–communist youth. Anarchists increased as the weeks went by and there were interesting projects of collectivization throughout New Castile. The old municipal authorities often continued alongside the Popular Front committees. Expropriation of industries and of small private businesses was exceptional. The shops and businesses of, for example, Talavera de la Reina, in the Tagus valley, might be covered with notices announcing 'here one works collectively'. But this indicated an agreement to distribute profits between owner and workers, not workers' control. In the country, in La Mancha as in New Castile, the large estates were all confiscated, and were run by the local branch of the UGT. There were numerous collectives, established in accord with the anarchist resolutions at their May congress, but they were not established everywhere, nor at once, and, even in *pueblos* where collectives were set up, it was unusual for the collective to be the sole economic unit: private persons were allowed (chiefly due to the support of the UGT or the com-

1. The nationalists paid the usual 3 pesetas a day to their soldiers as before July.

2. Alfonso Peña Boeuf, *Memorias de un ingeniero politico* (Madrid, 1954), p. 166f. Peña Boeuf became minister of public works under Franco in 1938 after he had been exchanged with a republican in nationalist hands.

munists) to continue to farm, and to carry on business, and, theoretically at least, anyone who had joined a collective could withdraw from it if he desired, taking with him goods to the value of those which he had when he entered. Both UGT and CNT (here, as in most places of revolutionary Spain) were, however, agreed on the superiority of collectivization to the distribution of land, both on economic and on social grounds.[1]

To the south, at Ciudad Real, the chief town of La Mancha, only one concern, an electricity plant, had been expropriated. Market, shops, and cafés carried on as before. The Austrian sociologist, Franz Borkenau, visiting this area in August, noted that, at one collective farm, the cattle seemed in good health, and that the wheat was harvested on time, being stored in the chapel. Before collectivization, the labourers had lived in Ciudad Real, and had come out for harvesting. Now they were settled in the manorial building. Food, though not plentiful, was described as better than before. Before the war, these same labourers had wrecked machinery brought in by the landowner, since they supposed that he was trying to bring down wages. Now a threshing-machine from Bilbao was welcomed and admired.[2] The general rule for collectivization was that land should not be held beyond the amount which could be cultivated without hired labour. Distribution of food could be only through the local committee. In some places, three free litres of wine might be distributed a week; in others, it might be double.[3] In some places, collectivists and individualists could live peaceably side by side; in one *pueblo* there might be two cafés, one where the individual peasant-proprietors went, one for the workers of the collective.[4] In some places the church might become a warehouse, in others a place for tranquil reflection.[5]

The revolution which centred upon Barcelona in July 1936 differed from that in the centre of Spain in being primarily anarchist. With

1. See below, p. 553f., for a detailed study of the collectives.

2. Borkenau, p. 149.

3. It was three litres in Albalate de Cinca, five quarts in Calanda (Teruel).

4. This again is Calanda (Teruel).

5. The former was common, the latter at Mazaleón (Aragon) (Agustín Souchy, *Colectivizaciones,* Barcelona, 1937, p. 87). (These instances are given here of what was occurring from July onwards, but the process was not complete till much later in the year.)

a requisitioned radio station, eight daily newspapers, innumerable weeklies and periodicals dealing with every aspect of society and continuous public meetings, the anarchist movement had really captured Barcelona. In that city alone, there were now 350,000 anarchists. The real executive organ in Barcelona, and, therefore, of Catalonia, was the Anti-Fascist Militias Committee, which had been formed on 21 July and upon which, as has been seen, the FAI and CNT were the most influential forces. Several representatives of the *Generalidad* were usually present at the meetings of the committee.[1] This committee sought to re-establish public order, organize production and food supply and, at the same time, put together an army to defend Barcelona and 'liberate' Saragossa. The committee's meetings were usually at night, since the members were busy doing other things during the day. Meanwhile, all the great industrial plant of Barcelona had passed to the CNT: the CAMPSA, the Ford Iberia Motor Company, the public works company known as El Fomento de Obras y Construcciones – all were anarchist directed. So too were the main services – water, gas and electricity. Barcelona thus became a proletarian town in a way that Madrid never did. Expropriation was the rule – hotels, stores, banks and factories were either requisitioned or closed. Those requisitioned were run by committees of former technicians and workers.[2] Food distribution, milk-pasteurization, even small handicrafts, were all collectivized. Account books were examined by the new managers with fascination. What waste, what profits, what corruption they seemed to show! And then (as a workers' committee on the Barcelona metro remarked) 'we set out

1. Though, as has been seen, all the Barcelona parties were represented on it, in approximate proportion to strength, as they were on its economic council (constituted 10 August) and the committee of education. On the 'patrol controls', responsible for public order and detentions, the anarchists had the commander, José Asens, and 325 out of the 700 men enrolled: the others were from the Catalan parties, the POUM and the socialists or communists.

2. The majority of Barcelona factory owners were either shot or had fled. Those who remained were chiefly those who had a good name for labour relations. The Ford and General Motors works were seized in Barcelona, in early August. After a protest by the American government, the Spanish government undertook compensation. In general, the republic tried not to offend other countries by requisitioning foreign concerns, and the CNT issued a list of eighty-seven British firms which were to be left untouched (Peirats, vol. I, p. 177).

on the great adventure!'[1] Since the large National Labour development building had been taken over by the FAI and CNT as headquarters, it seemed that nothing could go wrong.

Most industries were back at work by ten days after the rising. Public services were maintained by the anarchist unions, the electricity workers assuring the continuity of supply by guarding the dams and hydro-electric plants of the Lower Pyrenees, which provided Barcelona's power. Barcelona's sixty tram lines were run by their 6,500 anarchist workers and were soon running much as they were before the rising. Even so, an extraordinary variety of solutions was reached. In some places, the old wages, with numerous differentials, were maintained, in others a new uniform wage was established. The tramworkers of Barcelona sought a compromise, reducing the number of *different* wages to four. Differentials continued, however, for technicians and specialized workers and while, in prosperous factories, workers were probably better paid than before, in poor ones, they were often as badly paid as before. If a factory had plenty of stock and cash on hand at the time of the revolution, it would pay its way; if not, it soon declined. It seemed more difficult than people had assumed to organize a factory on anarchist lines if it required raw materials from sources outside anarchist control. If the raw materials came from abroad (and the cotton used in Barcelona factories mostly came from Egypt), the factories had to negotiate with the socialist dock workers and even with businessmen. Thus compromise, even centralization, began even in the first days of the revolution. Low stocks of raw materials and low funds also opened the way to state intervention. The Catalan government tried to regularize matters by, first, recognizing a workers' control committee for each large factory and then nominating an official delegate to sit on each such committee; the delegate was, however, to begin with, usually himself a worker who did little. Anarchist theory had not envisaged a situation in which they would gain power in some factories, but not destroy the state or their political opponents. The dictates of war

1. CNT–FAI bulletin no. 3 of 10 August, p. iv. See also Frank Mintz, *L'Autogestion dans l'Espagne révolutionnaire* (Paris, 1970); Josep María Bricall, *Historia económica de la Generalitat*, vol. I (Barcelona, 1970); Albert Pérez Baro, *Trenta mesos de collectivisme a Catalunya* (Barcelona, 1970).

also played a part: on 19 July, García Oliver instructed one of his anarchist comrades, Eugenio Vallejo, to create an armament industry in a city where no previous factories had made arms. The plan evidently required, from the start, collaboration between anarchists and other political movements, even though the chemical and metallurgical factories which were to make the arms were in anarchist hands. Here, too, the Catalan government intervened. (By October 1936, the *Generalidad* controlled fifty such factories in Barcelona and some 75 outside it.) Innumerable questions had also to be resolved with technical advice: could a lipstick factory really be reorganized to make shell cases? In addition, the anarchists had to collaborate with the banks, which were controlled by the UGT[1] – in practice that meant the communists. Thus, from the start of the war, the supporters of the concept of government – from the Catalan Esquerra to republicans, socialists and communists – had control of credit, even in the anarchist stronghold of Barcelona. Because of all these difficulties, the textile industry in Barcelona soon only worked three days a week. In order to overcome this, a national effort, organized by a vigorous government, was desirable. Thus, faced with an unprecedented situation, the anarchists of Catalonia improvised in the industries, of which they had become suddenly the masters, several different temporary solutions; though some worked adequately, the failure of those that did not pointed to unforeseen weaknesses in the anarchist 'Idea'.

A characteristic example of what happened was the collectivization of the Barcelona cinemas: all cinemas were grouped in a single enterprise, directed by a committee of seventeen men, of whom two were elected by a general assembly of workers, the fifteen others by workers of the different professional groups within the industry. Members of the committee received their normal salary but dropped their normal work, devoting themselves to administration. A three-quarters majority of the general assembly of workers was necessary to secure a dismissal. A month and a half of annual holidays were proclaimed, including two weeks in winter. During illness, a worker would get

1. The UGT bank clerks said (to the POUM actually), 'You can shoot us if you like but we will not give you the keys' (Manuel Benavides, *Guerra y revolución en Cataluña*, Mexico, 1946, p. 211).

full pay, and permanent invalids, 75 per cent of their old salary. Profits were devoted to building a school and a clinic.[1]

The revolution in Barcelona had other shapes too. As in Madrid, no one was to be seen in middle-class clothes. To wear a tie was to risk detention. *Solidaridad Obrera* even denounced the Russian foreign minister Litvinov as a bourgeois because he wore a hat. (The anarchist Hatters Union registered a protest.) Almost all the fifty-eight churches of Barcelona save the cathedral (preserved by order of the *Generalidad*) were burned. Some were ruined, others merely damaged. Much valuable petrol was wasted in an attempt to burn Gaudí's unfinished '*Sagrada Familia*', which was, alas, made of cement. By early August, whatever excitement there had been earlier at such scenes had died, and the destruction was carefully limited by the fire brigade. Church schools were shut: 'The revolutionary will of the people has suppressed schools of confessional tendency. Now is the turn of the new school, based on rationalist principles of work and human fraternity.'[2]

After the murder of Desiderio Trillas, president of the UGT dockers – presumably killed by anarchists – the FAI and CNT joined with other parties in denouncing the crime. Together, they threatened death to any who carried out indiscriminate shootings or looting: 'the Barcelona underworld is disgracing the revolution'. The FAI ordered its members to be vigilant so as to 'Smash the riff-raff! If we do not, the crooks will smash the revolution by dishonouring it.'[3] Several prominent anarchists were even shot, such as José Cárdenas, of the construction workers of Barcelona, and Fernández, president of the food syndicate, for having failed to 'overcome a moment of confusion and weakness' and killed a man and a woman who years before had denounced them to the police.[4] But at night, on the road out of Barcelona towards the Tibidabo mountain, shots continued to be heard. 'Fascists' continued to be arrested. A well-known extreme Left independent deputy and lawyer, Angel Samblancat, had, in the

1. Peirats, vol. I, pp. 364–9, gives decrees of collectivization. Cinemas and theatres were both open in early August, both collectivized, after a short gap.

2. Peirats, vol. I, p. 200.

3. CNT–FAI bulletin, 25 July. See also *Solidaridad Obrera*, 30 July and 31 July, qu. Payne, *The Spanish Revolution*, p. 227.

4. Peirats, vol. I, p. 182.

first days of the revolution, invaded the Palace of Justice at the head of the CNT–FAI militia, thrown out of the window legal documents, contracts, leases, crucifixes, and killed many lawyers and judges. Soon afterwards, however, Samblancat installed a revolutionary committee of justice, whose first act was to recall the officials and secretaries of the court.

*

The anarchists' domination in Catalonia placed them in an uneasy relationship with the Catalan government in what Azaña was to describe as 'a plot to annul the Spanish state'. The advance of Barcelona's militias, anarchists at their head, into Aragon, might be represented as a responsible defence of the central government. But there was still no discussion about it with the ministry of war in Madrid. There were other changes: given the weakness of the government in Madrid, the *Generalidad* was able to take over, without protest, the customs and the frontier guards, the railways and the docks, security at hydro-electric plants, the fortress of Montjuich and the Bank of Spain – even the right to issue money and pardons. All these powers, under the Catalan statute, belonged to Spain. Now, under the pretext that they were in danger of being usurped by the FAI, the *Generalidad* took them over. The University of Barcelona was rechristened the University of Catalonia. The *Generalidad*, in Azaña's words, 'took advantage of the military rebellion to finish with the state's power in Catalonia and then sought to explain everything by saying that the state did not exist'.[1] One Esquerra politician, José Tarradellas, thought that, since Catalonia had successfully defended herself against the military rising, she could wash her hands of Spain.[2]

On 9 August, a mass anarchist meeting was held at the Olympia Theatre in Barcelona to protest against the conscription by the Madrid government of the 1933 and 1934 classes of reserves to serve under regular officers: 'We cannot be uniformed soldiers. We want to be militiamen of liberty. To the front, certainly. But to the barracks

1. See Azaña's conversation in September 1937 with Carlos Pi y Súñer on this matter in Azaña, vol. IV, p. 796; and with Comorera in October 1937, *op. cit.*, p. 821.

2. Azaña, vol. IV, p. 707.

as soldiers not subject to the popular forces, certainly not!'[1] In protesting against the central government, the anarchists were thus joining hands with traditional Catalan separatism. But the *Generalidad*, fearing the consequences of legalized political armies, caught up in a maze of conflicting arguments, supported the idea of keeping the regular army, with officers named from above, and their political faith obscured. Companys was supported, on this, by the new united socialist party of Catalonia (PSUC). Though a socialist, Juan Comorera, became secretary-general of this party, the communists, by their superior efficiency, ruthlessness, and skill, dominated it. The PSUC even affiliated itself to the Comintern. Comorera, a blacksmith's son who had emigrated to Argentina in the twenties and returned in the thirties, had been Councillor for agriculture in the *Generalidad* in 1934 and had helped move the *rabassaires* to the Left in that year. He soon became a communist and even, within months, a member of the central committee of the Spanish communist party, along with another ex-socialist PSUC leader, Rafael Vidiella.[2] The Barcelona UGT, also under communist influence, increased its membership from 12,000 on 19 July to 35,000 at the end of the month, partly because of the help afforded by a party, or union, card to gain food, partly because of the urge towards association in revolutionary circumstances.

The PSUC favoured the 'army system' rather than that of the militia, since they had organized followers, and since their chief hope of influence was by infiltration into the officially recognized government. No party was in truth more interested in bringing political interests into the army, but they planned to do that from above. Formally, however, communist policy in Barcelona, as in Madrid, was that nothing should be done to jeopardize the winning of the war, while 'political adjustments between comrades' should await victory. The PSUC thus gave full support to the *Generalidad* over several reforms – the 15 per cent rise in wages, the return by the pawnshops of all articles pledged for less than 200 pesetas, and a forty-hour week.

1. CNT–FAI bulletin, 10 August. The document continues by recalling that the people in the French Revolution defied the world, but Napoleon's uniformed army led to Waterloo.

2. Bolloten, p. 113. Vidiella had once been an anarchist, being the CNT representative on the communist–anarchist–Esquerra discussions in 1925.

(Malraux in *L'Espoir* has a vivid account of the noise in Barcelona caused by the return, and sudden use, of the many sewing-machines previously in pawnshops.) The PSUC also made economic claims on behalf of the widows of dead fighters. All their attitudes were reformist, and conciliatory, in the sense that they were intended to improve conditions within the society that existed; the new society could wait.

On 31 July, Companys elevated himself from being formally president of the *Generalidad* – that is, the Catalan government – to become 'president of Catalonia'. That was one more step towards Catalan sovereignty, one more again upon which he did not consult the government in Madrid. Three members of the PSUC (Comorera, Vidiella, Ruiz) were asked to join the reconstituted *Generalidad* under Juan Casanovas, previously the president of the Catalan parliament. The anarchists threatened to leave the Anti-Fascist Militias Committee if the PSUC were to enter the government. The PSUC men withdrew and the *Generalidad* for the time remained composed of nine Esquerra members, and one each from the *rabassaires* and the more right-wing Catalan Action. 'I hand over the government to you,' Companys said grandly to Casanovas; who replied 'You hand over nothing, since there is nothing.'[1] The government tried to disarm anarchist militiamen in the 'patrol controls': an action which was furiously resisted by the CNT. 'Comrades,' the FAI, meantime, generously appealed on 5 August to the PSUC, 'together we have beaten the bloody beasts of fascist militarism. Let us be worthy of our victory by maintaining our unity of action until the final triumph. Long live the Revolutionary and Anti-Fascist Alliance.' Powerless in itself, the Catalan government, during the next weeks, by its endorsement of the Anti-Fascist Militias Committee, continued to encroach substantially on the authority of the government in Madrid. When, some weeks later, Prieto (by then a minister in Madrid) visited Barcelona, Colonel Díaz Sandino, Catalan counsellor of defence, greeted him as if he were the minister of a foreign power.[2]

Standing apart in Catalonia from anarchists, Esquerra and PSUC, were the POUM, the anti-Stalinist revolutionaries led by Catalan ex-communists. Their numbers also grew greatly. Some joined this party believing that it represented a mean between the indiscipline

1. Azaña, vol. IV, p. 702. 2. Azaña, vol. IV, p. 704.

of the anarchists and the strictness of the PSUC. Foreigners in Barcelona joined the POUM in the romantic supposition that it embodied a magnificent Utopian aspiration. Franz Borkenau noted the atmosphere of political enthusiasm among these émigrés, who clearly enjoyed the adventure of war and had complete faith in 'absolute success'. The POUM, with new headquarters in the Hotel Falcón in the Rambla, concentrated on pushing its comparatively unfamiliar name before the public, painting its initials in large letters on motor-cars and buses, and agitating for 'a government of workers only'. Though one of the founders, Maurín, was presumed (falsely) dead in nationalist Spain, the other leaders, who were all ex-communists from the twenties – Nin, Gorkin, Andrade, Gironella – all spoke frequently. The POUM youth movement, the JCI (Juventud Comunista Ibérica), seemed the most radical of all the Left's private armies and called continually for the 'formation of soviets', while ruthlessly killing 'enemies of the people'.

Catalonia as a whole and republican Aragon reflected the events in Barcelona. A political committee was formed in all *pueblos*. Power, as elsewhere, lay in the hands of the strongest party, regardless of formal representation. Thus the POUM predominated in the province of Lérida; the CNT elsewhere.[1] Usually, a red flag, decorated with a hammer and sickle, would be hung outside the town hall, indicating the magnetic attraction of Russia to all the proletarian parties, not only to the communists. The railways and public services were run by committees of the UGT and CNT. In most places, all local professional people and craftsmen had to take orders from the committee. Most churches were burned. In some places, particularly where the burning did not occur till August, and especially in the middle-class resorts along the Costa Brava, regret was marked. Borkenau observed sad women carrying to the pyres prayer-books, images, statues, and other talismans, which had been less an object of religious value than a part of familiar daily life. Only children seemed pleased, as they cut off the noses of statues before throwing them to the flames. The houses and land of the murdered or escaped bourgeoisie would be appropriated by the municipality. As else-

1. Sometimes, as in the village of L'Hospitalet, the CNT would take their hostility to the Esquerra and Catalan nationalist parties to the point of placing notices banning Catalan. (Jaume Miravitlles in *La Flèche*, 24 February 1939.)

where, the ruthlessness of the revolutionaries was tempered by streaks of generosity. For example, the French poet of the air, Antoine de Saint-Exupéry, then a correspondent for *L'Intransigeant*, succeeded in persuading a village revolutionary committee to spare the life of a monk who had been hunted in the woods. This secured, the anarchists shook hands excitedly with each other, and also with the monk, congratulating him on his escape.[1]

There were few large estates in Catalonia, and even anarchists were uncertain as to what should be done about the lands taken over. The eventual solution – not reached in most of Catalonia until the autumn – arranged that half the expropriated land should be run by the municipality, while the other half was divided among the poorer peasants. The Popular Front committee of the *pueblo* would receive half the rents, while half would be remitted. Revolution was less than complete in Catalonia, since both the Esquerra and the UGT could support the smallholders. Still, there was even there a lack of foresight in the peasants' treatment of bourgeois property. In Sariñena, a town between Lérida and Saragossa, where some members of the middle class (including the vet) had been spared, Borkenau watched the destruction of all the documents relating to rural property. A bonfire was set ablaze in the main square, the flames rising higher than the roof of the church, young anarchists throwing on new material with triumphant gestures.[2]

An amazing range of social and economic experiment was being tested in the countryside in Catalonia and Aragon as in Castile. In many places, for example, money was no longer in distribution. A careful account of what occurred at Alcora (Castellón) was given by an acute German observer, Hans Erich Kaminski:

Everyone can get what he needs. From whom? From the committee, of course. But it is impossible to provision 5,000 people from a single distribution point. Hence there are stores where, as before, one can satisfy one's requirements, but these are mere distribution centres. They belong to the whole village, and their former owners no longer make a profit. Payment is made not with money, but with coupons. Even the barber shaves in exchange for coupons, which are issued by the committee. The principle whereby each inhabitant shall receive goods according to his needs is only

1. Richard Rumbold, *The Winged Life* (London, 1953), p. 146.
2. Borkenau, pp. 93–4.

imperfectly realized, for it is postulated that everyone has the same needs ... Every family and every person living alone has received a card. This is punched daily at the place of work; hence no one can avoid working, for on the basis of these cards coupons are distributed. But the great flaw in the system is that, owing to the lack of any other measure of value, it has become necessary again to have recourse to money to put a value on labour performed. Everyone – the worker, the doctor, the businessman – receives coupons to the value of 5 pesetas for each working day. One part of the coupon bears the inscription 'bread', of which each coupon will purchase a kilo; another part represents a sum of money. But these coupons cannot be regarded as bank notes, since they can only be exchanged for goods and that only in a limited degree ... All the money of Alcora, about 100,000 pesetas, is in [the hands] of the committee. The committee exchanges the products of the community for other goods that are lacking, but what it cannot secure by exchange, it purchases. Money, however, is retained only as a makeshift ...

Nevertheless, money could be had from the committee if a peasant needed it to visit, say, a girl in the next village or a specialist doctor.[1] In all such places, an important role was played by the 'justice committees': in Lérida, a good example, this was composed by a third POUM, a third PSUC–UGT, a third CNT–FAI – the POUM doing so well because of their old strength in that town. The president and prosecutor were both chimney-sweeps.[2]

Down the coast at Valencia, the Speaker of the Cortes, Diego Martínez Barrio, who had fled there after failing to form a government in Madrid on 18–19 July, had organized a *junta* to control the five provinces of the Levante, which was more ineffective before the local committee than the *Generalidad* was before the Anti-Fascist Militias Committee. Martínez Barrio was even forced to live in the country, not in Valencia at all, after the surrender of the rebel officers in the barracks on 31 July. That success gave authority to the local CNT–UGT committee presided over by a left-wing officer belonging to the old UMRA, Colonel Ernesto Arín. Real power reposed in the hands of a revolutionary lieutenant, José Benedito, a member of

1. Hans Erich Kaminski, *Ceux de Barcelone* (Paris, 1937), pp. 118–22. Cf. also *Colectividades de Castilla* (Madrid, 1937); Agustín Souchy, *Entre los campesinos de Aragón* (Valencia, 1937), p. 92.

2. Broué and Témime, p. 123n. Manuel Buenacasa (*L'Espagne livrée*, reprinted Paris, 1971) gives a bloodcurdling account.

the Valencian autonomist Left party, and the chairman of the local defence committee. Yet, though the CNT was strong, dominating the port, and the transport and the building workers, Valencia was still more bourgeois than Barcelona, with many fewer expropriations. The anarchists of Valencia had mostly been *treintistas*, and the countryside had voted strongly for the CEDA in February. The UGT was influential among white-collar workers. The republicans, with a following among the lower middle classes and the richer peasants of the Valencian *huerta*, were divided between those who saw, in present circumstances, a chance for a Valencian separatist movement and the supporters of Azaña and Giral. The minute communist party in Valencia alone gave any support to the government delegation, headed by Martínez Barrio. It later gained support among the rich Valencian peasants, through its championship of the distribution of expropriated land to individual peasants against the anarchist plan of collectivization. Elsewhere in the Levante, anarchists and socialists disputed power in different villages. Alcoy, an old bastion of libertarianism, was anarchist, along with Jativa, Elche and Sagunto; while Alcira and Elda were socialist. At Castellón, Alicante, and Gandia, the two movements divided the authority.

In Andalusia, the revolution was anarchist in inspiration, without the focus which Barcelona provided for the revolution of Catalonia.[1] In most *pueblos*, old municipal councils merged with new committees. Control of roads and public services was shared by officials and militiamen appointed by the committee. Each town acted on its own responsibility. There was also hostility between the anarchist leaders, of cities such as Málaga and those of small *pueblos*. The former desired to intervene in the *pueblos*, and were resisted by the local leaders, who regarded that as an attack on their own rights.[2] The socialist agricultural union, the FNTT, despite their numbers, were pushed aside by the extremists: 'We in the socialist party were overwhelmed. What could we do? The people who took over thought only of violence. We were the strongest party here and yet we were helpless. We hardly ever met, to tell the truth. Those who took power had so little political consciousness that they robbed smallholders of the

1. See Ronald Fraser, *In Hiding*, pp. 133–4; see also Ronald Fraser, *The Pueblo* (London, 1973).

2. Julian Pitt-Rivers, *People of the Sierra* (London, 1954), pp. 18–19.

little they had.'[1] In many places, private property was abolished, along with the payment of debts to shopkeepers. In Castro del Río, near Córdoba (for years one of the great centres of anarchism in Spain),[2] a régime was set up comparable to that of the anabaptists of Münster of 1530, all private exchange of goods being banned, the village bar closed, the inhabitants realizing the long-desired abolition of coffee. 'They did not want to get the good living of those whom they had expropriated,' noted Borkenau, 'but to get rid of their luxuries.'[3] In many places in this region, the anarchists had taken the initiative against the authorities and instead, afterwards, of speaking of their resistance to the rebellion, would name this time that 'when the people rose against the *señoritos*'.[4] The great estates in this region continued often to be worked by their former labourers, who received no pay at all but were fed from the village store, according to their needs. (Some later complained that the new village committees behaved just as those in authority always did: 'they ate the ham'.)[5] Between the *pueblos*, an uncertain condition prevailed. The land was dotted with places where the rebel civil guard had abandoned their garrisons and, retreating to hill-tops, monasteries, and other easily defensible points, held out indefinitely, living as highwaymen by robbing from the neighbourhood. The longest surviving encampment of this kind was established by Captain Cortés of the civil guard in the monastery of Santa María de la Cabeza in the mountains of Córdoba. There were similar encampments of anarchist 'outlaws' inside rebel Andalusia, preying on the land and reverting to the banditry of which anarchism had been once in part a politicization.

The generally anarchist pattern of revolution in Andalusia was varied in Jaén, which had had a strong UGT following for several years, and at Almería, where the dock workers were chiefly communists. In Jaén, there was little social change. The civil guard was sent away, but the local committees organized their own militia, who patrolled the countryside in pairs, as the civil guard had done too. The committee usually took over from the landlord, and continued

1. Fraser, *The Pueblo*, p. 56.
2. See Díaz del Moral, p. 252ff.
3. Borkenau, p. 167.
4. Juan Martínez Alier, *La estabilidad del latifundismo* (Paris, 1968), p. 139.
5. Martínez Alier, p. 140.

to receive the landlord's half share from sharecroppers as discontented as before. In the straggling, stagnant town of Andújar, for example, though five of the middle class were killed, their land was left unexpropriated. The UGT left the administration of the large estates nearby to the municipality, with the result that the labourers worked the same hours as before for the same starvation wage. Committees running these villages were sometimes elected by Popular Assembly, sometimes named by the Popular Front parties.

The revolution in Málaga, controlled by the CNT and FAI, was characterized by its arbitrary inefficiency. Almost cut off from the rest of republican Spain (because of the nationalist hold on Granada, to the north-east), living under daily threat of aerial attack, with constant rumours that land attacks were about to be made upon it, Málaga was tense: 'They are going to destroy you, Málaga. Your vices have condemned you,' said an anarchist, watching the burning churches from a village outside.[1] Antonio Fernández Vega, the civil governor, 'a mere signing machine' before the victorious workers, seemed 'a pale Girondin, trembling before Jacobins in comparison with whom ours [it was the French journalist Louis Delaprée who spoke] were mere children'.[2] Eventually, the committee of public safety was recognized officially from Madrid and its president, a socialist schoolmaster Francisco Rodríguez, was named civil governor. This committee did not impose its authority on the province: Motril, Vélez Málaga and Ronda ran their own affairs under anarchist direction, the old municipal councils being brushed aside. But, when the anarchist militia occupied Puente Genil in Córdoba province, it was announced that, after the war, it would be annexed to Málaga. So provincial loyalty must have existed. In Ronda 'one did not collectivize, one did not share out, one socialized everything'.[3] In Málaga itself, meantime, a military command was set up by a group of sergeants, who proclaimed themselves colonels; and then a real colonel, Romero Bassart, of the *Regulares*, who had escaped from Morocco, became their chairman.[4]

1. Brenan, *Personal Record*, p. 289.
2. Louis Delaprée, *Mort en Espagne* (Paris, 1937), p. 70.
3. *España Libre*, 19 July 1947, qu. Lorenzo, p. 198.
4. R. Salas Larrazábal, vol. I, p. 288.

The republican territory along the north coast of Spain was cut off from Madrid and Barcelona by the columns operating under General Mola. Here three societies came into being, one centring on Bilbao and San Sebastián; one on Santander; and one on Gijón. In the former towns, and throughout the provinces of Vizcaya and Guipúzcoa, the Basque nationalists ensured the continuance of a middle-class social order. Both Bilbao and San Sebastián, and the territory around them, were controlled by committees of defence, but, on these, the Basque nationalists had a majority. Only the anarchists (with strength among the fishermen and builders) were inclined to make a stand against the Basques, who regarded the working-class parties with distrust. Hence, in the new Basque motorized police corps, no members of the left-wing revolutionary parties were permitted, though there were persons who might have preferred being on the side of the rebels. About five hundred persons were apparently murdered in the Basque provinces, apart from Colonel Carrasco and some officers and falangists who took part in the rising. The anarchists were mainly responsible. The Basque leader Irujo pointed out that, for several days, he and his colleagues were almost prisoners of the CNT who, in fact, had taken the lead in resisting the rising.[1] But, after the start of August, there was little persecution of the upper or middle class.[2] Priests went free and church services continued. Only two churches had been burned, in San Sebastián. Expropriation of capitalists' goods occurred only when they had taken part in the rebellion. The goods of such persons were handed over to a state board on which employees were represented, but which they did not control.

The only measures of social change in the Basque provinces were a decree forbidding anyone to be a director of more than one company (a blow at the Basque millionaires, though less at the bourgeoisie), the cut in rents by 50 per cent which obtained elsewhere in republican Spain, and the institution of a new public assistance board for those in need. The Vizcaya arms industry – the Eibar gun plants, the small-arms factories at Guernica and Durango, the Bilbao grenade and mortar factories – were naturally taken over by the Bilbao defence committee. The Basque nationalists also gained control of

1. Lizarra, p. 62.

2. Though 3,000 political prisoners were held in prison ships and fortresses, among them many women and children.

the financial structure of their provinces. New boards were formed to control the Basque banks.

Despite this moderation, the Basques came into conflict with the church.[1] The bishops of Vitoria and Pamplona, in a pastoral letter broadcast on 6 August, condemned the adhesion of the Basque catholics to the republican side.[2] The Basque priests, under the vicar-general of Bilbao, consulted together, and advised the Basque political leaders to continue to support the republic. The reasons for this advice were that there was no proof that the pastoral letter was authentic, since no copies of it had arrived; that the pastoral letter had not been promulgated with due formality, being merely broadcast; that there were suggestions that the bishop of Vitoria did not have full freedom of action; that the bishops could not know the truth of what was going on in the provinces of Guipúzcoa and Vizcaya; finally, that a change of attitude by the Basque nationalists would bring untold miseries upon many people and upon the church. Thereafter, the Basque priests continued in their defiance, remaining with their flocks, whose spiritual needs they continued to serve. They intervened on behalf of persons in danger from left-wing violence, especially their brethren in Asturias and Santander. The Basque catholic political leaders continued to support the republic and afterwards shared in its government. Their relations with Madrid were never good, distance confusing the problems of ideology. They justified their attitude generally by arguing that the four conditions named by St Thomas Aquinas as sanctioning a rebellion against the state did not exist, and that recent papal encyclicals had suggested that rebellion was never legal.[3]

Along the coast in Asturias, the situation was complicated by the resistance of the civil guard in the Simancas barracks in Gijón under Colonel Pinilla and by Aranda's defence of Oviedo. During the siege,

1. *Le Clergé basque*, p. 25f.

2. Text in Montero, pp. 682–7. The background of this letter is discussed in Iturralde, vol. II, pp. 302 and 328. For Múgica, see above, p. 287. Múgica later confirmed that he had signed the letter freely (see his letter to the *Gaceta del Norte*, of 25 July 1937, qu. Iturralde, vol. II, pp. 326–8). Later still he excused himself, since he did not know the facts (*Imperativos de mi conciencia*).

3. See the interview between Manuel Irujo, the Basque who later joined the republican government, and Prince Hubertus von Loewenstein (Hubertus von Loewenstein, *A Catholic in Republican Spain*, London, 1937, pp. 90–104).

however, relations between the UGT, CNT, and communist party in Gijón became closer even than those achieved in 1934. At the beginning, power was divided between rival authorities: the war committee of Gijón, presided over by Segundo Blanco of the CNT, and the Popular Front committee of Sama, led first by González Peña, the old socialist leader of 1934, and, afterwards, by another socialist, Amador Fernández. These authorities eventually united. Belarmino Tomás, a socialist deputy, became governor of the province of Asturias, with governmental powers delegated to him, as they had been, less effectively, to Martínez Barrio in Valencia. The important coal mines of Asturias were controlled by a council composed of a director, representing the state, certain technicians, a deputy director and secretary chosen by the Asturian mines councillor, and three workers. This director could not act without the workers' agreement.[1]

The siege operations against Aranda were still directed by the political leaders. Gijón was constantly shelled by the nationalist cruiser, the *Almirante Cervera*. Its people were poor, puritan, and confident of the future. A huge poster on the hoardings displayed a red Spain and, in the centre, a lighthouse giving a beam stretching over Europe. The legend ran: 'Spain will be a light to the world. *Viva* the Popular Front of Asturias!' At night, loudspeakers would bellow to empty streets false good news from faraway battlefields. Gijón, perched on the edge of the unfriendly Atlantic, gave the impression of being a lonely soviet all of its own.[2] As for Santander, that city was a far-flung outpost of the UGT, as its ancient position as Castile's only port might have suggested. Its defence committee, presided over by a certain Juan Ruiz, also acted almost independently from the central government in Madrid.

From the start of the civil war, the military tactics of these northern

1. See Jellinek (p. 300) and Koltsov (p. 127), describing visits to Gijón, a little later; see also C. Lorenzo, p. 172; and Fernando Solano Palacio, *La tragedia del norte* (Barcelona, 1938).

2. Jellinek, p. 415. Written from a Marxist point of view, this publication of the Left Book Club is invaluable for its detailed social and economic analysis of life in the republic. Jellinek was correspondent of the *Manchester Guardian* in Spain.

regions remaining faithful to the republic were hampered by separate political direction. The only thing they had in common was, after a few weeks of war, a lack of food. There was beer, cigarettes, cheese, and some fish, but little to eat. The symbolic figure of north Spain in late 1936 was the native of Gijón known as 'the man the cats are afraid of'. He could pounce on a cat from a distance of twenty yards. That night, there would be chicken on the menu for dinner.[1]

As for the old borders of republican Spain, the flight or murder of many carabineers caused the management of frontiers to fall into the hands of local committees. Some customs were run by the old officials under control of new committees. Thus, despite the formal demands of the Catalan government, the three main control points of the Catalan border with France were in the hands of the CNT – in particular the anarchist mayor of Puigcerdá, 'the lame man of Málaga', Antonio Martín, ran his local stretch of frontier as if it were private land, until his murder at communist hands, in April 1937.[2]

*

President Azaña, who appealed publicly on Radio Nacional on 23 July to Spaniards to rally behind the republic, not the revolution, later made a bitter condemnation of the 'rrrevolutionaries', as he spoke of them, through 'Garcés', one of the characters in his famous imaginary dialogue, *La velada en Benicarló*: 'Where was national solidarity? I saw it nowhere. The house began to burn in the roof; and the neighbours, instead of helping to put out the fire, gave themselves up to sacking the building, stealing whatever they could. One of the most miserable aspects of these events was the general dislocation, the assault on the state.'[3] The trouble was, though, that the house was collapsing, and Azaña, with Casares Quiroga, had been over-optimistic guardians of it in the weeks before. For the rest of the war, Azaña behaved as a passive man of letters, even if still President,

1. Thus Jellinek, in conversation, Geneva, 1960.

2. 'El cojo de Málaga' deserves a careful investigation. See below, p. 653. Equally independent were Ruca at Port Bou, and André Lerghaf and Sagaró at Le Perthus.

3. *La velada en Benicarló*, p. 426 (in *Obras*, vol. III); the speech of 23 July is in the same book, pp. 607–9.

cultivating, often over-obtrusively, the serenity of Montaigne in his château, while the countryside was aflame: a very different man from the haughty, sceptical, assertive orator of 1931.[1]

1. Azaña's head of military household in 1936, Major Casado, who would play a decisive part in the last weeks of the civil war (see below, p. 881) and who broadly shared Azaña's view of politics, in the end blamed Azaña most directly for the outbreak of the civil war; 'to decry, offend and depreciate the army . . . in order to gain the applause of the masses' was mad and provocative (see Casado, *Así cayó Madrid*, Madrid, 1968, p. 157).

19

The first campaign – the battles of Guipúzcoa, Aragon and the Guadarramas – the Alcázar at Toledo – a consideration of the balance of forces in July 1936 – arms from abroad?

By 22 July, meantime, there was war in Spain rather than rebellion, or resistance to it. Everywhere, the exultation which had followed the defeat (or the victory) of the rising gave way to a fear that armies were on the march against the *fête révolutionnaire* of the Left or of the Right. The militias of the unions and parties, even in the smallest towns, began to think of themselves as soldiers as well as street-fighters, alongside the police, assault guards and civil guard or regular army. Similarly, the generals organized 'columns' after the model of what they had been used to in the Moroccan Wars, to complete, as they hoped and supposed, the destruction of the revolution. Thus, as early as 19 July, Mola sent his adjutant, the Andalusian colonel, García Escámez, south with 1,000 men, mainly volunteers, two companies of *requetés* and one of falangists, to relieve Guadalajara. This he might have accomplished, if he had not halted to secure the victory of the rising at Logroño, where the military governor had been unwilling to commit himself. Mola had vehicles, petrol and men, but little ammunition: if he were to win, it had to be fast. As it was, this first striking-force of the war reached a point twenty miles from Guadalajara, before finding it had fallen to combined militias and regular troops from Madrid. So García Escámez withdrew to the north side of the Somosierra Pass, across the Guadarrama, the most easterly of the northern gates to Madrid. Here, the railway tunnel had been held for the nationalists by a group of young Madrid monarchists under the brothers Miralles, since 19 July.[1] Against them, republican forces which had earlier taken Guadalajara were now advancing.

1. Manuel Aznar, *Historia militar de la guerra de España* (Madrid, 1940), pp. 113–14. These young monarchists included the constitutionalist leader of later days, Joaquín Satrústegui.

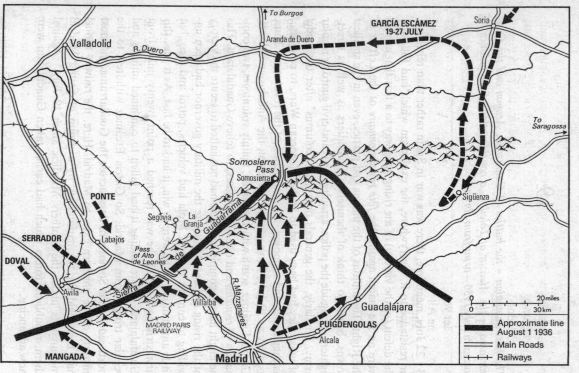

10. The fighting in the Guadarramas, July–August 1936

To the north-west of Madrid, at midnight on 21 July, a mixed column, perhaps two or three hundred strong, of regular soldiers and falangists, under Colonel Serrador (an ex-plotter of 1932) set out from Valladolid, also for Madrid via the Guadarrama, amid scenes of wild enthusiasm. It made for the western pass known as the Alto de León. This force was accompanied by Onésimo Redondo, the founder of the JONS at Valladolid, recently freed from gaol at Avila, and another young falangist leader later of importance, José Antonio Girón. The Alto de León had been occupied by a militia force from Madrid. The rebels realized the importance of holding their enemy beyond that point. Both these two passes, critical for the defence of Madrid, were won by the rebels on 22 July and 25 July respectively. Thereafter, shortage of ammunition caused Mola to halt. In the next few days, this shortage seemed desperate, and only a special consignment from Franco enabled him to hold on. At the same time, Mola had also dispatched three more columns from Pamplona under Colonels Beorlegui, Latorre, and Cayuela, *requetés*, falangists, and regular troops (the volunteers predominating) in the direction of the Basque provinces. These troops amounted to 3,430 men,[1] leaving 'in an atmosphere of fiesta more than of war'.

One thousand two hundred Carlists also went down to Saragossa from Pamplona. Their presence enabled the nationalists to undertake several punitive expeditions against surrounding Aragonese towns. No general offensive against Barcelona was contemplated. But two columns, on the other hand, set out from Barcelona to 'liberate' Saragossa. They were followed by others all along the front facing west. Perhaps 20,000 men left Barcelona for the 'front' in the first days of the war, some by train, for the railway-lines were soon in

1. Aznar, p. 128: *Cruzada*, XIII, pp. 529–30. The Beorlegui column of 2,000 men was: three companies of the (regular) regiment of América; a section of assault guards; two 'centurias' of *requetés*; four companies of *requetés*; two *tercios* of Falange; the machine-gun section (regular); the mortar section; and one 105 battery. Cayuela had 830 men, and Latorre had 600. During the first week of fighting, eleven columns were organized in Pamplona ranging between 200 and 2,000 in size. Seven left for Guipúzcoa, four for Madrid (De la Cierva, in Carr, *The Republic*, p. 196). Who were these Vendéans of the Spanish revolution? They were the peasant proprietors of Navarre, the sons of the bourgeoisie of Pamplona and Estella, and no doubt too of the working class of the region. Cf. too del Burgo, p. 23, and Luis Redondo and Juan de Zavala, p. 417.

good use, under control of the workers.[1] The first column of 2,500 anarchists was led by Durruti, to whom the success of the revolution had brought self-confidence and dreams of grandeur. This column set out on 24 July with such excitement that they were two hours away from Barcelona before discovering that they had forgotten their supplies. Thus it was that (as a propaganda pamphlet put it) '"The Free Man" was launched into the struggle against the fascist Hyena in Saragossa'. Durruti had as military advisers one of the heroes of 1934, Major Pérez Farras, and an ex-sergeant, José Manzana.[2] All the columns which set out from Barcelona so bravely had a political component: anarchist; Catalan or Esquerra; POUM; socialist and communist, usually combined. Famous anarchists of the past twenty years, renowned for astonishing crimes, came now to the front, in both senses of the word, as commanders. In addition to Durruti, there were, for instance, his old comrades of the *solidarios*: Domingo Ascaso (brother of the recently dead Francisco), Gregorio Jover, García Vivancos, and Antonio Ortiz, while García Oliver remained in Barcelona as the animator of all the columns. Another of the *solidarios*, Ricardo Sanz, arranged training for anarchist militiamen at the Pedralbes barracks.[3] The columns included regular soldiers as well: perhaps 2,000 out of the total 20,000 who went up into Aragon from Catalonia at this heady time.

By the beginning of August, the advanced positions of the republic were at Tardienta (the headquarters of 1,500 men of a PSUC column) and Siétamo, taken by the loyal Barbastro garrison, both near Huesca. The main POUM column of 2,000 men had their headquarters at Leciñena, to the north-east of Saragossa in the Sierra Alcubierre. Along the Ebro, at Osera and Pina, the anarchists were established under Durruti. At Montalbán, in the south, the carpenter, Ortiz, commanded a heterogeneous group, with anarchists predominating. Durruti's column, increased to about 6,000, was the most

1. Peirats says that 150,000 volunteered (vol. II, p. 135). Surely an exaggeration. Sanz has 20,000 (p. 83), and see also Colonel Martínez Bande, *La invasión de Aragón* (Madrid, 1970), p. 276. Who were they? Anarchists to begin with, afterwards other parties. Probably a very large number put their names down, fewer went, fewer still stayed.

2. Paz, pp. 331 and 340. The organization of the column is there described. Basically, the unit was the 'centuria' of a hundred men.

3. For Ricardo Sanz, see his *Los que fuimos a Madrid* (Toulouse, 1969).

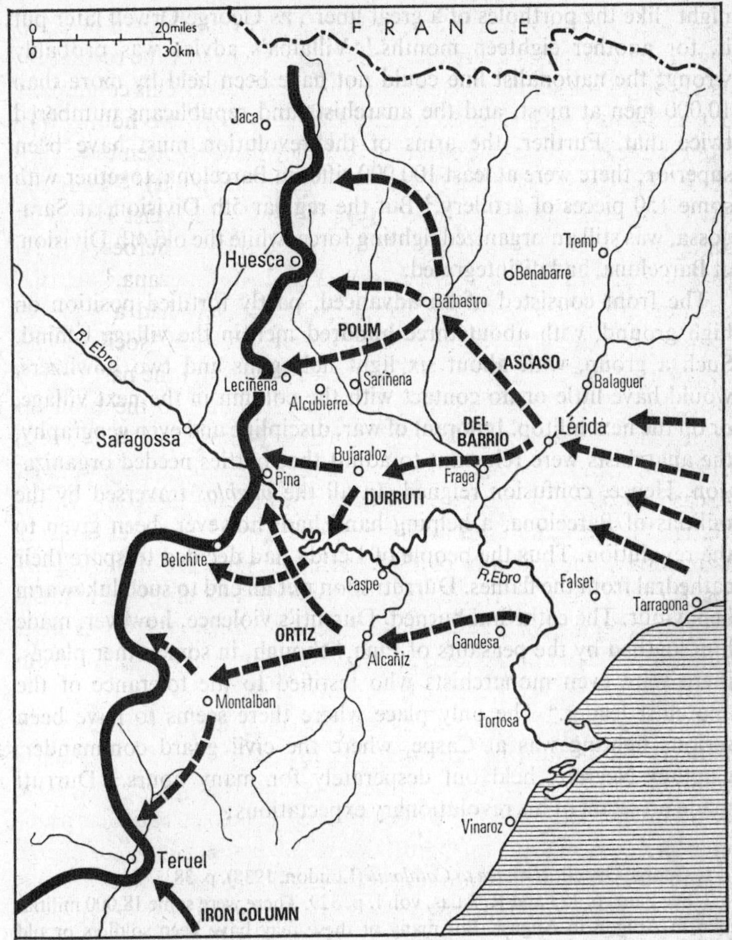

11. The Catalan invasion of Aragon, July–August 1936

formidable of these forces, having advanced through Caspe, Fraga, Peñalba to Bujaraloz, within striking distance of Saragossa. Here, Colonel Villalba, commander of the Barbastro garrison and now in official, if vague, command of the whole front, persuaded Durruti to halt for fear of being cut off; there, within reach of Saragossa, the column remained, the lights of the town twinkling tantalizingly at night 'like the portholes of a great liner', as George Orwell later put it, for another eighteen months.[1] Villalba's advice was probably wrong; the nationalist line could not have been held by more than 10,000 men at most, and the anarchists and republicans numbered twice that. Further, the arms of the revolution must have been superior; there were at least 100,000 rifles in Barcelona, together with some 150 pieces of artillery.[2] But the regular 5th Division, at Saragossa, was still an organized fighting force, while the old 4th Division, at Barcelona, had disintegrated.

The front consisted of an advanced, partly fortified position on high ground, with about three hundred men in the village behind. Such a group, with about six light field-guns and two howitzers, would have little or no contact with the column in the next village, or on the next hilltop. Ignorant of war, discipline and even geography, the anarchists were reluctant to admit that battles needed organization. Hence, confusion reigned. In all the *pueblos* traversed by the militias of Barcelona, a helping hand had, however, been given to the revolution. Thus the people of Lérida had decided to spare their cathedral from the flames. Durruti soon put an end to such lukewarm behaviour. The cathedral burned. Durruti's violence, however, made him loathed by the peasants of Pina,[3] though, in some other places, there were even monarchists who testified to the tolerance of the anarchist leader.[4] The only place where there seems to have been serious fighting was at Caspe, where the civil guard commander, Captain Negrete, held out desperately for many hours.[5] Durruti made no secret of his revolutionary expectations:

1. George Orwell, *Homage to Catalonia* (London, 1938), p. 38.

2. See Sanz, p. 123 and R. Salas, vol. I, p. 329. There were some 18,000 militiamen in Aragon in August. But many of these may have been soldiers or old soldiers. The nationalists in Saragossa probably had 4,000 men in the army, some 18 companies of civil guards and carabineers, some 1,500 Carlists, about 2,000 falangists, and perhaps 1,000 other volunteers in the first week. By 22 August, there were some 14,000 men on the nationalist side on the front from the Pyrenees to Teruel (Martínez Bande, p. 98).

3. Borkenau, p. 109.

4. The question is discussed by Jackson, p. 292; Paz, p. 337; and C. Lorenzo, pp. 146–7, and I received contrasting opinions in Saragossa.

5. For a ferocious picture, see Sebastián Cirac Estopañán, *Héroes y mártires de Caspe* (Saragossa, 1939).

It is possible [he told the Russian journalist Koltsov, at his headquarters in an abandoned country house between Bujaraloz and Pina] that only a hundred of us will survive, but, with that hundred, we shall enter Saragossa, beat fascism and proclaim libertarian communism ... I will be the first to enter Saragossa; I will proclaim there the free commune. We shall subordinate ourselves neither at Madrid nor Barcelona, neither to Azaña nor Companys. If they wish, they can live in peace with us; if not, we shall go to Madrid ... We shall show *you*, bolsheviks, how to make a revolution.[1]

The structure of the command was vague: theoretically under the Councillor of defence in the Catalan government, Colonel Díaz Sandino, the real military organizer in Barcelona was García Oliver. Colonel Villalba's authority did not run far. The commanders of columns attended, or were represented at, the 'Delegació del Front d'Aragó', together with some regular officers, but this was not effective. There were no reports to Madrid; tactical direction was nil.

Opposite, the nationalists were installed in similar positions, although their officers ensured military discipline. The *requetés* and falangists, headed by Jesús Muro, the local *jefe territorial*, were possessed of a fury as great as that of their opponents. They were further angered when a solitary republican bomber dropped a bomb which struck the famous effigy of the Virgin of the Pillar at Saragossa, but did not explode.[2] It was not simply a matter of religious outrage: the Virgin had been solemnly named captain-general of the city. Aviation played a modest part in these skirmishes: an occasional republican Fokker, Nieuport or Breguet clashed with nationalist machines of the same type, scarcely affecting the fighting but causing alarm.

In the centre of Spain, a different drama was under way. Faced with Mola's thrusts from over the Sierras, the republic and the revolution were defended by the remains of the regular army and by the militias, uneasily yoked together, and directed, equally uneasily, by a war ministry staffed by radical officers, assisted by some others of neutral or even secretly disloyal character. A large number of officers remained formally loyal to the republic, including numerous generals, and two commanders of divisions (one other remained

1. Koltsov, p. 29. See this interview analysed in Paz, pp. 362–3.

2. I saw this bomb, unexploded still, in the fender of Fal Conde's library in Seville in 1960.

in the republican zone to be dismissed). Of the officers loyal to the republic, probably half of them rationalized the accident of being in republican territory at the time of the rising into loyalty to the government. Others had become men of the Left, socialists, republicans, or even communists. Some were anarchist sympathizers. The politization of Spain had certainly affected the army. Among those who probably supported the government by chance rather than conviction was the easy-going General Miaja, commander of the infantry brigade in Madrid. Others felt bound to support the republic because of their oath to it, such as Major Vicente Rojo. Colonel Hernández Sarabia, a republican who had been chief of Azaña's military household in 1932, worked as general co-ordinator to the war minister, General Castelló, with Major Menéndez as his adjutant. Due to Castelló's melancholia at the turn of events,[1] Hernández Sarabia became in effect the war minister (he obtained the formal appointment in early August). General Riquelme, who had taken part in a famous conspiracy against Primo de Rivera in 1926, was appointed to general field command at Madrid, and attempted to gain a governmental hold over the militia forces by appointing loyal regular officers to lead them or at least advise their leaders. The two brothers Galán, Francisco and José María, lieutenants in the civil guard and carabineers respectively, both communists, brothers of the 'hero of Jaca', led the militia north to the pass at Somosierra, alongside anarchist columns led by prominent men of the CNT in Madrid, such as Cipriano Mera, or Teodoro Mora.

A further force advanced in the direction of Avila, to cut off that town from the pass at Alto de León. This was led by Colonel Mangada – the eccentric poet-officer (vegetarian, nudist and theosophist), well known in the army for his radicalism. Though he captured several *pueblos* where the civil guard had declared for the nationalists, Mangada did not get further than Navalperal, twelve miles short of his objective, since, though popular, he feared to lose communication with Madrid. His failure to advance upon the then poorly defended city of St Teresa was explained by the nationalists as being due to the appearance of the saint herself who allegedly (but surely untypically)

1. He soon gave up, and Hernández Sarabia (on 6 August) succeeded him. His melancholy was impelled by the death of his brother José at the hands of the anarchists in Estremadura (Sánchez del Arco, p. 65).

misled Mangada by saying that Avila was 'full of armed men'. Nevertheless, Mangada's advance was enough to cause his men to carry him in triumphal procession to the Puerta del Sol in Madrid, and to elect him to the rank of general. He was opposed by a force led brutally if incompetently by Major Lisardo Doval, and Doval's failure gave Mangada a reputation he scarcely deserved.[1]

In the meantime, the battles of the Alto de León and Somosierra, the first real conflicts of the civil war, were fought with extraordinary ferocity. The republic should have had the upper hand, for though the numbers of men must have been about equal, they had Madrid's three artillery regiments, and their closeness to Madrid made for logistic superiority. They possessed some 100,000 rifles and probably had an advantage in the air. The government had released by decree all soldiers from their duty to obey their officers (helping to leave the rebel officers without troops) and had then called for the formation, under regular officers, of twenty volunteer battalions which would include ex-soldiers, and which would fight alongside the militia. But difficulties between military commanders' and political leaders' interests were incessant. Thus the anarchists abandoned a post which controlled the reservoirs and water of Madrid, because of differences with the republican command. Only by chance was this not discovered.[2]

On both sides, prisoners were shot.[3] The aerial combats were slight, as in Aragon, and, indeed, it seemed little use having so many fighters as the republic had, if there were few enemy fighters to attack, and few bombers capable of exerting much effect on the battle on the ground.[4] The small number of nationalist aircraft had a definitely demoralizing effect. How many died in these days will never be known; for no one knows how many or who set out to fight: certainly not more than 5,000. Judging from the large numbers of regular

1. Antonio Cordón, *Trayectoria* (Paris, 1971), p. 242. The farouche character of Mangada's famous column, with an army of hangers-on from the cafés of Madrid (including prostitutes), caused it to seem a force out of the middle ages more than the twentieth century. His wife persistently importuned the ministry in Madrid for pens, waterproofs, even whistles.

2. Azaña, vol. III, p. 489.

3. Tagüeña, p. 128. Doctors on both sides had difficulties in preventing even the wounded from being shot on their stretchers.

4. See Hidalgo de Cisneros, p. 299.

officers who died on the republican side, captains of the civil guard or the assault guard, the militia losses must have been high, due to the confusion between militia groups and regulars, and also to the naïve courage of the militiamen. (The falangist, Onésimo Redondo, was killed by militiamen who had penetrated behind the lines, in an ambush at the village of Labajos on the Madrid high road.) On the republican side, Colonel Castilló, in command at Alto de León, was either killed by his own men or killed himself after his son had been killed in action. But it was not easy for an officer to lead a body of men who insisted on a show of hands before an attack. Both Captain Condés and Luis Cuenca, the men concerned in the death of Calvo Sotelo, found their own deaths here, with many others of their generation in the assault guards and in the socialist youth movement.

Like the armies which had gone out from Barcelona, the Madrid militiamen (probably in August 40,000 in all), were organized in columns of approximately three hundred men each. These assumed distinctive names, many of them evocative of old revolutions and far-off street-battles, such as 'Commune de Paris' or 'October No. 1'. Others took the name of contemporary political leaders, such as La Pasionaria. There were several battalions known as the Steel Battalion, so-called because it was assumed to be the picked corps of the union of political parties which had formed it. Columns organized by the war ministry were led by regular officers, but militia battalions were not. The most famous of the republican militia forces in the Sierras was that organized by the communist party, the Fifth Regiment.[1]

This force was based upon the communist militia, the MAOC; but others joined as a result of a recruiting drive led by La Pasionaria, the first headquarters being the Salesian convent of Francos Rodríguez in Madrid.[2] By the end of July, 1,000 members of 'the Fifth Regiment' had gone to the front.[3] It had its own reserves, system of

1. For this, see the books by Castro Delgado, Lister, *Nuestra guerra* (Paris, 1966), and Modesto; also the study of the Fifth Regiment by E. Comín Colomer, *El quinto regimiento* (Madrid, 1973); and Martínez Bande, *La ofensiva sobre Segovia* (Madrid, 1972), p. 18f.

2. Ibarruri, p. 285; Castro Delgado, p. 275.

3. Martínez Bande (*loc. cit.*, p. 19 fn. 5) estimates that the total in the Fifth Regiment eventually reached 22,250. *International Press Correspondence* (Inpreccor), vol. XVII, No. 6, 6 February 1937. But see R. Salas in Carr, *The*

supplies, and artillery. It also adopted the use of political commissars employed by the Red Army in the Russian Civil War, with the aim of making clear to the soldiers what they were fighting for. In theory, in the Fifth Regiment, as in the Red Army, commissars were attached to commanders at all levels down to that of company commander. Also, in theory, the counter-signature of commissars was necessary for every order. But neither of these stipulations was fulfilled. The first commander was a young communist named Enrique Castro Delgado.[1] But the moving spirits were the communist deputy for Cádiz, Daniel Ortega, and the Italian communist, Vittorio Vidali ('Carlos Contreras'). The latter was an indefatigable, ruthless and imaginative professional revolutionary. While, for instance, he early gained a reputation for shooting cowards, he also made the Fifth Regiment march in step by chartering the band of the Madrid UGT, under the direction of the composer Oropesa.[2] Under Carlos's guidance, certain famous military leaders appeared – notably Enrique Lister, once a quarryman, and Juan Modesto, an ex-woodcutter who had been an organizer of the MAOC since 1933 and a corporal with native troops in Morocco. Lister had been taken from Galicia while a boy to Cuba, had learnt politics on the building-sites of Havana, in the days of the dictator Machado, had joined the communists in an Asturian gaol in 1931, had spent three years in Moscow, following courses, and working on the underground, and had returned the previous September. Probably the men who really trained the Fifth

---

Republic, p. 187, where a figure of 15,000 in all is suggested for those *trained* by the Fifth Regiment. Other sources are Modesto, pp. 25–6 and Lister, p. 40. Salas (vol. I, pp. 222–3) argued that the Fifth Regiment's maximum was 3,500 (in October–November).

1. A romantic account of the organization is in Castro Delgado, p. 275f.

2. Lister, p. 67. Vidali, son of a workman of Monfalcone near Trieste, had been one of the animators of the 'Arditi rossi' of Trieste in the years of near civil war in Italy, emigrated to the USA and then to Mexico, went to a party school in Moscow, undertook a mission in Germany and had apparently been in Spain since 1934 as organizer of 'International Red Help'. Castro Delgado (p. 293) describes 'Carlos' as almost a monster, but there is no doubt of his competence. He came accompanied by his wife Tina Modotti, an Italian communist with whom he had been entangled in the mysterious affair of the murder of the Cuban communist Julio Antonio Mella in 1929. See P. Spriano, *Storia del partito comunista italiano* (Turin, 1970), vol. III, p. 86.

Regiment were a Portuguese exile, Captain Oliviera, and 'Captain Benito' Sánchez, one of the officers who had been condemned for rebellion after the events of 1934. Another communist leader to appear (though not in the Fifth Regiment) during the battles of the Sierras was Valentín González, 'El Campesino' (the peasant), being notorious for his beard, volubility and physical strength. His enemies said that his name, as well as his beard, was given to him by the communists to attract the peasants to the communist party. He himself said that he had been known by this sobriquet ever since the time when, aged sixteen, he had blown up four members of the civil guard in a lonely Estremadura sentry-box and then taken to the hills. Later he had fought in Morocco – on both sides, according to himself. He was a brilliant guerrilla leader, if probably not suited to his subsequent command of a brigade and a division.

The most celebrated incident of this period in the Spanish war occurred at Toledo. From Madrid, the minister of education, the minister of war, and General Riquelme had been furiously telephoning the 58-year-old infantry colonel, Moscardó, commander of the nationalist garrison still holding out in the Alcázar, in an attempt to persuade him to surrender. Finally, on 23 July, Cándido Cabello, a republican barrister in Toledo, telephoned Moscardó to say that if Moscardó did not surrender the Alcázar within ten minutes, he would shoot Luis Moscardó, the Colonel's 24-year-old son, whom he had captured that morning. 'So that you can see that's true, he will speak to you,' added Cabello. 'What is happening, my boy?' asked the colonel. 'Nothing,' answered the son, 'they say they will shoot me if the Alcázar does not surrender.' 'If it be true,' replied Moscardó, 'commend your soul to God, shout *Viva España*, and die like a hero. Good-bye my son, a last kiss.' 'Good-bye father,' answered Luis, 'a very big kiss.' Cabello came back on to the telephone, and Moscardó announced that the period of grace was unnecessary. 'The Alcázar will never surrender,' he remarked, replacing the receiver. Luis Moscardó was not, however, shot there and then, but was executed with other prisoners in front of the Tránsito synagogue on 23 August, in reprisal for an air raid.[1] This heroic

1. Moscardó did not know this till late September. The telephone call seems to have taken place despite some assertions to the contrary. The fact that the son was not killed for some weeks makes the story seem a little less dramatic.

tale became a legend in nationalist Spain. Subsequently, the accusation has been made that the telephone had been already cut by 23 July, and that no one recorded the telephone conversation at the time. Some exchange of this sort, nevertheless, assuredly occurred.

The Alcázar remained besieged. Though food was scarce, there was water and ammunition. The provisions were shortly supplemented by a raid on a nearby granary which brought back two thousand sacks of wheat. Horsemeat (there had been 177 horses in the Alcázar at the start of the siege) and bread were the basic diet in the Alcázar. As the days wore on, Moscardó became less the real leader in the siege than the colonel of the local civil guard, Pedro Romero Bassart. But Moscardó remained the heroic symbol. The number of attackers varied between 1,000 and 5,000, of whom many were 'tourists' of war, who drove out with their wives or girl friends from Madrid for an afternoon's sniping.[1] As for the hostages taken in with the defenders at the beginning, they were never heard of again, and all fifty of them must be supposed to have shared the fate of Luis Moscardó, on the other side of the lines.

While the Alcázar at Toledo continued to hold out, the Loyola barracks in San Sebastián surrendered to the Basques on 27 July, and the civil guard of Albacete were overwhelmed on 25 July. The officers

On the telephone call and the Alcázar generally, there is a large literature. See Herbert Southworth, *El mito*, p. 53f., for a fascinating inquiry, and also Antonio Vilanova, *La defensa del Alcázar de Toledo* (Mexico, 1963). Luis Quintanilla, *Los rehenes del Alcázar de Toledo* (Paris, 1967); and Cecil Eby, *The Siege of the Alcázar*. Cf. too Vila San Juan, p. 83f. De la Cierva, *Historia ilustrada*, I, p. 455, records a story of a man who heard the telephone call taking place. The telephone call between the Moscardós is one of the most famous incidents of the civil war. Equally pathetic was the fate of the son of General Cruz Boullosa, under-secretary for war from 14 May until 22 July. On 19 July, Cruz Boullosa discovered that his son, a cadet on holiday from the Alcázar, had made his way to Toledo to rally to the rising. The father secured the return of the son to Madrid, but the latter rallied to the rising in the Montaña barracks. The general telephoned Colonel Serra in the barracks and pleaded with him to let him go. The colonel said that that was up to the cadet in question and the son decided to remain with his comrades in the barracks. He was killed in the assault. (Cf. García Venero, *Madrid, julio 1936*, p. 383). Cruz Boullosa's brother was a general in the civil guard in Valladolid, and he himself was dismissed as disloyal in 1938. The interesting character in both these stories is, of course, the telephone.

1. See e.g. Lister, *Nuestra guerra*, p. 58.

in Valencia were also stormed in their barracks on 31 July, after a rising by NCOs and soldiers against them. Those who were not killed in the assault were tried and, in many cases, executed. The remaining points of nationalist resistance within republican territory were, therefore, Oviedo, the Simancas barracks at Gijón, the Alcázar, and one or two isolated spots in Andalusia.

At the same time, the dividing-line in Spain itself was being altered, in the south and in the north and north-east. The as yet few members of the Army of Africa, legionaries and *Regulares*, who had been transported across the Straits of Gibraltar, were enough to enlarge substantially the area dominated by General Queipo de Llano from Seville. Huelva, the whole of the southern coast from that port up to the Portuguese border, the once rich though now neglected land between Seville, Cádiz and Algeciras, and that between Seville and Córdoba, passed into nationalist hands, after a series of rapid marches by officers and men training in the Moroccan Wars.[1] Instead, therefore, of merely controlling in Andalusia a few cities where the rising had been successful, the nationalists held a compact territory striking a wound into the heart of the revolutionary south. As yet, Granada and several towns on the way to it were still beleaguered. But their relief did not seem distant. In all such towns or villages as were captured, bloody reprisals were enacted as atonement for the atrocities of the preceding days.

Between Barcelona and Madrid, the two main republican centres and fronts, the battle-line was uncertain. The column which had captured Guadalajara and Alcalá advanced to capture the cathedral city of Sigüenza. But further advances were precluded, as on the nationalist side, by a shortage of ammunition. From Valencia, a militia column drove north-west towards Teruel, the most southerly rebel town of Aragon. The civil guard, which formed part of that force, deserted to the nationalists as soon as they reached the front. Though Teruel was surrounded on three sides, and Major Aguado, its nationalist commander, was killed, no progress was made towards its capture. Here, as elsewhere, revolution occupied the militiamen as much as war. The confusion of the region was increased by the release of the common criminals of the Valencian penal establishment

1. Huelva had fallen to the nationalists after a delayed rising by the civil guard, whose officers had first refused to lead an expedition against Seville.

of San Miguel de los Reyes. These chiefly joined the CNT's Iron Battalion. One of the released convicts (aged thirty-four at the time of release, after eleven years of gaol) described how he and his comrades 'changed the mode of life in the villages through which we passed, annihilating the brutal political bosses who had robbed and tormented the peasants and placing their wealth in the hands of the only ones who know how to create it . . .' He added how the bourgeoisie (still in control of events, by his definition) plotted the Iron Battalion's later destruction, since 'they can be injured . . . by the wildly irrepressible desires we carry in our hearts to be free like eagles on the highest mountain peaks, like the lion in the struggle'.[1]

Yet, while rhetoric might inspire fighting hearts, the railways were as important in carrying men, and provisions, from cities to fronts and from one city to another. Behind the republican lines, the CNT strove to keep as many trains as before the war – a waste of resources, since there were fewer travellers and different needs.

Between these main battlefields, along the line of division soon referred to as a 'front', nearly 2,000 miles long, there were many gaps whence it was easy, from either side, to cross into the other Spain. Many refugees crossed secretly in these early weeks, from one 'zone' to another. Many 'loyal' civil guards joined their friends thus, others escaped by boat. Thus gradually the passions in Spain matured, or became debased, into a regular war.

*

The war which now began was in many respects a class war. But as usual in such circumstances, that meant in particular that the middle class was divided. There were innumerable instances of fathers and sons or brothers being on different sides. General Pozas, head of the civil guard and republican minister of the interior, had a brother who shortly became ADC to General Mola; Colonel Romero Bassart, military adviser to the militia in Málaga, had a brother who really led the defence of the Alcázar at Toledo; the brother of the commander of the republican fleet, Admiral Buiza, soon died in Andalusia fighting for the Legion. Hidalgo de Cisneros, soon to be the commander of the air force in the republic, also had a brother with

1. *Nosotros* (*Journal of the Iron Column*, 12–13, 15–17 March 1937); qu. Bolloten, p. 264.

Franco. Four Pérez Salas brothers were to be, in 1936, fighting in the republican army, a fifth was with the Carlists in Beorlegui's column. Franco himself, as has been said, sentenced a first cousin to be shot. (Another first cousin, Captain Hermenegildo Franco Salgado, and a brother of his own ADC, was the captain of the *Libertad*; he was murdered by his sailors at El Ferrol.) Carlos Baráibar, editor of *Claridad*, and Largo Caballero's adviser on military matters, had a brother who was an official in Franco's engineers. That list could be endlessly extended. The bourgeoisie certainly knew what the class struggle signified. Not only the bourgeoisie: Largo Caballero's misery at the (false) news that his favourite son had been shot on the nationalist side affected his judgement. Even Durruti had two brothers who were falangists. 'Almost everyone had someone on the other side,' remarked an old supporter of the CEDA, who fought ultimately for the Right, adding sourly though perhaps not accurately, 'the immense majority didn't want to fight for one side or the other'.[1]

The rebellion of the Right was in many ways a rebellion of youth. The establishment at the head of the *junta de defensa* of the 64-year-old General Cabanellas obscures the fact that Franco was the youngest general of a division, and that the leaders of the Falange were mostly twenty years younger than their enemies of the socialists or left republicans. Families were often divided in the civil war, but not in an obvious way by generations.

The total of men under arms in 1936 was, on paper, just over 100,000 in the army in the Peninsula and 30,000 in Morocco, together with 33,000 civil guards, 14,000 carabineers and 18,000 assault guards. But in Spain figures on paper are never the last word since, as usual, about a third of the conscripts were on leave: men would be called up in February, given three months' training, and then given leave at least for the summer, perhaps for the rest of their time of national service. Thus, the total really serving in the Spanish army was about 66,000, of whom some 34,000 were in the republican zone (together with some 12,000 'on leave') and some 32,000 in the rebel zone (along with 13,200 'on leave'). In addition, the Army of Africa, of some 30,000, was wholly with the rebels. Probably about 18,000 civil guards were with the government, against 14,000 with the rebels;

1. Fraser, *The Pueblo*, p. 41.

12,000 assault guards with the government, 5,000 with the rebels; and 4,000 carabineers with the government, 10,000 with the rebels. As for the air force, 3,000 were probably with the government and 2,000 with the rebels; while, in respect of the navy, the figures might be 13,000 loyal and 7,000 rebellious.[1]

Such estimates ignore the equally large numbers of men, also on both sides, who were 'loyal' or 'rebellious' only by accident of geography. Nor do men mean much, in modern war, if considered apart from their weapons, organization, leadership and training. For example, the 30,000 men in the Legion and in the Moroccan regiments were an excellent, if brutal, force if they could only be carried to the mainland. The conscripts on the Peninsula were often illiterate and as ignorant of discipline as were the anarchists. In addition, many of the regular officers and NCOs who sided with the republic were not African veterans, and hence had little combat experience. Out of about 12,000 officers who were either on active service or retired, about 7,000 probably sided with, or were available to, the rebels (including officers in the civil guard and including some 2,750 in Africa). Some 5,000 officers were in what became the republican zone of Spain at the beginning of the war. 1,500 of these were shot and another 1,500 dismissed from the army. Some 1,000 hid in embassies or elsewhere and perhaps escaped to nationalist Spain. About 1,000 serving officers (including over 20 generals) should in theory have been available to the government. There were also many retired officers, of whom some were happy to be asked to serve again in the army, even if some were disloyal.[2]

As for arms, there were probably over half a million rifles or portable arms in all in Spain and Morocco: the civil guard, assault guards and local police in the Basque country and Catalonia had about 100,000 rifles, the army about 400,000. The navy had some 30,000 rifles, the air force 6,000. These were mostly Mausers of 1893 vintage. There were also some 3,000 automatic rifles, made in Spain, of Trapote type, and 1,650 Hotchkiss machine-guns, bought from

1. I am grateful to Michael Alpert for his help in analysing these figures. See also R. Salas, vol. I, p. 185; Hills, p. 240; and Payne, *Politics*, p. 346, for contrasting figures.

2. For an amazing variety of estimates, see R. Salas, vol. I, p. 185; Hills, p. 240; De la Cierva, *Historia ilustrada*, pp. 201–2; and Azaña, vol. III, p. 487.

France. Of these, the government, after the rebellion, had probably a little over half the rifles (perhaps 275,000) and perhaps a third of the automatic weapons. No one knows how many militarily useful weapons there were before the war in private hands or in the hands of political parties. The government retained about 400 out of the 1,000 pieces of artillery in the country, as well as the arms factories at Trubia, Reinosa and Placencia de las Armas. All this artillery was old-fashioned, mostly made by Schneider, but nevertheless not easily co-ordinated: Howitzers ranged from 105 to 155 millimetre, cannon from 70 to 150 millimetre, coastal artillery was larger. But in the arms factories, ammunition and explosives plants (at Toledo, Murcia, Galdacano, Guernica, Eibar and La Manjoya), there were possibilities of renewal and new production. As for tanks there were but twenty of them in Spain in 1936: the rebels held on to eight of these, the republic twelve. By and large, the government did not lack weapons in 1936. What they lacked was military leadership, organization, workmanship and discipline.

There were some 400 aircraft in the country: about a hundred were civil aircraft, either private planes, or aircraft used for the post.[1] The navy had about one hundred aircraft, mostly seaplanes,[2] while the air force proper (a division of the army and commanded by regular army officers) had 50 fighters, 100 reconnaissance aircraft, and 30 light bombers.[3] Many (perhaps a third) of the military aircraft were in bad repair, were unarmed or could not fly for some other reason. In consequence, about two hundred serviceable aircraft turned out to be in government hands in July 1936, while the rebels had a few

1. There were 18 postal aircraft, large Douglases, belonging to LAPE (Línea Aero Postal Española).

2. One squadron of Dornier war seaplane bombers made in Cádiz; three squadrons of torpedo aircraft (Vickers Vildebeest, made by CASA in Getafe); one training squadron (Hispano-Suiza E.30 made in Guadalajara); one squadron of old Martinsydes; a flotilla of Savoia 62 reconnaissance aeroplanes from Italy; and a squadron of Macchis M.18 and some more Martinsydes in the naval air school for pilots in Barcelona.

3. The fighters were: Nieuports 52, made by Hispano-Suiza at Guadalajara, under French licence; three Hawker Spanish Fury fighters (reconstructed at Tablada in Spain); and six old naval Martinsydes. There were some ninety Breguet XIX reconnaissance aircraft, all that remained of a purchase from France arranged by Primo de Rivera. The bombers were a few Fokkers VII, some De Havilland Dragons, and some Douglas DC2s.

less than a hundred.[1] The government retained Spain's four fighter squadrons, based at Getafe and Barcelona, and one patrol squadron;[2] the rebels had no full squadrons, only about ten fighters, which chanced to be at one of the few airfields to fall into their hands. The ninety Breguet XIX reconnaissance aircraft were divided nearly equally between the two sides. The republic had five Fokker bombers, as opposed to the rebels' three (including the one which brought the first legionaries to Seville), and four De Havilland Dragon bombers, as opposed to the rebels' one (the aircraft which took the ill-fated General Núñez de Prado to Barcelona). The republic retained the four Douglas DC2s, and some Dornier Wal bombers bought by the army the previous year, as well as most of the naval aircraft. The postal aircraft and some fifty light aircraft remained with the government but the rebels had about a dozen useful sporting aircraft belonging to the Aeroclub of Andalusia. Reserves of bombs and munitions on both sides were negligible. Of air force pilots, there were some 150 republicans to about 90 nationalists, but the rebels could call on some private or retired fliers, and some others who could be quickly trained for the air.[3]

As for the navy, the government had there, it seemed, a greater superiority than in the other arms, since they held the old battleship *Jaime I*, three cruisers (the *Libertad*, the *Miguel de Cervantes* and the *Méndez Núñez*), twenty modern destroyers and twelve submarines. The rebels had only the *Jaime I*'s twin, the equally old battleship *España* then in dry dock, the cruisers *República*[4] (an old ship) and

1. De la Cierva (*op. cit.*, vol. I, p. 298) says 207 to the government, 96 to the rebels. See analysis in Jesús Salas, pp. 56–63; cf. also R. Salas, vol. I, pp. 194–5; Hidalgo de Cisneros, vol. II, p. 286; Miguel Sanchís, *Alas rojas sobre España* (Madrid, 1956), p. 8.

2. There were 50 Nieuports 52, 3 Hawker 'Spanish Furies' and the old Martinsydes.

3. See José Larios's *Combat over Spain* (London, 1966). De la Cierva (*op. cit.*, p. 300) goes rather too far in suggesting that the republican air force was headed by a 'handful of aristocrats', while their enemies were the most progressive officers in the country. Actually, Ramón Franco had been a powerful influence taking the air force towards the Left.

4. Later renamed the *Navarra*. Both the battleships *España* and *Jaime I* were of 15,500 tons and laid down before 1914. They carried 700–850 men. Of the cruisers, the *Libertad*, *Miguel de Cervantes* and *Almirante Cervera* were 7,500-ton ships, launched in the late 1920s. The 4,500-ton *Méndez Núñez* was launched in

Almirante Cervera, one destroyer, *El Velasco*, five gunboats, two submarines and some coastguard ships. The government's advantage was only apparent. The rebels had the main naval dockyard at El Ferrol, where two new cruisers, the *Canarias* and the *Baleares*, were nearing completion, along with Spain's only two minelayers. They had also a small naval base at Cádiz and a harbour at Algeciras. Against this, the republic had only the small naval building yard at Cartagena, and no dry-dock suitable for their cruisers: Mahon, in Minorca, had a floating-dock adequate for destroyers and submarines, but not for bigger craft. More important, the revolution in the fleet meant that the republic could count on only two admirals out of nineteen, two captains of ships of the line out of thirty-one, seven captains of frigates out of sixty-five, and only thirteen captains of corvette out of 128. These few officers were also demoralized by the murder of many of their comrades and the insecurity of their own position. But other matters favoured the republicans at sea. The ports of Barcelona and Bilbao could be fitted out to serve a navy, and they had over two-thirds of the merchant fleet of Spain (some 1,000 ships, many of which could be refitted for war).

If there were going to be a long fight, the republic seemed in a strong position from an economic point of view: they had most of industry, in Catalonia and the Basque country, the seat of Spanish clothing manufacture and of its iron and steel. In Asturias, they controlled the coal of the country, and they had the chemical and explosives plants. They had the gold reserves of the Bank of Spain. They had also the two cities of Spain with a population over a million (Madrid and Barcelona), and five out of the nine others which exceeded 100,000.[1] They perhaps controlled a population of some fourteen million, as opposed to ten with the rebels, and, while Burgos and Pamplona and perhaps some other cities in the north might be enthusiastic for the rising, Saragossa, Seville, Granada and Córdoba

---

1923 and the *República* (once the *Reina Victoria Eugenia*) with 4,800 tons was launched in 1920. The two new cruisers, *Baleares* and *Canarias*, were to be 10,000-ton ships, with a company of 765. Spain's navy was completed by 21 destroyers, 11 torpedo boats, 12 submarines, 9 coastguard sloops and 8 *guardapescas*.

1. Valencia, Málaga, Murcia, Bilbao, Cartagena. Saragossa, Seville, Granada and Córdoba were with the rebels.

were far from it. The government probably held two-thirds of the 200,000 motor-cars then in Spain, most of the 60,000 buses and lorries, most of the 4,000 railway engines and the 100,000 rolling stock. The cereal-growing areas of Spain were, on the other hand, almost equally divided, even if, after some weeks, nationalist advances would give the rebels two-thirds of the wheat-growing areas. The rebels had the sheep of Castile and Estremadura, the pigs of Galicia and Estremadura, as well as the beef cattle of Galicia and Castile. Cheese and butter production, the cotton, sugar, and potato regions, the flax, and the fishing industries, were also mostly with the rebels. The government had, on the other hand, the best olive- and wine-growing areas, of La Mancha and Catalonia (though not Rioja), and the fruit, rice and vegetable regions on the Mediterranean coast. The nationalists had much of the forests, including the corks of Estremadura and the wooded hills of Galicia; they had also the tin, the copper and the manganese which partially compensated for the republic's control of the iron. But republican Spain had Almadén, with its mercury. Republican Spain as it was at the end of July 1936 contributed 70 per cent to the budget, nationalist Spain only 30 per cent. The government controlled about 240,000 square miles, the rebels only 110,000. But the rebels' possession of Morocco, the two archipelagos of the Canaries and the Balearics (except for Minorca), together with most of the territory adjoining friendly Portugal, gave them a strategic advantage. On the other hand, the republic had the two main entry points for rail and road to France, as well as the north coast.

Both contestants, independently, began in this balanced, if tragic, situation, to think of procuring decisive help from abroad. Both, also independently, thought that this help could come best in the form of aircraft (though Mola was short of ammunition and could not advance in late July primarily for that reason). The aeroplane was the unknown factor. It seemed the weapon of the future. Hence the unfolding war became the first serious war in the air (as it had been the first rebellion of the telephone age).

20

Spain's relations with the rest of Europe – the republic and France – the republic and Russia – Franco and Hitler – condition of England

FOR many generations, Spain had played little part in international power politics, and foreign affairs had played a minor part in domestic politics. During the first years of the republic, Spain had been a conscientious member of the League of Nations, though Gil Robles had criticized the League's condemnation of Mussolini. Now, if the Spanish Civil War became an international crisis, if both sides were soon accusing the other of causing a foreign invasion, if cries of 'We don't want foreigners here' were to ring out as battle slogans in the lonely valleys of Aragon, and if nearly every foreigner who has written of the war records some Spaniard, on one side or the other, wishing that the 'foreigners' would leave the Spaniards to fight their own battles, it was the Spaniards themselves who, to begin with, sought aid from outside, not the powers of Europe who insisted on intervening.[1]

These appeals were the culmination of several generations of ambiguity in the feelings of Spaniards towards the outside world. Was Europe to be emulated, or kept at a distance? If the first, should the inspiration be martial Germany or peaceful England? Unamuno thought that to 'japonize' Spain would ruin all chances of national revival. Such 'Africanism' endeared Unamuno to the Right, which had looked on all reformers as frenchified (*afrancesado*) since 1808. But the Right were not consistent. Those who accused socialists of being 'anti-Spanish' spent the summers in Biarritz. If catholics saw an international plot in freemasonry, freemasons were equally justified in believing that those loyal to the church of Rome were concerned in as great a conspiracy directed by the true, as well as the black, Pope. The middle classes of Spain had, of course, strong commercial and financial connections with other countries. The famous

1. As recognized by Azaña in *El eje Roma–Berlín y la política de No-Intervención*, in Azaña, vol. III, p. 469.

International Telegraph and Telephone Company owned the Spanish telephone system.[1] Other American interests (totalling $80 million) were General Motors, Ford, Firestone Rubber, and some cotton stocks.[2] The British Río Tinto Company had extensive holdings in copper and pyrites, while the Tarsis Company of Glasgow also had large holdings in Spanish copper. The Armstrong Company owned a third of Spanish cork. The waterworks of Seville were also British-owned. Britain, the largest foreign investor, held about £40 million ($194 million) invested in Spain, out of a total of £200 million ($970 million) foreign capital in all.[3] The French controlled the lead mines at Peñarroya and San Plato, and had built the railways. Their total investment was about £28 million ($135 million). The Belgians also had large holdings in Spanish timber, tramways, and railways, and in the coal mines of Asturias. A Canadian company had organized the distribution of electricity in Catalonia. These, the most important of many foreign investments, were extensive interests in a country as little developed as Spain. The US, Germany, Britain and France provided respectively 34, 28, 22 and 12 per cent of Spanish imports and Britain, Germany, France and the US took 43, 26, 12 and 10 per cent of her exports. Spanish iron ore had been a standard item in the British iron and steel industry for many years – 57 per cent of Spanish production went to Britain in 1935 – and ore for Britain occupied most of the Spanish merchant marine. Then the Falange, for all its nationalism, was certainly no more representative of the Spanish tradition than, say, the anarchists; and, while there was an increase in Russian propaganda in Spain before the civil war, there was also much information about nazi Germany. The nazi party had a following of some 600 among the German colony in Spain, which numbered about 13,000.[4] The Spanish section of the

1. An American official of this company in the 1920s, Philip Bonsal (subsequently US ambassador in Cuba), says that the Andalusian landowners with whom he dealt were horrified at this invention, since they supposed that it would have the effect of 'allowing revolutionaries to talk to each other from city to city'.

2. Qu. Richard Traina, *American Diplomacy and the Spanish Civil War* (Bloomington, 1968), p. 62.

3. *Survey of International Affairs 1937*, vol. II, p. 170. See also Robert Whealey, in Carr, *The Republic*, p. 213 and note on p. 235.

4. *GD*, p. 483. See Buckley, p. 203, for a picture of German economic interests, and Viñas, *passim*, for a masterly analysis in depth. Some pro-nazi Spaniards,

German Labour Front had over fifty branches. German tourist offices and bookshops proliferated during the months before the civil war, though the nazis were chiefly active in checking the behaviour of German officials and diplomats. When so many 'solutions' to Spain's troubles were being canvassed, the example of nazi Germany, the disciplined enemy of decadent France, naturally exercised a powerful influence over the imaginations of young Spanish middle-class people; while several monarchist officers had good memories of relations with Germany in the 1920s.

In a broad sense, the Spanish Civil War was the consequence of the working of general European ideas upon Spain. Each of the leading political ideas of Europe since the sixteenth century has been received with enthusiasm by one group of Spaniards and opposed ferociously by another, without any desire for compromise being shown by either side: the universal roman catholicism of the Habsburgs, the absolutism of the Bourbons, French revolutionary liberalism, romantic separatism, socialism, anarchism, communism, and fascism. It was inevitable, therefore, that the war which began in 1936 should become a European crisis. As in the war of the Spanish Succession, the War of Independence, and during the First Carlist War, the prestige, the wealth and, in some instances, the people of the rest of Europe became, during 1936, intimately connected with the Spanish conflict. General European ideas had brought Spaniards to the pitch of war. European powers became entangled in the war at the Spaniards' request. The same great powers were then responsible for much of its course, above all for assisting one side or the other when they seemed to be losing. Throughout the civil war, the alternate repugnance and attraction which the rest of Europe has always had for Spain, and Spain for the rest of Europe, was reflected in the international implications of the fighting.[1]

*

such as Professor Vicente Gay, had received help from Germany to assist publishing their books on, admittedly, 'La Revolución Nacional Sindicalista' (Viñas, p. 169). The right-wing press also received subsidies; for example, Juan Pujol accepted 3–4,000 pesetas to put the nazi case in March's *Informaciones*.

1. See below, p. 463. A detailed consideration of the total effect of foreign intervention in the civil war will be found on p. 939ff. and in Appendix Three.

On the night of 19 July, José Giral, the new Prime Minister of the republic, sent a telegram, *en clair*, to the Prime Minister of France: 'Surprised by a dangerous military *coup*. Beg of you to help us immediately with arms and aeroplanes. Fraternally yours Giral.'[1] The fact that Giral sought to communicate direct with his French colleague is explained by the comradely manner of signature. For it seemed probable that Léon Blum, the new socialist French Prime Minister, was likely to be more sympathetic to an appeal for help than the Spanish ambassador in Paris, Juan Cárdenas, a diplomat of the old school.[2] (The latter's replacement by the Left Republican politician, Alvaro de Albornoz, had already been announced.)

Léon Blum, that passionate and sensitive Frenchman, had been Prime Minister of France only since 5 June, at the head of a ministry of socialists and radicals which enjoyed the support of the communists. Like the Spanish government, it had been formed as a result of a Popular Front electoral alliance. Though pacifist by inclination and anxious to proceed with the redress of social problems at home, Blum and his colleagues knew that the predicament of the Spanish republic was supremely important to France. For, at this time, in Paris, Lyon, and in all the cities of France, there were many street clashes between Left and Right, between the socialists or communists and fascist groups, such as La Croix du Feu and L'Action Française. Blum's sympathy for the republic was buttressed by strategic calculations, since a nationalist Spain would presumably be hostile to France. When, therefore, Blum received Giral's telegram, on the morning of 20 July, he summoned the foreign secretary, Yvon Delbos, and Edouard Daladier, his war minister. Both these men were radi-

---

A good summary of recent research on this topic is Robert H. Whealey, 'Foreign Intervention in the Spanish Civil War', in Carr, *The Republic*.

1. *Les Événements survenus en France 1936–1945, Rapport fait au nom de la Commission de l'Assemblée Nationale* (Paris, 1955), Témoignages I, p. 215. This was the account given of their tenure of office in France by the politicians of the thirties to a parliamentary commission of inquiry in 1946.

2. The rising brought semi-civil war to many Spanish embassies and legations abroad. In Rome, the ambassador Zulueta was thus barricaded in by his rebel chancery. In the end, however, all countries respected diplomatic practice and left diplomatic premises in republican hands, till they changed recognition. But probably only 10 per cent of the diplomatic corps of Spain supported the government (Julio Alvarez del Vayo, *Freedom's Battle*, New York, 1940, p. 261).

cals. Although they might have been supposed likely to sympathize less with the Spanish republic than the socialist members of the cabinet, they immediately agreed to help Giral.

Meantime, late on 19 July, Luis Bolín, on behalf of General Franco, still in the Dragon Rapide, and still piloted by the Englishman, Captain Bebb, flew to Biarritz and then on to Rome to make a formal request to the Italian government for twelve bombers, three fighters, and a certain number of bombs. This request by Franco was countersigned by Sanjurjo in Lisbon with what was probably his last signature before his death.[1] At the same time, a nationalist communiqué proudly announced that 'the interests of Spain are not alone at stake as our trumpet-call sounds across the Straits of Gibraltar';[2] while the British authorities in Gibraltar placed at the disposal of General Kindelán, the most senior air-force officer to side with the rebels, telephone lines upon which he and his friends could speak direct to Berlin and to Rome in subsequent weeks.[3]

On 21 July, the first reaction to the Spanish crisis also apparently occurred in Moscow. A joint meeting was held of the secretariats of the Comintern and Profintern (the body set up to coordinate communist activity in western trade unions). There was support for the idea of aid to the republic, and a new meeting was arranged for 26 July.[4] The reaction of Stalin and the Russian government towards the outbreak of the Spanish war (whatever part the Spanish communists had played before) was dictated by the question of how it would affect the current needs of Russian foreign policy. If, as in the case of China in 1926, communist opportunities would have to be sacrificed, then sacrificed they would be: the aims of communism could not be different from those of Russia. Fear of war had caused

1. Evidence of Luis Bolín. See Bolín's memoirs, p. 165.

2. *New York Times*, 21 July 1936.

3. Kindelán to Jackson, in Jackson, p. 248.

4. This derives from nationalist sources, deriving from documents discovered in Madrid after the end of the war. It may be seen in *Cruzada*, XXVIII, p. 99. The information appeared in 1937 in *I accuse France*, reprinted from *The Catholic Herald*, a pamphlet published in London by 'A Barrister'. The existence of the meeting was confirmed to Julián Gorkin by Albert Vassart, a metalworker who had been French representative in the ECCI (the Comintern executive). The ECCI secretariat was then: Dimitrov (general secretary), Togliatti, Manuilsky, Pieck, Kuusinen, Marty, and Gottwald.

Russia to emerge from her isolation of the late 1920s to enter the League of Nations in 1934, and to conclude the pact with France in 1935. Litvinov, the foreign minister, had spoken eloquently in the League for collective security.[1] A nationalist victory in the civil war in Spain would mean that France would be surrounded on three sides by potentially hostile countries. That would make it easier for Germany to attack Russia without fearing French attacks in her rear. For that reason alone, Stalin had a strong interest in the prevention of a nationalist victory.

The Spanish war admittedly afforded to the Spanish communist party, with its discipline, its skill at propaganda, and its prestige deriving from its connection with Russia, great opportunities, but at that time no one could foresee quite how powerful that party would grow. At the same time, overweening communist behaviour would alarm Britain and France. For that reason Stalin probably did not send orders to the Spanish communist party and his chief agents there, Codovilla and Stepanov, to make full use of every opportunity to gain control of the Spanish republic. He also hesitated about sending arms to Spain.[2] Stalin was then about to embark upon a new stage of the purge of the old bolsheviks. That perhaps caused the Russian dictator to listen with unusual attention to the leaders of the Comintern at this time. Dimitrov, Togliatti and Marty, to take only three of the most important international communists then in Moscow, must have had their own feelings as to what should be the communist reaction to the war in Spain. They could point out how, while Stalin delayed, Trotsky was already naming him 'liquidator and traitor of the Spanish revolution, abettor of Hitler and Mussolini'. With crablike caution, therefore, Stalin apparently reached one decision about Spain: he would not permit the republic to lose, even though he would not necessarily help it to win. The continuance of

1. Stalin perhaps kept the idea of an arrangement with Germany in the back of his mind if Litvinov should fail to secure an effective alliance with Britain and France.

2. It has been thought that a small number of red air force planes were shipped out of Odessa in July for Spain. This rumour derives from the memoir of one of the pilots, Achmed Amba, *I was Stalin's Bodyguard* (London, 1952), p. 27; also mentioned by Clara Campoamor, p. 174. No one saw these planes in the sky till later, however, and I think that it is improbable that they arrived before October. See below, p. 443. Amba, however, seems otherwise well informed.

the war would keep him free to act in any way. It might even make possible a world war in which France, Britain, Germany, and Italy would destroy themselves, with Russia, the arbiter, staying outside.[1] Thus the Russian government would support the agitation for aid to Spain, for the time being only in food and raw materials, and ensure that Russian factory workers made a 'contribution'. The Comintern representatives in Spain would be reinforced. The able, courteous, educated and ruthless leader of the Italian communist party in exile, Togliatti, for some time previously director of Spanish and Italian affairs in the Comintern, thus soon went to Spain, using the name 'Alfredo', as director of tactics of the Spanish communist party.[2] The Livornese communist Ettore Quaglierini occupied himself with the publications of the Spanish communist party and helped their fellow countryman, Vidali ('Carlos'),[3] as has been seen, with the projection of the Fifth Regiment as a model of military efficiency. One more communist international leader was the Hungarian, Ernö Gerö, 'Pedro' or 'Gueré', who became responsible for the guidance of the communists in Catalonia.[4] The Bulgarian Stepanov and Codo-

1. This would explain why Russia, and French communists, were so anxious that France would be drawn into the war on the side of the republic. Some support is given to this interpretation of Stalin's policy by Litvinov's reply to a question put by the French government as to what the Russian reaction would be to a general war arising from French intervention. While he admitted that the Franco-Soviet pact would impel Russian help to France, if the latter were attacked by a third power, 'it would be quite a different matter if war were to come as a result of the intervention of one of our countries in the affairs of a third'. (Statement made by Jules Moch, then sub-secretary of state, to Julián Gorkin.)

2. Togliatti himself (*Rinascita*, 19 May 1962) and the 'official' historian of the Italian communist party, P. Spriano, vol. III, p. 215fn. say (the latter having investigated the matter with some care) that Togliatti did not reach Spain until June 1937. Hernández, on the other hand, speaks of him as well established by August 1936, and Justo Martínez Amutio, *Chantaje a un pueblo* (Madrid, 1974), p. 236, speaks of him as being in Spain in the winter of 1936–7. As will be seen (see p. 709), there were good reasons for Togliatti trying to establish 'before history' his absence from Spain till that date. Perhaps he merely visited Spain for a short time in 1936.

3. See above, p. 323.

4. See José Esteban Vilaró's *El ocaso de los dioses rojos* (Barcelona, 1939); and Martínez Amutio, p. 317f. His real name was 'Singer'. Gerö had been 'instructor' in the French communist party in the late 1920s and early 1930s.

villa, the two Comintern representatives who had been in Spain for some years, remained.[1] The combination of a swiftly growing party and an inexperienced leadership gave special importance to the international functionaries. Men like Stepanov strutted across the stage of Spanish revolutionary history as if they were gods, disdainful of Spaniards, breathing mystery and power, but actually cynical, fearful of Stalin, and bureaucratic. Stepanov himself, protected by a staff of secretaries such as 'Angelita', a 'real demon, beautiful but cold and cruel', and 'Carmen the Fat', a Russian who became head of the cadre section of the united youth, established a virtual tyranny over the central committee of the party.[2]

The western European section of the Comintern, under its brilliant German communist chief, Willi Muenzenberg, was also active from its headquarters in Paris in linking the cause of the Spanish republic with the general anti-fascist crusade, which had been begun when the Soviet government had adopted the twin policies of the Popular Front and collective security.[3] The Spanish war was indeed a godsend to agitators for the Popular Front and the anti-fascist, hence pro-Soviet, cause. '*A notre secours, à votre secours,*' pleaded Romain Rolland, the French novelist whose activities expressed the short-lived alliance between literature, pacifism and friendship with Russia, '*au secours de l'Espagne!*'[4]

While these matters were being haltingly mooted in Moscow and Paris, Franco's agent, the journalist Bolín, had reached Rome, on 21 July. The next day, he and the Marqués de Viana, a monarchist

1. See Hernández, *Yo, ministro de Stalin en España*, p. 33ff. This unpleasant work of the leading communist renegade from Spain is the most intimate but also the most controversial source of communist policy in Spain. Other Italian communists in Spain from this time on were Pietro Ravetto from Biella and, according to Spriano (p. 215fn.), an NKVD shadow for Codovilla, whose name was Codevilla!

2. Martínez Amutio, p. 269f.

3. Koestler, *The Invisible Writing*, pp. 198, 313. Muenzenberg, previously known as the 'Red Hearst' of Germany, was a journalistic genius. With his gift for gathering duchesses, bankers, and generals, as well as intellectuals, in support of one or other of his causes, he really invented the fellow-traveller. His assistant in Paris was Otto Katz, *alias* Simon, a Czech who was also his guard. By July 1936, Muenzenberg was already beginning to quarrel with his bosses in Moscow, who found him too independent.

4. Qu. David Caute, *The Fellow Travellers* (London, 1973), p. 170.

(who had just come from ex-King Alfonso in Vienna), saw Count Ciano, the Italian foreign minister. Some years later, Ciano told Hitler that Franco had said that twelve transport aircraft would enable him to win the war in a few days.[1]

With Franco's first emissaries, Ciano was enthusiastic, but naturally Mussolini had to be consulted. It was not clear to the Duce what connection Franco had with the monarchist plotters to whom he, Mussolini, had pledged help in 1934.[2] Nor apparently did Franco know of the details of that arrangement. It was not until Mola sent the monarchist Goicoechea, the leading figure in the events of 1934, to Rome on 24 July, that the Italians agreed to listen seriously to the Spanish rebels.[3] But, also on 22 July, Franco made his first approach to Germany for help. On his behalf, Colonel Beigbeder, the ex-military attaché in Berlin, who had installed himself in the department of native affairs at Tetuán, sent a 'very urgent request' to General Kuhlenthal, German military attaché in Paris, accredited also to Madrid, for 'ten transport aircraft, with maximum seating capacity', to be purchased through German private firms and brought by German pilots to Spanish Morocco.[4] These were needed to supplement the old Breguets in getting the Army of Africa across the Straits. (Beigbeder was well aware of past German links with Spain in matters of arms supply. He and Kuhlenthal had travelled together in Morocco in 1935 and Kuhlenthal had known Franco since the time of the revolution in Asturias.)

The same day, a nationalist air force officer, Captain Francisco Arranz, accompanied by Adolf Langenheim, head of the nazi party in Tetuán, and Johannes Bernhardt, a nazi businessman of Prussian origin, met Franco and, the next day, set off with a private letter ('infantile' in style, according to Bernhardt) to Hitler to support Beigbeder's request. They travelled in a Junkers requisitioned from the Lufthansa at Las Palmas.[5] Bernhardt, an ex-sugar merchant from

1. Hitler's interview with Ciano at Brenner, 28 September 1940. *Documents on German Foreign Policy 1918–1945*, Series D (London, 1961), XI, p. 214.

2. Bolín, p. 168f.

3. See below, p. 352. Evidence of Luis Bolín. See also *Cruzada*, X, p. 126.

4. *GD*, p. 4.

5. See Viñas, p. 394f., and *Cruzada*, X, p. 127; cf. footnote to *GD*, p. 1. The letter did not appear in the files of the German foreign ministry and has not been published. Bernhardt described it to me in Buenos Aires in 1971. Mola also sent

Hamburg, ruined in 1929, had come to Morocco to seek a new life. In Tetuán, he was first employed by a company which sold kitchen stoves and other equipment to the Spanish garrison. He had in this way made friends in the officers' mess. Both he and Langenheim saw the possibilities of personal advantage, as well as German influence, in the sale of war material to the rebels.[1] Bernhardt was looking for a new outlet; a few months before he had contemplated going to Argentina.

In Paris, the Spanish ambassador, Cárdenas, meanwhile visited Léon Blum and, on behalf of Giral, made a request for 20 Potez bombers, 50 light Hotchkiss machine-guns, 8 Schneider 155 millimetre howitzers with munitions, 1,000 Lebel rifles, 250,000 machine-gun bullets, a million cartridges, and 20,000 bombs. Since the French arms industries had been nationalized, the purchase would need the approval of the French cabinet. To the surprise of Cárdenas, Blum agreed.[2] Now, almost at the same time, a telephone call was received in the Quai d'Orsay from Corbin, the French ambassador in London. Personally of the Right, Corbin was a faithful interpreter of English wishes. The British government, he said, was alarmed about the French reaction to the Spanish crisis. A meeting had previously been arranged in London for 23 and 24 July between the British, French, and Belgian foreign ministers to discuss a possible approach to Hitler and Mussolini for a new five-power treaty of collective security. Baldwin now wanted Blum to accompany his foreign secretary, Delbos, to England in order to discuss Spain. On the advice of Alexis Léger, the Martiniquais secretary-general of the Quai d'Orsay (later known as the Nobel prize-winning poet St Jean Perse, author of

---

the Marqués de las Marismas and the Marqués de Portago to Berlin. The Germans could not believe that Franco's and Mola's emissaries did not know each other and later instructed Arranz to repair to a particular café where Mola's men were also sitting. Only when the two Spaniards showed no sign of recognizing each other did they believe the lack of coordination between north and south in Spain. See, for this journey, José Escobar's *Así empezó . . .* (Madrid, 1974), pp. 110–11.

1. Testimony of Bernhardt. Langenheim was a mining engineer. See also Herbert Feis, *The Spanish Story* (New York, 1948), p. 280f., and Viñas, p. 364.

2. Evidence of Señor de Cárdenas. Cf. too *French Foreign Policy Documents 1936–1939* (hereinafter *FD*), vol. III, p. 52, which speak of a request for 20 aircraft, on 24 July. The other requests were named in the later list. See *FD*, p. 61.

Anabasis), Blum agreed.[1] Léger's nightmare was that Baldwin's Britain might turn away from a left-wing France to join Germany.[2] At the same time, Cárdenas, the Spanish ambassador in Paris, resigned (because of his nationalist sympathies) leaving two Spanish air-force officers, Ismael Warleta and Juan Aboal, to conduct the details of the arms transaction, until Fernando de los Ríos, the socialist professor and ex-minister, arrived from Geneva to take charge from them.[3]

On 23 July, the conference in London began in the morning. Blum arrived in time for luncheon. In the hall of Claridge's Hotel, Eden asked: 'Are you going to send arms to the Spanish republic?' 'Yes,' said Blum. 'It is your affair,' Eden replied, 'but I ask you one thing. Be prudent.'[4]

Now this advice by Eden naturally reflected the desire for peace felt by the British at this time. The leader of the opposition, Clement Attlee, might have voiced the sympathies of the Labour party for their Spanish comrades, when, on 20 July, he pledged 'all practicable support'; and the English middle and upper classes might favour the nationalists; but no politician in England argued that the country should actually involve itself on one side or another in the conflict. The question was, what kind of neutrality should be observed. The Labour party at first believed that neutrality meant that the republic should be allowed to purchase arms, from Britain as from elsewhere. Here they were in disagreement with the Conservative critics of the

government, such as Winston Churchill, who, though opposed to Germany and Italy as much as the opposition, did not immediately believe the Spanish conflict had any significance for Britain. Churchill

1. United States Foreign Policy (*State Department Papers*, henceforward referred to as *US D*), 1936, vol. II, pp. 447–9.

2. For Léger, see *The Diplomats 1919–1939* (Princeton, 1953), a symposium edited by Gordon Craig and Felix Gilbert.

3. Sanchís, p. 11. Cárdenas summoned the head of chancery, Cristóbal de Castillo, to apologize for leaving him with such problems. Castillo said that he would himself be resigning within a short while, though he would delay a day or two to make matters difficult for the republic. Cárdenas remained a further week in Paris to do what he could to prevent the dispatch of war material to the republic, by putting his friends at the British Embassy privately in the picture.

4. *Les Événements survenus*, pp. 216–17. But Eden specifically said that it was his recollection that Spain was not discussed (Anthony Eden, *Facing the Dictators*, London, 1962, p. 406).

himself was aghast by the revolutionary character of the republic, and wrote a few days later to Corbin to protest against French aid to the republic, and to urge 'an absolutely rigid neutrality'.[1] Eden at the foreign office attempted to secure this policy, both for Britain and for France, though Eden hated dictatorial governments. The supposition of the British was that the German remilitarization of the Rhineland in February, and the Italian conquest of Abyssinia, had satiated the dictators, who could now be induced to help create a new European order. In this design, the outbreak of 'the Spanish crisis' was, above all, an unwelcome interruption. Baldwin's instructions to Eden had been 'on no account, French or other, must he bring us into the fight on the side of the Russians'.[2] Eden's only move, in fact, had been to order British warships to Spanish ports to protect British lives.[3] He had also received the Spanish ambassador, López Oliván, and told him that there would be no ban on the export of civil aircraft to Spain and that, though a request for military material would have to receive a special licence, it would 'certainly be considered'.[4] The same day, 28 July, Eden told the British cabinet that the 'ordinary procedure' would be followed if either the Spanish government, or the rebels, wanted to buy arms; 'of course there was no question of intervention'.[5] Meantime, the first aircraft sold privately by British Airways to a representative of Franco, a certain Señor Delgado, of the Ibarrola Oil Company of Ceuta, had gone ahead: four Fokker passenger planes, at £38,000. But the French refused to let these leave Bordeaux when they stopped there to refuel.[6] On 31 July, however, the British government introduced a unilateral ban on arms shipments to Spain.

1. Winston Churchill, *The Gathering Storm* (London, 1948), p. 168. Churchill made his attitude very clear to the then newly appointed republican ambassador in London, Pablo de Azcárate, in October. On being presented to Azcárate by Lord Robert Cecil, Churchill turned red with anger, muttered 'Blood, blood, blood', and refused the Spaniard's outstretched hand. (MS memoirs of Pablo de Azcárate, made available to the author, Geneva, 1960.) Azcárate took over from López Oliván in August.

2. Thomas Jones, *Diary with Letters* (London, 1954), p. 231.

3. Eden, p. 401. By 24 July, nineteen ships, partly from the home fleet, partly from the Mediterranean fleet, were distributed around the Spanish coast.

4. Eden, p. 400; also *FO*/371/215/24/224–5.

5. *CAB* 23/85/130. 6. *FO* 371/205/24/243.

The British ambassador to Spain, Sir Henry Chilton, meantime had set up the British Embassy in a grocer's shop at Hendaye, on the French side of the International Bridge.[1] He was an unimaginative diplomat, of the old school: his American colleague, Claude Bowers, who was very republican in his sympathies, reported to Washington that everything Chilton did was 'intended to cripple the government and serve the insurgents'.[2] Chilton was also convinced that a victory for Franco would be better for Britain.[3]

English opinion was soon as inflamed by the Spanish war as it had once been by the French Revolution. The publisher Victor Gollancz's Left Book Club, which set out to publish a book each month against 'Fascism and War', had begun in May. This had been followed by the Right Book Club. Such literary commitment to politics was the reflection of the heavy social problems, as well as of general moral or international alarms caused by the lure of Russia, the decline of religion, 'the breakdown of standards' and the rise of Hitler. The official Labour opposition to Baldwin's government seemed ineffective. Able leaders such as Churchill and Lloyd George glowered in the political wilderness. The time was to be well expressed by W. H. Auden in his poem 'Spain 1937':

> Tomorrow, for the young, the poets exploding like bombs,
> The walks by the lake, the weeks of perfect communion;
> Tomorrow the bicycle races
> Through the suburbs on summer evenings. But today the struggle.

Another verse of the same poem now seemed apposite:

> What's your proposal? To build the just city? I will.
> I agree, or is it the suicide pact, the romantic
> Death? Very well, I accept, for
> I am your choice, your decision. Yes, I am Spain.[4]

1. The diplomatic corps had already left Madrid for the summer capital of San Sebastián before the rising. By 22 July they were all established, safe (after several adventures), in St Jean de Luz, the other side of the French frontier. The embassies in Madrid were in the hands of junior members of the diplomatic staff, or of consuls. There was, at this time, no German ambassador to Spain – none having been appointed since Count von Welczeck had left for Paris in April.

2. *USD*, 1937, vol. I, p. 224.

3. Qu. Dante Puzzo, *Spain and the Great Powers* (New York, 1962), p. 100.

4. Auden changed the lines of this excellent poem in subsequent editions, to diminish its militant intent.

Among intellectuals of the Left, Spain became the central point of life, work, and artistic inspiration. Stephen Spender wrote that Spain 'offered the twentieth century an 1848'.[1] Philip Toynbee, an undergraduate member of the communist party, recalled how the news of the Spanish war made him think that at last 'the gloves were off in the struggle against fascism'.[2] Rex Warner, also a republican sympathizer, wrote 'Spain has torn the veil of Europe'. Among most intellectuals, there was no difficulty in deciding which side in the war was 'right'. For Cecil Day Lewis, future Poet Laureate, the war was a battle of 'light against darkness'. Spain gave British intellectuals a sense of freedom, the thought of rubbing shoulders with the dispossessed in a half-developed country, above all the illusion that their 'action' could be effective.[3] 'Spain' seemed reality, England make-believe, scarcely to be roused from complacency save 'by the roar of bombs'.[4]

But society in general was divided: the *Morning Post*, *Daily Mail*, *Daily Sketch* and *Observer* supported the nationalists, and the *News Chronicle*, *Daily Herald*, *Manchester Guardian*, *Daily Express* and *Daily Mirror* were generally republican. *The Times* and *Daily Tele-*

1. Stephen Spender, *World within World* (London, 1951), p. 187.
2. Philip Toynbee, *Friends Apart* (London, 1954), p. 85.
3. Nancy Cunard and the periodical *Left Review* took a poll of English writers and asked them which side they 'backed'. Only five – among them Evelyn Waugh, Eleanor Smith, and Edmund Blunden – were for the nationalists. Ruby Ayres, Norman Douglas, T. S. Eliot ('I still feel convinced that it is best that at least a few men of letters should remain isolated and take no part in these collective activities'), Charles Morgan, Ezra Pound, Alec Waugh, Sean O'Faolain, H. G. Wells, and Vita Sackville-West were among the sixteen who declared themselves neutral. The remaining hundred writers committed themselves, many in passionate terms, in favour of the republic. These included Auden ('The struggle in Spain has X-rayed the lies upon which our civilization is built'), George Barker, Samuel Beckett (who commented simply, in capitals, in the well-loved style of *Godot*, 'UPTHEREPUBLIC!'), Norman Collins, Cyril Connolly, Alesteir Crowley, Havelock Ellis, Ford Madox Ford, David Garnett, Louis Golding, Lancelot Hogben, Laurence Housman, Brian Howard, Aldous Huxley, Storm Jameson, Dr Joad, Harold Laski, John and Rosamond Lehmann, Eric Linklater, F. L. Lucas, Rose Macaulay, A. G. Macdonnel, Louis MacNeice, Francis Meynell, Naomi Mitchison, Raymond Mortimer, John Middleton Murry, Sean O'Casey, V. S. Pritchett, Herbert Read, Edward Sackville-West, Stephen Spender, James Stephens, Sylvia Townsend Warner, Rebecca West, and Antonia White.
4. Orwell, p. 248.

graph tried to be impartial. *Punch* hailed the civil war, on 29 July, with one of Sir Bernard Partridge's well-known cartoons: a guitarist named 'Revolution' appears at the window of a sad woman in a Seville-like street. 'What, you again?' says she. The assumption was clearly that the Left had begun the war. On 12 August, Sir Bernard appeared less partisan. Against a back-cloth of burning cities, the damsel Spain is fought over by two bandits, communism and fascism. The former's head is tied in a kerchief. The latter wears a black hat. A more urgent or contemporary note was struck by Low's 'Turkish Bath' cartoon of 29 July in the *Evening Standard*. Under the headline 'Revolution at our Turkish Bath: Blimps Rise', Colonel Blimp, favourite butt of the Left, was depicted broadcasting a proclamation from the Hot Room.

In France, public opinion was even more bitterly concerned than in England. Most prominent French writers quickly took up a stand even if, like that of François Mauriac, it was one which they afterwards changed.[1] Spain was, after all, closer than it was to England, the communist party in France far larger and more serious. The wounds of the World War were greater. The Left in France saw Spain as the 'symbol of liberty in peril' and the 'prefiguration of our own future', in the words of André Chamson. The Right in France, who were more distinguished intellectually, more unconstitutional and more determined than in any other surviving democracy, saw Spain as the one country where communism was being resisted. The Camelots du Roi thought as Philip Toynbee did that the gloves were off, and 'against the revolution'. But the Left took the initiative in public opinion.

1. An excellent analysis is D. W. Pike's *Conjecture, Propaganda and Deceit* (Stanford, 1970).

21

Blum returns to Paris – de los Ríos – the anguish of Blum – Mussolini sends Savoias to Franco – Franco's emissaries in Bayreuth – Salazar – Muenzenberg at work – reactions across the Atlantic – the Italians crash

WHILE Eden and Blum were consulting in London, the humanist socialist, Fernando de los Ríos, the new temporary republican representative in Paris, called on Daladier, the French war minister, Pierre Cot, the air minister, and Jules Moch, under-secretary in Blum's private cabinet. The French undertook to supply pilots to fly the Potez bombers which the Spaniards had requested to Spain. 'A member of the French cabinet' also secretly told Count von Welczeck, German ambassador in Paris,[1] at much the same time, that France was preparing to supply the Spanish republic with weapons and bombers.[2] Welczeck reported this to Dr Hans Heinrich Dieckhoff, acting head of the German foreign office, a solemn career diplomat, who told the German Embassy in London to take up the matter with Eden.[3] Despite this, Dieckhoff informed the German war ministry that he thought the idea of helping Franco (Beigbeder's telegraphed request from Tetuán had by then arrived) 'out of the question'.[4] The German foreign ministry thus reacted to the Spanish crisis much as did the British. Help to either combatant would increase the danger of general war. By this time, Franco's messengers to Hitler had got no farther than Seville, where they were delayed by engine trouble.[5]

During the evening of 24 July, Léon Blum and Delbos returned to Paris. Waiting to meet them at Le Bourget was the silky radical minister, Camille Chautemps. He explained that the news of the government's decision to aid the Spanish republic had leaked out to

1. Welczeck had been ambassador in Madrid until the preceding April. He had been a friend of King Alfonso, an anti-nazi, a noted huntsman and a tireless man of the world.

2. *GD*, p. 4. 3. *loc. cit.*, n. 4. *op. cit.*, p. 7. 5. Viñas, p. 395.

the right-wing publicist, Henri de Kerillis (probably through Welczeck). Kerillis had already denounced the plan in the columns of *L'Echo de Paris*. 'No one can understand,' said Chautemps, 'why we are going to risk war on the behalf of Spain when we did not do so over the Rhineland.'[1] A radical revolt against the idea of aid to Spain was beginning. Both the first rumblings of this, and the memory of Eden's words, were in Blum's ears when, late that night, he saw de los Ríos, together with Daladier, Cot, Vincent Auriol (minister of finance), and Delbos.[2] De los Ríos pointed out to Blum that the civil war 'could not be looked upon as strictly national' because of Spain's strategic relation with Italy and Morocco. Blum still desired to help the republic. The contracts for the supply of aircraft were ready. But he did not want to act in the face of Eden's warnings. So he asked whether Spanish pilots could fly the aeroplanes to Spain. De los Ríos said that the shortage of pilots would make that impossible. Anyway, his government had hoped to be able to retain the services of the French pilots. At this, Daladier recalled a Franco-Spanish treaty of 1935. A secret clause of that provided that Spain would buy 20 million francs' worth of war material from France. De los Ríos and Blum agreed that the aircraft and other material should be shipped under this clause. Later still that night, de los Ríos was roused from bed by Pierre Cot, a radical professor of international law but drifting to the far Left through anti-fascism, who telephoned to ask him to come immediately to see him at his house. He did. Cot said that Delbos could not be cinvinced that French pilots could take the aircraft to Spain. Cot, therefore, had suggested that they should fly to the south of France and the aircraft would then be transported by Spaniards. This seemed a good compromise.

The next morning, 25 July, de los Ríos visited the French air ministry. All seemed favourable for the shipment. But, in the mean-

1. *Les Événements survenus*, p. 217.

2. The following is based on a letter from de los Ríos to Giral, a copy of which was stolen from the house of the Spanish consul general, Cipriano Rivas Cherif, in Geneva, and sensationally published at the end of 1936. See *Il Messaggero*, 10 December 1936 The letter may be seen in facsimile in Francesco Belforte, *La guerra civile in Spagna* (Milan, 1938–9), vol. I, p. 192. De los Ríos accepted its authenticity.

time, Castillo, the counsellor at the Spanish Embassy, refused to sign the appropriate papers. Barroso, the military attaché, also refused to sign the cheque paying for it. Both these men now resigned, on the ground that they would not be a party to the purchase of arms for use against their own people. They informed the press what they were doing.[1] The uproar was immediate. All the French evening papers, especially *L'Echo de Paris*, published sensational accounts of the 'arms traffic'. Lebrun, the President, warned Blum that he was leading France to war. Herriot, ex-Prime Minister and speaker of the chamber of deputies, did the same: '*Ah je t'en prie, mon petit, je t'en prie, ne vas pas te fourrer là-dedans!*'[2] The Prime Minister was torn. In the afternoon, the French cabinet met. Daladier and Delbos were the spokesmen for a refusal to Spain, Cot for acceptance. Eventually, the government announced in a communiqué that it would refuse the Spanish government's request for arms. But no hindrances would be placed in the way of private transactions, provided that the aircraft were not armed. Thus bombers were not to be sent. But these regulations were not kept. A quantity of military aircraft were secretly prepared. During the day, £140,000 in gold from the Spanish gold reserve arrived at Le Bourget as guarantee for the payment. Pierre Cot, the air minister, organized all these transactions, his *chef du cabinet*, Jean Moulin (the future hero of the Resistance), being charged to set up a team of specialists in matters of aviation to deal with the shipment. The young minister of sport, Léo Lagrange, also helped. The Byron of the age, André Malraux, then close to the communists, acted for a time as intermediary on behalf of the Spanish government,[3] applying 'the inventiveness of a great novelist to buying arms and gun-running'.[4] Malraux had visited Spain on 20 July, and had become convinced that the fate of the republic depended on air

1. Barroso, a friend of Franco whom he accompanied to London to George V's funeral as ADC, subsequently joined Franco's staff.

2. *Les Événements survenus*, p. 217.

3. Malraux had become world famous in 1934 with the publication of *La Condition humaine*. Malraux may never have been a communist, but he provided the motive for thousands of young men to become so.

4. Fischer, p. 334. Malraux believed then that Marxism was 'the only organism capable of opposing fascism with force'. See Walter G. Langlois, 'Aux Sources de l'Espoir', *La Revue des Lettres Modernes*, 1973, 5.

power.[1] Henceforward, the Spanish Embassy in Paris was a 'veritable caravanserai' where, at all hours of the day and during many of the night, individuals of every nationality came in and out offering all classes of arms, munitions, and aircraft, at all prices – with the somewhat gullible de los Ríos presiding over the arms purchase commission for a few weeks.[2]

In the more reserved atmosphere of Rome, on 25 July, Goicoechea, accompanied by Pedro Sáinz Rodríguez, the monarchist ideologue, arrived in Rome to support Bolín's requests for arms. The connection between the plotters of 1934 and the rebels of 1936 was satisfactorily explained to Count Ciano.[3] Mussolini was influenced by the rumours of French aid to the republic. Ciano was still enthusiastic in favour of helping Franco and his view prevailed. Italy arranged to send twelve Savoia 81 bombers to Morocco in the next few days. A telephone call from ex-King Alfonso, staying with the Princess Metternich in Czechoslovakia, to Mussolini hastened the shipment.[4] By this time, also, the arch-financier, Juan March,

1. Jean Lacouture, *André Malraux* (Paris, 1973), p. 227. Malraux went back to Spain in a Lockheed Orion belonging to the ministry of air in Paris on 25 July, as an informal observer for the French government, but also in his capacity as a president of the World Committee against Fascism and War. Malraux was piloted by the famous French flier, Edouard Corniglion-Molinier.

2. Azcárate, MS, p. 20. The effect of formal French non-intervention caused deep fissures and quarrels throughout the second International, of which the French socialist party was one of the leaders. The split in, for example, the Belgian socialist party (which at this time had a share in the government of Belgium) lasted until 1940.

3. *Cruzada*, X, p. 126. Bolín, pp. 170, 171. Attilio Tamaro (*Venti anni di storia*, Rome, 1952–3, vol. III, p. 200) says that Mussolini refused to send aid when twice asked by Franco and only agreed when he heard that Blum was helping the republic. This was probably a factor, not the decisive one.

4. Luca de Tena, p. 251. Of the aircraft, two later crashed (see below, p. 363). The French officials who investigated the crash alleged that one of the dead Italian pilots had received flying orders on 15 July. Apart from Mussolini's pledge and aid in 1934, there is no evidence of Italian aid before the rising; the papers on the dead pilot either contain a misprint, perhaps for 25 July; a deliberate forgery; or the pilot simply returned *from leave* on 15 July. Since the planes did not leave Sardinia for Morocco till 30 July, and since Franco had needed them from 19 July onwards, it is inconceivable that they were, as alleged, given flying orders before the rising. The document mentioning 15 July has never been published. It may never have existed.

had reached Rome, arranging credit for these first Italian shipments and coordinating other financial policies for the rebels.[1]

The motives of Mussolini in acting in this way were mixed. He was flattered to be asked. Aspiring to dominate the Mediterranean, he supposed that that ambition would be assisted by the establishment in Spain of a right-wing government. Such a 'new Spain' would draw off French troops from the Italian border and, in the event of a Franco–Italian war, help to prevent the passage of French troops in North Africa to France. The triumphant conquest of Abyssinia in April had left Mussolini both anxious to display his personality in some new way, and without any obvious place in which to do it. The Italians, he believed, had to be 'kept up to the mark by kicks on the shins'. 'When the war in Spain is over,' he later remarked, 'I shall have to find something else: the Italian character has to be formed through fighting.'[2] In 1936, Mussolini was in a mood of elation; on 24 October, he was to announce: 'At the close of the year 14 [of the fascist era] I raise a large olive branch. This olive branch rises from an immense forest; it is a forest of eight million bayonets well sharpened.'[3] The public reason for Italian intervention in Spain was that Italy was 'not prepared to see the establishment of a communist state' in Spain. It was also the reason which he privately gave to his wife Rachele.[4] Although, before July 1936, his propaganda had been more directed against the 'decadent' democracies than against communism, an even moderately left-wing government in Spain would be hostile to his designs. But it was still possible that internationally the Duce might draw closer to the bourgeois objects of his particular scorn than to Germany. His relation with Hitler was still undefined and exploratory. Here, as in his attacks upon communism, the Spanish crisis forced a change. The Spanish war would make Hitler and Mussolini allies. Later, Ciano told Cantalupo, his first ambassador in nationalist Spain, that the Duce had only 'very reluctantly

1. It was said that he bought a majority holding in the Savoia aircraft factory so as to be able to dominate the supply of bombers to Franco. See Fernando Schwartz, *La internacionalización de la guerra civil española* (Barcelona, 1971), p. 74. One can be sure that, whatever March did, he did it for profit.

2. Paolo Monelli, *Mussolini* (London, 1953), p. 141.

3. Eden, p. 424.

4. Rachele Mussolini, *My Life with Mussolini* (London, 1959), p. 91; Bolín's evidence.

agreed to lend Franco military support'.[1] King Victor Emmanuel always opposed the idea of aid but he was impotent.[2]

The diplomacy of Ciano, who played an important part in subsequent events, was violently anti-British without the fascination mixed with the hatred felt for Britain by Ribbentrop and even by Mussolini. When three falangists later described to him how all Spanish miseries, since the reign of Philip II, had been caused by England, Ciano encouraged them 'on this wise path', warning of 'the dangerous Anglomania of certain old stagers of diplomacy'.[3] His task during the Spanish war was made easier by the desire of the British government to achieve an Italian alliance. This increased Ciano's scorn for England, though he was friendly with Lord Perth, the roman catholic convert and ex-secretary-general of the League who was ambassador to Rome and who so far exceeded his government's instructions as to show himself to Ciano as 'a man who has come to understand, even to love fascism'.[4]

Also on 25 July, Franco's emissaries to Hitler, Captain Arranz, Bernhardt, and Langenheim arrived in Berlin. They had crossed with, and met, Mola's messengers to Mussolini at Marseilles airport. Franco's letter was given to Hitler through the foreign department of the nazi party. At the foreign ministry, both Dieckhoff, the acting head of the foreign ministry, and Neurath, the foreign minister, were repeating to their own satisfaction that deliveries of arms to aid the nationalists in Spain were impossible, since they would become known, and since 'there would be serious consequences to the German colony in Spain'.[5] Both the nazi party and Admiral Canaris, head of the Abwehr (that is, military intelligence), had other ideas. Canaris recommended Franco to his superiors as a 'tested man' who 'deserved full trust and support', and whom he had apparently met on visits to Spain.[6]

1. Roberto Cantalupo, *Fu la Spagna* (Milan, 1948), p. 62.
2. Attilio Tamaro, vol. II, p. 200.
3. Galeazzo Ciano, *Diaries 1939–1943* (London, 1947), p. 48.
4. Ciano, p. 206. Throughout this time, also, an Italian spy in the domestic service of Perth gained possession of the telegrams between Rome and England by fitting a removable false back to the ambassador's private safe. Ciano was thus able to act with unusual freedom in his relations with Britain.
5. *GD*, pp. 10–11.
6. Viñas plays down Canaris's role and he may be right to do so. Still, Canaris

Göring, chief of the Luftwaffe and of the German five-year plan, gave an account of what happened next at his trial at Nuremberg in 1946:

When the civil war broke out in Spain [testified the Reichsmarshal] Franco sent a call for help to Germany and asked for support, particularly in the air. Franco with his troops was stationed in Africa and ... he could not get his troops across, as the fleet was in the hands of the communists ... the decisive factor was, first of all, to get his troops to Spain ... the Führer thought the matter over. I urged him to give support under all circumstances: firstly, to prevent the further spread of communism; secondly, to test my young Luftwaffe in this or that technical respect.[1]

Spain gave the Luftwaffe, in fact, its first wartime activity.

Hitler agreed to see Langenheim and Bernhardt on the same evening, 25 July, at Bayreuth in the Villa Wahnfried after a performance of Siegfried.[2] Franco's letter to Hitler had requested merely ten anti-aircraft guns, five fighters and some other equipment. After the opera, Hitler demanded who Franco was, what he stood for, how he would be able to transport the army in Africa across the Straits of Gibraltar, and how he would pay his men, not to speak of Germany, if Hitler were to agree to assist him. The conversation lasted till two o'clock in the morning of 26 July. Hitler, to begin with accompanied only by Dr Kraneck, the head of the legal section in the nazi party's foreign department, the AO, ultimately agreed to help Franco in order 'to keep the Straits of Gibraltar from falling into communist hands'. Either on 26 July, or the next day, he decided to send Franco trans-

had been responsible for Spain placing her order in 1926 for submarines with a Dutch firm which was secretly financed by the German admiralty. Cf. F. Carsten, *The Reichswehr and Politics 1918–1933* (Oxford, 1966), p. 243. Franco later granted asylum and a pension to Frau Canaris after her husband's death in 1944. According to Ian Colvin, Canaris advised Franco as to how to resist Hitler's demands that Spain enter the world war (Ian Colvin, *Hitler's Secret Enemy*, London, 1957, p. 130). See also Karl Abshagen, *Canaris* (London, 1956), p. 112. Canaris had been in Spanish Morocco in 1916 where he had set up a supply base for German submarines, prepared a system of observation of allied ships in the Mediterranean and even allegedly directed risings against France. Canaris was a strong anti-communist.

1. International Military Tribunal, *The Trial of the Major War Criminals*, Nuremberg 1947–1949, ix, pp. 280–81.

2. Bernhardt to the author, Buenos Aires, 1971.

port aircraft, which Franco had not specifically asked for (though Beigbeder had). He also imposed conditions: German aid should go to Franco alone, so as to avoid conflicts between the different generals; and German assistance was to be defensive only, not offensive.[1] Later in the discussion, Göring, the war minister, General von Blomberg and a senior naval officer from Hamburg arrived.

Hitler later explained that he helped Franco in order 'to distract the attention of the western powers to Spain, and so enable German rearmament to continue unobserved'.[2] But, in 1941, Hitler said: 'If there had not been the danger of the Red Peril's overwhelming Europe, I'd not have intervened in the revolution in Spain. The Church would have been destroyed,' he added, not without relish.[3] He gave this as a reason for intervention to Ribbentrop on 27 July.[4] The Führer also thought that a nationalist success in Spain would establish a fascist power 'athwart the sea communications of Britain and France' – so adding a strategic reason for intervention.[5] In 1937, the Führer gave yet another explanation: Germany, who imported three-quarters of her ores, needed Spanish iron ore, and other minerals, and a nationalist government would maintain or increase sales to Germany, and a left-wing one might not.[6] This last point does not seem to have been urged by Bernhardt, though it must have been implicit, since Spain had exported iron to Germany for many years and the Germans had known of the potentials of Morocco since 1900. Canaris, who must have been consulted very soon, recalling his experience of the First World War, no doubt believed that German submarines could not refuel in war if the Spanish bases were in unsympathetic hands. Hitler, like Mussolini, was also pleased to be asked for help by Franco, and treated by another country, for the first time since he came to power three years before, as if he were indispensable. The part played by Bernhardt and, to a lesser extent, Langenheim, shows that the policy followed was that of the nazi

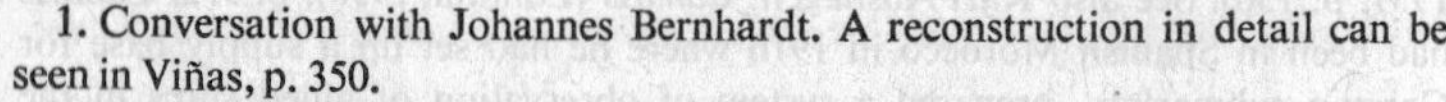
1. Conversation with Johannes Bernhardt. A reconstruction in detail can be seen in Viñas, p. 350.

2. Basil Liddell Hart, *The Other Side of the Hill* (London, 1948), p. 34.

3. *Hitler's Table Talk*, ed. by Hugh Trevor-Roper (London, 1953), p. 320.

4. Joachim von Ribbentrop, *Memoirs* (London, 1954), p. 59.

5. Liddell Hart, *loc. cit.* 6. See below, p. 736.

party, not that of the foreign ministry. This was the pattern of early nazi decisions: scepticism among professional diplomats, shared by the army; independent action supported by Germans in the country concerned; and quick decisions by Hitler, leading to early successes which made the diplomats' and generals' caution seem foolish.[1]

After the meeting at Bayreuth, a department in the German air ministry, special unit (*Sonderstab*) 'W', was set up by the state secretary of the air ministry, Erhard Milch, under General Wilberg, to superintend the recruitment of 'volunteers' and the dispatch of materials.[2] Two holding companies were also established, through which material from Germany to Spain would be sent, along with all payment or Spanish raw materials sent in exchange. These companies were HISMA (Compañia Hispano-Marroquí de Transportes), which was entirely under the direction of Bernhardt, with Franco's backing, and ROWAK (Rohstoff-und Waren-Einkaufsgesellschaft).[3] If a German trader wished to sell anything to Spain, he would have to sell it first to ROWAK; HISMA would market it in rebel Spain. A fleet of ships was assembled, and the navy instructed to provide protection. Twenty Junkers 52 (the tough, standard transport aeroplane or bomber of the Luftwaffe) and six Heinkels 51 (a less reliable fighter) were soon sent to Morocco, with eighty-six men, mostly Luftwaffe reservists: the first Junkers arrived on 29 July. Some of the former's engines were specially refitted to enable them to reach Spain, though half only went by air, half by sea.[4] At the same time, a 'tourist group' (Reisegesellschaftsunion) of Germans for Spain was set up under Major Alexander von Scheele, a veteran of the First World War who had once emigrated to the Chaco and had recently returned. The men left Hamburg for Cádiz on 29 July with the

1. See Karl Bracher, *The German Dictatorship* (London, 1970), p. 323.

2. Milch's diary for 26 July in David Irving, *The Rise and Fall of the Luftwaffe* (London, 1974), p. 48.

3. Captain Carranza, a retired army officer, was made a kind of formal partner to Bernhardt. Viñas prints the original contract of the company. ROWAK was not founded till later.

4. See Whealey, *loc. cit.* p. 215 and reference there; for the Junkers, see José Larios, *Combat over Spain* (London, 1966), p. 27; cf. evidence of General Warlimont, submitted to US Army Intelligence, 1945 (*UN Security Council Report on Spain*, 1946).

Heinkels and half the Junkers in the *Usamoro*. Milch bade them good-bye personally. They arrived on 1 August.[1] These were followed by engineers, other technicians, and some more fighters.[2] Scheele later became the military head of HISMA; Bernhardt, the general manager at Seville; and Colonel von Thoma, commander of ground troops and tanks, which began to arrive in about a month. Von Thoma and his officers set out partly to train the Spaniards, partly to gain battle experience themselves. He found, he says, the Spaniards quick to learn – and quick to forget.[3]

Henceforward, for two years and more, four transport aircraft were dispatched to Spain from Germany each week. Cargo boats were sent on an average every five days.[4] Bernhardt arrived back in Spain on the first Junker on 28 July. The nationalist commander in the air, General Kindelán, said to him: 'You are just a comedian trying to make money'. Bernhardt expostulated and told him to tell Franco of his suspicions. The Junkers immediately went into action to help the air lift. The next day or so, after the rest of the aircraft had arrived, Bernhardt had to go and tell both Queipo de Llano and Mola that the German help would go only to Franco. Queipo took the information with a laugh, while Mola's face fell; he knew what the news meant for him.[5]

These arrangements were made within a week of the request made to Hitler by Franco through the two Moroccan nazis. The German foreign ministry was taken by surprise. On 28 July, Dumont, at the Spanish desk in Berlin, was again minuting that the ministry was against intervention.[6] This view was shared by the war minister, Field-Marshal von Blomberg, and by General von Fritsch, the chief of staff. They thought Unternehmen Feuerzauber, 'Operation Magic Fire', as the Spanish adventure was officially known, militarily waste-

1. Viñas's dates.

2. There also were dispatched to Spain at this time twenty 20 mm anti-aircraft guns, two short-wave stations, some machine-guns, bombs, anti-gas equipment, stocks of aviation motors and medical equipment.

3. Liddell Hart, *op. cit.*, p. 98.

4. These figures derive from the nationalist historian of the war in the air, José Gomá, *La guerra en el aire* (Barcelona, 1958), p. 66. One hundred and seventy transport ships apparently made the journey to Spain during the entire war, chiefly leaving Hamburg.

5. Recollection of Johannes Bernhardt.

6. *GD*, p. 14.

ful. Ribbentrop, Hitler's special adviser on foreign affairs, shared these doubts.[1] Both the German foreign and economics ministries were, therefore, kept in the dark about HISMA and ROWAK until mid-October – though the finance ministry knew from the start, since it had to give ROWAK a credit of 3 million reichsmarks.[2] Nevertheless, the foreign ministry acquiesced without protest in the decisions taken against their advice.[3] When the Spanish government complained to the German counsellor in Madrid that German aircraft had been reported at Tetuán, the terse note 'not to be answered' was scrawled on the copy of the protest which arrived at the foreign ministry.[4] Everything was kept secret. The air ace Adolf Galland described how 'one or other of our comrades [in the Luftwaffe] vanished suddenly into thin air . . . After about six months he would return, sunburnt and in high spirits.'[5]

Nearly all the Germans who went to Spain, especially as pilots, were young nazis who believed that, in the words of one of their songs, 'We shall be marching onwards, if all else crashes about us: Our foes are the reds, the bolshevizers of the world.'[6] Most seem to have been genuine volunteers.

It was through Portugal that much German aid was arranged. The role played by that country in the Spanish War was simple. Less clerical than the Portuguese corporative régime, the Spanish nationalists stood for almost the same things as 'gracious Salazar', as the South African poet Roy Campbell would refer to the dictator in Lisbon.[7] The Portuguese government feared an invasion if the Left should win.[8] They were not tempted by the superficially attractive

1. Ribbentrop, p. 60. 2. *GD*, p. 114.
3. Ernst von Weizsäcker, *Memoirs* (New York, 1951), p. 112. 4. *GD*, p. 16.
5. Adolf Galland, *The First and the Last* (London, 1957), p. 23.
6. Wir werden weitermarschieren, wenn alles in Scherben fällt, Unsere Feinde sind die Roten, die Bolschewisten der Welt.
7. In his poem, 'The Flowering Rifle'. Campbell was caught in his house at Toledo by the outbreak of the revolution in that city. Narrowly escaping with his life (and that of his family), he later became one of the most ardent apologists for the nationalists, without, however, actually fighting for them. Southworth, *El mito*, p. 116f., makes a severe comparison between the version of 'The Flowering Rifle' published in 1939 and that of 1957.
8. Eden, p. 400. So Monteiro, Portuguese foreign minister, told Eden on 30 July, adding that he was afraid of a Spain which would be too closely linked with Germany.

idea of encouraging the disintegration of Spain into small caliphates.[1] The military aid which Salazar could give the nationalists was small. But he offered them other things as valuable: a place in which to plot; a refuge; and a means of communicating between their two zones at the start of the civil war. Nicolás Franco, the general's eldest brother, was permitted to establish his headquarters for the purchase of arms at Lisbon. The republican ambassador in that capital, the eminent historian and ex-foreign minister, Claudio Sánchez Albornoz, abandoned by his staff, swiftly became a prisoner in his own embassy. Salazar remarked on 1 August that he proposed to help the rebels 'with all available means' – including the intervention of the Portuguese army, if that should be necessary.[2] As a result, Spanish republicans who escaped into Portuguese territory were often handed over to the nationalists – such as, for instance, Andrés de Castro, a republican lawyer, with twenty-four fugitives from Vigo, who were shot on the International Bridge at Tuy.[3] The Portuguese press served the nationalists from the start. On 20 August, the German chargé d'affaires at Lisbon reported that war material brought from Germany in the steamships *Wigbert* and *Kamerun* had been dispatched onwards to Spain most smoothly. Salazar, he said, had removed 'all difficulties . . . by his personal initiative and handling of details'.[4]

The same day that Hitler agreed to help Franco, Gaston Monmousseau, the French communist railwaymen's leader and chief of the European office of the communist trade-union organization, the Profintern, apparently presided over a joint meeting of the executive committees of that body and of the Comintern.[5] It was decided that 1,000 million francs should be found to aid the Spanish government, of which the unions of Russia would contribute nine-tenths. The

1. The scheme was, however, examined and rejected. See Hugh Kay, *Salazar and Modern Portugal* (London, 1970), p. 86f.

2. Eventually 'several thousand' Portuguese volunteers fought for the nationalists. (Salazar, speech of May 1939, qu. Kay, p. 92.)

3. Iturralde, vol. II, p. 113.

4. *GD*, p. 53. Feeling against Portugal shortly became as strong as against Franco on the international Left. The novelist Louis Golding even agitated in England for a boycott on port.

5. The source of this statement is the same as in fn. 4, p. 338.

administration of the fund was to be carried out by a committee composed of Thorez, leader of the French communist party, Togliatti, La Pasionaria, Largo Caballero, and José Díaz.[1] An intense propaganda campaign in addition would be organized throughout Europe and America for aid to the republic. A large number of organizations for aid were set up, nominally humanitarian and independent, in fact dominated by communists. Paris, and Willi Muenzenberg, remained the centre of this activity. The most important of these groups was International Red Help, which had been active in assisting the revolutionaries of the Left in Spain since 1934. On 30 July, a huge meeting was held in the Salle Wagram in Paris at which Malraux, back from Spain, was the star speaker in a series of speeches which, punctuated by the '*Marseillaise*', '*La Carmagnole*' and '*La Jeune Garde*', called for 'volunteers and for contributions to aid Spain in her fight for liberty'. Afterwards, a Comité International de l'Aide au Peuple Espagnol was formed, of which Victor Basch was president.[2] This shortly had branches in nearly every country. For the time being, these organizations concerned themselves only with the provision of money, food, and medical supplies, not military aid. The committees' nominal leaders were usually distinguished, if innocent, but served by communist secretaries. But there was as yet no military aid from Russia. When the Spanish communists complained, Togliatti harshly remarked: 'Russia regards her security as the apple of her eye. A false move on her part could upset the balance of power and unleash a war in East Europe.'[3] At the same time, the (non-communist) International Federation of Trade Unions and the Labour Socialist International also met, in Brussels, on 28 July, deciding also to make an international financial

1. Nollau (p. 139) says that the Comintern executive (ECCI) set up a special committee on Spain composed of La Pasionaria, André Marty, Togliatti, André Bielov, and Stella Blagoyeva. The last two were cadre functionaries of the Comintern, possibly NKVD appointees: Stella Blagoyeva, a Bulgarian, finished her days as Bulgarian ambassadress to Moscow after 1945.

2. A Jewish polymath of Hungarian extraction. He and his wife were both murdered, being then over eighty, by the Gestapo in 1944. For the meeting, see Langlois, *loc. cit.*

3. Hernández, p. 36.

appeal for funds for Spain – though this met with limited success, £45,000 only being raised by September.[1]

*

The first reaction to the Spanish war was soon to be observed across the Atlantic.[2] Chile, Mexico, Argentina, Uruguay, Paraguay, and Cuba had received many recent immigrants from Spain, and all the countries of Latin and South America felt concerned by the events in Spain. There was strong feeling for the nationalists in Brazil and the Canadian province of Quebec, where, as in Spain, there were fascist organizations in a catholic background. The government of Chile was strongly pro-nationalist. The Mexican government from the start supported the Spanish republic, as might be expected from a country whose constitution had itself derived from a rising against clerical and aristocratic privilege. In Venezuela, Rómulo Betancourt's illegal reformist party, Democratic Action, took shape around the idea of support for the Spanish republic, while the Cuban Left felt as moved by the drama in Spain as by any event since their own revolution in 1933: Spaniards were highly important in the commercial life of Havana.

The United States were preparing to endorse the achievements of Roosevelt's first term of office in the presidential elections of 1936. International affairs then seemed far away to most Americans. Neutrality in all 'adventures' in Europe was the policy of both Republican and Democratic parties. During the Abyssinian crisis, in May 1935, a Neutrality Act had been passed in Congress, rendering it illegal for American citizens to sell or transport arms to belligerents, once the President had proclaimed there to be a state of war. Although this act was not meant to apply to civil wars, the American government behaved from the start of the Spanish conflict as if it did, although President Roosevelt had some sympathy for the republic – a point of view held much more vigorously by the American ambassador in Spain, Claude Bowers, a journalist and biographer (of Jefferson) by profession. Mrs Eleanor Roosevelt, Henry Morgenthau,

1. Report of 1936 TUC, quoted K. W. Watkins, *Britain Divided* (London, 1963), p. 153.

2. F. J. Taylor, *The United States and the Spanish Civil War* (New York, 1956), p. 39f.

secretary of the treasury, Henry Wallace, secretary for agriculture, Harold Ickes, secretary of the interior, and Sumner Welles, the assistant secretary of state, were also republican champions. But the secretary of state, Cordell Hull, had only sympathy for the cause of impartiality, and usually had his way. On the other hand, some companies such as the Texas Oil Company had a free hand to help Franco, as will shortly be seen.[1]

Public opinion in the US became, however, almost as moved by the Spanish war as it was in Europe. A torrent of propaganda poured from the Spanish government's information bureau in New York and from the 'Peninsular News Service', the nationalist headquarters in the same city. American newspapers took sides in the war with at least as great vehemence as did those in Britain and France. American catholics attacked reporters of republican sympathies and liberals attacked those who wrote in apology for the nationalists. On the *New York Times*, this discrepancy of view extended to two of its own newspapermen, W. P. Carney, who wrote from among the nationalists, and Herbert Matthews, among the republicans.[2] American socialist and liberal intellectuals took the cause of republican Spain to their hearts as they had never taken any foreign cause, and the relief and anti-fascist (pro-Soviet) organizations already in existence grew in strength.[3]

On 29 July, meantime, out of the first consignment of twelve Savoia 81 bombers[4] sent by Mussolini from Elmas (Cagliari), under Colonel Ruggero Bonomi, to help the nationalists, one made a forced landing at Berkane in French Morocco, one crashed at Zaida in Algeria, and a third crashed into the sea thirty miles offshore. An inquiry by General Denain, a former French air minister, showed that the aircraft had had their Italian colours painted out, had been fitted with four machine-guns, had left Sardinia at dawn, and had been manned by Italian air-force men in civilian clothes. A survivor admitted that the expedition was being made to assist the Spanish

1. See below, p. 417. Roosevelt was ignorant of Spanish politics: 'I hope that if Franco wins, he will establish a liberal régime,' he apparently told the subsequent republican ambassador, de los Ríos, over their first interview, in the summer of 1936 (Azaña, vol. IV, p. 630).

2. See Allen Guttman, *The Wound in the Heart* (New York, 1962).

3. See Caute, p. 139.

4. Savoia Marchetti 81.

rebels.[1] By that time, the other Savoias were at Franco's headquarters, under Bonomi, with a special friend of Mussolini's, the pilot Ettore Muti, among his men.

Now, earlier, on 29 July, the Quai d'Orsay had denied that the French government had sent any war material to the Spanish republic: and Blum and Delbos repeated the denial to the foreign affairs committee of the Senate on the 30th. On 2 August, there was a stormy meeting of the French cabinet. Cot argued that the proof of Italian help to the rebels showed that the policy of non-intervention had failed. Delbos, on the prompting of Léger and 'in consideration of the British position', argued that all countries who might aid one or other of the combatants in Spain should be approached for a general agreement on non-intervention. The cabinet announced that they had decided to appeal urgently to 'interested governments' – Britain and Italy in the first instance – for a 'Non-Intervention Pact'. This was welcomed by the British, who made it their business to ensure its success.[2] Nevertheless, despite these denials, and perhaps unknown to some of the French cabinet, Pierre Cot, Jean Moulin, Malraux and their friends were hastily already dispatching shipments to Spain of some of the newest military aeroplanes – including Marcel Bloch (Dassault) bombers built in 1935, Potez 54 bombers just entering into service and Dewoitine 371 fighters. These aircraft were flown to aerodromes in the south of France such as Montaudran (Toulouse) or Ubarière (Perpignan), where they were either taken over by Spanish pilots or flown to Spain by French pilots in reserve.[3] They were received at Prat de Llobregat, Barcelona, by Abel Guides, a French pilot nominated for the post by Cot. Altogether, by 8 August, some seventy aircraft had been sent, about forty or fifty from the government, about twenty or thirty through private arms dealers or impresarios, such as Malraux.[4] The first aircraft probably left on

1. *L'Echo de Paris*, 1 August 1936. Cf. Bolín, p. 172. Bonomi said in his book that he received the orders to go to Morocco on 28 July.

2. Note telephone call to Paris, 4 August (*FO* 371/205/26/23); conversations with the late Francis Hemming.

3. See Jean Gisclon, *Des avions et des hommes* (Paris, 1969), for an account of what happened to the seventeen Dewoitines flown to Montaudran.

4. The exact number, and of what make, is difficult to be certain about. The figure of seventy is Pierre Cot, *The Triumph of Treason* (Chicago, 1944), p. 343. See also Lacouture, p. 229; Salas Larrazábal, vol. I, p. 436; Sanchis, p. 11; and

31 July. It had not been, in the end, so easy to persuade the directors of the Breguet and Potez works to help the Spaniards, and only the directors of Dewoitine sent material with any enthusiasm, along with those at the Hotchkiss machine-gun works.[1] The value of this aid was anyway rather debatable since the Potezes, though they could carry 2,000 pounds of bombs, were slow: they could only go 100 miles an hour and could only operate with a crew of seven; they were hence nicknamed 'collective flying coffins'.[2] The Dewoitines (at 180 miles an hour) were faster than the Nieuports, but they arrived without armaments and were not easy to make ready for war. Recruitment of French technicians, as of pilots, followed. Specialized workmen, for example, were secured in France for the naval repair workshops at Cartagena and Valencia. The French radical politician, Senator Boussutrot, organized recruitment of pilots (some to be paid the enormous sum of 50,000 pesetas a month). The lives of these men were insured at 500,000 pesetas, with, appropriately, an insurance company of which Boussutrot was director.[3] At the same time, the four Fokker aircraft bought by Franco in England and held up at Bordeaux were returned whence they had come; and soon the

---

Les Evénements survenus, p. 219. The probable shipment was something like: 5 Bloch 210 bombers; 20 Potez 54 bombers (some being 540, some 543); 10 Breguet XIX reconnaissance planes; 17 Dewoitine 371 fighters; 2 Dewoitine 500 and 510 fighters; 5 Amiot bombers; and 5 Potez 25-A-2 bombers. Pike, pp. 44–6, has a list of 38 planes leaving Francazal (Toulouse) for Barcelona between 2 and 9 August; and 56 between 9 August and 14 October, from Montaudran, the neighbouring airfield owned by Air France. The latter included 6 Loire 46 fighters, and 1 Blériot Spad 510 fighter. There were probably more of the latter. Jules Moch, *Rencontres avec Léon Blum* (Paris, 1969), p. 146, speaks of another 13 Dewoitines going on 8 August.

1. Jesús Salas, p. 83.

2. A. García Lacalle, *Mitos y verdades: la aviación de caza en la guerra española* (Mexico, 1974), pp. 134–5.

3. Jesús Salas, p. 64, prints a contract with one pilot. The average junior Spanish officer's wage was 333 pesetas a month. Later, these huge sums for foreign aviators dropped by half, and, by the winter, volunteer pilots were paid 1,000 pesetas for every enemy shot down. The first 13 pilots were French (Darry, Valbert, Bernay, Thomas, Heilmann) but soon Englishmen appeared (Smith-Piggott, Doherty, Cartwright, Clifford, Collins) and later some Americans (Dahl, Tanker, Leider, Allison, etc.). All were mercenaries though all had, too, some political views.

imaginative André Malraux obtained the right to form and command in action an air squadron of foreigners. He collected together some twenty aircraft, mostly Potez 54 bombers, but also the one time private aircraft of the Emperor Haile Selassie of Abyssinia, a few mechanics, an interpreter, a transport manager, and a dozen pilots. Some of these were idealists, such as the communist commissar, Julien Segnaire, some were mercenaries. Most were French, but there were a few Italians and later some Americans, Germans and an Englishman. The 'Escuadrilla España', as Malraux called his squadron, was first based in Barcelona, then moved to Barajas outside Madrid, being active on the front in August in Estremadura; the pilots lived in Madrid.[1]

In the revolutionary columns on the ground there were also by August many foreigners, particularly German and Italian émigrés, communists and socialists, who had come to the 'Peoples' Olympiad' at Barcelona. Italian anarchists had been settled in Barcelona for many years, and some of them fought in the battle for the telephone exchange there. An Austrian anarchist died in the battle for the Atarazanas barracks, and perhaps two hundred foreigners took part in the fighting in July in Catalonia. The Italians soon formed themselves into the Gastone–Sozzi Battalion,[2] and the Germans, under Hans Beimler, a communist ex-deputy of the Reichstag, into the Thaelmann 'Centuria'.[3] A number of French and Belgians formed a Paris Battalion. These men (and some women) were of no particular political grouping, though communists predominated. In late August, another Italian group, the Giustizia e Libertà Column, led by the leader of the group of Italian social democrats of that name, Carlo

1. Malraux flew, though he had no pilot's licence. His task was to galvanize and to inspire. Many of his hangers-on at the Hotel Florida in Madrid made a bad impression. See Lacouture, p. 230; the novel by Paul Nothomb (Julien Segnaire), *La Rançon* (Paris, 1952), whose author appears in *L'Espoir* as 'Attignies'; Koltsov, p. 93; Pietro Nenni, *Spagna* (Milan, 1958), p. 196. A negative comment can be seen in Hidalgo de Cisneros, vol. II, p. 323f.

2. Gastone Sozzi was an Italian socialist killed by the Black Shirts.

3. Thaelmann had been a Hamburg harbour worker, whose hearty but semi-illiterate incoherence commended him to Stalin in the late twenties as a leader of the German communists. He was at this time in a concentration camp, where

he was later murdered (1944). Beimler had been imprisoned in Dachau and had escaped by strangling his SS guard and walking out in his clothes.

Rosselli, who had been active among Italian exiles in Paris since his own escape from a fascist gaol, fought near Huesca. The first English volunteers in Spain were Sam Masters and Nat Cohen, communist 'garment workers' from East London who were bicycling in France at the time of the rising. In Barcelona, they organized a 'centuria' named after the English communist, Tom Mann. The first Englishman who went to the front was apparently John Cornford, a twenty-year-old communist research student in history at Trinity College, Cambridge, the great-grandson of Charles Darwin and son of a professor of ancient philosophy.[1] Surprisingly, for a communist, he joined a POUM column on the Aragon front, at Leciñena on 13 August. This was because he had brought no papers with him proving his 'anti-fascist identity', and was thus refused membership of the PSUC column.[2] The first English volunteer to be killed was a woman, Felicia Browne, a communist painter, shot in Aragon on 25 August. Previously living on the Costa Brava, she had fought in the street-battles in Barcelona, whither she had gone to attend the People's Olympiad. Altogether these early 'volunteers for liberty' in Aragon or Catalonia probably numbered 1,000–1,500.[3]

Meantime, in the international game of chess which marked the diplomatic background to the civil war, some new moves were being made. Philip Noel-Baker, the foreign affairs spokesman of the British Labour party, arrived in Paris. Blum thought that a nationalist Spain would be a military threat to Britain as well as to France. Noel-Baker suggested that the British cabinet should be told that by the French. So Blum sent Admiral Darlan, the French chief of naval staff, to make an unofficial approach to Baldwin's government,[4] which was,

1. Cornford was accompanied (on a different part of the same Aragon front) by Richard Bennett, also from Trinity College, Cambridge. After a short while on the front-line, Bennett joined the Barcelona Radio Services and broadcast as 'Voice of Spain'.

2. *John Cornford, A Memoir*, edited by Pat Sloan (London, 1938), p. 199. See also P. Stansky and W. Abrahams, *Journey to the Frontier* (London, 1966), a memoir of Cornford and of another Englishman who went to Spain, Julian Bell. Cornford's resolution, and perhaps even more a famous resolute photograph of him, makes him the best known 'volunteer for Spain' of all, in England. His decision to go was fairly casual (Stansky and Abrahams, p. 314). He was a poet of rare promise.

3. Martínez Bande, *La invasión de Aragón*, p. 70.

4. *Les Événements survenus*, p. 219.

indeed, in need of accurate information. For the British Embassy in Madrid believed that it was only a matter of days before the capital would fall; and hence the government were not going to devote much attention to the plight of foreign nationals. The consul in Barcelona, Norman King, forecast economic collapse; while the ambassador at St Jean de Luz wrote that the contest was one of 'rebel versus rabble'. 'The situation is beginning to resemble that of the French Revolution, except that the rifle and the revolver have taken the place of "the Guillotine". The Scarlet Pimpernel is badly needed . . .',[1] he added. Daily, meantime, from republican Spain, and especially from Catalonia, other appeals were sent out for help:

> Workers and anti-fascists of all lands! We the workers of Spain are poor but we are pursuing a noble ideal. Our fight is your fight. Our victory is the victory of liberty. We are the vanguard of the international proletariat in the fight against fascism. Men and women of all lands! Come to our aid! Arms for Spain![2]

The government in Madrid were, however, also showing that they would not permit sentiment to come between them and their search for arms. On 2 August, Barcia, the republican foreign minister, asked a German businessman, Herr Sturm, of the Independent Airplane Association of Berlin, if Germany could sell them pursuit planes and light bombers, with bombs of a hundred or two hundred pounds. Payment would be in any currency requested, even in gold.[3] This request no doubt explains the continued politeness of the republican government at this time to Germany (the censorship even forbade the derogatory use of swastikas in cartoons), even though they must have known of the dispatch of war material by Germans to their enemies.[4] The German official, Schwendemann, who received the request, urged its dilatory handling, and not its straightforward rejection. A sea cargo of spare parts for aeroplanes and also lubricating oil for the engines, meantime, arrived in Morocco from Italy, on 2 August;[5] and, on 4 August, Admiral Canaris arrived secretly in

1. One soon appeared. See below, p. 477. *FO*, 371/205/26/83; 96; and 120; also 28/177.

2. CNT–FAI bulletin, 28 July. 3. *GD*, p. 20.

4. The republic also attempted to gain native troops from the fetid Spanish colony of Ifni, before it fell at the start of August.

5. R. Salas, vol. I, p. 441.

Rome, in order to coordinate German and Italian aid to Franco. He had a long talk with his opposite number in Italian military intelligence, Colonel Mario Roatta. That meeting marked the real beginning of the military collaboration which led to the future Axis.[1] Italy agreed to provide petrol, and to give permission to German aircraft to land *en route* between Germany and Spain.[2]

One other aspect of the internationalization of the Spanish Civil War should be noted. The 1930s were the great age of the foreign correspondent. From the end of July 1936, for two-and-a-half years, the best-known names in journalism were to be found south of the Pyrenees. Distinguished writers were hired by news agencies to represent them at the Spanish war. The journalists themselves were to write about Spain much that was inaccurate and much that was brilliant. But many journalists also wrote articles which were intended not so much to be commentary, as pamphlets aimed to help one side or the other. This was specially true of the republican side, for the nationalist press department had a harder task to excite enthusiasm among Anglo-Saxon correspondents. Among the republicans, journalists went into the lines, helped to train Spaniards in the use of machine-guns, and organized arms supply. A correspondent of *The Times* first pointed out to the Anti-Fascist Militias Committee that they could not win the war unless they found a way of feeding Barcelona.

*

No international action specifically caused the civil war, even if it is arguable that it would not have occurred had not the Left been oppressed by the fear of fascism, the Right by that of communism. No foreign power took the initiative to help either side. But those who were now drawn in, in one way or another, found it hard to disentangle themselves. Like Napoleon, they became bogged down in the quicksands of Spanish politics. The final breakdown of the European order thus began in July 1936 in Spain.

1. Whealey, in Carr, *The Republic*, p. 217, quoting German naval documents.
2. Viñas, p. 429.

22

The advance of the Army of Africa – Badajoz – the Tagus valley – the fall of Guipúzcoa – Varela in Andalusia – Miaja in Córdoba – Bayo in Majorca – Pinilla in Gijón – Aranda at Oviedo – the Alcázar – air raids

---

TWO campaigns soon altered the political complexion of Spain: the advance of the Army of Africa, commanded by Franco, northwards from Seville; and that of the Army of the North, under Mola, against the Basque province of Guipúzcoa.

The Germans supplied transport aircraft under Captain von Moreau to carry 1,500 men of the Army of Africa to Seville between 29 July and 5 August. Thereafter, 500 men were carried across daily. This was the first major 'air-lift' of troops in history.[1] Hitler later remarked that 'Franco ought to erect a monument to the glory of the Junkers 52. It is this aircraft that the Spanish revolution has to thank for its victory.'[2] Five Italian Savoia 81 bombers, with some other aircraft and surface craft, also covered a convoy of merchant ships which ferried about 3,000 men with equipment from Morocco to Spain on 5 August, 'the day of the Virgin of Africa'.[3] The republican

1. 12,000 men were flown to Spain from Africa in August and September in some 677 flights. After the end of September, the need for such airlifts ceased as Franco gained command of the sea. See below, p. 426. (Kindelán, in *Guerra de liberación*, Saragossa, 1961, p. 365.) Captain Alfred Henke was technical adviser to Franco on the airlift.

2. *Hitler's Table Talk*, p. 687. The very first airlift in the Spanish war was constituted by the modest flights of Fokkers and Dorniers from Tetuán to Seville carried out by Spanish pilots between 20 and 29 July, carrying 10 legionaries in each flight, 837 men between 20 and 31 July, according to J. Martínez Bande, in *La campaña de Andalucía* (Madrid, 1969), p. 36.

3. For a description of the day, the bands, Franco watching on the hill of El Hacho near Ceuta, and the arrival of the singing warriors, see Larios, p. 32, Bolín, p. 173, and Martínez Bande, *op. cit.*, p. 40f. The aircraft active on this day were the 5 Savoias, 3 Fokker Trimotors, a DC2 captured in Seville, 2 hydroplanes, 2 Nieuport fighters and a squadron of Breguets XIX (R. Salas Larrazábal, vol. I, p. 295). Cf. also the memoir by the Italian Colonel Bonomi on the Italians' role.

fleet, far more powerful than anything which the rebels could assemble, but incompetently led, retired to the harbours of Cartagena and Málaga. The republican seamen were probably also overawed by the presence of two of Germany's three battleships, the *Deutschland* and the *Admiral Scheer*, in the area. These victories of transport meant that a strong column could, therefore, be assembled at Seville, to march due north to cut off the Portuguese frontier from the republicans, to join forces with the Army of the North.

This army 'of Africa', as it very soon became known, was directed by Franco, who flew to Seville on 6 August, leaving Orgaz in command in Morocco. The column was led in the field by Yagüe, and, under him, Colonels Asensio, Delgado Serrano, Barrón, and Tella, with Major Castejón, all veterans of Moroccan warfare. Each of these officers commanded a *bandera*[1] of the Legion and a *tabor*[2] of *Regulares*, with one or two batteries. The whole force (almost all carried across the Straits by air and about 8,000 strong) travelled in detachments of a hundred strong, in lorries commandeered in Seville by Queipo de Llano, driven fast up the centre of the road. Eight Italian Savoias 81 and nine German Junkers 52 flown respectively by Italians and Germans gave the nationalists effective local command of the air, while volunteers from the aeroclub at Seville were active in reconnaissance and liaison missions. (Two flying-club pilots caused one group of militiamen to abandon their position by bombing them with melons.)[3] On arrival at a town, the lorries would halt, and artillery and aircraft would bombard it for half an hour. The legionaries and Moroccans would then advance. If there were resistance, a regular assault would be made. The militiamen might fight bravely while their ammunition lasted, and thereafter panic, with no discipline to prevent a rout: no one told them to spread out to defend a village. Afterwards, bodies of those killed in the revolutionary atrocities would be found, and, in reprisal, the leaders of left-wing parties who had remained would be hunted out and shot. Anyone would be liable to be shot who was carrying arms or whose shoulder bore the bruise of a recoil from a rifle. Few prisoners were made. The brutality

1. See above, p. 217 fn. 4. 2. A *tabor* was a battalion of 225 men.

3. Larios, p. 44. The republican air command concentrated – or, rather, split up – its still superior forces in the Sierras to the north of Madrid. See Jesús Salas, p. 64.

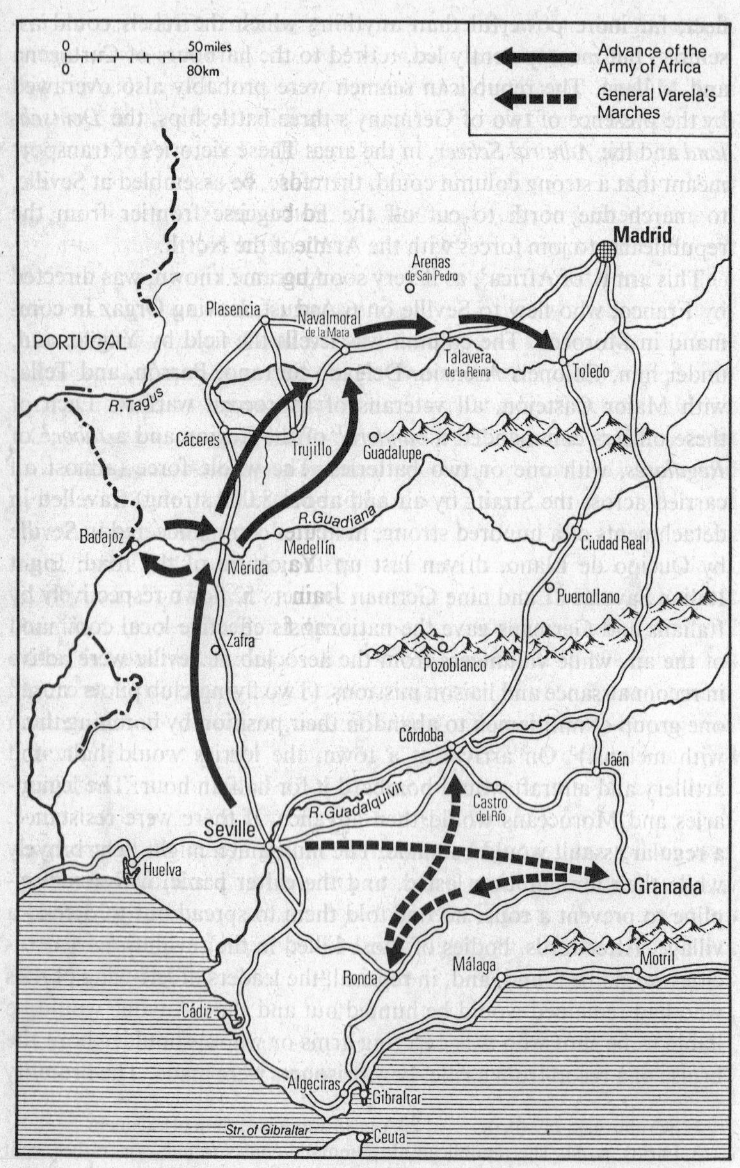

12. The advance of the Army of Africa, August–October 1936

of the Legion and the Moroccans was unexpected. The Moors – *los Moros* – had always been villains in Spanish fairy stories: they now became the focus of terror throughout southern Spain. The Portuguese press reported that 1,000 were even killed at the small town of Almendralejo.[1] A vast army of refugees fled before Yagüe's army northwards. Everywhere the killing of 'reds' would be accompanied by a re-opening of churches, masses, and baptisms of those born in the preceding month. In this way, Yagüe reached Mérida, with its magnificent Roman monuments, on 10 August, having advanced 200 miles in under a week. This was the kind of adventurous march in which Yagüe, by nature a *condottiere*, revelled. Hot-blooded, popular with his men, he in no way resembled the cold modern type of general on the German model whom Franco was coming to admire. Four miles south of Mérida, the militia gave Yagüe his first real contest of the war. The battle was fought over the river Guadiana before the town. A thrust by Asensio gained both bridge and town. The committee of defence of the city were executed – at their head, Anita López, the soul of anarchist resistance. Yagüe thus established contact with the northern zone of rebel Spain – though not as yet with any body of men organized as a fighting force. He also cut off the frontier town of Badajoz. Towards this, he next advanced with Asensio and Castejón, leaving Tella with a small force to hold Mérida. On 11 August, the Mérida militia, which had fled from the town and was now stiffened by 2,000 assault guards and civil guards from Madrid, launched a counter-attack. Tella held this off, enabling Yagüe, with Castejón and Asensio and about 3,000 men, to concentrate on Badajoz, though it is possible that the attack was a strategic error: it might have been better to press on to Madrid. Defending the town was Colonel Ildefonso Puigdendolas (previously in command of the column which captured Guadalajara), with some 8,000 inexperienced militiamen. Just before the attack, Puigdendolas had

1. *O Seculo*, 11 August 1936. The Portuguese press was, during the early months, frank in its comments on nationalist massacres. See Brenan, *The Spanish Labyrinth*, p. 225, and Southworth, *El mito*, p. 215, for comment. For this campaign, see also Aznar, p. 102f; Lojendio, p. 138f; Sánchez del Arco; and Harold Cardozo, *The March of a Nation* (New York, 1937); Cecil Gerahty, *The Road to Madrid* (London, 1937); and H. R. Knickerbocker, *The Siege of the Alcázar* (Philadelphia, 1936).

to expend material, energy, and confidence dealing with a mutiny of the civil guards.

The hot city of Badajoz is surrounded by walls and, from the east, whence Yagüe was advancing, is further guarded by the broad river Guadiana. After a morning's artillery bombardment, the attack was ordered in the middle of the afternoon of 14 August. The 16th Company of the 4th *Bandera* of the Legion stormed the Puerta de la Trinidad singing, at the moment of the advance, their regimental hymn proclaiming their bride to be death. At the first assault, they were driven back by the militia's machine-guns. At the next, the legionaries forced their way through, stabbing their enemies with knives.

The entry was made, although, of the assault force, only a captain, a corporal, and fourteen legionaries survived. At the same time, another column of legionaries assaulted the walls near the Puerta del Pilar. They made an entry there with less difficulty. The battle then went on in the streets. The two attacking forces met in the Plaza de la República beneath the shadow of the cathedral, and thereafter the town was lost. Hand-to-hand fighting continued until the night. Badajoz became a city of corpses. Battle and repression were indistinguishable since, once the town had been penetrated, there was no one to give orders either to continue or to cease fighting. Colonel Puigdendolas fled into Portugal. The legionaries killed anyone with arms, including militiamen on the steps of the high altar of the cathedral. The bull-ring became a camp of concentration. Many militiamen were shot and even more carabineers, on Yagüe's orders.[1]

1. The news of the 'massacre of Badajoz' was first given to the world by two French journalists, Marcel Dany and Jacques Berthet, and a Portuguese journalist, Mario Neves. Their account was later denied by Major McNeil Moss in *The Legend of Badajoz* (London, 1937), which was itself countered by Koestler in *Spanish Testament*, pp. 143–5. McNeil Moss got his story from two British volunteers for Franco (Captains Fitzpatrick and Nangle) who, however, only joined the nationalist army on 9 September. Inquiries by the author in Badajoz in 1959 left him convinced of the truth of the story as described above. The exact number of those killed will probably never be known. It may not be quite as many as 1,800 – the figure named by Jay Allen of the *Chicago Tribune*. Southworth's *El mito* (p. 123), contains new material on these events. There was certainly fighting inside the cathedral, as eye-witnesses separately testified to the author, and as is suggested anyway in nationalist accounts (e.g. Sánchez del Arco, *op. cit.*, p. 9). See Jay Allen's report published at the time in the *Chicago Tribune*

These executions continued into the next day, 15 August, and, at a lesser rate, for some time afterwards.[1] There was another burst of repression when Salazar handed over refugees who had fled across the border. This conquest sealed off the Portuguese frontier from the republican government.

On 20 August, Yagüe began a new advance, turning east towards Madrid. Tella advanced through Trujillo to Navalmoral de la Mata, which he occupied on 23 August. To the east, the valley of the Tagus stretched out with no serious natural obstacles. All the revolutionary collectives formed after the occupations of farms in March collapsed, without much fighting, though the collapse was followed by much killing. Asensio and Castejón advanced to the Tagus over the mountains of Guadalupe. Here the government's Estremadura army, under General Riquelme, with troops from Madrid, met them. A section of Asensio's column was nearly destroyed in the town of Medellín, by Malraux's air squadron[2] in its first serious engagement: the squadron had brought together two or three Potez bombers, one or two Breguets and a Douglas. But the militia on the ground were no match for the legionaries and Moroccans, who outmanoeuvred them, forcing them to retreat hastily from their position, or risk being cut off. Even the aircraft were little prepared for modern war (bombs had to be pushed from the windows of fighters). Nine thousand men retreated, including 2,000 anarchists who refused Riquelme's orders in battle and launched useless attacks in the San Vicente hills.

Asensio and Castejón joined Tella, therefore, at Navalmoral. After some days' rest, the advance began again on 28 August, along the northern side of the valley of the Tagus. Resistance was rare. The Army of Africa continued along the roads. The republican troops were unused to the battle conditions of this thirsty and barren valley.

(30 August 1936), reprinted in Robert Payne, *The Civil War in Spain 1936–1939* (New York, 1962), pp. 89–91; and J. T. Whitaker, 'Prelude to War' (*Foreign Affairs*, October 1942), p. 104f. A wholly false account of this massacre in which Yagüe was accused of having organized a fiesta at which the prisoners were shot before the wealth and beauty of Badajoz was published in *La Voz* of Madrid, 27 October 1936, and had a disastrous effect, causing reprisals in Madrid.

1. Yagüe did not intervene to prevent bloodshed. But, on Franco's orders, he did usually restrain the Moors from castrating corpses of their victims – an established Moorish battle-rite.

2. Malraux, pp. 99–105; Lacouture, p. 233.

There were desertions. The militia refused to dig trenches, on the ground that such an action was cowardly. The government could not risk losing all their men in a general engagement and, therefore, retreated all the time. About now, furthermore, the appearance of Italian Fiat fighters of the so-called Cucaracha group, faster than anything possessed by the republicans, reinforced the rebels' local control in the air.[1] On 2 September, the columns of the Army of Africa reached Talavera de la Reina, where 10,000 militiamen were established, with as much artillery as could be spared (as well as an armoured train), in a fine defensive position on the slopes before the town. At dawn on 3 September, Asensio and Castejón advanced to surround the town. The aerodrome and railway-station, some way out of the centre, were occupied. At midday, an assault was launched against the town itself, whose defenders by now had become thoroughly alarmed. In the early afternoon, after little street-fighting, Yagüe conquered Talavera. The under-secretary of war in Madrid, Hernández Sarabia, telephoned Talavera in the evening, to be answered by a Moroccan.[2] The last town of importance between Franco and Madrid had now fallen.

The completeness of this campaign of 300 miles in a month was a triumph for Franco, who had been criticized by some for selecting the western, longer route from Seville to Madrid, in place of the eastern, shorter and more normal one through Córdoba, La Mancha and Aranjuez. The campaign also consolidated Franco's position against both Mola and Queipo de Llano.

The second main campaign of August was that in the north. In late July, as has been seen, because of shortage of ammunition, Mola had been near to despair; even to suicide, on 29 July, reported his secretary. At one moment, he was down to 26,000 rounds of ammunition. Then Franco told him by telegram of the arrival of German and Italian aircraft, and sent him 600,000 cartridges.[3] Mola's plan, coordinated with Franco whom he met in Seville on 13 August, was

1. Hidalgo de Cisneros, vol. II, p. 299. These Fiat-Ansaldo fighters, the CR 32s, were the most used Italian fighter on the nationalist side in the civil war. They had begun to arrive by sea on 14 August and were based at the end of August on Cáceres.

2. Aznar, p. 174. It was Hernández Sarabia's last act as minister of war.

3. Iribarren, pp. 132, 135.

now to capture San Sebastián and Irún, thus cutting off the Basques from the French border at the western end of the Pyrenees. The columns of mainly Navarrese troops operating there were placed under the overall command of their countryman, Colonel José Solchaga. On 11 August, Major Latorre had taken the old Basque capital of Tolosa. A socialist who had prevented the local anarchists and communists from destroying the electricity centre in the town was for his pains shaved, except for a tonsure, and forced to run round the town crying, '*¡Viva Cristo Rey!*'[1] On the same day, Colonel Beorlegui seized Picoqueta, a key ridge commanding the approach of Irún. Telesforo Monzón, a prominent Basque nationalist politician, travelled hurriedly to Barcelona to seek aid. But the *Generalidad* could spare only 1,000 rifles. The Basques, therefore, confiscated the gold in the local branch of the Bank of Spain and other banks at Bilbao and sent it by sea to Paris, to buy arms on its credit. The first commander of republican forces in Guipúzcoa, Pérez Garmendía, fell into Beorlegui's hands; gravely wounded, Pérez Garmendía was briskly told by Beorlegui, an old friend, that it was fortunate he was about to die of wounds, since otherwise he would be shot as a traitor.[2]

The rebels moved some of their few naval vessels towards San Sebastián and Irún. The military governor, Lieutenant Antonio Ortega, in command at San Sebastián, threatened to shoot five prisoners for each person killed in sea bombardment, the prisoners in the town being many, and distinguished, due to San Sebastián's position as the summer capital of the country. The rebel ships, *España*, *Almirante Cervera*, and *Velasco*, nevertheless began to fire on 17 August. The population hid, but four people were killed, and thirty-eight wounded. Ortega executed eight civilian prisoners and five rebel officers. The naval bombardment continued on the following days, without causing panic. Irún and San Sebastián began also to be bombed daily, Junkers 52 being prominent among the attackers.

1. Iturralde, vol. II, p. 72.

2. *op. cit.*, p. 141. The brave, ruthless, simple giant, Beorlegui, was a man of character. Mola kept ringing him up but the colonel hated the telephone and persuaded Major Martínez de Campos to serve as go-between. 'You must take San Sebastián,' Mola would yell; 'Let him take Madrid,' Beorlegui would call back. See Martínez de Campos, p. 45. Beorlegui put up his umbrella in Oyarzún to protect himself from bombs (del Burgo, p. 206). See also Martínez Bande's official history, *La guerra en el norte* (Madrid, 1969), pp. 37–99.

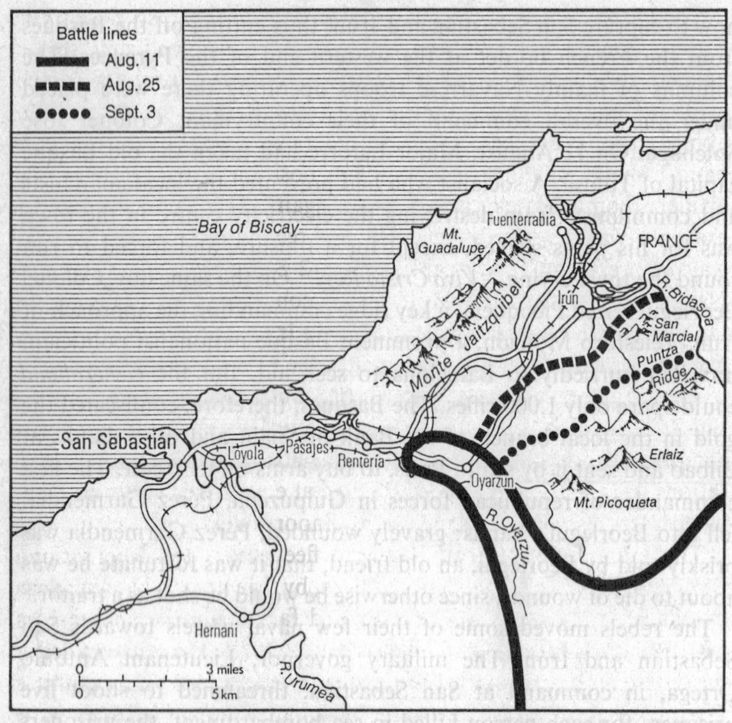

13. The campaign in Guipúzcoa, August–September 1936

On 26 August, the land assault on Irún began. The number of men involved was small: about 3,000 Basques and republicans, and nearly 2,000 nationalists. Beorlegui was, however, supported by nearly all the artillery upon which Mola could lay hands. He had also a small number of light German Panzer Mark 1 tanks, manned with machine-guns, and armoured cars. The Basques, on the other hand, were strengthened by a number of French and Belgian technicians sent by the French communist party,[1] and also by some anarchists from Barcelona. They had one regiment of artillery.

1. On his own admission in the Chambre des Députés on 16 March 1939, the French communist leader André Marty, member of the Comintern's central committee ECCI, future leader of the regularly organized International Brigades, was at Irún. For Marty, see below, p. 457.

The ensuing battle was fought in dazzling sunshine, so close to the French frontier that Beorlegui had to restrain his men from firing in an easterly direction. Day after day, there was a prolonged rebel artillery bombardment, followed by an assault, after the Basque lines appeared to be evacuated. The defenders would then return and, in hand-to-hand fighting, recapture the position. After a delay, the artillery bombardment would begin again. The Puntza ridge, for example, was destroyed, evacuated, and recaptured four times in this way before being finally captured, on 2 September. That day, the Navarrese also took the whitewashed convent of San Marcial, on the windy hill immediately commanding Irún, and the customs post at Behobia. The latter was surrounded, the men within fighting hand-to-hand to the last man, those who could having leapt into the Bidasoa to swim to France and to safety. Both sides fought with complete disregard of personal safety, putting the lie to those accusations of cowardice that both shouted at each other when the firing had ceased, at night, or during the afternoon's siesta.

The inhabitants of Irún began to flee across the International Bridge on the road to Hendaye. On foot, by wheelchair, by motor-car, by coach, by horse, with domestic and farm animals, with babies, with a few articles of cheap furniture or pictures, the refugees fled to the frontier, impelled by a blind panic, many in tears and penniless. The militiamen had hitherto been fed and urged on by their wives and families at home. Now they were alone, a rearguard who had nothing to defend. On 3 September, Beorlegui, having been visited the day before by the now anachronistic figure of Gil Robles, and commanding only 1,500 men, assaulted Irún. He was watched by spectators from the French side of the Bidasoa. The attack was not immediately successful. At two in the morning, however, the frontier village of Behobia was captured. Most of the defenders of Irún, including the committee in charge, fled to France before the sun rose. A detachment of anarchists from Asturias, together with some local communists and the French and Belgians, stayed last. The former set several parts of Irún ablaze. They also shot a number of the right-wing prisoners in Fort Guadalupe at Fuenterrabía, and then escaped, leaving the rest free to cheer Beorlegui the next day, as he occupied the ruined town. Beorlegui suffered a mortal wound in the leg in a final battle at the International Bridge, apparently from a group of

French communist machine-gunners. As for the refugees, those who wished to continue to fight – 560 men, including the French and Belgians – were sent off by train to Barcelona, where they attached themselves to the columns in Aragon. The rest were dispatched to camps in France.

This campaign handed over to the nationalists about 1,000 square miles of rich farm land, densely populated, with many important factories; it was also a victory of incomparable strategic importance, since its loss cut off the Basque nationalists, the Santanderinos and the Asturians from friendly France. The nationalists could also now travel by rail from Hendaye to Cádiz.[1]

Apart from their main strategic venture in the south of Spain, the nationalists mounted, in August, several forays to establish communications between Seville, Córdoba, Granada, Cádiz and Algeciras. The dashing son of a sergeant-major, General Varela, the ex-instructor of the Carlists,[2] drove across Andalusia with a *tabor* of Moroccans and relieved Granada.[3] The province of Málaga, though protected by mountains, was thus faced to the north as well as to the west by possible rebel advances. An attack on the city of Málaga was, however, called off. Varela was ordered north to defend the nationalist position at Córdoba, threatened on 20 August by a republican attack under General Miaja, briefly minister of war on the night of 18–19 July, now leading a detachment of republican troops from Madrid, along with some militiamen of Andalusia, numbering about 3,000. The attack reached the gates of Córdoba, which, under the nationalist Colonel Cascajo, might have fallen had it not been for the skilful use of Italian Savoia bombers. Then Miaja was beaten back, many men of the militia carrying rifles only for use against those stopping their flight.[4] Miaja's failure raised the question of his loyalty to the cause of the republic. Possibly, Miaja did not advance on Córdoba because Cascajo threatened reprisals on his

1. Martínez Bande, *op. cit.*, pp. 91–2.

2. See above, p. 129.

3. Luis María de Lojendio, *Operaciones militares de la guerra de España* (Barcelona, 1940), p. 108; Martínez Bande, *La campaña en Andalucía*, p. 73f.

4. Borkenau, p. 158; Martínez Bande, *op. cit.*, p. 61. Others fought bravely: one survivor recalls a whole battalion of volunteers from Alcoy being knifed by the Moors in their trenches (José Cirre Jiménez, *De espejo a Madrid* Granada, 1937, p. 20).

family who were there,[1] but more likely because he could not arouse his men to advance. It began then to be asked in Madrid, could any general or ex-regular officer be loyal?[2] Certainly, there was spying on a large scale. Miaja's adjutant, Captain Fernández Castañeda, was actually hoping to cross the lines and even then was doing his best to enable civil guards to escape from the republic (he himself escaped in February 1937).[3] Treachery, or at least ambiguity of loyalty, was indeed rife in Andalusia: 'There was a man in charge of the trench diggers,' recalled a schoolboy of the time, 'who had been sent from Málaga for the defence of the village and he was made one of the youth leaders. You'd hardly believe it, he turned out to be a leading falangist when the nationalists entered.'[4]

The republic launched some other initiatives in August. The Aragon front was quiet it is true, save from an attack on Huesca by Carlo Rosselli's group of Italian anarchists and social democrats of the Giustizia e Libertà Column, which received a baptism of fire at Monte Pelato in the Sierra de Galoche on 28 August – a skirmish in which their commander, the lawyer, Mario Angeloni, was killed.[5] More important, on 9 August, a Catalan and Valencian expeditionary force, under an air force captain, Alberto Bayo, and a civil guard captain from Valencia, Manuel Uribarri, arrived at Ibiza in a requisitioned liner (the *Marqués de Comillas*), two destroyers, a submarine, and six aeroplanes. The workers rose against the fifty men of the garrison and the island was returned to republican control. The socialist who was so bad an adviser to Largo Caballero, Luis Araquistain, and the communist poet, Rafael Alberti, were thereby released from gaol. Some days later, after a quarrel with Uribarri, Bayo arrived on the west coast of Majorca. This expedition was carried out under the authority of the *Generalidad*, and the ministry of war in Madrid seems not to have known much about it.

At dawn on 16 August, Bayo disembarked with about 8,000 men on the east coast near the small town of Porto Cristo, which was itself quickly occupied. But, after the success of the landing, the in-

1. Evidence of Francisco Giral. 2. Zugazagoitia, p. 110.

3. Taking with him, secretly, Ramón Serrano Súñer. Fernández-Castañeda eventually became a general in nationalist Spain.

4. Fraser, *The Pueblo*, p. 74.

5. Charles Delzell, *Mussolini's Enemies* (Princeton, 1961), p. 181. See also José Luis Alcofar Nassaes, *Spansky*, vol. I (Barcelona, 1973), p. 23.

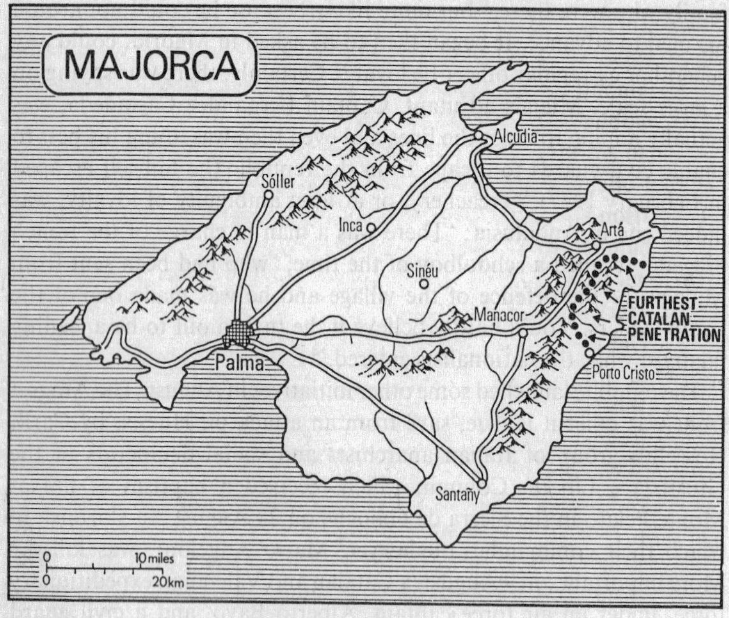

14. The invasion of Majorca, August 1936

vaders passed the morning indecisively. In the evening, six 75 millimetre guns and four of 105 millimetres were also disembarked, along with hydroplanes from Barcelona.[1] They established themselves about eight miles inside the island. Perplexity at their own success continued, so allowing the nationalists to gather themselves for a counter-attack. A small Italian air squadron which proudly called itself 'the Dragons of Death', of three Savoia 81 bombers, and a group of Italian Black Shirts, led by Arconovaldo Bonaccorsi, a fanatical fascist from Bologna with a red beard, known as the 'Conte

1. Figures in Guarner memorandum, p. 4. Originally, perhaps, only 2,000 disembarked but the total rose to about 8,000 probably (Martínez Bande, *La invasión de Aragón*, p. 141). The republic had made one other attempt at capturing Majorca: a destroyer anchored in the Bay of Pollensa, the captain landed alone, requisitioned a car and drove to Palma, where, in full uniform, he called on the military governor to surrender. The audacious request was rejected and the captain detained (see De la Cierva, *Historia ilustrada*, II, p. 40).

Rossi', arrived in their support,[1] together with three Fiat (CR32) fighters and some other nationalist aircraft. The Fiats, with Italian pilots (among them an excellent flier, named Cerestiato), outclassed their republican opponents. Henceforward, republican bombers were unable to get through to bomb Palma. On 3 September, a nationalist counter-offensive, led by Colonel García Ruiz, began. To begin with, the garrison had 1,200 men, 300 carabineers and civil guards together with a number of falangists, led by the Marqués de Zayas. This raised their total to 3,500. The Catalan expeditionary force, which had no medical service, field hospitals or adequate supplies, fled back to their ships. The invaders were demoralized by the aviation, but the decision to withdraw the bridgehead was taken unnecessarily. The retreat was covered, to some extent, by the deployment of the battleship *Jaime I*, outside the harbour, with some other republican naval vessels. The beaches were covered with corpses, but many militiamen managed to escape, leaving their arms. Many wounded billeted in a convent, however, were shot in the sight of the mother superior.[2] Few prisoners were spared execution. So the expedition came to an inglorious end, though Barcelona Radio announced: 'The heroic Catalan columns have returned from Majorca after a magnificent action. Not a single man suffered from the effects of the embarkation, for Captain Bayo, with unique tactical skill, succeeded in carrying it out, thanks to the morale and discipline of our invincible militiamen.'[3] Thereafter, Majorca remained for some months almost the private fief of the 'Conte Rossi' who, dressed in his black fascist uniform, relieved by a white cross at the neck, roared over the island in a red racing-car, accompanied by an armed Falange chaplain. It was now that the murders of working-class Majorcans reached their height.[4] Ibiza and Formentera, meantime, were abandoned. (The fate

1. Lojendio, p. 150; see too Elliot Paul, *The Life and Death of a Spanish Town* (New York, 1937); Jesús Salas, p. 98. Martínez Bande, *La invasión de Aragón*, has a useful chapter. This first Italian shipment to Majorca was financed by Juan March. See also the efforts of Mallorquin falangists, such as de Zayas, to buy arms direct in Rome for their island, reported in Martínez Bande, *La invasión de Aragón*, documento No. 3, p. 268f. For Bonaccorsi's part in assaulting the dissident fascist deputy, Misuri, in 1923, see Adrian Lyttleton, *The Seizure of Power* (London, 1974), p. 180.

2. Bernanos, pp. 111–12.

3. Qu. Jellinek, p. 405.

4. Dundas, p. 69ff. Georges Oudard (*Chemises noires, brunes, vertes en*

of Ibiza, a beautiful island, was appalling; the rebels first killed 55 in an air raid; the FAI then shot 239 prisoners; when the rebels finally returned, they shot 400.)[1]

In Asturias, meantime, the two battles for the Simancas barracks in Gijón and for Oviedo also continued into August. Only when the former had been reduced could the Asturian miners concentrate their numbers on Oviedo, where Colonel Aranda could not sally out of the town which he had held by such guile. His defence was made easier since Oviedo had been well equipped with armaments after the Asturias rising of 1934 – particularly machine-guns. Aranda had at his disposal some 2,300 men, including about 860 volunteers, mostly falangists. The siege of the barracks at Gijón was rendered more difficult by bombardment by the nationalist cruiser *Almirante Cervera* which lay off shore. The 180 defenders, on the other hand, were constantly lulled by broadcasts from Radio Club Lisbon, Corunna, and Seville, into false expectations that relief was on its way. The water supply of the defenders gave out, and the nightly smacking of lips by Queipo de Llano on Seville Radio turned several of the besieged half-mad. Still, they did not give in. Here, as less dramatically at Toledo, the sons of the colonel in command, the fanatical Antonio Pinilla, and of his second-in-command, Suárez Palacios, were brought by the militia to demand the surrender of the barracks. Pinilla refused. Eventually, the barracks were stormed by the miners using dynamite as their main weapon. Pinilla ordered no surrender even until the last moment. Finally, on 16 August, this commander sent a Roman message by radio to the nationalist warships off the town: 'Defence is impossible. The barracks are burning and the enemy are starting to enter. Fire on us!' The demand was obeyed, and the last defenders of the Simancas barracks died in the flames. Thereafter, the miners could lay close siege to Oviedo. Their

---

Espagne, Paris, 1938, p. 196f.), a pro-Right writer, noted, 'if Franco kept Majorca, it was thanks to the Italian aircraft'. Azaña, vol. IV, pp. 776 and 629, is specially contemptuous of this expedition for a 'Greater Catalonia', of which he was uninformed. De la Cierva, *Historia ilustrada*, vol. II, p. 83, says that there was virtually no repression in Majorca; perhaps Bernanos exaggerated, but everything points to there having been 'numerosísimas ejecuciones' as an informant told Azaña later (*op. cit.*, p. 737).

1. These details are described in Elliot Paul's book cited above.

military chiefs were the socialist miner, Otero, and the CNT steel-worker, Higinio Carrocera. Aranda lacked supplies, but the besiegers lacked almost all material except for their infernal dynamite. So neither side made a move. Aranda had to hold a whole city with enemies within as well as without with less than 3,000 men. His own cool but jovial personality was the mainstay of the defence,[1] but there also reappeared under his orders a captain of engineers, Oscar Pérez Solís, who had once been briefly secretary-general of the communist party though now a falangist, perhaps anxious in combat to purge himself of the indiscretions, bank robberies and murders which he had carried out for the communists ten years before.

At Toledo, the battle was intermittent. The resistance of the Alcázar maddened the militiamen besieging it, but their incompetence defeated only their own commanders: who themselves varied from a regular general, such as Riquelme, to the socialist painter, Luis Quintanilla. Rifle-fire went on all August from both sides. The well-trained defenders were good shots, and the militia made no attempt at an assault. Insults and boasts were exchanged through megaphones. Occasional bombs dropped made little difference at all to the defence of the ancient fortress, which had been thoroughly reinforced at the beginning of the century. The strongly catholic population of Toledo made the besiegers feel that they were surrounded by treason. The civilian authorities were, meantime, engaged in squabbling over the protection of the incomparable paintings in Toledo's churches and in the El Greco Museum. Although the defenders in the Alcázar possessed all the ammunition that they needed, there seemed little hope of their relief. They were cut off from the rest of Spain. There was no electricity, and the saltpetre off the walls was used for salt. The rebels conducted themselves, nevertheless, with serenity. Parades were taken, and the one thoroughbred horse inside was looked after as if in a stud. A fiesta in honour of the Assumption was even held in the cellars of the Alcázar, with flamenco dancing and castanets. Then, on 17 August, a nationalist aeroplane flew over them and dropped messages of encouragement from Franco and Mola and, more important, news. On 4 September, came the fall of Talavera de la Reina, only forty miles away down

1. See Oscar Pérez Solís, *Sitio y defensa de Oviedo* (Valladolid, 1938), *passim*; and a new study, Oscar Muñiz Martín, *El verano de la dinamita* (Madrid, 1974).

the Tagus.[1] The Alcázar received a message from the 'young women of Burgos': 'The heroic epic which your valour for God and Spain has written on our glorious Alcázar will be the pride of Spanish chivalry for ever. Gentlemen cadets, we are *señoritas* radiant with joy and hope and, like you, we are the New Spain of the glorious dawn.' (It was still widely believed that the Alcázar was held by cadets.)

The proximity of the nationalists to Madrid was soon expressed most vividly. On 23 August, the airport at Getafe was bombed and, on 25 August, Cuatro Vientos, an airport even nearer. On 27 and 28 August, Madrid itself was raided. Hans Voelckers, in charge at the German Embassy, described the raid on 27 August as being by three Junkers 52. 'Please arrange,' he asked Berlin, 'that, as long as Lufthansa traffic continues, no Junkers raid Madrid.' But, on 29 August, he had to complain again. Junkers 52 had dropped four heavy bombs on the war ministry, causing considerable damage and several deaths.[2] There was rising anti-German feeling in Madrid. Voelckers urged that the German Embassy and colony should leave.

The air raids caused the formation in Madrid of house committees in each block to organize listeners for the sirens which would be the signal to go down into the cellars. These committees also investigated the obscure texts of the government's housing decrees, and tried to give protection against illegal arrests. They were really a kind of local special constabulary in which the socialists and communists took the lead. Local communist branches also organized groups to paint the street lamps blue and secure a black-out. At that time of the year, nevertheless, a black-out was hard to enforce, since closed shutters made the rooms within intolerably hot. People were told to avoid the rooms facing the street and stay in inner rooms with candles. These experiences would become only too common to those who lived in other parts of Europe at the time of the Second World War. But, except for the modest alarms in the First World War, these raids on Madrid were the first of their kind to occur.

1. Borkenau, p. 147; *General Cause*, pp. 317–41.
2. *GD*, p. 61.

23

In pursuit of a Non-Intervention Pact – the USA holds off – trickery of Italy and of Stalin – arrival of the Russian mission – trickery of Germany – the Non-Intervention Committee

WHILE the republic was failing militarily, the diplomatic events of August marked as signal a defeat. On 3 August, Count Charles de Chambrun, the French ambassador at Rome, presented the French government's non-intervention plan to Ciano, who airily promised to study it.[1] Britain, on the other hand, accepted the idea in principle on its presentation, Eden giving his agreement from a holiday retreat in Yorkshire.[2] The same day, the German pocket-battleship, *Deutschland*, put into Ceuta, and Admiral Rolf Carls, in command, lunched with Franco, Langenheim, Bernhardt, and Beigbeder. An escort of falangists cried '*Heil Hitler!*'[3] That ship and the *Admiral Scheer* had been ordered to Spanish waters from Wilhelmshaven on 24 July. The next day, 4 August, André François-Poncet, French ambassador in Berlin, put the non-intervention plan to the Baron von Neurath, the German foreign minister, who answered that Germany had no need to make such a declaration. Neurath added that he knew that the French had delivered aeroplanes to the republicans. François-Poncet replied by claiming that the Germans had likewise supplied the nationalists.[4] In Moscow, the French ambassador made a similar approach to the Russian government, while, in Paris, the newly arrived republican ambassador, Alvaro de Albornoz, was again putting demands for Lebel rifles, Hotchkiss machine-guns, millions of cartridges, bombs, cannon, more Potez aeroplanes, and more Dewoitine fighters.[5] On 6 August, Ciano, having consulted Ulrich von Hassel, German ambassador in Rome, said that Italy agreed to the French plan. But he wanted to 'check all fund raising' for either side; to make the scheme cover all countries; and to establish a system of international control.[6] That day's *Pravda* announced that

1. Count Ciano, *Diplomatic Papers* (London, 1948), pp. 25–6. 2. Eden, p. 402. 3. *GD*, p. 27. 4. *ibid.*, p. 30. 5. *FD*, p. 120. 6. *GD*, p. 27.

the Russian workers had contributed 12,145,000 roubles to aid Spain. But the Russian government itself, like the Italian, agreed to the French non-intervention plan 'in principle', asking that Portugal should be asked to join the group of states subscribing themselves, and demanding that 'certain states' – Germany and Italy – should cease aid.[1] Nevertheless, on 7 August, François-Poncet was back at the Wilhelmstrasse (and Chambrun at the Palazzo Chigi) with a draft declaration of non-intervention, already accepted by Britain, Belgium, Holland, Poland, Czechoslovakia, and Russia, which would renounce all traffic in war material or aircraft. Neurath argued that such a thing would be difficult without a blockade: and what about the activities of the Comintern?[2] The same day, the British and French ministers in Lisbon asked Monteiro, the Portuguese foreign minister, to join the Non-Intervention Agreement. Monteiro, like Ciano, held his hand.[3]

All this time, the French frontier was open and new bombers and fighters, not to speak of pilots, were reaching the republic. But, on 8 August, the French cabinet changed their policy. A communiqué announced that, from 9 August, all export of war material to Spain would be suspended. This was explained as being due to the 'almost unanimously favourable' reply that the government had received to its ideas for non-intervention. In fact, the previous day Sir George Clerk, the British ambassador, had spoken, without instructions, to Delbos in strong terms. How could he reconcile the dispatch of French aircraft to Spain with the holding-up of the four Fokker aircraft at Bordeaux bound for the rebels from Britain? If France did not ban the export of war material to Spain, a common front with Britain on this whole matter would be much more difficult.[4] Further-

1. *The Times*, 7 August 1936.

2. *GD*, p. 323. 3. *USD*, 1936, vol. II, p. 485.

4. Alvarez del Vayo (*Freedom's Battle*, p. 70) reported the British ambassador's words much more strongly, and, though there is no evidence for other than the above in Sir George's account (Paris telegram No. 252 of 7 August) and in the French Documents (*FD*, vol. III, pp. 158–9), it is possible that he did speak specially vigorously: Hugh Lloyd Thomas, British minister in Paris, wrote privately to Sir Alexander Cadogan, under-secretary at the Foreign Office, that the ambassador's conversation with Delbos 'might well have been the factor which decided the government [in France] to announce the policy of non-intervention' (*FO*, 371/205/31/27). The French under-secretary, Pierre Vienot,

more, by this time, Admiral Darlan had returned from London. He had seen Admiral Lord Chatfield, who had told him that there was no point in making any approach to Britain about Spain, and, further, that Franco was a 'good Spanish patriot'. The British Admiralty were also 'unfavourably impressed' by what they had heard of the murder of the Spanish naval officers. Nothing should be done which allowed the spread of communism to Spain or, even worse, to Portugal. Darlan, therefore, reported that there was no possibility of Britain looking favourably on French aid to the republic.[1] Fear of offending England was the main reason why the French cabinet was thus brought, on 8 August, to reverse its decision of 2 August.[2] Blum bitterly regretted this. He nearly resigned, but his colleague, Auriol (who was in favour of the Spanish republic), and Fernando de los Ríos persuaded him not to do so. A Blum government would, after all, be better for the republic than any other.[3] On 9 August, Blum, in spite of everything, was cheered at a meeting at Saint-Cloud by a great crowd chanting 'Arms for Spain', while an aircraft traced the word PAIX in smoke across the blue summer sky. Both the socialist and communist French trade-union leaders were now committed to the policy which the crowd demanded. Léon Jouhaux, the socialist trade-union leader, and Thorez, the communist secretary-general, were as one in declaring that there could be no neutrality for 'the conscientious worker'. Since the dispatch of arms was forbidden, funds for clothing, food, and medical supplies for the republic were collected instead. In fact, so long as Pierre Cot remained minister of air (till June 1937), French airports were told to help republican aircraft. These breaches of non-intervention were officially excused as caused by 'errors of navigation'.[4] Some aircraft also continued to be sent directly from France. Fifty-six aircraft are

later told Thomas that the ambassador's 'timely words' had been most useful (*loc. cit.*, 29/215), and Delbos later said that he had 'listened' to the ambassador's appeal. The conventional view of the time was that 'Perfide Albion' had inspired non-intervention from the start.

1. *Les Événements survenus*, p. 219; *FD*, p. 130f, and *FO*, 371/205/27.

2. Pierre Cot, *op. cit.*, pp. 345–6.

3. De los Ríos convinced Blum with an eloquent description of the young militiamen fighting fascism in the sierras. Blum wept (Azcárate, p. 257).

4. Cot, pp. 353–4.

believed to have reached Spain between 9 August and 14 October from the Air France airfield at Montaudran.[1] The Catalan government succeeded also in getting some assistance, in both personnel and material, from France and Belgium, to help develop their munitions industry.[2]

While Blum was speaking at Saint-Cloud, the counsellor of the German Embassy in London was blandly assuring the Foreign Office that 'no war materials had been sent from Germany and none will be'.[3] But the Junkers, Heinkels, their pilots and technicians were already making an impact on the war in the south of Spain. The German consul in Seville appealed to the Wilhelmstrasse that these Germans should not appear in the streets in German uniform, since they were recognized and given 'great ovations'.[4] One Junker 52, however, made a forced landing in republican territory, where it was detained, with its crew. The next day, the German counsellor in Madrid, Schwendemann, on instruction from Berlin, demanded their release. The Spanish government refused. On 12 August, Neurath told François-Poncet that, until the Spanish gave up the aircraft ('merely a transport aeroplane'), Germany could not agree to a Non-Intervention Agreement.[5] But, on 13 August, Portugal accepted non-intervention in principle, reserving liberty of action if her border should appear threatened by the progress of the war. A few days before, the Spanish government had declared the Canaries and Galician provinces to be 'zones of war' and therefore subject to blockade. The Foreign Office said that they regarded the statement as one of intent: the fact of blockade was necessary before it could be internationally recognized.

The United States had by now also been called upon to take up an attitude to the Spanish war. On 5 August, after a meeting in the department of state, the secretary of state, Cordell Hull, allowed it to be generally known (though not announced) that his government favoured non-intervention.[6] On 10 August, the Glenn Martin Company, the leading aircraft firm in the US, asked what the government's attitude would be to the sale of eight bombers to the republic.

1. Pike, pp. 44–6, 48.
2. See Companys's letter to Prieto, 13 December 1937, qu. Peirats, vol. I, p. 136.
3. *GD*, p. 36. 4. *ibid*, p. 38. 5. *ibid.*, p. 37. 6. Traina, p. 50.

The acting secretary of state replied that such a sale 'would not follow the spirit of this government's policy of a "moral embargo" on arms to Spain'.[1] The State department next instructed Bowers, the American ambassador in Spain, to refuse even to join a mediation proposal suggested to the diplomatic corps at St Jean de Luz by the Argentinian ambassador.[2] American liberal opinion was shocked: 'Let us ask Jefferson where he stands on this issue!' The words might be those of Earl Browder, the American communist, but his sentiments were those of many democrats. Still, most Americans certainly supported the embargo. Mexico, meantime, alone of governments openly began to send a few arms to the republic. President Cárdenas would announce in September that he had sent 20,000 rifles and 20 million rounds of ammunition to the Spanish government.

The British and French pursuit of the chimera of non-intervention continued. Britain prohibited exports of war material to Spain on 15 August, after news had been received of flights of British aircraft from Croydon to rebel Spain.[3] Neurath gave a note to François-Poncet on 17 August agreeing, pending the release of the Junkers and the acceptance of similar obligations by all countries possessing arms industries, to ban arms shipments to Spain and suggesting that this ban should be extended to volunteers.[4] Ciano also took up this point with the French ambassador in Rome, but promised, before that question and that of funds were settled, that Italy would prohibit the export of arms.[5] This reversal surprised the French. It was caused by a realization that it would be possible, in the words of the German chargé at Rome, 'not to abide by the declaration anyway'.[6] On 24 August, with the future of the Junkers in Madrid still unsettled, Germany signed the declaration demanded by the French.[7] That day,

1. *USD*, 1936, vol. II, p. 474.

2. *ibid.*, p. 488. The first 'incident' for America arising out of the civil war was the accidental nationalist bombing of the US destroyer *Kane* while *en route* from Gibraltar to Bilbao to evacuate American citizens there. No damage was done and an evasive apology from Franco was forthcoming (Taylor, pp. 61–2).

3. This prohibition was first contingent on similar action by Italy, Germany, Russia, and Portugal; but it was implemented conditionally on the 19th (Eden, p. 403).

4. *GD*, p. 45. 5. Ciano, *Diplomatic Papers*, pp. 31–2. 6. *GD*, p. 60.

7. The crew of the Junkers had already been released. The aeroplane itself was destroyed in a nationalist air raid.

the British chiefs of staff presented an important paper, often subsequently referred to inside the British government, which argued that, for strategic reasons, Britain had to be on good terms with whoever won the war.[1]

Russia did not propose to be left out of these negotiations any more than the German foreign ministry wanted her to be. Given his desire for an alliance with France and Britain, Stalin wanted to be a party to all such discussions. On 23 August, Russia accepted the Non-Intervention Agreement and, on 28 August, Stalin issued a decree forbidding export of war material to Spain, in order to align the Soviet Union with the other powers. Russian officials showed even greater diffidence than usual during these negotiations, and Litvinov had to refer even insignificant details of wording of their government's adhesion to Stalin.[2] *Izvestia* turned many logical somersaults in denouncing neutrality as 'not our idea at all' and as 'a general retreat before fascist governments', yet explaining that the Russian acceptance of it was 'due to the fact that the French declaration aimed at the end of fascist aid to the rebels'.[3] The dilemma of Russian policy, desirous of pleasing France, while not appearing to desert the world revolution, was never more difficult. But Stalin's slowness is also explained by his preoccupation at that moment with the trial of the first group of Old Bolsheviks, which began on 19 August: Kamenev was condemned to death on 23 August, and Zinoviev some days later. Stalin's mind was thus on other things than Spain.

Moreover, at the very moment that Russia adhered to the Non-Intervention Agreement, diplomatic relations between her and the Spanish government were being formally, and indeed formidably, established.[4] An old revolutionary, Vladimir Antonov-Ovsëenko, who had commanded the Red Guard which stormed the Winter Palace in St Petersburg in 1917, and had later been a member of the first bolshevik government, arrived in Barcelona as consul-general on

1. C.O.S. 509 of 24 August 1936: 'A hostile Spain or the occupation of Spanish territory by a hostile power would make our control of the straits and use of Gibraltar as a naval and air base extremely difficult'.

2. *USD*, 1936, vol. II, p. 515. 3. *Izvestia*, 26 August 1936.

4. The republic had recognized Russia in 1933, but the rebellion of Asturias prevented an exchange of ambassadors. The exchange of ambassadors had been planned ever since February 1936, but only now occurred.

25 August. In the late twenties, he had been a prominent member of the Trotskyist opposition, but in 1928 he had capitulated to Stalin and had been afterwards a diplomat in Prague and Warsaw. The nomination of so experienced a revolutionary to Barcelona was a curious, and, as it turned out, an ironic step.[1] The competent Russian diplomat Marcel Rosenberg, ex-deputy secretary of the League of Nations, reached Madrid as ambassador on 27 August. Rosenberg brought with him a large staff, including a naval attaché, Captain N. Kuznetzov, an air attaché, Colonel Boris Svieshnikov, and a military attaché, General V. Goriev.[2] The chief Russian military adviser in Spain was the Latvian, General Jan Berzin, previously head of Russian military intelligence, a courageous man whose youth in Latvia had been spent fighting the Tsarist police. He played a brilliant role in the Russian Civil War. He was a tall, grey-haired man whom some mistook for an Englishman.[3] Antonov-Ovsëenko also had an economic adviser, Arthur Stashevsky, who was in effect a Russian economic attaché in Spain. He was a Pole, short and thick-set, married to a Frenchwoman, seeming to be an ordinary businessman, and had once also been Berzin's assistant. Other Russians included the writer, Ilya Ehrenburg, who came to Spain as *Izvestia* correspondent in late August, and busied himself with propaganda and even military activity as well as reporting.[4] Another Russian writer of eminence, Mikhail Koltsov, correspondent of *Pravda*, had arrived in Spain earlier, on 8 August.[5] These Russians were thus added to the ranks of influential communists already in Spain. The date of the arrival of these missions suggests that the double attitude ex-

1. For Antonov-Ovsëenko, see Isaac Deutscher, *The Prophet Armed* (London, 1954), p. 221, and *The Prophet Unarmed* (London, 1959), pp. 116–17, 160–61, 406.

2. For the arrival of Kuznetzov (afterwards admiral and supreme commander of the Russian navy), see his memoir in *Bajo la bandera de la España republicana*, a collection of Russian memoirs, published Moscow, ? 1967.

3. Walter Krivitsky, *I was Stalin's Agent* (London, 1963), p. 98. See also Elizabeth Poretsky, *Our Own People* (London, 1969), pp. 211–12. Berzin was born Ian Pavlovich Kuzis.

4. Ilya Ehrenburg, *Men, Years and Life* (London, 1963), vol. IV, p. 110. He had been in Spain earlier in the year.

5. Koltsov, pp. 9, 59. Koltsov speaks of the arrival on this day of a 'Mexican communist, Miguel Martínez', pseudonym for Koltsov himself. Koltsov was probably Stalin's personal agent in Spain, with on occasion a direct line to the Kremlin.

pressed in *Izvestia* was reflected in a double policy, showing that, as ever, Stalin intended to keep all courses open. The headquarters of the Russian mission in Madrid was the quiet Gaylord's Hotel, between the Prado and the Retiro Park.[1] As yet, no Russian military equipment was to be seen in Spain, though, at the very moment that Russia was formally 'banning the export of war material', Stalin was really approving it.[2]

Russia's double-dealing was matched by Germany. On 25 August, the day after Germany had signed the Non-Intervention Agreement, the war minister, Field-Marshal von Blomberg, summoned Colonel Warlimont, a promising and ambitious officer. The Führer, said Blomberg, was moving into an attitude of outright and explicit hostility to Russia. Hitherto, his anti-communism had been confined to Germany. Now it embraced the Comintern and all its works. His speech at the annual congress of the nazi party at Nuremberg in September would reflect that attitude. As a result, Blomberg went on, Hitler had decided to give substantial aid to Franco. Warlimont would lead the German contingent. On the 26th, Warlimont and Canaris visited the head of Italian military intelligence, Colonel Roatta, and then Roatta and Warlimont left for Tetuán, on an Italian cruiser. A German aircraft flew the two of them to Seville, where they talked to Queipo, and then to Cáceres, where they met Franco. Warlimont thereupon took up his duties.[3] Roatta returned to Italy but, in the course of the next month, about twenty light Ansaldo-Fiat tanks, including some fitted with flamethrowers and a quantity of Italian artillery of the reliable 65/17 millimetre model used in the First World War, were sent to Spain by Mussolini, along with 'specialists' in the use of this material, to act alongside the pilots of the Savoias and Fiat fighters already there.

While the other powers were thus busy arranging to break their words, Eden took up an Italian suggestion for a permanent group to supervise the working of non-intervention. After dispute as to its powers, a committee was arranged. This, deriving from the successful

1. For life in this hotel, see the brilliant Ch. 18 of Hemingway's *For Whom the Bell Tolls*.

2. See below, p. 441.

3. General Warlimont's affidavit to US military intelligence in 1946 (*UN Security Council Report on Spain*, p. 76).

ambassadors' conference at the time of the Balkan Wars, was to be convened at the Foreign Office in London. The first meeting was arranged for 9 September. Thus was born the Non-Intervention Committee, which was to graduate from equivocation to hypocrisy, and which was to last out the civil war.[1] Eden had returned to London on 16 August; Baldwin, however, had been ordered three months' rest, for medical reasons, and was away in South Wales. The cabinet 'did not meet', reported Eden later, 'from the end of July until the beginning of September, and the British policy was decided by the Foreign Office'.[2]

The Non-Intervention Committee met for the first time in London on 9 September. W. S. Morrison, financial secretary to the Treasury,[3] led the British delegation and took the chair. The other countries, represented by their ambassadors in London, included all the European countries except for Switzerland, which had banned the export of arms, but whose code of neutrality forbade her intervention even in a committee of non-intervention.[4]

The first meeting of the committee was concerned with 'the murky tide of procedure', in *Pravda*'s unusually accurate words. The representatives present agreed to give to Francis Hemming, a British civil servant in the cabinet office whose knowledge of Spain was confined to the butterflies of the Pyrenees and who became the commit-

1. Despite non-intervention, from this time the Foreign Office gave asylum to Spanish refugees from the 'Red Terror'; and within a matter of weeks the Embassy in Madrid (under George Ogilvie Forbes) comprised seven buildings. The change in British policy towards refugees was due to the consequences of a refusal to give refuge to the Marquesa de Balboa, with her twelve-year-old son (who was later shot). For the rest of the war, the embassies in the Spanish capital remained the home of several thousand upper- and middle-class Spaniards, some active members of the Fifth Column, others terrified and broken, all hungry, cold and pale, due to the lack of fresh air. There were later some exchanges of these refugees for republicans in nationalist hands.

2. Eden, p. 122.

3. 'Shakes' Morrison, as he was known, was a conservative politician and had been chairman of a cabinet sub-committee since early August coordinating non-intervention.

4. Non-Intervention Committee records in the Public Record Office, first meeting. Hereafter referred to as *NIC*. The Non-Intervention Committee was throughout serviced by the Foreign Office. Papers, documents, etc., were prepared by a British secretariat.

tee's secretary, the texts of the laws their countries had passed banning the export of arms. Apart from the British representative, the leading figures at the committee were Corbin, the French ambassador; Grandi, the fascist ex-foreign secretary of Italy whom Mussolini had transferred to the Embassy at London for not being satisfactorily fascist; and Maisky, the Russian ambassador. Ribbentrop (who became German ambassador on 30 October), and his second-in-command, Prince Bismarck, the grandson of the Iron Chancellor, took a less prominent part than Grandi to whom, indeed, they had been instructed to leave the running. Ribbentrop later described how difficult he found working with Grandi – 'an intriguer if ever there was one'.[1] Portugal, whose attendance the Russians had insisted upon, was not immediately represented. The Portuguese minister in Berlin said on 7 September (when the German ship *Usamoro* was refused facilities to discharge another cargo of arms for the nationalists at Lisbon due, it was thought in Berlin, to British influence) that she would not be represented until after a ban on volunteers.[2] Salazar apparently thought that to join the committee would to some degree imply a surrender of authority.[3] But the Portuguese need not have worried. Grandi had been instructed by Ciano 'to do his best to give the Committee's entire activity a purely platonic character'.[4] Ribbentrop later joked that a better name for the Non-Intervention Committee would have been 'intervention committee'.[5] The German attitude to the committee was more ambiguous than the Italian, because the German foreign office was so ill-informed as to what the war ministry and nazi party were doing. The German diplomats had not, indeed, decided whether real non-intervention would aid Franco or not. As for France and Britain, Bismarck reported that the first meeting of the committee left the impression that, for both countries, 'It is not so much a question of

1. Ribbentrop, p. 71. 2. *GD*, p. 77.

3. Kay, p. 95. Early in September, the crews of two Portuguese warships overpowered their officers and prepared to sail to join the republic. Salazar had them destroyed by gunfire.

4. *ibid.*, p. 75.

5. Ribbentrop, *loc. cit.* He added, in this apologia written in Nuremberg between the trial and the sentence, 'I often wished that this wretched Spanish Civil War would go to the devil, for it constantly involved me in disputes with the British government'.

taking actual steps immediately, as of pacifying the aroused feelings of the Leftist parties . . . by the very establishment of such a committee'.[1] From the start, the British and French governments were occupied less with the end of intervention on all sides, than with the *appearance* of such an end. In this way the flow of war material to the two sides in Spain might not be prevented, but, at the least, the extension of the Spanish war might be.

Britain accused Italy of landing aircraft in Majorca on 7 September.[2] On 12 September, Ingram, the British chargé in Rome, told Ciano that changes in the Mediterranean would 'closely concern the British government'. Ciano replied that no such alteration had occurred or was contemplated.[3] But Majorca was nevertheless an Italian stronghold throughout the civil war. The main street, the Rambla, in Palma, was renamed the Vía Roma, and statues of two Roman youths in togas with eagles on their shoulders stood at its entry. The Bay of Pollensa became an Italian naval base. War material poured into the island. The island was mined and refortified by Italians. The incident showed that Britain might protest when she felt her interests were threatened by some consequence of the Spanish war, but that she would not do so in respect of a simple breach of the Agreement. Yet, to give Baldwin's and Blum's Cabinets their due, both believed that their countries, and Spain, and European peace, would be best served by the prevention of military help to Spain. Both governments made every effort to keep the pact, even though in France this continued to make trouble for Blum. But, at this time, the majority of expressed opinion in both countries supported this policy. The Labour party in England even deplored the delay in bringing non-intervention into being. As for the communists, Thorez tried to persuade Blum to change his policy on aid to Spain on 7 September.[4] Despite his failure, he undertook that the communists would not vote against the government in the National Assembly. The Comintern sponsored in London a 'Commission of Inquiry into

1. *GD*, p. 84.
2. Lord Plymouth at meeting of the committee, 23 October 1936.
3. Eden in the House of Commons, 16 December 1936.
4. D. Cattell, *Soviet Diplomacy and the Spanish Civil War* (Berkeley, 1957), p. 24. La Pasionaria, Marcelino Domingo, and Jiménez de Asúa also failed to convince Blum in an audience about this time (Ibarruri, p. 305). But others were persuaded; for example, Edith Thomas wrote:

Alleged Breaches of the Non-Intervention Agreement in Spain'. Such respectable persons as Philip Noel-Baker, Lord Faringdon, Professor Trend of Cambridge, and Miss Eleanor Rathbone were members. The two secretaries were Geoffrey Bing and the journalist John Langdon-Davies, of whom the first, a young lawyer, was then a member of the communist party.[1] This was a typical communist tactic of those days, the favourite one, it would seem, of the inventive Willi Muenzenberg.

The second meeting of the Non-Intervention Committee occurred on 14 September, and set up a sub-committee, composed of Belgium, Britain, Czechoslovakia, France, Germany, Italy, Russia, and Sweden, to deal with everyday matters of non-intervention.[2] The smaller states even on the sub-committee were only too willing to follow the lead of the great powers and the real debates were confined to France, Britain, Germany, and Italy. The timidity before Hitler, and before all international responsibility, of the Scandinavian and (as they would now be called) the Benelux countries was indeed, in some ways, the most distasteful aspect of the diplomatic history of those days. But then, what could they do, if Britain continued with 'appeasement'? And 'appeasement' seemed the only safe policy for an empire already embarked on a long decline, however little she desired to admit it.

This meeting coincided with Pope Pius XI's first public reaction to the war in Spain. He spoke on 14 September of the republicans' 'truly satanic hatred of God' at Castelgandolfo to six hundred Spanish refugees.[3] The same day, a priest in Madrid who had sided with the republic, Father García Morales, adjured the Pope to denounce the

---

Pasionaria Pasionaria
il n'est plus temps que les hommes t'aiment
ils t'écoutent
comme ils écoutent le vent chanter . . .

1. Koestler, *Invisible Writing*, p. 323. Bing later went on to become a Labour MP and attorney general to President Nkrumah in Ghana. The Spanish republic said that they would accept 'real non-intervention'. By this they meant no legislation in any country preventing them from buying arms. This was rather different from, for example, the Labour party's view of non-intervention, which was that neither side should be able to get arms from abroad.

2. *NIC* second meeting.

3. Iturralde, vol. II, pp. 224–5.

rebels. Some days later, José Bergamín, the catholic apologist who edited *Cruz y Raya*, described the generals, bishops, Moors, and Carlists who were fighting the republic as being implicated in some 'fantastic mumming show of death'. Thus the Spanish Civil War caused a conflict within catholic consciences, if not the catholic church, throughout Europe and the world. Diplomatic manoeuvres were equalled by ecclesiastical. War within international opinion had also been declared. The conflict was by September 1936 thus no isolated Carlist war of the nineteenth century.

24

Republican defeats and their causes – massacre in the Model Prison – fall of the Giral government – Largo Caballero forms his ministry – fall of San Sebastián – the Alcázar

At the beginning of September 1936, Franco was at Talavera, and Mola was at Irún, threatening San Sebastián. The Majorcan expedition had failed. Saragossa, Huesca, Oviedo, and even the Alcázar at Toledo remained in rebel hands. In the south, much of Andalusia had been lost to the republic, as well as nearly all Estremadura. The brutality and experience of the well-armed Army of Africa was the chief explanation for the nationalists' success. Bravery might win street-battles, but was inadequate against legionaries and the *Regulares*. Only the Fifth Regiment among the militias knew anything of discipline. The remains of the regular army, the civil guard and assault forces still with the government seemed demoralized. The republic, with their purchases of French aeroplanes and their initial numerical advantage in aircraft, might often have enjoyed command of the air; but the mercenary French pilots were not of high quality, and the nationalists' concentration of their few, but impressive, new aircraft from Germany and Italy on the Estremaduran and Tagus fronts gave them superiority there. The young German pilots who flew these Junkers and Heinkels, alongside Spaniards, in the so-called squadron of 'Pedros and Pablos', were superior to their French counterparts. Political predilections also affected tactics. On the Talavera front, for example, the republicans had high hopes for an armoured train, that favourite development of the Russian Civil War. In Spain, that 'vital shovelful of coal that keeps a dying fire alive', as Trotsky had called his own train, proved useless. The Russian Civil War was nevertheless constantly recalled by the Spanish officers of the republic in search of some precedent for their own problems of leading a mass army.[1] Their troubles were not only in the fighting

1. Their followers were also influenced by a film of the Russian Revolution portraying the exploits of Chapaev, the guerrilla leader. As before the war, films

line. The ministry of war had as yet no real central staff, and the movement of militia forces from place to place entailed endless delays. The Catalan and anarchist forces still had no relation with the government in Madrid. There were few opportunities for rifle practice, and few rifles too for such training, since many workers continued to carry these weapons as symbols of liberty and because the political parties all kept back such a proportion of arms as they could for possible use against their friends. The CNT in Madrid, for example, were believed to possess 5,000 rifles at their headquarters. A food shortage also developed – this being due not only to the loss of Old Castile, but to the phenomenal waste of food at the front and the immediate consumption of food, including excessive slaughtering of herds, in many agricultural collectives.[1] Deep distrust prevented any understanding between communists and anarchists; La Pasionaria, on a delegation to France to seek arms as well as sympathy, with the ex-minister, Marcelino Domingo, was held up for a long time in Barcelona by the crippled FAI leader, Manuel Escorza, and Aurelio Fernández, chief of the 'Investigation Committee of Barcelona'.[2] The British and French governments' championship of Non-Intervention was also demoralizing, less because there was as yet any shortage of weapons than because Non-Intervention made the republic seem isolated.

In the capital, the consequent gloom resulted in gathering support for Largo Caballero, now virtually king of Madrid. Nearly every day he and Alvarez del Vayo visited the Sierra to exhort and be welcomed by the militiamen. They wanted, however, to dominate, and not simply enter, the government. They spoke of the need for a strong government, capable of overcoming the conflicting expressions of popular will throughout Spain. They and their followers coveted, too, a real proletarian administration. Even Prieto had complained in

made a great impression on the Spanish working-class – even Shirley Temple in *The Little Colonel*, which was also shown in Madrid at this time. Success was also enjoyed by Groucho Marx, who was represented as the President of 'Freedonia' in the film *Duck Soup*. Looking like any Spanish politician he remarked with a report in front of him: 'A four-year-old child could understand this report. Run out and find me a four-year-old child.'

1. For Madrid at this time, see Barea, pp. 569–70. 2. Ibarruri, p. 297.

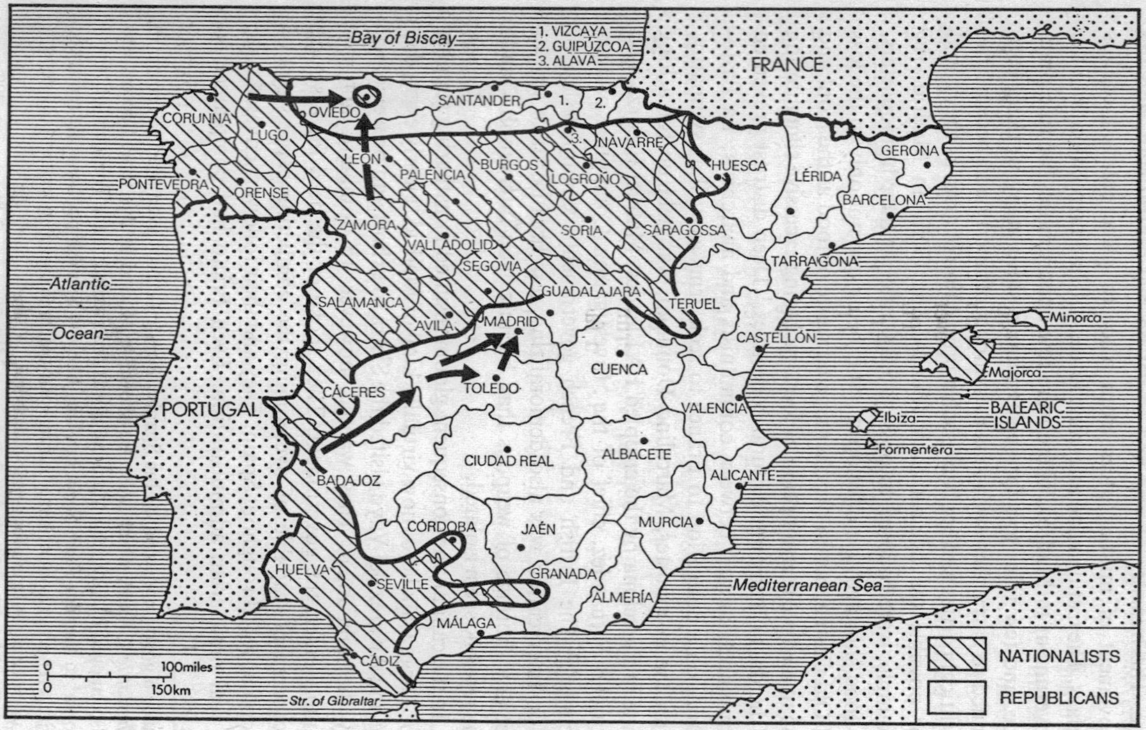

15. Division of Spain, August 1936

Informaciones that the reading of socialist newspapers was frowned on at the ministry of the interior. Prieto himself might have been an alternative Prime Minister, in August as in June; he worked incessantly for the service ministries, even though not a minister. The Italian socialist, Pietro Nenni, described him in shirt-sleeves, immersed in activity: 'He is nothing; he is not a minister; he is a deputy of a parliament in recess. But yet he is everything – the animator and coordinator of government action.'[1] Prieto had for a long time opposed the idea of his party taking over the government, still thinking it possible to influence Britain and France to help the republic if a wholly middle-class government were maintained. Retaining his dislike of Largo Caballero, Prieto realized, however, that he was the only possible successor to Giral.[2] He therefore suggested that socialist ministers should simply 'guide' the Giral government, as he himself was doing. The communists supported this policy.[3] Largo Caballero believed that that would compromise the socialists, as he now believed that their share in Azaña's government of 1931 had done, and help the anarchists. Largo wanted, in fact, to lead the government himself.

By this time, the atmosphere in the republic had been sensibly altered by the death of many of the political prisoners in the government's hands. In Barcelona, Generals Goded and Fernández Burriel were tried in early August. A retired officer who had become a lawyer was engaged to defend the two generals, who behaved with dignity. General Llano de la Encomienda and the civil guard general, Aranguren, bore witness against them. The two rebels were shot for rebellion in the fortress of Montjuich. The liberal members of the republican government agreed to confirm the death sentence with reluctance: many of them had known Goded well. A few days later, General Fanjul and Colonel Fernández Quintana, the rebels of the capital, were also shot after a court-martial in Madrid, the former after being married at the last moment to a widow who had been a

1. Nenni, p. 146.

2. See his interview of 25 August with Koltsov: 'He is an imbecile, a disorganizer . . . capable of taking all and everyone to ruin. But still he is the only man . . . capable of heading the new government.'

3. Ibarruri, p. 285.

messenger during the preparations for the rising.[1] They died before an appalling fate overcame their fellow-prisoners in Madrid. For, on 23 August, a fire broke out at the Model Prison.[2]

Was this caused by the three thousand political prisoners imprisoned there who attacked their guards with mattresses to which they had set fire as part of an attempt at an escape? Or was it the work of common criminals in the prison, stimulated by CNT militiamen, who had been searching for arms? The fair-minded judge, Mariano Gómez, who arrived shortly afterwards, thought that it was the first. But, at all events, the news that the political prisoners had rebelled spread in the city, at the same time as the 'massacre of Badajoz'[3] began also to be talked about. A crowd gathered, headed by militiamen on leave. They demanded that the building be stormed so as to massacre the political prisoners. Socialist politicians arrived to urge moderation. But the militiamen refused to listen. The prison staff fled. Forty prisoners were shot in the courtyard. Another thirty people were shot the next morning. The dead included such well-known ex-ministers as Manuel Rico Avello, Melquíades Alvarez, founder of the reformist party in 1912, under whose leadership many republican leaders had first ventured into politics, and Martínez de Velasco, leader of the agrarian party; as well as prominent falangists such as Fernando Primo de Rivera, brother of José Antonio, and Ruiz de Alda. Also killed in the Model Prison were Dr Albiñana, the leader of the nationalist party, Santiago Martín Bagüeñas, the police chief in Madrid until the Rising, General Capaz, and General Villegas, leader of the revolt in the Montaña barracks. Ruiz de Alda, shot by the 'republicans', was married to a daughter of Admiral Azarola, who had been shot by the 'fascists' in El Ferrol; while General Capaz, commander of western Morocco, 'hero of the Rif', had come in July to Madrid precisely to avoid having to declare himself one way or the other about the Rising. These murders appalled more than the 'fascists': Azaña and Giral were desolated, the former wishing that

1. She and her son by a previous marriage went with Fanjul's executor, to bury the general in the cemetery of Almudena. Both the son and the executor were murdered there (García Venero, *Madrid, julio 1936*, p. 364).

2. For two opposing accounts, see *The General Cause* and Borkenau (p. 127); see also 'Juan de Córdoba', *Estampas y reportajes* (Seville, 1939), p. 105, for Serrano Súñer's account of the events.

3. See above, p. 374.

he too had died, the latter weeping.[1] Where were the 'normal forces of order'? The minister of the interior, General Pozas, did what he could; others, who might have been expected to be present (such as the new director-general of security, Manuel Muñoz) were noticeably absent.

After these events, the ministry of justice established popular tribunals, intended to fill the gaps caused by the resignation, flight, or murder of the regular judicial authorities. These were composed of fourteen delegates from the popular front and the CNT, with three members of the old judiciary. Persons denounced to these tribunals were able to make some rough form of defence – though falangists were almost always shot, together, usually, with members of the CEDA or those who contributed to their funds. There continued to be anomalies and miscarriages of justice: thus, a doctor, denounced by a patient who owed him money, was able to disprove the charge and secure the indictment of the informer; while an ordinary tradesman, nevertheless, only at the last moment managed to escape being castigated as a spy by a creditor. 'Unauthorized' executions nevertheless continued, with somewhat diminishing ferocity. The two brothers, the Duques de Veragua and de la Vega, descendants of Columbus, were shot by militiamen, who were afraid that the popular tribunal might acquit them. At the end of August, the government told everyone to lock doors at 11 p.m., abolished nightwatchmen (*serenos*), instructed concierges to allow no one to enter houses, and to telephone the police if 'loud knocks indicate militiamen want to enter'.

On 4 September, Azaña bowed to the inevitable, accepted Giral's resignation as Premier, and asked Largo Caballero to form a government. Largo Caballero, the obvious choice for the succession, refused to take office unless the communist party also did so. He invited the

1. For Azaña's reaction, see his diaries, *Obras*, vol. IV, pp. 850–51, and Rivas-Cherif, *Retrato de un desconocido* (Mexico, 1961), p. 159. Azaña never recovered from these murders. Nor did he forgive the old 'monarchist without a king', Ossorio y Gallardo, who seemed to take such outrages in his stride: 'I don't justify anything. But this is in the logic of history!' (Azaña, vol. IV, p. 625). It was Ossorio, however, who persuaded Azaña not to resign: 'On the other side men are dying with your name on their lips'. Henceforward, Azaña remained less a President than the 'prisoner of being a republican symbol' (Azaña, vol. III, p. xxxviii).

anarchists to join: they refused. They were not ready to abandon their theoretical contempt for governmental power; instead, they wanted a national defence committee, with UGT–CNT representation only – power delegated from the collectives and regions directly – the full realization, that is, of the syndicalist state. That was unacceptable; debates within the CNT as to what attitude to have to these matters continued. Thus, at a meeting of federations of the libertarian movement of Catalonia, at the end of August, García Oliver, weary of talk, expostulated – 'Either we collaborate or we impose a dictatorship. Make a choice!'[1] The archpriest of opposition to the very idea of governmental authority was the crippled Manuel Escorza, whose only post was his membership of the peninsular committee of the FAI. Honest, implacable, inaccessible, bitter and ironical, Escorza dominated the discussions within the anarchist movement by sheer strength of will, as well as, as the communists pointed out, by his use of a private police force, which carried out to the full their master's orders of 'no quarter to fascists or neutrals'. While this spirit of a grand inquisitor lived on, the arguments of realism – that is, of alliance with the other parties – were difficult to put with success. On the other hand, the communists joined the central government. The Spanish communist central committee had opposed this, but Moscow, however, gave instructions to join.[2] The communists explained that civil war demanded unity against fascism and that the main tasks of the bourgeois revolution were already fulfilled. Accordingly, Hernández, editor of *Mundo Obrero*, became minister of education, and Uribe, a Marxist theorist, of agriculture. There were six socialists in the cabinet, including Prieto as minister of navy and air, and Alvarez del Vayo as foreign secretary. It would have been more appropriate to have given Prieto the ministry of war, but Largo wanted to control that more important ministry himself. It was also foolish to hand over the ministry of the interior, so important from the point of view of preventing the murders, to so incompetent a man as Angel Galarza, though he had had experience as director general of security during the early years of the republic. Juan Negrín, a *Prietista* socialist, became minister of finance; he had been professor of physiology at the University of

1. C. Lorenzo, p. 122. 2. Hernández, p. 139; Azaña, vol. IV, p. 821.

Madrid and had, though a deputy, distinguished himself principally in organizing the new university city outside Madrid. Luis Araquistain was given the post of ambassador in Paris, a post which involved the presidency of the republican Arms Purchase Commission in Paris.[1] The ambassador in London, López Oliván, a monarchist, now gave up his charge to join the nationalists. He was replaced by Pablo de Azcárate, deputy secretary-general of the League of Nations, who, being a high-minded liberal, seemed the best person to represent republican interests at the all-important London Embassy.

The republican cabinet was completed by two members of the Republican Left (including Giral, the ex-premier, as minister without portfolio) and one each of the Republican Union and the Esquerra.[2]

Largo Caballero, at the ministry of war, was supported by a new regular central staff organized by Major Estrada. Colonel Rodrigo Gil, an artillery officer of the old school, of marked left-wing views nevertheless, became under-secretary at the war office. Communist influence in the war ministry increased, since Major Estrada was about to join the communist party, and the chief of the technical secretariat was Antonio Cordón, another new communist, who controlled supplies.[3] Yet one more new communist, Major Díaz Tendero, the moving spirit in the pre-war UMRA, became the chief of a 'classification committee', whose task was to grade all officers in the republican zone by their political reliability: F for fascist, I for indifferent and R for republican were affixed to some 10,000 names; and all those with Rs were soon recalled to service. Similar reorganization, though on a smaller scale, came in the air force, where Prieto established a new general staff under Major Ignacio Hidalgo

1. Azcárate, MS., pp. 6–9. Araquistain, the principal inspiration of Largo's fatal turn to the Left before the war, was now himself turning to the Right.

2. The other Republican Left minister (of justice) was Mariano Ruiz Funes, minister of agriculture under Casares Quiroga and Giral. The Republican Union minister was Bernardo Giner de los Ríos, minister of communications, and the Esquerra minister, José Tomás y Piera, labour and health. On 16 September, Julio Just (Republican Union, ex-radical), a Valencian, became minister of public works and, on 25 September, Manuel de Irujo (Basque nationalist) became minister without portfolio.

3. See Castro Delgado (p. 545). For Cordón, see the engaging description in Martín Blázquez, p. 279. Cordón had been a regular army captain who had resigned under Azaña's law of 1932. See Cordón, p. 257.

de Cisneros, a regular air force officer and old collaborator of his, who had been in command of the air in Madrid since July.

This 'Government of Victory', as it was named, was the first in the West to include communists in the government.[1] Its purpose was to create strong government within the frame of republican legality. Largo Caballero, therefore, and the wing of the socialists who followed him, had, as a result of their experiences of the six weeks since the outbreak of war, greatly revised their political attitudes. Henceforward, there was little more mention in Largo's circle of the need for revolution. The watchwords were compromise and mobilization instead, total mobilization of all classes, including if possible the bourgeoisie, against the enemy. Largo Caballero sought in power an attitude to authority very different from the mood which he inculcated in his followers before the war.

His first task was to avoid defeat. To the alarmingly near Tagus front, Major (now Colonel) Asensio Torrado, one of the few able *africanistas* to stay loyal to the government, was dispatched to meet Yagüe, and his own namesake, Asensio of the Legion. The Gastone–Sozzi Column of Italian volunteers was transferred from Aragon to the Tagus, together with a new group of French volunteers, the '*Commune de Paris*' Column. Asensio Torrado attacked at Talavera. Disdainful of politics, lordly in manner, a complete professional officer, he brought order and discipline to the front, but he could not hold it. Though his men fought with courage and, this time, persistence, he could not manoeuvre to meet the fast-moving nationalist counter-attack. As other republican commanders had had to do so often, he was forced to choose between retreat and encirclement. His men made up his mind for him. They streamed back past his headquarters, leaving behind much material. But no immediate nationalist advance followed this new republican retreat. The advance from Seville had wearied even the Army of Africa. The nationalist general staff expected that, the closer their armies drew to Madrid, the stiffer would be the resistance.

In the pause while the main advancing column was reorganized,

1. Alvarez del Vayo, p. 203; Hernández, p. 47; Inprecorr, qu. Cattell, *Communism and the Spanish Civil War* (Berkeley, 1955), p. 56; Borkenau, p. 32; Martín Blázquez, p. 189. The communists also got the sub-secretaryships of education (Wenceslao Roces) and of health (Juan Planelles).

and Talavera established as a base of operations against Madrid, a newly equipped force under Colonel Delgado Serrano drove swiftly to the north to establish fighting liaison for the first time with the southernmost troops of Mola's Army of the North, Colonel Monasterio's cavalry force coming from Avila. A junction was made on 8 September at Arenas de San Pedro in the Gredos mountains. This cut off a large portion of republican territory to the west. The pacification of the area followed in the usual ruthless manner.[1]

The following day, the defenders of the Alcázar at Toledo received the news by megaphone from a militia-post in a house across the street that Major Rojo, ex-professor of tactics at the Academy of Infantry, wished to call with a proposal from the government. Since Rojo was known to Moscardó and others of the defending officers, he was received, during a ceasefire. He proposed that, in return for the surrender of the Alcázar, freedom would be guaranteed to all women and children inside. The defenders themselves would be handed over to court-martial. Moscardó refused these terms. In return, he requested Rojo to ask the government to send a priest to the Alcázar during another ceasefire. Rojo promised to pass on the request and departed, after chatting with the officers of the garrison, who unsuccessfully beseeched him to remain with them.[2] Then, during a three-hour truce, on 11 September, a suave priest, Vázquez Camarasa, who had escaped death in Madrid at the hands of the militia due to his liberalism, arrived at the fortress. Owing to the impossibility of hearing individual confessions, he gave a general absolution to Moscardó and the defenders. In a gloomy sermon, he spoke of the glory which the garrison would gather in the next world. He thus administered a kind of extreme unction to the defenders. Certain of the civil guards defending the Alcázar meanwhile talked with militiamen besieging them. The latter gave the defenders ciga-

1. It was at this point that the Army of Africa was joined by two ex-regular British officers, Lieutenants Nangle and Fitzpatrick. The former, who had been in the Indian Army, was a highly efficient officer. Fitzpatrick was a more romantic Irish soldier of fortune, who explained that he was driven to volunteer for Spain after seeing a famous photograph of militiamen seated on an altar dressed in priests' vestments. Both were given commissions in the Legion – the first foreigners to receive commissions who had not risen from the ranks. Fitzpatrick kindly permitted me to read his unpublished reminiscences of his experiences in Spain.

2. Aznar, p. 202.

rettes and undertook to take messages to their families. Vázquez Camarasa left, and the siege continued.[1] The republicans sought to end the resistance by burrowing under the walls from outside and planting a land mine under each of the two towers nearest the city. Civilians were evacuated from the city in preparation for the onslaught which was planned to follow the explosion. War correspondents were invited to Toledo, to watch the fall of the Alcázar, as if the occasion were certain to be a gala matinée.[2] Largo Caballero (for whom the Alcázar had become an obsession) refused an offer from José Díaz and Enrique Lister, the communist chiefs, to send the Fifth Regiment to Toledo; presumably he thought that he could win this battle without communist help – an early indication that the communists might find 'the Spanish Lenin' as difficult to manage as the 'moderates' had done.[3] On 18 September, the south-east tower was blown up, but the mine under the north-east one did not explode.

Before the decisive moments, as they seemed certain now to be, at Toledo, the rebels had some important victories elsewhere. Thus, on 13 September, the Basques surrendered the summer capital of San Sebastián to Mola without a fight rather than risk the destruction of its beautiful avenues. They also shot certain anarchists who wished to set the town ablaze before the entry of the enemy. Political prisoners (including the wife of the nationalist Colonel Solchaga) were escorted away – a generosity which contrasted with the nationalist treatment of the conquered town; for a black list was then read out of those suspected of being Basque nationalists and these or their relations (if they were absent) were captured and sent off to be imprisoned or shot in Pamplona.[4] But nationalist, particularly Carlist, tempers had been kept aflame by the discovery of the murder in the province of numerous prominent citizens such as Víctor Pradera and Honorio Maura, and mercy was silenced.

This defeat left all Guipúzcoa in rebel hands. It also led Prieto, the new minister of the marine, to send the main republican fleet from Cartagena and other Mediterranean ports to northern waters, on 22 September. This was accomplished, and the action certainly

1. Vázquez Camarasa left Madrid soon for Paris, disillusioned. For his future troubles, see Quintanilla, *Los rehenes del Alcázar*. He died in Bordeaux, in 1946.

2. Recollections of Henry Buckley and Lord St Oswald.

3. Ibarruri, p. 310.   4. Iturralde, vol. II, p. 224.

prevented a rebel blockade of the northern coast. But otherwise it did little for the war. In the south, meantime, General Varela embarked upon a new Andalusian march, to the north of the mountains sheltering the long coastal plain of Málaga. Making for Ronda, Varela occupied *pueblo* after *pueblo* without resistance. Ronda fell on 16 September. Queipo de Llano also captured the important mines of Peñarroya. These victories were followed by brutal proscriptions.

The battle soon broke out again in the Tagus valley. Once more, the militia fought with grim courage. This time, at Oropesa, they had even been persuaded to dig trenches. From these, however, they now refused to move, even when Yagüe sent forces on either side to outflank them. After a seven-hour battle, the militia were again forced to choose between retreat and encirclement. Once again, they chose the former, abandoning their defensive position at Santa Olalla, and also the larger town next to it, Maqueda, which fell to Yagüe, on 21 September. One of the animators of the past month's fighting, the Italian exile leader of the communist 'October No. 11' Battalion, Fernando de Rosa, one of the organizers of the socialist militia before the war, was killed.[1] In Oropesa, a group of the joint socialist youth fought to the end, led by the communist Andrés Martín in the church.[2] In all these battles, the professional skill of the legionaries, as well as the legend of their brutality, won the day, even though they were less numerous, and little better armed than their adversaries.

Now, however, a critical decision faced the nationalist command: should they relieve Toledo, which was now only twenty-five miles away; or continue to march on Madrid? The position of the Alcázar was now alarming. The defenders lived entirely in the cellars. They had run short of water and had to eat their mules and all but one of their horses – a thoroughbred racehorse who was tended till the end. On 20 September, five engines full of petrol were set up in the Hospital of Santa Cruz, and the walls of the Alcázar were sprayed with the inflammable fluid. Grenades were thrown to set it alight. A defender leapt out of the Alcázar and pointed the hose at the militia. The defender was killed, and the hose turned back to the Alcázar. In the afternoon, the petrol was set on fire, but no great damage was done. In the evening, Largo Caballero arrived in Toledo, to insist on the fall of the Alcázar within twenty-four hours. At last, he per-

1. Tagüeña, p. 134. 2. Ibarruri, p. 309.

mitted communist units under Major Barceló to enter the battle for Toledo: to no avail. The next day, Franco resolved to relieve the city. General Kindelán asked him if he knew that the diversion might cost him Madrid. Franco agreed that that was possible, but argued that the spiritual (or propaganda) advantage of relieving Moscardó was more important.[1] He was right: though unsentimental, Franco knew the importance attached to symbols in Spain. On 23 September, Varela, brought in from Andalusia to take command because Yagüe had opposed the diversion to Toledo, set out, with columns under Colonels Asensio and Barrón, to advance on the city from the north. The besiegers meantime laid a new mine beneath the north-east tower. Assault guards poured into Toledo from Madrid, to make the final onslaught. The mine was exploded on 25 September and the tower tumbled into the Tagus. But the solid rock foundations of the fortress could not be penetrated; and, while the government issued communiqués announcing the fall of the Alcázar, Varela reached a point only ten miles away.

On 26 September, the Army of Africa cut Toledo's road communication with Madrid. Escape for the republicans could only be to the south. In the morning of 27 September, the defenders saw the friendly army of Varela massing on the long barren hills to the north. At noon, an attack on Toledo from outside was launched. Once again, the training of the Army of Africa told immediately, although Toledo is easy to defend. The militia broke and fled, taking with them, however, most of the contents of the arms factory. In the evening, the defenders of the Alcázar heard Arabic words in the street below. The relief had arrived. There remained only the blood-bath that as usual attended the rebel capture of a town. Lieutenant Fitzpatrick, riding in with the Foreign Legion, reported that, in reprisal for the discovery of the mutilated bodies of two nationalist airmen outside the town, no prisoners were taken on entering Toledo, and that the main street was running with blood down the hill to the city gates.[2] Moroccans also killed the doctor and a number of wounded militiamen in their beds at the San Juan Hospital. Forty anarchists trapped in a seminary drank a vast quantity of anisette and set fire to the building in which they were hiding, burning themselves to

1. Kindelán, p. 123.
2. Fitzpatrick MSS.

death.[1] Varela entered the city on 28 September. Moscardó, parading before his men, informed him, saluting, that he had nothing to report, using the phrase *sin novedad* (as usual) which had served as the password for the rebels on 17–18 July. The besieged came out into the open air for the first time for two months; Archbishop Gomá returned to his archiepiscopal see, escorted by Moors; and prayers were offered to 'the subterranean Virgin of the Alcázar'.[2]

The military consequences of the relief of the Alcázar were, nevertheless, as Yagüe had feared. The republic were given time to reorganize before Madrid and were able, as will be seen, to secure substantial external assistance. Franco took his decision to divert to Toledo deliberately, however, and it is easy to imagine the obloquy in which he would have been held had he left Moscardó to his death.[3] No doubt, the emphasis given to the 'epic' of the Alcázar in subsequent propaganda derived from a desire to leave the impression forever that the decision was the right one.

1. Geoffrey Cox, *Defence of Madrid* (London, 1937), p. 54. This journalist (subsequently Sir Geoffrey Cox of Independent Television) was in Madrid at the time. Others have spoken of killings in this hospital. Certain unwounded militiamen took refuge in the hospital and so drew the fire of the Moors in that direction.

2. John Langdon-Davies, *Behind the Spanish Barricades* (New York, 1936), p. 257.

3. Kindelán, p. 23.

25

Nationalist Spain in August – the nationalist flag – great meeting in Seville – credit from Texas – Germans squabble – 'The Young General'

THE rebels had, by September, begun to imbue their movement with a heroic character which alone could justify the waging of war. Whereas their first communiqués in July spoke of the need for order and control of anarchy, people now talked of 'a crusade of liberation'. To sustain a war effort, to ensure that work continued in the shipyards and factories, to maintain morale, to justify executions, it was necessary all the time to make frenzied appeals to the past and to the spirit, and to excite civilian emotion through patriotic propaganda. Republicans of all complexions were denounced as 'reds'. Churches which had been empty before July filled every Sunday, while the controversy over which flag and which cry – '*Viva la República*' or '*Viva España*' – was resolved in favour of the old ways. (In the early weeks of the war, nevertheless, Left and Right had the same war cry: '*Viva España, y Viva la República*', Major Bayo said on landing in Majorca, just as did Franco in July.)[1]

On 15 August, the Feast of the Assumption, the monarchist flag was formally substituted for that of the republic. This action, of such great importance for the Carlists, was the only concession made to the Spanish monarchy in the war; and Mola's forces used the republican colours for some time longer. Nevertheless, in a solemn ceremony in Seville, Franco came forward on the balcony of the town hall, kissed the red and yellow flag many times and shouted across the packed square, 'Here it is! It is yours! They wanted to rob us of it!' Cardinal Ilundaín of Seville kissed the flag also. Then Franco went on: 'This is our flag, one to which we have all sworn, for which our fathers have died, a hundred times covered with glory'. He ended with tears in his eyes. Queipo de Llano spoke next, and went into a rambling discussion of the different flags which Spain had

1. Martínez Bande, *La invasión de Aragón*, p. 267; Franco, qu. Cabanellas, vol. I, p. 621.

had at different times. Finally, he compared the monarchist colours to 'the blood of our soldiers, generously shed, and the Andalusian soil, golden with harvests'.[1] He concluded with his customary references to 'Marxist rabble'. During this speech, Franco and Millán Astray, the founder of the Foreign Legion (who had just returned from Argentina), standing nearby, found it difficult to suppress their laughter. Afterwards, Queipo said that his intense emotion had prevented him from developing his speech as he had intended. Next to speak was General Millán Astray, a man from whom there seemed more shot away than there was of flesh remaining. He had now but one eye, one arm, and few fingers left on his one remaining hand. 'We have no fear of them,' he shouted, 'let them come and see what we are capable of under this flag.' A voice was heard crying '*¡Viva Millán Astray!*' 'What's that?' cried the general, 'No *vivas* for me! But let all shout with me "*¡Viva la muerte!*"' (Long live death!) The crowd echoed this famous slogan. He added, 'Now let the reds come! Death to them all!' So saying, he flung his cap into the crowd amid extraordinary excitement.

Millán Astray was an austere, dedicated fighter with a strong sense of honour. He had fought in the Philippines and had suggested the foundation of the Foreign Legion after a stay with its French version. Reckless to the point of folly, the 'glorious mutilated one' had, after being the Legion's first commander, resigned his commission in the heat of the Moroccan War as a protest against the insubordination of the *junteros* but had returned to command in the days of victory. Chancing to be in Argentina in July 1936 and not having been consulted by Mola, Millán Astray was apparently in two minds as to which side to support when the war began. But Franco's commitment decided him, and he remained throughout the war an influence on Franco, who relied on his judgement, though he never henceforth emulated his recklessness.

José María Pemán, the monarchist poet and writer, an old associate of Primo de Rivera's and one of the literary apologists for the 'movement', followed Millán Astray by comparing the war to 'a new war of independence, a new *Reconquista*, a new expulsion of the Moors!' The final exclamation sounded odd in a city from which an expedition

1. In *For Whom the Bell Tolls*, Pilar refers to the republican flag as 'blood, pus and pomegranate', and to the monarchist flag simply as 'blood and pus'.

of Moroccan soldiers had some days previously set out for the north to conquer Madrid, and whose public buildings and leading generals were even at that moment guarded by Moroccans. 'Twenty centuries of christian civilization,' continued Pemán, 'are at our backs; we fight for love and honour, for the paintings of Velázquez, for the comedies of Lope de Vega, for Don Quixote and for El Escorial.' While the crowd cheered him to the echo, he added: 'We fight also for the Pantheon, for Rome, for Europe, and for the entire world'. He concluded this successful oration by naming Queipo de Llano 'the new Giralda'.[1] Though this last comparison of the coarse-mouthed general with the enchanting Moorish tower next to the cathedral of Seville went a little far even for the crowds who cheered the speaker, such is the ease with which human beings can be brought to believe their own propaganda that active supporters of the nationalists in the Spanish Civil War came to accept such comparisons as valid. Words repeated for symbolic purposes after all achieve a new meaning. Thus Millán Astray in Pamplona a week later announced to a large crowd: 'Navarre! Pamplona! with profound reverence, I salute you! You will be the Covadonga of the new *Reconquista* of Spain and of Faith! You will be the cradle of national heroism! You will be – Navarre!'[2] Medieval names, shouted in an intoxicating manner, indeed for a time served the nationalists as a substitute for an ideology. As Millán Astray put it on another occasion: 'Castile! Permit me to say goodbye with a '*¡Viva Navarra!*' which is the same as to say, '*¡Viva España!*'

*

With a supply of military aid agreed from Germany and Italy after a week of war, the preoccupation of the rebels was how to secure credit for raw materials such as oil, the small native supply of which from the Canaries was hopelessly inadequate. They had also to improvise a new state structure, an undertaking which the 'reactionary' bankers of Spain accomplished with all the zest of institutional revolutionaries.

The republican possession of the Spanish monetary gold meant

1. Bahamonde, pp. 36–8. Pemán's speech appears in *Enciclopedia Universal Ilustrada*, 1936–9 Supplement (vol. II, p. 1404).

2. Del Burgo, pp. 158–9.

that the nationalists started the war with neither the backing for a currency nor the means of obtaining credit from abroad. The methods devised to deal with the situation were: a delay by the new authorities in paying interest on the national debt; a reduction of all superfluous costs of government; new duties to gain higher revenues – for example, a tax on civil servants' salaries – these had to work one day a week free – and a tax on bequests. The rest of the war was financed by internal financial mechanisms (loans, subscriptions, other taxes) and foreign aid.[1] Strict measures were imposed forbidding the export of national currency, fixing the peseta at the level which had obtained before the war. The only backing for this peseta was the expectation of a nationalist victory. The German agency HISMA, under Bernhardt's vigorous direction, however, helped to stabilize the nationalist currency. The export trade of the mines of Andalusia and of Morocco, together with the agricultural produce of the Canaries and Andalusia, also assisted. In addition, the financiers of Europe and America not only expected the nationalists to win, but desired them to. The collapse of investments in Russia had occurred too recently to be forgotten. Thus the matter of the oil supply was solved by the valuable long-term credit, without guarantee, accorded by the Texas Oil Company. Five tankers of the Texas Oil Company had been on their way to Spain at the time of the rising. They received orders from Captain Thorkild Rieber, the strongly pro-fascist president of the company (who visited nationalist Spain to talk with Franco and Mola in August), to deliver their goods to the nationalists. These shipments continued.[2]

Relations between the Spaniards and their German allies were not

1. Tamames, *Estructura*, p. 558.

2. The shipments were legal under the terms of the US Neutrality Act of 1935. After the US Embargo Act (see below, p. 575), some shipments were made by declaring that they were bound for France. The Texas Oil Company was fined $22,000. It made no difference; 344,000 tons of oil were delivered in 1936, 420,000 in 1937, 478,000 in 1938, 624,000 in 1939. The bill of $6 million was paid, and credit renewed (Feis, p. 269). See also Joseph L. Thorndike Jr, *Life*, 1 July 1940. Apparently, Texaco's decision derived from the action of an employee of CAMPSA, Juan Antonio Alvarez Alonso, who fled from Barcelona to Marseilles, where he found W. M. Brewster of Texaco (France) who put him in touch with Rieber, then in Paris. The CEDA government had changed their oil supplier from Russia to Texaco in 1935. (See Bolín, pp. 221–5, and Ramón Garriga, *Las relaciones secretas entre Franco y Hitler*, Buenos Aires, 1965, p. 164.)

straightforward. For example, the director of military supplies, Major von Scheele, quarrelled with the nationalist air commander, General Kindelán, at the end of August. Von Scheele supposed that the republicans' fast Breguet aircraft operating in Aragon would overwhelm the Germans, and Kindelán asked that the Heinkel fighters should be flown by Spaniards. Von Scheele replied that Spaniards would be incapable of flying them. The dispute had to be referred to Franco. There was also rivalry between the nazi Bernhardt and the soldier von Scheele, since the former treated von Scheele as a mere employee of his own, leaving the impression that he, Bernhardt, was Hitler's delegate to Franco. The latent quarrel between the nazi party and the German army was thus exhibited on Spanish soil. The German official, Eberhard Messerschmidt, on return to Germany from a visit to nationalist Spain, on behalf of the Export Cartel for War Materials, meantime urged his foreign ministry that the time was ripe to extract pledges from Franco with regard to Germany's 'future economic and perhaps even political influence' over Spain. He suggested a treaty to lay down a quota for deliveries of raw materials to Germany for a number of years. Bernhardt, anxious to ingratiate himself with Franco, opposed this. But Franco was later induced, against Bernhardt's advice, to start delivery of copper to Germany from the nominally British Río Tinto mines as part payment for war material.[1] Nor did the Germans see eye-to-eye with Franco ideologically. Captain Ronald Strunk, a German journalist and intelligence officer, later complained that he thought Azaña's policy of 'the middle way' superior to Franco's so-called 'saviour army', since that presaged a return of the old order, with landowners and a strong church.[2]

At this stage, Italian aid was limited to the supply of Savoia and Fiat aircraft flown by Italian pilots, some Fiat-Ansaldo tanks and other minor items of material. These were assimilated into the

1. *GD*, pp. 84–9.

2. *USD*, 1936, vol. II, p. 611. By the end of September, the Germans had carried 250,000 kilograms of war material and 13,500 troops from Morocco to Andalusia in Junkers and escorted these by Heinkel fighters; some 550 German troops were in Spain as opposed to some 400 Italians. See Whealey, in Carr, *The Republic*, p. 218, based on Luftwaffe papers. A big new arms operation from Hamburg to Spain began on 29 September under the name of 'Operation Otto'.

nationalist forces as technically members of the Foreign Legion. With them there were as yet no serious disputes.

Franco's position on the nationalist side had been enhanced during August. Partly this was the result of the successes of the Army of Africa, and the preoccupation of Mola with so many less spectacular campaigns. Partly, however, it was due to the relations which Franco had established with Germany and Italy. Both nations, especially the former, gained the impression that 'The Young General' was at the same time able and likely to be influenced by them. Juan March also liked Franco and that probably helped. Canaris spoke of Franco as warmly as did Johannes Bernhardt.

For the time being, however, nationalist Spain was without a single command. That became more and more inconvenient and, by the end of August, several generals – especially the commander of the air force, Kindelán – were speculating as to how to overcome the difficulty.[1] 'Cantonalism' had reached extremes in nationalist Spain almost as much as in the republic: for example, the military governor of Badajoz, Colonel Cañizares, having put on the blue shirt of the Falange, refused to collaborate with Queipo de Llano, remaining almost independent in his fief for months.[2] Would the Falange make the most of this opportunity? They did not, since they had not recovered from the blows that had fallen on them in July. They had been dragged into a rising with which many of the leaders were out of sympathy. Most of those leaders were now lost in republican Spain – possibly alive, probably dead. An army of new members were prancing about in blue shirts. These men and women often had no knowledge of the political ideas of José Antonio. Some were adventurers who had perhaps always secretly longed for a national crisis. Many were opportunists. Some came from the Left, and the then

1. Franco established himself on 26 August in a palace at Cáceres as a headquarters. In a cool drawing-room in this hot Estremaduran city he worked with his aides and his brother Nicolás, as political adviser. On two occasions, when visiting the Army of Africa at the front, he had to leave his motor-car to take refuge from a marauding republican aircraft.

2. Bahamonde, pp. 48–9. Cañizares, earlier a friend of Queipo de Llano, who had appointed him, quarrelled with him over the freedom of action to be allowed to the civil governor; he was not transferred till 1938. He was subsequently condemned to death by Queipo and only saved by Franco, with whom he had served in Morocco.

local chief in Segovia, Dionisio Ridruejo, later calculated that the Left accounted for 20 per cent of new members. Jesús Muro, the ex-member of Primo de Rivera's Patriotic Union, and provincial chief of Saragossa, had a bodyguard composed of one-time members of the CNT.[1] In addition, there were in the Falange ex-radicals, ex-CEDA members, and many who had taken no political position before.

On 29 August, the 'provincial chief' of Seville, Joaquín Miranda, a bull-fighter and ex-supporter of Miguel Maura, who had taken over nearly all the Andalusian parties, organized a meeting of the leading falangist survivors of the events of July.[2] There were also present Agustín Aznar, aged twenty-four, the head of the Madrid militia, who had directed the pernicious street-fighting in Madrid just before the war; and Andrés Redondo, brother of Onésimo, who, though not a falangist before the war, had assumed his brother's mantle in Valladolid, and now called himself 'territorial chief' of Old Castile. This was followed by a meeting of the national council of the Falange at Valladolid on 2 September. There Aznar, Rafael Garcerán (José Antonio's law clerk who had escaped from the Montaña barracks after it had fallen), and other associates from the old Madrid Falange, successfully argued for a 'provisional' seven-man *junta* of command to be set up with Manuel Hedilla, provincial chief in Santander, as chairman.

Hedilla was honest, unimaginative and, it seemed, incapable of full independent leadership. A former mechanic, he had had no formal education. He had some original ideas, and later would speak out against those of his colleagues who had murdered to settle personal accounts. Mola admired him for his resolution in Galicia at the time of the rising. Some saw in him a proletarian leader, who might raise Spanish fascism towards the heights; Aznar and Garcerán saw him as an effective, temporary chief until José Antonio was freed – their main preoccupation. This desire to keep a seat open for the absent José Antonio was the main reason for the failure of the Falange to take hold of the state.[3]

Gil Robles made a brief visit to nationalist Spain and to the front.

1. García Venero, *Falange*, p. 182.
2. There was an earlier meeting of surviving '*jefes provinciales*' on 2 August.
3. García Venero, p. 190f. The *junta* was Aznar, José Sáinz (New Castile), Jesús Muro (Saragossa), Andrés Redondo (Old Castile), and José Moreno

Narrowly escaping arrest by falangists in Burgos, he withdrew to Lisbon, where he spent the rest of the war, and many more years, in exile, conscious that his hour had passed, although, if he had remained in Spain, he could perhaps still have played a part, despite the number and the energy of his enemies among the monarchists and falangists.[1] 'Gil Robles is to blame for everything', José Antonio told the American reporter Jay Allen in his gaol in Alicante, and many others also thought that.

Among other contenders for authority if not power, ex-King Alfonso remained in central Europe and hesitated to support openly even his own friends in this struggle. Nor did anyone ask him to come back. His son, Don Juan, did attempt to come and fight. But he only got as far as Pamplona. There Mola virtually arrested him and escorted him back across the frontier on the explanation that his life was too dangerous to risk. Clearly, monarchy would have as difficult a path in the new Spain as democracy. Even so, by September the local Carlists were in semi-independent control of the province of Navarre, and were busy re-introducing religion to education there.

By this time, Franco as well as the commander of the nationalist navy, Captain Moreno Hernández, had joined the *junta* formed by Mola in July. A meeting of this committee occurred on 21 September, on an improvised airfield on the estate of a bull breeder, Antonio Pérez Tabernero, at San Fernando, near Salamanca. Generals Orgaz and Kindelán proposed the idea of a single command. Mola supported the suggestion with a fervour that raised doubts as to his sincerity. General Cabanellas was the only general who disliked the plan. Kindelán, supported by Mola, proposed that Franco should be the general at the head of the single command. That was agreed, though Cabanellas did not vote. The generals then separated. For about ten days, however, nothing more was done.[2] Kindelán was a monarchist and a friend of the King. He believed that Franco would

(Navarre), and the secretary Francisco Bravo (Salamanca). José Sáinz, actually the senior falangist present, never accepted that Hedilla had been nominated. See Gumersindo Montes Agudo, *Pepe Sáinz*, qu. Southworth, *Antifalange*, p. 140.

1. Gil Robles, p. 756. Actually, Mola told him to leave.

2. Kindelán, pp. 50–53; Iribarren, p. 216. This meeting was not held on 12 September, as sometimes said, probably because of a proof error in Kindelán's book. Present were Generals Cabanellas, Franco, Queipo, Saliquet, Mola, Dávila, Orgaz, Gil Yuste and Kindelán, and Colonels Montaner and Moreno Calderón.

in the end support a restoration. Others around Franco, pressing him and themselves forward at his headquarters in Cáceres, were his 45-year-old brother Nicolás; Yagüe, temporarily unemployed despite his victories in Estremadura, having given up his command over the decision to relieve Toledo; and Franco's old commander in the Legion, Millán Astray.

General Cabanellas continued for some days longer as president of the *junta*. He knew as well as anyone the differences between his fellow generals and must have seen that sooner or later they would have a bad effect on the war. He would, however, have preferred a *junta* of three generals so as to avoid the threat of a dictatorship.  Though he recognized Franco's military qualities, having commanded him in Africa, he suspected that he would never give up power if once he obtained it.[1] Consequently, Cabanellas sought to avoid the implications of the vote of 21 September. But by now, Franco, the victorious general in (if not of) the south, was the hope of all the middle class and all on the Right in a nation which, if anyone stopped to think of it, was plainly in full catastrophe. Calvo Sotelo, Sanjurjo, José Antonio, Goded, were either dead or unavailable. Mola was discredited by the failure of the conspiracy to achieve its objectives, and had been the bitter opponent of the republic who had treated him harshly; at the same time, he was looked on as a republican by monarchists. Queipo and Cabanellas had rebelled against Primo de Rivera. Only Franco had remained politically neutral in the past. Loyal to King Alfonso, Franco had worked for the republic. In mid-September 1936, furthermore, armies under his command were gaining victories. Mola had no sympathy at all for the Falange and its ideas, and, vigorous though he was, could not have made an appropriate Caudillo for the falangists, new or old. Many people too thought that he was still too much of a policeman. Queipo, with his rhetoric, his personalist approach, his bull-fighter friends and his nineteenth-century style, seemed a purely Andalusian leader, something of a figure of fun in Burgos and Salamanca, despised for both his coarseness of language and his republican past by the well-bred, conventional monarchist officers around Franco such as Kindelán.

During the next two weeks, Kindelán, working with Nicolás

1. As he told Kindelán on 28 September (Cabanellas, vol. I, p. 652 fn.).

Franco, the general's brother, and Colonel Yagüe, the best known combat commander, made considerable headway with their schemes. On 27 September, Yagüe appeared on a balcony in Cáceres to talk to a cheering crowd which had assembled to greet the news of the relief of the Alcázar. The colonel told the crowd that the Foreign Legion needed a supreme commander, and one whom they could trust.[1] Of course, Franco was the outstanding candidate, and the victory at Toledo was enough to decide waverers. Some maliciously said that the diversion to Toledo from the road to Madrid was decided upon by Franco to assist his political designs. Although Franco would, no doubt, have been capable of such an action, it is hard to believe that it was necessary, or that he could have been certain that it would have worked to his advantage. At all events though, the day after Toledo fell, on 28 September, the generals of the *junta* and some others travelled to Salamanca by air. On their arrival, Franco was hailed as 'Generalissimo' by an escort of falangists and Carlists ordered to act in this way by Nicolás Franco. To the assembled company of generals, Kindelán read a decree which he and Nicolás Franco had prepared. It stipulated that the armed forces should be subordinate to a generalissimo, who would also be head of state for the duration of the war. But this time the generals assembled were cool to the proposal. Why add political, to the military, responsibilities of the Generalissimo? Cabanellas said that he wished for time to consider the decree. The conference was suspended for lunch, after which, by a mixture of veiled menace and flattery – the details are not clear – Kindelán succeeded in establishing Franco as he wished. Yagüe, too, was present, and hinted that the Legion wanted Franco. Queipo and Mola did not go back to the meeting after the lunch. The draft of the decree, as accepted by the generals on the 28th, spoke of Franco as 'Head of Government of the Spanish state', without a time limit. But in the decree as published, Franco was named as assuming 'all the powers of the Spanish state'. Later, Franco, nevertheless, spoke of himself as Head of State in his decrees – from his first government order, in fact.[2] 'Why did you vote for Franco?'

1. See S. Payne, *Politics*, pp. 371–2.

2. See Cabanellas, vol. I, pp. 654–5, for the best account. What really happened at lunch is obscure despite the evidence of Kindelán (p. 54), and Dávila in *La Voz de España*, 1 October 1961.

Queipo de Llano was once asked by the monarchist, Vegas Latapié. 'And who else could we nominate?' Queipo answered, 'Cabanellas was impossible. He was a decided republican and everyone knew that he was a freemason. If we had named Mola, we should have lost the war. And I – I was greatly diminished in prestige.'[1]

Cabanellas had to sign the decree naming Franco as Generalissimo, but he did not do so before leaving Salamanca. He returned to Burgos alone, and decided to sign only after telephone conversations during the night with Mola and with Queipo. The former was cautious, but said that, if one faced facts, Franco had to be nominated. The latter spoke coarsely and was hostile. Cabanellas thought that he had to sign, in the interests of winning the war. He did so at midnight.[2]

On 1 October, Franco was installed in Burgos. Cabanellas handed over to him full powers of the *junta*, reading out a text slightly different once again from the published decree.[3] Franco gave his first public speech from a balcony on the town hall in Burgos on the subject of the future of Spain: the ballot box would be eliminated in favour of a 'better way of expressing the popular will'; labour would be guaranteed against the domination of capital; the Church would be respected, taxes revised, and the independence of peasants encouraged. In so far as the speech had any theoretical basis, it was founded on the more harmless aspects of the Falange's programme. Much more important were the exultant if quite untheoretical appeals to bellicose nationalism. To them the crowd in the square beneath the general responded with cries of 'Fran-co, Fran-co, Fran-co', as they had only a year before been crying 'Je-fe, Je-fe, Je-fe' for Gil Robles. Henceforward, posters all over nationalist Spain proclaimed the virtue of having 'One State, One Country, One Chief'. Franco began to be described as '*Caudillo*' – the Spanish for 'leader', or, should one say, Führer, or Duce. The remark 'Caesars are always victorious generals' was sporadically scrawled on the walls of nationalist Spain.[4] Franco maintained the ambiguity as to whether he was head of

1. Gil Robles, p. 776 fn. 2.

2. Cabanellas, p. 655. For the decree, see Díaz Plaja, pp. 249–50. A monarchist lawyer, Yanguas Messía, minister of foreign affairs under Primo de Rivera, drew up the decree in the end.

3. Cabanellas, p. 658. 4. Ansaldo, p. 78.

government or head of state, and if either for how long, so that monarchists could still fight for him. The Falange accepted this change without protest, for the time being. They had not been consulted, however, and those leaders most interested in keeping green the memory of José Antonio – Agustín Aznar, for instance – were angry. The Carlists had been preoccupied, at this moment, by the death of the old Pretender, Alfonso Carlos, in Vienna on 28 September. Last of the original line of Don Carlos, his remote cousin and nephew by marriage Prince Xavier would act as regent till a new member of the Bourbon dynasty could be found who would really pledge himself to '*Dios, Patria, Rey*', and the implacable principles of anti-democratic traditionalism. Fal Conde and other Carlist leaders, meantime, were on their way to Vienna for Don Alfonso Carlos's funeral, when Franco was gaining the 'crown' at Burgos.[1] One epoch of Spanish authoritarian politics ended as another began.

On 2 October, a new *junta técnica*, or provisional government, at Burgos, was named to carry on the nationalist administration, headed by an associate of Mola's, General Dávila, the officer who had ensured the success of the rising in Burgos. Nicolás Franco, a 'great friend of Germany' as the German diplomat Dumoulin reported,[2] stayed by his brother's side as 'secretary-general'. General Orgaz, 'resolute and irascible',[3] stayed as high commissioner in Morocco, with the Arabist Colonel Beigbeder as his secretary-general, an important job concerned with keeping the natives happy, and the supply of volunteers constant. The diplomat, José Antonio Sangroniz, another old friend of Franco's from Moroccan days, was in effect foreign minister, with the name of 'head of cabinet', while Juan Pujol, a monarchist journalist who had prepared Sanjurjo's manifesto in Seville in 1932, became chief of propaganda and press. He did not last long, however, and was replaced by Millán Astray.[4] Cabanellas,

1. See del Burgo, p. 267. Bizarre to say, the last Carlist Pretender of the old line was killed in a motor accident by an Austrian army lorry.

2. *GD*, p. 107.

3. Hoare, p. 145.

4. The *junta* was formally Dávila ('President'); governor general, Francisco Fermoso Blanco; secretary for war, General Gil Yuste; the presidents of commissions were Andrés Amado (finance); José López (justice); Joaquín Bau (commerce); Juan Antonio Suances (industry); Alejandro Gallo (agriculture);

as a sop, was given the title of inspector-general of the army. With Franco named as 'Generalissimo' (with his headquarters at Salamanca), the two main armies already formed, that of the north and that of the south, were confirmed in the names of Mola and Queipo de Llano. The latter, however, continued to do what he could to discomfit Franco, from his private kingdom of Seville. For his nightly broadcasts continued, though he had ceased to cry '*¡Viva la República!*' at the end of them.

*

On 6 October, Franco gave a reception for Count Dumoulin, the German counsellor in Lisbon, who had arrived with Hitler's congratulations on becoming Head of State. Franco expressed 'complete admiration' for Hitler and the new Germany. He hoped to be able to hoist his own flag beside the banner of civilization that the Führer had already raised, and thanked Hitler for 'his valuable material and moral help'. A dinner followed, attended by the highest-ranking German pilot in Salamanca, and by Nicolás Franco and Kindelán. Franco, reported Dumoulin, 'permitted not even a moment of doubt as to the sincerity of his attitude towards us, being very optimistic as to the military situation, counting on taking Madrid in the near future'. On the future political organization of Spain, Franco said that a restoration of the monarchy could not at present be discussed; but it was essential – 'though proceeding with kid gloves' – to create 'a common ideology among the co-fighters for liberation' – army, Falange, Carlists, orthodox monarchists, and CEDA;[1] and that indeed was beginning to take shape.

An equally important consideration so far as nationalist morale was concerned, was that the new cruiser *Canarias* had been completed at El Ferrol and brought into action, and that that single ship had transformed the situation at sea, as a naval battle off Gibraltar on 29 September had shown: the republican destroyer, *Almirante Fernández*, was sunk, the other republican vessels withdrew, and the

---

Romualdo de Toledo (education); José María Pemán (culture); Mauro Serret (public works); Nicolás Franco (secretary-general); and Francisco Serra (secretary-general of external relations). Sangroniz had been an official in the directorate general of Morocco in the 1920s.

1. *GD*, p. 105.

republican blockade of the Straits was at an end.[1] Henceforth, the balance of sea power was with the rebels, particularly when the other new rebel cruiser, the *Baleares*, entered into service as well. Given effective nationalist superiority in the air, the war seemed as good, or as bad, as over. But trouble was brewing internationally which destroyed this rebel optimism.

1. See account by the captain of the *Canarias*, Captain Francisco Bastarreche, *La guerra de liberación nacional* (Saragossa, 1961), p. 393f.

26

The anarchists in the Catalan government – Durruti still optimistic – the Council of Aragon – Basque autonomy – a new attack by the Army of Africa – commissars – Azaña leaves Madrid – sounds of battle in the Gran Vía

---

THESE changes among the rebels constituted a real *coup d'état* by General Franco, even though few noticed it as such, in the tumult of war and emotion which swept nationalist Spain after the relief of the Alcázar. On the revolutionary or republican side of the battle, changes were continuous, dramatic, tortuous but less decisive. No doubt a new state authority was there in the making but it arose hesitantly out of the ruins of the old régime and took many months more to be generally accepted.

On 27 September, the anarchists, having held the reality of authority in Barcelona since the rising, accepted it formally by entering the *Generalidad*; an intellectual anarchist, García Birlán, became responsible for health; Juan Domenech for supply; and Juan Fábregas became councillor for economics. The anarchists admittedly referred to the Catalan government as the 'Regional Defence Council', to avoid giving to their already alarmed followers the impression that they had joined a real government, but their entry into this new formal organization signified the failure of their previous effort to have the government of Madrid replaced by a National Defence Council. Ironically, this first entry of an anarchist movement into a position of political authority signified the beginning of the end of anarchism as a political force in Spain. The puritanical figure of the cripple Escorza here saw his influence waning; the star of the more realistic García Oliver rose.

The POUM also joined the *Generalidad*, its experienced leader, the controversial Andrés Nin, becoming councillor for justice. The PSUC leader, Juan Comorera, was in charge of public services. The PSUC's foothold was, however, still tenuous. Three Esquerra members (Tarradellas, prime minister; Ventura Gassol, education; Artemio Ayguadé, the interior) had the more important posts. Colonel Díaz Sandino, another 'Catalanist', was the councillor for defence. The Anti-Fascist Militias Committee, the driving-force of the first weeks after the defeat of the rising, was, however, dissolved on 1 October, and its sub-committees merged with the appropriate Catalan government departments. The FAI leader, Abad de Santillán, wrote later that 'Time and time again we were told that to get arms we would have to abandon the Anti-Fascist Militias Committee and enter the government'.[1] But this decision further disturbed the anarchist movement, even though García Oliver, as secretary-general of defence, ran the Aragonese army, and the anarchist Aurelio Fernández, secretary-general at the interior, was more powerful than his minister, Ayguadé. Another anarchist, Dionisio Eroles, still led the 'patrol controls', which survived as an independent source of anarchist power for months.[2] These reckless half idealists and half terrorists still terrified Barcelona, driving the middle class – shopkeepers, private businessmen, or even ambitious workers – more and more into the hands of the only shelter that seemed to be extended to them, the communists of the PSUC.

If relations between anarchists, communists and Catalan nationalists, not to speak of the POUM, were bad, contact hardly existed between Barcelona and Madrid. Yet there were accusations that Madrid was starving Catalonia: the Catalan Economic Council sent a mission to Madrid to ask credit of 800 million pesetas, another of 30 million to buy war material, another of 150 million francs to buy raw material; the requests were refused.[3] Nevertheless, Madrid complained of Catalonia's military inaction. The already legendary Durruti, however, preserved his idealism at the front. 'I do not expect any help from any government in the world,' he told a journalist, Pierre van Paasen. The Canadian replied: 'You will be sitting on a pile of ruins if you are victorious.' Durruti answered: 'We have always lived in slums and holes in the wall – we shall know how to accommodate ourselves for a time . . . We can also build. It is we

1. Abad de Santillán, p. 116.

2. Leval, p. 126. Cf. Benavides, *Guerra y revolución* (p. 132), for a description and an attack.

3. Peirats, vol. I, p. 216. Peirats, at this time editor of *Acracia* in Lérida, was one of the critics of the idea of participation.

who built the palaces and cities here in Spain and in America and everywhere. We, the workers, can build cities to take their place. And better ones – we are not in the least afraid of ruins. We are going to inherit the earth. The bourgeoisie may blast and ruin their world before they leave the stage of history. But we carry a new world in our hearts.'[1]

The presence of Durruti and the other anarchist columns in Aragon made possible there the establishment of a purely libertarian society. This was disturbing from the point of view of the central government, the Catalan government, the communists, and, indeed, of everyone apart from the CNT and FAI. But there was nothing that they could do about it. The collectives established in Aragon – the CNT later claimed that there were 450 of them – held a conference in late September, at Bujaraloz, near Durruti's headquarters. They set up a regional 'Council of Defence', composed of CNT members, and presided over by Joaquín Ascaso, a cousin of the famous anarchist killed in July. This had its seat at Fraga, and thence exercised supreme power over the whole of revolutionary Aragon.[2] Its organizers announced that rural Aragon had become the 'Spanish Ukraine' and that it would never be crushed by Marxist militarism, as the Russian anarchism had been in 1921.[3]

There was yet another fragmentation that autumn in the republican side. A rump meeting of the Cortes assembled to approve a statute of Basque autonomy. José Antonio Aguirre pledged the new Basque republic (to be known as Euzkadi), of which he was to become president, to stand by the government of Madrid 'until the defeat of fascism'.[4] On 7 October, all municipal councillors of the three

1. *Toronto Star*, 18 August 1936. Despite the fact that the journalist spoke of hearing 'cannon roaring at the front', this interview seems to have been held in Barcelona earlier. See Paz, p. 446. Durruti was shortly converted to the 'discipline of indiscipline'.

2. About this time, Durruti visited Madrid (on a fantastic mission, see below, p. 448) and told a reporter: 'I am against the discipline of barracks but also I am against the misunderstood liberty which helps cowards ... In war, delegates have to be obeyed' (Peirats, vol. I, p. 221).

3. Peirats, vol. I, p. 227; C. Lorenzo, p. 147. The character of this organization will be subsequently examined. See below, p. 556.

4. The Basque nationalist Irujo had joined the republican cabinet on 25 September (Lizarra, p. 99).

Basque provinces who could attend voted in the sacred village of Guernica for the presidency of the 'provisional government of Euzkadi' to govern during the civil war. Aguirre was elected almost unanimously. He then named a government, which was sworn in under the celebrated oak tree. The civil governor of Bilbao, and the presidents of the *juntas* of defence of Vizcaya and Guipúzcoa, who had exercised authority since July, handed over power to Aguirre. In his 'cabinet', there were four Basque nationalists, holding the key posts of the interior, justice, defence, and agriculture. The first Basque government included also three socialists, one communist (the secretary-general of the party in the Basque province, Astigarrabía, who was minister of public works) and one member each from the two republican parties. There were no anarchists in the cabinet. The new government's first action was humane. They evacuated 130 female political prisoners on the British ships *Exmouth* and *Esk* to France, through Dr Junod of the International Red Cross.[1] The Basque civil guard and assault guards were also reorganized, the former being altered into a people's guard under Luis Ortúzar. All this force were Basque nationalists, and all over six feet in height.[2]

This Basque government came into being only after some labyrinthine negotiations during which, on the one hand, Aguirre had to persuade Largo Caballero that a concession of this nature was the best way to get the Basques to fight; and, on the other, some Basque nationalists had toyed with the idea of exchanging autonomy as a return for supporting the nationalists, with whom they had contact through some of their members who, in Alava, had supported the rising.[3]

1. This arose from a harrowing incident. Bilbao had been bombed on 29 September. The consequent fury of the people of the city had caused the murder of a number of the political prisoners kept in three small cargo boats in the harbour of Bilbao. Afterwards, the Basque government released 130 women as part of an exchange previously agreed through Dr Junod. But when Dr Junod first returned to Bilbao, he did so without those children whom he had promised to bring back from where they had been on holiday near Burgos. For the nationalists had gone back on their word. The church bells of Bilbao were ringing, the mothers and the families of the children thronged the quay, when HMS *Exmouth* sailed in empty. The disappointment nearly caused the lynching of Dr Junod. But later forty children were sent back. The full exchange however was never achieved.

2. Aguirre, p. 29; evidence of Luis Ortúzar.

3. C. Lorenzo, p. 162; Iturralde, vol. II, p. 228.

The same day as the Basques achieved their ambitions, 7 October, the rebel offensive against Madrid was resumed. Yagüe, forgiven, returned to field command, though he was placed under Varela. The Army of Africa, now about 10,000 men, and still organized in its columns (under Colonels Asensio, Tella, Delgado Serrano, Castejón and Barrón) was now to act in the final onslaught on Madrid alongside the 10,000 falangists, *requetés* and regular soldiers delegated for the attack by Mola under General Valdés Cabanellas. (Mola was in supreme command of this army, but Varela took the day-to-day decisions, in conjunction with Franco and Yagüe.) There was also a cavalry column under Colonel Monasterio. The army, particularly the legionaries, was well fed, and well armed.

Yagüe probably expected the command but his relations with Mola were too bad to allow that. Instead, Varela was given the great opportunity. Impeccably dressed, always with white gloves, he was rumoured to keep his medals on when sleeping; certainly, one English journalist saw them on a silk dressing gown. General Mola announced facetiously that he would be taking a cup of coffee in the Gran Vía in the capital by 12 October. The Army of Africa soon captured San Martín de Valdeiglesias, and merged its offensive with that of Valdés Cabanellas at El Tiemblo. The militia fled towards Madrid and always along the road, making an easy target for nationalist aircraft with their machine-guns. Bayo, the commander of the ill-fated Majorcan expedition, tried somewhat unsuccessfully to harass the nationalist army by a series of guerrilla actions.[1]

Thus, although Mola did not keep his rendezvous in the Gran Vía (in whose Café Molinero a table was thereafter mockingly kept, with a reservation for him upon it in large letters), at the end of the first ten days of October the republic was faced once more with defeats on all sides. But Largo Caballero refused to mobilize Madrid's large building industry to dig entrenchments, on the ground that he had no shovels and no barbed-wire. He also thought that Spaniards might fight from behind trees, never from trenches.[2] The French journalist, Simone Tery, reported his expostulation: 'What, do you think that Spaniards can fight under the ground, like rats?'[3] In addition, his old friends in the builders' union in Madrid were reluctant to urge

1. Gregorio López Muñiz, *La batalla de Madrid* (Madrid, 1943), p. 5.

2. Fischer, p. 353.

3. Simone Téry, *Front de la liberté* (Paris, 1938).

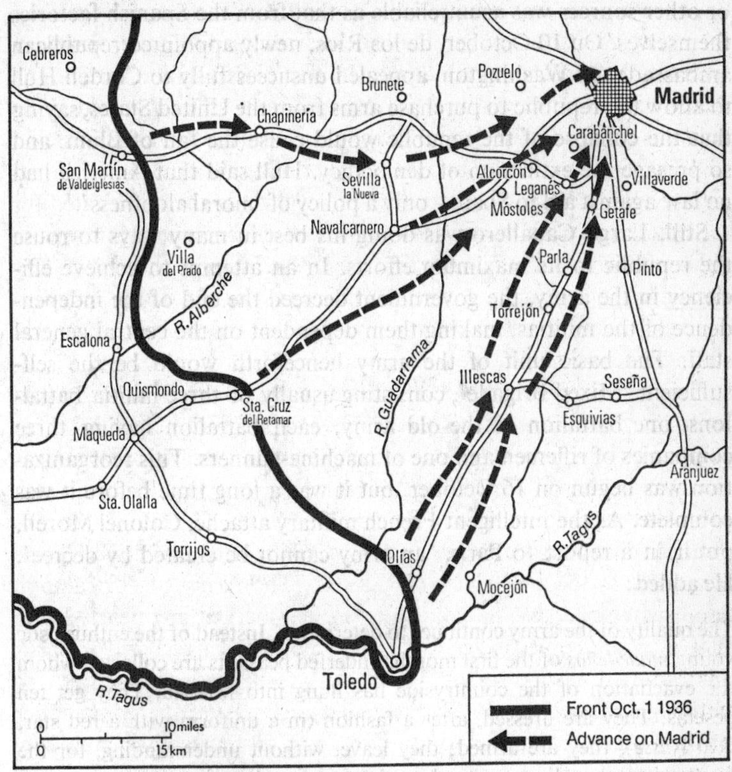

16. The advance on Madrid, September–November 1936

their members to build trenches after hours.[1] He did call up, on 30 September, the reserve classes of 1932 and 1933, but, to communist anger, he allowed the conscripts, if they were anarchists, to join CNT militia units. The communist leaders were now beginning to criticize the Prime Minister for what they thought his pedantry, his vanity, and his strange reliance on old and conventional generals.[2] Largo Caballero had not as yet made a single speech to the nation since he became Premier. He was a noble man and an honest man, everyone conceded, but he seemed not to be a war leader after all. Russian arms had not been arranged, while the supply from French

1. Jackson, p. 312. 2. Koltsov, p. 293.

or other sources was as unreliable as that from the Spanish factories themselves. On 10 October, de los Ríos, newly appointed republican ambassador at Washington, appealed unsuccessfully to Cordell Hull to allow the republic to purchase arms from the United States, saying that the collapse of the republic would cause the fall of Blum, and so presage the extinction of democracy. Hull said that America had no law against aid to Spain – only a policy of 'moral aloofness'.[1]

Still, Largo Caballero was doing his best in many ways to rouse the republic to its maximum efforts. In an attempt to achieve efficiency in the army, the government decreed the end of the independence of the militias, making them dependent on the central general staff. The basic unit of the army henceforth would be the self-sufficient 'Mixed Brigade', consisting usually of three militia battalions, one battalion of the old army, each battalion having three companies of riflemen and one of machine-gunners. This reorganization was begun on 16 October, but it was a long time before it was complete. As the intelligent French military attaché, Colonel Morell, put it in a report to Paris, 'an army cannot be created by decree'. He added:

> The quality of the army continues to deteriorate. Instead of the enthusiastic young *madrileños* of the first month, underfed peasants are collected whom the evacuation of the countryside has flung into Madrid. They get ten pesetas. They are dressed, after a fashion (in a uniform with a red star, *à la Russe*), they are armed; they leave, without understanding, for the front, where they discover, too late, that war is serious.[2]

To try to avoid this ignorance, the government, apparently on the suggestion of the Italian 'Carlos' (Vidali),[3] also established in all units the system of political commissars which already obtained in the communist Fifth Regiment. These were intended to maintain the militiamen's political faith in the cause after the disappearance of their own parties, and to diminish their suspicions of the regular

1. *USD*, 1936, vol. II, p. 536. By this time the nationalists were represented in Washington by the ex-ambassador in Paris, Cárdenas, who arrived in the USA at the end of August and who had weekly talks at the state department with the under-secretary, James Dunn – a career diplomat who, seventeen years later as US ambassador to Franco's Spain, finally concluded the US–Spanish bases agreement (evidence of Cárdenas).

2. *FD*, vol. III, p. 526. 3. Spriano, p. 87.

army officers. The idea derived from the commissars of the Red Army, more distantly from Carnot's regiments in 1794. The commissar's role was not well defined; he could be everything or nothing. This development of these 'theologians of the Red Army' or 'red almoners' (as the nationalists referred to them) turned out to be another victory for the communists. The organization was superficially fair to all parties: the socialist Alvarez del Vayo, for example, was commissar-general, the vice-commissars-general were Crescenciano Bilbao (a Prieto socialist); Antonio Mije (communist); Angel Pestaña (the old anarchist, now a syndicalist); Gil Roldán (anarchist); and Felipe Pretel (another socialist, and second-in-command of the UGT). In fact, Mije played a dominant part in respect of organization, while an ex-socialist youth leader, now a communist, José Laín Entralgo, became director of the training school for commissars near Valencia, which he made into a communist bastion. Both Alvarez del Vayo and Pretel were fellow-travellers, and Pestaña was shortly to be succeeded (through ill-health) by another socialist friendly with communists, García Maroto. Pestaña was anyway a man with no following at this time. Alvarez del Vayo, busy as foreign minister, in fact did little as commissar-general, Mije and Bilbao being the real managers of the corps.[1]

A few months later, the commissars seemed to be more assistant chiefs-of-staff than anything else: periodically they would 'be sent round by the party to . . . deliver some sort of political discourse . . . By this time, the political commissar was simply a go-between who was sent to headquarters to complain about rations etc. . . .'[2]

On the battlefield, in the north, the nationalist garrison in Oviedo, meantime, was relieved, by a column from Galicia, and after many privations – and, indeed, only just in time to prevent its fall to the Asturian miners, who had already penetrated into the town.[3] But the miners continued to press hard, if ineffectively, at Oviedo for another

1. There is a study of this office by Eduardo Comín Colomer: *El comisariado politico* (Madrid, 1973).

2. George Orwell, 'Notes on the Spanish Militias' in *Collected Essays, Journalism and Letters*, ed. by Sonia Orwell and Ian Angus (London, 1968), vol. I, p. 320.

3. On 15 October, García Escámez also entered Sigüenza by a sudden attack, north-east of Madrid. The militiamen hid in the cathedral and nationalist guns shattered part of that admirable building before they surrendered.

six months, since the garrison's link with the outside world was a thin neck of land.

General Varela soon launched the next stage of his assault on Madrid. On 15 October, the whole twenty-mile front was driven forward ten miles. The road junction of Illescas, half-way between Toledo and Madrid, fell on 17 October. Largo Caballero telephoned the town to speak to his commanding officer, to be answered, to his horror, by Varela. The next day, the weary republican militias, brutalized by the savagery of their Moroccan and legionary opponents, and only partly believing the assurance of their commissars that Russian help was coming, launched a counter-attack upon Castejón at Chapinería. Six thousand militiamen broke Castejón's lines, and surrounded the town by the morning of 19 October. Castejón then led a sally out of the town through its cemetery, and converted the republican counter-attack into another defeat. On 20 October, another republican attack, directed by Colonel Ramiro Otal, under Asensio Torrado (now a general),[1] with Majors Rojo, Mena, and Modesto, leading 15,000 men, was launched at Illescas, where Barrón was established with his Moroccans and legionaries. The republican forces were brought up to the front by double-decker Madrid buses visible across the flat land from Barrón's command post. Illescas was plastered by artillery bombardment, and the town surrounded. Monasterio's cavalry and Tella's column from Toledo were thrown into the battle. The nationalists outflanked the militiamen, who were driven back beyond their point of departure by 23 October.

The sound of battle could now be heard in Madrid. The government decided to move to a safer city. Their first choice was Barcelona, and President Azaña set off first, establishing himself in the parliament buildings in the Catalan capital. The government then changed their minds about leaving Madrid. Azaña remained where he was and the cabinet hastily announced that he had left for an extended tour of the front.[2] Henceforward, Azaña could be consulted only by telephone. He increasingly infuriated his ministers. He refused to listen to intelligence reports, which (not inaccurately) he named 'bad detective stories'. His sincerity impelled him to speak the truth, even

1. He had been promoted general after Talavera.

2. Azaña, vol. IV, p. 818. See Largo Caballero, p. 187, for a different account.

on telephone calls to other countries which could easily be tapped. When his cabinet expostulated, he would reply: 'I am not to blame that I am of an analytic spirit and you are not.'[1] Appalled by the murders and judicial assassinations carried out in the name of the republic, convinced that the republic would lose, contemptuous of Largo Caballero, Azaña now seemed more a liability than a leader.

In these nervous circumstances, a committee of the Popular Front and CNT was set up in Madrid to intensify the search for members of the Fifth Column. Illegal killings, which had almost ceased, broke out again. One so killed was Ramiro de Maeztu, once counted among the Generation of '98, later a theorist of Spanish monarchism, and another was Ramiro Ledesma, co-founder of Spanish fascism. Loyalty was everywhere suspect. Asensio Torrado was blamed for the defeat of Illescas, especially by the communists, but Largo Caballero admired him and insisted on giving him the post of under-secretary in the war office on 24 October, while General Pozas took command of the Army of the Centre.[2] Pozas, like many other non-political senior officers, was becoming more and more impressed by the communists. The same day, General Miaja, the old scapegoat for the collapse of the Córdoba offensive, was brought from Valencia and named commander in Madrid in succession to General Castelló, the ex-minister of war, whose mind was wandering. Miaja had denounced a recent rash of executions in Valencia, and he was apparently appointed to Madrid in order to save him from the consequences of that complaint.

The approach of battle to Madrid brought a measure of fraternity to anarchists and socialists in Catalonia. In Barcelona, at least, they sealed their differences, in a declaration of common purpose on 22 October, which was put into effect by a decree of the *Generalidad* two days later. While large firms (that is, those employing over 100 workers) and firms owned by 'fascists', were to be collectivized without compensation, plants employing between 50 and 100 workers (actually a majority of Barcelona's factories) could only be collectivized if that were requested by three-quarters of the employees. Still smaller firms were only collectivized at the owner's request, unless they were involved in war production. The *Generalidad* would have

1. Alvarez del Vayo, *The Last Optimist* (London, 1950), p. 173.
2. Largo Caballero, p. 186.

a representative on each factory council, and would appoint the council chairman on large collectives: and each collectivized plant would be run by a council chosen by the workers and have a two-year term of office. All collectives making the same things could be co-ordinated by one of fourteen councils of industry, which could also bring in private firms, where needed, in order 'to harmonize production'. This decree was, in fact, the culmination of a hundred other legislative acts on the subject of collectivization. It meant less a free hand to the anarchists than an effort by the state to standardize, and hence control, the process of collectivization. Some of the things for which the decree provided had already been achieved. Juan Fábregas, councillor for the economy, and also president of a still anarchist-dominated economic council of Catalonia (under the *Generalidad*, theoretically), a very new anarchist convert, was largely responsible. Coordination nevertheless remained in practice vague; there were no statistics and no records of sales. Cut off from raw materials and also from markets, the Catalan textile industry was running down.[1] The war industries were working but their transformation from peace-time uses was anything but easy.

The character of rebel Spain after three months of war was that of a new state, in which all the trends were towards centralization, unity and hence, in war, efficiency; in the republic, the institutions of the old state were laboriously being revived, while such innovations as were introduced spelled continued disunity and dissipation of resources. In rebel Spain, a group of able generals in their forties were ruthlessly seeking a new world; in republican Spain, a number of elderly politicians sought to hold on to a wreck which had already been scuttled. For the presence of so many young men in the army and in the communist and socialist parties, not to speak of the anarchist movement, should not delude the observer into thinking that the republic offered much of a chance for youth. The revolution did; but republic and revolution were two separate crafts.

1. See Carlos Semprún Maura, *Révolution et contre-révolution en Catalogne* (Tours, 1974), p. 110f, for a hostile critique by an anarchist.

27

The League – Russian aid – formation of the International Brigades – Kléber

THE annual assembly of the League of Nations had, meantime, met in Geneva. That organization was crumbling. Its faults were patent. Although, in 1936, the League was not twenty years old, and its permanent headquarters, with its huge, optimistic murals by the Catalan painter Sert, had not yet been opened, the undertaking seemed already something from another age. Never, even at the time of its splendour (such as after the admission of Germany in 1925), had the League lost the character of an institution dominated by the victors of 1919. Nevertheless, until 1935, it had carried out its role as the expression of a world-wide desire for peace comparatively successfully. It had made peace between Greeks and Bulgars in 1925. It ended the Colombo–Peruvian War of 1934. It had abstained from resolution, true, over Manchuria in 1931. But that mistake did not seem irreparable. In 1935, however, the League failed to take effective action over Mussolini's invasion of Abyssinia. It voted for sanctions, but not for any which had any effect. On 4 July 1936, even these had been abandoned. Mussolini's African adventure was tacitly condoned. The responsibility for all these retreats lay with the British and French governments, whose influence was supreme at the Palais des Nations. At the general assembly of 1936, the débâcle over Abyssinia had to be reviewed. But now there was also Spain. In the wings of the assembly, on 24 September, Eden persuaded Dr Monteiro to bring Portugal into the Non-Intervention Committee. In his speech in the general debate which opened the assembly, Eden, however, did not mention Spain at all. Dr Carlos Saavedra Lamas, the Argentinian president of the assembly, supported by other Latin American delegations, sought to prevent the republic's foreign minister, Alvarez del Vayo, from speaking on the civil war, since it was not on the agenda, though the general debate had usually been regarded as permitting discussion of anything. (Saavedra was prorebel.) But Alvarez del Vayo made his speech all the same, having been persuaded to be moderate by Eden. He deplored the fact that the Non-Intervention Agreement had placed his government on the same footing as the rebels: whereas, by international law, a government was entitled to buy arms abroad, while rebels were not. The republic would accept real non-intervention, but by that he meant freedom to buy arms.

This meeting at Geneva was not a happy one for the republic. It seemed evident that the Anglo-French policy was to subordinate Spain to the general European policies of these two governments. Azaña, Giral, Azcárate and all the 'liberals' in the government of the republic were disillusioned with England. Only Litvinov had spoken favourably for Spain. By that time, whether Litvinov knew it or not, Russia had decided to help Spain with arms as well as words. Indeed, the decision must have been taken some time in August since weapons began to reach Spain in mid-October.

The government of the republic had asked the Russian government to sell them arms while Giral was still Prime Minister. A delegation from Madrid apparently reached Odessa at the end of August.[1] By that time, it will be remembered, a strong Russian presence had been established in Madrid and Barcelona led by an experienced ambassador (Rosenberg) and an influential head of military mission (Berzin).[2] A few days later, a handful of Russian pilots started flying some of the new French aircraft which the republic had recently bought, 'in conditions of inferiority for us', making a considerable impression on their Spanish comrades: they were 'truly extraordinary pilots', Captain García Lacalle described them.[3] Some war material may also have arrived by late August, though none of it substantial – no Russian aircraft or tanks were to be seen till October.[4] Even with

1. Krivitsky (p. 110) speaks of 'three high republican officials' reaching Russia late in August. There is, surprisingly, as yet no other evidence for this visit but I incline to believe Krivitsky's testimony, even if his details are sometimes wrong.

2. See above, p. 392.

3. Letter to the author, July 1964. See G. Prokofiev in *Bajo la bandera*, p. 373. These pilots flew 'most of September' in Spain.

4. A German agent reported three Russian ships passing through the Dardanelles carrying 500 tons of war material and 1,000 of ammunition in September. See the files of the German military attaché at Ankara (annex to Report No. 4238 of the German military attaché, Ankara, 7 February 1938, and Annex 2

Britain and France backing non-intervention, there were alternatives to Russia in the US or in South America as suppliers of arms to the republic. But with German and Italian governmental assistance to Franco, a government, not just an arms manufacturer, was plainly desirable as a backer, and the Russian equipment was better qualitatively than anything to be found outside Britain or the US. Indeed, the Russian tanks and aircraft were as effective as, if not better than, anything in the world, as will be seen;[1] though neither Largo Caballero's nor Giral's cabinets knew that.

According to Walter Krivitsky, the Russian military intelligence 'resident' in The Hague, Stalin took a decision to help the Spanish republic on 31 August at a meeting of the Politburo in Moscow[2] and, from then on, both the Russian government and the Comintern, as well as their various secret and semi-espionage agents and organizations, began to prepare for a major military commitment. One reason for this decision was the mismanagement of the republican interests in Paris: the ambassador, Albornoz, de los Ríos, together with the socialist deputy for Granada, Dr Alejandro Otero, were all enlightened men, but they were not good arms smugglers. La Pasionaria (with a delegation from Madrid) visited Paris at the end of August and found that the telephone operator at the Embassy in Paris (who had been in the same post under the monarchist ambassador, Quiñones de León) told all the republic's secrets to the nationalist representatives in Paris.[3] At all events, Krivitsky in The Hague re-

to Report No. 7238 of 4 April 1938) which purport to be statements derived from a German agent with access to Turkish records of the amount of Soviet aid through the Dardanelles. (D. C. Watt discovered these valuable documents, see *The Slavonic and East European Review*, June 1960, pp. 536–41.) The German consul-general in Barcelona reported, on 16 September, that a reliable source told him that thirty-seven aircraft had been landed by Russians in Spain by boat a week previously (*GD*, p. 89) but no one saw them in the air until October. See also Gisclon, p. 123, for apparent confirmation of this. The French chargé in Turkey, however, reported that, from 15 August to 15 September, 'only four Russian or Spanish ships carrying 30,000 tons of oil to Spain were seen' (*FD*, p. 567).

1. See below, p. 445.

2. Other evidence, however, suggests that Stalin was not in Moscow on that day.

3. Ibarruri, p. 301.

ceived instructions (on 2 September, according to him) to mobilize all possible facilities for the shipment of arms to Spain from Europe.[1] About ten days later, on 14 September, there was a meeting in Moscow to arrange the shipment of aid from Russia direct to Spain. The meeting was held, ominously, in the Lubianka and present, it seems, were Yagoda, still for another week or so head of the secret police (NKVD); General Frinovsky, at the time 'commander of the military forces of the NKVD'; General S. P. Uritsky, chief of military intelligence in succession to Berzin who was in Spain as head of the military mission; and A. A. Slutsky, an 'amiable, courageous and humane' man who was chief of the foreign division of the NKVD. At this meeting, the NKVD was given an important supervisory role in the subsequent supply of arms and men in Spain, and it was agreed (or confirmed) that the superintending officer should be a certain Alexander Orlov (his real name was Nikolsky), a 'veteran officer' in the NKVD, who was also already in Spain.[2] The shipment of arms was to be the work of Uritsky who would set up a special agency to be directed by Captain Umansky, in Odessa; and this was shortly done.[3] But no one knew of this plan who did not absolutely have to: probably Litvinov, Rosenberg, Maisky and Koltsov remained in ignorance of these moves for weeks, as did the Comintern leaders (in Moscow or in Paris), most of whom continued to complain during September and early October that Stalin was continuing to 'betray the Spanish Revolution', in Trotsky's words from Nor-

1. Krivitsky, p. 111.

2. For the meeting, see Krivitsky, pp. 110–13. Orlov subsequently defected to the US, where he hid till Stalin's death and then gave evidence in various spy trials of the 1950s, as well as telling the Senate internal security sub-committee that his role in Spain had been to advise on 'intelligence, counter-intelligence and guerrilla fighting' (Hearings, part 51, 1957, p. 3422). He told Stanley Payne that he had been appointed to Spain on 26 August, and that he arrived there on 9 September. But for Orlov see Poretsky, p. 259.

3. Uritsky was the 36-year-old son of the founder of the Cheka murdered in 1918. Umansky (whom Krivitsky wrongly calls Oulansky) was one of the group of Jewish communists from Polotsisk in what used to be Austrian Galicia who played such an interesting part in Russian secret diplomacy and about whom the widow of one (Ignace Reiss-Poretsky) wrote so evocative a book (Elizabeth Poretsky, *Our Own People*, London, 1969). Krivitsky was another such. Umansky ('Misha') makes numerous appearances in Mrs Poretsky's study.

way.[1] The Spanish government did not know that Russia was going to help them with arms until a very short time before the ships carrying the material set off.

Russia had not embarked on adventures of this nature previously. She did not have a Mediterranean fleet. The supply routes would hence have to be kept secret. Given the geographical problems, and Stalin's own internal problems (if that is not too modest a word for the Purges, then beginning in the top ranks of the Old Bolsheviks), the scheme to assist the republic was a risky one, whenever the decision was taken.

The first cargoes to Spain from Odessa must nevertheless have been put on board at the end of September. Thus, the German chargé in Moscow, Tippelskirch, on 28 September wrote an interesting dispatch that an expert had noted that 'in the Black Sea harbour of Novorossik, access to the harbour area has been more severely restricted since the summer ...'. The same observer (presumably an agent of the German consul in Odessa) felt '... there was more than food in the heavy crates composing the cargo of the *Neva* which left Odessa for Spain ... So far, however, it has been impossible to obtain reliable reports of violation of the arms embargo by the Soviet government.'[2] Oil, yes. The republic had gone back to their old agreement with Russia (which the right-wing government had not renewed, in 1935) and Russia sent to Spain at least 30,000 tons of oil between 15 August and 15 September, 44,000 tons between then and 12 October.[3]

But Stalin continued to have misgivings about the decision to help the republic. To the Russian technicians and military experts whom he sent to Spain he gave the order 'stay out of range of artillery fire'.[4] Russian supply ships must have left Odessa about 4 October at latest. Even at that date the decision may not have been firm, as a tale told by a French anarchist, Pierre Besnard, suggests: on 2 October, he reached Madrid with two representatives of an (unnamed) international arms dealing consortium. Besnard, Durruti and Largo Caballero met these two men and heard what they had to say; Largo promised to put the idea of buying arms from this consortium to the cabinet that afternoon. The cabinet agreed, and the next day, 3 October, the details were worked out, Durruti again being present. On

1. See Hernández, p. 42; Fischer, p. 350. 2. *GD*, p. 100.
3. *FD*, vol. III, p. 567. 4. Krivitsky, p. 100.

4 October, Durruti was telephoned by the Russian ambassador, Rosenberg, who asked him to call on him; he could not do so since he had to return to the front. Some days later, Besnard was told that the republican government could not go through with the operation which he had initiated: the Russians had complained.[1]

The appropriate diplomatic arrangements were soon made for this new commitment. Thus in London, the Soviet chargé, Kagan, sent a note almost in the form of an ultimatum to Lord Plymouth, the new British representative on the Non-Intervention Committee. Alleging that Italian aircraft had flown legionaries to the Spanish mainland on 20 September, Kagan said, on 7 October, that, if such violations of the Non-Intervention Pact did not cease, Russia would consider herself free from her obligations under the agreement. 'If there is an agreement,' wrote Kagan, 'we want that agreement to be fulfilled. If the committee . . . can secure that . . . well and good. If it cannot, let the committee say so.'[2] The following day, 8 October, a Russian diplomat in Moscow told the American chargé that, unless the committee did show itself determined to bring about an immediate end of violations, Russia would withdraw, considering itself free to aid Spain with military equipment. This blunt change of policy infuriated the Foreign Office. 'What', they asked, 'can Russia hope to gain by throwing over neutrality at this time?' But the Russian action was supported on 9 October by the British Labour Party Conference, which passed a unanimous resolution declaring that Germany and Italy had broken their neutrality and calling for an investigation. That day, the meeting of the committee lasted seven hours, the exchange of accusations between Kagan and Grandi astonishing the other diplomats. Lord Plymouth pointed out to Germany, Italy and Portugal the allegations of aid made by the Spanish government at Geneva. Kagan accused Portugal of allowing its territory to be used as a nationalist base of operations, and demanded a commission to patrol the Spanish–Portuguese border. The Portuguese ambassador withdrew during the discussions of that Russian proposal, which he considered insulting.[3]

Russia now considered her position to be legally clear. At least

1. Speech of Pierre Besnard at the VIIth Congress of the AIT in Paris in 1937, qu. 'Andrés Suárez', *El proceso contra el POUM* (Paris, 1974), p. 22fn.

2. Cattell, *Soviet Diplomacy*, p. 44.

3. *NIS*, fifth meeting.

sixteen Russian and other ships passed through the Bosphorus in early October carrying arms for Spain.[1] The first to reach Cartagena was the *Komsomol*, carrying tanks, armoured-cars and some artillery, together with a group of tank specialists, headed by Colonel S. Krivoshein.[2] Perhaps, in all, a hundred tanks and a hundred aircraft arrived during these days, as well as a quantity of lorries, anti-aircraft guns, armoured-cars and other equipment, much of it new. The two types of Russian fighters sent to Spain, the I-15, a bi-plane known as 'Chato' or 'snubnose' in Spain, and the I-16, a new monoplane known in Spain as 'Mosca' (fly) (Rata to the nationalists), were the fastest in Europe, being in effect Russian versions of the American Curtiss and Boeing fighters.[3] The Chato had a maximum speed of 220 miles an hour, four machine-guns as well as the capacity to drop small 25-pound bombs.[4] The Mosca had only two machine-guns but was much faster, since its maximum speed was almost 300 miles an hour.[5] It also had a new device for swift climbing, a retractable undercarriage and a highly charged engine. Two groups of thirty-one aircraft each of these fighters were soon in service in Spain, almost all of them flown to begin with by Russian pilots. There also soon arrived three other aircraft: the SB-2 two-engined bomber, known as the Katiuska, built in 1933, which, since it had been designed as an 'interceptor' and could travel 250 miles an hour, did not require an escort;[6] the Natasha, another fast bomber;[7] and the Rasante, a low-flying bomber used for machine-gunning.[8]

1. See also (for approximate confirmation of the figure) *GD*, p. 126; *New York Times*, 24 October 1936.

2. Kuznetzov in *Bajo la bandera*, p. 179; also Krivoshein in the same, p. 319. Some ships were Russian, most Spanish.

3. 'I' was the letter indicating 'fast fighter' in the Russian air force and these two fighters were accordingly the 15th and 16th in the series. 'SB' meant bomber, 'R' reconnaissance. Both the Chatos and Moscas were designed by Polikarpov.

4. See García Lacalle, p. 561 (the improved model I-15 B came in reduced numbers, in 1938); Sanchís, p. 30f.

5. See García Lacalle, p. 565; Sanchís, *loc. cit.*

6. The Katiuska had a range of 900 miles, a bomb capacity of 1,700 pounds and had the same rapid rate of climb as the Mosca. See Sanchís, *loc. cit.* This bomber had a crew of three, two mobile machine-guns, one fixed, all 7.62 mm. Its bomb load was six Russian bombs of 70 kg and four of 10. It was inspired by the American 'Martin 139' and known as such in the nationalist zone.

7. The Natashas were bi-planes, 750 cv.

8. The Rasante, of 500 cv.

These aircraft were faster and technically superior to the German and Italian equivalents, though the sturdy Fiat fighter was still sometimes able to outmanoeuvre the Chato, and the Junkers 52 remained a useful pack-horse for transport, though less so for bombing. The Heinkels 51 were of much less use henceforth.

Within a short time the hundred or so new Russian aircraft in Spain would give the republic command of the air. Something similar happened in respect of the Russian tanks, sent to Spain at the same time. These ten-ton T-26 tanks were heavily armoured, cannon-bearing machines, of a more formidable type than the three-ton Fiat Ansaldos and six-ton Panzers Mark 1 against them, which had no cannon, only machine-guns.[1] Russian anti-tank guns (45 millimetre, based on the Vickers two-pounder) were also superior to any German models then available.[2]

Russian personnel in Spain numbered five hundred by 1 November. They were field officers, pilots, tank specialists or flying instructors, with some translators. The head of the mission remained General Berzin ('Grishin') who, as has been seen,[3] had arrived in Madrid in September. The head of the air force was Colonel Jacob Smushkevich ('General Douglas'). Largo Caballero later accused him of operating independently of the republican ministry of defence from the airbase of Los Llanos, and of being disdainful towards those Spaniards who were not communists.[4] His pilots included some, like Prokofiev, Kopets, and Schacht, who had been in Spain all September; and others who came now for the first time and who soon made themselves at home in the skies of Spain.[5] The future Marshals Malinovsky, Rokossovsky and Konev were all soon in Spain, as was General Kulik, 'the victor of Tsaritsin' in the Russian Civil War, who became an adviser to General Pozas, in command in the centre

1. The Russian T-26 tank weighed 10.5 tons and had a .45 mm gun and two twin machine-guns; the TB-5 (used from late 1937 only) had a .45 mm gun and four twin machine-guns. It weighed 20 tons. The Panzers were 6 tons with two machine-guns, and the Fiat Ansaldos were 3.3 tons and had one machine-gun. See *inter alia* R. Salas in Carr, *The Republic*, p. 187; also Modesto, p. 235.

2. Franco's ordnance factories copied them rather than the German equivalent.

3. See above, p. 393.

4. See Martínez Amutio, p. 85.

5. Largo Caballero, p. 206; Prokofiev, in *Bajo la bandera*, p. 380f.

of Spain.[1] Most of these Russians acted as 'advisers' to the republican commanders in their command posts, others stayed with technical arms, or in the headquarters of the Russian mission. The adviser in Madrid was to be the military attaché who had arrived in August, General Goriev, described by Ehrenburg as 'intelligent, reserved, and, at the same time, passionate – I could even call him poetical . . . everybody believed in his lucky star'.[2] The Russian tank base at Archena, a watering-place twenty miles inland from Cartagena, near Murcia, surrounded by olives, had a Spanish local organizer, Colonel Sánchez Paredes, who recruited tank drivers from the taxi and bus drivers of Madrid and Barcelona.[3] A fighter base and a bomber base for the Russians was established nearby at Alcantarilla. Other air bases were later organized at El Carmolí, near Madrid at Algete, and outside Alcalá de Henares, Some of these men came by sea, others by land – some even across central Europe.[4]

These deliveries of men and materials were not made by Russia as

1. Known as 'Kupper' in Spain. (Castro Delgado, pp. 457–8; Hernández, pp. 80–81.)

2. Ehrenburg, *Eve of War*, pp. 146–7. See also Modesto, p. 237; Ibarruri, p. 346; Lister, p. 76; and José Luis Alcofar Nassaes, *Los asesores soviéticos en la guerra civil española* (Barcelona, 1971), *passim*; and the Soviet history of the Second World War (*Istoriya Velikoy Otechestvennoy voyny Sovetskogo Soyuza 1941–5*), vol. I, pp. 112–13. According to El Campesino, Rokossovsky was charged with espionage in nationalist Spain – allegedly to discover for Stalin the character of certain German arms. Konev, under the name of 'Paulito', is said by El Campesino to have trained terrorists in Spain. Another Russian who directed sabotage and guerrilla war in nationalist territory (under Orlov, according to Orlov before the Congressional Sub-Committee in 1957) was Etingon (also known as Kotov). It was he who became the lover of the Barcelona communist Caridad Mercader del Río, and who picked out her son Ramón as a useful agent – later being used to murder Trotsky (see below, p. 447, fn. 4). Ehrenburg says Kotov 'inspired me with a certain mistrust' (*op. cit.*, p. 231). Krivitsky speaks of a General Akulov who was organizing military intelligence in Catalonia (*op. cit.*, p. 117); I suppose that Kotov and Akulov were the same.

3. R. Salas, vol. I, p. 533. De la Cierva, *Historia ilustrada*, vol. I, p. 399, has a tale of a Russian colonel (Krivoshein?) who is remembered in Archena for his help in restricting local repression.

4. See the memoir *Master of Spies* (London, 1975), p. 107, by the chief of the Czechoslovak military intelligence, Colonel Moravec, for an account of how Czechoslovakia helped 120 Russian officers through to Spain by giving them passports.

a friendly contribution to the revolutionary cause. They had to be paid for. This was done by the shipment to Russia of most of the gold which hitherto had guaranteed the Spanish currency, Spain's most valuable treasure. Spain had then the fourth highest gold reserve in the world. Some of this monetary gold had been sent to Paris to guarantee delivery of goods before the war, some in July. But most lay in the vaults of the Bank of Spain in Madrid.[1] Much of it was in coin – Louis d'or, sovereigns, dollars, as well as gold pesetas. In September, it had seemed desirable for the republic to remove this treasure 'to a safe place'. On 13 September, the cabinet gave authority to the new Prime Minister and finance minister, Largo Caballero and Negrín, to ensure this. The assumption apparently was that the gold would be taken somewhere in Spain; and it was taken by train to a large, well-guarded cave near Cartagena. Largo Caballero and Negrín, together with the latter's civil service under-secretary Méndez Aspe, soon decided that Russia was the safest place. Russia leapt at the idea, and Stalin's chief secret policeman in Spain, Orlov, was apparently placed in charge of getting it to Russia. Britain and France, the most logical places for the gold reserve, were the staunchest proponents of non-intervention, and it seemed risky to take the gold there.[2] It was not only the 'fascists' of whom Largo Caballero was afraid: Durruti had a plan to raid the Bank of Spain in early October, though he was talked out of it by Abad de Santillán.[3] Nevertheless, Largo Caballero and Negrín apparently told neither the President, Azaña, nor any other minister of their new plans. Azaña was, understandably, furious when he was told that the gold had left Spain; and Prieto wished to resign in protest, being dissuaded by Azaña from an action with which he himself sympathized.[4]

1. The total Spanish monetary gold was worth 2,367,000,000 pesetas (about $788 million). The quantity shipped to Russia was 1,581,642,000 gold pesetas worth ($500 million). The quantity sent to France in July was 470,000,000 pesetas worth ($155 million) to add to the 257,000,000 pesetas worth ($85 million) already there. See Appendix Seven.

2. Largo Caballero, pp. 203–4. For some details, see Martínez Amutio, p. 52f.

3. Paz, pp. 386ff, and Azaña, vol. IV, p. 705. Díaz Sandino and Abad de Santillán visited Azaña in September and told him that the anarchists wanted the gold in Barcelona; Díaz Sandino also suggested to Azaña that he should make himself dictator.

4. This is Prieto's story, as contained in articles collected later in *Convulsiones*,

Negrín shipped the gold to Russia on 25 October. It became a kind of 'current account', in Largo's words, on which the republic could draw to pay for their arms supplies and other purchases, including oil, from both Russia and elsewhere. Spanish wine, sugar and fruit, with some other goods, also helped the republic's balance in Russia. The details were arranged between Negrín and the Russian economic attaché, Stashevsky.[1]

This faery gold, as it later appeared to be, left for Russia in large boxes, being loaded onto four Russian steamers by sixty sailors who worked for three nights, while, during the day, they slept on the boxes containing it. The sailors were provided by the commander of the base at Cartagena, Captain Ramírez de Togores, without being told what they were doing. When the loading was finished, the under-secretary, Méndez Aspe, compared figures with Orlov. Orlov's figure was 7,900 boxes, Méndez Aspe's 7,800. The error was two lorry-loads, since each lorry had contained fifty boxes. Orlov did not tell Méndez Aspe of this divergence, since, if his count should prove to be correct, he might have had to be responsible for the lost boxes.[2] The Russian ships were guarded by the republican fleet as far as Algiers.[3] The arrival of the gold, or some of it, was seen by the German consul at Odessa who, on 6 November, noted the arrival of a grey ship of 4,000 tons, its name made illegible, which lay in Odessa roadstead without a flag, and which was unloaded at night.[4] When the gold reached Moscow, the counting was made to last for ever – so that

---

vol. II, pp. 132–41; it seems more reliable than the versions put out by Araquistain who was not there, or by Alvarez del Vayo, whose memory sometimes played him tricks (see Alvarez del Vayo, *Freedom's Battle*, pp. 286–7, and also Alexander Orlov in *Readers' Digest*, January 1967, and his evidence to the Senate Internal Security Sub-Committee). See Jackson, p. 318 fn. 8, for a suggestion that Prieto must have known and the article by the then Spanish ambassador in Russia, Marcelino Pascua, in *Cuadernos para el diálogo*, June–July 1968.

1. Martínez Amutio, pp. 58–9.

2. Orlov's details. El Campesino said later that he escorted the gold to Cartagena. In 1956, the receipt for the gold given by Russia to Spain, and handed by Negrín's heirs to the nationalist government, mentioned 7,800 boxes; either Méndez Aspe was right, or the Russian government accepted his figure, using the extra boxes for their own purposes.

3. Kuznetzov, in *Bajo la bandera*, p. 182f. Kuznetzov was permanently based in Cartagena.

4. *GD*, p. 128.

the four Spanish officials accompanying it remained in Russia as long as possible.[1] When their families in Spain grew anxious, they were sent to Russia also. They were not allowed to go free till 1938. Marcelino Pascua, the Spanish ambassador in Moscow, a socialist, doctor by profession and until now director-general of health, could do nothing for these unfortunate officials.[2] They were doubtless lucky not to have been turned to stone, as usually happens to human beings who enter the kingdom of giants. Eventually, they were allowed to go free – one being shipped to Stockholm, one to Washington, one to Buenos Aires. According to Orlov, Stalin celebrated the arrival of the gold with a banquet at which he announced, 'The Spaniards will never see their gold again, just as one cannot see one's own ears',[3] even though the official receipt said the Spanish republican government could re-export the gold when they liked.[4]

Meanwhile, on 21 September, the other part of Russia's help to Spain was begun when an NKVD agent named Zimin visited Krivitsky in The Hague, and a meeting was held in Paris with Krivitsky's colleagues posted in London, Stockholm and Switzerland. Zimin described the supreme importance of keeping Russia's name from being associated with the Comintern arms traffic. The first move, he said, was to set up an organization for the purchase of arms throughout Europe. Krivitsky, who was himself wondering at this time whether he could break away from his Soviet service, arranged the financial capital and the offices, and guaranteed profits.[5] Both he and Ignace Poretsky (Ignace Reiss), the NKVD chief in Switzerland, who worked with him on this, hoped obscurely that 'a victory for the Spanish Revolution would help to overthrow Stalin in Russia'. Agents, at a price, were easily found. These resembled characters in a spy story. There was, for example, a Dr Mylanos, a Greek, established in Gdynia. There was Fuat Baban, another Greek, the representative in Turkey of the Škoda, Schneider, and Hotchkiss firms, later arrested in Paris for selling drugs. And there was 'Ventoura. Of Jewish origin. Born Constantinople. Found guilty of a swindle

1. Prieto, *Convulsiones*, vol. II, pp. 131–3.
2. Martínez Amutio, p. 58.
3. Orlov, Senate Internal Security Sub-Committee, part 51, p. 3434.
4. *New York Times*, 10 January 1957.
5. Krivitsky, pp. 103–5; Poretsky, p. 150. Zimin is not otherwise identifiable.

in Austria. False passport. Lives with a woman in Greece. Domicile in Paris in a hotel in Avenue Friedland'.[1] It is such persons as these who must be pictured, during the rest of the Spanish war, carrying out their profitable missions behind the backs of the dignified gentlemen of the Non-Intervention Committee and supplying expensive, sometimes obsolete, weapons to the republican government's Arms Purchase Commission, with its headquarters in Paris, perhaps through the French communist party, the Spanish ambassador in Paris, or other agents.[2]

Around this Commission, a horde of unscrupulous profiteers clustered. Many of those involved became, in one way or another, corrupted whether or no they worked for the Comintern. Had the whole question of arms purchase been honourably carried on, many more weapons might have arrived in Spain, whatever happened to non-intervention. But perhaps the private arms traffic inevitably breeds corruption. A chain of import–export firms was nevertheless set up in Paris, London, Prague, Zurich, Warsaw, Copenhagen, Amsterdam and Brussels, with an NKVD member as a silent partner controlling funds. Arms were produced from Czechoslovakia, France, Poland, Holland and even Germany; from the latter country, the astute Admiral Canaris even secured the dispatch, through communist hands, of defective war material to the republic.[3] With the French frontier closed, the best way of transporting the arms was by

1. This derives from a German foreign ministry note of 8 October 1938, to the Spanish nationalist foreign ministry, quoted in *The International Brigades* (a nationalist propaganda pamphlet of the 1950s), p. 43.

2. Fischer, p. 371. Araquistain remained president of this till December, when his place was taken by Alejandro Otero. Otero returned to Spain in 1937 to succeed Colonel Pastor as under-secretary of the ministry of defence in charge of armaments. Dismissed in December 1937 by Prieto, he lived on in Paris selling arms on his own account. In April 1938, he was to become sub-secretary of defence – an appointment which Peirats compared to making Al Capone chairman of the Bank of Spain (*op. cit.*, vol. II, p. 147). The anarchists regarded Otero, socialist deputy for Granada and professor of gynaecology, as a profiteer pure and simple. On the other hand, when in charge of armament factories, he resolutely refused the SIM (the political police introduced into the republic late in the war, see below, p. 776) permission to enter those factories (Martínez Amutio, p. 327).

3. Though some genuine German material got through to the republic, and the nationalist ambassador in Berlin had to complain, that was not till 1938.

sea, consular papers being secured from British, Greek, Latin American or Chinese governments, falsely certifying that the goods were for those countries.[1]

*

Meantime, a third element in communist help to the republic began. How precisely it originated is a little obscure. Willy Muenzenberg, the propaganda chief of the Comintern in western Europe, visited Moscow in September.[2] He supported a suggestion apparently made by Thorez, the secretary-general of the French communist party, that some aid might also go to the republic in the form of volunteers raised internationally by foreign communist parties (though they would welcome non-communists) to add to those already in Spain fighting for the 'cause of liberty'. At the end of September, the central committee of the Italian communist party met in Paris in the presence of French communist leaders and of Codovilla, the senior Comintern representative with the Spanish party. They agreed that 'a column larger than that of Rosselli' should be organized from Italian anti-fascists to go to Spain.[3] In a day or two, the Comintern's executive took the decision to form, under their authority, a number of international columns out of all the many who wanted, or could be persuaded, or be sent, to go to fight for the republic. Luigi Longo, the Italian communist youth leader of some years before, had spent much of August and September in Spain, and he was charged to make the appropriate arrangements with the Spanish government.[4] Dimitrov, the Bulgarian communist who was secretary-general of the Comintern, is also said to have become enthusiastic for this idea.

No doubt, however, the Russian ministry of defence was concerned in the plan from an early stage, for the excellent reason that there was a precedent for this international force in the Red Army, during the Russian civil war. The designation 'International Brigade' had

1. Krivitsky, p. 103.

2. See Jurgen Schleimann, 'New Light on Münzenberg', *Survey*, April 1965. Muenzenberg was only able to return to Paris through the personal intervention of Togliatti. In 1937, he finally quarrelled with his chiefs, and left the party, to be murdered mysteriously in southern France in 1940. He was succeeded in Paris by the Czech Bohumil Smeral (the first leader of the Czech communist party during the early 1920s), who had none of his qualities.

3. Spriano, vol. III, p. 94. 4. Spriano, p. 130.

even been used, along with other names such as First International Legion of the Red Army, the International Red Army, and the First Revolutionary International Detachment. Into these forces in support of the revolution in Russia there had been pressed innumerable volunteers, or ex-prisoners of war from Austro-Hungarian or German or Bulgarian armies from out of the waves of men who had been washed into Russia by the First World War. Many of these men served in the Ukraine under no less a person than Antonov Ovsëenko, in 1936 now the Russian consul general in Barcelona. Some of them were even still available in sections of the Russian army. Presumably it seemed very convenient to Stalin if an experiment which had once been effectively tried out in one civil war might be employed again in another.[1] The Comintern had been concerned after all with armed insurrection in the 1920s and Togliatti, now so closely concerned with events in Spain, had written part of the Comintern's technical manual on the subject.[2]

In addition, many Italian, German and other exiles from fascist or right-wing authoritarian régimes, along with many others still in those countries, themselves longed for the outbreak of a real war against fascism:[3] 'We had a greater need of going to Spain than the Spanish republic had need of us', wrote one Italian exile, Emilio Lussu.[4] 'Oggi in Spagna, domani in Italia' was the famous cry of Rosselli, echoed by many others. Earlier in September, Randolfo Pacciardi, an Italian liberal republican émigré, had approached the Spanish government with the aim of forming an Italian legion in Spain, independent of political parties, to be recruited in Paris. But Largo Caballero opposed the idea.[5] Now, after new disasters on the battlefront, he altered his view. Luigi Longo, the prominent young Italian communist, Stephan Wisniewski, a Polish communist, and

1. See John Erickson, *The Origins of the Red Army*, in *Revolutionary Russia*, ed. R. Piper (Harvard, 1968), p. 251f. I am particularly grateful to Professor Erickson for his help in following up this reference. Tito was active in the Yugoslav international group in 1919.

2. See 'A. Neuberg', *Armed Insurrection* (London, 1970), p. 90.

3. Jacques Delperrie de Bayac, *Les Brigades Internationales* (Paris, 1968), p. 76.

4. Emilio Lussu, 'La Legione italiana in Spagna', *Giustizia e Libertà*, 28 August 1969, qu. Spriano, vol. III, p. 90.

5. Randolfo Pacciardi, *Il battaglione Garibaldi* (Lugano, 1948), pp. 17–19. For Pacciardi, see below, p. 482.

Pierre Rebière, a French communist, negotiated in Madrid on behalf of the Comintern on 22 October.[1] The three visited Azaña and Largo Caballero, who handed over responsibility to Martínez Barrio (then presiding over a committee to reorganize the army). It does not seem as if any one of these three republican politicians were enthusiastic for the idea, but they believed that the publicity at least would be good.

The formation of International Brigades then became the main work of the Comintern. Each communist party was instructed to raise a given number of volunteers. In many cases the prescribed figure was higher than local parties could attain. Most of the ablest leaders of the Comintern, not already involved in Spain, were employed in this way. The future Marshal Tito, Josip Broz, for example, was in Paris organizing, from a small left-bank hotel, the flow of recruits through his so-called 'secret railway', which provided passports and funds for East European volunteers, and the experienced Jules Humbert-Droz found himself doing the same thing in Switzerland.[2] Where the volunteer was not a communist, he was investigated by an NKVD representative and by a communist doctor – the latter at the French–Spanish border.[3] Many admittedly escaped this security checking, however, especially those who joined the volunteers in Spain or *en route*. Some adventurers in search of excitement joined – such as Nick Gillain, a Belgian, who later gave his reason for joining up as 'spirit of adventure, lassitude, and this rainy autumn

1. Luigi Longo, *Le Brigate Internazionale in Spagna* (Rome, 1956), p. 44. Cf. also pp. 18 and 27.

2. See Tito's declarations in *Life*, 28 May 1952, and Humbert-Droz's *Mémoires*, vol. II, p. 182. When, after the secret assassination of Gorkić and other leading Yugoslav communists in 1936, Tito became chief of the Yugoslav communist party, he supervised the dispatch of Yugoslavs. Tito denies having ever been in Spain but, in view of the surprising number of people who claimed to have seen him there, it seems possible that he at least visited the Brigades' headquarters for one reason or another. His reluctance to admit this is no doubt explained by some aspect of the Gorkić murder. Gorkić himself also for a time organized the dispatch of volunteers for the Brigades from Paris. One group of volunteers were betrayed to the Yugoslav police just before leaving the Dalmatian Coast: Gorkić was held responsible.

3. The fact that the Spanish republican government were under no illusions about the connection between the communist parties and the volunteers is attested by the advice of Spanish consuls to would-be volunteers to make contact with communist parties.

of 1936'.[1] About 60 per cent were communists before volunteering, and a further 20 per cent probably became communists during their experiences in Spain. From all countries (including Britain), 80 per cent of the Brigades were members of the working class.[2] Most were young men, though some of the Germans and Italians, militant refugees from fascist régimes, were veterans of the First World War. Many, especially among the French, were at that time unemployed[3] and many had experience of street-fighting against 'the fascists' in Berlin, Paris and even London. This was not the same as fighting the 'Moors', or the Foreign Legion, as they soon discovered. About 500 to 600 refugee communists were sent to Spain who had been exiles in Russia.[4] Among these were men such as Stern ('Kleber'), Zaisser (Gómez), Zalka ('Lukács') and Galicz ('Gal') who had fought in both the First World War and probably in the International Brigades in the Russian Army. They played a leading part in those in Spain.[5] An English communist volunteer aptly summed up the motives of his countrymen for volunteering by saying 'undoubtedly the great majority are here for the sake of an ideal, no matter what motive prompted them to seek one'.[6] Many volunteers regarded the battle which they were fighting in Spain as a first step in the struggle against the enemy at home; particularly the Italians, who were able to use Spanish radio stations to broadcast in Italian against Mussolini: 'the artillery of the loudspeaker', as 'Carlos' put it.[7] The Spanish war thus rejuvenated the Italian anti-fascist struggle. A Czech communist, such as Artur London, could regard his service in the International Brigades as part of the anti-nazi struggle in Central Europe.[8]

The central recruiting office of the Brigade was in the rue de Lafayette in Paris. Karol Świerczewski, a Polish colonel in the

1. Nick Gillain, *Le Mercenaire* (Paris, 1938), p. 7.

2. Approximate figure worked out after questioning of survivors.

3. Many unemployed Frenchmen from Lyon were dispatched into the Brigades.

4. Krivitsky, p. 112. 5. See below, p. 459.

6. Miles Tomalin MSS (unpublished diary), p. 7.

7. Italian language broadcasts from Valencia were directed by the communist, Velio Spano.

8. Artur London, a Czech, became vice-minister of foreign affairs before becoming one of the three victims of the 'Slansky trials' of 1949 to survive. See his *L'Aveu* (Paris, 1969), the film made of it by Costa Gavras, and also his dull, highly conventional *Espagne*... (Paris, 1966).

Russian service known as 'Walter', was military adviser, at the head of a *bureau technique* in the nearby rue de Chabrol. Świerczewski had fought in the First World War for Russia. He then took part in the Russian Revolution and Civil War, later becoming a professor in the Moscow Military School.[1] The theme of recruitment propaganda was the slogan that Spain should be 'the grave of European fascism'. Volunteers signed on without a contract and without knowledge of how long they would be fighting – an indefinite commitment which later led to trouble. From France, the volunteers were sent to Spain by train or boat. They then made their way, or were sent, to the new base at Albacete, half-way between Madrid and Valencia, surrounded by the dull wastes of La Mancha, and known for several centuries for the manufacture of knives.[2]

The first contingent of volunteers, five hundred strong, left the Gare d'Austerlitz, in Paris, by train 77 ('the train of volunteers') and travelled via Perpignan and Barcelona, to find on arrival on 14 October at Albacete that little preparations had been made. The barracks of the civil guard had been made over to them, but the rooms on the ground floor were still stained with the blood of those killed there on 25 July. The International Brigaders squeamishly preferred, therefore, to crowd into the rooms upstairs to sleep.[3] The first group were nearly all Frenchmen, with some Polish and German exiles from Paris. There were also some White Russians who hoped to use this roundabout method of returning to their own land. These new recruits were shortly afterwards joined by many of the foreign volunteers who had fought in Aragon and in the Tagus valley, including the remains of the German Thaelmann Centuria, some of the Italian Gastone-Sozzi Centuria, and the French 'Commune de Paris' Battalion. The young English poet, John Cornford, was among those volunteers (though he had returned home to England on sick leave after his fighting in August). The day after arrival at Albacete, all volunteers would be identified and registered. A clerk would ask if there were officers, non-commissioned officers, cooks, typists, artil-

1. He appears in *For Whom the Bell Tolls* as General Goltz.

2. See Longo, pp. 42–9; Max Wullschleger, *Schweizer Kämpfen in Spanien* (Zurich, 1939), pp. 21ff. Albacete was also within two hours' drive from Archena, the Russian tank base.

3. Gillain, p. 18.

lerymen, riders, or machine-gunners present. Many foolishly replied according to their ambitions rather than to their abilities. The volunteers were then organized in language groups, with appropriate names. The British volunteers were as yet too few to form a separate battalion and some were therefore put in with the Germans and some with the French.[1]

The supreme '*troika*' in command of the base was André Marty as commander, Luigi Longo ('Gallo') as inspector-general, and Giuseppe di Vittorio ('Nicoletti') as chief political commissar.[2] The two Italians were men of ability and humanity.[3] Marty lacked both. Catalan by blood, born in Perpignan, he was the son of a worker condemned to death in his absence for his part in the Paris Commune. He had first come to prominence in 1919 when, as a seaman-machinist, he had led the mutiny of the French Black Sea fleet in protest against orders received to support the White Russian armies. He became a communist later. His rise in the French communist party during the succeeding years was due to his record as '*le mutin de la mer noire*'. He owed his appointment at Albacete to his alleged military knowledge and to his favour with Stalin as one who had refused to take up arms against the struggling Soviet Union seventeen years before. He was a member of the seven-man directorate (secre-

1. Gillain, p. 18. These volunteers were soon supported by a British Medical Aid group including doctors and nurses. This originated as follows: Isobel Brown, the communist moving spirit behind the British Committee for the Relief of the Victims of Fascism (one of Muenzenberg's creations), was receiving many donations labelled 'Spain'. She, therefore, inspired the creation of a British medical aid committee, with non-communist, but left-wing, doctors as figureheads which dispatched the medical aid unit to Spain under the leadership of a socialist, a contemporary of Cornford's at Cambridge, Kenneth Sinclair Loutitt. The value of this and other medical units was considerable, since nearly all the army doctors of Spain were with the rebels. (As for the civilian practitioners, these seem to have been almost equally divided between the republicans and the nationalists.) See also *All my Sins Remembered* by Viscount Churchill (London, 1964). This peer led the British unit out to Spain.

2. Fischer, p. 367; Longo, p. 44. Longo later became secretary-general of the Italian communist party, a post he held from 1964 until 1969, when he became, and (1976) still is, president of the party.

3. Guiseppe di Vittorio, a labour organizer from Apulia and active in Italy against Mussolini earlier, was from 1945 to 1958 secretary-general of the General Confederation of Italian Labour, the communist trade union. Longo's *nom de guerre* was taken from the name of a famous and elegant matador, El Gallo.

tariat) of ECCI, the Comintern executive, and, given the importance of the Spanish venture, it was inevitable that one of that body should be the International Brigades' chief. By 1936, he was obsessed with fear of fascist or Trotskyist spies.[1] He was followed to Spain by his wife, Pauline – whom even he seemed sometimes to try and avoid. His appointment was one of Stalin's many errors of judgement even on small matters. Only Stalin himself had a more suspicious nature than André Marty. The chief of staff of the base was a crony of Marty's, a Parisian municipal councillor, Vital Gayman, who went in Spain by the common name of 'Vidal'.[2] Captain Alloca, an Italian tailor from Lyons, was in command of a cavalry base at the nearby town of La Roda, while a Czech, the able technician and future writer, Captain Miksche, set up an artillery school at Chinchilla de Monte Aragón.[3] The first infantry training commander at Albacete was a German journalist, Ernst Adam – not a communist – who afterwards moved to the front. He was succeeded by an incompetent Bulgarian who owed his appointment to his part in the explosion in Santa Sofia in 1923 – scarcely a very military operation.[4] Albacete soon became too full for all the trainees, and the neighbouring *pueblo* of Madrigueras was taken over by the Italians, Tarazona de la Mancha by the Slavs, La Roda by the French, and Mahora by the Germans. Another Bulgarian communist, Tsvetan Angelov Kristanov, who had been an emigrant in Russia from 1926 to 1936, ran the medical services of the International Brigades under the appealingly Scandinavian *nom de guerre* of Oskar Telge, with a staff of many nationalities beneath him,[5] and Marty's wife, Pauline, acted as inspector of the hospitals. Louis Fischer, the American journalist, nominally representing the *Nation* in Spain, acted first as quartermaster general, until he quarrelled with Marty, when his post was taken by yet another Bulgarian, Ljubomir Karbov.[6] The German Walter Ulbricht apparently organized a division of the NKVD

1. Ehrenburg, *Eve of War*, p. 167.
2. Marty's bodyguard was Pierre George, famous in the Second World War as 'Colonel Fabien'. See Fischer, p. 366, and *The International Brigades*, pamphlet issued by the Spanish foreign ministry, 1953.
3. Fischer, p. 379.
4. Comment by Ernst Adam (London).
5. Kristanov's identity was established for me by Victor Berck, to whom I am grateful also for other help.
6. Fischer, p. 366.

within the Brigades, where he investigated German, Swiss, and Austrian 'Trotskyists'.[1] The Brigade were provided with uniforms by the French communist party, including a round Alpine woollen hat. Discipline was enforced with an iron hand.

The Spanish people and the Spanish people's army have not yet conquered Fascism [Marty told the Brigade]. Why? Is it because they have lacked enthusiasm? A thousand times no. There are three things they have lacked, three things which *we* must have – political unity, military leaders, and discipline.[2]

When he spoke of military leaders, he indicated a short figure with grey hair, his overcoat buttoned up to his neck – 'General Emilio Kléber'. Kléber was now forty-one, apparently a native of Bucovina, then part of Roumania, at his birth Austria-Hungary. His real name was Lazar or Manfred Stern, his *nom de guerre* that of one of the ablest of the French revolutionary generals. In the First World War, he served as a captain in the Austrian army. Captured by the Russians, he was imprisoned in Siberia. At the Revolution, he escaped and joined the bolshevik party. After taking part in the Russian Civil War, and forming a part of International Brigades active there, he joined the Comintern military section. He was sent on confidential missions in the Chinese Wars and perhaps also to Germany.[3] Other rumours made Kléber one of the assassins of the Tsar, adviser to Haile Selassie, and to Luis Carlos Prestes in Brazil – a veritable Flying Dutchman of revolutionary war. Now appropriately he arrived in Spain, as the first leader of the first International Brigade. He was built up well by propaganda, as a 'soldier of fortune of naturalized Canadian nationality'. On being introduced to his future command by Marty, he stepped forward and gave the salute of the clenched fist, amid a roar of applause. Marty went on: 'There are some who are impatient, who wish to rush off to the front at once. These are criminals. When the first International Brigade goes

1. Ruth Fischer, *Stalin and German Communism* (Oxford, 1949), p. 500 n. Confirmed in Branko Lazitch's *Biographical Directory of the Comintern* (Stanford, 1973).

2. Esmond Romilly, *Boadilla* (London, 1971), pp. 72–3.

3. Krivitsky, p. 116. See also Andreu Castells, *Las Brigadas Internacionales* (Barcelona, 1974), p. 73f. This is much the best study of the Brigades. According to Castells, 'Kléber' came to Spain first in 1924!

into action, they will be properly trained men, with good rifles.' So the training at Albacete went on. The difficulties of language were surmounted. The different ways in which the nations carried out their left and right turns in drill were coordinated. Only the Germans, however, took drill seriously or were any good at it. Irishmen enlivened the dark barracks with doleful songs. In a dozen languages slogans were scrawled on walls: '*¡Proletarios de Todos Países! ¡Uníos!*' '*Proletarier aller Länder, vereinigt euch!*' '*Prolétaires de Tous Pays, Unissez-vous!*' '*Pracownic świata, łączüe się!*' '*Proletari di tutti i Paesi, Unitevi!*' 'Workers of the World, Unite!'

During the next few months, volunteers continued to stream into Albacete. The poet Auden[1] described the urgency of the appeal of Spain in words still irresistible:

Many have heard it on remote peninsulas,
On sleepy plains, in the aberrant fishermen's islands
 Or the corrupt heart of a city.
Have heard and migrated like gulls or the seeds of a flower.

They clung like burrs to the long expresses that lurch
Through the unjust lands, through the night, through the alpine
 tunnel;
 They floated over the oceans;
They walked the passes. All presented their lives.

On that arid square, that fragment nipped off from hot
Africa, soldered so crudely to inventive Europe;
 On that tableland scored by rivers,
Our thoughts have bodies; the menacing shapes of our fever

Are precise and alive. For the fears which made us respond
To the medicine ad. and the brochure of winter cruises
 Have become invading battalions;
And our faces, the institute-face, the chain-store, the ruin

Are projecting their greed as the firing squad and the bomb.
Madrid is the heart. Our moments of tenderness blossom
 As the ambulance and the sandbag;
Our hours of friendship into a people's army.[2]

1. He himself worked with an ambulance unit for a short while in 1937. See below, p. 609.

2. See comment on this poem, above, p. 346, fn. 4.

Some volunteers came by sea from Marseilles, some across the Pyrenees by secret paths unknown to, or unwatched by, the French police carrying out the orders of their non-interventionary government. Those who crossed the Pyrenees would stay one night in the old castle of Figueras. By both routes, nearly all went through Barcelona, or through Alicante, where they were greeted with enthusiasm by crowds shouting '*salud*', '*no pasarán*', and '*UHP*'. The streets would fill with Spaniards singing the 'International', 'The Young Guard', 'The Red Flag', or the 'Hymn of Riego', or all of them. The train onwards would stop at small stations, where peasants would press forward offering wine and grapes, giving the clenched-fist salute, and shouting '*¡Viva Rusia!*' Local communist and other Popular Front parties would crowd the platforms with the names of their villages inscribed on banners. Frequently the recruits would arrive drunk. One Irish recruit from Liverpool, who afterwards wrote a *Candide*-like description of his experiences, began on his first night at Albacete a saga of illnesses, drinking bouts and visits to the Brigade penitentiary that lasted for six months.

Not everyone was enthusiastic. The anarchists distrusted the International Brigades and gave orders to their militants who controlled the French frontier passes to oppose their entry. But 'after requests by international personalities', wrote a leading anarchist, 'we desisted, though continuing to believe that these persons were not wanted. Arms were needed, not men.'[1]

As the nucleus of the Brigades arrived in Albacete, Stalin telegraphed an open letter to José Díaz, the Spanish communist leader, published in *Mundo Obrero* on 17 October, saying that the 'liberation of Spain from the yoke of the fascist reactionaries is not the private concern of Spaniards alone, but the common cause of progressive humanity'. By late October organizations for aid to the republic had indeed sprung up in nearly every country in the world. Friends of Spain, Spanish medical aid committees, committees for Spanish relief were established everywhere. Behind them all lurked the shadow of the communist parties. Philip Toynbee, a communist at Oxford, described how his orders that term were 'to proliferate Spanish defence committees throughout the university, as a moth lays its eggs in a clothes cupboard'.[2] Spain also served other purposes: the leader of

1. Abad de Santillán, p. 175. 2. Philip Toynbee, p. 87.

the Indian congress party, Jawaharlal Nehru, writing for the Indian committee for food for Spain, pointed out, 'By sending a medical mission to China, by giving foodstuffs to the Spanish people, we compel the world's attention to our viewpoint.[1] Thereby, we begin to function in the international sphere, and the voice of India begins to be heard in the councils of the nations.'[2]

Göring in Berlin was meanwhile complaining that he did not have enough people to handle German deliveries to and from Spain. Hess then put the nazi party's foreign organization at his disposal for this, Eberhard von Jagwitz at its head. Jagwitz thenceforth worked directly under Göring, rooms being provided for him in the nazi party offices. It was only now on 16 October in fact that the German foreign and economic ministries heard of the existence of ROWAK and HISMA.[3] They swallowed their surprise. Bernhardt had arranged for a ship full of copper belonging to Río Tinto to be confiscated in Cádiz and sent to Hamburg. When Göring asked Bernhardt one day in October how German aid was to be paid for, Bernhardt could reply, 'There is a ship full of copper waiting for you.'[4]

The Non-Intervention Committee was still in being. But on 23 October, Maisky announced that Russia could no more consider herself bound by the Non-Intervention Agreement 'to any greater extent than any of the remaining participants' in the committee.[5] The upshot was Portugal's breach of diplomatic relations with the Spanish republic because of Russian charges against it. Russia did not, as her press had suggested was probable, now leave the committee. That may have been due to Litvinov's return from Geneva. He probably pointed out that an abandonment of the committee would mean a breach with France and Britain and, therefore, a blow to the policy of collective security. Lord Plymouth thereupon proposed the

1. There were, however, general relief funds which gave aid to both sides. The English General Relief Fund for Spain was supported by the archbishops of Canterbury and of Westminster, the chief rabbi, the moderator of the church of Scotland, and the free churches. It was formed in December 1936.

2. *Spain! Why?* (pamphlet by Nehru, London, 1937), p. 4. Nehru visited republican Spain in the course of the war.

3. *GD*, pp. 113–14.

4. Evidence of Johannes Bernhardt.

5. *NIS*, seventh meeting. Described in some detail by Ivan Maisky, *Spanish Notebooks* (London, 1966), pp. 45–57.

control of the supply of war material to Spain by, for example, establishing observers at Spanish ports who could report what they saw to the Committee.[1] This aristocratic voice of reason seemed, however, sadly inappropriate.

During these exchanges, the Italian foreign minister, Count Ciano, was paying an important visit to Berlin. He discussed Spain with Neurath and Hitler. These men agreed that Germany and Italy should accord the nationalists diplomatic recognition after the fall of Madrid. Neurath imagined that could be counted upon within a week. Both Germans and Italians denied vigorously to each other that they desired to take over any part of Spanish territory. They also exchanged rumours: Ciano said that he had heard nothing of the German report that 400,000 Russians were on their way to Spain. But he was all the same instituting an observation service between Sicily and Africa. In addition, Italy was finishing two submarines for the nationalists. No doubt the completed vessels would be useful in this Mediterranean vigil. This meeting brought the Germans and Italians close together on all matters. Within a week, Mussolini would for the first time use the phrase 'Berlin–Rome Axis' to describe that doomed friendship.[2]

Henceforth, in more ways than one, the Spanish Civil War would be more even than a European civil war: it would be a world war in miniature. For the Spanish war had broken out at a particularly critical moment not only in diplomacy, as has been seen, but in the development of armaments. By October 1936, the Junkers 52 and Heinkel 51 were familiar sights in Spanish skies. So were the Fiat fighter CR-32 and the French 'flying coffins' along with Dewoitines and Blochs. Soon the Russian aircraft of the newest new generation of aircraft, modelled on US precedents, would become equally familiar. The later famous Messerschmitt fighter and the much faster Heinkel 111, made with stressed skins, were already tested and would soon be seen in Spain. On the ground the panzer tanks and T26s from Germany and Russia would be in action in what the German tank commander General von Thoma would call 'a European Aldershot'.[3] Equally, the new German machine gun – the 'MG34' –

1. *NIS* (c), eighth meeting.
2. Ciano, *Diplomatic Papers*, pp. 60–61; *GD*, pp. 117, 122.
3. B. H. Liddell Hart, *The Other Side of the Hill*.

which entered service only in 1936 would be used in Spain as would the slightly older Russian Degtyareva Pekhotnii (DP). The new German 88 millimetre anti-aircraft gun – famous in the Second World War as the 'Eighty Eight' for use against tanks – was already in Spain by late October, alongside the still reliable Italian artillery of the First World War. Thus, in a country which until July had been technologically backward, the most modern designs in the most important of industries were employed to murderous effect. The rebellion of July 1936 thus thrust Spain into the twentieth century with, in the exact sense of the word, a vengeance.

BOOK THREE

WORLD WAR IN MINIATURE

'I do not know if it is irreverent or not. I believe not. But I am anyway convinced that if, from today onwards, some son of this blessed region of Navarre presents himself at the gates of heaven and says that he is from here, Saint Peter will enthusiastically say "Bravo! Carry on!"'

GENERAL MILLÁN ASTRAY in Pamplona

'Yesterday, thousands of men and women marched to the trenches singing. "The International" reached the enemy lines and made the mercenaries flee. The people of Madrid mounted guard around the city. Comrades, the hour is difficult. Despite that, we shall triumph. We shall triumph for ourselves, for our country and for the entire anti-fascist world.

Long live Madrid combatant and militant!
Long live our militias and our Fifth Regiment!
Long live the world struggle against fascism!
Long live new Spain, the Spain of the people!'

'COMANDANTE CARLOS' (Vittorio Vidali)

28

Arrival of Russian arms – the Condor Legion – the Fifth Column – the anarchists enter the government – Mola's plan of attack – the government leaves Madrid – General Miaja – massacre at Paracuellos – the battle of Madrid – the first International Brigades – Asensio crosses the Manzanares – fire raids – Boadilla, Lopera and the Corunna road

---

On 28 October, the diplomats met again in the gilded Locarno Room at the Foreign Office. Maisky repeated, with a plethora of double negatives, that those countries who considered it just to supply the Spanish government (that is, Russia) were 'entitled to consider themselves no more bound by the Non-Intervention Agreement' than did Germany, Italy, and Portugal.[1] The same day the British Trades Union Congress and Labour Party followed the Russians by dropping their support for non-intervention, following a meeting of the representatives of both the Second International and the Comintern in Paris on 26 October. Henceforth, 'Arms for Spain' was a cry which united the Left[2] in Britain as elsewhere. At the same moment, Largo Caballero was broadcasting over Madrid Radio:

> The time has come to deliver a death-blow [he began]. Our power of taking the offensive is growing. We have at our disposal a formidable mechanized

1. *USD*, 1936, vol. II, p. 546; *NIS*, eighth meeting. There is an interesting account of this meeting by Maisky, who is particularly good on the fear of the fascist powers shown by diplomats of smaller nations. Ivan Maisky, pp. 58–63.

2. At the Labour Party Conference, held that year in Edinburgh, 435,000 votes (against 1,728,000) had been cast (in the Labour Party's idiosyncratic method, the card vote) against the party line of support of non-intervention. The rebels included Sir Charles Trevelyan, Christopher Addison, Philip Noel-Baker and Aneurin Bevan. The conference was addressed with great eloquence by Jiménez de Asúa and Isobel de Palencia (mistaken by Hugh Dalton in his memoirs, *The Fateful Years: Memoirs*, vol. I, 1931–45, London, 1957, p. 99, for La Pasionaria). Isobel de Palencia, republican minister in Stockholm, wrote an account too in *I Must Have Liberty* (New York, 1940), p. 246. The national executive restrained the general ardour of the conference, however, by dispatching Attlee and Greenwood to consult with Chamberlain (acting Prime Minister) and to urge detailed inquiry into non-intervention breaches.

armament. We have tanks and powerful aeroplanes. Listen, comrades! At dawn, our artillery and armoured trains will open fire. Immediately, our aircraft will attack. Tanks will advance on the enemy at his most vulnerable point.[1]

Madrid had heard such optimistic predictions before. This time, however, Largo Caballero was speaking the truth: Russian tanks and aircraft had arrived.

The attack took place at dawn on 29 October. Fifteen T-26 Russian tanks, driven by Russians, led by a Lithuanian tank specialist in the Russian army, Captain Paul Arman (known as 'Greisser'), smashed into the nationalist cavalry.[2] These tanks were used in the new Blitzkrieg style propagated in Germany by Colonel Guderian and admired in Russia: massed together for a shock attack rather than, as favoured by the French, spread out in support of infantry,[3] even though the lack of mechanized vehicles for the infantry to follow blunted the point. A strange quixotic battle ensued between tanks and horsemen in the narrow streets of Seseña. Since Lister's new first Mixed Brigade, which had been allocated the task of providing the main assault behind the tanks, could not advance fast enough, the new monsters of the battlefield were forced to retire. Nevertheless, these tanks, heavily armoured and carrying heavy guns, were shown to be effective. One Russian tank was said to have destroyed eleven Italian ones. In addition, the Army of Africa had as yet only a few, bad, Italian, anti-tank guns. The same day, a squadron of Russian Katiuska bombers bombed Seville.[4]

1. *Solidaridad Obrera*, 30 October 1936.

2. Arman died as a general in the Second World War. The later Generals P. Batov and N. Voronov were also present in this day's fighting, the first as military adviser to Lister (who, like Modesto, knew a little Russian), the second as artillery adviser. It seems that it was at Seseña that the so-called 'Molotov cocktail' was

used for the first time, against the tanks by the legionaries (De la Cierva, *Historia ilustrada*, vol. I, p. 480). Lister tells us that the writer, Ramón Sender, acted for a time as his chief of staff in this battle but then abandoned the front precipitously (Lister, p. 82). See Batov's account in *Bajo la bandera*, p. 223f.

3. *GD*, pp. 123–5.

4. Jesús Salas, p. 126. In these Russian aircraft, the pilots were Russian, but bomb-droppers and machine-gunners were Spanish. The commander of this raid was a Russo-German, E. Schacht. See account by G. Prokofiev, *Bajo la bandera*, p. 378f.

The following day – though presumably without news of the Russian tank attack – the German foreign minister, Neurath, dispatched an instruction to Admiral Canaris, then in Spain where, under the name of 'Guillermo', he was enjoying himself driving fast about the deserted roads. 'In view of possibly increased help for the reds,' Neurath said, 'the German government does not consider the combat tactics of White Spain, ground and air, promising of success.' He therefore ordered Canaris to propose to Franco that Germany should send powerful reinforcements. If Franco wanted these, he would have to agree that they should be placed under a German commander responsible solely to him and guarantee that the war would be more systematically conducted.[1] Franco accepted these terms. On 6 November, the so-called 'Condor Legion', with Germany's 'most brutal-looking general' (as Hitler put it himself), Major-General von Sperrle, a senior air force general, as commander, and Colonel von Richthofen (cousin of the famous 'ace' of the Great War) as chief of staff, began to leave Germany for Seville under the code name exercise 'Rügen Winter'.[2] This force comprised about a hundred aircraft: a battle group of four bomber squadrons of twelve bombers each, a fighter group of the same strength, and a seaplane, reconnaissance, and experimental squadron. It was supported by anti-aircraft and anti-tank units, and two armoured units, of four tank companies, of four tanks each. This force amounted to some 3,800 men at the beginning, later to 5,000.[3] Richthofen, one of the two assistants to the head of the technical department in the Luftwaffe, was one of the architects of the growing German air force. He was 'a man of vision and resolution'. Although the Condor Legion was in some ways a revolutionary unit, its equipment and armament were still primitive. To begin with, aircraft flew mainly without radio. The machine-guns had to be reloaded by hand. The

1. *GD*, pp. 123–5.

2. Milch, the state secretary, saw off the first units on 6 November (Irving, p. 50). Sperrle had been responsible for all air operations, such as they were, under von Seeckt in the 1920s.

3. The tanks were commanded by Colonel von Thoma, who had been in Spain for three months training Spaniards. The fighters were commanded, to begin with, by Major von Merhard. The German air force at this time disposed of something over 1,200 combat aircraft (see Irving, p. 52 fn.).

bombers were Junkers 52. The fighters were still Heinkels 51. These heavy aircraft were all slower than Russian equivalents. There was also later attached to the Condor Legion a 'North Sea Group' composed of gunnery, mine, and signal specialists. These operated from the pocket battleships *Deutschland* and *Admiral Scheer*.[1] Since, at the beginning of the war, Franco had had only five signals officers, and no tanks, the technical value of this aid is self-evident. The use of a Heinkel 70, for photographic work inside republican territory, was another innovation. The Russian and German officers who, in the years before Hitler had come to power, had secretly trained together on the plains of White Russia, were now able to carry out other experiments in the larger battle-game of the Spanish war.

No doubt because of this new commitment, the nationalist generals seemed now supremely confident. For the final assault on Madrid, Mola established his headquarters at Avila. When asked by a group of foreign journalists which of his four columns would take Madrid, he replied that it would be that 'Fifth Column' of secret nationalist supporters within the city.[2] This unwise phrase was a justification for endless murders within the capital. A heavy bombing campaign against Madrid was mounted from 29 October onwards, partly to satisfy the German advisers who were curious to see the civilian reaction. The attack upon Getafe on the 30th was particularly severe. From that time onwards, every day until fighting began in the outskirts of the city on 6 November, one small *pueblo* after another described by journalists as a 'key' to Madrid was captured by the Army of Africa. On 4 November, the airport of Getafe fell. The same

1. *Völkischer Beobachter*, May 1939, qu. Toynbee, *Survey 1938*, vol. I, p. 358; Jesús Salas, p. 136.

2. The late Noel Monks, then of the *Daily Express*, described this conference to the author. Dr L. de Jong, the author of *The German Fifth Column in the Second World War* (London, 1958), has traced a reference to the Fifth Column in *Mundo Obrero* of 3 October 1936. But Lord St Oswald (at the time a reporter on the republican side) has a claim to have coined the phrase some weeks before, while the Army of Africa was still in the Tagus valley, and mentioned it in a dispatch (untraced) to the *Daily Telegraph*. He says the phrase was taken up by his fellow-reporters in the Telefónica in Madrid and from thence was carried to Mola across the lines by rumour. On the other hand, the phrase was also used about Russian supporters inside the fortress of Ismail beseiged by Suvarov in 1790.

day, the new Russian fighters (which first flew in combat on the 3rd) showed their superiority in dispersing a squadron of Fiat fighters which escorted some Junkers 52.[1]

Franco announced that the liberation of the capital was near, and told *madrileños* to keep to their houses, which 'our noble and disciplined troops will respect'. A threat that 'we shall know the guilty and only upon them will fall the weight of the law' accompanied these words.[2] Lists of persons to be arrested were made ready, and a municipal administration for the conquered city was formed. Lorries of food for the population were assembled only a little behind the artillery. Radio Lisbon even broadcast a description of Franco entering Madrid on a white horse.

On the republican side, despite the effectiveness of the Russian aircraft, and the high hopes of the day of the tank attack, there was gloom. The tanks, used again on 3, 4 and 5 November, had made little impact, partly because the Spaniards who were now manning them were baffled by their complexity. The streets of the capital were filled with refugees, cattle, and domestic animals. The government was then re-formed to include, in this crisis, the anarchists, just as the Catalan *Generalidad* had been re-formed a month earlier. The outstanding anarchist organizer in Catalonia, García Oliver, became minister of justice; Juan Peiró, the *treintista* who had spoken out so vigorously in July against the terror at the beginning of the war, became minister of industry; Juan López Sánchez, also a *treintista*, from Valencia, became minister of commerce; and Federica Montseny, an intellectual from Barcelona, became minister of health. These working-class leaders entered the government causing scarcely a ripple of surprise. The move had been urged ever since mid-September by the secretary-general of the CNT, Horacio Prieto, an unyielding 'realist' and advocate of collaboration.[3] The four an-

1. Two Russian fighter aerodromes were established near Madrid, one near Algete in the finca El Soto, under Major Richagov, and another at Alcalá de Henares; both were manned mostly by Russians, though there were some Spanish pilots, for example García Lacalle (*op. cit.*, pp. 174–5).

2. Valdesoto, p. 183.

3. C. Lorenzo, p. 224 (Lorenzo is Horacio Prieto's son). The four anarchists called on Horacio Prieto when they arrived in Madrid and asked for instructions; he said that the CNT was not the communist party, and would not seek to bind the ministers' freedom of action (*op. cit.*, p. 254). Horacio Prieto

archists had been previously elected as the appropriate members of their organization to join the government at a 'plenum' of the movement. The rest of the ministry, enlarged from thirteen to eighteen, remained much as previously. A Left republican, Carlos Esplá, active in preventing the rising at Valencia, became Spain's first minister of propaganda.[1] Azaña opposed the inclusion of the anarchists, but he was unable to exert any influence to prevent it.[2] In fact, since industry and commerce had previously been one department, and health had previously been simply a directorship-general, the number of anarchist portfolios was less than it seemed. García Oliver, the only anarchist ever to have held the portfolio of justice in any country, impressed even republicans by his efficiency.[3] But his obsession at the start of his tenure of office was to destroy the archives of convicts. This he did. It was later said that the compromising files had been burned in the air raid.[4] *Solidaridad Obrera* spoke of 4 November as 'the most transcendental day in the political history of the country', and announced that the government had 'ceased to be an oppressor of the working class'. Federica Montseny was after all the first female minister in Spanish history. The socialist Araquistain explained meantime from his embassy in Paris that the UGT had become converted to revolutionary socialism, and that the CNT now recognized the state as 'an instrument of struggle'.[5]

Peiró some weeks before had suggested how the government after victory should be a federal socialist republic – since, having admitted the collaboration of the other working-class parties, 'it would be neither just nor noble' to try and impose anarchist views by force on the future society.[6] But Federica Montseny was told by her father (an old anarchist propagandist, Federico Urales) that this step meant

---

had resumed his secretaryship-general shortly before the war, having resigned after the Saragossa conference in May.

1. The architect of the new University City in Madrid, Manuel Sánchez Arcos, was under-secretary.

2. Carlos Pi Sunyer, *La republica y la guerra* (Mexico, 1975), p. 419.

3. For example, Martín Blázquez, p. 298.

4. *General Cause*, p. 371, quoting from direct testimony.

5. *Socialist Review* (May–June 1938), vol. VI, no. 6, p. 17, qu. Cattell, *Communism*, p. 66.

6. Peirats, p. 233.

'the liquidation of anarchism. Once in power you will not rid yourselves of power.'[1]

How many reserves [she later remarked], doubts, internal anguishes had I to overcome personally in accepting this post! For others, a governmental post could be the goal and the satisfaction of measureless ambitions. For me, it was nothing less than a break with an entire life's work, which itself derived from the life's work of my parents.[2]

At the same time as the anarchists entered the government, the anarchist Council of Aragon, moving to Caspe, also opened their doors to receive representation of the other parties. Joaquín Ascaso was received by Largo Caballero, Companys and Azaña and the Council's powers were formally, if most reluctantly, accepted by the government. For the foreseeable future, republican Aragon would remain anarchist; but the seeds of its eventual destruction were already sown, since two communists, two members of the UGT, and a republican, were now present at its deliberations; and the republican member was Ignacio Mantecón, a strong communist sympathizer who soon became councillor of justice.[3] Still, for the time being, Aragon was virtually an independent state, even having commercial relations with the outside world. They had a police force, a production programme, tribunals – but, fatally for them, no army.

With a mixture of over-confidence and caution, meantime, Mola, Varela, and Yagüe delayed their assault on Madrid until dawn on 8 November.

The plan was that an arrow-like attack should be launched between the University City and the Plaza de España into the middle-class part of the city on the heights immediately above the valley of the Manzanares. The attack would entail a difficult climb up the hill covered by West Park, across the River Manzanares and the Casa de Campo. Of Yagüe's columns, the first, Asensio's, was to cross the Manzanares directly below the Paseo de Rosales, the long terrace-like street running along the top of West Park, and climb up to capture the Model Prison and the Don Juan barracks. Castejón was to cross to the left and establish himself at a student hall of residence known

1. Federica Montseny in a speech in Toulouse (*International Bulletin of the MLE–CNT in France*, September–October 1945); qu. Richards, p. 59.

2. Speech, 27 May 1937, qu. Peirats, vol. II, pp. 270–72.

3. Peirats, vol. I, pp. 228–9; C. Lorenzo, p. 151.

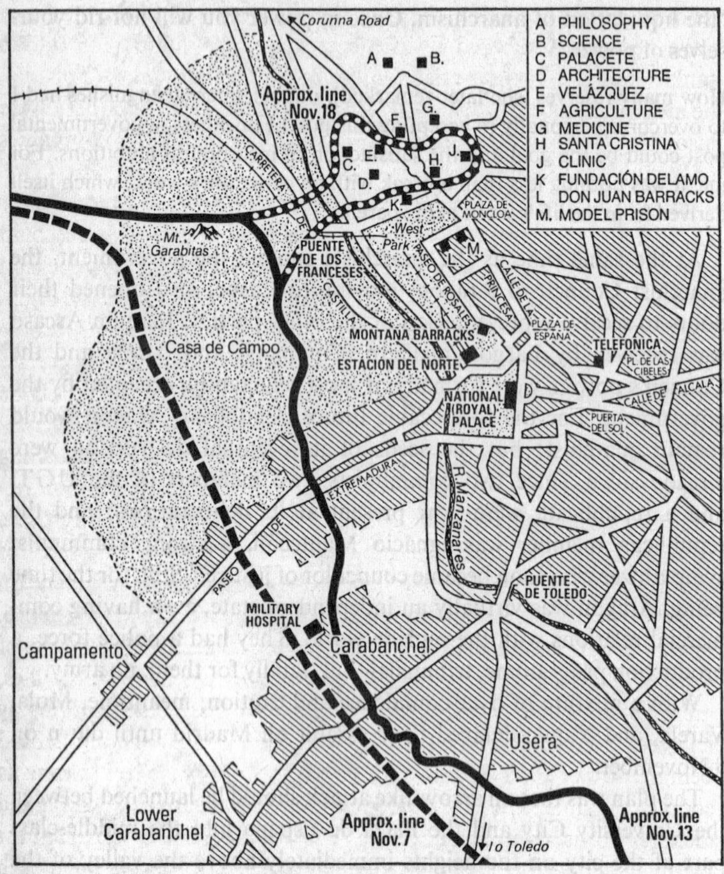

17. The battle of Madrid, November 1936

as the Fundación del Amo, on the Madrid side of the University City. Delgado Serrano, on the right, was to capture the Montaña barracks and bring the Royal Palace and the Gran Vía under fire. Barrón and Tella were to advance in the suburb of Carabanchel to try and suggest that the main attack was coming from the south.[1] These five columns, led by commanders all of whom had fought as young men in the Rif, were mostly composed of Moroccans and Foreign Legionaries.

1. López Muñiz, p. 25f.

Though, as has been seen, the latter were mainly Spaniards, they may have been outnumbered by the Moroccans. A number of Italian tanks – perhaps twenty – also fought, under Captain Oreste Fortuna, he and his men being technically a part of the Legion, and there were also some German tanks, under Colonel von Thoma – two companies of 'heavy' tanks, one of light.

Largo Caballero's government now decided to leave Madrid after all, and go to Valencia. It was announced that administration could not be carried on in a war zone. The postponement of this decision till now gave the government's withdrawal the appearance of flight. Further, Prieto had thought that like Azaña they should go to Barcelona, a more logical decision.[1] In the afternoon of 6 November, nevertheless, Largo Caballero suddenly told the commander of the Madrid Division, General Miaja, of the plan, and that he was henceforth in overall political, as well as military, control. The leading ministers, civil servants, and politicians of all parties thereupon left Madrid, taking with them all the government files, including those of the ministry of war.[2] The new anarchist ministers opposed this move, thinking that they had been brought into the government on false pretences, but they could do nothing about it; they left in silence, unable to communicate even with their followers.[3] Great convoys of vehicles covered the highways to Valencia, taking with them the files, archives and other materials of government.[4] The Russian Embassy left with other diplomats – the only Russian official staying behind being Orlov of the NKVD. Orlov said to Louis Fischer: 'Leave as soon as possible. There is no front. Madrid is the front.'[5] Miaja and General Pozas, commander of the Army of the Centre, were sent for by the under-secretary of war, General Asensio, who gave them each an envelope marked 'very confidential, not to be opened till 6 a.m.'.[6] Asensio then left for Valencia also. Miaja insisted that the orders be opened immediately. The two generals then discovered that the two

1. Prieto, *Convulsiones*, vol. II, p. 316.

2. The only under-secretaries left in Madrid were Fernando Valera, sub-secretary of communications, and Wenceslao Carrillo, of the interior (Lázaro Somoza Silva, *El general Miaja*, Mexico, 1944, p. 148).

3. Federica Montseny, speech 27 May 1937, qu. Peirats, vol. II, p. 272. See also comment in Prieto, *Palabras*, pp. 324–5.

4. Vicente Rojo, *España heroica* (Buenos Aires, 1942), p. 38. 5. L. Fischer, p. 369.

6. Koltsov, p. 189; Azaña (vol. IV, p. 860) records Miaja's account to him.

sets of instructions had been put in the wrong envelopes. Pozas was ordered to establish a new headquarters of the central army at Tarancón. Miaja was charged to set up a *junta* of defence with representatives of the Popular Front parties, to be responsible for Madrid and defend the capital in every way he could.[1] If he had to withdraw, he was to do so with his army intact and establish a new line near Cuenca, at the point which Pozas thought best.

The proposed *junta* was formed, and composed almost all of young men. Though proportionate, as stipulated, to the governmental parties, as in the *pueblos* of the first days of the war, power remained with the strongest group – in these circumstances, the socialist–communist youth and the communist party. The *Pravda* correspondent, Koltsov, busied himself with everything, organizing and choosing commissars, animating the ministry of war, attending meetings of the communist party central committee. General Goriev and the other Russian advisers also established themselves firmly, while the head of their mission, General Berzin, left for Valencia. A somewhat Russian tone came over republican propaganda as *Mundo Obrero* told its readers to 'emulate Petrograd'.[2]

A new general staff was set up in Madrid. Rojo, able, educated, cultivated, but pessimistic and with no popular touch, the officer who had visited the Alcázar during its siege, became chief of staff. A number of other young staff officers (Matallana, Estrada, Casado) were equally anxious to take advantage of an exciting opportunity to make their reputations.[3] All the commanders, and then the trade-union leaders in Madrid, were summoned to the war ministry. Miaja spoke to them in heroic terms, not concealing the gravity of the situation, and demanding that 50,000 more trade unionists be mobilized for the front. The chief of staff was, meanwhile, helped by luck: an Italian tank was blown up; in the pocket of a dead Spanish officer within was found Varela's battle plan for the next day.[4] The commanders returned to their men heartened, knowing at least that

1. Somoza Silva, p. 139; Largo Caballero, p. 235.
2. Barea, p. 174; Koltsov, pp. 184ff; Ehrenburg, *Eve of War*, pp. 146–7.
3. Rojo, p. 41. A more recent and detailed account can be found in Rojo's *Así fue la defensa de Madrid* (Mexico, 1967).
4. Rojo, *España heroica*, p. 44; Somoza Silva, p. 142. Text of this 'document which saved Madrid' is printed in Somoza Silva, p. 316.

Madrid would not fall without a fight. The first meeting occurred of the *junta* of defence of Madrid in the ministry of war: a group of enthusiastic young men, as eager to win glory as the officers. At their head, however, was the incongruous figure of Miaja, certainly surprised to find himself among them.[1] 'Loquacious, anecdotal, jumping from one subject to another',[2] he is not easy to judge. He was sympathetic, calm, easy-going, and lucky; but he was also incompetent and vain. He was short, resembled an amiable Franciscan priest in looks and had been as ambiguous in Madrid in July, as he had been unsuccessful in Córdoba in August.

Koltsov apparently took upon himself the dispatch away from Madrid of the more important political prisoners still remaining in the Model Prison (the total numbered over 1,000). Nearly all of these were butchered by their guards, officially while being 'transferred to a new prison', just short of the village of Paracuellos de Jarama a few miles beyond Barajas airport. During the following days many other executions occurred of political prisoners in Madrid, in that same bleak spot, at San Fernando de Henares nearby, and at Torrejón de Ardoz.[3] It is fairly clear that the leading police officials, from the new director of public order, Manuel Muñoz, downwards, were aware of these murders. It was left to an anarchist director of prisons, Melchor Rodríguez, subsequently appointed, to protest. These mur-

1. Somoza Silva, p. 316, prints the minutes of this meeting. The communists imposed a veto on the entry of the POUM into the *junta* and nothing the POUM leaders in Valencia could do could change this. Manuel Albar, socialist leader, told Enrique Rodríguez, the POUM *responsable* in Madrid, that the socialists had complained but had decided to accept matters 'because of the importance of Soviet aid'. Julián Gorkin came from Barcelona to argue the POUM's case – to no avail.

2. Azaña's view (*op. cit.*, p. 732).

3. Jesús Suarez Galíndez, *Los vascos en el Madrid sitiado* (Buenos Aires, 1945), p. 66; *General Cause*, p. 236; Koltsov, p. 192. G. Izaga, *Los presos de Madrid* (Madrid, 1940), p. 336 gives a horrifying nationalist account. Koltsov attributes the order to 'Miguel Martínez' who was, however, himself. Peirats blames José Cazorla (vol. II, p. 96). Christopher Lance, the English 'Spanish Pimpernel', had already brought about several successful escapes with great audacity, and would rescue over a hundred by using the ambulance unit financed by a Scottish philanthropist, as a secret transport from Madrid to the coast. Lance was eventually caught and held for months in unpleasant gaols. See his 'story' in Cecil Phillips, *The Spanish Pimpernel* (London, 1960); and Delmer, p. 345.

ders are to be explained by the atmosphere of panic which spread in Madrid at the fear that the capital might fall. The threat of disaster heightened emotions and the young men of the *junta* of defence who, knowing that they would die if Franco won, overlooked, where they did not sanction, brutality.

The cabinet narrowly escaped a similar fate. On the road to Valencia, several ministers were held up at Tarancón by the local anarchist committee. The local *responsable*, the anarchist Villanueva, had had orders from his comrades in Madrid to prevent all flight from the capital. 'You are cowards. Return to Madrid,' he said, 'at least leave your arms here.' They only got past with a written order from the CNT in the capital.[1] Such was the decay of the government at the moment when the Army of Africa was at the gates of Madrid.

Back in the capital, volunteers rallied to the defence because of the demands made for them by loudspeaker. Many of them were refugees from other parts of Spain. The mobilized carabineers, regular soldiers and militiamen, given extra fire by pamphlets, speeches, and poems proclaiming that those who did not believe in victory were cowards, carried out almost to the letter their orders not to retreat an inch. A sailor, Antonio Coll, earned fame by single-handedly destroying two tanks in the Usera suburb.[2] In the Casa de Campo, the nationalist advance which was planned to reach the Montaña barracks only reached the high ground known as Mount Garabitas. From thence a magnificent view, and also an artillery firing-point, can be gained across the valley, to Madrid. All the time, the republican commanders sent back appeals for more ammunition, or news that half their men had fallen. All the time, Miaja replied that reinforcements had been sent. But much of the organization of resistance, emanating from his cellar headquarters in the ministry of finance, derived less from Miaja

1. Alvarez del Vayo, *Freedom's Battle*, p. 208; Borkenau, p. 196; Eduardo de Guzmán, *Madrid rojo y negro* (Buenos Aires, 1939), p. 300. Pedro Rico, the popular mayor of Madrid, was also turned back. Returning to Madrid, he took refuge in the Mexican Embassy. He was not made welcome by the right-wing refugees whom he found there. But he now could not return to the town hall. He was afraid to go home. Despite his enormous girth, he was fitted into the boot of the car belonging to 'El Nili', the *banderillero* of Juan Belmonte, and driven to Valencia. Prieto secured his escape to France (*De mi vida*, vol. II, pp. 324–6). Prieto himself flew to Valencia.

2. Ibarruri, p. 334.

than from the Russian General Goriev whose office was a few doors away. Quite how much is a matter of speculation: each general has his friends among historians, as they had them among contemporaries.[1] It does seem, however, that another Russian, Major Voronov, was the inspiration in the artillery headquarters rather than the inspector-general of artillery, Colonel José Luis Fuentes, his Spanish chief.[2]

It was at this critical moment that the first units of the International Brigade marched along the Gran Vía towards the front. The first of these was a battalion of Germans, with a section of British machine-gunners, including the poet, John Cornford. The battalion was first named after its leader, an ex-Prussian officer, Hans Kahle, now a communist, but its name was then changed to the 'Edgar André' Battalion, in honour of a German communist, of Belgian origin, of that name, beheaded on 4 November by the nazis.

Secondly, there was the 'Commune de Paris' Battalion, composed of French and Belgians, under Colonel Jules Dumont, a French ex-regular officer but a long-standing communist who had been in Abyssinia and was known for his lectures on that theme.[3] Pierre Rébière was the commissar. The third battalion was the 'Dombrowski' Battalion, under a Pole, Boleslav Ulanovski, chiefly composed of socialist or communist Polish miners recently living in France and Belgium. All three groups included some survivors of those Germans, Frenchmen, and Poles who had fought in Aragon and in the Tagus valley. The entire Brigade (known as the 11th Brigade, since ten other new 'mixed brigades' had by then been formed in the republican

1. A portrait of Goriev appears in Castro Delgado, pp. 452–3. Louis Fischer (p. 377) describes him as 'more than any one man . . . the saviour of Madrid'. See also Ehrenburg (*Eve of War*, pp. 146–7) and Barea (pp. 289–90). De la Cierva, *Historia ilustrada*, vol. I, p. 492, takes a different view. Writers have usually divided the laurels between Miaja and Goriev according to their own inclinations.

2. Fuentes at first refused to see Voronov, then said that he could play no part since he did not know Spanish. Largo Caballero afterwards gave Voronov an equally bad impression, saying that republican Spain had no need of foreign arms (*Bajo la bandera*, p. 67). Voronov says that it was he who insisted that the republican artillery headquarters should be moved to the Telefónica (pp. 80–81), and he who protested against two hours being taken off for lunch by the artillery.

3. Described as Colonel 'Kodak', because of his pleasure at being photographed. Twenty years previously Dumont and 'Hans' had been facing each other in the German and French armies on the western front.

army) was commanded by the Hungarian, 'Kléber'. It had arrived after being cheered across La Mancha by peasants shouting '*no pasarán*' and '*salud*', to which its members had replied with a cry of '*Rot front*' and '*Les soviets partout*'. Now these apparently disciplined men, in corduroy uniforms and steel helmets, followed by two squadrons of French cavalry, greatly impressed the natives of Madrid, who had supposed the capital lost. Many thought that Russia was at last intervening. So the cry of 'Long live the Russians' rang from the balconies of the Gran Vía.

By the evening of 8 November, the Brigade was in position.[1] The Edgar André and Commune de Paris Battalions were sent to the Casa de Campo. The Dombrowsky Battalion went to join Lister and the Fifth Regiment at Villaverde.

It has been argued that the International Brigades saved Madrid. The British ambassador, Sir Henry Chilton, even assured his American colleague at St Jean de Luz that there were 'no Spaniards in the defending army of Madrid'.[2] This 11th International Brigade, however, comprised only about 1,900 men.[3] The 12th International Brigade, which arrived on the Madrid front on 13 November, comprised about 1,550.[4] This force was too small to have turned the day by numbers alone. Furthermore, the republican army had checked Varela on 7 November, before the arrival of the Brigade. It was Colonel Galán and Colonel Romero who held, with the 3rd and 4th Mixed Brigades, the rebels from crossing the Manzanares (ex-carabineers being important in the 3rd Brigade). The bravery and experience of the Brigades was, however, crucial in several later battles. The example of the International Brigades fired the populace of the capital with the feeling that they were not alone, that there was some substance for the stirring utterances of, say, Fernando Valera,

1. 'At dawn on 8 November, leaving for the Sierra, I saw a battalion of the first International Brigade in the Calle Ferraz' (Tagüeña, p. 140). So much for the strange statement by General Rojo (*Así fue*, p. 69) that these troops did not join the battle till 12 November. This distortion is discussed in R. Salas, vol. I, p. 584. See also Neruda's poem beginning 'Una mañana de un mes frío', in *Tercera Residencia* (Buenos Aires, 1961).

2. *USD*, 1936, vol. II, p. 603.

3. Cox, p. 144; Fischer, p. 373. Cf. Castells, p. 100f.

4. Fischer, *loc. cit.* Fischer being quartermaster presumably knew.

sub-secretary of communications, a republican deputy who, during the night of 8 November, proclaimed on Madrid Radio:

Here in Madrid is the universal frontier that separates liberty and slavery. It is here in Madrid that two incompatible civilizations undertake their great struggle: love against hate, peace against war, the fraternity of Christ against the tyranny of the church ... This is Madrid. It is fighting for Spain, for humanity, for justice, and, with the mantle of its blood, it shelters all human beings! Madrid! Madrid![1]

Most of the world, nevertheless, accepted the dispatches of the eminent journalists, such as Sefton Delmer, Henry Buckley, and Vincent Sheean, quartered in the Gran Vía or the Florida Hotels, who reported Madrid likely to fall.

The next day, 9 November, Varela, checked in the Casa de Campo, mounted a new attack, no longer a feint, in the Carabanchel sector. But the street-fighting baffled the Moroccans, who made no progress. They were excellent shots in the desert or in the open country, but less resourceful in the unfamiliar city. With the militiamen, the opposite was true: indeed, the republic's failure hitherto may be attributed to the unfamiliarity of the urban militiamen with the countryside. The republican artillery, moreover, numbered sixty pieces in Madrid and were well directed, the Telefónica building being an excellent observation post for Major Alejandro Zamarro, and the Russian adviser, Major Voronov.[2] In the Casa de Campo, Kléber assembled the International Brigade. In the misty evening, they launched an attack. 'For the revolution and liberty – forward!'[3] Among the ilex and gum trees, the battle lasted all night and into the morning of 10 November. By then, only Mount Garabitas in the Casa de Campo was left to the nationalists. But one-third of the first International Brigade was dead. Varela abandoned the direct attack on Madrid through the Casa de Campo. A sanguinary battle, however, continued in Carabanchel. Hand-to-hand fighting occurred in the Military Hospital. The bombing of the capital, which had been continuing intermittently since the start of the assault, was increased.

1. Somoza Silva, p. 183. This Valenciano would in the 1970s be Prime Minister of the Spanish republic in exile in Paris.

2. Voronov, in *Bajo la bandera*, p. 256.

3. Malraux, p. 322.

Incendiaries particularly were used, since fire was considered to be the best means of spreading panic. The government's bombers, meantime, had a success on the 11th in destroying much of Lieutenant Eberhard's Junkers and Heinkel squadron on the ground on the airfield at Avila.[1]

On 12 November, the continuing battle in Carabanchel convinced Goriev, Rojo, and Miaja that the next attack would be against the Madrid–Valencia highway. They accordingly sent to that sector of the front the new 12th International Brigade, comprising the Thaelmann, André Marty, and Garibaldi Battalions of Germans, 'Franco-Belges', and Italians. This Brigade was commanded by General 'Lukács', who was, in reality, the Hungarian novelist Mata Zalka. Like Kléber, he was a Hungarian officer who had served in the Austrian army in the First World War, had been captured by the Russians, had joined the Red Army, and had been by now a revolutionary longer than he had been a novelist. He had a Russian military adviser in Colonel Batov. The accomplished German communist writer Gustav Regler, handsome as Siegfried, was a commissar of the Brigade, though Longo, the Italian communist, held this post to begin with. Lukács also had two Bulgarian staff officers, Lukanov ('Belov') and Kozovski ('Petrov').[2] In this Brigade, the Thaelmann Battalion of Germans was led by the novelist Ludwig Renn, celebrated for his pacifist novel *Krieg* based on his experiences in the First World War. The Bavarian communist and ex-deputy, Hans Beimler, was his commissar. Attached to the battalion were eighteen Englishmen, including Esmond Romilly, an anarchic nephew of Winston Churchill. The Garibaldi Battalion of the Italians was led by the republican Randolfo Pacciardi.[3] The socialist ex-comrade of Mussolini, Pietro Nenni, was for a time a company commander, while seventeen nationalities in all were represented.

1. Jesús Salas, p. 133. Lieutenant Kraft Eberhard was the first German (nazi) officer killed in Spain.

2. Karlo Lukanov fought in the First World War, joined the communist party in 1919, fled to Austria in 1923 and went to Russia after a spell back in Bulgaria. After 1945 he was deputy prime minister of Bulgaria (1952–3) and later foreign minister. See, for this Brigade, Batov in *Bajo la bandera*, p. 228.

3. Pacciardi, a member of the republican party in Italy, came from the Maremma, and was a veteran of both the First World War and several fights in 1920–22 against the fascists. Since 1926, he had been in exile in France and Switzerland.

This force, despite its galaxy of talent of various kinds, was less well-prepared for war than the 11th Brigade had been. When the Brigade entered battle, commands were confused, since the language problem presented difficulties in giving orders. (Lukács was a less good linguist, as well as a less able commander, than was Kléber.) The Brigade had to fight when weary from marching ten miles. The artillery support was inadequate. Certain companies got lost. Once again, the Russian tank detachment failed to make adequate contact with infantry. Fighting went on all day; but the object of the attack, the hill in the geographical centre of Spain known as Cerro de los Angeles, remained impregnable. The counter-attack thus failed. Similarly, a major air offensive by the Russians on 13 November failed to drive the slower rebel aircraft from the skies.[1]

At the same time as the 12th International Brigade, Durruti also arrived in Madrid, with a column of 4,000 volunteer anarchists, having been persuaded to leave Aragon by Federica Montseny on behalf of the government.[2] He and García Oliver, minister of justice, desired an independent sector of the front on which to operate, and also new weapons; both requests were granted, after a fashion, though the rifles were Swiss 1886 models bought by Russia on the free arms market. Miaja agreed to allot to the anarchists the Casa de Campo. Durruti received orders to attack on 15 November, with all the republican artillery and aircraft in support. The orders given to him were confused, but they implied a frontal attack on the enemy: 'an imbecility,' thought another anarchist leader; 'they are looking for a defeat to discredit us . . . the communists cannot permit Durruti to be the saviour of the capital'.[3] At all events, when the hour came,

His nomination as leader of the Garibaldi Battalion was preceded by long discussions between him and the communists, sealed in a final agreement on 27 October, and marked by Pacciardi's agreement to have a communist, Antonio Roasio, from Biella, as commissar.

1. This was a famous battle, the most severe of 1936 in which 14 Fiats fought 13 Chatos over the Paseo de Rosales, and shot down several. A Russian pilot was lynched when he parachuted to Madrid, on the mistaken ground that he was a German.

2. Durruti had been reluctant to go. See Paz, pp. 418, 422, for numbers.

3. See Cipriano Mera, *Guerra, exilio y cárcel de un anarcosindicalista* (Paris, 1976), p. 86. Durruti was allocated a Russian 'adviser', known as 'Santi', whose real name was Mamsurov Jadji-Umar, a 'Caucasian', and future Russian general.

the machine-guns of the Moroccans – which they had, of course, not met before – so terrified the anarchists that they refused to fight. Durruti, furious, promised a new attack the next day. Varela chose this moment to advance once again, being covered now by the German Condor Legion for the first time.[1] Three times the van of Asensio's column reached the Manzanares, and three times it was driven back. Eventually, Asensio gained a foothold on the edge of the river beneath the Palacete de la Moncloa. After a heavy artillery and aerial bombardment, two Moroccan *tabors* and one *bandera* of legionaries charged across. They found that the column ahead of them (the Libertad column of Catalan socialists) had suddenly been withdrawn. But their replacements were not there. The nationalists' way up to the University City was almost clear. The heights were swiftly scaled. The School of Architecture and other neighbouring buildings were captured. The 11th International Brigade was sent from the Casa de Campo to defend the Hall of Philosophy and Letters. But more and more of the Army of Africa, including men from the columns of Delgado Serrano and Barrón, at the same time crossed the river.[2]

A bloody battle began in the University City. The babel of tongues, the frequent multilingual singing of the 'International', the insults exchanged between the nationalists and republicans, added to the macabre confusion. The marching songs of the German communists brought to the crumbling masonry of the laboratories and lecture halls a Teutonic sadness. Anarchists fraternized with men from the Brigade. Muffled commands sounded in the darkness addressed to men who had never seen the city which they had come to defend: '*Bataillon Thaelmann, fertig machen!*' '*Bataillon André Marty, descendez vite!*' '*Garibaldi, avanti!*'[3] Hours of artillery and aerial bombardment, in which neither side gave way, were succeeded by hand-to-

They did not get on well. In view of subsequent communist behaviour towards anarchists at the front, Merea's comment may well be a valid one. For speculation about Santi's role, see Eduardo Comín Colomer, *El comisariado político* (Madrid, 1937), p. 96.

1. The Condor Legion also bombed Cartagena, the port where Russian supplies usually came in, on this day.

2. Koltsov, p. 233.

3. Gustav Regler, *The Great Crusade*, translated by Whittaker Chambers (!) (New York, 1940), p. 4.

hand battles for single rooms or floors of buildings. In the still unfinished Clinical Hospital, the Thaelmann Battalion placed bombs in lifts to be sent up to explode in the faces of the Moroccans on the next floor; and, in that building, the Moroccans suffered losses by eating inoculated animals kept for experimental purposes. Great courage was shown on both sides. A company of Poles from the Dombrowsky Battalion resisted in the French Institute's Casa de Velázquez to the last man. An advance guard of Moroccans drove back Durruti's anarchists once again at the Plaza de la Moncloa, the first square inside Madrid proper, and began to fight their way along the Calle de la Princesa. Some even drove down the Paseo de Rosales to reach the Plaza de España. All were killed. But the rumour that 'the Moors are in the Plaza de España' was not easy to staunch. Miaja appeared on the battle-line to re-establish the courage of the militia. 'Cowards!' he cried, 'die in your trenches! Die with your General Miaja!'[1]

On 19 November, while the battle was still raging, Durruti was mortally wounded in front of the Model Prison. He died the next day in the Ritz Hotel, converted into a hospital for the Catalan militia. His death was said to have been caused by a stray bullet from the University City. It may also be that he shot himself by accident with his own rifle while getting out of his car. It was rumoured too that he was killed by one of his own men, an 'uncontrollable', who resented the new anarchist policy ('the discipline of indiscipline', since August advocated by Durruti) of participation in government, but of that there is no proof, nor is it likely.[2] Durruti's funeral in Barcelona was an extraordinary occasion. All day long, a procession eight to a hundred people broad marched down the Diagonal, the widest street in the city. In the evening, a crowd of 200,000 pledged themselves to carry out the dead man's principles. But the death of Durruti, at the age of forty, marked the end of the classic age of Spanish anarchism. An anarchist poet proclaimed that Durruti's

1. Antonio López Fernández, *Defensa de Madrid* (Mexico, 1945), p. 175.

2. Peirats, vol. I, pp. 245–6. The various possibilities are summarized in Juan Llarch, *La muerte de Durruti* (Barcelona, 1973). There is a colder summary of various versions in Jaume Miravitlles, *Episodis de la guerra civil espanyola* (Barcelona, 1972); and in Paz, p. 497, where the anonymous reviewer of James Joll's *The Anarchists* in *The Times Literary Supplement*, 24 December 1964, is taken to task. See also Angel Maroto, *Actualidad Española* (December, 1971).

nobility while living would cause 'a legion of Durrutis' to spring up behind him. He was wrong.

In the meantime, Franco, having apparently remarked before Portuguese journalists that he would destroy Madrid rather than leave it to the 'Marxists', embarked on the experiment of trying to bomb Madrid into surrender. The German officers of the new Condor Legion were interested to see the reaction of a civilian population to a carefully planned attempt to set fire to the city, quarter by quarter. The bombing included also buildings such as the Telefónica or the war ministry, whose destruction would cause special damage. The air raids were accompanied by artillery bombardment using incendiary grenades from Mount Garabitas. From 19 November until 22 November, the bombings by Savoias 81 and Junkers 52, especially at night, continued, and some 150 people were killed.[1] No city in history had then been so tested – though the attack was a foretaste of what would happen in a few years in London, Hamburg, Tokyo, and Leningrad – as commentators in Madrid at the time eloquently prophesied. Russian fighters were unable to maintain an effective reply at night. But the military and psychological effects of the air attacks were nugatory, since, as has almost always been the case with 'aero-psychological warfare', as it later became known, the bombing inspired greater hatred than it did fear. Only about a hundred houses were destroyed and the Telefónica remained. The Palacio de Liria, the town house of the Duke of Alba, was hit, but militiamen succeeded in carrying off most of the art treasures within.[2] The correspondent of *Paris Soir*, Louis Delaprée, wrote apocalyptically in his diary: 'Oh, old Europe, always so occupied with your little games and your grave intrigues, God grant that all this blood does not choke you'.[3] (He was himself mortally wounded in an aerial battle, a few days later, when flying home to complain that his editor had not published his most sensational dispatches.)[4]

1. J. Salas, *op. cit.*

2. In 1937, Sir F. Kenyon, former director of the British Museum, and James Mann, keeper of the Wallace Collection, visited republican Spain to report that the art treasures of the Prado and elsewhere in the republic were in excellent keeping.

3. Delaprée, p. 14.

4. Delaprée's plane was probably attacked by republican aircraft. Delaprée died a few days later in Guadalajara Hospital. Delmer (p. 324) says that the plane

The battle of the University City continued until 23 November. By this time, three-quarters of the area was in Mola's hands. The Clinical and Santa Cristina Hospitals, with the Institutes of Hygiene and Cancer, were his furthermost points of penetration. His advance towards the Plaza de la Moncloa was prevented by the continued defence in the Hall of Philosophy and Letters. The two almost exhausted armies now dug trenches and built fortifications. The nationalists realized that any further advance into Madrid would cost too much. The republicans understood that a dislodgement of their enemies would be equally costly. The Russian aircraft, though used timidly, with few long-distance bombing attacks, were adequate to give the republic full protection. A sombre meeting of nationalist commanders met at Leganés, on 23 November, under Franco's chairmanship. The rebel generals agreed that they should call off the frontal attack on Madrid. The next attacks would be attempts at encirclement. Thus there could be no hope for Mola of a cup of coffee in the Gran Vía's Café Molinero.[1]

The question of how many were killed in these famous battles in Madrid remains a matter of controversy. Though the deaths were fewer than might be supposed, given the 30–40,000 involved on both sides, the casualties on both sides probably amounted to about 10,000.[2]

Madrid now settled down to what was described as a siege, though only part of the city was invested. Measures continued against the Fifth Column, especially those suspected of firing at nights from 'phantom cars' – an act of sabotage planned by the last chief of the falangists in the Faculty of Medicine, Ignacio Arévalo, who was shortly killed. The police knocked one night at the Finnish Embassy in the Calle Fernando el Santo, to be refused admittance. From inside, someone opened fire (one policeman being hit). Finally breaking

---

was shot down by the republicans, since their counter-espionage wished to kill a suspected rebel agent, Dr Henry, of the Red Cross, who was also on board.

1. '*El café se le enfrió*
Y en Madrid no entró.'

2. R. Salas Larrazábal, vol. I, p. 625, gives the very low figure of 266 dead, 6,029 wounded for the defenders. He may not have found documentary proof for more deaths, but the figure is likely to be higher. Returns of deaths cannot be counted upon.

in, the police, headed by the young communist director of security, Serrano Poncela, and the ubiquitous Koltsov, found 525 Spanish bourgeois persons within. The Embassy officials, save one Spanish-born employee, had all left for Valencia.[1] Another characteristic event at the start of the winter was the murder of the Baron de Borchgrave, the Belgian chargé. He had persuaded several of his compatriots in the International Brigade to desert. One night, his body, with two others, was discovered outside Madrid.[2] By then, nearly all the embassies in Madrid had been removed to Valencia, the American one being the last; yet the situation remained diplomatically odd since, while the ambassadors lingered on at St Jean de Luz as if the summer were lasting forever, small staffs of officials remained in Madrid to look after right-wing refugees.

On 13 December, the nationalists sought to continue an offensive tentatively begun ten days earlier, aiming to cut off the republicans in the Guadarramas and ultimately to surround Madrid from the north.[3] The battle took the form of a struggle by the nationalists to reach the Madrid–Corunna road some miles short of El Escorial. General Orgaz, newly appointed supreme commander of the Madrid front in place of Mola, directed operations. Varela commanded in the field. Beneath him, were assembled 18,000 infantry and cavalry, organized into four mobile brigades under García Escámez, Barrón,

1. Koltsov, pp. 261–2. After this a false Embassy was opened under the national flag of Siam. The aim was to attract secret nationalists. Various persons (apparently only six) came to seek refuge. Their conversations were listened to by secret microphones, and they were later murdered.

2. It seems he was murdered by the special services' brigade of the ministry of war, then run by the anarchist Manuel Salgado, on the ground that before the war he had been representative of Mercedes in Madrid (*General Cause*, pp. 162–3).

3. In the beginning of this engagement Hans Beimler, the German commissar, had been killed – though probably not, as is sometimes alleged, liquidated by his communist comrades. See Gustav Regler, *Owl of Minerva* (London, 1959), p. 286, where his death is adequately described. The theory of murder is revived in Martínez Amutio, p. 240f. There it is bluntly stated that Beimler was killed for discrepancies with Moscow, and that nine members of the International Brigades were killed near Albacete to cover up his death. Beimler was replaced by Franz Dahlem, a communist deputy for the Reichstag in 1928, and German communist leader after the arrest of Thaelmann, described by Victor Serge as 'the toiler without personality, the militant without doubts ... the communist NCO' (Serge, *Memoirs*, p. 162).

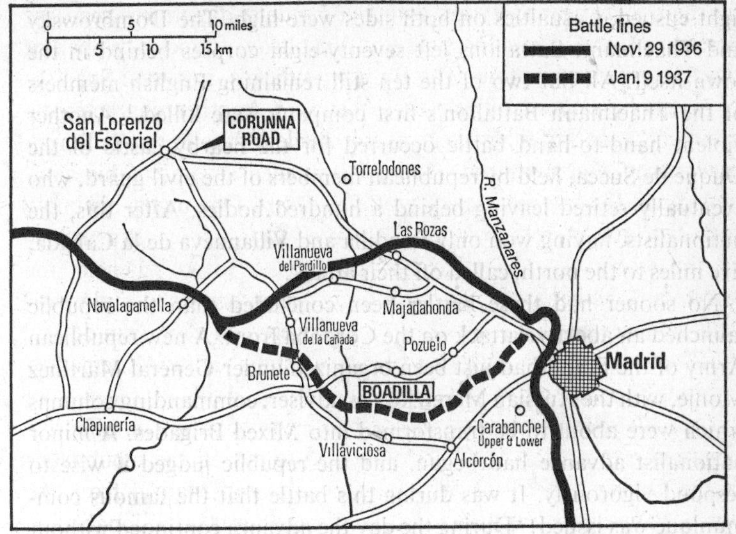

18. The battles of Boadilla and the Corunna Road, December 1936

Sáenz de Buruaga, and Monasterio.[1] The nationalists began, as usual, with a heavy artillery bombardment. On 14 December, the advance began on Boadilla del Monte, a lonely *pueblo* in the plain of Castile (though in fact less than twenty miles from Madrid) and dominated by a small monastery. By night, the town had fallen. The republican force there consisted of a series of heterogeneous battalions under Major Barceló, a republican army officer who, like many other regular soldiers, had joined the communist party since he was attracted by its discipline. A detachment of Russian tanks, under General Pavlov, recently appointed to take over command from Colonel Krivoshein of the tanks sent from Russia to Spain, and both International Brigades, were flung into the battle. (The two British volunteer groups attached to the Thaelmann and the Commune de Paris Battalions, Cornford's group and Romilly's, met for the first time beneath the ilex trees on the road to Boadilla.) The nationalists retired from Boadilla, and the Dombrowsky and Thaelmann Battalions entered it. Then the nationalists surrounded them. A terrible

1. López Muñiz, p. 56.

fight ensued. Casualties on both sides were high. The Dombrowsky and Thaelmann Battalions left seventy-eight corpses behind in the town itself. All but two of the ten still remaining English members of the Thaelmann Battalion's first company were killed.[1] Another violent hand-to-hand battle occurred for the nearby castle of the Duque de Sueca, held by republican members of the civil guard, who eventually retired leaving behind a hundred bodies. After this, the nationalists, having won only Boadilla and Villanueva de la Cañada, five miles to the north, called off their attack.

No sooner had these battles been concluded than the republic launched an abortive attack on the Córdoba front. A new republican Army of the South had just been organized under General Martínez Monje, with the Russian Meretzkov as adviser, commanding columns which were about to be transformed into Mixed Brigades. A minor nationalist advance had begun, and the republic judged it wise to respond vigorously. It was during this battle that the famous communiqué was issued: 'During the day the advance continued without the loss of any territory'. By this time, the British volunteers for the International Brigade had been numerous enough to permit the formation of a full British 'No. 1 Company', 145 strong, now attached to the French, Marseillaise, Battalion of the newly organized 14th International Brigade, commanded by the Polish General 'Walter' (Świerczewski).[2] These Anglo-Saxons were commanded by Captain George Nathan who, having risen to the rank of CSM during the First World War, had then become briefly an officer in the Brigade of Guards. He genuinely found himself as a leader in Spain – resourceful, brave as a lion, and respected by all.[3] One section of the British was composed of Irishmen who had all, it was said, 'ex-

1. Eight (out of the original eighteen) had been killed in their two previous actions, south-east of Madrid and in the University City. One of the survivors was Esmond Romilly, who shortly returned to England and who lived on to be killed fighting as a bomber pilot in the Battle of Britain. Romilly's *Boadilla* (reprinted London, 1971) is an inspired description of this battle.

2. A 13th International Brigade had also been formed and was at this time established before Teruel. It was chiefly composed of East Europeans. Its commander was a German communist, Wilhelm Zaisser, known as 'General Gómez', its political commissar a Pole (Ferry), and the chief of staff another German, Albert Schindler.

3. Nathan had been in Ireland in the early twenties. It seems that he was attached to the Black and Tans, and was a member of the so-called Dublin

perience of warfare in Ireland'. Their chivalrous leader, Frank Ryan, had been a radical member of the Irish Republican Army (IRA) since 1918.[1] The company left by train for the Andújar front on Christmas Eve and fought with the rest of the Brigade between 28 and 29 December, without success, to capture the small village of Lopera. In this battle died Ralph Fox, the commissar of the company, and communist poet.[2] Another promising English poet, John Cornford, was also killed, on the day following his twenty-first birthday.[3] In the same action died Pepe, 'El Algabeño', the aide of Queipo de Llano, bull-fighter turned falangist, and now column commander. The consequence of this action was the rebel capture of some 1,000 square miles of good land, some towns, and the hydro-electric station at El Campo.

After the failure of the action, André Marty appeared at General Walter's headquarters, and Major Gaston Delasalle, commander of the Marseillaise Battalion, was accused of spying for the nationalists, tried, and shot. The major died protesting his innocence, shouting imprecations at Marty and begging the intervention of the Alsatian Colonel Putz, the president of the council of war which had condemned him. If Delasalle was a spy for anyone, however, which seems doubtful, it would presumably have been for the government of France and not for Franco.[4]

*

Castle Murder Gang. As such, he was later identified as the murderer of the Lord Mayor and ex-Lord Mayor of Limerick (George Clancy and George O'Callaghan) in March 1921 (see Richard Bennett's article in the *New Statesman*, 24 March 1961).

1. Marcel Acier (ed.), *From Spanish Trenches* (New York, 1937), p. 113. For Ryan, see J. Bowyer Bell, *The Secret Army* (London, 1970), p. 189.

2. Fox was aged thirty-six when he died. In an introduction to a memoir published in his memory, Harry Pollitt claimed Byron as Fox's precursor in dying for a foreign cause (see Fox, p. 6). Byron seems to have been an obsession with Pollitt at this time. Having urged yet another poet, Stephen Spender, to join the communist party purely to be able to help over Spain, he advised him that the best way he could help the party was 'to go and get killed, comrade, we need a Byron in the movement'.

3. See Stansky and Abrahams, p. 384f, for an account of his death.

4. See Tom Wintringham, *English Captain* (London, 1939), pp. 83–6. According, however, to the not very reliable José Esteban Vilaró (*op. cit.*, p. 123) Delasalle had been a member of the Deuxième Bureau in 1919 at Odessa and there tricked

After Christmas, a new attempt was made by the nationalists to cut the Madrid–Corunna road. The columns engaged in the battle of Boadilla had been reinforced by new conscripted troops and falangists who had been trained by German officers at Cáceres. These were faced by a republican army reorganized on the Madrid front as an army corps (Miaja in command), with five divisions, led respectively by Nino Nanetti (an Italian communist who, arriving in Barcelona, had led a battalion of Catalan youth at Huesca in August), Modesto (the Spanish communist ex-NCO of Africa and the organizer of the Fifth Regiment) and regular Colonels Perea, Prada and José María Galán. The brunt of the nationalist attack was faced by Modesto's division, composed of new Mixed Brigades led by El Campesino, Luis Barceló, Cipriano Mera, and Gustavo Durán. Mera was the leading anarchist commander produced by the war, while Durán had been a composer – for films mostly – who had found himself as a commander, and had, before Christmas, been 'Kléber's' chief of staff.[1] On 3 January, the attack began. Barrón advanced

---

Marty in his first revolutionary exploit. See comments by Marty in the French Senate in March 1939, quoted by Pike, pp. 197–9. Delasalle was denounced by his commissar, the communist André Heussler, who was himself executed during the Resistance by his own comrades on a charge of treachery. See Delperrie and Castells, pp. 132, 163f, the best account of this incident. Marty was obsessed by spies but there were certainly some such. See, for example, the account by Henri Dupré of how he deceived Marty into giving him a post of confidence when he was in fact a Cagoulard in *La 'Légion Tricolore' en Espagne* (Paris, 1942). Dupré was shot in France as a collaborator in 1951. There were other spies: thus Leon Narvich, who presented himself in the Brigades as a Russian, an opponent of Stalin and the purges in Russia, was a provocateur of the NKVD. He was murdered by the friends of those whom he had betrayed in Barcelona in 1939.

1. Mauricio Amster, a Polish volunteer, then a communist, told me (in Chile, in 1971), that 'Kléber' had sent for him and told him that he wanted a chief of staff and desired to put to him three questions: did your father come from the middle class, were you once a social democrat, and did you desire to be a priest when you were young? To the first two questions, Amster answered yes. To the last he had to answer no. He did not get the job. Years later, in Santiago de Chile, by then an exile, he spoke with Durán, by then an official of the UN; and told him this story. Durán told him that he too had had this conversation with 'Kléber' but he had answered yes to all the questions. Such were the makings of a career in the world of 'Kléber'. Durán had in the weeks before the civil war been a leading figure in '*la Motorizada*', the motorized section of the socialist youth movement associated with Prieto.

along the road from Villanueva de la Cañada and, on 4 January, reached the first houses of Las Rozas, on the Madrid–El Escorial railway. On the right, García Escámez and Sáenz de Buruaga fought against tenacious resistance at Pozuelo. The advance was slow, since the number of summer villas in the area afforded good cover to the defenders. Kléber sent as reinforcements the Commune de Paris Battalion to Pozuelo and the Edgar André and Thaelmann Battalions to Las Rozas. On 5 January, after a day of inaction due to heavy fog, a new nationalist attack began. Bombing was followed by the advance of tanks and mobile artillery, then by the first two infantry waves, and then by more tanks. The republican front broke everywhere. This blitzkrieg attack was of interest to those German officers on the nationalist side who, with ruthless objectivity, continued to regard Spain as a 'European Aldershot'. A little earlier, at Pozuelo, six Russian armoured cars, with 37-millimetre guns based originally on German Rheinmetall design, had put twenty-five light German Mercedes tanks out of action – an occurrence which ultimately caused many modifications in German armament manufacture.[1] Now, the brigades of Barceló, El Campesino, and Cipriano Mera lost touch with each other, and munitions ran out. Miaja, in general command, was forced to send blank rounds to the front on the assumption that men who heard their rifles firing would go on defending themselves. He even staged a mock execution of deserters to prevent weakness in the trenches. The impending disaster caused the transfer of Lister's brigade from Madrid, and persuaded Largo Caballero to send the 14th International Brigade up from Córdoba.

But the nationalist advance continued. Orgaz's columns reached the high road at Las Rozas and beyond Pozuelo (though the town itself held on). But Orgaz's columns suffered heavy casualties from the machine-guns of the International Brigade. On the 6th, the Thaelmann Battalion was sent to hold out at Las Rozas, and not to retreat an inch farther. These orders were later revised, but by then

1. Tagüeña, p. 142. The Russian success was obtained with the armour-piercing shell soon adopted by Germany. Among those killed on 5 January was Guido Picelli, an Italian socialist, 'hero of the *giornata di Parma*' in 1922, at the head of two companies. See Spriano, p. 135, and, for a suggestion that he too was murdered by the communist police, Paz, p. 520, and Julián Gorkin, *El proceso de Moscú en Barcelona* (Barcelona, 1974), p. 54.

messages could not get through, since the battalion was surrounded. All day the Thaelmann Battalion held their ground, against tanks, aerial attack and infantry. The Moors – there was probably still a Moroccan majority in the nationalist assault force – stormed several of their trenches and bayoneted the wounded whom they found there. But the Germans did not give way. The next day, Kléber sent a new order to the battalion, to advance. The survivors had reluctantly to send back the following message: 'Impossible. The Thaelmann Battalion has been destroyed.'[1] Walter, leader of No. 1 Company of the Thaelmann Battalion,[2] had during this battle the eerie experience of coming upon the body of a Condor Legion pilot with whom he had once served in the same air squadron.[3]

By 9 January, the nationalists had conquered, at great cost, seven miles of the converted highway, from just beyond the last houses of Madrid at the Puerta de Hierro to Las Rozas. On 10 January, there arrived in Madrid the 14th and 12th International Brigades, including the British No. 1 Company, commanded now by Jock Cunningham, a communist since 1920 when he had been gaoled for leading a mutiny of the Argyll and Sutherland Highlanders in Jamaica.[4] Nathan commanded the Marseillaise Battalion in succession to the ill-fated Delasalle. A German group of the 14th Brigade asked for twelve hours' sleep after their forty-eight-hour journey following on their battles at Córdoba. Walter, their Polish commander, appealed to them: 'The government has called for the best troops. That is you. Or could there have been a mistake with regard

1. Lise Lindbaeck, *Internationella Brigaden* (Stockholm, 1939), pp. 87–90.

2. Not to be confused with the Polish General 'Walter'. (Walter Ulbricht, also in Spain for some time in 1937, was also, confusingly, known as 'Walter'.) Another international meeting at Las Rozas was that between the Russian Colonel Rodion Malinovski ('Malino'), who came to the front as aide to General Kulik ('Kupper'), with a White Russian, Captain Karchevski, who was fighting as chief of 'servicios' in the 14th International Brigade (*Bajo la bandera*, p. 15). (Karchevski was killed at Lérida in 1937.) Other White Russians, such as Colonel Boltin, accompanied by his 'pope', and Captain Rachewsky, fought for Franco.

3. Acier, p. 82.

4. Cunningham was a man of great physical strength, and, at a low level of command, possessed marked qualities of leadership. He was for a time nicknamed the 'English Chapaev' – after the guerrilla leader of the Russian Civil War – and, thanks to the Russian film then on in Madrid, there could not at that time have been a greater compliment.

to the 14th Brigade?' The recalcitrant troops went on to the front, this being perhaps the first time in history that a Polish commander has rebuked a German force. The next day, the republic counter-attacked in heavy mist (unusual in Madrid) and fierce cold. The 12th International Brigade reached Majadahonda and the 14th, Las Rozas – a battalion of the latter being lost in the mist and never being seen again. Russian tanks, led in person by General Pavlov, drove wildly about, destroying men but unable to gain ground. The battle continued till 15 January, when each side dug fortifications. Both had lost 15,000 men in ten days. Orgaz retained his seven miles of high-road, Miaja had prevented the isolation of the Sierras. The military stalemate thus appeared complete.[1] The rebels had observed that their opponents' power of resistance had increased and attributed that to the existence of 'foreign professional commanders'[2] as well as to discipline and new armaments.

The remainder of the 1,300-mile front was meantime quiet, since neither side had enough modern weapons for more than one battle at the same time. The republicans had men enough but many of these were, in the mind of the general staff, too unreliable (as in Aragon), too badly trained (as in the south), or too poorly armed (as along the Cantabrian coast). The fronts themselves still consisted in most places simply of 'a system of narrow trenches hewn out of the rock with primitive loopholes made out of piles of limestone'. Twelve sentries might be 'at various points in the trench, in front of which was the barbed-wire, and then the hillside slid down to a seemingly bottomless ravine: opposite lay naked hills'.[3] On every hill-top, in Aragon, for example, there seemed to be a knot of ragged, dirty men,

1. Regler, *Great Crusade*, pp. 219–41; Koltsov, p. 303. Koltsov's own role with the tanks in this battle seems to have been considerable. During this battle died Pablo de la Torriente Brau, a Cuban communist writer who had taken a great part in the struggle against Machado in his own country. See Teresa Casuso, *Cuba and Castro* (New York, 1960), p. 81.

2. López Muñiz, p. 64. Martínez Bande, *La lucha en torno a Madrid* (Madrid, 1968), estimates 6,000 republican casualties (dead 500) and 1,500 nationalist, in these battles.

3. Orwell, *Homage to Catalonia*, pp. 20–23. Orwell reached Barcelona at the end of December and joined a POUM column on the Aragon front, with whom he stayed till April. He returned to the front a month later but finally returned to England in June.

nationalist or republican, 'shivering round their flag', with bullets occasionally wandering between them – and sometimes voices, encouraging desertion, painting a rosy picture of the comforts to be had on the other side, and shouting insults. Nationalists would, indeed, desert, sometimes five a night, before a single company's sector. The republic offered every deserter from their enemies 50 pesetas, and 100 if they brought their arms with them – not admittedly a particularly enticing reward (the peseta was 36 to the pound sterling before the civil war). There were also instances of desertion by republicans though, at this stage in the war, the balance was probably in the republic's favour. In most cases the deserters, however, were men who had been caught in the wrong place at the start of the war, had pretended to belong to the side for which they were fighting to save their lives, and had been waiting, ever since, for an opportunity to cross the lines.

Dr Junod, the indefatigable humanitarian of the Red Cross, had established himself at St Jean de Luz in order to try to effect exchanges of prisoners, mostly persons apprehended at the beginning of the war rather than soldiers. Red Cross branch offices were set up in Salamanca and Valencia which communicated through Geneva. Lists of prisoners were compiled and, occasionally, individuals would be exchanged by Red Cross agencies between prisoners in one camp or the other and their relations. Giral, who became the republican minister in charge of the possible exchange of prisoners, proposed an exchange of 10,000 – but the nationalists were unhelpful, and only a few hundred were exchanged.[1] Friends and enemies rubbed shoulders in the Red Cross offices, irreconcilable even in their sorrow. Dr Junod told later the story of Isabella, a fierce monarchist, on behalf of whose brother he had pestered the republican authorities for months. At last the news came: 'Executed with ten others. Buried in the cemetery.' Tearless but deadly pale, she passed on her way out Carlota, whose fiancé had been missing. Each knew the story of the other. They saw each other and they understood at once. With the same movement of contempt and hatred, they avoided each other as they passed. But Carlota said afterwards: 'At least she can visit his grave. But I shall never know, never.'[2]

The character of the winter of 1936 in Spain was, however, best

1. Evidence of Francisco Giral. 2. Junod, p. 114.

expressed by the long convoy of lorries, laden with food brought by the nationalists to feed Madrid once it had fallen. Their contents slowly rotted in the snow and rain. A mile away, behind the republican lines, the people of Madrid stoically put up with rice, bread, and increasing hunger, the consequence of the killing of herds and immediate consumption during the first days of revolution, and of general economic dislocation, as well as the presence, in the republican zone, of a million refugees who had fled during the course of the autumn from one province after another.

29

The execution of José Antonio – Unamuno – nationalist Spain in the winter of 1936 – nationalist justice – economic condition of nationalist Spain – the church's attitude

THE repercussions of one event in particular extended over both sides of these battle lines. This was the trial of José Antonio. The decision to bring the leader of the Falange (who had now been in Alicante gaol since 6 July, remarkably well treated by an admiring prison staff) to trial seems to have been inspired by the fear that, if the 'military rebellion' were to collapse, one of their greatest enemies would go unscathed.

Plans for an exchange for José Antonio had failed; the government seem not to have been able to accept such an arrangement for fear of their own followers. An adventurous attempt to rescue José Antonio by means of a *coup de main* in Alicante had failed, though both the honorary German consul, Von Knobloch, and Admiral Carls, on the battleship *Graf Spee*, had been ready to help. The falangist leader of militias, Agustín Aznar, arrived in disguise in Alicante, on the German torpedo boat *Ildis*, sought to suborn the local CNT, but ultimately failed to find anyone in Alicante who would help him, even for 8 million pesetas.[1] Later, José Antonio made an offer to try to negotiate peace in the civil war by flying to Salamanca, leaving his relations in gaol as hostages against his return. The government refused, as the nationalist authorities no doubt would have done as well.[2]

José Antonio's trial was held correctly before a magistrate and he

1. These efforts are described in García Venero, p. 197f. See Southworth, *Anti-falange*, p. 145f, where José Antonio's last interview with a foreign journalist (Jay Allen) is published (reprinted from the *Chicago Tribune*, 9 October 1936). See also Jackson, p. 339, for what seems to have been another effort to save José Antonio, earlier on.

2. Letter to Martínez Barrio, quoted in F. Bravo Morata, *Historia de Madrid* (Madrid, 1968), vol. III, p. 208.

was able to defend himself by reading out editorials from *Arriba* to prove that his views differed from those of Franco or the monarchists. During the trial, a militiaman appeared as a witness for the prosecution. 'Do you hate the defendant?' asked José Antonio, who was defending himself. 'With all my heart', replied the witness. Dignified and eloquent throughout, the founder of the Falange was condemned to death. For his brother Miguel and his brother's wife, a similar sentence was asked. José Antonio, with the chivalry which his enemies have never denied him, appealed on their behalf. 'Life is not a firework one lets off at the end of a garden party', he concluded. As a result, they received terms of imprisonment. No such clemency was possible for José Antonio himself. Princess Bibesco, Asquith's daughter, who, as the wife of the ex-Roumanian minister in Madrid had been friendly with Azaña, telephoned the president to beg him to prevent the execution. Azaña gloomily answered that he could do nothing since he also was a prisoner,[1] though he had twice previously saved José Antonio's life by intervening with the civil governor of Alicante, Jesús Monzón.[2] According to Largo Caballero, the death sentence came up in the cabinet for confirmation on 20 November, but even as the discussion was going on, the news came of the technically insubordinate act of execution, the local bosses at Alicante having been afraid that the sentence would be commuted.[3] The anarchists had been opposed to the death sentence, since they granted that José Antonio was 'a Spanish patriot in search of solutions for his country'.[4] All the ministers apparently would have voted for the commutation of the sentence. Indeed, the execution of José Antonio was a boon to Franco in the long run, since he was the one other figure of real character on the Spanish Right who remained after the holocaust of July. But no action was taken against the Alicante

1. Ximénez de Sandoval, p. 617.

2. Monzón was a communist of good family from Navarre who earlier in the war had saved at least one old friend and ideological enemy, the Carlist conspirator, Lizarza, from certain death.

3. Largo Caballero, p. 21.

4. Abad de Santillán, p. 21, wrote: 'Spaniards of this stature, patriots such as he, are not dangerous, and are not to be found in the ranks of the enemy ... How much would the destiny of Spain have changed if an agreement between us had been ... possible, as Primo de Rivera desired.'

authorities; indeed, very many sentences were still carried out without governmental consultation.[1]

José Antonio was shot on 20 November in the prison yard in Alicante gaol, between two other falangists and two Carlists, who were also executed. His final request was that the patio in which he was to be shot should be wiped clean after his death 'so that my brother Miguel will not have to walk in my blood'.[2] At almost the same hour on the same day as José Antonio was shot, his contemporary, Durruti, was dying of wounds in the Ritz Hotel in Madrid. Two Spanish 'heroes of their time' died, leaving the way open to less generous successors. José Antonio left behind a will full of constructive ideas for a future Spain without rancour: it pleased Prieto but had no effect.

For a long time, this execution was not published in the nationalist press. He was referred to as *el ausente*, the 'absent one'. Since 1933, when names of falangist martyrs were read out at ceremonies, the Falange would cry *Presente*, 'Present', in imitation of a similar fascist rite. They would continue to call out 'Present' after the name of José Antonio, and many who knew that the *jefe* was really dead acted as if they thought he was not.

One other notable occurrence straddling the battle lines was the change of attitude of the most prominent intellectuals of pre-war Spain. Most of these had found themselves in republican Spain at the time of the rising. They signed a manifesto pledging support of the republic. The signatures had included those of the physician and historian, Dr Marañón; the ex-ambassador and novelist, Pérez de Ayala; the historian, Menéndez Pidal; and the prolific philosopher, José Ortega y Gasset: friends, founders even, of the republic of 1931. But the atrocities and the increasing influence of the communists caused all these men to take what opportunity they could find to flee

1. The cabinet had shown itself equally ineffective two months earlier when the radical ex-minister Salazar Alonso had been condemned to death by a revolutionary tribunal. The cabinet reprieved the condemned man but then went back on their decision, as a result of popular pressure.

2. The magistrate at the popular tribunal was Federico Enjuta Ferrán, a career magistrate. Years later he became a professor in Puerto Rico and was thrown by his pupils out of the window of a lecture hall and killed. This murder was never fully explained.

abroad. There, they repudiated their support of the republic.[1] A different course was taken by the Basque philosopher, Miguel de Unamuno, arch-priest of the Generation of '98. As rector of the University of Salamanca, he had found himself at the start of the civil war in nationalist territory. The republic had disillusioned him, he had admired some of the young falangists, and he gave money to the rising. As late as 15 September, he was supporting the nationalist movement.[2] But by 12 October his view had changed. He had become, as he said, later, 'terrified by the character that this civil war was taking, really horrible, due to a collective mental illness, an epidemic of madness, with a pathological substratum'.[3] On that date, the anniversary of Columbus's discovery of America, celebrated as the 'Day of the Race', a ceremony was held in the great hall (*paraninfo*) of the University of Salamanca. There was Dr Plá y Deniel, bishop of Salamanca;[4] there was General Millán Astray, the founder of the Foreign Legion, at the time an important if unofficial adviser to Franco. His black eye-patch, his one arm, his mutilated fingers made him a hero of the moment; and, in the chair, there was Unamuno, rector of the university. The meeting occurred within a hundred yards of Franco's headquarters, recently established in the bishop's palace in Salamanca, on the prelate's invitation. After the opening formalities, there were speeches by the Dominican, Father Vicente Beltrán de Heredia, and the monarchist writer, José María Pemán. Both delivered hot-tempered speeches. So did Professor Francisco Maldonado who made a violent attack on Catalan and Basque nationalism, describing them as 'cancers in the body of the nation'. Fascism, Spain's 'health-giver', would know how to exterminate both, 'cutting into the live healthy flesh like a resolute surgeon free from false sentimentality'. A man at the back of the hall cried

1. The novelist Pío Baroja fled from the republic to nationalist Spain, which he also abandoned.

2. He was reported as saying this in an interview in *Le Petit Parisien* of that date. On 12 August, the government of Madrid had deprived Unamuno of his rectorship for 'disloyalty', and on 1 September the Burgos *junta* had confirmed it.

3. Quoted Aurelio Núñez Morgado, *Los sucesos de España vistos por un diplomático* (Buenos Aires, 1941), p. 169f.

4. This prelate, it seems, had already used the word 'crusade' to describe the nationalist movement, in a pastoral letter of 30 September, *Las dos Españas* (see Abella, p. 177).

the Foreign Legion's motto: '*¡Viva la Muerte!*' (Long live death!). Millán Astray then gave the now usual rabble-rousing slogans: 'Spain!' he cried. Automatically, a number of people shouted 'One!' 'Spain!' shouted Millán Astray again. 'Great!' replied the audience. To Millán Astray's final cry of 'Spain!' his bodyguard gave the answer 'Free!' Several falangists, in their blue shirts, gave a fascist salute to the sepia photograph of Franco which hung on the wall over the dais. All the eyes were turned to Unamuno, who it was known disliked Millán Astray and who rose to close the meeting and said:[1]

All of you are hanging on my words. You all know me and are aware that I am unable to remain silent. At times to be silent is to lie. For silence can be interpreted as acquiescence. I want to comment on the speech – to give it that name – of Professor Maldonado. Let us waive the personal affront implied in the sudden outburst of vituperation against the Basques and Catalans. I was myself, of course, born in Bilbao. The bishop [here Unamuno indicated the quivering prelate sitting next to him], whether he likes it or not, is a Catalan, from Barcelona.

He paused. There was a fearful silence. No speech like this had been made in nationalist Spain. What would the rector say next?

Just now [Unamuno went on] I heard a necrophilistic and senseless cry: 'Long live death'. And I, who have spent my life shaping paradoxes which have aroused the uncomprehending anger of others, I must tell you, as an expert authority, that this outlandish paradox is repellent to me. General Millán Astray is a cripple. Let it be said without any slighting undertone. He is a war invalid. So was Cervantes. Unfortunately there are all too many cripples in Spain just now. And soon there will be even more of them, if God does not come to our aid. It pains me to think that General Millán Astray should dictate the pattern of mass psychology. A cripple who lacks the spiritual greatness of a Cervantes is wont to seek ominous relief in causing mutilation around him.

At this, Millán Astray was unable to restrain himself any longer. 'Death to Intellectuals!' '*¡Mueran los intelectuales!*' he shouted. 'Long live death.' There was a clamour of support for this remark from the falangists, with whom the simple, soldierly Millán Astray

1. Unamuno was at this time seventy-two. Next day, the Salamanca papers published the speeches of Pemán, Heredia, Francisco Maldonado and José María Ramos, but made no mention that Unamuno had even spoken.

had actually little in common. 'Down with *false* intellectuals! Traitors!' shouted José María Pemán, anxious to paper over the cracks in the nationalist front. But Unamuno went on:

This is the temple of the intellect. And I am its high priest. It is you who profane its sacred precincts. You will win, because you have more than enough brute force. But you will not convince. For to convince, you need to persuade. And in order to persuade you would need what you lack: reason and right in the struggle. I consider it futile to exhort you to think of Spain. I have done.

There was a long pause. Some of the legionaries around Millán Astray began to close in on the platform menacingly. Millán Astray's bodyguard pointed his machine-gun at Unamuno. Franco's wife, Doña Carmen, came up to Unamuno and Millán Astray and insisted that the rector give his arm to her. He did so and the two slowly left together. But this was Unamuno's last public address. That night, Unamuno went to the club in Salamanca, of which he was president. As the members, somewhat intimidated by these events, saw the rector's venerable figure ascending the stairs, some shouted out: 'Out with him! He is a red, not a Spaniard! Red, traitor!' Unamuno continued and sat down, to be told by a certain Tomás Marcos Escribano 'You ought not to have come here, Don Miguel, we are sorry for what happened today in the University but all the same you ought not to have come.' Unamuno left, accompanied by his son, the shouts of 'traitor' accompanying him. One minor writer Mariano de Santiago alone went with them. Thereafter, the rector rarely went out, and the armed guard that followed him were perhaps necessary to ensure his safety. The senate of the university 'demanded' and obtained his dismissal from the rectorship. He died broken-hearted on the last day of 1936.[1] The tragedy of his last months was a natural

1. See *Unamuno's Last Lecture* by Luis Portillo, whose translation of Unamuno's remarks this is. Published in *Horizon*, and reprinted in Cyril Connolly, *The Golden Horizon* (London, 1953), pp. 397–409. For another account see Emilio Salcedo's recent *Vida de don Miguel* (Madrid, 1964), p. 409f. I am grateful to Ronald Fraser for advice on details. There will never be full agreement on what was said and the tone in which it was said. I discussed this version with Luis Portillo, and with Ilse Barea who translated it. But see Pemán's account 'La Verdad de aquel día', *ABC*, 12 October 1965. One may well wonder why the Falange were present in such strength at the funeral.

expression of the tragedy of Spain, where culture, eloquence and creativity were giving way to militarism, propaganda, and death. Before long, there was even a concentration camp called 'Unamuno' for republican prisoners.[1]

*

Salamanca was now the centre of power in nationalist Spain. Franco slept, received and dined on the first floor of the episcopal palace and he worked with his staff on the second floor. The diplomatic secretariat headed by José Antonio Sangroniz, and the press and propaganda department, headed first by Juan Pujol, then by Millán Astray[2], were on the ground floor, while a radio telegraphic service was established on the top floor. The simplicity of this organization rendered it efficient. Apart from Franco himself, the important figures were his chief of staff, Colonel Martín Moreno; his brother Nicolás, who acted as political secretary; the legal adviser, Colonel Martínez Fusset; and one or two staff officers, such as Colonel Juan Vigón, a pro-German monarchist, and Major Antonio Barroso, the ex-military attaché in Paris. Influential also were Kindelán, the commander of the air force, and Admiral Juan Cervera, the 66-year-old sailor of experience, who became chief of staff of the navy. All these officers saw Franco daily – or rather, nightly, since Franco held a *tertulia* in his apartments most nights to discuss the war, usually with a general from the front also present: Varela, Yagüe, or some other *Africanista*.[3] Also in Salamanca, there were the German and Italian missions and diplomatic representatives, the headquarters of the Falange and some, though not all, of the government offices; the treasury, the new Bank of Spain, the ministries of justice and labour, were in Burgos. Salamanca was, however, the nerve centre of the

1. Miguel García, *Franco's Prisoner* (London, 1972), p. 25.

2. Luis Bolín, the ex-journalist of *ABC*, looked after the foreign press, along with Captains Aguilera and Rosales. All three were free with threats of execution to journalists whom they accused of being spies; others who worked in this section included the obscure writer, Vicente Gay, who succeeded Millán Astray; Agustín de Foxá, a clever falangist writer; José Ignacio Escobar, a monarchist journalist; and Eugenio Vegas Latapié, the monarchist writer.

3. See Admiral Juan Cervera's *Memorias de guerra* (Madrid, 1968), pp. 33–4, and Bolín, p. 219.

nationalist rebellion: to Salamanca, came the reports of the few diplomats which nationalist Spain as yet had officially (only the Marqués de Magaz in Berlin, García Conde in Rome), the private agents (Juan de la Cierva or the Marqués de Portago in London) and secret intelligence reports (particularly about ship movements and republican arms purchases) dispatched from the ex-monarchist ambassador in Paris, Quiñones de León, as well as such information as there was from spies in the 'red zone'.[1] The centralization of the nationalist command, and the concentration of power, in the willing hands of Franco became daily more striking, given the divisions in the republican zone. Loyal but unobtrusive generals such as Orgaz and Dávila played at least as great a part as more flamboyant and better known officers such as Varela, while the role of Admiral Cervera was considerable. Nephew of the unfortunate admiral who lost the Spanish fleet in the Spanish American War, older than any of Franco's other intimates, he was strong enough in character to insist on the importance of the sea in the conflict, and to ensure the purchase of naval supplies, such as mines (from Germany), or launches (from Italy), as well as money to set up new schools for naval technicians.

By the spring of 1937, the balance of power at sea lay with the nationalists, due chiefly to the neglect of this side of the matter by their opponents; and this, as much as military organization, was a determining element. The republican fleet based in Cartagena never sallied out into the Atlantic again after the end of September, leaving

1. See for this José Bertrán y Musitu, *Experiencias de los servicios de información del nordeste de Espana (SIFNE) durante la guerra* (Madrid, 1940). The SIFNE had been founded with a base in Biarritz in August 1936 by Mola and had, as its chief organizers, Quiñones de León, Colonel Bertrán y Musitu, and the Conde de los Andes. By the end of 1936, it had a good organization in Catalonia, based partly on ex-members of Primo de Rivera's Somaten, the old civil guard of Catalonia. Other organizations of espionage included several groups in France, such as the 'Mapeba' group directed by Nicolás Franco, several private persons and several effective organizations in Madrid such as the 'Organización Antonio', headed by Lieutenant Antonio Rodríguez Aguado, and several individuals in Miaja's headquarters, the military hospitals and later the School of Officers at Barajas. (See Vicente Palacio Atard, *La quinta columna*, in his *Aproximación histórica a la guerra civil española*, Madrid, 1970, p. 241f.)

the Cantabrian coast ill defended; a victory for the nationalists as great, if not so noticeable, as the advance of the Army of Africa to Madrid.

The nationalists were, however, adversely affected by other technical factors: namely, that the international telephone was controlled throughout the war by the republic. They had also only one of Spain's three cableheads at the beginning of the war: that at Vigo, whereas both those at Málaga and Bilbao were in republican hands. Communications from Salamanca to Vigo were bad. This meant that the nationalists' links with the outside world were less satisfactory than those of the republic. Journalists with the republican press were thus usually first with the news.[1]

Franco had now no rivals among his fellow generals and neither the falangists nor the Carlists were in a position to make any effective challenge to him, much less the old political parties. The falangists, the few 'old shirts' and the vast number of new ones, were still trying to find their political bearing. Few political parties, after all, have ever grown so fast as they – not even the communist party in the republic. From 75,000 as a maximum in July, they had, from whatever origin, nearly a million members at the end of the year. New falangist newspapers had sprung up everywhere. Hedilla, the new if temporary national *jefe*, worked hard to make of the vastly expanded movement a genuine party, but the demands of war prevented him from meeting with much success. The new *junta* of the Falange did found two small 'military schools' for militia officers at Salamanca and Seville but these were not successful. Their best units were taken over by the army proper. At the end of 1936, the movement claimed that it had sent 50,000 men to the front, with 30,000 in the rear – though those figures may have been exaggerated.[2] Actually, the Falange had more difficulties in their own ranks than they had with Franco. Some falangists were looking to Franco as a potential leader of a fascist Spain, and some hoped for much more from Hedilla. Others conspired with the Germans and Italians. Meantime, much the most remarkable falangist institution was the Auxilio de Invierno (Winter Help) founded in Valladolid by Mercedes Sanz Bachiller, the widow of Onésimo Redondo. It began in October in a single room in Valladolid as a centre for orphan children. Within a few months,

1. Bolín, p. 223. 2. Payne, pp. 145–7.

it had branches throughout nationalist Spain.[1] Since its title seemed too close to that of a similar nazi body in Germany, it changed its name to Auxilio Social (Social Help). Some of the staff of this organization were trained in Germany. One dour task was to look after the children of dead republicans or 'Marxists'. ('First the fathers are shot, then the children get charity' was a cynical comment.) These improvised social centres were nevertheless lively places, run by the wives and daughters of the rich, a little patronizingly perhaps, but with a dedication that, had it been geared to society before the war, would doubtless have rendered the war unnecessary.[2] Other bodies grew out of Auxilio Social. These included the Cocinas de Hermandad ('Brotherhood Kitchens'), organizations for making clothes for the destitute, and maternity homes. The 'Margaritas', the Carlist women's organization, also did much social work.

General Franco's only serious difficulties in the winter of 1936–7 were with the Carlists. On 8 December, the Carlist high command set up a 'Royal Military Academy' for the training of young officers in both military and ideological matters. Mola gave his approval. The Falange, after all, had two such centres of the military arts. But the initiators had not consulted Franco, who told General Dávila to inform the Conde de Rodezno that the creation of the Military Academy could only be considered an attempt at a *coup d'état*. Fal Conde, the Carlist supreme leader, the inspiration of the plan for the Academy, was ordered by Dávila to leave the country within forty-eight hours, unless he wished to appear before a war tribunal. The Carlist war *junta* considered this peremptory instruction on 20 December. They decided to agree, under protest, in order to prove their innocence of any attempt at a *coup*; and Fal Conde left for Lisbon, the favourite resort of right-wing exiles from Spain. Franco followed this with a decree uniting all the militias – Carlist, falangist and CEDA – and placing them all under an orthodox military authority.[3] Franco later told the German ambassador that he would

1. By October 1937 it had 711 branches; in October 1938, 1,265, and in October 1939, 2,847. It was a 'voluntary organization' though of course backed by the authorities.

2. See description of a visit in Julian Amery, *Approach March* (London, 1973), p. 99.

3. The above derives from Fal Conde's Archives, Seville, which I was able to consult thanks to Melchor Ferrer. See also del Burgo, p. 692.

have had Fal Conde shot had he not feared for the effects upon Carlist morale at the front.[1] The fighting spirit of the Carlists, indeed, could not be gainsaid. One *requeté* was apparently asked who should be told if he were to die. 'My father, José María de Hernandorena, of the Montejurra militia, aged sixty-five.' 'And if he should be killed too?' 'My son, José María de Hernandorena, of the Montejurra militia, aged fifteen.'[2] The Carlist movement, meantime, had itself expanded almost as much as the Falange and, since October, had been launching initiatives to influence the development of the nationalist state.

By January, the number of Peninsular volunteer battalions must have been a hundred. Many young middle-class Spaniards and ex-rankers, were under training at the twenty-two officers' schools, all aged between eighteen and thirty, all with a *bachillerato*, all with two months' experience of war and directed by General Orgaz, with the help of German instructors. These 'provisional officers' (*alféreces provisionales*), who had twenty-four days of training, were the core of the future nationalist army, despite their high death rate: 'provisional officer, certain corpse' was one macabre joke current in Burgos. Some 3,000 or 4,000 officers had been provided by Orgaz by the end of the winter of 1936–7.[3]

The commanders preferred to organize their recruits, as at the beginning of the war, in columns, not brigades, so that, in that way, they remained more old-fashioned than the republicans. During the spring, nevertheless, the first mixed brigades of the nationalist army, with ordnance, machine-gun and technical arms combined, began to be organized. By then, over 200,000 men were under arms in nationalist Spain: the Army of Africa reached 60,000, the *requetés* and falangists together numbered 120,000; and there were 25,000 cavalry, artillery, engineers and other services. Soon this army began to be organized loosely in divisions, with territorial names.

Some intellectual framework to these diverse efforts seemed in that time of ideologies desirable. Nicolás Franco favoured the creation of a 'patriotic party', such as Primo de Rivera's Patriotic Union. A

1. *GD*, p. 189.

2. This story may be apocryphal but, even if so, it expresses Carlist sentiment in this 'Fourth Carlist War', as they thought it.

3. De la Cierva, *Historia ilustrada*, vol. I, p. 440.

hundred ideas were canvassed: a Francoist Falange? 'Restoration?' words which went further than One Country, One State, One Leader. But how far could they go in the course of the war? On 27 February, the 'Royal March' became the national anthem of Franco's Spain. But the *Oriamendi*, the *Cara al Sol*, and the anthem of the Legion also had to be listened to standing up, in honour of the dead. Even so, with the red and gold flag, the change seemed encouraging to monarchists. But what monarchy? Surely not that of 1931, much less that of 1923. The 'new state' of Ferdinand and Isabella, whose emblem, the yoke and the arrows, was everywhere to be seen? The Moorish bodyguard outside Franco's headquarters, on the other hand, suggested a more eastern, grander style of authority than Spain had seen in its kings for generations. One political attitude, negative though it might seem, was constant: to kill the nineteenth century, 'liberal, decadent, masonic, materialist and Frenchified', and 'to return to impregnate ourselves with the spirit of the sixteenth century, imperial, heroic, proud, Castilian, spiritual, mythical and chivalrous'.[1] One sign of this new heroic attitude was the change in street names: nineteenth-century politicians, such as Castelar or Salmerón, disappeared as well as, naturally, '14 April' from the streets, which were taken over by 'Berlin', 'Labour', or 'San José'. In the no-man's land where propaganda, ideology, and battle cries became one, it was sometimes hard to know if these thoughts represented revolution or counter-revolution. There was a press campaign, for example, in favour of 'concision, rapidity, and an end to the spirit of procrastination'. The rehispanization of customs, names of hotels, and even of dishes became a fever in the minds of nationalist propagandists, who tried to insist that everything sounding foreign should vanish from the vocabulary: Russian salad became 'national' salad, *ragoût* disappeared from the menus, even the *tortilla a la francesa* lost its gallic name. (What should it become? Simply *tortilla*.)[2] That was the way to talk with 'an imperial accent'. There was a comparable drive to banish other 'liberal' ways of behaving: the full bathing-suit was *de rigueur* at two years old and for all men, there was 'war on the *decolleté* dress', and the short skirt. The sleeve had to go to the wrist, while all egalitarian manners and styles of address were severely

1. The words of Federico de Urrutia, quoted in Abella, p. 109.
2. See Abella, p. 119, for other diverting instances.

frowned upon. Anyone who said *salud* in republican style risked a visit from the police.

There were many other manifestations of the fascist counter-renaissance of which there were so many comparable examples in Italy and Germany under fascism and nazism.[1] Nationalist Spain was thus in the early stages of at least a cultural revolution. Three elements – conservatism, reactionary nostalgia and fascism – were alike present in the nationalist movement, but there was also Millán Astray's evangelical medievalism and his appeals for a return to chivalrous christianity. 'To me, *mutilados!*' he would bellow to the war-wounded, in his capacity as president of their association, just as once he had cried '*A mí la Legión*' to the Foreign Legion; and the men in wheelchairs and crutches would do their poor best to come to attention. The propaganda worked. Fighting for 'old Spain', against Russia, 'Marxismo', and masonry, many upper- and middle-class Spaniards found in 'the movement' something which almost did take them back to the days of the Crusades. The young Duque de Fernán Núñez, for example, who was killed on the Madrid front in November, wrote a classical last letter to his wife which expresses in mood the unreflective nobility of a paladin: 'Thus I am going, tranquil and constant, regretting only making you suffer . . . I hope [the children] may live in a world calmer and more normal than this, one where Manolo will continue the traditions of the house, practising virtue, duty and work, and knowing how to choose his friends.'[2] It may be, however, that young Manolo and his friends would have been already ranged in the ranks of nationalist Spain's equivalent of Mussolini's *balilla* or youth movement: under the name of *pelayos*, *cadetes* or *flechas*, the small boys of Salamanca, Seville and Burgos paraded these days in uniforms of the Falange, or the Carlists, with wooden rifles.

The church remained a fervent ally of the régime. Characteristic of the régime's propagandists was the depiction on nearly all its postage stamps of views of cathedrals, taking the place of the faces of republican or socialist leaders. Divorces and civil marriages concluded under the republic were annulled. Sermons were often close

1. Handel's oratorio *Israel in Egypt* was rendered *Mongol Fury* in Berlin.

2. A. de Castro Albarrán, *Este es el cortejo* (Salamanca, 1941), pp. 101–3. See also J. Luca de Tena, *Mis amigos muertos* (Barcelona, 1971).

to political harangues. Priests would often end their sermons with a '*¡Viva España!*' or a *viva* for the Generalissimo. One Sunday, in the monastery of La Merced at Burgos, during high mass, the priest broke off spontaneously in the middle of administering the sacrament.

O, you that hear me! [he said] You who call yourselves Christians! You are to blame for much that has happened. For you have tolerated in your midst, yea, and even employed in your service workmen banded together in organizations hostile to our God and our country. You have heeded not our warnings and have consorted with jews and freemasons, atheists and renegades, so helping to strengthen the power of the very lodges whose aim it was to hurl us all into chaos. Be warned of the tragedies of today! You should be to all these people – as we must all be – as fire to water... no dealings with them of any kind ... no pardon for criminal destroyers of churches and murderers of holy priests and ministers. Let their seed be stamped out – the evil seed – the seed of the Devil. For verily the sons of Beelzebub are also the enemies of God![1]

Catholics knew that hundreds of priests had been murdered in republican Spain, and believed that the numbers of the dead churchmen were greater even than they really were. There were few families too by now who had not had some relation, or close friend, shot on the other side of the battle-line. Further, the nationalist zone was increasingly reached by people who had got there after amazing journeys of great danger, and the stories of such people filled the papers.

There was a difference between the commitment of the Spanish hierarchy to the nationalist cause, and the attitude of the Vatican. True, when, in September, Pope Pius XI had received six hundred Spanish refugees from the republic, he had spoken of the 'satanic' behaviour of the godless in Spain.[2] But now, at the end of December, General Franco complained to the Italian ambassador, Cantalupo, of the Pope's attitude to the nationalist cause. His representative at the Vatican suggested to the Pope that he should publicly condemn the Basques. But Pius refused, perhaps due to the influence of Monsignor Múgica, the bishop of Vitoria. The furthest that the Pope would go would be to issue a condemnation of catholic cooperation with communists. He also complained of the execution of Basque priests by nationalist troops, and showed himself gloomy about

1. Ruiz Vilaplana, p. 191. 2. Speech on 14 September 1936.

Franco's prospects.[1] Presumably this attitude on the part of the Pope was caused by the relations of Franco with Mussolini and Hitler. But these Roman hesitations were only very rarely felt by most priests and catholics in Spain. For them, the 'crusade' was a holy war; the bishop of Salamanca had described communists and anarchists as sons of Cain, and the primate had designated the war as a punishment for the laicism and corruption imposed on the Spanish people by the political leaders: 'the jews and masons had poisoned the national soul with absurd doctrines, and tartar and mongol tales had been converted into a political system'.[2] There was a steady increase in attendance at church: in one village in Aragon, for example, in 1937 only 58 out of a population of 1,200 of an age to go to communion did not confess at Easter; in 1936, the figure had been 302.[3]

But there were nevertheless some dissensions within the church. The difficulties caused by the bishops of Pamplona and Vitoria have been described.[4] The bishop of Vitoria, Monsignor Múgica, had been now several months in Rome and, when news came that certain Basque priests who had sympathized with, or acted as chaplains to, the Basque nationalist forces had been shot, he wrote a full, reasoned and convincing report to the Pope.[5] He saw Pius XI on 24 November, and the subsequent papal representation to Franco was one reason why the shootings of Basque priests – there had already been fourteen of them – came to an end.[6]

All these priests had been shot precipitously without trial, and buried without coffins, funeral services, or official registration. One of those shot was a Carmelite monk, the rest parish priests; one of them, Father José Aristimuño, was an active Basque nationalist writer (though he had apparently opposed the alliance of Basque nationalism with the Left), and another a priest deservedly famous locally for his piety, Father Joaquín Arín, arch-priest of the little steel town of Mondragón.[7] Later, Cardinal Gomá tried to explain

1. *GD*, p. 267. 2. Cardinal Gomá, *El caso de España* (Pamplona, 1936), p. 12.

3. Lisón Tolosana, p. 232. Of course, as he dourly adds, by then many non-communicants might have fled or been shot. 4. See above, p. 286.

5. Letter published in *El clero vasco*, p. 365f. 6. See Monsignor Múgica's apologia, *Imperativos de mi conciencia* (Buenos Aires, 1945).

7. See Iturralde, vol. II, pp. 384f, 414. The names of the 14 were first published in nationalist Spain by Father Montero in 1961 (*op. cit.*, pp. 70, 77). Two subsequent shootings (Father Ituricastillo and Father Román de San José) occurred.

the deaths of these priests by saying that they had brought their troubles on themselves: a view which, expressed in an open letter to President Aguirre, brought another denunciation by Monsignor Múgica before the Pope. (He had already told Gomá to his face that Franco and his soldiers would have done better to have kissed the feet of the venerable Father Arín than to shoot him.)[1] A third letter, to Cardinal Pacelli, in March, would follow when the archbishop of Burgos, Manuel Castro, sought to excommunicate those priests of the Basque provinces who continued loyal to the Basque nationalist movement. Monsignor Múgica, each day more partisan, prevented that condemnation, and continued to support the Basque cause from Rome.

Similarly, the archbishop of Tarragona, Cardinal Vidal y Barraquer, saved from assassination by Companys, withdrew into a Swiss exile with a silence that everyone knew signified condemnation of atrocities on both sides in the war.[2] Finally, the crusaders had their disputes with those foreign catholics of distinction who, like Bernanos, Mauriac and Maritain ('the jew Maritain', nationalist propaganda inaccurately tried to call him) and those who, like the bishop of Dax in southern France, tried to mediate, or to arrange the exchange of prisoners. (The bishop of Dax went to Bilbao in September to try to comfort right-wing prisoners, who were confined in a horrible prison ship, more or less as hostages; subsequently, he sought to arrange an exchange. But the authorities in Salamanca could not accept that any authority of the church could have contact with the 'reds'.)

*

The nationalist leaders feared disturbances at the rear, and still caused to be shot many enemies of the régime as part of the *limpieza*, the 'cleaning' of Spain of its foreign imported diseases, including, haphazardly, prisoners. Of course, there were some guerrilla actions in, for example, Galicia or the Gredos mountains inspired by revolutionaries or government sympathizers who had hidden after the

1. Monsignor Múgica's second letter to the Pope is on p. 389 of *El clero vasco*, vol. II.

2. It was also said that the archbishop of Santiago de Compostela denounced the crimes of the falangists in Galicia.

nationalist conquest of the area concerned. Cantalupo, the first Italian ambassador to nationalist Spain, began his mission by asking for an end of the slaughter of prisoners. Franco told him that the shooting of prisoners had stopped.[1] That was not so. The failure of humane democracy in Spain had given power to one of the coldest-hearted men, a man intolerant of human foibles, humourless but able, calm and determined. One day that winter, Bernhardt was lunching with Franco (whom he admired). The question came up as to what to do with four militiawomen, captured, armed with rifles. Franco believed that all women captured in arms should be shot. 'There is nothing else to be done', he said, 'shoot them', without changing the tone that he would use for discussion of the weather.[2] To Colonel Faldella, chief of staff of the Italian troops who began to arrive in large numbers in the course of the winter, Franco made clear that his policy was not to defeat armies, but to conquer territory, 'accompanied by the necessary purges'.[3]

Two stages may be traced in the character of nationalist executions. At the beginning, shooting occurred without any judicial proceedings whatever. After a while, these terrible *autos-da-fé* of informal repression gave way to courts-martial, without, however, much greater guarantees for the victims, for the presiding judges were often young lieutenants who, after a while, thought no more of condemning men to death than 'shooting rabbits'.[4] The 'crimes' committed by some who were shot had been, it is true, sometimes odious; while some,

1. Cantalupo, p. 130.

2. Testimony of Johannes Bernhardt. The only persons to whom Franco showed mercy were his brother, the aviator, Ramón, sometime republican conspirator against the King, who was military attaché in Washington in 1936, and who delayed two months before throwing in his hand with the rebels; and Manuel Aznar, the editor of *El Sol* in Madrid, who had done much to help Azaña in 1931–2 and who, seen in militia uniform early in the war, later escaped to Saragossa, where he was arrested. Ramón Franco became commander of the air base at Palma, Aznar escaped being shot and, after much war journalism, ended up an ambassador of Spain. See García Venero, p. 243f. His military history, though Francoist, is the best of its kind. On good authority, Hills (p. 254) argued that Franco was inclined to shoot the leaders, pardon the followers, on the ground that the former should have known what they were doing.

3. O. Conforti, *Guadalajara* (Milan, 1967), p. 32.

4. As General Burguete said in a similar context in 1917. Cf. Dionisio Ridruejo, in Sergio Vilar, pp. 482–3.

such as republican officers, particularly of the civil guard, must have known that death was likely for them if they had opposed the rebellion. Spies and people who had taken part in church burnings, or killing in the republican zone, were likely to be executed in any such war. But the list of persons offered the last rites in the single gaol of Torrero, in Saragossa, is astonishing; not only were most people shot who had actively taken part in the republican war effort (for example, Colonels Encisco, one of the founders of the group of republican officers UMRA, and González Tablas, both captured at the front), but also Jaime Pérez, the grave digger of a small village (Blesa, Teruel), whose 'crime' was merely to have buried prominent people of the Right. Another man was shot because, when the legal records of Blesa were being burned, in the middle of the village street, he stirred the fire with a stick. Many complicated hatreds and conflicts of evidence came to light and were disposed of arbitrarily. Accusations might be made that so-and-so (a maid in a hotel, a bus conductor, or a soldier) had betrayed such-and-such a person of the Right. Once, a political commissar captured on the Teruel front was accused by a brother republican officer, also captured, of having killed a militiaman who had wanted to desert. The commissar had said that he had reported the lieutenant for theft, but nevertheless he was shot, telling the priest who gave him extreme unction that he blamed nobody for his death; society alone was evil.[1] Some unofficial executions also continued. The numbers of those who, in one way or another, were condemned and shot, continue to be difficult to estimate, but they could not have been much less than 1,000 a month, and sometimes, as when a republican city was captured, many more.

Innumerable republicans, revolutionaries and prisoners-of-war, Basque priests, separatists of every kind, found themselves in the crowded gaols of the nationalist rearguard, at the mercy of prison governors and warders who were often pedantic, frivolous, and cruel. Prisoners might be shot on the spot for giving a *viva* to the republic, they might be punished by having letters from their wives torn up, or be forbidden to receive letters from, or write to, fiancées. 'When hearts understand each other, bars do not exist', wrote one wife to

1. These and other instances can be seen in the diary of Father Gumersindo de Estella, in *El clero vasco*, vol. II, p. 289f.

a husband; the prison official asked the husband if he believed that any decent woman could write in such a manner.[1]

For those who escaped death or imprisonment, there was the risk, if the person concerned had been in any way a friend of the Left, of loss of employment. Civil servants had a hard time even if they had merely served the government between February and July 1936, unless they had taken a positive part at the time of the rising. Magistrates, schoolmasters, town clerks, even employees of the post office who continued in those tasks after July in the republican zone and were subsequently 'liberated' had, undoubtedly, a very difficult time securing their livelihood.[2]

A few voices were raised on behalf of toleration: one of them was Hedilla, the falangists' leader, in his Christmas speech of 1936: speaking to falangists who were concerned with investigations, he said, 'Prevent with all energy anyone from satisfying personal vengeances, ensure that nobody punishes or humiliates the man who, out of hunger or desperation, has voted for the Left. All of us know that, in many places, there were – and are – people of the Right who are worse than the reds ...' He ended this speech by opening his arms 'to the worker and to the peasant: let none of the social benefits achieved by the workers stay on the drawing board without producing an effect and without being converted into reality'.[3] But Hedilla was not in a position to put these fine thoughts into action. Furthermore, if Hedilla, and some others, such as Dionisio Ridruejo, the new head of the Falange in Valladolid, might think like that, many of his comrades in the Falange thought more of their requisitioned cars, their escorts (armed to the teeth), and their own political futures.

*

Economically, nationalist Spain was in fine fettle. Their peseta was quoted internationally at double the rate of that of the republic. They possessed nearly all the food that they needed, and were backed by most of the old Spanish financiers and bankers. Their credit continued good for essential supplies, including oil. During the winter of 1936–7, a new currency was printed by the firm of Gieselke in

1. See *El clero vasco*, vol. II, p. 144f.
2. Abella, p. 128.
3. Hedilla, in García Venero, *Falange*.

Leipzig, on the initiative of Johannes Bernhardt: this gradually superseded the old notes. It was backed simply by the will to victory on the nationalist side, and not at all by gold.[1] Control of prices was rendered formal on 13 October, and provincial committees to ensure this were established under the civil governors, with representatives of the Falange and the army. The branches of the National Bank of Spain at Burgos and at Seville acted as the central banks of the country. The funds available there to the rebel authorities (500 million pesetas) were supplemented by luxury taxes of 10 per cent on tobacco and wine, and also by a war tax on all incomes over 60,000 pesetas. Accounts of Popular Front parties were confiscated and the assets of some foreign companies taken over, if only temporarily. All debts owed to anyone in the republican zone were declared void, though debts, or interest owed there, had to be paid to the nationalist treasury. Externally, the nationalist peseta was fixed at 42.50 pesetas to the pound. These measures were much more effective than comparable measures in the republic but, even so, a modest inflation continued.[2]

It has been already suggested that, in August 1936, the area of Spain controlled by the rebels produced only about one-third of Spanish taxes. By December, the capture of San Sebastián and of the Tagus valley had increased the area 'liberated', but it still produced less than two-fifths of the national taxes before the war. At the same time, spending by the new authorities was running at a rate greater than a normal Spanish government in the whole country in time of peace. How was this money raised? First, the reliance on Germany and Italy for arms meant that the largest single item of essential equipment was secured, like oil, on credit (of course, that also had the effect of giving Germany and Italy, as well as Texas, a strong interest in Franco's victory). Second, subscription schemes played a great part, even if they sometimes degenerated into opportunities for intimidation. There were also constant appeals for gifts of jewellery, gold or cash: indeed, in November 1936, the authorities insisted on

1. Evidence of Johannes Bernhardt. The English firm of Bradbury and Wilkinson, which usually printed Spanish money, had been approached and refused. Thereafter, all currency in the republican zone was regarded as, and where necessary stamped as, invalid.

2. I am grateful to Mr Norman Cooper for help on these matters.

the exchange of all gold in private hands for cash.[1] It does not seem, however, that this raised much. But similarly, all foreign money in private hands or the hands of companies had theoretically to be handed over to a committee on foreign exchange. This stipulation affected foreign companies as well, except for German or Italian ones. Nearly all the money that was so collected in the early months of the civil war went into the hands of Bernhardt's HISMA. No money was allowed to be taken abroad by private citizens, interest on the national debt was suspended, while another scheme to raise money was the so-called *Plato Unico*, an innovation of Queipo de Llano's, copied from Germany, whereby clients at restaurants received one course, but paid for three, the balance being paid to the authorities. (It became in the end, however, merely a tax on meals.) Ineffective though this may have been, it was more successful than the days *Sin Postre* and *Sin Cigarro* (without pudding, and without tobacco).

Some of the subscription schemes had an odd air about them. What, for instance, is to be made of the appeals for money for a chalet for Colonel Cascajo, the tough political governor of Córdoba? Certainly, too, there must have been schemes which resulted in the immediate benefit of other officials, including perhaps the whisky-voiced Queipo de Llano.

No scheme for bonds was introduced in the course of the civil war. The consequence was that the rich, who invested little, merely increased their bank deposits. Private commerce naturally continued, though, since the shopkeeper class had been divided in politics before the civil war, many small undertakings and many small businesses were adversely affected. Booksellers, in particular, suffered, since books even distantly relating to forbidden themes were prohibited. This literary *limpieza* was extended to public libraries and schools. Huge fires were made of these books, many mistakes and countless arbitrary acts occurring, as usual on such demented occasions. Some blackmailing and protection rackets were carried on. Bars, cafés and other places of resort were supposed to close early,

1. In case the point was missed, one poster called out: 'Spaniard! Do not shake the hand of a man or woman who, after ten months of war, still wears a gold wedding ring which the country demands of her. That person is not a Spaniard.'

very early by Spanish standards, but these austere rules were more likely to be in force in the north than in Andalusia, where, in Queipo's unpredictable viceroyalty, a more free atmosphere prevailed. External commerce continued in the nationalist zone, but in January, each provincial governor was ordered to set up an import and export regulating committee to supervise all exports originating in areas under their control; another decree, of 22 January, forbade the export of all important goods (olive oil, wine, hides, wool, iron ore, pyrites, mercury, zinc and copper), unless approved by the newly organized National Committee on Foreign Commerce. This gave the nationalist authorities greater power over exports than any previous Spanish government, though, because of Queipo's presence, the export–import committee in Seville worked almost independently of Burgos.

Despite the Germans, trade with Britain continued to be important. Thus exports of sherry, other wines and pyrites would even show an increase in 1937 over 1935. A trade protocol confirming 'old links', in the most 'accidentalist' manner, was signed, in December 1936. Thereafter, a British commercial presence, in the shape of Arthur Pack, commercial counsellor at the British Embassy, was maintained in Burgos. This was an effective competitor to HISMA, and was more popular than the Italians' equivalent to HISMA, the Società Anonima Finanziere Nazionale Italiana (SAFNI), whose far from enterprising officials concentrated on trying to secure a favourable share when, and if, the nationalists should liberate the mercury mines in Almadén. Nevertheless, German–Spanish relations dominated the nationalist economy. For example, the British-owned Río Tinto Company, whose mines were occupied by the nationalist army in August (after months of labour disturbances), complained in mid-January that their copper was being requisitioned and sent to Germany. The Glasgow-owned Tharsis sulphur and copper mines similarly complained, as did the managers of iron and manganese mines in Morocco, in which there were substantial English interests. The British government subsequently complained to the German government, but the foreign ministry in Berlin were powerless, even ignorant, because of the influence acquired by Bernhardt and HISMA. There were some disputes between HISMA–ROWAK and the foreign ministry in January 1937, but Bernhardt came out of them, at the end, the master of Spanish trade, the nazi party achieving one more victory over the foreign ministry.[1]

One German assistance to General Franco remains to be noted: in December 1936 a huge Lorenz radio transmission plant arrived in Vigo from Hamburg, three times larger than any other in Spain. Henceforward, the voice of Salamanca and Burgos could be clearly heard throughout not only nationalist but republican Spain as well; and to begin with the voice of Queipo de Llano could be heard in particular: 'tonight I shall take a sherry and tomorrow I shall take Málaga'.[2]

1. See, for a discussion, Glenn T. Harper, *German Economic Policy in Spain* (The Hague, 1967), pp. 32–59.
2. See article *Cambio 16*, 15 September 1975.

30

Republican Spain – its political and regional fragmentation – Catalan industry – the communists and the republicans – the tribulations of Largo Caballero – republican reforms – a riot in Bilbao

In the winter of 1936–7, the republic seemed a united state only in the pages of the foreign press. Division characterized every institution and, while every party and every region seemed at loggerheads, there were also bitter quarrels within most parties. Of the parties, the communists, the new party of law and order, seemed both the most provocative and most self-confident of the different elements in the republican alliance. Their air of possessing the future, their dynamism, their political attitude of no-nonsense, and the prestige of Russian arms ('propaganda by sight', as González Peña put it) made them the obvious party for ambitious people to join. To the heavy tanks and fast fighters and bombers, there were soon added excellent new machine-guns. Many previously neutral army officers joined the communist party or came under their influence. Thus General Pozas, commander of the Army of the Centre, was already close to the party,[1] while Hidalgo de Cisneros, chief of the republican air force, who had never previously even thought about socialism, became a communist because he 'thought that they would contribute best to the struggle'.[2] The weakness, continued divisions, and ideological vagueness of the socialist party was another reason for communist success: old voters for that party joined the communists in droves. Largo Caballero might still be a socialist, but before the war, only a few months ago, had he not been the most pro-communist Spaniard of them all?

The anarchists, meantime, were falling out among themselves.

1. Zugazagoitia, p. 406.

2. Hidalgo de Cisneros, vol. II, pp. 317, 361. Barea (p. 720) wrote 'young officials of the various ministries . . . ambitious young men of the upper middle class who now declared themselves communists . . . because it meant joining the strongest group and having a share in its disciplined power'.

Many were critical of the entry of the four leaders into the government. Others criticized the government's move from Madrid, and accused their secretary-general, Horacio Prieto, of cowardice, for having let the ministers leave: an unjust accusation, since he had not been consulted. He resigned. That austere, proud, dry, uncompromising man was then replaced by Mariano Rodríguez Vázquez, an exuberant and athletic young building worker, with a powerful voice, who was the *protégé* of García Oliver.[1] Had Marx perhaps been right, some people asked, in suggesting that anarchism in practice degenerated into petty bourgeois behaviour?

Catalan socialists and communists were already almost indistinguishable in the PSUC. Elsewhere, many who did not formally join the party became in effect party members: among these were the deputies Margarita Nelken and Francisco Montiel (the treasurer of the UGT), Felipe Pretel (who also was a deputy commissar-general), and Edmundo Domínguez, the president of the Madrid *casa del pueblo* and secretary of the building workers. Many other members of the Madrid socialist party, left in the capital where the communists were, at this time, at their greatest strength, also accepted the language and style of communism, even if their loyalty to it was only skin-deep in many cases.[2] Communist numbers formally increased to 250,000 by the end of 1936.[3] Their championship of peasant ownership and opposition to revolution everywhere gained them ground. The Catalan writer, José Agustín Goytisolo, later wrote that his father joined the PSUC since, though a man of the Right, he wanted protection against the anarchists, who desired to take over the factory in which he worked as an engineer.[4] José Díaz was to tell the communist central committee in March that no less than 76,000 (almost a third) of party members were peasant proprietors and 15,485 (6.2 per cent) members of the urban middle class. There were thus more peasant proprietors than agricultural workers: an extraordinary situation. By June, the number of communists in Spain

1. C. Lorenzo, p. 155. 2. Castro Delgado, p. 475.

3. José Díaz, *Tres años de lucha* (reprinted Paris, 1970), pp. 289–90. The figure given by Díaz was 249,140, of which 87,660 (37.5 per cent) were industrial workers, 62,250 (25 per cent) agricultural workers, 7,045 (2.9 per cent) intellectuals and professional men.

4. In Sergio Vilar, *Protagonistas de la España democrática, la oposición a la Dictadura* (Paris, 1968).

would increase to nearly 400,000, of whom 22,000 were in Vizcaya and 64,000 in Catalonia. The united youth also increased greatly. So, too, did associates of communist front organizations, such as the 'Union of Girls', the 'Militia of Culture' and, above all, 'International Red Aid'. Against this vast increase in communist figures, the socialist party now numbered only 160,000, the FAI much the same number, and the anarchist youth about 100,000. The POUM may have had 60,000, at the outside. One reason for the communists' success was their formation in Catalonia of the GEPCI (Federation of Smallholders).[1] This organization infuriated the anarchists who realized it was a shelter for capitalists. Both anarchists and left-wing socialists also criticized the communist support for the small farmers of Valencia, many of whom had voted in the past for the Valencian autonomy movement, and some of whom had been members of the CEDA.[2] The communists claimed that over half their members were serving in the army: if true, that would mean that 130,000 out of the republican army of 360,000, at the end of March 1937, were communists.[3]

One use which the communist party made of its power was to establish itself deeply in the republican administration, to arrange that, through the agency of Orlov, the NKVD's tentacles should crowd out all private *checas*, both of the socialist-communist youth and others, and to prepare the way for the same onslaught on anti-Stalinist Marxists in Spain (such as the POUM) as was occurring in Russia.[4] The motives of the communists demand a little attention; for the POUM were not Trotskyists, Nin having broken with Trotsky on entering the Catalan government and Trotsky having spoken critically of the POUM. No, what upset the communists was the fact that the POUM were a serious group of revolutionary Spanish Marxists, well-led, and independent of Moscow. The POUM's leaders were all ex-communists, so that they could be regarded as traitors. In the whole of Spain, only the POUM newspaper *La*

1. Federación Catalana de Gremios y Entidades de Pequeños Comerciantes e Industriales. Figure given in *Frente Rojo*, 21 October 1937, qu. Bolloten, p. 83.

2. See Bolloten, pp. 192–3.

3. José Díaz, *Por la unidad, hacia la victoria*, speech of March 1937 (Barcelona, 1937), pp. 50–51.

4. Radek, Piatakov, and others were tried in Moscow between 23 and 30 January.

Batalla, and the CNT's *La Noche*, edited by members of the anarchist extreme group, the Friends of Durruti, mentioned the Purges in Moscow, for example; and the CNT eventually disavowed *La Noche*'s article. To most Spanish republicans, the Purges in Russia were allowed to seem an invention of fascist propaganda.[1]

The first move in the Spanish purge was the communist campaign to manoeuvre the POUM out of the Catalan *Generalidad* on the specious ground that the government should be one of unions, not parties. Nin, whose tenureship had been anyway controversial, at the councillorship of justice,[2] left on 16 December. The Catalan government was reconstituted, with the CNT getting four places (Herrera, Domenech, Isgleas, and Abad de Santillán) to the UGT's three (Comorera, Vidiella and Miguel Valdés – all PSUC members), the Esquerra's three (Tarradellas, Ayguadé, and Sbert), and the *rabassaires*' one (Calvet). Of these, Ayguadé, however, as councillor for the interior, was extremely close to the communists. The powerful figure of Comorera, secretary-general of the PSUC, came more and more to dominate this government. The anarchist Isgleas, nominally councillor for defence, did little.

The anarchists did not do much to defend the POUM, since they regarded the quarrel as just another internal Marxist squabble. Nin, though an ex-communist, was remembered as a renegade from the CNT. The Esquerra's lack of enthusiasm for the POUM was also well known; at the same time, the communists were by now (if only for the time being) Companys's close friends – not only against the revolution (POUM, CNT, and FAI), but against reaction. The latter needed to be guarded against as much as the former, since in the autumn of 1936, there was an attempt at a *coup d'état* by certain Catalan nationalists. The Estat Català leaders (most of whom were in Paris) had been expecting Franco's victory in Madrid.[3] They apparently wondered whether they might not try to negotiate an autonomous Catalonia in return for a recognition of Franco's victory

1. *La Batalla*, 27 January 1937, qu. Bolloten in Carr, *The Republic*; and *La Noche*, qu. Payne, *The Spanish Revolution*, p. 289.

2. For example Nin appointed as state prosecutor in Catalonia a semi *pistolero* named Balada 'who conducted trials as if he had been a slaughterman'. See Benavides, *Guerra y revolución en Cataluña*, p. 226.

3. For this party, see above, p. 132.

throughout the rest of Spain. The plotters also tried to gain the interest of certain disaffected anarchists. The story leaked out, Andreu Reverter, chief of police in the *Generalidad*, was found to be involved, as was Juan Casanovas, president of the *Generalidad*. The matter was hushed up: Reverter was arrested, on grounds of corruption; and Casanovas was allowed to leave quietly if hastily for Paris. Reverter was also secretly released, and was never heard of again. He may have been shot. He was replaced by a friend of Companys's, Martí Rouret, who himself soon gave way to a communist, Rodríguez Salas.[1]

This crisis anyway testified to the malaise between the central government and Barcelona. As has been seen, Catalonia had already profited from the military rising in July 1936 to carry out what had been in effect its own *coup d'état* over Madrid. An unresolved, and important, problem related to the position of Catalan industries, particularly war industries: the government of Catalonia insisted that the central republican government should deal only with them, and not directly with the industries concerned. Yet the *Generalidad* was far from efficient, and the needs of war were pressing.[2]

Thus the situation in Catalonia was one of unparalleled complexity: Companys and his friends in the Esquerra saw eye-to-eye with both the central government and the communists about how to deal with the anarchists and the POUM, on the need to end the terror in the rearguard, and on the desirability of ensuring state intervention in industry, rather than workers' control. They were opposed to the central government's (and the communists') ideas for centralizing the war effort. Beneath Companys's troubled eyes, in the meantime, the anarchists and the communists carried on daily clashes in the press. For example, *Solidaridad Obrera* wrote on 19 December that 'the scolding refrain [of the communists] "first win the war" pains us. That is a dessicated slogan, without substance, nerve or fruit. First win the war and make the revolution at the same time,

1. The Estat Catalá plot of November 1936 remains an obscure matter. Reverter is said by some to have been shot in prison. See Benavides, *Guerra*, p. 244, where it is said that Reverter was executed on the ground of having had his mother-in-law shot. See Payne, *The Spanish Revolution*, and Martínez Bande, *La invasión de Aragón*, p. 296.

2. See Azaña, *Obras*, vol. III, *Articulos sobre la guerra de España*, p. 508.

for the war and the revolution are cosubstantial, like sun and light.'

The communist plan was first to restore the power of the *Generalidad* against the anarchists and POUM, then to help the central government take over the *Generalidad.* Thus, in the winter of 1936, they agitated for the dissolution of the revolutionary committees, so as to place all executive organs of government under the *Generalidad* – in particular the control patrols under which innocent name anarchist leaders such as Dionisio Eroles, José Asens and Aurelio Fernández still terrorized Barcelona. Suspicion between the anarchists and the communists became acute in Barcelona at the start of January, after the latter persuaded Companys to appoint their secretary-general, Comorera, as food minister. Comorera abolished the bread committees, led by the anarchists, which had hitherto supervised the food supply of Barcelona. For a time, there was no state intervention in the food supply in Catalonia. Even rationing was delayed. This brought much hardship, since the price of bread had gone up far more than wages. There followed a bread shortage, partly caused by the inadequate harvest of the previous year, but attributed by the anarchists to Comorera's inefficiency. Comorera, however, gave out that his CNT predecessor, Domenech, had been far more incapable.[1] (The general price-index had gone up 40 per cent since June, and was increasing every month: 1937 would be a year of severe inflation.)[2] A poster war ensued, the anarchist posters demanding Comorera's resignation, while PSUC posters called for 'Less talk! Less committees! More bread!' and even 'All power to the *Generalidad*'. Meantime, bread queues, of 300 or 400 persons, outside closed bakeries, became a daily sight. Sometimes, when no bread could be distributed, assault guards had to disperse the queues with rifle butts.[3] All anarchist leaders, including the ministers in both the central government and the Catalan government, were disgusted by the communists' acceptance of the economy of controlled capitalism, but acquiesced.[4]

The 'normalization' of life in Barcelona (backed by both communists and Companys) was nevertheless a relief to many even of the working class. The sub-secretary of justice, Quero Morales, recaptured the Palace of Justice from the revolutionary tribunal headed

1. Peirats, vol. II, p. 163. 2. See below, p. 971. 3. Borkenau, p. 185.
4. See Juan López's speech on 27 May 1937 (qu. Peirats, vol. II, pp. 248–52).

by the bloodthirsty lawyer Samblancat, which had been there since July. Sbert, councillor for education in the *Generalidad*, had begun to reorganize primary schools on a conventional basis. Further change was similarly avoided in secondary and higher education due to the efforts of Professor Bosch Gimpera, at the University of Barcelona. There was also a slow re-establishment of municipal life, councils being named in place of the revolutionary committees, with an approximate ratio of three delegates for the anarchists, three for the non-revolutionary Left, and two for the PSUC (communists), with occasionally a place for the POUM.[1]

At the same time, on the national level, Largo Caballero persuaded the new anarchist minister of industries, Peiró, to cease pressing for the further collectivization of industries – on the ground that that would frighten foreign capital, though, of course, by the winter of 1936–7 most of the Catalan economy was collectivized, with factories working under the councils set up in October.[2] Many small shops had also been abolished in the interests of rationalization. Nevertheless, the system did not work as the Decree of October had provided.[3] Illegal collectivizations continued and many agreements for compensation were left unpaid. The general councils regarded as so necessary were not always set up. Many small undertakings demanded state help to get them out of economic difficulties. It was not altogether surprising that industrial output had dropped a third since June, and was continuing to drop.[4] The explanation of this was not primarily bad, or inexperienced, management: it was shortage of raw materials and of markets too. Anarchists were willing also to admit that the revolution had brought problems they had not dreamt of: the FAI leader, Abad de Santillán (then economic councillor in the *Generalidad*) wrote candidly:

> We had seen in the private ownership of the means of production, of factories, of means of transport, in the capitalist apparatus of distribution,

1. Bosch Gimpera, *Memorandum No. 1*, sent to the author, 1962.

2. Peirats, vol. II, pp. 262–3. 3. See above, p. 437.

4. See Bricall, *Generalitat*, p. 48. Bricall's table gives 100 as January 1936, 98 as June, 63 for November, and 69 for December. Other tables in this study suggest a drop in the industrial use of electricity in Catalonia from 40 million Kwh in June to 33 million in December (30 million in March), though household use of electricity was less markedly down in January 1937 as compared with 1936 (10.7 million Kwh in January 1936, 9.7 million in January 1937).

the main cause of misery and injustice. We wished the socialization of all wealth so that not a single individual would be left out of the banquet of life. We have now done something, but we have not done it well. In place of the old owner, we have substituted a half-dozen new ones who consider the factory, the means of transport which they control, as their own property, with the inconvenience that they do not always know how to organize . . . as well as the old.[1]

Though some new measures in social security were worked out – including accident and illness insurance, more rational pensions, and family allowances – the industrial syndicalism of Barcelona kept, unlike the rural anarchists, to individual wages, and did not experiment with family wages. These wages probably increased, it is true, in late 1936 by about a third over July. But the effect was ruined by the inflation, due to a fall in production, shortage of credit, as well as an influx of refugees from Castile and Aragon.[2] Later, anarchist ministers would complain bitterly that their ideas were rejected in the cabinet by the communists and republicans. Peiró, at the ministry of industry, said that the communists refused him money, opposed his decrees of collectivization, and thwarted him at every turn. On the other hand, they did prevent the return to private ownership of many enterprises already collectivized.[3]

The problems of anarchism at war could not have been predicted, nor could they be resolved. Consider energy: before the war, Barcelona's coal came mostly from Asturias. Now Asturias was cut off. England was a major exporter of coal: but, after the launching in September of the new nationalist cruiser, the *Canarias*, the republic had no longer command of the sea. Shortage of coal necessitated a reconsideration of transport and other industrial policies. Was it necessary to run as many trains as before the war? The CNT thought that it was. Yet by November they had had to modify that programme severely.[4] Similar problems affected the Catalan textile industry. Before the war, Catalonia had bought its cotton from Egypt,

1. Diego Abad de Santillán, *After the Revolution* (New York, 1937), p. 121.

2. Table in Bricall, pp. 116–17. Taking 1930 as 100, January 1936 was 161.5, June 162.6 and subsequent months were: July 165; August 167.9; September 172.9; October 182.3; November 191.1; December 197.6; January 1937, 209.7; February 227.1; and March 242.2. The spiral continued frighteningly throughout the year. See below, p. 973. Bricall's figures are for Catalonia.

3. For this debate, see C. Lorenzo, pp. 257–8.

4. See Leval, pp. 277ff.

the US, and Brazil; the wool it used came partly from Castile. Now the US and Brazil were inaccessible, the other side of Gibraltar, while Castile was mostly in the hands of Franco. Ships, mainly British ships, could still come from Egypt but even the Mediterranean was becoming less and less safe for republican merchantmen.

Catalonia had now three main types of management in industry; first, enterprises where the proprietor remained theoretically in his old place, but where the workers had elected a committee controlling the business. Most firms of this category were foreign-owned. Secondly, there were enterprises where the old proprietor had been replaced directly by an elected committee of workers. Thirdly, there were the 'socialized' enterprises, in which an effort had been made to rearrange the industry concerned. An example of this was the wood industry of Catalonia in which, under the aegis of the anarchist syndicate of wood workers, all the activities had been unified, from the cutting of the tree to the sale of the plank. But this gives a false impression of simplicity. In all large industries, and in industries important for the war, a state representative sat on the committee. He would be responsible for controlling credit, and sometimes raw materials. His role became more and more important, so that, in some enterprises (particularly the munitions factories), something close to nationalization would soon be achieved. Then the Decree of 24 October had given its approval to the survival of those private enterprises which employed less than a hundred workers. That meant the vast majority of Catalan enterprises. Despite the part played by the anarchist Juan Fábregas in its authorship, the real consequences of the Decree were to confirm the role of the petty bourgeoisie in business and, more important, to give the state an increasing responsibility for industry.[1]

The most important industry in Catalonia was, of course, the textile one (employing some 180,000 workers, over twice as many as any other single industry). Most factories were small. An effort was made to socialize this (that is, rationalize it under a single directorate), but many private undertakings survived, as well as some collectivized factories which refused to collaborate with any national, or regional,

1. Bricall indicates that the building industry, related to the wood trade, had dropped to 32 points in January 1937, in relation to 100 on the index in January 1936, and 69 in June.

plan. Meantime, the shortage of raw materials and of markets caused a three- or even a two-day week to be sometimes adopted (though, if that happened, workers would receive a four-day wage). An effort was made to standardize wages, resulting in an all-round cut, for ordinary workers as well as technicians, though the CNT explained that was counter-balanced by the new forty-hour week, the establishment of a fixed and permanent salary, and the abolition of piece-work.[1] But no effort was made to equalize wages between men and women. The industry seems to have been run by a veritable fiesta of committees organized in the pyramidical form beloved of the CNT: committee of shop floor, of zone, region and marketing, all elected by plenary assemblies of workers. This industry at the beginning had no governmental representation and refused it. The *Generalidad* responded by going to the strange length of importing material from France for the uniforms of their new army.[2] It was hardly surprising that this revolutionary textile industry should be producing less than half in January 1937 than it was in January 1936.[3]

As for the shipping companies, most of the larger ones (the Transatlantic Company, the Mediterranean Company) were now run by committees of both CNT and UGT. The Transatlantic Company had, in addition to three members each of these two unions on its committee, one representative each from the *Generalidad* and from the central government. The anarchist transport workers ran the trains, the underground and the bus services, though the UGT had representation on the committees of the two Catalan rail networks. On the other hand, the banks, after being run for a while by socialist bank clerks, were taken over by the *Generalidad*, while the telephone company was run by a committee of workers in each exchange.

Another important group of enterprises in Catalonia were the metallurgical plants. Some of these were foreign-owned, and, therefore, were run by workers' committees without any long-term collectivization. Others were collectivized, but not socialized, that is, they remained isolated enterprises – except, admittedly, for those needed

1. See *L'Oeuvre constructive de la révolution espagnole* (November 1936).

2. Semprún-Maura, p. 94.

3. Bricall's figure (*op. cit.*, p. 79): with January 1936 as 100, the figures were 71 in June and 60, 42, 54, 58, 41, 56, 49 and 40 in subsequent months, to February 1937.

by the war – and were, therefore, subject to interference by, in succession, the committee of militias, the *Generalidad* and the central government. Thus, the government delegate played a determining part in the Hispano–Suiza works, where armoured lorries, ambulances, hand grenades and machine-gun rests, among other items, were produced.[1] This was the only branch of industry which, in the winter of 1936, registered an increase in overall production in relation to the previous year.[2] The manufacture of machinery showed the sharpest increase.

Outside Catalonia, the central government was pursuing a similar policy. They sought to bring all major factories under state supervision, whether nationalized or privately managed. To ensure this, credit was made difficult for anarchist factories, and many other difficulties were put in their way by the government. Some mills, therefore, had to stop production, when cotton was exhausted. This occurred even though an anarchist, Peiró, was nominally at the ministry of industry. Peiró's plans for collectivization were rejected by Largo Caballero, and republican industry remained throughout the winter of 1936–7 unstandardized. Some factories were nationalized, some socialized and rationalized, some were in private hands, and some were in the hands of workers' committees, while both of the latter two categories had state representatives within them. All were short of raw material, spare parts and, except for war industries, markets: while Peiró found 11,000 demands for credit on his acceptance of office.[3]

At Valencia, arrangements in industry were more simple. Nearly all the factories and shops were directly managed by their workers. But the effect of the government's move to Valencia had been to give them, nevertheless, much more political control over the Levante, which, before November, had been almost independent. Ricardo Zabalza, who had led the socialist agrarian trade union (FNTT) in 1934, took over as civil governor and showed himself a decided cen-

1. Souchy, *Colectivizaciones*, p. 71.

2. Bricall (p. 79) has with January 1936 as 100, 67 for June 1936 and 85, 76, 96, 108, 70, 123 and 119 for subsequent months, these figures being kept up until the spring with its political crises. Chemicals were down by nearly 50 per cent in the winter of 1936–7 in relation to 1935–6.

3. Peirats, vol. II, p. 261.

tralist. The semi-independent committee of Valencia was stifled by the central government and it, and its most prominent member, the revolutionary Lieutenant Benedito, passed out of history after January 1937. Mayors began again, as in the past, to be nominated by the civil governor. Centralizing civil governors were appointed in as many places as possible.

In Madrid, hostility between the communists and anarchists had different implications. On the one hand, it was an aspect of the quarrel between Madrid and Valencia, and, on the other, of a dispute between the communists and Largo Caballero. After the battle of the Corunna high road, General 'Kléber' argued that the republic should attack, the International Brigades leading the offensive. But here 'Kléber' came up against the distrust which he had inspired in Miaja and other Spanish commanders. Largo Caballero, jealous of the prestige of La Pasionaria and other communists who had remained in Madrid during the fighting, even suspected that 'Kléber' wished to use the International Brigades to stage a communist *coup d'état* in the capital. The anarchists of Madrid supported Miaja, and indirectly, for the first time, Largo Caballero. Even so, 'Kléber's' tactical ideas might have triumphed had he not incurred the suspicion of André Marty. As a result, 'Kléber' left his command and temporarily went to live in a small hotel in Valencia. Thereafter, Miaja's reputation, whatever his real effect on the battles, grew daily. He was becoming extraordinarily popular in Madrid – and knew it. 'When I am in my car,' he told Zugazagoitia, 'women shout to me: "Miaja! Miaja! There goes Miaja!" I greet them and they greet me. They are happy and so am I.'[1] Miaja was not a political general. He did once tell Pietro Nenni that he liked the communists better than the socialists, because they were resolute: 'The socialists talk first, then act. If the communists talk, they do so after acting. Militarily speaking, it is an advantage.'[2] Later, it was suggested that he had become a party member. Actually, Miaja had the membership cards of all the political parties left in Madrid, including the joint youth movement, despite his sixty years;[3] and Azaña recalled him saying a few years before that, though he was certainly a republican, he could not work with socialists: they should all be shot.[4]

1. Zugazagoitia, p. 197. 2. Nenni, p. 171.
3. Malinovski, in *Bajo la bandera*, p. 21. 4. Azaña, vol. IV, p. 589.

The 'Spanish Lenin', meantime, was changing his whole view of politics. As Prime Minister, Largo Caballero had restored the authority of the state and, with the conventional General Asensio as under-secretary of war, had begun the reorganization of the army. The communists and the united youth, dominated by the communists, had helped him into power, and he had profited from the communist party's organizing skill. Still, he was disillusioned with communism. This may have begun when the communists, like Miaja, profited so greatly from the defence of Madrid. It did not help certainly that, on 21 December, Stalin sent a letter to him full of patronizing advice: the parliamentary method might be more revolutionarily effective in Spain than in Russia; even so, the Russian experience might be useful – hence the dispatch of certain 'military comrades' who had received orders to follow Spanish instructions and act as advisers. Stalin begged Largo Caballero 'as a friend' to report how successful the advisers had been, and even to say whether he found the ambassador, Rosenberg, satisfactory. The letter ended with the advice that peasants' and foreigners' property should be respected, that partisan forces should be formed behind the nationalist lines, that the small bourgeoisie should not be attacked, and that Azaña and the republicans should not be cold-shouldered.[1] But the culmination of Largo Caballero's resentment against Russia came in January when the Russian ambassador, Rosenberg, tried to influence him to dismiss General Asensio and make a number of other arrangement which the communists wanted. After two hours of animated conversation in which Alvarez del Vayo, as foreign minister, had also been present, Largo expostulated:

> Out you go, out! You must learn, Señor Ambassador, that the Spaniards may be poor and need aid from abroad, but we are sufficiently proud not to accept that a foreign ambassador should try and impose his will on the head of the Spanish government. And as for you, Vayo, you ought to

1. This letter was published for the first time in the *New York Times* on 4 June 1939, by the by then anti-communist Araquistain, ambassador in Paris, 1936–7. When this letter arrived in Largo Caballero's office, no one could read the illegible signatures. Codovilla, the Comintern agent, was summoned. He could not read the signatures either. It took a member of Rosenberg's staff of the Russian embassy to decipher the names of Stalin, Molotov and Voroshilov (Gorkin, *Canibales politicos*, p. 85).

remember that you are a Spaniard, and minister of foreign affairs of the republic, instead of arranging to agree with a foreign diplomat to exert pressure on your own Prime Minister.[1]

How ironic that the old trade unionist should reach a watershed in his political life in order to defend an officer who, though able, was deeply conservative! There were also similar scenes between Largo and the two communist ministers in the cabinet.[2]

Rosenberg in consequence soon left Spain (to be judicially murdered in Russia, along with most of his colleagues in the Russian diplomatic service). He was succeeded by the meeker figure of his chargé d'affaires, Gaikins. But it was evident, in early 1937, that the communists were dissatisfied with the Prime Minister whom they had previously supported so strongly. He refused to merge the socialist and the communist parties as the two youth movements had been merged, and as the communists were demanding all that winter. Marcelino Pascua, the Spanish ambassador in Moscow, even came to Spain with another message from Stalin, specially to press the idea of fusion. Largo still refused, though he was told that Stalin himself wanted him to continue as the leader of the united movement. Thus Largo was beginning to fight back against the communists in the winter of 1936–7, and they in turn to intrigue against him. Largo contemplated the dismissal of Alvarez del Vayo on grounds of disloyalty, obtained Azaña's support for that course, but hesitated and then withdrew at the last minute, though his words to Azaña had been strong: 'One of my ministers has betrayed me. He is a socialist. He is the foreign minister.'[3]

The trouble with complaining to Azaña was that the political moderation of the communist party in Spain had brought them a working alliance with the liberal republicans. The policy of Azaña and Giral, for example, insofar as one existed apart from the general aim of winning the war, was much the same as that of the communist party, in respect of both military strategy and economics. It was thus in language almost identical with that of La Pasionaria that Azaña, in one of his rare public appearances, at Valencia on 21 January,

1. This conversation was plainly heard outside the door by Largo's staff. See Ginés Ganga, in *Hoy*, 5 December 1942, qu. Bolloten, p. 273. See also Largo Caballero, p. 195.

2. Prieto speech in Mexico, 1946, qu. Bolloten, p. 223.

3. Prieto, *loc. cit.*

demanded 'a war policy . . . with only one expression – discipline and obedience to the responsible government of the republic'. Equally, the Prietista socialists, including Prieto himself, and the finance minister Negrín, looked to the communists as useful allies against not only Largo Caballero, whom they had so long disliked, but the whole policy of immoderate revolution, which they hated. They hated the POUM and the anarchists as much as the communists did. Furthermore, Russian military aid, and the incomparable *esprit* of the International Brigades, sustained the myth of 'Popular Front-ism', which they also continued to uphold. This working alliance between Azaña, Prieto and the communists might not be very profound, and it might not last long, but, as will be seen, it was enough to ruin Largo Caballero. At this time Prieto, to his subsequent embarrassment, even spoke in favour of the merger of the socialist and communist parties.[1]

Social and other reforms, Azaña and the communists could now agree, should await victory. It was the adoption of that policy which gave the communist party much of its attraction. At a national youth congress in Valencia in January, the secretary-general of the socialist-communist youth, Santiago Carrillo (the 'chrysalis in spectacles', as his enemies called him: he was only twenty years old), said, 'We are not Marxist youth. We fight for a democratic parliamentary republic.' *Solidaridad Obrera* named this 'reformist quackery': 'If the united socialist youth are neither socialist, communist, nor Marxist, what are they?' In fact, the united youth had not realized that its leaders had gone over so wholeheartedly to communism, and when it did, there were complaints – the secretaries in both Valencia and Asturias declining seats on the movement's national committee as a result.[2]

Yet when all these quarrels are understood, and this increasing stranglehold over the republic exercised by the opportunistic communists, Spanish and foreign, is taken into account, there were many ways in which this government of Largo Caballero was fumbling towards a better Spain. The war might be taking up most of the republican resources, but attention was being paid to education as never before. The number of new schools opened in 1937 would approach

1. Largo Caballero, p. 225.

2. See the letters quoted by Bolloten, *op. cit.*, p. 118. The Asturian united youth reached a working alliance afterwards with the anarchist youth.

1,000, many in the confiscated houses of the rich, and church schools had been converted into state or national schools ('New United Schools'). In 1937, there were to be 2,000 military schools, at which about 100,000 previously illiterate militiamen would learn to read.[1] In the agrarian collectives, there were usually several more teachers than before July 1936. A serious effort was made to insist on education for all, and most observers noticed that there were fewer children loitering disconsolately round the home than there were before. Several vocational or technical schools were founded, such as the agricultural University of Moncada (Valencia), where some three hundred pupils learned better agricultural techniques.[2] According to an anarchist account, there were 116,846 children in school in Barcelona in July 1937 compared with 34,431 in July 1936.[3]

In health, the first steps towards the socialization of medicine were also undertaken. The work of the anarchist councillor for health in Barcelona, García Birlán, and the director of health services whom he named, Dr Félix Martí Ibáñez, was outstanding. The 1,000 doctors of Barcelona, the 3,200 nurses, the 330 midwives, the 600 dentists, worked well and imaginatively.[4] Furthermore, the services offered, including operations, were free. Despite the demand for doctors and medical services at the front, there were over a thousand more beds for tubercular patients in the republic than in 1936. Later in 1937, compulsory inoculation for smallpox, diphtheria, and typhoid was instituted. By the end of 1937, there were as many child-welfare centres in republican Spain as there had been before the war in all Spain.[5] The devoted work of the foreign medical-aid organizations also radiated throughout the republic, setting new standards of hygiene and efficiency. Though García Birlán soon left the *Generalidad*, Federica Montseny, another dedicated and well-informed anarchist, remained as republican minister of health until well into 1937. Meantime, at the front, doctors such as Trueta, and the Canadian Bethune, introduced new methods of blood transfusion and treatment of wounds, which were to constitute a medical revolution.[6] One further innovation was that abortions were legalized by decree on 13 January – although they remained forbidden after three months of preg-

1. Figures in *Education in Republican Spain, 1938*. 2. Leval, p. 169.
3. *Libro de Oro de la Revolución Española*, qu. C. Lorenzo, p. 115.
4. Leval, p. 296. 5. Peirats, vol. III, p. 187. 6. See below, p. 550.

nancy – and such operations were carried out with proper medical help.[1]

Marriages were swift: in *Solidaridad Obrera* of 29 December 1936, the following paragraph appeared:

On Sunday morning, in the presence of numerous comrades, a simple and emotional scene occurred in the transport union, more for its libertarian significance than its social aspect. Two young people came together by free and spontaneous decision . . . Juan Freixas and Tomasa Costa . . . This union had one bond: love . . . the voice of our director, Liberio Callejas, sealed the union when he told them, 'In the name of liberty, stay united!'

Life in the republican prisons of the central zone, on the other hand, was no better than it was in those of Franco. Old gaols, such as that at Montjuich in Barcelona or the prison ships in the harbour, were overcrowded, the food scanty (rice and a piece of bread for lunch and for dinner, a little hot water with drops of coffee and perhaps another piece of bread at daybreak), and washing conditions primitive. As with the republicans and revolutionaries in Franco's gaols, many of the prisoners conducted themselves with exemplary heroism; and as in Franco's prisons, the gaolers were often petty, brutal and arbitrary. Nor were the people's tribunals as yet more honest courts of law than Franco's courts-martial were: prisoners were given little time to prepare their defence, they often had to accept a defence lawyer whom they had never known before the day of the trial, and the tribunal was still often composed of prejudiced persons themselves swayed by the enthusiasm of a crowd who might clap every time a death sentence was announced. In December, it is true, a governmental order announced that no one was to be executed before the sentence had been approved by four judges and afterwards by the cabinet, and gradually this order came to be carried out. Nevertheless, the shooting of 'rightists', officers, voters for the CEDA, priests, conspirators and innocent people continued during the winter of 1936–7 throughout republican Spain, though the role of the private gang became less, and that of the courts and of the government more pronounced. The main difference between the two

1. See the editorial of *Solidaridad Obrera* on 13 January 1937 (qu. Peirats, vol. II, pp. 116–17).

Spains on this score was that gradually the treatment of prisoners improved in the republic, the government being desirous of introducing humanity as well as regularity. In Franco's Spain any such desire is hard to detect. Melchor Rodríguez, a humane anarchist whom García Oliver appointed to be director-general of prisons, had no equivalent in Burgos or Salamanca. A self-taught philosopher, fearless and hostile to all terrorism, Rodríguez gained considerable moral authority. But the nomination subsequently led to the opening by the communists of their own gaols, without authorization or supervision, under the aegis of José Cazorla, the communist youth leader responsible for public order in Madrid.

García Oliver, the anarchist minister of justice, stood behind most such legal changes for the better. He made, on 31 January 1937, the most remarkable speech of any law minister at any time:

> Justice [he announced] must be burning hot, justice must be alive, justice cannot be restricted within the bounds of a profession. It is not that we definitely despise books and lawyers. But the fact is that there were [*sic*] too many lawyers. When relations between men become what they should be, there will be no need to steal and kill. For the first time, let us admit, here in Spain, that the common criminal is not an enemy of society. He is more likely to be a victim of society. Who is there who says he dare not go out and steal if driven to it to feed his children and himself? Do not think that I am making a defence of robbery. But man, after all, does not proceed from God, but from the cave, from the beast. Justice, I firmly believe, is so subtle a thing that to interpret it, one has only need of a heart.[1]

When he took office, he later said, there were no organs of justice. '. . . everyone administered their own justice. That was what has been called the *paseo*. I call it justice administered directly by the country in the complete absence of the traditional organs of justice.' Despite this unpromising beginning, he proceeded to establish a new code of laws. On 12 December, black-marketeering was made punishable by imprisonment. On the 22nd, a decree annulled all penalties for crimes committed before 15 July. On 28 December, a number of labour camps were created for nationalist prisoners – 'work and do not despair' being the motto over the gates. This innovation was an

1. Qu. 'Berryer', *Red Justice* (London, 1937).

improvement on the gaols. But libertarian anarchists of the past would have turned in their graves, particularly at the German-sounding motto. Court fees were also abolished, including fees for barristers. On 4 February, a decree gave women for the first time a legal identity, and another recognized as legal marriages the 'free unions' of militiamen killed at the front.[1] Anarchists had always believed in 'free union' as opposed to conventional marriage, with its virtual sale of brides in poorer places; but not in easy divorce. Federica Montseny, for example, did not oppose the family and she thought that children were often better educated at home than at school. She did believe in birth control, though thought that most women would be against it.[2]

*

The isolated northern republican territories remained apart from the quarrels of the south. They also remained remote from each other. Each of the three regions (Asturias, Santander, Vizcaya) had their own money, and even frontiers 'much more difficult to cross than an international one'. Once when General Llano de la Encomienda, the commander-in-chief in the north, desired to cross from Asturias into Santander, for both of which he was responsible, his car was searched and a cheese confiscated.[3]

In the coal mines of Asturias, management was in the hands of local councils, elected in the pits, themselves supervised by a labour committee, dependent on the provincial *junta*. The fishermen of Gijón were organized in an anarchist collective. The port at Santander was run by the socialists. In the Basque country, industry carried on normally. But each of these areas had their own difficulties. A manifesto issued in January by the provincial secretaries of the UGT and CNT in León, Asturias, and Palencia, vigorously attacked 'bureaucracy', indicating by its tone the menace that this was becoming even in such a small socialist state as Asturias. Asturias

1. García Oliver's speech, 27 May 1937 (Peirats, vol. II, pp. 252–8); see Cabanellas, vol. II, p. 1118.

2. Interview with Kaminski, *Ceux de Barcelone*, pp. 68, 74.

3. Report of Colonel Buzón Llanes, head of the 2nd section of the staff of the Army of the North, 21 November 1937, qu. Martínez Bande, *La guerra en el norte*, p. 247.

meantime was also still locked in a chronic battle against its own capital, Oviedo, still held by Aranda.

The Basque nationalists were trying to preserve their small territory from the extreme solutions of republican Spain. But it became more and more difficult to do so. On 4 January, a series of riots followed a German air attack on Bilbao carried out by the Condor Legion's Junkers 52. Two of these were shot down by Russian fighters. Two Germans parachuted to the ground. One was killed by a crowd infuriated by this wanton attack. The other was saved from a similar death by a Russian pilot. In the meantime, Bilbao turned mad with anger. The rage of the people was exacerbated by hunger, since few food ships had recently managed to penetrate the increasingly effective nationalist blockade. A furious mob, supported later by a battalion of UGT militia, marched to the buildings where the political prisoners of Bilbao were being kept. About 208 prisoners were killed in three separate gaols.[1] A similar outrage occurred, for a similar reason, in the prison ship *Alfonso Pérez*, off Santander: nearly 200 falangists, Carlists and supporters of the Right died there.[2]

Relations between the Basques and the central government were distant. No doubt the Basques might have tried to surrender on favourable terms if the republican government had not accepted their demands for autonomy. The visit of the republican fleet to Basque waters in September had helped morale and also brought arms. Later, though some Russian and further arms supplies did go to the north, they were irregular.[3] Aguirre had made himself commander-in-chief of the army in 'Euzkadi' – some 30,000 men – for all the world as if he were the head of an independent state's independent army; but Largo Caballero considered that force to be part of the republican army of the north, including the Basques with Asturias and Santander, nominally commanded by General Llano de la Encomienda, the somewhat reluctant victor of Barcelona in July. In 'Euzkadi', Basque was a joint official language with Spanish. Alone in the Basque provinces were the churches open in republican Spain. 'Euzkadi' remained dominated by a catholic and conservative

1. Del Burgo, p. 700.

2. García Venero, *Falange*, p. 151n; see Southworth, *Anti-Falange*, p. 124, and Steer, p. 110.

3. R. Salas, vol. I, pp. 369–70.

nationalist party which had been driven by calculation, circumstances and accident to ally with the revolutionary Left republic. Many Basques – including some sometime Basque nationalists – were fighting for Franco, and 'Euzkadi' only comprised Vizcaya. Most of Alava and Guipúzcoa were already Francoist. But morale was high in 'Euzkadi'. There were no problems with the communists, and the local communist leader, Astigarribía, was virtually a Basque nationalist. One Basque minister, it is true, Espinosa, of the Republican Union, was treacherously flown to the nationalists by a disloyal pilot and there executed in the course of the winter. Otherwise, forgetting a shortage of food, it would have sometimes been difficult to realize that the Basque country was at war.[1] But it was, as events were soon to show; and the poor production figures of the Basque arms industries would soon tell against the little republic.

*

In republican propaganda, two pictures were counterposed as if there were always potentially a civil war within the civil war: one picture, for foreigners, depicted Spanish democracy struggling against international fascism; the second picture, for consumption at home, showed the Spanish people at one pace only away from a new world: victory would lead to *vida nueva*.[2] The conflict was not easily resolved.

1. This comment ignores the unsuccessful Basque offensive in Alava mounted by General Llano de la Encomienda in December: it was held off by Colonels Iglesias and Alonso Vega. For the Basque experiment, see Stanley Payne, *Basque Nationalism* (Reno, 1975).

2. See for example 'Auca de la Lluita i del Milicia', No. 1, Edició del Comissariat de Propaganda de la Generalitat de Catalunya.

31

The people's army – communist influence – the Mixed Brigades – the communists in the air force – the navy – the revolution in field dressings

BY December 1936, the reorganization of the republican army was far advanced. The remains of the old army had been effectively merged with the militias, in the self-sufficient Mixed Brigade, two or three of which were supposed to form a division.[1] This was a feat of organization for which General Asensio, under-secretary of war, should take the credit. Several thousand regular officers, either from the retired or the active list in 1936, were, or were soon to be, implicated in the new army.[2]

This was said to number some 350,000 in the winter of 1936–7: of whom 85,000 were in the centre, 40,000 in Aragon, 30,000 and 20,000 in the southern and Levante zones, 40,000, 16,000 and 45,000 in the Basque country, Santander, and Asturias respectively, with perhaps 80,000 reserves.[3] But these figures were artificially inflated, with divisional paymasters receiving, corruptly, food and payment for many more men than were really present:[4] 20,000 militiamen in Aragon apparently received pay for 90,000, rations for 80,000 and,

1. For the creation of the Mixed Brigades, see Michael Alpert, *The Republican Army in the Spanish Civil War* (Reading University thesis, 1973). The Mixed Brigades were not numbered necessarily in order of completion but of commencement of organization: hence, at the end of December 1936, fifteen were in full service: the 1st, 2nd, 4th, 5th, 6th, 11th (International), 12th (International), 35th, 37th, 39th, 40th, 41st, 43rd, 44th, 50th and one unnumbered (E). Of these, four were commanded by militia leaders, the rest (except for the Internationals) by regular officers. The missing numbers were only contemplated. But soon militia commanders came forward.

2. 4,000 as a maximum.

3. R. Salas Larrazábal, vol. I, pp. 528–30.

4. Martínez Bande, *La invasion de Aragón*, p. 274, who published an admittedly unsigned report for the Catalan front; the *junta* of defence of Madrid on 12 December 1936, heard a report from Isidro Diéguez to this effect (see Alpert's thesis).

on the Madrid front, 120,000 rations were daily issued to 35,000 men. The food question was important: voluntary recruitment continued mostly perhaps because it was known that food was good at the front, while, in the cities, it was both difficult to get, and bad. Commanders did not report deserters with much enthusiasm, nor those absent without leave. Anxiety to maintain numbers made local commanders keen to avoid casualties. The 'useless riff-raff, amounting to 5 or 10 per cent, who are found in all bodies of troops, and who should be got rid of ruthlessly, were seldom or never got rid of'. Thus, George Orwell, a sympathetic observer. It is true that Orwell was stationed on that 'quiet section' of the quiet Aragon front (commemorated in John Cornford's fine poem *The Last Mile to Huesca*), and his remarks did not apply to shock units, such as Lister's brigade, nor to the International Brigades. But most of the republican army must have been as Orwell said it was.[1] 'I came to the conclusion,' Orwell went on, 'somewhat against my will, that, in the long run, "good party men" make the best soldiers, if they were working class particularly. In the POUM militia,' he added, 'there was a slight, but perceptible, tendency for people of bourgeois origin to be chosen as officers.' As for age, Orwell noticed that, 'while boys as young as fourteen are often very brave and reliable, they were simply unable to stand the lack of sleep'. The comment shows that many of the republic's soldiers (and no doubt Franco's army too) were young.[2]

Most of the Spanish war's long front lines were quiet. On the other hand, many republicans believed that, if they were captured, they would be shot; and if they were volunteers or officers, they usually would be. Few conscripts were shot on either side. Still, the danger concentrated the mind, and encouraged caution. All in the republican army were really understood by now to have joined up for the duration of the war. The International Brigade's volunteers could not choose their moment to withdraw, though some did, taking advantage (if they were from anti-fascist or democratic countries) of

1. Orwell, *Selected Writings*, vol. I, p. 325. Orwell joined the army in Barcelona. A small detachment of English volunteers for the POUM had been formed in England by Bob Edwards mainly of ILP members. Of these men 25 arrived in Barcelona on 12 January.

2. Conscripts were twenty to twenty-five years old in 1936, volunteers often younger.

their leaves to visit their embassies, and sometimes thereby finding the means to escape.

Men were kept in the front line for long periods – in Aragon five months continuously, sleeping indefinitely in discomfort in trenches. Thus the soldiers suffered from lack of sleep and were too tired to learn new things. The life of the troops was duller than it need have been: 'The few women who were in or near the line . . . were simply a source of jealousy. There was a certain amount of sodomy among the younger Spaniards,' Orwell drily recalled.[1]

The anarchists were aghast at all these developments leading to a new conventional army. The People's War schools, the Fifth Regiment's school in Madrid, and even the anarchists' own 'Bakunin' school in Barcelona, represented the end of an epoch. Was it possible for an anarchist to serve in the same unit as a communist, or a member of the bourgeoisie? To wear uniform, to obey orders from a central government? The libertarian youth spoke of the danger that the army would be scarcely different from the force that had rebelled in July: 'A shock force, knowing nothing of the cries of the cannon fodder for liberty, bread, justice'. 'We are not making war, but revolution,' said an editorial in *Acracia*.[2] The FAI demanded the suppression of the salute, equal pay for all in the army, newspapers at the front, and soldier councils, at all levels. *Solidaridad Obrera* grumbled about 'obsession of discipline', 'neo-militarism', and 'psychosis of unity'. The 3,000-strong Iron Column before Teruel (partly freed ex-convicts – perhaps 400) rebelled against the implications of the decree against militias.[3] Hitherto, the column had been paid *en bloc*. Now the men were to receive wages individually, from a paymaster in the ministry of war. The despair felt by these men at the prospect of having to obey orders; of having to refer to officers as *usted*, not the familiar *tú*; of having to expect insults from corporals and sergeants, such as they had known in the old bad days, was terrible. Many members of the group, perhaps several thousand,

1. Orwell, *Collected Essays*, vol. I, p. 523. Alpert comments 'perhaps dirt and scabies, or gonorrhea, from a quick trip to the city, were more characteristic than sodomy'.

2. Peirats, vol. I, p. 283. *Acracia* was Peirats' paper.

3. Martín Blázquez, p. 296. The pay in 1937 of an ordinary soldier was 10 pesetas a day; of a second-lieutenant, 25; a captain, 50; a lieutenant-colonel, 100.

deserted, rather than become 'robot-soldiers' – the rest, about 4,000, with great reluctance, voted on 21 March to accept militarization, as an alternative to dissolution.[1]

'One day,' wrote an ex-convict in the Iron Column, who had been condemned before the civil war to eleven years of imprisonment (for the murder of a *cacique*),

> one day – a day that was mournful and overcast – the news that we had to be militarized descended on the crests of the Sierra like an icy wind... I have lived in barracks and there I learned to hate. I have been in the penitentiary and it was there, strangely enough, in the midst of tears and torment, I learned to love, to love intensely. In the barracks, I was on the verge of losing my personality, so severe was the treatment and the stupid discipline they tried to impose upon me. In prison, after a great struggle, I recovered that personality... When, in the distance, I heard murmurs of the order for militarization, I felt my body become limp, for I could clearly see that the guerrilla fearlessness that I had gained from the revolution would perish.[2]

The anarchists realized that the communists intended to play a preponderate part in the new army, along with ex-regular officers. The leader of the communist Fifth Regiment, for example, Enrique Lister, was named to lead the first Mixed Brigade.[3] Perhaps these fears were exaggerated. Asensio, the under-secretary, Martínez Cabrera, the chief of staff, Llano de la Encomienda in the north and Martínez Monje in the south were not communists, nor were the leading defenders of Madrid, Miaja and Rojo. Still, the failure of the anarchists at the front, the delays caused by discussion of the political advantages of this or that attack, made the anarchists' position weak. Anarchists disliked regular officers as much as they did communists, and were naturally suspicious when the two showed signs of being in agreement.

1. C. Lorenzo, p. 188.

2. *Nosotros*, qu. Bolloten, p. 268. See also Fernando Claudín, 'Spain, The Untimely Revolution' in *New Left Review*, No. 74. The communist position is put in *Guerra y revolución en España 1936–1939* (Moscow, 1966), 3 vols. so far. The anarchist case is to be found in Vernon Richards, *Lessons of the Spanish Revolution*, where the dilemma is summed up as 'The "people in arms" won the revolution: the "people's army" lost the war.'

3. Lister had been appointed on 10 October and was succeeded in the Fifth Regiment by Modesto. The Regiment was dissolved on 21 January 1937.

For some months, militias survived, particularly in the south and in the Levante, where the new army commanders appointed by the republic had a hard time. But by and large the old groupings vanished. Battalion leaders became majors; 'century delegates' became captains. By the spring, Brigades 1–40 were complete; Brigades 101–115 were being trained; and 41–100 were in various stages of organization.[1] The Brigades were also swiftly organized in divisional units.

Some anarchists were active in the military reorganization, García Oliver himself being nominated by the government to direct the officer schools. He was also the anarchist representative on the Supreme War Council, created on 9 November under Largo's chairmanship. (The other members were Prieto, Julio Just and Alvarez del Vayo.)[2] Federica Montseny was also sympathetic to these changes; she had publicly deplored the hours lost in discussion at the front. But many other anarchists regretted their own leaders' acceptance of the forms of 'reaction'; particularly when García Oliver was referred to on the radio as 'His Excellency the minister of justice, Comrade García Oliver'.

As for Catalonia, the *Generalidad* formalized in Aragon what was in effect a separate army of its own in December. Three divisions were raised by conscription, and the old columns were converted into the regiments which the Catalans preferred to the brigade as the basic unit. The total nominally numbered some 40,000, though (as suggested earlier) probably the figure was much smaller; but they were certainly more numerous than the 20,000 or so nationalists opposite them, who would have been hard put then to resist a determined Catalan attack. The Catalan divisions retained their old political colouring under another heading. Thus, the anarchist militia was transformed into three divisions, ultimately led by new 'Majors'

1. Each brigade was to be 3,800 strong, including three battalions of about 500 men each, four batteries of three or four cannon, 120 machine-guns, 104 mortars, a stock of 2,200 rifles, and a communications and engineer detachment. In fact, this design was rarely achieved: most Mixed Brigades only had one machine-gun company.

2. Martín Blázquez (p. 299) was impressed with García Oliver's competence in organizing the officer schools.

Ortiz, Sanz, and Jover, all of them *guerrilleros* by way of preparation.[1] The POUM militia became the 29th Division, under the so-called Major Rovira; the PSUC militia became the 27th Division, under the communist militia leader, 'Major' José del Barrio; while the 'Maciá–Companys', or Catalan, column, became the 30th Division, under regular Major Jesús Pérez Salas. Most of these commanders had led those columns since July. The overall commander was Colonel Vicente Guarner, who was before the war a regular major.[2] Despite the 'militarization', the separate political colour of different units, nevertheless, persisted, and the government was never able to appoint its own nominees to command anarchist units: the defence committee of the regional CNT would give the government names from whom the commanders were to be chosen.

Uniforms were still non-existent, but most people wore corduroy knee breeches and a jacket with a zip. Training was rudimentary. Marksmanship was poor and rifle drill almost unknown. Grenades were still as liable to explode in the hands of the thrower as upon the enemy. In many places, there were no maps, range-finders for artillery, field glasses, or cleaning materials; and Orwell discovered, with the horror of a trained member of the Eton College Officer Training Corps, that no one in his POUM column had heard of a 'pull-through' with which to clean rifles.[3]

The Catalan War Industries Committee, presided over by Tarradellas, organized by Colonel Jiménez de la Beraza (director of the arms factory in Oviedo in 1934),[4] was being reasonably successful in gearing the industries of Catalonia to the manufacture of war material: for example, at the end of February 1937, these industries of Catalonia (which had been non-existent in July 1936) produced daily 500,000 rifle cartridges.[5] This committee had also had some success in concentrating production in plants with the best equipment, and closing and reorganizing several industries. But the far more important Basque war industries were a long way behind pre-war produc-

1. Militias commanders were theoretically not able to rise above the rank of major.

2. Guarner Memorandum, p. 5.   3. Orwell, *loc. cit.*

4. He had been sentenced to life imprisonment for failing to defend the factory.

5. Peirats, vol. II, p. 215.

tion, due partly to lack of raw materials, and partly to unsatisfactory management.

The republican army continued to be armed with rifles of different origins, about a third Mausers (that is, of the old army), a third Russian (the 'Mosin' type), and another third of varying makes, principally Mexican.[1] The variety in calibration caused many problems. The republicans had some hundred 37-millimetre Russian anti-tank guns, which they did not use well, and, by this time, much of the artillery they had had in July was depleted, thanks to ignorant misuse by the militia columns or by being left behind on the field, during retreat. Nevertheless, over the winter of 1936–7, schools of artillery at Chinchilla and at Almansa were opened: highly necessary, since a majority of artillery officers in July 1936 were on the nationalist side.[2]

The republican air force, because of its close relation with Russia, in respect of training and material, was more communist than the army was: its commander, Hidalgo de Cisneros, an aristocrat and *Prietista*, had, as has been seen, become a communist of the same kind as Cordón and other previously non-political army officers. (Hidalgo de Cisneros told his wife, Constancia de la Mora, granddaughter of the conservative politician Antonio Maura, the secret that he had joined the party; she replied that, some weeks earlier, she had done the same.[3]) Most of the Spanish pilots who went for a six-months training course in Russia knew how to fly well when they came back; many had also become communists. The Russian pilots under General Smushkevich were excellent propaganda in themselves, though between them, the Spanish pilots, and Belarmino Tomás, the commissar-general of the air, an anti-communist, there were continuous arguments.

1. This was the estimate of the acute French military attaché, *FD*, vol. V, p. 597.

2. Voronov (*Bajo la bandera*, p. 71) says 90 per cent. I think the figure lower though only 14 per cent were with the republic in 1938. By the winter of 1936, the old artillery of July 1936 was being replaced by French, English, and German, and some Russian artillery, as well as some Russian anti-aircraft batteries. Subsequently schools of artillery were also opened at Lorca and at Barcelona. The Barcelona school was later still merged with the one at Lorca, to the anger of the Catalans.

3. Hidalgo de Cisneros, vol. II, p. 123. Constancia de la Mora worked in the censorship department. See her *Doble esplendor* (Mexico, 1944).

In the navy, communism had been less successful. The commander, Admiral Buiza, his successor, Captain González Ubieta, and the commander of the flotilla of destroyers, Vicente Ramírez, were all career naval officers who did not develop any liking for the communist party. Bruno Alonso, the commissar-general of the fleet, was a *Prietista*, though he was ignorant of the sea. Two Russians captained republican submarines, a number of other Russian officers were attached as advisers to the senior officers, and the Russian naval attaché, Captain Kuznetsov, was always giving Prieto advice. But the Soviet pressure was not otherwise marked. This relative freedom from Russian or communist influence did not make for efficiency. Indeed, the republican fleet was a white elephant of the civil war, inactive and neglected. Much of the blame must go to Prieto, the minister responsible, who knew as little of the sea as did Bruno Alonso, and who trusted too much in these matters a personal secretary, Lieutenant Eduardo Merín (*El Papa Negro*), who breathed an air of omniscience, while being indolent, procrastinatory and possibly even treacherous.[1] Those naval officers who were technically loyal to the republic were many of them far from enthusiastic about the revolution; while many of the rank and file were anarchists. Captain Kuznetsov described a visit to the battleship *Jaime I* where he found at least three political meetings going on. 'Disputes and discussions never ceased,' the future commander-in-chief of the Russian navy commented sourly, 'the phrase "conquer or die" was heard everywhere, but the anarchists neither conquered nor died.'[2] This indiscipline among the men, ignorance among many of those promoted to command ships, and conflicting emotions in the hearts of the supreme commanders, were the reasons for the failure of the republican fleet. Buiza was reticent, brave but shy; González Ubieta had no desire to fight; Vicente Ramírez, an expansive Andalusian, laced his conversation with strong nautical expressions and hence was popular, but he could not create discipline; while the most effective officer was the conventional commander of the submarine flotilla, Remigio Verdía.[3]

1. Manuel Benavides, *La escuadra la mandan los cabos* (Mexico, 1944), p. 376.

2. *Bajo la bandera*, p. 142.

3. Russian officers who served with the republican fleet included S. Ramishvili (at Cartagena naval base); V. Drozd (with the destroyer flotilla); Nikolai Eguipko

The most important task of the republican fleet was admittedly less to fight Franco than to protect the route to Russia. Here the republic was more successful; between October 1936 and September 1937, over twenty large, mostly Spanish, transport ships made journeys from the Black Sea to Spain without difficulty.

In addition to the army, there survived, too, four armed police forces: the old civil guard, renamed the national republican guard; the assault guards; the carabineers, directed by the minister of finance to ensure the payment of customs on the frontier; and the corps of 'investigation and vigilance'. Of these, the republican guard and the assault guards played little part once the civil war was under way. They were less important than the local 'militias of the rearguard', many of which survived only too long, given the weakness of the well-meaning socialist minister of the interior, Angel Galarza. The carabineers were built up by Negrín over the winter of 1936–7, to do their work effectively, being nicknamed the '100,000 sons of Negrín', though there were no more than 40,000 of them. They were almost all socialists, not communists, insofar as that could be ensured. But the police proper and the corps of 'investigation and vigilance' did have substantial communist components, though the new director-general of security, Wenceslao Carrillo – he succeeded Muñoz – was a firm supporter of Largo Caballero. Still, the police chiefs of Madrid were either communists or friendly to them and the two chiefs of the intelligence department of the ministry of the interior, Juan Galán and Justiniano García, were both party members.

*

One series of innovations in the republican army in the winter of 1936–7 would ultimately affect the rest of the world. These were the changes in the treatment of war wounds introduced to begin with in Catalonia, under the inspiration of the then chief surgeon at the General Hospital in Barcelona, Josep Trueta. Trueta's innovations were the treatment of wounds and fractures by immediate surgery; the stitching of the edges of the wound; and the protection of the

and Burmistrov, commanders of two submarines; V. Alafuzov, on the cruiser *Libertad*; N. Ostriakov (killed at Sebastopol) and I. Proskinov, both with the diminutive fleet air arm.

injured part, and the giving of rest to the patient, by extensive use of plaster of Paris. These changes meant bringing the surgeon to the patient and not, as was usual in the First World War, the patient to the hospital. That change in itself saved many lives. The use of banks of preserved blood in the front line allowed surgeons to perform operations without delay. Doctor Durán-Jordà, director of the blood transfusion service of the *Generalidad* (subsequently of the republican army), was responsible for beginning this system, together with his Canadian assistant, the undisciplined, flamboyant, but heroic, Norman Bethune. Dr Bethune's mobile Spanish–Canadian blood unit first gave transfusions at the front on 23 December, 1936, in the University City: an event as important in the history of war as the almost contemporaneous flight for the first time over Madrid of the new German fighter, the Messerschmitt 109. Another of Trueta's innovations was the abandonment of the daily change of dressings and antiseptics, which had been for so long dreaded by the wounded. The consequence was that, in republican Spain, the number of deaths per casualty was much lower than it had been in France during the First World War, even though, to begin with, the medical services were not properly organized and sanitation was bad, while communication trenches (to get the wounded back) hardly existed.[1] Trueta also had some difficulties in getting his ideas accepted in the conventional republican army, though he ultimately succeeded in persuading Colonel d'Harcourt, the surgeon who was the head of the army surgical service, of their wisdom.[2] There was a particularly favourable change in respect of the incidence of gas gangrene, that

1. See J. Trueta, *Treatment of War Wounds and Fractures* (London, 1939); the *Principles and Practice of War Surgery* (London, 1943); *The Atlas of Traumatic Surgery* (Oxford, 1947); and the life of Bethune by Ted Allan and Sydney Gordon, *The Scalpel, not the Sword* (London, 1954), p. 102f. Bethune died in 1949 running a mobile operating unit with the Chinese communists. The antibiotic came in only in 1943. Trueta later became professor of orthopaedic surgery and traumatology at Oxford. See also Orwell, *Collected Essays*, vol. I, p. 323. Dr Manuel Bastos of Madrid had introduced the plaster cast and exposure by 'window' in Asturias in 1934.

2. The benefit of the government's move to Catalonia in late 1937 was considerable in this respect. Trueta's work was derived from that of Winnett Orr. Other important work in the civil war was done by d'Harcourt and Bofill, on frostbite and the use of sulphonamides in treatment, and also by González Aguilar in neurosurgical methods.

fatal disease of war – so much so that surgeons visiting Barcelona in 1938 began to think that Spain (or at least Catalonia) had no anaerobes, the carriers of that disease. But those with longer memories knew otherwise.

32

The land – agrarian collectives – did they work?

THE troubles between the anarchists and the communists over the army were compounded by worse difficulties still on the land. For the communists now openly gave support to the small farmer, while the anarchists, and many socialists in collaboration with them, championed agrarian collectives. These collectives were the romantic innovations of the Spanish revolution. They have dominated the imaginations of many in the years since that time. What were they like, how did they work, could they have survived, were they just?

There were perhaps some 2,500 collectives in republican Spain – a few hundred in Andalusia, about 450 in Aragon, about 350 in Levante, and in Castile perhaps 300. In Catalonia, there were only about 80; and, in the little pinch of Estremadura still with the republic, about 40.[1] By no means all these agrarian innovations were dominated by anarchists; there were some 800 socialist collectives, and about 1,100 had at least one or two socialists on their committees. Families who worked on agricultural collectives numbered nearly half a million, and the total land under collective management was nearly 9 million acres. Alongside the collectives, some 300,000 peasants had received land from the Institute of Agrarian Reform, the total having been handed over since 1932 being by now perhaps 1,500,000 acres; and there survived, of course, many private farmers, who desired to remain such, particularly in Catalonia and even in Aragon. Some places were wholly collectivized, most had a private element alongside the collective.[2] Some places even had two collec-

1. Figures in report of the Institute of Agrarian Reform, May 1938, qu. Payne, *The Spanish Revolution*, p. 241; also Leval, p. 80; figures are chiefly from anarchist sources and, therefore, perhaps over favourable to them. Other sources include A. Pérez Baró, *Trenta mesos de collectivisme a Catalunya* (Barcelona, 1970). Andalusia must have had 1,000 collectives during the war but, shortly, republican Andalusia was limited to Jaén and Almería. There had also been many more collectives in Estremadura.

2. See Peirats, vol. I, pp. 317–19.

tives, one anarchist, one socialist. In some places, a majority of the township had voted, when they took over the large estates near by, to work them as small farms. In Aragon, the collective was often the village itself. In the Levante, the collectives were more often partial undertakings, with only 40 per cent of the agricultural population organized communally.[1] In Andalusia, collectives might be formed on the confiscated private estates whose size and history gave rise to different problems to those occurring in Aragon. In fact, most of the land in collectives had previously been middle-sized, rather than very large estates, since the classic area of great estates of Estremadura and Andalusia had passed swiftly to the nationalists.

In Catalonia, in the country, the association of vinegrowers (*rabassaires*) expanded their organization to absorb all the independent peasants' associations in a single federation, which all such peasants were required to join. All land held on any form of tenancy was taken over by the cultivators. Barcelona might be, in the early months of the war, a triumph for collectivized industry; the countryside of Catalonia was a sea of smallholdings.[2]

Between a half to two-thirds of the entire country, was taken over during the first six months of the civil war.[3] As so often, unfortunately, with revolutionary schemes on the land, the revolutionaries thought in terms of numbers of acres rather than of types of crop. This was a weakness, since, whether revolution or reaction triumphs, a vineyard in La Mancha, an orange farm in the *huerta* of Valencia, and a poor mixed farm in Castile, are plainly different enterprises.

The collectives varied in size, between one with 5,000 members, such as that of Tomelloso (Ciudad Real) in the heart of the country of Don Quixote, which controlled wine vaults in which over four million gallons of wine could be stored, and Villas Viejas (Albacete), which consisted of two farms taken over by about twenty families (ninety-two persons) who worked there. To begin with, each collective adopted a separate statute of inauguration, with rules differing from place to place. Afterwards, a regional anarchist conference approved a model statute for all to copy. A general accounting system

1. Leval, p. 183.
2. Except for some collectives in the Ebro and in the market-garden area of the Llobregat plain.
3. Malefakis's figure, p. 386.

was also approved, and a national statistical section established. The collectives continued, however, to differ in character and regulations. In Aragon, as previously described, a congress of collectives had led to the formation of a regional council, directed by Joaquín Ascaso. Though, in other areas, councils were formed for other activities (production and rationing), nowhere else was there a powerful, independent anarchist-led council which rejected all external political authority.

Most collectives in villages or small towns were directed by an alliance of the UGT and CNT. Whatever differences there were at a national level between these two organizations, or between their leaders, in many small places, relations were good throughout the war. These UGT members were mostly people who had joined the socialist movement in 1931 or 1932 and who had played such an important part in agricultural politics before the war. Unlike the socialists in the towns, these rural socialists remained fairly free from communist influence. They had been, of course, revolutionary *Caballeristas* in the months leading up to the war.

The leading members of the local unions would declare the collective constituted, and name the 'delegates' to look after different branches of work – cattle, wine, oil, and so on, including statistics, transport, administration, and exchange. These men meeting together would constitute a council of administration of the collective, consisting of a president, secretary, vice-secretary, treasurer, and perhaps four other members. In some places, the council of administration was formed by vote of a 'general assembly' of the collective. The same 'delegate' could assume several jobs, always providing that he could carry out his own work in the fields: these men were not, above all, professional politicians or clerks. To rub that point home and show that one could not gain by being a delegate, members of the council of administration often received less pay than ordinary workers: for example, in Tomelloso, they got 11 pesetas a week less than the rest.[1] (This practice is one which might be emulated in other conditions.) The administrative delegate would, at the end of the year, tell the accountant of the region the balance of imports and exports into the collective. Surpluses, if any, were to go to the regional savings account, to help collectives which could not cover costs. The

1. *Campo Libre*, 11 September 1937.

money might also go to new purchases needed locally. All who joined the collective brought their land, farm implements, and stock. By no means all collectivists were landless persons hoping to have a share in the estates of the local landlord: some smallholders also joined. For example, Jaime Segovia, a young lawyer of Alcorisa (Teruel), helped to organize the collective there, despite his modest fortune;[1] and the farmer Vidal Cruz, president of the council of Alcázar de Cervantes, brought in four acres of his own land, together with two others he rented.[2] All the collectives maintained a treasury of their own: but even a prosperous collective would be unlikely to have more than 7 pesetas per member in cash on hand.

How far persons were forced into collectives is difficult to estimate. The communist press alleged that terror was general, even that 'known falangists' established themselves everywhere under the guise of being anarchists. By early 1937, small proprietors were able to carry on in most places without interruption, though they were forbidden to employ anyone, and, anyway in Aragon, were even forbidden to have their properties registered on the cadastral survey – 'in order to counterbalance the spirit of egoistic proprietorship'.[3] Relations between private peasants (often sustained by communist membership) and collectives improved throughout 1937.

The question of how far the collectives were socially successful, and how far they degenerated into the dictatorship of local bosses as closed in outlook as those whom they had expelled or killed, remains difficult to resolve.[4] The communist Lister was critical of the Council of Aragon in his memoirs: he depicted Ascaso arriving in Barcelona in a fleet of large cars, being received by banquets, while the average worker in his domain lived 'under an inhuman tyranny infinitely worse than before the anarchist revolution'. It was enough for the local committee to denounce a peasant family for it to be liquidated, and those who asked for the people concerned would be told they had 'passed over to the enemy'. In the time of *comunismo libertario*, he concluded, 'the Aragonese knew terror as an instrument

1. Leval, p. 88.

2. *Campo Libre*, 29 January 1938. Alcázar de Cervantes was the new name for Alcázar de San Juan.

3. Leval, p. 134.

4. Lister, p. 157.

of authority and organized crime . . . The enemies of all dictatorship established a rule which had nothing to compare, in respect of terrorist methods, with the most reactionary governments.' The anarchists themselves admit several defections: in Iniesta (Cuenca), for instance, the *individualistas* appear to have been strong. These people were not communists, but anarchists interested in the distribution of land. After the large properties had become the basis of the collective, the *individualistas* insisted on getting three-fifths of this land, together with about half the stock and farm implements. Eighty families remained in the collective afterwards and, evidently, they prospered – borrowing 13,000 pesetas from the regional headquarters – so that the number of families cooperating increased to two hundred by the end of 1937.[1] In Peñalba (Huesca), the outcome was less satisfactory. To begin with, in August 1936, the whole population, of 1,500, became part of the collective. But that was not popular, because the collective's chief task was to feed the Durruti column established near by. As a result, the majority of the population, when they had gathered sufficient courage, or when they realized that they would have communist backing, announced their intention to reclaim their property. A commission was entrusted to supervise the act of demolition, and did so satisfactorily. Five hundred persons were left to carry on the collective. Even so, there are further mentions of 'bad collectivists' who, when everything was provided free, tried to accumulate goods and then sell them or let them go bad.[2] What happened to such people is not always clear: in San Mateo (Castellón) and Serós (Huesca), it was explicitly provided that the general assembly of the collective could expel members for immorality[3] – though this power was never used. In many places, relations between private farmers and collectivists were cool and formal but not outright bad: at Calanda (Teruel), the birthplace of Buñuel, for instance, they had separate cafés.[4] Finally, at Fatarella (Tarragona), the small proprietors rose in arms against the CNT who wished to collectivize them; there were several dead before order was restored.[5] But was Lister, making all allowance for his exaggeration

1. *Campo Libre*, 18 December 1937.
2. Peirats, vol. I, pp. 321–2.
3. *ibid.*, pp. 334–5.
4. Souchy, p. 30.
5. Instance quoted by Broué and Témime, *op. cit.*

and bias, right in his condemnation of this experiment or not? It is necessary to explore some other sides of the problem before a verdict is reached.

The role of the 'general assembly' of the collectives varied. In some places, it was an active body, where the population was able, for a time, to guide the policy of the collective. At Ademuz (Valencia), for instance, a lovely village hung on a mountainside, the general assembly met every Saturday to discuss 'future orientations'.[1] In Alcolea de Cinca (Huesca), general assemblies were celebrated 'when they were needed'.[2] In Alcázar de Cervantes and in Granadella (Lérida), general assemblies elected the council of administration, but did little thereafter.[3] The collective of Cervera del Maestre (Castellón) was set up by 'agreement of an open assembly in the town square'.[4] Gaston Leval, a French anarchist, described visits to such general assemblies in Aragon where the arrangements adopted

> permitted the population to know, understand, and integrate themselves mentally in the society, to co-participate in the direction of public affairs, and responsibilities, so that recriminations and tensions – always produced when the power of decision is confined, without the possibility of reply, to certain individuals, however democratically elected – are absent.[5]

Considerable responsibility rested with secretaries to collectives, often chosen less for their political dedication than for their ability to read and write: thus, at one collective in upper Aragon, the secretary was for a time a university student and son of the local *cacique*, Vicente de Piniés, an ex-minister of the monarchy. (He later joined the army, crossed the lines in the middle of the battle, and became an ambassador under Franco.)[6]

A general judgement on the economic success of the anarchist collectives is particularly difficult to give. There were so many dif-

1. Peirats, vol. I, p. 336. 2. *ibid.*, pp. 311–13, 320.
3. *Campo Libre*, 29 January 1937. 4. Peirats, vol. I, pp. 333–4.
5. Leval, p. 220. Some of the urban or industrial collectives imposed a six-month limit on their council's duration. Leval gives an account of such a general assembly at Tamarite de Litera, Huesca (pp. 221–2). The meeting was held of 600 in the cinema, about 100 women, at 10 p.m.
6. Testimony of Jaime de Piniés, London, February 1973.

ferent varieties of agriculture. In some villages, for example, peasant families left on Monday mornings to work all the week in the hills with their goats and sheep and only return on Saturday night. Such statistics as exist give an increase in the production of wheat from Aragon and the centre of Spain, the main centres of collectives, and a decrease from Catalonia and the Levante, the stronghold of the peasant proprietors. This fact was seized upon by the anarchists: 'Peasants of Castile,' wrote a certain N. González, 'here you have conclusive proofs that the peasant collective is not a madness: it is the system where . . . production is greatest. This is the road, dear comrades, to follow . . .'[1] Alas, the trouble was that, even if there were indeed an increase of wheat, as these figures suggest, the increased consumption at the place of production, the decay of systems of transport and distribution, the increase of refugees and the greater demand for food made inevitable by the nationalist blockade, caused a shortage of food in all the cities of the republic except for Valencia.

Sometimes, the accounts of individual collectives are available. The following table gives those of Almagro, a town in La Mancha, of about 8,000 inhabitants, not far from Ciudad Real, a large centre for the wine industry.[2]

These figures show that the town of Almagro was scarcely keeping

1. *Campo Libre*, 9 October 1937.

	1936	1937	Difference
Catalonia	1,968,228	1,550,600	−417,628
Aragon	1,349,999	1,620,000	+270,001
Central Zone (i.e. Castile)	5,236,721	6,090,238	+853,517
Levante	1,293,942	1,197,216	−97,726
	9,848,890	10,458,054	+609,164

Figures in the ministry of agriculture's publication *Economía Política*, Publication 60, series C, No. 33. The 1936 figures take into account the production in the republican area only. The fact that the figures indicate a drop in production in Catalonia and the Levante suggests at least an intention of veracity, since this would hardly have been invented by a communist ministry of agriculture, with greater communist strength in those areas than in the centre and in Aragon.

2. *Campo Libre*, 2 October 1937. The slight error of addition in the right-hand top column is in the original. A *fanega* is a measure equivalent to 1.6 bushels and an *arroba* one equivalent to either 11.5 kilos or 4 gallons.

up with the inflation in the republic, which must have been, even in the country, something approaching 30 per cent between the dates mentioned. The anarchist reporter who visited the town on behalf

	Value of goods on 1 September 1936	Value of goods on 2 October 1937
Goods		
Mules	68,080 pesetas	91,150
Pigs	19,750	26,700
Sheep	70,000	74,000
Farm implements	140,500	150,405
Road-work implements	—	4,969
Carpentry	—	5,125
Cash in hand	—	4,336.74
Value of goods	298,330	356,686
Products		
Barley	3,400 fanegas	5,955 fanegas
Wine	500 arrobas	2,050 arrobas
Oil	600 arrobas	1,700 arrobas
Rye	80 fanegas	139 fanegas
Peas	60 fanegas	310 fanegas
Wheat	1,700 fanegas	900 fanegas
Maize	35 fanegas	—
Algarrobilla (bean)	160 fanegas	335 fanegas
Chick peas	4 fanegas	20 fanegas
Yeros (vetch)	70 fanegas	30 fanegas
Haba (bean)	20 fanegas	160 fanegas
Value of products	100,953 pesetas	158,726 pesetas
Total value of goods	298,330	356,686
and products	100,953	158,726
	399,283 pesetas	515,412 pesetas

Imports into the collective 1936–7: 375,577,84 pesetas
Exports from the collective 1936–7: 371,242.10 pesetas

Difference: 4,335.74 pesetas
Difference between value of 1936 and 1937: 116,129 pesetas

of the weekly *Campo Libre* also commented rather sharply that, though evidently the collective was doing well, it ought to try and save – not for itself, but for others in the region less prosperous. The collective of Almagro seemed to have forgotten that it was part of a federation. The comrades who formed the administrative council in Almagro were too proud. Nevertheless – and this was something apparently which by then could be said of the directors of few collectives – none of them smoked or drank. In this town, there was an anomaly: an anarchist flour mill, run by the workers, which was nevertheless not a part of the collective. Its products were of three qualities, described, in order of work, as 'FAI', 'CNT', and 'AIT'.[1] The collective was composed of 300 families, which, in the year from 1 September 1936, to 31 August 1937, each consumed 40 gallons of olive oil, 200 pounds of potatoes, and about 800 pounds of bread. About 430 litres of wine per family were drunk during the year – a modest amount, it might be thought, for consumption in the first year of revolutionary freedom. The church had been turned into a carpenter's shop. The town was notable for its lack of 'disorderly communists', and for good relations between the parties. The municipal council continued to exist, the anarchists holding six seats out of fifteen.[2]

Wages differed from collective to collective, the criterion really being the richer the collective, the better paid the workers. This was an ironic, if doubtless inescapable, conclusion to the libertarian dream. On the other hand, in many places, a little oil, wine, bread, even meat, were free, along with rent, electric light (where it existed), the use of a barber, medical advice and medicine. Wages usually varied according to the size, or needs, of the family. As has been seen, money was abolished altogether in many places, but, in most of them, after a few months, either a replacement for it was issued, in the form of vouchers (*vales* or *bonos*), or it reappeared as a 'usual wage', as elsewhere. For example, at Graus (Huesca), wages were first paid in vouchers: at the end of a month, these were replaced by tickets divided into points; then, because of the town's importance in the locality, at a crossroads, the peseta was reintroduced; and finally,

1. Alianza internacional de trabajadores.
2. *Campo Libre*, 2 October 1937.

the committee issued a local currency for use within the village, with varying payments according to needs.[1]

In a few places, especially remote ones where bad weather might be expected to cause shortages in winter, collectivists were permitted to keep a few animals of their own: in Piedras Menares (Guadalajara), for example, this was eighteen chickens and three goats;[2] in other places, communal dining-rooms were set up where bachelors could eat free, passers-by at the cost of a peseta.

Statistics sometimes point to a real rise in production, as for example on the collective of Miralcampo, set up near Guadalajara

1. *Wages in selected collectives*

	Working families, husband and wife	*Extra for working son*	*Extra for invalids living with family*	*Extra for minors*	*Bachelors*	*Widows*	*Retired couples*
Alcañiz	10	—	—	—	—	—	—
Alcázar de Cervantes	8	.50	—	—	—	—	—
Arganda	45 pw	—	—	7 pw	35 pw	25 pw	45 pw
Belvis de Jarama	8	—	—	—	—	—	—
	(plus produce; in harvest, 10 plus produce)						
Brihuega	(average wage among 125 families: 45 pw)				—	—	—
Cabañas de Yepes	45 pw	15 pw	12 pw	7 pw	32 pw	25 pw	—
Cervera del Maestre	6	3.50	—	1.50	—	—	—
Dosbarrios	45 pw	15 pw	12 pw	7 pw	32 pw	25 pw (32 pw if works)	—
Hospitalet de Llobregat	(average wage: 45 pw)			—	—	—	—
Huete	6 (factory worker got 12)			—	—	—	—
Iniesta	4	1	—	.50	—	—	—
Lérida	60 pw	10 pw	—	—	40 pw	—	—
Llombay	5	—	—	—	—	—	—
Madrid	12	12	—	10.20 (children between 16 and 18)			
				7.20 (,, ,, 14 and 16)			
	(also daily ration of greens valued at 2 pesetas)						
Meco	7.50	—	—	—	—	—	—
Monzón	9	4	—	3.50	—	—	—
Oriols	8	8	—	3 (children between 12 and 15)			
				1 (,, ,, 8 and 12)			
				3 (girls over 15)			
Perales de Tajuña	5	2	—	1	4	2.75 (for a spinster)	
Piedras Menares	8.50–9.50 (depending on size of family; payment goes up by .25 increases)						
Plá de Cabra	5	2 (for each member of family regardless of age)					
San Mateo	5	—	—	1.50	3	—	—
Tomelloso	6.50	6 (for first)					
		4.50 (for succeeding sons)		3	—	—	—
Villaverde	12	—	—	—	—	7.20	7.20
	(also daily ration of greens valued at 3 pesetas)						

(All wages in pesetas per day unless otherwise stated)

2. *Campo Libre*, 11 June 1938.

on land previously belonging to the Conde de Romanones.[1] There were also some radical improvements dictated or made possible by the demands of war and, perhaps, by the desire of the collectivists to prove the superiority of their system to all others. Time and again, there were reports of new model pig farms, new mills, and new roads. Land was often farmed in a more rational manner than before the war, irrigation extended, intelligent changes of production begun, hygiene improved, and sheds built. Many collectives bought new agricultural machinery. Schools increased, and the thirst for education by both young and adults was at least partially satisfied, in converted convents or palaces, by new schoolmasters, themselves finding learning difficult.

For innumerable workers, of course, the absence, death, or, in some instances, mere retirement of the old master class, of the priest, of the whole complicated apparatus of traditional catholic living, and of all the things that went with it, such as the subordination of women, sustained a persistent exhilaration, making up for such shortages as were caused by the war. Traditional life in Spain had been so often, in the small towns of Castile or Aragon, extraordinarily limited. Now the windows at least seemed open. The conquest of power by the workers had created problems, but much of the tedium of the old life had vanished, in a wealth of slogans, encouragements to harder work, revolutionary songs, old songs rewritten with modern words, radio broadcasts, and committee meetings, which gave the illusion, at least, that there was a political life in which the participation of all was possible.

1.

	1935–6	1936–7
Wheat	3,000 fanegas	7,000 fanegas
Barley	500 fanegas	2,000 fanegas
Wine	3,000 arrobas	over 4,500 arrobas
Melons	196,000 pesetas' value	300,000 pesetas' value
Alfalfa	80,000 pesetas' value	300,000 pesetas' value

ibid., 30 July 1937. The basis for 1935 figures is not known: were they real figures or those kept for tax purposes? In this instance, quite possibly the former, since the Conde's old manager and agent actually joined the council of administration.

From the government's point of view, the main practical disadvantage of collectives was that they paid no taxes; and, though the anarchists said that they 'judged it a sacred duty to take food directly to the front',[1] it arrived at irregular intervals, so that it could not be counted upon, and was often wasted. Nor, despite the presence of socialists in many councils of administration, could the collectives be counted upon to carry out governmental directives.

By December 1936, the chief officials of the ministry of agriculture, from the minister downwards, were communists. (Castro Delgado had moved from the Fifth Regiment to become director-general of agrarian reform, and the secretary-general was another communist – Morayta Núñez.[2]) This had the effect of causing many rural workers to assume that, though the master class was new, it was virtually the same as it had been before in all really important respects.

The fate of the collectives if the country had been at peace is difficult to estimate. For the very existence of the war and of the other revolutionary parties – perplexing though both seemed to the anarchists – may have been responsible for some of the success that the collectives had. The war sustained the sense of communal service. At the same time, the government's and the communists' backing of the small farmer meant that such people were usually certain of an ally in need, from the autumn of 1936 onwards: the local village council of administration could not go too far in bullying individuals to make them join or conform. (The communist minister of agriculture made a number of speeches promising the private farmer that his interests would be served by the communist party, and the message was heard: as has been pointed out, nearly one-third of party members were said to be peasant proprietors in February 1937.)

The only possible general conclusion is that the collective experience would have been a success or a failure depending on whether its managers were able, in peace, to accept the permanent existence of, and collaborate with, the state and private proprietors; and

1. Peirats, vol. I, p. 320.

2. Castro Delgado (pp. 379–82) recalled that his three priorities on taking over the Institute for Agrarian Reform were to destroy the agrarian reform teams staffed by socialists; to force employers to accept that the rhythm of war was different from that of peace; and to enrol as many people as possible for the communist party.

whether the state and the private proprietor could have brought themselves permanently to accept such enterprises as these Spanish kibbutzim alongside conventional social and economic ventures. Some anarchists, such as Horacio Prieto, were thinking along such lines, and some too were beginning to see that the merger of, say, twenty-five or fifty grocers' shops into one large collective store, as sometimes happened, was not necessarily a social advantage. The abolition of private locksmiths, shoemakers, furniture menders and cabinet makers often led to the disappearance of those essential crafts altogether. What would happen too to ensure that rich collectives handed over their excess produce for the benefit of poor ones, and how would the rural managements have secured the fertilizers, machinery, credit, and technical assistance which were needed by Spanish agriculture, whoever directed it? Thus, too many questions are unanswered to be able to say that these agrarian enterprises were successful *tout court*. Yet it is evident that they articulated the enthusiasms of many poor, but dedicated, men and women. They deserved neither the contempt of the communists nor the brutality of the nationalists, even if the ruthlessness and delusions of grandeur on the part of some of the anarchist leaders, such as Joaquín Ascaso, diminish the sympathy which might be otherwise universally felt for the idealistic autodidacts who worked in the system.

33

The nationalist blockade – German and Italian recognition of the nationalists – Spanish–Italian Agreement of 28 November – Spain before the League – the beginning of the Abraham Lincoln Brigade – the Non-Intervention Control Plan – the Embargo Law in the USA – the Mar Cantábrico

THE battles around Madrid in the winter of 1936–7 were international events as much as they were Spanish. Yet diplomats spoke as if Non-Intervention could be made to work. Thus on 12 November, Maisky, the Russian ambassador in London ('in a way a second loyalist ambassador in London'),[1] had happily remarked 'after weeks of aimless wandering, our committee . . . has elaborated a scheme for the more or less effective control of the Non-Intervention Agreement'.[2] For, on that day, a plan of Lord Plymouth's to discover breaches of the pact by posting observers at Spanish frontiers and ports was approved. Portugal, Germany and Italy argued that, before the plan could be put to the two Spanish contestants, control by air should be included. The near-impossibility of that suggested that these countries were concerned to prolong negotiations, rather than reach agreement. All this time, the German consul at Odessa, and newspaper correspondents at Istanbul, were reporting the shipment of arms from Russia.

The shipment of Russian military aid was, of course, noticed by consuls other than the German. On 15 November, Eden, in the House of Commons, bluntly announced that there were countries 'more to blame for the breach of non-intervention than Germany and Italy'. On 17 November, Eden was also faced with a new problem. The nationalists declared that they intended to prevent war material from reaching the republic, and, to do so, would stop and search ships

1. L. Fischer, p. 443.

2. *NIS*, eleventh meeting. 12 November 1936 was the day of Baldwin's famous admission to the House of Commons that he had 'been less than candid' to the electorate over rearmament for fear of losing the election.

on the high seas. Now, under international law, British ships could carry arms to Spain from foreign ports, and demand aid from the Navy, if interfered with, unless the interference were to occur within Spanish territorial waters, where the Navy was not entitled to follow. The British government regarded the action of such merchant ships 'contrary to the spirit, if not the letter', of the Non-Intervention Agreement. The Navy did not want to protect merchant ships carrying on such a trade.[1] If Franco were recognized as having belligerent rights in the civil war, interference would be legal. Though the British government would have liked to have made such an act of recognition (they believed that that would more easily keep Britain out of the conflict), the French opposed it. Eden wished neither to help Franco nor to offend France. But he would have liked 'to show a tooth in the Mediterranean'. On 22 November, in the cabinet, most ministers argued for belligerent rights, while Eden opposed them. Eden won, and the cabinet decided to let the Navy protect British ships while carrying ordinary cargo, but to forbid British ships to carry arms.[2] Actually, on 20 November, the Admiralty had told British warships that both Spanish navies could stop and search merchant ships for arms. Eden did not get that order cancelled till 25 November. It was fortunate for the British government that this did not leak to the press.[3]

Before this development had been digested, Germany and Italy announced their recognition of the nationalists as the government of Spain. Franco received the news by describing Germany and Italy, with Portugal and nationalist Spain, as bulwarks of culture, civilization, and Christianity in Europe. 'This moment', he added with a, for him, unusual superlative, 'marks the peak of life in the world.'[4]

1. Note by Eden to the cabinet, 21 November (in *CAB* 24/265).

2. Eden, p. 413.

3. Note to commander-in-chief, Mediterranean, 20 November 1936, from the foreign secretary.

4. This was on 18 November. The previous day Germany and Japan had affirmed their friendship in the Anti-Comintern Pact, ostensibly directed against communism but in reality an offensive military alliance. Italy joined a year later. On 24 November, the poet, Robert Graves, previously (like Bernanos) resident in Majorca, called on Churchill begging him to denounce German and Italian policy in the western Mediterranean:

But the situation was dangerous, for, on 21 November, an Italian submarine had entered the battle and torpedoed the republican cruiser, *Miguel de Cervantes*, off Cartagena.[1] On 27 November, the Italian ambassador in Paris told his American colleague, Bullitt, that Italy would not cease to support Franco, even if Russia were to abandon the republic – 'Franco's effectives being insufficient to enable him to conquer the whole of Spain'.[2] Mussolini was gambling all on a victory by Franco. He had just sent Anfuso, Ciano's principal secretary, and the chief of military intelligence, Colonel Roatta, to Franco, in order to suggest that Italy should send a division of Black Shirts to fight in Spain. In return, he wanted Franco to support Italy in her Mediterranean policy. Trade connections would be made as favourable as possible.[3] On 28 November, Franco agreed with this arrangement without enthusiasm, and the Black Shirts began to be fitted out. At that moment, Italy had sent to Franco altogether some 50 light Ansaldo-Fiat tanks, 50 pieces of artillery, about 24 Fiat fighters, 19 Savoia 81 bombers, and some Romeo 37 light bombers.[4] The tank specialists, who had been in action from 21 October till 26 November attached to the Legion, were now mostly withdrawn, leaving behind a rather demoralized group of Italian pilots under Captain Fagnani as the only Italians actually fighting for Franco, though what remained of the rest of the material was still there.[5]

Churchill: Both sides have imbrued their hands in blood. You wish for intervention? The country wouldn't stand it.

Graves: Not intervention in the sense of taking sides ... but of safeguarding British interest in the Mediterranean.

(Robert Graves and Alan Hodge, *The Long Weekend*, London, 1940, p. 411.)

1. It did not sink but, due to the lack of a good dry-dock in republican hands, was not repaired until 1938.

2. *USD*, 1936, vol. II, p. 576.

3. *GD*, p. 139; Ciano, *Diplomatic Papers*, pp. 75–7.

4. The IMAM Ro. 37 bis, to give it its full name, was a versatile aircraft of maximum 200 miles an hour at a height of 20,000 feet. It was used for observation, light bombing, machine-gunning from a low level, as well as aerial photography.

5. Fagnani even ordered the nationalist ace-pilot, Angel Salas Larrazábal, to be arrested when he refused an order not to fly over enemy territory in a Fiat. Salas did not suffer from this, but many Italian pilots had been killed and their aircraft destroyed by the Russians by now. See, *inter alia*, Emilio Faldella, *Venti mesi di guerra in Spagna* (Florence, 1939), p. 80. Other Italians with more elaborate

Meantime, the first German chargé to the nationalist government arrived at Burgos. This was General von Faupel, a corps commander in the First World War, an organizer of Frei Korps afterwards, who had spent most of the 1920s helping to reorganize the armies of Argentina and Peru. He was a strong nazi, a fluent Spanish speaker, having, since 1934, been director of the German Ibero-American Institute, and was much disliked by the German foreign ministry. Hitler had told him not to concern himself with military matters, and he took one man with him for propaganda, and one for the 'organization of the Falange'. From the start, he and his wife – 'gross, intelligent, and maternal' – were unpopular with the Spanish leaders.[1] Faupel, on the other hand, found Franco 'likeable', but 'incapable of measuring up to the needs of the situation'.[2] General Faupel was anti-religious, and hated the Spanish upper class – thinking that only a man of low birth could make a fascist revolution. Accordingly, his staff associated with, and encouraged, the more radical members of the Falange, particularly Manuel Hedilla.[3] Faupel wanted Hitler to carry out an anti-bolshevik crusade, in Spain and elsewhere; but Hitler had told him that Spain was 'a convenient side-show which occupied the great powers and left Germany free to pursue her aims in the east'.[4]

Faupel's first report to Berlin was to urge (with General von Sperrle, the commander of the Condor Legion, agreeing) that Germany should either now leave Franco to himself, or send additional forces. One strong German and one Italian division were all that were needed.[5] A concentrated combat force of 15,000–30,000 could, he said, easily break through the republican lines in overwhelming strength and so win the war. Dieckhoff at the foreign ministry warned against this, arguing that more than one German division would be

equipment, including thirty-eight tanks, had been incorporated into the Legion (Belforte, vol. I, p. 51).

1. Serrano Súñer, pp. 44–7. 2. *GD*, p. 159.

3. See below, p. 636. Faupel's opposite number in Berlin would be the Marqués de Magaz, once a member of Primo de Rivera's military directorate, who had lost a son in the Model Prison.

4. Whealey, in Carr, *The Republic*, p. 219, quoting from General Warlimont's interrogation.

5. *GD*, pp. 159–60.

needed and that, if such forces were sent, Germany and Italy would incur the same odium as the French had gathered in Spain in 1808. Shortly too, Germany and nationalist Spain would have to consider the question of payment, of German covetousness of Spanish ores, and other goods. A protocol extending the existing commercial treaty to 31 March 1937, and undertaking new negotiations before then, was, in fact, signed on the last day of 1936 by Faupel and an official of the nationalist diplomatic office.

Before that, Delbos, fearing that Italy was about to attack Barcelona, and aware that German help to Franco might be paid for in minerals,[1] proposed to Eden that they should ask Germany, Italy, and Russia for a 'gentleman's agreement' to cease the sale of arms and then mediate in Spain. Delbos also asked for support from Roosevelt. Bullitt, on receiving the request, took the opportunity to warn Delbos 'not to base his foreign policy . . . on an expectation that the United States would ever again send troops or warships or floods of munitions and money to Europe'.[2] The Non-Intervention Committee, meanwhile, agreed on 2 December (Portugal abstaining) to put Lord Plymouth's control plan to the two Spanish parties.[3]

On 4 December, France and Britain officially approached Germany, Italy, Portugal, and Russia on the subject of mediation. Eden suggested that the 'six powers most closely concerned' might call an armistice, send a commission to Spain and, after a plebiscite, set up a government under a group of men who had kept out of the civil war, such as Salvador de Madariaga, whom Eden had known and learned to respect at Geneva; Madariaga had been the Spanish representative during the last years of the republic and had been a permanent official of the League.[4]

There were thus now three Anglo-French plans for ameliorating the condition of the civil war; the control plan, the mediation proposal and a suggestion made by Lord Plymouth in the Non-Intervention Committee for giving priority to stopping volunteers going to Spain. On 6 December, while they were supposed at least to be considering these enlightened ideas, Mussolini, Ciano, and the Italian

1. *FD*, vol. IV, p. 89. 2. *ibid.*, p. 97; also *USD*, 1936, vol. II, pp. 578–81.

3. *NIS*, twelfth meeting.

4. *GD*, pp. 158–9; Eden, p. 416. Cf. Salvador de Madariaga, *Memorias (1921–36)*, Madrid, 1974, p. 374.

chiefs of staff met to plan the next stage in their aid to Spain.[1] The ubiquitous Canaris was also present, to tell the Italians that the German government desired to cut down participation in Spain as compared with Italy. The German war ministry had decided against Faupel's suggestion of sending complete units to Spain. Since Italy stood to gain diplomatically, surely it was up to Mussolini to give more help to Franco than Germany could afford. The next day, 7 December, Colonel Roatta was given the supreme command of all Italians in Spain, and a 'Spanish office' set up in the Italian foreign ministry to plan this new commitment.[2] The two naval staffs of the dictatorships also met in December and agreed that in general Italy would operate for Franco in the Mediterranean, and Germany concentrate on the Atlantic.

On 10 December, to the annoyance of Litvinov (who advised against taking the issue of Spain to the League) and of the French (who had not been consulted at all), Alvarez del Vayo put the republic's case before the League Council at Geneva. He could scarcely have expected that, after so many failures to take collective action, the League would be decisive over Spain; but at least the question was placed on the agenda. Alvarez del Vayo demanded that the League condemn Germany and Italy for recognizing the rebels. He pointed out that foreign warships had attacked merchantmen in the Mediterranean, that innumerable Moorish troops had been used, that the war in Spain was a general danger to peace, and that the Non-Intervention Agreement was ineffective. In the end, the Council urged the members of the League who were on the Committee in London to do their utmost to secure non-intervention, and commended mediation. Though Russia and Portugal declared their willingness to support any reasonable mediation plan, Germany and Italy, while offering support, said that they thought the idea unlikely to be accepted by either side. They were right: Spanish nationalist and republican newspapers both rejected mediation in editorials. The

1. *GD*, p. 165. The (London) *Observer*, under Garvin, a vigorous opponent of the republic, was foolish enough on this day to publish a dispatch saying there were 21,000 Russians in Madrid. Rumour thus fed on rumour, and truth seemed relative.

2. Mussolini's facsimile letter of appointment to Roatta is published in Alcofar Nassaes, *CTV*, facing p. 32.

mediation plan was dropped, Eden and Delbos pressing forward instead their less ambitious schemes. The republic accepted the control plan in principle on 16 December, at the same time setting out their familiar views on non-intervention, and reserving their right to reject the plan after further examination. The nationalists replied, on 19 December, by asking questions. These were considered by the Non-Intervention Chairman's Sub-Committee on 22 December, in an atmosphere of apprehension at the renewed possibility of general war.[1]

This alarm was caused by the news of the arrival of the first 3,000 Black Shirts in Cádiz, by the Spanish republic's seizure of the German vessel *Palos*, bound for nationalist Spain, and by the nationalists' sinking of a Russian supply ship, the *Komsomol.* In Paris, Delbos had a solemn talk with Welczeck. The French people wanted an understanding with Germany, he said.[2] The way to achieve that was collaboration in Spain. On Christmas Eve, 1936, the British and French ambassadors in Berlin, Rome, Moscow, and Lisbon insisted, over the heads of the Non-Intervention Committee, on the urgent need to ban volunteers from early in January. François-Poncet in Berlin added that the question had previously not seemed to France important enough to justify such an interference in personal freedom.[3] The prospects of this leading anywhere were hardly helped, however, when Blum was assured by the Italian minister that a period of Italian–French friendship could begin only if he allowed Franco to be installed in Spain. But Mussolini, added the diplomat, perhaps

1. *NIS*(c), seventeenth meeting. At an important meeting on 21 December, Hitler, Göring, Warlimont, Blomberg and Fritsch rejected more demands, pressed in person by Faupel, for the dispatch of three German divisions to finish off the war. See Gerhard Weinberg, *The Foreign Policy of Hitler's Germany* (Chicago, 1970), p. 297, basing himself on Warlimont's post-war testimony.

2. *G D*, p. 180.

3. *ibid.*, p. 186. The Germans believed that the British wanted only to safeguard their commercial interests in Spain. To this end, Faupel reported, not only did the commercial counsellor at the British Embassy, Pack, frequently visit Burgos to discuss such matters, but Chilton kept the nationalist authorities so well informed as to what was going on that the text of a statement to be made by Eden at 3 p.m. in the House of Commons was communicated to Franco by 10 o'clock in the morning of that day (*G D*, p. 181). This was not surprising, since Chilton was still very pro-nationalist. 'I hope,' he soon told Bowers, 'that they send in enough Germans to finish the war' (*U S D*, 1937, vol. I, p. 225).

with truth, hated Hitler and longed for an opportunity to break with him. An extension of this positive appeasement was seen in the Anglo–Italian 'gentleman's agreement' of 2 January 1937. This affirmed the independence of Spain and freedom of passage through the Mediterranean.[1] But the news of more Italian support for Franco put paid to any idea that this agreement would mean much. 'It seemed only too likely,' Eden later reflected, 'that Mussolini had used our negotiations as a cover plan for his further intervention.'[2]

'Armed tourists', as Winston Churchill named them, *commis-voyageurs en idéologie*, in the words of Colonel Morell, the French military attaché in Madrid, were undoubtedly now flocking into Spain.[3] On 15 January, a second expedition of 3,000 Italian Black Shirts and 1,500 technicians arrived in Cádiz. The Duce wanted his Italians in Spain for the glory of Italy and, therefore, did not want them mixed up in Spanish units, as Franco did. Franco gave way, with reluctance, for a time. By mid-January, Italians in Spain totalled 17,000.[4] These troops received two sets of wages: 2 pesetas a day from Franco, 20 lire a day from Mussolini. In Rome, other wages were nevertheless mentioned as an inducement to volunteers: 25 pesetas a day and 20,000 lire insurance.[5] Recruitment centres, meantime, were set up for Spanish volunteers in the larger provincial cities of Italy, particularly in poorer places, such as Bari, Cagliari or Naples. (There were also secret communist recruiting agents in Italy, for the International Brigades.) Not only that, but officials of the Italian railways were sent to Spain to reorganize the railways conquered by Franco. The Germans in Spain continued to number 7,000. All were paid only by Berlin.

On the last day of 1936, the American consul-general in Barcelona

1. It was expected that the agreement would lead to detailed negotiations, but these did not begin till 1938 (when they caused the fall of Eden – see below, p. 797).

2. Eden, p. 432. 3. *FD*, vol. IV, p. 71.

4. The Italian ministry of air noted on 23 January that 'by January, Italy had 211 pilots, 238 "specialists", 777 ground officers, 995 NCOs, and 14,752 troops'. (Qu. Cattell, *Soviet Diplomacy*, p. 4.)

5. *FD*, vol. IV, pp. 71 and 451. The dispatch on pp. 451–4 is helpful. See also *FD*, p. 563. Pay was thus over 175 lire a week, while a bricklayer in Rome would have got about 150 lire. Hourly wages for agricultural wages in Italy was 1 lira an hour. See Coverdale, *Journal of Contemporary History*, January 1974, p. 74.

estimated that 20,000 foreign volunteers for the republic had arrived by rail from France since October, 4,000 having passed through Barcelona and Albacete between Christmas and New Year's Eve,[1] while in Moscow, on 1 January 1937, seventeen Russian pilots were named 'heroes of the Soviet Union' for 'difficult government tasks' – that is, for Spanish service.[2] Thus war was carrying more and more men into Spain from all sides. Throughout, Russia made no public comment about her aid to Spain, but her tanks and aircraft were, of course, noted by all observers.

The first organized group of ninety-six Americans to volunteer for republican Spain left New York on 26 December.[3] It was actually an offence under American law for an American to enter the army of another state. But this did not apply to Americans who volunteered abroad; only to those who were recruited on American soil. From 11 January, US passports were normally marked 'Not valid for Spain'.[4] That made little difference, since from Paris onwards the volunteers could be looked after by the Brigades' now well-established organization. In fact, no prosecutions were ever made of US citizens volunteering for the republic.

1. *USD*, 1936, vol. II, p. 625. 2. L. Fischer, p. 387.

3. Edwin Rolfe, *The Lincoln Battalion* (New York, 1939), p. 18. This group arrived on 6 January at their base at Villanueva de la Jara, near Albacete, in the flat plain of La Mancha, whose bleakness recalled home to two from Wisconsin among them. Since they were accompanied by a number of Cubans, easy relations were soon opened with the villagers. The Cubans were led by Rudolpho de Armas, accompanied by the experienced communist leader, Joaquín Ordóqui, who was later, under Fidel Castro, to have a very strange history. Among them was a youthful communist, Rolando Masferrer, afterwards famous as a political gangster and senator. Other Cubans included some sixty members of the murdered labour leader Antonio Guiteras's paramilitary organization, Joven Cuba. A list of Cubans who fought in Spain would also include many of those who dominated the gangster politics of that island between 1933 and 1959.

4. The passports of these men may have played as great a part in history as the men themselves. For the NKVD secured the passports of many dead (and some alive) members of the International Brigade, and they were dispatched to Moscow: here a pile of nearly a hundred of them, 'mainly American', were observed by Krivitsky (*op. cit.*, p. 114). Then new bearers were issued with them, and entered America as, apparently, reformed citizens. One of these was probably the Catalan Mercader, the alleged murderer of Trotsky. See Robert Murphy, *Diplomat among Warriors* (London, 1964), p. 50, for an American diplomat's attempt to retrieve these passports.

The American 'moral embargo' on the sale of war material to Spain had been generally effective although some US material reached Spain through Mexico. On 28 December, Robert Cuse, a nationalized Latvian of the so-called Vimalert Company of Jersey City (probably an employee of the Russian government), applied for a licence to ship $2,775,000-worth of aeroplanes, aircraft engines and other parts to the Spanish government.[1] The state department had to grant the licence, but regretted that an American firm had insisted on its legal rights against the government's policy. Rightly fearing that the US government might quickly act to prevent shipment at all, Cuse began immediately to load his cargo on to the Spanish merchant ship *Mar Cantábrico*. The President, meantime, arranged that Senator Pittman and Representative McReynolds should introduce resolutions to ban shipments of arms to Spain into the two Houses of Congress when they reassembled on 6 January.[2]

On that day, in the Senate, only Senator Nye opposed the resolution. He argued that the embargo was unfair, since it harmed the republic more than it did the nationalists. Several members of the Lower House also criticized it. But the Senate passed the new law by 81 to 0 and the House of Representatives by 406 to 1. The dissentient, Representative Bernard, declared the act to be sham neutrality, since its effect was 'to choke off democratic Spain from its legitimate international rights at a time when it was being assailed by the fascist hordes'.[3] A technical error in the Senate, however, prevented the resolution becoming law until the 8th, and, on the 7th, the *Mar Cantábrico*, though with only part of Cuse's cargo, left New York in haste.

This was not the end of the adventure. Two American pilots, Bert Acosta and Gordon Berry, who had flown for the republic in the autumn at the high fees then offered, claimed that they were owed

1. The 'Vimalert enterprise' had sold aircraft engines to Russia in 1930 (Traina, p. 80).

2. This decision was apparently reached without discussion by the US cabinet. The secretary of the interior (*The Secret Diary of Harold Ickes*, London, 1955, p. 569) stated: 'I am sure that, if this question had been thrown to the cabinet for serious debate, there would have been opposition to it.'

3. Representative Bernard later introduced a resolution demanding support of the republic, suggesting at least equal restrictions against the governments of Germany and Italy.

$1,200 for their services. They persuaded the coastguard to serve a writ on the captain of the *Mar Cantábrico* in Long Island Sound.[1] But the writ turned out to apply only to the property of Prieto. So, accompanied by a coastguard cutter and aeroplane as far as the three-mile limit (in case the arms embargo should become law quicker than was expected), the *Mar Cantábrico* set off for Vera Cruz in Mexico, where she picked up a further cargo and sailed for Spain. Although then disguised as a British ship, the vessel was captured by the nationalist cruiser *Canarias* in the Bay of Biscay and the material on board commandeered. The Spaniards among the crew were executed.[2]

Franco announced that, over the Embargo Act, President Roosevelt had behaved like a 'true gentleman'. Germany also praised the Act. American communists protested, as did many liberal intellectuals in the United States. The Act did not cover oil. The President was begged by liberals at least to declare that, because of the presence of so many foreign troops in Spain, a state of war existed. Therefore, the liberals urged, the Neutrality Act of 1935 should be made to apply – so preventing any export of war material to Germany and Italy. Roosevelt was persuaded by Cordell Hull that such a declaration might increase the likelihood of general war. He, therefore, refrained from this step.[3] Some American equipment did reach Spain, however, through both Germany and Russia; for example, the T-26 tank had a 40-millimetre gun on it which was, to begin with, made in the US and sold to Russia.[4] Cuse's open challenge to the US government made things difficult for others in North America (such as the republican ambassador to Mexico, Félix Gordón Ordás) to find arms in the US more secretly.[5]

On 5 January, Portugal, and on 7 January, Germany and Italy,

1. The Spanish consul-general in New York later denied that any money was due to these men. Acosta was a famous flier, having flown with Admiral Byrd in the *America*, across the Atlantic in 1927.

2. Cervera, pp. 87–8; Senator Nye later accused the owners of a steamship company in New York of spying for Franco and causing the arrest of the *Mar Cantábrico*.

3. Taylor, pp. 75–95. There was also the catholic vote, upon which F.D.R. relied. Norman Thomas told the author that he felt this the most important reason for the embargo in F.D.R.'s mind.

4. Cervera, pp. 29–30; *FD*, vol. IV, p. 405.

5. See Gordón Ordás, *Mi politica fuera de España* (Mexico, 1965), vol. I.

answered the Anglo–French proposal on volunteers. (Russia had replied in the affirmative on 27 December.) The German note was drafted personally by Hitler. What was the point of by-passing the Non-Intervention Committee? Was it not unfair to make such a proposal now, when the republican side was so well supplied with foreign volunteers? But Germany would cooperate, provided that the plan was effectively controlled.[1] Eden, therefore, proposed to the British cabinet that they should offer the services of the Navy to supervise harbours round the Spanish coast, and be given rights to search. Baldwin, who before the discussion had approved Eden's idea, gave him no support; Hoare, First Lord of the Admiralty, severely criticized Eden, saying 'We are getting to a point when, as a nation, we are trying to stop General Franco from winning'. Hoare made 'every kind of technical argument' to invalidate Eden's plan: the Spanish coast was too long; too many ships would be needed; and the naval reserve would have to be called up. Other ministers took the same position, and the cabinet only gave authority for Eden to go ahead with an international, not a British, non-intervention plan. What Eden described as 'a truncated proposal', along these lines, was dispatched on 10 January.[2] Thus a good chance of a real non-intervention control was lost. From a paper circulated to the cabinet on 8 January, it became evident that Eden at least had come to see that 'The character of the future government of Spain has now become less important to the peace of Europe than that the dictators should not be victorious'.[3]

Germany, having seemed to be leaving the affairs of Spain all to Italy, suddenly took provocatory action. The German vessel *Palos* had been released after its seizure by the navy of the republic on 27 December, but one Spaniard on board was retained, along with a cargo of celluloid and telephones, on the ground that it was war material. Germany's demand for the release of the man and the material was not accepted. Neurath agreed to threaten 'sterner measures' if the demand were not immediately complied with. When

1. *G D*, pp. 210–12. 2. Eden, pp. 434–6.

3. Memorandum, 8 January, *CAB*/266. *CAB*/80(37) shows Eden to have been influenced by the requisitioning of the Tharsis Copper and Sulphur Co. and the Río Tinto Co., and the dispatch of pyrites and copper to Germany, whereas no copper had been received by Río Tinto at its refinery at Port Talbot since July.

it was not, three republican merchant ships were captured and two of them handed over to the nationalists. The bombardment of a port was kept for future use.

Another crisis followed. The French government heard, on 7 January, that three hundred Germans had landed in Spanish Morocco. The head of the Quai d'Orsay, Alexis Léger, reminded Welczeck, the German ambassador in Paris, of the Franco–Spanish Moroccan Agreement of 1912, forbidding the fortification of either Spanish or French Morocco against each other. Welczeck denied that there could be German troops in Spanish Morocco. The French press, meantime, became excited. Vansittart pledged British support to France if the reports should prove correct. The next day, French troops concentrated along the border of French and Spanish Morocco. Faupel reported to Neurath that there was a German unit in Melilla – a Spanish possession to which the Moroccan agreement did not apply – but nowhere else. Hitler, meantime, summoned François-Poncet and told him that Germany had no territorial ambitions in Spanish territory. The statement was given to the press, and the crisis died down. Colonel Beigbeder, now acting high commissioner in Morocco (in Orgaz's absence), told the French consul at Tetuán that, in fact, the Italians, not the Germans, 'were trying, under every pretext, to establish themselves in Spanish Morocco: they offered in profusion all that one could desire . . . he had refused'. He also said that, while some Germans had passed through Morocco, there were none there permanently, and none would be.[1] Beigbeder was an honest man and the French believed him. The incident thus passed into history as one more war scare, easily created and easily damped, in the chain of anxiety which destroyed the nerves of France between 1918 and 1939.[2]

But Morocco was playing a strange part in the civil war. Moroccan troops guarded General Franco, perhaps 50,000 Moroccan volunteers had been inspired, or cajoled, by the astute arabist, Colonel Beigbeder, to support the rising, yet negotiations had been begun between the republic and Moroccan nationalist leaders to bargain the independence of the protectorate in return for an end of their help for Franco. Before 18 July 1936, a 'committee of Moroccan

1. *FD*, vol. IV, pp. 457–9.
2. *USD*, 1937, vol. III, pp. 217ff; *GD*, pp. 215ff.

nationalist action' had sent a delegation to warn the government in Madrid of what was being planned by officers in the Army of Africa; but the government of Casares Quiroga neglected this, with every other warning.[1] After the rising, the same committee received representatives from the French Left and from the government in Madrid. The committee said that it would help to 'save democracy in Spain', providing that the republic would proclaim her support for the independence of Morocco from both France and Spain. Other demands were made such as that Spain should give arms to the nationalists and that France should embark on all necessary reforms in the sultanate. Abdel Kjalak Torres, leader of the reformist party, came to Barcelona in the autumn of 1936 to offer an alliance. The Catalans were interested, but Largo Caballero rejected the idea, for fear of making matters difficult for Léon Blum.[2] For Herriot, the French minister of the colonies, 'threatened terrible acts, if the republic were to give its support for such an enterprise which, in his opinion, was an act of madness'. Largo Caballero then merely offered 40 million pesetas to Abdel Kjalak Torres's committee to make propaganda for Spanish democracy, undertaking 'to behave well' in Morocco when they won. The Moroccans rejected this idea, but maintained relations with the Catalans.

Later, however, the republican government took other steps to try and stir up Morocco against Franco. For example, on 19 February 1937, they proposed to Britain and France concessions in Morocco favourable to both countries (perhaps an assignment of all Spanish Morocco to France) if they would change their minds over non-intervention.[3] Later still, Carlos Baráibar, by then Largo's under-secretary of state for war, would simply offer the Moroccans money to start a rebellion against Franco: they refused.[4]

On 14 January, Weizsäcker was telling a member of Ribbentrop's private information service that 'the Spanish adventure is to be abandoned. It is only a question of drawing Germany out of the affair gracefully,' he added.[5] Yet Göring admitted the same day that

1. Al-Lal el Fasi, *Los movimientos de independencia en el Mogreb árabe* (Cairo, 1948), p. 198.

2. Miravitlles, p. 119.

3. See Hernández, p. 75; Alvarez del Vayo, *Freedom's Battle*, p. 238.

4. Azaña, vol. IV, p. 66. 5. *G D*, p. 225.

Germany would never tolerate 'a Red Spain'.[1] Amid these conflicting attitudes, Göring, Mussolini, and Ciano met on 20 January, in Rome. They agreed that, now that Franco was 'amply supplied', Germany and Italy should support the Anglo-French plan to prevent volunteers entering Spain. The last military aid should be dispatched by 31 January. They also agreed that the civil war should under no circumstances be allowed to lead to world war. Schmidt, interpreter for Göring at this meeting, observed that both Germans and Italians spoke of their forces in Spain as if they were genuine volunteers – even to each other.[2] Weizsäcker also noted: 'Germany's goal, as well as Italy's, is in the first instance a negative one. We do not want a communist Spain.'[3]

Russian aid was also still aimed at preventing republican defeat. The intervention of forces large enough to ensure victory for either side in 1937 would have risked a general European war. Nobody desired such a war as a result of the conflict in Spain.

In fact, the Non-Intervention Committee was soon to achieve its own first real victory. On 28 January, General Faupel in Salamanca was told by the German foreign ministry that Germany desired 'as effective a control as possible to cut off Spain from supplies after it is established'.[4] This was soon agreed. There would be international observers on the non-Spanish side of Spanish frontiers, and on the ships of the non-intervention countries going to Spain. There would also be warships patrolling Spanish waters. Ribbentrop was instructed not to make air control a condition of acceptance of the control plan – for fear of ruining the prospects of agreement.[5] Grandi, too, was told by Ciano to be 'positive',[6] since Italian shipments to Spain had ceased. The stumbling-block was Portugal, who refused, for reasons of 'sovereignty', to accept international observers on her side of the Spanish frontier. Russia then said that she wished to participate in the naval patrol. She was offered an area off north Spain. Maisky suggested the east coast. That idea was rejected by Germany and Italy (who had been allocated that area) since they did not desire the Russian navy in the Mediterranean. Portugal agreed

1. *ibid.*, p. 226.

2. Paul Schmidt, *Hitler's Interpreter* (London, 1951), p. 62; Ciano, *Diplomatic Papers*, pp. 85–6.

3. Weizsäcker, p. 113. 4. *G D*, p. 237. 5. *ibid.*, p. 243. 6. *ibid.*, pp. 241–2.

to accept a number of British observers officially attached to the British Embassy in Lisbon, who would not be recognized as 'international controllers', and Russia, who anyway had very few ships to spare, agreed in the end not to insist on participating in the naval control. Perhaps she was persuaded to this conciliatory action by the capture just off Barcelona of a large cargo from Odessa in the old transatlantic liner, the *Marqués de Comillas*. The booty had been enormous.

The cost of a year's operation of the non-intervention scheme was estimated at £898,000. Britain, France, Germany, Italy and Russia would each pay 16 per cent (£143,680), while the other twenty-two countries divided the remaining 20 per cent.[1] The naval patrol would be undertaken by the four participants at their own expense. The scheme was finally agreed on 8 March. An international board, with Britain, France, Italy, Germany, and Russia (and later Poland, Greece, and Norway) represented, and with the Dutch Vice-Admiral van Dulm as chairman, would administer the scheme. Britain would be responsible for the Portuguese–Spanish frontier. One hundred and thirty observers, headed by a chief administrator (the Danish Colonel Lunn), would be on the French frontier, and 550 observers on ships sailing for Spanish ports, headed by Rear-Admiral Oliver, would supervise all unloading of cargoes. The naval patrol would be controlled by Britain from the French frontier to Cape Busto, at the north-west tip of Galicia, and from the Portuguese frontier on the Algarve to Cape Gata. France would patrol from Cape Busto to the Portuguese frontier, the Spanish Moroccan coast, Ibiza, and Majorca. Germany was to be responsible for the east coast of Spain from Cape Gata to Cape Oropesa, and Italy from Cape Oropesa to the French frontier. Minorca was also the responsibility of Italy. The setting up of the scheme, and the legislation needed in the various countries to ensure that their citizens complied, took until 20 April. The observers and the non-intervention patrol ships were by then in place. The non-intervention flag, two black balls on a white ground, waved hopefully henceforward off the harbours of Spain.[2]

1. Britain's 16 per cent was docked by £64,000, the estimated cost of the Portuguese frontier control. The background to the plan is described in Maisky's aptly titled chapter 'Words, words – and mountains of paper', *Notebooks*, p. 94f.

2. See *NIS*(c), twenty-second to fortieth meetings; *NIS*, fifteenth and sixteenth meetings.

34

The fall of Málaga and the battles of the Jarama and of Guadalajara

In the spring of 1937, three battles were fought in Spain: at Málaga, on the River Jarama near Madrid, and outside the city of Guadalajara, also close to the capital. The first, a skirmish only, was a victory for Franco; the second was a stalemate; and the third was a moral victory for the republic.

Málaga, with 100,000 inhabitants, is the chief city of a narrow plain running between the sea and the Sierra Nevada. Its superb climate and natural harbour have given it three thousand years of commercial eminence. At the start of 1937, the front, from a point on the coast twenty miles from Gibraltar, ran inland to Ronda and continued along the mountains to Granada. The republic thus held a coastal strip twenty miles wide, with Málaga as its centre. The only road linking the territory with the rest of republican Spain to the north was blocked by a flood at Motril. Málaga itself had been bombed and the workers had earlier destroyed the fashionable district of La Caleta. The town, therefore, presented an appearance of desolation. The authorities in Málaga had behaved as if they were a separate republic to the rest of Spain, and had organized themselves inadequately: hence it was said that the central government wished 'to hear nothing of Málaga'. But, formally, Málaga was under the care of the new republican Army of the South, headed by General Martínez Monje. He had a Russian adviser, Major Meretskov (a future marshal). His forces had begun to be organized as Mixed Brigades, but the process had not gone far.

A nationalist offensive began in this region on 17 January, directed by Queipo de Llano, leading their similarly named Army of the South. Colonel the Duque de Sevilla, a Bourbon and cousin of the ex-king, was in field command. He began by cutting off the westerly part of republican territory as far as, and including, Marbella, in the first three days. Next, troops from the garrison at Granada under Colonel Muñoz advanced to capture Alhama and the surrounding territory, to the north of Málaga. Both these two preliminary attacks were accomplished without resistance.

Though refugees from the newly lost territory crowded into the city and slept on the stone floor of the cathedral, the republican command at Málaga had no suspicion, apparently, that these events foreshadowed a general campaign. Nor was anything done to reinforce Málaga from Valencia. Since the road was cut at Motril, artillery could not, therefore, have been sent. Largo Caballero was anyway toying with the idea of an attack from the Madrid–Valencia road on the nationalists south of Madrid.

To the immediate north of Málaga, the mechanized forces of the Italian Black Shirts, nine battalions in all, rather more than 10,000 men, were now assembled under Roatta ('Mancini').[1] He had Colonels Emilio Faldella and Rossi as chief of staff and field commander respectively. (Roatta himself continued as chief of Italian intelligence while he was temporarily, as he supposed, in Spain.) Some of his troops were ex-fascists of the days of the march on Rome in 1922, most were new volunteers, though, as one of them later wrote, while all were legally volunteers, few were really so: they were '*voluntarios sin voluntad*'.[2] The Italian 'legionary' air force of 100 aeroplanes was in support. Unlike the pilots of July–August 1936 (who had worn Foreign Legion uniforms), these Italians had a uniform of their own, and operated entirely independently, so that they could, if possible, realize the glorious victory desired by Mussolini. Roatta had set up a base at Seville, where he gathered together his equipment, including many good lorries of Italian make, such as Fiat, Lancia and Isota Fraschini. His men had the same Mauser rifle used by the Spanish army, along with machine-guns, artillery and mortars of the First World War. Roatta at first had desired to mount an offensive from Teruel to the sea, but he had been talked out of the idea by Franco, who persuaded him to take part in the campaign for Málaga long coveted by Queipo de Llano.[3] Just before the campaign began, Mussolini told Franco that he could send no further aid after the forthcoming Non-Intervention Agreement on the end

1. His *nom de guerre* was taken from the surname of his wife. One of the young officers close to Marshal Badoglio, Roatta had been military attaché to France.

2. Letter from an officer of artillery to Alcofar Nassaes, in *CTV*, p. 58.

3. Kindelán, p. 63; Alcofar Nassaes, p. 64.

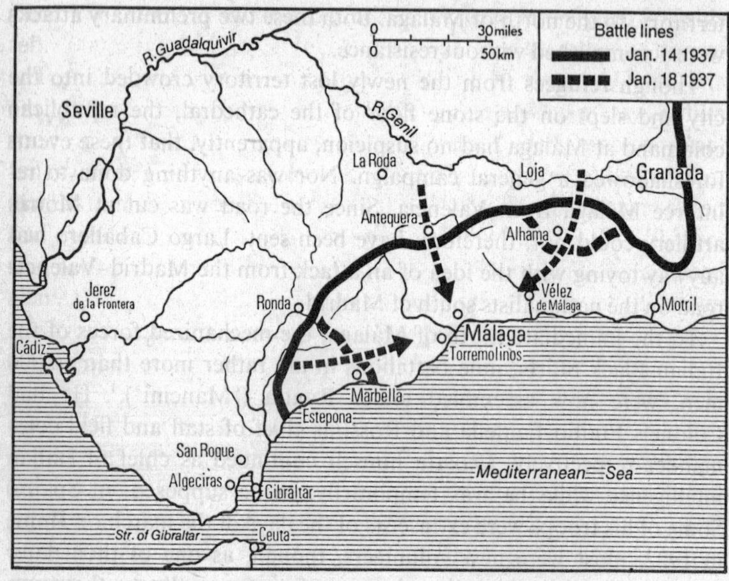

19. The fighting for Málaga, February 1937

of volunteers. Franco replied, on 25 January, that, since non-intervention control could not cover states such as Mexico, who were not party to the agreement, it should be rejected. He also gave a new list of war needs. Faupel and Roatta called on Franco to ask which of these were the most urgent. 'All,' said Franco. To secure this, the Generalissimo said that he would agree to set up a joint Italian–German general staff, consisting of five German and five Italian officers. The two allies went away to discuss this suggestion. Meanwhile, the Málaga campaign got under way.[1]

The republican commander at Málaga was Colonel Villalba, the turncoat of Barbastro, and recently transferred from Catalonia. A Russian colonel, who went under the name of 'Kremen', sat in Villalba's office trying to give him orders, but these were most unwelcome, and the communication between the two was slight. Nor was Villalba's understanding good with his supreme commander, Martínez Monje (who paid Málaga a short visit in January), or the

1. *G D*, pp. 231, 236.

chief of the general staff in Valencia, Martínez Cabrera. Villalba's troops numbered about 12,000, but he had only about 8,000 rifles and only 16 pieces of artillery.[1] Ammunition was very short. The militia were nevertheless confident, and warmly supported by the local peasants. For example, outside Málaga, in a *pueblo* too poor to have had large estates, Dr Borkenau was assured by a peasant that he was fighting for 'liberty'. In the city of Málaga itself, morale was low, discipline bad, brutality frequent. The political prisoners had been abominably treated in gaol. At the end of January, the communist deputy and commissar, Cayetano Bolívar, went to Valencia to explain to Largo Caballero the disorganization of the defenders: but Largo Caballero was not disposed to help, allegedly replying, 'Not a rifle nor a cartridge more for Málaga'.[2]

On 3 February, the attack on Málaga began in earnest.[3] Three battalions under the Duque de Sevilla advanced from the Ronda sector, meeting fierce resistance. On the morning of 5 February, the Italian Black Shirts began their advance. Panic developed in Málaga, partly because of the fear of being cut off. Villalba was unable to communicate a fighting spirit to the men of Málaga, and his conventional temperament was not such as to make him believe that a civilian population could fight to the death. In these circumstances, after the initial breakthrough, the nationalist advance continued with rhythmic regularity, along the roads. On 6 February, the Italians reached the heights of Ventas de Zafarraya, dominating the escape road to Almería. Roatta was wounded by one of the few shots fired in anger, though so lightly that he did not give up his command. Villalba ordered a general evacuation, believing the last moment to have been reached. In fact, the nationalists did not cut the road of retreat. They did not desire the fight of desperation upon which an encircled city would inevitably embark. The republican high command, the political and trade-union leaders, and others who feared the consequences of nationalist occupation, struggled to escape up the coast though the flood at Motril made the passage exceptionally difficult. The fortunate fled in the few available motor-cars, the re-

1. Martínez Bande, *La campaña de Andalucía*, p. 146.

2. Ibarruri, pp. 359–60.

3. The most careful account is Martínez Bande, *La campaña de Andalucía*, p. 139f.

mainder on foot. The *Canarias*, *Baleares*, and *Velasco* bombarded the town, but the republican fleet continued inactive.[1] In the evening of 7 February, the Italians reached the outskirts of Málaga. The next day, with the Spaniards under the Duque de Sevilla, they entered the desolate town. The Italians had lost 130 dead (4 officers) and 424 wounded.

There ensued the most ferocious proscription that had occurred in Spain since the fall of Badajoz. It was fired by the recollection of the 2,500 who had been killed in Málaga under the republic, the destruction of churches and the looting of private houses. Thousands of republican sympathizers were left behind, some being immediately shot, the rest imprisoned. One eye-witness alleged that 4,000 people were killed in the first week after the fall of the city. This may be an exaggeration. But certainly many were shot without trial on the beach, others after brief trial by the newly established council of war.[2] The only republican journalist left behind, Arthur Koestler, then of the *News Chronicle*, was imprisoned in Seville for several months, being much of the time under sentence of death as a suspected spy – an accusation for which there was some evidence.[3] The Italian ambassador, Cantalupo, at Franco's court complained that Italian troops had been discredited by the executions at Málaga, and Ciano ordered him to visit the town to see what was going on. He found rich women desecrating republican graves and later wrote to his master that he had personally secured reprieves for nineteen freemasons and the dismissal of two over-severe judges.[4] Among the loot was the alleged hand of St Teresa of Avila taken from a convent near Ronda, and found in the suitcase of Colonel Villalba. It was

1. Cervera, p. 73. 2. Bahamonde, p. 117.

3. He had been in Spain in August and posed as a nationalist sympathizer until recognized by a fellow German fighting for Franco. He was later exchanged, through the good offices of Dr Junod, for the beautiful wife of the nationalist pilot, Major la Haya. The British government intervened to help Koestler, because of his relationship with the *News Chronicle*, although Eden told the House of Commons he did not know what nationality Koestler was. He was, of course, Hungarian, and had been working for the Comintern in Paris since 1934. For the nationalist account of Koestler's case, see Bolín, p. 248f; for the Red Cross exchange, see Junod, p. 124.

4. Cantalupo, p. 137. One city prosecutor in Málaga was a young lawyer, Arias Navarro, who had been imprisoned for six months, and who now began a career which would end in his becoming Prime Minister of Spain in 1973.

dispatched to the headquarters of Franco, who henceforth kept it at his bedside.[1]

On the long coast road to Almería, nationalist tanks and aircraft caught up with the refugees. Many were shot. Many of those who escaped lay down exhausted and starving.[2] The attempted defence of this tragic exodus from the air was the last fight in which André Malraux's air squadron took part: the machines were by now mostly wrecked, the pilots mostly dead or wounded, and Malraux henceforth gave himself up to publicity, rather than combat, for the republic. The remains of the Escuadrilla España were integrated into the republican air force.[3]

This defeat led to the fall also, on 21 February, of Asensio Torrado, the under-secretary of war and Largo Caballero's favourite general, whom the communists accused of being in a Valencian night-club while Málaga was about to collapse. The two communist ministers in the government also complained that the cabinet had spent four hours discussing the problems of the glass industry at the height of the military crisis.[4] Largo Caballero had saved Asensio from disgrace in October when he had previously been pilloried as the 'general of defeat'; he was unable to do the same again, for the whole cabinet was ready to agree to his dismissal as a scapegoat, though he was no more blameworthy than many others.[5] Asensio was succeeded as under-secretary for war by Baráibar, editor of *Claridad*, an intimate of Largo's who, in the event, was no more helpful to the communists than Asensio had been. This affair was one more bone of contention between them and the 'Spanish Lenin'. It also caused a final quarrel between Largo Caballero and his old friend, Alvarez del Vayo, who supported the communists in this instance, as in most others.

Meanwhile, Queipo de Llano chafed at the restriction placed upon him by Franco that he should not proceed any further. It was an

1. Galinsoga, p. 285.

2. For the battle of Málaga, see Borkenau, p. 211f; Aznar, p. 339f; Koestler, *Invisible Writing*, p. 338f; T. C. Worsley, *Behind the Battle*, *passim*; Dr Bethune's diary in Ted Allan and Sydney Gordon, *The Scalpel, not the Sword* (London, 1954); R. Salas, vol. I, p. 803; Fraser, *In Hiding*, especially p. 149f.

3. Lacouture, pp. 247–8.

4. Ibarruri, p. 360.

5. The anarchists disliked Asensio as a disciplined opponent of libertarian activity on the battlefield. Prieto and the Left republicans disliked him because Largo Caballero admired him.

error, since the rest of eastern Andalusia, including Almería, could probably have been taken without much fighting. The capture of Málaga, however, gave the nationalists a Mediterranean port, thus enabling the blockade to be extended easily. The battle also cut the length of the front.

The defeat of Málaga coincided with a new nationalist offensive to the south-east of Madrid. The nationalists attacked in the valley of the Jarama with five mobile columns (now known to them as brigades) under Varela's direction, each with a regiment of Moroccans and Foreign Legionaries, under García Escámez, Sáenz de Buruaga, Barrón, Asensio, and Rada (the Carlists' old instructor), supported by six 155-millimetre batteries and a Condor Legion artillery group of new as yet untested 88-millimetre guns. The aim of the offensive was to cut the Madrid–Valencia highroad. It was undertaken along a ten-mile front running north to south from a line some hundred yards to the east of the Madrid–Andalusia highroad. The republicans had been planning an attack in the same area, but nothing had come of it, since Miaja was reluctant to let any troops leave Madrid to help General Pozas's army of the centre.

The attack, a surprise to the republic, began on 6 February. García Escámez drove furiously into the little town of Ciempozuelos, defended by the newly formed republican 15th Brigade, whose advance elements were overwhelmed. Rada advanced in the north to capture a 2,000 foot peak, La Marañosa, where two republican battalions fought almost to the last man. On 7 February, Barrón reached the junction of the Rivers Jarama and Manzanares, just short of the road junction at Vaciamadrid, bringing the Madrid–Valencia highroad under fire. The republican defence was hampered by a number of new Brigades, who had been intended to take part in the projected offensive, and now found themselves in retreat. On 8 February, Miaja sent the well-trained, and reorganized, 11th Division, now headed by the communist Lister, to aid General Pozas, the commander of the Army of the Centre. (Lister, in his memoirs, describes the Russian general Pavlov as the 'soul of republican resistance' during these days.)[1] Two republican defence commands were hastily put together,

1. Lister, p.100. Pavlov's aide, Kravchenko ('Antonio'), had been at the Lenin School in Moscow with Lister. Lister had Malinovski ('Malino') as his own adviser in this battle. Malinovski says that he had to give his advice very tactfully,

the first belonging to Miaja's army and commanded by the communist Modesto; the second, dependent on Pozas's Army of the Centre, was commanded by Colonel Burillo. On 9 February, the republican defence was reorganized all along the heights on the east bank of the Jarama. At dawn on 11 February, however, the nationalists succeeded in forcing the Jarama. A *tabor* of Moroccans (under Major Molero) silently worked their way in the dark to the Pindoque railway bridge, halfway between Ciempozuelos and San Martín de la Vega, another small white-washed village at the foot of the hills, where they knifed the sentries of the French André Marty Battalion (now of the 14th Brigade) one by one, while standing at their posts.[1] Immediately, the rest of Barrón's brigade crossed the river. The Pindoque Bridge was blown up by mines operated from the local republican command-post but, having risen a few feet in the air, descended on the same spot and so still afforded a crossing. The Italians of the Garibaldi Battalion, from high ground, concentrated their fire on the bridgehead and held up any further advance. Farther south still, Asensio had at dawn stormed San Martín de la Vega. Machine-guns held him up all day at the bridge there, but, at nightfall, he got across by a stratagem similar to that practised at dawn at the Pindoque Bridge. A detachment of Moroccans killed the Spaniards on guard. Asensio spent the night consolidating his position and, the next day, the 12th, stormed the heights of Pingarrón, on the other side of the river. Sáenz de Buruaga's brigade also crossed at San Martín and joined Asensio in the centre of the front. During the next two days, however, little further ground was gained by the nationalists, the 14th being a day of hard fighting without result.

Republican control of the air was meantime maintained over the battlefield, though the Condor Legion's 88-millimetre anti-aircraft batteries (their accuracy was phenomenal) limited the extent to which

so that Lister never really could feel that he was being dictated to (*Bajo la bandera*, p. 28). The Russian adviser to Pozas, Kulik, another future if ill-fated marshal ('Kupper' in Spain), also seems to have played a prominent, if negative, part. The anarchist 70th Brigade had Major Petrov as their adviser (sometimes acting as commander) and the future Russian Marshal Rodimstev ('Pablito') was with the 9th Brigade as a machine-gun expert.

1. See Martínez Bande, *La lucha*, p. 91; General Batov, in *Bajo la bandera*, p. 242.

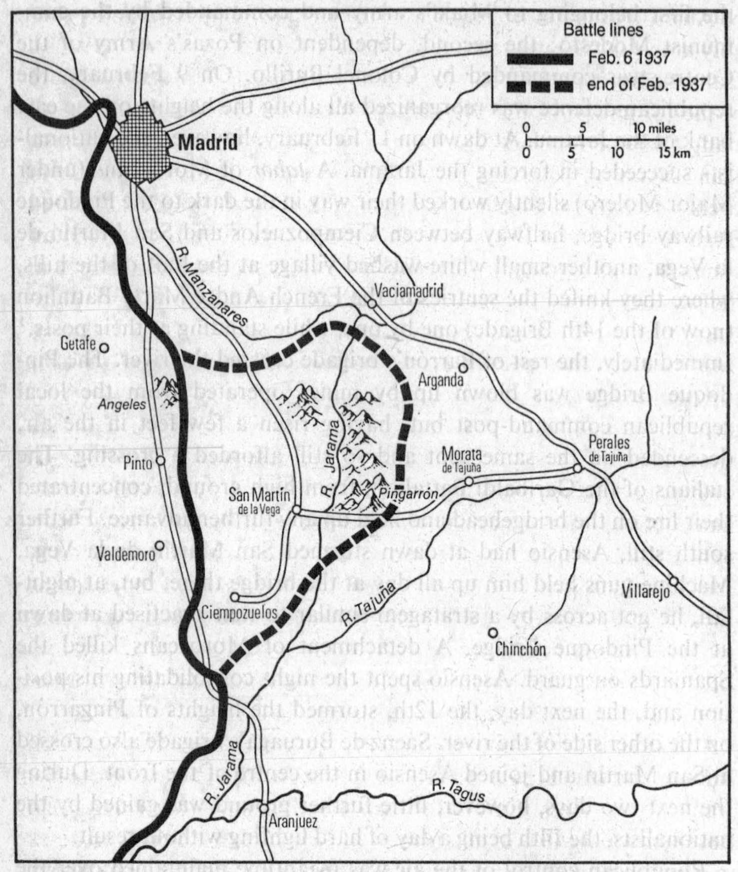

20. The battle of the Jarama, February 1937

this could be turned into a real help to an offensive.[1] Still, the old German Junkers were driven out of the sky by Russian *Chatos*, while the Russian tank brigade was concentrated before the town of Arganda in the north of the front.

This battle was the first fight of the 15th International Brigade, commanded by Colonel 'Gal' (Janos Galicz), a naturalized Russian,

1. García Lacalle refers to the precision of these anti-aircraft guns as '*the* revelation of the war' (p. 483).

of Austro-Hungarian birth, like 'Kléber' and 'Lukacs' (and probably active in the international brigades in the Red Army in 1919–20). Gal was incompetent, bad-tempered, and hated. The central figure in the formation of the Brigade, however, was the English chief of staff, Captain Nathan. The commissar was a French communist, Jean Chaintron ('Barthel'). The Brigade comprised volunteers from twenty-six nations. The first battalion of the Brigade were six hundred Englishmen of the Saklatvala Battalion – called after the Indian communist of that name who had been a member of parliament in the twenties, though usually known as the British Battalion. In command was the 'English Captain', Tom Wintringham, a communist from the middle class, an editor of the *Left Review* and military correspondent of the *Daily Worker*, an 'indefatigable military theorist', though with 'little actual experience of war'.[1] The political commissar was, first, David Springhall, a communist later famous for his part in a spy trial, and then an experienced and independent-minded Scottish communist, George Aitken. The company commanders and the political commissars were nearly all communists. The other battalions of the 15th Brigade were 800 mixed Balkans (including 160 Greeks), of the Dimitrov Battalion; 800 French and Belgians, of the 6th of February[2] (or Franco–Belgian) Battalion; and 550 Americans, the 'Abraham Lincoln Battalion', including a number of negroes, which was, however, still in training.

A number of Irishmen were tactfully divided between the Abraham Lincoln and the British Battalions.[3] Some of these men were, like Frank Ryan, members of the Irish Republican Army (IRA). To those knowledgeable of the ironies of Irish politics, it will come as no surprise that at that same moment an Irish group of volunteers (including other members of the IRA) were, by this time, also making their way to the front though on the nationalist side. Their com-

1. Jason Gurney, *Crusade in Spain* (London, 1974), p. 63; Wintringham, p. 16. The leader of the British Battalion in training had been Wilfred Macartney, a flamboyant journalist of the Left, who was not a communist – though he had been to prison for giving military secrets to Russia. He had to abandon command of the battalion because he was shot in the leg by Peter Kerrigan, commissar of the British in Spain, who was apparently cleaning his gun.

2. So named after the riots in Paris on 6 February 1934, but actually formed by coincidence on 6 February 1936.

3. Fred Copeman, *Reason in Revolt* (London, 1948), p. 83.

mander, General Eoin O'Duffy, headed an Irish fascist movement, the Blue Shirts. He doubtless hoped that the exploits of his six hundred men in Spain would bring him to political eminence in his own country. At this moment, they had completed training at Cáceres and had received orders to advance to the Jarama front.[1] Thus for some the Spanish Civil War must have been pre-eminently a war within the Irish Republican Army.

The British Battalion had borne the brunt of Asensio's and Sáenz de Buruaga's assault on 12 February. They defended the so-called Suicide Hill for seven hours against artillery and machine-gun fire from Pingarrón high above them, with a 'total lack of maps', and with perhaps three-quarters of the battalion never having held a loaded weapon in their hands before. It was a brave performance.[2] Nearly all the nationalist reserves were flung into the battle, while Lister, with his experienced 1st Brigade, arrived on the left of the British Battalion. A British volunteer, John Lepper, described the scene:

Death stalked the olive trees
Picking his men
His leaden finger beckoned
Again and again.[3]

The battle continued the whole of the 12th. The International Brigades suffered heavy losses, including most of their officers. Two hundred and twenty-five out of the original six hundred members of the British Battalion were left at the end of the day.[4] Wintringham, the battalion commander, was wounded, while Christopher Caudwell, a promising

1. Eoin O'Duffy, *Crusade in Spain* (London, 1938), p. 135. O'Duffy had been commissioner of the Irish Civic Guards till relieved of that post by De Valera in 1932. The Blue Shirts had been founded by ex-President Cosgrave after his defeat by De Valera in 1932. About half the rank and file, and nearly all the officers of O'Duffy's group in Spain were Blue Shirts. Those who were not were chiefly out-of-work adventurers. (See the pamphlet by Seumas McKee, *I was a Franco Soldier*, London, 1938.) For IRA membership see O'Duffy's book. At least one, Captain Diarmid O'Sullivan, had been in the rising of 1916.

2. See Gurney, p. 73.

3. Stephen Spender and John Lehmann, *Poems for Spain* (London, 1939), pp. 33–4.

4. Wintringham, p. 151f.

young communist writer, was among the dead.[1] One company of the British Battalion was tricked into capture by admitting to their trenches a group of Moroccans who advanced singing the 'International'.

It is easy to dwell on the exploits of the members of the International Brigades in this and other battles since their achievements are amply chronicled, since many men were courageous and since the fact of their presence was so unusual. But militarily more important at the Jarama were the Russian aircraft and tanks, which held the ground and controlled the air. Russian direction of the republican artillery was also important. The divisions between Generals Miaja and Pozas were responsible for some confusion, and only when Miaja was given equal rank to Pozas, as the commander of an army, that his reserve forces were fully committed.[2] Meantime, the legionaries and Moroccans, despite initiative and good leadership, were, by 16 February, driven into a defensive posture once they had captured the heights beyond the Jarama.

The front was not quite without incident. On 16 February, General O'Duffy's Irish nationalists had reached the Jarama front at Ciempozuelos. No sooner were they in position than they observed a force advancing towards them. The Irish officers concluded they were friends, and went to meet them. Eight paces from the captain of the advancing troops, the Spanish liaison officer with the Irish saluted and announced: '*Bandera Irlandesa del Tercio!*' The captain advancing drew his revolver, fired, and, in a few moments, the exchange became general. The Irishmen lost four killed, including the Spanish liaison officer. It then transpired that their opponents were indeed nationalists, from the Canary Isles. An inquiry was held, by which the Irish were held blameless and the Canary Islanders allotted all

1. His real name was Christopher St John Sprigg. He had written seven detective stories, five books on aviation, and three more works on philosophy and economics, including the famous *Illusion and Reality*, which put forward succinctly the Marxist view of aesthetics.

2. At the same time, the hated Colonel Gal was promoted to the rank of general, to command a division. He was replaced with the 15th Brigade by a Croat, Vladimir Čopić, a saturnine chess addict and musician, who had briefly been a communist deputy in Yugoslavia, and who later, under the name of 'Senko', had been one of the leading members of the Yugoslav communist party in Moscow.

responsibility. But thereafter the Irish were quartered at Ciempozuelos, and they saw little further action.[1]

Franco also had some difficulties with another ally: Italy. On 12 February, Roatta's chief of staff, Colonel Faldella, had come up from Andalusia and suggested another great Italian attack, so that they could add to the glory gained at Málaga. A large new contingent of regular Italian troops had arrived in Spain, under General Bergonzoli, in early February. What now about a thrust from Teruel to the sea? Faldella saw Major Barroso on Franco's staff, and, the next day, Franco himself. Franco complained bitterly:

First, I was told that companies of volunteers were coming to be included in the Spanish battalions. I agreed. Then I was asked to form Italian battalions and I agreed. Next, senior officers and a general arrived to command them, and, finally, already formed units began to arrive. Now you want to gather all these troops to fight together, under General Roatta, when my plans were quite different.[2]

Franco really wanted to distribute the Italians all over Spain. But he did not wish to antagonize Mussolini, so he again agreed. The Italians, volunteers and regular troops, would be allowed to form a single army under the name of CTV (Comando Truppe Volontarie) and fight on one front, though it would be to the north-east of Madrid, not where Roatta desired. Franco had still not given up hope of ending the war that winter by capturing the capital.

On 17 February, meanwhile, the reorganized republican army mounted a counter-attack. One division pushed Barrón back across the Valencia road. Another, from the north, crossed the Manzanares west of Marañosa. But an air combat on the 18th in which an increasingly famous nationalist air ace, Joaquín García Morato, played a decisive personal part, had temporarily given the nationalists aerial control. Under García Morato, the Italian Fiat fighters were showing themselves as good as the Chatos provided they were flown with courage and imagination, and at least eight Russian fighters were brought down.[3] At the same time, General Gal, the new divisional

1. O'Duffy, p. 157.

2. Conforti, p. 29. Roatta was promoted general after Málaga.

3. See Jesús Salas, p. 123, and Joaquín García Morato, *Guerra en el aire* (Madrid, 1940), p. 101. The caution of the Russian commanders – what would Stalin say if all these aircraft were lost? – caused them to hold their machines on the ground for the rest of this battle, thereby greatly assisting nationalist morale.

commander controlling the International Brigades, was unsuccessful in his attacks, on the 23rd and 27th, on the nationalists' front between Pingarrón and San Martín.

Here the Abraham Lincoln Battalion, 450 strong, saw their first action. Their commander was Robert Merriman, twenty-eight years old, the son of a lumberjack, who had worked his way through the University of Nevada to a lectureship at the University of California. He had come to Europe on a travelling scholarship to investigate agricultural problems. Alone of the Brigades, a majority of the Americans was composed of students. Seamen were the next largest group.[1] The Americans seemed innocent, beside the rest of the Brigades. They did not come from war-torn cities now ruled by dictators, as did many of their comrades. Few of them had served in the American army. They were younger than most of those in other Brigades. Yet they fought with great gallantry, without artillery cover, and quite as unprepared as the British had been a week previously. A hundred and twenty were killed, a hundred and seventy-five wounded. Among those killed was Charles Donnelly, a young Irish poet of promise.[2] Well might the survivors later sing, to the tune of 'Red River Valley':

> There's a valley in Spain called Jarama
> It's a place that we all know too well,
> For 'tis there that we wasted our manhood.
> And most of our old age as well.[3]

Henceforward, as had occurred in the battle for the Corunna road, each side was too strong to be attacked. Franco now tried to hasten the Italians to start their offensive to the north-east of Madrid in order to draw off the republican thrust, but they would not, or could not, hurry. Fortifications were, therefore, prepared. The battle of Jarama resulted in another stalemate, in which the republicans had lost land to the depth of ten miles along a front of some fifteen miles, but had retained the Valencia road. Both sides, therefore, claimed a

1. *Life* (iv, 28 March 1938, qu. Guttman, p. 98) estimated that 10 per cent of the American volunteers were jewish; 'I know what Hitler is doing to my people' was a normal explanation for volunteering.

2. Rolfe, pp. 57–71; Wintringham, p. 259.

3. Rolfe, p. 71. The best account of the Lincoln Battalion is Cecil Eby's *Between the Bullet and the Lie* (New York, 1969).

victory but both had really suffered a defeat. The republicans suffered more than 10,000 casualties (some 1,000 deaths, probably 7,000 wounded, some 3,500 sick), and the nationalists about 6,000.[1] The differences between the republican commanders, the toughness of the fighting, the sure sign that, even with substantial Russian aid (which, at least for a time, was technically superior to that of the nationalists), the war would be long, caused widespread gloom.

Franco's Italian allies were getting ready, as planned, to attack Madrid from the north-east. Their goal was Guadalajara, the capital of the province of that name, thirty miles from Madrid. They hoped that Orgaz would continue the Jarama offensive, and, if possible, meet the advance from the north-east at Alcalá de Henares, finally encircling Madrid. The attack on Guadalajara was undertaken on the right by the Soria Division under Moscardó, the hero of the Alcázar, with 15,000 fresh Moroccans, and some Carlists. On the left, 35,000 Italians fought under Roatta.[2] These were three divisions of fascist Black Shirts: the 'Dio lo vuole' Division, under General Rossi; the Black Flames, under General Coppi; and the Black Arrows, under General Nuvoloni. There was, too, the Littorio Division, a regular Italian army division, under General Bergonzoli. These were supported by 80 tanks and 200 pieces of mobile artillery, together with a chemical warfare company, a flame-thrower company, 8 armoured cars, 16 anti-aircraft guns, and 2,000 lorries. This force was accompanied by 50 fighters and 12 reconnaissance aircraft. The importance of the plan from Mussolini's point of view was that all Italians would act together, so that the victory to be gained would redound to the Italian credit.

1. The sources for this battle include Rojo, *España heroica*, pp. 54–69; Longo, pp. 208–38; Lister, p. 97f; Wintringham, p. 151f; R. Salas, vol. I, pp. 740–80; J. Salas, p. 160f; and Martínez Bande, *La lucha*, p. 73f.

2. Thanks to the kindness of Mr F. W. Deakin, then warden of St Antony's College, Oxford, I was able to see the report on Guadalajara sent to Rome by the Italian commander, General Roatta, in the library of St Antony's. There is a useful study of this battle by John Coverdale, *Journal of Contemporary History*, January 1974 ('The Battle of Guadalajara'). See also Lojendio, pp. 212ff; Aznar, pp. 380ff; Regler, *The Owl of Minerva*; Koltsov, pp. 350–53; Rojo, pp. 72–86; Longo, pp. 291–318; and Martínez Bande, *La lucha*, vol. III. The accounts of two Russian officers, Rodimstev and Batov, can be seen in *Bajo la bandera*. Italian accounts include that of Faldella.

The start of the offensive was accompanied by a bizarre proposal from Mussolini to Franco, put by the secretary of the fascist party, Roberto Farinacci, that Spain's troubles might, after the victory, be solved by the assumption of the Spanish throne by the Duke of Aosta, cousin of the King of Italy and grandson of the ill-fated Amedeo I, now viceroy of Abyssinia.[1] Out of those fighting, the Littorio Division, though a regular division of the Italian army, had been put together out of conscripted men, labourers who had desired to go to Abyssinia, many of them in their thirties or older, some not knowing where they were going to – perhaps to take part in the crowd scenes of the projected film *Scipio in Africa.* All concentrated in the new town of Littorio, under regular officers.[2] Though inexperienced as a unit, they had good equipment. All the Italian divisions were well provided with motor transport. Moscardó's Soria Division was only to be a reserve for the Italians, partly because it had to guard all the front.

Guadalajara in peacetime is a stagnant provincial capital commanding the gorge through which the river Henares runs swiftly down from the Guadarramas. The front was then held by the new republican 12th Division. It was broken at the first assault by Coppi's Black Flames Division, composed of trucks and armoured cars, operating the tactics later celebrated as the *Blitzkrieg.* At the same time, Moscardó broke through the republican lines on the Soria road. But in mid-morning, the temperature lowered, and rain fell. Sleet, ice, and fog followed. Many of the Italians were in colonial uniform, ready for the tropics. Their aircraft were unable to leave their improvised runways. The republican air force, in control of the air, on the other hand, broke the Italian morale almost at the start, General Smushkevich's headquarters being near by at Alcalá de Henares. The battle was indeed the occasion for 'the most rapid and orderly concentration of forces ever carried out by the republicans'.[3] The vile weather, as well as the fatigue of the men, prevented Orgaz from

1. Cantalupo, pp. 85–6, 147ff. Farinacci made no attempt to bring the ambassador Cantalupo into these discussions, and the two only met accidentally at a bull-fight. Farinacci had been known before the march on Rome in 1922 as the particularly brutal fascist *Ras* of Cremona.

2. Mussolini founded three towns of this name.

3. Rojo, *Así fue la defensa de Madrid*, p. 176; letter from García Lacalle, previously cited.

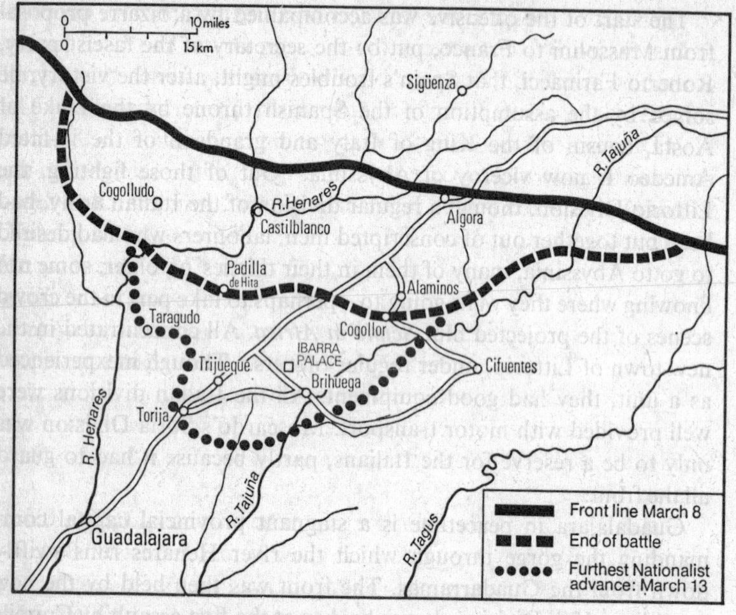

21. The battle of Guadalajara, March 1937

embarking on his attack in the Jarama valley. No doubt, a certain reluctance by him to help the Italians out of their difficulties played a part. On the next day, the 9th, the Italian advance began again, despite bad weather. Coppi's Black Flames entered Almadrones and then moved to the left flank to widen the gap in the republican lines, so capturing Masegaso. Nuvoloni and the Black Arrows took over in the centre, but the commander called a halt at night: a decision subsequently criticized, for it was crucial. Many of his men were either old or inexperienced in war, as well as being cold; and, as with all the Italian troops, the training had been bad. Moscardó, however, continued to advance and captured Cogolludo. The situation appeared for a time critical for the republic. This provided an opportunity for the communists to insist on the dismissal of another of their *bêtes noires*, Martínez Cabrera, republican chief of staff; he was replaced by Colonel Rojo, the chief of staff in the defence of Madrid. Though never a communist, Rojo was a competent technician, able to appreciate the military advantages of collaboration with the communist party. By the evening, a 4th Army Corps had been hastily assembled from the best republican regiments, under the overall command of Colonel Jurado, an able regular officer of artillery. The 11th Division, led by Lister, and including the German 11th International Brigade, and El Campesino's Brigade, was established in the woods along the road from Trijueque to Torija. Along the Brihuega–Torija road, the anarchist, Cipriano Mera, had established himself, with the 14th Division, which included Lukács's 12th International Brigade, headed by the Garibaldi Battalion. A third republican division, the 12th, was in the rear under a regular officer, an engineer, Colonel Lacalle. The old, partly walled town of Brihuega (a collective with 125 participating families) lay half-way between the two armies. Here, in 1710, the French General Vendôme had defeated Lord Stanhope, in the last engagement of the War of the Spanish Succession. Here again, an international battle occurred.

At dawn on 10 March, Brihuega fell to the advancing Italian Black Flames and Black Arrows under Colonel Enrico Francisci. Bergonzoli's Littorio Division of regular troops followed as a reserve. At the same time, Moscardó, advancing down the banks of the Henares, had reached Jadraque. Roatta was exuberant. At noon, the Garibaldi Battalion – accompanied by the formidable trio of Vidali (Carlos Contreras) as inspector-general of the whole front, Luigi Longo (Gallo), holding the same position for the International Brigades, and Nenni, who commanded a company in the battalion – advanced along the road from Torija towards Brihuega. They had no idea that Coppi and Nuvoloni had already taken that town. Reaching the so-called 'Palace of Don Luis', they advanced on foot, accompanied by a motor-cyclist patrol. Three miles short of Brihuega, this patrol encountered a motor-cyclist from Coppi's Black Flames who, hearing the Italian voices of the Garibaldi Battalion, asked if he were right in supposing that he was on the road to Torija. The Garibaldi motor-cyclists said that he was. Both groups returned to their headquarters. Coppi assumed that the Garibaldi Battalion's scouts were part of Nuvoloni's division. He continued to advance. Ilio Barontini, the commissar and acting commander of the Garibaldi Battalion, a Livornese communist, continued also.[1] He established his men in the

1. Pacciardi had been wounded at the Jarama.

vineyards on the left of the road, where they made contact with the similarly far advanced 11th International Brigade. Coppi's tanks now appeared. They were attacked by the machine-guns of the Garibaldi Battalion. The Black Flame infantry was sent in to attack. Two patrols of the opposing Italian forces met. The Black Flame commander asked why the other Italians had fired on him. '*Noi siamo italiani di Garibaldi*' came the answer. The Black Flame patrol then surrendered. But, for the rest of the day, the Italians fought a civil war of their own around a country house known as the Ibarra Palace. Vidali, Longo, and Nenni, meantime, arranged a propaganda campaign. Loudspeakers called out through the woods: 'Brothers, why have you come to a foreign land to murder workers?' Republican aircraft dropped pamphlets promising safe-conduct to all Italian deserters from the nationalists, with a reward of 50 pesetas. One hundred pesetas were pledged if they came with arms. Meantime in Rome, Count Ciano was assuring the German ambassador, Hassell, that Guadalajara was going well. 'Our opponents,' he added, 'are principally Russian.'[1]

The next day, the 11th, the battle began again. The Italian fascist commanders were favoured by an Order of the Day from Roatta instructing them to keep their men in the greatest exaltation. 'This is an easy matter,' went on Roatta, 'if they are frequently spoken to with political allusions, and are always reminded of the Duce, who has willed this conflict.'[2] The Black Arrows broke the front of Lister's 11th Division, capturing Trijueque, and began to drive fast in their armoured cars along the road to Torija. The Thaelmann Brigade received heavy casualties and might have suffered a serious blow to morale had it not been for the presence of mind of Ludwig Renn, their chief of staff. Rallying, they held the road to Torija from Trijueque. That to Trijueque from Brihuega was also held all day by the Garibaldi Battalion. Roatta ordered a day's rest. On the 12th, a storm permitted the republican bombers, rising from permanent runways, to pound away unmolested at the stationary Italian columns. The Black Shirts were machine-gunned from the air and bombed. Lister then ordered his division to counter-attack, a Russian

1. *G D*, p. 251.
2. *Spanish White Book* (Geneva, 1937), p. 275.

officer, Captain 'Pablito', the future Marshal Rodimstev, being particularly active at Lister's headquarters.[1] General Pavlov's Russian tanks attacked first, both T-26 and TB5 models – the latter, weighing 20 tons each, far more formidable than the 3-ton Italian Ansaldos. Trijueque was recaptured at bayonet-point by the Thaelmann and El Campesino Brigades. Many Italians surrendered. The republican attack continued along the road to Brihuega. The Garibaldi Battalion stormed their compatriots in the Ibarra Palace and captured it at nightfall. The following day, 13 March, the republican government telegraphed the League of Nations that documents and statements by Italian prisoners proved 'the presence of regular military units of the Italian army in Spain' in defiance of Article 10 of the Covenant of the League of Nations.[2] General Roatta dispatched his other two divisions, Rossi's Black Shirts and the Littorio Division, under Bergonzoli. These had been held in reserve to follow the initial breakthrough. Their use now meant that the original plan of Guadalajara had failed. Both attacks were beaten off. On the 14th, Pavlov's tanks drove up the road beyond Trijueque, towards the cathedral city of Sigüenza, captured much material, and might even have taken Sigüenza itself, had they been supported by mobile infantry. There was a pause in the battle for three days, on 15, 16 and 17 March. Roatta issued orders of the day, but made few preparations, pre-

1. Lister, p. 110. See Rodimstev's account in *Bajo la bandera*, p. 280f. Among those killed on this day was 'Consul General' (a rank in the fascist militias) Luizzi, ex-head of the Black Shirts of Udine. He was a battalion commander under Nuvoloni.

2. The documents captured at Guadalajara included many poignant letters from Italian wives and mothers to their serving sons or husbands. One wife wrote: 'What a beautiful honeymoon mine has been! Two days of marriage and twenty-five months of interminable waiting. First comes the country, I know, and afterwards love, but I am an egoist, and with reason, for you were one of the first volunteers to go to Africa, and are among the last to return. I pray God that one day He will make it possible for you both to serve the country and also provide bread for your family.' (Document No. 267 in the folio presented to the League of Nations.) A mother writes: 'Dear Armando, I can only pray that God and the saints keep you and if you return in good health we can go back to Rome and open the shop.' Other documents give lists of those shot as cowards for giving themselves self-inflicted wounds, and for bandaging themselves, when they had nothing wrong with them.

ferring to complain of the continued inactivity of Orgaz on the Jarama.[1]

On 18 March, the republicans on the Guadalajara front were put onto the offensive. The main thrust was led by Pavlov, who had sought to avoid the assignment, which had been insisted upon by Miaja.[2] It was a bad moment for the Italians: Roatta had that morning gone to Salamanca to ask Franco to permit him to call off the Guadalajara attack. Franco refused and insisted that now the attack had begun, it should be continued. The plans that he suggested to Roatta all called for continuation of the offensive. Roatta had just accepted one such plan, when his headquarters telephoned to say that the republic was counter-attacking. At half past one, over a hundred republican aircraft (Chatos, Moscas, Katiuskas, Natashas) attacked Brihuega. Heavy republican artillery-fire followed. At two o'clock, Lister's and Cipriano Mera's two divisions, with seventy of Pavlov's tanks, attacked, the one in the west, the second in the east, aiming to encircle the town. They had almost achieved this when the Italians received orders to retreat. They did so, so fast that the action was almost a rout, down the only road still open. The pursuit continued for several miles. Moscardó also was ordered to retreat to Jadraque.[3]

In this ill-named 'battle of Guadalajara', Mussolini's Italians reported that they lost only 400 killed, but they were not very truthful, and the figure was probably much higher. They may have lost as many as 3,000 killed, 800 prisoners-of-war, and 4,000 wounded. Moscardó's losses were insignificant. The republic lost about 2,000 killed, 400 prisoners and 4,000 wounded.[4] After the battle, apologists

1. Actually, several attempts at offensives were made in Orgaz's sector, without success. O'Duffy's Irishmen went into action for the first time on 13 March: the killed included Sergeant-Major Gaselee of Dublin and two *légionnaires* from Kerry.

2. The report of the meeting on 17 March which resulted in this nomination can be seen in Martínez Bande, *La lucha en torno*, pp. 154–73.

3. Regler, *The Great Crusade*, pp. 315ff. See Rodimstev, p. 306, Aznar, p. 113, and Conforti, p. 297.

4. See discussion in Coverdale, *op. cit.*, p. 67f. I follow Conforti's analysis, p. 376, for the republican losses, Martínez Bande's for the Italian losses and the Ufficio Spagna's for wounded and prisoners. Large quantities of Italian equipment were also captured: Lister says it reached 65 cannons, 13 mortars, 500

for the republic claimed it as a great victory over Mussolini. Ernest Hemingway, who arrived in Spain on 16 March, wrote, in a dispatch to the North American newspaper alliance: 'I have been studying the battle for four days, going over the ground with the commanders who directed it, and I can state flatly that Brihuega will take its place in military history with the other decisive battles of the world'.[1] Herbert Matthews, of the *New York Times*, reported that Guadalajara was to fascism what the defeat of Bailén had been to Napoleon.[2] Militarily, it would be more accurate to see the battle as similar to that of Jarama and the Corunna road. A nationalist attempt to complete the encirclement of Madrid was thwarted at the cost of twelve miles. But the retreat of the Italians, and the proof that organized Italian units were being used by the nationalists, was of considerable propaganda value to the republic. The battle had been intended as an exhibition of how the Italians could carry out modern techniques of war. But it in fact was an object lesson of how a mechanized attack should not be launched. Many tanks were left immobilized for hours for lack of fuel. The Italians had not maintained fighting contact with their enemies and had sought to operate without air cover, and without anti-aircraft protection.[3] The battalion commanders had no maps while even Roatta had only a Michelin road map (1 to 400,000 scale), whose lack of detail and of topographical information made it inadequate.[4] The role of the Russian advisers in this battle was considerable. Smushkevich ('Douglas') in the air, Pavlov with the tanks, Rodimstev with Lister, as well as Malinovsky, Batov and

---

machine-guns, over 3,000 rifles, 10 tanks. The 'Garibaldi' volunteers treated their Italian prisoners-of-war badly; did they kill them all? Possibly. (See Junod, p. 119.) See the inventory of the republican army published by Martínez Bande in *La lucha*, p. 227f.

1. Ernest Hemingway, 'The Spanish War', in *Fact*, June 1937. See Carlos Baker, *Ernest Hemingway* (London, 1969), p. 360f. The author of *Death in the Afternoon* thereafter took an active part in the war on the republican side, exceeding the duties of a mere reporter by, for instance, instructing young Spaniards in the use of rifles. The first visit of Hemingway to the 12th International Brigade was a great occasion, the Hungarian General Lukács sending a message to the nearby village for its girls to attend the banquet he was giving (Regler, *Owl of Minerva*, p. 298).

2. Herbert Matthews, *Two Wars and More to Come* (New York, 1938), p. 264.

3. García Lacalle, p. 239.

4. Coverdale, *op. cit.*, p. 72.

Meretskov: a galaxy of future 'heroes', even marshals, of the Soviet Union.

Guadalajara also had the effect of angering Mussolini so much that he declared that no Italians could return alive from Spain unless they won a victory. To Hassell, he blamed his Spanish allies who, he said, had 'hardly fired a shot during the decisive days'.[1] The senior falangist still alive, Fernández Cuesta, remarked to Angel Díaz Baza, a friend of Prieto's, sent to visit him in prison to talk of a compromise peace, that the Italian defeat at Guadalajara was the 'sole satisfaction he had experienced during the war'.[2] Nor was the discomfiture of the previously overweening Italian ally unwelcome to Franco and his high command. The gloom of Cantalupo, the Italian ambassador at Salamanca, became so great that he was soon recalled, after a posting of less than six months. There returned with him Generals Rossi, Coppi, and Nuvoloni, as well as the chief of staff, Colonel Faldella. But Roatta, more responsible than the others, remained in Spain, along with Bergonzoli, though General Ettore Bastico, a veteran of the Libyan and Abyssinian wars as well as the Great War, later replaced him as supreme commander in the field, and a well-known fascist organizer of the 1920s, Attilio Teruzzi, came to re-organize the 'volunteers'. The battle also led the general staffs of Europe (notably the French) to conclude that motorized troops were not as effective as had first been suggested. The Germans were restrained from drawing this conclusion by their contempt for the Italians as soldiers.[3]

The presence of organized Italian divisions at the battle of Guadalajara was discussed at the Non-Intervention Committee. On 23 March, the atmosphere of the committee had been excited by new reports that Italian troops had left in the *Sardegna* for Cádiz. Grandi said that he was unable to discuss the subject and, carried away by bad temper, added that he hoped that no Italian volunteer would leave Spain till the end of the war.[4] This candour caused consternation. The next day, Maisky accused Italy of 'ever-increasing military intervention', alleging that there were 60,000 Italians in Spain in mid-February (there were about 40,000), and that a commission

1. *G D*, pp. 258–60. 2. Zugazagoitia, p. 241.
3. F. Miksche, *Blitzkrieg* (Harmondsworth, 1944), p. 37.
4. Cattell, *Soviet Diplomacy*, p. 73.

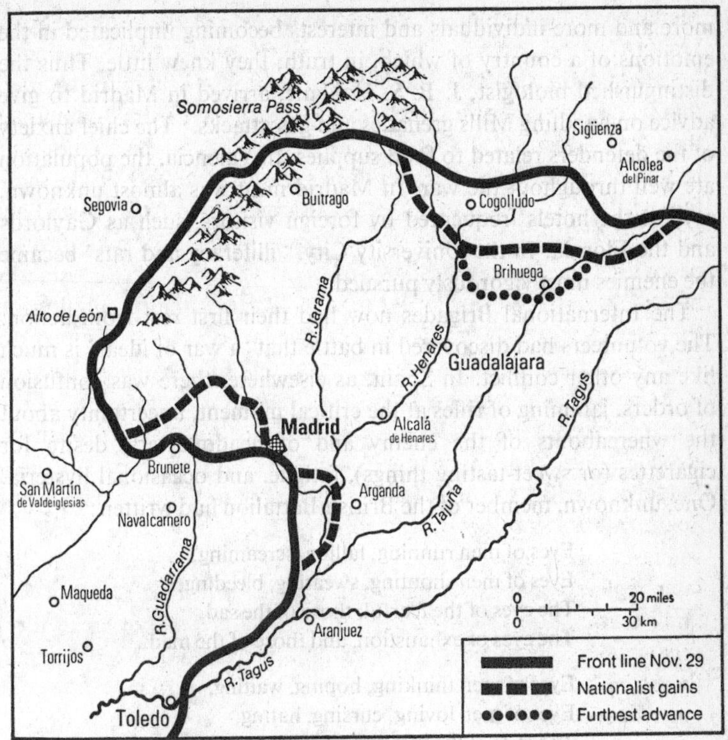

22. The battles around Madrid, November 1936–March 1937

should be sent to examine the matter on the spot.[1] Grandi's speech was discussed, in the meantime, in the chancelleries. German diplomats displayed tact. They appeared to want the control agreement to begin. Cerruti, the Italian ambassador in Paris, assured Delbos that Italy had no intention of breaking up non-intervention. By the start of April, the committee had been preserved, though it was not yet being used.

*

Guadalajara ended the conflicts around Madrid. Apart from intermittent bombardment, the front was quiet for months. The international shadows over the civil war, however, grew daily longer, with

1. *NIS*, nineteenth meeting.

more and more individuals and interests becoming implicated in the emotions of a country of which, in truth, they knew little. Thus the distinguished biologist, J. B. S. Haldane, arrived in Madrid to give advice on handling Mills grenades and gas attacks.[1] The chief anxiety of the defenders related to food supplies. In Valencia, the population ate well throughout the war. In Madrid meat was almost unknown, save at the hotels frequented by foreign visitors, such as Gaylords and the Florida. In the University City, 'illiteracy and rats' became the enemies most vigorously pursued.

The International Brigades now had their first rest from action. The volunteers had discovered in battle that 'a war of ideas' is much like any other conflict. In Spain, as elsewhere, there was confusion of orders, jamming of rifles at the critical moment, uncertainty about the whereabouts of the enemy and of headquarters, desire for cigarettes (or sweet-tasting things), fatigue, and occasional hysteria. One, unknown, member of the British Battalion had written:

Eyes of men running, falling, screaming,
Eyes of men shouting, sweating, bleeding,
The eyes of the fearful, those of the sad,
The eyes of exhaustion, and those of the mad.

Eyes of men thinking, hoping, waiting,
Eyes of men loving, cursing, hating,
The eyes of the wounded, sodden in red,
The eyes of the dying and those of the dead.

From the start, the wilder volunteers had met difficulties with the communist authorities, if only for drunkenness. But trouble was frequent.[2] Those who wished to return home were not permitted to

1. Haldane made three visits to republican Spain and henceforth he was in Britain a vigorous supporter of the 'Aid to Spain' movement, being then an 'open supporter' of the communists, though not yet a member, as he subsequently became (Ronald Clark, *JBS*, London, 1968, p. 115f.). For a picture of this scientist, 'pathetically anxious' to be of service, see Gurney, p. 77. Haldane's concern, and that of his wife Charlotte, in Spain had been begun by the enlistment of her sixteen-year-old son in the International Brigade. Mrs Haldane also visited Spain, but her main work was to act as matron for the reception of British volunteers for the International Brigades at the staging point in Paris.

2. Venereal disease was high among French volunteers, chiefly because no one had taken precautions against its spread. The British leaders gave lectures to their troops on contraception.

do so. Some complained that they had volunteered on the assumption that they could go home in three months' time. But they had no documents to prove it. Here the principles of a volunteer army fighting for ideals conflicted with military requirements. The punishment for attempted desertion or escape was at least confinement in a 're-education camp', for whose rigours idealistic, but easily disgusted, young men from Anglo-Saxon or Scandinavian countries were ill-prepared. But there were desertions all the same. The Foreign Office in London negotiated a settlement which exempted British volunteers from the death penalty if they were detected trying to desert, but that was several times imposed on perhaps as many as fifty others.[1] The communist leadership of the Brigades showed itself harsh to humanitarian needs, though the organizers, such as Marty in particular, lived well.[2] Uniforms were so scarce that the British Battalion seemed almost in rags.[3]

While some Anglo-Saxons became disillusioned, Eastern European volunteers continued to flow into Spain, many through Tito's 'secret railway'. Some were arrested on the way, since to volunteer for Spain was illegal in the non-intervention countries.[4] The right-wing governments of the Balkans and East Europe made every effort to enforce this. Nevertheless, the recruitment continued; in the universities or slums of central Europe or the Balkans, Spain seemed an exotic arena

1. Geoffrey Thompson, *Front Line Diplomat* (London, 1959), p. 118. Copeman recalled the execution later in the war of two British volunteers. See, for example, Eby, *Between the Bullet and the Lie*, for instances (also later in the war) of executions of Americans at the front. The number of Frenchmen shot by Marty's orders has always been a matter of speculation. See Delperrie, p. 778, for a summary of the evidence.

2. Though, in an effort to put the Popular Front policy fully into effect, cell meetings of the communist party inside the International Brigades ceased about this time for about nine months.

3. Nor were international relations inside the Brigades always happy. For instance, Gal, now a general, gave a banquet one night for the 15th Brigade. On his right at dinner he placed the new brigade commissar, George Aitken. On his left sat the new commander, Čopić. The chief of staff, Colonel Klaus, a Prussian who had fought as an officer in the First World War, was placed next to Čopić down the table. Klaus was so angry at this *placement* that in true German fashion he walked out and had to be brought back under armed guard. (Recollection of George Aitken.)

4. These laws were passed as part of the Non-Intervention Control Agreement.

with the liberty of the world in the balance; thus, while Tito continued to operate from Paris, the communist writer, Djilas, acted as controller in Belgrade of the flow of volunteers from Yugoslavia.[1] The base at Albacete became, in the spring of 1937, a power-house of communist leadership in East Europe ten years later. Most of the volunteers received, of course, from their Brigade journals and other reading matter, a mainly communist interpretation of the war and of the troubles of the republic: the POUM thus appeared in this literature, if at all, as no better than fascists.

Stephen Spender, the young poet who had been an active apologist for the republic, arrived at this time, in search of a former secretary, who had volunteered for the Brigades and who, being disillusioned, had tried to escape. For a time, it seemed that this man might be shot. In the style of a novel by Kafka, Spender dined with the commissars of the British Battalion who were his judges and who were persuaded to relent.[2] The *Candide*-like story of young Coope also shortly engaged the attention of England. He was a boy of eighteen, who volunteered for the Brigades after hearing a speech by the labour politician, Ellen Wilkinson, but who later escaped from them via a ship which left him in Greece. The boy's father went out to Spain to search for him and had to join the Brigade to do so.

The American battalions of the International Brigade were also visited by kind friends from home.[3] At one bedside, in a hospital financed by American sympathizers, Ernest Hemingway comforted a casualty by literary talk.[4] 'They tell me Dos Passos and Sinclair Lewis are coming over too', said a wounded American, a would-be writer. 'Yes,' said Hemingway, 'and when they come, I'll bring them

1. Vladimir Dedijer, *Tito Speaks* (London, 1953), pp. 106–8.

2. Spender, p. 212.

3. There were now two American battalions, the Abraham Lincoln Battalion, commanded by Martin Hourihan from Pennsylvania, and the George Washington Battalion, led by a Yugoslav American, Mirko Marković (Marcovich) – more Yugoslav, actually, than American.

4. The American Medical Bureau to Aid Spanish Democracy, headed by Dr Cannon of Harvard Medical School, had raised $100,000. For a time, the State Department refused, under the Embargo Act, to permit even doctors and nurses to go to Spain. Later, they relented. Another US fund was 'The North American committee to aid Spanish democracy', headed by Bishop McConnell. The two committees amalgamated in 1938.

up to see you.' 'Good boy, Ernest,' said the man in the bed, 'You don't mind if I call you Ernest?' 'Hell, no,' replied Hemingway.[1] This was a refreshing candour in the world of the International Brigades, where no one's name seemed to be truthfully given – to deceive whom was never clear, unless it was the republican Spaniards, for whom these Gómezes, Pablos, Martínezes, speaking in Slav accents, seemed to be playing a sinister game rather than a *ruse de guerre*.

The foreign-financed medical service, with their experienced and dedicated doctors, nurses and ambulance drivers, played almost as great a part as the International Brigades. Thus American medical aid had six hospitals in Spain, British medical aid, five. In these units, pacifists could serve the cause without a bad conscience, as could poets without military training. It was in one such unit that the best of the English poets of the day, W. H. Auden, served as a stretcher-bearer. But he went home 'after a very short visit of which he never spoke'.[2] Later, in June, a dependants' aid committee was formed in Britain for the welfare of the families of British volunteers in Spain. This was organized by Charlotte Haldane. Her secretarial staff were all communists, but the body was sponsored by uncommitted persons such as the sixty-year-old Red Duchess of Atholl (then a conservative MP, who later ruined herself politically by her championship of the republic),[3] Sir Norman Angell, Victor Gollancz, Professor Harold

1. Hemingway, *The Spanish War*. Hemingway shortly became busy assisting with the Dutch communist Joris Ivens's propaganda film, *The Spanish Earth*. The poet Archibald MacLeish, Dos Passos and Lillian Hellman were all involved in this (a successor to *Spain in Flames*, on which Hemingway had also worked, with Prudencia Pereda, a Spanish novelist in New York). Given these talents, it is surprising that the film was no better. (Dos Passos had just then had a great success with his recent novel *USA*.)

2. Spender, *World within World*, p. 247. See though Auden's article in the *New Statesman*, 20 January 1937. The experience of Auden in Spain is similar to that of Simone Weil. Both (unlike everyone else who visited Spain) were uninformative when they arrived home. Simone Weil, who spent some time in Catalonia in August–October 1936, underwent conversion as a result of her experiences. She had been appalled by the murders behind the republican lines.

3. Her Penguin Special, *Searchlight on Spain* (Harmondsworth, 1938), was the most successful of all the propaganda books on the Spanish war. In 1938, she resigned her conservative seat and stood as an independent conservative in protest against the government's non-intervention policy. She lost the ensuing by-election, despite the help of Gerald Brenan, Ch. 23 of whose *Personal Record* gives a vivid picture of the campaign.

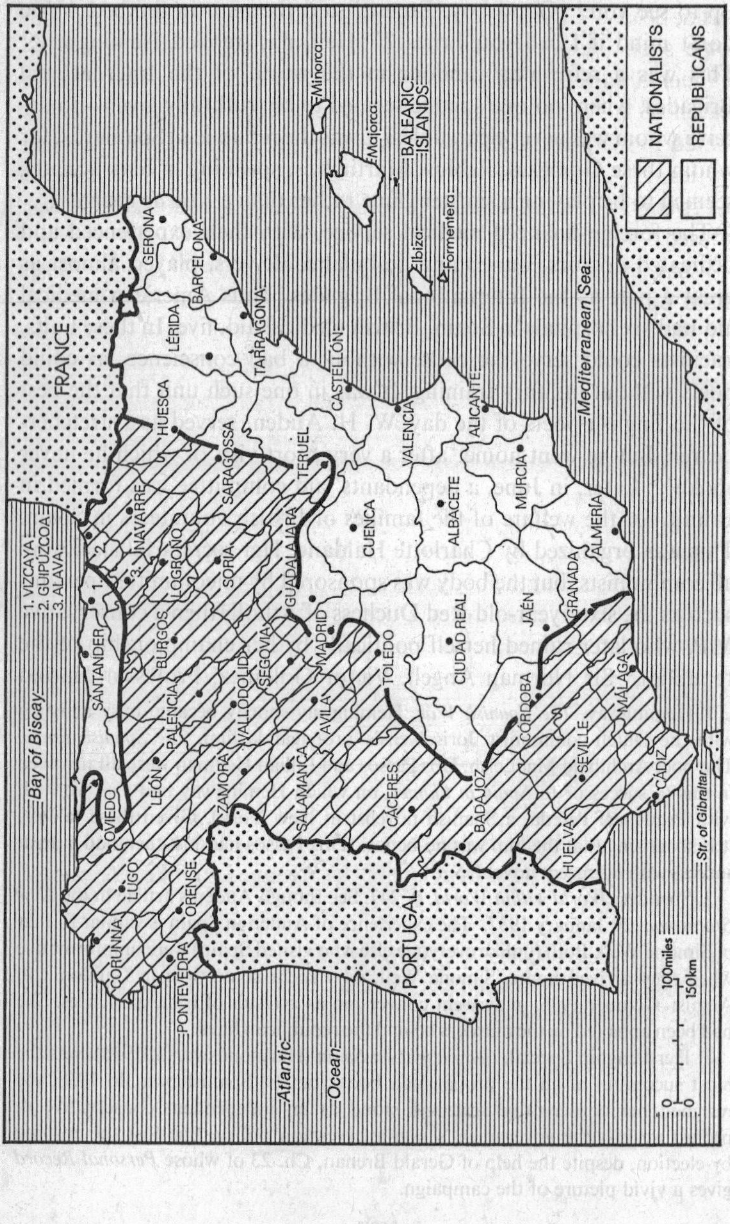

23. Division of Spain, March 1937

Laski, Sean O'Casey, H. G. Wells, and Sybil Thorndike; along with some social democratic labour politicians, such as Attlee or Emmanuel Shinwell.[1] Meanwhile, the United States government, in search of the purest neutrality, promulgated regulations which prevented the gathering of funds for one or other of the two Spanish parties, unless these were for *bona fide* relief purposes. But none of the twenty-six bodies which registered under these arrangements was refused a licence, and much money was found.

What was the reason for the passionate interest in the Spanish cause by so many who knew little of Spain before 1936? Virginia Woolf, when her nephew, Julian Bell, went to Spain, wrote:

I keep asking myself, without finding an answer, what did he feel about Spain? What made him feel it necessary, knowing, as he did, how it must torture Nessa [his mother] to go? . . . I suppose it's a fever in the blood of the younger generation which we can't possibly understand. I have never known anyone of my generation have that feeling about a war . . . And though I understand that this is a 'cause', can be called the cause of liberty and so on, still my natural reaction is to fight intellectually; if I were any use, I should write against it . . . Perhaps it was restlessness, curiosity, some gift that had never been used in private life and a conviction, part emotional about Spain . . . I'm sometimes angry with him; yet feel it was fine, as all strong feelings are fine; yet they are also wrong somehow; one must control feeling with reason.[2]

The answer to Virginia Woolf's question was that men such as Bell saw the Spanish war as a microcosm of European discontents, a way of fighting fascism, whether or no that dark cloud had reached their own land. Spain also assuaged a longing for action widely felt among the young for whom a civil war seemed, unlike the war of 1914–18, just.

1. Charlotte Haldane, *Truth Will Out* (London, 1949), p. 106. Gollancz and Laski were the directors, with John Strachey, of the famous Left Book Club, whose 50,000 members were a shadow political movement for the Popular Front in England.

2. Qu. Stansky and Abrahams, pp. 398–9.

35

The Basque campaign – the two armies – the bombing of Durango – Basque attempts at mediation – the blockade of Bilbao – Potato Jones – the Seven Seas Spray *– Guernica – Santa María de la Cabeza*

ON 22 March 1937, Franco put new plans to his air chief, General Kindelán. The front of Madrid would be reorganized defensively. Mola would embark on a campaign against the Basques, and would receive the bulk of the nationalist aviation and such artillery as could be spared.[1] This plan represented a stern realization that Madrid could not immediately be taken, and that the war could not be won quickly, even though, as a result of a vast recruiting campaign, the nationalists under arms would soon approach 300,000 men.[2] The republican northern territories were a tempting prize: not only were they politically divided and less well supplied than the centre, but they included the iron in the Basque country, and the coal in Asturias, as well as steel and chemical plants.[3]

In Mola's army, an essential role was played by the newly organized Navarre Division, whose men had been active in Guipúzcoa the previous year. This division comprised 18,000 men divided into four brigades led by Colonels García Valiño, Alonso Vega, Cayuela and Latorre. They were by now a match for the other older shock units of 'Foreign' legionaries (among whom some ex-anarchists and leftists were to be found, proving their loyalty by exposure to danger).[4] Many thought that Bilbao could be taken within three

1. Kindelán, p. 76.

2. About March 1937, republican and nationalist troops theoretically numbered about 110,000 to 80,000 in both the north and the centre, about 80,000 to 30,000 in Aragon, and 60,000 to 50,000 in Andalusia and Estremadura (F.Ciutat, qu. Payne, *The Spanish Revolution*, p. 330). But see p. 542 above for qualifications to these figures.

3. See report published in Martínez Bande, *Vizcaya* (Madrid, 1971), p. 223f.

4. Apparently, in early 1937 one group of CNT in the Legion tried to rebel and release the prisoners in Saragossa. The plot miscarried and all were shot (see Payne, *Politics*, p. 390).

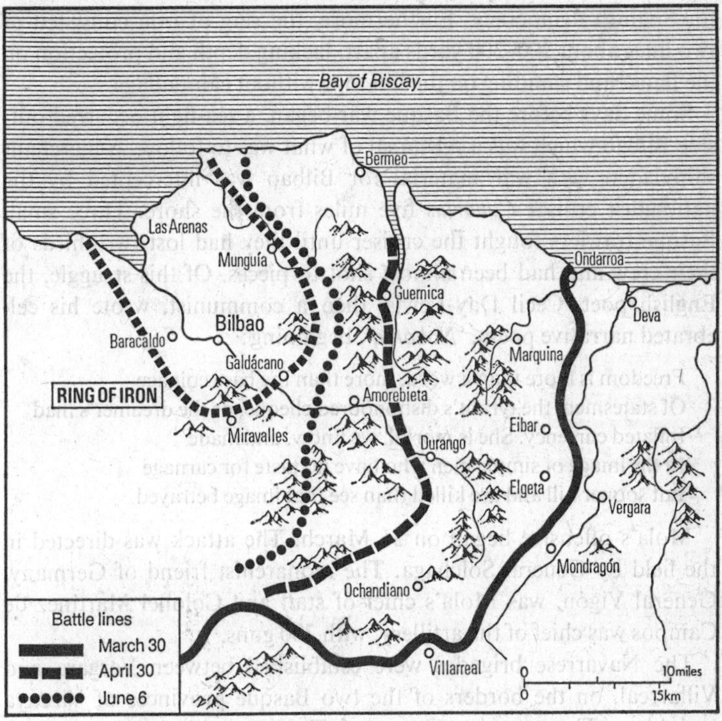

24. The campaign in Vizcaya, March–June 1937

weeks of the start of operations. For Mola knew the deployment of his enemies, through the treachery of Major Alejandro Goicoechea, a Basque officer, who had taken part in the building of Bilbao's defences, the so-called 'ring of iron', and who had driven over to the nationalists in his motor-car early in March.[1] No doubt he also knew something of the lack of contact and understanding between the Basques and the republican government in the centre: the Basques were, after all, fighting for independence, not for the revolution or

1. See his report in Martínez Bande, *op. cit.*, pp. 229–38. He later became famous in Franco's Spain as an engineer of another sort: he designed the Talgo, the low-slung Madrid–Irún express train. He was luckier than his assistant, Captain Pablo Murga, who had been shot as a spy in November 1936. (See Martínez Bande, *La guerra en el norte*, pp. 161–2.)

for Spanish democracy. Furthermore, the ring of iron consisted of two lines about 200–300 yards apart, lacking depth and protection on the flank, and standing on the hill tops without camouflage.

Some days before the Basque war began, a sea-fight occurred outside Bilbao which was a rehearsal of what was to follow. A merchant ship laden with war material for Bilbao was intercepted by the nationalist cruiser *Canarias* five miles from the shore. Three small Basque trawlers fought the cruiser until they had lost two-thirds of their crew and had been almost shot to pieces. Of this struggle, the English poet, Cecil Day-Lewis, then a communist, wrote his celebrated narrative poem, '*Nabarra*', beginning:

> Freedom is more than a word, more than the base coinage
> Of statesmen, the tyrant's dishonoured cheque, or the dreamer's mad
> Inflated currency. She is mortal, we know, and made
> In the image of simple men who have no taste for carnage
> But sooner kill and are killed than see that image betrayed.

Mola's offensive began on 31 March. The attack was directed in the field by General Solchaga. The monarchist friend of Germany, General Vigón, was Mola's chief of staff and Colonel Martínez de Campos was chief of the artillery, with 200 guns.

The Navarrese brigades were established between Vergara and Villarreal, on the borders of the two Basque provinces of Vizcaya and Alava. They were heavily armed. Together with them were a new force, the Black Arrows, numbering 8,000 Spaniards with Italian officers, headed by Colonel Sandro Piazzoni. In support, 80 German aircraft were assembled at Vitoria, and another 70 Italian and Spanish planes at other northern nationalist aerodromes.[1] The nationalist fleet, including the old battleship *Jaime I*, the cruisers *Canarias* and *Almirante Cervera*, and the destroyer *Velasco*, could establish, with many smaller vessels, an effective blockade.

1. Aznar, p. 397. The Condor Legion at this time was composed of (1) a combat group of two squadrons of Heinkels 51 and one of the new fast Messerschmitts 109, and one or two fighters; the commander of this group was von Merhard; (2) a bomber group of two squadrons of Junkers 52 and Heinkels 111, commanded by Major Fuchs; (3) a squadron of reconnaissance aircraft commanded by Major Kessel; (4) a squadron of light bombers (Henschels 123); (5) a squadron of Heinkel 59 seaplanes; (6) a squadron of Junkers 52, for transport; (7) anti-aircraft batteries. The Legion continued to have altogether 100 aircraft. Sperrle remained the commander. (Jesús Salas, pp. 212–13.)

The republican Army of the North was still commanded by General Llano de la Encomienda, the loyal commander of the army in Barcelona in July 1936. He was pessimistic of victory, since, though his charge covered the republican forces along the Cantabrian coast, there was still no unity at all among the Basques, Asturians, and Santanderinos, nor even the pretence of it. The commissar-general of the army was the Asturian socialist, González Peña: the commissar in the Basque country, the Basque communist deputy, Jesús Larrañaga; in Asturias, the anarchist Francisco Martínez; and in Santander, Antonio Somarriba, a socialist. This coalition did not work. Even the communist Larrañaga was at the mercy of conflicting opinions, since the Basques distrusted him as a communist, the communists as a Basque who even, unlike Aguirre, spoke Basque in his family. The inspector-general of the Army of the North, General Martínez Cabrera, the recently dismissed chief of staff, did not have a good name. Largo Caballero had privately assured the Basques that the Army of the North did not really exist and that he recognized the Basque army, the 'army of Euzkadi' which was nominally a part of Llano de la Encomienda's command, as the main military organization in the north of Spain.[1] Llano de la Encomienda had been forced to the humiliation of sending a telegram asking the Prime Minister whether that was indeed so. He moved his headquarters to Santander in February and had little thereafter to do with the day-to-day business of the campaign. His troops altogether theoretically numbered 150,000. In theory, too, he had over 250 pieces of artillery, but they were divided, with 75 in Vizcaya, 130 in Asturias and 50 in Santander. He had a few T-26 Russian tanks, and a few Renault tanks from France, but these were fewer than those of their opponents. Against the strong nationalist navy, the republic in the north could call on only two destroyers off shore and three submarines. The Basques had only about 25 to 30 aircraft. Republican bombers in the centre of Spain had too short range to help the

1. Twelve questions put by Llano de la Encomienda to Aguirre on 9 January are published in R. Salas, vol. III, p. 2840. Question No. 7 was characteristic: 'the clothing and equipment belongs to Euzkadi or to the Army of the North? If it is of the latter, can the central staff intervene in its distribution?' The Basque section of this army numbered 36,000 in March, being increased ultimately to 100,000 by June (Martínez Bande, *Vizcaya*, p. 36).

northern battlefield from there and they were not moved. (Some fighters, however, were soon dispatched.) The equipment of the armies of the north was not as good as it might have been, considering that the republic controlled the arms factories of Trubia, Eibar, and Reinosa, the munitions and explosive plants of Galdacano, Guernica and La Manoya, not to speak of the several steel plants of Vizcaya. But levels of production there had fallen, not risen, in the war.

The Basques had raised forty-six infantry battalions, totalling about 30,000. Of these, twenty-seven were Basque nationalists (these being known as *gudaris*), eight socialists, the remainder mixed communists, socialist-communist youth, left republicans, and anarchists. This army was attended by a corps of almoners, composed of eighty-two priests, whose duties, unique in the republican army, were to celebrate mass, to watch the *gudaris*' morality, to be present at the last moments of the dying, and to 'form the minds of the conscripts in the christian tradition'. There were also about ten battalions of Asturians, who were very unpopular with the Basques due to their thefts of cattle, their seduction of Basque girls and even occasionally their murderous behaviour: thus the priest of Abadiano was apparently shot by the Asturians as they passed through.[1]

Mola issued a preliminary ultimatum reminiscent of the Athenians' threat to Melos: 'I have decided to terminate rapidly the war in the north: those not guilty of assassinations and who surrender their arms will have their lives and property spared. But, if submission is not immediate, I will raze all Vizcaya to the ground, beginning with the industries of war.'[2]

On 31 March, this threat, intended to have psychological importance, began to be put into practice. Junkers 52 of the Condor Legion bombed the country town of Durango, a road and railway junction between Bilbao and the front. One bomb killed 14 nuns in the chapel of Santa Susana. The Jesuit church was bombed at the moment the priest was communicating the Body of Christ. In the church of Santa María, the priest was killed while elevating the Host. The rest of the town was also bombed and machine-gunned. 127 civilians, including 2 priests and 13 nuns, were killed that day, and 121 died later in hospitals.[3]

1. Martínez Bande, *Vizcaya*, p. 135.
2. Qu. Aznar, vol. II, p. 133. 3. Steer, p. 162.

Durango had previously been known as the town where Don Carlos had decreed, in 1834, that all foreigners taken in arms against him should be executed without trial. From 1937, it enjoyed the equally cruel renown of being the first defenceless town in Europe to be mercilessly bombed.

The same day, after heavy and well coordinated air and artillery bombardment, the nationalist Colonel Alonso Vega advanced on the right of the front to capture the three mountains of Maroto, Albertia, and Jarindo. North of Villarreal, in the centre of the front, violent fighting occurred in the suburbs of Ochandiano. This battle continued until 4 April. Forty to fifty aircraft bombed the town each day. The Navarrese nearly encircled it. Terrified of being cut off and so falling alive into the hands of the enemy, the Basques withdrew, leaving six hundred dead. Four hundred prisoners were taken. After 4 April, there was a pause in the offensive, due to heavy rain. Mola reorganized his troops for the next phase of the campaign, which had already seemed likely to be longer than he had at first prophesied. General von Sperrle complained.[1]

The Basques fortified their new positions, and made further adjustments to the ring of iron. The tactical use of aerial bombardment, however inaccurate, had caused much alarm, and increased the hatred against Germany. More men were mobilized, and some further war material arrived, so that, by 10 April, the Basques had 140 pieces of artillery.[2] The arrival of General Goriev, the outstanding Russian officer in Spain, as military adviser, with some other Russian personnel, did not, however, seem to improve matters, despite Goriev's high reputation in Madrid.[3]

On 6 April, the nationalists announced that they would prevent food supplies from entering republican ports in north Spain.[4] The

1. Alcofar Nassaes, p. 112; see also Sancho Piazzoni, *Las tropas Flechas Negras* (Barcelona, 1942). *G D*, p. 269.

2. Martínez Bande, *Vizcaya*, p. 35.

3. Koltsov, p. 397; Castro Delgado, p. 517f. There were also serious disputes within the Basque communist party: Astigarrabía and Urondo (director of public works) were closer to the Basque government's policy than others outside the government, such as Ormazábal, Larrañaga, and Monzón (Ibarruri, p. 388; Castro Delgado, p. 525).

4. British ships carried most of the trade to and from Spain. British exports to Spain fell during 1937. Coal exports went down by 37 per cent, machinery by

British steamer *Thorpehall*, with a cargo of provisions for Bilbao from Santander, was accordingly stopped five miles off shore by the nationalist cruiser *Almirante Cervera* and the armed trawler *Galerna*. Eventually, the *Thorpehall* was allowed to pass, since the nationalist vessels showed a disinclination to quarrel with two British destroyers, HMS *Blanche* and *Brazen*, which hastened to the scene. This event raised in an acute form the whole matter of blockade. In the early part of the war, the republican government had declared a blockade of certain ports of nationalist territory. The British had considered that the declaration applied to far too large a territory and, 'in order to be valid', blockade 'had to be effective'.[1] Thus, if a Spanish warship had stopped any merchantmen on the high seas, Britain would have regarded the action as incorrect. British ships would have to be protected against such interference. Britain furthermore only recognized a three-mile limit off the coast, whereas Spain insisted on six miles. The complexity of the situation was such that naval orders were amended so often as to place an intolerable burden on junior officers of the Navy.

The announcement of this new nationalist blockade exacerbated the complexity of the position of the British government. By international law, a blockade (including the right of search on the high seas) could be carried out by recognized belligerents. But because they did not wish to subject British merchantmen to search by Spanish naval vessels, Baldwin and his ministers were opposed to the recognition of the two Spanish warring parties as belligerents. The situation was further complicated by the fact that many foreign vessels flew British flags to try to avoid detention and secure protection. As the British cabinet were aware, many merchantmen were

---

90 per cent, motor-cars by 95 per cent, cutlery by 90 per cent (figures for all Spain, since the Board of Trade did not separate statistics for the two Spains). British imports, however, increased, except in respect of nuts and potatoes. For those British persons who worried about their investments in Spain, that genius *manqué* of the epoch, Brian Howard, on the Left if an aesthete, wrote a poem urging them to

> Spare a thought, a thought for all these Spanish tombs,
> And for a people in danger, grieving in breaking rooms,
> For a people in danger, shooting from falling homes.

1. *FO*, 371/205/33.

'virtually blockade-runners who took the risk for the high freights'.[1] But the nationalists now had command of the seas. If, therefore, belligerent rights were granted, it would be nationalist naval vessels that would mostly be doing the intercepting, and British merchantmen which would mostly suffer. But if belligerent rights were not accepted, British merchant ships would be entitled to ask for the aid of the Royal Navy if they were interfered with (outside the Basque territorial waters). How much less trouble, therefore, it would be if there were no British merchant ships going to Basque ports at all!

This last reflection, perhaps made subconsciously, probably disposed the captain of HMS *Blanche* and the commander-in-chief of the Mediterranean fleet to conclude that the nationalist blockade was effective. Sir Henry Chilton reported the same from Hendaye. There were similar reports: not only was the nationalist navy outside Bilbao able to prevent the entry of all merchantmen; but Basque territorial waters were mined. Thus (reported Chilton and the Navy) it would be dangerous for British merchant ships to try to enter Bilbao. Inside the three-mile limit, of course, the Royal Navy had no right to protect merchantmen. Since the Basques had lost command of the sea, attacks might be carried out against British ships within the territorial waters. So the Admiralty instructed all British merchant vessels, within a hundred miles of Bilbao, to repair to the French fishing port of St Jean de Luz, and to await further orders. The following day, Chilton was told by Major Julián Troncoso, the nationalist military governor of Irún, on instructions from Burgos, that Franco was determined to make the blockade effective. The voyage of four British merchantmen known to be bearing food cargoes and now at St Jean de Luz would, in particular, be prevented by force. Meantime, more mines would be laid across Bilbao harbour.[2] This determined statement reached London on the morning of Saturday 10 April. It caused Baldwin to summon the cabinet for Sunday. Back from their weekends, then came, among others, Duff Cooper, secretary of state for war, Sir Samuel Hoare, the First Lord of the Admiralty, Sir John Simon, the Home Secretary, and Eden,

1. *CAB*, 23/88, meeting of 7 April, remark of Runciman, president of the Board of Trade.

2. Nationalist note of 9 April, referred to by Eden in the House of Commons, 19 April (*Hansard*, House of Commons, vol. 322, col. 1404).

the Foreign Secretary. As a result, the Board of Trade 'warned' British ships not to go to Bilbao, and intimated that the Navy could not help them if they tried to do so. The Admiralty also sent the battleship *Hood*, pride of the fleet, to 'somewhere in the neighbourhood of Bilbao, in order that the British forces in that region might not be inferior to those of General Franco'. Baldwin explained, to an angry House of Commons on the following Monday, that there were risks against which it was impossible to protect British shipping.[1] The government was concerned less with the abstract principle of the freedom of the seas than the important matter of the 60,000 tons of iron ore which normally Britain imported from Basque ports.[2] In fact, the ports themselves of northern Spain were free of mines and there was reason to suppose that they would continue to be, for mines would hinder the nationalists' own use of the ports in the event of their victory. But the approaches to the ports had been mined.

Throughout the following week, there was uproar in Parliament. All that spring, Spain had been an incessant topic for question-time and for debates on foreign affairs. Eden and his lieutenant, Cranborne, had been hard pressed both by labour and liberal sympathizers of the republic and by the handful of conservatives who supported the nationalists. Had the government heard of the arrival of new Italian divisions at Cádiz? How many Russians were there at Madrid? How many British volunteers had been killed? To these questions, the government had professed ignorance of exact information. They had also been carrying on secret negotiations with the nationalists so as to ensure for themselves the produce of British-owned mines in the rebel zone, provided that they did not sell pyrites to France.[3] Now the British interest in Spain reached a climax. Eden defended non-intervention, in a speech at Liverpool:

> A broad gain remains. The policy of non-intervention has limited and bit by bit reduced the flow of foreign intervention in arms and men into Spain. Even more important, the existence of that policy, the knowledge that many governments, despite all discouragement, were working for it, has greatly reduced the risks of a general war.[4]

1. Eden, p. 462; *CAB*, 15/37, 11 April 1937 (*Hansard*, House of Commons, vol. 322, col. 597).

2. *CAB*, 16(37): meeting on 14 April 1937.

3. *CAB*, 23/87.

4. Anthony Eden, *Foreign Affairs* (Speeches) (London, 1938), pp. 189–90 (speech of 12 April).

Privately, Eden 'definitely wanted the republic to win'.[1] On 14 April, Attlee moved a vote of censure. The British government, the greatest maritime power in the world, had given up trying to protect British shipping; yet the Basques had said that the mines in Bilbao harbour had been cleared, and that at night armed trawlers (aided by searchlights) protected the port. (This information came from a telegram which he had had from Aguirre.) Where did the government gain its information of the dangers? Did it do so from 'those curious people, our consular agents, who seem so silent on the question of Italian troops landing'? Sir John Simon, the Home Secretary, next argued that if British ships were to be allowed to go to Bilbao, there would have to be mine-sweeping. That would constitute 'a full dress operation of war'. Sir Archibald Sinclair, the liberal leader, argued that the government's acceptance of the nationalist blockade spelled intervention. The Germans, after all, he said, recalling incidents of the winter, had always looked after *their* ships. Churchill spoke next, and, reiterating his Olympian detachment from either side in the war, indulged in a day-dream of mediation through 'some meeting in what Lord Rosebery once called a "wayside inn", which would give the chance in Spain of peace, of law, of bread and of oblivion'. Then indeed these 'clenched fists might relax into the open hands of generous cooperation'. Harold Nicolson, for the National Labour party, described the refusal to risk British ships in Basque waters as a 'bitter pill. It is not pleasant. It is a potion which is almost nauseating', but it had to be accepted. Noel-Baker suggested that it was the first time since 1588 that the British seemed to have been afraid of the Spanish fleet. Eden ended the debate by saying that, if British merchant ships were to leave St Jean de Luz, and so disobey the Board of Trade, they would be given naval protection as far as the three-mile limit. 'Our hope is that they will not go, because, in view of reports of conditions, we do not think it safe for them to go.'[2]

The masters of the merchantmen at St Jean de Luz were growing

1. So he confided to his private secretary, Oliver Harvey (John Harvey, *The Diplomatic Diaries of Oliver Harvey 1937–1900*, London, 1970, p. 34).

2. All this debate, which was punctuated by points of order, cries of 'withdraw', and other interruptions, is to be seen in *Hansard*, House of Commons, vol. 322, cols. 1029–142. See Harvey, p. 39. 'It is very difficult to get facts out of the Admiralty', Eden's private secretary added.

impatient. Their cargoes (for which they had been paid handsomely)[1] were rotting. Three vessels, all commanded by Welsh captains named Jones (therefore differentiated from their cargoes as 'Potato Jones', 'Corn Cob Jones', and 'Ham and Eggs Jones'), gained notoriety by pretended attempts to set out from port. 'Potato Jones', whose potatoes concealed weapons and whose motives were material, gained a sudden, if unmerited, reputation, from a series of breezy answers to a reporter of the *Evening News*, as a rough salt in the Conradian tradition. But it was not he (he delivered his cargo in Valencia) who broke the Bilbao blockade. First, the 'Red Dean' of Canterbury, Dr Hewlett Johnson, a prominent and restless apologist for Russia, and now the republic, sailed from Bermeo, near Bilbao, to St Jean de Luz, on a French torpedo boat, without mishap; and told the *Manchester Guardian* so. Then the *Seven Seas Spray*, a merchant vessel with a cargo of provisions from Valencia, sailed out of St Jean de Luz, at ten o'clock at night on 19 April, ignoring messages from the shore. Her master, Captain Roberts, turned a blind eye to the warnings of a British destroyer ten miles off the Basque coast. The captain of the destroyer told Roberts that he must proceed at his own risk, then wished him luck. In the morning, the *Seven Seas Spray* reached Bilbao, without having seen either mines or nationalist warships. As this vessel moved slowly up the river to dock, the captain and his daughter standing on the bridge, the hungry people of Bilbao massed excitedly on the quay, and cried 'Long live the British sailors! Long live Liberty!'

The British Admiralty now admitted its former error. For the truth about Bilbao was as Attlee had described it in the debate: the blockade at Bilbao was ineffective.

Other ships moored at St Jean de Luz, therefore, set out for Bilbao. One of these, the *MacGregor*, while ten miles out, was ordered to stop by the nationalist cruiser, *Almirante Cervera*. The *MacGregor* sent an SOS to HMS *Hood*. Her commander, Vice-Admiral Blake (who had disbelieved in the story of mines), requested the *Almirante Cervera* not to interfere with British ships outside territorial waters. The *Almirante Cervera* replied that Spanish territorial waters extended six miles. Admiral Blake said that Britain did not recognize

1. Special profits (up to 100 per cent more than usual) were earned by British shipowners who ran the risk of helping to provision the republic.

this claim, and told the *MacGregor* to proceed, if she wished. The *MacGregor* did so. A few yards short of the three-mile limit, the armed trawler *Galerna* fired a shot across the *MacGregor*'s bows. HMS *Firedrake* ordered the *Galerna* not to attack a British ship. From the coast, the Basque shore-battery loosed a salvo, and the *Galerna* withdrew. No further attempt was made to prevent British shipping from arriving at Bilbao, although the blockade continued.

What was the explanation of this curious incident in the history of shipping? Eden was no doubt telling the truth when he told the House of Commons, in passing, on 20 April, that 'if I had to choose in Spain, I believe that the Basque government would more closely conform to our own system than that of Franco or the republic'. (In his memoirs, Eden later wrote that 'from the early months of 1937, if I had to choose, I would have preferred a government victory'.)[1] But the Admiralty and Sir Samuel Hoare, who desired to avoid all trouble with Franco, apparently gave incorrect information to the cabinet. Some at least of the Admiralty's information derived less from a careful examination of the facts than from the nationalist warships themselves. The *Daily Telegraph* of 20 April published an interview with a nationalist, Captain Caveda, who remarked how pleasant it had been to work with the British fleet 'on questions arising from the blockade of Bilbao'. Sir Samuel Hoare at the Admiralty seems to have been pleased to accept the false information and to act precipitately upon it.

*

On 20 April, a new nationalist advance began in Vizcaya. When the artillery and aerial bombardment had ceased, and the Basques came up from the shallow trenches in which they had sheltered, they heard the Navarrese machine-guns from the rear. Once more, as at Ochandiano, the cry was 'we are cut off'. Many defenders retreated while they still could. Before the village of Elgeta, however, among the lion-shaped hills of Inchorta, good deep trenches had been dug. Led by the militia Major Pablo Belderrain, the Basques here held off the attack. But two CNT battalions withdrew. This defection completed the collapse. The Basque commanders now longed to retreat to the prepared trenches of the 'ring of iron'. Constant bombing blocked

1. Eden, *Facing the Dictators*, p. 441.

roads and prevented movement. The general staff in Bilbao displayed a laxness that brought accusations of treachery. On 24 April, all the heights on that section of the front chosen for the offensive fell to the colonel in command of the 1st Navarrese Brigade, Rafael García Valiño. Belderrain had to fall back from Elgeta. An atmosphere of panic persisted. Artillery did not know where to fire. Trenches were evacuated. General defeat for the Basques thus seemed imminent six days after the renewal of Mola's offensive. A new crisis now, however, followed: Guernica.

Guernica was a small town of the Basque province of Vizcaya, lying in a valley six miles from the sea and twenty from Bilbao. With a population of 7,000, Guernica seemed at first sight to fit undramatically into a hilly countryside of friendly villages and isolated farmhouses. It had been badly damaged by the French in the Peninsular War. It had nevertheless been celebrated, since before records began, as the home of Basque liberties. For the 'parliament of Basque senators' used to be held before Guernica's famous oak tree while in the church of Santa María the Spanish monarchs, or their representatives, used to swear to observe Basque local rights. (The oak was also a sanctuary for Basque debtors in the old days.) On 26 April 1937, Guernica lay ten miles from the front, and was crowded with refugees and retreating soldiers.

At half-past four in the afternoon, a single peal of church bells announced an air raid. There had been some raids in the area before, but Guernica had not been bombed. There were no air defences of any kind. At twenty minutes to five, a single Heinkel 111 (a new fast German bomber, with a metal frame, capable of carrying 3,000 pounds of bombs), flown by Major von Moreau, bombed the town, disappeared and returned with three other similar aircraft.[1] These Heinkels were followed by three squadrons of the older spectres of the Spanish war, Junkers 52 – twenty-three aircraft – some new Messerschmitt BF-109 fighters[2] and some older fighters, Heinkels 51. The fighters were to escort the bombers but also to machine-gun at

1. These Heinkels had begun to arrive in Spain in February. They would replace the Junkers 52. Their first use had been a raid on Barajas and Alcalá de Henares on 9 March. Von Moreau was an 'ace' pilot who had successfully dropped supplies into the Alcázar at Toledo in September 1936.

2. See below, p. 678, for this aircraft.

a low level all people they saw. Incendiary, high-explosive and shrapnel bombs together weighing 100,000 pounds were dropped by several waves of aircraft. Forty-three aircraft altogether took part, the Junkers being led by Lieutenants von Knauer, von Beust and von Krafft. The centre of the town was left destroyed and burning. The Basque parliament house (*casa de juntas*) and the remains of the famous oak, lying away from the centre, nevertheless remained untouched.[1] So was the arms factory outside the town. Many people, perhaps as many as a thousand, were killed, though subsequent events make it impossible to be quite certain how many.[2] Many others were maimed or injured in other ways. It is possible that some Italian aircraft joined in the last stages of the bombing.

This story was attested by all witnesses, including the mayor of the town, and the British Consul, as well as by foreign correspondents – principally English – who were in the Basque country at the time.[3] But Bolín, the chief of the foreign press sections at Salamanca, said on 27 April that the Basques had blown up their own town.

On 28 April, Durango and, on 29 April, meantime, Guernica, fell

1. For these details, see Gordon Thomas and Max Morgan Witts, *Guernica* (New York, 1975), pp. 206–13. The authors had access to the diary of Von Richthofen, the chief of staff of the Condor Legion, and other Condor Legion memories. The oak was destroyed in the Napoleonic wars but there was a stump and new shoots thereafter.

2. See *Le Clergé basque*, pp. 151–3, and Vicente Talón's *Arde Guernica*, the first edition of which (Madrid, 1970) was an important break-through in the writing of contemporary history in Spain. Talón's account is accepted in R. Salas, vol. II, p. 1386 and p. 2864f. (vol. III). For a general study of the impact of Guernica, see Herbert Southworth's *La Destruction de Guernica* (Paris, 1975). An account remarkably free of varnish can be seen in Martínez Bande, *Vizcaya*, p. 106f. The number of persons killed is extremely difficult to establish. Estimates vary from 1,600 to 100. Talón discusses the figures (p. 91f.) and suggests 200. But even the nationalist commission of inquiry suggested that 70 per cent of the houses were totally destroyed, 20 per cent seriously damaged, and only 10 per cent left moderately well off. Perhaps 1,000 died.

3. See Appendix Eight for the British Consul's report. The Basque account was confirmed by conversations which I had in Guernica in the summer of 1959 and with Father Alberto Onaindía, who was present. I also discussed Guernica with Noel Monks, of the *Daily Mail* and Jesús María de Leizaola. In 1945, the Basque government in exile attempted to bring a case against Germany at the Nuremberg War Crimes Tribunal. The attempt was unsuccessful, since no events which occurred before 1939 were taken into account at Nuremberg.

to the nationalists, without much resistance. General Solchaga executed the captured Basque commander, Colonel Llarch, with three of his staff, after a summary court martial. Foreign journalists with the nationalists were told, and shown, that, while 'a few bomb fragments' had been found in Guernica, the damage had been mainly caused by Basque incendiarists, in order to inspire indignation.[1] On 4 May, a new nationalist report said that Guernica naturally showed signs of fire after 'a week's bombardment by artillery and aircraft'. It agreed that Guernica had also been intermittently bombed over a period of three hours. Ten days later, the word 'Garnika' was found in the diary for 26 April of a German pilot shot down by the Basques. The pilot explained, unconvincingly, that that referred to a girl whom he knew in Hamburg. Some months later, another nationalist report admitted that the town had been bombed, but alleged that the aeroplanes were republican. The bombs, it was said, had been manufactured in Basque territory and the explosions caused by dynamite in the sewers. But in August a nationalist officer admitted to a reporter from *The Sunday Times* that Guernica had been bombed by his side:[2] 'Certainly we bombed it and bombed it and *bueno* why not?' Years later, the German air ace, Adolf Galland, who shortly afterwards joined the Condor Legion, first admitted that the Germans were responsible.[3] He argued, however, that the attack was an error, caused by bad bomb sights and lack of experience. The Germans, said Galland, were trying for the bridge over the river, missed it completely, and by mistake destroyed the town. That idea is supported by other Germans including some who took part in the raid.[4] The wind, they said, caused the bombs to drift westwards. In fact, Guernica was a military target, being a communications centre close to the battle line, almost within sight indeed of the nationalist columns some miles to the south. Retreating republican soldiers could only escape westwards with any ease through Guernica, since the bridge just outside across the river Oca was the last one before the sea. But if the aim of the Condor Legion was primarily to destroy the bridge, why did von Richthofen not use his supremely accurate

1. For the visit of foreign journalists between 29 April and 3 May see Southworth, p. 90.
2. Virginia Cowles, *Looking for Trouble* (London, 1941), p. 71.
3. Galland, p. 26.
4. Thomas and Witts, p. 212.

Stuka dive bombers, of which he had a small number at Burgos? Why too was such a specially devastating expedition mounted? At least part of the aim in his mind (if not in his diary) must have been to cause the maximum panic and confusion among civilians as well as among soldiers. The use of incendiary bombs proves that some destruction of buildings or people other than the bridge must have been intended, even though von Richthofen may not have known that the fires would spread so fast through Guernica's narrow streets and even though dust and smoke from the explosions caused by the Heinkels may have prevented the pilots of the Junkers from seeing the bridge clearly or perhaps at all. The well-attested machine-gunning of people running out of the town could hardly be part of the business of destroying the bridge.

The diary of von Richthofen also makes clear that Colonel Juan Vigón, Mola's chief of staff, knew of the raid beforehand: the two are said to have conferred on both 25 and 26 April 'without reference to higher authority'.[1]

At the same time, however, it is fair to recognize that the raid was a part of combined operations closely connected with the campaign under way; and that there is no direct evidence that the Germans knew of the importance of Guernica in the minds of the Basques, nor that any nationalist Spanish officers, who would of course have known of Guernica's place in the Basque mind, knew the raid would be so horrifying. There is no evidence even that Vigón knew that the raid would be so devastating, nor that Franco, Mola or even Sperrle discussed the planned raid beforehand: at that time, as will be seen, Franco was very preoccupied indeed with the problems of the Falange and Hedilla.[2] Mola, it is said, was shocked when he got to Guernica on 29 April.[3] It has also been suggested that Franco was furious with the Germans when he knew of the consequences of the raid.[4] That may very well be so since there were no similar raids later on in the Basque country of a Guernica type and indeed the Condor Legion never again attempted anything in the nature of 'area bombing' of defenceless towns.[5]

1. Thomas and Witts, pp. 197–8.

2. See below, p. 641. 3. Martínez Bande, p. 110. 4. See Hills, p. 281.

5. The Italian raids on Barcelona in 1938 were against a city with some air defences. But see below, p. 806.

An international controversy raged over Guernica. The painter Picasso had, earlier in the year, been commissioned to paint a mural for the Spanish government building at the World's Fair in Paris.[1] He now began work on a representation of the horrors of war expressed by the destruction of Guernica, in a painting which is probably his best known of all.[2] Exhibited in Paris in 1937 for the first time, it went to the Metropolitan Museum in New York. Shock at what they had done, and anxiety about the repercussions, meantime, caused the nationalist command and the Germans to mount an elaborate campaign of concealment. No such concentrated raid had after all occurred before. Propagandists on both sides took up positions from which they never departed. If one correspondent of *The Times*, George Steer, was prepared to write so explicitly on the Basque side of the story, James Holburn, the correspondent of the same English paper on the nationalist side, wrote, when entering the city with the baggage train of Solchaga: 'the few craters I inspected were caused by exploding mines'.[3] Twenty Basque priests, of whom one was an eye-witness of the bombing, and including the vicar-general of the diocese, wrote to the Pope telling him who had destroyed Guernica. Two of them, Fathers Pedro Menchaca and Agustín Isusi, preceptor of Vitoria and priest of Santos Juanes in Bilbao, went to the Vatican with this letter. It was delivered, but they were only received by Cardinal Pacelli, the papal secretary of state, on the condition that they did not mention the subject which had brought them to Rome. When they were received, the two Basques could not restrain themselves from speaking of Guernica, and Pacelli, coldly remarking 'The Church is persecuted in Barcelona', showed them to the door.[4]

1. Though he had not lived in Spain since 1903, Picasso in 1936 accepted the (honorary) post of director of the Prado and reported on the condition of the paintings which had been removed from Madrid to Valencia. In January he had etched a series of satirical strips, 'The Dream and the Lie of General Franco', in the style of the Aleluyas for which Spanish politics had been known since the eighteenth century – and revived during the civil war.

2. Guernica was an international journalistic water-shed in the civil war. Thereafter, for instance, *Time* magazine, *Life*, and, after a while, *Newsweek* took the side of the republic (Guttman, pp. 61–2).

3. *The Times*, 5 May 1937.

4. Evidence of Father Alberto Onaindía. The priest who collected the signa-

The nationalist story of this event was maintained for a generation. Those who told the story at the time, such as Captain Luis Bolín, lived on.[1] It was only when they had died, or had ceased to be influential, and when government documents began to be available, that, in 1970, the admission was made that Guernica was bombed from the air.[2] Even then, it continued to be often maintained that the Basques had finished what the Germans had merely begun.[3]

On 30 April, ten days after the international non-intervention control had begun and when the British Foreign Secretary had therefore believed that he would have been free for a while from considering what he thought of as the 'War of the Spanish Obsession', Eden told the House of Commons that the cabinet were considering what could be done to prevent another Guernica. In the Condor Legion itself, 'great depression' followed the attack.[4] On 4 May, Lord Plymouth suggested to the Non-Intervention Committee that it should call on both Spanish parties not to bomb open towns. Ribbentrop and Grandi disingenuously argued that the subject could not be discussed apart from a consideration of the general humanitarian aspect of the war. Maisky protested against this extension of the area of debate.[5] A conference of Church of England leaders, including William Temple, archbishop of York, made a formal protest to Eden against the bombing of non-military targets. The crisis served to divert attention from the very large shipments of military equipment which were then coming to the republic from Russia.[6] Similarly, on 29 April, Franco had signed an agreement to buy from Italy two old submarines, the *Archimedes* and the *Torricelli*, to supplement his fleet. This also passed unnoticed.

The Basque collapse behind the destroyed city, meantime, was staunched, although the fishing port of Bermeo was captured on 30 April by the Black Arrows, numbering 4,000. On this day, Basque

---

tures, Father Fortunato de Unzueta, wrote an account of how this letter was prepared, in *El clero vasco*, p. 244f.

1. It appears nevertheless that he was transferred from his post immediately. Bolín's memoirs were only published in 1967. His Appendix III and Ch. 33 are, I fear, untrue.

2. In Talón's *Arde Guernica*.

3. See De la Cierva, *Historia ilustrada*, vol. II, p. 158.

4. Galland, *loc. cit*.

5. *NIS*(c), forty-ninth meeting.

6. R. Salas Larrazábal, vol. II, p. 1561.

morale was given a fillip by the destruction of the battleship *España*, apparently by one of the rebels' own mines off Santander, the crew being saved. On 1 May, Mola attacked all along the front. The Italians in Bermeo were surrounded, and forced to beg relief. Bombing had now lost some of its terror for the Basque militia, since they had observed that the noise it caused was worse than its effects.

*

While Guernica occupied the headlines, events almost as dramatic were occurring in the Sierra Morena, the magnificent range of mountains which divides the tableland of Castile from Andalusia. On two mountain tops around the shrine of Santa María de la Cabeza, 250 civil guards from Jaén, most of their families, 100 falangists, and about 1,000 members of the bourgeoisie of Andújar had held out for the rising for nine months. Throughout most of the early part of the war there had been no attack launched against this nationalist enclave in the heart of republican Spain. Indeed, for some time, the Popular Front committee of Andújar had been uncertain whether the civil guard in the sanctuary were friends or enemies. After living in this equivocal security for some time, and after they had gathered a good supply of food, the rebels decided that it was morally impossible not to let the 'reds' know where they stood. So they dispatched a letter by hand giving a declaration of war. Major Nofuentes, who wanted to surrender, was deposed from command in the sanctuary, though his life and that of certain other pro-republican officers was respected. A siege then began. A captain of the civil guard, Santiago Cortés, whose wife and family were political prisoners in Jaén, led the defenders. Carrier pigeons communicated news and exultant messages to the nationalists at Seville. Nationalist pilots, such as the brilliant Major Carlos de Haya, trained specially in order to drop supplies into the small area which was being defended – a technique which they found to be similar to dive-bombing. Altogether 160,000 pounds of food were sent from Seville and 140,000 from Córdoba. More delicate supplies (such as medical appliances) were dropped by turkey, a bird whose flight is heavy, majestic, and vertical. Inside the sanctuary, schools and hospitals were improvised. Although a force of Queipo de Llano's was only about twenty miles away at Porcuna (captured on 1 January 1937) the nationalists made no real effort to relieve the garrison.

In early April, the republic decided to crush this island of resistance, and dispatched a large force under the communist deputy, and now lieutenant-colonel, Martínez Cartón. After fierce fighting, the small encampment of defenders was divided into two. Lugar Nuevo, the smaller encampment, sent its last pigeon to Captain Cortés to say that it could no longer hold out. Torrential rain followed and, during the night, Lugar Nuevo was evacuated without loss, all the defenders, including two hundred women and children, being taken into the sanctuary. Next, Franco gave permission to Cortés to surrender should resistance become impossible. He also gave orders for the evacuation of women and children, under the guarantee of the Red Cross officers, who had recently arrived. But Cortés and the defenders, inflamed by the passions which it had been necessary to arouse in order to carry on resistance, doubted the power of the Red Cross to fulfil the task. The defenders were surrounded by 20,000 republicans. Doubts arose. The attack began again. Cortés was wounded on 30 April, and sent a last message by carrier pigeon, while, on 1 May, the republican army broke into the sanctuary. Cortés's last orders to his men were: 'the civil guard and the Falange die, but do not yield'.[1] The sanctuary burned. Flames engulfed the Sierra. Eventually, the majority of the women and children were taken away in lorries, and the remaining defenders taken prisoner. Cortés died of wounds in hospital. Cortés took with him to the grave the secret of where the effigy of the Virgin of La Cabeza itself had been buried for safe-keeping.

1. The best book on this event is Julio de Urrutia, *El cerro de los héroes* (Madrid, 1965), a passionate work of investigation. The heroes did not receive their due reward in nationalist Spain.

36

Negotiations between Carlists and falangists – the Hedilla affair – the murder of Goya – the decree of unification – Serrano Súñer

DURING the spring of 1937, the two embattled Spains were consolidated. Henceforth, the country contained what seemed to be more two states than a single one divided by class. Franco, on the one hand, achieved a crushing victory over the falangists and the Carlists, the two movements which alone had survived. The nationalist cause was strengthened by the crisis of April 1937, and the authorities in Salamanca were everywhere respected, though such men as Queipo in Seville and Cañizares in Badajoz had much freedom of action. The consolidation of power in the republican zone of Spain was a more drawn-out affair and, although the state emerged victorious, the victory brought demoralization, so that it was pyrrhic.

The crisis behind the nationalist lines stretched back to the preceding winter when the Carlist 'delegate-general', Fal Conde, had been exiled by Franco to Portugal.[1] The Carlists had been angry at the harsh measure. This discontent on the part of the Carlists struck a responsive note in the breasts of certain falangists out of sympathy with General Franco. Fal Conde in Lisbon received an invitation from the Falange to discuss the idea of a unification between the two parties. The invitation was accepted.[2] After all, the two parties agreed on the diagnosis of Spain's troubles, even if they differed on the cure.

These negotiations lasted three weeks. They produced no results.[3]

1. See above, p. 507.

2. All the above and the following derived from the Carlist Archives, Seville. The falangists taking part in the discussions were Sancho Dávila, Pedro Gamero del Castillo (a leading 'new shirt' of Seville), and José Luis Escario. The Carlists were Fal Conde, the Conde de Rodezno, and José María Arauz de Robles. Hedilla, the provisional head of the Falange, knew of the negotiations but disapproved of them (*GD*, p. 268). He did not know of the part played by Dávila (García Venero, *Falange*, p. 324). Another who played a part was José María Valiente, sometime leader of the CEDA youth, and now a Carlist.

3. The most remarkable document was a series of 'bases for a union' of the

The Carlists concluded that the falangists were aiming at consuming the whole nationalist movement. The two parties, therefore, parted, amicably, at the end of February. The way to a resumption of discussions was to be kept open by the amenable Conde de Rodezno. But the idea of the unification of the two parties was taken up by General Franco himself, who had heard of these developments, presumably through Rodezno, whose principled support for the old cause had always been tempered by ambition, and a dislike of Fal Conde, as was seen in the talks with Mola before the war. Since he had assumed power, Franco successfully manipulated the disparate supporters of the national movement as if they had been the warring chieftains of the Rif during his early manhood. Would not a simple unification, from above, lead to that amalgamation of ideologies of which he had hopefully spoken to the German diplomat Dumoulin five months before?[1]

One other influential person supported this plan: Ramón Serrano Súñer, the Generalissimo's thirty-six-year-old brother-in-law, who before the war had been the CEDA's deputy for Saragossa and a vice-president of that movement. This ambitious lawyer had escaped from republican Spain. Though he had been Franco's closest associate in political circles, the rising had surprised him in Madrid. He had been imprisoned in the Model Prison, where he had observed the shooting of his friends, Fernando Primo de Rivera and Ruiz de Alda. His hatred of the republicans was also sharpened into continuous rage by the death of his two brothers at their hands. Since they had died partly because they had been refused asylum in the French Embassy, he nursed a particular passion against France, bolstering his growing contempt for democracy. These appalling experiences marked him for life. There was now little left of the politician of the CEDA which he first had been. His speech at the famous rally of the JAP, in the sleet, at El Escorial, in April 1934, had anyway been a fulmination against the degeneracy of democracy. He had been a friend, since their days at the university, of José

---

two groups, included in a falangist note of 1 February. By this, the Falange would 'agree to install, at an opportune moment, a new monarchy, as a guarantee of the continuity of the national-syndicalist state and as the basis for its imperium. The new monarchy would break all links with the liberal monarchy.'

1. See above, p. 426.

Antonio.[1] Henceforward, this dandy with prematurely white hair and blue eyes, was the dominant influence on his brother-in-law. The easy-going Nicolás Franco, with his unpunctuality, and odd working hours, became less and less important until he was quietly posted away as ambassador to Portugal. Serrano Súñer owed his political success to his cleverness, powers of decision, ruthlessness, and his charm; but while he pleased a small circle, he alienated the masses. He seemed sensitive, revengeful, arrogant and mercurial – 'quick as a knife in word and deed', a British opponent would say of him – as much a contrast to the reserved Franco as to the expansive *bon-homme*, Nicolás Franco.[2] The close relations between Franco and Serrano were maintained by their two wives, Zita and Carmen, who met constantly. Thus began in Spain the rule of what was referred to as *Cuñadismo* – brother-in-lawship.

To begin with, the *Cuñadísimo* (supreme brother-in-law) had no official position. From the moment of his arrival in Salamanca on 20 February, Franco used him as a political guide. Serrano occupied himself in trying to find some theoretical and, if possible, juridical, basis for the new nationalist state. He wanted to save his brother-in-law from setting up a military and personal régime in the style of General Primo de Rivera; equally, he did not want a party state. He had interviews with monarchists, falangists, churchmen, and generals. He saw Cardinal Gomá, the Conde de Rodezno, and General Mola. Afterwards, he took a walk one day with Franco, in the garden of the bishop's palace at Salamanca. He told the Generalissimo that his discussions suggested that none of the existing parties in nationalist Spain met the needs of the moment. Even so, something would have to be done. The army was the basis of the existing power. But 'a state of pure force', he said, could not be indefinitely prolonged. The national movement had been in the beginning a negative reaction against the 'criminal weakness' of the republican government, and against the menace of a communist

1. Serrano Súñer was not a member of the Falange before 1936. His escape from the republican zone was thanks to his move to a clinic, and his subsequent escape thence with Miaja's ex-chief of staff on the Córdoba front. The republican minister without portfolio, Irujo, was responsible for his move to the clinic (see Lizarra, p. 125) on the initiative of Dr Gregorio Marañón.

2. Hoare, p. 56. Hoare compared him to Stendhal's Count Mosca (p. 167).

revolution. A return to parliamentary government was impossible. 'In other places, thanks to an intelligent series of conventions, democracy may give effective results. But, in Spain, it has been amply indicated that it is only possible in a raw or explosive shape, and in a form leading to suicide.' Here surely was an opportunity of creating a state free of all commitments, precedents, and burdens, a state truly new, the sole state of this kind which had ever been able to appear. Was not the position in Spain in 1937 really much as it had been in the fifteenth century (as the now murdered Carlist, Pradera, had put it) at the start of the reign of the catholic kings?[1]

All new ideas on the Spanish Right seem to lead back to Ferdinand and Isabella. So it could not have been surprising to Franco when Serrano spoke to him in this style, one spring afternoon in 1937. This was the first of many such talks between the two men. Franco busied himself with studying the statutes of the Falange, of which, of course, he was not a member. He read José Antonio and Pradera. But, even in the militarist society of 'White Spain', political life was not quite dead. There were many underemployed falangists anxious for preferment. Six months of strutting about with armed escorts was enough. They wanted power. In March, those falangists who had taken the lead in the abortive negotiations with the Carlists now plotted the overthrow of Hedilla, the provisional leader of the Falange. This was the so-called Madrid group, all friends or relations of Primo de Rivera's, of whom the prominent members were Agustín Aznar; Rafael Garcerán, José Antonio's law clerk who had managed to make himself secretary of the *junta* of the Falange; José Moreno, *jefe provincial* in Pamplona; and Sancho Dávila, a cousin of José Antonio's, who had escaped from a republican gaol to lead the Falange in Andalusia. These men were admirers of José Antonio, and, like many others, kept up the fiction of refusing to accept the rumour that he was dead. (There were stories that he was alive: in England, in hiding in Alicante, already secretly in nationalist Spain. His death had not been announced and some believed that he was indeed still alive.) They disliked Hedilla, for they thought that he was trying to establish himself as the new leader, and one of an excessively proletarian type. These men had little following, but they were influential in Salamanca.

1. Serrano Súñer, pp. 29–31.

Hedilla, who was not yet thirty-five years old, had been living in Salamanca since October, with his family, attempting to organize the still growing movement. Most of the rank and file of the 'old shirts' supported Hedilla, as did most of the provincial chiefs of the northern provinces, as well as the intellectuals in the movement. The expanding falangist press also looked to Hedilla: though *FE*, of Seville, preferred Sancho Dávila. Hedilla responded sympathetically to the pressures which sought to make him a national leader; but he did not create these pressures. Both he and his supporters looked towards Germany rather than to Italy for inspiration, and the German ambassador, Faupel, had set out to cultivate a nazi spirit among them. Hedilla had some political gifts; for example, when José Andino, the falangist leader in Burgos, had diffused a speech of José Antonio's on Castile Radio against the orders of Vicente Gay, head of the Generalissimo's press department, and had been arrested, Hedilla had patiently negotiated his release.[1] On the other hand, he was tactless: he allowed a journalist, Víctor de la Serna, to publish an excessively laudatory article about him, and he once unwisely kept Serrano Súñer waiting in his anteroom. He had also offended some by his interventions in favour of mercy in the case of people who would otherwise have been shot;[2] and the Italian ambassador, Roberto Cantalupo, had tried to use him as a go-between to limit the repression.[3] Hedilla's efforts, meantime, to establish the Falange as a serious movement separate from the army were thwarted, partly since many thought it prudent to remain friendly with both him and Franco's headquarters; and partly because the military had all the resources. One trivial but important difficulty was that the telephone lines were controlled by the military and a call from Valladolid to

1. For this, see García Venero, *Falange*, p. 317. The event occurred on 2 February. The speech had contained such phrases as 'we do not want a Marxist revolution. But we know Spain does need *the* revolution.' The speech had been an attack on both Left and Right in the elections of 1936.

2. The case made for him by García Venero, *Falange*, p. 237f, appears convincing, though Southworth (*Antifalange*, p. 159) is right to warn that what distressed him was the number of those shot without trial, rather than those shot at all.

3. Cantalupo, pp. 117–18; García Venero, *Falange*, p. 249; and Southworth, *Antifalange*, p. 160. Italian fascists were often shocked by Spanish conservatives' brutality.

Salamanca which was not about a military matter might mean a wait of ten hours.

If the opposition to Hedilla had come from the 'Madrid group' it would not have been serious. But the opposition to him within the movement was stiffened by a number of professional men – engineers, lawyers, 'technocrats' – who wished to convert the Falange into the single doctrine-less, pragmatic party of a new authoritarian state. They too had backed the idea of negotiations with the Carlists (a characteristic representative of this group, the engineer José Luis Escario, had been on the falangist delegation to Lisbon). Serrano Súñer gave support to these men: neither he nor Franco desired to have another centre of authority, whether expressed by Hedilla or anyone else.

With all these developments Hedilla was out of sympathy. In early April, he went up from Salamanca to Vitoria to visit Fal Conde's provisional successor as national delegate of the *requetés*, José Luis Zamanillo, and the two of them agreed that, if there were any unification of Falange and Carlism, they would have nothing to do with it, and would say so. Almost at the same time, however, Franco was talking with Rodezno and some other Carlists about the idea of a formal unification of all the parties, movements, and sub-groups, of nationalist Spain. It was a very military suggestion: who else but a general would even consider a unification of such contrasting kinds of men into a single movement, as if they were indeed merely the freebooting gangs of armed men that their enemies believed them to be? Still, Rodezno recommended the scheme to his followers. The news of this reached Hedilla while still in the north. He announced that he would convoke a national council of the Falange on 25 April. His falangist opponents, Dávila, Aznar, and Garcerán, then denounced him for 'making monstrous propaganda on behalf of himself ... gearing his activity towards the creation of personal followers ... showing evident ineptitude, worsened by illiteracy ...'.[1] They declared that the continued absence of José Antonio demanded, according to the statutes of the party, a rule by a triumvirate, and accordingly took over, physically, the movement's offices in Sala-

1. Angel Alcázar de Velasco, *Serrano Súñer en la Falange* (Madrid, 1940), pp. 64–6.

manca, with the connivance of other falangists in the city, and perhaps of Franco and Serrano Súñer. Hedilla accepted the *fait accompli*, but went to Franco to complain: he only saw Franco's staff officer, Colonel Barroso. But the 'rebels' were received by Franco. Hedilla next ordered the local Falange in Salamanca, headed by Ramón Laporta, to re-occupy the movement's offices and he asked the commandant of the nearby Pedro Llen school for falangist officers, the Finnish fascist Major von Haartman, to send a unit of his cadets to assist. Von Haartman (who had arrived to fight against communism the previous October and who owed his post at Pedro Llen to the German ambassador) insisted on a written order, but when he received it, his cadets marched in and the offices of the Falange were returned to Hedilla, without bloodshed, in the middle of the night.[1] The building quickly filled with Hedilla's friends, among them Hans Kroeger, the nazi party representative on Faupel's staff. Precisely what happened next is open to doubt. Von Haartman recalled that Hedilla ordered him to detain the insurrectionary falangist leaders, while Hedilla himself said that he wanted the triumvirate to come and talk with him, and sent out emissaries with that intent. The evidence seems to suggest that the mission was an offensive one.[2] At all events, the head of the falangist militia in Santander, José María Alonso Goya, a devoted friend of Hedilla, went with a posse of armed men to Sancho Dávila's pension in the Plaza Mayor. Goya knew all these men and had even been in the Model Prison in Madrid with Sancho Dávila. But when he arrived at the latter's lodging, a brawl began. Goya and one of Sancho Dávila's friends (the bodyguard Peral) were killed. The civil guard arrested all others involved, including Dávila. Within a few hours, Garcerán was also arrested, when another Hedillista gang was about to break into his house. The civil guard had followed all these events closely. Von Haartman was arrested too.[3]

1. Haartman's memoir, qu. Southworth, *Antifalange*, p. 197.

2. The conflict of evidence is summarized in Southworth, *op. cit.*, p. 198 and pp. 219–24.

3. See *Cartas entrecruzadas entre el Sr D. Manuel Hedilla Larrey y el Sr D. Ramón Serrano Súñer* (Madrid, 1947). See also L. Pagés Guix (possibly a pseudonym for Garcerán), *La Traición de los Franco* (Madrid, 1938); Payne, *Politics and the Military*, pp. 166–7; and García Venero, *Falange*, p. 372f.

Hedilla called a meeting of the Falange's national council for 18 April. Present on that occasion were the surviving leaders of the movement, except Dávila, who was in gaol. Hedilla made a speech justifying his time as provisional leader, and requested a new vote on the subject of who was to be the chief henceforth. In the ballot, Hedilla was chosen, by ten against four, out of twenty-two votes; the rest were blank papers. Hedilla went to Franco to tell him that his position had been confirmed. Franco said that he was pleased: it was, he said, what he had hoped would happen. He persuaded Hedilla to appear on the balcony with him. There were cheers and *vivas* for both. Franco made what *ABC* the next day described predictably as 'a magnificent speech, inspired by the most pure ideas and sentiments of the Spanish tradition'. The three preparatory phases, Franco explained, of the new Spain were the Spain of the catholic kings, of Charles V and of Philip II. Since 1598, however, it had been downhill all the way. On 19 April, Hedilla dismissed the only member of the rebel 'triumvirate' out of gaol, Aznar, from the headship of the militias. This act seemed to be underwritten by Franco, since Aznar and all his followers, including bodyguards, were sent to the front. Hedilla appeared to have won, but, at eight o'clock in the evening, he received, at his home, the text of a decree which Franco proposed to issue later that night on Radio Nacional, forcibly uniting the Falange with the Carlists. At midnight, the decree was issued, incorporating all groups which were supporting the nationalist side, including the monarchists. Franco would be the leader, adding that title to that of Head of State and commander-in-chief. The new party would have the portmanteau name of Falange Española Tradicionalista y de las JONS.[1] As well as keeping Hedilla in ignorance of his plans, Franco had consulted neither Fal Conde nor the Carlist regent Xavier de Bourbon-Parme. The aged widow of old Don Alfonso Carlos (herself a veteran of the Second Carlist War in the 1870s) wrote to Fal Conde on 23 April: 'It is an infamy that has been done to us. With what right ...?' The Carlist War Council was not

1. García Venero, *Falange*, p. 394. The text is in Díaz Plaja, pp. 398–401. The witty Agustín de Foxá referred to the monstrously entitled party as the 'Compañia Internacional de Coches Camas y de los Grandes Expresos Europeos'. It was written some days before – no doubt before 16 April (see Escobar, p. 178).

officially told what had happened by Franco till 30 April.[1] The four Carlists included by Franco in the proposed new political secretariat of the movement (Rodezno, Dolz de Espejo, Arellano and Mazón) were known compromisers with the army. Many Carlists, who gained far less than their due from the new 'movement' simmered with rage but, for the moment, kept their protests to silent disapproval.

But what, it will be asked, of General Mola, the commander of the Army of the North, the old conspirator of Pamplona? He was present on 18 April on the balcony of Franco's headquarters at Salamanca. But he only expressed himself by a petty objection to the use, in the decree, of a verb not registered by the Spanish Academy.[2] Queipo de Llano was also summoned from Seville and his adhesion reluctantly obtained. From all over Spain, meantime, servile congratulations reached Franco by telegram. He had brought off a second *coup d'état*.

Hedilla was allocated a place on this new political secretariat. He refused. Those who accepted were all unimportant in the movement.[3] Franco tried to persuade him, through emissaries. He continued to refuse, on the advice of Pilar Primo de Rivera, of Aznar (whose motives must have been mixed), of Ridruejo, the young poet who was provincial chief in Valladolid, and the German ambassador, all of whom still had hopes for an independent Falange of 'old shirts'. A telegram was sent to all provincial chiefs in nationalist Spain which (apparently written by José Sainz) told them that, to avoid possible wrong interpretations of the decree of unification, they were only to follow orders received directly from the supreme command.

1. Carlist Archive. The official party uniform henceforth consisted of the blue shirt of the Falange and the red beret of the Carlists. Neither party liked the compromise, and the falangists put the Carlist beret into their pockets whenever they could. On one celebrated occasion, a group of falangists with bare heads were greeted by the Carlist Rodezno in ordinary clothes. Asked why he was so dressed, the old cynic answered: 'It is because I cannot put my blue shirt into my pocket...' (Ansaldo, p. 78).

2. Serrano Súñer, p. 42.

3. They were José Luis Escario, the 'technocrat'; Colonel Gazapo, the rebel officer of Melilla at the beginning of the war, active in Saragossa since, a falangist since about May 1936; Miranda, the Seville chief; Giménez Caballero, an early Spanish fascist, expelled by José Antonio and recently readmitted; López Bassa, an *arriviste*, from Majorca; and Pedro González Bueno, another (very) 'new shirt'.

This was later considered to be an act of defiance of Franco, but apparently Hedilla did not know that it had been sent. The circumstances were ambiguous enough for misunderstanding to be almost inevitable. During the next day or two, Hedilla went from person to person seeking advice: perhaps there was more genuine misunderstanding and his actions seemed like plotting to the Generalissimo and his advisers. The nazi leader, Kroeger, offered to Hedilla to ensure his safe conduct to Germany, and the local fascist, Guglielmo Danzi, offered a similar safe conduct to Italy.[1] Hedilla refused. Aznar, meantime, was arrested on charges relating to the events of the night of 16 April.

On 25 April, Hedilla was also arrested and placed in Salamanca gaol.[2] There he was charged with the illegal detention of Dávila; with the illegal use of government lorries to carry the cadets of Pedro Llen to Salamanca; and with causing the laboratory of the Faculty of Science at the University of Salamanca to be transformed for his personal benefit, in order to manufacture a gas which, in its turn, would have enabled him to assault the Generalissimo's headquarters.[3] These bizarre trumped-up charges enabled the régime to keep him in gaol while other prominent falangists were also arrested and charged with one act of subversion after another. On 1 May, all the provincial leaderships (*jefaturas*) of the Falange were abolished and, in June, while some falangists were released, Hedilla was newly charged, with the murder of Peral, Dávila's bodyguard, and with trying to overthrow the Caudillo. In the foundation of his charge Franco's legal adviser, Colonel Martínez Fuset, and the new commander of the civil guard in Salamanca, Major Lisardo Doval, of sinister memory in Asturias, played a prominent part, both seeing the falangists as dangerous 'reds'. Hedilla was condemned to death, but his sentence commuted. There were some public demonstrations in support of Hedilla, but those who took part in them were arrested as 'reds' and disappeared into gaol for many months. Several other prominent falangists were similarly charged, receiving long sentences

1. See Southworth, *Antifalange*, p. 213.

2. There appears no truth in the story put out by Cardozo, p. 308, that Franco was personally challenged by Hedilla.

3. García Venero, *Falange*, p. 406. This was the very time when the Guernica attack of 26 April was being conceived and carried out.

which were in the end all commuted. Few of them, however, played any subsequent part in Spanish politics.[1] Other more accommodating falangists served Franco willingly, often with enthusiasm.

This clash between fascism and authoritarian conservatism was won by the latter because of Franco's contempt for ideas; and, to be honest, many of the 'ideas' which he smashed were un-thought-out, second-rate and second-hand, as a great many are in the century of mass culture, in Spain and elsewhere.

So ended the so-called 'Hedilla plot', in which Hedilla was almost the only person not to have conspired: yet he was to spend the next four years in detention, hunger and discomfort.[2] The treatment of Hedilla by Franco is another example of the latter's coldness of heart, in this case shown to one who had helped the cause a good deal in the first months of the war. It was a bizarre moment, as well as a tragic one for Hedilla, since, the very day of his arrest, the new salute, with the arm extended, with the palm facing outwards, was adopted as a national salute for formal occasions. This 'dialectic of fists and pistols', in José Antonio's words, had been won by those who had the most of the latter.

Serrano Súñer became secretary-general of the new movement. He palliated the different sections of the political Right, in particular those falangists who gathered in the drawing-room in Salamanca of Pilar Primo de Rivera.[3] Pilar Primo de Rivera, who had been herself restless in the spring of 1937, became the presiding figure in Auxilio Social from October 1937. General Monasterio, a cavalry officer, and one of Gil Robles's aides as war minister, took on the post of commander of the militias – an honorific post, since Carlist and falangist militiamen were all integrated in the army.

Franco considered that, since Serrano was a man without followers and owed everything to himself, he would be easily manageable.

1. An exception was José Luis Arrese, who was condemned to death in Seville for helping Hedilla but became, nevertheless, secretary-general of the movement in 1941.

2. His vexations were added to by his fellow prisoners who were 'reds' and who naturally hated him.

3. Gil Robles, ex-leader of the CEDA, announced his support for Franco, but he spoiled the effect by aligning himself at the same time with the (orthodox) monarchists. He remained in exile, taking no part in politics (though he occasionally helped with arms traffic), and did not return to Spain till 1957.

Indeed, no dispute between the two seems to have occurred till after the end of the civil war. Serrano remained isolated, distrusted and feared. He was strongly, even passionately, pro-German, though he was disliked by the German ambassador. As a one-time prominent member of the CEDA, Serrano had old friendships with a large number of people on the Right of Spanish politics. He was quite an old hand in Spanish politics, but was well prepared to create a 'new state'. This was,

what it is convenient to name the authoritarian state, the unique type of modern state which appears expedient, the only form of society which can carry out the re-education and reorganization necessary for the political life of Spain. Perhaps, in its outward form, this state offers some resemblance to régimes already adopted by certain other peoples, but what, truly, varies from people to people is the dogma which covers this form, and the spirit with which it is obeyed. There can, as in totalitarian Russia, be a complete divergence between government and governed. The form can, as in the case of Germany, have an immoral side. We, on the other hand, have nothing to do with such doctrinal points. Our position derives from our national tradition and our confessional faith. We reject political relativism and political agnosticism. Outside the vast field left to discussion and doubt, there exist permanent truths, certainties, of which political life is composed, and which give limits to governmental action. These are the great and unchanging principles which affect the 'to be or not to be' of the country and of the whole of civilized society.[1]

Serrano sought an ideology which would 'absorb Red Spain, our great ambition and our great duty' and he supposed that the Falange would do this more than would traditionalism. The main achievement of the April decree was, however, not to give the new state a structure, but to remove the necessity for political speculation at least until the war was won.

Franco's allies, Generals Faupel and Roatta, met to discuss these developments. The latter now thought that, unless Germany and Italy intervened to exercise a decisive influence both on operations and on the development of Spanish society, the war could not be won. Faupel gave to Franco a Spanish translation of the nazi labour law. He suggested that he should embark on similar social legislation, and

1. Serrano Súñer, p. 38. This text was written in 1947 and the mention of the 'immoral' side to German practice was thus a post-1945 reflection.

offered to place appropriate 'experts' at his disposal. The Italian fascist representative, Danzi, gave Franco a draft constitution for Spain on the Italian model. But the Generalissimo paid attention neither to Danzi nor to Faupel.[1] Serrano Súñer said that these schemes and their inspirers would have been more welcome if the latter had taken the trouble to translate what they had to say into Spanish.[2]

*

Meantime, what of the monarchy? Franco told *ABC*, the monarchist paper, his ideas, later in the year: 'If the moment comes for a restoration,' the new monarchy would have to 'be very different from what fell on 14 April . . . the person who incarnates it must come as a pacifier.' But that meant that the return of monarchy would be delayed: delayed a long time.[3] The only monarch in Spain would be Franco. Surrounded by an escort of Moroccans, greeted with reverence by all who met him, the title of sultan would indeed have been a more appropriate one for the new conqueror, if it did not suggest to the modern ear a certain regard for the pleasure of life. Perhaps 'Caesar', much used by nationalist propaganda in 1937, would actually be appropriate.

During 1937, Franco's position received further buttressing; a decree of 4 August, obliging all serving officers to affiliate to the FET de las JONS, stated that the Caudillo would designate his own successor. Franco began to appear dressed as an admiral, as well as a general. At the same time, the walls of nationalist Spain were covered with posters crying '*Franco, Caudillo de Dios y de la Patria*', and with photographs of the 'smiling general',[4] while new books often contained a pious dedication to Franco, such as 'paladin of the new epics, present and future, of western christian civilization'.[5] The

1. *GD*, p. 274. 2. Serrano Súñer, p. 49.

3. *ABC de Sevilla*, 19 July 1937.

4. At least one man, a pastry-cook from Estremadura, Fernando Gordillo Bellido, unwisely used the back of one of these posters for a different purpose: to write a letter renewing a subscription to a journal. He was arrested, tried, and gaoled for six years and a day, and met another innocent man, Hedilla, in the gaol of Las Palmas (García Venero, *Falange*, p. 444).

5. W. González Oliveros, in *Falange y Requeté orgánicamente solidarios* (Valladolid, 1937), as qu. Cabanellas, vol. II, p. 939. González Oliveros became civil governor in Barcelona after the war.

propagandists of the new Spain of the era of Franco were the bellicose priest from Navarre, Father Izurdiaga; the 'proto-fascist', Giménez Caballero; and Eugenio D'Ors, once a radical Catalan republican, student of the Free Institute, now a fervent falangist. (He once remarked: 'the Spaniards love a uniform, provided it is multiform'.) During early 1937, the press department of the Generalissimo continued to be directed by Vicente Gay, the alcoholic, anti-semitic professor from Valladolid. New polemical 'Franquistas' – the word began now to be used – included the monarchist journalist, Joaquín Arrarás, who would soon publish Franco's first biography; the police writer Mauricio Carlavilla, an expert on the relation between '*Anti-España*' and homosexuality; and 'El Tebib Arrumi', a doctor turned journalist, whom Franco had known in Morocco, and who was the headquarters' official reporter.[1] Gay's assistant was Ramón Ruiz Alonso, the ex-CEDA deputy for Granada who had been implicated in Lorca's death.[2] Other intellectuals of the Right came forward to fill posts as rectors of universities, directors of new institutes and newspapers. It was a wonderful time for all those disgruntled, or unsuccessful, writers who had failed during the republic due, as they purported to believe, to the 'jewish-Marxist-masonic conspiracy for the capture of patronage' in the universities or for favour in the arts.

1. 'El Tebib Arrumi' was Víctor Ruiz Albéniz who had worked for eight years as a doctor at the Monte Uixan mines. For a general picture of press relations in Salamanca, see Southworth, *La Destruction*, p. 63f.

2. Gay was succeeded soon by Major Arias Paz of the corps of engineers.

37

The communists condemn Largo Caballero – a new Catalan government – the May Days in Barcelona – the Estremadura offensive – the campaign against the POUM – the fall of Largo – Negrín's government – state of the armies

THE political crisis in Franco's Spain caused the death of two people only, even if it resulted in the imprisonment of many. It did not affect the war. The almost concurrent crisis in republican Spain, of greater complexity, more important for Spain and the European socialist movement, caused the death of several hundred, damaged morale, and prevented the republic from launching any offensive which would have taken advantage of their enemies' preoccupation with the north.

The republic's crisis was the consequence of the emergence, since July 1936, of a new force in Spanish politics: namely, the communist party, a movement sustained by Russia's diplomatic and military help, guided by a group of experienced international communists, and supported by many members of the middle class. For this was no ordinary communist party. If its propaganda harked back to the Russian revolution, its practice suited, and reflected the desires of, the small shopkeepers, small farmers, taxi drivers, minor officials and junior officers who joined it between July 1936 and the end of the year, without reading much Marx or knowing much of Russia, in the hope of finding protection against anarchism and lawlessness. The communists stood for a disciplined, left-of-Centre, bourgeois régime, capable of winning the war, with private industry limited by some nationalization, but not by collectivization, or workers' control. That desire for protection accounted for the complaisance of many middle-class politicians towards the communists during this spring – certain protection in republican Spain, against anarchists, and possible international protection, against Franco. Prieto, too, hostile always to revolution, with the right-wing socialists, was still a firm supporter of collaboration with the communists. Companys, despite his knowledge that communism spelled centralism, preferred to use the Catalan communists of the PSUC, well organized by Juan Comorera, against the anarchists who had helped Catalan separatism in the past and whom he, Companys, had so often defended. It had previously been shown how many army and air force officers, for technical reasons, preferred the communists to the other parties and how, while some joined the party explicitly, many others looked on it with sympathy. The astonishing, apparently endless, series of triumphs since July 1936 of the self-confident communists seemed to some a sure token that they possessed an elixir for continuous success.

Against this new political force was ranged – though that suggests a non-existent formality – a heterogeneous gathering. There were the left-wing socialists, headed by Largo Caballero, still the Prime Minister, increasingly resentful of communist infiltration into the organs of the state and of communist arrogance. There were some officers and officials, such as General Asensio, who had kept their heads, failed to surrender to the emotions of the mass and were shocked by the communists' cynicism. There were the increasingly isolated revolutionary communists of the POUM, whose emotions were to be chronicled so well by George Orwell (at that time serving with the POUM militia in Aragon); and there was the anarchist movement, though this was divided – it was a long way, intellectually, from the small group of nationally influential anarchists, such as the CNT's secretary-general, Mariano Vázquez, and the four anarchist ministers who had been convinced of the need for authority of some sort at least while the war lasted, to those who still, and independently, controlled the forces of public order in Catalonia. There were also the anarchists who ran half Aragon as 'the Spanish Ukraine'; and there were the anarchists in the factories of Barcelona, who resented the stealthy way in which the state had mastered the revolution, through the manipulation of credit, raw materials and the insistence on the priority of war production; for, during the spring, the communists were able to enhance successfully the role of the state delegate in all the larger factories.

In the unfolding drama, ordinary people, non-political workers or secret sympathizers with the nationalists, were in a weak position, since the censorship was in communist hands, and often prevented truthful versions of events being known. Under the excuse of the needs of war, less and less accurate knowledge of what was happening was available to good republicans, while their picture of the outside world became almost as narrow as that in the zone of Franco. Meanwhile, the economic position was steadily worsening: in May 1937, food prices in Barcelona were almost double those of July 1936.[1] Most factories indeed were running down. Only the metallurgical industries, in which war production was concentrated, showed an increase over July 1936.[2] The industrial use of electric power in April 1937 was down 27 per cent on what it had been in the same month of 1936.[3] Wages meantime had risen only 15 per cent over July 1936[4] – a stability in one part of the economy due to the fact that strikes, at which both UGT and CNT had been such expert practitioners, were unthinkable.

The political crisis in the republic came to a head in May 1937, but its roots need to be sought in the events of the previous winter. Thus, at their annual conference on 21 February, the FAI threatened that their ministers would be withdrawn from the government unless the Aragon front, still manned mainly by anarchists, were supplied with arms.[5] Some time during the spring, the FAI seized a shipload of arms in Barcelona harbour. Largo Caballero brought up the matter in the cabinet and asked the anarchist ministers to surrender the arms. García Oliver said that he would give up the arms if the government gave the anarchists some aeroplanes. Largo accepted this without protest.

The communist party held a conference from 5 to 8 March at Valencia.[6] The speeches were extremely moderate in tone, save on the subject of the POUM. Díaz praised the republicans of Azaña's persuasion for participating in the 'anti-fascist movement hand-in-hand with the proletariat'. He denied that the republic stood for a battle against religion. He left open the question of whether confiscated estates should be collectively, or individually, run. But he, and all speakers, urged speed in unifying the army, and organizing in-

1. Bricall, p. 137.

2. Surprisingly, April 1937 was the best month in the metallurgical industry for many months.

3. 29,228,088 kW in comparison with 40,265,603 in 1937 (Bricall, p. 55).

4. I quote Jackson's figure (*op. cit.*, p. 365).

5. FAI minutes, published Barcelona 1937. Qu. Cattell, *Communism*, p. 110. (La Pasionaria to Azaña, in Azaña, vol. IV, p. 820.)

6. An imaginative description appears in Castro Delgado, pp. 475–80.

dustry for war. Otherwise, he added 'the government will cease to be the government'.[1] Lister, increasingly depicted as the most popular commander in propaganda, and his commissar, Santiago Alvarez, became members of the central committee.[2] As for the POUM, their leaders were vilified. With Trotsky, they had recently spoken of 'Stalinite Thermidorians' who had established in Russia 'the bureaucratic régime of a poisoned dictator'. They also insisted that they were fighting for socialism against capitalism, and that 'bourgeois democracy in this country' had had its day – dangerous attacks on the communists' defence of 'the democratic republic'.[3] The POUM had even suggested that Trotsky be invited to make his home in Catalonia. Díaz denounced the POUM as 'agents of fascism, who hide themselves behind the pretended slogans of revolutionaries to carry out their major mission as agents of our enemies in our own country'. The few POUM newspapers and radio stations outside Catalonia were seized, as harmful to the war effort. During the spring, the POUM leaders became more and more apprehensive. They were mostly ex-communists who had in some cases known Moscow well in the 1920s. Nin had known the Russian consul-general in Barcelona, Antonov Ovsëenko, when he had been a follower of Trotsky. Undoubtedly, from Stalin's point of view, he knew too much. The minister responsible for press and propaganda, Carlos Esplá, explained to Gorkin: 'At this time we cannot have polemics with the Russians.' His deputy warned the POUM that he thought the communists were preparing their physical suppression.[4]

A committee of liaison between communists and socialists had meantime been created. This dangerous step, as Largo Caballero thought it, was counterbalanced by his own reassignment of a number of the communist officers – 'communistoid' (as their enemies called them) – to remote fronts. This plan included the dispatch of the chief of personnel, Major Díaz Tendero, to the north.[5] Díaz Tendero had attacked Largo Caballero anonymously in a military journal as senile and therefore incapable of directing the war. During March – when the Russian military advisers and senior communist officials were at their most influential, following the victory of Guadalajara – the

1. Díaz, *Por la unidad*, pp. 13–15. 2. Lister, p. 106.
3. *The Spanish Revolution* (POUM newspaper), 3 February 1937.
4. Gorkin, *El proceso de Moscú*, p. 45. 5. Martín Blázquez, p. 320.

Comintern's directors of the Spanish communist party evidently resolved to destroy Largo Caballero once and for all.

The communists had by then also probably got wind, through Alvarez del Vayo, of a scheme of Largo Caballero's whereby a settlement of the war would be internationally sought and guaranteed, giving bases to Italy, mines to Germany, in return for the total exclusion of Russia's influence: this idea was apparently put to the great powers of Europe by Araquistain, the ambassador in Paris, who fully shared Largo Caballero's views on the subject of communist influence. Nothing came of the scheme, just as nothing had come of the plan to stir up trouble for the nationalists in Morocco, by sponsoring an independence movement there. At all events, Largo Caballero seemed busy on the international scene,[1] in a way which might be to Russia's disadvantage, and he had obliquely attacked the communists by publicly saying that his feet were surrounded by 'serpents of treason, disloyalty and espionage'.

An astonishing meeting of the Spanish communist party executive was shortly held, attended by Marty, Codovilla, Stepanov, Gerö, Gaikins (the Russian chargé) and apparently even Orlov, of the NKVD. One of these – it is obscure who[2] – announced that Largo Caballero should be removed from the premiership. Díaz and Hernández protested. Díaz added that Spanish communists should not always have to follow the lead of Moscow. Fear or ambition kept the other Spaniards from speaking. Stepanov said that it was not Moscow but 'history' which condemned the Prime Minister, for his defeatism and for his defeats. Marty agreed. Díaz called Marty a bureaucrat, and Marty growled that he was a revolutionary. 'So are we all', said Díaz. 'That remains to be seen', answered Marty. Díaz told Marty that he was a guest at meetings of the Spanish communist

1. See above, p. 579, where this idea is first discussed; and Payne, *Spanish Revolution*, pp. 271–2.

2. Hernández (p. 66), from whom comes our knowledge of this meeting, says that it was Togliatti who proposed the destruction of Largo Caballero. Togliatti himself (*Rinascita*, December 1962) denied that he was in Spain until June 1937 and there is such general agreement that he was in Moscow until then (see Spriano, *op. cit.*, p. 215 fn. 1) that we must admit that Hernández must be wrong. It is possible that Togliatti could have come to Spain on a special mission, as stated before. (See p. 340 above.) See further discussion in Giorgio Bocca, *Palmiro Togliatti* (Rome, 1973), p. 285f.

party. 'If our proceedings do not please you,' said Díaz deliberately, 'there is the door.' Uproar followed. Everyone stood up. La Pasionaria shrieked 'Comrades! Comrades!' Gerö sat open-mouthed in surprise. Only Orlov seemed imperturbable. Codovilla tried to calm Marty. Such scenes were unheard of at meetings of communist parties. Eventually, Díaz was brought to accept the proposal if the majority voted for it. Díaz and Hernández were alone in voting against. One Comintern representative next said that the campaign to destroy Largo Caballero should begin at a meeting in Valencia, and blandly suggested that Hernández should make the keynote speech. As for the next Premier, Juan Negrín, the finance minister, would be the best choice. He was less obviously pro-communist than Alvarez del Vayo, who was anyway foolish, and less potentially anti-communist than Prieto. Hernández soon made his speech, in the Cinema Tyris, Valencia. Largo Caballero asked for his resignation. Hernández said that he was in the government as a communist representative and, if he left, the communists would all withdraw. Largo Caballero vacillated, asked the communists for another man in place of Hernández, but, in the end, did nothing.

The tension in the streets in Barcelona between the anarchists and the POUM, on the one hand, and the government and PSUC, on the other, was equally acute. Companys's lieutenant, Tarradellas, wanted to fuse all the Catalan police into one body, thereby above all dissolving the control patrols which were still directed by the CNT. In this matter, as in so many others, the aims of the communists, and those republicans or Catalans, who placed the efficient conduct of the war above all else, once more coincided. Problems had been continuous since January. There had been many murders in both Barcelona and Madrid, with anarchists killing communists and *vice versa*, squabbles over control on committees, and in industries, sudden attempts by communists at intimidation. In March, a communist group stole twelve roughly-made tanks from an anarchist depot, by forging an order from an anarchist commissar.[1] When, on 26 March, Tarradellas forbade any police to have political affiliations, and ordered all political parties to hand over their arms, the anarchists resigned from the *Generalidad*. The succeeding governmental crisis lasted so long that the Plaza de la República became nicknamed

1. Peirats, vol. II, p. 172.

the Plaza 'of the permanent crisis'.[1] The anarchist youth, meanwhile, inspired by the implacable cripple Escorza, explained that they could not, and would not, die for that 'pretty April democracy [of 1931] that used to deport us . . . the tragic alternative is, as it was in the First International: either state or revolution'.[2] The fact was, however, that José Asens, the anarchist chief of the control patrols, had arrested and killed innumerable people without cause and still terrified Barcelona. Other anarchist patrols inspired private 'expropriations', which were no better than thefts.[3]

Eventually, on 16 April, the agile Companys formed a new government of much the same complexion as before. The main difference was that the important communist minister of supply, Comorera, moved to the portfolio of justice.[4] The parties kept their arms, the control patrols survived, and nervousness in Barcelona continued. The anarchist ministers in the government at Valencia had done their best to restrain their Barcelona comrades, but only lost influence with their own followers, over whom they had anyway slight authority.

On 25 April, the anarchist paper, *Solidaridad Obrera*, published a determined attack on José Cazorla, the communist commissar for public order in Madrid. He had closed the anarchist newspaper there simply because it had printed a denunciation by Melchor Rodríguez, the anarchist prison director, of the communists for retaining a private prison and interrogation chamber. The ensuing scandal resulted in a communist setback: Largo Caballero dissolved the entire Madrid defence *junta*, which, as has been seen, was dominated by the communists. He handed back the administration of the capital to a town council representing all the parties. Also on 25 April, a

1. Now renamed Plaza San Jaime.

2. *Ruta*, journal of JLC (Catalan anarchist youth), 25 March 1937.

3. 'Uncontrollables' at the CNT's orders robbed the *Generalidad* of 18,000 pounds of flour, 5 lorry-loads of wheat, 40 of potatoes: *Solidaridad Obrera* defended them. See report in Martínez Bande, *La invasión*, p. 278.

4. The new government consisted of Tarradellas (Premier), Sbert (culture), and Ayguadé (internal security), all of the Esquerra; Isgleas, Capdevila, Domenech and Aurelio Fernández (of the CNT, getting defence, economy, public services, and health); Miret, Vidiella and Comorera (of the PSUC, getting food, labour and justice); while Calvet (*rabassaires*) was responsible for agriculture. The appointment of a *pistolero*, such as Aurelio Fernández, could scarcely have inspired confidence.

prominent communist in Barcelona, Roldán Cortada, was found dead, presumably shot by anarchists. The same day in Puigcerdá, the east Pyrenean frontier town, a clash occurred between the carabineers and the anarchists of the local collective. Negrín, the finance minister, had decided to end the anomaly whereby that important frontier was controlled by the CNT. The Puigcerdá collective had become a centre for spying, false passports and secret escapes, and the mayor, Antonio Martín, was believed to keep his own cattle while insisting on collectivization for others. He was as much an eccentric as a smuggler, more a man of action than an anarchist. Nevertheless, after a violent clash, apparently provoked by the carabineers, he and several of his followers were killed.[1] Negrín had less difficulty in resuming governmental control over the other customs posts.

Open fighting in Barcelona began to be feared between anarchists and POUM on the one hand and the government and the communists on the other.[2] The communists were said to have devised a new slogan: 'Before we capture Saragossa, we have to take Barcelona.' Arms were gathered and buildings secretly fortified, both sides fearing the other would strike first. The Voroshilov (previously Atarazanas) and Pedrera barracks were the communist citadels. The Marx barracks were the stronghold of the POUM. The CNT held out at the Chamber of Commerce. A week passed. People began to say that the murder of Roldán Cortada had been a communist provocation to justify a police action in anarchist quarters of Barcelona: the rumours survive to this day, for Cortada, once a friend of Largo

1. I am grateful to Mariano Puente for his help in elucidating this obscure brawl. See also Benavides, *Guerra y revolución en Cataluña*, p. 405f, where the accusation is made that Martín and his men were attempting to extend their area of control, over the village of Bellver on the road to Seo. The collective had 170 members, with a salary of 50 pesetas per man, 35 per woman. See *La Révolution prolétarienne*, 25 June 1937. Martín has his defenders.

2. This was the impression of George Orwell, who returned to Barcelona from the front on 26 April – he had been serving with the POUM column (*Homage to Catalonia*, pp. 169ff). His account of the following riots, marvellously written though it is, is a better book about war itself than about the Spanish war. But see Cruells, *Mayo sangriento* (Barcelona, 1970), pp. 41, 52. Auden commented in 'Spilling the Spanish Beans' (*New English Weekly*, 29 July 1937, qu. Orwell, *Collected Essays*, vol. I, p. 269) that 'the Spanish government (including the semi-autonomous Catalan government) is more afraid of the revolution than it is of the fascists'.

Caballero, was known to be against the growing spirit of 'pogrom' in the PSUC.[1] The first of May, traditionally a day of rejoicing, was quiet, since the UGT and CNT agreed that processions would be sure to lead to trouble. On 2 May, Prieto telephoned the *Generalidad* from Valencia. The anarchist operator answered that there was no such thing as a government in Barcelona, only 'a defence committee'. The government and the communists had believed for some time that the CNT tapped their calls, which they were in a position to do. Perhaps they just listened. Communists have never liked being eavesdropped on. On 2 May, a call from Azaña to Companys was interrupted by the telephonist, who said that lines should be used for more important purposes than a talk between the two presidents.[2] In the afternoon on 3 May, the chief of the police in Barcelona, Eusebio Rodríguez Salas, went to the Telefónica, and visited the censor's department on the first floor, intent on taking over the building. That seemed a provocation, since the anarchist committee's control of the Telefónica was 'legal', according to the *Generalidad*'s own decree on collectivization. The anarchist workers opened fire from the second floor down the stairs to the censor's department. Rodríguez Salas telephoned for aid. The civil guard appeared, also two FAI police leaders, Dionisio Eroles (now head of the anarchist commissariat) and José Asens (who had succeeded Eroles as chief of the control patrols). Eroles persuaded the CNT workers not to shoot again. They gave up their arms, but fired their spare ammunition through the windows. A crowd had by now gathered below in the Plaza de Cataluña. It was at first assumed that the anarchists had captured the police chief. The POUM, the Friends of Durruti, the Bolshevik-Leninists (a small group of real Trotskyists headed by a gifted journalist, Grandizo Munis), the anarchist youth, took up positions. Within a few hours, all the political organizations had brought out their hidden arms and had begun to build barricades. Shop owners hastily shuttered their windows.[3]

1. José Peirats, *Los anarquistas en la crisis política española* (Buenos Aires, 1964), pp. 241–3; Felix Morrow, *Revolution and Counter-revolution in Spain* (New York, 1938), p. 87.

2. Miravitlles, p. 141.

3. Some still think that the plot was carefully worked out; suggestions supporting this conspiracy theory are contained in Krivitsky (p. 128) who wrote that, on 2 May, he met (presumably in Holland) an important Spanish communist,

Until this moment, the communists in Barcelona had gained their ends chiefly by a mixture of intimidation and common sense. Their political tactics had the support of both the *Generalidad* and the republican government at Valencia. Ayguadé, the Catalan councillor for public order (in effect, minister of the interior), admired Comorera and was thus close to the communists. They probably thought that the Telefónica would have been easily captured. An open clash with the CNT in Barcelona was one contest which the communists could not have been sure of winning. The communist party had embarked on the destruction of Largo Caballero, with all his prestige among the working class in Spain. That task required their undivided attention. Largo Caballero was having some success in his drive against the communists. A decree of 17 April, restricting the commissars' powers and requiring the appointment of all commissars to be personally approved by himself, had angered them as much as the dissolution of the Madrid *junta* of defence had. The communists would have taken more trouble, and taken men from the front, if they had planned a *coup* in Barcelona. But once the shooting had begun, they might be expected to reap the fullest advantage from what was happening – in particular, to discredit the POUM, whom they proposed no doubt to destroy one day if they could. The POUM, especially the POUM youth (Juventud Comunista Ibérica – JCI),

---

one 'García', head of 'the loyalist secret service', who had been sent to Moscow for a holiday by Orlov, who wanted him 'out of the way'. But who is this 'García'? Victor Serge (*op. cit.*, p. 335) speaks of a discussion in March in Brussels with someone who had been told by a 'prominent Spanish communist' that in Barcelona 'they're getting ready to liquidate thousands of anarchists and POUM militants'. There are anarchist suspicions of a visit to Paris on 26 April by Comorera, and his alleged talks with the Estat Català leaders in exile there (Peirats, *La CNT*, vol. II, p. 215). Abad de Santillán talks of a prediction, also in Brussels, by the Spanish ambassador, Ossorio y Gallardo, that the CNT and FAI would soon be finally dealt with. Gorkin (*The Review* of the Imre Nagy Institute for Political Research, October 1959) claims that the Comintern's man in Catalonia, Ernö Gerö, 'provoked in 1937 the famous May Days in Barcelona ... the great provocator of Budapest in 1956 [thus] held his dress rehearsal'. Azaña, on the other hand, in his diary later, censured Ayguadé for 'giving battle without having prepared for it', (vol. IV, p. 577), and, in his *La insurrección libertaria y el 'eje' Barcelona–Bilbao* (vol. III, p. 514), rightly says that 'all the elements were present for a conflagration in Barcelona, without the "novelesque" explanation of a "foreign power" being involved'.

and the 'Bolshevist-Leninists' had meantime issued many appeals during April in favour of continuing the revolution, of the immediate dissolution of the Cortes, and the establishment of a constituent assembly, based on collectivist committees. The anarchist youth and an extreme anarchist 'groupuscule' which called themselves 'The Friends of Durruti' found these ideas acceptable.[1]

The communist party later alleged that the crisis had been caused by the agents of Franco in the CNT and, above all, the POUM. Documents were said to have been found in hotels in Barcelona proving it. It has admittedly since become known that Franco told Faupel, the German ambassador at Salamanca, on 7 May, that he had thirteen agents in Barcelona. One of them had reported that 'the tension between the communists and anarchists was so great that he could guarantee to cause fighting to break out there'. Franco said that 'he had intended not to use this plan until he began an offensive in Catalonia but, since the republicans had attacked at Teruel[2] to relieve the Basques, he had judged the present moment right for the outbreak of disorders in Barcelona. The agent had succeeded, within some days of receiving such instructions, in having street-fighting started by three or four persons.'[3] But spies are boastful, and that one may have attributed the spontaneous outbreak of the fighting to his own intrigues. Franco must also have been anxious to suggest the efficacy of his intelligence service to the Germans.

In the meantime, CNT representatives visited Tarradellas, and Ayguadé. The two councillors promised that the police would leave the Telefónica. The anarchists went on to demand the resignations of both Rodríguez Salas and Ayguadé. That was refused. By night-

1. Who were the 'Friends of Durruti'? Young *FA Iistas*, such as Pablo Ruiz, Careño, Eleuterio Roig and, above all, Jaime Balius, who had disliked the politics of the CNT since November. The real old friends of Durruti, the *solidarios* and the men around the journal *Nosotros*, were, however, not friendly to the 'Friends of Durruti'. The ideas of the latter can be seen in the journal *El Amigo del Pueblo*. They were, as Lorenzo says (p. 269), bolshevik anarchists, in the sense that they wanted to capture power, not the dissolution of the state. They were Leninists, perhaps, without being Marxists, if that is possible. Another dissident group had been formed around the journal *Acracia*, edited in Lérida by José Peirats.

2. A minor attack which had no consequences.

3. *GD*, p. 286. Cruells, p. 47, argues that Franco's agents did little beyond supply information to the nationalists.

fall, therefore, Barcelona was a city at war. The PSUC and the government controlled Barcelona to the east of the Rambla. The anarchists controlled the area to the west. The suburbs were all with the CNT. In the centre of the city, where union and political headquarters were near to one another in requisitioned buildings and hotels, machine-guns were placed on roofs, and firing began along the housetops. All cars were shot at by both sides. Yet at the Telefónica, a truce had been agreed, and the telephone exchange itself, the nerve of the civil war from first to last, was working. The police on the first floor even sent sandwiches up to the CNT above. Several police cars, however, were blown up by grenades dropped from roofs. Any journey by car was dangerous.[1] What worsened the situation was that the CNT and FAI were no longer coherent; the revolutionary torch had been seized by their extremist followers, or by the anarchist youth.[2] In the evening, the POUM leaders proposed to the confused anarchist leaders in Barcelona an alliance against communism and the government; the anarchists refused.[3]

On 4 May, Barcelona was silent, save for machine-gun and rifle fire. Shops and houses were barricaded. Bands of armed anarchists attacked assault guard, republican guard, or government buildings. These were followed by communist or government counter-attacks. The atmosphere was that of 19 July 1936. The angles of fire were almost the same as on that epic day. Once again, the police fired against their late comrades in arms, in July the soldiers, now the anarchists. In the meantime, the political leaders of the anarchists, García Oliver and Federica Montseny, broadcast an appeal to their followers to lay down arms and return to work. Jacinto Toryho,

1. Richard Bennett (with Barcelona Radio) described to me how at this time his door in Barcelona was opened by two men carrying bombs who bluntly asked him: 'Whose side are you on?' 'Yours,' he wisely answered. Another witness of these events was Willy Brandt, representing Norwegian newspapers in Spain from February to May 1937. Sympathetic to the POUM though critical of their excesses, Brandt returned to Norway deeply critical of the communists (see Terence Prittie, *Willy Brandt*, London, 1974, p. 34).

2. There was some possibility of some sectors of the CNT, especially the FIJL, going over to the POUM. See Wildebaldo Solano, *The Spanish Revolution: the Life of Andrés Nin* (London, no date), p.18. Wildebaldo Solano was secretary-general of the POUM youth movement.

3. Julián Gorkin, *Caníbales políticos*, p. 69.

editor of *Solidaridad Obrera*, did the same. The ministers then travelled to Barcelona, with Mariano Vázquez, secretary of the national committee of the CNT, together with Pascual Tomás and Carlos Hernández Zancajo, of the UGT executive committee. All wished to avoid an engagement against the communists. Federica Montseny explained later that the news of the riots had caught her and the other anarchist ministers completely by surprise.[1] Nor had Largo Caballero any wish to use force against the anarchists. Units of the anarchists' 26th Division (previously the Durruti Column), under Gregorio Jover, assembled at Barbastro to march on Barcelona. On hearing García Oliver's speech, they stayed where they were. The nearby 28th Division, the old Ascaso Column, however, and perhaps also the POUM Division under Rovira, were only restrained from marching on Madrid by the action of the head of the air force on the Aragon front, the communist Major Alfonso Reyes, who threatened to bomb the column if it marched on.[2] The spirit of Romance lived on, however, in Barcelona: 'Before renouncing the struggle against fascism, we will die in the trenches; before renouncing the revolution, we will die on the barricades.'[3] Thus the anarchist youth.

Inside the *Generalidad*, Tarradellas, backed by Companys, continued to refuse the anarchists' demands for the resignation of Rodríguez Salas and Ayguadé. But, on 5 May, a solution was reached. The Catalan government resigned, being replaced by a 'provisional council', in which Ayguadé did not figure.[4] The anarchists, the Esquerra, the PSUC and the *rabassaires* would each be represented. But confused firing, nevertheless, continued, raking along the empty broad streets, and bringing death to those who ventured out of their refuges. Two leading Italian anarchist intellectuals, Camillo Berneri and his collaborator, Barbieri, were mysteriously murdered.[5] The

1. Peirats, *La CNT*, vol. II, p. 274.

2. Ibarruri, p. 377. This story is also told by Hidalgo de Cisneros, vol. II, p. 210, who says that anarchists and *POUMistas* had already left the front.

3. Semprún Maura, p. 219.

4. Members were Sesé (UGT), Valerio Mas (CNT), J. Pons (*rabassaires*), and Martín Faced (Esquerra).

5. Who by? The two Italians were arrested, by presumably PSUC or *Generalidad* police, on 5 May, as 'counter-revolutionaries'. They were never seen again. Berneri was working on a dossier listing relations between Italian fascism and

Friends of Durruti issued a pamphlet announcing that a revolutionary *junta* had been formed. All responsible for the attack on the Telefónica would be shot. The national guard had to be disarmed while the POUM, having 'established itself beside the workers', had to be given back a place in the government. *La Batalla* republished this manifesto without comment. The atmosphere of alarm was heightened by the arrival of British destroyers in the bay, which the POUM feared, for no reason, might begin a bombardment.[1] Actually, the British feared that the anarchists were 'getting the upper hand . . . and evacuation of foreigners was being considered'.[2] On this day, there was also fighting in Tarragona and other cities along the coast.[3] During the night, Companys and Largo Caballero had a telephone conversation, in the course of which Companys accepted the Prime Minister's offer of help to establish order.[4]

On 6 May, a truce proclaimed by the anarchists was observed all morning. But appeals to return to work were disregarded, out of fear, not from obtuseness. In the afternoon, fighting began again. Police and Esquerra volunteers attacked anarchist buildings. A number of civil guards were blown up in a cinema by 75-millimetre artillery, brought by members of the libertarian youth from the coast. Antonio Sesé, the communist general-secretary of the Catalan UGT, and a

---

Catalan nationalism (Peirats, *La CNT*, vol. II, p. 198). He had become a kind of intellectual centre for the backers of 'revolution without delay', and, as Semprún Maura puts it, was an 'obvious target for the Russian-directed secret police'. Italian anarchists had been active in Barcelona for a generation. Spriano (p. 209) assumes that the murder of Berneri was an example of 'Stalinist methods introduced into Spain'. Berneri had only two days before publicly regretted, on Barcelona Radio, the death of Antonio Gramsci, in magnanimous terms (*op. cit.*, p. 154). See the testimony of Giovanna Berneri, widow of Camillo, in *Lezioni sull'antifascismo* (Bari, 1962), p. 190f.

1. Orwell, with a POUM firing-post, shared this fear.

2. *CAB*, 20(37) of 5 May.

3. *Solidaridad Obrera*, 14 May 1937. Some thirty or forty anarchists were killed in Tarragona, more in Tortosa. In both places, the fighting began, as at Barcelona, with a would-be police take-over of the telephone exchanges (Peirats, *La CNT*, vol. II, p. 342). In Gerona, and Lérida, where the CNT or the POUM had complete control, there were no incidents; everywhere else in Catalonia, where the PSUC or the Esquerra had influence, there was fighting.

4. Angel Ossorio y Gallardo, *Vida y sacrificio de Companys* (Buenos Aires, 1943), p. 210.

member of the new provisional council of the *Generalidad*, was killed on his way to take up his appointment (perhaps accidentally, since all moving cars were shot at, though possibly as a reprisal for the death of the anarchist, Domingo Ascaso, killed earlier on). In the evening, two republican destroyers, followed by the battleship *Jaime I*, arrived with armed men from Valencia. The reluctance of Largo Caballero to act in the crisis had been overcome by Prieto. Four thousand assault guards, led by Colonel Emilio Torres, an anarchist sympathizer (sometime military adviser to the Tierra y Libertad Column), also arrived from Valencia by road, having overcome risings at Tarragona and Reus on the way, with some bloodshed: local anarchists had blown up road and railway bridges to prevent the passage of the column.[1] On 7 May, the CNT appealed for a return to 'normality'. The presence of assault guards from Valencia in the streets ensured that this occurred. On 8 May, the CNT broadcast: 'Away with the barricades! Every citizen his paving stone! Back to normality!' The Barcelona riots were over. A contemporary press estimate of the casualties was 500 killed and 1,000 wounded.[2] The *Generalidad* was again reconstituted, on the basis of just one representative each from the UGT (the communist Vidiella), the CNT (Valerio Mas), and the Esquerra (once again Tarradellas). Some responsible for deaths were later tried – but only those in Tarragona, and they did not receive death sentences, only terms of imprisonment.[3]

Throughout these anxious days, President Azaña had remained in his palace in Barcelona, undisturbed by the fighting though apprehensive. For months, he wrote in his diary, he had done nothing save count the minutes until his (invariably gloomy) predictions were fulfilled. He summed up these days in Barcelona as

> revolutionary hysteria passing from words to deeds, in order to murder and steal; ineptitude of the rulers, immorality, cowardice, calumnies,

1. Sanz, *Los que fuimos*, p. 145.

2. Peirats (hereafter always *La CNT*), vol. II, p. 206. Abad de Santillán (p. 138) speaks of 1,000 dead, and several thousand wounded. The anarchist leaders regretted afterwards that they had secured this ceasefire, since it led to their final surrender before the communists (Abad de Santillán, p. 140f).

3. Peirats, vol. II, p. 346. Mas had been secretary of the CNT in Catalonia. He was succeeded in that post by Dionisio Eroles, and he soon afterwards by Juan Domenech.

shooting by one trade unionist or another, presumption by foreigners, insolence of separatists, disloyalty, pretence, empty talk by those who had failed, exploitation of the war to make money, negative approach to those desiring to organize an army, paralysis of the war operations, little puppet states (*gobiernitos*) of petty bosses in Puigcerdá, La Seo, Lérida and so on. Companys talks idiocies about giving battle to the anarchists, but he has not the means.[1]

Prieto – the only minister who tried to do anything to protect Azaña – often telephoned, offering escort to a warship in the harbour. But that would have demanded vigorous physical action on Azaña's part, even a risky journey out of doors. 'Don Manuel', wrote Zugazagoitia uncharitably, 'prefers four days of intermittent fears and uncertainty to four minutes of resolution.' During these four days, he nevertheless finished *La Velada de Benicarló* (The Evening at Benicarló), a brilliant but pessimistic dialogue on the reasons for, and character of, the civil war which he had begun to write two weeks before the rising.[2]

*

The 'May Days' of Barcelona showed that the anarchists could not be counted upon to respond as one to any situation: a gulf stretched between the anarchist ministers, busy trying to win the war, and the anarchist youth. Such previously powerful influences as the cripple, Escorza, had lost their control over their followers. The crisis showed that there would be no truce between the POUM and the communists. The *Generalidad*, the communists, and the central government showed themselves ready to act together, by force if necessary, against 'extremists'. Finally, May in Barcelona marked the end of the revolution. Henceforward, it was the republican state which was at war with the nationalist state, rather than revolution against fascism. The new director of public order in Barcelona, José Echevarría Novoa, soon restored normality to most of the prisons and court proceedings, doing away with the arbitrariness which had

1. Azaña, vol. IV, p. 575. Of the government that he formed in February–May 1936, only two people (Giral and Casares), as he noted bitterly were in Spain: the rest had gone into exile or were, safely, ambassadors.

2. Zugazagoitia, p. 213. Martínez Bande, *La invasión*, p. 282, prints the text of Azaña's telephone conversations with the ministry of war and subsequently with Prieto.

characterized the anarchist control over much of the judicial system. Unfortunately, however, the communists were thereby able to embark more easily on their more limited, but for those concerned no less ruthless, crusade against the POUM and other Marxist heretics.

The 'May Days' led, too, to the last stage of the communist attack upon Largo Caballero. The relationship between the Prime Minister and the communists had been made worse than ever by a dispute on strategy. Several republican officers of the high command proposed to test the new republican army by launching an attack in Estremadura, towards Peñarroya and Mérida. They rightly believed that the nationalists had few resources in that region, and that they might thereby divide the enemy territory into two.[1] Largo Caballero supported the idea. The communists opposed it. The Russian chief adviser, General 'Grigorovich', whose real name was Stern and who had replaced Berzin,[2] together with his colleague, the adviser to the Army of the Centre, General Kulik, proposed instead striking down from the republican positions along the Corunna road towards the little town of Brunete, cutting off the nationalists in the Casa de Campo and the University City.[3] Miaja, under communist influence, declared his disapproval of the Estremadura plan.[4] Finally, when the republican officers proved recalcitrant, the Russian advisers threatened to deny the republic use of their aircraft for the proposed offensive.[5] Nevertheless, Largo convinced himself that the plan which he wanted would go ahead. Another difficulty between the Prime Minister and the cabinet was the former's determination to go ahead

1. The Estremadura plan (drawn up by Colonel Alvarez Coque) is printed by Martinez Bande in *La ofensiva sobre Segovia*, pp. 237–40, and discussed there on p. 53f.

2. Berzin was recalled and executed in Russia as part of the purge of the Soviet army. This Stern should not be confused with Stern, the real name of 'Kléber'.

3. Hernández, pp. 80–81.

4. Casado, pp. 71–3.

5. *ibid.* A state department memorandum (sent from Valencia) estimated that at this moment the republic possessed 460 aircraft. Of these, 200 were said to be Russian fighters, 150 Russian bombers (bi-motor Martin type), and 70 Russian observation planes (Cattell, *Communism*, p. 228). See also Jackson, p. 372 fn., where the views of Llopis, Largo's cabinet secretary, and Julio Just, minister of public works, are compared with those of Prieto as to the practicality of the scheme.

with his old idea of arousing Spanish Morocco against Franco by 'distributing money among some prominent Moors'.[1]

This military quarrel merged into the larger communist feud with Largo Caballero. Galarza, the weak minister of the interior but an enemy of the communists, was denounced by the communists for permitting the Barcelona crisis to arise – for failing 'to see the open preparations for a counter-revolutionary putsch'.[2] (There existed neither 'preparations' nor a 'counter-revolutionary putsch', and Galarza had no jurisdiction in Barcelona over internal order, which was in the hands of the Catalan counsellor, and friend of Comorera, Artemio Ayguadé.) On 11 May, the POUM's Valencian paper *Adelante* compared the government, because of its repressive measures, to one led by Gil Robles. Inter-city telephone calls were then forbidden – a measure often used in Spanish crises in internal order from 1909 onwards – and a stricter press censorship introduced. The Esquerra and the communists in Barcelona began to campaign for the 'municipalization' of urban transport, which meant destroying the tram, bus, and metro collectives. On 13 May, the government once again ordered the surrender of all arms, except those held by the regular army, within seventy-two hours. The Barcelona civil guards, PSUC, and assault guards began to round up arms. Finally, also on 13 May, at a cabinet meeting in Valencia, Jesús Hernández and Uribe proposed the punishment of those responsible for the May Days, the POUM and CNT, as well as the cancellation of the Estremadura offensive.[3] Largo Caballero called the communists 'liars

1. Azaña, vol. IV, p. 594. Baráibar subsequently gave a report on this project to Azaña (*op. cit.*, p. 613) in which he assured the President that the rising was a 'matter of days – when the religious fiestas come to an end'. Azaña believed rightly that similar sums were being spent in Morocco by the nationalists. There was also a plan for Moorish women to be paid to go to Spain to persuade their husbands in Franco's army to throw down their arms: 'We make a Moroccan adaptation of Lysistrata,' said Azaña grimly!

2. Largo Caballero says that the communists wanted to be rid of Galarza since he was, at that time, investigating the loyalty of General Miaja and Colonel Rojo, found to have been members of the UME before the war (*op. cit.*, p. 218). Whether they were or were not members has not been fully disclosed. They certainly had no record of left-wing opinions before 1936.

3. For this crisis see Peirats, vol. II, pp. 238ff; Cattell, *Communism*, pp. 153ff; Largo Caballero; Alvarez del Vayo, *Freedom's Battle*, p. 212; Gorkin, *Caníbales políticos*, Araquistain, and Hernández. I consulted Señor de Irujo, Señor Alvarez

and calumniators' and said that he was, above all, a worker, who could not dissolve a brotherhood of fellow workers, unless there were proofs against them. The anarchist members of the cabinet supported the Prime Minister and argued that the riots in Barcelona had been provoked by the 'non-revolutionary parties'. The two communists walked out of the meeting. Largo Caballero tried to continue but the communists were soon followed by Giral, Irujo, Prieto, Alvarez del Vayo, and Negrín. Prieto said that the government could not continue without the communists. Largo Caballero was left in the cabinet room with two of his old friends, Galarza and Anastasio de Gracia, and four new ones – the anarchist ministers. The anarchists suggested to Largo that the government continue without the communists and the right-wing socialists, but the old Prime Minister refused. The cabinet crisis was thus open. Largo went to Azaña, who was delighted to receive his resignation. But he did not accept it immediately. Some time that day, Hernández, on behalf of the communists, proposed to Negrín, the finance minister, that he should become Prime Minister. Negrín answered that he would do so if his party accepted the idea, adding that he was unknown and not popular. Hernández said that popularity could be created. If there were one thing which the communist party could do well, he added, it was propaganda. Negrín protested that he was not a communist, and Hernández answered that was 'all the better'.[1] At the same time, Prieto also apparently desired Negrín to be Premier, since Negrín had been for many years one of his friends.[2] The next day, 14 May, Largo Caballero repeated his resignation to Azaña. The President asked the Prime Minister to remain in office until after the planned military operation – either at Brunete or in Estremadura. Largo Caballero agreed and began to plan a cabinet without the communists. So great a break with the past administration would have

del Vayo and Señorita Montseny, present at this cabinet. See also Azaña, vol. IV, p. 595, for Largo's contemporary report.

1. Hernández, pp. 86–8. Krivitsky says that, as early as November 1936, Negrín had been 'picked' by Stashevsky as the next Premier (*op. cit.*, p. 119).

2. No evidence exists that Prieto had reached a formal agreement with the communists prior to this meeting, though allegations to that effect are put forward by Bolloten (*op. cit.*, pp. 311–12).

needed, in effect, a new executive. In consequence, Largo Caballero, supported by the executive committee of the UGT, approached the anarchists with the idea of forming a purely trade-union cabinet, of CNT and UGT. The way to the pure syndicalist state seemed thus to be opened. At this point, however, Negrín, Alvarez del Vayo, and Prieto told Largo Caballero that the government could not do without the communists because of the need for Russian aid. The communists were now a power, too, in their own right. The right-wing of the socialists, inspired by Prieto and directed by the secretary-general of its executive, Ramón Lamoneda (at that time, a philo-communist), achieved what they had been wanting for many years: the removal of Largo Caballero. Since Azaña's Left republican party shared the views of the *Prietistas*, it was obvious that Largo Caballero did not have enough support for maintaining a government.[1]

The communist party did admittedly send a message to Largo Caballero naming their conditions for support of a government headed by him. All problems of war would be dealt with by a supreme war council. The Prime Minister would cease to be war minister. All the ministers would have to please all parties supporting the government (Galarza would therefore have to be dismissed). A chief of staff would plan the war. The political commissars would be responsible only to the war commissariat, though that body would be responsible to the war minister and war council. These conditions were rejected by Largo Caballero. He hoped to fight the communists and to use the ministry of war, purged, as a base. He was fully supported by his old anarchist enemies. Azaña, however, sought a compromise candidate. Prieto had always seemed to him mercurial and too controversial, since his enmity with Largo Caballero was so longstanding, so personal and so well known. Negrín, whom the communists had by now let it be known that they would support, stood out as the obvious choice. The communists thought Prieto unsuitable on the ground that they would be unable to influence him as they thought that they could influence Negrín.

*

1. Lamoneda's letter of refusal to back Largo Caballero is printed in Peirats, vol. II, p. 246. See also Largo Caballero, pp. 217–18. Lamoneda had been temporarily a communist in 1920. See above, p. 118.

Juan Negrín came from a prosperous middle-class family of the Canary Isles. He was forty-eight. The family owned much of the centre of Las Palmas, and were religious: Negrín's mother lived many years at Lourdes, and his only brother was a monk. Trained as a doctor in Germany, he had been a pupil of the Nobel prizewinner for medicine, Ramón y Cajal, one of the most remarkable of Spaniards, whom he succeeded, when still young, as professor of physiology at the University of Madrid. He had had much to do with the organization of the University City. Married to a Russian, the language in his household was French. He also spoke both English and German. He was thus thoroughly a European. He did not join a political party, and had had little interest in politics, till the last years of Primo de Rivera's dictatorship, when he joined the socialist party. Though he became a deputy under the republic, he did not take an active part in politics till the civil war. Almost the only political act which was remembered of him during the republic was his vote in 1932, in his party group, against a reprieve for General Sanjurjo.[1]

Despite this lack of political experience, Negrín was named minister of finance by Largo Caballero in September 1936. His enterprise in the university recommended him for this arduous post. He was also known to be indefatigable and generous (he had personally helped to finance the library of the Medical School and its laboratory). In July and August 1936, he had helped many people escape from the revolutionary *checas*. He disliked Largo Caballero and had done his best to avoid cabinet meetings over which he presided. At that time, he was a follower of Prieto.[2] But he hardly ever made a speech in the Cortes and was still politically unknown. In the ministry of finance, he was a successful administrator. He handled the complicated questions of paying for Russian aid with skill, and established good relations with the Russian economic attaché, the Pole, Stashevsky. But he was a man without a personal following, and without any apparent political prejudices, though the anarchists knew him as a vigorous enemy of collectivization: he had refused credit for collectivist projects suggested by anarchist ministers. The anarchists also

1. Zugazagoitia, p. 138. Cf. an exchange with Azaña on this in 1938 in Azaña, vol. IV, p. 875.

2. Álvarez del Vayo, *The Last Optimist*, p. 228. Prieto's own description of him can be seen in *Convulsiones*, vol. II, p. 219f.

accused him of building up the carabineers as a private army under the ministry of finance. This, however, had been done by Negrín to ensure that the government received proper customs dues: it was a force now headed by the chemist, Dr Rafael Méndez, a colleague at the university. Negrín was a man of the *grande bourgeoisie,* a defender of private property, even of capitalism. This fact, combined with his efficiency and his academic background, seemed likely to recommend him to Britain and France and caused him to be accepted, without question, by many disparate groups, as the new leader of the republic. The much more politically experienced politicians of the republic (by no means only the communists) thought it would be comparatively easy to influence Negrín. He had failed to prevent inflation in the first nine months of the war, but he had been at least competent in his ministry, unlike the disorderly Alvarez del Vayo.

At the start of his premiership, Negrín told Azaña that, if he were to be Prime Minister, he would be so 'one hundred per cent'.[1] He insisted on so being for the rest of the war. The management of the war demanded different arts from the management of the Cortes, and Negrín was successful where his rivals failed. His arrogance, the inevitable consequence of the entry of such a first-class brain into politics, however, made him ten enemies a day. Other politicians were furious that a newcomer to politics should behave so dictatorially towards them, and be so contemptuous of their intrigues, and ambitions, as well as so intolerant of their failures. Members of Negrín's cabinet were angered by his irregular habits of eating and drinking, and of calling conferences at all hours. Others accused Negrín of a lack of those Roman virtues which they said were necessary to win the war, and of having indeed Roman vices of gluttony and a taste for excess. No doubt, the new Prime Minister was incapable of working with a team of ministers, especially a coalition of such disparate individuals as was necessary in the republic. But he was a man for whom personal freedom was a passion. He was also insistent on his right to personal privacy. There was no sign that his lavish living, his pleasure in the company of women, and his gargantuan eating and drinking interfered with his work. Largo Caballero reported that, sometimes, when he sent for Negrín, he was

1. Statement to me by Julio Álvarez del Vayo, Geneva, 1960.

told he was abroad; Largo said nothing, thinking that it was to do with arms purchases. In fact, Largo later alleged, Negrín was chasing about France with girls in fast cars under an assumed name.[1] One should take such remarks with reserve since they were made by a puritan of seventy about a *bon viveur*. Yet Prieto recalls him dining two or three times the same night in different places.[2] 'Never have I seen his equal,' said Azaña, of his appetite.[3] Nevertheless the President was initially pleased: 'When I speak with the head of the government,' he wrote in his diary on 31 May, 'I no longer have the impression that I am speaking with a dead man . . . that is an advantageous innovation.'[4] Later, Azaña became disillusioned. Negrín and he lived in different worlds; Azaña was looking back, wondering what had gone wrong, and who was the most responsible; Negrín, with no political past, thought only of the present or the future. The relation between the President, who theoretically could dismiss the Premier, and the Premier, who had a duty to listen to the President's advice though not to accept it, went through vicissitudes. 'Karamazov', Besteiro described the Prime Minister, in November 1938; at that time he alone believed in victory.[5]

The policy of Negrín as Prime Minister was one of a realistic opportunism. A moderate socialist with a predilection for 'planning', he was ready to make any political sacrifice to win the war. This led him, as it had led Largo Caballero, into close relations with Russia, since, as before, Russia remained the main source of arms. Furthermore, its realism made the Spanish communist party, throughout Negrín's ministry, the most useful political group in Spain. Thus Negrín had to accept things from the Russian military advisers, and from the Spanish communist party, which he disliked. As minister of finance, Negrín had been specially concerned with the dispatch of the Spanish gold to Moscow. His consequent relations with Russia resembled those of Faust with Mephistopheles.

It would be wrong, however, to conclude that Negrín was a mere instrument of Russian policy. Few politicians have successfully used

1. Largo Caballero, p. 204.

2. Prieto, *Convulsiones*, vol. III, p. 220.

3. Azaña, vol. IV, p. 867.

4. Azaña, vol. IV, p. 603. On the other hand, by 16 June, he was criticizing Negrín's 'juvenile optimism' (*op. cit.*, p. 620).

5. Azaña, vol. IV, p. 894.

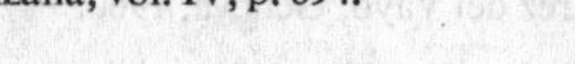

a communist party, and not been later swallowed by it. But in the 1930s and in Spain, the possibility did not seem so far-fetched. Negrín's personal self-confidence and his ebullient but secretive nature led him to think that he could slough off the communist connection when it was necessary. When, from the early summer of 1938, he was seeking peace with the nationalists, he did not confide in the communists nor in anyone else. It would be foolish to suppose that so independent-minded an intellectual, with so bad a temper, could be subservient to anyone. While Largo was referred to by the Russians as 'comrade', Negrín insisted on being named 'Señor Presidente'.[1] Negrín had no close relations with the leaders of the Spanish communist party and he disliked La Pasionaria. Indeed, despite the eclipse of the anarchists, the communists increased their power less under Negrín than they had under Largo. Hernández said later that a time would have come when they would have had to 'liquidate' Negrín.[2] La Pasionaria later spoke of Negrín's 'dark thoughts' and alleged that, so far from Negrín being a tool of the communists, they, the communists, were victims of his wrong judgement.[3]

This war was a mortal struggle in which most Spaniards had lost close friends or relations in appalling circumstances. No quarter would be offered to the vanquished. Negrín's main mistake was to have allowed his disdain for revolutionary folly to cause him to overlook communist repression of the revolutionaries. Negrín was here naïve; the communist-dominated SIM (Servicio de Investigación Militar), for instance, was to build a set of private prisons, unearthed by the nationalists after their victory.[4] Negrín denied that these could have existed, and said that the reports were nationalist propaganda. Ten years later, he admitted that he had been wrong.[5] Negrín was,

1. That is Presidente del Consejo, the Spanish equivalent of Prime Minister. Recollection of Alvarez del Vayo (Geneva, 1960).

2. Hernández, p. 135. This may have been said because Negrín from an early stage placed hope in a world war which he thought inevitable, but which Stalin was always trying to stave off.

3. Ibarruri, p. 437. Togliatti said in 1962 that he met Negrín once only in Spain, in March 1939.

4. For the SIM see below, p. 759.

5. Negrín denied the existence of the torture chambers to Henry Buckley in Perpignan in 1939, and admitted his error to the same journalist in 1949 (Mr Buckley's evidence to the author).

however, surrounded by the wrecks of the reputations of men like Azaña, the 'strong man of the republic', and 'the Spanish Lenin', Largo Caballero. The anarchists were crushed in spirit by the discovery of the realities of political life. Negrín assumed heavy responsibilities when becoming Prime Minister. He made mistakes. But for the rest of the civil war, this energetic physiologist, with the disorderly private life, represented the spirit of the Spanish republic.[1]

Negrín's cabinet owed much to Azaña in its composition. It included two socialists besides the prime minister – Prieto, who brought together the war, navy and air ministries, in a single ministry of national defence, and Prieto's protégé, Zugazagoitia, the minister of the interior. Negrín kept the ministry of finance himself, and the communists, Hernández and Uribe, retained their ministries of education and agriculture. Azaña's old friend, the ex-prime minister of July 1936, Giral, and Giner de los Ríos, republicans, became foreign minister and minister of communications and public works. The Basque Irujo became minister of justice and a Catalan, Jaime Ayguadé, brother of the ex-Catalan councillor, became minister of labour. Thus, no members of Largo Caballero's wing of the socialist party were included in the government. Araquistain, Largo Caballero's chief remaining supporter, even resigned from the Embassy in Paris. He was replaced by Ossorio y Gallardo, the 'monarchist without a king', civil governor of Barcelona in 1909, since 1936 ambassador in Brussels, who, it was hoped, would as a catholic please the French Right.[2] Alvarez del Vayo remained chief political com-

1. Negrín was also skilful with foreign journalists, while Largo Caballero told Azaña that 'he did not believe in the reality of the outside world' (*Obras*, vol. IV, p. 617). See Juan Marichal, 'La significación histórica de Juan Negrín', *Triunfo*, 22 June 1974, who concluded that 'in few men of European history of the last century and a half has there been – as was the case in respect of Dr Negrín – such a fusion of intelligence and character, of moral integrity and intellectual capacity'. Bolloten's hostile view (p. 300) is, I believe, wrong. See Cabanellas, vol. II, p. 970, for a balanced view.

2. The most influential republican representative in Paris during Negrín's government was the arms-purchase chief, Dr Alejandro Otero, helped by the American journalist, Louis Fischer, ex-quartermaster of the International Brigades, interpreter of Russia for the US in the 1920s, who from the Lutetia Hotel directed an organization for the purchase of arms and the diffusion of

missar and Spanish representative at Geneva. He left the foreign ministry with irritation.[1] The ex-lieutenant of carabineers who had been governor of San Sebastián in the early days of the war, the communist Colonel Antonio Ortega, succeeded Wenceslao Carrillo as director-general of security: a bad appointment. The communists also retained other critical positions in the police and Major Díaz Tendero returned as personnel chief in the army. Negrín asked the anarchists to join the cabinet but they refused, saying that they had not provoked the crisis, which they considered 'unwise, inopportune, and harmful to the conduct of the war'. To join Negrín, they said, would prove a 'lack of nobility'. On 27 May, the four anarchist ex-ministers gave addresses denouncing communist and Left republican opposition to the revolutionary changes in society which they had advocated. The anarchist rank and file heard in detail of the quarrels of Juan Peiró with Negrín over the state seizure of the salt mines of Sallent, of López's frustrations at the ministry of commerce, of Federica Montseny's honest doubts about the anarchist role in government.[2] Thereafter, the CNT and FAI continued to collaborate with the government, but no longer exercised responsibility for its actions. They did not withdraw from either the army or the ranks of the bureaucracy. Their leaders realized that only Franco would profit from such action; and, after the May Days in Barcelona, this lesson was borne in on even the anarchist youth, even the comrades of those who had been killed in the fighting in May. Many anarchists continued to suppose that their day would come after the victory, when their numbers might be expected to tell. There was, in consequence, a certain abdication of vitality on their part, and certain members (including the secretary-general, Mariano Vázquez) became regarded as supporters of Negrín.[3] Anarchist strength was far too great for there to be any question of their total 'liquidation', as there

---

republican propaganda. Perhaps one should note too the activities of French communists in Toulouse. See discussion in Pike, p. 128, on the role of Jean Marcel Blanc and the Bar Gambetta.

1. Julio Just was also angry to be leaving his ministry of public works: 'personally, and as a Valencian' (Azaña, vol. IV, p. 603).

2. Texts in Peirats, vol. II, pp. 248–77.

3. *ibid.*, p. 281.

might be with the POUM: the movement claimed over two million members in April 1937.[1]

The anarchists' formal loss of power continued in the early summer. The Barcelona control patrols were dissolved on 7 June. Other changes in the Barcelona police handed over effective control to proved non-anarchists – the pro-communist Colonel Ricardo Burrillo becoming director-general of security in Catalonia. General Pozas took over command of the Catalan army; he seems to have actually joined the communists (PSUC). The FAI lost their share in the posts on the popular tribunals, on 25 May, on the ground that, unlike the CNT, they were not a legally constituted body and, therefore, could not be represented in the institutions of the republic. All CNT-FAI committees in Catalonia by now were replaced by municipal councils. In June, the anarchists, of their own accord, dropped out of the *Generalidad*, after a series of political intrigues which repelled them. The still agile Companys (and the PSUC) had determined to introduce the distinguished rector of the university, Dr Pedro Bosch Gimpera, a brilliant anthropologist, of Acción Catalana, to the new government: but the anarchists were hostile to this extension of 'Catalanism'. Also they now believed that all real authority in republican Spain rested with Negrín. They were right in that, since Negrín's carabineers had recovered the customs, and there was no Catalan councillor for defence, after the nomination of Pozas as captain-general of Catalonia. Catalan police, even Catalan firemen, were transferred elsewhere in Spain.[2]

1. Circular No. 12 of the national committee of the CNT of April 1937, qu. Lorenzo, p. 275 fn. 43. Of the total claimed of 2,178,000, 1,000,000 were allegedly in Catalonia.

2. This resumption of governmental power in Catalonia was the consequence of an explicit, firm governmental decision urged in particular by Azaña (*op. cit.*, pp. 604–5). The new Catalan government was composed only of PSUC and Esquerra with three councillorships each, Acción Catalana and *rabassaires*, with one each: Sbert (interior), Tarradellas (finance), Pi y Súñer (culture), all of the Esquerra; Vidiella (labour), Serra Pamiés (supply), and Comorera (economy) – PSUC; Bosch Gimpera (justice) of Acción Catalana, and Calvet (agriculture), of the *rabassaires*. Of Companys's former moderate colleagues of the beginning of the war, only two – Tarradellas and Pi y Súñer, remained: all the others, old friends such as Espanya, Gassol, and Escofet – had been forced into exile in France; or had fled there. Twelve ex-councillors of the *Generalidad* were in Paris, according to Azaña (*op. cit.*, p. 624).

Meantime, the ex-president of the council, Largo Caballero, whose fall had been so swift as to be hardly believable, returned to the secretariat of the UGT, where he was to be safe a few more months, surrounded by those who, as he believed, were 'clean, pure members of society, members of my own class – people who might make mistakes, but who act in good faith'.[1]

The government of Largo Caballero between September 1936 and May 1937 had successfully incorporated the revolution within the boundaries of the state. When Largo Caballero took office, the orders of the central government could often do no more than endorse *faits accomplis* by regional forces. When he left, orders from Valencia were customarily fulfilled. In order to achieve this victory for state power, Largo had been forced to welcome the communist party as an executive organization. A year previously, he could have accepted this. But the realities of political power, the evolution of the communist party itself and the value which he placed upon his own independence, caused him to repudiate the communists. He could, as he knew, have become the leader of a united socialist–communist party. He was unwilling to unite his own party with the communists, and, thereafter, they abandoned him. Thus, in his last hours as Prime Minister, his only supporters, by a paradox, were the anarchists against whom he had fought all his life and whose influence he had systematically reduced during the previous eight months. Equally paradoxically, the forces ranged against Largo were the moderate socialists and the communists, united in their desire to restrict the further progress of the revolution. A year previously, the same executive of the socialist party which now opposed Largo Caballero – headed by González Peña and Lamoneda – had tried to manoeuvre the supporters of Largo out of control of the party precisely because they feared him, and them, to be too close to the communists. This change can only be understood if it is recalled that for Prieto, as well as for the communists and for Azaña, the chief disturbing factor within the republican camp remained the anarchists, with their surviving cantonalist suspicion of the very idea of the state.

Largo Caballero, despite his obstinacy, vanity, and lack of imagination, was a man of integrity, simplicity and courage who was easily tricked by the communists, who had at their disposal large resources

1. Largo Caballero, p. 229.

of public relations. Largo's dignified departure from the prime ministership marked the end of a whole era in Spanish politics; in terms of efficiency, the change from the plasterer to the professor of physiology could only be for the best. But Negrín could never be so popular in the Spanish working class as Largo Caballero had been.

BOOK FOUR

THE WAR OF TWO COUNTER REVOLUTIONS

'Perhaps the only ones who are not tired of the war are the combatants.'

MANUEL AZAÑA to Marcelino Pascua
13 August 1937

'The ivory tower is no place for writers who have in democracy a cause to fight for. If you live, your writing will be better for the experience gained in battle. If you die, you will make more living documents than anything you could write in ivory towers.'

ANDRÉ MALRAUX in Hollywood
November 1938

38

New war in Vizcaya – Besteiro in London – the mediation proposal – the Deutschland *incident – the German fleet at Almeria – the Huesca and Segovia offensives – death of Mola – the fall of Bilbao – the collective letter of the Spanish bishops – controversy in France – persecution of Basque priests*

THE new republican state over which Dr Negrín presided was a far more formidable one than that which Largo Caballero had inherited from Giral. It had what seemed on paper to be powerful armies: Miaja, with five army corps, in the Army of the Centre; Colonel Morales Carrasco, a regular colonel of engineers, in command of an Army of the South; General Pozas, commanding the Army of the East (including Catalonia and Aragon); and the embattled Army of the North, under General Llano de la Encomienda. The majority of commands in the field were held by ex-regular officers, though some of these, as has been seen, were now politically minded – mostly, like Colonel Cordón (now chief of staff to Pozas) or Major Ciutat (chief of staff to Llano de la Encomienda), communist; but there were some who were anarchist in outlook, such as Major Perea, commander of the 4th Army Corps. The most prominent commanders who had not been in the army before 1936 were the communist militia leader, Modesto, in command of the 5th Army Corps, and some of the divisional commanders (such as Lister, Ortiz, Sanz, Trueba, Mera, Jover, and Rovira). Several International Brigade commanders were also to be found in control of divisions (Hans Kahle, 'Walter' and 'Gal'). Thanks to Russia, the equipment was almost adequate; thus the Army of the Centre had some 100,000 rifles for its 180,000 men. There were altogether 450 batteries, with 1,680 cannon in all. The trouble with this equipment was that the pieces of artillery were various, little of it reached far, and heavy artillery was scarce. Many still had to use a great diversity of charges: for example, the reliable old 77-millimetre Krupp field gun was made to use twenty-two different sorts of projectile. Nevertheless, the republic did have a formidable tank force now led by the Russian General 'Rudolf'. It had about 125 T-26 tanks and over 100 armoured cars.

Opposed to this, the nationalist army, with Germany and Italian artillery was probably gun for gun superior to that possessed by the republic, and their tanks, though much less formidable, were better organized and used with greater imagination.

In the air force, the republic still had technical and numerical superiority, over all, but the first would not last much longer, and neither was true of the northern front. The republicans had about 450 aircraft, commanded by Hidalgo de Cisneros; 200 were fighters (150 Russian) and 100 bombers (60 Russian). Fighters in the central zone were still led by a Russian (Colonel 'José'), while most of the squadrons of Chatos, and all those of the Moscas, were flown by Russians. But, from May 1937, Spanish pilots trained in Russia were taking the Russians' place.[1] Other aircraft still included some of the Blochs, Dewoitines, and Nieuports from France of the early days of the war (though the republic had lost 150 aircraft since July 1936) and there were also a few Bristol Bulldogs bought in England, as well as some Letovs and others newly bought in France.

In comparison, the nationalists had a little less than 400 aircraft: about 150 had Spanish pilots; 100 German, in the Condor Legion; and about 120 Italian, in their 'legionary air force'. The Fiat CR-32 was still the characteristic fighter of both the Italian and Spanish services. New aircraft, however, from both Germany and Italy, in particular the Savoia 79 bomber, from Italy, the Heinkel 111 bomber, and above all the famous Messerschmitt 109, came, in the summer of 1937, to dominate their Russian opponents, being faster, lighter, and having greater firepower. The Messerschmitt, for example, had a top speed of over 350 miles an hour, a high rate of climb, bullet-proof fuel tanks, and a theoretical range of 400 miles – a considerable improvement over the Russian aircraft which had served so well during the winter of 1936–7 (even if the range was in practice much less than 400 miles).[2]

1. R. Salas Larrazábal, vol. II, p. 1194.

2. The ME 109 had two fixed machine-guns in the cowlings, and two 20 mm. cannon in the wings. Their radio equipment was bad in comparison with British.

This technical superiority was already evident in naval matters. The republic had abandoned any attempt to intervene in the Straits. Though the republican fleet was still larger than that of their enemies, their lack of officers with experience kept the ships in harbour. Several submarines had been lost, and the north coast was effectively blockaded. Azaña at least realized that: 'No war can be won in the Peninsula if one does not dominate the sea, particularly if the French frontier is closed or hostile.'[1] The overall command of the republican navy soon passed to Captain Luis González Ubieta, in place of Admiral Buiza, but, save for one fortunate encounter in 1938, the new commander was no better than the last one: Prieto's *éminence grise* in the admiralty, Lieutenant Merín, kept his cautious hand over the fleet.

Prieto did, however, suppress Largo Caballero's Supreme War Council, confirm the able Colonel Rojo as chief of staff, and create four sub-secretaries of defence (Fernández Bolanos, Benjamín Balboa, Camacho, and Pastor) in respect of the army, navy, air force and armaments, none of whom were communists.[2] Prieto's design, largely achieved, of balancing communists with republicans or anti-communist socialists did not, however, have always the results for which he hoped. For example, the appointment of Colonel Visiedo as head of fighter operations 'balanced' the communism of Colonel Hidalgo de Cisneros, chief of the air force; but Visiedo seems to have been one of those 'geographically loyal' only to the republic and, in consequence, very cautious.[3]

Negrín's government included five men (Prieto, Zugazagoitia, Irujo, Uribe, and Hernández) from the Basque provinces.[4] There the front was continuing to crumble. On 18 May, the priest of Amore-

But these weaknesses were not apparent against the Russians over Spain. More Messerschmitts 109 were ultimately built than any other in the history of aviation – 33,000. It had been designed by Willy Messerschmitt in 1935 and was made by Bayerische Flugzeugwerke at Augsburg. Several types of this plane were tested in Spain – the 109B-1, 109B-2, C-1, D, E-O, and later, E-1.

1. Azaña, vol. IV, p. 620.

2. This balance of forces in May 1937 derives from R. Salas Larrazábal, vol. I, p. 1084f; Voronov, in *Bajo la bandera*, p. 128; Cattell, *Communism*, p. 228; and Sanchís, *passim*.

3. See García Lacalle, p. 388, for instances of Visiedo's obstructionism.

4. Prieto was born in Oviedo, but went to Bilbao as a boy.

bieta, Father San Román Ituricastillo, crossed the lines on a private mission of conciliation: a risky thing to do, at the best of times. The nationalists shot him, and announced that he had been killed by the 'reds'.[1] The Basques were now almost back to the 'ring of iron'. The bombing continued, the Condor Legion experimenting now with the idea of dropping incendiary bombs on woods to force the Basques to leave their positions. The assumption by Aguirre of the command in chief of the Basque army corps in the field confused matters further with Llano de la Encomienda. Aguirre wrote to Prieto that the latter was the 'personification of incompetence', incapable of understanding the Basques and excessively influenced by the communists, notably his chief of staff, Major Ciutat, an able officer, but apparently anti-Basque.[2]

Aircraft sent to the help of the Basques from Valencia via France were meantime held up at Toulouse by Colonel Lunn of the Non-Intervention Patrol Commission. (The republic expected that friends in Air France would have refuelled the aircraft and sent them on their way.) They were then returned to Valencia, with their machine-guns confiscated. Eventually, on 22 May, the risk was taken of sending fighters across nationalist Spain to Bilbao. Seven arrived safely and, in the next few weeks, some fifty aircraft were sent from the republic to the north; forty-five arrived – some Moscas, Chatos and some Natasha bombers.[3] In addition, the British agreed to join the French in escorting Basque refugee ships (including British merchant ships), once they were outside the Spanish three-mile limit. The first refugees to be evacuated were children, to be divided among those who agreed to look after them. The CGT in France agreed to take 2,300, while Russia undertook the care of communist children. A Basque children's relief committee in England, supported by the British branch of the roman catholic church, accepted 4,000 children. These, after being carefully examined by doctors from the ministry of health, were boarded at a camp in Stoneham in Hampshire. The authorities in Burgos protested, believing that these steps implied that the Basques were preparing to destroy Bilbao. But the evacuation of 'our brave

1. Iturralde, vol. II, p. 425.

2. Martínez Bande, *Vizcaya*, p. 128f.

3. R. Salas, vol. II, pp. 1382–3; Francisco Tarazona, *Sangre en el cielo* (Mexico, 1960), p. 132.

expeditionary infants', as the Bilbao press described those who went away, continued without difficulty.[1]

Perhaps in the knowledge of the difficulties between the Basques and the republican government in Valencia, several new unofficial proposals were now made to the Basque government for a separate peace. Such ideas had been unofficially put forward throughout the winter. The most important new plan derived from the Argentinian ambassador to Spain, then established, with the rest of the diplomatic corps, at St Jean de Luz. He suggested to the Pope that he should try to arrange a separate peace. As a result, Cardinal Pacelli, secretary of state, about 12 May, sent a conciliatory telegram to Aguirre, suggesting terms for peace in the northern provinces. Unfortunately, the telegram was dispatched *en clair*. The post office in Paris, seeing a communication for Spain, sent it to Valencia, where it fell into the hands of the republican government. Largo Caballero did not raise the question in the cabinet. Instead, he sent a bitter telegram denouncing the Basques for trying to arrange a separate peace. The Basque government, not knowing of the misdirection in Paris, concluded that the affair was a manoeuvre of the communists to discredit them. The Basque minister of justice, Leizaola, therefore, sent a telegram couched in such strong terms that Prieto, reading it, thought that it demanded that he should be shot.[2] In this state of misunder-

1. Yvonne Cloud, *Basque Children in England* (London, 1937); Steer, p. 263. Britain made a proposal to the Basques that they should name a series of neutral zones which would be guaranteed against attack. The republican government protested against Britain's act in thus dealing with the Basques as if they were a regular government.

2. See *Revue des deux mondes*, 10 February 1940. That article falsely alleged that the Basque government had begun negotiating direct with Franco. The above account was told to me by Leizaola, who confirmed the account in Aguirre, pp. 34–6. It has been slightly corrected by that in Largo Caballero (p. 206), e.g. the Basques said that a meeting of the republican cabinet was secretly held without the Basque minister Irujo being present. The telegrams from Faupel to Berlin giving a version of the tale current in Salamanca should be discounted. In March 1937, another *démarche* had been made to secure a mediated peace – this time by Mussolini through his consul in San Sebastián, the Marquis of Cavaletti, 'perhaps by establishing an Italian protectorate over the Basque provinces!' Aguirre rejected the proposal (Aguirre, pp. 31–3). See also the discussion in Martínez Bande, *La guerra en el norte* (Madrid, 1969), p. 60f. and that in the biography of Cardinal Gomá by Antonio Granados (Madrid, 1969, p. 155f).

standing, the relations between the Basque and republican governments remained throughout the rest of the war. Meantime the Pope also approached Cardinal Gomá in the same sense as he had approached Aguirre. Gomá went to Mola and Mola telephoned Franco and limited guarantees were indeed offered to the Basques by the nationalists. But nothing came of this.

The dealings between the Basques, Cardinal Gomá, the Pope and Mussolini were not the only efforts being made to end at least part of the slaughter in Spain. For Anthony Eden had been visited in London by the socialist reformist, Besteiro, who had represented the republic at the coronation on 12 May of King George VI. Besteiro came to Eden on behalf of the melancholy Azaña, begging the British Foreign Secretary to mediate. Azaña had suggested that, after a withdrawal of foreign volunteers, the great powers should then impose a settlement on Spain.[1] The idea was one with which Eden had himself toyed. The new British chargé at Valencia, John Leche, reported, however, that the hatred in Spain was such that mediation would not now prosper.[2] Eden persevered. The British ambassadors at Rome, Berlin, Paris and Moscow, and the minister at Lisbon, approached the foreign ministers in those capitals in the sense that Azaña had suggested.[3] On 19 May, Bastiniani, Ciano's second-in-command at the Palazzo Chigi, angrily complained to Hassell that Eden's plan was typical of 'the British desire to prevent a fascist victory at all costs'.[4] Franco told Faupel that an armistice and free elections would mean a 'leftist government' and mark the end of White Spain. He 'and all nationalist Spaniards would rather die than place Spain in the hands of a red or a democratic government'. Serrano Súñer also believed that a compromise of any sort would 'leave open the door to a return to that state of affairs which had made war inevitable'.[5] The Generalissimo added that he could well believe therefore that the republic might accept mediation. The British, said Franco, wanted an armistice, since they had advanced

1. Madariaga, *Memorias*, p. 416. Azaña (vol. IV, p. 588) confirms that this was a personal peace mission of his own, with which Largo Caballero had nothing to do. Largo commented adversely, in his memoir (p. 199). See comment by Jackson, p. 442f.

2. *USD*, 1937, vol. I, p. 295.

3. *GD*, p. 291. 4. *ibid.* 5. Serrano Súñer, p. 70.

large sums to the Basques.[1] Franco and Faupel agreed how much trouble was caused by the Vatican. In consequence, Franco had insisted to Cardinal Gomá, the archbishop of Toledo, that no mention should be made in Spain of the recent encyclical, *Mit brennender Sorge*, delivered against nazi Germany, and read in German churches in March.[2] Geoffrey Dawson, editor of *The Times* in London, was, meanwhile, anxiously wondering how he could calm Germany's feelings over his paper's reporting of Guernica: 'No doubt they [the Germans] were annoyed over Steer's first story of the bombing of Guernica, but its essential accuracy has never been disputed and there has not been any attempt here to rub it in . . . I did my utmost, night after night, to keep out of the paper anything that might have hurt their susceptibilities.'[3] On 24 May, Ciano told the American ambassador that Eden's armistice plan was unfair, since Franco was about to enter Bilbao.[4]

Eden arrived in Geneva for the League of Nations Council and the British delegation which he led there openly confessed that the armistice plan had failed.[5] Indeed, nothing more was heard of it. On the 28th, the League Council considered a Spanish complaint about Italian intervention. Alvarez del Vayo spoke eloquently. He doubted whether non-intervention control would prevent the influx of material and agreed to the withdrawal of volunteers. Litvinov supported him. Delbos and Eden proclaimed their 'fervent belief' that they had made progress since the previous December, when the Council had last considered Spain. Their policy both at the conference table and in the corridors was, as ever, to keep the discussion in a low key so as not to drive the Germans or Italy from impatience out of the Non-Intervention Committee.

In that body in London, Grandi was busy raising a new incident, that of the Italian cruiser *Barletta*. This vessel, part of the Italian contribution to the non-intervention patrol control, had been sheltering in Palma, in Majorca. It could not have been carrying out its patrol duties there, since Majorca was a French responsibility. Nor could its presence in Palma have been innocent. During a republican air raid, on 24 May, on the island, the *Barletta* was hit. Six Italians

1. This was not true, though Britain had extensive financial interests in Bilbao.
2. *G D*, p. 295. 3. *History of The Times*, vol. IV (London, 1952), p. 907.
4. *U S D*, 1937, vol. I, p. 302. 5. *ibid.*, p. 303.

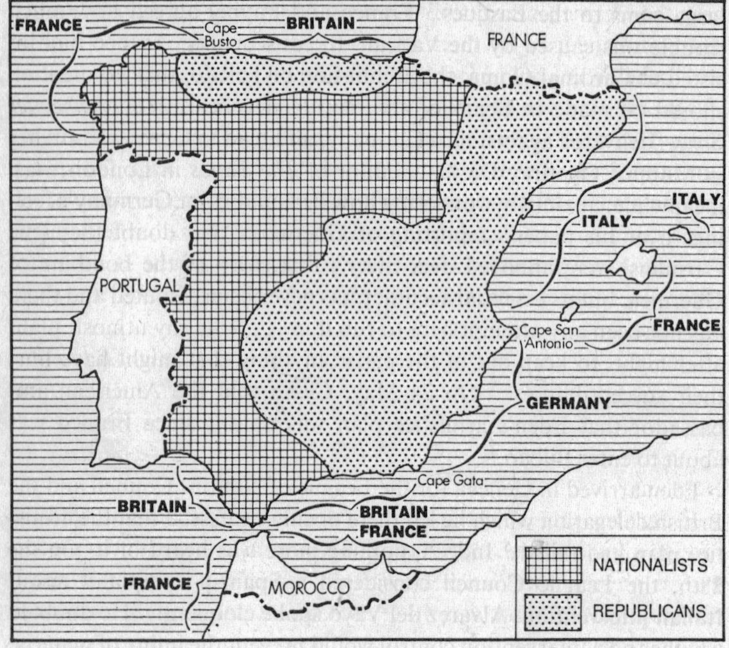

25. Naval Non-Intervention Patrol

were killed. The Non-Intervention Committee suggested a safety zone might be found for all naval patrol vessels in Palma.[1] The next day, the League Council formally regretted that its resolution of December had not been carried out, welcomed the control plan, urged the withdrawal of volunteers, condemned the bombing of open towns, and approved such humanitarian acts as Britain and France had undertaken in respect of the Basque children. These pious sentiments were doomed to remain as aspirations. For the same day a new naval incident occurred in the Balearics.

The ministry of defence at Valencia had pointed out that international naval patrol could not be exercised inside Spanish territorial waters. Palma harbour was a known centre of nationalist arms shipment. The republicans would, therefore, continue to attack it. On 26 May, the air raid on Palma had been repeated, and bombs fell

1. *NIS*, twenty-second meeting.

near the German patrol ship *Albatross*, also lying off duty in Palma. The commander of the German naval patrol protested: repetition of such behaviour would produce 'counter-measures'.

That evening, the German battleship *Deutschland* lay at anchor off Ibiza. Two republican aircraft, at first unidentifiable against the dying sun, appeared overhead and dropped two bombs. One fell in the seamen's mess, killing twenty-three and wounding seventy-five of the ship's company. The other hit the side deck and caused little damage. The affair was witnessed by the republican fleet, then out on a rare sortie. In consequence, the Germans at first thought that they had been attacked by destroyers.

The republican ministry of defence claimed that the *Deutschland* had fired first at the aeroplanes, who thereupon retaliated. This was untrue. 'Reconnaissance aircraft', which the ministry claimed them to be, do not carry bombs.[1] The aircraft were, in fact, flown by Russians.[2]

Hitler flew into a rage at the death of so many Germans, and the foreign minister Neurath passed six hours with him seeking to moderate his anger.[3] The *Deutschland* itself sailed to Gibraltar where it disembarked the wounded. Nine more died, bringing the death-roll to thirty-one.[4]

At dawn on 31 May, the Germans took their revenge. The pocket battleship *Admiral Scheer* and 4 destroyers appeared off Almería, and fired 200 shots into the town, destroying 35 buildings and causing 19 deaths. Germany also decided to withdraw from the non-intervention discussions, and from the naval patrol, until she had received 'guarantees against the repetition of such incidents'. Italy would act

1. Blum told the American ambassador that his information was that the Germans were telling the truth (*USD*, 1937, vol. I, p. 309).

2. See Prokofiev, in *Bajo la bandera*, p. 401, and García Lacalle (p. 212), where it is suggested that the Russians confused the *Deutschland* for the *Canarias*. See Azaña, vol. IV, p. 611, where he points out that the fact was surprising, since 'the Russians observe a most rigorous discipline and their chiefs, like their government, know that they must avoid any conflict with the Germans'.

3. *USD*, 1937, vol. I, p. 317; *GD*, p. 297f. See also François-Poncet's dispatch of 3 June (*FD*, vol. VI, p. 22).

4. The *Deutschland*'s victims were looked after by the governor of Gibraltar, General Sir Charles Harington, whose preoccupation hitherto in the Spanish war had been how to restore the Royal Calpe Hunt to its ancient glory. Meets had been resumed after the fall of Málaga.

likewise.[1] In Berlin, Sir Nevile Henderson, recently arrived as British ambassador, begged Neurath 'not to do the reds the compliment of expanding the Spanish situation into a world war'.[2] Even Cordell Hull summoned the new German ambassador in Washington, Dieckhoff. With his usual caution, the secretary of state told him that the United States desired Germany 'to make peaceful adjustments' of its Spanish difficulties.[3] In Valencia, the republican cabinet met. Prieto suggested that the republic should bomb the German fleet throughout the Mediterranean. This, he admitted, might start a world war but that was worth risking, since it would draw off German aid from Franco. This audacious proposal was characteristic of Prieto. Negrín said cautiously that Azaña would have to be consulted. That gave all the ministers time to consult their consciences – and their friends. Hernández and Uribe went to the central committee of the communist party. The proposal flung the Comintern advisers into a fine flurry. Codovilla went to the Soviet Embassy. Moscow[4] was consulted by wireless; and Moscow answered that Russia had no desire for world war. Prieto's plan should, therefore, at all costs be defeated. But Azaña also opposed Prieto's plan. He said 'we must ensure that *Deutschland* is not our *Maine*'.[5] A real war against Germany might, after all, have brought the annihilation of the republic before Britain and France could be induced to help them. The 'incident' of Almería, therefore, was allowed to be forgotten.[6]

There was another occasion when a world war was nearly provoked by the republic. The dismembered body of a republican pilot was dropped onto the airfield at Barajas near Madrid, with scornful comments made in Italian. The incensed republican air force wished to take off to bomb Rome. Hidalgo de Cisneros, the commander, announced that he would accompany his men. But once again the republican cabinet restrained the impetuous. The advantage to the republic of a general conflict was always equivocal if it were to arise from the Spanish war. It is unlikely that Britain and France would have wanted to assist the republic if they could have helped it. This

1. *NIS*, fifty-third meeting. 2. *GD*, p. 299. 3. *GD*, p. 302.

4. *La Casa* (home) was the Spanish communists' word for Moscow.

5. Azaña gives an account (vol. IV, pp. 611–13). See also Hernández, p. 114.

6. The account by Hernández is generally confirmed by Prieto in the preface to the Mexican edition of *Como y porqué salí del Ministerio de Defensa Nacional.*

was a preoccupation of Russia, who knew that, if she sent to Spain enough arms to win the war for her allies, a world war would probably follow, with Britain and France neutral, if not aligned against her.

The incident at Almería marked the beginning of bad relations between Prieto and the communists. Previously, during the destruction of Largo Caballero, these had prospered, out of convenience. Prieto had been shortly afterwards approached by Uribe and Hernández, who had suggested daily conferences with them. Prieto replied that the communists could discuss matters with him at the cabinet meetings, not with him alone. Thereafter, though the *Prietistas* remained at one with the communists on some issues – how to treat Largo Caballero, how to restrain the anarchists – their friendship began to slacken, as friendships with communists often do.[1]

Bad weather, meantime, had been holding up Mola's operations against Bilbao. Inside that city, a new general staff arrived from Valencia (to act beside the Russian Goriev) under General Gámir Ulíbarri, to replace Llano de la Encomienda as a 'promise of efficiency'. Gámir took over as supreme Basque commander, while Llano de la Encomienda was asked to hold onto the command of the army in the Asturias and Santander. Gámir, a military theorist, had once been director of the School of Infantry at Toledo and, since the start of the war, republican commander at Teruel. This able officer was indeed able to achieve greater efficiency in the Basque general staff. That was odd, since his chief of staff, Major Lamas Arroyo, would have liked to have fought for the nationalists, despite the fact that he had earlier been chief of staff to the ill-fated Puigdendolas, of Badajoz, and to General Walter; he had fought in most of the main battles of the war but was disloyal in inclination if competent in action. The explanation for the greater efficiency of the Basques under Gámir was really that Aguirre had been prevailed upon to withdraw from his commandership in chief.[2] During May, many more men had been called up. A new shipment of Czech arms,

1. Prieto, *Convulsiones* I, pp. 152–3. The first communist complaint against Prieto was during the forthcoming battle of Brunete, when Uribe and Hernández told Negrín that the minister of defence was re-allocating commands to their disadvantage.

2. See R. Salas Larrazábal, vol. II, p. 1395.

including 55 anti-aircraft guns, 30 cannons, and 2 squadrons of Chato fighters, also arrived at the start of June. Other commanders came up from Madrid – among them, the gifted Italian communist Nino Nanetti, who had distinguished himself with the 12th Division at Guadalajara.

The republican government now undertook two offensives in other parts of Spain to draw the nationalist fire from Bilbao. The first was an attack against Huesca, on the Aragon front. This was carried out by the reorganized Catalan army, which, since the May riots, had been under more rigid central control. Led by General Pozas, the attack was unsuccessful. The republicans outnumbered their opponents, who were well entrenched in the town, though hard pressed and almost besieged. There were 1,000 republican casualties, mainly anarchists, in the two weeks which the attack lasted. They included too the gay General Lukács who was killed by a shell.[1] These Italians were observed in their train singing 'Bandiera Rossa' on the way to the front by the recently wounded George Orwell. From his hospital train he saw

> window after window of dark smiling faces, the long tilted barrels of the guns, the scarlet scarves fluttering – all this glided slowly past us against a turquoise-coloured sea . . . The men who were well enough to stand moved across the carriage to cheer the Italians as they went past. A crutch waved out of the window; bandaged arms gave the red salute. It was like an allegorical picture of war – the trainloads of fresh men gliding proudly up the line, the maimed sliding slowly down.[2]

The other attack at this time was on the Segovia front. On 31 May, General Domingo Moriones, with three republican divisions (under José María Galán, Walter, and Colonel Barceló respectively), broke through the nationalist lines at San Ildefonso. The attack reached La Granja before being halted by Varela, with units transferred from

1. See account given by Gustav Regler, who was wounded at the same time (Regler, *The Owl of Minerva*, p. 312). So was the Russian General Batov (*Bajo la bandera*, p. 100). See *Historia y vida*, December 1969. The nationalist air ace García Morato killed Dr Heilbrunn, doctor of the 12th International Brigade, not Lukács. Lukács was succeeded as commander by the Bulgarian Kosovski ('Petrov').

2. Orwell, *Homage to Catalonia*, p. 260. This campaign is well described in Martínez Bande, *La gran ofensiva sobre Zaragoza* (Madrid, 1973), pp. 39–74.

Barrón's division south of Madrid. The attack occasioned a quarrel between General Walter and Colonel Dumont, his subordinate of the 14th International Brigade, the attacking force, as to who was to blame for the ultimate reverse.[1] Since Dumont was supported by the French communists, Walter could do no more than protest against Dumont's vanity and inefficiency. The Russian air force in support of the republic was not only ineffective, but bombed republican positions.[2] The failure of these two offensives sealed the fate of Bilbao.

There was one further preliminary to the final act of the Basque campaign. The death occurred on 3 June of General Mola. The aeroplane in which he was flying crashed on the hill of Alcocero, near Burgos. Mola used aeroplanes a great deal and there is nothing to prove foul play even though, for many years afterwards, a colonel sat in Valladolid, with two loaded pistols before him on his table, waiting till he found out who killed his son, Captain Chamorro, the pilot of the aircraft. Faupel described Franco as 'undoubtedly relieved by the death of Mola'. The Generalissimo's last words on his brother-in-arms were: 'Mola was a stubborn fellow! When I gave him orders differing from his own proposals, he often asked, "Don't you trust my leadership any more?" '[3] The eclipse of the 'Director' of the conspiracy of the preceding year removed one more general with a

1. Our Lady of the Fuencisla, patron saint of Segovia, was later named a full field-marshal for her part in the defence of the town. This was when Varela had become minister of war in the nationalist cabinet in 1942. The news caused Hitler to say that he would never under any circumstances visit Spain (*Table Talk*, p. 515).

2. See Tagüeña, p. 152, for an honest description. Martínez Bande, *La ofensiva sobre Segovia y la batalla de Brunete* (Madrid, 1972), pp. 61–100 gives useful information. See also Gillain, p. 57f, for a mordant description of the troubles between Walter and Dumont. The republic also misused a company of Russian T-26 tanks. Martínez Bande publishes a report on the battle by Walter and Galán (*op. cit.*, p. 246f.). This was the republican offensive described by Hemingway in *For Whom the Bell Tolls*. He suggests that it was betrayed but, due to Marty's obstinacy, was allowed to continue. The action of this book covers 'the sixty-eight hours between Saturday afternoon and Tuesday noon of the last week of May 1937' (Baker, p. 225). Hemingway himself, oddly enough, was by then back in New York, campaigning to raise funds for the republic.

3. *G D*, p. 410. One allegation at the time was that Mola had been killed by the Germans because he had protested against the bombing of civilian targets. The protest and alleged outcome are equally unlikely.

political position of his own. Mola had been a man of decision, nervous and outspoken, who, though a republican all his life, had taken to the Carlist cause when posted to Pamplona, and the Carlists to him, so warmly, that his death was a bad blow for them.

General Dávila, head of the administrative *junta* at Burgos, who resembled Mola in his views, succeeded as commander of the Army of the North. He was a bureaucratic general, in height even shorter than Franco, but 'pure, austere and Spanish', as Admiral Cervera recalled him. General Gómez Jordana succeeded Dávila at Burgos. A member of Primo de Rivera's governments, son of an officer whose name in Morocco was legendary for knowledge of, and interest in, the Moroccans, himself high commissioner of Morocco under the King, he was already old, and, therefore, recommended himself as being beyond personal ambition. Although a monarchist, he regarded himself as a liberal. In truth, he was a man of an age far from that of fascism, communism, and the industrial revolution. Courteous, loyal, indefatigable, and honest, he was later, as foreign secretary, to do much to commend Franco's régime to foreign ambassadors.

On 11 June, the Army of the North returned to the attack. The preliminary artillery bombardment by 150 pieces, accompanied by aerial bombing of both the Condor Legion and Italian aircraft, was heavy, and the shock broke the Basque defenders of the last high point before the 'ring of iron'. By nightfall, Colonels García Valiño, Bautista Sánchez, and Bartomeu, with three out of the six Navarrese brigades, had reached this famous line of defences. All night, the bombardment continued. Incendiary bombs dropped in a cemetery and caused a fiery resurrection of the dead.[1] General Gámir had

1. Martínez de Campos, p. 221. The army of the nationalists in the north had now been reorganized. The expanded old 6th Division, with headquarters at Burgos, had been renamed, what it already was in reality, the 6th Army Corps (General López Pinto in command) divided into two divisions. The first division, under Solchaga, comprised six Navarrese Brigades, the first four of them formed on the basis of the old Carlist volunteer columns, being commanded as on 31 March, the two new ones being headed by Colonels Bartomeu and Bautista Sánchez. The chief of staff remained Vigón, the artillery continued to be under Martínez Campos. On 23 May, this division was renamed the 61st (Navarrese) Division, that is, the 1st Division of the 6th Army Corps. See Martínez Bande, *Vizcaya*, pp. 124–5.

probably about 40,000 men in all, of whom some were Asturianos or Santanderinos and, therefore, unreliable; while about half the other units were socialist or communist in political flavour and therefore unable to share fully in the Basque nationalist adventure breathed by those brigades whose names were '*Arana Goiri*', '*Itxar Kundia*' or '*Sukarrieta*'.[1]

On 12 June, after the batteries and more aircraft (perhaps seventy bombers in action that day) had pounded away at the 'ring of iron' for several hours, Bautista Sánchez's brigade attacked at the spot where the defence system had hardly been constructed at all. The treachery of Major Goicoechea had no doubt suggested this point for the assault, at this weak point of Monte Urcullu. The attack followed the artillery bombardment. The defenders could thus hardly tell when firing from tanks succeeded the shelling. Confusion, smoke, movement was suddenly everywhere. Once again, Basque units found that they were in danger of being surrounded, and hastened to retreat. By dusk, Bautista Sánchez had broken the Basque lines on a front half a mile long. He was only six miles from the centre of Bilbao. The nationalists could shell Bilbao as well as bomb it.[2] On 13 June, all the Basques beyond the 'ring of iron' were withdrawn inside. Their morale had suffered a shattering blow: thereby proving the psychological unwisdom of an elaborate, fixed system of defence. In Bilbao, many prepared to flee to France. A conference was held at the Carlton Hotel, at which Aguirre asked the military commanders if Bilbao could be defended.[3] The chief of artillery, Guerrica Echevarría, thought that it could not. The Russian General Goriev advised resistance. Another Russian adviser, Colonel Golmann, and a Frenchman, Monnier, were also firm. Gámir said nothing. During the night of 13–14 June, the Basque government decided to defend Bilbao. Prieto gave precise orders from the ministry of defence to that effect. Industrial and other establishments useful to the enemy were to be destroyed. But as many as possible of the civilian popu-

1. Martínez Bande, *La guerra*, pp. 154–5. The divisional and brigade organization was weak.

2. See del Burgo, p. 900, and Martínez Bande, p. 172.

3. Steer, p. 307; R. Salas, vol. II, p. 1403; Martínez Bande, *Vizcaya*, pp. 288–90, prints the notes of the chief of staff, Lamas, at this conference. Steer's account is excellent. The Russian Koltsov was in Bilbao too, though not at this meeting.

lation were evacuated to the west, towards Santander. This foreshadowed the abandonment of the city.

On 14 June, the Alsatian Colonel Putz, who had previously commanded the 14th International Brigade, took over command of the 1st Basque Division. The Italian Nino Nanetti was given a division also. Nevertheless, the flight of refugees from Bilbao went on all day, and the road to Santander was machine-gunned by the Condor Legion. Two vessels full of refugees were captured by the nationalist fleet. The Basque government withdrew to the village of Trucios, in western Vizcaya. They left behind a *junta* of defence for Bilbao composed of Leizaola (the minister of justice), Aznar (socialist), Astigarrabía, and Gámir. The government's withdrawal was a reasonable act; less so the flight of Navarro, the chief of the navy off Vizcaya, the chief of artillery, Guerrica Echevarría, and others in the last ships available. On 15 June, thanks to Putz, a line at least was presented to the advancing Carlists and Italians: Belderrain was in the north, Putz in the centre, and, in the south, Nino Nanetti. It was again at a point where the treacherous Major Goicoechea had revealed the fortifications to be incomplete that the next attack was made. Nanetti's men broke and fled across the river Nervión, without blowing up the bridges behind them. They thus laid open the road to Bilbao. The next day, 16 June, Prieto telegraphed to Gámir to hold Bilbao at all costs, especially the industrial region of the town. But the Fifth Column had begun to fire indiscriminately into the suburb of Las Arenas. An anarchist group silenced this outburst. There was, however, no aerial bombardment: the nationalists had learned a lesson from Guernica; while Leizaola discovered, and quashed, a plan to burn the city.[1] Throughout the day, the nationalist advance continued. Putz's division incurred heavy casualties. On 17 June, the field headquarters of these two commanders were in the centre of Bilbao. During that day, 20,000 shells dropped on the city. High points and isolated houses changed hands several times. A few factories were evacuated, some more partially evacuated, the rest abandoned. Within Bilbao, men and material were transported along the railway line and the last two roads towards Santander. These routes

1. See Víctor de Frutos, *Los que no perdieron la guerra* (Buenos Aires, 1967), p. 119. Frutos was a commander of a brigade. For Leizaola, see Sancho de Beurko, *Gudaris, recuerdos de guerra* (Buenos Aires, 1956), p. 90.

were now beginning to come within artillery range of the advancing Black Arrows. In the evening, Leizaola chivalrously arranged for the delivery to the enemy of political prisoners in Basque hands to avoid leaving them without guards in the last stages of the resistance. He also prevented the communist and anarchist battalions from blowing up the university and the church of San Nicolás, which they had thought would make good enemy machine-gun nests. The nationalists had now gained all the right bank of the river Nervión from the city to the sea and most of the left bank as far as the railway bridge. At dusk on 18 June, the Basque units were ordered to evacuate their capital. In the morning of 19 June, the last of them did so. At noon, nationalist tanks made a preliminary reconnaissance across the Nervión, to find Bilbao empty. The Fifth Column, the opportunists, and the secret agents emerged, to hang red and yellow monarchist flags from their balconies. A crowd of two hundred nationalist sympathizers gathered to sing and shout. A Basque tank appeared from nowhere, dispersed the crowd, tore down, with bursts from its guns, three flags from the balconies, and drove along the last road of escape. Between five and six o'clock in the evening, the 5th Navarrese Brigade, under Bautista Sánchez, entered the city and placed the monarchist flag on the town hall.[1]

Thus ended the experiment of the Basque republic, Euzkadi, whose political leaders transferred themselves, a government-in-exile, to Barcelona. General Gámir preoccupied himself with withdrawing as many troops as he could towards Santander, losing as he did so, in an aerial attack, the new Italian commander of his second division, Nino Nanetti.[2] His tasks were easier since Franco made no serious effort to follow up the capture of Bilbao quickly, as his air chief Kindelán complained.[3] The nationalists had lost some 30,000 casualties since March, including 4,500 deaths; Gámir estimated a total of 35,000 casualties for the republic, of which 10,000 would have been the maximum for deaths.[4]

1. Aznar, pp. 425–6; Steer, pp. 336–71.

2. See unpublished MSS of Colonel Lamas, qu. Martínez Bande, *Vizcaya*, p. 198 fn. 317.

3. Kindelán, p. 86.

4. Martínez Bande, *La guerra*, pp. 219–20; Basque official casualty figures for June were lost. For April and May, they were 7,344 and 8,793. 14,000 total casualties for June would be quite likely.

Franco had learnt his lesson from the 'senseless shootings' after the fall of Málaga. He forbade large troop detachments from entering Bilbao, so avoiding excesses.[1] Immediate reprisals did not occur, and few civilian prisoners were made. But the conquerors made immediately every effort to extinguish Basque separatist feelings. Schoolmasters were dismissed unless they could positively prove at least their political neutrality. The Basque tongue was officially forbidden. Within a fortnight, Herr Bethke, of ROWAK, had visited the iron mines, blast furnaces, and rolling mills of Bilbao. He found them undamaged. Work could continue to provide for future offensives.[2] Ores sent in the past to Britain, particularly to the Steel Company of Wales, were diverted.[3] So, too, were the important chemical works at Galdacano, the only factory in Spain capable of the manufacture of artillery shells. Vizcaya had half the production of explosives in all Spain. The fall of Bilbao also meant that all three of Spain's principal cableheads for telecommunications were in Franco's hands (the others were Vigo and Málaga).[4]

The news of the fall of Bilbao was given by a priest to the Basque refugee children in England at their main camp at Stoneham (Hampshire). The assembled children were so appalled that they fell upon the bringer of such bad tidings with stones and sticks. Three hundred children out of the 3,500 broke out of the camp in grief-stricken purposelessness.[5]

*

The fall of Bilbao intensified an already heated world-wide controversy over the religious implications of the Spanish Civil War. The

1. *G D*, p. 409. 2. *ibid.*, p. 412.

3. The Germans were prepared to negotiate over this later with Britain and, by the end of 1937, iron ore exports to Britain were back to normal.

4. The naval significance of the fall of Bilbao is well described by Admiral Cervera (*op. cit.*, p. 170), whose blockade had so contributed to the victory. The naval shipyards, supplies of anchors, cables, chains and so on were of great service.

5. Cloud, p. 8. Something of the life of these camps was given to the author by Víctor Urquídi, who worked in them when a student at the London School of Economics. The Basque children formed themselves a committee, he recalls, 'to fight corporal punishment'; and when a dentist came, he arrived to find the camp empty: the children had fled.

tone of the dispute had been set in January when *Osservatore Romano*, the Vatican periodical, had ruminated: 'To a militant conception of life, struggle for a doctrine is a holy war . . . only liberal agnosticism, with its conception of tolerance in theory, as well as in practice . . . can be shocked by ideological struggles.'[1] But, despite this, the republican affiliation of the Basques, 'the most Christian people in Spain',[2] made catholics look to their loyalties. In the spring, two eminent French catholics, François Mauriac and Jacques Maritain, had issued a pro-Basque manifesto. Dr Múgica, Bishop of Vitoria, in Rome, wrote supporting the French manifesto even if he still refused to give his name publicly to the defence of the Basques:[3] he kept his protests to the Vatican, where, however, his views had an effect. The destruction of Guernica strengthened the hands of those whom the right-wing French catholic press dubbed the '*chrétiens rouges*'. On 15 May, two Spanish Dominicans in Rome, Father Carro and Father Beltrán de Heredia, published a violent pamphlet denouncing the idea 'prevalent in too many catholic homes' that one could be neutral in the Spanish Civil War. For that meant giving equal rights to 'the murderers, the traitors to God, and to the Fatherland'. Sin, like crime, had no rights. The archbishop of Westminster described the war as 'a furious battle between christian civilization and the most cruel paganism that has ever darkened the world'.[4] The Pope officially declared all those priests who had been murdered to be martyrs. Claudel thereupon wrote his ode '*Aux Martyrs Espagnols*', as a verse preface to a pro-nationalist book by Juan Estelrich, a Catalan but Francoist diplomatic agent in Paris. On 1 July, Maritain replied with an article in *La Nouvelle Revue française*, in which he described those who killed the poor, 'the people of Christ', in the name of religion, as being as culpable as those who killed priests by hatred of religion.[5]

1. *Osservatore Romano*, 8 January 1937.

2. *La Guerre d'Espagne et le catholicisme*, a pamphlet by Vice-Admiral H. Joubert in answer to the article of 1 July by Maritain (Paris, 1937), p. 26.

3. Iturralde, vol. II, pp. 318–19. Nevertheless, the bishop by this time recognized privately that he was wrong, and later was to do so publicly.

4. Qu. Father Bayle, SJ, *¿Qué pasa en España?* (Salamanca, 1937).

5. Maritain's position is to be found in his preface to Alfredo Mendizábal, *Aux origines d'une tragédie* (Paris, 1937). See also Ch. 8 'Católicos Antitotalitarios' of Southworth's *El mito de la cruzada*. For Claudel's ode, see above, p. 271.

That day the Spanish hierarchy, led by Cardinal Gomá, archbishop of Toledo, took the unusual step of dispatching a joint letter to the 'Bishops of the Whole World'.[1] They explained that they had not wished an 'armed plebiscite' in Spain, though thousands of christians 'had taken up arms on their personal responsibility to save the principles of religion'. They argued that the legislative power since 1931 had sought to change 'Spanish history in a way contrary to the needs of the national spirit'. The Comintern had armed 'a revolutionary militia to seize power'. The civil war was, therefore, theologically just.[2] The bishops recalled the martyred priests and comforted themselves with the reflection that, when their enemies who had been fascinated by 'doctrines of demons died under the sanction of law, they had been reconciled' in their vast majority to the God of their fathers. In Majorca, only 2 per cent had died impenitent; in the southern regions no more than 20 per cent. The bishops concluded by naming the national movement 'a vast family, in which the citizen attains his total development'. Despite this, they added that they 'would be the first to regret that the irresponsible autocracy of parliament should be replaced by the more terrible one of a dictatorship without roots in the nation'. They finally reproved (though in words moderate enough to suggest that they sought a compromise) the Basque priests for not having listened 'to the voice of the Church'. This letter was signed by neither the archbishop of Tarragona (in exile in Switzerland), nor by the bishop of Vitoria.[3] The latter prelate denied from Rome that there was a religious free-

1. Published in London by the Catholic Truth Society. It seems probable that the letter was written on the suggestion of General Franco. It was drafted by Cardinal Gomá and circulated for signature by the bishops.

2. Father Ignacio Menéndez Reigada added, in *La guerra nacional española ante la moral y el derecho* (Salamanca, 1937), that the rising had been 'not only just but a duty'.

3. The bishop of Orihuela was ill, so his representative signed on his behalf. The archbishop of Tarragona, though refraining from commenting on the attitude of the Spanish Church in the civil war, never made any public statement of his position. He never returned to Spain, however, and, dying in exile in the Chartreuse convent near Zurich, had inscribed on his tomb the laconic epitaph reminiscent of that of Hildebrand: 'I die in exile for having too much loved my country.' Cardinal Segura, shortly to return to Seville from Rome, was apparently not asked to sign the letter.

dom in nationalist Spain (even the Germans had complained about persecution of protestants),[1] nor was it true that death sentences were only administered after trial.[2] Despite this championship by their bishop, the Basque priests were accused before the Pope by the Spanish hierarchy of having acted as politicians and of carrying arms. The Basque clergy replied that no Basque priest had ever been affiliated *qua* priest to the Basque nationalist party and that none, not even the corps of almoners, had carried arms.[3] But, on 28 August, the Vatican formally recognized the 'Burgos authorities' – as the British Foreign Office referred to them – as the official government of Spain. An apostolic delegate, Monsignor Antoniutti, was dispatched to the Castilian capital. Henceforward any catholic who sided with the republic or who even, like Maritain, preached that the church should be neutral, became technically a rebel against the Pope. But until late 1938, the rebels still felt a little aggrieved towards the Vatican, since the Pope did not accord them full recognition, and did not send a nuncio, only an apostolic delegate.

The pamphlet war continued during the rest of the Spanish conflict, above all in France. Accusations of espionage, or that foreigners were plotting with right- or left-wing terrorist groups, were made daily.[4] Mauriac continued his articles in favour of the republic. Charles Maurras replied, in *L'Action française*, by proclaiming that the church was the only real International. Bernanos soon published *Les Grands Cimetières sous la lune*, which gave so terrible an account of the nationalist repression in Majorca. A right-wing writer replied with *Les Grands Chantiers au soleil*. A Jesuit priest, Juan Vilar Costa, who had sided with the republic, founded a catholic institute for religious studies, to give the republic a better name than it had previously among the world's catholics. He also published a clever book, *Montserrat*, commenting on the Spanish bishops' letter. In Liège, a characteristic prayer of the exiled Spanish priests to the Virgin of the Pillar appeared:

> To You, O Mary, Queen of Peace, we always return, we the faithful sons of Your best-loved Spain, now vilified, outraged, befouled by criminal bolshevism, deprived by Jewish Marxism, and scorned by savage com-

1. *G D*, p. 236. 2. *Le Clergé Basque*, p. 10. 3. *ibid.*, pp. 33–8.
4. See Southworth, *El mito*, p. 235; Pike, pp. 130–32.

munism. We pray You, tears in our eyes, to come to our help, to accord final triumph to the glorious armies of the liberator and reconqueror of Spain, the new Pelayo, the Caudillo! *Viva* Christ the King![1]

In England, judgements were almost as elated: for example, the prominent catholic apologist Douglas Jerrold, who, a year previously, had constituted a small link in the chain leading to the rising, wrote in his autobiography, *Georgian Adventure*, of a visit to Franco: Franco might 'not be a great man, as the world judges, but he is certainly something a thousand times more important – a supremely good man, a hero possibly; possibly a saint'.[2]

In America, the Basque priests relied upon protestants for active championship. But polls suggested that only four out of ten American catholics were with the bishops. Opinion was so cautious that a project to bring certain Basque children to America was dropped as risking neutrality.[3] Certainly, fear of alienating the catholic vote was a main factor in Roosevelt's decisions.[4] In the Basque provinces themselves, persecution had started. 278 priests and 125 monks (including 22 Jesuits) suffered deprivation, imprisonment, or deportation to other parts of Spain.

In July 1937 the 'Second International Writers' Congress', 'a travelling circus' of writers, was held at Valencia, Barcelona and Madrid, intended as a culmination to these controversies. The declared purpose was to discuss the attitude of intellectuals to the war. One concealed aim, however, was to condemn André Gide who, in his recent book, *Retour de l'URSS*, had attacked the Soviet Union, where he had been received as a friend of the government. This congress was attended by Hemingway, Spender, Pablo Neruda, Nicolás Guillén, and most of the leading literary apologists for the republic. Others present included Julien Benda, André Chamson, Ilya Ehrenburg, Ludwig Renn, and Eric Weinert (of whom Weinert and Renn had both served in the International Brigades). The congress was

1. Antonio Berjón, *La Prière des exilés espagnols à la Vierge du Pilier* (Liège, 1938).

2. Jerrold, p. 384. For the controversy in England over Guernica, see Southworth, *La Destruction*, *passim*.

3. Taylor, p. 157.

4. See p. 576 n 3 below.

dominated by Malraux, 'with his nervous sniff and tic', who defended Gide from the accusations of being a 'Hitlerian fascist'.[1] The delegates drove about in Rolls Royces and talked with the Spanish poets of the war – Rafael Alberti, Altolaguirre, Bergamín, Antonio Machado, and Miguel Hernández. Of these, Rafael Alberti was the most prolific: there were few editions, for example, of *Volunteer for Liberty*, the paper of the 15th International Brigade, which did not contain one of his verses. The best new poet was, however, probably Miguel Hernández, a member of the Fifth Regiment at the start of the war. He was a shepherd who had been taught to read by a priest in the hills through examples of sixteenth- and seventeenth-century writing. The outbreak of the civil war inspired in him a sudden outburst of poetic activity. For example:

The winds of the people sustain me,
Spreading within my heart.
The winds of the people impel me,
And roar in my very throat . . .

I come not from a people of oxen,
My people praise
The lion's leap,
The eagle's straight swoop,
And the strong charge of the bull
Whose pride is in his horns.

Hernández was representative of a whole generation of young socialists or communists who believed that they were fighting for liberty in Spain. Most of them would not have put up with Stalinism for a minute had they known what it involved. They were scornful of defeatism and, rather than rendered political by the war, were made military by it.[2]

1. Lacouture, p. 253; Spender, *World within World*, p. 496; see also Koltsov, p. 431,Ehrenburg, *The Eve of War*, p. 408, and *Left Review*, September 1937.

2. See Claude Couffon, *Miguel Hernández et Orihuela* (Paris, 1963, translation, slightly altered, by A. L. Lloyd, in Spender and Lehmann, *Poems for Spain*, p. 37). See an interview with his widow in *Triunfo*, 4 January 1975. Hernández's father-in-law had been a member of the civil guard and had been shot, quite gratuitously, by the anarchists in the summer of 1936.

A speech by Bertolt Brecht was read at the congress.[1] As on many occasions of this kind, the national anthems of the different nations were played, so that the English poet, Stephen Spender, found himself at Barcelona giving the salute of the clenched fist while the band trumpeted 'God save the King'. Azaña refused to give the closing address. He thought that nobody important had come from abroad, and that the Spanish delegation was 'no more lucid' than the foreigners were.[2]

1. He shortly wrote his play *Señora Carrara's Rifles*, satirizing the idea of neutrality, on the model of J. M. Synge's *Riders to the Sea*. The theatrical effectiveness of the play is not diminished by the playwright's mistake in giving his characters Italian, instead of Spanish, names.

2. Azaña's contemptuous description is in his diaries (*op. cit.*, vol. IV, p. 672).

39

The fall of the POUM – arrest and murder of Nin – consequences and morals

DURING the summer, Irujo, the minister of justice, was doing his best, with Negrín's encouragement, and the collaboration of the Catalan councillors, to revive conventional justice: regular judges sat as chairmen of popular tribunals, prison directors were appointed from the old career service rather than by political affiliation, the biretta returned to the court, as did the republican flag over the law court building. Such radical revolutionary lawyers as Angel Samblancat and Eduardo Barriobero lost their positions of terrifying power in Barcelona. Many who had at first greeted the revolution with enthusiasm welcomed these setbacks to it. For these acts were important victories of justice over the rule of force, predictability over arbitrariness. But there was a dark side to these occurrences. Ever since the formation of Negrín's government, the communists had concentrated upon the persecution of the POUM. Its leaders were accused of fascism and of conspiring with Franco. The work of persecution, including arrest, interrogation, and torture, was mainly carried out by foreign communists. The Spanish communists, not knowing and not daring to guess the truth, observed what was going on and cravenly applauded, thereby causing the demoralization of the republican cause in a way which they perhaps never fully realized. Did the catholic communist José Bergamín really believe that Nin, Gorkin and Andrade were spies? It is impossible to believe. Yet he wrote that he thought the POUM leaders had no right to any defence.[1] The *Prietista* wing of the socialists and even the left republicans connived at these actions in a way which damaged them also. Beset by problems of war and its cruelties, they read the ac-

1. Qu. 'Max Reisser', *Espionaje en España* (Paris, 1938), p. 12. It never became clear who wrote this book or in what language it was first written. The Spanish translator was Arturo Perucho, director of *Treball*, a PSUC paper and ex-sub-editor of Juan March's *El Imparcial*.

counts of the alleged treachery by the POUM, and gave the benefit of the doubt – to the accusers, not the accused.

In April, the communist-controlled police in Madrid had unearthed a conspiracy by the Falange. One of the conspirators, named Castilla, was induced to become an *agent provocateur*. Castilla prevailed upon another falangist in the capital, Golfín, to prepare a fraudulent plan for a military rising by the Fifth Column. Golfín did this, and he, and his plan, were then apprehended. Next, someone, probably Castilla, forged a letter of extreme innocence purporting to be from Nin, the outstanding leader in the POUM, to Franco, on the back of Golfín's plan. At about the same time, another genuine falangist, José Roca, who kept a bookshop in Gerona, was unmasked by the Catalan communists. Roca's task in the Fifth Column was to pass on messages to a hotelier in the same town, named Dalmau. One day, sometime in May, a well-dressed individual called at the bookshop, left some money for Roca, and a message for Dalmau, and asked if he could leave a suitcase in the shop for three days. Roca agreed to his request. Not long after, the police arrived to carry out a search. Naturally, they came upon the suitcase which, when opened, was found to contain a pile of secret documents all sealed, curiously enough, with the stamp of the POUM military committee.[1]

It was upon these documents, the letter from Nin to Franco, and the suitcase found in Gerona, that the communist case against the POUM rested. All were forgeries.

By mid-June, the communists judged their position strong enough to take final action. They had secured the banning of the POUM's paper, *La Batalla*, on 28 May. Antonov-Ovsëenko, Berzin, and Stashevsky, the most prominent Russians who had been in Spain since August 1936 (as consul-general in Barcelona, chief of the military mission and economic councillor), were all recalled in June 1937

1. This account derives from what Golfín and Roca told the POUM leaders when they met in prison. See Gorkin, pp. 252–3 and 258–60. The *provocateur* Castilla was allowed to escape with his life and a certain amount of money to France. The chief Catalan police agent acting for Gerö, Victorio Sala, once a member of the POUM, later broke with the communists, whom he has since accused of atrocious crimes. The documents were published in *Espionaje en España*. The communist point of view can be seen in the pamphlet by the French communist journalist, Georges Soria, *Trotskyism in the Service of Franco* (New York, 1938).

to Moscow and vanished forever: Stashevsky had unwisely visited Moscow in April and complained to Stalin of the recklessness of the Russian secret police's activity in Spain. But doubtless his fate was settled before that anyway.[1] On 12 June, in Russia, Marshal Tukhachevsky and seven other senior Russian generals were shot for 'intrigues with Germany'. It could thus hardly have been a surprise to the communist minister of education, Jesús Hernández, when, on 14 June, he was told by Colonel Antonio Ortega, the director-general of security, that the GPU chief in Spain, Orlov, had given orders for the arrest of all the leaders of the POUM.[2] Hernández went to Orlov, who insisted that the cabinet should be told nothing of the matter, since the minister of the interior, Zugazagoitia, and others, were friends of those detained. There was proof, Orlov added, of the POUM's connection with a fascist spy-ring. Hernández went to Díaz, who was furious. Together, they went to the communist party headquarters, where a quarrel occurred. Díaz and Hernández denounced the foreign 'advisers'. Codovilla suggested smoothly that excess of work was making Díaz ill. Why did he not take a holiday for a while? In Barcelona, meanwhile, on 16 June, on the orders of the new head of public order there, the *comunizante* Colonel Ricardo Burillo, the POUM headquarters at the Hotel Falcón was closed. It was immediately turned into a prison. The POUM itself was declared illegal, and forty members of its central committee arrested. Rovira, the commander of the 29th POUM Division, on the Aragon front, received a telegram to go to Barcelona to the headquarters of

1. Krivitsky, p. 125, confirmed to John Erickson by a former Russian officer. His French wife and daughter also vanished at the same time from Paris (Poretsky, p. 212). According to Krivitsky, Stashevsky approved the actions of the GPU against the 'Trotskyists' in Russia but thought that they should respect legally constituted parties in Spain. He left Russia happily thinking he had convinced Stalin of this view. Antonov-Ovsëenko was appointed people's commissar for justice and told to return to Russia to take up those duties: a joke typical of Stalin. He never arrived at his post. Some suggest that he had come to like the Catalans too much for his safety (see Miravitlles, p. 195f.).

2. Ortega had been a sergeant of carabineers before 1936, and had commanded republican forces at Irún in August. By mid-1937 he was a communist. For all the following see Hernández, pp. 124–6. An account of events from the POUM side is given in Gorkin, *El proceso*, pp. 102ff. See also Katia Landau, *Le Stalinisme en Espagne* (Paris, 1938) for horrible stories.

the Army of the East: on arrival, he was arrested.[1] Small POUM battalions at the other fronts were disbanded. Andrés Nin was taken off separately, and his friends all found themselves in underground dungeons in Barcelona or in Madrid. All members of the POUM went in fear of arrest, since Stalin's habit of visiting the alleged crimes of the leaders upon friends and families was well known. The communist newspapers screamed accusations against those whom their party had arrested, but did not bring to trial. A rumour then spread that Andrés Nin had been murdered in prison. Nin had once been Trotsky's secretary, had worked in Russia throughout the 1920s until he had left it, and Stalinist communism, through disillusionment with its methods, and he was precisely the kind of individual whom Stalin desired dead.

Negrín sent for Hernández. He asked Nin's whereabouts. Hernández said that he knew nothing. Negrín complained that the Russians were behaving as if Barcelona were their own country. What would happen in the cabinet that afternoon when Nin's disappearance would be raised? Hernández promised to investigate. Codovilla told him that Nin was being interrogated. The cabinet meeting followed. At the door, journalists asked for news of Nin. Inside, Zugazagoitia demanded if his jurisdiction as minister of the interior were to be limited by Russian policemen. Prieto, Irujo, and Bernardo Giner supported this protest. Hernández and Uribe replied that they knew nothing of Nin. No one believed them, not realizing that there could be secrets even among communists. Negrín then suspended the discussion until all the facts were known.

Had they been able to purchase and transport good arms from US, British, and French manufacturers, the socialist and republican members of the Spanish government might have tried to cut themselves loose from Stalin. But the non-intervention of the British, French, and American governments meant that the alliance with Russia could not be broken. Since the gold had already gone to Moscow, there was also little possibility of being able to buy elsewhere.

A widespread campaign in Spain and abroad now began asking 'Where is Nin?' Nin, after all, was one of the internationally best known people in the Spanish revolutionary movement. The CNT

1. R. Salas, vol. II, p. 1294.

national committee sent a protest to the government, on 28 June, complaining that they needed very good evidence before they could believe that people such as Nin, Gorkin and Andrade were fascists, just as they would need proof to believe such an accusation against Miaja: 'We beg, in the name of justice, constitutional legality and the right of all citizens, defended and represented by their own democracy, that the political persecution against the POUM cease.'[1] Negrín begged the communist party to end the discreditable affair. The Spanish communists, who were in a scarcely better position to answer these questions than their questioners, replied that Nin was no doubt in Berlin, or Salamanca. In fact, he was almost certainly already dead. It seems that Nin had first been taken by car from Barcelona to Orlov's own prison, in the dilapidated ex-cathedral city of Alcalá de Henares, Azaña's birthplace and Cervantes's, but now almost a Russian colony. He there underwent the customary Soviet interrogation of traitors to the cause.[2] His resistance to these methods was amazing. He refused to sign documents admitting his guilt and that of his friends. Orlov was at his wits' end. So were Bielov and Vittorio Vidali who apparently were his colleagues in the actual interrogation of Nin. What should they do? Orlov himself went in deadly fear of Yezhov, the insensate chief of the GPU. Eventually, according to Hernández later, the Italian Vidali (Carlos Contreras) suggested that a 'nazi' attack to liberate Nin should be simulated. So, one dark night, probably 22 or 23 June, ten German members of the International Brigade assaulted the house in Alcalá where Nin was held. Ostentatiously, they spoke German during the pretended attack, and left behind some German train tickets. Nin was taken away and murdered, perhaps in El Pardo, the royal park just to the north of Madrid. His refusal to admit his guilt probably saved the lives of his friends. Stalin and Yezhov perhaps planned a trial in Spain on the model of the Moscow trials, with a paraphernalia of confessions; if so, they were thwarted, though, during subsequent months, the remaining POUM leaders were subjected to interro-

1. See Peirats, vol. II, p. 334; the CNT statement is printed in full in Martínez Bande, *La invasión de Aragón*, pp. 293–7.

2. R. Salas, vol. II, p. 1294. Others believe that he was taken to Russia to be killed there. Orlov, in the 1950s, tried to put the blame on a certain 'Bolodin', sent from Russia (Miravitlles, p. 193). Did he exist?

gation and torture in, for example, the convent of Saint Ursula in Barcelona, 'the Dachau of republican Spain' as one of its survivors of the POUM described it. Although Nin was the only member of the POUM's leadership to be killed, a number of international sympathizers with it also died in mysterious circumstances: these included Erwin Wolf, half-Czech, half-German, another ex-secretary of Trotsky, who was kidnapped in Barcelona, and never seen again; the Austrian socialist, Kurt Landau; Marc Rhein, the journalist son of the old menshevik leader, Rafael Abramovich (Abramovich himself made two fruitless journeys to Spain to discover what had happened); José Robles, sometime lecturer at Johns Hopkins University, Baltimore, perhaps killed because he had been interpreter to the disgraced General Berzin;[1] and, perhaps, 'Bob' Smilie, the English journalist, son of the miners' leader of that name, who had come to Spain on behalf of the British Independent Labour party and died apparently of appendicitis, in a prison to which he had been sent without justification.

What did the members of the republican government think of this affair? It is hard to be certain: Negrín told Azaña that Nin had been detained and freed by German agents within the International Brigades. Was that not a little novelesque? asked Azaña. Not at all, Negrín said. The same sort of thing had occurred in respect of several Russian advisers at Gaylord's Hotel, who had been poisoned by nazi spies. Azaña noted this 'fact' in his diary without comment.[2] The question is open whether, on the one hand, Negrín suspected the truth, and misled Azaña; or whether Negrín was deceived by the communists. It seems likely that the first was the case: and that Negrín knew it to be 'a dirty business', as he put it to Hernández.[3] Both Azaña's and Negrín's attitudes to the POUM were conditioned by their irritation with what they believed to be a provocative group

1. Robles, an exile in the US from Spain for some years, had been a friend of Dos Passos, who took up his cause. He was murdered because he knew too much. It was Hemingway's cynicism over Robles's fate that broke the friendship between Dos Passos and Hemingway.

2. Azaña, vol. IV, p. 692. Although Casares Quiroga later explained the false basis of at least the story of the poisoning.

3. *op. cit.*, p. 99. Hernández is the only ex-communist (or communist) to mention this explanation of Nin's death, though Santiago Carrillo has now accepted that he was 'killed in our zone' (*Demain Espagne*, p. 57).

of revolutionaries who they thought were damaging the war effort. Nin's councillorship of justice in Catalonia had scarcely been distinguished by a nice concern for humanity towards the 'bourgeoisie', and a comment by a member of the POUM, Manuel Casanova, on the party's activities at Lérida in 1936 is a reminder that that party 'knew how to hate'.[1] This of course does not justify, but it helps to explain, the opinions of the President and the Prime Minister.

The affair of the POUM caused, in the world of communism, as great an intellectual controversy as the Basque priests did in the similarly theological world of Roman Catholicism. In some cases, the same men who protested against the Pope's treatment of Basque priests protested against Stalin's treatment of the POUM: for example, Mauriac, Jean Duhamel and Roger Martin du Gard wrote to the republican government to protest against the trial of the POUM, and to implore them to permit rights of defence. Ilya Ehrenburg, the one Russian writer of his generation apart from Pasternak who survived the purges in Russia and who had, as has been seen, been much in Spain, wrote in *Izvestia*:

> I must express the sense of shame which I now feel as a man. The same day that the fascists are busy shooting the women of Asturias, there appeared in the French paper a protest against injustice . . . But these people did not protest against the butchers of Asturias but rather against the republic who dares to detain fascists and *provocateurs* of the POUM.[2]

Ehrenburg, alas, knew only too well how innocent were those who died in the purges, as his subsequent memoir shows.[3] Meantime, George Orwell, in trying to defend the POUM in liberal England, found his articles refused by Kingsley Martin, the editor of the *New Statesman*.[4]

1. Casanova, p. 23.
2. *Izvestia*, 3 November 1937, qu. Suárez, p. 54 fn.
3. 'Destroyed for no reason at all by their own people', he says of Goriev, Antonov-Ovsëenko, Berzin and Stashevsky (*op. cit.*, p. 176).
4. For this controversy, see George Orwell, *Collected Essays*, vol. I, p. 363, and Kingsley Martin's memoirs *Editor* (London, 1938), p. 226. Orwell later made the somewhat surprising admission, in a letter to Frank Jellinek, the *Manchester Guardian* correspondent, that he agreed that 'the whole business about the POUM has had far too much fuss made about it and that the net result of this kind of thing is to prejudice people against the Spanish government' . . . 'Actually', he added, 'I've given [in *Homage to Catalonia*] a more sympathetic account of the "POUM" line than I actually felt, because I always thought they were

The republican government were doing their best to escape from the trap into which, through excessive reliance on the Russians, they had fallen. Irujo, the Basque nationalist minister of justice, named a special magistrate, Miguel Moreno Laguía, to act as a judge in the case of Nin. Moreno Laguía did detain a number of policemen who, he thought, were involved, among them a certain Vázquez. A unit of assault guards arrived to release him, while he was in the judge's custody. When the judge protested, the guards sought to arrest him also. The judge let Vázquez go. Irujo, Prieto and Zugazagoitia threatened to resign unless Moreno were confirmed. Later, the cabinet transferred the director-general of security, Ortega, who had been responsible for the original arrest of Nin, to a field command, and eventually replaced him by Carlos de Juan, the chief prosecutor of the republic. Judge Moreno Laguía continued vainly looking for Nin, while Nin's companions remained months more in gaol before being brought to trial,[1] and his presumed murderers continued in influential positions. During the latter part of 1937, a number of the POUM rank and file were also quite ruthlessly and illegally shot, after summary courts-martial manned by the communists.[2] According to Gorkin, meantime, there were about 1,500 'antifascist prisoners' – anarchists, *POUMistas*, others – in the Model Prison in Valencia in late 1937.

The crimes against the POUM were acts of barbarity carried out in Spain by Spanish and foreign communists at the behest of the republic's only, and over powerful, ally, Russia. The POUM had few friends, in Spain or outside. The repression against this party was sanctioned by most supporters of the Popular Front, and was scarcely a cause of complaint even by the anarchists. Azaña, Negrín, and Prieto, to name only three representative men, were plainly

---

wrong ... But ... I think there was something in what they said, though no doubt their way of saying it was tiresome and provocative in the extreme.' Orwell also pointed out that communism at that time had an attraction in western countries to the rich, while Trotskyism 'has no appeal to anyone with over £500 a year'.

1. See below, p. 865. Moreno Laguía was a friend of Azaña, with whom he was in touch (*Obras*, vol. IV, p. 828).

2. Among those executed were José Cullares, José Navarro López and Marciano Mena. Cf. Casanova, p. 23.

worried by the case of Nin, though the latter two perhaps less by the outrage itself than by the effect caused outside Spain. Azaña, and with him thousand of others, regarded the death of Nin and the suppression of the POUM as an acceptable exchange, in time of war, for the virtual end, under communist police, of the undisciplined killings of the first months, and for the embourgeoisement of, and the state's capture of, the revolution. They had no sympathy with the revolutionary aims of the POUM, no personal feeling for Nin. There were accusations made at the time, which have not been substantiated or fully disproved, that certain POUM leaders, as well as anarchists, had taken care to place money or valuables which they had seized in the early days of the revolution in France.[1] Azaña looked on Russia as 'the man whom one admits to society because it is impossible to do otherwise, but who is the friend of nobody'.[2] But the crime reverberates through the years, as do all the contemporaneous crimes in Russia. Thereafter, in fact, the communists in Spain were more circumspect. No other major political personality was detained. This was no doubt due to the full-time presence of the astute Togliatti as chief representative of the Comintern in the Spanish communist party from the summer onwards.[3] Still, there were many people unjustly in gaol for the remainder of the civil war and even the lawyer of the leaders of the POUM, Benito Pabón, found himself so threatened that he fled the country; he went as far as he could to escape the vengeance of the communists and settled in the Philippines.

1. Cf. Benavides, *Guerra*, p. 229. 2. Azaña, vol. IV, p. 618.

3. When precisely, one cannot help wishing to ask? The POUM leaders were arrested on 16 June. Togliatti had thus a good reason for wanting it to be established that he was not in Spain until after 16 June and for having his friends (Vidali, Berti, Longo) repeat it to P. Spriano (vol. III, p. 215). The reasons for leaving Moscow were no less compelling. Togliatti was certainly in Spain when, in August, a circular was issued stating that newspapers which criticized the Soviet Union would be suspended indefinitely. (Circular of 14 August, qu. Broué and Témime, p. 284.)

40

The Battle of Brunete – Santander – the Ebro – end of the Council of Aragon – the fall of Asturias – end of the war in the north

AFTER the capture of the Basque provinces, General Franco paused before falling upon Santander, the next republican centre in the north. The republic then launched its long-discussed diversionary offensive in the centre. That, as might be expected, was the communist choice of Brunete. Two army corps had been gathered, under the overall command of Miaja. These were the 5th Army Corps, led by Modesto, and the 18th Army Corps, led by Jurado, an artillery column. The former comprised Lister's 11th Division, El Campesino's 46th Division, and Walter's 35th Division, while Jurado's corps included Gal, with the 15th Division (the 11th and 14th International Brigades). In reserve, Kléber returned to command the 45th Division and Gustavo Durán, Kléber's chief of staff during the winter, commanded the 39th Division. The communist influence in this army was extensive. They had five out of six divisional commanders; one army corps commander; and the commissars of the two army corps were communists (Delage and Zapiraín). So was Miaja's commissar – Francisco Antón. This army numbered 85,000. It was supported by 40 armoured cars, 300 aircraft, 130 tanks and over 220 field guns. The aim was to advance towards the stagnant village of Brunete (population 1,556, in 1935) from the north of the El Escorial–Madrid road so as to cut off all the besiegers of the capital from the west.[1] Rojo, the chief of staff of the army, expected

1. Rojo, *¡ Alerta los pueblos!* (Buenos Aires, 1939), p. 104; *España heroica*, pp. 87ff; Lister, p. 132; Aznar, p. 435; López Muñiz; Castro Delgado, pp. 541ff; Longo, pp. 371–97. In writing of this battle I drew on the memories of Malcolm Dunbar, Giles Romilly, George Aitken, and Miles Tomalin, who fought here with the British Battalion. On general matters of interpretation, see R. Salas Larrazábal (*op. cit.*, vol. II, p. 1215f). Particularly significant is his note (fn. 9, p. 1275) in which he criticizes the Russian Malinovsky, present as an adviser, for ignoring, in his memoir (*Bajo la bandera*, p. 37f), the role of Colonel Matallana in the preparation of the offensive. Martínez Bande, *La ofensiva sobre Segovia*,

the republicans to achieve these aims before Franco's reinforcements could arrive.

The 15th International Brigade, led by the Croat communist Čopić, was used in this battle as a shock force,[1] along with the 11th Brigade of Germans, now led by Colonel Staimer, and the 13th, chiefly Slavs and French, led by the Italian communist 'Krieger' (Vincenzo Bianco). The latter included a number of Spaniards. Later on, Pacciardi's Garibaldi 12th Brigade, mainly Italians, played a part.[2] Russian advisers were, of course, present, among them General Stern (Grigorovich) as senior adviser, and Smushkevich, still at the head of the air mission. Numerous Russian pilots were still with the republican air force. The planning of the attack was the responsibility of Matallana, new chief of staff to Miaja.

The nationalists were surprised by the offensive of Brunete, perhaps because it had been discussed in the cafés of the republic for months. On the line which was to bear the brunt of the attack there were certain depleted elements of the 71st Division, mainly falangists, and about 1,000 Moroccans. After being exhorted, on the eve of the attack, by Prieto and La Pasionaria, the 11th republican Division under Lister struck at dawn, on 6 July, after a heavy artillery and aerial attack. Within a few hours, they had advanced nearly ten miles and surrounded Brunete.

Miaja's equivalent, as nationalist commander in the centre, was Saliquet, but General Varela was made supreme field commander for

---

p. 103f, gives a good general survey. R. Salas Larrazábal prints the battle-order of the International Brigades in vol. IV, pp. 3434–3572. See, too, R. Casas de la Vega, *Brunete* (Madrid, 1967).

1. The British Battalion in this brigade was commanded by Fred Copeman, an ex-sailor who had been concerned in the so-called naval mutiny of Invergordon in 1931. According to his own account, Copeman did not become a communist till he had left Spain. He was, nevertheless, so closely associated with the party that this made no difference. The British Battalion was itself one of three regiments, commanded by Nathan, alongside three others commanded by Mihály Szalvai ('Chapaev'). Szalvai became a general in post-war Hungary.

2. See Longo, p. 291. Only the 14th (French) International Brigade was quite inactive in this engagement among the 'Internationals'. Staimer – 'Colonel Richard' – was yet one more important German communist to lead a brigade in Spain. 'Krieger' had succeeded another German, Zaisser ('Gómez'). Staimer had been head of the woodworkers' union in Germany and chief of the *Rot Front* organization in northern Bavaria in 1932.

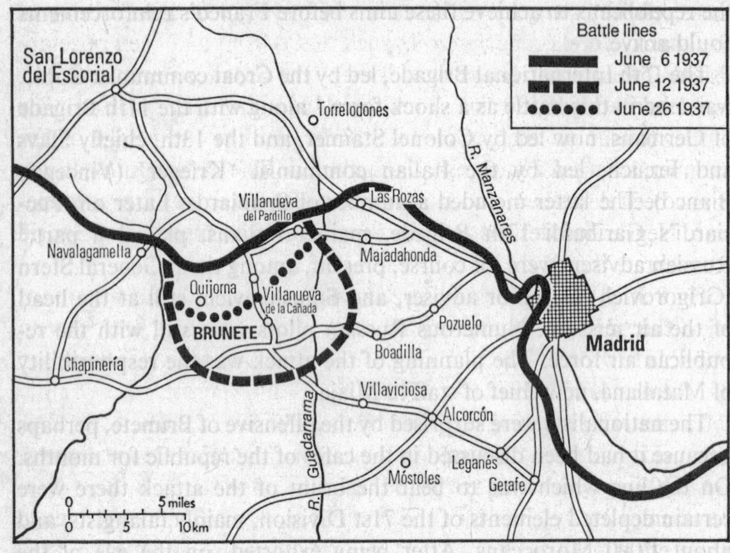

26. The battle of Brunete, July 1937

the defence and counter-attack. Several divisions were transferred to the Brunete front and the Condor Legion and heavy artillery were dispatched from the north.[1] So were Colonels Alonso Vega's and Bautista Sánchez's 4th and 5th Navarrese Brigades. The transfer of these reinforcements was carried out very quickly: a real triumph of planning. When they arrived, Brunete was in the hands of Lister. The garrison of the nearby village of Quijorna was still, with courage, resisting El Campesino. Villanueva de la Cañada, Villanueva del Pardillo, and Villafranca del Castillo also held out against the 15th Brigade, most of the defenders being young falangist volunteers from Seville. Though the first of these fell the next day to the British, the advance was slowed by confusion. Brigade upon brigade were sent through the small breach in the nationalist lines, and became mixed up with each other. The known communist background to the attack caused republican officers and non-communists to grumble about the direction of the battle. The chief of staff of the operation, Casado, who had been critical of it, retired ill in the middle. Eighty tanks were

1. Galland, p. 27.

unsuccessfully flung at Villafranca.[1] By midnight on the first day of the attack, Varela reported to Franco that a front had been re-established. Twenty-four hours later, thirty-one battalions and nine batteries had arrived in reinforcement of the nationalist position. The battle, fought on the parched Castilian plain at the height of the summer, assumed a most bloody character.[2] The battle against thirst, it has been described, and it is obvious that water was a preoccupation. Negrín had desired to hold a special cabinet meeting in Madrid to celebrate the victory: Azaña dissuaded him.[3]

On 8 July, El Campesino, egged on by being told that his troops were the best in the republican army and that they must set an example to the rest, reached the last houses of Quijorna.[4] That village fell the next day. Villanueva del Pardillo and Villafranca del Castillo fell in the early morning of 11 July. But Boadilla, constantly attacked, was held by Asensio. In the Condor Legion, Messerschmitt fighters (ME 109) appeared on the battle front here for the first time. Outnumbered by the Russians' Chatos, they seemed, however, much more effective. The Heinkel 111 bomber was also as effective as it had been in the north of Spain, particularly at night, though the Russian fighters were also here used at night, for the first time.

By 13 July, the offensive stage at Brunete was over. Henceforward, the republicans would be attempting to defend the positions which they had won. On 15 July, after further fierce fighting around Boadilla, orders were given for trenches to be dug. The republic had gained a pocket of land about eight miles deep by ten wide. Lister was two miles south of Brunete on the road to Navalcarnero. At the end of this battle, the gallant English Major Nathan of the gold tipped baton was killed.[5] The reason for the republican failure to

1. Miksche, p. 38. 2. Aznar, p. 443; López Muñiz, p. 171.

3. Azaña, vol. IV, p. 678.

4. It is perhaps of more than social interest that, on the night of 8 July, Hemingway, Martha Gellhorn, and Joris Ivens dined at the White House to explain what they thought the US should do to help Spain (F.D.R. papers, Hyde Park, File 422A).

5. He was mortally wounded by a bomb. In his last moments, he ordered those around him to sing him out of life. At nightfall, he was buried in a rough coffin beneath the olive trees near the River Guadarrama. A funeral oration was pronounced by the brigade commissar, George Aitken. Gal and Jock Cunningham, two tough men who had been jealous of Nathan, stood listening with tears run-

continue their offensive when all was in their favour has been much discussed. The responsibility lay with the lack of imagination and initiative shown in battle by junior and middle-rank officers. Republican training, under Russian inspiration, or that of elderly regular officers, was much more old-fashioned than that afforded to the nationalists at their new academies under the aegis of the Germans. The nationalists' provisional officers, *alféreces provisionales*, were often well educated young men of the upper class, used to the country (and to shooting game). They were now, as on other occasions, more effective as soldiers than even clever working-class young men from the city, intellectuals or workers, not to speak of elderly regular officers, who had spent years in dull garrisons reading French books on drill. Not for the first time, victory went to those who could think of war as hunting carried on by other means. The republic were also short of non-commissioned officers. Given an army as conventionally organized as the republican one, good corporals and sergeants are as important as staff officers. They were not available. The strictness of discipline and the absence of political intrigues and arguments in the nationalist army also played a critical part.

At a higher level, the nationalists can be faulted over Brunete, for Franco suspended his offensive in the north, in order to regain a ruined Castilian village of little strategic value. He sought to avoid the psychological damage of losing territory. That was Franco's approach throughout the war: it was a political, rather than a military, reaction. At the same time, Miaja, in supreme command, was, as expected, slow in his reactions.[1]

On 18 July, divisions under Sáenz de Buruaga attacked on the left, under Asensio on the right, and under Barrón towards Brunete itself in the centre. On this day, the Condor Legion began to dominate the skies of Castile, and shot down twenty-one republican aircraft.[2]

---

ning down their cheeks. Evidence of George Aitken. See also Steve Nelson, *The Volunteers* (Leipzig, 1954), pp. 166–9.

1. One might also note the remarks of Colonel Menéndez against Modesto, Lister, Mera, El Campesino and other militia leaders: 'Modesto is the only one of them who knew how to read a map. The others, in addition to not knowing how, don't think it necessary.' (Azaña, vol. IV, p. 712.)

2. On the 18th Julian Bell, another English hero of his own time, nephew of Virginia Woolf, was killed, aged twenty-nine, at Villanueva de la Cañada, when

Henceforth, the balance of air strength in the centre of Spain remained with the nationalists. The battle continued between 19 and 22 July, in awful heat under an implacable sun, with thirst a characteristic of both sides.[1] On 24 July, Asensio and Sáenz de Buruaga broke the lines of the republic on the flanks. Barrón broke through in the centre to recapture Brunete, save its cemetery, where Lister maintained himself until the 25th. Varela wished to pursue the republicans to Madrid. But Franco restrained him, pointing to the prior need of concluding the war in the north.[2] The republic retained Quijorna, Villanueva de la Cañada, and Villanueva del Pardillo, at a cost of 20,000 casualties and about 100 aircraft. The nationalists lost 23 aircraft, and 17,000 casualties.[3]

The battle may be regarded as similar to that of Jarama, Guadalajara, or the Corunna road, in reverse. Both sides claimed a victory. The battle certainly delayed the attacks in the north. The republicans gained an area of about four miles deep along a front of ten miles. But they failed to attain their objectives. In fact, the republican army lost so much valuable equipment, and so many veteran soldiers, that the battle of Brunete should be regarded as a defeat for them. It was also a setback to the communists who had sponsored it. The appearance of the Messerschmitts, along with the new Heinkels 111 and the new Savoias 79, marked the end of republican air superiority, which had done so much to guarantee Madrid: for these new fast monoplanes, with their stressed-skin construction, were more than a match for the Russians.[4]

The losses of the International Brigades were particularly heavy at

---

driving an ambulance for the British medical aid unit. He had been in Spain a month. (See Quentin Bell, *Julian Bell*, London, 1938, p. 176, and Stansky and Abrahams, pp. 399–413.)

1. See R. Salas Larrazábal, vol. II, p. 1254 and references; Jesús Salas, pp. 227–35.

2. Kindelán, p. 99. Juan Ignacio Luca de Tena, then Varela's ADC, gives an account of this conversation which implied that Franco's reasons for stopping Varela's advance on Madrid derived from his fear of Varela getting too much glory (Luca de Tena, pp. 205–6).

3. For the casualties see Casas de la Vega, p. 362f; Martínez Bande, p. 231; R. Salas Larrazábal, vol. II, p. 1256. Miaja told Azaña on 9 August that the republic lost 1,800 dead and 17,000 wounded (Azaña, vol. IV, p. 732), while Giral reported that half the 'wounded' were either deserters or malingerers.

4. R. Salas Larrazábal, in Carr, *The Republic*, p. 181.

Brunete. The Lincoln and Washington Battalions lost so many men that they had to be merged. Among the Americans who fell was Oliver Law, the Negro commander of the Lincoln Battalion. There was also insubordination among the Brigades. Captain Alocca, in command of the Brigades' cavalry, deserted in the face of the enemy and drove to the French frontier. Returning later to Madrid, he was shot for cowardice. The British Battalion, which had been reduced to about eighty men, grumbled about returning to the battle. The 13th Brigade, mainly Poles, absolutely refused to return. Its commander, 'Krieger' (Vincenzo Bianco), sought to re-establish himself by brandishing his revolver. Pointing this weapon at one of the mutineers, he ordered obedience. The other refused. 'Think well of what you are doing,' returned the colonel. 'I have.' 'For the last time!' 'No,' answered the mutineer. The colonel shot him dead. The men became furious and 'Krieger' himself narrowly escaped death. The mutineers set off for Madrid and were only subdued after the arrival of some assault guards with tanks. The Brigade thereafter had to be thoroughly re-organized and 're-educated'.[1]

Military theorists were later at pains to point out the tactical significance of the battle of Brunete for the use of the tank. The Czech Captain Miksche, for example, who commanded a group of batteries on the republican side, later reflected, in his theoretical study, *Blitzkrieg*, that the republican tanks were unsuccessful since they were used spread out in support of infantry, in accord with French theories; but Varela, on the insistence of the German von Thoma, concentrated his tanks to find a tactical thrust-point (*Schwerpunkt*) and so gained the day. In fact, the republic always used all their

1. See report of Colonel Matallana printed in De la Cierva, *Historia ilustrada*, vol. II, p. 242. The commander of the Garibaldi Battalion, Pacciardi, now abandoned Spain, disillusioned with communism in the brigades. Nenni agreed with him over this and returned to Paris, the 'Garibaldis' henceforth being commanded by Carlo Penchienati (a communist who later broke with the party) and subsequently Arturo Zanoni, a socialist. See Pacciardi, pp. 239–40 and 161, and Spriano, p. 223. Arthur Horner, then president of the South Wales miners, succeeded in extracting a pledge from the Brigade authorities that leave should be given to members of the Brigades. But this was never fully implemented. During his visit Horner was briefly imprisoned in Barcelona because a Moorish flag was found in his luggage and he was accordingly denounced as a monarchist (Arthur Horner, *Incorrigible Rebel*, London, 1960, p. 159).

armour dispersed, artillery and aircraft as well as tanks, and von Thoma's experiments could only be on a small scale since he had so few vehicles to bring up infantry to support the tanks.[1] Neither side conducted itself well in details: three hundred men of El Campesino's column were surrounded and taken prisoner. They were all later found dead, with their legs cut off. El Campesino shortly captured a *tabor* of Moroccans. Four hundred of them were shot. The birth of a new Spain? Azaña asked himself on hearing the news. On the contrary the old Spain, with all its warts, was preferable.[2]

Two weeks later, the nationalists renewed their offensive in the north. The Army of the North was still led by Dávila. The Italians, under General Bastico, were grouped as the Littorio Division, the Black Flames, and the March 23rd Division led respectively by Generals Bergonzoli, Frusci and Francisci.[3] The six experienced Navarrese brigades, under Solchaga, were commanded by Colonels García Valiño, Muñoz Grandes, Latorre, Abriat, Alonso Vega and Sánchez González respectively. (The two last had returned from the Brunete front.) Muñoz Grandes, who had been the first commander of the assault guards in 1931, had escaped from Madrid, early in the year. An old friend of Franco's in Morocco, as was Alonso Vega, this austere officer now began a successful military career. To these were added two brigades of Castilian volunteers, under General Ferrer, anxious to win back Castile's only port, the splendid watering place of Santander. Another group were the Spaniards and Italians, the Black Arrows, some 8,000 men, led by Colonel Piazzoni. There were thus probably some 25,000 Italians engaged in the ensuing battle. The Army of the North comprised 90,000 in all. Before this campaign, Franco transferred his headquarters from Salamanca to Burgos, the Italian General Bastico at his side.[4] Dávila had at his

1. Miksche, p. 171. This controversy over the use of tanks can be traced back to their first operational use, in the battle of Cambrai on the Western Front in 1917. Neither side in the civil war had enough lorries to enable motorized infantry to take advantage of the initial breakthrough.

2. Azaña, vol. IV, p. 698.

3. The date 23 March commemorated the foundation of the fascist movement in Italy in 1919.

4. The most careful account of this battle is Colonel Martínez Bande's *El final del frente norte* (Madrid, 1972). One can also still consult with profit Aznar, pp. 466–75.

disposal some 70 aircraft of the Condor Legion, 80 Italian aircraft and 70 Spanish machines, together with a seaplane flotilla.

The 14th and 15th Republican Army Corps were the nucleus of the defence of Santander. Generals Llano de la Encomienda and Martínez Cabrera had been sent back discredited to the central zone, and General Gámir was now the supreme republican commander, while the two army corps were led by Colonels Prada and García Vayas. This force was supported by some 50 batteries, 33 fighters and bombers, and 11 reconnaissance aircraft. The republican army numbered 80,000. The bare figures give an inaccurate idea of the disproportion of the forces. Except for 18 Russian fighters, Gámir's aircraft were slow and old. The nationalists' air support included the latest German models, which were being used to test their efficiency. The same was true of their artillery. Relations between Santander and Asturias were no better than they had been when the Basques had been fighting alongside in Guipúzcoa, though the remains of the old Basque army were present alongside the Santanderinos. They were in bad fettle and morale had not been improved by rumours, firmly based, that they might surrender to the Italians, in return for their lives.[1]

The campaign began on 14 August. The battle lines lay across the Cantabrian range, whose highest points were in the hands of the republic. The field of war was thus, throughout the campaign, of rugged beauty. The republicans were overwhelmed by the aerial bombardment. On the first day of the attack, the front in the south was broken. The Navarrese brigades rolled up the foothills of the Cantabrians. Reinosa, with its armament factory, was captured on 16 August. Gámir and his Russian advisers disputed over whether or no Colonel García Vayas, chief of the 15th Army Corps, who had held Santander since the very beginning of the war, and was popular in the city, should be relieved by Colonel Galán, one of the famous group of communist brothers. Compromise was reached, but the front broke. Many were captured. Next, backed by their own weight of artillery, tanks, and aircraft, the Italian Black Arrows broke the

1. For these abortive efforts which involved a secret meeting between Fr Onaindía and the Italian military attaché near Algorta (Vizcaya) on 25 June and the former's subsequent journey to Rome to illuminate Ciano – utterly ignorant of the Basque problem – see S. Payne, *Basque Nationalism*, p. 280.

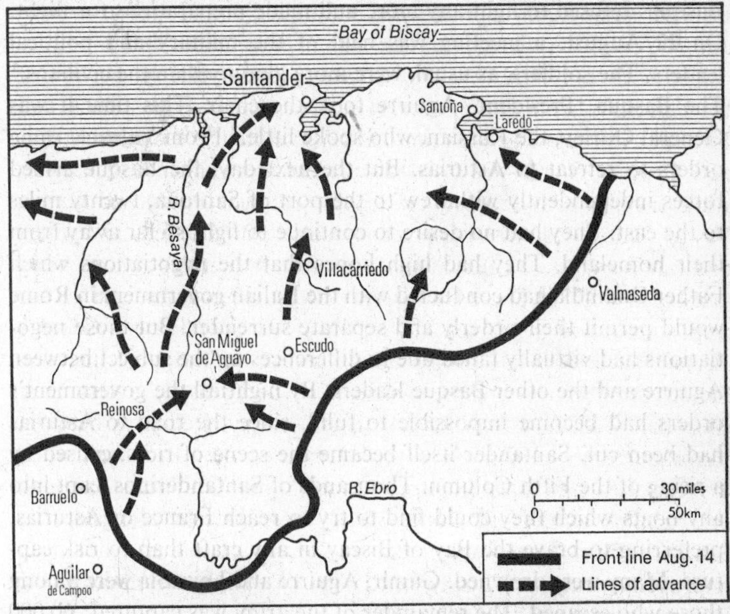

27. The Santander campaign, August 1937

front by the sea on 18 August. The March 23rd Division, in the centre, captured the critical pass of Escudo. Henceforward, there was no real front. The army of Santander retreated steadily. The Basques fought better for Santander than the Santanderinos had for Bilbao, but even they could not maintain their hold.[1] In Santander itself, the factories and the port were closed, so that workers could be free to build fortifications. Once again, a Spanish city became filled with the cattle, the domestic animals, and the few personal belongings of peasants flying from the battle raging round their homes. Many Santanderinos (perhaps a majority) longed for Franco's victory – it was a conservative city which had thrived because of its use as a resort by the Spanish aristocracy. The Basque émigré government, as it had now become, again occupied itself with evacuation. Many

1. Aguirre had wanted to move all the Basque forces to the Catalan front in order to advance on Navarre from the rear(!); the idea had been rejected in Valencia (Aguirre, pp. 59ff).

Basques refused to fight any more and made preparations for flight. On 22 August, a meeting was held of the military and political leaders. The soldiers, as usual, were more gloomy than the civilians.[1] The Basque 'President' Aguirre took the chair. This time it was General Goriev, the Russian, who spoke little.[2] From Valencia came orders to retreat to Asturias. But the next day, the Basque armed forces independently withdrew to the port of Santoña, twenty miles to the east. They had no desire to continue to fight so far away from their homeland. They had high hopes that the negotiations which Father Onaindía had conducted with the Italian government in Rome would permit their orderly and separate surrender. But those negotiations had virtually failed due to differences on the subject between Aguirre and the other Basque leaders. By nightfall the government's orders had become impossible to fulfil, since the road to Asturias had been cut. Santander itself became the scene of riots, caused by a rising of the Fifth Column. Thousands of Santanderinos leapt into any boats which they could find to try to reach France or Asturias, preferring to brave the Bay of Biscay in any craft than to risk capture. Many were drowned. Gámir, Aguirre and Leizaola were among those who escaped. The remainder of the army was captured; 60,000 prisoners were made – the largest single victory in the civil war.[3] The deputy for Santander, Ramón Ruiz Rebollo, was one of the last to leave. He survived to give a harrowing description of 100,000 people on the quays the night before the rebels arrived.[4]

Two Basque officers went from Santoña to negotiate the Basque surrender with the Italian commander, Colonel Farina, commander of the Black Arrows, in whose hands the Basques rightly judged themselves safer than in those of Franco. An agreement was reached. The Basques would surrender, deliver their arms to the Italians, and maintain order in the areas which they still held. They had already freed the 2,500 prisoners in the gaol of Santoña. The Italians would

1. Castro Delgado, p. 539.

2. For an account of this depressed gathering, see Gámir, p. 84; Zugazagoitia, vol. II, pp. 307–8; and the report of Major Lamas, quoted in Martínez Bande, *op. cit.*, p. 78 fn. 85.

3. Martínez Bande has a sad picture of many of these men sitting in the local bull-ring (*op. cit.*, facing p. 104). Some 30,000 were Basques, 20,000 Santanderinos.

4. Azaña, vol. IV, p. 782.

guarantee the lives of all Basque fighters. The Basques then agreed to surrender without further conditions. They tried, but failed, to secure more general assurances.[1] In the event, many Basques refused to surrender and did their best to escape. A subsequent attempt by a Basque nationalist politician, Juan Ajuriaguerra (who, unlike Aguirre, had been concerned with negotiations with Italy from the spring onwards), at further negotiations with General Roatta was subsequently disowned by the nationalist high command.[2] Meantime, Dávila and his army entered Santander. The Italians entered Santoña and the Italian Colonel Fagosi took over the civil administration. The British vessels *Bobie* and *Seven Seas Spray* stood by in Santoña harbour ready to carry refugees to France. But no instructions came to begin any shipment. On 27 August the commander of the *Bobie*, a French captain named Georges Dupuy, and Costa e Silva, a Brazilian non-intervention observer on the *Seven Seas Spray*, received permission from the Italians to embark all those in possession of a Basque passport. The embarkation therefore began. But at ten in the morning, Italian soldiers surrounded the ships and the waiting Basques with machine-guns. Colonel Fagosi informed Dupuy and Silva that no one was to leave Santoña, foreign or Basque. All the Basques on board the two ships were ordered to disembark. The ships were then searched by five falangists. At dawn, the next day, 28 August, Dupuy saw those who had so briefly been his passengers being marched as prisoners along the road towards the prison of Dueso. Colonel Farina had been disowned by his chief of staff, Major Bartolomé Barba.[3] The ships of hope then raised anchor, some refugees hiding in the machinery. Those left behind were treated simply as prisoners of the nationalists. Summary trials and executions followed.

Mussolini nevertheless telegraphed his congratulations to the Italian commanders. The text of that telegram and the names of its

1. Martínez Bande, *op. cit.* (p. 97) publishes a facsimile of the act of surrender and the full document (pp. 228–9). See also General Piazzoni's account on pp. 230–42, and S. Payne, *Basque Nationalism*, p. 285, for discussion on Father Onaindía's account.

2. Steer, pp. 388–90. This account is confirmed by Jesús María de Leizaola. See however R. Salas, vol. II, p. 1460f, and Martínez Bande, *op. cit.*, pp. 93–4.

3. He had been head of the U M E in pre-war days and had escaped from Valencia in August 1936.

addressees were published in the Italian papers on 27 August. For the first time the Italian public could know the names of their commanders in Spain: Roatta, Bergonzoli, Teruzzi, Bastico: new heroes of the new Italy! Ciano instructed Bastico to secure 'guns and flags captured from the Basques'. He recorded in his diary 'I envy the French their Invalides and the Germans their Military Museum. A flag taken from the enemy', added this fellow-countryman of Leonardo, 'is worth more than any picture.' The next day he wrote: 'This is the moment to terrorize the enemy. I have given orders for the aircraft to bomb Valencia.'[1] Mussolini's Spanish allies, however, were not so enthusiastic about the part played in these engagements by Italian troops: 'Only an enemy without a command or cohesion, and in numbers insufficient to cover the fortifications constructed, could give way before an offensive as magisterially conceived . . . but as incompetently carried out as that of the legionaries.' Thus Colonel Urbano, in a special report to the nationalist general staff.[2]

The Germans in Spain were quarrelling among themselves. Sperrle, commander of the Condor Legion, and Faupel, the ambassador, hated each other. Sperrle even refused to see Faupel when he called to see him at San Sebastián. Sperrle also publicly criticized the monopoly held by HISMA, so encouraging the Spaniards to criticize it too. Franco even asked, through Sperrle, to have Faupel replaced, partly because of his intrigues with the Falange, chiefly because of his heavy-handed arrogance.[3]

Franco received the news of the capture of Santander while attending to the start of another republican diversionary offensive, this time on the Aragon front. This was undertaken by the Catalan army – now reorganized, hispanized and renamed the Army of the East – commanded by General Pozas. Under him were 'Kléber', with the 45th Division, Colonel Trueba (an intelligent autodidact), with the 27th, and the communist Major Modesto's 5th Army Corps, comprising the 11th, 46th and 35th Divisions led respectively by Lister,

1. Ciano, *Diaries 1937–8*, p. 5. The correspondent of *The Times* who described the nationalist capture of Santander was Philby.

2. Martínez Bande, *op. cit.*, p. 245f.

3. *GD*, p. 434. This recurred in mid-August. Sperrle was himself also shortly recalled (though not as has been claimed for his part in Guernica), being succeeded in command of the Condor Legion by General von Volkmann.

El Campesino, and Walter. These had been transferred from Brunete. Walter's division included four International Brigades (not the 14th, because of his quarrel with Dumont).[1]

Opposing this array was General Ponte, in charge at Saragossa, General Urrutia at Huesca and General Muñoz Castellanos at Teruel. The front was not continuous, since only strategic heights were fortified. The Aragon front had been neglected. It was an area where the nationalists had not undertaken extensive fortifications.

The Aragon offensive had plainly another purpose. This was the communists', and the central government's, desire to break the Council of Aragon. Here, as in so many other matters, communist and 'liberal' supporters of the republic were as one. The moderate socialists fully supported the policy which followed: indeed, Prieto gave the orders on 4 August, though his motives in sending Lister's division of 11,000 men to do the work may be open to question: did he hope to kill two birds with one stone?[2] Azaña was delighted; one of the 'councillors of Aragon' was an ex-chauffeur of his.[3]

This Council of Aragon, presided over by Joaquín Ascaso, had outraged both the Catalan and the central governments. Ascaso, an anarchist who had escaped from Saragossa, was a dynamic, violent

1. While the Croat Čopić remained leader of the 15th Brigade, Steve Nelson, a shipyard worker from Philadelphia, of Slovene origin, despite his name, was brigade commissar, in succession to Aitken who had returned home. These appointments signified a period of American predominance in the 15th Brigade. There was even some American resentment when the post of chief of operations in the Brigade went to Malcolm Dunbar, an efficient young Englishman who three years before had been 'leader of an advanced aesthetic set at Cambridge'. Three British brigadiers (Copeman, commander at Brunete; Tapsell, commissar; and Cunningham, chief of staff) returned to England, with a specific purpose in mind – to discuss the nature of communist control over the British Battalion. A quarrel ensued at the central committee of the communist party. Cunningham never went back to Spain, being accused of 'fascism'. He left the party. The other two returned. The Brigade had been enlarged by the addition of the Mackenzie-Papineau Battalion, formed from Canadians previously with the Americans. This was named after the two Canadian leaders of the revolt of 1837 against Britain. Less than a third of the Battalion were Canadians, the remainder being American. The commissar was Joe Dallet, a longshoreman of New York, of rich family who had joined the republic to throttle the evidence of his early sheltered life. These details suggest how Spain seemed the world's testing ground for other things than heavy tanks, Messerschmitts, and anarchist experiments.

2. Lister, p. 152. 3. Azaña, vol. IV, p. 614.

and unscrupulous man.[1] Many of the collectives had been socially successful, but they had made too ineffective a contribution to the war. Complete figures for the economic performance of the region under the anarchists are difficult to establish; but the production of coal in the mine at Utrillas, near Montalbán, for example, was only a tenth of normal.[2]

In late July, the communists had begun one of their ominous and intimidatory press campaigns against Ascaso. Carabineers confiscated food lorries passing from one collective to another. The communists, the UGT and the socialists set up a new organization, the Aragon Council, at Barbastro, which asked the government to establish a new 'federal government' of Aragon. On 11 August, after the harvest was in – a very important element in the situation – the Council of Aragon was dissolved, José Ignacio Mantecón being named governor-general of the three Aragonese provinces. An old member of the Council of Aragon himself, Mantecón was a left republican then on the brink of joining the communists. Immediately the decree was published, the 11th Division under Lister was sent 'on manoeuvres' to Aragon. Ascaso and the anarchist members of the Council of Aragon were detained (Ascaso on a charge of smuggling jewels). Six hundred other anarchists throughout Aragon were arrested. Those peasants who had successfully held out of collectives took over many of those experiments by assault, 'carrying away and dividing up the harvest and farm implements'.[3] The offices of the CNT regional committee were taken over, and their files and records seized. Other communist army units took over collectives in the valley of the Ebro and upper Aragon. Anarchist troops at the front desired to attack the communists when the news came slowly and confusingly through to them, but they were restrained. The anarchist divisions with their old home-made tanks and motley weapons were infinitely less well equipped than were Lister's men with their Degtyareva machine-guns. The CNT national leadership did what they could to

1. C. Lorenzo, p. 139. According to Juan Sapiña (Azaña, *Obras*, vol. IV, p. 635), deputy for Castellón and director-general of mines, he went about with an escort of 24 men. His secretary had once been on the staff of Juan March.

2. Azaña, vol. IV, p. 685, also p. 744.

3. See J. Silva, qu. Bolloten, in Carr, *The Republic*, p. 375. See Negrín's account to Azaña (Azaña, vol. IV, p. 733).

avoid executions, but it was a measure of their decline that they could do no more. Indeed, by this time, vigorous defenders of CNT–FAI principles such as Abad de Santillán or Escorza were increasingly left out of the deliberations of these movements. Mariano Vázquez, the secretary-general of the CNT, had become almost a *Negrinista* and so had many of the anarchists who held positions under the government. Some anarchist newspapers, so far as they could, denounced the communists' actions, though not naming precisely what they had done. They resorted to general criticism of Russian practices and published articles describing the economic and social benefits of the collectives.[1] Later, to try and save the next crop, some Aragonese collectives were actually restored, but about a third of them were destroyed, and those which were revived were less self-confident than they had been, while many anarchists remained in prisons or camps until the end of the war.

The ensuing Aragon offensive was partly conceived to remove the bad impression created by these events, partly to ensure the continuance in the front line of the anarchist divisions and partly to justify a general reinforcement of that area with military units of the non-anarchist sections of the republican army. The main aim, however, was to draw away the main nationalist effort from the north.

On 24 August, the republican attack began at eight points without aerial or artillery preparation. Three attacks were made north of Saragossa, two between Belchite and Saragossa, and three to the south. The republic had 80,000 troops, 100 tanks and perhaps 200 aircraft. The two villages of Quinto and Codo, north of Belchite, were the first to fall. The Ebro was crossed near Fuentes del Ebro, and Mediana fell on 26 August.[2] Nevertheless, the tenacity of the nationalist garrisons, with little air cover, astounded the attackers,

1. See *Campo Libre* in August and September 1937. There is a bitter account of this by the leader of the 26th Division, Ricardo Sanz, in Ch. XII of his *Los que fuimos a Madrid*. Mantecón later told Azaña that Lister wanted to shoot the councillors but he, Mantecón, had restrained him: I know what would have happened: he would have put the blame on me and posed himself 'as defender of the people'. (Azaña, vol. IV, p. 897.)

2. The 15th International Brigade played a major part in these battles. The British Battalion's Irish commander, Daley, died of wounds, to be succeeded by Paddy O'Daire. Thompson and Dallet, commander and commissar of the Lincoln Battalion, were killed, Nelson the brigade commissar wounded.

who included the best troops in the republican army, and also surprised many prominent foreign and Russian military leaders, headed by General Stern (Grigorovich) and the new Russian air force commander, General 'Montenegro'.[1] Belchite held out the longest.[2] When the republicans at last entered Codo, which had been defended by some 300 Carlists against the republicans' 2,000, they found the slogan scrawled on the wall 'when you kill a "red", you will have a year less in purgatory'.[3]

The small, well-fortified town of Belchite (its population had been 3,812 in 1935) had an extraordinary fascination for the republic, whose troops had been watching it for months. The siege was harsh but the defence vigorous. The defenders' water supply was cut off. They could hardly have felt better for the knowledge that, according to military manuals, they were demonstrating 'the use of the island of resistance, organized for all-round defence'. The heat was appalling. The nationalist mayor, Ramón Alfonso Trallero, was killed with a rifle in his hands on the walls of the city. But the nationalist command did not make the mistake that they had made at Brunete: they did not abandon their offensive in the north to save a small town in the centre. In the end, substantial air support was sent down; but, at the beginning, they had only fifteen aircraft (Heinkels). Soon 40 nationalist fighters, 20 bombers and 20 supply aircraft, were to be seen in Aragon, of which the bombers were Savoias 79, the fighters Fiats commanded by the air ace García Morato. The 13th and 150th nationalist divisions of Barrón and Sáenz de Buruaga were also dispatched from the Madrid front to meet in Aragon those same picked units led by Lister, Walter, and El Campesino, against whom they had fought in Castile. Barrón held up the republican advance north of Saragossa. Sáenz de Buruaga sought to relieve Belchite, now ten miles behind the republican front lines. But Belchite surrendered on 6 September. The republic now returned to the defensive. After one reckless dash by Lister, into Fuentes del Ebro, using new BT-5

1. Montenegro's real name does not seem to have come out. See Azaña, *op. cit.*, p. 687 for estimate of his quality. The best general survey of this battle is Martínez Bande's *La gran ofensiva*, p. 77f.

2. Aznar, p. 504; Castro Delgado, p. 560. For this battle, I was assisted by Malcolm Dunbar.

3. Buenacasa, p. 9. This *POUMista*, present at the battle, pays tribute to the high Carlist morale.

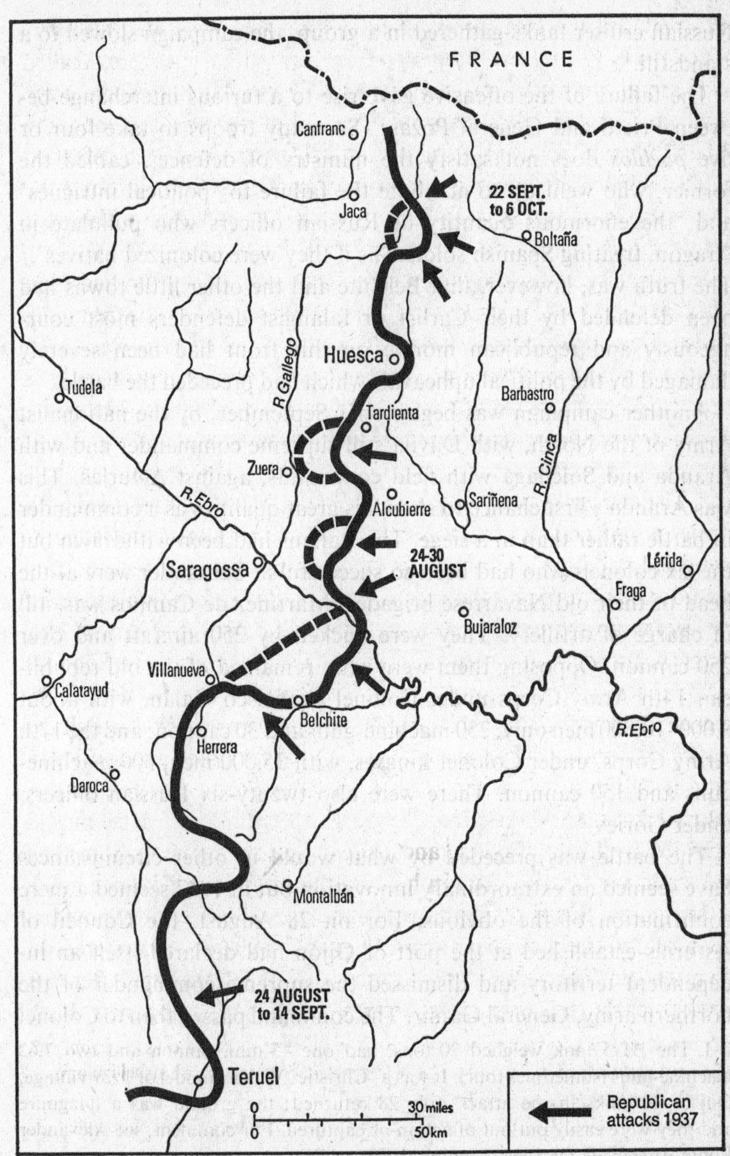

28. The Aragon offensive, August–October 1937

Russian cruiser tanks gathered in a group, the campaign slowed to a standstill.[1]

The failure of the offensive gave rise to a furious interchange between Prieto and General Pozas: 'So many troops to take four or five *pueblos* does not satisfy the ministry of defence', cabled the former, who went on to attribute the failure to 'political intrigues' and 'the enormous quantity of Russian officers who pullulate in Aragon, treating Spanish soldiers as if they were colonized natives'.[2] The truth was, however, that Belchite and the other little towns had been defended by their Carlist or falangist defenders most courageously and republican morale on this front had been severely damaged by the political upheavals which had preceded the battle.

Another campaign was begun on 1 September, by the nationalist Army of the North, with Dávila still supreme commander and with Aranda and Solchaga with field commands, against Asturias. This was Aranda's first chance to show his great qualities as a commander in battle rather than in a siege. The Italians had been withdrawn but the six colonels who had been so successful at Santander were at the head of their old Navarrese brigades. Martínez de Campos was still in charge of artillery. They were backed by 250 aircraft and over 250 cannon. Opposing them were what remained of the old republican 14th Army Corps under Colonel Francisco Galán, with about 8,000–10,000 men only, 250 machine-guns and 30 cannon; and the 17th Army Corps, under Colonel Linares, with 35,000 men, 600 machine-guns and 150 cannon. There were also twenty-six Russian officers, under Goriev.[3]

The battle was preceded by what would in other circumstances have seemed an extraordinary innovation but in 1937 seemed a mere confirmation of the obvious. For on 28 August, the Council of Asturias established at the port of Gijón had declared itself an independent territory and dismissed the supreme commander of the northern army, General Gámir. The command passed then to Colonel

1. The BT-5 tank weighed 20 tons, had one 45 mm. cannon and two 7.62 machine-guns (sometimes four). It was a 'Christie' Vickers model of 1929 vintage. Out of 40 tanks in the attack only 28 returned: the ground was a quagmire and they were easily put out of action or captured. For comment, see Alexander Foote, *Handbook for Spies* (London, 1953), p. 18.

2. Telegram quoted by R. Salas Larrazábal, vol. II, p. 1324.

3. Ehrenburg, p. 147.

Adolfo Prada, a regular officer who had commanded a column at Madrid and was now almost a communist. He had done his best to reorganize his army of ten divisions. His chief of staff was the able Major Ciutat, a communist of the new wave, who had also served Llano de la Encomienda in that capacity. Political power was concentrated in the hands of the socialist miners' leader Belarmino Tomás, who was vain, ambitious and extravagant. The politics of 'the republic of Asturias' was almost enough 'to create fascists', Colonel Prada himself later reported, adding that 'even boys of ten were imprisoned, if their fathers were fascists, and even girls of sixteen, if they were pretty'.[1]

The nationalist advance, to begin with, was slow. The Leonese mountains provided magnificent defence positions for this old heart of revolutionary Spain. Vertigo was a weapon of war in the hands of the defenders. Oviedo was, of course, already nationalist but it was still almost besieged, and the mining towns near by were still revolutionary. The absence of the Condor Legion, then on the Aragon front, prevented the swift victory of machine over nature that had characterized the battle for Santander.[2] At all events, by 14 October, after a six-week battle, several of the highest points of the Leonese mountains remained with the republic, despite the low morale in their armies, where most people knew that victory and escape were alike improbable. According to Prada himself, the province outside the mining towns was right-wing by inclination, and 85 per cent of the soldiers came as a result of conscription. The most practical hoped that winter would come early and delay the nationalists' advance. But cold affected the republican soldiers first. Flight was difficult, since the nationalists commanded the sea; the mountains represented the only hope for many. Morale was further lowered by the escape of prominent men (the mayor of Gijón, for example) in such foreign boats as they could find. Colonel Prada even had to order three brigade commanders and six battalion commanders, with another dozen officers, to be shot in order to maintain discipline.[3]

1. Azaña, vol. IV, p. 846f. (Prada's report to the President).

2. For this campaign, see Martínez Bande, *El final del frente norte*, p. 109f.

3. Prada reported this to Azaña personally (Azaña, *op. cit.*, p. 847). He said that the '*gobiernín*', as Azaña contemptuously referred to the Council of Asturias, refused to admit that, in Asturias, there could be a Fifth Column. Belarmino Tomás,

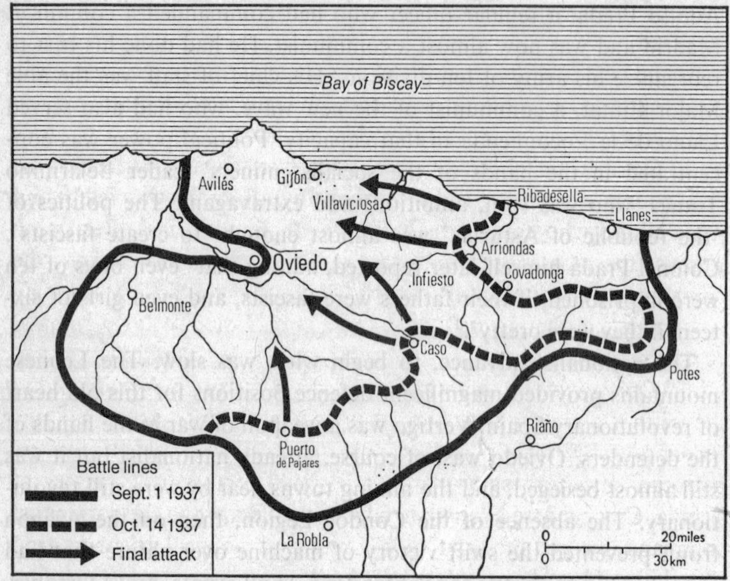

29. The Asturias campaign, September–October 1937

Suddenly, in the course of one week, Asturias was lost and won. The Condor Legion returned from Aragon. On 15 October, Aranda and Solchaga effected a junction at the mountain town of Infiesto. Panic spread among the Asturians. The Council for Asturias held an emergency meeting. A proposal was made that, in return for allowing the army to embark, the Asturians would not destroy the industry of the town. But there was no fleet to enable this proposal to be put into practice. Henceforward, in contrast with the earlier weeks of the campaign, resistance was feeble. The advance continued as swiftly as the nationalists could manage. The Germans in the Condor Legion tested the idea of 'carpet bombing'. Galland and his friends flew in close formation, very low, up the valleys, approaching the enemy from the rear. All bombs were then simultaneously released on the Asturians' trenches.[1] The republican aerial response was negligible:

'entirely subservient to the CNT', said: 'In red Asturias, there are no fascists'. But, even in 'red' Avilés, the Fifth Column had attacked a brigade, causing many casualties.

1. Galland, p. 30.

most of the Russian pilots and most experienced Spanish ones had vanished.

At the next and last meeting of the Council, the orders of Negrín were found to be to resist to the end. The communists Juan Ambou and Avelino Roces were ready for this, but, in the Council of Asturias on 17 October, the military commanders were so pessimistic that the only course seemed to be that of flight by all means possible;[1] and leave all did who could – including, in an English boat, Belarmino Tomás; the most prominent local anarchist, Segundo Blanco; the commander, Colonel Prada, Major Ciutat and others. The Russian advisers left in the few available aeroplanes. Colonel Galán escaped in a fishing boat. The armies disintegrated. Many were killed at sea. On 20 October, when Aranda was still twenty-five miles from Gijón, the Fifth Column acted. One group demanded unconditional surrender. Another seized certain buildings by force. Twenty-two republican battalions surrendered. The head of the arms factory at Trubia, Colonel José Franco, handed over the town to the nationalist command, secured the safety of two hundred political prisoners, and gave himself up; he was later tried and shot.[2] At the last minute, Prieto gave orders for the last republican ship in the harbour of Gijón, the destroyer *Ciscar*, to leave. The head of the Russian mission complained. No agreement was reached. The next day, Prieto learned, to his surprise, that the *Ciscar* had been sunk: General Goriev and Colonel Prada had insisted on going back on his order.[3] On 21 October, Aranda and Solchaga's forces entered Gijón. A ferocious proscription followed. Though the whole northern front disappeared, several thousand men maintained themselves in the Leonese mountains until March, so delaying new offensives by the nationalist armies. Among those left behind in the Cantabrian hills was said to be General Goriev, allegedly saved by a Russian aeroplane later in the year.[4]

1. The minutes of the last meeting are published in *Independent News*. (See Broué and Témime, p. 380.)

2. The details of his trial were followed in nationalist Spain with great interest.

3. Prieto, *Convulsiones*, vol. II, p. 60; cf. Azaña, vol. IV, p. 830.

4. An abortive attempt had been made to rescue Goriev by Abel Guides, the star pilot in Malraux's squadron who afterwards had joined the republican air force. Guides made three flights but was shot down and killed on the fourth. See Ehrenburg, *Eve of War*, p. 147. Saved in Asturias, from Franco, nothing

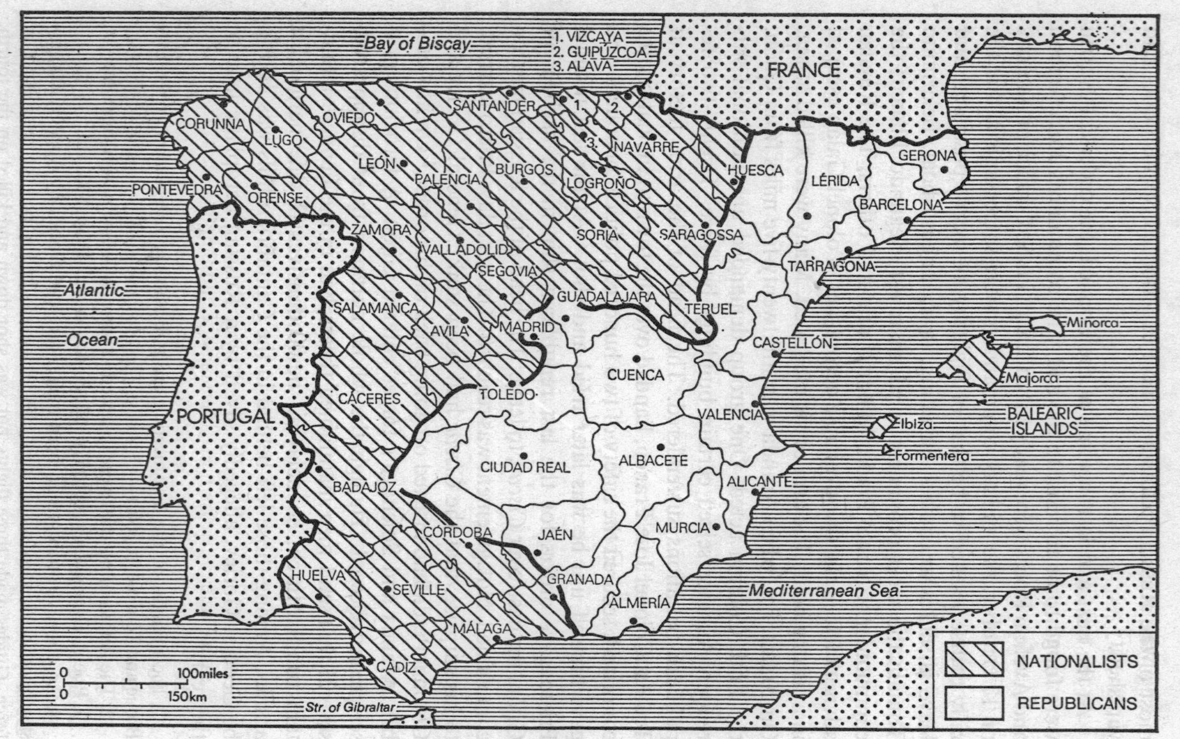

30. Division of Spain, October 1937

The war in the north had been remarkable for the nationalist superiority of aerial and artillery armaments. Yet neither in the Basque, the Santander, nor the Asturias campaigns did superior technology cause the nationalist victory. The existence of three almost independent states on the republican side, with quite different theories of government, was the fatal source of weakness. General Llano de la Encomienda was never able to establish a unity of command. Nor was his successor Gámir Ulibarri. There was also defeatism on the republican side, more than outright treachery (as can be seen from the poor information which the nationalists had in respect of enemy movements). Republican aerial support was poor at the beginning in the Basque country, but in June a substantial number of aeroplanes were made available: unfortunately, these were wasted, despite the valour of many young Spanish pilots who had been trained in Russia (actually in Armenia).[1]

The long campaign since March had brought to the nationalists the Asturian coal fields and the industries of Bilbao, particularly the arms industries. From now on, the nationalists could make their own ammunition. The campaign gave the nationalists 11,600 square miles of land; 1½ million people – including many war prisoners who were put to work in concentration camps; 36 per cent of national production, 60 per cent of national coal production, and nearly all the steel of Spain. The victory also enabled the nationalist navy to be concentrated in the Mediterranean. Finally, it freed 65,000 men of the Army of the North, and its armaments, to fight in the south.

The republican army in the north had, since May 1937, lost probably 33,000 dead, some 100,000 prisoners, and over 100,000 wounded. The nationalist losses included 10,000 dead and 100,000 casualties in all.

---

could save Goriev from his own government. Returning to Russia, he was shot. For the further struggles of *guerrilleros* in Asturias, between 1937 and 1948, see A. Saborit, *Asturias y sus hombres* (Toulouse, 1964).

1. The communist party tried to place a good deal of blame on the shoulders of the secretary of the communist party of Euzkadi, Astigarrabía, who was condemned by a plenum of the central committee for having supported too warmly the 'reactionary and bungling policy of Aguirre' (*Campo Libre*, 27 November 1937).

41

Further surprising contortions in the Committee of Non-Intervention – the Leipzig *incident – German economic pressure on Franco – the Italian submarine campaign – Nyon – back to the League of Nations – the Committee in the autumn – the British volunteer plan*

THE Spanish Civil War remained throughout 1937 the main international crisis, an irritant to the democracies, an opportunity to the dictators. During the summer and autumn, however, the diplomatic side of the conflict followed a specially tortuous path. As usual, a critical role was played by Britain who continued all these months to seek, above all, an agreement with Germany. Her Spanish policy was at all times subordinate to this vain, but comprehensible, aim. The policy was pursued with even greater energy after May 1937, when Stanley Baldwin gave way as Prime Minister to Neville Chamberlain.

After the bombardment of Almería, the British and French foreign secretaries, Eden and Delbos, procured the return of Italy and Germany to naval patrol. The two Spanish contestants were asked to refrain from attacking foreign warships and to name safety zones for refuelling patrol ships. The republic, however, condemned the whole control system for treating them on the same level as the nationalists, and demanded the freedom to carry out 'legitimate acts of war', such as air attacks in Palma, without 'Almería incidents'. Russia, fearing an international coalition against her, announced that patrol should be a matter for all powers on the Non-Intervention Committee. Ciano, fearing a German *rapprochement* with England, complained to Berlin (as did Ribbentrop in London) at being told, at the last minute, of a projected visit by the German foreign minister, Neurath, to Britain.[1] Mussolini, meanwhile, boasted to Hassell on the 12th that England still underestimated him. In any war between him and England, the leopard (Italy) might be defeated in the end, but the lion (England) would be severely wounded in the process.

No sooner had the Germans, with the Italians, agreed to return to non-intervention, than the captain of the German patrol cruiser

1. *GD*, p. 339.

Leipzig reported that, on 15 June, three torpedoes had been fired at his ship off Oran. They did not register hits. Then, on 18 June, the same captain alleged that either another torpedo had glanced the ship's side or that the cruiser had come into contact with part of the submarine. This news reached Hitler at a bad moment. He had just returned from a memorial service to the sailors killed on the *Deutschland.* He demanded, first, that Neurath cancel his proposed visit to London; secondly, he wanted a demonstration of protest by the fleets of all the naval patrol powers.[1] The republic denied responsibility for the attack. Prieto offered to give Eden all facilities for an inquiry into the incident: Eden, who had believed Germany's story over the *Deutschland*, accepted Prieto's denial. Germany and Italy refused an inquiry. Eden, reported Azcárate to Valencia, 'could not hide his shame and disgust at Germany's behaviour'.[2] Nevertheless, nothing could make the Non-Intervention Committee agree. Germany and Italy withdrew from the naval patrol, though remaining in the committee.[3] It seems unlikely in fact that the *Leipzig* was attacked.

Negrín and Giral, his foreign minister, visited Paris.[4] Blum had been defeated, to be succeeded as Prime Minister by Chautemps, the radical socialist. Blum, however, was vice-premier and Delbos still at the foreign ministry. The two Spaniards set out to try to persuade this government to end non-intervention. Russian help to the republicans, they said, had been reduced, firstly because of the nationalist blockade in the Mediterranean, secondly because of the closing of the French frontier, and thirdly, from the start of July, because of the war between China and Japan, in which Stalin had decided to help the former. The idea that, by buying arms from the democracies, he could detach himself from Russia and from the communists naturally played its part in Negrín's mind. The question of how he would now have paid, however, is obscure.

1. *GD*, p. 366.

2. Azcárate, p. 80. In a foreign affairs debate in the House of Commons on 25 June, Chamberlain, making his first speech as Prime Minister, described Germany's behaviour over the *Leipzig* 'as showing a degree of restraint that we ought to recognize'. On non-intervention, he said: 'Each side is being deprived of supplies of material of which it feels itself in urgent need'. (*Parliamentary Debates*, vol. 325, col. 1586.)

3. *NIS*(c), fifty-fifth and fifty-sixth meetings.

4. Azaña, vol. IV, p. 654, gives a report by Negrín of this journey.

The republican position had been rendered worse still by the Portuguese abandonment of control, until the naval patrol was restored. Britain and France, after Germany and Italy had left the naval patrol, offered to carry out all of it themselves, with neutral observers on board their ships. Grandi and Ribbentrop alleged that that would be excessively partial. They proposed that belligerent rights, including the right of search on the high seas, should be granted to both Spanish parties, as a substitute for naval patrol.[1] This favoured the nationalists. So far from it being acceptable to the French, Chautemps and Delbos were considering following Portugal's example, and abolishing all frontier control. Negrín and Giral thought that was a good second-best to an end to non-intervention. But the French reliance on the British prevented this. The French ministers realized that any breach with Britain would merely help Italy. The tragic actor in the drama remained Léon Blum: '*je n'en vis plus*,' he would murmur, appalled, to his friends in the Second International, such as Nenni or de Brouckère.[2]

The nationalists, meantime, sent a note to all foreign powers, threatening that those countries (England and France, for example) who did not agree to grant belligerent rights 'should not be surprised' if Spain were henceforward economically closed to them.

The British and French governments were laboriously patching up again the elaborate fabric of non-intervention. The Non-Intervention Board estimated that forty-two ships escaped inspection between its start in April and the end of July. Nor was the air route covered. The control board could not prevent the dispatch of military supplies in ships flying a Spanish or a non-European flag. German, Italian, and Russian material continued to flow into Spain, the German ships flying a Panama flag; a fact overlooked by the Non-Intervention Committee.

The nationalist debt to Germany had attained 150 million reichsmarks. For what purpose? Certainly simplifying the question, Hitler announced, in a speech at Würzburg on 27 June, that he supported Franco in order to gain possession of Spanish iron ore. In 1937, Germany was to import 1,620,000 tons of iron from Spain, 956,000 tons of pyrites, 2,000 tons of other minerals. During July, the Ger-

1. *NIS*(c), fifty-seventh meeting. 2. Nenni, p. 83.

mans, because of the crisis over Brunete, were able to elicit from the nationalists some economic concessions.[1] In a document signed by Jordana and Faupel on 12 July, the Spaniards promised that they would conclude with Germany their first general trade agreement, would tell Germany of any economic negotiations with any other country, and give most-favoured-nation treatment to Germany.[2] This was supplemented by a declaration, on 15 July, that both countries would help each other over the exchange of raw materials, food, and manufactured goods.[3] On the 16th, Spain agreed to pay its debts for war material in reichsmarks, with 4 per cent annual interest. As guarantee of the debt, raw materials would be sent to Germany. Germany would participate in Spanish reconstruction and redevelopment.[4] The monopoly companies HISMA–ROWAK, still directed by Johannes Bernhardt, would continue to control German–Spanish economic relations. The German foreign ministry did not like this arrangement but they knew of the prestige which Bernhardt had in nazi party circles and could not hope to break his authority.

These good relations were a contrast with those between the nationalists and the Italians. The Italian commanders still wanted to use their troops in a decisive action where they could win 'a great triumph'. Danzi, the fascist director in Spain, had apparently 240,000 pesetas a month to spend on propaganda for the legionaries. But, said Faupel, everyone really knew that the battle of Bilbao had been decided by German fliers and anti-aircraft batteries, not by the Italian forces on the ground. Franco himself had recently described the history of Italian troops in Spain as a 'tragedy'.[5]

Back in London, the deadlock in the Non-Intervention Committee seemed complete. On 9 July, the Dutch ambassador proposed that Britain should reconcile the opposing points of view.[6] After consulting the cabinet, Lord Plymouth accepted the task. On 14 July, he sent

1. B. Klein, *Germany's Economic Preparations for War* (Cambridge, Mass., 1959), p. 41, discusses. See also Harper, p. 65. Germany's total iron ore imports in 1936 were 9.2 million tons. Germany needed these imports to sustain her steel industry. She had imported ore from Spain before; for example, in the 1920s Spanish imports accounted for one quarter of German imports. But a great deal of German imports from Spain in 1937 and 1938 were vegetables, fruit and wine (more, in fact, in terms of marks than minerals).

2. *GD*, p. 413. See Harper, p. 52f. 3. *GD*, p. 417. 4. *GD*, p. 421.

5. *GD*, p. 410. 6. *NIS*, twenty-fourth meeting.

to the committee a British 'compromise plan for control of non-intervention'. Naval patrol would be replaced by observers at Spanish ports. There would also be observers on ships. On land, the control system would be restored. Belligerent rights at sea should be granted when 'substantial progress' had been made in withdrawal of volunteers. Germany accepted the plan 'as a basis for discussion'.[1] Delbos was angry. Britain, he complained, was now midway between France and Italy, instead of cooperating with France.[2] Azaña emerged from his lonely eminence to denounce the plan, as helping Franco. Belligerent rights, he said, could only favour the nationalists, and a partial withdrawal of volunteers would enable Franco to dispense with the inefficient Italians; the republic would have to give up invaluable members of the International Brigade. Count Grandi, however, succeeded in evading any real consideration of the British plan. He demanded that the points in it be discussed in numerical order. Thus belligerent rights which, by hasty drafting, had been placed prior to volunteers, would have been discussed first. Maisky wanted to talk of volunteers first. On the 26th, Britain asked for other governments' views in writing. Léger in Paris complained that the British 'were prepared to accept anything rather than have a showdown'.[3]

Eden who was still Foreign Secretary under Chamberlain had begun by welcoming the new Prime Minister's interest in foreign affairs, for Baldwin had been bored by the subject. Eden had also thought Chamberlain agreed with him before he was Premier. Nevertheless, under Chamberlain, the British government were to seek the appeasement of Hitler and Mussolini more vigorously than they had done under Baldwin. The change of emphasis was seen in the olive branch sent in the form of a private letter suggesting 'talks' from Chamberlain to Mussolini on 29 July.[4] Mussolini was anxious to

1. *NIS*, twenty-sixth meeting.

2. *USD*, 1937, vol. I, p. 360. This remark was made at a lunch at which the new British ambassador in Paris, Phipps, and Bullitt were present.

3. *USD*, 1937, vol. I, p. 366.

4. Ciano, *Diplomatic Papers*, p. 132; Churchill, *Gathering Storm*, p. 189; Eden, p. 445. The letter was written without Eden's knowledge. The Spanish government seemed to ignore this change. Azaña, who had regarded the British as a malign influence over Spanish affairs, was assured by Azcárate on 16 August that the British government did not know what it wanted. 'There is nobody in the

secure British recognition of his conquest of Abyssinia. Spain, for Chamberlain, was a troublesome complication which should, if possible, be forgotten. This now seemed possible. Even Eden told Delbos that he hoped Franco would win, since he thought that he could reach agreement for an eventual German and Italian withdrawal.[1] On 6 August, Maisky asked pointblank in the Non-Intervention Sub-Committee if Germany and Italy would agree to the withdrawal of all volunteers on the two sides in Spain. He received only a vague answer.[2] During the rest of August, there was only one non-intervention meeting. This was on the 27th, when it was concluded that the naval patrol did not justify its expense and that, therefore, the British idea for observers at ports should be substituted for it.[3]

But there were new alarms. The flow of material to the republic from Marseilles, through the Straits of Gibraltar as well as from Russia, seemed formidable. Nationalist agents in Bucharest, Algiers and Gibraltar, as well as in Berlin and Rome (in collaboration with Germany and Italy), were worried.[4] Rumours of the extent of Russian aid to the republic caused Franco to send his brother Nicolás to Rome and to ask the Italian fleet to strike against Russian, Spanish republican, and other vessels in the Mediterranean.[5] Mussolini agreed. He would not use surface vessels, but submarines, 'which would raise a Spanish flag if they had to surface'.[6] (Mussolini had the largest submarine fleet in the world at that time: 83 submarines to the French 76 and British 57.)[7] As a result, Russian, British,

political world of these countries who makes plans on a long distance.' 'It would cost me a lot of work to believe that the British Empire is governed by fools,' Azaña replied (Azaña, *op. cit.*, p. 738).

1. *USD*, 1937, vol. I, p. 369. This was no doubt a hasty aside by Eden, for the Foreign Secretary was generally sympathetic at this period to the republic. That at least is his own account, confirmed by a hostile witness like Hoare in *Nine Troubled Years*.

2. *NIS*(c), sixty-second meeting.

3. *NIS*(c), sixty-third meeting.

4. Cervera, p. 111.

5. *GD*, p. 432.

6. This visit occurred on 4 August (*ibid.*, p. 433).

7. *Jane's Fighting Ships 1936*. The Italian navy was strong in comparison with France, having 6 battleships to France's 7, 29 cruisers to 16, 64 destroyers and flotilla leaders to France's 60. (British figures for comparable craft were 15, 52 and 175, with 57 submarines, plus 5 aircraft carriers.)

French, and other neutral ships, as well as Spanish vessels, were soon attacked in the Mediterranean by Italian submarines and by Italian aircraft operating from Majorca. A British, a French, and an Italian merchant ship were bombed on 6 August near Algiers. On 7 August, a Greek ship was bombed. On the 11th, the 13th, and the 15th, ships of the republic were torpedoed. The British tanker *Caporal* was attacked on 10 August. On 11 August, the republican tanker *Campeador* was sunk south of Malta by two Italian destroyers: surface ships were used several times. On the 12th, a Danish cargo boat was sunk: Vansittart complained to the Italian chargé, Guido Crolla, saying he knew 'for a fact that those aeroplanes were based on Palma'.[1] A Spanish merchant ship, the *Ciudad de Cádiz*, was sunk leaving the Dardanelles on 14 August, and another, the *Armuro*, was sunk on the 19th. On 26 August, a British ship was bombed off Barcelona. On 29 August, a Spanish steamer was shelled by a submarine off the French coast. A French passenger steamer reported that she was chased by a submarine into the Dardanelles. On the 30th, the Russian merchantman *Tuniyaev* was sunk at Algiers, on its way to Port Said. On 31 August, a submarine attacked the British destroyer *Havock*. On 1 September, the Russian steamer *Blagaev* was sunk by a submarine off Skyros. On 2 September, the British tanker *Woodford* was sunk near Valencia. 'Three torpedoings and one prize,' Ciano remarked in his diary on that day, 'but international opinion is getting very worked up, particularly in England, as the result of the attack on the *Havock*. It was the *Iride*,' the Italian foreign secretary admitted – though only to himself.[2]

The nationalists, who had had no submarines at the start of the war, now had two, sold to them by Italy. A number of other Italian vessels had been made available to the nationalist command, as 'legionary' submarines; while some other Italian submarines were acting on their own, Italian, orders. The *Tuniyaev* had thus been sunk by a 'legionary'. The *Iride* was, however, under Italian orders.[3] (Italy had also sold the nationalists six old destroyers and an old cruiser, the *Taranto*.)[4] The British cabinet was still loath to take action: it was represented that the dispatch of British naval vessels to the

1. Eden, p. 457. The British had apparently also broken the Italian naval cypher.
2. Ciano, *Diaries 1937–8*, pp. 7–8. 3. See Alcofar Nassaes, *CTV*, p. 150.
4. Cervera, p. 186.

Mediterranean would provide Italy with more targets.[1] Many British merchantmen were, as the cabinet knew, secretly carrying arms as well as food to Spain; and their motives were commercial as a rule, not idealistic. The freedom of the seas was one thing; the freedom of Jack Billmeir, the Newcastle shipping millionaire, to make a fortune another. But British imports of mineral ore from Spain were still considerable, and could not be done without.

Eden persuaded the cabinet to send more destroyers to the Mediterranean. Chamberlain also agreed to Delbos's suggestion for a conference of 'interested powers'. On 6 September, all states with Mediterranean frontiers, except Spain, together with Germany and Russia, were invited by Britain and France to a conference, on the 10th. This was to be held at Nyon, not far from Geneva, where it was not proposed to hold it for fear of angering Italy, who associated the city of Calvin with the League's condemnation of her Abyssinian expedition. 'The full orchestra,' Ciano now noted, 'the theme: Piracy in the Mediterranean. Guilty – the fascists. The Duce is very calm.' García Conde, the Spanish nationalist ambassador in Rome, brought Ciano a message from Franco saying that, if the blockade lasted throughout September, it would be decisive. 'True', Ciano admitted, but he nevertheless ordered Admiral Cavagnari to suspend it, until further orders.[2]

The Russian chargé in Rome, Helfand, accused Italian submarines of sinking the merchant ships *Tuniyaev* and *Blagaev*. He claimed irrefutable evidence of Italian guilt – 'from intercepted telegrams, I expect', wrote Ciano airily, doubtless recalling the use which he himself made of that source of information.[3] Ciano disclaimed responsibility and disputed the right of Russia to make such a judgement. Both Italy and Germany proposed that the Non-Intervention

1. Eden, p. 461.

2. Ciano, *Diaries 1937–8*, p. 9. The blockade was nearly successful as it was. Whatever credence one can give to the incomplete figures reported by the German military attaché at Ankara, he clearly *reflects* the truth when he reports no Russian material reaching Spain at all during September by the sea route. On the other hand, substantial supplies did get through in August. See Azaña, *op. cit.*, p. 733. Stalin had pointed out to Pascua the advantages of the home manufacture of armaments in order to save the ruinous costs, which, after all, could not be endless: the gold might not last.

3. *ibid.*, p. 11.

Committee, rather than a special conference, should handle the matter. But Eden and Delbos pressed on with their arrangements. Churchill and Lloyd George, from the south of France, wrote to Eden that now was 'the moment to rally Italy to her international duty'.[1]

The conference followed, with Italy and Germany absent. It was successful. First, Delbos and Eden proposed that the Mediterranean should be patrolled by warships of all the riparian states, with Russia (and Italy) allotted the eastern Mediterranean. But the smaller countries had no warships to spare for this task, and did not wish to risk war. So it was decided that the British and French fleets should patrol the Mediterranean west of Malta and attack any suspicious submarine. This was decided on the first day of the conference. The agreement was signed on the 14th.[2] Mussolini was furious, and Litvinov spoke of his pleasure at an international agreement 'with very considerable backing'. Churchill wrote to Eden that the agreement had shown the possibility of British and French cooperation. Further arrangements, between naval experts, were planned to consider attacks by aircraft. Ciano sent a note requesting 'parity of duties' for Italy with all the other states of Nyon. The wits in the Café Bavaria at Geneva suggested that the 'unknown statesman' – Mussolini – should erect a monument to the 'unknown submarine' in Rome. On 17 September, the Nyon conference's naval experts gave to the naval patrol the same power against aircraft that they had already against submarines. Warships which attacked neutral ships would be counter-attacked by the patrolling navies, regardless of whether they were in Spanish territorial waters. On the 18th, the French and British chargés in Rome gave Ciano the texts of the Nyon Agreements, and asked for an interpretation of his request for 'parity'. They thus made possible the return to friendly relations with Italy which Chamberlain desired.

The same day, Negrín was before the League of Nations Assembly requesting that its political committee examine Spain. As usual, only Litvinov and Mexico supported the republic. Eden claimed that non-intervention had stopped a European war: echoing Baldwin a year

1. Churchill, p. 191.
2. Eden, p. 465. See minutes of this meeting in *FD*, vol. VI, p. 730f.

before, he compared non-intervention to a leaky dam, 'better than no dam at all'.[1] Negrín wished France to send 400 or 500 officers or NCOs to help the republic and asked for that.[2] He also talked, and got on good terms, with Eden, who said that British public opinion did not want Franco to win. The cabinet, he said, was divided. Chamberlain was afraid of communism and the government were unable to take a strong line until rearmament was complete.[3] Italy meantime was invited to send experts to Paris to 'adjust' the Nyon Agreement in accordance with Italian wishes. Ciano, therefore, felt that he had achieved a triumph. On 27 September, the British, French and Italians began naval talks in Paris. Italy was allotted a patrol zone between the Balearic Islands and Sardinia, and in the Tyrrhenian Sea. This enabled Italy to continue sending supplies to Majorca without fear of being watched. Also on the 27th, the League's political committee did take up the question of Spain. Alvarez del Vayo spoke with eloquent bitterness at the news of Italian reinforcements to General Franco. Walter Elliott, the British representative, persuaded the committee to omit any denunciation of Germany and Italy from the resolution to be put forward. But that document did refer to the 'failure of non-intervention', to the consideration of ending it (unless an agreement could be reached on the withdrawal of volunteers in 'the near future') and to the 'existence of veritable foreign army corps on Spanish soil'. However much the British might dislike such candour they could hardly object. For Mussolini, even while the resolution was being discussed, was publicly mourning the deaths of thousands of Italians on Spanish soil, during his visit to Germany – where he was overwhelmed by the signs which he had seen of German preparedness for war. Privately, the Duce told Hitler that, Nyon or not, he would continue torpedoing. He boasted that he had already sunk nearly 200,000 tons of ships.[4] These remarks gave an ironic

1. Baldwin used the metaphor in 1936 (Keith Middlemas and John Barnes *Baldwin*, London, 1969, p. 967).

2. *FD*, vol. VI, pp. 824–5.

3. Azaña, vol. IV, p. 805. The republicans failed, as they had wished, to get Spain re-elected as a member of the League's Council. Chile offered to arrange enough votes to ensure that, provided the asylees in the embassies were released. This idea was rejected with contempt.

4. *Documents secrets du ministère des affaires étrangères d'Allemagne 1936–43*, vol. III, p. 22 (Moscow, 1946).

quality to the apparently successful end, on 30 September, of the naval talks in Paris, Italy now being included in the Nyon patrol.

It was hard now to represent the Nyon conference as exactly a triumph of 'strength'. Notes were prepared in the Foreign Office and in the Quai d'Orsay to invite the 'pirate now turned policeman' (as Ciano boasted himself to be)[1] to general talks on Spain. This was put to Ciano on 2 October. The same day, the carefully drafted resolution of the League was passed. Alvarez del Vayo only agreed to the vagueness of the phrase 'in the near future' on the understanding that Britain and France needed ten days to see if Italy would reply amicably to their invitation. But Franco now wanted more, and not fewer, 'volunteers'. The Italian troops had proved their usefulness in the campaigns in the north. But Franco did want General Bastico recalled, for his subordinate's impertinence during the Santander campaign in going so far as to negotiate individually with the Basques.

Franco was at the time preoccupied with the case of Harold Dahl, a former US air force pilot, who had enlisted in the republican air force. He had been forced to bail out over nationalist territory. A court-martial there sentenced Dahl, and two Russian pilots, to death for 'rebellion'. The US government had to exert itself, and an American colonel who had fought in Morocco by Franco's side telegraphed to his ex-comrade in arms to appeal for clemency. The death sentence was later commuted to life imprisonment.[2]

On 10 October, Ciano told Eden and Delbos that he could not act over Spain without Germany. So far from wishing to settle the situation in Spain, Ciano was wondering whether he could dispatch some regular Alpine troops there – 'to break through to Valencia'.[3] He also responded to Franco's request over the command by naming General Mario Berti as the new commander of the Italian troops in Spain in succession to Bastico. When, at the end of October, a ceremony was held for the presentation of medals to men who had fought in Spain and to the widows of those who had fallen, Ciano 'examined his conscience' to ask if this blood had been shed in a good cause. 'Yes, the answer is yes,' he comforted himself, 'at

1. Ciano, *Diaries 1937–8*, p. 15.
2. But Dahl returned to America in 1940.
3. Ciano, *Diaries 1937–8*, p. 18.

Málaga, at Santander, at Guadalajara, we were fighting in defence of our civilization and our revolution!'[1]

The French reaction to Ciano's refusal to talk without consulting Germany was to consider opening the Pyrenean frontier fully to the passage of arms for the republic. Eden persuaded Delbos to go back first to the Non-Intervention Committee. Delbos said that if an agreement were not reached on volunteers within one week, France would open her frontier.[2] For the blockade of the Mediterranean was now almost complete; the sinking of the supply ship *San Tomé* had been a serious blow.[3] On 15 October, Eden told Grandi that this new appeal to the committee was 'a last attempt'. He told a conservative audience at Llandudno that his patience with Italian intervention in Spain was 'well-nigh exhausted'. Some days earlier, the Labour Party Conference, meeting at Bournemouth, had denounced non-intervention; Sir Charles Trevelyan, a rebel in 1936, introduced this year's special resolution. (The Trades Union Congress some weeks before had followed the same line.)[4]

On 16 October, the Non-Intervention Sub-Committee at last met again. Between then and 2 November, the British plan of July, which had proposed the grant of belligerent rights subject to the withdrawal of a 'substantial proportion' of volunteers in Spain, became the basis for discussion. After prolonged, wearisome, and confusing negotiations, in which the patient Eden played an important role, this plan was accepted. The two Spanish parties were to be asked for their cooperation, to accept two commissions to number the foreigners in their zones, and to put the withdrawal into effect.[5] In the meantime, since more than a week had passed since Delbos made his stipulation, the French frontier was left open for the passage of arms by night. Eden cryptically told Delbos, 'Don't open the frontier but allow to pass what you want'.[6] Thenceforward, in Blum's words, 'we voluntarily and systematically shut our eyes to arms smuggling and even

1. *ibid.*, p. 26.
2. *USD*, 1937, vol. I, p. 420. Here, as so often, the best source for French policy is in these reports by the American ambassador in Paris.
3. Azaña, vol. IV, p. 823.
4. Watkins, p. 186.
5. *NIS*, twenty-eighth meeting; *NIS*(c), sixty-fourth to seventieth meetings.
6. Azcárate, p. 122.

organized it'.[1] On 28 October, Azcárate talked with Eden in the House of Commons. Azcárate urged firmness.

EDEN: What you want is a preventive war against Italy.

AZCÁRATE: No, simply a clear political line which, if maintained with energy and determination, would be enough to calm the intemperance of Mussolini.

EDEN: It is not easy to decide that line.

AZCÁRATE: With respect to Spain it is easy: it is to make certain that the UK preserves Spain free from foreign entanglement and free from a fascism which would interfere with British strategic interests.

Eden [reported Azcárate] heard me with his head low, saying that it was easier for me to say this than for him to convince his colleagues. I asked him what the republic ought to do to give a guarantee that there was no communist danger in Spain. Eden merely agreed that it would be unreasonable to insist that the two communists leave the government.[2]

At this time, despite Azcárate's reservations, Eden was 'very anxious to find a way of helping Valencia'.[3]

The real motives of the intervening countries were becoming clear, at least to themselves. On 5 November, Hitler, while unfolding his desire for a war of extermination against Britain and France to an alarmed Neurath, Blomberg, and Beck, said that, in the Spanish war, 'from the German point of view, a hundred per cent Franco victory is not desirable. We are most interested in the continuance of the war.'[4] Only thus, he went on, could the Italian position in the Balearic Islands – important from the strategic point of view – be preserved. A little earlier, a Russian general had told Orlov, the NKVD representative, that the Politburo had adopted a policy much the same

1. *Les Événements survenus en France*, p. 219.

2. Azcárate, pp. 129–30.

3. Oliver Harvey, *Diplomatic Diaries* (London, 1970), p. 49. Cf. also B. H. Liddell Hart, *Memoirs* (London, 1965), vol. II, p. 136.

4. This was the celebrated 'Hossbach Memorandum' (*Nuremberg Trials*, vol. XXV, pp. 403–14). It was also the time when the Germans in Spain were becoming excited over the Spanish mining project – see p. 618. For discussion as to its validity, see A. J. P. Taylor, *The Origins of the Second World War* (London, 1961), p. 131, and Alan Bullock, 'Hitler and the Origins of the Second World War', *Proceedings of the British Academy*, 1967.

as that proposed by Hitler: that is, that it would be best if the war in Spain dragged on and tied Hitler down there.[1] Thus, for mutually hostile reasons, the two leading powers on the edge of the Spanish war reached the same conclusion. Not long before, even the British Foreign Secretary had made a slightly different judgement: British interests, Eden had told the cabinet at the end of September, would be best served by a stalemate. It was against British interests that Franco should win, while he was dependent on German aid. Prolongation of the war by six months would increase the strain on Italy.[2]

On 6 November, Italy joined Germany and Japan in signing their so-called Anti-Comintern Pact. Although Ciano desired this to remain a 'pact of giants', he planned to bring Franco's Spain in, so as to link the 'Axis to the Atlantic'. On 20 November, Franco accepted the British 'volunteer' plan in principle. He made reservations about the proposed commission's powers to guarantee the withdrawal. He suggested that the withdrawal of 3,000 volunteers would constitute the 'substantial withdrawal' upon which belligerent rights would be conditional. The figure no doubt occurred to Franco since precisely that number of Italian troops were now withdrawn, regardless of agreements, because they were sick or unreliable.[3] On 1 December, the republic also accepted the plan – though for different reasons: Azaña and Giral hoped that acceptance might mean the suspension

1. A. Orlov, *The Secret History of Stalin's Crimes* (New York, 1953), pp. 241–2. Orlov names this soldier 'General N'. Can one trust Orlov's testimony? Where it coincides with, or does not contradict, other evidence, it seems acceptable. Araquistain made the same point in *La Prensa* (Buenos Aires), 12 July 1939: Stalin did not wish to win the war because that would have exasperated Hitler, nor to lose it because, once it was over, Hitler would have more freedom to carry on his aggression in East Europe and against the Soviet Union. On the other hand, Spain for Russia was a secondary affair compared to her friendship with Britain and France, as Azaña and Pascua realized (Azaña, vol. IV, p. 734).

2. *CAB*, 35(37), 27 September 1937. At a subsequent meeting Chamberlain had said that it did 'not matter to us which side won, so long as it was a Spanish and not a German or Italian victory' (*CAB*, 37(37), of 13 October 1937). Louis Fischer also described how a certain Colonel Clark of the war office asked him: 'In your opinion would it be better if Franco won quickly or if Spain remained an open wound through which the poisons of Europe could escape?' (*op. cit.*, p. 457).

3. *GD*, p. 550.

of hostilities, which would thereafter not be renewed. Azaña had, for a long time, been placing hopes in the idea that a withdrawal of volunteers might lead eventually to an armistice. Negrín agreed that the start of a volunteer plan would mean suspension of fighting, and liked the idea because, at worst, it would give the republic time to re-group.[1]

1. Azcárate, p. 120.

42

Franco's Spain on the way to victory – ill-behaviour of the Italians – Germany's quarrels with Franco over mines – the nationalist army – Franco's first government

DURING the lull which followed the Asturias campaign, the stability of both Spains seemed such as would preserve a stalemate. Compared with the 'lyrical illusion' and the chaos, the mood of euphoria and massacre of July 1936, the coherent organization of two Spains, each with armies larger than any in Europe save that of France, was astonishing. War had in both zones forged order, though it was not one of which any man of peace could feel proud. Dionisio Ridruejo, the young falangist, disciple of Serrano Súñer, poet, and propagandist of the nationalist régime, reflected later that the war was the time in modern history when the Spanish people participated most fully in their own destiny;[1] but that destiny was greatly affected if not determined by weapons from abroad.

However politically conscious its people may have been, nationalist Spain (now two-thirds of the whole country) remained a military society. The aristocratic General Gómez Jordana still headed the *junta técnica* at Burgos, the provisional government, free from bureaucracy, which wielded all the administrative power. Its departments were spread about several cities. Serrano Súñer, with vague powers, but no governmental post or title during 1937, was the political leader. An unconvincing but serviceable falangist past was created for him, his friendship with José Antonio at the university emphasized. His powers were not limited by the new national council,

1. Dionisio Ridruejo, *Escrito en España* (Buenos Aires, 1962), p. 34. This young poet and orator, briefly provincial chief of Valladolid but coming from Segovia, denounced Franco for arresting Hedilla, became director-general of propaganda under Serrano, his mentor, in early 1938. Why was he not detained for his *démarche* before Franco? The answer must be that his youth, eloquence, sincerity, promise and charm ensured him the protection both of General Monasterio, head of the united militias, and of Serrano, whom he met in the *tertulias* of Pilar Primo de Rivera.

whose forty-eight members were named on 2 December. This body remained more advisory in character even than most such portentously named organizations. It resembled the Italian fascist grand council, since its members, their duties legislative, were nominated by Franco. There were three women on the council – Pilar Primo de Rivera, Mercedes Sanz Bachiller, widow of Onésimo Redondo, the founder of Auxilio Social, and María Rosa Urraca Pastor, the Florence Nightingale, though known as *la Coronela*, of nationalist nurses. There were six generals (Queipo, Dávila, Jordana, Yagüe, Monasterio and Orgaz), two colonels (Beigbeder, high commissioner in Morocco, and Gazapo), twenty old falangists (among them Fernández Cuesta, Sancho Dávila, Agustín Aznar, and José Antonio Girón), and eleven old Carlists (including Rodezno and Esteban Bilbao). The remainder of the list were monarchists, conservatives or technicians of various sorts. The Carlist, Fal Conde, was asked to be a member. He refused and remained in proud but ineffective exile.

The new 'national movement' (the Falange Española Tradicionalista) developed little during 1937. Did it exist at all, who were its members, where were its offices? It was the instrument of Serrano Súñer, but what was that? Fascist, corporativist, militarist or 'Francoist'? The movement had, admittedly, officers, if it lacked an ideology. Thus the FET chief of press and propaganda at Salamanca was Father Fermín Yzurdiaga, the falangist priest from Pamplona – a hybrid suitable for the hybrid party. Beneath him were Dionisio Ridruejo, chief of propaganda, and a Carlist, Eladio Esparza, press chief. Later, Serrano Súñer substituted Antonio Tovar, another 'old shirt', for Esparza. The mood of the Falange was now one of subservience to the army: *Arriba España*, the party paper, had a slogan 'For God and Caesar' on its front page. Apart from propaganda, the FET did little. It seemed to be a 'parallel state' but it was more a bureaucracy of sinecures. Nothing changed in this respect when, in October, Raimundo Fernández Cuesta, secretary-general of the Falange before the war, was exchanged from a republican gaol for Justino de Azcárate, brother of the ambassador in London. Prieto, alone of republican ministers, opposed this exchange, for who, he asked, was Justino de Azcárate? Some republicans hoped that Fernández Cuesta might create difficulties with the Falange if he were returned to Burgos. He did not do so, however, and de Azcárate was of no service to the republic, since, severely shaken by his imprisonment, he stayed in France.[1] Fernández Cuesta became secretary-general of the new united movement in Burgos. He lacked the energy to be a rival to Serrano Súñer, and the dream of Prieto and some others that he might found a '*Falange Española Auténtica*', to divide the movement in nationalist Spain remained a fantasy.[2]

The Carlist representatives who stayed on the national council were all of the moderate wing who, following Rodezno, had accepted the Decree of Unification. On 5 December, Prince Xavier, the Carlist regent, condemned those who took the oath which was demanded by the council without asking his permission. He followed this with a journey to Spain, his usual headquarters being in France. In San Sebastián, he told Serrano Súñer that it was wrong to try and give to Spain a Gestapo on the German model. In Burgos, he told Franco: 'If it were not for the *requetés*, I doubt whether you would be where you are.' These remarks were not well received. The Prince went on a tour of the battlefronts. Having met a welcome in Seville, he reached Granada before he was ordered to leave Spain. He had another interview with Franco, who told him: 'You are waging a campaign in favour of monarchy.' The Prince replied: 'I have not spoken a word of politics. But my name is Bourbon. And, after all, I thought you also were a monarchist.' 'Much of the army is for a republic,' answered Franco, 'and I cannot ignore that state of mind.' 'I believe that the main reason why you want me to leave Spain is that the Germans and Italians insist,' said Prince Xavier. Franco surprisingly agreed, by saying: 'If you remain in Spain, Your Highness, neither the Germans nor the Italians will give us any more war material.' Prince Xavier, therefore, left Burgos for France, remarking, 'Do not forget that I am the last link between you and the *requetés*; nor that I shall always work for Spain, but never for you personally.'[3] In fact, the Falange and the Carlists remained apart, in all senses save

1. I benefited from discussion with Justino de Azcárate (Caracas, 1973).

2. Prieto, *Palabras*, pp. 235–6. Prieto was perhaps misinformed by 'Luis Pagés Guix' who put out a version of the events of Salamanca under the title of *La Traición de los Franco*. For commentary see Southworth, *Antifalange*, and De la Cierva, *Historia ilustrada*, vol. II, p. 293.

3. From an unpublished series of notes for a life of Prince Xavier de Bourbon-Parme in the Carlist Archives at Seville.

formally: the two youth movements never merged, and Xavier remained an exile.

During the winter of 1937–8, the nationalists created a conventional cabinet. On 1 February, of this Second Triumphal Year, Franco became president of the council, with the Conde de Gómez Jordana vice-president and foreign minister. Gómez Jordana's aristocratic style had made a good impression on foreigners – particularly the English: 'a man of another age', Serrano spoke of him disdainfully.[1] Dávila, keeping command of the Army of the North, was minister of defence. General Martínez Anido, the notoriously brutal and embattled civil governor of Barcelona after 1917, and a member of Primo de Rivera's cabinets, returned from abroad at seventy-five, to be minister of public order. The other members of the government were non-military. Andrés Amado, a friend of Calvo Sotelo's, became finance minister. A naval engineer, Juan Antonio Suances, an old friend of Franco, became minister of industry and commerce.[2] The Carlist, Rodezno, became minister of justice, Sáinz Rodríguez, the monarchist intellectual, minister of education. The most powerful member of the cabinet was Serrano Súñer, minister of the interior, even though he had public order subtracted from it. He was also secretary-general of the movement. Fernández Cuesta, the only 'old shirt' in the government, was minister of agriculture, in addition to his honorific post of secretary-general of the national council. Pedro González Bueno, an engineer and characteristic 'technocratic' member of the new Falange, became minister of labour. The last member of the cabinet, Alfonso Peña y Boeuf, minister of public works, was also an engineer, who had played no previous role in politics. Of these ministers, four – Serrano, Fernández Cuesta, Suances, and Peña y Boeuf – had escaped from republican Spain during the war and thus at least knew what they were fighting against. Three were ex-

1. Serrano Súñer, p. 136. It is also a little doubtful whether all Englishmen liked his style of not getting to his office till eleven in the morning. That offended Sir Philip Chetwode (see below, p. 854).

2. Suances had been a friend of Franco since their childhood at El Ferrol. Both had wanted to be naval officers, but only Suances was accepted. Suances later became director of a partly British-owned company engaged in building ships for the Spanish navy. He resigned in 1934 because he was unable to bring about the nationalization of the British share. He escaped from Madrid after the start of the civil war – and had been employed at Burgos in naval construction.

collaborators of Primo de Rivera (Martínez Anido, Andrés Amado and Jordana). Amado and Sáinz Rodríguez had been monarchists, Rodezno was the only Carlist, Serrano Súñer the only *CEDAista*, two were falangists (Fernández Cuesta and González Bueno) and two friends of Franco (Peña and Suances). Not one of these new men had been a minister under the republic, even in the right-wing régimes, and only Rodezno and Serrano Súñer had been deputies. Colonel Beigbeder was confirmed, meanwhile, as high commissioner in Morocco.[1] The cabinet took an oath of allegiance to Franco and to Spain in the romanesque monastery of Las Huelgas: 'In the name of God and His holy evangelists, I swear to fulfil my duty as minister of Spain with the most exact fidelity to the Head of State, Generalissimo of our glorious armies, and to the principles which constitute the nationalist régime in service of the destiny of the country.' *Sotto voce*, Rodezno remarked to Sáinz Rodríguez, after taking the oath: 'What no one can now take from us is the rank of ex-minister – the most important thing to be in Spain'.[2]

One omission was Queipo de Llano. He was unable to understand falangism, and disliked seeing falangists getting good jobs in the new régime. Gradually, though not yet entirely, his private fief in Seville was to be taken away from him. By the middle of 1938, he was no more than military commander in the south. Serrano was busy organizing a more predictable method of governing Spain than his. Queipo was angry at his exclusion, and brought an end to his broadcasts. Nationalist Spain was duller thereafter. Thousands of Spaniards had listened to him every night at 10 p.m.[3] and believed all that he had said. In the republican zone, he had also been heard – there was no interference – with either apprehension or enthusiasm. Barcelona Radio had often inaccurately accused him of being drunk. 'Well why not,' he bellowed in answer. 'Why shouldn't a real *hombre* enjoy the

1. He had held this post since April 1937. For a discussion of Beigbeder's astute rule see Charles Halstead, 'A somewhat Machiavellian face', *The Historian*, November 1974.

2. Serrano Súñer, p. 123.

3. For two nights, Queipo had changed to 10.30 p.m. This was, he told his hearers, because a delegation of Sevillian girls had complained that his broadcasts at ten o'clock gave them only half an hour at their window with their *novios*. So Queipo changed his time, thereby disrupting nationalist radio programmes: for all stations were linked with Seville Radio for Queipo.

superb quality of the wine and women of Seville?' He was taxed with his republican past. He replied that he had thought at one time that the republic could solve the problems of Spain. Now the future lay with Franco. But, he assured his listeners, if he should see that Franco was not acting in Spain's best interests (an eventuality he considered impossible), his patriotism was such that he would fight even the Caudillo. This reflection was not popular at Salamanca. His farouche personal insults to 'the jew Blum', Doña Manolita (Azaña) or English journalists such as Nöel Monks (whom he accused of being intoxicated when he wrote for the *Daily Express* that Guernica had been bombed), or Miaja, whom he despised, or Prieto, of whom he had been once a friend, were part of the folklore of rebel Spain. What entranced his hearers was his custom, at the end of an attack on the 'rabble' for one vice or another, of introducing an irrelevant message, such as, 'And now, if my wife and daughter who are in Paris happen to be listening, I should like to say I hope they are well and to assure them that we here in Seville are thinking of them. Buenas noches, señores!'[1] Actually, this early practitioner of radio propaganda was an efficient administrator. He had done his best to expand the textile industry of Seville, and he tried to develop chemicals. He also arranged for the distribution of seed and favourable loans to farmers. He tried to protect tenant farmers by introducing a moratorium on mortgage payments and distributed estates belonging to republicans to peasants loyal to the nationalist cause. (Some land was given too by very large proprietors such as the Duke of Alba, to help Queipo's agrarian reform.) Queipo was also responsible for growing rice in the delta of the Guadalquivir to make up for the loss to the nationalists of the famous Valencian rice fields, at Albufera: 240,000 acres were converted in the marshes.

Two other omissions in the cabinet were Nicolás Franco and Sangroniz, the controllers of the nationalist household for eighteen months since October 1936. Neither was friendly with Serrano Súñer, who disliked their old-fashioned methods; and neither was protected by Franco, for whom gratitude was never a virtue. Nicolás Franco went to Lisbon as ambassador, Sangroniz to Caracas.

1. There is a good study of Queipo as propagandist in Dundas, *Behind the Spanish Mask*, p. 59f.

The nomination of Martínez Anido as minister of public order was calculated to strike dread into the minds of all republicans. Yet either through senility or conservatism, Martínez Anido was one of the more humane of Franco's ministers. Like Gómez Jordana, a man of another epoch, he despised fascism, and insisted on trials by military tribunals; so that few, henceforth, were executed in nationalist Spain '*por la libre*'.[1]

Among the bourgeoisie of nationalist Spain, there was no slackening in enthusiasm for the 'crusade'. The leaders might not be on such good terms as they made out. The defeated might be maltreated. But this was war, was it not, and these ugly matters were the obverse side of one's own sacrifices. The currency was fairly stable, food prices had not risen much, and stocks would have been adequate to provision all republican Spain. The spectre of hunger in the cities did not exist. Even coal was now in ample supply. Thus, away from the front, middle-class life could be carried on without much interruption. Bullfights had been resumed in the summer, and the regular *ferias* were held.[2] In the evening, one would, as of old, walk up and down the main street of the town at the hour of the *paseo*, and notice perhaps a number of uniforms. There would be posters encouraging patriotic service. One would hear news of so-and-so's daughter, working with the Auxilio Social. The national lottery had been re-established. One would have to give, before the evening was out, at a café or in the cinema, a contribution to war victims or to subsidize state meals or to aid refugees. As the evening progressed, war might seem nearer. At ten o'clock, there would be Queipo de Llano on the radio in cafés, private houses or, if one were able to find a table, in one of the crowded restaurants. Then, at midnight, there would be the daily communiqué, the list of casualties and of prisoners: and then, with the 'Royal March', to bed.

1. Statistics of those '*pasados por las armas*' thus must somewhere exist. For Martínez Anido, see Cabanellas, vol. II, p. 945.

2. Most prominent bull-fighters of the time (Marcial Lalanda, 'Manolo' Bienvida) were with the nationalists. The great Manolete was in the nationalist army on the Córdoba front, though he began to draw attention during the season of 1938. For a discussion see Rafael Abella, 'Toros en la Guerra Civil', *Historia y vida*, January 1975. Some corridas were held in the republic, mostly as benefits for hospitals or schools, despite the opposition of the anarchists.

As for the lives of the combatants, the pilot Ansaldo, now returned to the war after recovering from his injuries in the air crash in which Sanjurjo died, gave one account of a day on the northern front:

8.30 a.m.	Breakfast with the family.
9.30 a.m.	Departure for the front. Bombardment of enemy batteries. Machine-gunning of trenches and convoys.
11 a.m.	A little golf at Lasarte . . .
12.30 p.m.	Sun-bath on Ondarreta beach and short swim in the calm sea.
1.30 p.m.	Beer, shrimps, and conversation in a café.
2 p.m.	Luncheon at home.
3 p.m.	Short siesta.
4 p.m.	Second war mission, similar to that of the morning.
6.30 p.m.	Cinema. Old but fine film of Katharine Hepburn.
9 p.m.	Aperitif at the Bar Basque. A good 'Scotch'. Animated scene.
10.15 p.m.	Dinner at Nicolasa's, war songs, company, enthusiasm . . .[1]

Ansaldo here reflected the most dramatic side to the civil war, since the air continued still to be one part of war where brave or clever individuals fighting in single combat could have an effect. In the course of the war, a series of nationalist air heroes had made great reputations: Carlos de Haya, a giant, who had flown Junkers most of 1937, and who was shot down by a Chato in early 1938, after 300 sorties; Angel Salas Larrazábal, who had 618 sorties in the war, including 49 aerial combats – the highest figure for pilots on his side; and, the most famous of all, Joaquín García Morato, who had 511 sorties, 56 combats, and shot down 40 enemy aircraft. Small, brave, sympathetic, García Morato was the hero of the nationalist aviation.[2]

If 'heroes' had come to the papers, saints were back in the schools. The year 1937 had seen the rehabilitation of religious teaching in schools. In April, all schools were ordered to have images of the Virgin. All pupils were, as in the past, before the coming of the republic, to repeat, on reaching and leaving school, an Ave María. The crucifix reappeared in the schoolrooms. Staff and pupils were obliged to go to mass on festivals. Readings from the gospel were to be given once a week. The catholic church permeated every aspect of Spanish nationalist culture. Monsignor Antoniutti, the new apostolic delegate, had resolved many problems of the relations between church and state in Spain: thus Cardinal Segura, expelled from the

1. Ansaldo, p. 74. 2. J. Salas, pp. 458, 459 and 462–3.

republic as primate, returned as archbishop of Seville, after the death of Archbishop Ilundaín. Segura was, from the start, almost as intransigent to the new Franco régime as he had been with the republic, refusing, for example, to have the names of dead falangists put on the cathedral walls, and holding himself aloof from the collective madness of war propaganda.

War brought many radical changes. A decree of 7 October obliged all fit women between the ages of seventeen and thirty-five who were not occupied by their families, war-work, or hospital duties, to undertake social service. A certificate of social service became essential to secure employment for Spanish women. The war thus brought change to women among nationalists, as well as republicans, as occurred during all wars of the century. 'Women in the service of Spain', '*Frentes y hospitales*', 'Work of assistance to the Front', were some of the organizations to which eager women lent their labour, encouraged by slogans that told them that each stitch was a minor victory against the cold which tortured those at the front.

Largely under German inspiration, the nationalist régime was developing the ideology-less, aseptic 'interventionism' of the First World War: permission had to be sought to set up new factories, the function of the state was defined as to 'discipline production', even if banks and public companies were relieved of the need to hold shareholders' meetings, or ensure a public audit of their books. Factories concerned with war production, including the steel and iron works in the Basque country, were placed under military control, and made to supply the armies with the cutlery, plates, uniforms needed, as well as war material. Food, soap and textiles were 'syndicalized', in the so-called vertical syndicates, under the direction of the state. No strikes or collective bargaining were permitted. Industry was reorganized in branches according to category. Nationalist agricultural policy was the work of a national wheat council, the SNT (Servicio Nacional del Trigo), and then the SNRET (Servicio Nacional de Reforma Económico Social de la Tierra), set up respectively in August 1937 and April 1938. The first sought to control prices and distribution of wheat and other agricultural produce. Sales by farmers were prohibited; the SNT bought produce from farmers at fixed rates, reselling it to authorized millers or bakers. Cultivation of land over and above the previous year's harvest was banned – a measure which led some farmers to close production. Even so, wheat was exported to Germany. Since, during 1937, more and more of the republic was captured, the surplus disappeared. Prices of bread were nevertheless stable. Oil, fruit, meat and some other foods were similarly organized. The SNRET was intended to reform agriculture by irrigation, modernization and mechanization, not redistribution. Another task was to hand back land to its old owners, according to a suspension of the institute and laws of agrarian reform. Was this a totalitarian state? Its enemies said so, as did some of its own friends. Father Menéndez Reigada, for example, wrote a catechism in which one exchange ran, in answer to this very question, 'The Spanish state is totalitarian if one understands that word correctly'. 'But what is a totalitarian state?' 'A totalitarian state is one in which the state must intervene in all manifestations of social life . . .'[1]

*

The nationalist army now numbered 500,000 men. This was less than the republican army at the same time. Some eleven classes of reserves had been called up. These men included not only deserters from the republic, but many captured in the republican zone, even soldiers, and then made to change sides. In the winter of 1937–8, all these troops had mostly become reorganized into divisions. They slowly lost most of the territorial significance of their regional names. Although there was conscription, the number of volunteers was great: perhaps 100,000 Carlists, and over 200,000 falangists.[2] These large forces were still organized in three main assemblies: the Army of the North, under Dávila; of the Centre, under Saliquet; and of the South, under Queipo de Llano. Two hundred battalions and seventy batteries (commanded by General Orgaz, the efficient organizer of military academies) formed the reserve.

Since the nationalists' material was bought abroad, there was no need of local arms factories (apart from explosive and ammunition plants), but Hispano Suiza had established a new factory in Seville, which dealt with repairs to, and reconstruction of, the Fiat fighters, and, of course, the arms and explosives factories of the north made a substantial contribution to reducing the régime's debt to Germany.[3]

1. *Catecismo patriótico español* (Salamanca, no date).

2. See De la Cierva in Carr, *The Republic*, p. 200.

3. See Jesús Salas, p. 339.

Forty thousand of the nationalist troops were at this time probably Moroccan, a similar number Italian, while the German personnel perhaps numbered 5,000. But those 5,000 were important out of all proportion to numbers. The Army of Africa, both Foreign Legion and *Regulares*, were now divided up among the rest of the army. While the commanders who had made their name in the advance on Madrid remained in the central zone, those responsible for the victories in the north, such as García Valiño or Alonso Vega, were high in the list of potential commanders of armies.

The nationalist command had also by this time a powerful intelligence section, headed by Colonel José Ungría, who had been on Miaja's staff in Madrid until the war, and who had subsequently escaped from the capital. A sometime student of the École Supérieure de la Guerre at Paris, and military attaché there in the early 1930s, Ungría brought together all the separate intelligence services of the nationalists, Fifth Columnists, and foreign agents into a single organization at first known as the SIM (Servicio de Información Militar), and then the SIPM (Servicio de Información y Policía Militar) established in November 1937.[1] This concerned itself with espionage and counter-espionage as well as intelligence. By mid-1938, it had as many as 30,000 people working for it, with spies in the officers' school at Barajas in Madrid, as well as several spy rings in Catalonia, run by secret falangists and monarchists. Over a hundred people were said later to have passed daily between Catalonia and France to give information.[2] (The republic's military intelligence was headed by the confusingly similarly named Colonel Domingo Hungría, who commanded the 14th Army Corps of '*guerrilleros*' which was specially active behind the nationalist lines in the autumn of 1937. There was, however, no urban guerrilla movement in such cities as Saragossa, Burgos or Seville: the activities of these commandos, apparently with the Russian Colonel Rokossovsky as adviser, were confined to roads, railways lines and rural communications.)[3]

1. The SIFNE of Bertrán y Musitú was merged with the SIPM in February 1938.

2. Cf. J. M. Fontana, *Los Catalanes en la guerra de España* (Madrid, 1951), pp. 161–2 for the spy rings of Luis Canos, José María Velat, Manolo Bustenga and Carlos Carranceja; pp. 336–7 for the story of Clariana, the double spy, shot in Irún.

3. See Palacio Atard, *La quinta columna*, p. 261f; 'El Campesino' alleges Rokossovsky's role, otherwise undocumented.

By 1938, many people were escaping from the republican zone as much out of opportunism as from idealism. These persons might receive the question 'Why did you not cross before?' on their arrival at Irún. Such people were carefully investigated. So were those who crossed from the republican front to the other side. If they had no friend or relation who could vouch for them, they might easily pass months or even years in labour battalions, working for 2 pesetas a day.[1] On the other hand, large numbers of accepted refugees were to be found in all the large cities of nationalist Spain, battening on relations and reinforcing the prejudices of the authorities.

Endlessly throughout 1937, all manner of slogans had been flung at Spaniards between Cádiz and Hendaye. The blue shirt of the Falange received eulogies from Giménez Caballero, poems on 'imperium' were written by Pemán, innumerable books exultantly described days at the front. What too would Francoist Spain have been like without 'For Spain, one, great and free', 'For God and Caesar', 'For the Fatherland, Bread and Justice' or 'We have the vocation of empire'? 'Franco commands, Spain obeys' ran another motto, and a poster showed Franco saying 'My hand will be firm, my pulse will not tremble'. The new triptych 'Service, Brotherhood, Hierarchy' took the place of 'Liberty, Equality and Fraternity'. In the newspapers or in books, the men of the republic were reviled, and Joaquín Arrarás's comments upon stolen sections from Azaña's diaries of 1932 and 1933 set, in *ABC* and, later, in book form, a new low standard of personal invective. The falangist magazine *Fotos* published a gallery of 'illustrious savages' (the politicians of the republic), while the Navarrese civil governor of Corunna, José María de Arellano, made arrangements for the removal from all documents, from the register of births to the list of the college of lawyers, of the 'hateful name' of Santiago Casares Quiroga.[2] Anti-semitism, latent behind right-wing Spanish propaganda for years, grew steadily out of sympathy with Germany, despite the lack of grounds for it; Juan Pujol, the journalist who was once a friend of Azaña's, and was press chief to Franco for a time, embarked on the dangerous argument that Companys was the descendant of converted jews, while newspapers

1. Abella, p. 134.
2. *ibid.*, p. 268.

even alleged that 'an enormous part of the Catalan population is jewish'.[1]

*

On 7 March, the nationalists promulgated their 'labour charter'. This marked the culmination of innumerable discussions within the régime, and was very much a compromise.[2] Many of the proposals sounded admirable. Conditions of work were to be regulated. A minimum wage was guaranteed, accompanied by social insurance, family allowances, and holidays with pay. Labourers' wages were raised, and peasant families were to be allowed a plot of land adequate for their primary needs. Tenant farmers were to be safeguarded against eviction. Most of these aims remained, however, in the realm of aspiration. In practice, as in Italy under Mussolini, the old oligarchy never lost their economic mastery, despite the newness of their government's pretensions. The only sections of the charter which were fully applied were those guaranteeing private property and threatening that acts which disturbed production would be regarded as treason.

The economic life of the country was to be controlled by the 'vertical' syndicates, whose officials were to be falangists. These prescribed a hierarchy of assemblies rising from local corporations in each district to five national chambers of agriculture, shipping, industry and commerce, public and national service, and culture, and ultimately to a national corporative assembly. These ideas were influenced by Mussolini's *Carta del Lavoro* of 1927 and by Hitler's Law of National Labour of 1934, but their effect on the economy was, in fact, slight. Few businessmen paid more than token attention to the whole scheme. More important was the Press Law of April, by which the state assumed control of the Spanish nationalist press. Only registered journalists would be allowed to practise this craft, just as

1. Pujol, *Cuando Israel Manda*, in *ABC de Sevilla*, 20 December 1936, qu. *Catalunya sota el règim franquista*, vol. I (Paris, 1973), p. 136; *Domingo* (San Sebastián), 21 March 1937.

2. The origins of the labour charter are discussed in Payne, *Falange*, pp. 186–7. The author was González Bueno, with help from Ridruejo and other young falangists.

only registered newspapers and periodicals would be allowed to appear. *El Debate*, for example, the main paper of the CEDA, would never appear again, nor would the Carlists' *Época*. The press would be an instrument of the state. Article 18 of the Press Law forbade all writings which threatened the prestige of the régime, placed obstacles in the way of the government, or 'stirs pernicious ideas among the intellectually weak'. This broad definition secured the subservience of the press for many years. Monarchist, militarist, clerical and extreme conservative ideas were all more and more expressed with a coating of fascism.

Another innovation was 'Plan 38', an educational reform introduced by Sáinz Rodríguez, the new minister. It put Spanish secondary state education firmly under the Church, leaving the question of universities to be decided after the war. (Universities were suspended during the war on both sides, along with other luxuries.) The obese Sáinz Rodríguez did not last long as minister of education. His indiscretions were great; greater still was his reluctance to apologize for them. He was dismissed, and followed others of a different epoch, such as Lerroux and Gil Robles, into a Lusitanian exile. Under Sáinz Rodríguez, state primary education had been formally reorganized, beginning with a purge of teachers and a substitution of traditional courses by four elements – those of religion, patriotism, civic and physical education. Physical education was supposed to concentrate on specifically Spanish sports. The details of the other three elements were decided by the teacher. Hence, the purge was the most important part of the programme. In teaching, as in politics, it is the man who counts, not the theory. School-teachers who practised in the new Spain of Ferdinand and Isabella had to make a sworn declaration to the glorious national movement, had to swear that they had never belonged to any political party associated with the Popular Front, nor to any separatist party, nor to the old teachers' association affiliated to the UGT. If they had spent any time in the 'red zone', they had to make an affidavit describing their activities there. They had also to procure a certificate of their religious, moral, political and social conduct before, and during, the national movement, by their parish priest, as well as a similar certificate, on the same subject, from the commander of the local garrison or 'delegate of public order'. A report of the mayor had also to be procured, and the would-be teacher had finally to appear personally before an academic, civil or military interviewing authority. Having passed these hurdles, the teacher underwent a course telling him the true principles of education.[1] Practice, no doubt, made these difficulties more easily overcome than might seem likely, but almost nobody of left-wing or liberal inclination was to be found in the nationalist state's educational service in 1938.

The fight against frivolity, and France, continued: 'Spanish Woman', a manifesto of the 'catholic ladies of Seville', appealed,

In these grave moments for the country, your way of life cannot be that of frivolity, but austerity; your place is not in the theatres, the *paseos*, the cafés, but in the church and the hearth. Your ornaments cannot be inspired by the dirty fashions of treacherous and jewish France, but the modesty and *pudeur* of christian morality ... Your duty is not to procure for yourself an easy life, but to educate your children, sacrificing your pleasures and helping Spain.[2]

Just as, in republican Spain, conservatism, reaction and christianity survived in embassies, in hiding, or in inconspicuous discretion, so did revolution and radicalism continue within the shadows of those well protected castles, half ancient, half new, which were the institutions of the Francoist state. Political life survived after a fashion in prisons, and one should not forget the scenes such as described by the Basque priest, Father Gumersindo de Estella, in his prison diary:

3 February, 1938. Thursday. Present at two executions. One called Francisco Espinosa, native of Callosa de Segura (Alicante). Soldier of the republican army, fallen prisoner at Celadas (Teruel). Did not wish to confess. He said that religion had been falsified by the rightists, that he who killed by shot would die by shot, and that soon the rightists would all be killed themselves. The other was a man of thirty, good physique. Made prisoner at Santoña. Native of Funes (Navarre), but lived in San Sebastián. Confessed, heard mass and received communion. This unhappy man had been in the labour battalion in San Juan de Mozarrifar, he said something against Franco, was detained and condemned to death. Felt panic before the idea of death and above all on seeing the picket of soldiers. Begged for chloroform, but they did not give it to him. They were both executed at seven in the morning in the cemetery. This last was called Florián Lacarra Iñigo.[3]

1. Abella, pp. 308–9. 2. Qu. Abella, p. 325. 3. *El clero vasco*, vol. II, p. 293.

Franco had few political difficulties but his régime did have some with his allies. Admittedly, the Italians in Spain established good relations with the Spaniards. Common temperament and similarity of tongue made for frequent close associations, including illegitimate children and marriages. Nevertheless, the Mixed Brigades of Italians and Spaniards, much used after Guadalajara, all met difficulties from a reluctance of the Italians to give up pasta, and difficulties over language in commands.[1] Ciano's secretary, Anfuso, returned from Spain in mid-October to tell his master that the Italian troops in Spain were tired, and that Franco could hardly wait for them to go away, though he needed Italian artillery and aircraft. Ciano supposed that the Generalissimo 'must be jealous of our success'.[2] The arrogance of the Italian officers and troops, however, especially in San Sebastián, angered all Spaniards with whom they came into contact. There was also a squabble in respect of the bill for the two submarines sold by Italy to Spain, which had not been paid.[3] These difficulties, however, were smoothed over by the dispatch of 100,000 tons of Spanish steel to Italy.[4] But Mussolini was still owed 3 billion lire for war material at the end of November, with no prospect for an early settlement of the debt.[5] He told Ribbentrop on 6 November

> We have established at Palma a naval and an air base: we keep ships permanently stationed there and have three air fields. We intend to remain in that situation as long as possible . . . Franco must come to understand that, even after our eventual evacuation, Mallorca must remain an Italian base in the event of a war with France [so that] . . . not one Negro will be able to cross from Africa to France by the Mediterranean route.[6]

Presumably this assurance in respect of a European war assuaged the Duce for his unsatisfactory ally in Burgos. There was, indeed, now also a nationalist naval base at Palma, directed by Admiral Moreno, concerned with preventing Russian ships reaching Spain. The three nationalist cruisers were based at Palma, as were four destroyers bought in Italy, and the old *Velasco*; three gunboats, two mine-sweepers, the two submarines bought from Italy and the Italian 'legionary' submarines. This base in the coming year was able to assure General Franco an almost complete naval blockade of the

1. Abella, pp. 291–2.
2. Ciano, *Diaries 1937–8*, p. 22.
3. *ibid.*, p. 32.
4. *ibid.*, p. 37.
5. *G D*, pp. 512–16.
6. Ciano, *Diplomatic Papers*, p. 144.

republican coast. There were also in Palma some fifty aircraft: a squadron of Heinkels from the Condor Legion, an Italian group of Savoias and Fiat fighters, and a Spanish squadron.

The nationalists had some difficulties too with their German friends. These were not personal ones, for the latter kept to themselves. The Condor Legion even lived in a special train, which they moved from front to front to avoid having to mix with Spaniards. They might occasionally sally out to reserved tables in restaurants, or special brothels, but few knew Spanish. The instructors in military academies became better acquainted with Spain. Germany was now affording to the nationalists credit of 10 million reichsmarks a month, of which 4 million was for war materials, 5½ million for other exports, and 350,000 cash credit. There was no sign that the Spaniards were in any hurry to pay these debts. Also, German financiers were becoming fearful lest Britain should buy the iron. The officials of HISMA and ROWAK, under Bernhardt's influence, had been concentrating their attention on the Montana project, designed to guarantee to Germany a steady supply of Spanish minerals. The project aimed at German control of seventy-three Spanish mines. The new German ambassador, the Baron von Stohrer (who succeeded the unpopular Faupel), advised that German interest in Spain must be 'the deep penetration' into agriculture and mining. The former question solved itself since, whatever happened, Spain would have to find a market. The mines, on the other hand, were more difficult. Upon them, all German diplomatic, military, and cultural efforts had to be based.[1] 'The solution', he added, 'would have to be forced, if it could not be obtained by reasonable means.' On 9 October, however, a decree issued by the Spaniards nullified all titles to mines obtained since the start of the civil war. The Germans anxiously asked the meaning of this. Nicolás Franco (who was still in office then) replied that only a fully-fledged Spanish nationalist government could conclude so important a matter as the Montana project. Nothing now was done. Göring and Bernhardt became impatient.[2]

1. Stohrer, a professional diplomat, had been intended as ambassador in Madrid in early 1936. He had served there before, as a secretary during the First World War, busy sabotaging allied interests. He was a brilliant linguist, a tall commanding figure 'with a remarkable knowledge of Spain' (Hoare, p. 44).

2. For all the above see *G D*, pp. 496–503 and 541–2.

Impatience changed to suspicion when Britain, the rival in peace and the probable enemy in war, exchanged diplomatic agents with Franco – for commercial reasons: for Sir Henry Chilton retired, leaving the chargé in Valencia, John Leche, to be named minister with the republic. Sir Robert Hodgson (whose knowledge of Spanish and experience as an official agent in Russia in 1921 recommended him for the difficult post) went to Burgos on 16 November as agent.[1] The British cabinet hoped that, in addition to looking after commercial interests, Hodgson's mission would secure information about German and Italian military experiments.[2] The Duke of Alba went to London in a complementary capacity. Eden was hostile to the idea of receiving Alba and only consented when the Spaniards demanded his reasons – which he did not give.[3] (After some months, Alba and his staff became legally diplomats at least: in March 1938, the Duke was excused from a legal requirement to take a driving test, on Foreign Office application.)[4] Furthermore, in November, a British naval vessel, the *Galatea*, made a courtesy visit to Beigbeder, high commissioner of Morocco, and the red and gold flag was thus hoisted onto a British ship: a similar thing had also occurred in Palma. On 2 December, Stohrer complained to Franco that England had received considerable concessions from Spain, and demanded an explanation, for Germany wanted the lion's share of the ore of Bilbao and Asturias, as well as an unlimited concession to buy scrap. Otherwise, she would have to 're-examine her attitude' to the Spanish nationalist government. Franco described the German allegations as 'fabrications', saying that he was surprised that Britain paid so little attention to Spain. The delay over the Montana project, said Franco,

1. The British mission was unpopular. 'It was assumed', Sir Robert Hodgson said, 'that we were against the movement and "*España, una, grande, libre*". This was proved by our obstinate denial of belligerent rights and by the continued description in the British press of the nationalists as insurgents.' Hodgson did not have an interview with Franco till 1 February 1938. (Sir Robert Hodgson, *Spain Resurgent*, London, 1953, pp. 84–5.)

2. *CAB*, 12(37). Hodgson's mission had been suggested first in March.

3. The French government did not establish even these limited relations with nationalist Spain. All they did, as *L'Action française* ironically commented, was to restore the *Sud Express*, the main daily train from Paris to Hendaye. But Charles Maurras was received in Salamanca 'not even as a diplomat, but as a Head of State'.

4. *News Chronicle*, 30 March 1938, qu. Watkins, p. 68.

was due to his lack of copies of previous laws, of archives, and of trained officials.[1] Still, the question of a formal contract was left to *mañana.*

At the New Year, Franco received a personal message from Mussolini. The Duce wanted to continue to send Italian aid, but could it not be used in accordance with its quality – in engagements in which decisive results could be expected?[2]

The Baron von Stohrer was, meantime, telling Berlin that, if Franco were to win by military methods, Germany would have to send not only more material, but many more technicians and officers with general staff training.[3] Ciano was worried. He feared 'a republican offensive to push back the whole nationalist front'. What would happen to the Italian expeditionary force then? 'Either we strike the first blow,' he mused on 14 January, 'or skilfully disengage ourselves, and rest content with having inscribed on our banners the victories of Málaga and Santander.'[4] By the end of the month, an air of frenzy had come over Ciano – preoccupied as he was with Hitler's designs on Austria, and his master's more distant ones on Albania. 'We *must*', he wrote, 'get to the end of the Spanish adventure.'

In Burgos, the German diplomats argued about their mines. Gómez Jordana told Stohrer on 25 January that he had to stand by old Spanish laws in dealing with the matter because 'the mentality of the Spanish people is such that it tends to call members of previous governments to account for its actions . . . One never knows what might happen,' he added, with the wisdom of an old monarchist. Sangroniz – this was before his appointment to Caracas – told the ambassador the next day:

> I want to tell you that it was not correct to arrange the matter as Germany wanted to do. It was a psychological error to alarm and, in a sense, mobilize the interested parties, and the entire Spanish administration, by the purchase of numerous mining rights. This aroused opposition, which would not have appeared if Germany had purchased only a few to begin with.[5]

It was not the first time that the German nation had been discomfited by greed.

1. *GD*, p. 522. 2. Ciano, *Diaries 1937–8*, p. 62. 3. *GD*, p. 553.

4. Ciano, *Diaries 1937–8*, pp. 64–5. By then the republicans had captured Teruel. See below, p. 792.

5. *GD*, p. 470.

The Germans and Italians were not the only ones who, at the instructions of their governments, as much as from their own will, came to nationalist Spain to fight. Some volunteers – there were probably 1,000 of them in the winter of 1937–8 – came from Portugal and, from the ranks of the restless Right in the rest of Europe, others came too, anxious to fight against communism, or for religion, or monarchy, or the 'immense salutary revolution' that one of the characters in the French fascist Drieu la Rochelle's novel *Gilles* saw the Francoist cause to be.[1] These included French *camelots du roi* such as the Baron de la Guillonière, who had enlisted with the Carlists and who died in Vizcaya; or Colonel Bonneville de Marsagny, who, with a number of white Russians, enlisted in the Legion; and one or two Englishmen or Irishmen, some remaining from O'Duffy's ill-fated blue shirts, some volunteers on their own.[2] There were also volunteers from Spanish America. Finally, there were the Moroccans, whose role in the nationalist army continued to be important.

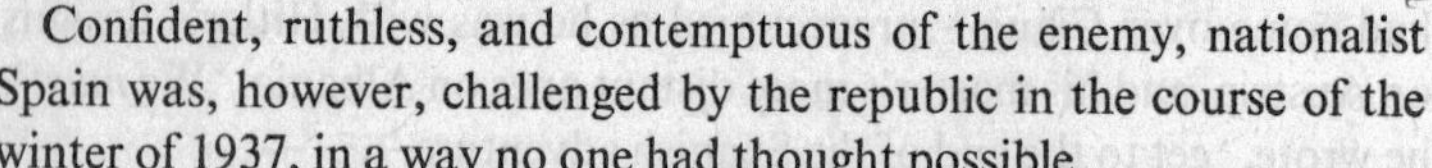

Confident, ruthless, and contemptuous of the enemy, nationalist Spain was, however, challenged by the republic in the course of the winter of 1937, in a way no one had thought possible.

1. Drieu la Rochelle, *Gilles* (Paris, 1967), p. 490.

2. Such as Captains Fitzpatrick, Nangle and Peter Kemp whose *Mine were of Trouble* (London, 1957) is an excellent picture of life in the Legion.

43

The republic faces a second winter of war – Azaña, Prieto, Negrín – the eclipse of separatism – Prieto and the communists – the armed forces – Negrín and the communists

WHERE the new politicians among the nationalists were dreaming of fascist innovation inspired by the remote past, the old statesmen of the republic exchanged doomed memories. Where did it all go wrong, would it have been different if Alcalá Zamora had not been President, was it the fault of Lerroux? The nationalists were optimistic; pessimism was widespread in the republic.

Azaña had been gloomy since the war began. By the autumn of 1937, he believed defeat to be inevitable and had begun even to discuss, with old collaborators such as Martínez Barrio, what ought to be done in such circumstances. Mexico might be friendly, but one could not imagine the emigration there of a million or two million republicans or socialists. France might close the frontier. 'For lack of a far-sighted policy, are we to remain here, abandoned to the horrible reprisals of the rebels?' Martínez Barrio believed that, for the working class, if all were lost, the defeat would be a temporary setback and, in one way or another, they would pursue their class interests: 'For the republicans, it would be the end of everything, since one cannot imagine that, in twenty or even thirty years, a liberal republic will return to Spain; and thank God if we can find a corner of the world in which to finish our lives.' It was all very well to speak of a Numantian spirit but, at the last minute, the 'Numantinos' would disappear.[1] Azaña was looking for peace, but a real peace; 'Because, one does not have to rack one's brains to imagine a funereal peace reigning over Spain after the defeat of the republic, and the execution of the republicans.' Thus Azaña spoke to Giral. All these politicians found themselves contemptuous of, but uncertain how to

1. Numantia, a hill fortress near Soria, resisted Rome until the end in 134–133 B.C. In fact, there was no possible escape for the defenders since Scipio Aemilianus had drawn continuous entrenchments round the town.

treat, the 'unquenchable optimism', as Giral put it, of Negrín. Azaña, Martínez Barrio, Prieto, perhaps all the ministers, except for Negrín and the communists, believed that the republic could now not win the war militarily, but they realized that they could not abandon those millions of Spaniards, who supported the republic, to their fate. The persecution after the end of the fighting in the north, Azaña and Martínez Barrio agreed, was a prefigurement of what would happen in the rest of Spain, if the republic failed to negotiate peace. Many older republicans were even gloomier: Nicolau d'Olwer, the first finance minister of the republic in 1931, now thought that what suited Spain best was a régime such as that of Primo de Rivera. 'What would happen', Pi y Súñer, the Catalan councillor for education, wondered nervously, 'if the nationalists were to make a tremendous offensive with all their forces and enter Catalonia? Have the general staff envisaged that?' Martínez Barrio thought that appeals to fight 'to the last man and to the last peseta', had less and less appeal. Everyone was tired of the war, thought Giral, a tireless foreign minister who brought efficiency to a ministry which Alvarez del Vayo had left in such disorder that, to begin with, Giral had had, he said, to look in the newspapers for details of the British control plan (Azaña reassured him such things were a 'tradition of the house').[1]

Prieto too was weary of the war, of the politics of socialism, of his new enemies and his old enemies alike: 'I don't care if the two parties merge or not,' he once told Hernández and Uribe, 'because once the war is over, in whatever way, I have resolved, if I save my skin, I shall finish my political life once and for all. I will take a passage in the first boat which sets out for the furthermost Spanish-speaking country.'[2]

Negrín, with his 'tranquil audacity', alone had any hope. He believed that even a compromise peace could only be achieved if there were a plainly visible possibility of victory. The French frontier was now open to the passage of arms, due, Negrín believed, to his own diplomacy. A good linguist and well-travelled man, he saw the salvation of the republic in Geneva, Paris or London. His association with Azaña was complicated, but the constitutional relationship was not easy. In the autumn of 1937, they seemed personal friends. The

1. All the above conversations derive from Azaña's diaries.

2. Azaña, vol. IV, p. 786.

two agreed on policy towards Catalonia, and towards the CNT, but, while Negrín was the motor of the war effort, Azaña was only a gilded observer, his role limited to disputing with Negrín over nominations for appointments. Years before, when dining with Azaña and Araquistain, Negrín had said that Spain 'required a dictatorship under democratic rules which would prepare the people for the future'.[1] Now he had his chance to put this idea into effect. He governed by decree. Decrees had to be counter-signed by Azaña. That did not ensure the survival of democracy, for there was no means of challenging the government, save by the use of pressure groups; or by intimidation. The occasional meetings of the Cortes were lifeless. The press, in Azaña's admission, appeared written all by the same hand, usually 'combative and untutored'.[2]

Negrín's first priority was to end the geographical disunion of the republic. By late 1937, much had been done in this respect, but the civil governor of Cuenca could still complain that his province was like the Rif: 'there are no roads, no telephones. I cannot get into touch with many *pueblos*. The province is roamed by columns of irregular militiamen.' Two of this governor's predecessors had fled their posts, afraid for their lives. A number of anarchist columns battened on the *pueblos*, making no contribution to the war. The governor began his tenure of office camping in an official residence from which all the furniture had been stolen.[3] General Hernández Saravia found, if anything, a greater confusion a little to the north, when he took over the command at Teruel, with his new Army of the Levante.[4]

The greatest challenge to republican authority was still that offered by the Catalans, although the 'normalization' of life in Catalonia had gone on throughout the year: as councillor for the interior in the *Generalidad*, Antonio Sbert had gone far to re-establish good standards of public order, while Pi y Súñer (councillor for education) and Bosch Gimpera (councillor for justice and in charge of higher education) revived the rule of reason in their respective spheres, despite brushes with the central government. All sentences of death by any court were now reviewed by the government. Courts of justice, high courts, courts of appeal, the College of Lawyers, the College of Public

1. Azaña, vol. IV, p. 107.
2. *ibid.*, p. 794.
3. Gómez Lobo to Azaña, *op. cit.*, p. 748.
4. See below, p. 788.

Notaries, the Registry General of Births, Deaths, and Marriages, were all operating. A restoration of bourgeois standards, such as had driven socialists and anarchists to revolution? No doubt, but now more and more people were realizing, too late, that the old, despised bourgeois republic was the best friend that they would ever have.[1] Sentences given in 1936 were reconsidered, while the crimes of the early days of the war began also to be investigated, to the fury of the CNT, who found such prominent anarchists of the revolutionary summer as Barriobero, Aurelio Fernández and even Sánchez Roca, García Oliver's under-secretary when he had been minister of justice, under interrogation and even in gaol.[2] The communists also complained when the Catalan police interrogated members of the PSUC. Vidiella, the communist councillor for labour, protested that the police could not investigate such 'revolutionary acts'. Nevertheless, they continued to do so, though communists found it easier to escape retribution than anarchists did.

Still, Catalonia remained a state within a state. Azaña could not forgive the Catalans' capture, when the republican government had been so weak, of so many undertakings which belonged to the Spanish state;[3] and Negrín believed that the intervention, not just of the state but the Spanish state, was essential if Catalan industry were to make its maximum contribution to the war effort. As it was, despite Companys's subsequent assurances in a long letter of 13 December, Catalan industry was well below the levels that it had attained before 1936.[4] Even the metallurgical sector of industry, which had experienced a spurt forward in the winter of 1936–7, had fallen back in 1937–8 to a level not only lower than what it had been in early 1936, but below that level which it had reached in the worst years of the depression. The overall index of industrial production in November 1937 was scarcely half that of June 1936.[5] The figures in the war industries could not, of course, be compared with pre-war indices, but in almost every sector the production was less than it

1. This sad image is Christopher Seton-Watson's in relation to pre-fascist Italy.
2. García Oliver demanded to the state prosecutor, Eduardo Ortega y Gasset, that Fernández be released, adding 'we do not make requests twice'. Ortega fled the country.
3. See above, p. 299.
4. Qu. in Ossorio y Gallardo, p. 207.
5. 53 compared to 98 in June 1936, with January 1936 as 100 (Bricall, p. 96).

could have been, and in most instances far less.[1] Shortage of raw materials and the irregularity of supply, as well as a market shrinking with every rebel victory, was responsible, while Comorera, the communist councillor for industry, had ensured that the Catalan government delegate played a bigger and bigger part in all factory committees. Negrín was, however, determined to settle the problem of authority once and for all and, with the support of Azaña, though against the arguments of the communists, decided to move the seat of government from Valencia to Barcelona.[2]

This was done in the autumn of 1937, with deliberate lack of consideration for Catalan susceptibilities. Negrín requisitioned buildings of his choice as ministries, ignored Companys's offers to provide accommodation, and avoided all contact, written or personal, with him. He even stopped Companys from going to the opera by denying him a seat in the presidential box at the Liceo. Negrín established himself in the Pedralbes Palace, while Azaña followed him back to the Catalan capital.

These actions infuriated the *Generalidad*. They were to them the culmination of 'a sustained and systematic drive to diminish the authority of the Catalan government'. On all other matters, the government, they thought, was vacillating, and disorganized; it only seemed firm when it had to do with Catalonia. Young Catalans at the front did not know for whom they were fighting. These were the views of Carlos Pi y Súñer to Azaña in a formal complaint in September. The state, Pi went on, owed Catalonia 70 million pesetas for war services. Catalonia paid for the army of Aragon, but received no recompense, Catalan police had been dismissed, while a special intelligence service had been introduced which adversely affected Catalonia. The Catalans regarded the Army of the East as one of occupation, and feared that the communists were planning a military dictatorship. The heroic myth of Madrid's resistance, they complained, was simply used to justify centralism. The state's services of public order in Catalonia were not coordinated with the activities of the Catalan government. At the same time, the communists in Catalonia were supported by the central government, and tried to absorb everything. The Catalans wished to be assured that, once peace were re-established, they could

1. Bricall, p. 70.
2. See e.g. Azaña, *op. cit.*, p. 760.

recover their own régime.[1] Azaña assured his visitor that nobody had thought of suppressing the *Generalidad*. The once agile Companys seemed, however, at this time, at the end of his resources: to most people, he seemed ill, to Prieto mad, to Negrín, worthless. He protested his desire to resign but his friends assured him that there was nobody to replace, him; and, indeed, Tarradellas and Comorera, his closest collaborators, seemed to Prieto 'miserable *canaille* incapable of a noble reaction',[2] though they were competent men.

The Basques, after their defeat, were in no position to give similar trouble. Their leaders had moved, it is true, to Barcelona and had set up an 'emigré government'. Azaña laughed disdainfully at Aguirre's airs, particularly when he spoke of a 'Barcelona–Bilbao Axis', to coordinate the aims of the separatists. But a consequence of the transfer was that catholic services were again held in the Catalan capital, at the Basque headquarters. In July, Irujo, minister of justice, proposed the reopening of churches. The council of ministers gave permission for services to be held in private homes licensed by the government. In October, the ministry of finance excepted religious silver and jewels from the law providing for the delivery of all other precious stones and materials to the government to help finance the war – though, admittedly, much of it had already gone. By the winter, 2,000 priests had returned from exile to Barcelona. These went about in lay dress, though (from March 1938) they were not, as heretofore, called up for military service, but drafted into the medical corps. The Vatican, additionally, did not wish the formal re-establishment of religion in the republic. That might have weakened the catholic purity of Franco's cause. Cardinal Vidal i Barraquer was apparently willing to return to his cathedral at Tarragona but was refused permission by the Pope to do so.[3]

*

The triumph of Negrín and the central government over the Catalans left behind frustration. Prieto was concerned with a similar problem

1. Carlos Pi y Súñer to Azaña, in Azaña, vol. IV, pp. 790–801.

2. *op. cit.*, p. 802; also p. 760.

3. Alvarez del Vayo, *The Last Optimist*, pp. 317–18. The vicar-general of Barcelona forbade the opening of any church and allowed it to be known that he would refuse licences to priests who heard mass. (Evidence of Señor Irujo.)

of authority. It will be remembered that Prieto, in his determination to oust Largo Caballero, had been willing to use the communist party to that end. He had even for a time advocated the unification of the socialist and communist parties. The courage, realism, and reliability in war of the communist party, during the winter of 1936–7, had led him to a tolerant attitude to the communists once he knew that he and they saw eye-to-eye over Largo, and indeed over the anarchists. Nevertheless, the affair of Nin and the POUM had shattered this confidence. Several incidents during his first month at the combined ministries of defence had led him to conclude as early as the end of June that communist policy was to capture 'all the resources of the Spanish state'.[1] Prieto clashed with the Russian advisers over the disposal of a Messerschmitt 109 which had fallen almost undamaged into republican hands. The communists wanted to give this aircraft to the Russians, while Prieto insisted on showing it first to the French.[2] During the Aragon offensive in August, Prieto complained of the manners, as of the competence, of the Russian advisers, and found himself thwarted, as has been seen, by Russian behaviour over the destroyer *Ciscar* at Gijón.[3] In the autumn, Prieto began a considered manoeuvre to restrict communist influence, even in the army: thus, officers were forbidden to engage in political proselytization, or to attend party meetings. In November, Alvarez del Vayo was replaced as chief political commissar by a friend of Prieto's, Crescenciano Bilbao. Alvarez del Vayo had made of the commissariat of war an 'almost wholly communist' organization.[4] Many of the commissariats at the fronts were abolished, despite protests by communists. That meant the transfer of Antón, commissar-general of the Army of the Centre, to a regular battalion. This young man, who, before the civil war, had worked as a railway clerk, was secretary of the Madrid party. He was said to be the lover of La Pasionaria, twenty years his senior, and certainly he occupied a house with her and Togliatti in Madrid.[5] Antón was a Spanish workers' leader of the new bureaucratic generation. How different from Julián Ruiz, the Asturian miner whom La Pasionaria had married when young,

1. Azaña, vol. IV, p. 638.
2. *Convulsiones*, vol. II, p. 65f.
3. See above, p. 731.
4. Prieto's words to Azaña, *op. cit.*, p. 638.
5. *Convulsiones*, vol. II, p. 34; Hernández, pp. 99–100; Castro Delgado, p. 201; El Campesino, *Comunista*, p. 86f.

and by whom she had two grown-up sons! Prieto's order caused bad blood between him and La Pasionaria, with the upshot that Antón left his post as commissar but never went to the front. The communist party also dominated the various republican police forces and had the prisons filled with their own special enemies, as well as more genuine enemies of the republic. George Orwell in February 1938, on return from Spain, estimated there to be 3,000 political prisoners in their gaols and probably that is a reasonable estimate if, however, there are taken into account the anarchists and others arrested, as mentioned above, for revolutionary crimes of the early days.[1] Those POUM leaders who, unlike Nin, were still alive, had not yet been brought to trial. Orlov's men were still at work, while, more important still, there was a new counter-espionage body, the SIM (Servicio de Investigación Militar). The purpose of this organization of deserved ill-repute was to restrict the activity of 'uncontrollables', anarchist or otherwise. It was for that reason that Prieto, pressed by Russian 'technicians', agreed to establish the SIM in the first place.[2] Prieto hoped thereby to coordinate all the 'intelligence' services at work in the republic – some run by the army, some by the ministry of the interior, one by the Basques, one by the Catalans – nine, at least, in all.[3] He appointed a socialist friend, Angel Díaz Baza, to be the first SIM chief. That sympathetic man was, however, not the right person to direct a secret service in a civil war. A sometime leader of the left republican youth, Prudencio Sayagües, previously second-in-command, took over provisionally – he, in the early days of the war, had led a reckless counter-espionage service in the war ministry.[4] But problems continued: Prieto ordered the arrest of a communist major of militias, 'El Negus', who had travelled around Catalonia seeking support for a movement to remove Prieto from the ministry of defence. But it turned out, in the end, that it was not the SIM who

1. George Orwell, letter to Raymond Mortimer, 9 February 1938.

2. *Convulsiones*, II, pp. 56–7.

3. Manuel Uribarri, *El SIM de la República* (Havana, 1942). Carlos de Juan, the new director-general of security, did his best to cut the size of, and remove the politics from, the police (there were 4,000 more police in the republic in mid-1937 than there were before the war in the whole Peninsula. Azaña pointed out that the 'problem' was common to both zones, as 'one now refers to them' (*op. cit.*, p. 835).

4. *The General Cause*, p. 161.

carried out the arrest, but the communists, into whose dungeons the offending major passed – and indeed was never heard of again. Prieto was furious.[1] Then came problems over the local chiefs of the SIM. One of the military successes of the war, a socialist intellectual militia officer, once chief of staff to 'Kléber', and commander of a division at Brunete, was named to command the SIM in Madrid. Prieto learned that he had nominated mostly communists to his staff and transferred him back to active service. A Russian 'technician' complained to Prieto. Prieto refused to reinstate the man concerned and his relations with the Russians worsened.[2] The officer was followed in Madrid by Angel Pedrero García, who had been with García Atadell in the odious 'dawn patrol' and, more recently, leader of one of the small counter-espionage forces which the SIM had been founded to get rid of.

The overall director of the SIM after Sayagües was Colonel Uribarri, a socialist officer who had commanded a guerrilla column in the Sierra de Gredos in October 1936 and who had begun the war as a loyal captain of the civil guard in Valencia. He had also been commander on the Toledo front, where he lived, according to Lister, like a feudal baron, 'his headquarters a nest of spies', with daughters of local landlords the sweethearts of his staff.[3] To begin with, he served Prieto loyally in the SIM, describing to his chief how yet another Russian had tried to get him to consult directly with him. Afterwards, the communists seem to have manipulated Uribarri's personality. Exhausted by work, he let the SIM become precisely what Prieto had sought to avoid – a communist political police force. Here, as in so many aspects of the civil war, events played into communist hands. Only they were persistent enough to organize an efficient secret police. At all events, the SIM began soon to employ all the vile tortures of the NKVD: cells were made so small that prisoners could hardly stand, being paved with bricks set on edge. Powerful electric lights were available to dazzle, noises to deafen, baths to freeze, irons

1. Prieto in *Yo y Moscú* (Madrid, 1955), p. 156. No one ever heard what happened to El Negus, even when his policy became that of the party itself.

2. Prieto, *Convulsiones*, vol. II, pp. 22, 57, and *Yo y Moscú*, p. 189. Orlov, still head of the GPU in Spain, thought of assassinating Prieto; he was dissuaded by Hernández (see *Convulsiones*, vol. II, p. 117).

3. Lister, p. 125.

to burn, and clubs to beat. The SIM was responsible for the murder of several conscripted into the republican army, not merely the cowardly and inefficient, but also those unwilling to follow the orders of communist commanders. Local chiefs of the SIM, such as Appellániz in Valencia, or Francés in Andalusia, showed themselves brutal whether or no they were technically communists (Appellániz was an ex-post office official turned policeman). Many of the SIM leaders were members of the socialist communist youth such as Santiago Garcés who ultimately succeeded as the national head of the movement: one of the many whose dubiously legal activities before the war had helped bring the conflict about and to whom responsibility and power brought neither wisdom nor humanity.[1]

It was, however, apparently not the SIM, but a section of the republican army, which was responsible for a distasteful scheme in Madrid. A tunnel had been dug to run from a house in the suburb of Usera towards the nationalist lines. A number of nationalist sympathizers, including several sheltering in embassies, paid to avail themselves of this escape. When they arrived at the tunnel, clutching a few valuables and keepsakes, they were shot down. Sixty-seven people were duped by this tunnel of death.[2]

The SIM's judicial counterpart were the military tribunals established for summary trials of spying and other crimes. The setting up of these bodies led, in January 1938, to the resignation of the Basque-born minister of justice, Irujo. He remained minister without portfolio, being replaced at the ministry of justice by the president of the UGT executive, Ramón González Peña, the hero of Asturias in 1934 and the strong *Prietista* of early 1936. Thereafter, the tribunals worked under summary procedure, without normal guarantees for the defence of the accused. Evidence consisted of reports made by the special police, or the SIM.[3]

1. Martínez Amutio, pp. 211, 228.

2. *The General Cause*, p. 304. The army unit in question was the 36th Mixed Brigade, commanded by Justo López de la Fuente, who, returning to Spain in the 1960s, died in gaol because of this. There was a similar scheme in Russia during their civil war. Cf. Angelica Balabanoff, *Impressions of Lenin* (Ann Arbour, 1964), p. 108.

3. For a description of these arbitrary tribunals on which the ignorant and malevolent often sat as judges, see G. Avilés, *Tribunales rojos* (Barcelona, 1939), *passim*. Hard though such books are to credit, they are impossible to reject.

It is reasonable to denounce the injustice and illegality of these courts, but the plan was that no death sentences were to be carried out save after approval by the cabinet and, by and large, that was held to, except for those shot in the front line for desertion or cowardice in the face of the enemy.[1] During 1938, some 240 death sentences would be passed and the security tribunals passed another 725. But many of these were not carried out. Probably less than 1,000 were shot behind the republican lines in the course of 1938.

*

The republican army now theoretically numbered nearly 750,000. There were 1,500 pieces of artillery, including anti-aircraft guns. This enormous organization cost 400 million pesetas a month, larger than the entire national budget before the war. The non-political, or politically ambiguous, Vicente Rojo, promoted to general in November 1937, was still the efficient, if pessimistic, chief of staff. The Army of the Centre was still commanded by Miaja; that of the Levante, by Hernández Saravia; and that of the East, by Pozas. Two inactive armies, of Andalusia and of Estremadura, were commanded by Colonels Prada and Burillo, the former being the last commander in the north, the latter the *comunizante* aristocratic ex-commander of assault guards. Hidalgo de Cisneros, at the head of the republican air force, now had some 200 fighters, 100 bombers, and another 100 reconnaissance or other aircraft. This gave the republic a superiority in numbers of fighters, not of bombers. Most were now flown by Spanish, rather than Russian, pilots, but Russia still had an air mission, at whose head 'Montenegro' had been followed by a similarly unidentified Colonel 'José'.[2] The fleet remained inactive. After he had lost one convoy from Russia on 7 September, due to the resilience of the captain of the nationalist cruiser *Baleares*, Buiza lost his job as admiral in charge, and was succeeded by Captain González de Ubieta. But the naval position continued to worsen. Morale remained low, initiatives were rarely taken and the republican fleet, unlike the nationalist one, was a veritable white elephant of the war.

The International Brigades were formally incorporated into the

1. An exception was during the collapse in Aragon in early 1938. See below, p. 801.

2. R. Salas Larrazábal, vol. II, p. 1560.

republican army. Officially, the Brigades took the place of the Foreign Legion in the old Spanish army. Careful attention was by now paid to discipline and dress. A five-point justification of the salute even appeared in *Our Fight*, a weekly paper published in English by the 15th International Brigade:

(1) A salute is the military way of saying 'hello'.
(2) A salute is the quickest way for a soldier to say to an officer, 'What are your orders?'
(3) A salute is not undemocratic: two officers of equal rank, when meeting on military business, salute each other.
(4) A salute is a sign that a comrade who has been an egocentric individualist in private life has adjusted himself to the collective way of getting things done.
(5) A salute is a proof that our Brigade is on its way from being a collection of well-meaning amateurs to a steel precision instrument for eliminating fascists.[1]

Early in 1938, these admonitions were followed up by an appeal to all to learn Spanish. *Volunteer for Liberty* described this 'our anti-fascist duty'.

The Brigades were finding it harder to gain new recruits from abroad. Thus the party in Italy had set out to recruit first 400 a month, then 100 or 150. In the winter of 1937–8, this fell to 68, 77 and 34 in December, January and February.[2] Volunteers returned home disgruntled. The liquidation of the POUM created a deservedly bad impression. The Brigades were more and more filled by Spanish volunteers. A crisis was also brewing in the Brigade organization. Vital Gaymann, the French manager of the base at Albacete, had been accused of embezzlement. He left for Paris. He and his henchmen apparently had taken many of the volunteers' personal effects.[3] His successor was 'Gómez' (Zaisser), who had earlier led the 13th International Brigade. This appointment intensi-

1. Qu. in William Rust, *Britons in Spain* (London, 1939), p. 98. These instructions were not confined to the International Brigades. Pamphlets on 'Leadership' were also published in considerable numbers, e.g. *El Mando* by 'General W.W.W.'.

2. Spriano, p. 226. Other figures for 1938 from Italy were 27, 34, 47 and 35 in March and following months.

3. Gurney, p. 53.

fied the quarrel between German and French communists at Albacete. Karpov, the Bulgarian quartermaster-general (in succession to Louis Fischer), and a French communist, Grillet, with his wife, were also accused of embezzlement. The Grillets were intimates of Pauline Marty. At last, the cry came that Marty himself had '*volé les soldats de la Liberté*'. The scandal grew so that the great man had to go to Moscow to justify himself. He did not return to Spain for some time.[1]

Another scandal affected the generals associated with Largo Caballero: Asensio, Martínez Cabrera, and Martínez Monje. After the fall of Gijón, they were arrested, with Colonel Villalba of Málaga, prior to charges of treason. They were all innocent, however, and their release was achieved.[2]

It would have been militarily wiser if the republic had worried less about potential spies than about such matters as the shortage of lorries in their reserve. The shortage was caused as much by neglect as by destruction in battle.[3] Disillusion, meantime, affected the whole of the army, not simply the International Brigades; in this second winter of war, fatigue, shock and demoralization were frequent, as can be seen from the number of cases brought against those who withdrew from the battle without permission or were would-be deserters.[4] A great many did desert, nevertheless. While the republic had organized a modern army if anything sooner than their opponents had done, they also had reproduced the bureaucracy, and the jealousies, which characterized the old army: Miaja, for example, was strong enough to be able to insist that his reserves should not be taken from him to fight outside the central zone.

As to arms, thanks to Russia, the essentials were now being acquired, though, as Prieto put it to the US chargé, Stalin feared that what all the world already knew would soon be discovered – namely, that he was selling arms to the republic. The republic, Prieto pointed out, had to pay the full market-price for goods. Apart from Russia, the republic bought from intermediaries and adventurers. All

1. *The International Brigades* (pamphlet, Madrid, 1953), p. 21.

2. Asensio became military attaché in the US, Martínez Cabrera military governor in Madrid.

3. Azaña, vol. IV, p. 683.

4. R. Salas Larrazábal, vol. II, p. 1583.

of them, Prieto complained, exacted vast profits.[1] In the centre of these gun-runners and idealists, Comintern agents and gangsters, the American journalist, Louis Fischer, continued to direct the chain of arms-purchasing bodies from the Hotel Lutetia in Paris, in conjunction with Colonel Pastor. They sent some two hundred expeditions of material to Spain from France in the nine months between 1 July 1937 and 1 April 1938.[2]

Negrín's difficulties continued with both the *Caballerista* socialists and the anarchists. Largo had offended his successors by speeches in Paris and in Spain. Nevertheless, his supporters had been edged out of *Claridad*, the Madrid socialist paper, which had done so much to press his cause in early 1936. On 1 October, the UGT, after an undignified squabble, expelled Largo Caballero and his friends from their executive on the technical, if unworthy, ground that the branches which supported him had not paid their subscriptions.[3] The event was yet one more proof that war belittles as often as it ennobles. On 19 October, the ex-Premier made a speech at Madrid criticizing Negrín's conduct of the war. The government had permitted this speech on the assumption that Largo Caballero would appear foolish. The speech was, however, a dignified self-defence, without bitterness.[4] His further activities were prohibited. The director-general of security, Carlos de Juan, himself telephoned Largo Caballero to stop him going to Alicante for another speech, on the ground that all large meetings were being banned. Largo complained, to no avail.[5]

1. *USD*, 1938, vol. I, pp. 149–50. The arms profiteers at the expense of the republic came from all classes. Who in those days had not heard of the English peer who, having received payment from the republic for a cargo of ammunition, sold it again to the nationalists?

2. R. Salas Larrazábal, vol. II, p. 1619.

3. The meeting had been convoked at the last minute, on dubious grounds (Largo Caballero, p. 236).

4. Text in Peirats, vol. II, pp. 382–93.

5. The new executive of the UGT included Ramón González Peña (president); Edmundo Domínguez (vice-president); Rodríguez Vega (secretary-general); Amaro del Rosal Díaz (assistant secretary); and Felipe Pretel (treasurer). Both Domínguez and Pretel had once been supporters of Largo, but they were now *Negrinistas*. Such are the consequences of power. The old *Caballerista* executive continued in existence, disputing the validity of the new. After some months, negotiations were begun between the two, the skilful diplomacy of the French union leader, Léon Jouhaux, being used to begin the conversations. Eventually a

The communist party had continued, in the summer of 1937, to press for unification between socialists and themselves, and a working pact between the two parties was made public on 17 August. This repeated the war aims of Negrín's government, adding the sinister comment that the extreme revolutionary Left should be purged. But this, and another, later, declaration, by all five Popular Front parties on 10 October, made no other concession to the communists. At the end of October, Negrín ended the discussions about prospective unity, saying that such a rigid framework was more suitable to nationalist, than to republican, Spain. This rebuff was not offset by the communist success in November in establishing, by a moderate programme, an alliance of all the youth movements, including the anarchists (the Alianza Juvenil Anti-Fascista – AJA). The socialists could not object, since their youth had long ago been swallowed up. Though the new body had no policy, its very formation was an indication that the anarchist youth had learned a lesson in the May riots. They were no longer the spearhead of an unofficial opposition. (The collapse of Asturias had also destroyed the schismatic branch of the united youth there.)

On 1 October, the Cortes met for one of their six-monthly meetings held to preserve the form of democracy. Ghosts dominated: twenty-eight members had been murdered in the early part of the war in the republican zone, at least double that number had been shot by the rebels, and probably one hundred of the members elected in 1936 were pursuing rebellion against the republic only too successfully. Many republican deputies were abroad, like Marcelino Domingo or Albornoz, either as ambassadors or in exile. Among the two hundred or so present were several radicals and one member of the CEDA. Portela Valladares, the weak Prime Minister during the elections of 1936, attended. He had first rallied to Franco and escaped death at the hands of the anarchists. Now he described how Franco had tried to persuade him to declare a state of war after the elections. He was an ambiguous man, and his speech on this occasion did not enhance his reputation. The communists, who claimed 300,000 members,

compromise was reached, and four of the Largo Caballero wing (Zabalza, Díaz Alor, Belarmino Tomás, Hernández Zacajo) joined the executive. But they did not do so as officers, and Largo Caballero himself remained outside. See Peirats, vol. II, pp. 393–4.

apart from the PSUC (about 64,000) and the united socialist-communist youth, suggested new elections, though without much enthusiasm. Certainly, their parliamentary representation did not reflect their strength.

The most serious criticism of the government came from those members of the CNT who still hoped to forge a syndicalist state out of the civil war. They concentrated, however, during the autumn and winter of 1937–8 on preserving what independence they possessed rather than expanding it – above all, to maintain their reduced numbers of agrarian collectives. Congresses of the CNT discussed what was to be done, both in September 1937 and in January 1938. Although suggestions for reform were canvassed, covering all aspects of the republican economy, most ideas put forward sought the improvement of the existing state of affairs; the millenarian aspect of anarchism had almost vanished. What was left seemed no more than a federalist movement, without effective national organization, which gave general, if grudging, support to the government. Under the influence of the realistic ex-secretary-general of the CNT, Horacio Prieto, anarchists were persuaded to accept the idea of nationalization of large industries and banks in exchange for collectivization of small ones, and on the land, as well as the 'municipalization' of local services. But they did not go as far as Horacio Prieto wanted, and form a political party emanating from the CNT, as the socialist party emanated from the UGT.[1] The occupation of Aragon by Lister's troops had been followed by similar, but less successful, efforts to destroy collectives in La Mancha and in Castile, generally undertaken by the communist troops of El Campesino. There was also an ugly incident in Barcelona, in September 1937, when new inter-party fighting was only just avoided when the armed forces tried to take over the headquarters of the rationing syndicate, where arms were still hidden: 8,000 bombs, hundreds of rifles, machine-guns, millions of cartridges were discovered.[2]

In the winter of 1937–8, many collectives persisted, even in Aragon, in republican Spain, though rumours were incessant that they were all about to be abolished. But their faith had gone. Anarchist newspapers still criticized government and communists, and they did so in almost every issue. 'Today, more than in the time of the dictator-

1. C. Lorenzo, p. 84. 2. *ibid.*, p. 312; Azaña, vol. IV, p. 802f.

ship [of Primo de Rivera]', someone signing himself 'An Atheist' wrote in *Campo Libre*, 'mediocre, drunken and arrogant men announce that they are absolute masters of Spain.'[1] Another issue of the same paper placed the communists on the same plane as Machiavelli and Ignatius Loyola.[2] 'From Christ to Durruti', ran another article, 'political power, no matter what its name, has satisfied itself by murdering the preachers of doctrines.'[3] During the winter, the censorship became increasingly rigorous; *Solidaridad Obrera* was banned for several days simply for placing white spaces instead of a censored article: no paper was supposed, by word or omission, to indicate the censor's activity. To most anarchists, the leadership of the socialist party seemed identical to the 'other Marxists', the communists. The old UGT, on the other hand, was different, and collaboration between them and the CNT was good at local level. The shoemakers' collective at Lérida, the chocolate cooperative of Torrente in Valencia, the flour mills of Valencia itself, the general collectives at Jativa or Mas de las Matas, continued to function and, if there were no pressing government interest, did so as independently as at the beginning of the war.

The Institute of Agrarian Reform reported in late 1937 that 5.8 million acres of land had been expropriated by reason of abandonment of political responsibilities; 4.8 million acres, for reasons of 'social utility', the 1935 law being put to use, ironically, by the republic; and 3 million provisionally occupied. This was a total of nearly 13 million acres or almost a quarter of the cultivable area in the republican zone.[4] According to one report, 100,000 more acres of cereals were sown in 1937–8 than in 1936–7, but hands were lacking to bring it in. The same report said that the tractors were not being managed properly: the government's capacity to help was limited by the failure of peasants to declare the number of machines which they possessed, for fear of confiscation.[5] But the government never found the means to persuade or to force the collectives or the peasants to

1. *Campo Libre*, 20 November 1937.
2. *ibid.*, 27 November 1937.
3. *ibid.*, 18 December 1937.
4. The total cultivable area was 60 million acres.
5. *Imprecorr*, 17 May 1938, p. 145. The same report says that the Institute of Agrarian Reform spent 200 million pesetas in credit and aid to peasants between July 1936 and 31 December 1937.

deliver, rather than consume, the fruits of what seems to have been sometimes a higher production.

As 1937 drew to its end, there were innumerable rumours of attempts to arrange a compromise peace. Angel Ossorio y Gallardo, republican ambassador in Paris, was said to be in touch with certain monarchists in that city. Angel Díaz Baza, Prieto's friend, maintained relations at Hendaye with Troncoso, the nationalist military governor of Irún.[1] In practice, however, Franco had never any intention of making concessions. One other contact was through the Red Cross. Dr Junod, helped by the British Embassy at Hendaye, succeeded in arranging the exchange of small groups of prisoners. But this hardly made any inroad upon the thousands now in Spain. Even most of those who had taken refuge in foreign embassies in Madrid at the start of the war were still held there. In January 1938, most were transferred to Valencia with the embassies concerned and, a little later, 500 persons who had taken refuge in the French Embassy were sent away. There remained, however, over 2,000 left in embassies in Valencia.[2]

*

Most anarchists regarded Negrín as the living symbol of counter-revolution. Yet, despite the surviving disorders and disquiet within, Negrín's government had achieved a degree of unity which was itself a revolution in Spanish history. Negrín's aim was to create a strong state, capable of holding out, if not of winning the war, against another of the same strength. He also sought to restrict agrarian collectives; reduce workers' control and replace it by nationalization or state management; encourage owners of capital and the petty bourgeoisie, and compensate, ultimately, those whose capital had earlier been confiscated. Land reform was continued, but the ministry of agriculture gave no credit or technical help to agrarian collectives, unless they had been recognized by the state. This was a reasonable

1. Pike, p. 129. The last was an unsuitable contact: Troncoso, an important link in nationalist intelligence, was arrested in Bayonne for organizing a group, including an Italian fascist, the Marquis di Maraviglio (editor of the Rome paper *La Tribuna*), whose aim was to capture the republican submarine C-2 when it docked in Brest.

2. A. Toynbee, *Survey, 1937*, p. 391.

social democratic solution to the problem of Spain at war. Negrín was fighting for democracy and liberty, even if he came to rely on communists (many of whom were only fair-weather communists) to support him. Those who were fighting for revolution, of whatever character, never forgave him. Nor did those who fought for Catalan or Basque separatism. Thus, he had many enemies – not least those indicated by Colonel Prada, the able and realistic last commander of the Army of the North, to Azaña: 'The trouble with this war', the colonel said, 'is that almost nobody tells the truth of what he sees and knows, while many responsible people are actually incapable of rendering account of what they have seen.'[1]

1. Azaña, vol. IV, p. 848.

44

Teruel – Attlee with the British Battalion – Colonel Rey d'Harcourt – Paul Robeson sings – El Campesino surrounded – break-through in Aragon – the way open to Barcelona – Alonso Vega reaches the sea

AFTER the capture of Asturias, Franco's plan was to attack Guadalajara, and then move on to Madrid. This plan never matured. The Generalissimo's plans were discovered. According to one recent account, a republican spy apparently disguised himself as a shepherd, crossed the lines and copied down the plan in the enemy command post.[1] Whether or no that it true, the republic instead launched their own offensive, at Teruel, on 15 December, a week before the Guadalajara attack was due to begin. Teruel was chosen since it was thought not to be strongly held; its capture would give a shorter line of communications between New Castile and Aragon, and threaten the road to Saragossa. Like Belchite, Huesca, and Saragossa itself, Teruel was also a town which had fascinated the republic since the start of the war. Prieto perhaps hoped to use the capture of Teruel as a position of strength, from which to try and arrange an armistice. The attacking Army of the Levante was under Hernández Saravia. He had reorganized that army almost from scratch, for, when he had taken up the command, the republican lines were twenty miles from those of the enemy, he himself had no car to take him around, and there was nothing to eat at headquarters. The different units were casually billeted on the *pueblos* of lower Aragon and lived off them.[2]

Hernández Saravia's army in December totalled about 100,000 men, composed of the 18th Army Corps under Colonel Fernández Heredia, one of the regular officers who had helped to defend Madrid in 1936, the 20th under Colonel Menéndez, another old member of

1. So De la Cierva says (*Historia ilustrada*, vol. II, p. 328), though he says the spy was Cipriano Mera – a story of which the latter does not speak in his own book.

2. Azaña, vol. IV, p. 812.

Azaña's prewar 'black cabinet', and the 22nd under Colonel Juan Ibarrola, a Basque officer of the civil guard who had hitherto fought in the north. A devout catholic, Ibarrola worked well with the communists as many conservative army officers did. His Army Corps included Lister's 11th Division, selected for the first attack.[1] The Russian General Stern (Grigorovich) was as ever the adviser for this campaign, and played an important part in its execution.

Teruel is the bleak, walled capital of a poor province, with a population of 20,000. Each winter, it records the lowest Spanish temperature of the year. The town is celebrated for the glum legend of the *Lovers of Teruel*, which often attracts those who desire a melancholy theme for a short ballet. This gloomy history was a suitable background for the atrocious battle of Teruel, which lasted for over two months.

On 15 December 1937, with snow falling, and without artillery or aerial preparation (so as to avoid giving notice of his intentions), Lister began his attack. He and Heredia set out to surround the town.[2] This they did by advancing immediately to the ridge on its west side known as La Muela de Teruel – Teruel's tooth. By the evening, the encirclement was accomplished. The commander of the garrison at Teruel, Colonel Rey d'Harcourt, withdrew his defences into the town. On the 17th, he gave up attempting to maintain a foothold on La Muela. Franco, however, did not decide until 23 December to suspend the Guadalajara offensive with which his German and Italian advisers urged him to continue. But the Generalissimo decided that he could not afford the political failure of abandoning a capital of a province. The attack had been a surprise in nationalist Spain: however much the communists might fear espionage, there was little of it in the region of Teruel that was of

1. Aznar, p. 549. The command was as follows: 22nd Army Corps (Ibarrola) – 11th Division (Lister) and 25th Division (Vivancos); 20th Army Corps (Menéndez) – 68th Division (Trigueros) and 40th (Nieto); 18th Army Corps (Heredia) – 34th Division (Etelvino Vega) and 64th (Martínez Cartón). Tanks (both T-26s and BT-5s), artillery and sapper units were attached to each Army Corps.

2. The best journalistic accounts of this battle from the republican side were by Henry Buckley and by Herbert Matthews in *Two Wars and More to Come* (New York, 1938). See also Lister, p. 171f; R. Salas, vol. II, p. 1637f. Lojendio, Azñar, and Villegas are sources for the nationalist counter-offensive.

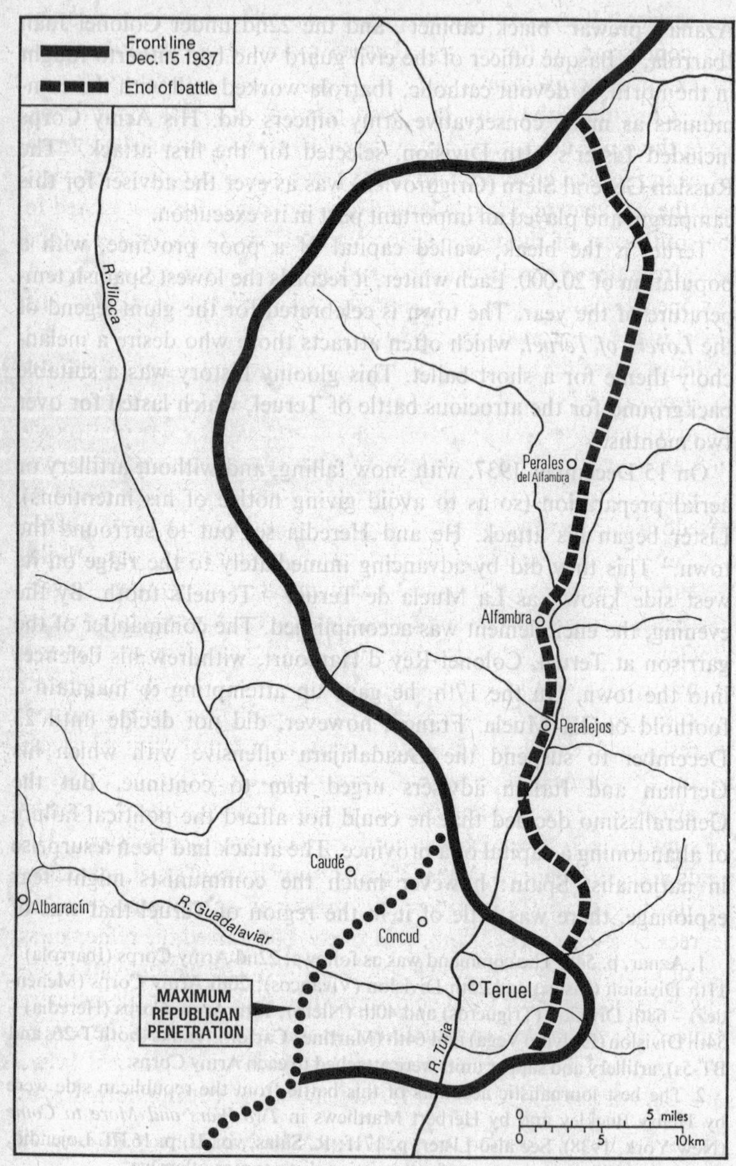

31. The battle of Teruel, December 1937–February 1938

any service.[1] But, as at Brunete, Franco was determined not to make any concession to his enemy: thus he mounted a frontal counter-attack, on a narrow front.

By Christmas, the town had been penetrated by the republicans, while the 4,000 defenders (half were civilians) had established themselves in the civil governor's office, the Bank of Spain, the seminary, and the convent of Santa Clara. These buildings were clustered in the south part of the town. Ciano babbled on 20 December: 'The news from Spain is not good. Franco has no idea of synthesis in war. His operations are those of a magnificent battalion commander. His object is always ground, not the enemy.'[2]

Franco's counter-offensive to relieve Teruel could only begin on 29 December. Rey d'Harcourt was telegraphed to 'trust in Spain as Spain trusts in you', and to defend at all costs. After a day of artillery and aerial bombardment, Generals Varela and Aranda, the experienced *Africanista* of the drive on Madrid, and the 'hero of Oviedo', with newly organized Army Corps, known as 'of' Castile and 'of' Galicia, advanced. Their supreme commander was Dávila. Beneath the two generals in field command were the famous Navarrese brigades, now converted into divisions. They were protected by the Condor Legion, whose personnel by this time had begun to weary of the constant changes of front.[3] The republican lines were pushed back, but did not break. Inside the town, Rey d'Harcourt maintained his resistance. On New Year's Eve, with the weather worsening, the nationalists made a supreme effort, reaching La Muela de Teruel in the afternoon. The city could now be easily shelled, but the republicans maintained their defence until visibility was non-existent. The roads and the engines of all machines of war froze. Teruel, maintaining its reputation for bad weather, registered a temperature of 18 degrees below zero. Men who, at Brunete, had cursed the remorseless sun of Castile, now went down with frostbite. The nationalists probably suffered the most from cold since their lack of a textile industry reduced the warm clothes available. The sewing 'women in the service of Spain' had not made enough winter clothing. A blizzard lasted four days, leaving behind four feet of snow and cutting both armies

1. See Kindelán's report on the republican air force, 8 February 1938, qu. R. Salas, vol. II, p. 1624.

2. Ciano, *Diaries 1937–8*, p. 46. 3. Galland, p. 32.

off from their supply depots. Six hundred vehicles were snowbound between Teruel and Valencia. In the meantime, fighting continued inside the city itself. Prieto had insisted that civilians among the nationalists should not be harmed. This excluded the use of large land mines. Nevertheless, the republicans flung grenades into the ruined cellars of the buildings in which the shivering defenders clustered. By New Year's Day 1938, the defenders in the convent and hospital of Santa Clara were dead. On 3 January, the civil governor's residence fell. The remaining defenders now had no water, few medical supplies, and little food. Their defences were piles of ruins. Yet they maintained themselves till 8 January, when the weather still prevented a nationalist attack. The artillery had, however, begun again, with heavy snow on the ground. Colonel Rey d'Harcourt, with the bishop of Teruel at his side, soon surrendered. A simple soldier, he was accused by the nationalists of both military errors and of treason. His surrender seemed too rational an act for the mood of Franco's new Spain. But he had resisted longer than might have been supposed humanly possible. After his surrender, the civilian population of Teruel was evacuated. The republicans became the besieged and the nationalists the besiegers. As for the bishop, Prieto wished to have him escorted to the frontier and freed there: a majority of the cabinet were against that humane proposal and both he and the colonel were held in gaol.[1]

On 17 January, Aranda and Varela sought to capture the high ground around the city. Heavy Italian artillery prepared the way for the advance. After an hour's fighting, with overhead combats between Fiats and Russian fighters, the republican line broke. On the 19th, for the first time, the International Brigades under General Walter were flung into this battle.[2] Slowly the republicans continued

1. Prieto, *Palabras al viento*, p. 220. Both were later shot. See below, p. 881.

2. The International Brigades had rested during the early part of these operations. It was early in December that the British Battalion had received a visit from the Labour leaders Attlee, Ellen Wilkinson and Philip Nöel-Baker. A dinner was given, at which Attlee promised to do his utmost to end the 'farce of non-intervention', and Nöel-Baker recalled how Britain had sent 10,000 men to assist the Spanish liberals in the Carlist Wars. Henceforth, the No. 1 Company of the British Battalion was known as the 'Major Attlee Company'. Attlee wrote back: 'I would assure [the Brigade] of our admiration for their courage and devotion to the cause of freedom and social justice. I shall try to tell the comrades at home

to retreat, and the heights of La Muela were lost. But on 25, 26, and 27 January, Hernández Saravia launched holding counter-attacks all along the front to the north of Teruel. There was much war-weariness and even rebelliousness among the republican combatants; some fifty men, of whom three were sergeants, were shot for rebellion on 20 January by the commander of the 40th Division, Andrés Nieto, at Rubielos de Mora.[1] On 7 February, a nationalist attack began north of Teruel towards the River Alfambra, where the republican defences were weak, since their main army was concentrated in the city of Teruel. This battle lasted two days. The front was pierced by three attacks. Monasterio's cavalry swept all before it in the most spectacular cavalry charge of the civil war, perhaps the last great cavalry action in the history of war.[2] Aranda and Yagüe, the latter with a reconstituted 'Army of Morocco' advanced with equal swiftness. By 7 February, the victory was complete, and achieved before Hernández Saravia had managed to send any reinforcements. In these two days, the republic lost 500 square miles, 7,000 prisoners, 15,000 other casualties, and a vast amount of material – munitions, arms, and ambulances. Those who were not cut off fled in disorder, and were machine-gunned from the air as they did so.

The last battle for Teruel began on 17 February. Yagüe on this day crossed the Alfambra and, advancing south along its east bank, cut off the city from the north. On the 18th, he and Aranda began a movement of encirclement, like that carried out in December by the republicans, several miles from the city.

By 20 February, republican road and rail communications to Valencia were threatened on both sides. Teruel itself was being penetrated by other nationalist units. Hernández Saravia gave orders for withdrawal. Most of the republican army was out of danger before the retreat was cut off, but again they left behind much material. 14,500 prisoners were taken. In these battles, the nationalists

of what I have seen. Workers of the World unite!' The singer, Paul Robeson, was a visitor too. As for those for whom 'home' meant France, the winter of 1937–8 was notable for the publication of Malraux's *L'Espoir*. Azaña commented: 'Ah, these Frenchmen! Only they would think of making a civil guard into a philosopher!'

1. R. Salas, vol. II, pp. 3050–51.

2. Save certain Russian actions near the Caspian in 1942.

had only a slight aerial advantage, so far as figures are concerned: the republicans had 120 fighters against 150 nationalist machines; 80 bombers against 100 nationalist; with other aircraft balanced about 100 to 110. But rebel morale, willingness to take risks, and training remained superior to that of their enemies. Casualties as at Teruel are difficult to estimate. It seems that the nationalist relief army lost about 14,000 dead, 16,000 wounded and 17,000 sick during the fighting. Those within numbered 9,500 and were all dead or prisoners by February. Republican casualties are practically impossible to estimate but it would be surprising if they were less than half as much again as those of their enemies.[1]

Among those surrounded in Teruel were El Campesino and the 46th Division. They managed, however, to force their way out through the enemy lines. This bearded man of action later claimed that he was left in Teruel to die by Lister and Modesto, his rivals among the communist commanders. He also reported that Teruel itself was starved of ammunition by General Grigorovich, and allowed to fall, in order to discredit Prieto.[2] Lister, on the other hand, alleged that El Campesino fled the battle.[3] This dispute, no longer military but political, rumbles on across the years, and is difficult to resolve. El Campesino has a bad memory, but his communist rivals often had bad consciences.

The fighting in early 1938 was accompanied by heavy bombing raids on Barcelona. On 6 January, Prieto proposed an agreement banning the aerial bombardment of rearguard towns on both sides. The nationalists replied that Barcelona would continue to be bombed unless its industries were evacuated. Then Seville and Valladolid were bombed by the republicans on 26 January. These raids were against Prieto's instructions, being ordered by Hidalgo de Cisneros.[4] In their turn, they caused a further nationalist raid on Barcelona on 28 January, killing 150. This air attack was launched by Italians from Majorca without consulting any Spanish commander. With satis-

1. See Martínez Bande, *La batalla de Teruel* (Madrid, 1974), p. 227.

2. El Campesino, *Listen, Comrades* (London, 1952) p. 11; *Comunista en España*, pp. 65–70. See Prieto's review of this book reprinted *Convulsiones*, vol. II, pp. 110–11.

3. Lister, p. 301.

4. Prieto, *Yo y Moscú*, pp. 197–200.

faction, Ciano read a melodramatic account of the raids: 'I have never read a document so realistically horrifying. Large buildings demolished, traffic interrupted, panic on the verge of madness, five hundred wounded. Yet there were only nine Savoias 79, and the whole raid lasted one and a half minutes.'[1]

There was also now a new burst of submarine activity in the Mediterranean, carried out by the two nationalist submarines bought from the Italians. On 11 January, the Dutch merchantman *Hannah* was sunk. Two unsuccessful attempts were made on British ships on 15 and 19 January. On 1 February, the British ship *Endymion*, with a cargo of coal for Cartagena, was torpedoed and sunk, ten lives being lost, including that of the Swedish non-intervention observation officer on board. The *Endymion* was a known smuggler, having offered to carry coal to the nationalists also. But Eden told Grandi that the British Navy reserved the right to destroy all submerged submarines in its patrol zone. This had some effect, and, for a time, no further submarine sinkings were reported. Sporadic aerial attacks continued on merchant ships, bringing supplies to the republic. The Admiralty nevertheless established a degree of friendship with Admiral Moreno, the commander of the nationalist fleet, at Palma, who told them where the 'legionary' and the nationalist submarines were at work.[2]

The international scene, never still, was, meantime, changing fast in the spring of 1938. The ceaseless activity and indecision of the Non-Intervention Committee seemed the only constants. Lord Plymouth, in reply to Franco's suggestion that belligerent rights should be granted after 3,000 'volunteers' were withdrawn, proposed it after the withdrawal of three-quarters of them. But Plymouth was not inclined to be hasty. The German representative Woermann (most of the time Ribbentrop's understudy) described the work of the committee in late January as

1. Ciano, *Diaries 1937–8*, p. 72. Eden promised Azcárate to try to intervene with Franco against these raids (Azcárate, p. 209). While it presumed that this *démarche* was being considered, the republicans refrained from reprisals. But later, after Eden had resigned, Britain said that she had never taken any initiative in the matter.

2. Eden, p. 571. The captain of the *Sanjurjo*, who was responsible for the attack on *Endymion*, was relieved of his command on return to harbour.

unreal, since all participants see through the game of the other side, but only seldom express this openly. The non-intervention policy is so unstable, and is such an artificial creation, that everyone fears to cause its collapse by a clear 'no', and bear the responsibility. Therefore, unpleasant proposals are talked to death, instead of rejected. It proved tactically clever to bring up belligerent rights at the same time as volunteers [he added], since that made it possible to drag out the discussion again and again.[1]

Woermann thought Britain was interested in the volunteers' scheme only because it seemed the best way of removing Italy from the Balearics. Volunteers, he comforted his superiors, could not be withdrawn before May – and further delays would always be possible. Thus, with justified bitterness, the English communist Edgell Rickword satirized the committee in his poem 'To the Wife of any Non-Intervention Statesman':

Permit me, Madam, to invade,
Briefly, your boudoir's pleasant shade:
Invasion, though, is rather strong,
I volunteered, and came along.
So please don't yell or make a scene
Or ring for James – to intervene.

The German foreign ministry (the expert there on Spain now being Weizsäcker) replied to Woermann with equal cynicism. German policy was to prevent a republican victory (not necessarily to secure a nationalist one). Its aim was to gain time, deferring 'for as long as possible the time when we might have to commit ourselves to a fundamental decision'.[2]

Lord Plymouth, the indefatigable peace-maker, soon presented new ideas for the withdrawal of volunteers. The powers should choose between a proportionate and a numerical withdrawal. 20,000 or 15,000 men might represent a figure to be regarded as 'substantial'.[3] Grandi and Woermann commented politely. More important talks were now going on in London than these, between Grandi, Eden, and Chamberlain. It became clear that these were indeed three-sided. Relations between Eden and Chamberlain had been bad since the latter's damper, in Eden's absence in January, to President

1. *GD*, p. 564. 2. *ibid.*, p. 573. 3. *NIS*(c), eighty-third meeting.

Roosevelt's plan for a general conference for peace.[1] Eden desired to make negotiations for an Anglo–Italian Agreement conditional on the withdrawal of at least some volunteers from Spain. Chamberlain thought that this insistence would waste too much time. On 18 February, Grandi refused to discuss separately the volunteers in Spain. He suggested 'general conversations' in Rome which would also discuss British recognition of the Italian empire in Abyssinia. Chamberlain agreed. Eden did not. So the latter resigned, with his under-secretary of state, Lord Cranborne, on the 20th, to the delight of Ciano and Mussolini – and also (according to Ciano) of Lord Perth.[2]

Shortly afterwards, on 6 March, the republic received the unexpected encouragement of a victory at sea. The main nationalist fleet, led by the cruisers *Baleares*, *Canarias* and *Almirante Cervera*, were sailing past Cartagena, at midnight on 5 March, in convoy with some merchant ships, on their way south from Palma. The republican cruisers *Libertad* and *Méndez Núñez*, and the destroyers *Lepanto*, *Sánchez Barcáiztegui*, and *Almirante Antequera*, under the direction of Captain González Ubieta, came broadside against this over-confident nationalist force. The republican destroyers loosed torpedoes and left the scene. The *Baleares* was hit amidships and blew up. HMS *Kempenfelt* and *Boreas*, on non-intervention patrol near by, picked up 400 out of the 1,000 who were aboard and took them to the *Canarias*. The nationalist admiral, Manuel Vierna, went down with his ship, accompanied by 726 officers and men.[3] The sinking of the *Baleares* nevertheless did not interfere with the nationalist control of the sea around Spain.

*

Franco had prepared his next offensive into Aragon. The attacking army would be commanded by Dávila, with Franco's staff adviser, Colonel Vigón, as his chief of staff. Solchaga, Moscardó, Yagüe, and Aranda would command army corps, and so would the Italian General Berti. Divisions under García Escámez and García Valiño, now recognized as the outstanding younger commanders, would

1. Eden, p. 549f.
2. Feiling, p. 337; Eden, pp. 380–82; Ciano, *Diaries 1937–8*, p. 78.
3. Cervera, p. 226.

form the reserve. Varela, with the Army of Castile, would hold himself ready in the wings of the general attack, at Teruel. The Condor Legion also held itself in readiness. As for the German tanks, Franco wanted to parcel them out among the infantry – 'in the usual style of generals who belong to the old school', von Thoma scornfully recalled. 'I had to fight . . .' he said, 'to use the tanks in a concentrated way.'[1] But the nationalists had nearly two hundred of them and, as it happened, tactics scarcely mattered.

The attack, preceded by heavy artillery and aerial barrage, began on 7 March. The best troops of the republic were weary after Teruel. Their material was exhausted: half the men lacked even rifles. The Aragon front was broken at several points on the first day. The republicans had anticipated a new deadlock as after Brunete. Their front line troops had had no combat experience. Yagüe advanced down the right bank of the Ebro, sweeping all before him. On 10 March, Solchaga's Navarrese won back Belchite. The 15th International Brigade were the last out of that dead town which fell easily, despite fortifications specially designed by the Russian Colonel Bielov ('Popov'), who turned out more of an NKVD specialist than an engineer.[2] The Italians encountered momentary stiff resistance at Rudilla, and then, with the Black Arrows leading, broke through the line. 'It is full speed ahead,' crowed Ciano in Rome.[3] Lister wanted to cover his own responsibility by shooting some of those who commanded troops falling back. Since they were communists, this matter came up, it seems, at discussions within the communist party. The sentences were carried out, an Italian communist Marcucci ('Julio')

1. The Condor Legion now had two Messerschmitt 109 groups of four squadrons; two Heinkel 51 groups of two squadrons; a reconnaissance group of Heinkels and Dorniers 17, of three squadrons; four bomber groups of three squadrons of Heinkels 111 and Junkers 52. Fighters and reconnaissance groups were of nine aircraft, bomber groups of twelve. The tank corps under von Thoma now comprised four battalions, each of three companies with fifteen light tanks a company. This was accompanied by thirty anti-tank companies, with six 37-mm. guns apiece.

2. The now veteran American Major Merriman was killed in the retreat. Merriman was succeeded by the English Malcolm Dunbar. A Brooklyn art student, Milton Wolf, took over the Lincoln Battalion. The commissar of the British Battalion, Wally Tapsell, was killed near Belchite. He had been an outspoken critic of the changes of front in the communist policy towards Spain.

3. Ciano, *Diaries 1937–8*, p. 87.

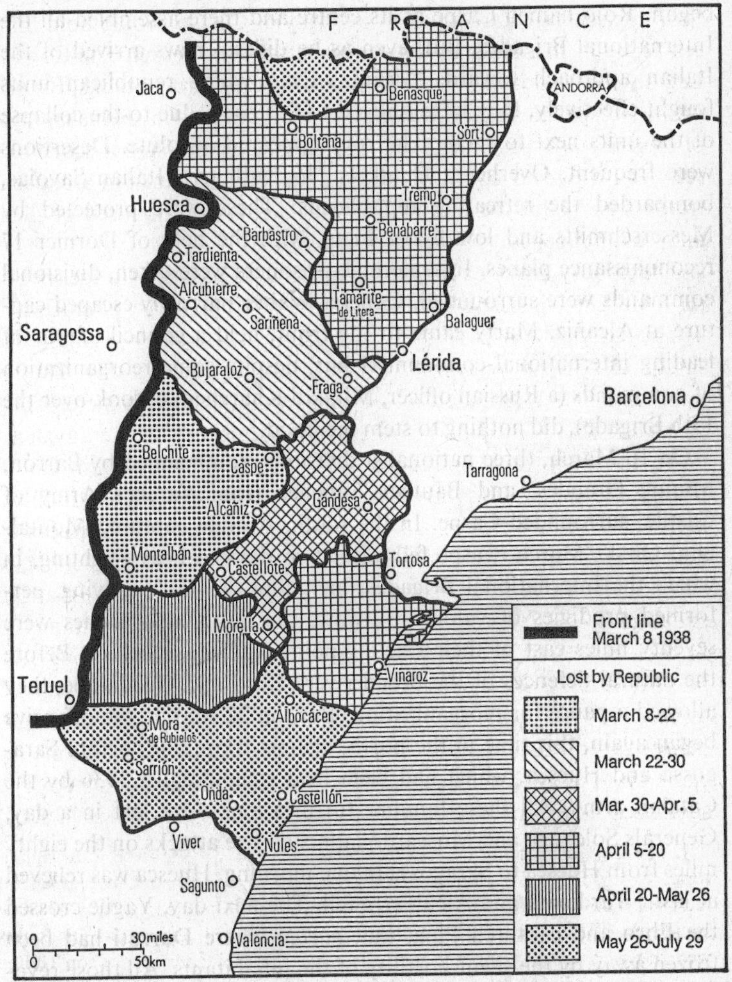

32. The campaigns in Aragon and the Levante, March–July 1938

killing himself in Madrid in protest or perhaps in fear that, by his complaint at the central committee, he would himself be killed.[1] Aranda had to endure harder fighting, before breaking through, on 13 March, to capture Montalbán. The defence had, however, hardly

1. Martínez Amutio, p. 266.

begun. Rojo named Caspe as its centre and there assembled all the International Brigades. But, even as he did so, news arrived of the Italian approach towards Alcañiz. Even where republican units fought effectively, they were obliged to fall back, due to the collapse of the units next to them. The rout appeared absolute. Desertions were frequent. Overhead, Heinkels 111, with new Italian Savoias, bombarded the retreating republicans. These were protected by Messerschmitts and low flying Fiats, with the help of Dornier 17 reconnaissance planes. Innumerable prisoners were taken, divisional commands were surrounded. General Walter narrowly escaped capture at Alcañiz. Marty came to the front, held a council of war of leading international communists but, despite some reorganization of commands (a Russian officer, Mikhail Kharchenko, took over the 13th Brigade), did nothing to stem the flood.[1]

On 16 March, three nationalist divisions, commanded by Barrón, Muñoz Grandes, and Bautista Sánchez from Varela's Army of Castile, surrounded Caspe. In the south, Aranda captured Montalbán. On 17 March, Caspe fell, after two days of heavy fighting, in which the International Brigades, including the 15th, rallying, performed prodigies of valour. By now, the nationalist armies were seventy miles east of their starting-point eight days before. Before the natural defences of the broad rivers Ebro and Guadalupe, they allowed a pause for reorganization. But, on 22 March, the offensive began again, this time in the north, against those lines before Saragossa and Huesca, which had been held since August 1936 by the Catalan army. All these familiar fortifications were lost in a day. Generals Solchaga and Moscardó launched five attacks on the eighty miles from Huesca to Saragossa in one morning. Huesca was relieved at last.[2] Tardienta and Alcubierre fell. The next day, Yagüe crossed the Ebro and captured Pina, that *pueblo* where Durruti had been frozen away by the silent hostility of the inhabitants. All those revolutionary Aragonese villages which, in August 1936, had given birth

1. Cf. Castells, p. 311f.

2. Julian Amery, *Approach March*, p. 92, recalls a macabre scene in the cemetery outside Huesca, relieved now by the nationalists, in which skeletons and decomposing corpses, along with freshly dead men, had been arranged in a dance of death to welcome the enemy. (Amery, a future English politician, visited nationalist Spain in the spring of 1938 as a student.)

to such a varied political anthropology were now captured. Pursued by machine-gun fire from the air, the inhabitants of these collectives fled east, where they joined an all-too-familiar stream, with their cattle, chickens, and carts carrying furniture. For, if deserters were now chiefly men who left the republic for the rebels, the refugees from rebel victories were countless. On 25 March, Yagüe captured Fraga, and then entered the golden land of Catalonia. At Lérida, the next town, El Campesino's division made a brave and militarily valuable stand for a week. To the north, Moscardó entered Barbastro. Further north still, Solchaga was pinned down in the Pyrenees. As they wound their way through the valleys, his columns presented an easy target to republican artillery and aircraft. To the south, however, Aranda, García Escámez, Berti, and García Valiño drove across the high plain known as the Maestrazgo, in southern Aragon, before preparing to advance to the Mediterranean. The fronts hardly existed. There were isolated acts of resistance by one or other of the republican units, as well as confusion, breakdown of communication, suspicion of treachery. Anarchist commanders (such as Miguel Yoldi, of the 24th Division) found themselves starved of munitions. Others (such as Máximo Franco, of the 127th Brigade) were arrested, due simply to communist distrust of anarchist leaders. Marty travelled about from headquarters to headquarters looking for traitors: he could not prevent the virtual disintegration of the International Brigades. There were a great many arbitrary executions, sometimes of officers in front of their men, but usually, as a certain Captain Joaquín Frau put it, the 'terror from enemy attacks from the air was greater than that inspired by the pistols of our own officers'.[1] In general, the campaign seemed lost. It is unclear where the rout would end. While superior artillery and good leadership played its part in

1. It is hard to sort out the accusations of treachery, cowardice, attempted murder, which fill the works of anti-communist writers of this period – e.g. Peirats, vol. III, pp. 102f and 251f. A number of commanders were bound to be dismissed in consequence of these defeats. A number of others were evidently shot, partly for political or even personal reasons. Several of the most discreditable occurrences happened in Andalusia, where there could be no excuse that the stress of defeat compelled it. Anarchists did not accept murders by communists without protest: thus the famous guerrilla fighter, Francisco Sabater ('El Quico'), shot a communist captain and commissar as a reprisal for being placed in an exposed part of the front (Téllez, p. 17).

these rapid nationalist advances, air superiority was the most notable cause of victory. The plains of Aragon provided easy landing fields. Aeroplanes thus could carry out the one-time functions of cavalry in driving republican units from their positions, as in a charge. From these battles, the Germans learnt much about the use of fighters for the support of infantry; the Russians more reluctantly did the same.[1]

On 3 April, Lérida and Gandesa fell to the nationalist armies. One hundred and forty British and American members of the 15th International Brigade were taken prisoner. The remains of the Brigade had however, held back Yagüe for several days, permitting regroupment and some withdrawal of material.

On 3 April, Aranda's troops saw the Mediterranean. A few days later, the Italians almost reached the sea at the mouth of the Ebro. They were held up at Tortosa by stiff resistance from Lister. Colonel Gastone Gambara, in field command of the Italians, reported differences with the Spanish. Ciano for once agreed that his countrymen were not blameless. 'So often Italian officers show a stubborn and provincial intolerance, explicable only by their ignorance of the world,' he remarked.[2] To the north, the advance of the nationalists continued into Catalonia. By 8 April, Balaguer, Tremp, and Camarasa had fallen. This cut Barcelona off from her hydro-electric plants in the Pyrenean waterfalls. The effect on the declining industry of Barcelona was severe. The old steam-generating plants of the city had to be put back to work. But no attack on Catalonia was launched: Franco diverted his main effort towards the sea. This was probably a strategic mistake. His decision was perhaps taken to avoid an extension of the conflict, for his intelligence is said to have reported the likelihood of French intervention if 'the Germans' should reach the Pyrenees.[3] Even so, Yagüe knew that there was nothing much between himself and Barcelona. It was a blow to him, as to others, to have to turn away from the enemy capital. Still, by April it did seem that the end of the war must be near. On this day, Good Friday,

1. The nationalist pilots sometimes thought of air battles in the same terms as a bull-fight. Some would refer to the stage of actual battle by the bull-fight cry '*¡Al toro!*' The motto of the famous nationalist air ace, García Morato, was '*Vista, suerte y al toro*' – good eyes, good luck and at the bull.

2. Ciano, *Diaries 1937–8*, p. 99.

3. De la Cierva, *Historia ilustrada*, vol. II, p. 354. The rumours are not confirmed. For another, less charitable view, see below, p. 938.

Alonso Vega, leading the 4th Navarrese Division, took Vinaroz, a fishing town known for its lampreys. He was thus able to make the sign of the Cross on the shores of the Mediterranean. His men waded out into the sea in exultation. The republic was cut in two. García Valiño's forces turned north and cut off numerous republicans in the northern Maestrazgo. By 19 April, Franco held forty miles of the Mediterranean. This series of victories, following the anxious moments over Christmas at Teruel, did suggest that, as Serrano Súñer said in a speech on 3 April, 'the war approaches its close'.[1]

1. Qu. Abella, p. 312.

45

Negrín in Paris – Blum's second government – opening of the frontier – raids on Barcelona – Mussolini's satisfaction – the SIM's murders – Negrín and Prieto – a riot in Barcelona – the fall of Prieto – Negrín's new government

---

THE collapse of the Aragon front caused Negrín to fly to Paris to demand that the French government re-open the frontier, closed since January, when the premier Chautemps had formed a government without the socialists. Originally, Negrín had wanted to say that the republic was about to launch a great counter-attack which, if well supplied by French arms, could sweep back the enemy. He was talked out of that idea by Prieto, who thought that he should tell the truth, and say that only an instant delivery of arms could stave off defeat.[1] Negrín arrived in the French capital at an opportune moment.[2] For France, like the rest of Europe, was occupied by Hitler's rape of Austria on 12 March, when those Junkers 52 which had played such an important part in the early days of the civil war, flew again, to carry German soldiers to Vienna.[3] On 10 March, Chautemps's ministry had fallen, for no good reason save that the Prime Minister did not like foreign crises. Blum formed his second government, with the enlightened Joseph Paul-Boncour as his foreign secretary. Chamberlain noted that the new French government was one 'in which one cannot have the slightest confidence'.[4] It was certainly weak. It was also outspoken. Even the cautious René Massigli, political director at the Quai d'Orsay, went so far as to call non-intervention 'a farce'.[5] Pierre Comert, director of information at the Quai d'Orsay, was overheard to say, 'We will avenge Austria in Spain'.[6] (Hitler had, however, told Schuschnigg, the Austrian chancellor, that if he

1. Zugazagoitia, vol. II, p. 82. 2. Alvarez del Vayo, *The Last Optimist*, p. 300.

3. Hitler used the ex-commander of the Condor Legion, Sperrle, as a physical menace at his famous interview with Schuschnigg.

4. Feiling, p. 347. 5. *USD*, 1938, vol. I, p. 163.

6. Robert Brasillach, *Histoire de la guerre d'Espagne* (Paris, 1939), p. 397.

did not yield to German demands, Austria would become 'another Spain'.)[1] At a meeting of the French national defence committee, on 15 March, Blum suggested that the French send an ultimatum to Franco. This would state: 'If, within twenty-four hours, you have not renounced the support of foreign forces, France will . . . reserve the right to take all measures of intervention which she judges useful.' General Gamelin pointed out, however, that the general staff did not have a separate plan of mobilization for the south-west of France. Daladier said that world war would follow any French intervention in Spain. Léger, still secretary-general of the Quai d'Orsay, remarked that intervention would be a *casus belli* for Germany and Italy, while Britain would break with France.[2]

On 17 March, the French cabinet agreed to Negrín's request to open the frontier.[3] Blum wept in sympathy with the republic as arms, purchased from Russia, private adventurers, the Comintern, and some even in France herself, began to flow across the Pyrenean frontier into Spain. But further steps were rejected.[4] The idea that a French motorized corps might go to the aid of Catalonia was disallowed by the chiefs of staff when they realized that such a step would be accompanied by general mobilization. Blum was assured by Colonel Morell, the French military attaché in Barcelona, '*Monsieur le Président du Conseil! Je n'ai qu'un mot à vous dire: un roi de France ferait la guerre.*'[5] But Ribbentrop was right when, on 21 March, he told the Italian chargé in Berlin, Magistrati, that France would not

1. Schuschnigg, *Ein Requiem in Rot-Weiss-Rot*, p. 37, qu. Churchill, *Gathering Storm*, p. 205.

2. This meeting is described in Maurice Gamelin, *Servir* (Paris, 1946–7), vol. II, pp. 322–8. See also Georges Bonnet, *De Washington au Quai d'Orsay* (Geneva, 1946), p. 77.

3. Their resolution was perhaps helped by the appearance of a news story that a military rising had taken place against Franco at Tetuán. This was the fabrication of the Comintern propaganda department in Paris carried out by Otto Katz and Claud Cockburn. The fraud aimed to give the impression that Franco might still be defeated and that, therefore, it was worth the French effort to open the border. (Claud Cockburn, *Crossing the Line*, London, 1956, pp. 27–8.) (I am grateful to Claud Cockburn for help here and elsewhere in this book.)

4. L. Fischer, pp. 451–2, suggests that a crucial talk between the British ambassador Phipps and Paul-Boncour tipped the balance. Phipps is said to have protested against the proposals to mobilize.

5. *Les Événements*, p. 253.

intervene in Spain without Britain's support. (He doubted that Chamberlain 'was bent on a policy of adventure'.)[1] But there were some members of the British government who were perturbed: also on 21 March, Captain Liddell Hart, the military historian who was then a special adviser to the war office, wrote a memorandum to Hore-Belisha, the British secretary of state for war, in which he concluded that, 'A friendly Spain is desirable, a neutral Spain is vital... from a strategical point of view, the political outcome of the present struggle is not, and cannot be, a matter of indifference to us.'[2] But what could be done? The question of volunteers in Spain had brought Eden's quarrel with Chamberlain to a head, but seemed otherwise certain to remain unresolved – as France at least hoped that it would be. Halfway through this 'Second Triumphal Year',[3] the Generalissimo would not mind losing the Italian infantry, said the Marqués de Magaz, his courteous ambassador in Berlin; but he required the Condor Legion and the Italian 'specialists' (particularly the pilots in Majorca) till the end of the war. Mussolini as usual was worrying why his precious infantry was not used more, so he pettishly ordered the air force in Majorca to cease operations till it was.[4] For this reason, Barcelona enjoyed, at the start of March 1938, peace from aerial attack. Bruno Mussolini, the Duce's son, was then withdrawn from the air force engaged in Spain, after twenty-seven sorties. He had volunteered to take part, but withdrew, on Franco's suggestion, when (it was falsely reported) special efforts were undertaken by the republic to shoot him down.[5] Negrín meantime left Paris, convinced that Prieto had misled him as to the right policy.

On 16 March, Barcelona was again heavily bombed by the Italians. The German ambassador in Salamanca, Stohrer, reported the effects as 'terrible. All parts of the city were affected. There was no evidence

1. *G D*, p. 622. Ribbentrop succeeded Neurath as German foreign minister in February.

2. Basil Liddell Hart, *The Defence of Britain* (London, 1938), p. 66.

3. It had become customary in nationalist Spain to date public decrees and even private letters by the terminology Year I, Year II, after the rising of 18 July 1936, in the style of fascist Italy. (In Rome, 1937 was the Year XV.)

4. Ciano, *Diaries 1937–8*, p. 80. Ciano was almost frantic: 'Franco must exploit his success. Fortune is not a train which passes every day at the same time. She is a prostitute who offers herself fleetingly and then passes on to others.'

5. Rachele Mussolini, p. 71.

of any attempt to hit military objectives.'[1] The first raid came at about ten o'clock in the evening. Six Hydro-Heinkels (flown by German pilots) flew across the city at 80 miles an hour and 1,200 feet up. Thereafter raids by Savoias as well followed at three-hourly intervals until three o'clock in the afternoon of 18 March. There were seventeen raids in all. About 1,300 were killed and 2,000 injured.[2] Ciano reported that, as with the raids in February, orders for the raids were given by Mussolini and that 'Franco knew nothing about them'. Stohrer reported Franco furious.[3] The Italians now had three aerodromes on Majorca which depended on the air ministry in Rome and whose pilots were able to act independently of the nationalist high command.[4] On 19 March, indeed, the Generalissimo asked for their suspension, for fear of 'complications abroad'. This did not prevent Ciano from lying to the American ambassador in Rome that Italy had no control over Italian aircraft operating in Spain. Mussolini, thinking, like his own ex-General Douhet, aircraft could win a war by terror, declared his delight that the Italians 'should be horrifying the world by their aggressiveness for a change, instead of charming it by the guitar'.[5] The republic had the fighters to repel these attacks, but internal rivalry and jealousy prevented them from making the most of their material. Demoralization was considerable until the fighters were withdrawn from the front and organized as a coastal defence force under Major García Lacalle.[6]

The consternation abroad was considerable. Meetings of protest were held in London.[7] The most eloquent protest was George

1. *G D*, p. 625.

2. Report of US military attaché, Colonel Fuqua (Claude Bowers, *My Mission to Spain*, New York, 1954, p. 376).

3. *G D*, p. 626.

4. See Cervera, pp. 317–18; and Kindelán, p. 19. The German Hydro-Heinkels of Palma were known as 'Negrillas', the Italians, Legionaries.

5. Ciano, *Diaries 1937–8*, pp. 91–2.

6. For an account in Barcelona, see Horner, p. 160.

7. A public letter of protest was signed by a mixed group of eminent Englishmen, including both archbishops, Cardinal Hinsley, the Lord Chief Justice, the chairmen of ICI and Lloyds, Lords Horder and Camrose, the headmasters of Rugby and Haileybury, Maynard Keynes, and many others. H. G. Wells gave his name to one of these protests. The nationalist agent, the Duke of Alba, wrote to him in astonishment that so great a writer should have such truck with the 'rabble'.

Barker's fine poem 'Elegy for Spain'. Even Cordell Hull abandoned his customary caution to express horror 'on behalf of the whole US people'. But indiscriminate raids on republican towns continued from time to time. The contribution which they made to the nationalist cause was probably not, however, worth the trouble which they brought. For instance, the petrol-storage station in Barcelona was attacked thirty-seven times before it was hit. Nor did the attacks interfere seriously with the loading and unloading of republican supply ships in Mediterranean harbours.

*

At this period of military crisis, the loathsome SIM came into its own in Barcelona. Designed to find spies, it also sought 'defeatists', defined as those guilty of profiteering, food-hoarding, or robbery. Summary trials before the special tribunals (*tribunales de guardia*) followed these charges. The SIM apparently also undertook a brief private murder campaign of vengeance against some of the PSUC's critics in Barcelona, particularly anarchists. Forty people had been 'taken for a ride' before the government intervened to end this development. The special prisons of the SIM in Barcelona, especially that in the convent of San Juan, nevertheless remained full of strange tortures which might have been devised by the ghost of Edgar Allan Poe. A spherical room painted in black, with a single light at the top, gave a feeling of vertigo. Some cells were so small that one could not sit down. Such tortures were applied indiscriminately to nationalist and republican (or anarchist and POUM) prisoners, particularly the latter. 'During the last year of the civil war,' the then councillor of justice in the Catalan government, Bosch Gimpera, recalled, 'we spent a good deal of the time struggling against the military tribunals and the SIM.'[1] Difficulties arose over the composition of the *tribunales de guardia*, since the presiding judge found himself without power *vis-à-vis* other members of the court, who always included a military officer and a member of the SIM itself. Many cases were held by these *tribunales* which should have been tried by the ordinary courts.[2] The SIM did discover a number of genuine agents; in the spring of 1938, they found a list of the Falange which operated in

1. In a letter to the author.

2. Bosch Gimpera, Memorandum No. 5.

Catalonia. 3,500 persons were detained and, after interrogation which included torture, proof of espionage was detected.[1]

On his return from Paris, Negrín found Barcelona heavy with gloom. The fountainhead of the defeatism was, as he expected, Prieto. Stretched in his armchair in the ministry of national defence, he would blandly announce to journalists and sycophants, in the tone of a victor: 'We are lost!' Prieto infected everyone with this pessimism, including the easily influenced but hard-working foreign minister, Giral, who even expressed his gloom to the French ambassador, Labonne. (Admittedly, Giral was in close touch with Azaña who was even more gloomy than Prieto was.) Almost before Negrín had returned, therefore, the French government was thus being informed by their representative in Barcelona that any war material which they might allow to be sent to Catalonia might fall into the hands of Franco – or Hitler. It required all Negrín's skill to convince Labonne that he, at all events, was resolved to fight on. But what was to be done with Prieto?[2] A cabinet meeting had been arranged for 16 March, the day of the worst bombing in Barcelona, at the Pedralbes Palace in Barcelona, under Azaña's chairmanship. Before it began, Negrín spoke to both Prieto and Zugazagoitia, Prieto's friend, the ex-editor of *El Socialista*, and minister of the interior, and begged them to support him if, at the meeting of the cabinet, anyone should mention negotiations. Both agreed to do so, thinking that the Prime Minister himself was going to propose mediation. Prieto suggested that republican funds abroad might be blocked so as to help those forced into exile after peace. Negrín hastily replied 'all that is taken care of'.

At a preliminary meeting of ministers before the cabinet, Negrín

1. See Peirats, vol. III, pp. 280 and 288. According to one report, the SIM had 6,000 agents in Madrid alone, with a budget of 22 million pesetas. The SIM shortly went into a period of disorganization – its chief, Colonel Uribarri, escaping to France with a good deal of money. His extradition, though demanded, never occurred. His successor was Santiago Garcés, previously of the socialist youth, a confidant of Prieto, who had been in the murder-car at the time of the death of Calvo Sotelo. Another prominent member of the SIM, Maxim Schneller, head of its 'Foreign Section', seems to have been a double spy and fled to France (see Delmer, p. 356, where there is a description of a visit to the SIM's prison ship, *Uruguay*, in Barcelona harbour).

2. Alvarez del Vayo, *The Last Optimist*, p. 301.

said that he understood that some of the ministers were for peace. No one replied. Giral, the foreign minister, said that Labonne, the French ambassador, had offered the members of the government a refuge at the French Embassy in the event of collapse. The republican fleet, Labonne had added, could sail to Bizerta or to Toulon. This last point made everyone angry, for they thought that the French were thinking only of themselves, desiring to remove from the Mediterranean a potentially hostile fleet in nationalist hands. The ministers then moved into Azaña's room. There, the angry noise of a great multitude could be heard moving towards the palace. A demonstration was being held to protest against surrender, and Prieto. Organized by the communists and supported by one or two prominent *Negrinistas*, including even Mariano Vázquez, the secretary-general of the CNT, the crowd carried banners on which were written 'Down with the treacherous ministers!' and 'Down with the minister of national defence!' The gates of the Pedralbes Palace gave way, and a large Barcelona mob arrived beneath the french-windows of Azaña's room. Prieto, the object of the crowd's anger, could thus hear La Pasionaria, his particular enemy, haranguing her followers. Negrín persuaded the crowd to go away, having reassured a delegation headed by La Pasionaria[1] that the war would go on. Prieto later accused the Prime Minister of organizing this demonstration. Yet Prieto could not have made headway with negotiations. For the nationalists would only have accepted unconditional surrender. That would have included the freedom to exterminate the 'absolute enemy' – the phrase used by Serrano Súñer to describe every shade of left-wing opinion, from liberal to anarchist.[2]

Ten days later, at a meeting of the socialist party executive, on 26 March, in his own house, Negrín belittled the differences between Prieto and the communists. Zugazagoitia intervened. 'Don Juan,' he said, 'masks off! At the front, our comrades are murdered because they refuse to accept communist commands. As for Don Indalecio,

1. Other members of the delegation were Pretel (UGT); Vidarte (socialist); Santiago Carrillo (united youth); Serra Pamiés (PSUC); and Guerrero (FAI) (Ibarruri, p. 395).

2. The above derives from Prieto, *Epistolario Prieto y Negrin* (Paris, 1939); Prieto, *Convulsiones*, vol. II, p. 37; Alvarez del Vayo, *The Last Optimist*, p. 123; Zugazagoitia, p. 400.

look at the articles in the *Frente Rojo* and *La Vanguardia* by "Juan Ventura", a *nom de plume* of the minister of education!'[1] *La Vanguardia*, a republican paper which supported Negrín, had that day named Prieto an 'impenitent pessimist'. Negrín answered that he needed both the communists and Prieto. The next day, *Frente Rojo* published another article by Hernández, suggesting Prieto's dismissal. Zugazagoitia protested, at a cabinet meeting that night, that that had been published after the censor had struck it out. Hernández replied that a minister could not be censored by officials. Negrín calmed both the opponents.[2]

Prieto's prestige, along with his own self-confidence, had much diminished after the fall of Teruel, even though his friends assured him that Teruel had been abandoned by the communists in order to discredit him. The truth of these allegations may never be disentangled, though a conscious plot to abandon Teruel can be discounted. But the communists' manoeuvre against Prieto had certainly begun some weeks before. On 24 February, Hernández's first article appeared in *Frente Rojo*, denouncing 'the defeatists'. The decision by the communists to launch a deadly campaign of propaganda against the defence minister must have been taken shortly before that.

According to Jesús Hernández, the Bulgarian Comintern representative, Stepanov, had just been to Moscow. Russia, he said, was ready to send a great deal of new aid to Spain, provided the mercurial Prieto were ousted. Thereafter, a policy of grim resistance to the end would have to be followed. Hernández argued that Prieto was the only man for that policy, since only he could gain the support of the communists, the CNT, and the UGT. But Togliatti said that Prieto had to be dislodged while Negrín would have to become almost a dictator.[3] A number of speeches, by La Pasionaria, Miguel Valdés (a communist in Catalonia) and Hernández followed, attacking Prieto.

1. i.e. Jesús Hernández. For confirmation of communist murders at the front, see Peirats, vol. III, pp. 102–30. The CNT and FAI sent a complaint on this question to Prieto on 25 March.

2. Prieto, *Yo y Moscú*, p. 38.

3. Hernández, p. 159. This was scarcely a happy time in the world communist movement: Bukharin and his fellow victims, including Yagoda and Grinko, the commissar of finance who had received the Spanish gold in 1936, were tried between 2 and 13 March 1938.

On 28 March, a gloomy meeting occurred of the war council, a committee of the cabinet set up to run the war with soldiers, politicians and civil servants present. Prieto's despondency seemed to affect everyone. Negrín assured the generals that they retained at least his confidence. The next day, while El Campesino was battling unsuccessfully for Lérida and the 15th International Brigade for Gandesa, the republican cabinet met in Barcelona. Again, Prieto (in Negrín's words) 'with his suggestive eloquence, his habitual pathos', demoralized the cabinet, by falsely representing the conclusions of the previous day's meeting of the council for war.[1] On the night of 29–30 March, 'a painful and violent struggle surged up' within the mind of Negrín. Negrín visited the front often, often talked with soldiers, and knew that, whatever one's private thoughts, defeatism like cowardice should never be shown. As a result, he decided to transfer Prieto from the ministry of defence, though if possible retaining him in the government.[2] In the morning, Negrín telephoned Zugazagoitia, and asked him whether Prieto would like to leave the ministry. Zugazagoitia relayed the inquiry to Prieto who wrote a letter of resignation.[3] The executive of the socialist party visited Prieto to consult him as to what course to follow, but he gave no lead. Another visit was from a commission of the CNT, composed of Horacio Prieto, Segundo Blanco, and Galo Díez (a veteran anarchist, now secretary of the CNT national committee). Horacio Prieto and Segundo Blanco were both leading exponents of CNT–UGT collaboration, which had been sealed in a joint statement of aims ten days before.[4] They told Prieto that, despite 'the enormous ideological differences which divide us', they had no wish to see him removed from the ministry of defence.[5] These three men were disillusioned with communist conduct; they believed that the war was lost, and that the peace should be made as soon as possible. A national anarchist meeting was soon held. All agreed that it was desirable to back Prieto and finish with Negrín; but opinions differed as to what

1. Prieto, *Yo y Moscú*, pp. 39–40. Prieto said later he merely told the meeting the 'fascists would inevitably reach the Mediterranean'.

2. Prieto, *Epistolario*, p. 24.

3. Qu. in Prieto, *Yo y Moscú*, p. 43f.

4. See C. Lorenzo, pp. 291 and 313. A liaison committee had been formed with Horacio Prieto president and Rodríguez Vega (socialist) secretary.

5. *ibid.*, pp. 176–7.

to do next. Horacio Prieto had the candour to say that the republic was becoming a Russian puppet; that negotiations were essential; that Franco's military superiority was assured and that, if nothing were done, he would soon be able to dictate his own conditions. Pandemonium followed. The ex-councillor in the *Generalidad*, Juan Domenech, rhetorically replied that the war would never end while a tree of Catalonia still stood and while there was a man of the FAI able to stand behind it. Mariano Vázquez, the friend of Negrín who was secretary-general of the CNT, agreed. Never had the movement seemed more divided. The meeting appropriately ended without a conclusion.[1]

The only explanation of this crisis is that Negrín, without communist encouragement, had determined to move Prieto from the ministry of national defence because of his defeatism. He wanted Prieto to become minister without portfolio or of public works and railways. But Prieto refused these posts (he had wanted railways to be controlled by the ministry of defence) and so left the government. Prieto later explained that he left the ministry since he was weary of the communists. He described his arguments with that party over matters of strategy and tactics. He explained how certain shipping companies had been founded to purchase arms abroad, but were later used for making commercial profits for the communists.[2] The weakness of his argument was that he could not suggest that a social or military policy different from that of the communists would have been more advantageous. Indeed, until recently, his policy, and communist policy, had been close in outlook. He did not explain what stratagem, other than one of friendship with Russia, could have been followed when Russia remained the only sure source of war material and when Russia already had the gold reserves of Spain. Nor did he suggest what else could be done other than carry on the war if the

1. C. Lorenzo, p. 315.

2. Shipping companies created in England by the republican government were those of Howard Tenens Ltd, the Prosper Steamship Co., the Burlington Steamship Co., 'Southern Shipping', and the Kentish Company. The Enterprise Maritime, also created by the republic, was registered at Marseilles. The Mid Atlantic Company was formed to charter other ships and was run by a Basque nationalist and a socialist under the direction of the Spanish Embassy in London. Prieto's son Luis was financial attaché. The Tyneside millionaire Billmeir was the hidden hand behind many such ventures.

nationalists should offer only unconditional surrender. After all, his own negotiations for peace with Franco had made little headway. The truth seems to be that Prieto was exhausted by the war as well as by his own difficulties with the communists. His last service as a minister, however, was to dissuade Azaña from resigning also.[1] He subsequently busied himself with journalism, seeking, through a variety of friends abroad, to negotiate with the nationalists.[2]

The communists had their own crisis at this moment. The Russians wished the Spanish communists also to withdraw from Negrín's government. The communist caucus assembled in its customary atmosphere of jealousy and cigarette smoke. Did Moscow want the republic to lose, demanded Hernández? The Bulgarian Stepanov replied that this move was aimed to convince English and French public opinion that the communists were not interested in the conquest of power in Spain. If, as seemed likely, European war came, a Russian alliance with Britain and France would thereby be easier to achieve.[3] Moscow's orders were, however, partially obeyed; Uribe remained at the ministry of agriculture but Hernández left the ministry of education to become commissar-general of the Armies of the Centre and South, a post of potential power. This superficial change in the cabinet was compensated for by the return of the communist apologist, Alvarez del Vayo, to the foreign ministry. Other communists also received important positions: for example, Carlos Núñez Maza became under-secretary for air; Antonio Cordón, under-secretary for war; Pedro Prados, chief of staff of the navy; Colonel Eduardo Cuevas, director-general of security; Marcial Fernández, director-general of carabineers; and Hilario Arlandis, who, almost alone of the first generation of Spanish communists, was still a party member,

1. Prieto, *Palabras al viento*, pp. 282–3.

2. See, for example, Amery, pp. 108–9. Prieto was offered the post of ambassador to Mexico. No doubt Negrín wanted him out of the way. Azaña was furious. That led to a major quarrel between the two, since Azaña desired to keep Prieto as a possible Premier. Prieto refused. See Azaña, vol. I, pp. 881–3. Eventually, much later in the year, Prieto agreed to be 'special ambassador' to the inauguration of President Aguirre Cerda of Chile. He went to Santiago, made innumerable brilliant speeches, and was in exile already when the war ended.

3. Hernández, pp. 166–8. On 18 March, Russia proposed a 'grand alliance' within the League against Hitler. This was rejected by Chamberlain.

was director of the school for commissars, while the commissar general, Bibiano Ossorio y Tafall, though formally a left republican, was really a communist puppet.[1]

Negrín, meantime, dropping the portfolio of finance, became minister of defence as well as Premier. The finance ministry went to his previous under-secretary, Méndez Aspe, a civil servant by career. The other socialists in the cabinet, apart from Negrín, were González Peña, minister of justice, and Paulino Gómez Saez, minister of the interior. The latter had always been a Prietista, but the communists maintained their hold on the police services under his authority. The Basque Irujo remained minister without portfolio and the Catalan Jaime Ayguadé remained as minister of labour. The government was strengthened by the entry into it of Segundo Blanco, an anarchist leader who had escaped from Asturias, and took the unimportant post of minister of education and health. The anarchists agreed to this support of Negrín (as they had supported Largo Caballero in the heroic, now far-off, days of November 1936) because of the serious military danger: on 30 March, a FAI circular had urged all members to rally to the government in the hour of need, while CNT leaders had similarly sent out messages, calling for the mobilization of 100,000 volunteers. Actually, Blanco's ministry did not loom large in the war; and Blanco, previously a critic of Negrín and the communists, soon became very friendly with the Prime Minister. Blanco's presence in the government may have helped to limit further communist persecution of anarchists at the front and elsewhere. Other posts went to republicans – Giral (minister without portfolio), Giner (transport), and Antonio Velao (public works). The ex-minister of the interior, Zugazagoitia, became secretary-general of defence, a nominal post: Zugazagoitia would complain that to discover what was going on, he had to read the newspapers.

Negrín, on Rojo's suggestion, created, out of the remains of the armies defeated in Aragon, and in the moment for recovery that Franco's turn southwards left to him, a new 'Army of the East' (Grupo de Ejércitos de la Región Oriental) under the command of Azaña's loyal friend, Hernández Saravia, who had led the advance on Teruel. The word 'Catalonia' played no part in these large gather-

1. Castro Delgado, p. 659.

ings of men. Miaja was given the supreme command of the Army of the Centre (Grupo de Ejércitos de la Región Central).

*

The republic, despite appearances, was not beaten. A show of working-class unity was once more patched up.[1] On 18 March, the UGT and CNT had signed an agreement marking a further retreat from anarchism. Industry would be subject to central economic planning. Collectivization henceforth would be voluntary. The UGT agreed to try to persuade the government to cease trying to dissolve existing agricultural collectives, and to support workers' control in those industries which desired it. Both unions agreed that their tasks were to promote greater production. In fact, collectivization was still everywhere giving way to state control. The government increasingly appointed 'mediators' as supervisors of those concerns still run by committees of workers. The economics ministry would then try to provide such concerns with the raw materials which they needed. The same degree of collaboration between the Catalans and the central government still did not exist even in show: a letter from Companys to Negrín dated 25 April catalogued numerous grievances. The leading one was that, though the enemy had penetrated Catalan territory, there was no Catalan in the higher ranks of the ministry of war, nor in the supreme war council. The army fighting on the Catalan front was commanded by Castilians. Nor were documents relating to the conduct of war sent to the Generalidad (as they had been in the time of Largo Caballero). Companys demanded that the Catalan statute should be amplified to deal with war needs. He received no answer to this letter and matters continued as before.

Administrative arrangements for the bisection of the republican territory, long feared, were now being put into effect. The International Brigades' base at Albacete was transferred to Barcelona. A submarine mail service was established between Barcelona and Valen-

1. This agreement and the negotiations leading up to it are described in full in Peirats, vol. III, p. 62f. A committee to coordinate UGT–CNT activities was set up under two anarchists (Horacio Prieto and Roberto Alfonso) and two from the UGT (Rodríguez Vega and César Lombardie). During April, the CNT gave other backing to the government, the ex-minister Peiró becoming commissar-general of electricity (*op. cit.*, p. 124).

cia, along with a passenger and freight service. Republican leaders regularly flew over the rebel lines between their bases. The consequences of the bisection were less serious than might have been supposed. Daladier's new French government (which in April succeeded Blum's second short-lived administration)[1] also opened the canals of south France to enable the republic's vessels to pass from the Mediterranean to the Atlantic.

The collapse of the Aragon front had brought to a head yet one more crisis in the republic which had been grumbling on for months. In some ways a problem in personal relations, the clash between Negrín and Prieto was a matter of temperament. But that in itself went to the heart of the divisions, ideological and political, which beset the uneasy republican coalition. The difficulty was that, by this time, communist policy, however effective in organizing professional Spain and the remains of the liberal bourgeoisie to fight against fascism, had drained much of the spirit from the republic: Orwell, writing in February 1938, had explained that, on his return to England after fighting with the POUM, 'a number of people had said to me with varying degrees of frankness that one must not tell the truth about what was happening in Spain and the part played by the communist party because to do so would be to prejudice public opinion against the Spanish government and so aid Franco'. Orwell added that he did not agree since he held 'the outmoded opinion that in the long run it does not pay to tell lies'.[2]

1. Though this mainly radical socialist cabinet stood to the right of those of Blum and Chautemps, it was supported by the socialists.

2. Letter to the editor of *Time and Tide*, 5 February 1938. Orwell had pointed out earlier that the war produced a 'richer crop of lies than any event since the Great War of 1914–1918'. ('Spilling the Spanish Beans', in *New English Weekly*, 29 July 1937.)

46

The campaign in the Maestrazgo – Yagüe and Negrín in search of compromise – the US and the Embargo Act – renewed crisis in the Mediterranean – German ambiguities – the nationalists halted before Valencia

---

YET the war was far from over. It is true that the recent nationalist advances had won back huge tracts of valuable territory. In the Pyrenees, Generals Solchaga, Moscardó, and Yagüe had advanced as far as the River Segre and its tributary, the Noguera Pallaresa, which runs up to the French border. They had, however, to leave for weeks one republican division unconquered under Antonio Beltrán, nicknamed 'El Esquinazado' (The Dodger), in the Valle del Alto Cinca, up against the frontier.[1] The course of the river Ebro from the junction with the Segre to the sea presented a natural line of defence for Catalonia upon which the republicans swiftly improved by fortifications. At the mouth of the Ebro, the Italians, frustrated of their desire to be first of nationalist troops to the Mediterranean, were held up at Tortosa till 18 April. Though the town then at last fell, the Italian troops were good for fighting for a while. On the south side of the nationalist salient to the sea, their advance was also greatly slowed. Here Varela sought to press down from Teruel across the dull plain of the Maestrazgo. A breach of the republican lines was made at the first assault. But, immediately, the weather changed to continuous rain. This helped the defenders, who were also reinforced by new weapons, especially fighters and anti-aircraft guns – part of

1. A local politician, Beltrán had been prominent in 1930 in the rising of Jaca and had been the left republican administrator of a state housing project in Canfranc. He had become a 'communist' in the war. See Prieto, *Convulsiones*, vol. II, p. 203, for his future adventures in Russia, his return to France with the *maquis*, his subsequent deportation to Corsica, his break with the communists, his work with US intelligence after 1945 in Spain, the US and Mexico, where, like many another Spanish hero of our time, he died in poverty, having quarrelled with his US masters. The Dodger's nickname was inherited from his father and grandfather, famous Canfranc smugglers.

the consignment brought in from France. The advance was halted altogether on 27 April. On 1 May, in one more attempt to clinch the victory which had seemed so short a while ago to promise so brightly, General Aranda mounted a new assault twenty miles to the east of Varela and fifteen miles from the Mediterranean. In between Varela and Aranda, General García Valiño led a mobile force to press forward whenever the two flanks were held. But along all three lines of advance, the fighting was hard. The slow pace of the advance caused new political murmurings inside nationalist Spain. These were not staunched by news of a successful bombing raid by thirty-four bombers of the Condor Legion on the port of Cartagena which further damaged the republican fleet's low morale.

A thwarted hope of triumph manufactures resentment. Franco was criticized by his comrades for not attacking Catalonia. Yagüe, speaking on 19 April at a falangist banquet at Burgos, commemorating the anniversary of the unification, praised the fighting qualities of the republicans and termed the Germans and Italians 'beasts of prey'. He also said:

> In the gaols, comrades, there are thousands and thousands of men who suffer. And why? For having belonged to a party or to a syndicate. Among these men there are many honourable and hard-working people who, with a little kindness, might be incorporated into the movement. We must be generous, comrades, we must have a great soul and know how to forgive. We are strong and we can permit ourselves this luxury. I ask the authorities . . . to look again at these people's dossiers and, in returning these men to their homes, return to them also benevolence and tranquility, so that we can banish hatred.

He pleaded too on behalf of the unfortunate Hedilla and the old shirts in gaol, 'the initiators of our movement'.[1] This generous

1. The text of this speech was published only in the *Diario de Burgos*, 19 April 1938. It is reprinted in García Venero, *Falange*. Yagüe was approached by Prieto in the spring of 1938 through Jakob Altmaier, a German journalist and socialist refugee and an unnamed Austrian monarchist, to try and secure a compromise peace. By the agreement, Franco and Negrín were to form a coalition government with Prieto, Gil Robles, and other 'moderates'. There would be a plebiscite in two years on the monarchy. See Amery, pp. 108–9. Altmaier had been a socialist leader in Frankfurt during the revolution of 1919 and in World War II worked in British intelligence. See also Prieto, *Palabras*, p. 237, where it is implied that Negrín prevented him from negotiating as much as he might.

speech resulted in Yagüe's temporary relief of his command of the 'Army of Morocco'. He had hoped for a fascist 'rejuvenation' of Spain but, instead, the septuagenarian, Martínez Anido, controlled home affairs, the Italians were bombing Barcelona, and the war seemed to be going on for ever. A fortnight later, the old shirts were antagonized anew by a decree which permitted the Jesuits to return, and which enabled them to behave virtually independently of any state sanction.

It was in this atmosphere, superficially more hopeful for the republic, that, on 1 May, Negrín issued a thirteen-point declaration listing the war aims of his government. Negrín's points stipulated the need for absolute independence for Spain; the withdrawal of foreign military forces; universal suffrage; no reprisals; respect for regional liberties; encouragement of capitalist properties, without large trusts; agricultural reform; the guaranteed rights of workers; the 'cultural, physical, and moral development of the race'; establishment of the army outside politics; renunciation of war; cooperation with the League of Nations; and an amnesty for enemies. The programme, designed for its international propaganda value as well as a blueprint for mediation, was much more moderate than the anyway moderate programme of the Popular Front. Any constitutional politician of the lost age of innocence under the restoration could have subscribed to Negrín's points. The CNT were not consulted beforehand, but the UGT–CNT committee of collaboration approved the statement warmly. The FAI did not, its 'Peninsular committee' (on which the cripple Escorza still exerted an influence) denouncing it as a return to the *status quo* before July 1936.[1] Where now were the *illusions lyriques*, the uncompromising dreams of Durruti, Isaac Puente and the other leaders at the Saragossa conference of May 1936? Negrín's government, at the end of April, was even attempting to conciliate foreign capital, by decreeing the dissolution of the CNT's hydro-electric combine and the return of the companies to their previous owners. (The companies, confident of Franco's victory, ignored this.)

1. See Circular No. 17 of the FAI, issued 3 May. Qu. Peirats, vol. III, p. 118. The thirteen points were discussed at a cabinet meeting on 30 April. Segundo Blanco said the CNT should be consulted. Negrín decided that was impossible since the British Embassy had to receive the document the same day, and it was, after all, primarily a statement for foreign consumption (*op. cit.*, p. 119).

But none of the controversial points had a chance of winning approval from Franco, who had no intention of making concessions. While Franco lived, there was no chance of securing the disappearance of the army from Spanish politics.

It appears, nevertheless, that, almost from the time that he had become Prime Minister, Negrín, that subtle and elusive personality, had been attempting to achieve peace by negotiation. He had tried to make contact with the Vatican in August 1937.[1] He had already had meetings with the German ambassador in Paris, Count Welczeck. He also sought mediation through a cousin of Serrano Súñer, but again he was unsuccessful. It is hard to blame Negrín for continuing the war when there was no alternative save unconditional surrender. From now on, Negrín placed his hopes in the outbreak of a general European war in which, he supposed, Spain's troubles would be subsumed. Azaña, meantime, told Negrín that he had felt 'since September 1936, a "dispossessed President". When you formed a government, I believed, at first, I could breathe again, and that my opinions would be at least heard. It has not been so. I have to suffer in silence.'[2] The two men continued to differ: Azaña continued to look backwards to speculate on where he had gone wrong in the early 1930s; Negrín, with no political past, continued to look forward. Negrín, with the day-to-day business of maintaining morale at the front, nerved himself to radiate optimism; Azaña, with little to do, could only bitterly reflect.

Franco liked neither Negrín's nor Yagüe's ideas: 'Whoever desires mediation', he said, in a speech on 6 June, 'serves the "reds" or the hidden enemies of Spain.' He added, for good measure, that the war was the 'coronation of a historic process of struggle of the fatherland against the "anti-patria"', and to make peace now would ensure a new war later.[3] A major press campaign was mounted in nationalist Spain against those who demanded mediation: 'In the name of the

1. Azaña, vol. IV, p. 845.

2. Azaña, *op. cit.*, p. 877. This conversation had been on 22 April, arising from Negrín's desire for Azaña's signature to 45 death penalties. Azaña was reluctant. Negrín thought it essential, to avoid *paseos*, to save life. Negrín reminded Azaña that he had himself regretted that he had pardoned Sanjurjo in 1932. (Negrín himself had been in favour of shooting Sanjurjo, though he had liked him personally; Azaña had disliked Sanjurjo personally but had supported his reprieve.)

3. Franco's speech, qu. Abella, p. 328.

destiny of Spain, its martyrs and heroes, the fatherland demands the unconditional victory of Franco.'

*

The international prospects in the spring of 1938, unlike the military situation in Spain itself, were increasingly discouraging for anti-fascists. Chamberlain was pressing on to anticipate and, therefore, resolve further German demands in central Europe, particularly in Czechoslovakia. On 16 April, he achieved his Anglo–Italian Mediterranean Pact. Italy undertook to withdraw her troops from Spain once the war was over. Though only then would the pact come into force, the two countries agreed to guarantee the *status quo* in the Mediterranean. Perth, noted Ciano, was moved. He said: 'You know how much I have wanted this to come about.' 'It is true,' added Ciano, 'Perth has been a friend – witness dozens of reports which are in our hands.'[1] Azcárate sent a protest to the Foreign Office expressing horror that the exchange of letters between Italy and Britain should accept Italian troops in Spain till the end of the civil war – while Britain was maintaining the Non-Intervention Pact, not to speak of a plan for withdrawal of volunteers.[2] *Pravda* denounced the Anglo–Italian Pact as giving its blessing to Mussolini in 'his war against the Spanish people'. Even Churchill echoed the same, in a letter to Eden: 'A complete triumph for Mussolini, who gains our cordial acceptance for his fortification of the Mediterranean against us, for his conquest of Abyssinia, and for his violence in Spain.' The conservative opponents of Chamberlain came, during the next weeks, to be almost republican sympathizers.[3]

1. Ciano, *Diaries 1937–8*.

2. Azcárate, p. 153. The republican ambassador added that thereafter 'shame and indignation' at British policy caused the republic to keep relations with the UK to a minimum.

3. W. Churchill, *The Gathering Storm*, p. 221. Churchill, for instance, was brought to have an amicable conversation with the republican ambassador, Azcárate, showing sympathy for the republic, after dinner at the Soviet Embassy. The conversion of Churchill to the republic was the work of his son-in-law, Duncan Sandys, who visited Barcelona in the spring of 1938. But Churchill's 'republicanism' was always realistic. Thus, he told a Buenos Aires newspaper: 'Franco has all the right on his side, because he loves his country. Also Franco is defending Europe against the communist danger – if you wish to put it in those

There was no sign whatever that Italy had any intention of keeping the Non-Intervention Agreement any more than in the past. Three hundred more Italian officers went to Spain on 11 April. For her part, Germany concluded that an early nationalist victory would prevent action over the volunteer plan. The foreign ministry, therefore, instructed their London Embassy to agree to any 'formula' that they could think of for the withdrawal of volunteers. Hitler wanted to withdraw the German troops in Spain. The Austrian air force needed guidance, and 'our soldiers cannot learn any more'.[1] Franco suggested that the Condor Legion might be withdrawn, provided that the aircraft, anti-aircraft guns, and other equipment were left behind for the Spanish pilots, whom the Germans had trained to fly. Alongside this mood of German restlessness, the republic was able to profit for a time from a new French mood in the spring of 1938. The new Prime Minister, the dour peasant, Daladier, told the American ambassador in Paris, Bullitt, that he had opened the French frontier as wide as possible for the Spanish republican benefit. Russia, he said, had agreed to send three hundred aircraft to Catalonia, provided that the French transported them across France. Daladier did this in large lorries, even though 'he had to cut down trees along the roads of Aquitaine to let the wings pass'.[2] 25,000 tons of war material crossed the Pyrenean frontier in April and May. No progress, not surprisingly, was made in the discussions which Daladier's foreign secretary, Georges Bonnet, had begun with Italy, on the model of Chamberlain's. The talks were broken off when, on 15 May, Mussolini announced that he did not know what could come of them, since the two countries were 'on different sides of the barricades' in Spain. Bonnet, however, was conservative and cautious. He proved to be no friend to the republic.

On 13 May, Alvarez del Vayo again appeared before the Council of the League and demanded that those countries which, in October, had resolved that non-intervention should be reconsidered if it were not shortly made effective, should now enact that reconsideration. Chamberlain's new Foreign Secretary, Lord Halifax, pressed for a

terms. But I – I am English, and I prefer the triumph of the wrong cause. I prefer that the other side wins because Franco could be an upset to British interests.' (*La Nación*, Buenos Aires, 14 August 1938.)

1. *GD*, p. 635. 2. *USD*, 1938, vol. I, pp. 192–3.

vote. He was anxious to concentrate on the crisis in Czechoslovakia.[1] His own private secretary, Harvey, whom he had inherited from Eden, wrote: 'neither he nor Chamberlain had such an abhorrence of dictatorship as to overcome their innate mistrust of French democracy, and its supposed inefficiency'.[2] Some delegations at Geneva, such as those of China and New Zealand, who might on this occasion have supported Spain, did not have time to consult their governments. When the vote came, on the same day that the matter had first been raised, only Spain and Russia voted for the resolution calling for action. Britain, France, Poland and Romania voted against, while the other nine states of the Council abstained. The number of abstentions reflected the increasing sympathy felt for the republic, because of the worsening position in Europe.

There was some pressure upon the American government to end their embargo on arms to Spain. The columnist, Drew Pearson, remarked that 'Washington has seen all kinds of lobbying . . . but seldom before has [it] seen people spend money to come from all over the country in a cause from which they would receive no material benefit'.[3] The former secretary of state (and future secretary for war), H. L. Stimson, and the ex-ambassador to Germany, William Dodd, signed a petition against the embargo. Einstein and other interested scientists joined the campaign. Resolutions were introduced in Congress proposing the end of the embargo by Representative Byron Scott and Senator Nye. On 3 May, the secretary of state, Cordell Hull, met his advisers in the state department to consider Senator Nye's resolution.[4] Hull and the officials agreed that they need not intervene to prevent the passage of the resolution. A planned 'leak' about this appeared in the *New York Times* on 5 May. Immediately, the new, catholic American ambassador in London, Joseph Kennedy, telegraphed his alarm lest this measure should cause an extension of

1. On 10 May, Ivone Kirkpatrick told Prince Bismarck that 'If the German government would advise the British government confidentially what solution of the Sudeten German question they were striving after . . . the British government would bring such pressure to bear in Prague that the Czechoslovak government would be compelled to accede to German wishes.' (*G D*, Series D, vol. II, doc. no. 1511.)

2. Harvey, p. 124. 'My colleagues are dictator-minded', Eden had often said.

3. *New Orleans States*, 9 May 1938, qu. Taylor, p. 169.

4. R. J. Bendiner, *The Riddle of the State Department* (New York, 1962).

the civil war. The catholics in the United States made passionate protests against help to 'bolshevists and atheists'. Roosevelt, on a fishing holiday in the Caribbean, told Hull to delay and, when he returned to Washington, the decision to end the embargo was reversed. At the end of May, a letter from Hull told Senator Pittman that the Spanish Civil War was 'more than a civil war' and so could not be treated simply as such.[1]

Litvinov was complaining in Geneva to Louis Fischer, still acting as arms purchaser for the republic: 'Always defeats, always retreats.' 'If you gave them five hundred more aircraft, they could win the war,' said Fischer. Litvinov protested that such a consignment would help Russia more in China than in Spain. He anyway had no aircraft. 'I merely hand on diplomatic documents,' he added. But he promised to ask his master. (This was a bad time for him: nearly all his ambassadors in the Russian foreign ministry had recently been arrested.)[2] But, even if he had procured five hundred aircraft, it would have been difficult to get them to Spain. For, on 13 June, Daladier, under pressure from Britain, again closed the frontier.[3] The months during which arms supplies could freely be brought to the republic were thus at an end, though, before the frontier was closed, Miles Sherover, the Polish-born businessman who was now purchasing agent in the US for the republic, and indeed general manager of the republican interests there, managed to ship substantial

1. Taylor, p. 174; Traina, p. 134f; Bendiner, pp. 59–62; *USD*, 1938, vol. I, pp. 183–95. The German ambassador in Washington reported to Berlin that the British influence was the decisive factor (*GD*, pp. 656–7). Arthur Krock told me (9 January 1963) that, so far as he could recall, Hull or Welles gave him the information on which he had based this article, and that that was the policy his informant then wished to achieve. Ickes (vol. II, p. 390), says Roosevelt told him on 9 May that 'to raise the embargo would mean the loss of every catholic vote next fall and that the democratic members of congress were jittery about it and didn't want it done'. This confirms the impression of Norman Thomas, with whom I discussed this matter in 1962. Jay Allen in *The Christian Science Monitor* later alleged that Cardinal Mundelein of Chicago telephoned Roosevelt on a later occasion to dissuade him from raising the embargo (Traina, p. 213). Krock's son was apparently one of the very few Americans fighting for Franco.

2. L. Fischer, pp. 468–70. Litvinov himself had, for many months, a suitcase packed ready to take with him to gaol as his wife recalls.

3. Harvey, p. 157: 'The French are getting increasingly restive as a result of having closed their frontier as a result of our urging,' Harvey wrote on 2 July.

supplies through the so-called 'Hanover Corporation'; most of these were lorries, cars and lorry engines.[1] A month later, the first chamber of the French Court of Appeal decided that certain gold belonging to the Bank of Spain, which had been deposited in France at Mont de Marsan, belonged to 'a private society' and could not therefore be remitted to the republic. This was another reverse, though some material continued to pass. The Mediterranean route was now almost completely unused.

On the nationalist side, new Italian forces were being dispatched to Spain, from 1 June onwards. Ciano assured Millán Astray and a party of Spanish pilots visiting Rome that, 'notwithstanding all committees, Italy will not abandon Spain until the nationalist flag is flying from the loftiest towers of Barcelona, Valencia and Madrid'.[2] Given that mood in Rome, it was scarcely surprising that the British government soon had, reluctantly, to return to the 'Spanish question'. On 18 May, the House of Lords had discussed the Anglo–Italian Agreement; the Foreign Secretary, Halifax, had said of the Italian undertakings: 'We . . . do accept these assurances and believe that they will be honourably carried out.'[3] But this remark was followed by a further outbreak of nationalist bombing of republican Spain. There were raids on Valencia and other Mediterranean coast towns, none of which had much in the way of anti-aircraft guns.[4] On 2 June, Granollers, a town of no military significance, twenty miles north of Barcelona, was bombed. About a hundred people (mainly women and children) were killed. Halifax protested to Burgos and to the German ambassador in London, Dirksen, though he added 'that he knew that this was a very delicate matter and he wished *at all events* to avoid creating any ill feeling in Germany'.[5] Sir Nevile Henderson begged Weizsäcker to use German influence to secure an end of these indiscriminate attacks.[6] Ciano was similarly approached by Perth. So was the papal secretary of state by the British minister to the

1. Traina, p. 168. Sherover had first made news by selling $60m of Soviet American Security bonds between 1931 and 1935. He had been commercial agent for the republic since 1936. In conversation in 1975, Sherover confirmed that Roosevelt anyway gave him to understand that it was the catholic vote which affected him.

2. Ciano, *Diaries 1937–8*, p. 123.

3. *Speeches on Foreign Policy, 1934–9* (London, 1940), p. 164.

4. Cf. Thompson, p. 122f. 5. *G D*, p. 684, Dirksen's italics. 6. *ibid.*, pp. 684–5.

Holy See. Ciano, bland as ever, promised to do what he could. ('Actually,' Ciano assured the German ambassador Mackensen, 'we have, of course, done nothing, and have no intention of doing anything either.')[1] Cardinal Pacelli explained that the Vatican was constantly using its influence in one way or another with Franco.[2] Eventually, Britain proposed that a special commission should investigate such attacks, to see if they were really directed at military targets. None of the countries whom Britain approached (the US, Sweden, Norway, Holland) to share in the scheme was willing. Britain, therefore, sent two officers of her own to carry out the inquiry. Though they reported that the bombing must have been often aimed at non-military targets, nothing came of their conclusions.

The situation was exacerbated by further attacks upon British ships in Spanish waters. By this time, most seaborne trade with the republic was carried in British-owned ships. Others decided that the risk of being bombed, or seized, was too great. Many of these ships, however, were British only in name – many being Greek, registered in nominally British companies, through the agency of men such as Jack Billmeir, whose Stanhope Shipping Company now had some thirty-five ships trading with the republic. Between mid-April and mid-June, 22 British-registered ships (out of 140 then trading with the republic) were attacked in Spanish waters. Eleven were either sunk or seriously damaged. Twenty-one British seamen died, as did several Non-Intervention Committee observers. Chamberlain's cabinet, according to Sir Alexander Cadogan, the permanent under-secretary at the Foreign Office, was 'almost distracted'.[3] Daily, the British government was attacked in the House of Commons for permitting this sorry state of affairs. Most of the ships were sunk in harbours and the Navy found it thus hard to counter the action. The subtle vocabulary of R. A. Butler, parliamentary under-secretary at the Foreign Office, was taxed to explain why the government would not permit the export of anti-aircraft guns to republican Spain, nor the merchant ships to carry their own arms. Yet it became evident that the attacks were deliberate. Several conservatives, such as Duncan Sandys, were at one with the socialist Nöel-Baker in protesting against the ignominy of the position. The rising star of the left,

1. *GD*, p. 683. 2. *USD*, 1938, vol. I, p. 208.

3. *USD*, 1938, vol. I, p. 215. He succeeded Vansittart on 1 January 1938.

Aneurin Bevan, evoked memories of what Clive of India would have done, and Lloyd George demanded reprisals by bombing Italian air bases in Majorca.[1] Churchill said:

I think it could be perfectly safely said to General Franco, 'If there is any more of this, we shall arrest one of your ships on the open sea' . . . I can quite understand undergoing humiliation for the cause of peace. I would have supported the government, if I felt that we were making towards greater security for peace. But I fear that this abjection is woefully misunderstood abroad. I fear that it will . . . actually bring us nearer to all those dangers which we desire above all things to withhold from our people.[2]

Lord Cecil of Chelwood resigned the conservative party whip in the House of Lords because of the government's ineffectiveness. The archbishop of York, Dr Temple, with other prelates, pleaded for 'effective action'. Chamberlain noted in his diary: 'I have been through every possible form of retaliation, and it is absolutely clear that none of them can be effective unless we are prepared to go to war with Franco . . . of course, it may come to that, if Franco were foolish enough.'[3] On one occasion, in the cabinet, he suggested that Britain seize Minorca in protest; 'The difficulty of this,' the cabinet minutes acidly noted, 'was that Minorca was owned by the government.'[4]

The nationalists eventually suggested that Almería might be made a safety zone for shipping. This idea was rejected both by the republic and by the Committee of British Shipowners, since only a seventh of the shipping then frequenting republican ports could be accommodated in Almería. The situation was permitted to continue. The British ship *Dellwyn* was sunk off Gandia in the sight of a British warship. 'The first time in history,' mourned Bowers, the American ambassador and a devoted friend of democracy.[5] Prieto, in a speech at Barcelona, reflected,

1. *Parliamentary Debates*, vol. 337, col. 1011 (21 June 1938).
2. *ibid.*, col. 1387 (23 June 1938).
3. Feiling, p. 352.
4. *CAB*, 27(38), on 1 June.
5. *USD*, 1938, vol. I, p. 231. One reaction was Low's cartoon of 16 June, in which he caused Colonel Blimp to remark: 'Gad sir, it is time we told Franco that, if he sinks another hundred British ships, we shall retire from the Mediterranean altogether.'

Who would have thought it possible, we who, in our study of international relations, have come across mention of the arrogance and pride of England, who would not tolerate the least harm to its material interests, nor an attack on the lives of one of its subjects? Yet here, in our cemeteries, are the bodies of English sailors who have paid with their lives for the confidence they had in the protection of the Empire.

The continuance of attacks caused Lord Perth to tell Ciano that he feared that Chamberlain 'might fall if the raids continued'.[1] The raids were, apparently in consequence, called off from the start of July. The crisis had made for bad relations between the nationalists and their allies. For, if Germany and Italy denied responsibility, they were placing it upon Franco. Stohrer was instructed to tell Franco that Germany had expected that he would have protected the Condor Legion from odium. But some Germans were being indiscreet themselves. On 12 July, the *News Chronicle* published a report of a lecture by General von Reichenau, the ambitious nazi commander of the German 4th Army Group, on 'The German attitude towards events in Spain': 'two years of real war experience', said Reichenau, 'have been of more use to our yet immature Wehrmacht, to the offensive power of the people, than a whole ten years of peaceful training could have been'. The British cabinet had the lecture circulated to them, and those ministers who read it could see that in aerial, tank and anti-tank warfare the Germans had gained much from their Spanish experience.[2] 'Spain has taught us particularly valuable lessons in the use of motor vehicles in war', said von Reichenau. Lord Halifax suggested that the British should 'draft an appeal to the contending sides to stop the war. Such an appeal would, of course, be based on grounds of humanity, Christianity and so forth . . . it would not be likely to succeed, but it would strengthen the moral position of His Majesty's government.'[3]

The Germans were, in fact, this summer engaged in a serious quarrel with Franco. Franco signed the Spanish mining law before showing it to von Stohrer. Concessions included to please the Ger-

1. Ciano, *Diaries 1937–8*, p. 132.
2. See *CAB* (163) 38. For Reichenau, see R. J. O'Neill, *The German Army and the Nazi Party 1933–1939* (London, 1966), p. 194. The lesson the Germans had drawn was that Franco did not have enough motor vehicles to enable Blitzkrieg.
3. *CAB*, 32 (38) of 13 July.

mans permitted 40 per cent foreign capital investment, and the possibility of exceptions, higher than this percentage, in Morocco. The law satisfied Germany, but not the manner of its publication. Von Stohrer coldly demanded whether he was no longer *persona grata.* He was told that Franco was busy. Von Stohrer demanded whether he could not spare half an hour to see the German ambassador. Later, he was received by Gómez Jordana, who explained how he and Franco had championed Germany in their cabinet, and had even gained amendments in Germany's favour. Enemy propaganda, he added, would have claimed that Germany had forced concessions if Franco had received the ambassador just before the decree was published. 'But Spanish nationalist newspapers never report when I call,' von Stohrer pointed out. With bad temper, Germany accepted the apology, as well as the concessions.[1] During the next few weeks, German relations with Franco were excessively complicated; Germany even seems to have toyed with the idea of making its half-formulated desire to prolong the war in Spain into a reality by selling equipment to the republic, and German nazi negotiators secretly met Negrín, as will be seen.

During these weeks of continuous international crisis, the nationalist offensive in the Maestrazgo and along the Mediterranean continued with painful slowness. The republic, its forces commanded by General Leopoldo Menéndez (under the overall command of Miaja), resisted with skill and valour. The Condor Legion's commander, General Volkmann, reported that its material was exhausted.[2] The republicans had, on the other hand, received from Russia numerous new Moscas, including the so-called 'Supermosca', with four machine-guns and high speed; from France, forty Canadian Grumman fighters.[3] Thus only on 14 June did Castellón, sixty miles south of Vinaroz, fall to Aranda, after several days of ferocious fighting in its suburbs. Forty political prisoners were murdered and the town sacked before the last republican units left. The nationalists hence-

1. *GD*, pp. 675–81. For commentary, see Harper, p. 98f.

2. *GD*, p. 689.

3. According to R. Salas (vol. II, p. 1870), the republic refused to buy from the US the T-6 fighter, which would have had a considerable effect. But how would they have paid, and was it desirable to change from one supplier to another in mid-war?

forward had a large Mediterranean port in El Grao de Castellón. They were also only fifty miles north of Valencia. But, despite the fact that García Valiño's experienced troops (now an army corps) had joined Aranda, Solchaga and Varela, a military stalemate was reached, eight miles north of Sagunto. The only nationalist success now obtained was General Iruretagoyena's conquest of El Esquinazado's enclave in the Valle del Alto Cinca. The Pyrenean town of Bielsa fell on 6 June. Four thousand men escaped into France.[1]

*

In mid-June it was no longer suggested in Spain that the war would soon be over. The optimism of the spring had vanished. War weariness was everywhere. According to von Stohrer, 'the terror practised at present in the nationalist zone by Martínez Anido' was 'unbearable, even to the Falange'.[2] Negrín, speaking in Madrid on 18 June, said that not one more second of war could be tolerated if Spain's existence as a free country was to be preserved. The bishop of Gerona wrote a letter to Companys, on 28 June, from nationalist territory, in which he argued that the republic should surrender, since Franco's army had triumphed in over half Spain and, therefore, President Companys, as a good democrat, should recognize this 'majority principle'.[3] Abroad, Litvinov announced that Russia would be only too glad to withdraw from Spain on the basis of 'Spain for the Spaniards', while Ilya Ehrenburg in *Pravda*, on 17 June, stretched out the 'hand of conciliation' towards the old Falange, whom he surprisingly named 'Spanish patriots'. Already the Russian military mission was much smaller than it had been before. Azaña had an interview with the British chargé, John Leche, in the Museum of Vich, in which he once again urged a mediation in Spain which would include a plebiscite, following a cease-fire.[4] Azaña was more and more critical of the judicial procedures being practised in his name: of the supreme tribunals, he noted desperately: 'lack of guarantees. Incompetence of illiterate judges. Impolitic cruelty . . . a few boys condemned to death for singing a song. The informer did not know what he was doing. Bad treatment: one blind, one deaf.' But Negrín

1. Aznar, p. 704; Buckley, p. 375. 2. *GD*, p. 711.
3. Professor Bosch Gimpera gave me a copy of this letter.
4. Evidence of Professor Bosch Gimpera.

still believed that a few exemplary punishments would win as much as battles.[1]

On 27 June, Maisky agreed to the plan for the withdrawal of volunteers worked out in the Non-Intervention Committee. Two commissions were to be sent to Spain, the first to enumerate the foreigners, the second to supervise their withdrawal. The cost, estimated at between £1,750,000 and £2,250,000, would be borne by the non-intervention countries.[2] The plan was sent for comment to the two sides in Spain. The nationalist attitude was expressed by Jordana. He explained that 'a way must be sought of strengthening Neville Chamberlain's position by accepting the plan in principle, but, by skilful reservations and counter-proposals, to win as much time as possible to prosecute the war in the meantime'.[3] The minds of all were best expressed by Maisky (inculpating his own country) when he said that 'the whole demeanour of the interventionist powers compels me to doubt whether the actual evacuation of the "volunteers" will take place'.[4]

On 5 July, the nationalist army in the Levante began a great effort to force a way to Valencia.[5] Nine hundred cannon and four hundred aircraft were now concentrated in that zone. García Valiño pressed down from the north outside Castellón, but here the Sierra de Espadán reached almost to the sea and the republican forces, led by the astute Gustavo Durán and General Menéndez, could not be dislodged. On 13 July, Varela, with Berti and three Italian divisions, alongside Solchaga's Navarrese, attacked southwards from Teruel. The armour of the Italians decided the first days of the battle, but the republican resistance was again well organized. A force of carabineers held out for a long time at Mora de Rubielos. Then Sarrión fell, and, with it, the republican positions along the Sierra de Toro. The front now began to crumble in a fashion reminiscent of what had happened in Aragon. The nationalist tourist bureau, recently opened,

1. Azaña, *op. cit.*, p. 880.
2. *NIS*, twenty-ninth meeting; *NIS*(c), ninety-third meeting.
3. *GD*, p. 725.
4. Cattell, *Soviet Diplomacy*, p. 119.
5. Ansaldo, p. 63, says that this attack was the result of a personal initiative of Franco. Certain alarmists in nationalist Spain were convinced that the Germans were at the back of this campaign, in order to prolong the war.

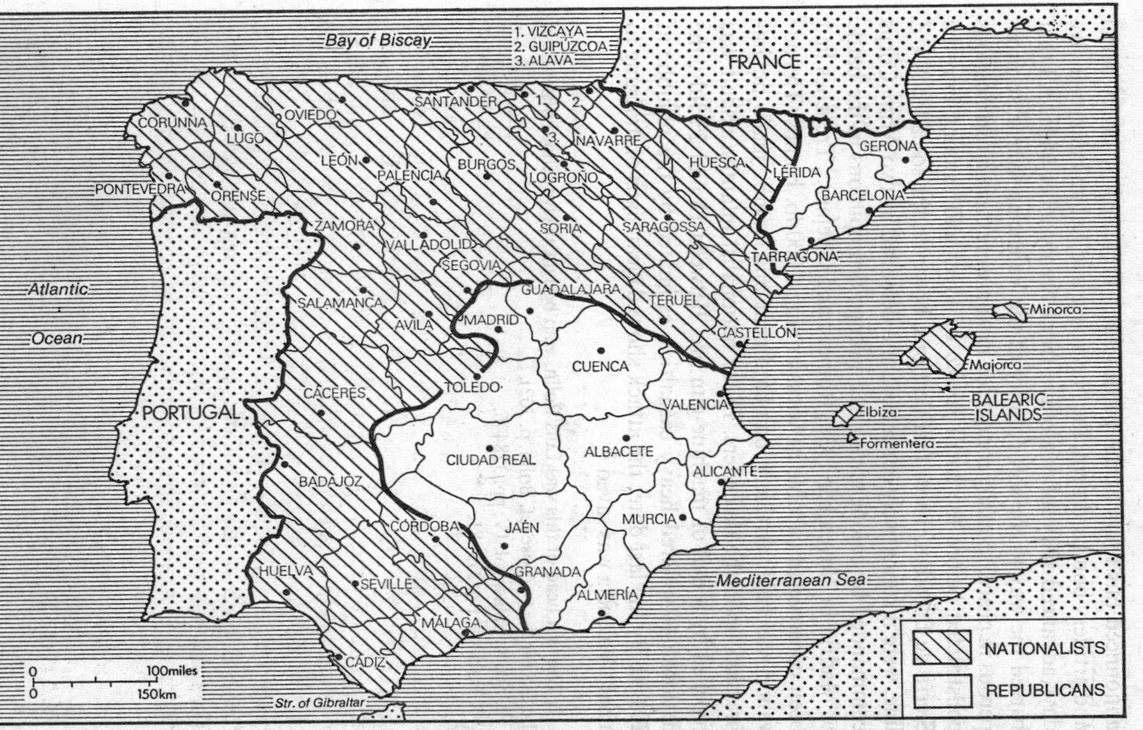

Bay of Biscay
1. VIZCAYA
2. GUIPÚZCOA
3. ALAVA
FRANCE
CORUNNA
LUGO
OVIEDO
SANTANDER
NAVARRE
LEÓN
PALENCIA
BURGOS
LOGROÑO
HUESCA
LÉRIDA
GERONA
BARCELONA
PONTEVEDRA
ORENSE
ZAMORA
VALLADOLID
SORIA
SARAGOSSA
TARRAGONA
SEGOVIA
GUADALAJARA
TERUEL
Atlantic
Ocean
SALAMANCA
AVILA
MADRID
CASTELLÓN
Minorca
Majorca
BALEARIC ISLANDS
Ibiza
Formentera
CUENCA
TOLEDO
CÁCERES
PORTUGAL
VALENCIA
CIUDAD REAL
ALBACETE
ALICANTE
BADAJOZ
CÓRDOBA
JAÉN
MURCIA
HUELVA
SEVILLE
GRANADA
ALMERÍA
Mediterranean Sea
MÁLAGA
CÁDIZ
0 100miles
0 150km
Str. of Gibraltar
NATIONALISTS
REPUBLICANS

33. Division of Spain, July 1938

announced bus tours of the battlefields.[1] Protected by heavy aerial and artillery bombardment, the Navarrese and Italian infantry in five days advanced sixty miles along a front twenty miles wide. All that barred the way to the soft country of the Valencian *huerta*, so prosperous in peace, so easily conquered in war, were certain fortifications constructed before the small *pueblo* of Viver and running into the Sierra de Espadán. These fortifications, however, the so-called XYZ line, were imaginatively conceived, and defended by two Army Corps commanded by colonels who had won golden opinions in the battle of Madrid in November 1936, Romero and Güemes.[2] Trenches had been constructed capable of withstanding 1,000-lb. bombs. The advance was held. Artillery bombardment and bombs made no impression upon the defenders. Every nationalist infantry assault was repelled by a hail of machine-gun fire. Between 18 and 23 July, the nationalists suffered heavy casualties, estimated by the republic at 20,000. By the last date, the attack showed clear signs of dragging to a halt. Valencia was saved.[3]

1. The first head of this was Luis Bolín, who bought twelve school buses from the US for the purpose (cf. Bolín, p. 302).
2. See R. Salas, vol. IV, pp. 3284–6.
3. Buckley, pp. 379–81.

47

The battle of the Ebro – advance to Gandesa – the war of attrition – the crisis of August – the Munich crisis and Spain – withdrawal of the International Brigades – the League of Nations Commission – Sir Philip Chetwode in Spain – the battles on the Caballs – the Mediterranean Agreement

---

ON 24 July 1938, Negrín told the republican war council in Barcelona that Valencia would be lost unless there were a diversionary attack elsewhere. General Rojo, chief of staff, therefore, proposed to attack to the north of the nationalists' salient to the Mediterranean. The plan was to force a passage across the great River Ebro at several points, about seventy miles from the sea, in order first to confuse communications between the nationalists in the Levante and in Catalonia and secondly, if possible, restore land communications between Catalonia and the rest of republican Spain. To carry out this scheme, a new 'Army of the Ebro' had been constituted under Modesto, consisting of the 5th Army Corps under Lister, the 12th under Etelvino Vega and the 15th under Manuel Tagüeña. The 18th Army Corps, under José del Barrio, was in reserve. This force of 80,000 men was to be supported by 70–80 field batteries, and 27 anti-aircraft guns. The republicans' air support had been much improved, thanks to the Supermosca and Superchato fighters manned by Spaniards who had been trained in Russia. All the proposed leading commanders of the Army of the Ebro were communists, corps commanders and divisional commanders alike, as well as, of course, Modesto. Indeed, these commanders met regularly, as party members, with the directorate of the party.[1] The anarchists held only two brigade commands out of twenty-seven in the whole Army of the Ebro.[2] They were not, however, anything like so badly represented as that in other armies. For example, Colonel Perea, commander of the Army of the East, had always been sympathetic to the anarchists, while, of the five armies of the central zone, under Miaja, only one (the unimportant

1. Lister, p. 220. 2. Peirats, vol. III, p. 230.

Army of Estremadura) was led by one who could be called even a communist sympathizer, Colonel Burrillo.[1] The others may not have been anarchists, but they were not communists. In addition, the communists were not united: Modesto and Lister, the two outstanding military successes of the war, were on bad terms. Modesto was a sarcastic, despotic Andalusian, sometimes brutal, rarely candid, but a real military leader, with no political gifts or ambitions. Lister was a warm-hearted and ambitious orator, with a strong sense of friendship, undisciplined, and ready to lend himself to any propaganda activity, which he carried out well; sometimes harsh, he also tolerated innumerable mistakes by his subordinates if he liked them.[2] In addition, many new communists were really bourgeois in all but name. Other successful communist commanders had had their political attitudes formed exclusively by the war. No one knew what views they would have afterwards. The chief of staff of the army, Rojo, continued to seem to the anarchists all too tolerant of the communists, but he was a technician pure and simple. Bernal, the chief of transport, was a known anti-revolutionary. The socialist chief of administration of the army, Trifón Gómez, was a follower of Prieto's, and had even been removed from the party directorate in 1934 when Largo Caballero began his move to the left. Colonel Jurado, the artillery officer, now in charge of anti-aircraft, was thought by some to have backed the republic by accident. Manuel Albar, in charge of coordination of the different commissariats, and Alfonso Játiva, the sub-secretary of the navy, were men of Prieto. So too were Belarmino Tomás, the new commissar of the air, and Zugazagoitia, the secretary-general of defence – though his job scarcely existed.[3] Many other assignments in the ministry of war were still held, as they had been under Prieto, by politically neutral professional officers rather than by communists. For example, artillery was still directed by Colonel Fuentes, the officer who had seemed so anti-Russian to Major Voro-

1. These were the Armies of the Centre (Casado), the Levante (Hernández Saravia), of 'Manoeuvre' (Menéndez) and Andalusia (Moriones).

2. For an excellent pen-picture of the two, see Tagüeña, p. 187.

3. It is interesting that a job was found for Tomás, who had been so unsuccessful but so presumptuous in the presidency of the Council of Asturias. The nationalists would have hesitated at such an act of kindness rewarding incompetence.

nov in November 1936; Colonel Montaud, one of the commanders of the Basque army, directed communications; Doctor José Puché, rector of the University of Valencia, a friend of Negrín, was head of the army medical corps; only Major Azcárate, a cousin of the ambassador, who controlled the engineering corps, and Colonel Sánchez Paredes, the tank specialist, could be regarded as close to the communist party. The sub-secretary in charge of arms purchase, the enigmatic socialist deputy for Granada, Alejandro Otero, seemed, on the other hand, a capitalist of wide imagination. The communist-led units received the lion's share of the best arms; but they were the offensive ones. They also seem to have been the best commanders, though that is a difficult matter to judge.

In the Army of the Ebro, the rise of Manuel Tagüeña, still under thirty, but in command of an Army Corps, with no military experience before 1936, was symbolic of the large number of young men, chiefly communists, or members of the united youth, who gained field command in the later stages of the civil war.[1] His communism was that of a patriotic fighting-man, not that of an 'ideologue'.

These reorganized armies held on in republican Spain throughout 1938. The recovery after the defeats of the spring was a great achievement. The opening of the French frontier in March was partly responsible. The calling up of new classes of reserves was also important, as was the provision of new officers' schools. The recovery was also the stubborn work of embattled men, most of them under twenty-five, who knew that they stood to lose all, including their lives, unless they worked until they dropped.

It was rash of the republic, with the French frontier once more closed, to embark upon an offensive, in the summer of 1938, as the examples of Brunete, Belchite, and Teruel might have suggested to them. The pattern of those battles – the early success of the attack; containment by nationalist reinforcements, hurried from other

1. An active member of the socialist youth before the war, Tagüeña fought in the Sierra in July and in the Tagus front in September, in Madrid in October, succeeding Fernando de Rosa, and became, in the winter of 1936–7, one of the first commanders of a Mixed Brigade. He joined the communist party in November 1936. His great success had been in the Aragon front in retreat in March.

fronts; and a nationalist counter-attack – was indeed followed in the battle of the Ebro, though on a larger scale, and with more terrible consequences than in those other engagements.[1]

Still, at a quarter past midnight on the night of 24–25 July, with no moon, the crossing of the Ebro began. Units under Tagüeña started to cross the river between Mequinenza and Fayón. Lister and the 5th Army Corps began to cross at sixteen points in the great arc between Fayón and Cherta, notably at Flix, Mora la Nueva, Miravet, and thirty miles to the south, at Amposta, near the sea. Ninety boats (each of which carried 10 men), 3 pontoon bridges, and about 12 others, had been assembled. The armoured accompaniment consisted of 22 T-26 tanks and 4 companies of armoured cars, armed with machine-guns, not cannon. More material would follow across the bridges, once these could safely be swung across the river. The first unit across in Lister's Corps was the Hans Beimler Battalion of the 11th International Brigade, reconstructed, composed of Germans, Scandinavians and Catalans, whose commanders led the way with a cry of 'Forward, sons of Negrín!', in unfamiliar accents.[2] The river Ebro is at Mora some hundred yards wide and runs through a fairly steep gorge.

The other side of the river from Mequinenza to the sea was guarded at this time by the Army of Morocco, to whose command

1. For the battle of the Ebro, see Luis María Mezquida, *La batalla del Ebro* (Tarragona, 1963–7); Julián Henríquez, *La batalla del Ebro* (Mexico, 1944); and the versions given by Tagüeña, Lister, Martínez de Campos, Kindelán, Rojo and Henry Buckley in their often-cited books. For the battle plan, see R. Salas, vol. IV, pp. 3287–97. Mezquida's volumes have the merit of incorporating a large number of personal testimonies from junior ranks. For an impression of the war in the air, see García Lacalle, p. 381f. For an odd recent eye-witness account, see Francisco Pérez López, *A Guerrilla Diary of the Spanish Civil War* (London, 1972). See also R. Salas, vol. II, p. 1967f. I benefited from discussing this battle with the then Colonel Martínez de Campos and Manuel Tagüeña, and from correspondence with Colonel García Lacalle.

2. *Reconquista* (newspaper of the Army of the Ebro). The preparation of this offensive is well described in Tagüeña, p. 200f. Equally important, in these first days of the battle of the Ebro, was the reconstituted French 14th Brigade, led by Marcel Sagnier, commissar Henri Tanguy. See Delperrie de Bayac, p. 354f. The pontoon bridges and inflatable rubber boats were bought in France. Did the French military advise on their use, as implied by General Barroso to Hills (p. 319)? There is no evidence.

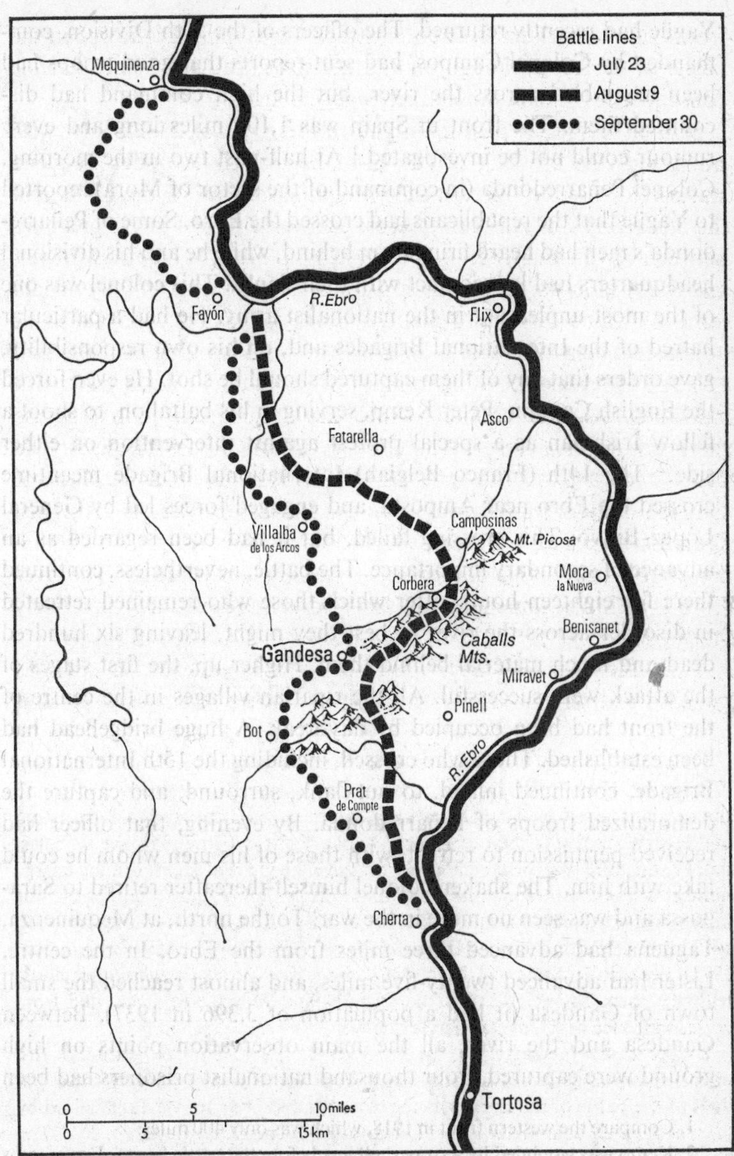

34. The battle of the Ebro, July–November 1938

Yagüe had recently returned. The officers of the 50th Division, commanded by Colonel Campos, had sent reports that good troops had been assembled across the river, but the high command had discounted them. The front in Spain was 1,100 miles long and every rumour could not be investigated.[1] At half-past two in the morning, Colonel Peñarredonda (in command of the sector of Mora) reported to Yagüe that the republicans had crossed the Ebro. Some of Peñarredonda's men had heard firing from behind, while he and his divisional headquarters had lost contact with their flanks. This colonel was one of the most unpleasant in the nationalist army. He had a particular hatred of the International Brigades and, on his own responsibility, gave orders that any of them captured should be shot. He even forced the English Captain, Peter Kemp, serving in his battalion, to shoot a fellow Irishman as a special protest against intervention on either side.[2] The 14th (Franco–Belgian) International Brigade meantime crossed the Ebro near Amposta, and engaged forces led by General López Bravo. This crossing failed, but it had been regarded as an advance of secondary importance. The battle, nevertheless, continued there for eighteen hours, after which those who remained retreated in disorder across the river as best they might, leaving six hundred dead and much material behind them. Higher up, the first stages of the attack were successful. All the riparian villages in the centre of the front had been occupied by daybreak. A huge bridgehead had been established. Those who crossed, including the 15th International Brigade, continued inland, to out-flank, surround, and capture the demoralized troops of Peñarredonda. By evening, that officer had received permission to retreat, with those of his men whom he could take with him. The shaken colonel himself thereafter retired to Saragossa and was seen no more in the war. To the north, at Mequinenza, Tagüeña had advanced three miles from the Ebro. In the centre, Lister had advanced twenty-five miles, and almost reached the small town of Gandesa (it had a population of 3,396 in 1937). Between Gandesa and the river, all the main observation points on high ground were captured. Four thousand nationalist prisoners had been

1. Compare the western front in 1918, which was only 400 miles.

2. Kemp was wounded by a stray shell just before the battle began. For months previously he had been facing a one-time contemporary of his at Trinity College, Cambridge, Malcolm Dunbar, chief of staff to the 15th International Brigade.

taken, many desertions following. Franco ordered the heavy reinforcement of the region by the divisions of Barrón, Alfredo Galera, Delgado Serrano, Rada, Alonso Vega, Castejón (from Andalusia), and Arias. Colonel Martínez de Campos recorded in his diary that, while with his artillery in the Sierra de Espadán, he suddenly received orders to 'halt the movements begun . . . the enemy has crossed the Ebro'.[1] Franco at first considered permitting an advance so deep as to allow a pincer movement which would destroy the whole republican army. He was talked out of this, but kept the bridges under bombardment; he determined not to make any advance by infantry until artillery and aircraft had established complete command.

The main battle occurred at Gandesa. This town was assaulted by Lister, day and night, during the hot days of the Aragon summer. On 1 August, the 15th International Brigade launched their most fierce attack upon Hill 481, named by them 'The Pimple', immediately before Gandesa. Once again the death-roll was heavy, as it had been inside Gandesa, during fighting for that town in March. Among those killed was Lewis Clive, socialist councillor in South Kensington, and David Haden Guest,[2] a young communist philosopher from Cambridge. By 2 August, the republican advance had been contained. The front lay straight from Fayón to Cherta, along the base of the Ebro's arc, but scooping eastwards to leave the nationalists with Villalba de los Arcos and Gandesa. In the north, the pocket between Mequinenza and Fayón was ten miles at its widest. The republic began to dig trenches. Yagüe showed himself as gifted an organizer of defence as of advance. He was calm throughout. Nevertheless, technical weaknesses were probably the reasons for the republic's failure to advance further. An iron bridge across the Ebro for the passage of heavy tanks took far too long to establish. The republican infantrymen had to go to the front on foot, because of a shortage of lorries. Furthermore, the nationalists were able to complete their defences of Gandesa, including trenches, without republican bombing, at a time when most of the nationalist fighters were still at Valencia (the bombers had been brought up, and were busy bombing the Ebro bridges). Modesto had wanted to bomb Gandesa but he

1. Martínez de Campos, p. 154.

2. Haden Guest had been the inspiration of a whole generation of communists at Cambridge. Clive had rowed for Oxford University in the early 1930s.

was thwarted by Colonel Visiedo, the chief of operations in the air ministry: Colonel García Lacalle, the republic's fighter commander, who proposed the bombing, believed Visiedo, a conventional officer, to be little less than treacherous in this negative attitude but then accusations of treachery were almost as frequent as those of Trotskyism in the republican camp.[1] On 14 August, the HISMA chief, Bernhardt, nevertheless, had to telegraph Göring for more ammunition for the invaluable 88-millimetre anti-aircraft guns, to meet the 'acute military danger'.[2] The orders issued by Lister and Tagüeña remained – 'vigilance, fortification and resistance'. These words were repeated throughout the following weeks. Officers and men were shot for retreating. Sergeants were ordered to kill their officers if they gave the command to retire without written orders from above. 'If anyone loses an inch of ground,' Lister ordered, 'he must retake it at the head of his men or be executed.'[3]

Franco never permitted even a tactical setback to go unchallenged. He determined to press the republic back from the territory which it had won. Almost all the nationalist air force was concentrated on the Ebro: some three hundred aircraft altogether. Franco was criticized in this decision at the time by other generals such as Aranda. But the decision was his and characteristically so. Franco's tactics were to make an intense artillery and aerial attack upon a given point, small in area, so that resistance would be impossible. Then an attack would be carried out by small bodies of men – perhaps only two battalions. The nationalist artillery commander was Martínez de Campos, who had been commander of artillery throughout the campaign in the north. The battle of the Ebro became, under his direction, a major

1. Letter from Lacalle, July 1964.

2. *GD*, p. 735. Immediately before the start of the Ebro battle, the Spanish nationalist ambassador in Berlin, the Marqués de Magaz, had complained that the German government were selling arms to the republic. Rifles at £1 a piece and also aircraft had been sold by Germany nominally to China and Greece, in fact to republican Spain. Magaz alleged that Göring knew of the transaction, wishing to prolong the civil war by this trickery. After two months, Germany denied that their government was implicated. (Documents quoted in *The International Brigades*, p. 44.)

3. Aznar, pp. 744–5, prints several republican orders later captured which show that this threat was often carried out.

artillery contest – the only occasion when in Spain the classic formula 'artillery conquers the ground, infantry occupies it' was fully applied.  The first nationalist counter-attack in this manner came on 6 August, when Delgado Serrano reconquered the northern pocket between Mequinenza and Fayón. The republic left behind 900 dead, 1,600 rifles, and over 200 machine-guns. On 11 August, Alonso Vega and Galera mounted a counter-attack against the Sierra de Pandols, the blue slate mountains in the south of the front. By the 14th, Lister had surrendered the high point of Santa Magdalena. On the 19th, another counter-attack was launched, by Yagüe, on the republican position on the north side of Mount Gaeta, with softer, undulating slopes, overgrown with ilex trees. This was also ultimately successful. On 3 September, an attack was made by the two army corps of Yagüe and García Valiño (the latter transferred from the Levante, and now in command of an 'Army of the Maestrazgo') composed of the divisions of Galera, Delgado Serrano, Arias, and Mohammed 'el Mizzian' – the one Moroccan officer (he was a nephew of one of Spain's once most truculent enemies) who rose to be a divisional commander in the nationalist army. Gandesa was partially relieved, and the nationalists also recaptured the village of Corbera in the cultivated valley between the Pandols and Mount Gaeta. In this way, the republic lost, after six weeks, about 120 square miles of the land which it had won. But these bare statements give an inaccurate picture of the relentless battle fought in the August heat. All day and every day the nationalist aeroplanes, sometimes two hundred at the same time, circled over the republican lines, with hardly any interference from the inadequate anti-aircraft defences and badly managed fighters of their opponents. Many of their Moscas and Chatos were destroyed, many were damaged, and many pilots were either dead or wounded; by this time, most of the best Russian pilots had been withdrawn. Nor had the republican command integrated the air force with the army's needs. The republican local command of the air had been eclipsed by the start of August. That more than cancelled the advantage gained from their possession of the high ground. During the counter-offensive, the nationalist aircraft dropped 10,000 pounds of bombs every day. But the republican engineers, who repaired the bridges under bombardment, were tenacious. This period of the 

battle was perhaps most remarkable for the difficulty found in hitting small targets: five hundred bombs were needed to destroy one pontoon bridge.

*

The republic was jubilant for some time after the Ebro attack. Even Azaña was for a time persuaded that the tide had turned. The crisis over Czechoslovakia also threatened a general European conflict, in which the Spanish war would presumably have been subsumed, as Negrín wanted. These favourable events did not, however, prevent a damaging governmental crisis. Fifty-eight death sentences for espionage or sabotage were pending, and were matters for dispute within the cabinet. The condemned were members of the espionage ring of a falangist named Villalta, which had recently been broken. As a result, Negrín demanded that all courts dealing with espionage and other crimes relating to the war should be placed under the ministry of war. He wanted that ministry also to deal with port administration; and finally he wanted the outright nationalization of the war industries. Now there certainly was confusion in the arms industries, sometimes the fault of the workers, sometimes of the state organization.[1] In addition, the activities of the SIM in Catalonia had led to complaints, by Companys and others, that this police force was breaking the Catalan statute. The inconclusive result of this controversy had led Negrín to the decree of militarization. As for the scheme for nationalization, many were, really, partially unemployed – more so than before 1936[2] – while many collectivized industries needed help: 'collectivized factory requires capitalist partner' ran an advertisement in a Barcelona factory.[3] Many ministers (most of the non-communists) opposed the policies of Negrín. The Basque and Catalan ministers in the central government, Ayguadé and Irujo, thought that they should resign. The crisis lasted many days.[4] The censorship prevented the reason for these two ministers' attitudes

1. See Peirats, vol. III, pp. 197–205.

2. The average in Barcelona was 80,000 compared with 50,000 in January 1936.

3. Qu. Azaña, vol. III, p. 511.

4. On 9 August, Prieto attacked Negrín before the national committee of the Spanish socialist party. The speech was published as 'How and why I left the ministry of defence'. See *Yo y Moscú*, pp. 137–227.

becoming widely known: the most important newspaper in Barcelona, *La Vanguardia*, which defended Negrín, explained them as separatist plots. War commissars even let it be known that the *Generalidad* was backing a separatist revolt.[1] Then Negrín left Barcelona for several days, no one knowing where he was. He had decided to precipitate a crisis, fearing that Azaña was thinking of sending for Julián Besteiro, who had stayed on in Madrid virtually as a private person, to form a government of mediation or surrender. But Azaña believed that, once a truce were reached, even if temporary, neither side would be able to resume the battle.[2]

At length, Negrín arrived at the house of Companys, and asked himself to dinner. He told Companys that he was tired of not receiving adequate backing in Catalonia, and that he had decided to retire from politics in order to go to a biology congress at Zürich. He would before that present his resignation to Azaña, recommending that Companys should succeed him as Prime Minister. Companys, taken aback, tried to persuade Negrín to stay at his post. Negrín said that he realized that he had failed to establish good relations with Catalonia and admitted that he lacked subtlety. The conversation ended indecisively. The next day, Tarradellas and Sbert, the two senior members of the Esquerra in the *Generalidad*, both went to see Negrín. They assured the Prime Minister that they desired to arrange matters amicably with him. But Negrín seemed resolved to retire, saying to Sbert, 'Tomorrow you will see how all this can be arranged. I shall be very happy in Zurich with the biologists.' This was a political sleight-of-hand by Negrín, not really an attempt to find a successor. Companys was not a viable successor: adroit political manager that he once had been, he had by then lost many of his old Esquerra friends to the PSUC, others to exile, while he himself had lost heart after the government had moved to Barcelona. He was a broken man. Immediately afterwards, Negrín began telephoning around Barcelona, and formed a new ministry, leaving out Ayguadé and Irujo. For them, he substituted José Moix (a communist, though an anarchist

1. A secret FAI circular of September 1938 pointed out that of 7,000 promotions in the army since May, 5,500 had been communists (Peirats, vol. III, p. 225).

2. Zugazagoitia, pp. 438–40. See comment by Jackson, p. 457. By that time, Azaña's diary is too fragmentary for much use to be made of it.

until March 1933, when he had been expelled over an ideological dispute) and Tomás Bilbao (a Basque, member of a minority Basque party, Basque Nationalist Action, until then consul in Perpignan, and a strong *Negrinista*). The other ministers were the same as in April. Segundo Blanco, the anarchist, remained, though, in the eyes of his CNT comrades, he was already 'one more *Negrinista*'.[1] Negrín next went to Azaña, giving him the list of the new ministry, saying that, since this was a partial crisis, he had not felt it necessary to consult him; but that, if he wanted to reject the new ministry, he would have to bear in mind that Negrín had the army behind him (hundreds of telegrams had allegedly arrived from army commanders telling him of their support). Negrín then submitted the decrees in his original programme, which had led to the crisis, to Azaña. Azaña rejected the one militarizing the tribunals, but accepted those approv- the death sentences and nationalizing the arms industries. Thirteen out of the fifty-eight death sentences were carried out. The nationalization did not, however, alter the circumstances in the industries themselves.[2] Surprisingly enough, Negrín did go to Zurich to his congress of physiologists; with results that will be seen later.[3]

This continued compromise with the communists has damned Negrín. His personal secretary, Benigno Rodríguez, was a party member, having once been the editor of *Milicia Popular*, the organ of the Fifth Regiment. Yet, in August 1938, as before, he had had little alternative save to sup with the devil. His attempts to secure a mediated peace – which he had concealed from the communists – had been fruitless. The only victory that Franco would envisage was a total one. The only hope for the republic still seemed to be to continue to resist, until the general situation in Europe should explode. In the meantime, the most tenacious advocates of the policy of resistance remained the communists. There was no alternative to employing their services. Negrín did not take the communists into his confidence in his search for a negotiated peace. His political aim

1. Zugazagoitia, p. 90.

2. The above owes much to Professor Bosch Gimpera. See also Zugazagoitia. I also discussed the event with Irujo. The rumour that at this time the Basques and Catalans sought a negotiated peace by asking the help of Bonnet and Halifax is false (it is reported as a fact in *USD*, 1938, vol. I, p. 239).

3. See below, p. 848.

was that of Stalin himself – to be willing to play a double-game. To do this against the communists may be dangerous, but it might have been successfully achieved in so unorthodox a country as Spain.

Meantime, the republic had accepted the British volunteer plan in principle. But they made reservations. They wished, for example, the Moroccans in the nationalist army to be classified as foreign volunteers, that 'technicians' should be withdrawn first, and that non-intervention should be made watertight by aerial control. The republic also deplored the grant of belligerent rights under the plan. The nationalists, for their part, demanded an immediate grant of belligerent rights, and the withdrawal of 10,000 volunteers from each side afterwards. But that could not be supervised internationally, since 'foreign observers would usurp, in a humiliating way, the sovereign rights of Spain'. The Non-Intervention Committee's secretary, Francis Hemming, was then sent off to nationalist Spain to persuade Franco to change his mind. This nationalist note, as it stood, amounted to rejection. Azcárate wrote a personal letter to Vansittart, pointing out the injustice of maintaining non-intervention at all, when Germany and Italy were party to Franco's rejection of the volunteer plan. The French–Spanish frontier had been closed in June in order to help persuade Franco to accept the plan'. Could the frontier at least not be re-opened? Vansittart never answered.[1]

General Berti was now talking to Franco on Mussolini's orders. The Italians in Spain numbered at that time 48,000. Italy was willing to do almost anything to help: either to send two or three more divisions to Spain, or 10,000 more men to make up for losses, or withdraw partially or totally. Franco chose a partial withdrawal.[2] So Mussolini decided to concentrate the Littorio and March 23rd Divisions into one large division and withdraw the other Italians. Britain's attention could be drawn to this, and Ciano could argue that the Anglo–Italian Agreement should be put into effect.[3] But Mussolini was angry with the Generalissimo over the Ebro battle. 'Put on record in your diary,' Mussolini thundered to Ciano, 'that

1. Azcárate, p. 174. Azcárate thought that Halifax saw the injustice of the discrimination, but could do nothing to counter Chamberlain's desire not to offend Italy.

2. *G D*, pp. 765–6.

3. This plan was not accepted by Franco till the end of September.

today, 29 August, I prophesy the defeat of Franco . . . The reds are fighters, Franco is not.'[1]

The republican offensive across the Ebro naturally caused gloom in nationalist Spain. Defeatism was talked, even at Burgos. The falangists were murmuring against both Franco and Martínez Anido. Stohrer reported scenes between Franco and his generals, 'who do not carry out attack orders correctly'. The Generalissimo was as alarmed by the Czech crisis as Negrín was elated. The possibility of a general war, and one which he might have to fight against France, caused him to send 20,000 prisoners to work on border fortifications, in the Pyrenees and in Spanish Morocco. No one told Franco the Führer's intentions. German aid temporarily stopped in mid-September, due to their needs in central Europe, The Marqués de Magaz, nationalist ambassador in Berlin, was admittedly assured, on 19 September, that there would be no changes in German policy to Spain, even if war did come.[2] But, a week later, Franco was still angry. Were Spanish ports needed by Germany for supply?[3]

The General Assembly of the League, meantime, assembled, for the last time, as it turned out, at Geneva. Negrín and Alvarez del Vayo once more put the Spanish case. They left behind them the war at its grimmest. For, after the capture of Corbera, the battle of the Ebro had become an exercise in endurance. The front remained stationary, though active, until the end of October. Negrín himself (unknown to the communists, as to the Basques or Catalans) now embarked upon a new project of compromise. On 9 September, when ostensibly in Zurich with his conference of physiologists, he secretly met an emissary of Hitler (probably Count Welczeck, the German ambassador in Paris) in the Sihl forest outside Zurich.[4] But there was

1. Ciano, *Diaries 1937–8*, p. 148. 2. *G D*, p. 742. 3. *ibid.*, p. 747.

4. The US consul-general in Geneva reported that Negrín's discussion was with the Duke of Alba (*US D*, 1938, vol. I, p. 239). Bosch Gimpera and Juan Negrín junior told me explicitly that it was a German. Negrín also told this to Prieto's secretary, Víctor Salazar (*Convulsiones*, vol. III, p. 2222), with the clear intention that he should pass on the news. It is difficult to believe that Hitler's emissary, whoever he was, said, as Prieto reported, that Hitler was willing to transfer his support to Negrín from Franco on the condition that Negrín set up a nazi-style state. Perhaps it should be added that Negrín always had a line open to Berlin, through the singer Emerita Esparza, who travelled several times from Barcelona to Berlin in the course of the war, staying with Negrín in the Pedralbes Palace in Barcelona. Was she a spy? For whom?

no possibility of compromise while Franco was in power. Ten days later, Mussolini, nevertheless, concluded that a mediated peace in Spain was inevitable, and that he would thus lose his '4 billion lire of credit'.[1]

The Duke of Alba, the nationalist agent in London, was told at the Foreign Office that the French would take no action against Spain in a general war if Franco were to declare himself neutral. Otherwise, if war came, there would be an immediate attack on Morocco and across the Pyrenees. Franco made the declaration desired of him.[2] 'Disgusting!' remarked Ciano, 'enough to make our dead in Spain turn in their graves!'[3] In pursuance of the same policy, the Generalissimo also announced, as a sop to France, that no German and Italian units would be permitted within eighty miles of the French frontier. Franco was usually realistic.

The conference of Munich followed. The fate of Czechoslovakia is well known. As for Spain, Mussolini (roaming the room with 'his hands in his pockets', as Ciano described him, 'his great spirit always ahead of events and men . . . He has already passed on to other things') told Chamberlain that the swift withdrawal of 10,000 men would 'create the atmosphere' for the start of the Anglo–Italian Agreement. He added that he was 'fed up' with Spain where he said (untruthfully) that he had lost 50,000 men, and was weary of Franco, who had thrown away so many opportunities of victory. Chamberlain, delighted with his success in 'solving' the Czech problem, suggested a similar conference to 'solve Spain'. The two sides could be called on to observe a truce, while the four Munich powers would help to work out a settlement.[4] News of this leaked out, and caused the republic to fear that it was about to suffer the same fate as Czechoslovakia. Franco did not like the idea either.

Hodgson, the British agent in Salamanca, told Stohrer, however, that Britain was intending to mediate in Spain.[5] Stohrer had himself questioned whether compromise might now not be in Franco's favour, when his troops were being 'bled white on the Ebro'. But the Generalissimo himself, sitting next to Stohrer at dinner on 1 October,

1. Ciano, *Diaries 1937–8*, p. 159.
2. *G D*, p. 479. Salazar had urged Franco to this attitude. See Kay, p. 117.
3. Ciano, *Diaries 1937–8*, p. 163.
4. Ciano, *Diaries 1937–8*, pp. 167–8; Feiling, p. 376.
5. *G D*, p. 754.

talked only of the Führer's triumph at Munich. He was silent when the ambassador suggested that the 'Czech method' might be the model for the solution of other international questions.[1] On 2 October, Negrín (distressed by Munich and the evidence it offered for the weakness of the old democracies)[2] broadcast a speech declaring that Spaniards must come to an understanding with each other. He demanded publicly whether the nationalists desired to carry on war until the country was destroyed. The speech made clear to the world for the first time Negrín's aspiration to seek a negotiated peace. But Hodgson's attempts – aimed at 'compromise, with the appearance of complete victory' – were as unfruitful as all similar proposals had been. On 4 October, Schwendemann, at the Spanish desk in the Wilhelmstrasse, admitted that Germany's 'negative aim' of preventing a communist Spain could be achieved by compromise. So could their economic interests. But, he added, 'a strong Spain leaning towards Germany' could only be secured by Franco's victory.[3] On 6 October, Jordana repeated to Stohrer that a compromise would mean that the whole civil war would have been fought in vain. The republic must be forced to capitulate.[4] A nationalist pamphlet published in Paris declared that 'the civil war itself was caused by the attempt at mediation between the rival forces of Spain embodied in the republic'.[5] Far from considering compromise, Franco was demanding from Germany shipments of 50,000 rifles, 1,500 light and 500 heavy machine-guns (one month's German production of machine-guns), and 100 75-millimetre guns. These, he assured the Germans, would give victory. The Germans were willing, on condition of the formal recognition of all their mining rights. But the matter was not agreed until November.[6]

After Munich, Stalin meantime had despaired of being able to arrange an alliance with France and Britain against Hitler. From October, Russia toyed increasingly with the only other solution open to her to avoid being involved in war: friendship with Hitler, at the democracies' expense. It was a policy which Stalin had probably contemplated as a possibility, even at the most enthusiastic moment

1. *G D*, p. 756. 2. Comment of Francisco Giral.
3. *G D*, p. 758. He had been counsellor in Madrid in 1936.
4. *ibid.*, p. 760. 5. *Médiation en Espagne* (Paris, 1938).
6. *G D*, pp. 776, 784–6. See below, p. 860.

of the Popular Front.[1] This change had an effect on the Spanish war. Russian spokesmen had suggested that they would be pleased to withdraw from Spain.[2] Hence Stalin's agreement that, before the final understanding in the Non-Intervention Committee on volunteers, the International Brigades should be withdrawn.[3]

The role of the Brigades was now over. They had ceased to be effective propaganda for the republic, and the seasoned men who had composed the early Brigades had mostly been killed, or had left Spain. A majority of those in the Brigades were now Spanish, some volunteers, but some of them men from prison, work camps, and disciplinary battalions. Several even of the officers in command of foreign volunteers were also Spanish. The 15th Brigade, for example, was led by the Spanish Major Valledor.[4] Admittedly, Colonel Hans Kahle, leader of the first International Brigade in Madrid in 1936, was still in action, in command of a division at the front. But his troops, like those of his colleague, the equally experienced General Walter, were Spaniards. Even the Lincoln Battalion comprised a three-to-one majority of Spaniards.[5] Thus Negrín was able, without military risk, to propose at Geneva, during the Munich crisis, the withdrawal of all foreign volunteers in republican Spain. He asked the League to supervise this step. In so doing, he demonstrated his contempt for the Non-Intervention Committee, and gave a fillip to the spirits of the League. The secretary-general of the League, the usually cold anglophile Avenole, was unable to repress his delight.

1. See above, p. 339. On 25 December 1937, a French journalist, Luciani, representing several French papers in Moscow, had been summoned by Litvinov, to be told that the Kremlin had 'established contacts' to initiate a German–Russian *rapprochement*. Litvinov told Luciani to tell his ambassador. But though he did so, no one took the message seriously. See *Le Monde*, 19 February 1969, qu. Suárez, p. 25.

2. See above, p. 831.

3. The number of Russians in Spain had diminished, for Spanish pilots had been trained to fly the aircraft the Russians had given them: the Russian military mission seems to have been much smaller; and even Orlov, the NKVD representative, had defected, on 12 July 1938, fleeing first to Canada, then to the US (see his testimony before the internal security sub-committee of the Senate, 14–15 February 1957: *Hearings*, p. 3421).

4. A leader of the revolt in the Asturias in 1934, Valledor had also fought in Asturias in 1936–7. He had escaped from nationalist Spain in 1938.

5. Rolfe, p. 234.

'A master-stroke!' he exclaimed, when meeting Azcárate in the corridors of the Palais des Nations. On 1 October, it was agreed that the League should supervise the withdrawal, through a commission of fifteen officers, headed by a general. Russia now diminished the propaganda appeals on behalf of the republic, but they continued to send military equipment, in diminished quantities. With the French frontier closed once again, it was difficult to make sure that any aid would arrive. The sea route (even that between Marseilles and Barcelona) was impracticable.

The grim battle of the Ebro continued. Franco prepared his main counter-attack. On the republican side, 'Resist – Resist' continued to be cried by the commissars. The battle was still continuing when the International Brigades were withdrawn. Their last action was on 22 September, when the 15th Brigade went into battle for the last time. The British Battalion once again suffered heavy casualties. The son of the American writer, Ring Lardner, who had been among the last Americans to enlist, was killed in this battle.[1] At a parade of farewell to the Brigades at Barcelona on 15 November, Negrín and La Pasionaria spoke words of thanks. La Pasionaria's speech revived for a moment all the ideals of those who had cared so much for the Spanish cause in the heroic days. First, she addressed the women of Barcelona:

Mothers! Women! When the years pass by and the wounds of war are staunched; when the cloudy memory of the sorrowful, bloody days returns in a present of freedom, love, and well-being; when the feelings of rancour are dying away and when pride in a free country is felt equally by all Spaniards – then speak to your children. Tell them of the International Brigades. Tell them how, coming over seas and mountains, crossing frontiers bristling with bayonets, and watched for by ravening dogs thirsty to tear at their flesh, these men reached our country as crusaders for freedom. They gave up everything, their loves, their country, home and fortune – fathers, mothers, wives, brothers, sisters, and children – and they came and told us: 'We are here, your cause, Spain's cause is ours. It is the cause of all advanced and progressive mankind.' Today they are going away. Many of them, thousands of them, are staying here with the Spanish earth for their shroud, and all Spaniards remember them with the deepest feeling.

1. Vincent Sheean, *The Eleventh Hour* (London, 1939), p. 237.

Then she addressed the assembled members of the Brigades:

Comrades of the International Brigades! Political reasons, reasons of state, the welfare of that same cause for which you offered your blood with boundless generosity, are sending you back, some of you to your own countries and others to forced exile. You can go proudly. You are history. You are legend. You are the heroic example of democracy's solidarity and universality. We shall not forget you, and, when the olive tree of peace puts forth its leaves again, mingled with the laurels of the Spanish republic's victory – come back![1]

The parade heaved with controlled emotion: it was true, surely, as Pietro Nenni reflected, that, all unknowing, they had 'lived an *Iliad*'.[2] The crowds cheered beneath large photographs of Negrín, Azaña – and Stalin. Flowers were thrown. Slightly less than half the 10,000 volunteers then in the International Brigade began to leave by boat and rail for France, for home, wherever it might be. The League of Nations Commission, led by the Finnish General Jalander, the British Brigadier Molesworth, and the French Colonel Homo, counted 12,673 foreigners in the republican forces. Some had assumed Spanish nationality. By mid-January, 4,640 men of 29 nationalities had left Spain. Of these, 2,141 were French, 407 British, 347 Belgian, 285 Poles, 182 Swedes, 194 Italians, 80 Swiss, and 54 Americans. Another 6,000 – Germans, Yugoslavs, Czechs, Hungarians – remained, knowing that their homes would not welcome them, to be engulfed in the catastrophe in Catalonia, perhaps to encounter hardships greater than they had known in the war.[3]

One other commission was also in Spain during this, for democrats, distressing autumn. In October 1937, the republic had proposed to the British that they should negotiate the exchange of those Spanish civilians who desired to leave nationalist territory, for nationalist

1. From a pamphlet printed in Barcelona 1938. The same day, Colonel Ramón Franco, who had been for some time aerial commander of the nationalists in the Balearics, was shot down and killed in his hydroplane (J. Salas, p. 384).

2. Nenni, p. 172.

3. 305 members of the British Battalion were greeted, amid excitement, at Victoria Station on 7 December by Attlee, Sir Stafford Cripps, William Gallacher, Tom Mann, and Will Lawther. Sam Wild then gave the battalion its last dismissal. The Dependants' Aid Committee looked after the families of those killed as best it could.

prisoners in republican hands. A commission led by Field-Marshal Sir Philip Chetwode, a hero of the First World War, was arranged to visit Spain to effect a general exchange of prisoners, though Chetwode was not allowed to set off till September 1938. The commission was not successful. It secured several small-scale exchanges, such as that of 100 British prisoners in nationalist hands for 100 Italians held by the republic. When Sir Philip returned to London at the end of the war, he claimed that he had persuaded the republic to stop executing their prisoners and that he had gained the remission of 400 death sentences by General Franco. The latter achievement appears genuine, the former less so, since the republican government had already promulgated it.[1]

*

On 30 October, the nationalist counter-offensive began on the Ebro. The point of attack was the one-mile wide northern stretch of the Sierra de Caballs. For three hours after dawn, the republican positions were subjected to bombardment by 175 nationalist and Italian batteries, as well as over a hundred aircraft. A hundred republican fighters made no impression upon this aerial armada. Then the Army Corps of the Maestrazgo under García Valiño went into the attack. Mohammed el Mizzian, with the Navarrese of the 1st Division, captured republican positions abandoned during the bombardment. The battle on the heights of the Caballs continued all day, but, by night, these mountains were in nationalist hands, including nineteen fortified positions and the republican defence network. The nationalists claimed 1,000 prisoners and 500 dead, as well as 14 aircraft. The loss of the Caballs was a terrible blow to the republic, since it commanded the whole region.

Worse was to follow. On the night of 1–2 November, Colonel Galera, an officer who had begun the war as a commander of *Regulares*, stormed the Pandols, the only high point remaining to the republic. On 3 November, advancing through the village of Pinell,

1. Toynbee, *Survey*, (London, 1938), vol. I, pp. 392–3. The secretary to this commission was Noël Field, ex-State department official, League official and future victim, or hero, of the cold war. He already was, or considered himself, in 1938 a Russian agent. See Flora Lewis, *The Man Who Disappeared* (London, 1965).

he reached the Ebro. The right flank of the nationalist army had now achieved its objectives. On 7 November, Mora la Nueva on the river bank fell. The nationalists launched a massive attack towards the hill known as Mount Picosa. In this sector, the republic had entrenched itself with skill. After the fall of Mount Picosa, the pressure of the nationalist armour convinced the republic that the battle of the Ebro was as good as lost. By 10 November, only six republican batteries remained west of the Ebro. With deliberation, the last republican defence points were abandoned. The hill village of Fatarella fell on 14 November, to Yagüe. The last stages of the conflict were delayed by the first snows of winter falling upon a battlefield which had earlier been rendered intolerable by the heat of summer. On 18 November, Yagüe entered Ribarroya, the last republican bridgehead. The intrepid Anglo-Saxon reporters, Hemingway, Buckley, Matthews, and Sheean, were among the last to cross the river, Hemingway rowing hard in a small boat.[1] Controversy reigns over the number of casualties in this battle. Both sides probably lost about 50,000 to 60,000, with deaths numbering 6,500 among the nationalists, and probably between 10,000 and 15,000 among the republicans. Both sides lost many aeroplanes, the republic between 130 and 150 – which they could not replace.[2]

The same day that the last republicans left the right bank of the Ebro, 16 November, the Anglo–Italian Agreement came into being, now that the 10,000 Italians, of whom Mussolini had spoken at Munich, had been withdrawn from Spain. The Italians remaining in

1. Hemingway had gone back to America earlier in the year, having finished his bad play, *The Fifth Column*, in the Hotel Florida. One night in the summer, however, the friends of the republic were happy to hear on the wireless the announcement: 'The writer, Ernest Hemingway, has suddenly left his home in Key West. He was last seen in New York, boarding a ship, without hat or baggage, to rejoin the Spanish republican troops at the front.' (Regler, *Owl of Minerva*, p. 298.) Hemingway was disillusioned with 'the carnival of treachery and rottenness on both sides' by now (Baker, p. 401). See his *The Denunciation* and *The Butterfly and the Tank*.

2. Lister, p. 214; Tagüeña, p. 261; R. Salas, vol. II, p. 2021, and vol. IV, p. 3303. The latter gives deaths at 4,007, wounded 37,712, and ill 15,238, a total of 56,957. It would be reasonable to suppose that 10 per cent of the wounded and sick later died.

Spain would be about 12,000 men of the Littorio Division, consisting of picked men, to be commanded by the temperamental and fascist-minded General Gambara. Berti, who had been a successful commander, and Piazzoni (the 'Papa of the Black Arrows') were withdrawn. There remained pilots, the tank corps, and artillerymen, as well as officers and NCOs to command four mixed divisions of Spaniards.[1] Ten thousand returning men were welcomed at Naples on 20 October. King Victor Emmanuel and the populace greeted them without warmth. But Ciano soon forgot his consequent annoyance when he received from Franco, as a souvenir, a painting by Zuloaga of *The Oldest Requeté*, with a pleasant background of war and flames.[2] Chamberlain now judged that the long-sought Anglo-Italian Agreement could come into force.

A fortnight later, in the House of Commons, Eden recalled how Lord Perth had said, when the agreement was signed in April, that a settlement of the Spanish question was a 'prerequisite' for its entry into force. Now, Eden said, there had been no such settlement, only an arrangement at the expense of Spain. Such a remark was shown to be justified when, in the House of Lords, on 3 November, Halifax announced that Mussolini had 'made plain that, whether Britain approved or not of his reasons, he would not be prepared to see Franco defeated'. The previous day, the Spanish Civil War had even flared up in the North Sea. Seven miles off Cromer, a nationalist armed merchantman, the *Nadir*, sank the *Cantabria*, a steamer used by the republic for food supplies.[3] Eleven British ships, furthermore, had been attacked in republican ports during the month of November; yet now, on 16 November, here in Rome was Lord Perth

1. Gambara, a young officer in the First World War, had fought in Ethiopia as chief of staff to Bastico. He was to become chief of staff to Graziani in 1943 in Mussolini's ill-fated republic of Salò. The Cuerpo de Ejército Legionario under Gambara consisted of the Littorio Division (General Bitossi), the Frecce Nere (Colonel Babini), the Frecce Azzurre (Colonel la Ferla), the 'Flechas Verdes' (Colonel Battisti), and an artillery section, headed by General D'Amico. The corps had some 58 batteries (Aznar, p. 609). The Italians comprised now 26,000 NCOs and men, 2,000 officers (Belforte, p. 118). See Alcofar Nassaes, *CTV*, p. 176.

2. Ciano, *Diaries 1937–8*, pp. 180–81.

3. *The Times*, 5 November 1938.

'moved', as the master-toady Ciano put it, at this last act in appeasing Italy.[1]

1. The aim of the Anglo–Italian Agreement was to wean Italy from Germany. Halifax wrote to Sir Eric Phipps in Paris: 'Although we do not expect to detach Italy from the Axis, we believe the agreement will increase Mussolini's power of manoeuvre and so make him less dependent on Hitler and, therefore, freer to resume the classic Italian role of balancing between Germany and the western Powers' (*British Foreign Policy*, 3rd series, vol. III, No. 285). Mussolini's response was to launch a renewed campaign for the cession of the French territories of Nice, Savoy and Corsica.

48

The two Spains compared after the end of the Ebro campaign – misery and moderation – the end of the POUM – the campaign in Catalonia – the collapse – the fall of Barcelona

AT the end of the battle of the Ebro, nationalist morale had naturally again risen. It was sustained by press, radio and literary campaigns, which continued to drench the country in half-fascist, half-monarchist and wholly-catholic propaganda. The paintings of Sáenz de Tejada, for example, or Teodoro Delgado, seemed a right-wing parody of those staunch, clenched-fisted, forward-looking workers and fighters seen on republican posters. Radio Nacional de España, directed by the falangist Antonio Tovar, had a different objective, since it was aimed at the secret nationalists or Fifth Column in republican Spain, as much as at the enemy.[1] Expansively entitled journals such as *La Ametralladora* (The Machine-Gun), *Jerarquía* (*Revista Negra de la Falange*) (Hierarchy), or *Vertice* (The Vertex) published the cartoons, poems, stories, arguments, and drawings of the new régime's new or rediscovered artists and writers, for a large audience. The purges of civil servants, schoolmasters, university professors and doctors continued, as more and more territory was captured. 'The prisons', wrote the German ambassador Stohrer, 'are overflowing as never before. In the prison here [i.e. at Salamanca], which is intended for forty persons, there are supposed to be about 1,800 at the present.'[2] In September, the nationalists announced that they had taken 210,000 prisoners since the war began, of which 134,000 were at 'liberty' –

1. This psychological war is excellently analysed in Abella, p. 369f. This radio station in Salamanca was directed by Jacinto Miquelarena, whose brief '*Comentarios*' were well edited. The ex-radical socialist, Joaquín Pérez Madrigal, had an amusing programme entitled '*La Flota Republicana*'. He also gave details of the menus in the restaurants of Salamanca designed to make mouths water in Barcelona. Whether that had a good effect on the half-starving anti-republicans in republican territory is doubtful. See his nine volumes of apologia, dangerously entitled *Memorias de un converso* (Madrid, 1943).

2. *GD*, p. 796.

usually in the army, or some kind of 'national service'. The rest were dead or in prison. There were bouts of executions of so-called spies, one running into several hundreds.[1] The Falange and the clergy grumbled at each other, though they did not openly quarrel. The cult of José Antonio, begun on the second anniversary of his death (20 November 1938), had no effect on this. But despite his Jesuit training, Serrano Súñer had not successfully bridged the gap between these two departments of Spanish society. The final text, for instance, of the new Secondary Education Law of 20 September 1938 seemed an uneasy compromise between Falange and church: one hour a week was for 'the patriotic formation of youth', while there would be two hours' religious teaching. Whereas catholicism was declared 'the essence of Spanish history', of the two foreign languages which could be studied, one could be either German or Italian. But in general the catholics, through their leadership in the ministries of justice and education (the Conde de Rodezno and Sáinz Rodríguez), won where religion was concerned: all secular rights were cancelled, the state was tied to catholicism, and non-catholic churches were given few facilities.[2] A nuncio, Monsignor Cicognani, had come to Spain to replace the apostolic delegate, Monsignor Antoniutti, in June 1938, while the nationalist ambassador in Rome was the lawyer, José Yanguas Messía, who had been foreign minister under Primo de Rivera. One more man of the old directorate thus found himself being used in the new tyranny.

The economic situation in nationalist Spain was a little less favourable than it had been a year previously. There was food for those who could buy it, but wages had not kept up with prices, despite the price control. Due to difficulties of transport, prices varied wildly

1. One alleged plot concerned the British consul in San Sebastián, Harold Goodman, in whose suitcase secret nationalist documents were found. Was it a police plant or an attempt by the republic to gain information? A servant killed himself; perhaps, therefore, the latter. Thompson, p. 145, considered the Gestapo responsible: 'what spy would draw a trench system on a sheet?'

2. Payne, *The Spanish Revolution*, p. 193. Yet this catholicism had strange bedfellows: '*Caminos de la guerra española; caminos del imperio hispano; caminos del Islam; trinidad que resulta en la sola meta del afán sin horizontes*'. Thus Antonio Olmedo in *ABC de Sevilla*, 5 April 1938. (Paths of the Spanish war; paths of the Spanish empire; paths of Islam; trinity resulting in the sole goal of struggle without end.)

from district to district. Inflation had brought prices up from a level of 164 in 1935 (with 100 in 1913) to 212 in 1938. Meat had increased some 80 per cent, vegetables, wine and oil, nearly 50 per cent, and textiles about 40 per cent; wages had only risen about 20 per cent in general since 1935. Manufactured goods were almost non-existent, though production in essential industries had increased during 1938. The output of iron ore from Vizcaya, for example, reached 154,000 tons in 1938, in place of 115,000 in the last year of peace – a substantial increase too on what was produced in early 1937 under the Basque republic. Movement in the port of Bilbao increased by 50 per cent over peace-time.

González Bueno, minister of syndical organization, had meantime set up a skeleton of new state unions (*sindicales*) throughout Spain. But 'syndical' control of labour and of the economy existed only on paper. The nationalist economy was, in the main, a banker's one, with continuous governmental intervention, production stimulated by war, wages kept steady by terror. Share prices on the nationalist-held Bilbao stock exchange were rising; while, internationally, the nationalist peseta was quoted at 100 to the pound in late 1938, with the official rate still 42.50 (the republican peseta was then over 500 to the pound).

The nationalist government, needing new war supplies badly, had, meanwhile, agreed to the German conditions for fulfilment of their latest request. German capital would be permitted to participate in Spanish mines to the extent of a basic 40 per cent. But 60 per cent would be permitted in one mine and 75 per cent in four others. These enterprises, grouped in the so-called 'Montana' project, of which the artful Bernhardt was the chairman, concentrated on mines which were not working well at the time; the German interest in 1938 was an insurance against the day when Germany would not be able to make a direct exchange of weapons for ore.[1] Bernhardt picked his Spanish partners well, so that he knew that they would accept German leadership. In Morocco, where the Spanish mining law did not apply, German participation was permitted up to a 100 per cent. Spain agreed to pay all the expenses in Spain of the Condor Legion and to import 5 million reichsmarks' worth of mining machinery.

1. *GD*, pp. 795–6. The date of the agreement was 19 November. See Harper, p. 112.

That would enable Franco to contemplate a new offensive immediately, and so strike the republic at the moment when they had exhausted their supplies. This aid was the consequence of the German realization that, after Munich, nothing which they did in the Spanish war would cause Britain and France to go to war. Had it not been for it, a compromise peace, or perhaps, more likely, a permanent division of Spain (such as divided Germany, Korea and Vietnam after 1945), might have been inevitable. The new aid admittedly did not arrive until the New Year, but the knowledge that it was on the way enabled the nationalists to act swiftly.[1]

The nationalist army had doubled during the year to total over a million. All healthy men between the ages of eighteen and thirty-one were in the army, and many more besides as volunteers. This host was organized in three main armies – that of the south, and inactive, under Queipo; that of the Levante, the main inspiration of the next campaign, under Orgaz; and that of the centre, preparing for an attack on Madrid, under Saliquet. The two last generals were 'Francoists'. Queipo alone was in any way likely to think independently.[2]

On the republican side, the successful withdrawal from the right bank of the Ebro masked the destruction caused. After all, the nationalists had taken three months to win back what they had lost in two days. But discontent seethed. The anarchist historian, Peirats (then a second-lieutenant in the army), has described how the police network now seemed to control the whole army, SIM agents being everywhere, their methods, as ever, being characterized by a mixture of sadism and incompetence, some of their chiefs being quite new men: the SIM chief in the 119th Brigade, for example, who had powers of life and death in that unit, was only nineteen in late 1938.[3] By this time, a million men had probably been mobilized in the republic as

1. See comment by Harper, p. 117, and Salas Larrazábal in Palacio Atard, p. 123. In 'Spilling the Spanish Beans' Orwell wrote 'though the war may end soon or may drag on for years, it will end with Spain divided up either by actual frontiers or into economic zones'.

2. The nationalist army was composed of sixty-one infantry divisions (840,000 men), 15,323 cavalry, 19,013 artillery, 119,594 auxiliary services, 35,000 Moroccans (with Spanish officers), 32,000 CTV (half Spanish), and 5,000 Condor Legion: Total – 1,065,941. (Bolín's figures, p. 349.)

3. Peirats, vol. III, p. 278.

well since July 1936. The class of 1919, men aged forty, would soon be called to the colours (the nationalists had not had to go beyond the class of 1927).

Thus altogether 8 per cent of the Spanish population in late 1938 was either in the army, or a prisoner. If the peace-time history of the republic was the history of the nation's 'politicization', the war was characterized by its 'militarization'.

On 30 September, the six-monthly session of the Cortes was held, this time at San Cugat del Vallés. Attacks against Negrín were made, by the Catalan (Esquerra) deputy, Miguel Santaló, and the Basque ex-minister, Irujo. The former alleged that at the time of the August crisis, newspapers friendly to Negrín had misrepresented the decree which militarized the tribunals as being a decree affecting the harbour. Both he and Irujo pointed out that the republican government was bound, legally and morally, to consult the Catalan government.[1]

As for religious freedom, private celebration of mass had been permitted for some time. Two thousand priests were privately active in Barcelona in 1938, protected by the SIM against the anarchists.[2] There were no priests active even privately in the central zone. From August, priests were, however, allowed to tend to spiritual needs in private both in prisons and at the front. Irujo proposed a corps of almoners for the army and suggested the opening of a church in Barcelona. He and the councillor for justice in Barcelona (Bosch Gimpera) again asked Father José María Torrent, vicar-general of Barcelona, to open at least one church; but Father Torrent refused to allow this. The vicar-general made further difficulties. It was difficult for these churchmen to collaborate with a régime which had been denounced as satanic by orthodox catholics, and which had, at the least, failed to prevent the murder of so many of their brethren. On 17 October, a funeral procession even passed through Barcelona in memory of a dead Basque officer. Further unsuccessful efforts were made to try to secure the return of the archbishop of Tarragona, Cardinal Vidal i Baraquer. On 9 December, a commissariat of religion was finally set up, to provide ministers for the armies, and Dr Jesús Bellido, professor of medicine in the University of Barcelona,

1. *Diario de Sesiones*, 30 September 1938.
2. Lawrence Fernsworth, *New York Times*, 23 March 1938, qu. Jackson, p. 458.

became the commissar-in-chief. The outbreak of the Catalan campaign prevented this from being put into effect.[1]

Food was now short in the republic. In Madrid, half a million persons lived, during the winter of 1938–9, on a daily issue of two ounces of lentils, beans or rice, with an occasional ration of sugar or salt cod. Lentils, the commonest food, were named Dr Negrín's 'little victory pills'. Average rations of republican troops had shrunk: from 1⅔ pounds of bread a day in 1936 to less than a pound in 1938, just over half a pound of meat to a third, and the ration of vegetables was also down.[2] The republic had to buy much of its food from abroad and supplies were irregular, because of the continued bombing of supply ships. Sir Denys Bray, the Indian civil servant who headed the League's mission on refugee relief, reported that the whole population of the republic were living on minimum rations, while even those were not being distributed. In Barcelona, where there were a million refugees in addition to the normal population, the problems were appalling. An International Commission for the assistance of child refugees, founded by the Quakers in December 1937, could help only 40,000 out of 600,000 child refugees, though they were being financed by seventeen governments.[3] The cost of giving a third of these children one meal a day throughout the winter was estimated as nearly £150,000. Many diseases appeared, such as scabies and pellagra; and deaths from malnutrition doubled between 1937 and 1938.[4] The Quakers' mission did help to alleviate the worst tragedies. The nationalists, meantime, sought to point the contrast between the hungry republic and their own territory, by an air-raid of loaves of bread on Barcelona. (The republicans replied with an air-raid of shirts and socks, to demonstrate their alleged superiority in manufactured goods.) The work on the fields in the republic continued, but in many places at greatly reduced momentum: in Cuenca, for instance, only 14 per cent of the land reserved for cereals could

1. A. Toynbee, *Survey*, 1938, vol. I, pp. 271, 389.

2. The exact figures here were 700 grammes of bread dropping to 400, 250 of meat to 150, 200 of vegetables to 180.

3. Bosch Gimpera, Memorandum No. 2.

4. See discussion in Jackson, p. 447, and also Norah Curtis and Cyril Dilby, *Malnutrition* (London, 1944), p. 46f.

be sown, due to shortage of hands.[1] In the republican zone, the wheat harvest had reached 130 million bushels.[2] Trifón Gómez, the realistic socialist who was commissary-general in the army, believed it to be less; but even what there plainly was, was quickly and mysteriously dispersed. Since the government was slow to pay, the peasants did not deliver their goods. Disorganization in the largely communist-managed ministry of agriculture, as well as the collectives, who neither paid taxes nor cooperated with rationing, was thus to blame for what went wrong with the republic's food supply.[3]

Even in manufactured goods, the republic was in a bad position. The chief cause was the shortage of raw materials due to the blockade. But what about Spanish production, and, in particular, the output of the Catalan war industry over which there was such argument? Despite all the communists' efforts, the change over from textiles and chemicals to armaments was difficult; one type of aircraft only was developed, a copy of the Chato, of which 169 were built in 1938 though never used. Monthly arms production in December 1938 was 1,000 rifles and 10 million bullets; 700,000 grenades and 300,000 artillery shells; 80,000 mortar grenades and 100 mortars.[4] Otherwise, all depended on Russia. Overall industrial production in Catalonia was only a third of what it had been in July 1936, and prices had risen 300 per cent since then. Between November 1937 and November 1938, there was an inflation of almost 200 per cent.[5] A more telling statistic was the collapse of the use of electricity during 1938, itself a consequence of the loss of the hydro-electric plants. In September

1. *Campo Libre*, 14 January 1939, gives the following figures for sowing in the season 1938–9:

Cuenca:	170,000 hectares
Toledo:	200,000 hectares
Madrid:	69,010 hectares
Granada:	117,000 hectares (67,000 wheat)
Córdoba:	39,330 hectares (15,800 wheat)
Jaén:	74,700 hectares (45,000 wheat)
Albacete:	204,690 hectares (119,230 wheat)

2. 8 million quintals.

3. See conversation between Trifón Gómez and Azaña, Azaña, *op. cit.*, vol. IV, p. 900.

4. Soviet army records, qu. Payne, *The Spanish Revolution*, p. 344.

5. Bricall, pp. 48 and 101.

1938, the last month for which statistics seem available, the industrial use of electricity was half that for September 1937, while that itself was probably half normal use.[1] The political decay of the anarchists before the communists was also responsible for the economic failure of the republic. That decay was not halted, may even have been hastened, by the holding of a national conference of anarchists of all tendencies – the CNT, FAI and FIJL (anarchist youth) – in October 1938; the proposal was again made for the translation of the FAI into a regular political party. The idea was rejected. Horacio Prieto again put forward his ideas for 'collaborationist' anarchism, whereby nationalization, collectives and private property would co-exist.[2] But these ideas seemed treacherous to most delegates. Only in one sphere, indeed, was the republic still able to preserve its optimism. This was education.

I have visited [reported the French poet and flier Antoine de Saint-Exupéry], on the Madrid front, a school installed 500 metres from the trenches, behind a small wall, on a little hillock. A corporal was teaching botany. He was carefully peeling away the petals of a poppy. Around him were gathered bearded soldiers, their chins sunk in their hands, their brows knitted in the effort of concentration. They did not understand the lesson very well, but they had been told: you are brutes, you have only just left your holes, we must save you for humanity. And with heavy feet they were hurrying towards enlightenment.[3]

The survival of this ardent spirit, and much cultural activity due to the stimulus of war, led a French journalist, Raymond Laurent, to say: 'You are fighting for the noble cause of humanity as much as for the security of France itself.'

That view was no longer still held by the leaders of the POUM, who, except, of course, for the murdered Nin, were at last brought to trial in October 1938. Not long before, the real falangists who had been implicated in their affairs had also been tried. Thirteen of those, including the agents Golfín, Dalmau and Roca, were shot for what, given the circumstances of a civil war, was genuinely espionage. When the POUM leaders came to the tribunal, however, the case against them collapsed. Republican ministers and ex-ministers, headed by

1. *ibid.*, p. 55.

2. These and other moderate ideas were launched by Horacio Prieto in Abad de Santillán's journal, *Timón*, in August 1938. See discussion in C. Lorenzo, p. 294.

3. Antoine de Saint-Exupéry, *Terre des hommes* (Paris, 1939), p. 210.

Largo Caballero and Zugazagoitia, gave evidence in the POUM's favour. Gironella, the young leader who had organized the POUM militia in July 1936 (as well as the POUM cavalry, barracks, anthem and band), addressed the prosecutor, to the general scandal, as Vishinsky. Arquer caused difficulties by insisting on testifying in Catalan. A real representative of Trotsky, Grandizo Munis, declared that the POUM were in no way Trotskyists. The judgement found the POUM to be true socialists, and absolved them of treason and espionage. Five leaders, including Gorkin and Andrade, were, however, condemned to various terms of imprisonment for activities at the time of the May crisis of 1937, and for other revolutionary activities prejudicial to the war effort.[1]

A word should be spared to consider the personal aspect of the war; in the republic, men who a few years before were simply unknown students, workers or agitators, had risen to high positions. The old leaders – Azaña, Largo Caballero, Prieto, Martínez Barrio – had sunk in repute, being replaced by a new group of younger men. The change in the status of this latter group affected private lives. Rumours circulated everywhere: so-and-so was drunk at his command post, so-and-so had left his wife and was living with a new woman. It is more odd that the upheaval was not greater, considering the change in status of many military leaders and other officials of the republic. Some, like Cipriano Mera, had announced that, after the war, they would go back to their old professions – in Mera's case, masonry.[2] But many, even many anarchists, were proving themselves competent administrators. Negrín was a republican equivalent of Franco in the sense that, being of the generation of men unknown before the war, he could use this new personnel, without prior commitments.

The German ambassador, Stohrer, concluded a general analysis of the Spanish situation at this time with the percipient comment that

1. Gorkin, pp. 268–80; Peirats, vol. III, pp. 297–300. See also Suárez's general account of the trial. One of the POUM leaders, Rey, was freed. He was shot by Franco after the end of the war. After the end of this trial, three leading anarchists – Federica Montseny, Abad de Santillán and García Birlán – visited Azaña to denounce Negrín as a dictator and demand a change of government. But Azaña, as usual, would do nothing definite, though agreeing with his visitors. (Peirats, vol. III, p. 318.)

2. He did eventually do so, in France.

mutual fear was the reason for the continuance of the war. No prominent man on either side had illusions as to what would happen to him if he were caught by his enemies. Franco had told an American correspondent that he had a list (with witnesses) of a million persons on the republican side who were guilty of crimes. The German ambassador believed, nevertheless, that the opportunity for a negotiated peace might suddenly come.[1] At the same time, Adolf Berle, the banker who had become assistant secretary of state in the US, was telling President Roosevelt how compromise might be achieved in Spain. He proposed an Inter-American approach at the forthcoming conference of South American countries at Lima. The plan was never carried forward, due to quarrels among the South Americans and to the cautious spirit of Cordell Hull. But Cuba, Mexico and Haiti declared themselves, for different reasons, in favour of an approach such as Roosevelt had contemplated.[2]

In fact, the chances of compromise were remote. The nationalists had even refused to countenance a proposal by Negrín in August that each side should suspend the execution of military prisoners for a month.[3] Even on the question of the removal of volunteers (a touchstone for his pacific intentions), Franco was unyielding. He would accept no such agreement unless he first were granted belligerent rights. In the meantime, with his new German arms assured, he was preparing a new offensive to follow the battle of the Ebro, just as the run-away Aragon campaign had followed the battle of Teruel. The best nationalist divisions were assembled all along the line from the Pyrenees to the Ebro and the sea. These were, from north to south, a new 'Army of Urgel', under Muñoz Grandes; the Army of the Maestrazgo, under García Valiño; and the 'Army of Aragon', under Moscardó. Then came the Italian General Gambara's four divisions. Farther to the south, there was the 'Army of Navarre', under Solchaga, and Yagüe, with the 'Army of Morocco'. This 'Army of the North' was, as ever, led by the competent bureaucrat, General Dávila, and consisted of 300,000 men, being supported by 565 pieces

1. *GD*, p. 796.

2. *USD*, 1938, vol. I, p. 255. I discussed the failure of this plan with A. A. Berle in 1963.

3. Though the Chetwode commission (see above, p. 854) persuaded the nationalists to delay 400 executions.

of artillery. The nationalist air force had 500 aeroplanes, enough to command in the air.[1] Franco himself established his headquarters (it had always the code-name 'Terminus') in the castle of Pedrola, north of Lérida.[2] The offensive, planned for 10 December and postponed till the 15th, was finally decided for the 23rd.[3] The apprehension was great that the attack on Barcelona would involve much fighting.

The republican battle lines in Catalonia were commanded by Hernández Saravia. Beneath him were the Armies of the East and of the Ebro, under Colonels Perea and Modesto respectively. These forces numbered 300,000. 360 pieces of artillery were available, as were 200 tanks and armoured cars (mostly T-26 tanks which were beginning to seem very heavy and ineffective). But many of these items were in bad repair. Aircraft numbered barely 80, and most of the pilots, though enthusiastic, were inexperienced.[4] The republican army in Catalonia also suffered from a shortage of ammunition and above all of faith in victory. Negrín himself was, as he confessed, 'spiritually and physically' tired.[5] Rojo, chief of staff, on the other hand, believed that Franco needed months in which to prepare a general attack, and the republican leaders hence were toying, when attacked, with a plan to disembark a brigade at Motril, which would march to Málaga and raise Andalusia. This was combined with another republican attack, in Estremadura. But both Miaja and his chief of staff, Matallana, now promoted a general, refused. The government in Barcelona had to accept this defensive insubordina-

1. J. Salas has (p. 432) 197 fighters, 93 'aviones de cooperación', 179 bombers.

2. Franco's headquarters staff in 1938 was directed by the now General Francisco Martín Moreno, beneath whom were Colonels Villanueva, Ungría, Barroso, Villegas and Medrano (organization, information, operations, services, maps): the essential if forgotten men in the organization of Franco's war. Cervera and Kindelán continued as chief of staff of the navy and head of the air force, while Generals García Pallasar and García de Pruneda directed the artillery and the engineers. See Martínez Bande, *Los cien últimos días de la república* (Barcelona, 1972), p. 39.

3. Aznar, pp. 814–15.

4. García Lacalle, p. 445. Many aircraft were short of machine-guns.

5. Zugazagoitia, p. 447. The English editor Kingsley Martin told Negrín in December that Churchill had 'changed his mind' over the Spanish republic. 'Too late', said Negrín. (Kingsley Martin, p. 136.)

tion. Possibly, the reluctance of Matallana derived from treachery.[1] On the other hand, Rojo's action in transferring thirty-six aircraft to the central zone weakened Catalonia.[2] Before this, Negrín had sent the chief of the air force, Hidalgo de Cisneros, to Moscow for a replenishment of arms: 250 aircraft, 250 tanks, 4,000 machine-guns, and 650 pieces of artillery. The cost was to be the then huge sum of $103 million, though the republic's credit in Russia apparently stood at less than $100 million. Hidalgo de Cisneros saw Voroshilov, Molotov and Stalin, and, despite Voroshilov's comment, 'Are you going to leave us without any weapons to defend ourselves with?', the shipment was agreed. It was sent from Murmansk in seven ships, to Bordeaux. But it arrived late; and the French government did not hasten its onward shipment.[3] Little of it had reached Barcelona by January.

On 23 December, the attack began, after the nuncio had vainly requested a truce for Christmas in the name of the Pope.[4] The assault was launched by the Navarrese and the Italians, across the River Segre, fifteen miles north of its junction with the Ebro at Mequinenza. The crossing made, the surprised defenders – a well-equipped company of carabineers – were deserted by their officers. The front was thus broken, at the first moment of contact. Higher up the Segre, in the foothills of the Pyrenees, Muñoz Grandes and García Valiño also broke the republican lines. These breaches caused the abandonment of the line of the Segre. At Barcelona, the attack was at first thought a minor one, but soon Lister's 54th Army Corps was thrown into the

1. See the accusations in De la Cierva, *Historia ilustrada*, vol. II, pp. 474–5. Matallana certainly was in touch with the nationalists two months later.

2. García Lacalle, p. 431.

3. See Hidalgo de Cisneros, vol. II, pp. 445–52. García Lacalle, by then head of the republican fighters, urged this visit in November. Hidalgo agreed, and undertook to go. Weeks later, which seemed like years, Lacalle returned from the front and found him still there. Hidalgo explained that he had not gone because Negrín and he had thought that the under-secretary, a communist of long standing, Núñez Maza, should go. Lacalle returned to the front, picturing yet again an emissary to be already in Moscow. Weeks later, which again seemed like years, Lacalle returned to find Núñez Maza still in Barcelona because he believed this to be a manoeuvre by Hidalgo to remove him from his job. Hidalgo de Cisneros then went: too late. (Letter from García Lacalle, July 1964.)

4. See Buckley; Alvarez del Vayo, *Freedom's Battle*, p. 262f; Aznar, p. 816f; Rojo, *España heroica*; Lojendio, p. 547f.

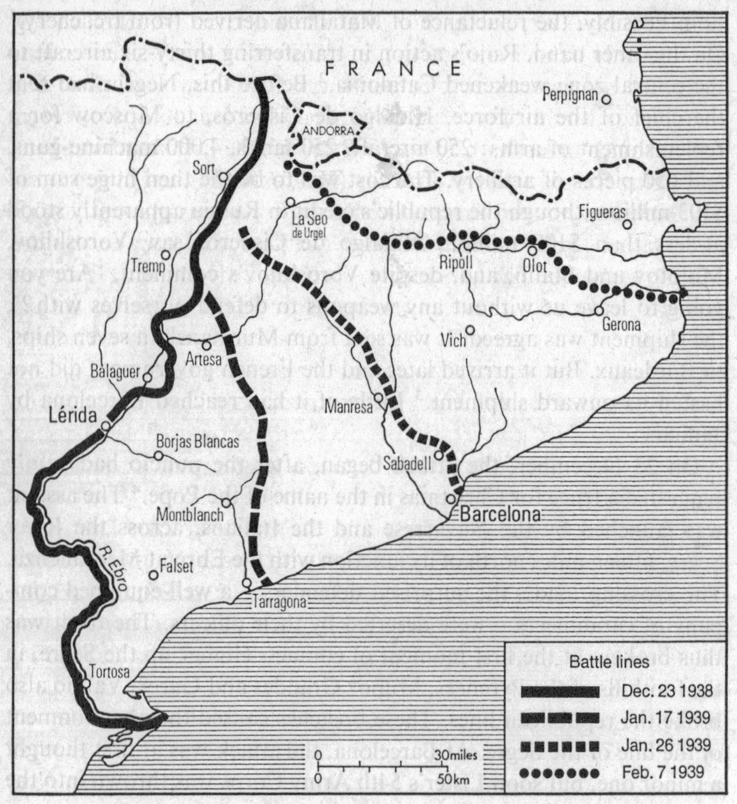

35. The campaign in Catalonia, December 1938–January 1939

battle, to try to hold the attack. With headquarters at Castelldans, in the first line of hills east of the Segre, Lister maintained himself for a fortnight.

On 3 January 1939, the nationalist armour eventually told against Lister, who was forced to abandon his line of defence to the Italians. In the north, García Valiño and Muñoz Grandes, supported by Moscardó, captured the communications centre of Artesa de Segre. On 4 January, the wrecked town of Borjas Blancas fell to the Navarrese and Italian armies. The front was open. Gambara was wounded, but he did not abandon his command. Several Italians were captured by Lister, however, to be shot after interrogation.[1] Ciano, noting that the only danger seemed the possibility of French intervention, instructed his ambassadors in Berlin and London to say that that contingency would bring 'regular' Italian divisions to Spain – even if this should 'unleash world war'.[2] But, with the British cabinet bent on making friends with the dictators (Halifax told Ciano in Rome on the 12th that he hoped Franco 'would settle the Spanish question'),[3] there was no likelihood that Daladier's cabinet would act to save the Spanish republic. The republican commander-in-chief, Hernández Saravia, informed Azaña that he had only 17,000 rifles left for all Catalonia.[4] If that were so – and Hernández Saravia was an honest man – it indicates the confusion in the armies, since there should have been far more than that number of arms available. The battle of Catalonia became a rout. The reorganized Italian mobile divisions astonished the republicans. Too late did Rojo try to get men and material sent up by boat from Valencia. Uselessly did the government extend the draft to men of forty-five. Successive defence lines (L.1, L.2, L.3) were hardly manned. The only successful counter-measure of the republic was a diversionary campaign on the borders of Andalusia and Estremadura. This advance ('Plan P', as Rojo knew it) was led by General Escobar, the civil guard colonel of 1936 in Barcelona, with Colonels Ibarrola and García Vallejo, in command of large if not very disciplined armies; the other armies of the central zone, led by General Moriones and Colonel Casado, also began some local actions. The territory occupied was quite large, but militarily that meant little. For, on 14 January, a sudden and imaginative advance by Yagüe from Gandesa along the Ebro took him to the sea to capture Tarragona. There he met Solchaga, with his Army Corps, proceeding north along the coast. The first mass for two-and-a-half years was held in the cathedral, while the proscription began in the city.

The French government opened the frontier again to allow into Catalonia some of the new war material bought in Russia, but it was too late. The streets and squares of Barcelona were filled with refugees. The city wore a desperate air. Soldiers, bourgeoisie, and anarchists thought only of how they could escape to France. Air raids

1. A. Santamaria, *Operazione Spagna, 1936–1939* (Rome, 1965), p. 115.
2. Ciano, *Diaries 1939–43*, p. 5. 3. *ibid.*, p. 10.
4. Alvarez del Vayo, *Freedom's Battle*, p. 262; Azaña, vol. IV, p. 907.

were continuous, especially on the port. These aimed to destroy vessels which might assist those who desired to flee. The government, preoccupied with the question of evacuating children, did not move until the last moment. In one of the last entries in his diary, Azaña recorded a visit to Hernández Saravia's headquarters: 'Enormous disaster. The army has disappeared. The men of the Ebro [collapse] almost without fighting. Worse than April.'[1]

The battle drew nearer to Barcelona, with little fighting; the advance was almost as fast as the advancing columns could have managed had there been no opposition at all. On 24 January, Yagüe, by the sea, Solchaga, twenty-five miles inland, and Gambara, seven miles farther to the north, had reached the Llobregat, the river which runs roughly from north to south to flow into the Mediterranean a few miles to the west of Barcelona. The same day, García Valiño captured Manresa, and turned north-east to attempt to cut off Barcelona from the border. Negrín, Azaña, the government, the communist leaders, the chiefs of the army and of the civil service now moved from Barcelona to Gerona, along with the Catalan and émigré Basque governments. (Azaña was left to shift for himself.)[2] In the Catalan capital, there was no spirit of resistance, and the communist demand that the Llobregat should become 'the Manzanares of Catalonia' was mere persiflage. The republican chief of staff, Vicente Rojo, remarked that, 'though not exhausted by suffering and hunger, the people were tired of the war'.[3] The Catalan capital could have been defended, and García Lacalle, the commander of the republican fighters, expressed to his chief an astonishment that it was not, which was felt everywhere in the air force.[4] The central government's feud with the *Generalidad* paid its toll, since it had broken Catalonia's desire to resist the nationalist armies. The communist campaign against the POUM and anarchists had had the same effect.[5] Those foreigners who remained either joined the flood of

1. Azaña, vol. IV, p. 906.

2. Azaña, vol. III, p. 537. According to Azaña, the government left behind all the papers relating to foreign affairs and to espionage in nationalist Spain. This was fatal for many.

3. Vicente Rojo, *¡Alerta los pueblos!* (Buenos Aires, 1939), p. 173.

4. García Lacalle, p. 490.

5. 'In killing the revolution, the anti-fascist war was killed too.' Thus M. Casanova, in *Cahiers de la quatrième internationale* (Paris, 1971), p. 5.

refugees, which fled north, or tried to find a ship to take them off. The streets of the great city were filthy after the flight of the municipal cleaners. Mobs began to pillage food shops.

In Rome, Barcelona was held so certainly to be lost that Lord Perth was already asking Ciano to try to prevent reprisals by the nationalists.[1] In France, a debate raged for a week in the National Assembly, in the course of which Daladier and Bonnet said that it was too late to try to save Spain, while Blum and the united Left, including the communists, denied that all was lost. Yet Blum's criticism of the Daladier government for continuing even now to maintain non-intervention could have applied to his own government, at least after February 1937. On 25 January, Yagüe, followed by Solchaga and Gambara, crossed the Llobregat. Resistance was isolated, and without plan. By the following morning, the north and west of Barcelona had been invested. The Navarrese and Italians established themselves on Mount Tibidabo and Yagüe on Montjuich (where he liberated 1,200 political prisoners). At midday, the occupation of the city began. On the first tank which entered Barcelona, a laughing German jewess was perched, giving the fascist salute. She had recently been in the women's prison at Las Cortes as a Trotskyist.[2] The incongruity of the spectacle gave a mocking commentary to the *vivas* of triumph at the 'liberation' of Catalonia. The streets were empty. Almost half a million persons had left for the north by all means possible. By four o'clock, the main administrative buildings were occupied, untouched by incendiaries. In the evening, those citizens of Barcelona who had all the time secretly supported the nationalists came into the streets to rejoice.

Others came out with a different purpose: there were five days of *paseos*, during which the surviving falangists of the city, embittered by suffering, killed whom they liked with impunity.[3] General Gambara, commander of the Italian troops, reported to Ciano that Franco had 'unleashed in Barcelona a very drastic purge'. Mussolini, hearing that many Italian exiles had been captured, and asked for his views,

1. Ciano, *Diaries 1939–43*, p. 15.

2. Junod, p. 133.

3. Cabanellas, vol. II, p. 1047; Cabanellas speaks of 10,000 shot between 26 and 31 January, 25,000 other executions later on. He gives no evidence for these figures. He may be right.

said, 'Let them all be shot. Dead men tell no tales.'[1] There followed a more regular procedure carried out by councils of war organized by the new military governor, General Alvarez Arenas, who was also responsible for the full restitution of the old order: de-nationalization, de-collectivization, new bank notes, new salutes, the washing off of posters and slogans and, under the orders of Colonel Mut, the 'withdrawal' of all Marxist, anarchist and Catalan separatist books. Henceforth, Catalans would speak 'the language of empire'.[2] New newspapers or old ones came out anew, *Vanguardia* as *Vanguardia Española*: one of its collaborators, Carlos Sentís, described the collapse of Catalonia as simply the 'end of a gangster film'. It was to innumerable people the end of a world, as well as of a dream. Catalan autonomy was rescinded; the dancing of the *Sardana*, the Catalan national dance, banned; and the Catalan tongue (henceforward referred to always as a 'dialect') prohibited as an official language. Those who published even business prospectuses in Catalan were fined, Spanish had to be used in churches on all occasions, and even Catalan christian names were prohibited. Shortly afterwards, an order came to remove the inscriptions, on tombs in the cemetery of Montjuich, commemorating Durruti, Ascaso and the anarchist schoolmaster Ferrer, shot in 1909. Catalonia had finished with all that, as with fifty years of vigorous cultural endeavour.

It had not gone forwards to fascism, however; when Ridruejo, director-general of propaganda, arrived with propaganda for the Falange written in Catalan, it was confiscated. He was not permitted to hold a series of meetings in favour of reconciliation between conquerors and conquered; and the military governor, Alvarez Arenas, told him that the gravest problem 'was to . . . restore altars to the city'.[3] The Bible, not José Antonio, gave the text for the punishment of the old 'red city', seat of anarchism and separatism, which had, like Sodom or Gomorrah, to be 'purified'.[4]

1. Ciano, *Diaries 1939–43*, p. 34.
2. Abella, p. 401.
3. Ridruejo, in Sergio Vilar, p. 485.
4. Cf. 'El Tebib Arrumi', qu. *Catalunya sota* . . . p. 147. This book contains a full analysis of the persecution of Catalanism in 1939.

49

The flight from Catalonia

THE conclusion of the campaign of Catalonia was not an offensive but a victory parade, preceded by a flight. The world was astonished at the swiftness of the collapse, which had been caused by war-weariness as much as by the depletion of men and material on the Ebro. Duncan Sandys expressed the views of many sympathizers with the republic (or at least the enemies of Franco's allies) when he urged upon the ambassador in London, Azcárate, that some further resistance was necessary in upper Catalonia for the world to suppose that the war was not over.[1] Henry Stimson, ex-secretary of state, wrote a long letter to the *New York Times* citing legal and political reasons for lifting the embargo on arms to Spain.[2] A correspondence on the subject ensued, none the less passionate for being too late to be of assistance. The White House received a letter saying: 'For God's sake! Lift that embargo on Spain. Look what happened to us!' The signature was 'Ghost of Czechoslovakia'.[3] On 27 January, at a cabinet meeting, President Roosevelt said that the embargo 'had been a grave mistake . . . The President said that we would never do such a thing again . . . He agreed that this embargo controverted old American principles and invalidated established international law.'[4] But this did not then help. Nor was it much comfort to the republic to know that, in England, seventy-two persons out of a hundred questioned in a public opinion poll supported them, against only nine for Franco.[5]

*

1. Azcárate MS. 2. On 23 January.

3. F.D.R. papers, Hyde Park. The same point of view was urged in a book by Allen Dulles and Hamilton Fish Armstrong of *Foreign Affairs* (*Can America Stay Neutral?*).

4. Ickes, p. 569.

5. From an unpublished Ph.D. thesis, *The Spanish Civil War*, by H. J. Parry of the University of California, qu. Taylor, p. 195. There were three other polls of

Catalonia to the north of its capital was in disorder. The republican government had made no provision for the crisis which now occurred; the state fell apart; and the minister of the interior was himself reduced to try, pistol in hand, to regulate the traffic on the main road to France.[1] The government, including Azaña, moved north from one temporary residence to another, quarrelling as they went. The head of the fighters in Catalonia, García Lacalle, had no idea of the whereabouts of the commander of the air force, Hidalgo de Cisneros.[2] The flights from Irún, Málaga, Bilbao – all those movements of a terrified population – paled into insignificance when compared with the flight from Catalonia along what even the Baron von Stohrer recognized to be a 'road of suffering'.[3] This was a movement of panic, for only a small percentage of those who fled would have been in mortal danger if they had remained in Catalonia. But the whole of Catalonia seemed to be on the move – and many of those who were fleeing were already refugees, from Estremadura or Andalusia. The traffic jam of official and private cars and lorries was continuous. All the towns on the way to the French border were filled. At night, the pavements were choked with hunger-stricken, shivering human beings, of all ages. Characteristic of the chaos was the fate of the prisoners who were members of the POUM – Gorkin, Andrade, Gironella and others. Their captors who were members of the SIM had wanted to leave them behind in Barcelona to the tender mercies of Franco. Then, however, most prisoners were moved northwards. At a certain point near the French border, their gaolers placed themselves at their disposal. Once in France, they were, however, first turned back to go to Spain. Only some days later did they escape in truth, hurrying out of the road when by chance they saw the judge

British opinion, collected by the British Public Opinion Institute, during the civil war. In January 1937, 14 per cent considered that the Burgos *junta* should be considered the true government of Spain, against 86 per cent who did not. In March 1938, 57 per cent considered themselves in sympathy with the government, 7 per cent with Franco and 36 per cent neither. In October 1938, the answers were much as in the previous March.

1. So Martínez Barrio told Azaña, in Azaña, vol. III, p. 541.
2. García Lacalle, pp. 494–5.
3. *GD*, p. 844.

who had condemned them, José Gomís, passing in a black car. The refugees' difficulties were worsened by aerial attacks from the Condor Legion, apparently against Franco's wishes.[1]

At first, the French government had refused, for political as well as for financial reasons, to permit the entry of the refugees. France had already spent 88 million francs on aid to Spanish refugees since the start of the war. They proposed instead a neutral zone on the Spanish side of the frontier, where refugees could be maintained by foreign relief. The nationalists, however, refused to consider this plan. So the French government permitted the opening of the frontier, at first only to civilians and wounded men. Under these conditions, the first crossings began at midnight on 27–28 January. Fifteen thousand crossed on 28 January. On the succeeding days, this figure was exceeded. In the first week of February, it became evident that the retreating republican army had no intention, and no means, of resisting the nationalist advance, despite the arrival of two new squadrons of I-15 B fighters (Superchatos) from Russia.[2] The French, therefore, were faced with a choice between permitting the entry of the soldiers, or resisting them by force. On 5 February, the French government decided to admit the army, subject to the surrender of their arms. Thus, to the 10,000 wounded, the 170,000 women and children, and the 60,000 male civilians who had crossed since 28 January, there were added 220,000 men of the republican army, between 5 and 10 February. Even so, the nationalists captured some 60,000 prisoners.[3]

The frontier was a scene of tragedy. The fugitives were worn out. Their clothes were damp from rain and snow. Yet there were few complaints. Crushed by disaster, the majority of the Spanish republicans walked erect into exile. Children carried broken toys, the head of a doll or a deflated ball – symbols of a happy childhood

1. Hills, p. 324, speaks of anger between Kindelán and the German military attaché, Baron von Funck, on this matter.

2. They were soon sent off to Toulouse.

3. Figures are discussed in Pike, pp. 213–14. Basing himself on the Mexican Embassy in Paris, De la Cierva gives a figure of 527,800 exiles from Spain between February and late April 1939. Azaña (vol. III, p. 534) has 220,000. Alvarez del Vayo (in Azaña, vol. III, p. 553) said a total of 400,000 crossed. Sir John Simpson, *The Rufugee Problem* (London, 1939), has 270,000 soldiers, 170,000 civilians and 13,000 ill – a total of 453,000.

which they had lost. At the border, what laughter, what happiness! But what disillusion![1]

The Spanish side of the frontier was controlled by a certain José Ramos, head of one of the murderous revolutionary tribunals of the early days in Barcelona, afterwards commandant of the gaol at Ordenes. He behaved as a brigand.[2] On the French side of the frontier, a camp was opened as a clearing centre at Le Boulou. There was no shelter, though most of the women and children were removed, along with some wounded soldiers, to other parts of France. Families were separated who had never before been apart, even in the disaster of the flight. Camps were established at Argelès, at St Cyprien, at Barcarès, and at four smaller places in the area, for the reception of the republican army. These were simply open spaces of sand dunes near the sea, enclosed by barbed-wire, from which the inmates were prevented from leaving by force. Men dug holes for themselves like animals, to find some shelter. There were eventually fifteen camps, guarded by Senegalese and members of the *garde mobile*. Some refugees crossed the border with a handful of earth which they had taken as they left their villages. One *garde mobile* forcibly opened one of these clenched hands and scattered the earth of Spain in disdain into a French ditch.[3] Among those who crossed was a phantom gathering of international volunteers who had been regrouped (or had regrouped themselves) under the direction of a Pole (Henrik Torunczyk): among them were still Ludwig Renn, Heinrich Rau, Mihály Szalvai (the Spanish Chapaiev) and the Italian, Giuliano Pajetta, as well as André Marty. Malraux, who had been filming *L'Espoir* in Catalonia, was there: '*c'était toute la révolution qui s'en allait*'. True, and the hopes for 'anti-fascism' outside received a harsh setback.[4]

In the camps, for ten days, there was no water or food supply, and those wounded who stayed with their comrades were left uncared for.

1. Howard Kershner, *Quaker Service in Modern War* (New York, 1950), p. 24.

2. *La Dépêche* (Toulouse), 3 March 1939, qu. D. W. Pike, *Vae Victis!* (Paris, 1969), p. 14.

3. Regler, *Owl of Minerva*, p. 321. See Pike, *Vae Victis!*, pp. 216–17.

4. Giuliano Pajetta had been the youngest commissar in the International Brigades. A young communist from Turin at fourteen, he had been arrested, fled to France and then to Russia and had been in Spain almost since the beginning. Such old warriors in Spain as Longo, Vidali and Togliatti also left Catalonia. (Spriano, p. 271.)

Among these was the great poet Machado, who shortly died in a pension at Collioure, due to the recurrence of an asthmatic complaint, exacerbated by the pains of the evacuation.[1] Food was later secured, but there was no sanitation or shelter, and meagre medical services. The French government was criticized for permitting these conditions but the difficulties of providing for about 400,000 refugees at short notice were, after all, herculean. France was never given much recognition for admitting the refugees at all. No doubt the French government hoped, by neglect, to force as many as possible of the refugees to throw themselves on Franco's mercy. But callousness was also shown by persons comfortable in America or England: Herbert Matthews, for example, was told by the editor of the *New York Times* not to send him too many emotional reports of the conditions of the camp.[2] The cost of providing for one refugee was 15 francs a day and, for the wounded, 60 francs. The French government gave 30 million francs for this purpose early in February. At the same time, they not unnaturally asked other governments to help with the burden. The Belgians agreed to accept 2–3,000 Spanish children, but to begin with the British and Russian governments would not accept any refugees. Russia's attitude was widely commented on; particularly in the right-wing French press. Later, Britain agreed to the entry of a selected number of leaders, and Russia gave £28,000 for aid to the refugees, Britain £50,000 to the Red Cross for work in the camps.[3] There were inevitably several settlements of private scores in these camps. In the camp at Argelès, for example, Astorga Vayo, of the hated SIM, sometime commandant of a large republican prison camp at Omells de Nagaya in Lérida, was one day greeted by several acquaintances from earlier in the war.[4] He walked with them for a while discussing

1. The new republican ambassador in Paris, Marcelino Pascua (transferred from Moscow), tried to get Machado to Paris, but his attempt failed due to the gravity of Machado's state (letter to the author from Marcelino Pascua).

2. Regler, *Owl of Minerva*, *loc. cit*. For sympathizers with the republic, the care of the refugees was the last and most painful of the 'causes' of the Spanish war. See Nancy Cunard, *Manchester Guardian*, 17 February 1939, and Ch. XV of Nancy Mitford, *The Pursuit of Love*.

3. A. Toynbee, *Survey*, vol. I, pp. 397–9.

4. Astorga's method of maintaining discipline had been to shoot five people for every prisoner who escaped. See for an account Juan Pujol in *Historia y vida*, January 1975.

old times. Suddenly he realized that they had led him to an unfrequented part of the camp. Before him he observed a deep trench dug beneath some pine trees. He turned in dismay. His companions smiled grimly. They buried him alive.[1]

*

Meantime, on 1 February, a rump of sixty-two members of the Cortes, elected almost three years before with such enthusiasm, met in a dungeon of the old castle of Figueras, the last town in Catalonia short of the border. Diego Martínez Barrio sat at a table draped with the flag of the republic. Negrín made a speech naming only three conditions for peace: a guarantee of Spanish independence; a guarantee of the right of the Spanish people to choose their own government; and freedom from persecution. Nobody opposed these conditions, although it was certain that they would not be accepted by General Franco, and that, therefore, the government was, in effect, recommending the continuance of the war.[2] The Cortes broke up. Its members left for France. Some, indeed, had spent the previous night there. Alvarez del Vayo and Negrín approached Ralph Stevenson and Jules Henry, the British and French ministers, to try and arrange with the nationalists a mediation on the conditions of the speech at Figueras. The diplomats agreed to try and do so. Negrín added that, if the terms were rejected, the republic would continue the war from Madrid.[3] He had long before resolved to do that. Alvarez del Vayo busied himself with the safe conduct from Figueras of the paintings of the Prado. They were taken in lorries to Geneva, where they were held on behalf of the Spanish people by the secretary-general of the League. The refugees stood aside, while the canvases of Velázquez, Goya, Titian, Rubens passed. Azaña (echoing one of the characters in his *Velada en Benicarló*) remarked to Negrín that all notions of monarchy and republic were not worth a single Velázquez. Negrín agreed.[4] Neither, of course, believed it.

1. Gorkin, *Caníbales políticos*, p. 237; and Pike, *Vae Victis!*, p. 53.

2. *Diario de Sesiones*, No. 69, February 1939. See the description of the scene in Zugazagoitia, p. 508f.

3. *USD*, 1939, vol. II, pp. 739–40.

4. Alvarez del Vayo, *The Last Optimist*, p. 294; Azaña, vol. III, p. 554.

The Navarrese and Italian advance continued irresistibly. Gerona fell on 5 February, after incendiary bombing which infuriated the retreating republicans into a show of resistance. On the same day at daybreak, Azaña, Martínez Barrio and Companys left Spain. Azaña's departure was banal. The car in which Martínez Barrio was travelling broke down and blocked the road. Negrín personally tried to push it aside. To no avail: the President had to leave Spain on foot. Negrín and Azaña said goodbye at Las Illas, just in France. Then Negrín returned for a few hours more to Spain; Azaña went on into exile.[1] Several nationalist prisoners were murdered. They included Colonel Rey d'Harcourt, the hero of Teruel, and the bishop of Teruel with him.[2] Marty was only narrowly forestalled in an attempt to shoot a number of his old staff at Albacete, who might, so he feared in his narrow insanity, tell the world of some of his maniacal acts.[3] To the west, García Valiño entered the old cathedral city of Vich. As the nationalists now suspected, the last resistance was over in Catalonia. The last-minute replacement of Hernández Saravia by Jurado as commander-in-chief was of no avail. The new general was experienced but nobody could recreate a front. (Hernández Saravia had desired to dismiss Modesto and give his command to the anarchist-minded Colonel Perea. Negrín and Rojo opposed that.)[4] While Sir Robert Hodgson, on behalf of Britain, was putting Negrín's peace points to the nationalists, four Army Corps were advancing towards the French frontier. On 8 February, the Navarrese entered Figueras. The same day, their advanced units came into contact with the rearguard of the retreating republicans. On 9 February, Solchaga and Moscardó reached the French frontier, the former at Le Perthus, the latter in the mountains of Nuria. By the 10th, the whole frontier was lined by the nationalist armies. Earlier in the day, Modesto had led the last

1. Azaña's account is in his letter to Ossorio, 28 June 1939, in *Obras*, vol. III, p. 552f.

2. *The General Cause*, p. 178.

3. Regler, *Owl of Minerva*, p. 325.

4. Earlier tension between Rojo and Hernández Saravia is expressed in a note of a meeting between them published by R. Salas, vol. IV, p. 3345. Saravia had been quite isolated from his troops for over two weeks, being kept informed only by the fighter commander, García Lacalle, where the enemy was. See García Lacalle, p. 495.

units of the Army of the Ebro into France. It was at this moment that Giménez Caballero, the first fascist in Spain, then serving under Moscardó as a 'provisional lieutenant', recalled Louis XIV's famous boast, and made the exuberant proclamation to his men: 'At last, there are the Pyrenees!'

50

Negotiations for peace – General Franco's conditions – French and British recognition of Franco – Colonel Casado's coup *– flight of Negrín – the civil war within the Civil War – communist abnegation – unsuccessful negotiations with Burgos – scenes on the Mediterranean coast*

AFTER the fall of Catalonia, the world concluded that the Spanish war was over. The nationalist peseta rose on the Paris Bourse to seventy times the value of the republican.[1] Inside nationalist Spain, no more was heard of plots of assassination. At Chicote's bar, in San Sebastián (the most 'normal' of the nationalist cities), pessimists had once been the most fashionable clients. Now optimists discouraged even those who laughed at notices announcing 'Keep quiet, be careful, enemy ears are listening'. One could go to the cinema (to see, for example, the Italian fascist monumental historical film, *Scipio in Africa*, or one of the new Spanish documentaries – *España Heroica*, or *Los Conquistadores del Norte*, or even Clark Gable and Jean Harlow in *Seas of China*) with an easy conscience. The question of the relationship between the régime and the church was discussed by Serrano Súñer in a press conference on 6 February. (He was now minister of public order as well as of the interior after the death of the aged General Martínez Anido, on 24 January.) While praising catholic tradition, he proposed a division of powers, especially in education. He also demanded the right of episcopal presentation which the state had enjoyed since the Concordat of 1851. But Serrano Súñer did not have his own way in everything. Cardinal Segura, now archbishop of Seville, had denounced the Falange as irreligious, and deplored the influence of the nazis. A little

1. The real value was nearer the unofficial rate of 100 to the pound than the fixed one of 42. The *vales*, issued by municipalities, by Popular Front committees, and by the *Generalidad* in the early days of the war (nick-named 'pyjamas', because they could only be used at home) were no longer accepted.

later, the primate, Cardinal Gomá, returned to the matter more discreetly (as was his custom) in his Lenten pastoral letter, in which he criticized 'exaggerated nationalism'. A decree of 15 December had, meanwhile, given back to the royal family the property and rights of citizenship taken from them by the republic. King Alfonso and his son Juan announced that they wished to be regarded as 'soldiers of Franco', until further orders.

The nationalist régime was now also courted by those who previously had scorned it. The French government, for example, dispatched Senator Bérard to Burgos to negotiate diplomatic relations. Bérard was treated coldly. Jordana demanded, first, recognition *de jure*, the return of republican ships in French waters, of Spanish art treasures taken by the republic to France, and of Spanish money in France. The nationalists refused to pay anything for the upkeep of the republican refugees in southern France, or to approve the French government to reimburse their expenses in this matter from Spanish assets in France.[1]

The government of the republic now assembled in Toulouse. Negrín and Alvarez del Vayo arrived there, on 9 February, from Figueras, to discover the rest of the cabinet waiting for permission from the French authorities to fly to Valencia. After a brief cabinet meeting in the Spanish Consulate, the difficulties over transport were smoothed over. Negrín and Alvarez del Vayo flew to Alicante in an aeroplane belonging to Air France. They found the military leaders of central Spain low in spirit.[2] This mood was exacerbated by the fact that, the same day that Catalonia fell, Minorca also surrendered. Franco had let it be known in London that he would occupy Minorca without Germans or Italians. Three battalions of the republican garrison then rebelled against Negrín, and the captain of one of them telephoned his brother, the head of the shipyard at Pollensa in Majorca, to send over envoys to negotiate the surrender. As a result, the British cruiser HMS *Devonshire* brought negotiators from Majorca to Port Mahon. Its captain helped to negotiate the surrender of the island and transported six hundred republicans, led by the commander, Luis González Ubieta, the recently retired chief of the

1. Madariaga, *Spain*, p. 431.
2. Alvarez del Vayo, *Freedom's Battle*, p. 275.

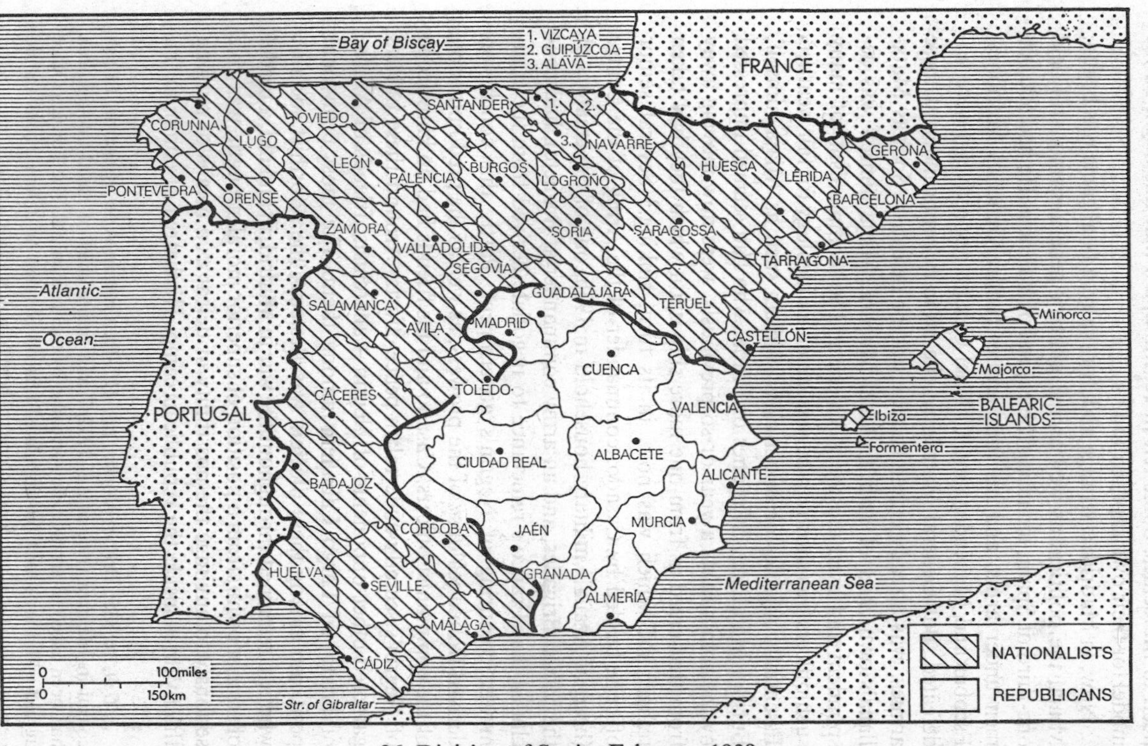

36. Division of Spain, February 1939

fleet, to Marseilles. Some felt in central Spain that this might be the model for their own capitulation.[1]

Now, in Madrid, a strange and, for many, a fatal game was begun. Miaja, the political as well as the military generalissimo, still held one-third of Spain, including the capital of Valencia. He had 500,000 men under arms, and his four armies (under Generals Moriones, Escobar and Menéndez, and Colonel Casado respectively) were undefeated. But General Matallana, the military commander of these armies, was already either treacherous or defeatist. So was Matallana's own chief of staff, Colonel Muedra. Miaja himself was despondent and lived mostly in Valencia. The 'communism' of many such officers was shown to be very much an ideology for fair weather. Essentially middle- or upper-class soldiers such as Miaja himself, Burillo, Matallana, Moriones or Prada, who had seemed impressed by the communists a year or so previously, were now moving away from that creed as from one more ship upon which they had taken refuge, and which was now, in its turn, sinking.[2] Several senior officers, headed by Casado, commander of the Army of the Centre (head of Azaña's military household in 1936, one of the creators of the Mixed Brigades, and an army commander at Brunete), had concluded that Franco's reluctance to negotiate derived from the communist colouring of Negrín's government. Partly this conclusion derived from a jealousy of the prowess, as well as the predominance, of the communist officers. Casado and his friends had no knowledge of Negrín's secretly undertaken peace efforts. Around these officers gathered other opponents of Negrín – anarchists, friends of Azaña, of Prieto, of Largo Caballero among them. The most prominent politician among these plotters was Besteiro, the reformist socialist who had remained throughout the war in Madrid, ill and old, a model of stoicism who, from a position of superior moral strength, was able seriously to envisage the possibility of defeat as a means of purging the rivalries inside the republican camp. His hatred of communism,

1. *GD*, p. 835; Bruno Alonso, pp. 117–18. Captain Alan Hillgarth, British consul in Majorca (vice-consul 1932–7 and future chief of naval intelligence), had been asked to arrange the surrender by the nationalists. The Foreign Office agreed with the request but stipulated that no German or Italian troops should be allowed on the island for two years. These conditions were kept.

2. Guy Hermet, *Los comunistas en España* (Paris, 1971), p. 30.

and his contempt for the revolutionary terror, caused him to underestimate the nationalist repression and the evolution of 'Francoism' during the war.[1] The plot might have been unsuccessful had it not been for the anarchists, who received instructions from Mariano Vázquez, their secretary-general, now in France, to prepare for the acceptance of the nationalists' victory. Vázquez had become a friend of Negrín, as has been seen, but the one anarchist who had found himself as an effective army commander, Cipriano Mera, commander of the 4th Army Corps under Casado, was far from it. (The other three corps commanders under Casado – Barceló, Ortega and Bueno – were communists.) A handful of members of the CNT in Madrid, such as the journalist García Pradas, Eduardo Val and Manuel Salgado, pressed Mera forward. Meantime, Miaja, the Generalissimo of central Spain, had decided that there was no further point in continuing the war; the republic would lose in the end, even if it fought on another year. The nationalist spy organizations, a real Fifth Column, were also secretly active, probing, through trusted intermediaries, the loyalty of Casado, of Matallana, of Muedra (Matallana's chief of staff) and of other officers. Casado had already embarked by early February on correspondence with the chief of Franco's intelligence in Burgos, Colonel Ungría.[2] The negotiations between Casado and Burgos envisaged a guarantee of life to those army officers who laid down their arms 'and who had not committed crimes'.[3] Casado also exchanged letters with an old friend, General Barrón, an army commander with Franco. Casado, the nerve of the plot, was able, cultivated, austere and hard-working: he lived as simply as if he were the most junior soldier, and worked as if he were the commander-in-chief.[4] He also had been in touch since late 1938 with Denys Cowan, the British liaison officer of the Chetwode commission in Madrid. Probably acting unofficially on behalf of the

1. Saborit, *Julián Besteiro*, p. 410.

2. The decisive part was played by the head of the spy ring, 'Antonio' (called after Antonio de Luna, a university professor). Professor Julio Palacios, an agent of 'Antonio's', was instructed to make contact through intermediaries with Casado in January. (From an unpublished 'Memoria' by Palacios, qu. Martínez Bande (*Los cien últimos días*, 1972, p. 119). Colonel Bonel in Toledo also played an important part in negotiations between Madrid and Burgos.

3. Martínez Bande, *op. cit.*, p. 120.

4. Zugazagoitia's comment in his book, *Historia de la guerra en España*, p. 546.

British Government, Cowan was clearly interested in bringing the war to an end.[1]

The communists had, for a long time, been suspicious of Casado. He had opposed the Brunete offensive in 1937. Daniel Ortega, the communist deputy, a commissar of the Fifth Regiment in the early days, who worked in Casado's headquarters, had told La Pasionaria earlier in the year of his suspicions of Casado.[2] Casado knew of Azaña's attempts at a mediated peace, through Besteiro. Casado's wife, an influence on him, was suspected by some of treachery, though defeatism was probably the explanation. Casado is known at one point to have suggested that, if Negrín had insisted on a 'Numantian struggle' to the bitter end, and resolved that all should be lost rather than surrender, he would have continued, though reluctantly, to back him: what Casado and his friends found understandably unacceptable was a public Numantian posture with, at the same time, preparation for flight (the 'Numantinos, with aeroplanes and secret accounts in Switzerland', as Azaña spoke of them).[3] Casado's headquarters was in the dilapidated old estate of the family of Osuna outside Madrid near Barajas: the Alameda, so charmingly portrayed by Goya. In this delightful palace, with its wonderful statues, staircases and lawns, Casado planned the end of the war.[4]

In Madrid, the commanders had been for a long time out of con-

1. Ibarruri, p. 429. There persists a rumour that Casado was paid by the British government to try and bring the war to an end. This unlikely story seems disproved by the manner in which he was received when he arrived in Britain at the start of April. Broué and Témime (p. 261) suggest that Cowan initiated the plot. I feel that that was a survival of the old French respect for '*l'intelligence*', which it has not always merited.

2. The following account of the end of the war in Spain and the *coup* of Colonel Casado is pieced together from, chiefly, the narrative of Colonel Casado himself (confused and contradictory though it is, his second edition is different from his first), Castro Delgado, La Pasionaria, Bruno Alonso, Alvarez del Vayo, García Pradas *(Cómo terminó la guerra de España)*, Wenceslao Carrillo (*El último episodio de la guerra civil española*, Toulouse, 1945), and Jesús Hernández. Also Negrín's speech in the Cortes Committee in Paris on 31 March; Bouthelier *(Ocho días)* and Edmundo Domínguez *(Los vencedores de Negrín)*. Martínez Bande's *Los cien últimos días de la república* is a sober careful account, as is usual with that author, and gives information about Casado's contacts with Burgos. See also Mera's memoirs, p. 193f.

3. Prieto recalls this in *Convulsiones*, vol. II, p. 83.

4. Martínez Bande, *Los cien últimos días*, p. 82.

tact with their government. All were tired of fighting. The policy of resistance was only urged by the communist party – whose leaders in Catalonia and on the Ebro, Lister and Modesto, with Togliatti, had also returned to Spain from Toulouse. While many commanders such as Rojo, Hernández Saravia, Jurado, Perea, Pozas and others remained in France, the veteran communist leaders of the Army of the Ebro came back too.[1] One professional officer, Jesús Pérez Salas, who had fought through the war, recalled later that anxiety as to what sort of political system there would be, even if the republic were to win, was then widespread.[2] Meanwhile, from 8 to 11 February, the communists in Madrid held a conference, at which many allegations of defeatism were heard.[3] The CNT, FAI and anarchist youth also met, and even had a meeting in Valencia, with Negrín, to discuss the situation. Negrín caused unnecessary anger when he refused to receive the new secretary of the FAI, José Grunfeld, with the explanation that 'he was not Spanish'.[4] At this point, some anarchists in the Peninsula backed the idea of continued resistance; but from France, where many of the leaders now were (and remained), instructions came which accepted defeat, and tried to plan for the evacuation of other anarchist leaders from central Spain.[5]

Alvarez del Vayo flew from Madrid to Paris to persuade Azaña to return to Spain also. But Azaña told him: 'My duty is to make peace. I refuse to help, by my presence, to prolong a senseless battle. We must secure the best possible guarantees, and then conclude, as soon as we can.' Alvarez del Vayo gave up his task as useless.[6]

Negrín reached Madrid on 12 February. That same day, he had an interview with Casado lasting four hours.[7] Casado, speaking of the hunger and lack of fuel in Madrid, said that the war must be brought to an end. Negrín promised to send fifteen days' worth of

1. Tagüeña, p. 304. Díaz had been in Moscow since November (Spriano, vol. III, p. 272).

2. Pérez Salas, p. 232. 3. Ibarruri, pp. 436–7.

4. Peirats, vol. III, p. 353. He was an Argentinian.

5. The instructions dated 10 February were signed by Mariano Vázquez of the CNT and Pedro Herrera of the FAI (*ibid.*, p. 356). Cf. Juan López, *Una misión sin importancia: memorias de un sindicalista* (Madrid, 1972).

6. Alvarez del Vayo, *Freedom's Battle*, p. 278f.

7. Casado says this was 25 February. I accept Martínez Bande's view that it was not. Mera confirms, p. 194.

provisions. Casado replied with further complaints. He had no transport. Britain and France had abandoned the republic. The fall of Catalonia had cut the anyway diminished raw materials of the republic by 70 per cent. Many troops had no shoes and no overcoat. There were only forty aircraft to serve his army, little artillery, very few automatic weapons. The nationalists had 32 divisions south of Madrid, with masses of artillery, tanks, and 600 aircraft. Negrín told Casado that Russia was sending 10,000 machine-guns, 600 aircraft and 500 pieces of artillery. They were now in Marseilles and, despite the difficulties, would soon reach Spain. The peace negotiations with Franco, he added, had failed. Casado said that these Russian supplies would never arrive, since the only route was the well-guarded one across the sea from Marseilles to Valencia. He beseeched Negrín to begin negotiations again, and offered his own services in assistance. Negrín accepted the offer. He added that he would have no hesitation in removing the communist party from the government if it should be necessary. He told Casado that he would promote him to the rank of general. Negrín later met the leaders in Madrid of the Popular Front parties. He was vague about his general aims. Casado saw the same politicians, and before them vented his irritation against the communists. Some communists in Madrid, such as Tagüeña, Domingo Girón (the local organizer) and Pedro Checa, began to prepare against the threat of a military conspiracy, rumours of which they had heard.[1] A communist party delegation headed by La Pasionaria called on Negrín: 'If the government is ready to go on with the fight, the communist party will back it; if the government wants to make peace proposals, the communist party will not be an obstacle'. Negrín said that he saw continued resistance as the only possible course of action. Yet he seemed a man 'overwhelmed by events who, having spent his forces in a difficult struggle against the currents of surrender, was allowing himself to be dragged to the bottom all the same, trying to maintain a fragment of honour'.[2]

Negrín's policy in February 1939 has been the subject of controversy. He wished to fight on. But in private, it is alleged, he made sure that he and his friends had safe routes for escape. Did he, in fact,

1. Tagüeña, p. 306.

2. Ibarruri, p. 440. The other communists included Checa, Delicado and Isidro Diéguez.

while presenting a front of resistance to the end, secretly welcome Casado's conspiracies as justification to himself to escape? Was he outmanoeuvred, or did he allow himself to be outmanoeuvred? Did he know of Casado's (and Matallana's) secret dealings with Franco, and if he did, why did he not arrest them? In retrospect, the communists, on whom he relied more and more, considered his conduct a 'contradiction and incomprehensible'; while he reaffirmed his decision to resist, he did nothing to organize resistance.[1] Negrín seems in truth to have been undecided. He desired peace but knew, better than Casado, that Franco's terms were harsh. Until the collapse in Catalonia, he had had an army behind him. Now, in the centre of Spain, he found himself not only undecided, but with an untried, possibly disloyal army, headed by officers whose loyalty was certainly questionable. Yet he knew too that the communist commanders, even if effective, had their first loyalty to the party. Negrín's conduct of affairs during this month invites questions; but his position was not enviable. His only strategy was to await the holocaust of a world war. His tactics could only be (and there he did see eye-to-eye with the communists) to be the last to abandon the fight.

On 16 February, Negrín held a meeting of republican military leaders in a hanger at Los Llanos aerodrome, just south of Albacete.[2] There were present several veteran commanders of the republican army – men who, as captains or majors, had rallied to the republic in July 1936 and who now held, some of them, if precariously, the *bâtons* of general officers. To them Negrín spoke for two hours. He described the failure of his peace negotiations of the last month. He also described how, since May of the previous year, he had been seeking peace on honourable terms, through intermediaries. He said that now there was no other course but resistance. Next to speak was General Matallana who argued that it was madness to continue to fight. He appealed to the humanity of the Prime Minister to bring an end to the war. Generals Menéndez, Escobar and Moriones, commanders of the Armies of the Levante, Estremadura and Andalusia respectively, agreed with Matallana. All of them regular officers before 1936, they represented in their own lives, in an acute form,

1. Ibarruri, p. 427.

2. R. Salas, vol. IV, pp. 3392–8, gives Camacho's report. I accept the dating of Martínez Bande which dates this meeting 16, not 27, February.

the tragedy of the war: they were loyal to the government, hostile to revolution. Admiral Buiza, commander of the navy (he had been reappointed to that post to succeed González Ubieta), reported that a commission representing the crews of the republican fleet had decided that the war was lost, and that the nationalist air attacks would soon force the fleet to leave Spanish waters, unless peace negotiations were begun. Negrín told Buiza that the leaders of the commission should have been shot for mutiny. Buiza said that, while, in principle, he agreed with Negrín, he had not so acted, because he personally agreed with the commission's views. Next, Colonel Camacho spoke on behalf of the air force. He said that he had only three squadrons of Natasha bombers, two of Katiuskas and twenty-five Chatos or Moscas. He also proposed peace. But he did say that the air force had enough petrol for a year's more war. General Bernal, military governor of the naval base at Cartagena, spoke likewise. Miaja, the 'hero of Madrid', complained that he had not been permitted to speak. Negrín now gave him the floor, saying that he had wanted him, as commander-in-chief, to speak last. Surprisingly, Miaja demanded resistance at all costs. Thereupon, Negrín summed up, without making firm suggestions as to the action to be followed; but he let it be understood that, since negotiations had failed, the war would have to continue.[1] There were some who afterwards wondered whether Negrín's action in only summoning officers known to be pessimistic did not indicate that the Prime Minister was already himself pessimistic. Why too did he fix the government at the small undistinguished manufacturing town of Elda, twenty miles inland from Alicante, so far from Madrid, if he wanted really to go on fighting? It was suspiciously near to the coast in case escape should be necessary. The communist high command, now almost openly under the chairmanship of Togliatti, had, on the other hand, set up their headquarters near by, in the beautiful palm forest at Elche, and the same question might have been asked of them too.[2] It seems likely that, while Casado, Matallana and the other officers in Madrid

1. Casado, p. 121; cf. Benavides, *La escuadra*, p. 451.

2. Attacks on Negrín's way of life in this last stage of the Spanish republic were made by Casado (p. 135) and García Pradas (p. 34). Was he really surrounded by chorus girls, were there really crates of champagne? Or is this the imagination of puritans?

were conspiring with anarchists and the politicians in Madrid, Negrín had reached the conclusion that some kind of temporary dictatorship under himself with communist support was necessary to ensure the continuance of the war. Casado, Matallana, Escobar and other officers who were not in agreement with the prime minister would be promoted to positions of no importance.

The situation in Madrid was indeed now terrible, as Casado had said. Negrín perhaps did not quite realize how bad it was. The Quaker International Commission for the Assistance of Child Refugees reported that the average food supply was such that even if the existing level were maintained, it could not support life for more than two or three months more. There was no heating, hot water, medicines or surgical dressings. These conditions defeated such international help as was being mobilized. 'Food for Spain' funds were being gathered in England. Gifts were made by several governments. The governments of Canada, Norway and Denmark bought surplus food supplies and gave them to Spain. Belgium gave about £10,000 worth of food, Sweden £75,000 (in addition to an earlier £50,000). The French government agreed to send 45,000 tons of flour to the republic, though not as a gift. The United States sent 600,000 barrels of flour through the Red Cross. But this cargo was shunted about the Mediterranean from one port to another before being finally delivered. The shipowners also attempted to make the bill for transport of the flour as large as possible, justifying themselves by saying that, each time a port was named for delivery, it fell to the nationalists. Thus the hungry children of the republic waited three months after delivery of the US flour at Le Havre. The Quaker commission, meantime, continued to give aid to territory conquered by the nationalists, though they insisted on strict conditions for it.[1] The nearer the republic drew to its end, however, the greater international interest there was in its fate – especially in the United States. Madrid was a strange, silent city whose inhabitants knew that, if the war were to continue, their hour of trial had come round again. Newspapers continued a bland optimism which no one felt, as did the radio services, which continued under Negrín's direction.

Under cover of secrecy, Casado was continuing his negotiations with Burgos. His plan was to arrest and hand over to Franco many

1. Kershner, p. 47.

communist and other leaders, and he even apologized that he would not be able to prevent the flight of some.[1] Colonel Ungría at Burgos received a full description of Negrín's meeting at Los Llanos. Two colonels on Casado's staff, Garijo and Muedra, also contemplated handing over the army in the central zone, without more ado.

*

On 13 February Franco, meantime, concentrated the mind of those inclined to work for surrender by promulgating a decree applying to all guilty of 'subversive activities' from October 1934 until July 1936, as well as to those who since had 'opposed the nationalist government in fact or by vexatious passivity'. This gave a broad licence for vengeance. The issue of reprisals was the most important one for the republic. If guarantees against them had been given, the republic would have made peace a year before. Azcárate was still pressing the British government to put Negrín's last three points as an armistice to Franco. Otherwise, the republicans were saying, Franco would be responsible for a continuation of the bloodbath. On 17 February, Azcárate and Alvarez del Vayo, still in Paris, telegraphed to Negrín to suggest that freedom from reprisals should be made the only condition of peace, and to allow them to put this to Lord Halifax for transmission to Franco. Halifax had proposed this simple condition to Azcárate. Due to telegraphic delays (attributed subsequently by Azcárate and Alvarez del Vayo to the wilful interference of Casado), Negrín's affirmative reply did not reach Paris until 25 February. Halifax, meantime, on 22 February, had given up waiting for the agreement to his proposal. He began to arrange an unconditional recognition of the nationalist government.[2] Chamberlain had three days earlier confided to his diary: 'I think we ought to be able to establish excellent relations with Franco, who seems "well disposed to us" '.[3] Long before that, on 18 February, Franco had ended all ideas of a conditional peace, whether put by Britain, or France or by any republican. 'The nationalists have won,' he declared, 'the

1. Martínez Bande, p. 121.

2. These facts were related to the author by Azcárate. They are described on p. 221 of his unpublished memoirs. Cf. also Alvarez del Vayo, *Freedom's Battle*, p. 285.

3. Feiling, p. 394.

republicans must, therefore, surrender without conditions.' Franco had stated in November 1938 that there could be no question of an amnesty: 'Those who are amnestied are demoralized'. He believed in 'redemption through the penalty of labour'. Those who were not to be executed would have to 're-educate' themselves by work in labour camps.

On 20 February, Casado was visited by an agent of Franco's intelligence, Colonel José Centaño de la Paz, who had been, throughout the war, chief of a precision instrument factory belonging to the republican army at Aranjuez, but also, since 1938, head of a spy-ring, known as 'Lucero Verde'. He and Manuel Guitián, also an agent of Burgos, called on Casado at the Alameda and were received with enthusiasm; Casado made to them exaggerated promises as to what he could do, saying he could hand over the Army of the Centre by 25 February. He promised to go to Negrín and demand his resignation. Centaño then produced a written guarantee for the lives of career officers in the republican army who had committed no crime and who laid down their arms. 'Magnificent, magnificent!' said Casado. Centaño had reported to Burgos favourably of Casado before and had spoken of him as an anti-communist second to none.[1] During another discussion, on 22 February, Casado left Centaño the impression that he could realize his plan of surrender 'with complete success and with all security': these words being written in capitals in the report. Casado, meantime, begged the nationalist high command to delay any offensive.[2]

Franco dispatched on the 22nd a telegram to Neville Chamberlain assuring him that his own patriotism, his honour as a gentleman, and his known generosity were the finest guarantees for a just peace. He later announced that the tribunals to be set up after the republican surrender would deal only with criminals – 'reprisals being alien to the nationalist movement'.[3] This bland remark, along with the telegram to Chamberlain, was considered by Britain to be the only condition obtainable for her recognition of the nationalist government.

In the meantime, Casado banned the publication of the com-

1. Martínez Bande (*op. cit.*, pp. 124–6) quotes Centaño's report. Casado in his book says that he only met Centaño in March and that his visit was a surprise. This seems not to have been true.

2. Martínez Bande, *op. cit.*, p. 126. 3. Azcárate, *loc. cit.*

munist paper *Mundo Obrero* on 23 February, because of a manifesto due to appear in it which attacked Largo Caballero for leaving Spain, and which urged continued resistance. Uribe, the communist minister of agriculture, in Madrid, protested. Casado still refused to permit publication. The following day, the manifesto was circulated by hand. Casado recalled it so far as was possible. Negrín returned to Madrid on 24 February, and Casado tried to persuade him that the right course was capitulation. He was unsuccessful, as he must surely have realized would be the case. He had clearly promised to Franco more than he could give. Franco himself disliked the idea of 'treating' with any new council of defence which might include a politician such as Besteiro. He was anyway receiving reports from such officers as General Jurado, now in France, and even General Matallana, still in overall command of the Armies of the Centre, as to where the resistance would be least if an attack were to be launched.[1]

On 26 February, Senator Bérard completed his mission in Burgos. All the nationalist demands were accepted. France and nationalist Spain would live together as good neighbours, cooperate in Morocco, and prevent all activities directed against the security of each other. The French government undertook to return to Spain all Spanish property taken to France against the wishes of its true owners. This would include £8 million in gold kept in Mont de Marsan as security for a loan made in 1931. The Bank of France had refused to return this to the republic, although the loan had been repaid. All other republican possessions in France, all battle, merchant and fishing vessels, works of art, vehicles and documents, were also to be sent to Spain. In return, the nationalists agreed to receive a French ambassador at Burgos.

Thus the official recognition by France and Britain could occur on 27 February. Chamberlain read out Franco's telegram on 22 February to the House of Commons. Both the Liberal and Labour parties opposed recognition and forced a debate. Attlee condemned Chamberlain's devious way of agreeing the act of recognition with Daladier before telling the House of Commons.

We see in this action [he concluded] a gross betrayal of democracy, the consummation of two and a half years of the hypocritical pretence of non-

1. Martínez Bande, *op. cit.*, p. 128.

intervention and a connivance all the time at aggression. And this is only one step further in the downward march of His Majesty's government in which at every stage they do not sell, but give away, the permanent interest of this country. They do not do anything to build up peace or stop war, but merely announce to the whole world that anyone who is out to use force can always be sure that he will have a friend in the British Prime Minister.

Chamberlain answered this by saying that General Franco had given pledges of mercy and that, short of war, Britain could never enforce any conditions on him. There followed, as often in the course of the Spanish war, a heated exchange between Sir Henry Page Croft, a conservative supporter of General Franco (it was he who, a year before, had described Franco publicly as 'a gallant christian gentleman'),[1] and Ellen Wilkinson, a fervent friend of the republic. Eden supported the government from the back benches, saying that to delay recognition might prolong the war. Yet other conservative back-benchers, such as Vyvyan Adams, deplored unconditional recognition. The communist Gallacher also suggested that the Prime Minister should be impeached.[2]

Azcárate paid a final melancholy visit to Lord Halifax to ask Britain to try still to secure some guarantee of moderation by Franco as a condition of recognition.[3] Russia denounced the falsity of 'the capitalist policy of capitulation before the aggressor' but took no other action. No act of recognition of Franco was prepared in Washington, but most other countries now followed the lead of Britain and France.

Back in Madrid, the anarchists were holding a meeting. Instructions from their secretary general Vázquez in France to back any effort to end the war were accepted. There was some discussion of the idea that Negrín was contemplating a *coup d'état* within the state. The CNT resolved to resist such an idea, which could lead to a communist dictatorship. The CNT now was, however, little more

1. Qu. Watkins, p. 118.

2. The opposition, ever since they had decided in October 1936 that non-intervention was a 'farce', had actively supported the Spanish republic, and had had good relations with Azcárate at the Spanish Embassy.

3. Later he handed over the Spanish Embassy in London to the Foreign Office who delivered it to the Duke of Alba. Similar scenes were taking place in other capitals.

than a large working-class pressure group without clear goals though resolved to oppose the communists.[1] In Burgos, a new message was received from Madrid saying that a '*junta* of liquidation' of the war would be set up the next day, and that Besteiro and Colonel Ruiz-Fornells, chief of staff of the Army of Estremadura, would go to any aerodrome that the nationalists specified in order to arrange the surrender. Franco replied that he still would not treat with any civilians. There could only be unconditional surrender, except for the guarantees already promised to the army officers. He would not treat with Besteiro. One or two officers could come if they desired.[2] Franco was not going to offer the republic the luxury of an honourable peace; nor did he want those who wished to get away to be able to do so. This delayed Casado's *coup d'état* for several days.

The following day, 28 February, after the news of the recognition of Franco by Britain and France, Azaña, in Paris, resigned from the presidency of the republic. The permanent committee of the Cortes assembled at La Pérouse, a famous restaurant on the Quai des Grands Augustins, and Martínez Barrio assumed Azaña's duties, as provided under the constitution of 1931. But he had no intention of returning to Spain. The civil governor of Madrid, José Gómez Ossorio, meantime, told Casado that he had received orders for his relief. Negrín, however, assured Casado, by telephone, that he had *not* ordered his relief, and summoned him to Elda for a meeting on 2 March, with Matallana. The two officers drove down the 260 miles in the morning. Negrín proposed the reorganization of the general staff. Matallana and Casado would become heads of the 'general' and of the 'central general' staff respectively. Both officers repeated their arguments against further resistance. Casado, with the communists Modesto and Cordón, were to be named generals, while two officers on Casado's staff, Muedra and Garijo, were to become respectively sub-secretary of the army and adjutant to Miaja. All these appointments had been agreed at a meeting of the cabinet during the night of 28 February. Casado and Matallana argued against reorganization. After the meeting, they drove north to Valencia. There they met Miaja, General Menéndez and Colonel Ruiz-Fornells. Casado described to these officers his determination to rebel against the government and to make peace. All promised support, but

1. García Pradas, p. 82. 2. Martínez Bande, *op. cit.*, p. 128.

warned against the communist party. Nevertheless, Casado made a similar approach to Hidalgo de Cisneros, whom he knew to be a communist, the next day at lunch outside Madrid. Presumably he supposed that the air leader's loyalty to his old friends was greater than that to his new comrades. 'Only we generals can get Spain out of the war', said Casado, who, according to Hidalgo de Cisneros, had already given orders for his new insignia as a general to be placed on his uniform. 'I give you my word,' he added, 'that I can get better terms from Franco than Negrín ever can. I can even assure you that they will respect our ranks.' Hidalgo asked how this was and Casado said that the British representative in Madrid (presumably Denys Cowan) had arranged everything with Franco. Hidalgo thought that Casado was romancing, but told Casado to go and see Negrín.[1] Hidalgo de Cisneros told Negrín of this interview. But Negrín did nothing. He faced the new challenge with temporary but fatal passivity.[2]

At much the same hour, Admiral Buiza at Cartagena summoned the commanders of the ships and the political commissars. He told them that a *coup d'état* against Negrín was being prepared and that a national council of defence would be formed, representing the armed forces, all trade unions and political parties. No one at the meeting objected, and Buiza concluded that agreement had been achieved. Twenty-four hours later, Paulino Gómez Saez, the socialist minister of the interior, arrived to tell the commanders that the government had been told what Buiza had said the previous day, and that it was determined to prevail. In Madrid, Casado continued plotting and received the support of most of the non-communist political colonels, and of the non-communist political parties. He prevented the circulation of the *Diario Oficial* of 3 March, which named the changes in command decided on by Negrín. General Martínez Cabrera (military governor of Madrid), Vicente Girauta (director-general of security) and in particular Angel Pedrero García, chief of the SIM in Madrid, also pledged their support. The SIM's surprising support for Casado was of great importance. Casado told Cipriano Mera to make ready to take over the central army in his place. A telegram arrived from Negrín summoning Casado to another con-

1. Hidalgo de Cisneros, pp. 463–4; Alvarez del Vayo, *Freedom's Battle*, p. 291.
2. Jackson, p. 474, is perceptive on this moment of 'passivity'.

ference at Elda. Casado telephoned Matallana, who was with Negrín, that he would not go because he feared arrest. Negrín was told that Casado's health prevented him from making so long a road journey again. Negrín sent his private aeroplane to fetch him. Meanwhile, all the communist leaders who had arrived from France clustered together at Elda, expecting to be given work by Negrín; Cordón was to be secretary general of defence, Jesús Monzón his secretary, Francisco Galán to command the naval base at Cartagena; and the military governors of the important coastal provinces of Valencia, Murcia and Alicante were to be succeeded by Lister, Etelvino Vega and Tagüeña.

The next day, 5 March, saw the culmination of the plots in Madrid. In the morning, the head of Barajas airport informed Casado that Negrín's Douglas aircraft had landed. Casado gave orders that the pilot should be sent home. At noon, Negrín once more telephoned to Casado. The colonel said that his health made it impossible to leave Madrid. Negrín, brushing this aside, said that he needed Casado immediately, regardless of health. Another aeroplane would arrive at six in the evening to take several cabinet ministers, who were at Madrid, to Elda. Casado, said Negrín, should travel with them. Casado answered that he would 'arrange matters' with the ministers.

Negrín's nomination of 'Paco' Galán to command the naval base at Cartagena now fired strange events in that port (some fifty miles away from the government). First, General Bernal, the military governor till then, passively agreed to hand over to Galán.[1] The officers of the artillery, under Colonel Gerardo Armentía, came out to protest. There was similar indignation in the fleet. Admiral Buiza and Commissar-General Alonso contemplated attacking the city.[2] Next, a Fifth Column of falangists emerged, headed by Colonel Arturo Espá, of the coastal artillery regiment. Supported by mobs wishing to show enthusiasm for the victors of the civil war, they surrounded the artillery barracks. A retired officer living in the city, General Rafael Barrionuevo, proclaimed himself military governor, in Franco's name. A regiment of marines joined the falangists, and, together, they proceeded to take over the naval radio station. From

1. Bruno Alonso, *La flota republicana y la guerra civil de España* (Mexico, 1944), pp. 136–7. Galán took over from Bernal on the night of the 4th.

2. *ibid.*, pp. 141–3.

thence, they sent demands for reinforcements to Cádiz. Colonel Armentía surrendered to the Falange, and shortly afterwards killed himself. Admiral Buiza then ordered the fleet to sea (including the three remaining largest ships, the cruisers *Miguel de Cervantes*, *Libertad* and *Méndez Núñez*, and eight destroyers), with Galán's agreement since he, Galán, sought sanctuary on board the *Libertad*, after having been briefly detained by the chief of staff of the base, Colonel Fernando Oliva. Galán resigned. Negrín appointed the naval under-secretary, Antonio Ruiz, to succeed him.[1] The communist ex-minister, Jesús Hernández, acting on his own responsibility as commissar-general of the army, dispatched the 4th Division, including a tank unit from the base at Archena, under a securely loyal communist officer, Colonel Joaquín Rodríguez, who had begun his war career in the Fifth Regiment, to help Cartagena. By mid-afternoon, both the falangist and the anti-communist rising had been suppressed. A nationalist warship, the *Castillo de Olite*, which arrived with 3,500 soldiers on board, was sunk when it came to reinforce the falangists.[2] The other nationalist naval vessels were held back in time. But the republican fleet remained at sea, and, indeed, gave itself up to the French, who requested Buiza to surrender in Bizerta. Thus the republic lost its three cruisers, eight destroyers and many small craft.[3]

In Valencia, something similar occurred: General Aranguren, the military governor, declined to hand over to Lister and, with General Menéndez of the Levante Army, prepared to resist with force. La Pasionaria and Manuel Delicado who had been in Murcia drove up to Elda to report on what had occurred at Cartagena: on their way, they were fortunate to escape arrest by a squad of assault guards acting for the socialist governor of Murcia, Eustasio Cañas, who had given orders for the arrest of communists, in support of Casado.[4]

In Madrid, six ministers of Negrín's cabinet – Giner, Velao, Paulino Gómez, Segundo Blanco, Moix and González Peña – were lunching in the central government building. They were joined for

1. Bruno Alonso, p. 146. 2. Some 1,200 died.

3. For this day's events in Cartagena, see Manuel Martínez Pastor, *Cinco de marzo 1939* (Madrid, 1971). There is also Luis Romero's non-fiction novel *Desastre en Cartagena* (Madrid, 1971). Galán wrote an account in *España republicana* (Buenos Aires, March–April 1968).

4. Ibarruri, p. 450.

coffee by Casado, who later said that each minister privately expressed to him his despair at Negrín's policy. Casado explained that he had no intention of accompanying them to Elda. Giner, who had been minister of communications throughout the war, telephoned to Negrín to suggest a postponement of the cabinet. Negrín answered so fiercely that the ministers set off immediately, though without Casado. At seven o'clock, Negrín telephoned Casado yet again, ordering his presence. Casado replied that he would come if the situation were no worse. Half an hour later, Casado moved his headquarters to the treasury, an easily defended eighteenth-century building of distinction in the Calle Alcalá, near the Puerta del Sol. There he met Besteiro. The anarchist 70th Brigade under Bernabé López, from Mera's Army Corps, established itself around the building. Casado allowed himself to be named president of the new national council, after Besteiro had declined (he agreed to act as foreign secretary). Casado later gave way to Miaja who, through fatigue, gloom, realism and opportunism, was shortly persuaded to join the plotters. Casado then took upon himself the portfolio of defence. The other members of the council were Wenceslao Carrillo, the socialist ex-director general of security under Largo Caballero; González Marín and Eduardo Val, of the CNT; Antonio Pérez, of the UGT;[1] and Miguel San Andrés and José del Río, both republicans. None were well known except for Besteiro. These men, nevertheless, took respectively the portfolios of the interior, finance, communications, labour, justice and education. Sánchez Requena, a member of Pestaña's unsuccessful syndicalist party, was secretary. This *junta* broadcast a manifesto at midnight on 5–6 March:

Spanish workers, people of anti-fascist Spain! The time has come when we must proclaim to the four winds the truth of our present situation. As revolutionaries, as proletarians, as Spaniards, as anti-fascists, we cannot endure any longer the imprudence and the absence of forethought of Dr

1. Antonio Pérez, a railway worker, was a socialist, a follower of Prieto. He had been a member of the executive committee of the socialist party. A rump of this body had met to discuss what to do, and had been forced (according to its vice-president Edmundo Domínguez) to back the council by a vote achieved by a packed meeting. Neither Domínguez nor the secretary of the UGT, Rodríguez Vega, had wanted to accept the post in the council, and so Pérez did – against his will.

Negrín's government. We cannot permit that, while the people struggle, a few privileged persons should continue their life abroad. We address all workers, anti-fascists and Spaniards! Constitutionally, the government of Dr Negrín is without lawful basis. In practice also, it lacks both confidence and good sense. We have come to show the way which may avoid disaster: we who oppose the policy of resistance give our assurance that not one of those who ought to remain in Spain shall leave till all who wish to leave have done so.

The plotters were on shaky ground: Negrín's government was legally constituted. As events were to show, too, Negrín's policy had logic behind it, and the council were unable to fulfil the promise in the last sentence.

Besteiro, Casado and Mera spoke. The first demanded the support of the legitimate power of the republic which, he added, was now nothing more than 'the power of the army': strange echo of the sort of speech that might have been made by Franco in 1936.[1] Casado concentrated on an appeal to all in the trenches, on both sides. 'We all want a country free of foreign domination. We shall not cease fighting till you assure us of the independence of Spain,' he added, for Franco's benefit, 'but, if you offer us peace, you will find our Spanish hearts generous.'[2]

Negrín was presiding over a cabinet meeting at Elda. Matallana was with him, though whether as a prisoner or as an adviser was obscure. At all events, it appears that it was he who answered a telephone-call from Casado. 'Tell him I have revolted,' Casado said. Negrín took the telephone: 'What is going on in Madrid, General?'[3] 'I have revolted,' answered Casado. 'Against whom? Against me?' 'Yes, against you.' Negrín told him that he had acted insanely. Casado answered that he was no general, but a plain colonel, who had done his duty as 'an officer and as a Spaniard'. Once again in the Spanish Civil War, the telephone provided the technical basis to the drama.[4] The telephone rang often that night between Elda and

1. Saborit, *Julián Besteiro*, p. 411. The writer, Julián Marías, came forward to act as Besteiro's secretary.

2. Casada, p. 150. Mera had wanted to arrest Negrín and take him to Burgos!

3. An echo of Casares Quiroga's question, so long before, to General Gómez Morato: 'What is going on in Melilla?' (see above, p. 217).

4. Alvarez del Vayo, *Freedom's Battle*, p. 224. There are other versions of this conversation. See García Pradas, p. 75.

Madrid; Negrín tried to find someone to arrest Casado. But no one would.

Next day, Casado arranged that Miaja should come to take over as president of the national council. He told General Menéndez to tell Negrín that, unless Matallana, under arrest at Elda, were released within three hours, he would shoot the entire cabinet. Matallana was released – though not before he had (falsely) declared himself at Negrín's disposal in respect of the revolt at Cartagena. Meantime, Casado appointed the anarchist, Melchor Rodríguez, deservedly famous as a humane director of prisons, to be mayor of Madrid, ordered the red stars to be stripped from the uniforms of the army, and suppressed all the recent promotions. But Miaja became lieutenant-general, a rank abolished by Azaña in 1931.

Negrín wavered. Jesús Hernández arrived at Elda to ask what was to be done. 'For the moment,' said the Prime Minister, 'nothing. We are thinking of what to do.' This deliberation continued all day. The Russian advisers, however, knew very well what to do. Hernández drove north to the headquarters of General Iaborov, in the Valencian farm 'El Vedat', and found it in disorder and the general, who had succeeded General Maximov as head of the Russian military mission, in a high state of excitement. 'We are leaving, we are leaving,' he told Hernández without ceremony.[1] Sub-Commissar Castro Delgado and Commissar Delage secretly left Madrid to ask the communist leadership if they ought to order the communist-led divisions to march on the capital. They discovered La Pasionaria, Lister and Modesto in a splendid country house near Elda, run as a hotel by the poet Alberti and his wife, María Teresa León. Also present were Pasionaria's secretary, Irene Falcón, Tagüeña (escaped from Madrid) and some others. Indecision reigned, in an atmosphere of unreality. Handsome meals were served. Members of the central committee and commissars paced about, like week-end guests in a country house, uncertain precisely what to do with their time. Alberti walked sadly under the trees outside. Togliatti was deciding what to do.[2]

1. Hernández, p. 197. Iaborov's (or Berov's) fate, origin and character are unknown. Lister mentioned him in passing. He and his staff no doubt left that day, with their records.

2. Castro Delgado, p. 731; Tagüeña, p. 312.

Even if Stalin desired to abandon Spain to its own resources, the Spanish communists could surely not contemplate, after such expense of energy, that an unknown colonel should take over authority, ignoring the communist party. Yet the alternative course seemed the risky one of using against him the communist-led divisions around Madrid, together perhaps with the guerrilla units under communist orders (the 14th Corps, under Major Domingo Hungría). The project seemed uncertain, since many republicans, who would not otherwise have taken sides at all, would rally to Casado if there were to be a civil war within the Civil War. Commanders such as Burillo, Prada, Camacho and Pedrero, of the SIM, had shown themselves to be friends of the communists of the moment only. Miaja, with his reputation inflated by communists, was also shown to be less than loyal to his mentors.

Negrín was thus in a difficult position. Doubtless he was aware that Casado would not hesitate to arrest him if he could, and leave him in gaol to be handed over to Franco, if he did not shoot him himself. He was a politician without a party, as well as a war leader without an army. The once immensely powerful *Negrinistas* had been reduced to a small group of ministers sitting, like their leader, in a country house, wondering how they could get to Paris. The great communist party now seemed to have dwindled to a group of leaders who, having antagonized the revolutionaries by their counter-revolution, had outraged the bourgeoisie by their cruelty, opportunism and mendacity. Now they were almost alone: leaders with no followers.

Negrín made last-minute attempts to prevent strife. The anarchist minister of education, Segundo Blanco, whose loyalties in the crisis were ambiguous, made an unsuccessful effort at compromise. Casado, on the other hand, was attempting to secure the arrest of the government, and of the communist leaders, to offer to Franco, no doubt, as prizes. Chaos prevailed throughout republican Spain. The commanders of the different armies were once again the effective rulers. No one knew the whereabouts of his colleagues. Party or union membership seemed irrelevant. At the small air base at Monóvar, a few miles away from Elda, Negrín, his staff and the communist leaders assembled. There were Alvarez del Vayo, Uribe and Moix, of his government; Hidalgo de Cisneros, the air chief; Lister, Tagüeña and Togliatti. La Pasionaria flew off to France, with the Navarrese communist Monzón.[1] Hidalgo de Cisneros telephoned a message calling on the *junta* at Madrid to settle its differences with Negrín. Until half past two in the afternoon, the small band waited at the airport for Casado's answer. The central committee of the communist party held its last meeting: Togliatti told the few members present that the national council of defence was the only government in Spain, that to fight it was to begin another civil war, and that the only recourse was to save the greatest number of communists.[2] A manifesto was put out to this effect, written by Togliatti.[3] Alvarez del Vayo played chess with Modesto. Lister, charged to organize the defence of the airport with some eighty *guerrilleros* only, while the government was leaving, heard that it was beginning to be surrounded.[4] They heard too that Alicante had passed to Casado, and that Etelvino Vega, Negrín's newly appointed military governor there, had been arrested. They waited no longer, giving up Spain for lost. Jesús Hernández, Togliatti and Pedro Checa stayed behind to try and organize a semblance of a communist party in clandestinity. At three o'clock in the morning, the three last aeroplanes of Negrín's government left the little airport: two set off for France, the other, which had less capacity, went to Africa. Before setting off, the communist from Seville, Manuel Delicado, pressed into the hand of each refugee a pound note.[5]

*

Back in Madrid, however, the cause of resistance (to whom? to Franco, to Casado or to both?) was not yet lost. If the government and the communist leaders had fled, the communist-led divisions around Madrid were of a mind to fight. They almost certainly received no approval from the party leaders to do so, for communications were cut. It was not the first time that a communist party has taken two contradictory policies at the same time. Barceló moved in with his 1st Army Corps to close all the entrances to the capital. He

1. Ibarruri, pp. 453–4; Tagüeña, p. 318. 2. Tagüeña, p. 316.

3. The manifesto is, it seems, printed in R. Salas, vol. IV, p. 3414. Togliatti's authorship was attested by Ettore Vanni, *Io, comunista in Russia* (Bologna, 1948), pp. 6–18, qu. Spriano, vol. III, p. 272. Vanni was then the director of the Spanish communist daily of Valencia, *Verdad.* He subsequently broke with communism.

4. Lister, pp. 256–7. See, too, Castro Delgado, p. 733.

5. Alvarez del Vayo, *The Last Optimist*, p. 316; Lister, p. 257.

occupied the ministries at the end of La Castellana, the Retiro Park and the old headquarters of the Army of the Centre at the Alameda. Three of Casado's colonels and a socialist commissar were shot.[1] Colonels Bueno and Ortega sent troops from the 2nd and 3rd Army Corps to support Barceló. Thus most of the centre of Madrid passed into communist control. Only a few government buildings were in the hands of the Casadistas. Nevertheless, there was much confusion, and the only members of the central committee still in Spain (Togliatti, Checa, with Jesús Hernández and the youth leader, Fernando Claudín) were for many hours out of contact with the armies around Madrid, being held for a time prisoners by the SIM at Monóvar.

In the afternoon, Mera's mostly anarchist 4th Army Corps marched to relieve Casado, now holding out in the south-easterly suburbs. His 12th Division, led by Liberino González, captured Alcalá and Torrejón. Mera rapidly assumed the role of strong man in Casado's party, being backed by his second-in-command, the socialist major 'Paquito' Castro.[2]

Throughout 8 March, fighting continued in Madrid. The communists remained in control. In the rest of Spain, Jesús Hernández succeeded in dispossessing Ibarrola from the command of the 22nd Army. Togliatti, Checa and Claudín joined him near Valencia after many difficulties. In the meantime, communists were everywhere being arrested, their party offices seized and a general campaign of persecution opening against them.

The other three armies (of the Levante, Estremadura and Andalusia) held their fire; though their commanders (Menéndez, Escobar and Moriones) had verbally pledged support to Casado, they could not have known of the reaction of their men if orders had been given to move on Madrid.[3] There was some fighting in most places. Of these generals, only Menéndez would have preferred to surrender to Franco than fight Casado. In Madrid, the extent of the communist victory was such that, if they had wished, they could have dictated terms. But, abandoned by their political leaders, and apparently out

1. These were Colonels López Otero, José Pérez Gazzolo and Alfredo Buznego, and Commissar Peinado Leal (Martínez Bande, *op. cit.*, p. 220).

2. W. Carrillo in *El Mundo* (Mexico, 1 September 1944, qu. Bullejos, p. 226).

3. For all this see Togliatti's letter to the communist leaders abroad published in *Histoira internacional* (Madrid, February 1976).

of touch with Togliatti at important moments, they did not know what to do. On 9 March, Matallana told one of Franco's agents with whom he was in contact, 'almost with tears in his eyes', that he hoped Franco would launch a general offensive, in order to prevent Madrid falling to the communists.[1] As a result of political indecision, however, the communist commanders almost waited to be defeated. Barceló clearly would have liked to launch a final assault on the council of defence. But his men were tired.

The following day, the communist Colonel Ortega came forward to offer to mediate between the two sides in this new civil war. (It had been he who, as director of security in 1937, had been responsible for the arrest of Nin.) During the last week or two, his loyalty too to his adopted party had been distinctly weak. According to the communists, however, this offer was made because of renewed nationalist attacks.[2] Casado agreed to this mediation. In the meantime, there was a cease-fire, with the two groups still facing each other in postures of hostility. Nationalists in Madrid, meantime, reported in gloomy terms: 'Casado appears unable to control the situation.' The nationalists had advanced some way, during the fighting in Madrid, across the Casa de Campo towards the Manzanares. By 10 March, the communists were, in effect, surrounded in the city which they had assaulted and their leaders beginning to contemplate withdrawal.

On 11 March, the communists were driven out of their positions, and many of Barceló's and Bueno's men passed to Casado. In the end, most of their commanders were captured and were ready to make peace. Army units led by officers in favour of the *junta* had surrounded Madrid. Casado stipulated that all units should return to their positions of 2 March. Prisoners taken were to be given up, commanders would be dismissed. This would leave Casado free to make his own nominations for the three communist army corps. In return, Casado pledged himself to free all 'non-criminal' communist prisoners, and to listen to the points of view of the communist leaders. Thus ended the civil war within the Civil War; some 230 had been killed, some 560 wounded.[3] The contestants had included groups from all the old columns which had sallied out so bravely in

1. Martínez Bande, p. 212.
2. Ibarruri, p. 455. Miaja may have suggested it.
3. R. Salas, vol. II, p. 2318. Ramos Oliviera, vol. III, p. 392, says 1,000.

July 1936: even the remains of the Iron Column could be found in the 12th Division under Liberino González.

The communists agreed to try to secure a cease-fire. If there were no reprisals, they would act as previously against the nationalist 'invaders'. Togliatti, back in touch, apparently, encouraged Barceló to this compromise, on the telephone from Alicante. In the same morning of 12 March, the communist forces returned to their positions of 2 March. On the following day, military tribunals nevertheless met and sentenced Barceló, his commissar José Conesa and some others to death. The sentences on Barceló and Conesa (an old member of the socialist youth and a commissar on the central front since October 1936) were carried out immediately. They were acts of retribution more than of justice. No other death sentences were carried out – though some others were gaoled. Some anarchist tribunals were privately mounted against the communists. Outside Madrid, General Escobar and the Army of Estremadura crushed communist resistance in Ciudad Real directed by the communist deputy Martínez Cartón. Menéndez, still at the head of the Army of the Levante, prevented the 22nd Army Corps, now controlled by Hernández, from moving upon Valencia.

*

Negrín and the communists disposed of, Casado turned to his negotiations with Burgos. Both he and Matallana had remained daily in contact with Franco's representatives during the communist week, the '*Semana Comunista*' as it was described. Once free to act again, they told their new friends that they were ready to go on whatever day Franco wished to Burgos. But, on 16 March, the message came back that Franco was only interested in unconditional surrender.[1] Casado had only to send one officer with full powers, or two at most, and they should not be outstanding leaders. While the national council considered this discouraging document, Casado himself planned the retreat of the Army of the Centre to the Mediterranean, and the expatriation of those who wished to leave. It must have been clear to the colonel that there was little hope of serious negotiation. His

1. Martínez Bande, *Los cien últimos días*, p. 221. These telegrams went from Colonel Ungria in Burgos to Colonel Bonel, in La Torre de Esteban Hambrán (Toledo), who communicated with Centaño and other agents in Madrid.

task, therefore, was to gain time so as to allow those who wanted to escape to do so. During the ensuing fortnight, many managed to do this. But the means of escape were few, even for those who managed to reach the east-coast ports. The council, meantime, also agreed to send junior officers, as Franco desired, to Burgos; and on 19 March, Franco agreed to negotiations on that basis. He and the nationalist command had been busy with the redeployment of their armies, to be ready for a new offensive, should it be necessary.

The two junior emissaries named for negotiation by the republic were Colonels Garijo and Leopoldo Ortega, both of whom had been on the staff of the Army of the Centre for most of the war. These two officers left for Burgos by air in the morning of 23 March, accompanied by Centaño and two other members of Franco's intelligence service. The conditions which they brought with them were not even discussed by Colonels Gonzalo and Ungría, their nationalist co-negotiators, who merely handed them a document for transmittal to Casado. The nationalists' document provided for the flight of the republican air force to nationalist aerodromes on 25 March. As for the army, there would have to be a cease-fire on all fronts, on 27 March. Commanding officers, with white flags, were to come to the nationalist lines, with documents describing the position of their forces. In addition, Franco named two ports on the Levante for the expatriation of those who wished to flee. He did not mind if British ships transported these refugees, and would put no difficulties in the way of the departure of these ships. But there was to be no pact, no signature of any document naming the concessions. The council of defence, Garijo then said, was not interested in saving criminals, but he wanted to know if the concept of crime in the nationalist mind corresponded to legislation before 18 July, if responsibility was to be considered collectively, if the benevolence which would affect officers who surrendered would also affect civilians, and if the safe conduct to those who wanted to leave could be assured. How many might want to leave? Perhaps 4,000, said Garijo; 10,000, thought Ortega.[1] On 25 March, after anguished discussions in the council of defence,

1. For this first interview, at the aerodrome at Gamonal near Burgos, see Martínez Bande, *Los cien últimos días*, p. 229. During the course of a conversation on 23 March, Colonel Ungría said that the professional officers in the republican army had prolonged the war; Colonel Garijo spiritedly replied that

Garijo and Ortega returned to Burgos, to demand that the terms should after all be put in writing and that a delay of twenty-five days should be granted for the expatriation of those who wished to leave. The latter point was refused but the former was accepted. Garijo began to draw up such a document. There were some other points at issue. At six o'clock, however, Colonel Gonzalo bluntly announced that negotiations were considered broken off because the republican air force had after all not surrendered. Garijo and Ortega flew back to Madrid. The air force was, of course, important, if only because, by its offices, people could escape: on 25 March itself six aircraft flew from central Spain, carrying to France officials and others who feared reprisals.[1]

Thus ended Casado's ill-fated attempt to secure a more honourable end to the war than Negrín had been able to achieve. By his action, he had ruined the possibility of further republican resistance, although, for many of those who had taken part in the war on the republican side, continued fighting, however despairing, would have been more advantageous than unconditional surrender into the hands of nationalist justice. Had the republic lasted intact, with Negrín and Casado still in one camp, for even so short a time as two weeks longer, their international position might have altered. On 15 March, Hitler marched into Prague. Even Chamberlain spoke in protest, on 18 March. By the end of the month, the Anglo-French guarantee to Poland had transformed the international situation. A united republic could have taken advantage of the opportunity thus opening out. All that can be said for Casado is that his negotiations gained time for many republican leaders, though not for the rank and file, to escape. Meantime, the UGT executive, that unreliable body, which had played so curious a role in the history of the civil war, held a last meeting at Valencia: the discussion ended in uproar, dissension and fears of violence.[2] The same day, Togliatti and Jesús Hernández left Cartagena for Mostaganem, in Algeria, by air.[3]

---

the republic had lost the war only because those officers had not been allowed to do as they wanted. Further, if the professionals had had a cause in which they really believed, it was doubtful if they would have lost.

1. For the second conference at Gamonal, see Martínez Bande, *Los cien últimos días*, p. 246f.

2. Domínguez, *op. cit.*

3. Spriano, vol. III, p. 272.

Early in the morning of 26 March, Casado telegraphed to Burgos to announce that the air force would be surrendered the next day. In reply, Franco announced that the nationalist armies were about to advance. He demanded that units in the republican front line should show a white flag before the start of artillery and aerial bombardment.[1] Yagüe, once again in Estremadura where he had won his first laurels in the war, advanced in the Sierra Morena. All day, the advance continued. Pozoblanco fell at noon, Santa Eufemia at dusk. Thirty thousand prisoners and 2,000 square kilometres were captured during the course of the day. In hundreds of villages, white flags were raised and, in towns, red and gold ones. At four in the afternoon, Franco broadcast those 'concessions' which his two colonels had put forward at Burgos on 21 March. They sounded well enough. The council of defence met at six o'clock in the evening. Miaja, once a symbol, now a cypher, presided, but Casado was the effective chairman. Nobody suggested further negotiations. The council decided not to order resistance to the nationalist advance and to permit all who wished to return home. So there followed the self-demobilization of the republican army. The men abandoned the front for their homes, and their officers did not stop them. This spontaneous act, all along the front, was not halted by a description, on Madrid Radio, by the council's secretary, José del Río, of the true story of the negotiations at Burgos.

On 27 March, a new nationalist advance began from Toledo. The Navarrese, under Solchaga, the Italians, under Gambara, and the Army of the Maestrazgo, under García Valiño, made a free passage of the Tagus. Here, as in the south, the republic abandoned the front. During the day, their Army of the Centre disintegrated. Matallana, in general command of all these forces, told Casado that several units had gone over to the nationalists, and that soldiers of both sides were embracing each other in the Casa de Campo. By nine in the evening, the staff only of the first three army corps remained. Casado told the members of his council to leave for Valencia, whither Miaja had already gone. Various anarchists belatedly wished to continue resistance. At ten o'clock, representatives of the UGT, the socialist party, the republican union and the CNT broadcast appeals for calm. Then, when not a single republican soldier remained in the front line save

1. Aznar, p. 845.

in the Guadalajara sector, Casado ordered Colonel Prada, the new commander of the Army of the Centre, and the officer who had commanded in Asturias at the end, to negotiate surrender with the nationalist commander in the University City. That officer accepted a rendezvous with the nationalist commander at the Clinical Hospital. Casado telegraphed to President Lebrun to beg that all republicans who wanted should be able to land in France (if they got there). He made the same request to President Cárdenas of Mexico. Next, he told Matallana to authorize retreats by all the republican armies in the manner of that of the central army. Then he flew to Valencia. He and his wife passed over streams of lorries and groups of republican soldiers going home. Santiago Carrillo was the last of the communist leaders to leave Madrid, on this same 27 March.[1] Behind in Madrid, Besteiro remained, enigmatic and resigned, along with Rafael Sánchez Guerra, now political secretary to Casado as he had once been to President Alcalá Zamora. The creeping optimism of Besteiro's tubercular condition caused him to anticipate fair treatment just as, at the beginning of the war, Casares Quiroga's tuberculosis had persuaded him of too optimistic an interpretation of the events in the summer of 1936. On behalf of Matallana, Colonel Prada surrendered the Army of the Centre at eleven o'clock. Another nationalist army broke through the Guadalajara front, to meet those forces advancing from Toledo. In the capital itself, the Fifth Column emerged from its hiding places. At midday, the nationalist 1st Army, under General Espinosa de los Monteros, who had for a time been a refugee in the French Embassy before being exchanged, entered Madrid, and occupied the government buildings. There was scarcely any resistance: almost the only casualty was the aged anarchist journalist, Mauro Bajatierra, who engaged in a single-handed battle with the police who came to arrest him in his house. General Matallana was the most senior officer to hand himself over to the enemy, knowing that his life was guaranteed. Behind Espinosa, there followed both the representatives of Auxilio Social, and two hundred officers of the nationalist army's Juridical Corps, with lorry-loads of documents relating to crimes allegedly committed in the republic. '*¡Han pasado!*' (they have passed), cried the rapidly assembling pro-nationalist crowds. Those right-wing Spaniards who had passed the

1. Guy Hermet, *Les Espagnols en France* (Paris, 1967), p. 168.

war behind the blinds of foreign embassies soon emerged into the light of day for the first time for two and a half years, blinking, with faces pale as ghosts. On the other fronts, in Estremadura, Andalusia and the Levante, mass retreats were also taking place.[1]

Casado arrived at Valencia. He cabled the British government, begging them to send ships to take off 10,000 refugees to Oran or Marseilles, but they had neither the desire nor the means to help on so large a scale. At Valencia, at Alicante, at Gandia, at Cartagena and at Almería, perhaps 50,000 republicans gathered, clamouring for expatriation. But the ships of the Mid-Atlantic Company, the republican shipping line, established in London, refused to help, arguing that they had not been paid. The desertion of the republican fleet now told against thousands of republican soldiers and politicians. At noon the next day, 29 March, Casado, established in the old captaincy-general, was visited by the Valencian Fifth Column, who demanded their own immediate establishment in the administrative buildings. The town was now running with persons making the fascist salute. Casado appealed for calm over Valencia Radio, and left for Gandia, where he embarked in the British naval vessel *Galatea*. He was only enabled to do so since the Foreign Office, realizing the enormous tragedy of the situation, instructed its somewhat hesitant consul there, Godden, to interpret his instructions 'in as wise and generous a manner as possible'.[2] During the day, Jaén, Ciudad Real, Cuenca, Sagunto and Albacete were occupied by the national-

1. One who observed the entry of Franco's armies into Madrid was the eldest son of the US ambassador in London, Kennedy. The young Joseph Patrick Kennedy had arrived in Barcelona in January, having written a doctoral thesis at Harvard on 'Intervention in Spain'. When Barcelona fell, Kennedy left for Valencia and thence to Madrid, technically designated as press attaché to the US embassy in Paris. In Madrid, Kennedy was both arrested by an anarchist patrol and entered into contact with the Fifth Column. He remained in the capital until early April. By inference, his mission must have been both official and secret.

2. British Foreign Office papers, P.R.O. The captain thought that Casado and his party were 'fit persons for embarkation in one of HM ships'. He did not think that the 300 'armed communists', who suddenly appeared on the quay, were so. Altogether the British Navy took off some 650. There were at least ten times that number left behind. Martínez Bande *Los cien últimos días*, p. 287) suggests that there were between 10,000 and 20,000 at Alicante. (I am grateful to Michael Alpert for his help in framing this interpretation. See his article in *Sábado Gráfico*, April 1975.)

ists. On 30 March, Gambara's Italians entered Alicante, and Aranda entered Valencia, by then under the control of the Falange. Women and children ran forward to kiss the hands of the conquerors, while roses, mimosa and laurels were flung from balconies of the middle class. On 31 March, Almería, Murcia and Cartagena were occupied. In all these coastal towns, thousands of those who had wished to leave their country were captured by the advancing armies. The scenes of fear before the nationalists' entry were pitiful to see. There were several suicides. General Franco, suffering from a cold in Burgos, was at last informed by an aide that the nationalist troops had occupied their final objectives in the early evening of 31 March. 'Very good,' he replied without looking up from his desk, 'many thanks.'[1] The serenity with which he received the news of his victory was an appropriate commentary on his method of achieving it.

1. Díaz de Villegas, p. 384. Another reaction was Mussolini's comment to Ciano, pointing to an atlas open at the map of Spain; 'It has been open in this way for nearly three years, and that is enough. But I know already that I must open it at another page.' Ciano, *Diaries 1939–43*, p. 57. Italy attacked Albania the following week (6 April).

CONCLUSION

'In class wars, it is the side that wins who kills most.'

GERALD BRENAN, *South from Granada*

'Irony, which exists in everything, appears in a striking manner in the modern history of Spain, since it is "francoism" which has realized the communist programme – that is "the bourgeois revolution". Certainly, like the ailing daughter of old syphilitics, this bourgeois revolution, born late, has not had, from its strange sisters, the gift of a cultural and social renewal, the increase of democratic liberties or the disappearance of ancestral prejudices ... But, to use the language of modern Marxists, the economic basis of the bourgeois revolution has been created – even though Spanish Marxists deny it ...'

CARLOS SEMPRÚN MAURA,
Révolution et contre-révolution en Catalogne

51

Conclusion

THE outstanding matters arising out of the Spanish war were soon settled. On 26 March, Spain had adhered to the Anti-Comintern Pact, and, on the 31st, a five-year treaty of friendship between Spain and Germany was signed at Burgos by Gómez Jordana and the Baron von Stohrer. Also on the 31st, a Non-Aggression Pact was signed between the new Spain and Portugal. Already too, Marshal Pétain, who had been French commander in Morocco in 1925, had arrived at Burgos as French ambassador. Serrano Súñer ordered the people off the streets and the shutters down to greet him. His reception by his ex-comrade-in-arms was icy, rendered more so by the French government's delay in handing over the republican fleet gathered at Bizerta. He and Franco anyway had never been friends.[1] The studied insults to Pétain from the régime would have maddened anyone else: as it was, Pétain kept his temper and consoled himself by saving from the police a republican who took refuge in his embassy garden in San Sebastián.[2] Spanish *objets d'art* and money taken to France by the republic, together with arms, aircraft and rolling stock, were soon returned to Spain. The paintings from the Prado were sent back to Madrid from Geneva, after a brief exhibition.

On 1 April, the United States recognized the nationalist régime. Russia was thus the only major power which had not done so. The American ambassador, Bowers, received, on returning home to Washington, the bitter consolation of being told by Roosevelt that he thought that, after all, the embargo policy had been wrong. On 20 April, the Non-Intervention Committee, which had not met since

1. But Pétain's biographer, Maître Isorni (*Philippe Pétain*, Paris, 1972, p. 397f.) says Franco had 'admired Pétain in 1925'.

2. *ibid.*, p. 419. Pétain's British colleague was Sir Maurice Peterson. See his *Both Sides of the Curtain* (London, 1950), pp. 153–235. He too had a difficult time.

July 1938, solemnly dissolved itself.[1] On 19 May, a nationalist victory parade was held in Madrid. General Gambara's Italians occupied a place of honour. On 22 May, the Condor Legion held a farewell parade at León. Four days later, the German officers and men embarked at Vigo for Hamburg. On 31 May, 20,000 Italians set off from Cádiz. Both Germans and Italians were fêted in their own countries: on 6 June, Hitler reviewed 14,000 members of the Condor Legion in Berlin. The Italians were welcomed at Naples by Ciano and King Victor Emmanuel. Escorted to Rome by a detachment of Spaniards, a further victory parade there was received by Mussolini and watched from a balcony by King Alfonso XIII. Tears sprang to Alfonso's eyes as the soldiers of his fatherland, 'distant but victorious', marched past. By the end of June, the evacuation of German and Italian military forces from Spain was complete.

As for the republican refugees from Mediterranean ports, many found asylum hard to come by. Eventually, after waiting on British or French ships in Marseilles or North African ports in disagreeable conditions, most found themselves on French soil, along with those 400,000 or more who had earlier fled from Catalonia. Many, perhaps 50,000, refugees and soldiers, soon agreed to go to nationalist Spain. Most leaders found reasonable lodging, but the rest remained in the concentration camps of southern France. By April, conditions there had improved. Food supplies were now almost adequate. Sanitation and medical services were no longer non-existent. There had been no large-scale epidemics. But the inmates still had nothing to do save wait. They were not allowed to leave, being officially 'interned'. Their general situation remained purgatorial.

The leaders of the exiles were by this time quarrelling. On 31 March, Negrín gave a hotly contested account of his activities since the fall of Catalonia to a pathetic meeting of the permanent committee of the Cortes in Paris. Martínez Barrio, Araquistain, La

1. *NIS*, thirtieth meeting. At this meeting, Francis Hemming arranged to pay back to member governments a proper proportion of the surplus funds in the committee's account; he arranged that he should be commissioned to write a survey of the work of the committee – a book which, however, never appeared; it was agreed that 'no facilities ought to be given to outside persons' to look at the committee's documents – another provision which was not kept; the idea of an 'old comrades' association', of those who had served in non-intervention patrol, was also approved – similarly without effect.

Pasionaria, disputed, the latter proclaiming that her hands had 'neither blood nor gold upon them'.[1] At the same time, the ship *Vita* left Boulogne for Mexico, piled with precious stones and other treasures, mainly confiscations from nationalist sympathizers at the start of the civil war.[2] Negrín was dispatching this hoard for the safe-keeping of the Mexican President Cárdenas, in order to finance the republic in exile. When, however, the *Vita* arrived in Mexico, Prieto, who had remained in South America after the inauguration of the new Chilean President, was there to receive it. He persuaded Cárdenas that he had a title to the treasure. This was a questionable manoeuvre. He set up a committee of the permanent committee of the Cortes, the JARE (Junta de Auxilio a los Republicanos Españoles) to administer the funds in question. Negrín, maintained nevertheless as Prime Minister in exile, by a narrow majority of the same permanent committee, placed the funds which he had saved in the SERE (Servicio de Emigración para Republicanos Españoles), administered by Dr Puché, the head of the army's medical corps and rector of the University of Valencia, a friend of his. This group was increasingly compromised in the eyes of the world because of its support by the communist party. But the two groups, which quarrelled fiercely, did transport about 25,000 republican refugees to South America, especially Mexico and Argentina. (Perhaps 50,000 Spaniards in all went eventually to South America.) Most of the rest remained in southern France, to be eventually absorbed in the community of that area. Many of the able-bodied were shortly employed in the construction of French fortifications. Others, perhaps 100,000, returned to Spain in the course of 1939. In time, the French government made all male foreigners eligible for service in their army: the chief of the republican fleet, Admiral Buiza, for example, was to enter the Foreign Legion.[3] By July, the population of the concentration camps had fallen to 230,000.[4] Russia welcomed about 2,000 Spanish communists, along with the 5,000 or so Spanish children whom they

1. *Diario de Sesiones*, 31 March 1939.

2. The Spanish republicans were alleged by their enemies to have carried away enormous funds and money abroad. Most of this, however, had been used for the purchase of arms.

3. Bruno Alonso, p. 156.

4. At least 70,000 in Barcarès, 40,000 in Argelès, 30,000 in Saint Cyprien. See Pike, p. 55. At Gurs, there were 7,000 ex-Brigade members.

had accepted in the course of the war.[1] Two hundred republican leaders, including Casado and Menéndez, were accepted in Britain.[2] But in 1940, there were still some 350,000 Spaniards in France, many of them about to be dispatched to work for the Germans or even to extermination camps.[3] If one should acknowledge the generosity of France in receiving such a large quantity of refugees, one should note also the surprising narrowness of French officials, police, and politicians, towards the majority of Spaniards who fled there.[4]

A study of life in the French concentration camps in southern France scarcely shows human nature at its best. The quarrels among communists and anarchists in the war were not forgotten, nor were espionage, treachery and murder.[5] Some 4,700 are supposed to have died in the camps, while the Italian communist Chedini is said to have followed his assassination of Italian anarchists in Spain by suggestions for a list of 'undesirables' to the French authorities.[6] The communists once again obtained control, some Germans preferred to return to Germany than stay where they were, being apparently betrayed by a double-agent named Stephen Maas, while some Italian communists even preferred the risk of a return to Spain to remaining in France.[7]

In Spain the victors were naturally exultant. In Madrid, for example, the middle-class population and the conquering army surged into the streets at night, filling the restaurants, the bars, eating and drinking up everything, while the officers of the army's juridical corps went patiently about their bloody business of arrests, investigation and listening to informers. (In Madrid there were few unauthorized killings, unlike Barcelona.) At last, priests could wear their birettas again in Madrid, civil guards their three-cornered hats, Carlists their red berets. Streets quickly had their names changed; Alfonso XII Street became itself again after being, during the republic, Alcalá Zamora Street and then Agrarian Reform Street. 'Rights of the Child Street' had as short a shrift as the 'Street of

1. For a description, see Tagüeña, p. 300f.

2. See Eugene Kutischer, *The Displacement of Population in Europe*, Studies and Reports Series D, no. 8 (Montreal, 1944, ILO), p. 44.

3. See below, p. 949.

4. This theme is well treated in Cabanellas, vol. II, p. 1119f.

5. Hermet, *Les Espagnols*, p. 28.

6. Pike, p. 68. 7. *ibid.*, p. 72.

the United Socialist Youth Militias of the Home Front' (Calle de la Milicias de Retaguardia de la Juventudes Socialistas Unificadas). But it was perhaps surprising to find Marshal Joffre Street in Barcelona becoming Bourbon Street. A flood of atrocity stories filled the newspapers and bookshops, while liberal or 'Marxist' books were ordered to be taken from even the private shelf. Symbolic book-burnings of Marxist books were carried out in large cities. A wave of victorious propaganda broke over the country leaving to the defeated, even if they had their lives, scarcely their private thoughts, much less their jobs. The tone was given in a broadcast on Radio Nacional on 2 April: 'Spaniards, on the alert! Peace is not a comfortable and cowardly rest in front of History . . . Spain remains on a war footing.'[1] It was an accurate statement. For, as expected, a terrible proscription was undertaken. The already overcrowded prisons were supplemented by vast camps in which republican politicians, soldiers and officials were herded, often being brutally treated, and held for, in some cases, years. Many were sentenced to death by courts-martial and, though that penalty was often commuted, the term of imprisonment would always be thirty years. Often, it is true, the sentence would be reduced to ten years, though some might be under a death sentence for two years. The new secretary-general of the UGT, Rodríguez Vega, who managed to escape from Spain in late 1939, estimated that some two million persons had passed through the prisons and concentration camps of Spain by 1942, many to work for years of hard labour, some on the monstrous mausoleum, the Valley of the Fallen, an ugly building intended to rival the Escorial in the Guadarramas and to house the dead of the civil war; and most being forced to give the fascist salute daily.

Many were shot. Crimes committed in republican Spain were investigated, and those allegedly responsible for the 'revolutionary excesses' of 1936 were hunted down, the survivors from republican gaols being anxious to help the business of identification. The summer of 1939 was a fiesta for the informer, for the vengeful and for the bloodthirsty.[2] The ruthlessness of the conquerors was sustained by a middle class which had known that they had only narrowly escaped

1. Abella, p. 416

2. See Georges Conchon's brilliant novel, *La Corrida de la victoire* (Paris, 1960).

extinction. The absence of magnanimity which characterized the end of the war was the more complete since the deteriorating international situation silenced the anyway enfeebled voice of the world's liberal opinion. The terror in the war had been increased by propaganda; the revolutionaries had indeed done many abominable things; those who had come out alive from a republican gaol or an embassy were in no mood for forgiveness; and in the minister of the interior, Serrano Súñer, they had an appropriate spokesman, for his own experiences, as has been seen, were such as to make him close his eyes to pity.

In addition to those shot for revolutionary crimes (the burning of a church would be counted as meriting a death sentence as much as the murder of a banker), numerous republican officers, officials and other responsible persons were executed. The numbers of those who died at the end of the war (and the shootings continued until into the 1940s) have been variously estimated, sometimes the figure being added to those killed in the nationalist zone during the war itself, sometimes also implicating those who, like Besteiro or the poet Miguel Hernández, died from neglect in gaol.[1] (Besteiro, who remained in Madrid to receive the victors, realized how he had miscalculated the mood of Franco's Spain when his efforts at mediation brought him a thirty-year sentence.) Ciano, visiting Spain in July 1939, reported 'trials going on every day at a speed which I would call almost summary . . . There are still a great number of shootings. In Madrid alone, between 200 and 250 a day, in Barcelona 150, in Seville 80.'[2] (Seville had been in nationalist Spain throughout the war: how could there be still enough people to shoot at this rate?) Of course, Ciano was an outsider, whose view could not have been formed from personal observation. Still, his figures have a ring of truth about them: thus the civil governor of Albacete, Martínez Amutio, described how, out of 36 tried with him at Almansa (Albacete) in December 1939, 32 were shot.[3] One witness speaks of 2,000

1. For Miguel Hernández, see a vivid interview with his widow, in *Triunfo* (Madrid), January 1975.

2. Ciano, *Diplomatic Papers*, pp. 293–4.

3. Testimony to the author by Martínez Amutio, civil governor of Albacete till March 1939.

shot at Ocaña (Toledo), an important gaol in central Spain.[1] There seem to have been three hundred executions a week in Barcelona in May.[2] The Basque nationalists claimed that 21,780 Basques died in the post-war repression.[3] Could the over-all figure have approached the much-quoted one of about 193,000 named in 1944 to Charles Foltz, an American journalist, by an unidentified official of the ministry of justice?[4] It is improbable; perhaps the figure lists the number of death sentences passed, without noting the sentences which were commuted. Perhaps the figure included all those shot in nationalist Spain during, as well as after, the war? The history of the twentieth century, despite its energy for statistics and its appetite for exactness, is unfortunately full of murky statistics of this vagueness, and it would be wiser no doubt to leave the matter unresolved, for the contempt of the present rather than for, as yet, the judgment of history. The history of Spain since 1939 is scarcely a matter for historians, even if it is barely believable that the contemporary politics of a western European state should leave undecided a matter of this type. There seems no doubt whatever that tens of thousands of Spaniards died in the months following the war.

Among those about whose death there is no doubt were Generals Aranguren and Escobar, the civil guard commanders in Barcelona at the beginning of the war; General Martínez Cabrera; Colonel Burillo; the communist director-general of security, Colonel Antonio Ortega; his namesake, the communist commissar, Daniel Ortega; the socialist youth leader, José Cazorla; the President of Catalonia, Luis Companys; the minister of the interior, Julián Zugazagoitia; the anarchist minister of commerce, Juan Peiró; Prieto's secretary, Cruz Salido – the last four of whom were shot when handed over by the gestapo in occupied France after 1940. Most of those concerned in Colonel Casado's *coup*, including anarchists, survived, as did some who, like Cipriano Mera, were only captured later. The co-founder of the

1. Sergio Vilar (p. 227), quoting a communist, Miguel Núñez, who spent twelve years there.

2. *Catalunya sota . . .*, p. 242.

3. Astillara, *La guerra de Euzkadi*. Mera lists 500 by name executed in Madrid prison while he was there in 1941–44, p. 288.

4. Charles Foltz, *The Masquerade in Spain* (Boston, 1948), p. 97.

POUM, meantime, Joaquín Maurín, continued in gaol.[1] Comorera, the communist leader in Barcelona, however, risked too much when he returned to Spain of his own free will in 1956. Arrested and tried, he died in gaol some years later. But the leaders of the republic mostly escaped to an often disagreeable, impecunious or sad exile, while it was the rank and file, the mayor of the small village not the lord mayor, the secretary of the small collective rather than the commander-in-chief, who suffered the worst consequence of this brutal persecution.

The responsibility for the repression lies first with the local supporters of the nationalists whose hatred and fury could only be contained by death sentences imposed by the summary courts. In addition, the director of prisons, Máximo Cuervo Radigales, of the military legal corps, and Colonel Martínez Fuset, head of that corps, probably fanned the flames. The ministers of the interior, justice and war might have attempted to limit ruthlessness but they did not. Ultimately responsible was Franco, who confirmed more death sentences than any other statesman in the history of Spain but who could have exercised a decisive influence for magnanimity. A sharpness was given to the repression by the deliberate recruitment of police and security forces from among those who had been in republican gaols, or who had otherwise suffered.[2]

The Spanish Civil War exceeded in ferocity many wars between nations. The losses in lives from all causes, taking into account deaths from malnutrition in the republic, as well as those shot after the war, must have been about 500,000.[3] As in many wars, the number of those killed in action or who died of wounds afterwards, was a modest part of the dead: probably not much more than 200,000 (say,

1. See, for the repression, Juan M. Molina, *Noche sobre España* (Mexico, 1958); Miguel García, *I was Franco's Prisoner* (London, 1972); Ronald Frases, *In Hiding*. A lurid account is by the Paraguayan chargé d'affaires, Arturo Bray, *La España del brazo en alto* (Buenos Aires, 1943), and there is the graphically entitled *24 años en la cárcel* (Paris, 1968) by Melquesidez Rodríguez Chaos.

2. See *Catalunya sota . . .*, p. 242.

3. The first edition of this book (1961) was among the first to suggest that the until then accepted figure of a million dead was an exaggeration. Note that attempts to reach a figure by demographic analysis have given figures as far apart as 800,000 (Jesús Villar Salinas, *Repercusiones demográficas de la última guerra civil española*, Madrid, 1942) and 560,000 (Pierre Vilar, *Histoire*, p. 117).

90,000 on the nationalist side, 110,000 on the republican) or 10 per cent of the total combatants.[1] Murders or executions behind the lines account perhaps for another 130,000 (75,000 nationalist, 55,000 revolutionary or republican, including executions in prison camps, at the front line or as a result of tribunals after 1936).[2] It would be reasonable to allow 10,000 for deaths by aerial bombardment, perhaps 25,000 for deaths by malnutrition or other diseases attributable to the war, together with 100,000 deaths from execution or other causes subsequent to the war (either in or out of gaol).[3] If one supposes a permanent emigration of 300,000 (that is, people who left and who did not get back), Spain may be supposed to have lost nearly 800,000 people in the civil war, including the flower of the new generation.

*

The cost of the war, including both internal and external expenditures, was named later by the nationalists at 30,000 million pesetas ($9,375 million).[4] The chief real cost was in labour, due on the one hand to the deaths and permanent disabilities caused, and on the other to the permanent exile of so many persons at the end of the war. It would be a hard task, however, to measure the exile of, say,

1. As a result of more careful analysis of each battle's figure, I have scaled this down from my last edition. Jackson's arguments appear convincing here (p. 526f.), and they coincide with De la Cierva (vol. II, p. 221f.). R. Casas de la Vega, *Las milicias nacionales en la guerra de España* (Madrid, 1974) calculates 17,015 killed or died of wounds out of a total of 160,000–170,000 falangist volunteers in the war.

2. See pp. 265 and 270 for reasons for these calculations and other conflicting evidence. De la Cierva puts this figure at merely 50,000, 25,000 each, neatly enough (*Historia ilustrada*, vol. II, p. 221). I would like to think that he is right but I fear he is optimistic. Jackson, I fear, underestimates the republic's murders and overestimates those of the rebels.

3. I include here as war dead those who, like Julián Besteiro, or Miguel Hernández, died in gaol as a result of the war. Whereas Jackson has this figure of 50,000 above suggested, he gives a figure of 200,000 for post-war reprisals. See p. 925 above. De la Cierva, *op. cit.* (vol. II, p. 223) says 50,000 should be regarded as the maximum. Cabanellas (vol. II, p. 1112) ventures 300,000.

4. *Boletín Oficial del Estado*, 4 August 1940, qu. Sarda, *El Banco de España 1931–1962*, has 22,740 million pesetas among the republicans, 10,000 million among the nationalists (pesetas of 1935). The former high figure is at least partly to be attributed to the high cost of personnel in the republican army.

the poet Juan Ramón Jiménez or the death of Lorca in terms of pesetas. 4,250 million pesetas' worth of damage nevertheless was done to property during the course of the war. 150 churches were completely destroyed and 4,850 damaged, of which 1,850 were more than half destroyed. 173 towns were so badly damaged that the Generalissimo 'adopted' them – his government, that is, undertook to pay the cost of restoration. 250,000 houses were so badly ruined as to be uninhabitable. Another 250,000 were partially damaged.[1] This damage was much less than what happened to France in the Great War of 1914–18. As for the practical consequences, the victors refused to recognize money issued by the republican government after 18 July 1936: notes issued before then, however, could be exchanged for new pesetas at par. Cash deposits in banks made before 18 July 1936 were also paid in full in new pesetas. Bank accounts used in the republic after 18 July 1936 became subject to investigation, and out of 9,000 million pesetas in bank accounts in the republican zone at the end of the war, only 3,000 million survived the investigation.[2]

As for the productive part of the economy, the factories of Bilbao and Barcelona lived through the war almost untouched. The irrigation system around Valencia was not harmed. While Spain lost a third of her livestock[3] and much farm machinery, farmland and farm buildings also suffered less than might have been expected. Still, land sown in 1939 showed a big drop in comparison with 1935.[4] The war was hard on the railways: 1,309 engines (42 per cent of those existing

1. Report of the Dirección General de Regiones Devastadas, 1943. This was some 8 per cent of the total houses of the country.

2. Tamames, *Estructura*, p. 559.

3. Tamames, *La república*, p. 357, prints these figures:

	Cattle	*Sheep*	*Pigs*
1933	597,000	2,926,000	382,000
1941	291,000	1,977,000	191,000
Reduction average	34.3%	32.7%	50.6%

4. Eight million hectares of wheat in comparison with 11 million in 1935. Of course in some areas specially hit, such as that in which the battle of the Ebro was fought, the losses were greater: Mezquida (vol. I, p. 162) gives, for example, figures showing that, whereas in 1935 there were 5.4 million vines in Gandesa, over 2 million had been lost by 1939. The *vendimia* took many years to recover its old production.

in 1936), 30,000 goods wagons (40 per cent of 1936), and 3,700 passenger carriages (70 per cent of 1936) were destroyed. Lorries were scarce, but roads were in good condition. A third of the merchant marine was lost (70 ships or 220,000 tons). Stocks of raw materials and of food were low. The beginning of the Second World War, in September 1939, six months after the end of the Spanish war, prevented Spain from making up these losses from abroad. The situation was worsened by a long succession of droughts. The years of privation following the war (especially 1941–2) were thus known as the 'great famine'. Agricultural production in 1939 was down 21 per cent, industrial production some 31 per cent, national income 26 per cent, and income per head 28 per cent.[1]

The archaeological and artistic collections in Catalonia emerged from the war almost unscathed, due to the care of the Catalan government. There were no major artistic losses in central and southern Spain either. Much priceless private and ecclesiastical jewellery, however, disappeared. A few important treasures were taken abroad by the republican government in 1939, and handed to the League of Nations with the Prado paintings, but all were returned. Of the places and works of art destroyed, the church of Santa María del Mar, the Gothic church in Barcelona, the Plaza de Zocodover in Toledo, and the Infantado Palace in Guadalajara, were the worst artistic losses.

*

The end of the civil war closed an epoch in Spanish history. Nearly all the main actors of the past turbulent half-century were either dead or in exile. Many institutions and ideals had been swept away. The 'liberals' and the catholic politicians of the republic had been pushed unceremoniously to the side even before the start of the war. Now the great working-class parties of Spain had also been overwhelmed, along with their wild, generous, and violent dreams, as well as their

1. Figures in Tamames, *La república*, p. 357. Thus, if 1929 represents 100:

	1935	*1939*
Agricultural production	97.3	76.7
Industrial	103.3	72.3
Income per head (1929 pesetas)	1033	740

often inspired experiments, such as the collectives in both town and on the land. The Basque and Catalan leaders were separated by exile from their own dearly loved regions, as well as from Castile. What deaths, too, there had been among the victors! Who could forget the thirteen murdered bishops, at the head of the army of six thousand ecclesiastical ghosts. The exuberant Sanjurjo, the conspirator Mola, the brilliant Calvo Sotelo, José Antonio Primo de Rivera with all his charm, Onésimo Redondo, the fascist from Valladolid, Ledesma, with his Hitlerian quiff, the eccentric Maeztu, the Carlist philosopher Pradera – all had died, and had died violently. None of the vanquished parties in the civil war had suffered such a toll of deaths among their leaders as the Falange[1] – unless the poets, among whom the slaughter had also been terrible, are reckoned a party: for the God-fearing humanist Unamuno was dead of grief in Salamanca; García Lorca lay in an unknown grave near Granada; Machado died an exile in a pension at Collioure; while Miguel Hernández was soon to die in Alicante gaol. Beyond all these deaths of celebrated men, there rose the mass spectre of those many thousands of warriors, known and unknown, who too had died, many giving their lives for causes which, on both sides, they had come to believe were noble; while many others had died without idealism, for causes for which they had fought without hope.

The causes themselves were also dead by 1939. The three great quarrels which had led to the war – those of region, church, and class – had spent themselves, being transmuted in the strife from passionate conflicts between irreconcilable extremes into opportunistic battles for victory, or survival, at all costs. If liberalism and freemasonry had been exorcized, the church had been wounded by the Falange. Yet most of the social aspirations of the Falange had vanished just as completely as had communism, anarchism, and socialism. The defeat of Basque and Catalan separatism did not mean that the monarchists or Carlists were able to impose their views. Upon the heaped skulls of all these ideals, in the dust of the memory of so much rhetoric, one more cold-hearted, dispassionate, duller, and greyer man survived triumphant, as Octavius survived the civil wars in Rome. Caesar and Pompey, Brutus and Antony, Cato and Cicero –

1. Sixty per cent of pre-civil-war Falange members are said to have been killed in the conflict (estimate by Payne, *The Falange*, p. 212).

all, with all their genius, lacked the minor talent of being able to survive: Franco was the Octavius of Spain.

Franco's achievements in the civil war were considerable. As supreme commander of the nationalist forces his duties were strategic or political, never tactical – though he was often at the front. He had no opportunities to show himself (or risk his reputation) as a field commander. His task was to decide in what region a new offensive should be, to be certain that an offensive did not begin till all was ready, to halt a counter-attack (as at Brunete) when it had accomplished its task, and to ensure, through the aid of such efficient but undramatic officers as Dávila, or Orgaz, or Barroso, that the right equipment arrived on the right front at the right time. He was careful to give supreme field commands to men such as Saliquet who, being old-fashioned and indeed old, could never be a rival to him. German officers serving with Franco, such as von Thoma, found him conventional. But in his caution, patience, and puritanism he resembled von Thoma's future conqueror at El Alamein – Montgomery.

As a supreme commander, Franco showed none of the recklessness for which he had been known as a young man in Morocco. Unlike von Thoma, Franco had no interest in military innovations *per se.* Perhaps his greatest military success was political. Political leaders were to General Franco merely divisional commanders, while military affairs also had their political or psychological significance; hence the decision to relieve Toledo and Brunete, the reluctance to accept *faits accomplis* at Teruel and the Ebro. He established himself as the political leader of the most passionately concerned country in the world by a contempt for political passions. He was no orator: a suitable visitation, it might perhaps be thought, on a country which had suffered from a surfeit of rhetoric. Alcalá Zamora, Azaña, Prieto, Calvo Sotelo, Gil Robles, Melquíades Alvarez and La Pasionaria were admirable speakers, with a real feeling for the ring of words: Franco initiated for Spain an age of statistics in which language was used to disguise, rather than to convey, thought. 'Down with the intellectuals', the cry of Millán Astray, Franco's mentor in that amoral but effective corps, the Foreign Legion, was an all too appropriate cry in a country where the old political life, inspired by French-educated men of letters, with their endless *tertulias* in cafés in Madrid and their cult of eloquence, had so tragically failed.

The political alliance which he achieved among his followers was the chief reason for his victory. No doubt he was assisted in providing a theoretical basis for that by Serrano Súñer, whose pre-war sympathy for a radical, right-wing system, even if it was not fascism, had been sharpened by his black experiences in the Model Prison. (To have seen humanity on that summer night of August 1936, in Madrid, was something to concentrate the mind only too greatly, as Azaña realized at the time.) The unity of the movement was itself the source of the propaganda which made it possible to mobilize a million men in the 'crusade'. But Franco's calm, effortless, professional superiority first obtained for him the leadership of the nationalists long before Serrano Súñer had escaped from a republican prison, and then enabled him to maintain himself. There were almost as many possible fissures in the nationalist side as there were among the republicans. The delay in obtaining victory, and the incessant disappointments, gave many opportunities for the nationalist alliance to collapse. Doubtless agreement between Falange, church, monarchists, Carlists, and army was made easier by a certain class desperation, a greater appreciation of the disastrous consequences of defeat than existed on the republican side, perhaps by a greater cynicism which led these disparate groups, like Franco himself, to believe that there were no political aims so important that victory might be jeopardized in obtaining them. But it was Franco who turned this desperation, these fears, and this cynicism into engines of war. These negative emotions were supported by much positive enthusiasm from a right wing led in the war by its extremists, who were delighted to think that the old politics of public debate and lip service to French liberalism were over at last. This extreme right, monarchist rather than falangist, was both better supported and more determined than their enemies, abroad and in the republic, supposed. Franco and his foreign minister, the Conde de Gómez Jordana, also showed themselves clever diplomatists in ensuring adequate German and Italian aid without surrendering to the dictators of those countries more than an admittedly large number of mining rights.

If political unity helped the nationalist victory so much, disunity among the republicans was a prime cause of their defeat. That made the political anthropology of republican Spain, particularly at the early stages, a peculiarly fascinating study. Nowhere, too, were republican voices more discordant than in attributing responsibility for the defeat. Some blamed the communists for strangling the 'revolution' by their own quest for power. Some argued that, though many Spanish communists sought victory as passionately as they said they did, Stalin was afraid of the consequences of a republican victory, and, from a certain stage, did what he could to ensure its defeat. Madariaga many years ago argued that the divisions within the socialist party made the civil war inevitable; and the political errors of judgement of Largo Caballero, a good trade-union organizer without vision, were at the heart of the problems of the republic in the months before the conflict. The Spanish socialist party was indeed a microcosm of Spain itself: the revolutionary urban youth, the militant young countrymen of the FNTT, the social democrats of Prieto, the uncertain leadership of Largo, the technocratic professionalism of Negrín, the theoretically 'pure' Marxism but practical sweet reasonableness of Besteiro, all contained visions of what Spain might be: the clashes between them were destructive of what Spain had already achieved, in particular what had been achieved to liberate Spaniards. Nowhere in the world has the idea of the class struggle been more destructive of the very class the concept was first devised to help than it has been in Spain.

The anarchists believed that the war would have been won if the proletarian revolution had been fully carried out in its first days. But in those areas where revolution was put before military preparation, such as west Andalusia and Estremadura, the Army of Africa cut through its enemies as a knife cuts butter. The fighting between anarchists and communists began early; throughout the spring of 1937, communists were shooting anarchists and POUMistas. This unedifying stanza in the epic of the Spanish revolution culminated in the May Days. There followed the communist repression of the Council of Aragon. Finally, the war ended, bizarrely, as it had begun, with a dedicated professional officer rising against the government to avoid communism. The republic was thus much hampered by the disputes between those who supported it. Even when the communists, through superior logic and skill, had gained a prominent position, the silent suspicion which they inspired sapped morale. The 'golden century' of Spain had been wracked by the hatred between old christians and jewish converts. Similarly, the intellectual renaissance of the Spanish working class in the twentieth century was dominated by equal tension between Marxists and Bakuninists, to give communism and anarchism an appropriately personal colouring. (The 'liberals' backed first the one, then the other.) Did all the parties feel so strongly about their own policies that defeat itself seemed preferable to a surrender of the purity of their individual views? It would be more truthful to say simply that no one was able to forge a real unity out of the republican warring tribes as Franco was able to do among the nationalists. Politicians spoke of the petty caliphates of the early middle ages to describe the political, as well as the territorial, divisions of the republic: General Llano de la Encomienda's lost cheese on the 'frontier' between Asturias and Santander was a symbol of the disunity.[1] Negrín did his best. But such a policy meant making use of the communist party. The non-intervention policy of the western democracies forced Negrín to a dangerous reliance on Russia. It would have been inconceivable not to have used the fighting qualities of the communists. But some aspects of communist behaviour, in particular their inhumanity and untruthfulness, poisoned the lifeblood of the republican cause.

A real revolutionary state, such as Russia became in 1919, rather than a revolutionary anarchist society, might, it is true, have made war more effectively. But that would have necessitated the capture of power by a communist party stronger and even more ruthless than that which did exist; and such a thing would have been even less to the anarchists' liking. Further, given the character of Europe at that time, not to speak of Spain, it is doubtful if a revolutionary republic would have been allowed to enjoy its triumph peacefully.

How easy to feel sympathy for the anarchist leaders in their dilemmas during the war! Anarchism had a creative and original contribution to make to Spanish society. No doubt, an anarchist revolution of a full-blooded style was impossible unless a much higher percentage of the population were favourable.[2] But a less full-blooded revolution could perhaps have existed alongside a mixed society. Anarchists simply killed too many people at the beginning of the civil war. It was also the moderate Juan Peiró who wrote, in October 1938, that, 'on the first day after the military victory' over fascism, the libertarian struggle would begin again against Marxism

1. See above, p. 539. 2. This is discussed on p. 564.

and the middle class. He nevertheless 'hoped to avoid a civil war among the Left'; a scarcely comforting remark, after two years of conflict.[1] To some extent, too, the anarchists, who were nothing if not honest, created their own enemies. People who had never read a word of Marx joined the communists since they sought security against the anarchist gangs of July 1936, in which hardened criminals worked hand in hand with idealists. The bourgeois members of the Spanish communist party defended their property through that party; they were not negligible. From the angle of the 1970s, and the modern industrial state of huge corporations, as from the state enterprises of modern Russia, the petty bourgeoisie of old Spain, with the numerous small firms, do not seem the worst enemies that the Spanish working class has ever had.

Tragically, the one department of republican politics where Negrín, with backing from Azaña, was able to bring unity – the relation of central with autonomous authority in Catalonia – brought disillusion. It was also an error not to maintain, or revive, constitutional life. The Prime Minister should have been regularly and rigorously questioned in the Cortes, once order had been restored. The lack of a vigorous democratic life reflected on the efficiency, as well as the good name, of the republic. The opposition should have been able to question the successive ministers on the conduct of the war even if elections would have been difficult.

Franco was fortunate: if the Czech crisis had led in 1938 to a world war, rather than to Munich, a French army might have intervened to save the republic. Had it not been for Colonel Casado's *coup d'état*, the war might have lingered on into the summer of 1939. The Anglo-French guarantee to Poland came at the end of March and their pursuit of the Russian alliance began in May. It will be thus seen how close Negrín was to realizing his aim of drawing the logical conclusion from the fact of foreign intervention in the conflict, and subsuming the Spanish, in the European, civil war.

Franco was obstinate in opposing the idea of mediation. A compromise peace would almost certainly have been welcomed by a majority of Spaniards had they been consulted at any moment after August 1936. Azaña and Negrín began to pursue this chimera from the middle of 1937. It goes without saying that such a compromise

1. C. Lorenzo, p. 236.

would have saved thousands of lives as well as factories, rolling stock, and agricultural production figures. The saving of life as such was never an important consideration for Franco, who profited from his victory to carry on with his odious policy of *limpieza*: the 'cleaning up' of Spain from the doctrines which he considered evil. Franco and Serrano Súñer considered that their alliance with Germany and Italy was bringing them into touch with the wave of the future, which seemed likely then to triumph in Europe. The *limpieza* did not work: 'French' ideas have long since returned to Spain, along with *ragoût*, Marxists, anarchists, and even democrats. A mediated peace would thus not only have been humane: it would have recognized the possibilities open in the long run to Spain in the twentieth century in a way which Franco's pursuit of the absolute monarchy could not, either in the war or the peace of exhaustion that followed. If the nationalists had not made evident their desire to execute many people after their victory, the war could have been brought to an end a year before it did.[1] But with '*anti-España*', they wanted no compromise, any more than they had wanted one with Abd-el-Krim; and the 'crusade of liberation' was indeed fought as if it were a great colonial war, led by men such as Sanjurjo, Mola, Kindelán, Varela, Yagüe and Franco himself whose political imaginations had been formed in the sun of Morocco. The tragedy, or irony, was that it was an imperial war carried out at home. The 'language of empire' in the mountains of Aragon sounded a strange tongue.

The Pyrenees make Spain and Portugal almost more an island than a peninsula. Sea power is certain to affect a Spanish war. At the beginning, the republic had most of the fleet. The nationalists brought the two new cruisers *Canarias* and *Baleares* to Gibraltar in September 1936 and, though they lost their only battleship, the *España*, off Santander in April 1937, dominated the Cantabrian coast as well in that summer. The republic's only battleship, the *Jaime I*, blew up in June 1937. Though the republic continued to have three cruisers until the end of the war, not to speak of fourteen destroyers, the nationalists maintained their superiority, with four ex-Italian destroyers and two new destroyers of their own. When the *Baleares* was sunk in March 1938, it was almost made up for by the *Navarra*, converted from the old *República*. Altogether, the nationalists sank

1. A point made by Abad de Santillán, *Por qué perdimos*, p. 15.

48 republican merchant ships (to the republic's capture of 22) and 44 foreign (some 240,000 tons), and captured 202 republican merchant ships and 23 foreign ones (330,000 tons – together with 150,000 tons of cargo confiscated).[1] In respect of all small ships, the nationalists always had an advantage, except for submarines. The nationalists were able, with their allies' help, to impose a successful blockade. The history of the republican fleet is inglorious; that of the nationalist, distinguished. The republicans were so short of officers that they never took advantage of their superiority in numbers of vessels. They were also short of oil at sea in the last year (though not in the air force).

The republic also began the war with an advantage in the air. In the first two or three months, whatever the numbers were, the Junkers, Fiats and Savoias from Germany and Italy were superior in practice to the French help to the republic. The large consignments of Russian aircraft, particularly Moscas and Chatos, gave the republic an aerial superiority in the winter of 1936, but in 1937 Messerschmitts, new Heinkels and new Savoias tipped the balance back. The Russian aircraft were also used conservatively, often timidly by both Russians and their Spanish pupils. They lost many. In the north, and during most of 1938, the nationalists had overwhelming aerial superiority, but, during the early stages of the battle of the Ebro, the new Russian Supermoscas and Superchatos made an impression. The rebels used about 1,300 planes in the war, the Left probably about 1,500.[2] These were substantial figures: the German air force in 1937, for example, numbered only about 2,000 while the British and French had about 1,500 and 3,000 respectively.[3]

The history of the Spanish war of revolution is partly the history of the abuse of technology: the Buick in which García Lorca travelled to his death at Viznar, the cars which 'took people for a ride' – sad euphemism borrowed from films – on the republican side, the telephone on which Moscardó spoke to his son and the telephone build-

1. Cervera's figures (Cervera, p. 422). Slightly different figures were given by Admiral Bastarreche in his contribution to the seminars in the University of Saragossa (*Guerra de liberación*, Saragossa, 1961, p. 422).

2. R. Salas, vol. IV, p. 3422. A detailed analysis of foreign aid follows in Appendix VII.

3. *FD*, vol. VII, p. 377.

ing which the communist police determined to capture in Barcelona were the bric-à-brac of a half industrialized society in which power was ultimately gained by the men whose use of these gadgets was more adroit. Queipo de Llano's successful use of the microphone with his graphic language was symbolic of how old Spain triumphed, with new weapons.

Franco's army was better organized, all things considered, than that of his enemies. Political unity gave him unity of command. Nationalist forces were more disciplined than their opponents and their logistical arrangements excellent, as seen in the ease with which reserves were moved from one front to another. German technical training, particularly in signals, played a considerable part there. But equally important was the availability of so many middle-class young men as *alféreces provisionales*, provisional lieutenants, whose education made them more effective than the junior republican officers. The republican achievement in assembling an army at all was considerable. But they failed to make as much use as they might have done of the regular officers available to them. The militias of the people's army alike were effective and heroic in defence, often unimaginative in attack. The failure of the militia on the Aragon front against a thin nationalist line makes nonsense of the anarchist complaints on the subject of a regular army. On the other hand, the people's army did turn out to be as conventional and as bureaucratic as the anarchists feared.[1] In the end, General Matallana was probably right when he told Negrín in 1939 that 'though the army had learned some defensive tactics, they were incapable of retreat or counter-attack'.[2] Franco's deficiencies were less organizational than errors of judgement; time and again, at Brunete, Teruel and the Ebro, he insisted on fighting for the few miles that had been lost rather than cut his losses or seek to turn the enemy's flank. These frontal counter-attacks were wasteful in terms of lives, as they always are in war. His greatest strategic mistake was probably not to have advanced on Barcelona in April 1938. Is it possible that he, as his enemies (particularly monarchists) have suggested, prolonged the war deliberately, to ensure his own political advantage? It seems improbable; as over

1. Many instances of this are given in Alpert's excellent thesis.

2. Qu. Carr, *Spain*, p. 689. Matallana's loyalties might be suspect; his tactics were sound.

Toledo in 1936, Franco could not have known that such a risky decision would have benefited him in the end. In April 1938, the international situation might have caused things to turn out badly for him. If there had been world war over Czechoslovakia, at the time of Munich, Spain would surely have been swept into it, with Franco's Spain surely in the front line. Franco's decision not to attack Barcelona until he had destroyed the republican army in the south was fully in character, and indeed can be justified on political as well as strategic grounds.[1] Nobody could have known that Barcelona would fall without a fight.

The financial management of the war was a success for the nationalists, a disaster for the republic. The former paid for their war effort by delaying the interest both on the national debt and on most of the new debt due on the war; by ruthlessly reducing unnecessary spending; by new taxes; by the establishment of a new Bank of Spain, which lent to the nationalist authorities 9,000 million pesetas; and, of course, by foreign aid, which was not paid for until afterwards. The republic had recourse to similar financial methods (for example, the delay on interest on debt) but they undertook a formidable expansion of the currency, vast governmental spending, with substantial inflation, as well as severe rationing which did not prevent considerable scarcity of food from late 1937 onwards.[2]

Foreign intervention was, of course, of great importance in the war, as could easily be seen if one were to look up, for example, at the sky over Brunete or the Ebro, covered as it then was with aircraft made in Russia, Germany and Italy. The same thing could be seen as Hotchkiss and Degtyareva machine-guns clashed with Bredas and Mausers. The fuel-bearers in the conflict interacted and it is not satisfactory, in order to reach an estimate of their significance, simply to add up what they severally gave or sold.[3] There were many occasions when the timing of certain foreign supplies was critical. First, the supply of Junkers 52 by Germany in July 1936 helped Franco to lift the Army of Africa across the Straits of Gibraltar. To say simply that

1. Even Azaña later commented (letter to Ossorio, 28 June 1939) that he was surprised that Franco did not go for Barcelona in March 1938 (vol. III, p. 537).

2. See, on this subject, Tamames, *La república*, p. 341; Carlos Delclaux, *La financiación de la cruzada* (University of Deusto, unpublished thesis, 1950).

3. See Appendix VII, for a full inquiry.

the nationalists would have lost the war had it not been for that begs too many questions. Some troops had been flown over before the Junkers arrived and, sooner or later, the rebels would have discovered the incompetence of the republican fleet; as indeed they did, when they gained control over the Straits at the end of September with the action of the *Canarias*. Still, the war would have taken a different course if the Army of Africa had not reached the mainland so fast. This help had a greater effect than the simultaneous purchase of aircraft by the republic from France, whatever the quantity or quality of the latter. The Junkers 52 ('iron Annie') cast its shadow over much of Europe between 1936 and 1945, never more than when it did so over the sea separating that continent from Africa in 1936.

The impact of other men and equipment in the first three months of the war is less easy to judge. In a country without any tanks to speak of before July, the few Panzers Mark I which came from Germany and the light Fiats from Italy certainly were more impressive than the huge CNT tanks, home-made in Barcelona. In the summer of 1936, the French aircraft – Potez, Dewoitines and Blochs – were faster than the Heinkels and Junkers 52 of the Germans but they were handled less well and, already in the late summer, the Italians' Fiat fighter – the CR32 – was showing itself a dependable new weapon in the air. The first Ansaldo tanks from Italy with light machine-guns were seen at the fall of Irún. But they were not decisive in that action.

The second important occasion in respect of foreign intervention was in November 1936, when the Russian assistance to the republic, the arrival of the International Brigades, and the organized support of international communism, helped to save Madrid. Here the critical time was the start of November, when the heavy T-26 tanks, together with the Mosca and Chato fighters, dominated the battlefields.[1] The Russians also sent many of their old 'Pulemet Maxim' machine-guns which were very reliable and also the lighter Degtyareva Pekhotnii (DP), a very good gun of its class. These were much more serviceable than the Hotchkiss medium machine-guns bought from France. Russian advisers also probably played a positive part, though it is very difficult to know exactly how much help they were.

1. La Pasionaria (in *They Shall Not Pass*, p. 348) says that 'without the Soviet tanks and aeroplanes, the defence of Madrid would have been impossible'.

Thirdly, the material sent by Mussolini and Hitler in 1937 probably prevented a collapse of nationalist morale when the rebel generals failed to capture the capital. The Condor Legion became a really revolutionary force, in service of the counter-revolution admittedly, in the course of 1937. New, light Messerschmitt 109 fighters and Heinkel bombers, together with the new Savoia 79, won the air back for the nationalists from Brunete onwards, and the Panzers and Fiat Ansaldo tanks recovered the initiative. Probably equally important was the powerful German anti-aircraft '88' (88-millimetre Flak 36), which remained the backbone of German defence from the moment that it first began to be effectively used in Spain in the winter of 1936–7. The new German 'Maschinengewehr 34' (MG 34) also made a considerable impact as a 'general purpose machine-gun' – more so than the Italian equivalent, the Breda 30.

Fourthly, the opening of the French frontier to Russian and other foreign aid staved off defeat for the republic in the spring of 1938, after the success of the nationalists' Aragon campaign.

Finally, if Franco had not exchanged so many mining rights for German arms in the autumn of 1938 he might not have been able to launch the Catalan campaign at Christmas of that year.[1] Had it not been for that, his army would have been as badly provided after the battles of the Ebro as was the republican army. In that case, the war might have ground to a *de facto* halt along the battle lines.[2]

The German government knew by late 1938 that the fears which she had entertained earlier of a spread of the war in Spain into 'a European conflagration' were groundless, however flagrant a breach she might commit of the Non-Intervention Pact. For, after the Munich settlement, it seemed that Britain (and France) would never go to war over a European issue. This impression was confirmed by the carrying into effect in November 1938 of the Anglo–Italian Agreement. The Germans were also encouraged to think that they could act with impunity by the cooling of Russian interest in Spain in the autumn of 1938, and indeed by various gestures, especially after Munich, by the Russian government towards Germany herself. But until Munich, German policy had been to refuse to commit

1. The shipment is described in detail on pp. 850 and 860 above.

2. For a contrary view, see R. Salas's essay in Palacio Atard, *Aproximación histórica a la guerra civil española* (Madrid, 1970).

enough forces or war material to Spain to secure the triumph of their nationalist protégés. The Germans believed that such a commitment would have risked the expansion of the Spanish war into a European one. Indeed, Germany and Russia shared, throughout the civil war, a disinclination to risk a general war breaking out over Spain: once Russia became committed to the republic, in October 1936, any general war resulting from the Spanish conflict would surely have implicated her also. So Stalin had followed a policy similar to that of Hitler: prevention of his protégés' defeat, without ensuring their victory; for to ensure a republican victory would have meant the commitment of troops and material on a scale which would have risked general war.

All the first four occasions when intervention was critical were defensive ones, when the intervening powers sought to prevent the defeat of one side or the other. That was one reason why the war lasted so long. Hitler and Stalin both found good reasons to justify to themselves the continuance of the war. They could test new military ideas and new equipment. For each of them, victory might bring as many difficult questions as defeat. If the civil war were to continue, such questions could be postponed. Mussolini, who sought glory in Spain, was dissatisfied. He sent as many troops as he could – too many, as his weakness at the time of the Anschluss showed. If either Germany or Russia had sent as many men to Spain as Italy did, a European war would have followed. But 50,000 Italian troops were neither numerous enough to win the war for Franco, nor to shock Europe into a general conflict. The last critical intervention, in late 1938, marked a policy of full commitment to the rebels by Germany in the knowledge that, if France (and Britain) did not fight for Czechoslovakia, they would not do so for Spain. In addition while, throughout the war, the republic were persistently trying to ensure supplies or to convert their plants into war factories, nationalist supplies were more regular. Reliance on Germany and Italy avoided the need for a large war industry.

Technology and diplomacy interacted. The Spanish civil war was a conflict in the time of the 'stressed skin' revolution in the design of aircraft as much as it was one of ideologies. It was a war of revolutionary ideas in propaganda and means of communication, in which foreigners played as much a part as they did in the battles proper.

In a long war in the age of industry, supplies of energy are as important as arms. The Texas Oil Company and, to a lesser extent, Standard Oil of New Jersey, gave much help to Franco by their substantial supplies on credit. Nearly 3½ million tons of oil were apparently delivered by these companies to the rebels during the civil war; while the republic imported 1½ million tons, mostly from Russia.[1] The US also sent some army lorries, at prices lower than were available from Germany or Italy: 12,000 lorries came from Ford, Studebaker and General Motors, while 3,000 came from Germany and Italy. The oil compensated for the lack of coal in the nationalist zone until the conquest of the Asturias in late 1937. (The war stimulated a drive towards the use of oil in industry, on the railways, and in shipping, which continued afterwards.) Nationalist commerce, meantime, was intelligently, if piratically, undertaken, with Franco able to sell where he wanted, without worrying about pre-war arrangements. Had the republic been able to purchase arms from, say, Britain, the US, and France then the war would have taken a different course, though it is fair to question whether the equipment from France at least would have been as good as that from Russia. The I-15 fighter was better than the Breguet, the Degtyareva than the Hotchkiss machine-gun and the T-26 and BT-5 tanks more powerful if more clumsy than the French equivalents. The British government really sustained the policy of non-intervention, though it had been proposed by Blum. The French governments were too fearful of Germany to risk a breach with Britain. The head of the Quai d'Orsay, Alexis Léger, pointed out that a breach would have been inevitable if the Popular Front government in France had really become embroiled on the side of its ideological comrades in Spain.[2] The French frontier was, therefore, only open for shipment of arms to Spain for short periods.[3] The British were, meantime, determined to prevent a general war from following from the civil war, though there was an undercurrent of sympathy for Franco in

1. De la Cierva, *Historia ilustrada*, vol. II, p. 326; Feis, *loc. cit.* Exact figures seem to be 3,471,383 and 1,504,239 respectively.

2. See above, p. 344.

3. 17 July–8 August 1936; c. 20 October 1937–January 1938; 16 March–13 June 1938; and in January–February 1939. Aircraft certainly crossed the frontier between August and October 1936 also.

parts of the government and the Foreign Office (not Anthony Eden, however). Most Englishmen responsible for foreign policy wished that Spain would somehow vanish. When it was clear that the Non-Intervention Pact was being disregarded, it was cynical to insist on its maintenance. That cynicism brought the British government as little credit as it did advantage. A general war which broke out over Spain in 1936, 1937, or 1938 would have been fought in circumstances more favourable for the western democracies than that which came in 1939 over Poland. The alternative to the 'farce of non-intervention' was (as it was to Munich, to the reoccupation of the Rhineland, and to German rearmament) to stand firm and denounce the breach of the agreements. That policy had a chance of upsetting the dictator without a war. But, for reasons which derived from the worsening British economic position stretching back to the 1890s, it was not tried until September 1939 when the British Empire went to war for Poland. The battles in Spain were thus decided by the commodity of the discussion in the Non-Intervention Committee a thousand miles away. Eden became gradually aware of the unwisdom of appeasement, though in August 1936, when non-intervention began, he had, according to his own account, 'not learnt that it is dangerous to offer gestures to dictators, who are more likely to misinterpret than to follow them'.[1] It was hard for him to understand people who signed an agreement without intending to honour it. Before 1914, it would not have been done.

General von Thoma, commander of the German tank detachment in the civil war, later spoke of Spain as the 'European Aldershot'.[2] The battle experience gained for Germany by the two technical arms, tanks and aviation, was valuable. So, too, were the iron and other ores that Franco's victory in the civil war made available to Germany. Blum, justifying, at his trial at Riom in 1942, the dispatch of French aircraft to Spain, also spoke of the Spanish war as a 'test for French aviation'. But the French drew the wrong lessons from the war in

1. Eden, p. 403.

2. See Liddell Hart, *The Other Side of the Hill.* The value of Spanish combat experience for German fliers needs some qualification: the Condor Legion were more heavily tested in the Second World War than in Spain, and possibly Spain's lessons were less relevant to the skies of Britain.

Spain. They even believed a German émigré writer, Helmut Klotz, who, after a few weeks in Spain, wrote in his book, *Les Leçons militaires de la guerre civile en Espagne*, that the tank had been mastered by the anti-tank gun. The French general staff ignored the mechanized warfare which had been tested in Spain. This was to their disadvantage when Guderian's Panzer divisions streamed across their northern plains in 1940. The Russians also drew false conclusions from their Spanish experience, though Prieto later described the Russians too as treating Spain as 'a real-life military academy'.[1] General Pavlov told Stalin that the Spanish war proved that tank formations could not play an independent operational role.[2] He may have given that advice to escape being branded as an admirer of Marshal Tukhachevsky, who had had faith in such formations. The large Russian army of heavy tanks was, probably in consequence, in 1939 distributed as an infantry support force. The success of German light tanks in Poland and France led to a change back to Tukhachevsky's system, but that came too late for the opening of the Russo–German war in 1941.

Both the Italian and Yugoslav communists found their time in Spain of inestimable help in the partisan fighting in their own countries in 1944–5. Even the British learned something: the *Illustrated London News* showed the way with an examination of the effects of the air raids in Barcelona entitled a 'Study in Human Vivisection'. Copeman, ex-commander of the British Battalion of the International Brigade, found himself, within a few months of the end of the war in Spain, lecturing to the Royal Family at Windsor on air-raid precautions.[3] Medicine generally gained enormously from the new methods of treatment of war casualties introduced into Spain

1. Prieto, *Yo y Moscú*, p. 140.
2. B. Liddell Hart, *The Soviet Army* (London, 1956), pp. 316–17.
3. Many mistakes nevertheless crept into the calculations of the British government in respect of the likely effects of an aerial attack on London deduced from the raids on Barcelona in March 1938. The officials worked out that seventy-two casualties might be caused by one ton of bombs. Later, however, in all the raids on Barcelona, an average of 3.5 persons per bomb was reported killed. This new casualty ratio was not substituted in the British home office plans for the earlier, more drastic figures. (R. Titmuss, *Problems of Social Policy*, London, 1950, *Official History of the War*, pp. 13–14.) I was grateful to the late Christopher Bennett for drawing my attention to this.

by the republican army.[1] Henceforth, in wars people have died from gunshot wounds in hundreds where previously they died in thousands.

The general implications of the Spanish Civil War in the rest of the world cannot, however, be measured in precise ways. Outside Spain, the war looked, at least at first, when all the parties of the Left seemed to be cooperating, the moment of hope for a generation angry at the cynicism, indolence, and hypocrisy of an older generation with whom they were out of sympathy. The struggle gave birth to a burst of creative energy in many countries (as well as in Spain on both sides) which can be argued as comparable in quality to anything produced in the Second World War. The civil war destroyed the political hopes of a whole generation of Spaniards; but the war was also part of the twentieth-century renaissance in Spain. The civil war is symbolized nevertheless as much by the heroic actions before Madrid, as by the gathering together in the same angry gaols of dissidents on both sides: 'we were 400 prisoners, mixed FAI, anarchist youth, priests, deserters, some officers, common criminals, vagabonds, drunks, homosexuals'.[2] Thus a sometime prisoner in a camp run by the SIM in Catalonia. Similar gatherings of dissident falangists, alongside anarchists, communists and freemasons, might be found in nationalist Spain. Crusades give opportunities for heroism as for brutality. But Nin and Hedilla were alike sacrificial victims of orthodoxy. The civil war had moments of glory. But it was essentially a terrible tragedy and interruption in the life of a European people – the one major European people, it might be gloomily remembered, that before 1936 was too poor to have a modern armament industry.

1. See above, p. 550.

1. *Historia y vida*, January 1975.

Epilogue

SPAIN took years to recover from the civil war. She will never do so completely, for the war transformed the country. The First World War numbed its participants, particularly France, for a generation. The nazis' murders will never be forgotten in Germany, nor will the persecutions under Lenin and Stalin in Russia be forgotten by Russians. The Spanish Civil War was the Spanish share in the tragic European breakdown of the twentieth century, in which the liberal heritage of the nineteenth century, and the sense of optimism which had lasted since the renaissance, were shattered.

This is not the place to say in detail what the cold general did with his victory. Caudillo, Head of State and of government, king in all but name, Franco ruled regally, according to no theory save his own style of compromise, developed during the civil war, between Falange, Church, army, monarchists and industry, and sustained by a public cult of himself which owed more to the twentieth century than to that of Ferdinand and Isabella. Franco continued to treat his allies as if they were Moroccan tribes such as he had met in his youth. Procrastination was his most frequent policy, etiquette a constant preoccupation, a desire for personal power his only ideology. The romantic, authoritarian, and catholic monarchism, expressed in the leading articles of Ramiro de Maeztu's *Acción Española* before 1936, influenced his rule more than the fascism of José Antonio did. Spain became legally a monarchy in 1947, but Juan, heir of King Alfonso XIII (who died in Rome in 1941), waited in vain for twenty years more before Franco named Juan Carlos, Juan's son, as his heir as Head of State in 1969. While Spain remained politically fairly immobile for over thirty years after the end of the civil war, she underwent an economic and social revolution, so that the country became one of those which, like Germany and Japan, will be seen to have had its industrial revolution under the aegis of an authoritarian right-wing régime. For many years, the censorship continued in Spain to be as rigorous as it had been since the beginning of newspapers.

Franco outlived most of his comrades-in-arms and most of his colleagues in his early governments. Some of the generals of the crusade had their days as ministers.[1] Others did not.[2] Among civilians, Serrano Súñer remained the most powerful man in Spain after Franco until 1942. Then dismissed, he became politically unimportant: a meteoric career thus ended at forty. A few falangists, such as Raimundo Fernández Cuesta, or José Antonio Girón, who were known at the time of the civil war, played a part in subsequent governments, as did some Carlists, such as the Conde de Rodezno or Esteban Bilbao. But Franco was adept at finding new men. The old hero of the 'old shirts', Manuel Hedilla, and the old hope of the Spanish democratic Right, Gil Robles, lived on alike ignored: the former was only freed from gaol in 1941, the latter remained in exile until 1957. Once Spain became theoretically a monarchy again in 1947, Franco reinvigorated the nobility by giving several new titles; notably, it is true, to the ghosts of Mola, Calvo Sotelo and José Antonio who, long in their graves, became dukes. To the dead dukes, however, were added several live marquises: Queipo de Llano (a life-long republican), Dávila, Saliquet, Admiral Moreno, and Juan Antonio Suances, while Generals Yagüe, Varela, García Escámez, Vigón and Kindelán, with Admiral Juan Cervera, in the end received posthumous marquisates. There were, too, several new counts, some alive, such as the new Conde del Alcázar de Toledo (Moscardó), the new Condesa del Castillo de la Mota (Pilar Primo de Rivera), and General Martín Moreno, and many dead ones, such as Onésimo Redondo, Víctor Pradera, the air ace, García Morato, and Juan de la Cierva.[3] The creation of a dead nobility was one of Franco's most generous deeds.

Partly from poverty, more from policy, Spain never entered the world war by the side of Hitler, who said, when he asked for the payment of his 400 million reichsmarks due to him, that Franco made him feel 'almost like a jew, who wants to make business out of the holiest possessions of mankind'.[4] Goethe defined genius as knowing

1. Such as Yagüe, Muñoz Grandes, Varela, Alonso Vega, García Valiño, Martín Alonso, Dávila, Orgaz, Vigón and Barroso.

2. The less fortunate included Kindelán, Aranda, Saliquet, and Queipo de Llano.

3. The strange affair of Franco's titles is expounded in Appendix I to Vila San Juan, p. 472f.

4. Documents on German Foreign Policy, vol. XI, p. 213. It is a great achievement to have made Hitler feel jewish. Spanish proposals to Germany to enter the

where to stop. That was only the most obvious way in which Franco differs from the popular image of the expansionist fascist dictator. He despised publicity, even if, unlike his neighbour, the monkish Salazar, he liked show. Hitler and Franco met at Hendaye in 1940. The meeting was not a success, though what was said remains controversial. Hitler later said that he found Franco so difficult that he would prefer to have three or four teeth out than have another such interview.[1] Nevertheless when Germany attacked Russia, the 'Blue Division' of 47,000 falangist volunteers, under Geneal Muñoz Grandes, fought by the side of the Germans. Throughout the early part of the war, nationalist Spain supplied Germany with submarine bases, monitoring services, war material, and even air bases,[2] while the agency into which HISMA, ROWAK, and the Montana project had been grouped together, SOFINDUS (Sociedad Financiera Industrial Ltda), continued to control German–Spanish economic relations.[3]

As for the defeated, history, as Auden prophesied, has said alas, but has given 'neither help nor pardon'. Many, it is true, fought for the French Resistance, or the Red Army – perhaps 10,000 died in concentration camps.[4] Perhaps 25,000 republican Spaniards were killed in the Second World War.[5]

The republican leaders passed their years of exile quarrelling over their phantom power, and over the financial assets remaining to them. Negrín died in 1956 in Paris, leaving to the Spanish government in his will, several documents relating to the Spanish gold sent to Russia. In 1945, he resigned as Prime Minister in exile, in the hope

---

war in 1940 were: Germany to deliver to Spain between 400,000 and 700,000 tons of grain; all the fuel and equipment which the Spanish army needed, and artillery, aircraft, special weapons and troops needed to conquer Gibraltar. Germany was also to agree to hand over to Spain all French Morocco, together with Oran, and help her secure revision of the southern frontier of Rio de Oro.

1. Paul Schmidt, *Hitler's Interpreter* (London, 1951), p. 193.

2. U N Security Council *Report on Spain*, 2, 76.

3. German assets in Spain amounting to $55 million were finally liquidated in May 1948 by agreement with Britain, France, and the United States.

4. Lister, p. 241.

5. Pike discusses figures, in *Vae Victis!*, p. 114. The figure of republicans dead may be less. There were certainly over 10,000 in Mauthausen, of whom 2,000 returned.

of uniting all the exiles. Others succeeded him. Martínez Barrio maintained himself as President of the republic in exile, which post he held till his death in 1962. He was succeeded as President in exile by Jiménez de Asúa, the socialist lawyer, who died in 1970. Prieto died in Mexico, in 1962. Alvarez del Vayo, still an optimist, was expelled from the Spanish socialist party for his over-close friendship with the communists and was still living in 1975. Largo Caballero died a broken man in Paris in 1946, after four years in a German concentration camp. Azaña died in 1940 in the Grand Hotel du Midi, Montauban.[1] Of the republican generals, Miaja, Riquelme, Pozas, Jurado and many others died in exile, while Rojo and Casado returned to die in Spain in the 1960s.[2] Bayo, hero of the Majorcan expedition of 1936, lived to train Fidel Castro's followers in guerrilla warfare to attack another, larger island. The anarchists, despite schisms, maintained a flourishing organization among the émigrés in southern France. Of the first rank of leaders, Federica Montseny, García Oliver and Ricardo Sanz were still living in 1976, in France or in Mexico.

The Spanish communist party was for many years directed by Santiago Carrillo, secretary-general and the ex-secretary-general of the united socialist youth. La Pasionaria was for thirty years president of the party. Díaz fell from a window in Tiflis in 1942, after he had lost his job to La Pasionaria. Modesto, Uribe, Castro Delgado, and Jesús Hernández, all died in the 1960s, as did General Cordón in 1972. Hernández and Castro Delgado both eventually left the party and both wrote books sufficiently malicious to be published quickly in nationalist Spain. So too did another disillusioned, once famous, communist, Valentín González, 'El Campesino', who rejected the discipline with which he was required to conduct himself in Russia. After many adventures, he escaped from Russia through Persia. Tagüeña left the party and died in Mexico in 1972. Most of the leaders of the POUM such as Julián Gorkin and Joaquín Maurín

1. There remains a controversy as to whether Azaña died in the church; the balance of the evidence seems negative, though he was visited by Monsignor Theas, the bishop of Montauban, in his last hours. Azaña's widow told her husband's two biographers (Professor Sedwick of Florida and Cipriano Rivas-Cherif) two conflicting accounts (see Sedwick, p. 236).

2. Matallana, who handed over the republican armies of the centre, was tried, imprisoned, and died aged only fifty-eight in Madrid in 1952.

lived for many years in exile, the latter only dying in 1973. Of the Basque leaders, Aguirre died in 1960, to be succeeded as president of the Basque government in exile by Leizaola. The conscience of Catalonia was for many years maintained by José Tarradellas, titular president of the *Generalidad*. Others who died in exile and who played a part in this history included Alcalá Zamora, who died in Buenos Aires in 1949. Lerroux returned to Spain to die, in 1949. The victors' ban extended to all those who had done anything to create Catalan or Basque nationalism even if, like Francisco Cambó, they had given money to the nationalist cause: Cambó died in Buenos Aires in 1947 having been forbidden to return to Spain till that date.[1]

The republicans were naturally grieved when, at the end of the Second World War, Britain and America did not turn their arms against General Franco. Their bitterness continues. Those Spanish exiles in France who had fought with the *maquis* against the Germans attempted, between 1945 and 1949, in a struggle whose history remains to be written, to stage a return to Spain by guerrilla warfare, without success. Finally, the plight should not be forgotten of the war-injured in exile, who have never benefited from state pensions and have often lived the remainder of their lives in bad circumstances, relying on private charity.

The leading Germans and Italians who befriended the nationalists all vanished in the Second World War. Of their followers, the Baron von Stohrer remained ambassador in Madrid till dismissed by Ribbentrop in 1942, for failing to prevent the fall of Serrano Súñer. General von Faupel and his wife committed suicide in 1945, when the Russians entered Berlin. Among the generals, von Sperrle, von Thoma and von Richthofen commanded with distinction in the Second World War and the first subsequently was tried as a war criminal. Galland, who flew over three hundred sorties in his Messerschmitt 109 with the Condor Legion in Spain, became, with Mölders, who succeeded him in his Spanish posting, the most well-known German pilots in the battles for Britain and France. On the other

1. This persecution which included exclusion from any form of public office affected not only members of the Lliga who had gone abroad but many who had worked actively for the nationalists in the war, such as Bertrán y Musitu, one of the Lliga's founders who had organized Franco intelligence in France, and the millionaire shipowner, the Conde de Ruiseñada.

hand, the astute Johannes Bernhardt lived on in Spain until 1950 and then went to Argentina.[1]

Among the Italians, General Roatta served as Mussolini's chief of staff, was disgraced, and escaped to Spain from hospital while awaiting trial as a war criminal. He returned to die in Italy, in 1968. Bastico, Berti and Bergonzoli all fought in Africa, Bastico becoming governor of Libya in 1941; Berti commanded the artillery in Ethiopia and died in 1960; Bergonzoli, the 'electric whiskers' of Wavell's advance, was captured in Benghazi in 1941, and lived on Lake Maggiore for the rest of his life. Gambara fought in Libya and Yugoslavia, in the Second World War, becoming chief of staff to Graziani in the republic of Salò, and died in Rome in 1962. Bonaccorsi, the 'Conte Rossi', fought in Somalia and also died in 1962. Grandi, having helped to overthrow his master, lived for many years a businessman in Mexico.

Among the Russians who came to Spain, Berzin, Stashevsky, Antonov-Ovsëenko, Goriev, Gaikins, Rosenberg and Koltsov were all either executed or died in concentration camps. Berzin, Koltsov and Antonov-Ovsëenko were subsequently rehabilitated, much good that did them. Their deaths were regretted as a mistake, in passing, by Khrushchev in his speech denouncing Stalin in February 1956, at the twentieth party congress of the communist party of the Soviet Union.[2] The tank general, Pavlov, was shot by Stalin in 1941, when he had lost his army in the first weeks of the German advance. General Kulik was also shot in 1941, for foolishness over Red Army equipment. General Stern (Grigorovich) commanded the first Red Banner Army in 1938 against the Japanese at Changkon ferry and fought in Finland; he too was shot in 1941. Rychagov, a leading pilot in Spain, who fought in the Red Banner Army, at Lake Khason,

1. I met him in Buenos Aires in 1972, an exile from two countries, nostalgic for the east Prussia of his youth, a symbol of the German gamble for world power which ended so tragically.

2. 'Very grievous consequences, especially in reference to the beginning of the war, followed Stalin's annihilation of many military commanders and political workers during 1937–41 . . . during this time, the cadre of leaders who had gained military experience in Spain and in the Far East was almost completely liquidated.' (Bertram Wolfe, *Khrushchev and Stalin's Ghost*, New York, 1957, p. 174). Here, at least, Khrushchev exaggerated.

against the Japanese, was shot for failures against the Luftwaffe. On the other hand, Krivoshein, Voronov, Rodimtsev, Yakushin, Batov, Meretskov, Malinovsky, Konev, and Rokossovsky, with Admiral Kuznetzov, all ex-Spanish veterans, all rose to eminence in Russia; Kuznetzov commanded the Russian fleet throughout the Second World War and again after 1953. Malinovsky became minister of defence under Khrushchev. He, along with Voronov, became a marshal. Etingon, who began his career as 'Kotov' in Barcelona, as a director of counter-espionage, was shot, with his then chief Beria, in 1953.[1] Orlov lived for many years secretly, a valued defector and respected US citizen.[2] General Krivitsky, that much-quoted witness, was found shot in the Hotel Bellevue, Washington, on 10 February 1941.[3]

Among foreign communists who fought in Spain, the magnetic Kléber was executed in Russia before 1939, Gal and Čopić soon afterwards. In the late 1940s, all communists from Eastern Europe who had fought in Spain came under the cloud of Stalin's suspicion. The then Hungarian foreign secretary, Laszlo Rajk, commissar of the Rakosi Battalion in the 13th International Brigade, 'confessed', at his trial in 1949, that he went to Spain, on behalf of the police of Admiral Horthy, 'with a double purpose: to find out the names of those in the Rakosi Battalion . . . and . . . to bring about a reduction of the military efficiency of the Rakosi Battalion. I should add that I also carried on Trotskyist propaganda in the Rakosi Battalion.'[4] After Rajk's execution, many veterans of the Spanish Civil War in Eastern Europe were arrested, and some shot. After the death of

1. For Etingon, see Isaac Don Levine, *Mind of an Assassin* (London, 1960); Orlov's testimony to the Senate; P. Deriabin and F. Gibney, *The Secret World* (London, 1960), p. 187.

2. He was a great help to the FBI in several cases of 'espionage', notably those of the Soble brothers and Zbrowsky.

3. The question of whether this was another murder by Stalin or a suicide was never established.

4. *Laszlo Rajk and his Accomplices before the People's Court*, p. 6. The recollection of the Czech volunteers in Spain is the backcloth to Artur London's trials: '*nous voilà, six vétérans de la Guerre d'Espagne réunis. Mais où est notre enthousiasme d'autrefois?*' (*L'Aveu*, p. 16). To have been a member of the International Brigades was as bad as having intervened in Russia against the bolsheviks in 1919.

Stalin in 1953, these old 'volunteers for liberty' were, however, rehabilitated. They were released from prison too, if they were still alive. Such men were soon to be found in important positions; Mehmet Shehu (sometime in the 12th International Brigade) became President of the Albanian government and Enver Hodja was also a veteran of the Brigades; Raiko Damianov, vice-president of Bulgaria; Josef Pavel, the last commander of the Dimitrov Battalion, was Dubček's minister of the interior in 1968; Pal Maleter, who fought under Lukács, was the heroic minister of defence in Hungary in 1956 whom Khrushchev executed. Twenty-four Yugoslavs who fought in Spain became generals in the Yugoslav army. Most distinguished themselves in the partisan war under Tito, the organizer of the 'secret railway' to Spain. General 'Walter' (Świerczewski) was minister of defence in Poland between 1945 and 1947, when he was murdered by Ukrainian partisans. Gerö, the Hungarian of many aliases who ruled the communists in Catalonia, became deputy premier of Hungary and Khrushchev's tool in the Hungarian revolution of 1956. Ferenc Múnnich, another political commissar of the Rakosi Battalion, became president of Hungary, after an ambivalent career in Hungarian politics since 1945. Togliatti and Luigi Longo (the latter having led the partisans in north Italy in 1943–4) for many years ruled the Italian communist party, while Giuseppe di Vittorio was secretary-general of the CGT in Italy till his death in 1958. Vittorio Vidali ('Carlos Contreras') was for years a senator, and leader of the communists in Trieste. Codovilla returned to Buenos Aires, where he died in 1972. Pacciardi, of the Garibaldi Battalion, and of the Italian republican party, served as defence minister in the coalition cabinets of de Gasperi. Nenni, leader of the Italian socialists, became vice-president of Italy. Hans Kahle died as police chief of Mecklenburg in 1952, while Franz Dahlem was purged in 1953 after the June rising in Berlin. Heinrich Rau, sometime chief of staff of the 12th Brigade, became deputy premier of East Germany. General 'Gómez' (Wilhelm Zaisser) was five years East German minister of state security before being disgraced in July 1953. General Staimer, as Colonel 'Richard', commander of the 11th Brigade, became chief of police in Leipzig. In the French Resistance there died many ex-volunteers of the International Brigade: Colonel Dumont, Pierre

George ('Colonel Fabien'), Colonel Putz, Pierre Rebière, Joseph Epstein (Colonel Gilles in the Resistance) and Major François Bernard; while Henri Tanguy – 'Colonel Rol-Tanguy' – the last commissar of the 14th Marseillaise Battalion, was among the liberators of Paris in 1944.[1] Marty was expelled from the communist party in France, before he died in 1955.

Of the surviving American members of the International Brigade, many fought in the Second World War. These men were, however, suspect in the eyes of the administration. It was not until late in the war that they were even permitted to go abroad.[2] After the war, in the era of McCarthy, any connection with the Spanish cause came to be regarded as subversive. The Abraham Lincoln Battalion itself was declared so in 1946, after their last reunion had been addressed by General Walter.[3] That body of veterans continued to be persecuted until the 1960s in a way which brought the liberal state into disrepute. Miles Sherover, however, the republican commercial agent in the US, was to be found in the 1970s prospering in Venezuela, and in Israel too.

Few of the Anglo-Saxon ex-combatants in Spain gained high positions in their own lands. The only British member of parliament in post-war years who fought in Spain was Robert Edwards, once a captain in the POUM Battalion in Aragon. Some of his comrades in the International Brigades, however, could for years be found in important positions in the trade-union movement. Will Paynter, for many years general-secretary of the mineworkers, for example, was British commissar at the base at Albacete.[4] Copeman left the communist party early in 1939. Later, he joined in turn the roman catholic church, the Labour party, and the Moral Re-armament

1. See Delperrie de Bayac, p. 390, for further news of French volunteers. Some were on the other side. Thus the Cagoulard, Henri Dupré, worked for the nazis and was shot in 1951.

2. *Volunteer for Liberty*. Introduction to bound edition of files (New York, 1946), p. 3.

3. See Taylor, pp. 113–15.

4. The role of Jack Jones and Bert Ramuelson, both ex-Brigade volunteers, in British trade-union politics in the 1970s is well known. Ramuelson, a Polish immigrant to Canada, fought with the Mackenzie-Papineau battalion. Jones was wounded at the Ebro.

Association. Jock Cunningham, after finding his military qualities rejected by the British army because of his rebellious past, wandered for many years over the face of Britain as a casual labourer. Frank Ryan, the Irish leader in the International Brigades, spent some years in a Spanish prison before being released to work for the Germans. He died after strange adventures in a tubercular sanatorium in Leipzig in 1941,[1] while Malcolm Dunbar, chief of staff of the 15th International Brigade, walked out to sea to a watery suicide in 1963.

*

Now, after many years, Spain itself enjoys a prosperity much higher than it did before the civil war. The death rate has fallen and the country enjoys an increase of real income at least double that of 1931–5.[2] But freedom of speech was for many years limited. Some lingered in prison for years for political reasons. For all its economic and social changes, Spain faces an uncertain political future. The civil war casts a long shadow over the present and even the future. Spain thus remains in travail. But freedom will one day come and, when it does, the Spaniards will at long last pay heed surely to Azaña who, with all his egotism, sectarianism and pessimism, nevertheless rose, in despair, to magnanimity and wisdom, which he did not attain when in power, and who closed a speech, at the height of the civil war, by saying:

> When the torch passes to other hands, to other men, to other generations, let them remember, if they ever feel their blood boil and the Spanish temper is once more infuriated with intolerance, hatred, and destruction, let them think of the dead, and listen to their lesson: the lesson of those who have bravely fallen in battle, generously fighting for a great ideal, and who now,

1. Evidence of Wing Commander Sir A. James, honorary first secretary in the British Embassy in Madrid. (Confirmed by the Ryan family. See too *The Irish Times*, 9 April 1975.)

2. These figures derive from *La Renta Nacional de España en 1959 y Avance del 1960* (Madrid, 1960). Agricultural production *per capita* was beginning to reach 1931–5 levels by 1958. Real agricultural wages were much the same in 1958 as in 1935. (See Tamames, *Estructura*, pp. 44–6.) The point of breakthrough for industry, however, when Spaniards were better off than before the war, was 1952–3.

protected by their maternal soil, feel no hate or rancour, and who send us, with the sparkling of their light, tranquil and remote as that of a star, the message of the eternal fatherland which says to all its sons: Peace, Pity, and Pardon.[1]

1. Manuel Azaña, at Barcelona, 18 July 1938. Miguel Maura, the most independent of politicians, described (*op. cit.*, p. 225) a tragic visit to Azaña in exile in a small village in Savoy: 'All had gone under for him during those most distressing days of the civil war. His obvious talent had gauged the pettiness of ambitions, the superficiality of dreams of power and of popularity, which perhaps once had been the aim of his ambitions, and his ideal. Disenchanted, sad, but, I repeat, with a judgment more clear and lucid than ever, he sketched for me a picture of what the last three terrible years had been morally for him. In that harsh moment, I had before me a man superior to all human praise, possessions, a humanity almost superhuman because of its disinterest and its renunciation of vanity and ambition.' Azaña was still barely sixty, but died the next year.

protected by their maternal soil, feel no hate or rancour, and who send us, with the sparkling of their light, tranquil and remote as that of a star, the message of the eternal fatherland which says to all its sons: Peace, Pity and Pardon.'[1]

1. Manuel Azaña at Barcelona, 18 July 1938. Miguel Maura, the most independent of politicians, described (*op. cit.*, p. 225) a tragic visit to Azaña in exile in a small village in Savoy: 'All had gone wrong for him during those most distressing days of the civil war. His obvious talent had gauged the pettiness of ambitions, the superficiality of dreams of power and of popularity, which perhaps once had been the aim of his ambitions, or his ideal. Disenchanted, sad, but, I repeat, with a judgement more clear and hard than ever, he sketched for me a picture of what the last three terrible years had been mentally for him. In that harsh moment I had before me a man superior to all human passions, possessing a humanity almost superhuman because of its disinterest and its renunciation of vanity and ambition.' Azaña was still barely sixty, but died the next year.

APPENDICES

Appendix One

The Spanish Bourbons and the Carlist Claim

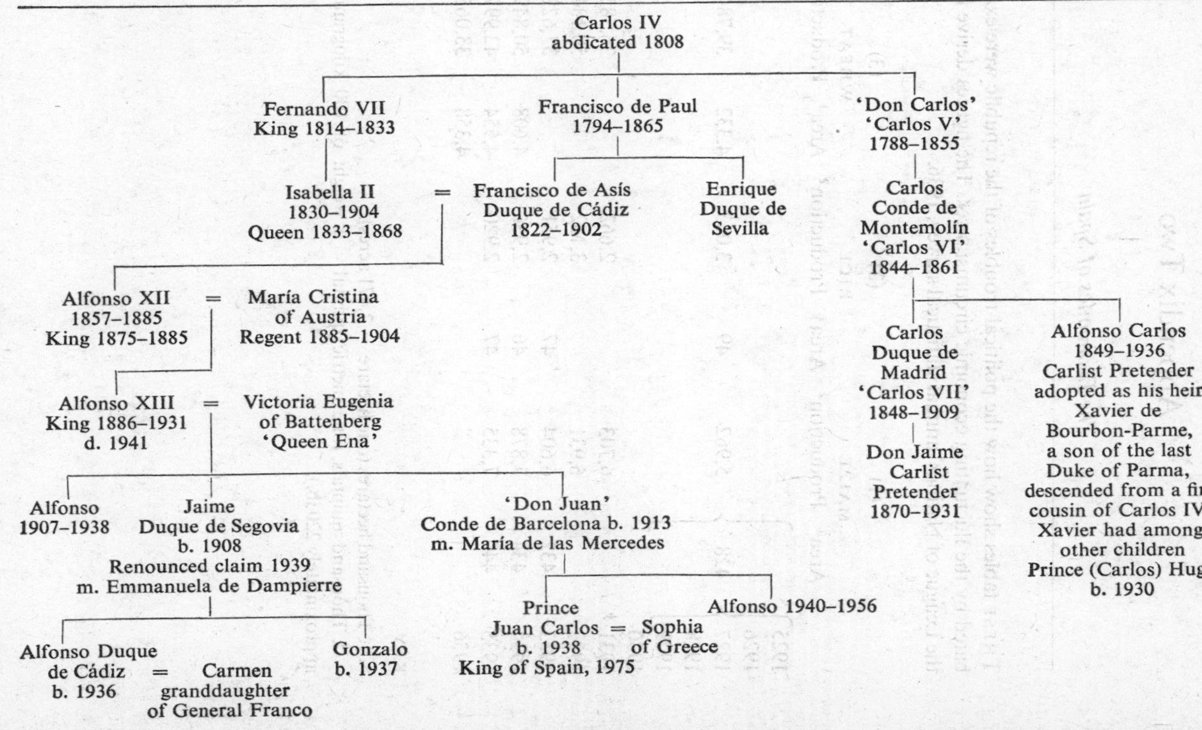

Carlos IV
abdicated 1808
Fernando VII
King 1814–1833
Francisco de Paul
1794–1865
'Don Carlos'
'Carlos V'
1788–1855
Isabella II
1830–1904
Queen 1833–1868
=
Francisco de Asís
Duque de Cádiz
1822–1902
Enrique
Duque de
Sevilla
Carlos
Conde de
Montemolín
'Carlos VI'
1844–1861
Alfonso XII
1857–1885
King 1875–1885
=
María Cristina
of Austria
Regent 1885–1904
Carlos
Duque de
Madrid
'Carlos VII'
1848–1909
Alfonso Carlos
1849–1936
Carlist Pretender
adopted as his heir
Xavier de
Bourbon-Parme,
a son of the last
Duke of Parma,
descended from a first
cousin of Carlos IV.
Xavier had among
other children
Prince (Carlos) Hugo
b. 1930
Alfonso XIII
King 1886–1931
d. 1941
=
Victoria Eugenia
of Battenberg
'Queen Ena'
Don Jaime
Carlist
Pretender
1870–1931
Alfonso
1907–1938
Jaime
Duque de Segovia
b. 1908
Renounced claim 1939
m. Emmanuela de Dampierre
'Don Juan'
Conde de Barcelona b. 1913
m. María de las Mercedes
Prince
Juan Carlos
b. 1938
King of Spain, 1975
=
Sophia
of Greece
Alfonso 1940–1956
Alfonso Duque
de Cádiz
b. 1936
=
Carmen
granddaughter
of General Franco
Gonzalo
b. 1937

Appendix Two

The Economics of Spain

THESE tables show how the political troubles of the republic were exacerbated by the fluctuating economic circumstances. The figures derive from the League of Nations' annual statistical survey, 1936.

	(1) MAIZE		(2) RICE		(3) WHEAT	
	Area[1]	Production[2]	Area[1]	Production[2]	Area[1]	Production[2]
1925–1929	428	5,962	49	3,063	4,332	39,784
1930						
1931		6,703		2,662		36,585
1932		6,931		3,182		50,134
1933	432	6,604	47	2,951		37,622
1934	434	7,878	46	2,936	4,608	50,849
1935	440	7,335	47	2,920	4,554	42,997
1936					4,358	33,065

KEY

1. Thousand hectares (one hectare = 2.471 acres).
2. Thousand quintals (one metric quintal = a weight of 100 kilogrammes, approximately 220 lb.).

	(4) SUGAR CANE Production	(5) WINE Production (*million hectolitres*)	(6) OLIVE OIL Production
1926	92	15.4	2,301
1927	99	27.6	6,656
1928	116	21.5	1,914
1929	134	24.3	6,601
1930	169	17.7	1,149
1931	176	18.6	3,511
1932	175	20.6	3,488
1933	157	19.2	3,102
1934	184	21.2	3,130
1935	198	16.0	4,398
1936	180		

	(7) WOOL Production (*1,000 metric tons*)	(8) SILK Raw	(8) SILK Artificial
1925			112
1926	38.6		
1927	38.1	83	143
1928	38.1		502
1929	37.6		900
1930	36.3		1,523
1931	34.9	44	1,639
1932	35.4	42	2,160
1933	35.4	38	2,295
1934	33.1	30	2,526
1935	29.9	34	2,722

	(9) SALT Production (1,000 metric tons)	(10) COAL Production (1,000 metric tons)
1927	979	6,563
1928	983	6,371
1929	1,079	7,108
1930	1,038	7,120
1931	889	7,091
1932	959	6,854
1933	929	5,999
1934	762	5,932
1935		7,017

	(11) COKE Production (1,000 metric tons)		(12) ELECTRICITY (million KWh)
	Ovens	Gasworks	
1926	832 (combined)		1,708
1927	714	161	1,849
1928	681	204	2,370
1929	768	216	2,433
1930	676	233	2,609
1931	503	248	2,681
1932	369	243	2,795
1933	427	248	3,066
1934	486	250	3,198

	(13) MANGANESE (1,000 metric tons)	(14) PYRITES (1,000 metric tons)	(15) LEAD ORE (1,000 metric tons)
1926	44.9	3,655	216
1927	36.9	3,611	196
1928	13.7	3,625	177
1929	17.9	3,867	181
1930	16.8	3,417	164
1931	17.9	2,594	151
1932	2.6	2,125	137
1933	2.8	2,219	115
1934	3.8	2,072	102
1935	1.3	2,286	104

	(16) LEAD (*1,000 metric tons*)	(17) ZINC ORE (*1,000 metric tons*)	(18) IRON ORE (*1,000 metric tons*)
1926	149		3,191
1927	144	132	4,972
1928	131	122	5,785
1929	143	145	6,559
1930	123	160	5,525
1931	110	112	3,190
1932	105	92	1,760
1933	88	95	1,815
1934	72	79	2,094
1935	63	83	2,633

	(19) STEEL (*1,000 metric tons*)	(20) COPPER ORE (*1,000 metric tons*)	(21) COPPER (*1,000 metric tons*)
1926	668	49.5	23.9
1927	671	50.7	28.7
1928	777	54.2	27.8
1929	1,003	63.7	28.5
1930	925	58.4	23.0
1931	645	54.0	25.7
1932	532	35.0	15.6
1933	507	44.0	17.3
1934	647	30.0	13.8
1935	580	30.0	10.8

	(22) NEW VESSELS LAUNCHED	(23) MOVEMENT OF SHIPPING (Entry) (*million tons*)	(Clear)
1926	26		
1927	23		
1928	12		
1929	37	18	27
1930	25	18	28
1931	48	17	23
1932	11	16	23
1933	18	15	23
1934	18	15	23
1935	3	16	22

	(24) IMPORT–EXPORT (Special Trade) (*metric tons*)		(25) IMPORT–EXPORT (Merchandise) (*million pesetas*)	
1926	4,127	7,088	2,148	1,605
1927	5,602	10,285	2,576	1,887
1928	6,634	11,432	3,004	2,118
1929	7,131	11,533	2,737	2,108
1930	5,862	9,955	2,447	2,300
1931	4,809	6,693	1,176	961
1932	5,133	5,180	975	738
1933	4,105	6,159	835	669
1934	4,892	6,587	855	611
1935	5,048	6,364	878	583

	(26) VALUE OF PESETA (*as percentage of gold parity* 1929)	(27) INDEX NO. OF SHARES AND INDUSTRIAL PRODUCTION (100 = 1929) SHARES		PRODUCTION
1929	100			
1930	79.5			98.6
1931	65.0	84.4		93.2
1932	54.8	65.1		88.4
1933	56.8	56.0		84.4
1934	55.3	57.6		85.5
1935	55.3	63.1[1]		86.9
		65.7	(1936 Jan.)	
		64.9	Feb.	
		60.9	March	
		59.9	April	
		58.6	May	
		58.1	June	
		57.8	July	

1. Highest figure during the republic = November 1935, when it was 67.3.

(28)

SAVINGS BANK DEPOSITS
(at end of each year)

	POST OFFICE	SAVINGS BANK
	(million pesetas but note change of value of peseta, Table 26)	
1928	239	1,608
1929	252	1,703
1930	265	1,882
1931	278	2,014
1932	298	2,158
1933	318	2,320
1934	338	3,778
1935	370	

Appendix Three

The International Brigades

Brigades	*Battalions*	*Principal initial composition*
11 (formed October 1936) (Hans Beimler, subsequently Thaelmann)	1 Edgar André	German
	2 Commune de Paris (later transferred to the 14th Brigade)	French–Belgian
	3 Dombrowsky (later transferred to 12th, 150th, and 13th Brigades)	Polish Hungarian Yugoslav
12 (formed November 1936) (Garibaldi)	1 Thaelmann (transferred to 11th)	German
	2 Garibaldi	Italian
	3 André Marty (Franco–Belgian) (transferred to 150th, 12th, and 14th)	French–Belgian
13 (formed December 1936)	1 Louise Michel (transferred to 14th)	French–Belgian
	2 Chapiaev (transferred to 129th Brigade)	Balkan
	3 Henri Vuillemin (transferred to 14th)	French
	4 Mickiewicz (Palafox)	Polish
14 (formed December 1936) (Marseillaise)	1 Nine Nations Battalion (transferred to Commune de Paris)	
	2 Domingo Germinal (mostly Spanish anarchist youth)	
	3 Henri Barbusse	French
	4 Pierre Brachet	French

15	(formed February 1937) (eventually Lincoln–Washington)	1 Dimitrov (transferred to 129th and then 13th)	Yugoslav
		2 British	British
		3 Lincoln, Washington, Mackenzie–Papineau	US
		4 Sixth of February (transferred to 14th)	French
150	(formed June–July 1937)	1 Rakosi	Hungarian
		2 (transferred to 13th)	
129		1 Mazaryk (attached to 45th Division)	Czechoslovak
		2 Dajakovich	Bulgarian
		3 Dimitrov	Yugoslav Albanian
	(in the 86th Brigade)	An international battalion commanded by Colonel Morandi	

Appendix Four

Exchange Rates to the £

	January 1930	*January 1936*	*January 1939*	*May 1939*
$	4.86	4.93	4.64	4.68
Franc	134.21	174.00	176.00	176.00
Lira	92.46	61.80	88.00	88.00
Peseta	25.22	36.00	100–200*	42.00
Mark	20.43	12.22	11.55	11.63

* Republican peseta

Source: *The Times*

Appendix Five

The Life and Death of the Peseta on the Tangier Exchange
(to the Pound Sterling)

	Republican Peseta	*Nationalist Peseta*	
1936			
June	36		
July (1st two weeks)	36		
	43		
August	55		
September	57		
October	63		
November	77		
December	116		
1937			
January	115	76	These were overprinted
February	114	76	
March	152	88	
April	134	122	
May	147	76	New notes henceforth
June	158	74	
July	217	81	
August	221	76	
September	246	86	
October	212	79	
November	226	85	
December	226	87	

1938	*New Valencia notes*	*Old Valencia notes*	*Nationalist Peseta*
January	425	219	91
February	510	306	95
March	530	353	102
April	533	246	97
May	708	272	108
June	635	254	110
July	635	291	113
August	681	288	126
September	917	338	145
October	983	346	144
November	1,083	379	173
December	1,462	450	172
1939			
January	2,132	488	177
February	2,391	448	126
March	13,538	386	129

Source: C. Delclaux, *La financiación de la cruzada*, University of Deusto thesis (1950, unpublished), p. 108.

Appendix Six

Catalan Industrial Production 1936–8

	1936	*1937*	*1938*
January	100	70	60
February	98	58	60
March	97	66	60
April	94	69	41
May	95	65	30
June	98	68	32
July	82	71	37
August	64	68	31
September	73	66	33
October	69	60	
November	63	53	
December	69	58	

General Index of Wholesale Prices, Barcelona 1936–1938 (100=1913)

	1936	*1937*	*1938*
January	168.8	223.7	434.4
February	168.2	244.4	457.7
March	167.2	266.5	524.5
April	169.1	294.3	530.1
May	170.6	297.6	547.9
June	171.9	303.7	551.6
July	174.7	315.8	554.2
August	178.9	322.7	554.2
September	183.1	342.7	556.9
October	194.4	358.8	562.3
November	202.9	375.4	564.4
December	209.6	389.1	564.7

Source: Bricall.

Appendix Seven

An Estimate of Foreign Intervention in the Spanish Civil War

IT will have been obvious from the text of this book that the efficacy and character of foreign help to one or other of the two Spains did not depend on numbers of aircraft or men. Nor did it depend on the amount that each side spent abroad or received from abroad as gifts (though the gifts were not enough to make very much difference: all the main intervening powers were paid in one way or another for their help in respect of war material).

A reckoning is nevertheless desirable. First, as regards money: broadly speaking, the republic spent everything which they had, and a little more. The nationalists had nothing to begin with, but obtained a lot on credit. The consequent bills were paid in full, though, in respect of Italy, final payment was not made till 1967.

Republican spending abroad was an intricate series of gambles, with Russia acting as the bank. The figures will probably never be sorted out until Russian archives are open. A tentative conclusion can, nevertheless, be reached. The Spanish gold reserve in July 1936 amounted to 700 tons of gold, much of it in coin (particularly sovereigns). This treasure was in the hands of the government, and was worth $788 million (£162 million).[1] At the end of the war, all this had been spent, except for $48 million deposited in Mont de Marsan in France; while in addition to the gold actually sent to Russia – about $500 million worth (1,582 million gold pesetas or £100 million) – the Soviet government claimed that they were owed another $50 million.[2] Spanish exports from the republic probably brought in another $100 million, which was also consumed, largely on war supplies, and largely spent in Russia. Finally, the republic sent abroad a large quantity of confiscated jewels, gold, silver and other valuables, gaining thereby $14 million in the U S alone in 1938.

1. On the basis of tons being metric tonnes, represented by 32,150 troy ounces fine. Converted on the basis of $4.8666 to the dollar, and the early 1936 rate for the peseta.

2. *Pravda*, 5 April 1957. In 1939, the story was current that the republic owed Russia $120 million (see L. Fischer, p. 346). It will be remembered that Hidalgo de Cisneros obtained $85 million worth of arms in late 1938 after Stalin had told him that the republic's credit was exhausted. See above, p. 869. Apparently, $35 million was paid soon, hence the outstanding bill of $50 million.

All in all, it would seem likely that the republic may have spent abroad something over $900 million between 1936 and 1939, most of it on arms and most of it in Russia.[1]

The main suppliers to the nationalists were of course the Germans and the Italians, though the help of the Texas Oil Company and other oil companies should be taken into acount: the above Russian figures, after all, include the bills for Russian oil delivered to Spain.

German military aid to Franco was valued at 540 million reichsmarks, that is, £46¼ or $225 million (1,955 million pesetas by the 1939 exchange of 42¼ pesetas to the pound). Of this total, 88 million reichsmarks were spent on salaries and expenses, for which Germany did not ask the Spaniards to pay; 124 million was spent on direct deliveries to Spain; and 354 million spent on the Condor Legion.[2] The Spaniards later agreed to accept a debt of 378 million reichsmarks, along with a bill for compensation to Germans who suffered losses in Spain of 45 million reichsmarks. These debts were paid off in full between 1939 and 1945 by minerals, vegetables, fruit and other goods delivered to Germany in those years, by the costs of the Blue Division (a unit mainly of falangists sent to the Russian front in 1942 under General Muñoz Grandes), and by various settlements between Spain and the allies in 1945. Of the exports sent by Spain to Germany during the civil war itself, 48 per cent was food and vegetables, and only 27 per cent minerals.[3]

Italian aid to Franco was estimated by Ciano in 1940 at 14,000 million lire (£157¼ million or $766 million – 6,646 million pesetas).[4] But in the

1. This figure is obtained by considering the total gold reserve of $788 million, deducting the $48 million left in France, adding the $50 million allegedly owed to Russia, adding also the value of exports and allowing something for the valuables exported. It is not wholly clear how the money was physically spent, but Delclaux (*La financiación de la cruzada*, p. 75) gives this list of recipients of moneys from the Bank of Spain up till 1 January 1938: to Russia, 663 million pesetas; Mont de Marsan, 350 million pesetas; Fernando Shaw, Alfredo Palacios, Antonio Cruz Marín, all in London, respectively 11, 16 and 34 million pesetas; Gordón Ordás, the ambassador in Mexico, 64 million pesetas; de los Ríos, the ambassador in Washington, 175 million; Araquistain and Albornoz, both ambassadors in Paris, 194 and 210 million respectively; Mendez Aspe, the head of the Treasury, 400 million; and anonymous (!), 100 million.

2. Figures in *G D*, p. 892. See also *G D*, vol. XI, pp. 329–30. See also Whealey in Carr, *The Republic*, p. 219, and Angel Viñas, 'Los costos de la guerra civil' in *Actualidad Económica*, August 1972.

3. Southworth, *Antifalange*, p. 178.

4. To Hitler in conversation (*G D*, p. 933). These thousand millions are of course billions in the US.

end Italy sent a bill for only about half that – 7,500 million lire (£84¼ million, $410 million, or 3,560 million pesetas) which corresponds with other estimates in the course of the war. After further haggling, the Italian and Spanish governments agreed in May 1940 on a figure of 5,000 million lire (£56¼ million, $273½ million, and 2,373½ million pesetas), the payment to be made over twenty-five years, beginning in 1942.[1] The payments were to be by instalments, beginning with 80 million lire in 1942, and ending with 300 million lire in 1967, while the debt carried an interest at the beginning of ¼ per cent, and at the end of 4 per cent.[2] These payments were made in full, the Italian government after 1945 being as good a creditor as its fascist predecessor, even when Togliatti and the communists were in the administration. No doubt the Italians were much the most generous of those who intervened in Spain, since the bill which was settled by Franco did not take into account a good deal of military activity by the Italian armed forces which was not charged for. Hence possibly Ciano's originally much larger estimate, though probably that was inflated.

Nationalist expenses abroad should also take into account about $10 million spent in the US on oil, and perhaps another $10 million in that country and elsewhere on items such as buses or medical supplies all of which, of course, have a military use.

Total nationalist spending abroad, all of it on credit, must thus have been about $635 million if the figure of 7,500 million lire is considered as representing a reasonable estimate of Italian aid rather than the sum eventually paid. If 14,000 million lire were accepted, then the nationalists would be said to have received $981 million.

It is naturally tempting to place these figures beside that of republican spending of $900 million and conclude that international involvement in Spain was at least as great on the side of the government as on that of the rebels – or even greater.[3] Such an account would, however, be misleading. The equation put in those simple terms does not take account of the differences between the Russian, German and Italian economies, nor the differences between the economies of the two Spains. It is not at all clear whether the Russians gave anything like value for money, and indeed the notion of value in considering Russian prices for items such as tanks and aircraft is somewhat farcical. The huge discrepancy in different estimates for what Italy made available merely points out the fact that this sort of sum will always leave room for speculation. Russian transport costs were high. Nor can the value of a gold reserve be precisely rendered in terms of ordinary money, particularly not one which was then one of the largest

1. Agreement of 8 May 1940. 2. Delclaux, p. 65.
3. This is done by Jesús Salas in his *Intervención extranjera*, p. 510.

in the world. A more useful reckoning is that which is made possible by a rough knowledge of the numbers of different pieces of equipment, though even there a simple enumeration of numbers of aircraft does not tell anything like the whole story.

Nevertheless it is useful to know that Spain received from abroad something between $1,425 million and $1,900 million. It might also be pointed out that those who backed their side with credit – Germany and Italy – had that much more incentive to go on with their support of all kinds in order to recover payment eventually, while those who sold assistance for cash – Russia – could at least be content that they had received money for value. Some would also add that those who insisted on payment may have doubted the likely success of their side, whilst those on extended credit were confident of it.[1]

AID TO THE NATIONALISTS

Germany

German strength in Spain reached about 10,000 at its maximum, though 14,000 veterans attended the Condor Legion parade in Berlin in May 1939. The Germans who helped the nationalists probably exceeded 16,000, of whom many were civilians and instructors.[2] About 300 Germans died in Spain. The Condor Legion numbered 5,000 men. This important, well-led, experimental tank and aircraft unit was accompanied by thirty anti-tank companies. Colonel von Thoma, who commanded the tank corps, told the Americans in 1945 that he took part in 192 tank engagements during the war.[3] These Panzer Mark I tanks were not effective against the larger Russian ones in 1936 and 1937. The total number sent to Spain was probably about 200. The German shipments were delivered in about 180 separate voyages. The Germans sent about 600 aircraft to Spain including 136 Messerschmitts 109, 125 Heinkels 51, 93 Heinkels 111 and 63 Junkers 52.[4]

1. I am particularly grateful to Peter Robeson, of Baring Brothers, who kindly helped me on these sums and their interpretation.

2. Manfred Merkes, *Die deutsche Politik im Spanischen Burgerkrieg*, 2nd edition (Bonn, 1969) has a total of 15,990 men sent to Spain including non-military personnel but leaving out those who went in mid-1937, for which he obtained no data.

3. Liddell Hart, *The Other Side of the Hill*, p. 126.

4. Actually 593, according to Jesús Salas's figures in his *Intervención extranjera*, p. 439. These figures take precedence over his own and his brother's previous estimates (in e.g. Palacio Atard, p. 201) or other estimates, e.g. Gomá or De la Cierva. The heavy Junkers 52 (bombers) and small Heinkels 51 (fighters) were the

Any reckoning of German help to Franco should consider also the help given in military academies, signals equipment and training made available, as well as the advice given on a hundred small but crucial matters of military organization. The 88 millimetre anti-aircraft gun was also a major contribution by Germany and probably stopped the republic making use of their aerial superiority in the spring of 1937.

Italy

Italian forces in Spain at their maximum numbered between 40,000 and 50,000 and perhaps a total of 75,000 went to Spain altogether.[1] The Italians lost more than 4,000 dead in Spain,[2] and perhaps a quarter of their effective military equipment there too.[3] For Italy sent to Spain about 660 aircraft, of which the most important were the 350 Fiat CR.32 fighters and the 100 Savoias 79. There were also some 70 Romeos 37 and 64 Savoias 81.[4] Perhaps 150 Italian tanks were sent to Spain, all either 3½ ton Fiat Ansaldos, armed with 7 millimetre machine guns, capable of a speed of twenty-five miles an hour, with two men on board; or heavier flame throwers, carrying 125 litres of petrol and able to throw them 60–70 yards.[5]

---

mainstay of the early days; the fast Messerschmitts 109 (fighters) were used in 1937. The medium-range Heinkel 111 was Germany's most modern bomber. Other aircraft bought from Germany included 31 Dorniers 17 (a bomber in its day faster than most of the world's fighters), 33 HEs 45, and 20 HEs 46. J. Salas (*La guerra*, p. 209) tells us that five models of the famous Stuka (Junkers 87) went to Spain in 1937 but were not much used. One was in action at Teruel in February 1938 and one was apparently shot down in January 1939 (García Lacalle, p. 485).

1. In the spring of 1937 there were some 35,000 Italians in the CTV, perhaps 10,000 in the Legion, the *Flechas* and in the legionary air force. See Payne, *Politics*, p. 327; and Alcofar, *CTV*, p. 189. Higher figures were given at the time, because of the confusion caused by the units of Spaniards led by Italian officers and NCOs.

2. Alcofar, *CTV*, p. 189. 3,785 are buried at the monastery of San Antonio, Saragossa, 372 in the cemetery of Puerto del Escudo, and there were some other isolated deaths. Cf. Belforte, p. 228, and Conforti, p. 416. But there were also some Italian airmen and others killed who were not part of the CTV.

3. Estimate of Denis Mack Smith, *Mussolini as a Military Leader* (Reading, 1973), p. 9.

4. R. Salas's figure (*op. cit.*, p. 3420) and J. Salas's *Intervención extranjera*, p. 435, which I prefer to the announcement by the Stefani News Agency in 1941, qu. *New York Times* 28 February 1941 (763 aircraft). Higher figures for the number of Fiat CR.32s have been given.

5. Stefani figures; Alcofar (1972) criticizes (p. 190).

Other equipment included about 800 pieces of artillery (the excellent 65/17 millimetre 1916 model),[1] which seem to have been all left in Spain. The Italian artillery was well directed by officers experienced in the First World War, headed by General Ettore Manca. The Italians probably also dispatched some 1,414 aircraft motors, 1,672 tons of bombs, 9 million rounds of ammunition, 10,000 machine-guns and automatic rifles, 240,000 rifles, seven million rounds of artillery ammunition, and 7,660 motor vehicles.[2] According to estimates in the Italian press in 1939, Italian pilots flew 135,265 hours in the war, participated in 5,318 air raids, hit 224 ships, and engaged in 266 aerial combats, in which they brought down 903 aeroplanes. 5,699 officers and men and 312 civilians of the Italian air force were also allegedly engaged at different times. Ninety-one Italian warships and submarines are believed to have taken part in the civil war. The latter are said to have sunk 72,800 tons of shipping. Italian engineering, signalling and even cryptography did their bit, including schools of 'Radio Transmission' in Valladolid, Miranda de Ebro and Palencia.[3] There were two large Italian military hospitals at Valladolid and at Saragossa, each with 1,000 beds or over, and some smaller hospitals, with three hospital trains. The general equipment and organization of the Italian units, bad in 1937, recovered in 1938 and the rations and conditions were probably superior to those of the Spaniards.[4]

Portugal, Ireland, France etc.

Other foreign governmental assistance included that of Portugal whose help was, at the beginning of the war at least, incalculable, for geographical rather than military reasons. Several thousand Portuguese volunteers fought in the Foreign Legion and in some other units.[5] Six hundred Irishmen fought for the nationalists under General O'Duffy. Their losses were

1. Cantalupo and Belforte (p. 164) speak of 800 pieces. See Whealey in Carr, *op. cit.*, p. 221; *Forze armate*, June 1939; and comment by R. Salas, vol. II, p. 2370, and J. Salas, *Intervención extranjera*, p. 490.

2. Stefani News Agency in 1941. See slightly lower figures in J. Salas, *Intervención extranjera*, p. 490.

3. Alcofar, *CTV*, p. 191.

4. Belforte, p. 183.

5. See Martínez Bande, *La lucha*, p. 110 fn. 122; De la Cierva, *Leyenda y tragedia de las brigadas internacionales* (Madrid, 1973), p. 101; and Kay, p. 92. Apparently, the 'Viriato' Brigade of Portuguese volunteers offered by General Raúl Esteves, one of the founders of Salazar's revolution, never set off as a separate unit but even so the Portuguese who did go were called 'Viriatos'. In a previous edition I spoke of 20,000 volunteers from Portugal: this probably was an exaggeration. For the experiences of a Portuguese 'flier' with Franco, see José Sepúlveda

negligible. Some right-wing Frenchmen volunteered for the *requetés* and the Legion – accorded the right to wear a thin tricolour ribbon across their shoulder strap, and commanded by a Colonel Courcier, of the Spahis[1] – as did some Latin Americans and White Russian exiles and others. The numbers could not have been more than 1,000 at most. Few Anglo-Saxons fought for Franco.[2]

Other help to the Nationalists

At least 75,000 or so Moroccan 'volunteers', Spain's sepoys, fought for Franco and played a very prominent part in the early days.[3] The nationalists also bought some fifty or so aircraft from countries other than Germany or Italy (a few Dragons and Fockers).

AID TO THE REPUBLIC

Russia

The republic bought about 1,000 aircraft from Russia, perhaps 300 from other sources, principally France.[4] Of these, almost 400 were Chato

Velloso, *Páginas do diario de un aviador na guerra de España* (Lisbon, 1972). General Spinola, famous in 1974 in Portugal, acted only as an observer in a mission; he never fought.

1. See above, p. 768.

2. These seem to have included only four Americans (the 'electrical genius' Stanley Baker, the pilot Patriarca, shot down over the republic in 1936, the son of Arthur Kroch of the *New York Times*, and Captain Guy Stuart Castle) and perhaps twelve Englishmen (Captains Fitzpatrick and Nangle, who served in the Legion; Peter Kemp; a certain Patrick Campbell; Rupert Bellville, who fought with the falangists in Jerez in 1936; two deserters from the Royal Marines, 'Stewart' and 'Little'; two other deserters, from HMS *Barham*, Wilson, who emigrated to Canada, and Yarlett, who died of wounds; and some other Englishmen who fought in Andalusia in the Legion). Half of these seem to have been at least partially Irish.

3. The British consul general in Tangier estimated 70,000 Moroccans had gone to the war by June 1938. (See Halstead's article on Beigbeder in *The Historian*, November 1974 and De la Cierva, *Historia ilustrada*, vol. I, p. 472).

4. These are Jesús Salas's figures on p. 429 of his *Intervención extranjera* and pp. 3418–19 of vol. IV of his brother's book. The commander of the Katiuskas, Colonel Leocadio Mendiola, now in Mexico, says that there were only 62 of them and the commander of the Natashas, Major José Romero, says that there were only 93 of them. García Lacalle, in a letter to me, says that the overall figure was nearer 500, of which 300 were fighters, 220 bombers. However, I accept the Salas figures on the basis of their documentation.

fighters, almost 300 Moscas, with perhaps 100 Katiuska bombers, 60 Rasantes and 113 Natasha bombers. From France, the principal items were the 42 Dewoitines 371, the 40 Potez 54 and the 15 March Blochs 210.[1] Total purchases of aircraft from France must have been anywhere between 100 and 150. Other purchases included 40 Aeros 101, 10 Letovs, 14 Vultees A1, 11 Bristol Bulldogs, 20 De Havilland Dragons, and 28 Koolhovens FK51 from Holland, and a squadron of 40 Grumman fighters from the US: with good radios, otherwise unsatisfactory for war;[2] and certain aircraft engines enabling aircraft to fly at a great height. Total aircraft from countries other than Russia may have been about 320, giving a total of 1,320 aircraft in all.

It is less easy to make estimates of republican purchases of other items of equipment. According to the German military attaché's reports from Istanbul on the basis of reports from agents in Istanbul, in some 164 shipments (71 Spanish, 39 British, 34 Russian, 17 Greek and 4 other), between September 1936 and March 1938, Russia sent by sea some 242 aircraft, 703 cannon, 27 anti-aircraft guns, 731 tanks, 1,386 lorries, 69,200 tons of war material and 29,125 tons of ammunition. In addition, 920 officers and men came that way, apparently, together with at least 28,000 tons of petrol and 32,000 of crude oil, 4,650 tons of lubricants, together with some other items, such as 450 tons of clothing, 325 of medical stores, 100 rifle machine-guns, 500 Howitzers, and 187 tractors.[3] Doubtless there were further shipments, though the blockade made the Mediterranean very difficult or even impossible in the next months. As for land shipments, the nationalist headquarters made various estimates: one, of October 1938, suggested that between July 1936 and July 1938, some 200 cannon, 200 tanks, 3,247 machine-guns, 4,000 lorries, 47 artillery units, 4,565 tons of ammunition, 9,579 vehicles and 14,889 tons of fuel had come in.[4] This aid was supplemented later. It came, no doubt, from the Comintern's arms purchase agencies, the republic's assessment commission in Paris and directly from Russia. In quantity, the republic's foreign supplies were probably as great

1. Many other figures can be found even in R. Salas in Palacio Atard, p. 200. The republic built or assembled Moscas and Chatos in Barcelona; the nationalists found 200 of these in Barcelona, 100 in Alicante. See also Sanchís, p. 35; Gomá, p. 58; De la Cierva, *Historia ilustrada*, vol. II, p. 313. William Green and John Fricker, *The Air Forces of the World* (New York, 1958), p. 249, thought that Russia sent 550 I 15s, 475 I 16s, 210 2B-2s, 130 R-5 reconnaissance and 40 R2.

2. Letter from Colonel García Lacalle, July 1964. One at least of these Grummans did good service as a pioneer in military aerial photography.

3. See D. C. Watt, 'Soviet Aid to the Republic' in *The Slavonic and East European Review*, June 1960.

4. *The International Brigades*, p. 123; cf. too Alpert, p. 309.

as those of the nationalists (in some items greater), but the quality was various. Furthermore, much was wasted or left behind on the battlefield. The variety of calibration of the rifles pinpointed the disadvantages of getting help from so many different places. The nationalist forces had a regiment of Russian tanks by the end of the war, along with a quantity of Russian machine-guns. Both sides were short of lorries; lack of transport may have been the deciding factor in the ultimate failure of the republic's attack on the Ebro front.

The tanks made available by Russia to Spain probably numbered 900, the pieces of artillery 1,550, the armoured cars 300, the machine-guns 15,000, automatic rifles 30,000, mortars 15,000, rifles 500,000, lorries 8,000, along with 4 million artillery projectiles, 1,000 million cartridges and 1,500 tons of gunpowder.[1] The Russian tanks were mostly T-26s, some TB-5s, both being much heavier, better armed, faster and more formidable though less manoeuvrable than the German or Italian tanks available to the nationalists. But they benefited the republic less than they should have done.

The International Brigades

The total number of foreigners who fought for the Spanish republic was probably about 40,000, about 35,000 being in the International Brigades, which probably never exceeded 18,000 at any one time.[2] There could

1. I have taken these estimates from J. Salas's *Intervención extranjera* (p. 476), and from *Solidaridad de los pueblos con la república española* (Moscow, 1972), though I think the figures of artillery may well be high.

2. Wintringham, p. 37; Rolfe, p. 8. Vittorio Vidali (Carlos Contreras) has given the figure as 35,000 (*Il Contemporaneo*, vol. IV, July–August 1961, p. 284). Soviet army archives, qu. Payne, *Spanish Revolution*, gives 31,237. The analysis in the useful study by Andreu Castells, *Las brigadas*, is impressive; it leaves us with 59,380, but the evidence is weak: where does the writer's figure of 15,400 Frenchmen come from? Why trust a Russian book better than an Italian one for Italian participation? The Spanish foreign ministry's pamphlet, *The International Brigades* (published 1952), though presenting a great deal of interesting material, exaggerated with an estimate of 125,000 – a figure (a guess?) which seems first to have appeared in Lizón Gadea, *Brigadas internacionales en España* (Madrid, 1940), p. 11. R. Salas, vol. II, p.21 44, also argues, implausibly, that the figures were 120,000. De la Cierva, *Historia ilustrada*, vol. I, p .404, has 80,000. La Pasionaria and her colleagues (*Guerra*, vol. II, p. 234) says 30,000 to 35,000 and Delperrie de Bayac (p. 386) also has 35,000. Perhaps Salas and De la Cierva went wrong in including Spanish volunteers for the Brigades as if they were foreigners.

hardly have been less than another 10,000 doctors, nurses, engineers, and others from abroad in addition. The largest national group of volunteers were the 10,000 or so French, of whom 1,000 were killed.[1] Germany and Austria together contributed perhaps 5,000, of whom 2,000 died.[2] The number of Poles, including Ukrainians in what after 1945 became part of Russia, may also have been about 5,000.[3] Italy came next with 3,350.[4] The United States contributed about 2,800. Of these, about 900 were killed.[5] There were about 2,000 British volunteers, of whom about 500 were killed and 1,200 wounded – a high percentage;[6] about 1,000 Canadian volunteers, 1,500 Yugoslavs,[7] 1,000 Hungarians, 1,500 Czechs, and 1,000 Scandinavians, of whom 500 were Swedes.[8] Seventy-six Swiss were killed.[9] The other volunteers came from what was claimed to be fifty-three

1. *L'Epopée de l'Espagne* (Paris, 1957), p. 80. This booklet names the number of French members of the Brigades as 8,500. But one of its authors told me that he distrusted the sources of his own information and that the figure should have been higher.

2. Alfred Kantorowicz, *Spanisches Tagebuch* (Berlin, 1948), p. 15.

3. This was Maciej Techniczek's figure to Castells, with which I agree.

4. Togliatti, in his history of the Italian communist party, says the figure was 3,354, of which 3,108 were combatants. 1,819 were communists, 310 socialists, republicans or members of the 'Justice and Liberty', and 1,096 non-party but 'mostly recruited from our organizations'. Togliatti adds that about 600 Italians were killed (356 communists), 2,000 wounded, and 100 taken prisoner – presumably shot (Togliatti, *Le Parti communiste italien*, Paris, 1961, p. 102). The discrepancy between Togliatti's and the Russian Military Archives' figure, mentioned above, suggests the unreliability of the latter. Perhaps the Russians cut out the non-communists. Social origins suggested of figures known: 1,471 industrial workers, particularly from metallurgical industries, only 254 peasants, 69 professional people, including 19 lawyers. But of 1,412 combatants the social origins were not known. Sociological categories of this sort are anyway misleading. 102 combatants from Italy in Spain were over sixty, most were between thirty and forty-five years old. Considering only communists, the most 'Garibaldine' were Venetians: 309 from Venetia Euganea, 225 from Venetia Giulia. 145 were Tuscans. See Spriano, vol. III, pp. 227–9.

5. Rolfe, p. 7.

6. Rust, p. 210. Neal Wood, *Communism and British Intellectuals* (London, 1959), p. 56, however, says that there were 2,762 British volunteers, 1,762 wounded and 543 killed. He may be right, but no one else would give such exact figures.

7. Tito, in his remarks to *Life* (28 April 1952). Dedijer, p. 108, gives the Yugoslav figure as 1,500 volunteers, 300 wounded, 'almost half killed', and 350 interned in France after the collapse of Catalonia.

8. *Clarté* (Stockholm), No. 2 of 1956, p. 2.

9. Wullschleger, pp. 39–42.

nations.[1] Ninety Mexicans probably fought in Spain.[2] As to Russians in Spain, the maximum at one time was 700, the total number being probably between 2,000 and 3,000.[3] Perhaps 1,000 Russian pilots flew in Spain.[4]

One should also not ignore the 47 million roubles' worth of 'gifts' from Russian workers in August 1936 and a fund reaching some $10 million from private and other organizations abroad. If one is to be pedantic, one should also remember that such services as the International Brigades and the voluntary medical missions presented no expenses to speak of in respect of foreign exchange. Over two million dollars' worth of aid was collected by American relief bodies.

Mexico sent 20,000 rifles, 28 million cartridges and 8 batteries with some lorries and aircraft. This was not a gift however: it was paid for even though much of this equipment was second-rate.

1. Longo, p. 34. A recent study by I. Persiguer, *Participación de polacos antifascistas en la guerra de España*, in I. Maisky, *Problemas de la historia de España* (Moscow, 1971) speaks of 30,000 Slavs in Spain. I believe this to be an exaggeration.

2. Lois Elwyn Smith, p. 200.

3. See *Istoriya velikoy otechestvennoy voyny Sovyetskogo Soyuza 1941–5*, vol. I, pp. 112–13; this gave a figure of 557 Russian 'volunteers' as being in Spain presumably sometime in 1937, of whom 23 were military '*asesores*', 49 instructors, 29 gunners, 141 pilots, 107 tank crews, 29 naval personnel, 73 interpreters and 109 'technicians', signallers, and doctors. The number of Russian NKVD 'specialists' remains a mystery. But Largo told Azaña in 1937 that there were then 781 Russians in Spain (Azaña, vol. III, p. 477). See also Hidalgo de Cisneros to Bolloten, in Bolloten, p. 125. Lister says 2,500 (*op. cit.*, p. 265). R. Salas, vol. II, pp. 2151–3, says over 20,000. See Alpert, pp. 287–9. Jesús Salas (*Intervención extranjera*), p. 453, guesses 12,000 without documentary evidence. De la Cierva, *Historia ilustrada*, vol. II, p. 314, has 5,000. La Pasionaria and her colleagues (*Guerra y revolución en España 1936–1939*, vol. II, p. 235) say 2,000, never more than 600–800 at a time.

4. Jesús Salas, *La guerra*, p. 286.

APPENDIX SEVEN

SUMMARY

Probable figures for foreign intervention in the civil war.

	Men	Aircraft	Tanks	Artillery (pieces)
Nationalists				
From Germany	*c.* 17,000	*c.* 600	200	1,000 (estimate)
„ Italy	*c.* 75,000	*c.* 660	150	1,000
„ Others	*c.* 75,000 (Moroccans)	4		
		c. 1,264	*c.* 350	*c.* 2,000
Republicans				
From Russia	*c.* 2,000–3,000	1,000	900	1,550
„ Others	35,000 (International Brigades) 5,000 (Other) 10,000 (Non-combatant volunteers from abroad)	320		
		c. 1,320	*c.* 900	*c.* 1,550

Appendix Eight

Guernica

(i) *Letter about Guernica from the British Consul, R. C. Stevenson, addressed to the British Ambassador, Sir Henry Chilton at Hendaye.*

British Consulate,
Bilbao,
28th April 1937.

Dear Sir Henry,

On landing at Bermeo yesterday I was told about the destruction of Guernica. I went at once to have a look at the place and to my amazement found that the township normally of some five thousand inhabitants, since the September influx of refugees about ten thousand, was almost completely destroyed. Nine houses in ten are beyond reconstruction. Many were still burning and fresh fires were breaking out here and there, the result of incendiary bombs which owing to some fault had not exploded on impact the day before and were doing so, at the time of my visit, under falling beams and masonry. The casualties cannot be ascertained and probably never will, accurately. Some estimates put the figure at one thousand, others at over three thousand. An inhabitant who went through it all, told me that at about 4 p.m. three machines appeared overhead and dropped H.E. and incendiary bombs. They disappeared and ten minutes later a fresh lot of five or six machines came and so on for several hours, until after seven. All told he estimates the number of planes at fifty. After two or three visits panic seized the population. Men, women and children poured out of Guernica and ran up the bare hillsides. There they were mercilessly machine gunned, though with little effect. They spent the night in the open gazing at their burning city. I saw many men and women erring through the streets searching in the wreckage of their houses for the bodies of their dear ones.

In the afternoon I saw Monzón who appeared stunned by the catastrophe. He asked me what could be done for the women and children of Bilbao. I told him that evacuation on the scale suggested, he mentioned a quarter of a million, was beyond the task of man where so little comprehension was shown abroad, and where there was no organization extant for tackling and carrying out such a scheme. I told him what was felt in France over the refugee problem. I mentioned Russians, Poles, Italians, Germans and Jews all of whom had inundated France in hundreds of thousands during the past two decades. Moreover, the scheme depended on Salamanca which commanded the seas and Salamanca had not yet replied to the suggestion put to it by you that the liner *Havana* and the yacht *Goiseko Izarra* should be left unmolested on their proposed voyages between Bilbao and French ports.[1] He saw the reason of it all, but nevertheless asked me if I could not think of some solution. To this I replied that I had sought one during several hours, but that I could only suggest surrender. This he said was impossible. I conjured before his eyes a picture of Bilbao destroyed in the same way with no earthly chance for more than a fraction of the population, today about half a million, escaping destruction. No, and again no. I told him I sympathized with him, that his judgement was dimmed by passion, that resistance against overwhelming odds was useless, that I would put the members of the Government, senior officials and leaders of the Basque Nationalist Party on a destroyer. But of no avail. He said surrender was impossible whatever the consequences. Today I covered the whole ground again with the President, but found there the same resistance to the idea of surrender. The President asked me whether I thought there was a possibility of the British and French Governments intervening. I said that if there were intervention I could not conceive it on any basis other than surrender. You will have read his appeal to the civilized world in the press.

I feel I have gone far enough in this regard. I can obviously not persuade them to surrender, at least not at present. I dare say, human nature being what it is, my suggestion will find an echo some time, if only then it is not too late. How in the event of an evacuation I shall proceed, I have not thought out yet. With bombers overhead, with extremist elements on the war path, with thousands of men, women and children running amok, all wanting passage, with the impossibility of keeping secret the plans for such an evacuation, I cannot see how it is to be carried out successfully.

That the morale here has gone down there cannot be any doubt. My friend, Eguía, the 'First Lord of the Basque Admiralty' but without a seat in the Cabinet, told me today that he feared the home front would break up if the bombardments of civilian centres and the military reverses continued.[2] I cannot but think he is right. After all, there are three political groups in Bilbao, the Basque Nationalists, the Left Wingers, and the sup-

1. This belonged to the Basque millionaire, Ramón de la Sota. Built at Troon in 1904, its 1,266 tons made it one of the largest private yachts afloat. For de la Sota, see below, p. 988.

2. J. de Eguía, head of the Basque navy.

porters of Franco. The first will die or be shot according to whether they fight or surrender; the second will either run away, to Santander or Gijón, or surrender in the hopes of saving their necks, as the rebels will exhaust their capacity for executions on the Basques; the third may form a 'fifth column'. Which of these possibilities will materialize is in the lap of the gods. Probably a bit of each, and there is no saying how the rebels will act when they find themselves at the open gates of a major city. Eguía told me further that rumours of an attempt of the extremists to seize power were current and growing in insistence. You will thus see that the situation here is decidedly critical and that deterioration may set in any day.

The official denials of Salamanca respecting the bombardment of Guernica lend colour to the belief that whatever the physical courage of the rebels they will not have the moral courage to carry out their threat to raze Bilbao. Many people build fresh hopes on this slender chance. It is also argued that a Bilbao, destroyed, will bring Franco no nearer victory as he then will be without the industrial plants he so much needs.

All the foregoing is just a series of impressions of which I have had so many during the past thirty-six hours that I cannot form an opinion. I have, though, strong views on the question of evacuation of women and children, even if it is only a few thousand and if anything can be done in this respect before it is too late, so much the better. Is there any hope of a favourable reply from Salamanca? Both Casterán and I feel that something ought to be done to bring about realization of the *Havana* project without any conditions of hostages, leaving it to us to get out a reasonable percentage of womenfolk of rebels.

I am being pestered night and day by people wishing to leave. The public had come to look on British destroyers as a public utility and are quite incredulous when I tell them it's all over. I have, however, arranged, with the President's permission, to put on board our destroyer twelve people, Señora de la Sota, who herself belongs to a Royalist family, and her children and the Aburtos, who are half Basque, half rebel. Ramón de la Sota won't leave, notwithstanding my entreaties. I told him that he was at the head of the list of 'personas fichadas' and that his failure to get out whilst the going is good might cost him his head, for I cannot conceive that the rebels will take into account that for the past nine months his house has been full of political refugees, who through his influence have not only been saved from imprisonment and possibly death, but also got passports and permits to leave in our destroyers.

I hope this has not been too long.

Yours sincerely,

(Signed) R. C. STEVENSON

(ii) *The Foreign Office minutes on this paper deserve to be reproduced too:*

This is an interesting account.

Mr Stevenson decided to use his influence to persuade the Basques to surrender: I don't think that there is any risk that the Basques will have thought that HMG were trying to exercise pressure: it was clearly a personal matter.

J. A. MALCOLM,
5/5.

A very interesting account of Mr Stevenson's visit to Guernica and of his conversations with Basque authorities. On another paper I had suggested that Mr Stevenson might have been going too far in suggesting surrender to the Basque authorities and of promising ahead to evacuate the Gov[t].

On Sir G. Mounsey's instructions I telephoned to Hendaye this morning in order to tell Mr Stevenson not to repeat his advice to the Basques. Mr Stevenson had, however, left for Bilbao this morning. Sir H. Chilton told me that he had made it quite clear to Mr Stevenson last night that he should not repeat his advice, and that the latter quite understood the position.

Is it necessary, in this case, to telegraph to Mr Stevenson direct?

D. HOWARD,
5/5.

I spoke in the same sense to Mr Stevenson on the telephone as he had in mind some arrangement about the Basque Gov[t]. surrendering and our agreeing to take them on board our ships. I told him he must not pursue this any further. It was liable to lead us into all manner of complications.

We had better send a telegram to confirm our views, for record purposes, though I have no doubt Mr Stevenson understands our wishes now.

G. M. (SIR GEORGE MOUNSEY)
5.5.37.

I agree.

A. E. (ANTHONY EDEN)
May 6.

Lord Cranborne
Sir R. Vansittart,

I am not sure whether it has been sufficiently clear in the minutes on these papers what is actually proposed about any evacuation of the Basque Gov[t].

What we wish to make quite clear to Mr Stevenson is that he should on no account make any arrangements with the Basque Gov[t]. for giving them refuge on a British ship, in advance of any emergency occurring.

On the other hand we would wish to let our naval authorities at Bilbao have the same discretion as they have received at Barcelona and elsewhere in Spain: viz. that if and when an emergency does occur, and members of the Basque Govt. whose lives are in imminent danger actually seek refuge on one of our ships, they should not be refused access.

This can surely hardly be construed into intervention on our part. It is not pre-arranged – as is the despatch of food-ships and evacuation of civilians – and it amounts to an act of humanity to individuals whose lives would otherwise be sacrificed. If they were brought to this country they would of course be asked to give certain assurances as to their neutral behaviour while here.

G. M. (SIR GEORGE MOUNSEY)
7.5.37.

This seems all right, if there is no pre-arrangement. But I do feel it is intensely important not to give the German and Italian Govts an excuse for saying that we have intervened, and with all deference to Sir G. Mounsey, I see a difference between protecting Br. ships, food or otherwise, *outside* Spanish territorial waters or of evacuating Basque women and children, and taking on to Br. warships a Govt. which has actually been in charge of the conduct of the war and has been defeated. This comes, to my mind, far nearer intervention. S. of S. shld see.

C. (LORD CRANBORNE)
7.5.

I agree.

G.
8/5

The evacuation of the Basque govt., if such a situation arises, is going to be a very difficult and delicate thing. This dft. telegram commits us to nothing and can of course go. But what if Mr Stevenson is faced with an emergency application? It is clear that little is now needed to make Signor Mussolini throw non-intervention to the winds. We cannot obviously go in and fetch the Basque govt. out. But if they get out of territorial waters on their own and reach a British ship on the high sea, is that ship to refuse to take them? I think it cannot refuse – though that may be enough for Mussolini. I suggest however that this sh[d]. be Mr Stevenson's general attitude.

R. V. (SIR ROBERT VANSITTART)
May 10.

Bibliographical Note

The Spanish Civil War, and its origins, has by now a large bibliography. See J. García Durán, *Bibliografía de la guerra civil española* (Montevideo, 1965), or Ricardo de la Cierva *et al.*, *Bibliografía sobre la guerra de España* (Madrid, 1968). Neither are, or could be, complete; and both already betray their age. Some errors of the latter are pointed out by Herbert Southworth, 'Los Bibliófobos', *Cuadernos de Ruedo Ibérico*, No. 2. A good bibliographical essay on modern Spanish history is contained in Raymond Carr, *Spain 1808–1939* (Oxford, 1966). Other bibliographical material can be found in the series of *Cuadernos bibliográficos de la guerra de España 1936–1939* (published by the University of Madrid, 1966 onwards).

I. COLLECTIONS OF DOCUMENTS

The most important texts of the Republic are contained in María Carmen García Nieto and Javier M. Donézar, *Bases documentales de la España contemporánea*, vols. 8 and 9, La Segunda República (Madrid, 1974). Texts for 1936 can be seen in Ricardo de la Cierva, *Los documentos de la primavera trágica* (Madrid, 1967). For the war, there is Fernando Díaz-Plaja, *La guerra de España en sus documentos*, 2nd ed. (Barcelona, 1966).

II. INTRODUCTORY

(1) The best history of modern Spain is that of Carr (see above). For an admirable introduction to the twentieth century, see Gerald Brenan, *The Spanish Labyrinth* (Cambridge, 1943). Other general works include Manuel Tuñón de Lara, *La España del siglo XX* (Paris, 1966), and Antonio Ramos Oliviera, *Politics, Economics and Men of Modern Spain* (London, 1946); both emphasize economics. The first half of Salvador de Madariaga's *Spain* (London, 1946, and subsequent editions) remains useful.

(2) The best political history of the Restoration is Melchor Fernández Almagro, *Historia política de la España contemporánea*, 2 volumes (Madrid, 1959). For the Institución Libre de Enseñanza, see the book of that name by Vicente Cacho (Madrid, 1962). For Alfonso XIII, see Julián Cortés Cavanillas's *Alfonso XIII* (Madrid, 1959). For the war in Morocco, see David Woolman, *Rebels in the Rif* (London, 1969). For 1909, see Joan Ullman, *The Tragic Week* (Cambridge, Massachusetts, 1968). For

the dictatorship of Primo de Rivera, see Juan Velarde Fuertes, *Política económica de la dictadura* (Madrid, 1968): there is no satisfactory political study nor even a biography. For the Army throughout the period, see Stanley Payne's *Politics and the Military in Modern Spain* (Stanford, 1967).

(3) A useful general analysis of constitutional issues is Carlos Rama, *La crisis española del siglo XX* (Buenos Aires, 1960).

III. THE EARLY HISTORY OF WORKING CLASS MOVEMENTS

(1) For anarchism, see Casimiro Martí's excellent *Los orígenes del anarquismo en Barcelona* (Barcelona, 1959); Josep Termes, *Anarquismo y sindicalismo en España* (Barcelona, 1972); Anselmo Lorenzo, *El proletariado militante* (Mexico, 1940, and other editions), a personal account: José Díaz del Moral's famous *Historia de las agitaciones campesinas andaluzas – Córdoba* (Madrid, 1929); the first volume of José Peirats, *La CNT – la revolución española* (Toulouse, 1951); and Diego Abad de Santillán, *Contribución a la historia del movimiento obrero español*, 2 volumes (Mexico, 1962). Useful or interesting information on anarchism can also be found in the work of Joan Ullman (see above, section II (2)); in Joaquín Romero Maura's meticulous study of the Barcelona working class movements in the early years of the century, *La rosa del fuego* (Barcelona, 1974); and dotted about the three volumes of Maximiniano García Venero, *Historia de las Internacionales en España* (Madrid, 1956). Brenan (see above, section II (1)) is excellent on Andalusian anarchism, and such works as Angel Pestaña, *Lo que aprendí en la vida* (Madrid, 1932), Manuel Cruells, *Salvador Seguí, el Noi del Sucre* (Barcelona, 1974), and Abel Paz, *Durruti: le peuple en armes* (Paris, 1972), add personal views. The best introduction to anarchism as an international phenomenon is James Joll, *The Anarchists* (London, 1964). See also Joaquín Romero's article 'Anarchism To-day: the Spanish Case' (*Government and Opposition*, vol. 5, No. 4, Autumn, 1970).

(2) Socialism is less well served, though see Gerald Meaker's excellent *The Revolutionary Left in Spain, 1914–1923* (Stanford, 1974), Julián Zugazagoitia's *Pablo Iglesias* (Madrid, 1926), the slight *Mis recuerdos* of Largo Caballero (Mexico, 1954), and Andrés Saborit's episodic *Julián Besteiro* (Buenos Aires, 1967).

(3) The unimportant history of the communists before 1936 is well introduced by Meaker (see above, section III (2)) and chronicled at enormous length in E. Comín Colomer, *Historia del partido comunista en España*,

3 volumes (Madrid, 1965). See also José Bullejos, *Europa entre dos guerras* (Mexico, 1944), Enrique Matorras, *El comunismo en España* (Madrid, 1935), V. Reguengo, *Guerra sin frentes* (Madrid, 1954), and the appropriate chapters in Jules Humbert-Droz, *Mémoires*, 3 volumes (Neuchâtel, 1969–1972).

(4) For a general survey, see Stanley Payne's uneven *The Spanish Revolution* (New York, 1970).

IV. THE REPUBLIC

(1) Among comprehensive studies, Joaquín Arrarás's *Historia de la segunda república española*, 4 volumes (Madrid, 1956–1964), is the most detailed; it favours the Right. The first half of Gabriel Jackson's *The Spanish Republic and the Civil War* (Princeton, 1965) is a warm-hearted and well-written account, favouring the liberals. José Plá's *Historia de la segunda república española*, 4 volumes (Barcelona, 1940–1941), can still be read with profit. The essays in Raymond Carr's *The Republic and the Civil War in Spain* (London, 1971) include interesting revisionist arguments.

(2) The best study of the fall of the monarchy and the formation of the republican movement is in S. Ben-Ami's *The Origins of the Second Republic* (Oxford Ph.D, 1974).

(3) Jean Bécarud's *La Deuxième République Espagnole* (Paris, 1962) is good on elections. See also on that theme José Venegas, *Las elecciones del Frente Popular* (Buenos Aires, 1942), and a meticulous modern study, Javier Tusell's *Las elecciones del Frente Popular*, 2 volumes (Madrid, 1971). There is, too, Manuel Ramírez Jiménez, *Los grupos de presión en la segunda república española* (Madrid, 1969). There is no study of foreign policy other than the *Memorias (1921–1936)* of Salvador de Madariaga (Madrid, 1974).

(4) The economic history of the republic can be studied in Alberto Balcells *Crisis económica y agitación social en Cataluña 1930–1936* (Barcelona, 1971), and in the first half of Ramón Tamames's *La república, la era de Franco* (Madrid, 1973) – a provocative work of political economy.

(5) Edward Malefakis's *Agrarian Reform and Peasant Revolution in Spain* (New Haven, 1970), is far the best study of agrarian problems. There is much illuminating material in three studies of three very different villages: Julian Pitt-Rivers's *People of the Sierra* (London, 1954), Gerald Brenan's *South from Granada* (London, 1957), and Carmelo Lison Tolosana's *Belmonte de los Caballeros* (Oxford, 1966).

(6) The liberal challenge is badly served by historians or memoir-writers, apart from Manuel Azaña's unique diary contained in volumes III and IV of his *Obras completas* (Mexico, 1966), and in the stolen pages edited by Joaquín Arrarás in 1938 as *Memorias íntimas de Azaña* (Madrid, 1939). Two lives of Azaña also help a little: Cipriano de Rivas-Cherif's *Retrato de un desconocido* (Mexico, 1961), and Frank Sedwick's *The Tragedy of Manuel Azaña and the Fate of the Spanish Republic* (Ohio, 1963). See also Miguel Maura's *Así cayó Alfonso XIII* . . . (Mexico, 1962), and Marcelino Domingo's *Mi experiencia del poder* (Madrid, 1934).

(7) The best general study of the Spanish Right is that by Richard Robinson, *The Origins of Franco's Spain* (Newton Abbot, 1970), and there are useful memoirs by José María Gil Robles (*No fue posible la paz*, Barcelona, 1968) and Joaquín Chapaprieta (*La paz fue posible*, Barcelona, 1971). Alejandro Lerroux's *La pequeña historia* (Madrid, 1963) is not trustworthy. The most informative life of Calvo Sotelo is that by Aurelio Joaniquet (Santander, 1939). The monarchists are studied in Santiago Galindo Herrera, *Los partidos monárquicos bajo la segunda república* (Madrid, 1956) and, much more critically, by Paul Preston in several analyses (e.g. *The Spanish Right under the Second Republic*, Reading, 1971, and 'The Moderate Right and the Undermining of the Second Spanish Republic', *European Studies Review*, vol. III, no. 4 (1973)). Monarchist nostalgia can be seen in José María Pemán, *Mis almuerzos con gente importante* (Madrid, 1970), or Juan Ignacio Luca de Tena, *Mis amigos muertos* (Barcelona, 1971). Javier Tusell gives a methodical study of the CEDA in his *Historia de la democracia cristiana en España*, 2 volumes (Madrid, 1974). See also José Gutiérrez Ravé's *Antonio Goicoechea* (Madrid, 1965).

(8) The Carlist revival is represented by Luis Redondo and Juan de Zavala's *El requeté* (Barcelona, 1957), and Jaime del Burgo's *Conspiración y guerra civil* (Madrid, 1970). For a balanced general study, see Martin Blinkhorn, *Carlism and Crisis in Spain* (Cambridge, 1975).

(9) The best history of the Falange is the work of that name by Stanley Payne (Stanford, 1961). Also worth exploring are David Jato, *La rebelión de los estudiantes* (Madrid, 1953), Felipe Ximénez de Sandoval's life of José Antonio – the *Biografía apasionada* (Barcelona, 1941) – Francisco Bravo's *Historia de la Falange Española de las JONS* (Madrid, 1940), and *Hacia la historia de la Falange* by Sancho Dávila and Julián Pemartín (Jerez, 1938). José Antonio's complete works have appeared in various editions, e.g. *Obras completas* (Madrid, 1942). (For the Falange in the war, see below, section VII (1).)

(10) For the working class movements under the republic, there is little to add to the list in section III (1) to (3) above. On anarchism, the works of Peirats, Abad de Santillán, García Venero, Brenan and Paz might be supplemented by John Brademas's *Anarcosindicalismo y revolución en España 1930–1937* (Barcelona, 1974). Prieto's various essays of journalism (in *Convulsiones de España*, 3 volumes (Mexico, 1967–1969), *De mi vida*, 2 volumes (Mexico, 1965–1970) or *Palabras al viento* (Mexico, 1942)), give the moderate socialist attitude.

(11) Regional problems under the republic have been inadequately studied. Unlike the struggle for autonomy, the working of the Catalan *Generalidad* has not received much attention. E. Allison Peers's *Catalonia Infelix* (London, 1937), though old, is still the only introduction in English. There is an unsatisfactory life of Companys by Angel Ossorio y Gallardo: *Vida y sacrificio de Companys* (Buenos Aires, 1943). See for general background García Venero's *Historia del nacionalismo catalán* (Madrid, 1967) and Jesús Pabón's *Cambó*, 3 volumes (Barcelona, 1952–1969), the best political biography in Spanish. The Lliga has received extensive treatment in Isidre Molas's *Lliga Catalana* (Barcelona, 1972). Balcells (see above, in section IV (4)) deals in detail with the economy. As for Basque nationalism, Stanley Payne's *El nacionalismo vasco* (Barcelona, 1974) is a good, short, rather sceptical, introduction, which replaces García Venero's *Historia del nacionalismo vasco* (Madrid, 1945), though that contains useful information.

(12) The church under the republic is dealt with competently by José Mariano Sánchez in *Reform and Reaction* (Chapel Hill, 1964), and more passionately by Juan de Iturralde in *El catolicismo y la cruzada de Franco* (Bayonne, 1955). See also Arxiu Vidal i Barraquer, *Església i estat durant la segona república espanyola 1931–1936*, vol. I (Montserrat, 1971). There is, of course, material on this subject in Gil Robles's, and others', memoirs.

V. THE CIVIL WAR AS A WHOLE

General works include the second half of Gabriel Jackson's book (see section IV (1) above) and of Raymond Carr's collection. A general history from a Trotskyist angle is Pierre Broué and Émile Témime's *La Révolution et la guerre d'Espagne* (Paris, 1961). Julián Zugazagoitia's *Historia de la guerra en España* (Buenos Aires, 1940, subsequent reprints) is a vivid account by a Socialist minister. More critical of the republic is Ricardo de la Cierva's handsome but uneven *Historia ilustrada de la guerra civil española*, 2 volumes (Barcelona, 1970). The same author's general history of the war has not as yet (1976) reached the stage of combat. Robert

Brasillach's *Histoire de la guerre d'Espagne* (Paris, 1939) is a period piece only. The enormous *Historia de la cruzada española*, 35 folios (Madrid, 1940–1943), directed by Joaquín Arrarás, is useful on the rising. Guillermo Cabanellas's *La guerra de mil días* (Barcelona, 1973) is a well-written if prickly account by a socialist son of General Miguel Cabanellas, whose part is here well presented.

VI. MILITARY, NAVAL AND AIR ASPECTS

(1) There is as yet no adequate study of the creation and character of the nationalist army. Numerous autobiographies and memoirs have, however, been written by or about commanders in that force: among the first, General Kindelán's *Mis cuadernos de guerra* (Madrid, 1945), General García Valiño's *Guerra de liberación española* (Madrid, 1949) and General Martínez de Campos's *Ayer, 1931–1953* (Madrid, 1970). Among the second are José María Pemán's life of General Varela, *Un soldado en la historia* (Cádiz, 1954), the biography of Mola by his ADC, Colonel José María Iribarren (*El general Mola*, Madrid, 1945), and numerous lives of Franco. Of the latter, the most balanced is J. W. D. Trythall's *Franco* (London, 1970) and the liveliest that by 'Luis Ramírez' (*Francisco Franco*, Paris, 1964). Brian Crozier's *Franco* (London, 1967) is uncritical. There are some interesting insights in George Hills's *Franco* (also London, 1967). The life of Yagüe by Juan José Calleja (*Yagüe, un corazón al rojo*, Barcelona, 1963) avoids all the difficult subjects.

(2) The monumental study of Ramón Salas Larrazábal on the Republican Army (*Historia del ejército popular de la republica*, 4 volumes, Madrid, 1974) is a mine of information and publishes many interesting documents in the appendices. More manageable and less *parti pris* is Michael Alpert's *The Republican Army in the Spanish Civil War* (Reading Ph.D., 1973). Memoirs by republican officers are legion: for example, General Vicente Rojo's *Alerta los pueblos* (Buenos Aires, 1939), *Así fue la defensa de Madrid* (Mexico, 1967) and *España heroica* (Buenos Aires, 1942); Julián Henríquez Caubín's *La batalla del Ebro* (Mexico, 1944); José Martín Blázquez's well-written *I Helped to Build an Army* (London, 1939); Colonel Casado's unreliable tale of his *coup d'état*, *The Last Days of Madrid* (London, 1939); and the testimony of five senior communist officers – Enrique Lister's *Nuestra guerra* (Paris, 1969), Juan Modesto's *Soy del quinto regimiento* (Paris, 1969), Antonio Cordón's *Trayectoria* (Paris, 1971), Manuel Tagüeña's excellent *Testimonio de dos guerras* (Mexico, 1973), and Ignacio Hidalgo de Cisneros's *Memorias*, 2 volumes (Paris, 1964).

(3) The two earliest military histories, Manuel Aznar's *Historia militar de la guerra de España* (Madrid, 1940) and Luis María de Lojendio's *Operaciones militares de la guerra de España* (Barcelona, 1940) are still useful for the nationalist army, but much the most satisfactory general military history is now that contained in the numerous volumes edited by Colonel Martínez Bande for the Servicio Histórico Militar (Madrid, 1968 onwards), even though they are excessively discreet about many aspects of nationalist decision-making. There is also much interesting information in Salas Larrazábal (see (2) above).

(4) Naval matters are covered encyclopedically in José Luis Alcofar Nassaes's *Las fuerzas navales en la guerra civil española* (Barcelona, 1971). See also, for the nationalist operations, Admiral Cervera's *Memorias de guerra* (Madrid, 1968) and Admiral Moreno's *La guerra en el mar* (Barcelona, 1959). A republican naval memoir is Bruno Alonso's *La flota republicana y la guerra civil de España* (Mexico, 1944) and a suggestive journalistic account can be found in Manuel Benavides's *La escuadra la mandan los cabos* (Mexico, 1944). The Russian contribution to the republic's naval presence is well summarized in Admiral Kuznetsov's contribution to *Bajo la bandera de la España republicana* (Moscow, probably about 1970).

(5) The best history of the war in the air is Jesús Salas Larrazábal's *La guerra de España desde el aire* (Barcelona, 1969). See also General José Gomá's *La guerra en el aire* (Barcelona, 1958). A republican pilot's view is contained in Colonel Andrés García Lacalle's *Mitos y verdades* (Mexico, 1974). Less comprehensive is F. Tarazona's *Sangre en el cielo* (Mexico, 1960). The Escuadra España receives epic treatment in Malraux's wonderful novel, *L'Espoir* (Paris, 1937). Other still interesting memoirs by republican fliers are the books by Oloff de Wet, *Cardboard Crucifix* (Edinburgh and London, 1938), and F. G. Tinker, *Some Still Live* (New York, 1938). Nationalist memoirs include those of J. García Morato's episodic *Guerra en el aire* (Madrid, 1940), Juan Antonio Ansaldo's *¿Para qué?* (Buenos Aires, 1951), and José Larios's *Combat over Spain* (London, 1966).

Technical information can be found in Salvador Rello's four little volumes, *La aviación en la guerra de España* (Madrid, 1969–1971), or Miguel Sanchís's *Alas rojas sobre España* (Madrid, 1956).

There are many accounts by both German and Italian fliers for Franco (for example, Max von Hoyos, *Pedros y Pablos*, Munich, 1941) and some by Russians (see the memoirs in *Bajo la bandera*, mentioned in (4) above). See too Jean Gisclon, *Des avions et des hommes* (Paris, 1969).

(6) The military conspiracy and the Rising are described exhaustingly in Arrarás's *La cruzada* (mentioned in V above). See for this also Antonio Lizarza's *Memorias de la conspiración* (Pamplona, 1954), Felipe Bertrán Güell's *Preparación y desarrollo del alzamiento nacional* (Valladolid, 1939) and the account by Mola's chauffeur, B. Félix Maíz, *Alzamiento en España* (Pamplona, 1952). The first volume of De la Cierva's *Historia* (see V above) draws together many of the threads and there is useful comment in the works earlier cited of Robinson, Gil Robles and Stanley Payne (*Politics and the Military*). Luis Bolín's *Spain, the Vital Years* (London, 1967) contains evidence on Franco's activities. The work of del Burgo (see above, section IV (8)) is interesting on Carlist attitudes. See García Venero's *Madrid, julio 1936* (Madrid, 1973) for the débâcle there. Luis Romero's *Tres dias de julio* (Barcelona, 1967) is a clever attempt to recreate the first days of the war.

(7) Separate battles are described in the books of Martínez Bande (see above, para. (3)). See, however, also Robert Colodny, *The Struggle for Madrid* (New York, 1958) for the fighting round the capital; Esmond Romilly, *Boadilla* (new edition, London, 1971) for an account of that battle; Olao Conforti, *Guadalajara* (Milan, 1967); R. Casas de la Vega, *Brunete* (Madrid, 1967) and *Teruel* (Madrid, 1975); Luis María Mezquida, *La batalla del Ebro*, 2 volumes (Tarragona, 1963), and the same author's *La batalla del Segre* (Tarragona, 1972), and Henríquez Caubín's book on the Ebro previously cited (see para. (2) above). For Guernica, see Gordon Thomas and Max Morgan Witts, *Guernica* (New York, 1975), an exciting account which, however, leaves some questions unanswered. Colonel Martínez Bande's *Los cien ûltimos dias de la república* (Barcelona, 1972) throws light on nationalist intelligence at the end of the war, as does José Bertrán y Musitu's *Experiencias de los servicios de información del nordeste de España* (*SIFNE*) (Madrid, 1940). Cecil Eby's *The Siege of the Alcazar* (London, 1966) is the most balanced account of that incident. Julio de Urrutia, *El cerro de los héroes* (Madrid, 1965) is a careful though passionate account of Santa María de la Cabeza. Luis Romero's *Desastre en Cartagena* (Madrid, 1971) tells the tale of the revolt in that city in March 1939.

VII. NATIONALIST SPAIN

(1) The political history of nationalist Spain awaits its historian and he, the papers. In the meantime, some information can be derived from the various lives of Franco and Ramón Serrano Súñer's *Entre Hendaya y*

Gibraltar (Madrid, 1947). Hedilla's life as told to, and edited by, Maximiniano García Venero (*Falange*, Paris, 1967), is interesting, especially when read in conjunction with Herbert Southworth's commentary *Antifalange* (Paris, 1967). Hedilla's subsequent correction of García Venero has appeared as *Testimonio de Manuel Hedilla* (Barcelona, 1973). Dionisio Ridruejo's *Escrito en España* (Buenos Aires, 1962) has passing references to the war. On the Falange, the work of Payne (see section IV (9) above) remains the best introduction. The works previously cited of Ansaldo (see section VI (5) above), del Burgo (section IV (8)) and Bolín (section VI (6) above), are helpful.

(2) Far the best social history of nationalist Spain is Rafael Abella's *La vida cotidiana en la España Nacional* (Barcelona, 1973). Some contemporary journalistic accounts throw light: for example, Eddy Bauer, *Rouge et or* (Neuchâtel, 1939).

(3) The repression in nationalist Spain is amply chronicled in Antonio Bahamonde's *Memories of a Spanish Nationalist* (London, 1939), on Seville, Antonio Ruiz Vilaplana's *Burgos Justice* (New York, 1938), Jean Flory's *La Galice sous la botte de Franco* (Paris, 1938), *Franco's Rule* (London, 1937), and *El clero vasco frente a la cruzada franquista* (Bayonne, 1966).

(4) The economic side of the 'crusade' can be found in Carlos Delclaux's thesis *La financiación de la cruzada* (Deusto, thesis unpublished,) and J. R. Hubbard's article, 'How Franco Financed His War', *The Journal of Modern History* (December, 1953). See also, if you can find it, Juan Sardá's 'El Banco de España (1931–1962)' in *El Banco de España* (Madrid, 1970), and Glenn T. Harper, *German Economic Policy in Spain* (The Hague, 1967).

(5) The victors sought to prove the legality of their rebellion in *Dictamen de la comisión sobre la ilegitimidad de poderes actuantes en el 18 de julio de 1936* (Barcelona, 1939).

(6) Post-war repression is covered in *Catalunya sota el règim franquista* (Paris, 1973), Melquesidez Rodríguez Chaos, *24 años de la cárcel* (Paris, 1968), Miguel García, *I was Franco's Prisoner* (London, 1972), Arturo Bray, *La España del brazo en alto* (Buenos Aires, 1943) and also Ronald Fraser, *In Hiding* (London, 1972).

VIII. THE POLITICS OF THE REPUBLICANS DURING THE CIVIL WAR

(1) For general studies of the republic, see Diego Sevilla Andrés, *Historia política de la zona roja* (Madrid, 1954) and Burnett Bolloten, *The Grand*

Camouflage (London, 1961). For a personal but informed view at the time, see Franz Borkenau, *The Spanish Cockpit* (London, 1937).

(2) The vanishing centre is not well covered. See, however, the diaries of Azaña previously cited (section IV (6)), the autobiography of Angel Ossorio y Gallardo, *La España de mi vida* (Buenos Aires, 1941) and Azaña's famous dialogue, *La velada en Benicarló* (in volume III of his *Obras completas*, several other editions). Casado's memoir (section VI (2) above) expresses the frustration of a loyal army officer.

(3) The socialists also lack a detailed analysis. But see the works of Largo Caballero, Zugazagoitia, Prieto and Saborit (on Besteiro) previously cited. Julio Alvarez del Vayo wrote several autobiographies, of which the most useful is *Freedom's Battle* (New York, 1940). See also Justo Martínez Amutio, *Chantaje a un pueblo* (Madrid, 1974), and the last volume of Antonio Barea's *The Forging of a Rebel* (New York, 1946).

(4) On the anarchist experience in the civil war, see Diego Abad de Santillán, *Por qué perdimos la guerra* (Buenos Aires, 1940) and José García Pradas, *Cómo terminó la guerra de España* (Buenos Aires, 1940) – both personal accounts. The most useful survey is that in José Peirats, *La CNT en la revolución española*, 3 volumes (Toulouse, 1951–1953), which has much interesting documentation. On the 'politics' of anarchism, see César Lorenzo's *Les Anarchistes espagnols et le pouvoir* (Paris, 1969) and Vernon Richards's *Lessons of the Spanish Revolution* (London, 1953). On the revolution, see F. Mintz's *L'Autogestion dans l'Espagne révolutionnaire* (Paris, 1970) and Gaston Leval's *L'Espagne libertaire* (Paris, 1971). See also Cipriano Mera's *Guerra, exilio y cárcel de un anareco-sindicalista* (Paris, 1976), 'El movimiento libertario español', supplement, *Cuadernos de Ruedo Ibérico* (Paris, 1974), Albert Pérez Baró, *Trenta mesos de colectivisme a Catalunya* (Barcelona, 1974), and Ricardo Sanz, *Los que fuimos a Madrid* (Toulouse, 1969). The previously cited books of Brademas, Paz (section III (1)), Borkenau and Bolloten are helpful and Juan Peiró's *Perull a la reraguarda* (Mataró, 1936) testifies to anarchist realism at the time. A recent work by Carlos Semprún Maura, *Révolution et contre-révolution en Catalogne* (Tours, 1974) makes some good points.

(5) The communists have, or have provided themselves with, an ample bibliography. The two most serious historical analyses are D. T. Cattell, *Communism and the Spanish Civil War* (Berkeley, 1955), and Burnett Bolloten, *The Grand Camouflage* (London, 1961). Communist memoirs include the books of La Pasionaria (Dolores Ibarruri), *They Shall Not Pass* (London, 1967), Hidalgo de Cisneros, Lister, Cordón and Modesto (cited

in section VI (2) above). Some information can also be found in Santiago Carrillo's *Demain Espagne*, a conversation with Régis Debray and Max Gallo (Paris, 1974). Ex-communists who have criticized their old comrades are Jesús Hernández, *Yo, ministro de Stalin en España* (Madrid, 1954), Enrique Castro Delgado, *Hombres made in Moscú* (Barcelona, 1965) and El Campesino (Valentín González), whose books are *Comunista en España y anti-Stalinista en la URSS* (Mexico, 1952) and *Listen, Comrades* (London, 1952). Manuel Tagüeña's book (cited above section VI (2)) approaches the theme with serenity. Criticism of or comment on the communists in the civil war can be found everywhere in political studies or memoirs of the civil war. See in particular the books of Barea, Martínez Amutio and Borkenau (cited above, in (1) and (3) and also see the paragraph below on Russia (IX (7)).

(6) Catalonia. Bricall's *Política económica de la Generalitat* (Barcelona, 1970) is a major contribution to the economic history of the war. Most of the anarchist accounts have valuable information, in particular the books previously cited of Semprún Maura, Abad de Santillán and Pérez Baró. Manuel Benavides's *Guerra y revolución en Cataluña* (Mexico, 1946) is a vivid account favourable to the PSUC. See now Carlos Pi Sunyer, *La república y la guerra* (Mexico, 1975) and Frederic Escofet, who gives a good account of 19 to 20 July 1936 in *Al servei de Catalunya i de la república*, 2 volumes (Paris, 1973). George Orwell's *Homage to Catalonia* (London, 1938) brilliantly evokes the scene in May 1937. See also the life of Companys by Ossorio y Gallardo (cited section IV (11) above). Azaña's diaries have ample comment. For right wing views of Catalonia under the republic, see F. La Cruz, *El alzamiento la revolución y el terror en Barcelona* (Barcelona, 1943) and José María Fontana, *Los catalanes en la guerra de España* (Madrid, 1951).

(7) On the Basques, G. L. Steer's *The Tree of Gernika* (London, 1938) is an exciting account of the war in Vizcaya, very pro-Basque. A. de Lizarra's *Los vascos y la república española* (Buenos Aires, 1944) gives the views of Manuel de Irujo. José Antonio Aguirre's *De Guernica a Nueva York pasando por Berlin* (Buenos Aires, 1944) does not help much. A military study is Sancho de Beurko, *Gudaris, recuerdos de guerra* (Buenos Aires, 1956). See also Stanley Payne's history.

(8) For the POUM, see George Orwell, *Homage to Catalonia* (London, 1938), Joaquín Maurín's *Revolución y contrarevolución en España* (second edition, Paris, 1966) and Julián Gorkin's *Caníbales políticos* (Mexico, 1947). A new version of Gorkin's story had appeared as *El proceso de Moscú en Barcelona* (Barcelona, 1974). A recent essay is Andrés Suárez's

El proceso contra el POUM (Paris, 1974). Katia Landau's *Le Stalinisme en Espagne* (Paris, 1938) exposes the communist persecution of the POUM. Grandizo Munis's *Jalones de derrota* (Mexico, 1948) is a well-written view of the failure of the revolution, from a roughly *POUMista* angle. See also Manuel Casanova, *L'Espagne livrée* (reprinted Paris, 1971).

(9) The appalling circumstances in which many lived behind the lines are vividly described in such works as *The General Cause* (a report on the mass law suit which followed the war undertaken by the victors, Madrid, 1943, and reprinted). See too Father Montero's book, *La persecución religiosa en España* (Madrid, 1961), Pilar Millán Astray's *Cautivas: 32 meses en las prisiones rojas* (Madrid, 1940), Agustín de Foxá's novel, *Madrid, de Corte a checa* (San Sebastián, 1938), the trial reported in the book entitled *Por qué hice las chekas de Barcelona* (Madrid, 1940) by Rafael López Chacón, and some of the POUM's attacks on the communists (e.g. the works cited by Julián Gorkín, Katia Landau and Manuel Buenacasa).

(10) The economic history of the Republic demands more careful study than hitherto made. But see the works of Bricall, Semprún Maura, Mintz, Delclaux, Sardá and Stanley Payne (*The Spanish Revolution*) cited above.

IX. INTERNATIONAL IMPLICATIONS

(1) There is much interesting material in Jesús Salas Larrazábal's *Intervención extranjera en la guerra de España* (Madrid, 1974). There are short diplomatic accounts by P. A. M. van der Esch, *Prelude to War* (The Hague, 1951) and Dante Puzzo, *Spain and the Great Powers 1936–1941* (New York, 1962). Fernando Schwarz's *La internacionalización de la guerra civil española* (Barcelona, 1971) is suggestive. N. J. Padelford's *International Law and Diplomacy in the Spanish Civil War* (Cambridge, Mass., 1939) is still the best survey of the legal issues. A. J. Toynbee, with V. M. Boulter and Katherine Duff, still give the best study of the war as an international problem in *The Survey of International Affairs 1937*, volume II, and for 1938, volume I (London, 1938 and 1948 respectively). The Red Cross representative in Spain, Marcel Junod, has a good section in his *Warrior without Weapons* (London, 1951). Herbert Southworth's *La Destruction de Guernica* (Paris, 1975) is an illuminating study of press reactions. (I was fortunate to have access to the memoirs and papers, as yet unpublished, of Pablo de Azcárate, the Republican ambassador in London in 1936–1939.)

(2) The International Brigades have been widely written about. Almost every country in the world has their special history. The best general history is the encyclopedic if indigestible work of Andreu Castells, *Las brigadas*

internacionales en la guerra de España (Barcelona, 1974). See also Jacques Delperrie de Bayac, *Les Brigades internationales* (Paris, 1968), and Vincent Brome, *The International Brigades* (London, 1965). Colonel Martínez Bande's *Brigadas internacionales* (Barcelona, 1972) is less impressive than his other work and Ricardo de la Cierva's *Leyenda y tragedia de las brigadas internacionales* (Madrid, 1969), slight. The appendix in Ramón Salas Larrazábal's *Historia del ejército popular de la república*, volume IV (Madrid, 1974), is interesting.

(3) Britain and the Civil War is investigated by K. W. Watkins's *Britain Divided* (London, 1963). British foreign policy is considered by Anthony Eden's worthy *Facing the Dictators* (London, 1962) and *The Diplomatic Diaries of Oliver Harvey* (London, 1970). British diplomats in Spain who make a contribution include Sir Robert Hodgson (*Spain Resurgent*, London, 1953), Sir Geoffrey Thompson (*Front Line Diplomat*, London, 1959) and Sir Samuel Hoare (*Ambassador on Special Mission*, London, 1946). The best background to British diplomacy at that time is Keith Middlemas's *Diplomacy of Illusion* (London, 1972). British intellectual reaction to the war is captured by Peter Stansky and William Abrahams, *Journey to the Frontier* (London, 1966), a study of John Cornford and Julian Bell. The best books by British participants are Esmond Romilly's *Boadilla* (London, 1971), John Sommerfield's *Volunteer in Spain* (London, 1937), Tom Wintringham's *English Captain* (London, 1939), George Orwell's book earlier cited, and Jason Gurney's *Crusade in Spain* (London, 1974). See also Carmel Haden Guest, *David Guest: a Scientist Fights for Freedom* (London, 1939). A survey of the British volunteers can be found in William Rust's *Britons in Spain* (London, 1939); it is uncritical.

The only work of a British volunteer for Franco is Peter Kemp's vivid *Mine were of Trouble* (London, 1957).

Irish involvement with the nationalists is commemorated by General O'Duffy's *Crusade in Spain* (London, 1938).

(4) French foreign policy and the Spanish civil war is exposed in the several volumes of foreign policy documents published as *Documents diplomatiques français 1932–1939*, 2nd series, 1968 onwards (volumes III to VII). See also the account given by Léon Blum in *Les Événements survenus en France* (Report of the parliamentary commission of inquiry into the causes of the defeat in 1940, published Paris, 1955). There is also material in Pierre Cot's *The Triumph of Treason* (Chicago, 1944), Georges Bonnet's *De Washington au Quai d'Orsay* (Geneva, 1946) and General Gamelin's *Servir* (Paris, 1946–7). An excellent survey of the propaganda war in France is D. W. Pike's *Conjecture, Propaganda and Deceit and the Spanish Civil War* (Stan-

ford, 1970). Maître Isorni's *Philippe Pétain*, 2 volumes (Paris, 1972) has an interesting chapter on Pétain and Spain. Malraux's *L'Espoir* (Paris, 1937) has incomparable passages.

The part of French volunteers for the republic is summarized in *L'Épopée d'Espagne* (Paris, 1957). See also Henri Dupré, *La 'Légion Tricolore' en Espagne* (Paris, 1942) for suggestions that not all Marty's fantasies were unfounded.

(5) On Germany and the civil war, the foreign policy documents Series D, volume III, are invaluable. German policy is analysed in Manfred Merkes, *Die deutsche Politik im Spanischen Bürgerkrieg* (Bonn, 1969), and Glenn Harper (in the book cited in section VII (4) above). There are some accounts by fliers in the Condor Legion, for example General Galland's *The First and the Last* (London, 1957). A brilliant recent study is Angel Viñas's *La alemania nazi y el 18 de julio* (Madrid, 1974).

For the Germans who fought for the Republic, see Gustav Regler's excellent *The Owl of Minerva* (London, 1959), Ludwig Renn's *Der Spanische Krieg* (Berlin, 1955) and Alfred Kantorowicz's *Spanisches Tagebuch* (Berlin, 1948) and *'Tschapaiew', das Bataillon der 21 Nationen* (Berlin, 1956).

(6) Italian diplomacy towards Spain can be studied in Ciano's *Diaries 1937–1938* (London, 1952) and *1939–1943* (London, 1947), and *Ciano's Diplomatic Papers* (London, 1948). See also Roberto Cantalupo, *Fu la Spagna* (Milan, 1948). The military intervention is summarized in José Luis Alcofar Nassaes, *CTV: los legionarios italianos en la guerra civil española* (Barcelona, 1972), and there is still point in looking at older accounts such as Ambrogio Bollati's *La Guerra di Spagna*, 2 volumes (Turin, 1937, 1939), or Francesco Belforte, *La guerra civile in Spagna* (Milan, 1938). There are also some accounts by Italian volunteers' for Franco, such as Emilio Faldella's *Venti mesi de guerra in Spagna* (Florence, 1939) or Sancho Piazzoni's *Las tropas flechas negras en la guerra de España* (Barcelona, 1942), and Ruggero Bonomi's *Viva la muerte* (Rome, 1941). On the left, there are books by Randolfo Pacciardi (*Il battaglione Garibaldi*, Lugano, 1948), Luigi Longo (*Le brigate internazionale in Spagna*, Rome, 1956), Pietro Nenni (*La Guerre d'Espagne*, Paris, 1959), Giovanni Pesce (*Un garibaldino in Spagna*, Rome, 1955) and Carlo Penchienati (*Brigate Internazionale in Spagna*, Milan, 1950). The best background to the politics of the left is in Paolo Spriano's *Storia del partito comunista italiano*, volume III (Turin, 1970).

(7) The best study of Russian policy is still D. T. Cattell's *Soviet Diplomacy and the Spanish Civil War* (Berkeley, 1957), although it does not take into consideration the large collection of recent Russian memoirs. The most

important of these is *Bajo la bandera de la España republicana* (Moscow, about 1970). For Russian diplomacy, there is Ivan Maisky's *Spanish Notebooks* (London, 1966), for unofficial war and diplomacy there is Mikhail Koltsov's *Diario de la guerra de España* (republished Paris, 1963) and Louis Fischer's *Men and Politics* (New York, 1963). See also Walter Krivitsky's *I Was Stalin's Agent* (London, 1963) and Ilya Ehrenburg's memoirs, volume III, *The Eve of War 1933–1941* (London, 1963). Obviously, many of the studies of communism are also helpful in interpreting Russian policy.

(8) The volumes of US Foreign Policy documents in their *Foreign Relations* series (1936, volume II; 1937, volume I; 1938, volume I; 1939, volume II, Washington, 1954–1956) are interesting. See also the memoir by the US Ambassador, Claude Bowers, *My Mission to Spain* (New York, 1954). For oil policy, see Herbert Feis, *The Spanish Story* (New York, 1948). Analyses of US foreign policy towards Spain can be found in Richard Traina, *American Diplomacy and the Spanish Civil War* (Bloomington, 1968), and F. J. Taylor, *The United States and the Spanish Civil War* (New York, 1956).

There are many personal accounts of American volunteers in Spain; among them are Steve Nelson, *The Volunteers* (Leipzig, 1954), Edwin Rolfe, *The Lincoln Battalion* (New York, 1939), and Alvah Bessie's *Men in Battle* (New York, 1939). The most balanced account of the Abraham Lincoln battalion is that of Cecil Eby, *Between the bullet and the lie* (New York, 1969), but see Arthur Landis's *The Abraham Lincoln Brigade* (New York, 1967) to warm the heart.

Ernest Hemingway's famous novel *For Whom the Bell Tolls* (New York, 1940) is often illuminating. Many American journalists wrote interestingly at the time; among them see the books of Herbert Matthews, *Two Wars and More to Come* (New York, 1938), and H. R. Knickerbocker, *The Siege of the Alcazar* (Philadelphia, 1936).

The intellectual impact of Spain on the US is considered in Allen Guttman's *The Wound in the Heart* (New York, 1962).

(9) Other countries affected by the Spanish Civil War include Mexico, about whose involvement see Lois Elwyn Smith, *Mexico and the Spanish Republicans* (Berkeley, 1955); Switzerland, for which see Max Wullschleger, *Schweizer Kämpfen in Spanien* (Zurich, 1939); Cuba, for which see Raúl Roa, *Pablo de la Torriente Brau y la revolución española* (Havana, 1937); as well as most of the central European countries. Some indication of the importance of the conflict for the Czechs, for example, can be seen in Artur London's *L'Aveu* (Paris, 1969). For very detailed studies in most

East European countries about their numbers and participation see Castells's bibliography. Portugal's role can be studied in *Dez anos de política externa* (*1936–47*), vol. III (Lisbon, 1965).

X. MISCELLANEOUS

For surgical innovations due to the civil war, see J. Trueta, *Treatment of War Wounds and Fractures* (London, 1939). María Rosa Urraca Pastor's *Así empezamos* (Bilbao, 1940) gives the memoirs of a leading nationalist nurse ('*La coronela*').

The third volume of F. Bravo Morata's *Historia de Madrid* (Madrid, 1968) and Vicente Ramos's *La guerra civil en la provincia de Alicante*, 3 volumes (Alicante, 1974), begin what will, no doubt, be a library of local histories.

Ian Gibson's *The Death of Lorca* (London, 1973) illuminates the atmosphere of Granada in 1936.

XI. LITERARY CONSEQUENCES

For an introduction, see Aldo Garosci's *Gli intelletuali e la guerra di Spagna* (Turin, 1959); Guttman (see above, section IX (8)); Frederick Benson, *Writers in Arms* (New York, 1967); and Stanley Weintraub's well-written *The Last Great Cause* (London, 1968). A Reading thesis by Hilary Footit is good on French right wing reactions (*French Intellectuals and the Spanish Civil War*, Reading Ph.D., 1972). Enrique Súñer, *Los intelectuales y la tragedia española* (San Sebastián, 1937) gives a nationalist reaction, on which there is valuable information in the work of Abella (section VII (2) above). Herbert Southworth's *El mito de la cruzada de Franco* (Paris, 1963) stirs up nationalist standards of scholarship. See now *Les Écrivains et la guerre d'Espagne* (Paris, 1975).

XII. THE CHURCH IN THE CIVIL WAR

See, for an anti-Franco polemical work of scholarship, Juan de Iturralde, *El catolicismo y la cruzada de Franco*, 2 volumes (Bayonne, 1955). For the Basque priests, see *El clero vasco frente a la cruzada franquista* (Bayonne, 1966). The 'anti-crusade' gets further consideration in the Bishop of Vitoria (Dr Mateo Múgica)'s *Imperativos de mi conciencia* (Buenos Aires, no date) and *Montserrat, glosas a la carta colectiva de los obispos españoles*, written by Fr J. Vilar Costa (Barcelona, 1938). See, for French Catholic support for the republic, Georges Bernanos, *Les Grands Cimetières sous la lune*

(Paris, 1938) and Jacques Maritain, *Sobre la guerra santa* (Buenos Aires, 1937).

For the orthodox defence of the church, see Cardinal Gomá's *Pastorales de la guerra de España* (Madrid, 1955) and many pamphlets such as Fr Ignacio Reigada, *La guerra nacional española ante el moral y el derecho* (Salamanca, 1937). Reasoned defence of the church can be found in Luis Carreras, *The Glory of Martyred Spain* (London, 1939). A full consideration of the persecution of the church under the republic is in Fr Antonio Montero's book cited above (para. VIII (9)). There is some useful material in Antonio Granados's *El cardenal Gomá* (Madrid, 1969).

XIII. NOVELS

Some of the novels dealing with the Spanish war and its origins are: Georges Conchon, *La corrida de la Victoire* (Paris, 1960); Camilo José Cela, *Vísperas, festividad y octava de San Camilo del año 1936 en Madrid* (Madrid, 1969); Pío Baroja, *Aurora roja* (Madrid, 1929); José María Gironella, *Los cipreses creen en Dios* (Barcelona, 1956); Agustín de Foxá, *Madrid, de corte a checa* (San Sebastián, 1938); Ernest Hemingway's *For Whom the Bell Tolls* (New York, 1940); Angel María de Lera, *Las últimas banderas* (Barcelona, 1966); André Malraux, *L'Espoir* (Paris, 1937); Henri de Montherlant, *Le Chaos et la nuit* (Paris, 1963); Gustav Regler, *The Great Crusade* (New York, Toronto, 1940); and Ramón Sender, *Seven Red Sundays* (London, 1936).

XIV. FILMS

Some films are: *Madrid '36* (1937, made by Buñuel); *L'Espoir* (1939, made by Malraux); *La Guerre est finie* (1964), Semprún's brilliant reconstruction of exile politics; *Mourir à Madrid* (1962), Rossif's reconstruction; *The Spanish Earth* (1938), made by Joris Ivens, Hemingway, Lillian Hellman, Dos Passos – unsuccessful; *The Spirit of the Beehive* (1974), beautiful if lowering.

Select Bibliography

The following lists books, articles and other matter referred to in the footnotes, apart from newspapers and periodicals; and also some other books consulted which are of use. The criterion for inclusion at all is often the significance of the volume or pamphlet as typical of its sort: thus the historical value of *The Bishop of Chelmsford Refuted* is not great; but it and other pamphlets are interesting in themselves.

ABAD DE SANTILLÁN, DIEGO, *Por qué perdimos la guerra* (Buenos Aires, 1940); *La revolución y la guerra en España* (Buenos Aires, 1937).

ABELLA, RAFAEL, *La España nacional* (Barcelona, 1973).

ABERRIGOYEN, IÑAKI DE (IGNACIO DE AZPIAZU), *Sept mois et sept jours dans l'Espagne de Franco* (Paris, 1938).

ABSHAGEN, KARL, *Canaris* (London, 1956).

ACEDO COLUNGA, FELIPE, *José Calvo Sotelo* (Barcelona, 1959).

ACIER, MARCEL (ed.), *From Spanish Trenches* (New York, 1937).

AGUIRRE Y LECUBE, JOSÉ ANTONIO DE, *De Guernica a Nueva York pasando por Berlín* (Buenos Aires, 1944).

ALBA, VÍCTOR (PEDRO PAGÉS ELÍAS), *Histoire des républiques espagnoles* (Vincennes, 1948).

ALCALÁ GALIANO, ALVARO, *The Fall of a Throne* (London, 1933).

ALCÁZAR DE VELASCO, ANGEL, *Serrano Súñer en la Falange* (Madrid, 1940).

ALCOFAR NASSAES, JOSÉ LUIS, *CTV: los legionarios italianos en la guerra civil española* (Barcelona, 1972); *Los asesores soviéticos en la guerra civil española* (Barcelona, 1971); *Las fuerzas navales en la guerra civil española* (Barcelona, 1971).

ALCOLEA, RAYMOND, *Le Christ chez Franco* (Paris, 1938).

ALLAN, TED, *The Man who Made Franco* (article) (Colliers, 1947).

ALLAN, TED (and GORDON, SYDNEY), *The Scalpel, Not the Sword* (London, 1954) (Life of Doctor Norman Bethune).

ALONSO, BRUNO, *La flota republicana y la guerra civil de España* (Mexico, 1944).

ALPERT, MICHAEL, *The Republican Army in the Spanish Civil War, 1936–1939*, Reading 1973 (unpublished).

ALVAREZ, RAMÓN, *Eleuterio Quintanilla (vida y obra del maestro)* (Mexico, 1973).

ALVAREZ DEL VAYO, JULIO, *Freedom's Battle* (New York, 1940); *Give Me Combat* (New York, 1973); *The Last Optimist* (London, 1950).

AMBA, ACHMED, *I was Stalin's Bodyguard* (London, 1952).

SELECT BIBLIOGRAPHY

AMERY, JULIAN, *Approach March* (London, 1973).

ANSALDO, JUAN ANTONIO, *¿ Para qué ? . . . (De Alfonso XIII a Juan III)* (Buenos Aires, 1951).

Anuario Estadístico de España (Madrid, 1931).

ARAQUISTAIN, LUIS, *El comunismo y la guerra de España* (Carmaux, 1939).

ARENILLAS, JOSÉ MARÍA, *The National Question and the Socialist Revolution in the Basque Country* (Leeds, 1972).

ARMILLAS GARCÍA, LUIS, *Rutas gloriosas* (Cádiz, 1939).

ARMIÑÁN, JOSÉ MANUEL DE and LUIS DE, *Epistolario del dictador* (Madrid, 1930).

ARMIÑÁN, LUIS DE, *Bajo el cielo de Levante* (Madrid, 1939).

ARNAL, MOSÉN JESÚS, *Por qué fui secretario de Durruti* (Andorra, 1972).

AROCA SARDAGNA, JOSÉ MARÍA, *Los republicanos que no se exilaron* (Barcelona, 1969).

ARRARÁS, JOAQUÍN, *Franco* (Buenos Aires, 1937); *Historia de la segunda república española*, 4 vols. (Madrid, 1956–64).

ASENSIO TORRADO, General, *El General Asensio: su lealtad a la república* (Barcelona, 1938).

ATHOLL, KATHARINE, Duchess of, *Searchlight on Spain* (Harmondsworth, 1938).

ATTLEE, C. R. (with ELLEN WILKINSON, PHILIP NOEL BAKER, JOHN DUGDALE), *What We Saw in Spain* (London, 1937).

AUB, MAX, *Campo cerrado* (Mexico, 1943).

AUCLAIR, MARCELLE, *Enfance et mort de García Lorca* (Paris, 1968).

Authors Take Sides (London, 1937).

AVILÉS, GABRIEL, *Tribunales rojos* (Barcelona, 1939).

AYERRA, MARINO, *No me avergoncé del Evangelio* (Buenos Aires, 1958).

AZAÑA, MANUEL, *Obras completas*, 4 vols. (Mexico, 1966–8).

AZCÁRATE, PABLO DE, *Memoirs* (unpublished).

AZNAR, MANUEL, *Historia militar de la guerra de España (1936–1939)* (Madrid, 1940).

AZPILIKOETA, ——— DE, *Le Problème basque vu par le cardinal Gomá et le président Aguirre* (Paris, 1938).

BAHAMONDE Y SÁNCHEZ DE CASTRO, ANTONIO, *Memoirs of a Spanish Nationalist* (London, 1939).

BAILEY, GEOFFREY, *The Conspirators* (London, 1961).

Bajo la bandera de la España republicana (Moscow, ?1970).

BAKER, CARLOS, *Hemingway: the Writer as an Artist* (Princeton, 1952).

BALBONTÍN, JOSÉ ANTONIO, *La España de mi experiencia* (Mexico, 1952).

SELECT BIBLIOGRAPHY

BALCELLS, ALBERTO, *Crisis económica y agitación social en Cataluña (1930–1936)* (Barcelona, 1971).

BALK, THEODORE, *La Quatorzième* (Madrid, 1937).

BALLESTEROS, ANTONIO, *Historia de España*, 8 vols. (Barcelona, 1919–36).

BARÁIBAR, CARLOS DE, *La guerra de España en el plano internacional* (Barcelona, 1938).

BARCIA TRELLES, AUGUSTO, *La política de no-intervención* (Buenos Aires, 1942).

BARCO TERUEL, ENRIQUE, *Valle del Jarama (Brigada Internacional)* (Barcelona, 1969).

BARDOUX, JACQUES, *Chaos in Spain* (London, 1937).

BAREA, ARTURO, *The Forging of a Rebel* (New York, 1946).

BARMINE, ALEXANDER, *One Who Survived* (London, 1945).

BAROJA Y NESSI, PÍO, *Ayer y hoy* (Santiago de Chile, 1939).

BARRIOBERO, EDUARDO, *Un tribunal revolucionario* (Barcelona, 1937).

BARTLETT, V., *I Accuse* (London, 1937).

BASALDÚA, PEDRO DE, *El dolor de Euzkadi* (Barcelona, 1937); *En España sale el sol* (Buenos Aires, 1946).

BAUER, EDDY, *Rouge et or* (Neuchâtel, 1939).

BAYLE, FR. CONSTANTINO, *¿ Qué pasa en España ?* (Salamanca, 1937).

BEAUFRE, General ANDRÉ, *The Fall of France, 1940* (London, 1965).

BÉCARUD, JEAN, *La Deuxième République espagnole 1931–1936* (Paris, 1962).

BÉCARUD, JEAN (and LAPOUGE, GILLES), *Anarchistes en Espagne* (Paris, 1969).

BELFORTE, FRANCESCO, *La guerra civile in Spagna* (Milan, 1938).

BELL, QUENTIN (ed.), *Julian Bell; Essays, Poems and Letters* (London, 1938).

BEN-AMI, S., *The Origins of the Second Republic* (Oxford thesis, 1974).

BENAVIDES, MANUEL, *El último pirata del Mediterráneo* (Madrid, 1933); *Guerra y revolución en Cataluña* (Mexico, 1946); *La escuadra la mandan los cabos* (Mexico, 1944).

BENDINER, ROBERT, *The Riddle of the State Department* (New York, 1962).

BERJÓN, ANTONIO, *La Prière des exilés espagnols à la Vierge du Pilier* (Liège, 1938).

BERNANOS, GEORGES, *Les Grands Cimetières sous la lune* (Paris, 1938).

BERNERI, CAMILLO, *Mussolini à la conquête des Baléares* (Paris, 1937); *Guerre de classe en Espagne* (Paris, 1938).

BERNERI, GIOVANNA, *Lezione sull'antifascismo* (Bari, 1962).

'BERRYER', ———, *Red Justice* (London, 1937).

BERTRÁN GÜELL, FELIPE, *Preparación y desarrollo del alzamiento nacional* (Valladolid, 1939).

BERTRÁN Y MUSITU, JOSÉ, *Experiencias de los servicios de información del nordeste de España (SIFNE) durante la guerra* (Madrid, 1940).

BESSIE, ALVAH CECIL, *Men in Battle* (New York, 1939).

BETHUNE, NORMAN, *Le Crime de la route Málaga–Almería* (Publicaciones Iberia, no date).

BEUMELBURG, WERNER, *Kampf um Spanien, die Geschichte der Legion Condor* (Berlin, 1940).

BEURKO, SANCHO DE, *Gudaris, recuerdos de guerra* (Buenos Aires, 1956).

BIHALJI-MERIN, OTO (MERIN, PETER), *Spain Between Death and Birth* (New York, 1938).

BILAINKIN, GEORGE, *Tito* (London, 1952).

Bishop of Chelmsford Refuted, The (London, 1938).

BLANKFORT, MICHAEL, *The Brave and the Blind* (New York, 1940).

BLEY, WULF, *Das Buch der Spanienflieger* (Leipzig, 1939).

BLINKHORN, MARTIN, '"The Basque Ulster": Navarre and the Basque autonomy question under the Spanish Second Republic', *The Historical Journal*, XVII, no. 3 (1974) pp. 595–613.

BLOCH, JEAN RICHARD, *España en armas* (Santiago de Chile, 1937).

BLYTHE, HENRY, *Spain over Britain* (London, 1937).

BOLÍN, LUIS A., *Spain, the Vital Years* (London, 1967).

BOLLATI, AMBROGIO, *La guerra di Spagna sino alla liberazione di Gijón* (Turin, 1937); *La guerra di Spagna dalla liberazione di Gijón alla vittoria* (Turin, 1939).

BOLLOTEN, BURNETT, *The Grand Camouflage; the Communist Conspiracy in the Spanish Civil War* (London, 1961).

BONET, JOAQUÍN ALONSO, *¡Simancas! Epopeya de los cuarteles de Gijón* (Gijón, 1939).

BONNET, GEORGES, *De Washington au Quai d'Orsay* (Geneva, 1946).

BONOMI, RUGGERO, *Viva la muerte, diario dell' 'Aviación de El Tercio'* (Rome, 1941).

Book of the XVth Brigade, The (Madrid, 1938).

BORKENAU, FRANZ, *The Spanish Cockpit* (London, 1937).

BORRÁS Y BERMEJO, TOMÁS, *Checas de Madrid* (Barcelona, 1956).

BOTELLA PASTOR, V., *Así cayeron los dados* (Mexico, 1959); *Por qué callaron las campanas* (Mexico, 1953).

BOUTHELIER, ANTONIO (with MORA, JOSÉ LÓPEZ), *Ocho dias de la revuelta comunista* (Madrid, 1940).

BOWERS, CLAUDE, *My Mission to Spain* (New York, 1954).

BRACHER, KARL, *The German Dictatorship* (London, 1970).

BRADEMAS, JOHN, *Anarcosindicalismo y revolución en España (1930–1937)* (Barcelona, 1974).

BRASILLACH, ROBERT, *Histoire de la guerre d'Espagne* (Paris, 1939).

BRAVO, FRANCISCO, *Historia de la Falange española de las JONS* (Madrid, 1940).

BRAVO MORATA, FEDERICO, *Historia de Madrid*, vol. III (Madrid, 1968).

BRAY, ARTURO, *La España del brazo en alto* (Buenos Aires, 1943).

BRECHT, BERTOLT, *Die Gewehre der Frau Carrara*, in *Gesammelte Werke*, vol. 3 (Frankfurt, 1967).

BREDEL, W., *Rencontre sur l'Ebre* (Paris, 1950).

BRENAN, GERALD, *Personal Record* (London, 1974); *South from Granada* (London, 1957); *The Spanish Labyrinth* (Cambridge, 1943).

BRERETON, GEOFFREY, *Inside Spain* (London, 1938).

BRICALL, JOSEP MARÍA, *Política económica de la Generalitat (1936–1939)*; *Evolució i formes de la producció industrial* (Barcelona, 1970).

BRISSA, JOSÉ, *La revolución de julio en Barcelona* (Barcelona, 1910).

BROCKWAY, FENNER, *The Truth about Barcelona* (London, 1937).

BROME, VINCENT, *The International Brigades, Spain, 1936–1939* (London, 1965).

BROUÉ, PIERRE (and TÉMIME, ÉMILE), *La Révolution et la guerre d'Espagne* (Paris, 1961).

BROWDER, EARL (with LAWRENCE, BILL), *Next Steps to Win the War in Spain* (New York, 1938).

BUCKLEY, HENRY W., *Life and Death of the Spanish Republic* (London, 1940).

BULLEJOS, JOSÉ, *Europa entre dos guerras* (Mexico, 1944).

BULLOCK, ALAN, 'Hitler and the Origins of the Second World War' (*Proceedings of the British Academy*, LIII, 1967; Raleigh lecture).

BURGO, JAIME DEL, *Conspiracion y guerra civil* (Madrid, 1970).

BUSCH, ERNST (ed.), *Kampflieder*; *Battle-songs*; *Canzoni di guerra*; *Chansons de guerre*; *Canciones de guerra de las brigadas internacionales* (Madrid, 1937).

BUSTAMANTE Y QUIJANO, RAMÓN, *A bordo del 'Alfonso Pérez'* (Madrid, 1940).

BUTLER, Lord, *The Art of the Possible* (London, 1971).

BUTLER, J. R. M., *Lord Lothian* (London, 1960).

CABANELLAS, GUILLERMO, *La guerra de los mil días*, 2 vols. (Barcelona, 1973).

CABANILLAS, ALFREDO, *Hacia la España eterna* (Buenos Aires, 1938).

CABEZAS, JUAN ANTONIO, *Asturias, catorce meses de guerra civil* (Madrid, 1974).

CACHO VIU, VICENTE, *La Institución Libre de Enseñanza* (Madrid, 1962).

CACHO ZABALZA, ANTONIO, *La Unión Militar Española* (Alicante, 1940).

CALLEJA, JUAN JOSÉ, *Yagüe, un corazón al rojo* (Barcelona, 1963).

CAMPBELL, ROY, *Flowering Rifle* (London, 1939).

CAMPESINO, EL: see GONZÁLEZ, VALENTÍN.

CAMPOAMOR, CLARA, *La Révolution espagnole vue par une républicaine* (Paris, 1937).

CANTALUPO, ROBERTO, *Fu la Spagna* (Milan, 1948).

CAPA, ROBERT, *Death in the Making* (New York, 1938).

CARDOZO, HAROLD G., *The March of a Nation* (New York, 1937).

Carlist Archives, Seville: these were papers, letters and other matter in the possession of Manuel Fal Conde, shown to me by Melchor Ferrer.

CARR, RAYMOND (ed.), *The Republic and the Civil War in Spain* (London, 1971); *Spain 1808–1939* (Oxford, 1966).

CARRASCAL, G., *Asturias, 18 julio 1926, 21 octubre 1937* (Valladolid, 1938).

CARRERA, BUENAVENTURA, *L'Europe aveugle devant l'Espagne martyre* (Paris, 1939).

CARRERAS, LUIS, *The Glory of Martyred Spain* (London, 1939).

CARRERO BLANCO, LUIS, *España y el mar* (Madrid, 1962).

CARRETERO, JOSÉ MARÍA, *Nosotros los mártires* (Madrid, 1940).

CARRILLO, SANTIAGO, *Demain Espagne* (entretiens avec Régis Debray et Max Gallo) (Paris, 1974).

CARRILLO, WENCESLAO, *El último episodio de la guerra civil española* (Toulouse, 1945).

CARRIÓN, PASCUAL, *La reforma agraria de la segunda República* (Barcelona, 1973).

CARSTEN, FRANCIS, *The Reichswehr and Politics 1918–1933* (Oxford, 1966).

CASADO, SEGISMUNDO, *The Last Days of Madrid* (London, 1939).

CASANOVA, MANUEL, *L'Espagne livrée* (Paris, 1971).

CASARIEGO FERNÁNDEZ, JESÚS EVARISTO, *Flor de hidalgos* (Pamplona, 1938).

CASAS DE LA VEGA, R., *Brunete* (Madrid, 1967).

CASTELLS, ANDREU, *Las brigadas internacionales de la guerra de España* (Barcelona, 1974).

CASTILLO, JOSÉ DEL (with ALVAREZ, SANTIAGO), *Barcelona, objetivo cubierto* (Barcelona, 1958).

CASTRO ALBARRÁN, ANICETO DE, *Este es el cortejo . . . héroes y mártires de la cruzada española* (Salamanca, 1941).

CASTRO DELGADO, ENRIQUE, *Hombres made in Moscú* (Barcelona, 1965).

Catalunya sota el règim franquista, vol. I (Paris, 1973).

Catholic church in Spain. Joint letter of the Spanish bishops to the bishops of the whole world concerning the war in Spain (London, 1937).

CATTELL, DAVID TREDWELL, *Communism and the Spanish Civil War* (Berkeley, 1955); *Soviet Diplomacy and the Spanish Civil War* (Berkeley, 1957).

CAUTE, DAVID, *The Fellow Travellers* (London, 1973).

CELA, CAMILO JOSÉ, *Vísperas, festividad y octava de San Camilo del año 1936 en Madrid* (Madrid, 1969).

CERVERA VALDERRAMA, Admiral JUAN, *Memorias de guerra 1936–1939* (Madrid, 1968).

CHAMSON, ANDRÉ, *Rien qu'un témoignage* (Paris, 1937).

CHAPAPRIETA, JOAQUÍN, *La paz fue posible* (Barcelona, 1971).

CHAVES NOVALES, MANUEL, *A sangre y fuego, héroes, bestias y mártires de España* (Santiago de Chile, 1937).

CHOMSKY, NOAM, *American Power and the New Mandarins* (London, 1969).

Christ or Franco? An answer to the Spanish episcopate (London, 1937).

CHURCHILL, WINSTON, The Second World War, vol. I: *The Gathering Storm* (London, 1948).

CÍA NAVASCUÉS, POLICARPO, *Memorias del tercio de Montejurra* (Pamplona, 1941).

CIANO, Count GALEAZZO, *Diaries 1937–1938* (London, 1952); *Diaries 1939–1943* (London, 1947); *Diplomatic Papers* (London, 1948).

CIERVA, RICARDO DE LA, *Historia de la guerra civil española* (Madrid, 1969); *Historia ilustrada de la guerra civil española* (Barcelona, 1970); *La historia perdida del socialismo español* (Madrid, 1972); *Leyenda y tragedia de las brigadas internacionales* (Madrid, 1969); *Los documentos de la primavera trágica* (Madrid, 1967).

CIRAC ESTOPAÑÁN, SEBASTIÁN, *Héroes y mártires de Caspe* (Saragossa, 1939).

CIRRE JIMÉNEZ, JOSÉ, *De Espejo a Madrid con las tropas del general Miaja* (Granada, 1937).

CLARK, RONALD, *J.B.S.: The Life and Work of J. B. S. Haldane* (London, 1968).

CLAUDÍN, FERNANDO, *La crisis del movimiento comunista* (Paris, 1970); 'Spain, the Untimely Revolution', *New Left Review*, no. 74.

Clerge basque, Le, Rapports présentés par des prêtres basques aux autorités ecclésiastiques (Paris, 1938).

CLÉRISSE, HENRY, *Espagne 36–37* (Paris, 1937).

Clero vasco frente a la cruzada franquista, El (Bayonne, 1966).

CLEUGH, JAMES, *Spanish Fury; the Story of a Civil War* (London, 1962).

CLOUD, YVONNE, *Basque Children in England* (London, 1937).

COCKBURN, CLAUD, *Crossing the Line* (London, 1956).

COLÁS LAGUÍA, EMILIO, *La gesta heroica de España* (Saragossa, 1936).

Colectividades de Castilla (Madrid, 1937).

COLMEGNA, HÉCTOR, *Diario de un médico argentino en la guerra de España, 1936–1939* (Buenos Aires, 1941).

COLODNY, ROBERT, *The Struggle for Madrid* (New York, 1958).

COLVIN, IAN, *Hitler's Secret Enemy* (London, 1957).

COMÍN COLOMER, EDUARDO, *El comisariado político en la guerra española 1936–1939* (Madrid, 1973); *El Quinto Regimiento de Milicias Populares* (Madrid, 1973); *Historia del partido comunista de España*, 3 vols. (Madrid, 1965); *La república en el exilio* (Barcelona, 1957).

Communist Atrocities in Southern Spain, The (Preliminary, Second and Third Reports, in English, London 1936; Fourth and Fifth Reports, in Spanish, Burgos 1937).

Communist International, Report of the VIIth World Congress of the (London, 1936).

CONCHON, GEORGES, *La Corrida de la Victoire* (Paris, 1960).

CONFORTI, OLAO, *Guadalajara* (Milan, 1967).

CONILL Y MATARÓ, ANTONIO, *Codo: de mi diario de campaña* (Barcelona, 1954).

CONNOLLY, CYRIL, *The Condemned Playground* (London, 1945); *The Golden Horizon* (London, 1953).

CONQUEST, ROBERT, *The Great Terror* (London, 1968).

CONZE, EDWARD, *Spain Today* (London, 1936).

COPEMAN, FRED, *Reason in Revolt* (London, 1948).

CÓRDOBA, JUAN DE (JOSÉ LOSADA DE LA TORRE), *Estampas y reportajes de retaguardia* (Seville, 1939).

CORDÓN, ANTONIO, *Trayectoria (recuerdos de un artillero)* (Paris, 1971).

CORNFORD, JOHN, see SLOAN, PAT.

COT, PIERRE, *The Triumph of Treason* (Chicago, 1944).

COUFFON, CLAUDE, *A Grenade, sur les pas de García Lorca* (Paris, 1962); *Miguel Hernández et Orihuela* (Paris, 1963).

COVERDALE, JOHN, 'The Battle of Guadalajara', *Journal of Contemporary History* (January, 1974).

COWLES, VIRGINIA, *Looking for Trouble* (London, 1941).

COX, GEOFFREY, *Defence of Madrid* (London, 1937).

CREAC'H, JEAN, *Le Cœur et l'épée* (Paris, 1958).

CROZIER, BRIAN, *Franco* (London, 1967).

CRUELLS, MANUEL, *El 6 d'octubre a Catalunya* (Barcelona, 1971); *Mayo sangriento: Barcelona 1937* (Barcelona, 1970).

Cruzada: Historia de la cruzada española, 35 folios (Madrid, 1940–43).

Cuadernos de Ruedo Ibérico: 'El movimiento libertario español' (Paris, 1974).

CURTIS, NORAH (and DILBY, CYRIL), *Malnutrition* (London, 1944).

DAHMS, HELMUTH, *Der Spanische Bürgerkrieg 1936–1939* (Tübingen, 1962).

DALTON, HUGH, *The Fateful Years: Memoirs 1931–1945* (London, 1957).

DÁVILA, SANCHO (and PEMARTÍN, JULIÁN), *Hacia la historia de la Falange, primera contribución de Sevilla* (Jerez, 1938).

Déclarations des gouvernements européens au sujet des affaires d'Espagne (summary of documents in typescript in the Rockefeller Library of the Palais des Nations).

DEDIJER, VLADIMIR, *Tito Speaks* (London, 1953).

De julio a julio (by J. García Oliver etc.) (Barcelona, 1937).

DELAPRÉE, LOUIS, *The Martyrdom of Madrid* (Madrid, 1937).

DELCLAUX, CARLOS, *La financiación de la cruzada*, University of Deusto thesis (1950, unpublished).

DELMER, SEFTON, *Trail Sinister* (London, 1961).

DE LOS RÍOS, FERNANDO, *Mi viaje a la Rusia Soviética*, 2nd ed. (Madrid, 1970).

DELPERRIE DE BAYAC, JACQUES, *Les Brigades Internationales* (Paris, 1968).

DERIABIN, P. (and GIBNEY, F.), *The Secret World* (London, 1960).

DESANTI, DOMINIQUE, *L'Internationale communiste* (Paris, 1971).

DEUTSCHER, ISAAC, *Stalin, a Political Biography* (London, 1949); *The Prophet Armed* (London, 1954); *The Prophet Unarmed* (London, 1959); *The Prophet Outcast* (London, 1963).

DE WET, OLOFF, *Cardboard Crucifix* (Edinburgh and London, 1938).

DÍAZ, JOSÉ, *Por la unidad, hacia la victoria* (Barcelona, 1937); *Tres años de lucha* (Paris, 1970).

DÍAZ DE ENTRESOTOS, BALDOMERO, *Seis meses de anarquía en Extremadura* (Cáceres, 1937).

DÍAZ DE VILLEGAS, JOSÉ, *Guerra de liberación; la fuerza de la razón*, 1st ed. (Barcelona, 1957).

DÍAZ DEL MORAL, JOSÉ, *Historia de las agitaciones campesinas andaluzas: Córdoba* (Madrid, 1929).

DÍAZ NOSTY, BERNARDO, *La comuna asturiana* (Madrid, 1974).

DÍAZ-PLAJA, FERNANDO, comp., *La guerra de España en sus documentos*, 2nd ed. (Barcelona, 1966).

Dictamen de la comisión sobre la ilegitimidad de poderes actuantes en el 18 de julio de 1936 (Barcelona, 1939).

DIEGO, Capitán de, *Belchite* (Barcelona, 1939).

Documents diplomatiques français 1932–1939, 2e série (Paris, 1968).

Documents on German Foreign Policy 1918–1945, Series C, vols IV (London, 1962) and V (London, 1966); series D, vols III (London, 1951) and XI (London, 1961). (Note: *GD* in footnotes refers to Series D, vol. III.)

Documents secrets du ministère des affaires étrangères d'Allemagne, vol. III (Moscow, 1946).

DOLGOFF, SAM, *The Anarchist Collectives; Workers' Self-management in the Spanish Revolution, 1936–1939* (New York, 1974).

DOMÉNECH PUIG, ROSENDO, *Diario de campaña de un requeté* (Barcelona, no date).

DOMINGO, MARCELINO, *La experiencia del poder* (Madrid, 1934).

DOMÍNGUEZ, EDMUNDO, *Los vencedores de Negrín* (Mexico, 1940).

DUCLOS, JACQUES, *Mémoires 1935–1939* (Paris, 1969).

DUMONT, RENÉ, *Types of Rural Economy* (London, 1957).

DUNDAS, LAWRENCE, *Behind the Spanish Mask* (London, 1943).

DUPRÉ, HENRI, *La 'Légion Tricolore' en Espagne* (Paris, 1942).

DURÁN JORDÁ, FREDERICK, *The Service of Blood Transfusion at the Front* (Barcelona, 1937).

DUVAL, MAURICE, *Les Espagnols et la guerre d'Espagne* (Paris, 1939); *Les Leçons de la guerre d'Espagne* (Paris, 1938).

DZELEPY, ELEUTHÈRE, *Britain in Spain* (London, 1939); *The Spanish Plot* (London, 1937).

EBY, CECIL D., *Between the Bullet and the Lie* (New York, 1969); *The Siege of the Alcazar* (London, 1966).

EDEN, ANTHONY (Earl of AVON), *Facing the Dictators* (London, 1962).

Education in Republican Spain (London, 1937).

EHRENBURG, ILYA, *The Eve of War* (*Men, Years and Life*, vol. IV) (London, 1963).

EISNER, ALEXEI, *La 12a Brigada Internacional* (Valencia, 1972).

ELSTOB, PETER, *Spanish Prisoner* (New York, 1939).

L'Épopée de l'Espagne; brigades internationales, 1936–1939 (Paris, 1957).

ERICKSON, JOHN, *The Soviet High Command* (London, 1962).

ESCH, PATRICIA A. M. VAN DER, *Prelude to War: the International Repercussions of the Spanish Civil War, 1936–1939* (The Hague, 1951).

ESCOBAL, PATRICIO P., *Death Row: Spain 1936* (Indianapolis, 1968).

ESCOBAR, JOSÉ IGNACIO, (Marqués de VALDEIGLESIAS), *Así empezó . . .* (Madrid, 1974).

ESPERABÉ ARTEAGA, ENRIQUE, *La guerra de reconquista española* (Madrid, 1939).

ESPINA DE SERNA, CONCHA, *Luna roja, novela de la revolución* (Valladolid, 1939); *Princesas del martirio* (Barcelona, 1940).

ESPINAR, JAIME, *'Argelés-sur-Mer' (Campo de concentración para españoles)* (Caracas, 1940).

ESTEBAN INFANTES, General, *General Sanjurjo* (Barcelona, 1957).

Evenements survenus en France 1936–1945, Les, Rapport fait au nom de la Commission de l'Assemblée Nationale; Temoignages, vol. I (Paris, 1955).

FALDELLA, EMILIO, *Venti mesi de guerra in Spagna* (Florence, 1939).

FARMBOROUGH, FLORENCE, *Life and People in National Spain* (London, 1938).

FD: see *Documents diplomatiques français.*

FEILING, KEITH, *The Life of Neville Chamberlain* (London, 1946).

FEIS, HERBERT, *The Spanish Story* (New York, 1948).

FERNÁNDEZ ALMAGRO, MELCHOR, *Historia de la república española, 1931–1936* (Madrid, 1940).

FERNÁNDEZ ARIAS, ADELARDO, *Madrid bajo 'el terror', 1936–1937* (Saragossa, 1937).

FERRARA, MARCELLA and MAURICIO, *Palmiro Togliatti*, French translation (Paris, 1955).

FERRARI BILLOCH, FRANCISCO, *¡¡Masones!! Así es la secta, las logias de Palma e Ibiza* (Palma, 1937).

FERRER, MELCHOR, *Documentos de don Alfonso Carlos* (Madrid, 1950).

FERRER, SOL, *Francisco Ferrer* (Paris, 1962).

FIDALGO CARASA, PILAR, *A Young Mother in Franco's Prisons* (London, 1939).

FISCHER, LOUIS, *Men and Politics* (New York, 1941); *The War in Spain* (New York, 1937).

FISCHER, RUTH, *Stalin and German Communism* (Oxford, 1949).

FITZPATRICK, Captain NÖEL, *Memoirs* (unpublished).

FOLTZ, CHARLES, *The Masquerade in Spain* (Boston, 1948).

FONTANA, JOSÉ MARÍA, *Los catalanes en la guerra de España* (Madrid, 1951).

FONTERIZ, LUIS DE (pseud.), *Red Terror in Madrid* (London, 1937).

FOOTE, ALEXANDER, *Handbook for Spies* (London, 1953).

FOOTIT, HILARY, *French Intellectuals and the Spanish Civil War* (Reading Ph.D., 1972).

FORBES, ROSITA, *The Sultan of the Mountains* (New York, 1924).

FORELL, FRITZ VON, *Mölders und seine Männer* (Graz, 1941).

FOSS, WILLIAM, *The Spanish Arena* (London, 1938).

FOX, RALPH, *A Writer in Arms* (London, 1937).

FOXÁ, AGUSTÍN DE, *Madrid, de corte a checa* (San Sebastián, 1938).

FRASER, RONALD, *In Hiding: The Life of Manuel Cortes* (London, 1972); *The Pueblo* (London, 1973).

FRUTOS, VÍCTOR DE, *Los que no perdieron la guerra* (Buenos Aires, 1967).

FÜHRING, HELMUT HERMANN, *Wir funken für Franco* (Gütersloh, 1941).

FULLER, General, *The Conquest of Red Spain* (London, 1937).

GALEY, JOHN H., 'Bridegrooms of Death: a Profile Study of the Spanish Foreign Legion', *Journal of Contemporary History*, vol. IV, No. 2 (1969).

GALÍNDEZ SUÁREZ, JESÚS, *Los vascos en el Madrid sitiado* (Buenos Aires, 1945).

GALINDO HERRERA, SANTIAGO, *Los partidos monárquicos bajo la segunda república* (Madrid, 1956).

GALLAND, ADOLF, *The First and the Last* (London, 1957).

GALLO, MAX, *Spain under Franco: A History* (London, 1973).

GAMELIN, MAURICE, *Servir* (Paris, 1946–7).

GAMIR ULÍBARRI, General, *De mis memorias* (Paris, 1939).

GANNES, HARRY (with THEODORE 'REPARD'), *Spain in Revolt* (London, 1936).

GARATE, JOSÉ MARÍA, *Mil dias de fuego* (Barcelona, 1972)

GARCÍA, JOSÉ, *Ispaniia Narodnogo fronta 1936–1939* (Moscow, 1957).

GARCÍA, MIGUEL, *I was Franco's Prisoner* (London, 1972).

GARCÍA ALONSO, FRANCISCO, *Así mueren los españoles* (Buenos Aires, 1937).

GARCÍA ARIAS, LUIS, *La política internacional en torno a la guerra de España 1936* (Saragossa, 1961).

GARCÍA LACALLE, ANDRÉS, *Mitos y verdades: la aviación de caza en la guerra española* (Mexico, 1974).

GARCÍA MERCADAL, JOSÉ, *Aire tierra y mar* (Saragossa, 1938?–40).

GARCÍA MORATO, JOAQUÍN, *Guerra en el aire* (Madrid, 1940).

GARCÍA PRADAS, JOSÉ, *Cómo terminó la guerra de España* (Buenos Aires, 1940).

GARCÍA SERRANO, RAFAEL, *Diccionario para un macuto* (Madrid, 1964).

GARCÍA VALIÑO, RAFAEL, *Guerra de liberación española. Campañas de Aragón y Maestrazgo* (Madrid, 1949).

GARCÍA VENERO, MAXIMINIANO, *Falange en la guerra de España: la unificación y Hedilla* (Paris, 1967); *El general Fanjul* (Madrid, 1967); *Historia de las Internacionales en España*, 3 vols. (Madrid, 1956–7); *Historia del nacionalismo catalán*, 2 vols. (Madrid, 1967); *Historia del nacionalismo vasco* (Madrid, 1945); *Madrid, julio 1936* (Madrid, 1973).

Garibaldini in Ispagna (Madrid, 1937).

GAROSCI, ALDO, *Gli intellettuali d la Guerra di Spagna* (Turin, 1959).

GARRACHÓN CUESTA, ANTONIO, *De África a Cádiz y de Cádiz a la España Imperial* (Cadiz, 1938).

GARRIGA, RAMÓN, *Las relaciones secretas entre Franco y Hitler* (Buenos Aires, 1965).

GARTHOFF, R., *How Russia Makes War* (London, 1954).

G D: see *Documents on German Foreign Policy 1918–1945.*

General Cause, The: see Spain, Tribunal supremo.

GEORGE, ROBERT ('ROBERT SENCOURT'), *Spain's Ordeal* (London, 1938).

GERAHTY, CECIL, *The Road to Madrid* (London, 1937).

GIBSON, IAN, *The Death of Lorca* (London, 1973).

GIL MUGARZA, BERNARDO, comp., *España en llamas, 1936* (Barcelona, 1968).

GIL ROBLES, JOSÉ MARÍA, *Discursos parlamentarios* (Madrid, 1971); *No fue posible la paz* (Barcelona, 1968).

GILBERT, MARTIN, *A Century of Conflict; essays presented to A. J. P. Taylor* (London, 1966).

GILLAIN, NICK, *Le Mercenaire* (Paris, 1938).

GIMÉNEZ CABALLERO, ERNESTO, *¡Hay Pirineos! Notas de un alférez en la IV^a de Navarra sobre la conquista de Port Bou* (Barcelona, 1939).

GIRONELLA, JOSÉ MARÍA, *Los cipreses creen en Dios* (Barcelona, 1956); *Un millón de muertos* (Barcelona, 1961).

GISCLON, JEAN, *Des avions et des hommes* (Paris, 1969).

GODED, MANUEL, *Un 'faccioso' cien por cien* (Saragossa, 1939).

GOMÁ ORDUÑA, JOSÉ, *La guerra en el aire* (Barcelona, 1958).

GOMÁ Y TOMÁS, ISIDRO, Cardinal, *Pastorales de la guerra de España* (Madrid, 1955).

GÓMEZ ACEBO, JUAN, *La vida en las cárceles de Euzkadi* (Guipúzcoa, 1938).

GÓMEZ BAJUELO, GIL, *Málaga bajo el dominio rojo* (Cádiz, 1937).

GÓMEZ CASAS, JUAN, *Historia del anarco-sindicalismo español* (Madrid, 1968).

GÓMEZ MÁLAGA, JUAN, *Estampas trágicas de Madrid* (Avila, 1936).

GÓMEZ OLIVEROS, Major, *General Moscardó* (Barcelona, 1955).

GONZÁLEZ, VALENTÍN, ('EL CAMPESINO'), *Comunista en España y anti-Stalinista en la URSS* (Mexico, 1952); *Listen, Comrades* (London, 1952).

GONZÁLEZ OLIVEROS, WENCESLAO, *Falange y requeté orgánicamente solidarios* (Valladolid, 1937).

GONZÁLEZ RUIZ, FRANCISCO, *J'ai cru en Franco, procès d'une grande désillusion* (Paris, 1937).

GORDÓN ORDÁS, FÉLIX, *Mi política fuera de España*, 2 vols. (Mexico, 1965–7).

GORKIN, JULIÁN, *Caníbales políticos; Hitler y Stalin en España* (Mexico, 1941). Republished, with notes, as *El proceso de Moscú en Barcelona* (Barcelona, 1974); 'My Experiences of Stalinism', *The Review*, no. 2, October 1959 (Imre Nagy Institute for Political Research).

GOTT, RICHARD (and GILBERT, MARTIN), *The Appeasers* (London, 1963).

GRANADOS, ANTONIO, *El cardenal Gomá* (Madrid, 1969).

GRAVES, ROBERT (and HODGE, ALAN), *The Long Week-end* (London, 1940).

GREAVES, HAROLD, *The Truth about Spain* (London, 1938).

GREENE, HERBERT, *Secret Agent in Spain* (London, 1938).

GROSS, BABETTE, *Willi Muenzenberg: Eine politische Biographie* (Stuttgart, 1967).

GROSS, MIRIAM, *The World of George Orwell* (London, 1971), (contains an essay by Raymond Carr).

GUARNER, Colonel VICENTE, *Papers* (unpublished).

GUÉRIN, DANIEL, *L'anarchisme* (Paris, 1965).

Guerra y revolución en España 1936–1939 (Moscow, 1966).

GUEST, CARMEL HADEN, *David Guest: a Scientist Fights for Freedom* (London, 1939).

GURNEY, JASON, *Crusade in Spain* (London, 1974).

GUTIÉRREZ RAVÉ, JOSÉ, *Antonio Goicoechea* (Madrid, 1965); *Gil Robles, caudillo frustrado* (Madrid, 1967).

GUTTMANN, ALLEN, *The Wound in the Heart; America and the Spanish Civil War* (New York, 1962).

GUZMÁN, EDUARDO DE, *El año de la victoria* (Madrid, 1974); *La muerte de la esperanza* (Madrid, 1973); *Madrid rojo y negro; milicias confederales* (Buenos Aires, 1939).

HALDANE, CHARLOTTE, *Truth Will Out* (London, 1949).

HALIFAX, Lord, *Speeches on Foreign Policy 1934–1939* (London, 1940); *The Fullness of Days* (London, 1957).

HAMILTON, THOMAS J., *Appeasement's child* (London, 1943).

HANIGHEN, FRANK (ed.), *Nothing but danger* (London, 1940).

HARPER, GLENN T., *German Economic Policy in Spain* (The Hague, 1967).

HEDILLA, MANUEL, *Testimonio* (Barcelona, 1973).

HELSBY, CYRIL, *Air raid Structures and A RP in Barcelona Today* (London, 1939).

HEMINGWAY, ERNEST, *For Whom the Bell Tolls* (New York, 1940); *The Fifth Column* (Harmondsworth, 1966); *The Spanish War* (London, 1938).

HENDERSON, Sir NEVILE, *Failure of a Mission* (London, 1940).

HENRÍQUEZ CAUBÍN, JULIÁN, *La batalla del Ebro* (Mexico, 1944).

HÉRICOURT, PIERRE, *Les Soviets et la France, fournisseurs de la révolution espagnole* (Paris, 1938?).

HERMET, GUY, *Les Espagnols en France* (Paris, 1967); *Los comunistas en España* (Paris, 1971).

HERNÁNDEZ, JESÚS, *La Grande Trahison* (Paris, 1953).

HIDALGO DE CISNEROS, IGNACIO, *Memorias*, 2 vols. (Paris, 1964).

HILLS, GEORGE, *Franco: the Man and his Nation* (London, 1967).

HIRIARTIA, J. DE, *Le Cas des catholiques basques* (Paris, 1938 ?).

'HISPANICUS', (pseud.) (ed.), *Foreign Intervention in Spain* (London, 1938).

HITLER, ADOLF, *Hitler's Table-Talk 1941–1943* (London, 1953).

HOARE, Sir SAMUEL, *Ambassador on Special Mission* (London, 1946).

HOBSBAWM, ERIC, *Primitive Rebels* (Manchester, 1959).

HODGSON, Sir ROBERT, *Spain Resurgent* (London, 1953).

HORNER, ARTHUR, *Incorrigible Rebel* (London, 1960).

HOSKINS, KATHARINE BAIL, *Today the Struggle; literature and politics in England during the Spanish Civil War* (Austin, 1969).

HOYOS, GRAF MAX VON, *Pedros y Pablos; fliegen, erleben, kämpfen in Spanien* (Munich, 1941).

HUBBARD, JOHN R., 'How Franco Financed His War', *The Journal of Modern History* (December, 1953).

HUIDOBRO PARDO, LEOPOLDO, *Memorias de un finlandés* (Madrid, 1939).

HULL, CORDELL, *Memoirs*, 2 vols. (New York, 1948).

HUMBERT-DROZ, JULES, *Mémoires*, 3 vols. (Neuchâtel, 1969–72).

I Accuse France, by 'A Barrister' (London, 1937).

IBARRURI, DOLORES, *et al.*, *Guerra y revolución en España 1936–1939* (in progress, 3 vols. 1967–71); *They Shall Not Pass: the Autobiography of La Pasionaria* (Translation of *El único camino*) (London, 1967).

ICKES, HAROLD, *The Secret Diary of Harold Ickes* (London, 1955).

INGE, W. R., *Dean Inge indicts the Red Government of Spain* (London, 1938).

International Brigades, The See Spain, Office of Information.

International Committee for the application of the agreement regarding Non-Intervention in Spain. Stenographic notes of proceedings, 1st to 30th meetings: of the Chairman's Sub-Committee; and of the technical sub-Committees (complete set in the Public Record Office, London).

International Military Tribunal: The Trial of the Major War Criminals, 37 vols. (Nuremberg, 1947–9).

IRIBARREN, JOSÉ MARÍA, *El general Mola* (Madrid, 1945).

IRVING, DAVID, *The Rise and Fall of the Luftwaffe* (London, 1974).

ISORNI, JACQUES, *Philippe Pétain*, 2 vols. (Paris, 1972).

Istoriya Velikoy Otechestvennoy voyny Sovetskogo Soyuza, 1941–1945, vol. I (Moscow, ?).

ITURRALDE, JUAN DE, *El catolicismo y la cruzada de Franco*, 2 vols. (Bayonne, 1955).

IZAGA, GUILLERMO ARSENIO DE, *Los presos de Madrid; recuerdos e impresiones de un cautivo en la España roja* (Madrid, 1940).

IZCARAY, JESÚS, *Madrid es nuestro* (Madrid–Barcelona, 1938).

JACKSON, GABRIEL, *A Concise History of the Spanish Civil War* (New York, 1974); *Historian's Quest* (New York, 1969); *The Spanish Republic and the Civil War 1931–1939* (Princeton, 1965).

Jane's Fighting Ships (London, 1936).

JATO, DAVID, *La rebelión de los estudiantes* (Madrid, 1953).

JELLINEK, FRANK, *The Civil War in Spain* (London, 1938).

JERROLD, DOUGLAS, *Georgian Adventure* (London, 1937).

JIMÉNEZ DE ASÚA, LUIS, *Anécdotas de las constituyentes* (Buenos Aires, 1942).

JOANIQUET, AURELIO, *Calvo Sotelo, una vida fecunda* (Santander, 1939).

JOHNSON, Dr HEWLETT, *Report of a Recent Delegation to Spain* (London, 1937).

JOHNSTONE, NANCY J., *Hotel in Flight* (London, 1939).

JOLL, JAMES, *Intellectuals in Politics* (London, 1960); *The Anarchists* (London, 1964).

JONG, Dr L. DE, *The German Fifth Column in the Second World War* (London, 1958).

JORDAN, PHILIP, *There is No Return* (London, 1939).

JOUBERT, Vice-Admiral H., *La Guerre d'Espagne et le catholicisme* (Paris, 1937) (pamphlet).

JUANES, JOSÉ, *Por qué fuimos a la guerra* (Avila, 1937).

JUNOD, MARCEL, *Warrior without Weapons* (London, 1951).

KAMINSKI, HANS ERICH, *Ceux de Barcelone* (Paris, 1937).

KANTOROWICZ, ALFRED, *Spanisches Tagebuch* (Berlin, 1948); *'Tschapaiew', das Bataillon der 21 Nationen* (Berlin, 1956).

KAY, HUGH, *Salazar and Modern Portugal* (London, 1970).

KEMP, PETER, *Mine were of Trouble* (London, 1957).

KENYON, Sir FREDERIC, *Art Treasures of Spain* (London, 1937).

KERSHNER, HOWARD, *Quaker Service in Modern War* (New York, 1950).

KESTEN, HERMANN, *Les Enfants de Guernica* (Paris, 1954).

KINDELÁN, General ALFREDO, *Mis cuadernos de guerra* (Madrid, 1945).

KIRK, H. L., *Pablo Casals* (New York, 1974).

KIRKPATRICK, Sir IVONE, *Mussolini, Study of a Demagogue* (London, 1964).

KLEIN, BURTON, *Germany's Economic Preparations for War* (Cambridge, Mass., 1959).

KLOTZ, HELMUT, *Les Leçons militaires de la guerre civile en Espagne* (Paris, 1937).

KNICKERBOCKER, H. R., *The Siege of the Alcázar* (Philadelphia, 1936).

KNOBLAUGH, H. EDWARD, *Correspondent in Spain* (London and New York, 1939).

KOESTLER, ARTHUR, *Dialogue with Death* (New York, 1942); *The Invisible Writing* (London, 1954); *Spanish Testament* (London, 1937).

KOLTSOV, MIKHAIL, *Diario de la guerra de España* (Paris, 1963).

KORTA, ADAM (with HOPMAN, M.), *Karol Świerczewski* (Warsaw, 1954).

KRIVITSKY, WALTER, *I was Stalin's Agent* (London, 1963).

KUTISCHER, EUGENE, *The Displacement of Population in Europe* (Montreal, 1944).

LACOUTURE, JEAN, *André Malraux* (Paris, 1973).

LA CRUZ, FRANCISCO, *El alzamiento, la revolución y el terror en Barcelona* (Barcelona, 1943).

LAMO DE ESPINOSA, E., *Filosofía y política en Julián Besteiro* (Madrid, 1973).

LANDAU, KATIA, *Le Stalinisme en Espagne* (Paris, 1938).

LANDIS, ARTHUR H., *The Abraham Lincoln Brigade* (New York, 1967).

LANGDON-DAVIES, JOHN, *Behind the Spanish Barricades* (New York, 1936).

LARGO CABALLERO, FRANCISCO, *Mis recuerdos, cartas a un amigo* (Mexico, 1954).

LARIOS, JOSÉ (Duque de LERMA), *Combat over Spain* (London, 1966).

LAST, JEF, *The Spanish Tragedy* (London, 1939).

Laszlo Rajk and his Accomplices before the People's Court: a transcript of the Rajk trial (Budapest, 1949).

League of Nations, *Rapport de la Mission sanitaire de la Société des Nations en Espagne, 28 décembre 1936 – 15 janvier 1937* (Paris, 1937); *Yearbook 1936* (Geneva, 1937).

LEHMANN, JOHN, *The Whispering Gallery* (London, 1955).

LEÓN, MARÍA TERESA, *Contra viento y marea* (Buenos Aires, 1941).

LERROUX, ALEJANDRO, *La pequeña historia* (Madrid, 1963).

LEVAL, GASTON, *L'Espagne libertaire 1936–1939: L'œuvre constructive de la révolution espagnole* (Paris, 1971); *Né Franco né Stalin: la collettività anarchiche spagnole nella lotta contro Franco e la reazione Staliniana* (Milan, 1955).

LEWIS, FLORA, *The Man Who Disappeared – the Strange History of Noël Field* (London, 1965).

LEWIS, WYNDHAM, *Count Your Dead: They Are Alive!* (London, 1937).

Libro de oro de la revolución española, 1936–1946 (Toulouse, 1946).

LIDDELL HART, Sir BASIL, *The Defence of Britain* (London, 1938); *Memoirs*, 2 vols. (London, 1965); *The Other Side of the Hill* (London, 1948); (ed.), *The Soviet Army* (London, 1956).

Lieder der spanischen Revolution (Moscow, 1937).

LINDBAECK, LISE, *Internationella Brigaden* (Stockholm, 1939).

LINDSLEY, LORNA, *War is People* (Boston, 1943).

LISÓN TOLOSANA, CARMELO, *Belmonte de los Caballeros* (Oxford, 1966).

LISTER, ENRIQUE, *Nuestra guerra, aportaciones para una historia de la guerra nacional revolucionaria del pueblo 1936–1939* (Paris, 1966).

LIZARRA, A. DE, *Los vascos y la república española, contribución a la historia de la guerra civil 1936–1939* (Buenos Aires, 1944).

LIZARZA, ANTONIO, *Memorias de la conspiración* (Pamplona, 1954).

LIZÓN GADEA, ADOLFO, *Brigadas internacionales en España* (Madrid, 1940).

LLARCH, JUAN, *La muerte de Durruti* (Barcelona, 1973).

LLORENS, JOSEP MARÍA, *La iglesia contra la república española* (Vieux, 1968).

LLOYD GEORGE, DAVID, *Spain and Britain* (London, 1937).

LLUCH VALLS, FRANCISCO, *Mi diario entre los mártires, cárcel de Málaga, año 1937* (Granada, 1937).

LODOLI, RENZO, *I legionari* (Milan, 1970).

LOEWENSTEIN, Prince HUBERTUS VON, *A Catholic in Republican Spain* (London, 1937).

LOJENDIO, LUIS MARÍA DE, *Operaciones militares de la guerra de España, 1936–1939* (Barcelona, 1940).

LONDON, ARTUR, *L'Aveu* (Paris, 1969); *Espagne* (Paris, 1966).

LONGO, LUIGI, *Le brigate internazionale in Spagna* (Rome, 1956).

LÓPEZ, JUAN, *Una misión sin importancia* (Madrid, 1972).

LÓPEZ BARRANTES, RAMÓN, *Mi exilio* (Madrid, 1974).

LÓPEZ CHACÓN, RAFAEL, *Por qué hice las chekas de Barcelona* (Madrid, 1940).

LÓPEZ FERNÁNDEZ, ANTONIO, *Defensa de Madrid* (Mexico, 1945).

LÓPEZ MUÑIZ, GREGORIO, *La batalla de Madrid* (Madrid, 1943).

LÓPEZ SEVILLA, ENRIQUE, *El partido socialista obrero español en las cortes constituyentes de la segunda república* (Mexico, 1969).

LORENZO, ANSELMO, *El proletariado militante* (Mexico, no date).

LORENZO, CESAR M., *Les Anarchistes espagnols et le pouvoir* (Paris, 1969).

LOVEDAY, ARTHUR FREDERIC, *World War in Spain* (London, 1939).

LOW, MARY, *Red Spanish Notebook; the first six months of the revolution and civil war* (London, 1937).

LOZANO, JESÚS, *La segunda república: imágenes, cronología y documentos* (Barcelona, 1973).

LUCA DE TENA, JUAN IGNACIO, *Mis amigos muertos* (Barcelona, 1971).

LUNN, ARNOLD HENRY MOORE, *Spanish Rehearsal* (New York, 1937).

LUSSU, EMILIO, 'La Legione italiana in Spagna' (*Giustizia e Libertà*, 28 August 1969).

MACK SMITH, DENIS, *Mussolini as a Military Leader* (The Stenton Lecture, University of Reading) (Reading, 1973).

MacROBERTS, NOEL, *A.R.P. lessons from Barcelona* (London, 1938).

McCULLAGH, FRANCIS, *In Franco's Spain: being the experiences of an Irish war correspondent during the great civil war which began in 1936* (London, 1937).

McGOVERN, JOHN, *Terror in Spain, how the Communist International has destroyed working class unity, undermined the fight against Franco, and suppressed the social revolution* (London, 1938?); *Why the bishops back Franco* (London, 1936).

McCKEE, SEUMAS, *I was a Franco Soldier* (London, 1938).

McNEILL-MOSS, GEOFFREY, *The Epic of the Alcazar* (London, 1937).

MADARIAGA, SALVADOR DE, *Spain, a Modern History* (London, 1946); *Memorias (1921–1936)* (Madrid, 1974).

MAEZTU, RAMIRO DE, *En vísperas de la tragedia*, prologue by J. D. Areilza (Madrid, 1941).

MAISKY, IVAN, *Spanish Notebooks* (London, 1966).

MAÍZ, B. FÉLIX, *Alzamiento en España, de un diario de la conspiración* (Pamplona, 1952).

MALAPARTE, CURZIO, *¡Viva la muerte!* (Special number of 'Prospettive') (Rome, 1939).

MALEFAKIS, EDWARD E., *Agrarian Reform and Peasant Revolution in Spain: Origins of the Civil War* (New Haven, 1970).

MALRAUX, ANDRÉ, *L'Espoir* (Paris, 1937).

MANCISDOR, JOSÉ MARÍA, *Frente a frente* (Madrid, 1963).

MANN, THOMAS, *Avertissement à l'Europe*; preface d'André Gide (Paris, 1937).

MANNING, LEAH, *What I Saw in Spain* (London, 1935).

MARAÑÓN, GREGORIO, *Libéralisme et communisme; en marge de la guerre civile espagnole* (Paris, 1938).

MARICHAL, JUAN, 'La significación histórica de Juan Negrín' (*Triunfo*, 22 June 1974).

MARINELLO, JUAN, *Hombres de la España leal* (Havana, 1938).

MARITAIN, JACQUES, *Sobre la guerra santa* (Buenos Aires, 1937).

MARRERO SUÁREZ, VICENTE, *La guerra española y el trust de cerebros* (Madrid, 1961).

MARTÍ, CASIMIRO, *Los orígenes del anarquismo en Barcelona* (Barcelona, (1959).

MARTIN, CLAUDE, *Franco, soldat et chef d'état* (Paris, 1959).

MARTIN, J. G., *Political and Social Changes in Catalonia During the Revolution* (Barcelona?, 1937).

MARTIN, KINGSLEY, *Editor* (London, 1938).

MARTÍN ARTAJO, JAVIER, *No me cuente Ud. su caso. Recuerdos* (Madrid, no date).

MARTÍNEZ, CARLOS, *Crónica de una emigración (la de los republicanos españoles en 1939)* (Mexico, 1959).

MARTÍNEZ ABAD, JULIO, *¡17 de julio! La guarnición de Melilla inicia la salvación de España* (Melilla, 1937).

MARTÍNEZ ALIER, JUAN, *La estabilidad del latifundismo* (Paris, 1968).

MARTÍNEZ AMUTIO, JUSTO, *Chantaje a un pueblo* (Madrid, 1974).

MARTÍNEZ BANDE, Colonel JOSÉ MANUEL, *La guerra en el norte* (Madrid, 1969); *Brigadas internacionales* (Barcelona, 1972); *El final del frente norte* (Madrid, 1972); *La batalla de Teruel* (Madrid, 1974); *La gran ofensiva sobre Zaragoza* (Madrid, 1973); *La invasión de Aragón y el desembarco en Mallorca* (Madrid, 1970); *La lucha en torno a Madrid* (Madrid, 1968); *La marcha sobre Madrid* (Madrid, 1968); *La ofensiva sobre Segovia y la batalla de Brunete* (Madrid, 1972); *Los cien últimos días de la república* (Barcelona, 1972); *Vizcaya* (Madrid, 1971).

MARTÍN BLÁZQUEZ, JOSÉ, *I Helped to Build an Army; civil war memoirs of a Spanish staff officer* (with an introduction by F. Borkenau) (London, 1939).

MARTÍNEZ DE CAMPOS, CARLOS (Duque DE LA TORRE), *Ayer, 1931–1953* (Madrid, 1970).

MARTÍNEZ PASTOR, MANUEL, *Cinco de marzo 1939* (Madrid, 1971).

MARTY, ANDRÉ, *Volontaires d'Espagne: douze mois sublimes!* (Paris, 1937).

MATORRAS, ENRIQUE, *El comunismo en España* (Madrid, 1935).

MATTHEWS, HERBERT, *The Yoke and the Arrows; a report on Spain* (New York, 1961); *Two Wars and More to Come* (New York, 1938).

MATTIOLI, GUIDO, *L'aviazione legionaria in Spagna* (Rome, 1940).

MAULVAULT, LUCIEN, *Glaïeul noir* (Paris, 1938).

MAURA, MIGUEL, *Así cayó Alfonso XIII . . .* (Mexico, 1962).

MAURÍN, JOAQUÍN, *Revolución y contrarevolución en España* (Paris, 1966).

MAURRAS, CHARLES, *Vers l'Espagne de Franco* (Paris, 1943).

MEAKER, GERALD, *The Revolutionary Left in Spain, 1914–1923* (Stanford, 1974).

Medical aid unit in Spain, The story of the (London, 1936).

MENDIZÁBAL VILLALBA, ALFREDO, *Aux origines d'une tragédie: la politique espagnole de 1923 à 1936* (Paris, 1937).

MENÉNDEZ REIGADA, IGNACIO, *La guerra nacional española ante la moral y el derecho* (Salamanca, 1937).

MERKES, MANFRED, *Die deutsche Politik im Spanischen Bürgerkrieg*, 2nd ed. (Bonn, 1969).

MEZQUIDA, LUIS MARÍA, *La batalla del Ebro*, 2 vols. (Tarragona, 1963–7); *La batalla del Segre* (Tarragona, 1972).

MIDDLEMAS, KEITH (and BARNES, JOHN), *Baldwin, A Biography* (London, 1969); *Diplomacy of Illusion* (London, 1972).

MIGUEL, FLORINDO DE, *Un cura en zona roja* (Barcelona, 1956).

MIKSCHE. F. O., *Blitzkrieg* (Harmondsworth, 1944).

MILLÁN ASTRAY, PILAR, *Cautivas: 32 meses en las prisiones rojas* (Madrid, 1940).

MINNEY, R. J., *The Private Papers of Hore-Belisha* (London, 1960).

MINTZ, FRANK, *L'Autogestion dans l'Espagne révolutionnaire* (Paris, 1970).

MIQUELARENA, JACINTO, *Cómo fui ejecutado en Madrid* (Avila, 1937); *El otro mundo* (Burgos, 1938).

MIRAVITLLES, JAUME, *Episodis de la guerra civil espanyola* (Barcelona, 1972).

MITCHELL, Sir PETER CHALMERS, *My House in Málaga* (London, 1938).

MITFORD, JESSICA, *Hons and Rebels* (London, 1960).

MOCH, JULES, *Rencontres avec Léon Blum* (Paris, 1970).

MODESTO, JUAN, *Soy del quinto regimiento* (Paris, 1969).

MOLA, EMILIO, *Obras completas* (Valladolid, 1940).

MOLINA, JUAN, *Noche sobre España* (Mexico, 1958).

MONELLI, PAOLO, *Mussolini. An intimate Life* (London, 1953).

MONTERO, ANTONIO, *La persecución religiosa en España* (Madrid, 1961).

MONTERO DÍAZ, SANTIAGO, *La política social en la zona Marxista* (Bilbao, 1938).

Montserrat, glosas a la carta colectiva de los obispos españoles (Barcelona, 1938). (The author was J. Vilar Costa.)

MONTSERRAT, VICTOR, *Le Drame d'un peuple incompris. La guerre au pays basque* (Paris, 1938).

MORA, CONSTANCIA DE LA, *In Place of Splendor; the autobiography of a Spanish woman* (New York, 1939).

MORAVEC, FRANTISEK, *Master of Spies* (London, 1975).

MORENO, Admiral, *La guerra en el mar* (Barcelona, 1959).

MORROW, FELIX, *Revolution and counter-revolution in Spain* (New York, 1938).

MUGGERIDGE, MALCOLM, *The Thirties* (London, 1940).

MÚGICA, Dr MATEO (Bishop of Vitoria), *Imperativos de mi conciencia* (Buenos Aires, 1945).

MUNIS, GRANDIZO, *Jalones de derrota: promesa de victoria, España 1930–1939* (Mexico, 1948).

MUÑIZ MARTÍN, OSCAR, *El verano de la dinamita* (Madrid, 1974).

MUÑOZ DIEZ, MANUEL, *Marianet, semblanza de un hombre* (Mexico, 1960).

MUSSOLINI, RACHELE, *My Life with Mussolini* (London, 1959).

Nazi Conspiracy in Spain, The (London, 1937). (The author was Otto Katz.)

NEHRU, JAWAHARLAL, *Spain! Why?* (London, 1937).

NELSON, STEVE, *The Volunteers* (Leipzig, 1954).

NENNI, PIETRO, *Spagna* (Milan, 1958).

NERUDA, PABLO, *España en el corazón, himno a las glorias del pueblo en la guerra (1936–1937)* (Santiago de Chile, 1938).

NIN, ANDRÉS, *Los problemas de la revolución española* (Paris, 1971).

NOLLAU, GUNTHER, *International Communism and World Revolution* (London, 1961).

NONELL BRÚ, SALVADOR, *Así eran nuestros muertos del laureado Tercio de Requetés de Ntra. Sra. de Montserrat* (Barcelona, 1965).

NORMAN, JAMES, *The Fell of Dark* (London, 1960).

NORTH, JOSEPH, *Men in the Ranks, the story of 12 Americans in Spain* (New York, 1939).

NOTHOMB, PAUL (JULIEN SEGNAIRE), *Le Rançon* (Paris, 1952).

Nuevo Ripaldo enriquecido con varios apéndices (Madrid, 1927).

NÚÑEZ MORGADO, AURELIO, *Los sucesos de España vistos por un diplomático* (Buenos Aires, 1941).

Nyon Conference, 1937, *International agreement for collective measures against piratical attacks in the Mediterranean by submarines* (London, 1937).

O'DONNELL, PEADAR, *Salud! An Irishman in Spain* (London, 1937).

O'DUFFY, EOIN, *Crusade in Spain* (London, 1938).

L'Oeuvre constructive de la révolution espagnole, CNT–AIT (Barcelona, 1936).

O'NEILL, CARLOTA, *Una mexicana en la guerra de España* (Mexico, 1964).

O'NEILL, R. J., *The German Army and the Nazi Party 1933–1939* (London, 1966).

ORLOV, ALEXANDER, *Evidence at Senate Internal Security Sub-committee*, (14 February 1957).

ORTEGA Y GASSET, JOSÉ, *España invertebrada* (Madrid, 1922).

ORTIZ DE VILLAJOS, CÁNDIDO, *De Sevilla a Madrid, ruta libertadora de la columna Castejón* (Granada, 1937).

ORWELL, GEORGE, *Collected Essays*, vol. I (London, 1968); *Homage to Catalonia* (London, 1938).

OSSORIO Y GALLARDO, ANGEL, *Julio de 1909, declaración de un testigo* (Madrid, 1910); *La España de mi vida, Autobiografía* (Buenos Aires, 1941); *Vida y sacrificio de Companys* (Buenos Aires, 1943).

OUDARD, GEORGES, *Chemises noires, brunes, vertes en Espagne* (Paris, 1938).

OYARZÚN, RAMÓN, *La historia del carlismo* (Madrid, 1969).

PABÓN, JESÚS, *Cambó*, 3 vols. (Barcelona, 1952–1969); *Palabras en la oposición* (Seville, 1935).

PACCIARDI, RANDOLFO, *Il battaglione Garibaldi* (Lugano, 1948).

PADELFORD, N. J., *International Law and Diplomacy in the Spanish Civil War* (Cambridge, Mass., 1939).

PAGÉS GUIX, LUIS, *La traición de los Franco* (Madrid, 1938).

PALACIO ATARD, VICENTE, *Aproximación histórica a la guerra civil española* (Madrid, 1970).

PALENCIA, ISOBEL DE, *I Must Have Liberty* (New York, 1940); *Smouldering Freedom* (New York, 1945).

PALMER, NETTIE, *Australians in Spain* (Sydney, 1948).

PAMIÉS, TOMÁS, *Testamento de Praga* (Barcelona, 1970).

PAUL, ELLIOT HAROLD, *The Life and Death of a Spanish Town* (New York, 1937).

PAUL-BONCOUR, J., *Entre deux guerres* (Paris, 1946).

PAYNE, ROBERT, *The Civil War in Spain, 1936–1939* (New York, 1962).

PAYNE, STANLEY, *Falange* (Stanford, 1961); *Basque Nationalism* (Reno, 1975); *Politics and the Military in Modern Spain* (Stanford, 1967); *The Spanish Revolution* (New York, 1970).

PAZ, ABEL, *Durruti: le peuple en armes* (Paris, 1972).

PEERS, EDGAR ALLISON, *Catalonia Infelix* (London, 1937); *The Spanish Tragedy, 1930–1936; Dictatorship, Republic, Chaos* (London, 1936); *Spain in eclipse, 1937–1943, a sequel to The Spanish Tragedy* (London, 1943).

PEIRATS, JOSÉ, *La CNT en la revolución española*, 3 vols. (Toulouse, 1951–1953); *Los anarquistas en la crisis política española* (Buenos Aires, 1964).

PEIRÓ, JOAN (JUAN), *Perull a la reraguarda* (Mataró, 1936).

PEMÁN, JOSÉ MARÍA, *Mis almuerzos con gente importante* (Madrid, 1970);

Poema de la bestia y el ángel (Madrid, 1939); *Un soldado en la historia (Vida del General Varela)* (Cádiz, 1954).

PENCHIENATI, CARLOS, *Brigate Internazionale in Spagna* (Milan, 1950).

PEÑA BOEUF, ALFONSO, *Memorias de un ingeniero político* (Madrid, 1954).

PÉREZ BARÓ, ALBERT, *Trenta mesos de collectivisme a Catalunya* (Barcelona, 1970).

PÉREZ DE OLAGUER, ANTONIO, *El terror rojo en Andalucía* (Burgos, 1938).

PÉREZ FERRERO, MIGUEL, *Drapeau de France; la vie des réfugiés dans les légations à Madrid* (Paris, 1938).

PÉREZ LÓPEZ, FRANCISCO, *A Guerrilla Diary of the Spanish Civil War* (London, 1972).

PÉREZ MADRIGAL, JOAQUÍN, *Aquí es la emisora de la flota republicana* (Madrid, 1939); *Augurios, estallido y episodios de la guerra civil* (Avila, 1937); *Memorias de un converso*, 9 vols. (Madrid, 1943).

PÉREZ MORÁN, DOMINGO, *¡A éstos, que los fusilen al amanecer!* (Madrid, 1973).

PÉREZ SALAS, JESÚS, *Guerra en España (1936 a 1939)* (Mexico, 1947).

PÉREZ SOLÍS, OSCAR, *Sitio y defensa de Oviedo* (Valladolid, 1938).

La persecución religiosa en España (Buenos Aires, 1937).

'PERTINAX', *Les Fossoyeurs de la France* (Paris, 1946).

PESCE, GIOVANNI, *Un garibaldino in Spagna* (Rome, 1955).

PETERSON, Sir MAURICE, *Both Sides of the Curtain* (London, 1950).

PHILBY, KIM, *My Silent War* (London, 1968).

PHILLIPS, A. V., *Spain under Franco* (London, 1940).

PHILLIPS, CECIL, *The Spanish Pimpernel* (London, 1960).

PIAZZONI, SANCHO, *Las tropas Flechas Negras en la guerra de España* (Barcelona, 1942).

PIKE, D. W., *Conjecture, Propaganda and Deceit and the Spanish Civil War* (Stanford, 1970); *Vae Victis!* (Paris, 1969).

PINI, G., and SUSMEL, D., *Mussolini*, 4 vols. (Florence, 1953–5).

PITCAIRN, FRANK, pseud. (COCKBURN, CLAUD), *Reporter in Spain* (Moscow, 1937).

PITT-RIVERS, JULIAN, *People of the Sierra* (London, 1954).

PLÁ, JOSÉ, *Historia de la segunda república española*, 4 vols. (Barcelona, 1940–41).

PONS PRADES, EDUARDO, *Un soldado de la república* (Madrid, 1974).

PORETSKY, ELIZABETH, *Our Own People* (London, 1969).

PRADERA, VÍCTOR, *El estado nuevo* (Pamplona, 1934).

PRATS Y BELTRÁN, ALARDO, *Vanguardia y retaguardia de Aragón* (Buenos Aires, 1938).

PRIESTLEY, J. B. (and WEST, REBECCA), *Spain and Us* (London, 1936).

PRIETO, INDALECIO, *Convulsiones de España*, 3 vols. (Mexico, 1967–9); *De mi vida*, 2 vols. (Mexico, 1965–70); *Cómo y porqué salí del Ministerio de Defensa Nacional, intrigas de los rusos en España* (Mexico, 1940); *Epistolario Prieto y Negrín* (Paris, 1939); *Palabras al viento* (Mexico, 1942); *Yo y Moscú* (Madrid, 1955).

PRIMO DE RIVERA, JOSÉ ANTONIO, *Obras completas* (Madrid, 1942).

PRITTIE, TERENCE, *Willy Brandt* (London, 1974).

PUZZO, DANTE, *Spain and the Great Powers, 1936–1941* (New York, 1962).

QUEIPO DE LLANO, ROSARIO, *De la cheka de Atadell a la prisión de Alacuás* (Valladolid, 1939).

QUINTANILLA, LUIS, *All the Brave* (New York, 1939); *Los rehenes del Alcázar de Toledo* (Paris, 1967).

RAMA, CARLOS, *La crisis española del siglo XX* (Buenos Aires, 1960).

'RAMÍREZ, LUIS', *Francisco Franco: historia de un mesianismo* (Paris, 1964).

RAMÍREZ JIMÉNEZ, MANUEL, *Los grupos de presión en la segunda república española* (Madrid, 1969).

RAMÓN-LACA, JULIO DE, *Cómo fue gobernada Andalucía* (Seville, 1939).

RAMOS, VICENTE, *La guerra civil 1936–1939 en la provincia de Alicante*, 3 vols. (Alicante, 1974).

RAMOS OLIVIERA, ANTONIO, *Politics, Economics and Men of Modern Spain 1808–1946* (London, 1946).

REDONDO, LUIS (and ZAVALA, JUAN DE), *El requeté; la tradición no muere* (Barcelona, 1957).

REGLER, GUSTAV, *The Great Crusade* (New York, Toronto, 1940); *The Owl of Minerva* (London, 1959).

REGUENGO, V., *Guerra sin frentes* (Madrid, 1954).

RELLO, SALVADOR, *La aviación en la guerra de España*, 4 vols. (Madrid, 1969–71).

RENN, LUDWIG, see VIETH VON GOLSSENAU.

La Renta Nacional de España en 1959 y Avance del 1960 (Madrid, 1960).

REPARAZ, ANTONIO, *Desde el cuartel general de Miaja al santuario de la Virgen de la Cabeza* (Valladolid, 1937).

RESTREPO, FÉLIX, *España mártir* (Bogotá, 1937).

Revolución de octubre en España, La (Madrid, 1934).

RIAL, JOSÉ ANTONIO, *La prisión de Fyffes* (Caracas, 1969).

RIBBENTROP, JOACHIM VON, *Memoirs* (London, 1954).

RICHARDS, VERNON, *Lessons of the Spanish Revolution, 1936–1939* (London, 1953).

RIDRUEJO, DIONISIO, *Escrito en España* (Buenos Aires, 1962); *Poesía en armas* (Barcelona, 1940).

'RIEGER, MAX', *Espionnage en Espagne* (Paris, 1938).

RIESENFELD, JANET, *Dancer in Madrid* (New York, 1938).

RÍO CISNEROS, AGUSTÍN DE (with PAVÓN PEREIRA, ENRIQUE), *Los procesos de José Antonio* (Madrid, 1969).

RIVAS-CHERIF, CIPRIANO DE, *Retrato de un desconocido: vida de Manuel Azaña* (Mexico, 1961).

ROA, RAÚL, *Pablo de la Torriente Brau y la revolución española* (Havana, 1937).

ROBINSON, RICHARD, 'Calvo Sotelo's Bloque Nacional and its Manifesto' (University of Birmingham, *Historical Journal* 1966, vol. x, No. 2); *The Origins of Franco's Spain* (Newton Abbot, 1970).

ROCKER, RUDOLF, *Extranjeros en España* (Buenos Aires, 1938); *The Tragedy of Spain* (New York, 1937).

RODRÍGUEZ CHAOS, MELQUESIDEZ, *24 años en la cárcel* (Paris, 1968).

RODRÍGUEZ TARDUCHY, EMILIO, *Significación histórica de la cruzada española* (Madrid, 1941).

ROJAS, CARLOS, *Por qué perdimos la guerra* (Barcelona, 1970).

ROJO, VICENTE, *¡ Alerta los pueblos! Estudio político-militar del período final de la guerra española* (Buenos Aires, 1939); *Así fue la defensa de Madrid* (Mexico, 1967); *España heroica* (Buenos Aires, 1942).

ROLFE, EDWIN, *The Lincoln Battalion* (New York, 1939).

ROMANONES, Conde de, *Y sucedió así* (Madrid, 1947).

ROMERO, EMILIO, *La paz empieza nunca* (Barcelona, 1965).

ROMERO, LUIS, *Desastre en Cartagena* (Madrid, 1971); *Tres días de julio* (Barcelona, 1967).

ROMERO MAURA, JOAQUÍN (with PRESTON, PAUL, VARELA ORTEGA, JOSÉ and RUIPEREZ, MARÍA), 'Para la historia de la república española' (*Revista Internacional de Sociología*, July–December 1972).

ROMERO-MARCHENT, JOAQUÍN, *Soy un fugitivo* (Valladolid, 1937).

ROMILLY, ESMOND, *Boadilla* (London, 1971).

ROOSEVELT, F. D., Papers (unpublished, Hyde Park, New York).

ROS, FÉLIX, *Preventorio D* (Barcelona, 1939).

ROSENSTONE, ROBERT A., *Crusade of the Left; the Lincoln Battalion in the Spanish Civil War* (New York, 1969).

ROSSELLI, CARLO, *Oggi in Spagna, domani in Italia* (Paris, 1938).

ROUGERON, C., *Les Enseignements aériens de la guerre d'Espagne* (Paris, 1940).

ROY, M. N., *Memoirs* (Bombay, 1964).

RUDEL, CHRISTIAN, *La Phalange* (Paris, 1972).

RUIZ ALBÉNIZ, VÍCTOR, *Del Ebro al Mediterráneo (febrero–abril del 38)* (Madrid, 1941).

RUIZ VILAPLANA, ANTONIO, *Burgos Justice; a year's experience of nationalist Spain* (New York, 1938).

RUMBOLD, RICHARD, *The Winged Life. A Portrait of Antoine de Saint-Exupéry, Poet and Airman* (London, 1953).

RUST, WILLIAM, *Britons in Spain* (London, 1939).

SABORIT, ANDRÉS, *Asturias y sus hombres* (Toulouse, 1964); *Julián Besteiro* (Buenos Aires, 1967).

SAINT-AULAIRE, AUGUSTE, comte DE, *La Renaissance de l'Espagne* (Paris, 1938).

SAINT-EXUPÉRY, ANTOINE DE, *Terres des hommes* (Paris, 1939).

SALAS LARRAZÁBAL, JESÚS, *Intervención extranjera en la guerra de España* (Madrid, 1974); *La guerra de España desde el aire* (Barcelona, 1969).

SALAS LARRAZÁBAL, RAMÓN, *Historia del ejército popular de la república*, 4 vols. (Madrid, 1974).

SALAZAR ALONSO, RAFAEL, *Bajo el signo de la revolución* (Madrid, 1935).

SALAZAR, OLIVEIRA, Dr, *L'Alliance anglaise et la guerre d'Espagne* (Lisbon, 1937).

SALCEDO, EMILIO, *Vida de don Miguel* (Madrid, 1964).

SALTER, CEDRIC, *Try-out in Spain* (New York, 1943).

SÁNCHEZ, JOSÉ MARIANO, *Reform and Reaction; the politico-religious background of the Spanish Civil War* (Chapel Hill, University of North Carolina Press, 1964).

SÁNCHEZ DEL ARCO, MANUEL, *El sur de España en la reconquista de Madrid* (Seville, 1937).

SÁNCHEZ GUERRA, RAFAEL, *Mis prisiones* (Buenos Aires, 1946).

SANCHÍS, MIGUEL, *Alas rojas sobre España* (Madrid, 1956).

SANTAMARIA, A., *Operazione Spagna 1936–1939* (Rome, 1965).

SANZ, RICARDO, *El sindicalismo y la política: los 'solidarios' y 'nosotros'* (Toulouse, 1966); *Figuras de la revolución española: Buenaventura Durruti* (Toulouse, 1944); *Los que fuimos a Madrid, Columna Durruti, 26 división* (Toulouse, 1969).

SANZ Y RUIZ DE LA PEÑA, N., *Romance de la muerte de Pepe García, 'el Algabeño' (1937)* (Valladolid, 1937).

Saragossa, Universidad de, *La guerra de Liberación Nacional* (Saragossa, 1961).

SARDÁ, JUAN, 'El Banco de España 1931–1962', in *El Banco de España* (Madrid, 1970).

SAROLEA, CHARLES, *Daylight on Spain; the answer to the Duchess of Atholl* (London, 1938).

SCHAPIRO, LEONARD, *The Communist Party of the Soviet Union* (London, 1960).

SCHLAYER, FELIX, *Diplomat im roten Madrid* (Berlin, 1938).

SCHLEIMANN, JURGEN, 'New Light on Münzenberg' (*Survey*, April 1965, London).

SCHMIDT, PAUL, *Hitler's Interpreter* (London, 1951).

SCHWARTZ, FERNANDO, *La internacionalización de la guerra civil española* (Barcelona, 1971).

SEALE, PATRICK (and MCCONVILLE, MAUREEN), *Philby, the Long Road to Moscow* (London, 1973).

SECO SERRANO, CARLOS, *Historia de España: época contemporánea* (Barcelona, 1962).

SEDWICK, FRANK, *The Tragedy of Manuel Azaña and the Fate of the Spanish Republic* (Ohio, 1963).

SEMPRÚN MAURA, CARLOS, *Révolution et contre-révolution en Catalogne* (Tours, 1974).

SENDER, RAMÓN, J., *Counter-attack in Spain* (Boston, 1937); *Requiem por un campesino español* (Buenos Aires, 1961); *Seven Red Sundays* (London, 1936); *The War in Spain* (London, 1937).

SERGE, VICTOR, *Memoirs of a Revolutionary* (London, 1963).

SERRANO SÚÑER, RAMÓN, *Entre Hendaya y Gibraltar* (Madrid, 1947).

Servicio Histórico Militar, *Historia de la guerra de liberación*, vol. I (Madrid, 1945).

SETON WATSON, CHRISTOPHER, *Italy from Liberalism to Fascism* (London, 1967).

SEVILLA ANDRÉS, DIEGO, *Historia política de la zona roja* (Madrid, 1954).

SHEEAN, VINCENT, *Not peace but a sword* (New York, 1939); *The Eleventh Hour* (London, 1939).

SILVA, General CARLOS DE, *Millán Astray* (Barcelona, 1956).

SIMPSON, Sir JOHN, *The Refugee Problem* (London, 1939).

SINCLAIR, UPTON, '*No pasarán*' *(They shall not pass)* (London?, 1937).

SLOAN, PAT (ed.), *John Cornford, a Memoir* (London, 1938).

SMITH, LOIS ELWYN, *Mexico and the Spanish Republicans* (Berkeley, 1955).

SOLANO, WILDEBALDO, *The Spanish Revolution: the Life of Andrés Nin* (London, no date).

SOLANO PALACIO, FERNANDO, *La tragedia del norte* (Barcelona, 1938).

Solidaridad de los pueblos con la república española (1936–1939) (Moscow, 1972).

SOMMERFIELD, JOHN, *Volunteer in Spain* (London, 1937).

SOMOZA SILVA, LÁZARO, *El general Miaja (biografía de un héroe)* (Mexico, 1944).

SORIA, GEORGES, *Trotskyism in the Service of Franco: facts and documents on the POUM* (London, 1938).

SOUCHY, AGUSTIN, *Colectivizaciones. La obra constructiva de la revolución española* (Barcelona, 1937); *Entre los campesinos de Aragón* (Valencia, 1937).

SOUTHWORTH, HERBERT R., *Antifalange* (Paris, 1967); *El mito de la cruzada de Franco* (Paris, 1963, also French edition); *La Destruction de Guernica* (Paris, 1975).

Spain, *Guernica; being the official report of a commission appointed by the Spanish national government to investigate the causes of the destruction of Guernica on 26–28 April, 1937* (London, 1938); Foreign Ministry, *La agresión italiana. Documentos ocupados a las unidades italianas en la acción de Guadalajara* (Valencia, 1937); Office of Information, *Las brigadas internacionales; la ayuda extranjera a los rojos españoles* (Madrid, 1948); *Appeal by the Spanish government. White book published by the Spanish government and presented to the Council on 28 May 1937* (Geneva, 1937); *Documents on the Italian intervention in Spain* (London, 1937); Tribunal supremo. Ministerio fiscal, *The general cause, the red domination in Spain, preliminary information drawn up by the ministry of justice* (Madrid, 1946); Servicio Histórico Militar, *Síntesis histórica de la guerra de liberación, 1936–1939* (Madrid, 1968).

SPENDER, STEPHEN *World within World* (London, 1951); (with LEHMANN, JOHN (ed.)), *Poems for Spain* (London, 1939).

SPERBER, MURRAY A., comp., *And I remember Spain; a Spanish civil war anthology* (London, 1974).

SPIELHAGEN, FRANZ, *Spione und Verschwörer in Spanien* (Paris, 1936).

SPRIANO, PAOLO, *Storia del partito comunista italiano*, vol. III *(I fronti popolari, Stalin, la guerra)* (Turin, 1970).

STACKELBERG, KARL GEORG, Freiherr VON, *Legion Condor; deutsche Freiwillige in Spanien* (Berlin, 1939).

STANSKY, PETER (and ABRAHAMS, WILLIAM), *Journey to the Frontier* (London, 1966).

STAVIS, BARRIE, *Refuge; a one act play of the Spanish war* (New York, London, 1939).

STEER, GEORGE LOWTHER, *The Tree of Gernika: a field study of modern war* (London, 1938).

STEWART, MARGARET, *Reform under Fire; social progress in Spain 1931–1938* (London, 1938).

STRONG, ANNA LOUISE, *Spain in Arms, 1937* (New York, 1937).

'SUÁREZ, ANDRÉS', *El proceso contra el POUM* (Paris, 1974).

SÚÑER, ENRIQUE, *Los intelectuales y la tragedia española* (San Sebastián, 1937).

SWAFFER, HANNEN, *A British Art-critic in Republican Spain* (Madrid, 1938).

SZINDA, GUSTAV, *Die XI Brigade* (Berlin, 1956).

TAGÜEÑA, MANUEL, *Testimonio de dos guerras* (Mexico, 1973).

TALÓN, VICENTE, *Arde Guernica* (Madrid, 1970).

TAMAMES, RAMÓN, *Estructura económica de España* (Madrid, 1969); *La república, la era de Franco* (Madrid, 1973).

TAMARO, ATTILIO, *Venti anni di storia* (Rome, 1952–3).

TANGYE, NIGEL, *Red, White and Spain* (London, 1937).

TARAZONA, FRANCISCO, *Sangre en el cielo* (Mexico, 1960).

TAYLOR, A. J. P., *The Origins of the Second World War* (London, 1961).

TAYLOR, FOSTER JAY, *The United States and the Spanish Civil War* (New York, 1956).

TÉLLEZ, ANTONIO, *La guerrilla urbana en España: Sabater* (Paris, 1972).

TENNANT, ELEONORA, *Spanish Journey* (London, 1936).

TERMES, JOSEP, *Anarquismo y sindicalismo en España: La primera internacional 1864–1881* (Barcelona, 1972).

TÉRY, SIMONE, *Front de la liberté, Espagne 1937–1938* (Paris, 1938).

THARAUD, JÉRÔME, *Cruelle Espagne* (Paris, 1937).

THOMAS, GORDON (and WITTS, MAX MORGAN), *Guernica* (New York, 1975).

THOMPSON, Sir GEOFFREY, *Front Line Diplomat* (London, 1959).

'*The Times*', *History of*, vol. IV (London, 1952).

TINKER, FRANK GLASGOW, *Some Still Live* (New York, 1938).

TITMUSS, RICHARD, *Problems of Social Policy* (London, 1950).

TOGLIATTI, PALMIRO, *Le Parti communiste italien*, translation (Paris, 1961).

TOMALIN, MILES, *Diaries* (unpublished).

TOMLIN, E. W. F., *Simone Weil* (Cambridge, 1954).

TORRIENTE BRAU, PABLO DE LA, *Peleando con los milicianos* (Mexico, 1938).

TORYHO, JACINTO, *La independencia de España* (Barcelona, 1938).

TOYNBEE, ARNOLD, *Survey of International Affairs*, 1937, vol. II (with V. M. Boulter) (London, 1938); 1938, vol. I (with Katherine Duff) (London, 1948).

TOYNBEE, PHILIP, *Friends Apart* (London, 1954); *Spain Assailed* (with Gilles Martinet, etc.: a student delegation to Spain) (London, 1937).

TRAINA, RICHARD P., *American Diplomacy and the Spanish Civil War* (Bloomington, 1968).

TRAUTLOFT, HANNES, *Als Jagdflieger in Spanien* (Berlin, 1940).

TREND, J. B., *The Origins of Modern Spain* (Cambridge, 1934).

TROTSKY, LEON, *The Spanish Revolution (1931–1939)* (New York, 1973).

TRYTHALL, J. W. D., *Franco: A Biography* (London, 1970).

TUÑÓN DE LARA, MANUEL, *La España del siglo XX* (Paris, 1966); *El movimiento obrero en la historia de España* (Madrid, 1972).

TUSELL, JAVIER, *Historia de la democracia cristiana en España*, 2 vols. (Madrid, 1974); *Las elecciones del Frente Popular*, 2 vols. (Madrid, 1971).

ULLMAN, JOAN, *The Tragic Week, A study of anticlericalism in Spain 1875–1912* (Cambridge, Massachusetts, 1968).

United Nations Security Council, *Report on Spain* (New York, 1946).

United States Government, *Foreign Relations of the United States:* 1936 (vol. II); 1937 (vol. I); 1938 (vol. I); 1939 (vol. II). (Washington, 1954–56).

URIBARRI, MANUEL, *La quinta columna española* (Havana, 1943).

URRACA PASTOR, MARÍA ROSA, *Así empezamos (memorias de una enfermera)* (Bilbao, no date).

URRUTIA, JULIO DE, *El cerro de los héroes* (Madrid, 1965).

USD: see United States Government.

VALDESOTO, F. DE, *Francisco Franco* (Madrid, 1943).

VALVERDE, JUAN TOMÁS, *Memorias de un alcalde* (Madrid, 1961).

VANNI, ETTORE, *Io, comunista in Russia* (Bologna, 1948).

VANSITTART, Lord, *The Mist Procession* (London, 1958).

VEGA GONZÁLEZ, ROBERTO, *Cadetes mexicanos en la guerra de España* (Mexico, 1954).

VEGAS LATAPIÉ, E., *El pensamiento político de Calvo Sotelo* (Madrid, 1941).

VELARDE, JUAN, *Política económica de la dictadura* (Madrid, 1968).

VENEGAS, JOSÉ, *Las elecciones del Frente Popular* (Buenos Aires, 1942).

VICENS VIVES, JAIME, *Aproximación a la historia de España* (Barcelona, 1962).

VIDAL I BARRAQUER, ARXIU, *Església i estat durant la segona república espanyola 1931–1936*, vol. I (Montserrat, 1971).

VIETH VON GOLSSENAU, ARNOLD ('LUDWIG RENN'), *Der Spanische Krieg* (Berlin, 1955).

VIGÓN, JORGE, *General Mola, el Conspirador* (Barcelona, 1957).

VILA SAN JUAN, JOSÉ LUIS, *¿ Así fue? Enigmas de la guerra civil española* (Barcelona, 1972).

VILANOVA, ANTONIO, *La defensa del alcázar de Toledo* (Mexico, 1963).

VILAR, PIERRE, *Histoire de l'Espagne* (Paris, 1952).

VILAR, SERGIO, *Protagonistas de la España democrática, la oposición a la dictadura 1931–1969* (Paris, 1969).

VILARÓ, JOSÉ ESTEBAN, *El ocaso de los dioses rojos, Barcelona, Perthus, Argelés, París, Méjico* (Barcelona, 1939).

VILLALBA DIÉGUEZ, FERNANDO, *Diario de guerra, 1938–1939* (Madrid, 1956).

VILLAR, MANUEL, *El anarquismo en la insurrección de Asturias* (Valencia, 1935).

VILLAR SALINAS, JESÚS, *Repercusiones demográficas de la última guerra civil española* (Madrid, 1942).

VILLARÍN, JORGE, *Guerra en España contra el judaísmo bolchevique* (Cadiz, no date).

VIÑAS, ANGEL, *La Alemania nazi y el 18 de julio* (Madrid, 1974).

VOROS, SANDOR, *American Commissar* (Philadelphia, 1961).

'W.W.W., General', *El mando* (Barcelona, 1937).

WALL, BERNARD, *Spain of the Spaniards* (New York, 1938).

WARNER, GEOFFREY, *France and Non-Intervention in Spain, July–August 1936* (International Affairs, April 1962).

WATKINS, K. W., *Britain Divided* (London, 1963).

WATSON, KEITH SCOTT, *Single to Spain* (London, 1937).

WATT, D. C., 'Soviet aid to the Republic', *The Slavonic and East European Review* (June 1960).

WEIL, SIMONE, *Ecrits historiques et politiques* (Paris, 1960).

WEINBERG, GERHARD, *The Foreign Policy of Hitler's Germany. Diplomatic Revolution in Europe* (Chicago, 1970).

WEINTRAUB, STANLEY, *The Last Great Cause: the intellectuals and the Spanish Civil War* (London, 1968).

WEIZSÄCKER, ERNST VON, *Memoirs* (New York, 1951).

WHITAKER, J. T., 'Prelude to War' (*Foreign Affairs*, New York, October 1942).

WINTRINGHAM, THOMAS HENRY, *English Captain* (London, 1939).

WOLFE, BERTRAM, *Khrushchev and Stalin's Ghost* (New York, 1957).

WOOD, J. K., *The Long Shadow* (unpublished MSS, Harrogate).

WOOD, NEAL, *Communism and British Intellectuals* (London, 1959).

WOODCOCK, GEORGE, *Anarchism* (London, 1963).

WOOLMAN, DAVID, *Rebels in the Rif* (London, 1969).

WOOLSEY, GAMEL, *Death's other Kingdom* (London, New York, 1939).

WORSLEY, CUTHBERT, *Behind the Battle* (London, 1939).

WULLSCHLEGER, MAX, (ed.), *Schweizer Kämpfen in Spanien* (Zurich, 1939).

XIMÉNEZ DE SANDOVAL, FELIPE, *José Antonio, Biografía apasionada* (Barcelona, 1941).

YZURDIAGA, FERMÍN, *Discurso al silencio y voz de la Falange* (Salamanca, 1937).

ZAYAS, Marqués DE, *Historia de la vieja guardia de Baleares* (Madrid, 1955).

ZUGAZAGOITIA, JULIÁN, *Historia de la guerra en España* (Buenos Aires, 1940); *Pablo Iglesias* (Madrid, 1926).

ZYROMSKI, JEAN, *Ouvrez la frontière!* (Paris, 1936).

ZAYAS, Marqués DE, *Historia de la vieja guardia de Baleares* (Madrid, 1955).

ZUGAZAGOITIA, JULIÁN, *Historia de la guerra en España* (Buenos Aires, 1940); *Pablo Iglesias* (Madrid, 1936).

ZYROMSKI, JEAN, *Contre la frontière* (Paris, 1939).

Index

NOTES:

1. Where only one of the surnames of a Spanish person is known (see note 2 on page 4), that surname precedes all instances of where both are known.
2. Officers are normally given ranks which they held on 18 July 1936, or higher ranks later obtained.
3. Spanish towns and villages are given with their provinces. Thus: Covadonga (Oviedo).
4. The following abbreviations are used:

A: Anarchist (CNT, FAI)
Abp: Archbishop
Alb: Albanian
Arty: Artillery
B: Basque
Be: Belgian
Bp: Bishop
Br: British
Bulg: Bulgarian
C (and com.): Communist
Car: Carlist
Cat: Catalan
Col: Colonel, Lieut Colonel
Con: Conservative
Cub: Cuban
Cz: Czech
Dan: Danish
Dip: Diplomatic
Dir: Director
Du: Dutch
Ed: Editor
Eng: English
F: Falange
Fas: Fascist
FR: Father
Fr: French
G: German
Gov: Governor
Gen: General
Hu: Hungarian
IB: International Brigade
Ir: Irish
It: Italian
Lab: Labour
Ld: Lord
Lieut: Lieutenant
LR: Left Republican
Maj: Major
Min: Minister
M, Mon: Monarchist
N, Nat: Nationalist in civil war
P: *POUMista* (see page xiii)
Pol: Polish
Port: Portuguese
Prof: Professor
R, Rep: Republican in civil war
Rad: Radical
Ru: Russian
S, Soc: Socialist
Sp: Spanish
Sw: Swiss
UR: Republican Union Party
US: United States
v: von
vol: Volunteer
Yug: Yugoslav

Abad de Santillán, Diego (*b.* 1897) (A), councillor of *Generalidad*, 270n3, 524, 654n3; meeting with Companys, 248; and Anti-Fascist Militias Committee, 250; and anarchist movement, 429, 448n3, 725; on José Antonio, 499n4; on revolution's lack of achievement, 527–8; denounces Negrín, 866n1
Abadiano (Vizcaya), 616
ABC, M. newspaper 53, 57, 59, 141, 504n2, 639, 644, 760; suspension, 58, 102; London correspondent, 203; as *ABC de Madrid*, 292n2
ABC de Sevilla, 272n1, 859n2
Abd-el-Krim, Mohammed (1882–1963), Leader of the rebels of the Rif, 24–5, 27 and n2, 936
Aboal, Maj. Juan (*b.* 1893) (R), 344
Abraham Lincoln Battalion, 574n3, 591, 595, 608n3, 716, 725n2, 798n2, 851; declared subversive, 955
Abramovich, Rafael (*b.* 1880), Ru. Menshevik leader, 706
Abriat, Col. (Com), 717
Aburtos (family), 988
Abyssinia, 479; Italian conquest, 345,

Abyssinia – *contd*
353, 439, 597, 739, 741, 797, 822, 856n1; U S neutrality, 362; the League and, 439
Acción Castellana, right-wing group, 59
Acción Catalana (Acció Catalá), 45n1, 250 and n2, 672 and n2
Acción Católica, 105–6
Acción Española, legal M. paper, 59; influence on Franco, 947
Acción Nacional (Popular Action), 55n2, 57; purpose, 55–6
Acción Popular, 107; core of CEDA, 108
Acosta, Bert, U S airman, 575–6, 576n1
Acracia, CNT newspaper, 656n1; and a conventional army, 544
L'Action Française, 337
L'Action Française (newspaper), 151, 697, 766n3
Adam, Ernst, G. vol. in I B, 458
Adams, Vyvyan (1900–51), Eng. Con. politician, 897
Addison, Christopher (later Ld. Addison) (1869–1951), 469n2
Adelante (P O U M newspaper), 663
Ademuz (Valencia), 558
Admiral Scheer (G. battleship), 371, 387, 470, 685
Aerial reconnaissance, 981n2
Agadir, 231n1
Agrarian Party, Castilian landowners, 59
Agrarian Reform, Institute of, 84, 106, 146, 169; settlements under, 170, 553; collectives in R. Spain, 553 and n1; Castro Delgado as Dir.-Gen., 564 and n2; suspension under Franco, 758; expropriation of land, 785; aid to peasants, 785n5
Agrarian Reform Law, 83–5, 91, 100, 101n, 148, 155; abandonment, 127; settlements in 1934, 130; reforms in 1936, 161; fresh impetus, 169, 170; under N., 284 and n3
Agrarians, 6, 107; 1936 elections, 151, 156, 162n2; military training, 151
Agriculture, new legislation, 72–3; conditions in Spain, 78ff., 131, 169, 202; reform ideas, 79–80, 82–5; main problems, 80–83; tenant farmers, 82–3, 131, 761; 1932 revolts, 103; wage inflation and, 170; under Second Republic, 188, 189; in war, 553; backing for small farmers, 564; N. wartime policy, 757–8, 761; in R. area, 785–6, 863–4, 864n1; losses due to war, 928 and n4; 'great famine' period, 929; present productivity, 956n2
Aguado Martínez, Maj. Virgilio (1900–36) (N), commander at Teruel, 326
Aguilera, Capt. Gonzalo (N), press officer, 504n2
Aguirre Cerda, Pedro, Pres. of Chile, 814n2
Aguirre y Lecube, José Antonio (1904–60) (B), Pres. of 'Euzkadi', 430, 431, 513, 540, 621, 774; and monarchists, 89; youth movement (*Mendigoixales*), 89n; cabinet, 431; and Basque army, 680, 687; and a separate peace, 681 and n2; defence of Bilbao, 691; Santander campaign, 719n, 720; *d.*, 951
Aid to Spain, 606n1
Air force, nationalist, 342, 358; numbers, 321; equipment, 330–31; command of the air, 371, 376, 715, 718, 937; aeroclub volunteers, 371; Italian and German reinforcements, 376 and n1, 678; and Messerschmitts, 678 and n2, 713, 715, 775; superiority of, 400, 678–9; and Madrid offensive, 432, 481–2, 483, 593; and Mola's Basque campaign, 612, 614; bombs Durango, 616–17; and Guernica, 626, 628; assault on Bilbao, 690–91, 692; battle of Brunete, 713, 714–15; creation of heroes, 756; renewed bombing of R. cities, 826–7; and battle of the Ebro, 841, 842, 843, 854–5; Catalonia campaign, 868; and value of foreign aid, 941
Air force, republican, 371n3, 587; first bomb, 319 and n2; equipment, 330–31; capabilities, 375, 400; reorganized, 407–8; and control of the air, 446, 937; success at Avila airfield, 482; anti-aircraft batteries, 548n2; Russian aid and equipment, 548 and n2, 662n5, 678, 830 and n3, 835; communist influence, 548; defence of Madrid, 589, 597, 600, 602; Basque campaign, 615–16; superiority of, 678, 779; bombs *Deutschland*, 685; and Barajas incident, 686; battle of Brunete, 713; defence of Santander, 718; strength (1937–38), 779; internal rivalry, 807; coastal defence force, 807; French aid, 830 and n3, 835; impotence at Ebro, 843, 854; Catalonia campaign (1938–9), 868; peace proposal, 892, 911, 912
Air force, Spanish, 100, 142; oath of allegiance, 58; in Moroccan wars, 203n2; and military rising, 217, 219, 246; armaments, 329; numbers and make of aircraft, 330 and nn1, 3

INDEX

Air France, 364n4, 390, 884
Air-raids, foretaste of the future, 486; fail to achieve submission, 486, 807; and Messerschmitts, 109; over Madrid, 551; bombardments, 794; Br. government mistake in bomb/casualty ratio, 945 n3. *See also under individual cities*
Aitken, George (*b.* 1894) (R), Eng. vol. in I B, 591, 607n3, 710n, 713n5; returns home, 723n1
Aizpún Santafé, Rafael, CEDA minister of justice, 134n1
Ajuriaguerra, Juan (*b.* 1904) (B), 721
Akulov, Gen. (Ru. officer), military intelligence in Catalonia, 447n2
Alafuzov, V. (Ru. naval officer), 549n3
Alas Argüelles, Prof. Leopoldo (*d.* 1936), execution, 266
Alauch, Carmen, 10n1
Alava (B. province), 87, 132, 262, 614; illiteracy, 56; in rising, 236–7; population of, 237n1; Francoism in, 541; unsuccessful offensive in, 541n1
Alba, Duque de (Jacobo Stuart Fitzjames y Falcó) (1870–1953), N. agent in London, 754, 766, 807n7, 897n3; Madrid Palacio de Liria, 486; reported meeting with Negrín, 848n4; talks with Foreign Office, 849
Albacete, 241, 255, 325; I B base, 456 and n2, 457, 459–60, 461, 488n3, 574, 608, 780–81, 816, 955; '*troika*' command, 457; communist power-house, 608; German/French quarrels, 781; Nat. occupation, 915, 924
Albalate de Cinca (Saragossa), 126n2, 294n3
Albania, 767, 954, 969
Albar, Manuel (S), 477n1; commissariat coordinator, 836
Albatross (G. patrol ship), 685
Alberti, Rafael (*b.* 1902) (C), poet, 699; release from Ibiza, 381; country house, 904
Albertia, Mt., 617
Albiñana y Sanz, Dr José María (1883–1936) (F), founder of 'Nationalist' party, 100; death, 404
Albornoz y Liminiana, Alvaro de (1879–1954) (R), Rad Min., Amb. in Paris, 337, 387, 441; in Azaña's cabinet, 36, 38, 42n2; and Bank of Spain, 975n1
Albufera (Valencia), rice fields, 754
Alcalá de Guadaira (Seville), 326
Alcalá de Gurrea (Huesca), 126n2
Alcalá de Henares (Madrid), 36, 247, 447, 596, 597, 624n1; prison, 103, 705; Russian aerodrome, 471n1
Alcalá Zamora, Niceto (1877–1949), Pres. of the Republic (1931–36), 58n2, 76, 84, 130, 147, 171–2; character, 33, 194, 931; following, 72, 153; resignation, 76; distrust of rivals, 125 and n, 126, 134, 149; denounced by L R, 134; and Fanjul, 149; impeachment, 172, 221; last years, 172n1; *d.* in exile, 951
Alcampel (Huesca), 126n2
Alcañiz (Teruel), 800
Alcantarilla (Murcia), Ru. fighter-bomber base, 447
Alcázar, the (Toledo), siege of, 246–7, 247n1, 324–6; hostages, 246–7, 247n1, 409–10, 411–13; telephone call at, 324n1; 'sightseers', 325; N. relief, 385–6, 400, 412, 413; Franco and, 412, 423; bloodbath, 412; results, 413
Alcázar de San Juan (Alcázar de Cervantes), 272, 556 and n2, 558
Alcázar de Velasco, Angel (*b.* 1909) (F) 206n3
Alcira (Valencia), 305
Alcocero hill (Burgos), 689
Alcolea de Cinca (Huesca), 558
Alcora (Castellón), 303–4
Alcorisa (Teruel), 126n2, 556
Alcoy (Alicante), 305, 380n4
Alcubierre (Huesca), 800; Sierra de, 316
Alfambra (river), 793
Alfaro Polanco, José María (*b.* 1906) (F), 195n2
Alfonso XII, King of Spain (1857–85) (King 1875–85), accession, 14; death, 16; and the army, 91
Alfonso XIII, King of Spain (1886–1941) (King 1886–1931), 7, 89, 920; abdication, 3, 32; regency, 16; and First World War, 21, 22; and Moroccan wars, 24, 25 and n, 93; and Primo de Rivera, 26, 28, 29; 'trial', 26n1; attempts to govern, 29–30; in exile, 32, 96, 109, 130, 342, 352, 421; and Segura, 47; army adherents, 57, 59, 91; supports the republic, 58; attempted murder, 68, 132; pact with Carlists, 96; monarchist group, 151–2, 205; and Franco, 422, 884; death, 947
Alfonso Carlos, Don (1849–1936), Carlist pretender, 96, 97, 167n3, 205, 239; death, 425; his widow and Franco, 639

Alfonso Pérez (prison ship), 540
Alfonso Trallero, Ramón (*d.* 1937) (N), Mayor of Belchite, 726
'El Algabeño' (N), bullfighter, 283; *d.* in battle (1937), 491
Algeciras, 212, 231, 255, 326, 332, 380; military rising, 223, 241
Algeria, 449, 739, 911
Algete (Madrid), 447; Ru. aerodrome, 471n1
Algorta (Vizcaya), 718n
Alhama (Saragossa), 582
Alhucemas Bay, Sp. landing, 98, 140
Alianza Internacional de Trabajadores (AIT), 561 and n1
Alianza Juvenil Anti-fascista (AJA), 783
Alianza Obrera, 133, 135 and n2
Alicante, 242, 251, 273n5, 305, 421, 906, 909; R. refugees, 914 and n2; It. entry, 915
Alicante prison, 11, 183, 251, 498; and José Antonio, 499–500
Allen, Jay (*b.* 1900), US journalist, 374n, 421, 498n1
Alloca, Capt. (*d.* 1937), Fr. vol. in IB, 458, 716; shot for desertion, 716
Almadén (Seville), 333; copper mines, 519
Almadrones (Guadalajara), 598
Almagro (Ciudad Real), agricultural collective, 559–61
Almansa (Albacete), 924; artillery school, 548
Almendralejo (Badajoz), Moorish massacres, 373 and n
Almería, 21, 242, 251, 553n1, 585; murder of bishops, 270n4; communism, 306; bombardment of, 685–7, 734; suggested safety zone at, 828; R. refugees, 914; N. occupation, 915
Almirante Antequera (R. destroyer), 797
Almirante Cervera (N. cruiser), 253, 310, 331n4, 332, 377
Almirante Fernández (R. cruiser), 426
Almirante Valdés (R. destroyer), 227
Alonso, Bruno (1888–) (S), commissar of R. fleet, 900; ignorance of the sea, 549
Alonso Goya, José María (*d.* 1937) (F), 638
Alonso Vega, Col. (later Gen.) Camilo (1889–1970) (N), 237 and n1, 759; and military rising, 237, 541n1; Navarrese brigade leader, 612, 712, 717, 803; civil war campaigns, 617, 712, 803; and Ebro, 841, 843; in Franco's ministry, 948n1
Altea (Alicante), 275–6, 276n1
Altmaier, Jacob (1889–1963), G. peace intermediary, 819n
Alto de León Pass, 315, 320; battle of, 321, 322
Altolaguirre, Manuel (R), poet, 699
Alvarez, Santiago (C), pol. commisar, 649
Alvarez Alonso, Juan Antonio, employee of CAMPSA, 417n2
Alvarez Arenas Romero, Gen. Eliseo (*b.* 1882) (N), and Catalonia, 874
Alvarez Buylla, Capt. Arturo (1895–1936), Acting High Commissioner of Sp. Morocco (1936), 205–6, 217
Alvarez Buylla, Plácido, minister (1936), 179n
Alvarez Coque, Col. (1877–) (R), Estremadura plan, 662n1
Alvarez y González, Melquíades (1864–1936), politician, leader of Democratic Progressive party, 404, 931
Alvarez del Vayo, Julio (1891–1974) (S), Ambassador, foreign minister, commissar-general, 116, 388n4, 402, 435, 664, 775, 814; and collaboration with bourgeoisie, 110 and n1; and army rising (1936), 172; and Codovilla, 200n3; cabinet posts, 406, 533, 650, 670–71, 770; on Spain at Geneva, 439–40, 571, 683, 743, 744, 823, 848; dismissal planned, 534; on war council, 546; communist disapproval, 651; replacement, 775; and a mediated peace, 880, 894; and Prado paintings, 880; and Azaña's resignation, 889; leaves Spain, 905–6; expulsion from socialist party, 950
Amadeo I, Duke of Aosta, King of Spain (1845–90), 14, 597
Amado, Andrés (N), min. of finance (1938) in Franco's cabinet, 425n4, 752, 753
Amba, Achmed, Ru. pilot, 339n2
Ambou, Juan (C), Leader in Asturias, 731
América, regiment of, 315n
American International Telegraph and Telephone Co., monopoly, 28
American Medical Aid Fund to the Spanish Republic, 608n4
Americans in Spanish Civil War, *see* US citizens
Amery, Julian (*b.* 1919), Con. politician, visits 'Social Help', 507n2; at Huesca cemetery, 800n2
D'Amico, Gen., It. artillery commander, 856n1

INDEX

Amnesty, 1936 decrees, 161
Amorebieta (Vizcaya), 679–80
Amposta (Tarragona), 838, 840
Amster, Mauricio, Pol. vol. in IB, meeting with Kléber, 492n1
Anarchist Brigades, 588n, 658, 724, 801, 835, 902
Anarchist Youth, *see* Federación Iberica de Juventudes Libertarias (FIJL)
Anarchists, 11, 26n3, 30, 40; organization of, 6, 65, 68; anti-government activity, 16, 19 and n2, 61–2; reaction to Russian Revolution, 22, 23, 67; and violence, 24, 61, 63, 275–6, 276n1, 278–9; disputes of, 24, 61, 63, 66, 73–4, 521–2, 647, 813; ideologies of, 39, 60–62, 66, 71, 136, 181–2, 192, 279, 526, 528, 539; and communism, 40, 67 and n3, 402, 483 and n3, 646, 660n2, 661–2, 724–5, 865, 933–4; and the church, 54, 61 and n, 269; and the state, 60, 69, 249; protest at industrialization, 61, 63; assassination attempts, 63, 69; rationalist schools, 64; in First World War, 65–6; power over working classes, 66, 190; CNT/*Pistolero* warfare, 66 and n2; eclipse under Primo de Rivera, 67–8, 71; legendary warriors, 68; membership and numbers, 70 and n, 110, 249, 293, 671–2, 672n1; *treintista* movement, 73–4, 180, 193n1, 471; deportations, 78; outbursts of 1933, 103–5, 110; and Profintern, 117; imprisonments, 145, 162; and 1936 elections, 154–5; and 'libertarian communism', 180, 181–3, 249; oppose an organized army, 181, 544–5, 546, 547; and Azaña's government, 193; song '*Hijos del pueblo*', 195–6, 196n1; and military rising, 223, 225n2, 232–3, 234, 236, 248; executions by (1936), 259; efforts to stop, 277, 279, 298–9; and factory organization, 296–7; 'outlaw' encampments, 306; troops in civil war, 316 and n1, 318, 320, 321, 329; and Caballero's government, 406, 435; enter Catalan government, 428, 471; political commissars, 435; and Spain's gold reserves, 448 and n3; and Otero, 451n2; join Madrid government, 471–3, 475, 522; volunteer forces, 483, 484; and Durruti's death, 485; end of Spain's classic age, 485–6; opinion of José Antonio, 499; problems thrown up by war, 528, 544, 934; failure at the front, 545 and n2; champion agrarian collectives, 553, 557, 559; dislike of Asensio Torrado, 587n5; ministers/youth division, 661; and Largo Caballero, 664; and Negrín, 666–7, 671, 786, 812, 815, 866n1, 889; advocacy of revolutionary change, 671, 934; loss of power, 671–2; pro-Prieto, 812; national conference (1938), 865; instructed to accept Nat. victory, 887, 889, and n5; and resistance, 889, 912; and Casado's conspiracy, 902; and defeat, 933; contribution to Sp. society, 934; emigré organization in S. France, 950
Andalusia, 23, 28, 58 and n, 90, 170, 255, 519; anarchism, 24, 61, 62, 63, 66, 67, 69, 81, 99, 103, 801, 933; drug case, 27–8; unemployment (1931), 47, 81; and *obrero consciente*, 62; the *pueblo*, 69–70, 305–6; *latifundia*, 80, 81; socialism, 81, 105; Carlism, 97, 129; 1936 elections, 157; and military rising, 177, 220, 221–3, 227, 241, 269; Falange atrocities, 263, 265n5; attacks on the church, 269; murder gangs, 274, 279; anarchist inspired revolution, 305–6, 933; in civil war, 326, 380, 400, 411, 914; questionable loyalty, 381; mining resources, 417; agricultural collectives, 553 and n1, 554; flight of refugees, 876
Andes, Conde de los (Francisco Moreno y Zulueta) (1881–1963) (M), and SIFNE, 505n
Andino, José (F), Leader in Burgos, 636 and n1
Andrade, Juan (*b.* 1898) (P), 118n2, 302, 876; alleged espionage, 701, 705; trial, 866
André Marty Battalion, 482, 484, 968; XIVth Brigade, 589
Andrés, Joaquín de, headmaster, execution, 266
Andújar (Jaén), 307, 491; Popular Front, 630
Anfuso, Filippo (*b.* 1901), It. fascist official, 568, 764
Angell, Sir Norman (1874–1967), man of letters, 609
Angeloni, Mario (*d.* 1936), It. vol., *d.* at Monte Pelato, 381
Anglo-Italian Agreement (1937), 797
Anglo-Italian Mediterranean Pact (1938), 941; terms, 822; reactions to, 822 and nn2, 3, 849; Br. belief in, 826; implementation, 855–6; aims, 857n

Anguera de Sojo, José Oriol (1878–1956), CEDA min. of labour, 134n1
Anguiano Mangado, Daniel (*b.* 1882) (S), 118n2; in Russia, 116
Annual, battle of (1921), Sp. defeat, 24–5, 27
Ansaldo, Maj. Juan Antonio (1901–58) (M), airman, 100; fetches Sanjurjo from Lisbon, 254, 756; a day on the northern front, 756
Anti-Comintern Pact (Germany/Japan), 567 and n4; joined by Italy, 567n4, 747; Sp. adherence, 919
Anti-Fascist Militias Committee, 301; beginning in Barcelona, 249, 295, 369; representatives, 249–50, 250n2, 295n1; main tasks, 250, 295; dissolution, 429
Antón, Francisco (C), Commissar, 710, 775; and La Pasionaria, 775
Antona, David (A), and military rising, 247
Antoniutti, Mgr Ildebrando (1898–1967), Apostolic delegate, 697, 756; replacement, 859
Antonov-Ovsëenko, Vladimir (1884–1937), Ru. Consul-general, Barcelona, 392–3, 453, 649; disappearance, 702–3, 703n1, 707n3, 952
La Antorcha (C. periodical), 118n
Aosta, Amadeo Duke of (1898–1942), Viceroy of Abyssinia, 597
Appellániz, Lorencic (*d.* 1939) (C), SIM interrogator, 778
Aragon, 25, 54, 105, 202, 326; libertarian communism, 126, 430, 473; Right/Left battles, 127–8; 1936 elections, 157; in military rising, 238–9; attacks on the church, 269, 272, 302; POUM/UGT/CNT political power, 302; socio-economic experiments, 303–4; minor skirmishes of civil war, 381; collectives, 430, 553–9 *passim*, 724, 801; anarchist Council of Defence control, 430 and n3, 473, 647; independent state, 473; conditions at the front, 495–6, 544; refugees in Barcelona, 528; R. army, 542, 546; arrest of anarchists, 724
Aragon: republican offensive (1937), 688, 703, 710, 722–3, 725–6, 727–8 (map), 727; opposing army, 723; anarchist divisions, 724; republican forces, 725; Ru. armaments, 728 and n1; behaviour, 775
Aragon: nationalist offensive (1938), 779n1, 797–803; army commanders, 797–8; use of tanks, 798; republican rout, 798, 800, 801; It. troops, 798–9, 800, 802; aerial bombardment, 800, 802; causes of victory, 801–2; reaches the Mediterranean, 802–3; division, 802
Arana, Sabino de (1865–1903), founder of Basque nationalism, 88, 89n
Aranda (Burgos), 310; nationalist atrocities, 258
Aranda Mata, Col. (later Gen.) Antonio (1888–) (N), 236; and military rising, 236, 240, 254; defence of Oviedo, 309–10, 384, 385, 791; Asturias offensive, 728, 730, 731; battle of Teruel, 791, 792, 793; Aragon offensive, 797, 799, 800, 801; Pyrenean campaign, 819, 830–31; enters Valencia, 915; dropped by Franco, 948n2
Aranguren Roldán, Gen. José (1875–1939) (R) 901; in Barcelona, 235, 249, 403; execution, 925
Aranjuez, 184, 376, 895
Araquistain Quevedo Luis (1886–1959), Amb. in Paris, 110 and n1, 407, 451n2; ed., *Leviatán*, 133n2, 200n3, *Claridad*, 200; and military rising, 172; *Cabalieristas*, 178, 381, 407 and n1, 650; anti-communist, 200 and n3; political changes, 200n3; release from Ibiza, 381; on UGT and CNT, 472; resignation, 670; receives money from Bank of Spain, 975n1
Arauz de Robles, José Maria (*d.* 1937) (Car), 632n2
Archena (Murcia), Ru. tank base, 447 and n3, 456n2
Archimedes (It. submarine), 629
Arellano, José Maria de (Car), 760; and Car/F. secretariat, 640
Arenas de San Pedro (Avila), 409
Arévalo, Ignacio (*d.* 1936) (F), 487–8
Arganda (Madrid), 590
Argelès, refugee camp, 878, 879–80
Argentina, 362, 391, 681, 921
Argüelles, Sgt. Jesús (*d.* 1935), execution, 146n2
Arias Navarro, Carlos, Municipal prosecutor, Málaga, 586n4
Arias Paz, Maj. (1899–1965), press officer, 645n2; ordered to the Ebro, 841, 843
Arín, FR Joaquín, shot by nationalists, 512, 513
Arín Prado, Col. Ernesto (*b.* 1875) (R), of Valencia committee, 304

Aristimuño, Fr José (*d.* 1936) (B), shot by nationalists, 512
Arlandis, Hilario (C), sculptor, 118; in Moscow, 117; and school for commissars, 814–15
Arleguí y Bayonés, Gen. Miguel (1858–1924), Dir. Gen. of Security (1923), 26
Arman, Capt. Paul ('Greisser') Ru. officer, leads tank offensive, 468; death, 468n2
Armas, Rudolpho de, Cub. volunteer, 574n3
Armentia Palacios, Col. Gerardo (*b.* 1890) (R), artillery officer in Cartagena, 900; suicide, 901
Arms Purchase Commission (R), 407, 451
Armuro (R. merchant ship), 740
Army of Africa, 93, 326, 933; headquarters, 177; summer manoeuvres (1936), 200, 205; Franco in command, 203, 255, 370, 419; ignorance of mainland rising, 205–6; *Africanistas* in command in Spain, 231, 242; Moorish troops, 241; numbers serving, 328; transport to Spain, 342, 370 and n1, 371, 939–40; to join forces with Army of the North, 371 (map), 372, 373, 375; brutality, 400; and advance on Madrid, 408–9, 432, 470, 478, 484; British volunteers, 409n; relief of Alcázar, 412–13; column commanders, 432; poor armaments, 468; numbers in 1936–37, 509; Moroccan plans, 579; division among 1937–38 army, 759
Army of Andalusia (R), 779, 836n1, 907
Army of Aragon (N), 380, 430, 867, 891
Army of Castile (N), 798, 800
Army of Castile and Galicia (N), 791
Army of Catalonia (R), 779, 800
Army of the Centre (N), 758, 861
Army of the Centre (R), under Pozas, 437, 475–6, 521, 588–9, 662, 677; under Miaja, 775, 779, 814, 816, 835–6, 907; Mediterranean retreat, 909; disintegration, 912; surrender, 913
Armies of the Centre, 835–6, 836–7
Army of the East (R) (including Aragon and Catalonia), under Pozas, 677, 704, 722, 773, 779; re-created by Negrín, 815, 835, 868
Army of the Ebro (R), 835, 868; communist and anarchist forces, 835–7
Army of the Ebro (N), 881–2
Army of Estremadura (N), 891; (R), 836, 907, 909
Army of the Levante (N), 832, 843, 861, 891; (R), 771, 779, 788, 836n1, 907, 909
Army of the Maestrazgo (N), 843, 854, 867, 912
Army of 'Manoeuvre' (R), 836n1
Army of Morocco (N), 793, 820, 838, 840, 867
Army of Navarre (N), 867
Army of the North (N), under Mola, 370–72, 409, 426, 539n3; under Dávila, 690 and n, 717, 728–31, 733, 752, 758, 867
Army of the North (R), under Llano de la Encomienda, Basque contribution, 615–16; nationalist bombardment, 616–17; subsequent commands, 687, 787; casualties, 733
Army of the South (N), under Queipo de Llano, 426, 582, 758, 861
Army of the South (R), 490, 582, 677, 814
Army of Urgel (N), 867
Arnedo (Logroño), civil guard incident, 78
Arquer, (P), trial, 866
Arranz y Monasterio, Capt. Francisco (*b.* 1897) (N), emissary to Hitler, 342, 354
Arriba España (F), 499, 750
Arrarás, Joaquín (N), 'Franquistas', 645; and Azaña's diaries, 760
Arrese y Magra, José Luis (*b.* 1905) (F), assists Hedilla, 642n1
Arrieta, Lucius (Car), 203n3
Artesa de Segre (Lérida), 870
Ascaso, Francisco (*d.* 1936) (A), 248, 316, 430
Ascaso, Joaquín (A), 555, 556, 723; 'Council of Defence', 430, 473, 723–4; character, 723–4; detention on smuggling charge, 724
Ascaso Budría, Domingo (*d.* 1937) (A), 68; deportation, 78; in civil war, 316; death, 669, 874
Asens, José (A), 295, 526; anti-fascism, 250n2; terrorism, 652; and control patrols, 654
Asensio Cabanillas, Col. (later Gen.) José (1896–) (N), and military rising in Tetuán, 217, 224; Spanish campaigns, 371, 373, 375, 376. 408; at Alcázar, 412; and Madrid offensive, 432, 482, 588–9, 592; battle of Brunete, 714–15
Asensio Torrado, Col. (later Gen.) (1892–) (R), under secretary for war

Asensio Torrado, Col. – *contd* (1936–7), 713; campaigns, 408, 436 and n1, 437, 475; supported by Largo Caballero, 533–4, 587, 781; reorganizes the army, 542, 545; unpopularity, 587n5; and communist cynicism, 647; accused of treason, 781; military attaché US, 781n2
Assault guards (*Asaltos*), 139, 156, 172, 206; anger at falangist murders, 206–7; and military rising, 232, 233, 234, 236, 240, 245, 246; their numbers, 249, 328, 329; in civil war, 373, 550; demoralization, 400; and relief of Alcázar, 412; quell Barcelona May Days, 660
Astigarrabía, Manuel (B), 121, 431; communist leader, 541, 617n3; Bilbao *junta* of defence, 692; and 'Euzkadi', 733n1
Astorga Vayo (*d.* 1939), prison official, death, 879 and n4, 880
Astoy Mendi (prison ship), 271
Asturias, 9, 90, 133, 380; mining resources, 21, 161, 310, 335, 528, 539, 612, 733; workers on Moscow underground, 124n; in military rising, 236, 255; revolutionary situation at, 309–10; economic advantages, 332 and n1; battles of Gijón and Oviedo in, 384, 539–40; united youth of, 535 and n2, 783; republican army, 542, 616; lack of unity, 615; relations with Santander, 718; nationalist offensive, 728, 729–33, 730 (map); declares itself independent, 728–9, 729n3, 730–31; nationalist acquisitions, 733
Asturias: 1934 revolution, directed by miners, 136, 138n, 139 and n; working class alliance (UHP), 136 and n2, 138, 139, 191; Comintern reaction, 137; revolutionary committees, 138, 139; repression, 140, 142–4; casualties, 143 and n2, 144 and n1; repercussions, 144, 145–6, 151, 155, 384; death penalties, 146–7; release of prisoners, 160
Atholl, Katherine, Duchess of (1874–1960), 609 and n3; *Searchlight on Spain*, 609n3
Attlee, Maj. Clement (later Earl) (1884–1967), and support for republican Spain, 344, 611; and blockade, 621, 622; visits IBs, 792n2; London greeting, 853n3; condemns Chamberlain, 896–7
Auden, W. H. (1907–73), poet, pro-republic, 347n3; experiences in Spain, 460n1, 609 and n2; on Spanish government, 653n2; 'Spain 1937', 346–7, 346n4, 460
Augustinian order, schools, 52, 75–6; El Escorial, 277
Aunós Pérez, Eduardo (1894–1967), and José Antonio, 167
Auriol, Vincent (1884–1966), Fr. Soc., 350, 389
Austria, attacked by Hitler, 804–5
Auxilio Invierno ('Winter Help'), 506–7, 507n1
Auxilio Social ('Social Help'), 507, 642, 750, 913
Avenol, Joseph Louis Anne (1879–1955), Sec. Gen. of League of Nations, 851–2
Avila, 240, 320, 321, 409, 470; bombing of airfield, 482
Ayamonte (Huelva), 100
Ayguadé Miró, Artemio (Cat.), Councillor for Internal Security, Catalonia (1936–7), 428–9, 663
Ayguadé Miró, Dr Jaime (1882–1943) (Cat.), minister (1938–39), 524, 652n4, 654n3; anti-fascism, 250n2; and communism, 524, 655; and May Days, 656–7, 658; in Negrín's cabinet, 670, 815, 844–5
Ayres, Ruby M., 347n3
Azaña y Díaz, Manuel (1880–1940) (R), minister of war, prime minister and president of the republic, xix, xx, 11, 36, 54n3, 85, 86, 104, 121, 140, 418, 532; literary accomplishments, 36 and n2; background and character, 36–7, 38, 52, 56, 76, 92, 194; eloquence, 37, 49n4 (quoted), 134 and n1, 290, 299, 931, 956–7; hostility to church and army power, 38, 76, 92; alliance with socialists, 38–9, 128; adherents, 38, 59n5; freemason, 42 and n2; and catholicism, 49 and n4, 53, 950n1; and riots of May 1931, 57, 59n5; and the army, 58n5, 92–3, 175, 205; 1931 constitution, 76; 1932 Carlist conspiracy, 99, 100; in low esteem in Cortes, 105, 106; resignation (1933), 106, 107; and revolution, 128, 132, 133n2; arrest and imprisonment, 136 145, 147n2, 154, 499; restores Republican Left, 151, 154, 157, 165; declares a 'state of alarm', 159, 161; asked to form a government, 160; composition, 161, 661n1; and economic affairs, 161–2; opposition alliance, 165; disregards Franco's warning, 167 and

n1; inability to maintain order, 168, 171; and José Antonio, 168, 499; elected President (May 1936), 178; ignores great depression, 186; and the republic's difficulties, 194; foresees disasters ahead, 228, 229; in republican Spain, 277, 283, 311–12; responsibility for war, 312n; grief at Model Prison deaths, 404–5, 405n; persuaded not to resign, 405n; and assault on Madrid, 436–7; anger at removal of Spain's gold reserves, 448; and anarchists, 472, 473; war policy, 534–5; and May Days conspiracy, 655n3, 660–61; and Largo Caballero, 663n1, 664; opinion of Negrín, 668 and n4; and his cabinet, 670; peace mediation plan, 682 and n1, 888, 935; and *Deutschland* incident, 686; Bilbao *junta of defence*, 612; on Writer's Congress, 700 and n2; and Nin's disappearance, 706–7, 708–9; and Council of Aragon, 723; and British non-intervention plan, 738 and n4, 737–8; defeatism, 769, 782, 845; relations with Negrín, 771, 814n2, 821 and n2, 831–2, 866n1; and Catalonia, 773, 872, 876; leaves Spain, 881, 889; resigns from Presidency, 898; death in Montauban, 950; did he die in the church?, 950n1; speech on the Civil War (18 July 1938), 956–7; 'El cojo de Málaga', 311n3; *Mi rebelión en Barcelona*, 154; *La velada en Benicarló*, 276, 311 and n3, 661

Azarola y Gresillón, Admiral Antonio (*d.* 1936) (R), minister of marine, commander of naval base, El Ferrol, 253; execution, 266, 404

Azcárate, Maj. Gumersindo de (1878–1938) (R), controller of engineering corps, 837

Azcárate y Florez, Justino de (R), foreign min., 228; exchanged, 750–51

Azcárate y Florez, Pablo de (1890–1971) (R), amb. in London, 407, 440, 847 and n1; encounter with Churchill, 345n1; and *Leipzig* affair, 735; on Br. government, 738n4; and Anglo-Italian relations, 746; and Anglo-Italian Pact, 822 and n2; and freedom from reprisals in peace negotiations, 894; hands over Sp. Embassy, 897n3

Aznar, Agustín (F), 420 and n3; and Franco, 425, 640; attempted rescue of José Antonio, 498; and Hedilla's overthrow, 635, 637, 639; arrest, 641; member new national council, 750

Aznar, Admiral Juan Batista, Prime Minister, 31

'Azorín' (José Martínez Ruiz) (1873–1967), 35n3

Baban, Fuat, 450

Babini, Col., It. officer, 856n1

Badajoz, 77, 194, 241, 632; peasant revolt, 170; battle of, 373, 374; 'massacre', 374 and n1, 375, 404, 586

Badía, José (*d.* 1936) (C), murder, 179n

Badía, Miguel (*d.* 1936) (C), terrorist, and *escamots*, 132; murder, 179n

Badoglio, Marshal (1871–1956), 583n1

Baena, José (C), 118n2

Bahamonde y Sánchez de Castro, Antonio, chief of propaganda to Gen. Queipo de Llano, 259n2, 286n3; on Andalusian murders, 265n7

Bajatierra, Mauro (*d.* 1939) (A), 913

Baker, Stanley, U S vol. 980n2

Bakunin, Mikhail (1814–76), 40, 191; anarchist ideas, 16, 60, 62; Spanish emissary, 60; dispute with Marx, 61, 934; anarchist school in Madrid, 544

Balada, state prosecutor in Catalonia, 524n2

Balbo, Marshal Italo (1896–1940), 100

Balboa, Benjamín, sub. sec. defence, 679

Balboa, Marquesa de, refugee, 395n1

Balbontín, José Antonio (*b.* 1893) (C and L R), Deputy and lawyer, 123

Baldwin, Stanley (later Earl) (1867–1947), prime minister of England (1935–7), 395, 397, 734; and Spanish crisis, 343–4, 345, 367–8; silence on rearmament, 566n2; fails to support Eden, 577; and belligerent rights, 618; boredom with foreign affairs, 738; on non-intervention, 742–3

Baleares (N. cruiser), 331n4, 332, 427, 586, 779, 797, 936

Balearics, the, 161, 166, 743, 796; Mola's plan and, 173, 175; military rising, 242, 255; atrocity casualties, 265; nationalist possession, 333; return to republic, 381; abandoned, 383; naval incident, 684

Balius, Jaime (A), a 'friend of Durruti', 656n1

Balmes Alonso, Gen. Amadeo (1877–1936), shot dead, 212; funeral, 217

Bank of Spain, 377, 517, 791; gold of, 332, 448, 974n1, 975n1; removal for 'safety' to Russia, 448–9; personal recipients of money from, 975n1

Baráibar, Carlos de (S), ed. *Claridad*, 328, 587; and Morocco, 579, 663n1; under sec. of war, 587
Barajas (airport). 366, 477, 624n1, 686, 888, 900; School of Officers, 505n, 759
Barba Hernández, Maj. Bartolomé (*b.* 1895), 721; and U M E, 166n1, 241; hatred of Azaña, 166n1; and rising, 241, 251; in the war, 721n2
Barbastro, 126n2, 270n4, 584, 658, 724, 801; in rising, 238–9; loyalist garrison, 316
Barbieri, Francesco (*d.* 1937) (It. A), murdered, 658 and n5
Barcarès, refugee camp, 878
Barceló Jover, Maj. Luis (1896–1939) (R), 887; trial of rebel officers, 248; battle for Toledo, 412; loses Boadilla, 489; battle for Corunna road, 492, 493; Segovia offensive, 688; resistance in Madrid, 906–7, 908; execution, 909
Barcelona, 10, 21–2, 89, 136, 270 and n4, 574, 928; 1909 Tragic Week, 10 and n1, 16–19, 64, 65, 191, 211; industrial development of, 16, 21, 27, 188, 648 and n2; anarchism and, 22, 47, 63–7, 69, 70n, 73, 110, 232–3, 248, 294–9, 428, 429, 647, 659, 672; working-class violence in, 23–4, 54; counter-terrorism in, 23; 1931 elections, 31, 45; and the problem of Catalonia, 46, 63, 64; illiteracy in, 56; in military rising, 168, 209, 210 and n1, 214, 232–6, 248, 269; People's Olympiad, 233, 366, 367; republican forces, 233 and n3, 326; organization of revolution, 250, 294–9; exhibition of exhumed Salesian nuns, 272; priests and nuns killed, 273; economic council, 295n1; social services, 295n1, 536; 'patrol controls', 295n1, 301, 526, 651, 652, 672; takeover of industrial plants, 295 and n2; wage differentials, 296; collectivization, 297–8, 298n1, 437–8; church burning, 298; P O U M membership, 302; and early campaigns, 315, 316, 318; its port facilities, 332; Russian presence at, 392–3, 440; bad contact with Madrid, 429, 525; anarchist/socialist agreement (Decree of October), 437, 521, 529; welcomes volunteers, 461; funeral of Durruti, 485; anarchist/communist division, 526, 651, 653; conditions in the city, 526–8, 648, 863, 871–2; industrial syndicalism, 528; artillery school, 548n2; aerial bombardments, 627n5, 794, 806–7, 808, 809, 871–2; Anarchist-P O U M/government-P S U C war, 651, 653 and n2, 654–6; May Days conspiracy, 654 and n3, 655–60, 933; appeals for armistice, 657–8, 658n2; repercussions, 661–2, 663, 671; punishment of instigators, 663–4; seat of Catalan government, 773; resumption of catholic services, 774 and n3; inter-party fighting, 784; cut off from Pyrenean hydro-electricity, 802; submarine mail service to Valencia, 816–17; government leaves for Gerona, 872; nationalist occupation of, 873; post-war killings in, 873 and n3, 924, 925; bomb/casualty ratio in air raids, 945n3
Barcelona: Atarazanas Barracks, 236, 248, 366, 653; Cataluña, Plaza de, 232, 233, 234, 235, 654; Chamber of Commerce, 296, 653; Escuela Moderna, 64; Falcón Hotel, 302, 703; Montjuich Fortress, 63, 299, 403, 537; Palace of Justice, 299, 526–7; Paralelo, 34; Pedralbes Barracks, 233, 269, 316; Palace, 773, 809, 810; Pedrera Barracks, 653; Puerta de la Paz, Plaza, 232; Radio Services, 367n1, 383; the Rambla, 232, 233 and n3, 302, 657; San Andrés barracks, 236, 248; San Juan convent, 808; Telefónica, 654, 655, 656; University, 299, 527; Voroshilov Barracks, 653
Barcelona Traction Co. ('La Canadiense'), 44, 66
Barcía Trelles, Augusto (1881–1961) (R) foreign min. (1936), 179n
Barham, H M S, 980n2
Barker, George (*b.* 1913), poet, pro-republic, 347n3; 'Elegy for Spain' 807–8
Barletta (It. cruiser), part of patrol control, 683–6
Barńes, Francisco (L R), min., 179n
Baroja y Nessi, Pio (1872–1966), novelist, 35n2, 190, 501n1
Barontini, Ilio (C), It. officer in Spain, 599–600
Barrera Luyando, Gen. Emilio (1869–1943) (N), Capt. Gen. of Barcelona, co-ordinator of 1932 conspiracy, 99, 247n2; and armed insurrection (1936), 165, 247 and n2
Barrio, José del (C), 250n2; 'Maj.' Catalan Division, 547; 18th army corps, 835
Barriobero Herrán, Eduardo

(1880–1939) (R), Rad. lawyer, 701; imprisonment, 772
Barrionuevo, Gen. Rafael (N), and Cartagena takeover, 900
Barrón y Ortiz, Col. (later Gen.), Fernando (1892–1952) (N), 371, 432, 689; and military rising, 224; and Alcázar, 412; Madrid offensive, 432, 436, 474, 484, 488–9, 588–9, 594; battle of Corunna Road, 492–3; battle of Brunete, 713–14; siege of Belchite, 726; Aragon offensive (1938), 800; ordered to the Ebro, 841; minister under Franco, 948n1
Barroso y Sánchez-Guerra, Maj. Antonio (*b.* 1893), military attaché Paris 1936, on Franco's staff, 351 and n1, 504, 594, 638, 868n2, 931
Bartomeu y González Longoria, Col. (later Gen.) Maximiano (*b.* 1888), commander Navarrese Brigade, 690 and n
Baruela, José Antonio (F), 279 and n2
Barzona (C), 291
Basch, Victor (*d.* 1940), 361
Basque Children's Relief Committee, England, 680, 694 and n5
Basque Communist Party, 617n3
Basque Nationalist Action, 846
Basque Nationalists, 88, 97, 190; catholicism, 88–9; reaction to anti-clericalism, 90; alliance with socialists and the Left, 132; elections (1936), 153, 156, 162n2; and military conspirators, 175, 237; atrocities against, 262–3, 512; middle class social order, 308; financial control, 308–9; cut off from Spain, 380, 540; treatment by conquerors, 410; and people's guard, 431; and Army of the North (*gudaris*), 616; defence of Bilbao, 691; Mid-Atlantic Shipping Co., 813n2
Basque Provinces, 9, 21; separatist aspirations, 17, 86–90, 132, 613, 694, 774, 930; and Second Republic, 32, 88; relations with the church, 53n2, 87 and n3, 309, 698, 774; and Carlist wars, 88; abolition of local rights (1839), 88; industrialization, 88, 332, 539; achievement of 'Concierto Económico', 89, 132; relations with central government, 132, 193 and n2, 309, 540, 613, 681; in military rising, 236–8, 255, 308; motorized police corps, 308; political prisoners, 308n2; character of revolution, 308; Mola's campaigns, 370, 612–14; Francoism, 541; R. army, 542; war industries, 547–8; possession of iron and coal, 612, 694; communist disputes, 617n3; conditions at the front (retreat), 679–80; evacuation of refugees, 680–81; proposals for separate peace, 681 and n2, 682; withdrawal of government to Trucios, 692; trade relations with Britain, 694 and n3; emigré government in Barcelona, 774
Basque Republic (Euzkadi), creation, 430–31; and female political prisoners, 431 and n; reorganization of civil and assault guards, 431; Aguirre as commander in chief, 540, 615n; catholic–conservative domination, 540–41; recognized army, 615 and n; a government-in-exile (Barcelona), 693
Basque Statute, 89–90, 90n1, 97, 430
Basques, forces engaged in civil war, 378, 379, 410, 718, 719–20; independence goal, 613; lack of unity, 615; in Negrín's government, 679; under Gámir, 687–8; christianity, 695; clergy dispute with the Vatican, 697; attempted embarkation, 721; deaths in post-war repression, 925; leaders in exile, 930; their fate, 951
La Batalla (P O U M paper), 659; mentions Stalin's purges, 523–4; banned by communists, 702
Basterrechea y Díaz de Bulnes, Admiral Francisco (*d.* 1962) (N), 937n1; Capt. of *Canarias*, 427n
Bastico, Gen. Ettore (*b.* 1876), It. commander in Spain, 722, 856n1; replaces Roatta, 604; battle of Brunete, 717; to be recalled, 744; later career, 952
Bastiniani, Giuseppe (1899–1961), It. dip., 682
Bastos, Dr Manuel, Rep. physician, 551n1
Batet Mestres, Gen. Domingo (1872–1936), Gen. in command of VIth Division, Burgos, 136; meeting with Mola, 211–12; arrest, 238; execution, 266; address to his executioners, 280–81
Batov, Col. (later Gen.), military adviser to Lister, 468n2; to 'Lukács', 482, 603; wounded at Huesca, 688n1; eminence in Russia, 953
Battisti, Col. Emilio (*b.* 1889) (It.), 856n1
Bau y Nolla, Joaquín (M), Deputy, and Calvo Sotelo's murder, 207; and *junta técnica*, 425n4

Bautista Sánchez, Gen. Juan (N), commander Navarrese Brigade, 690 and n, 712; Bilbao offensive, 690–91, 693; battle of Brunete, 712; Aragon offensive, 800
Bavaria, *Rot Front* organization, 711n2
Bayo Girón, Capt. Alberto (1894–1967) (R), and Ibiza, 381; invasion of Majorca, 381–2, 383, 414; guerrilla tactics, 432
Bayreuth, Villa Wahnfreid, 355
Beaufre, Gen. André, in Morocco, 94
Bebb, Capt., pilots Franco's aircraft, 204 and n2, 212 and n3, 338; flight map, 213
Beceite (Teruel), 126n2
Beck, Gen. Ludwig (1880–1944), 746
Beckett, Samuel (*b.* 1906), pro-republic, 347n3
Behobia (Guipúzcoa), 379
Beigbeder Atienza, Col. (1890–1957), arabist, 218; and military rising in Tetuán, 217, 218, 226; Moroccan reputation, 218, 425, 753 and n1, 766; intermediary, 342, 349, 387; and German/Italian troops in Sp. Morocco, 578
Beimler, Hans (1895–1936), G. Com. vol. in I B, 366, 482; Dachau prisoner, 366n3; theories of his murder, 488n3
Belchite (Saragossa), 798; siege of, 725, 726, 837–8
Belderrain Olalde, Maj. Pablo (B), 623, 692
Belgium, 201 and n1, 335, 378; non-intervention, 388, 390, 398; arms traffic, 451; accepts Sp. children refugees, 879; and I B, 968
Bell, Julian (1908–37), Eng. writer, ambulance driver in Spain, 367n2, 611, 714n2; death at Brunete, 714n2
Bellido, Dr Jesús (R), Professor of Medicine, University of Barcelona, 862–3
Belligerent rights, 567, 618, 736, 738; and withdrawal of volunteers, 795, 847
Bellver (Lérida), 653n1
Bellville, Rupert (*d.* 1962), Eng. adventurer, 980n2
Belmonte, Juan (1902–62), 478n1
Beltrán, Col. Antonio ('El Esquinazado') (*d.* 1960) (R), Pyrenean outpost, 818, 831; later career, 818n
Beltrán de Heredia, FR Vincente (*b.* 1885), at Salamanca University meeting, 501, 502n
Benavente, Jacinto (1866–1954), 35n3
Benda, Julian (1867–1956), 698
Benedito Lleo, Lt. José (R), power in Valencia, 304–5
Bennett, Richard, Eng. journalist, vol. in Spain ('Voice of Spain'), 367n1; Barcelona Radio, 657n1
Beorleguí y Canet, Col. Alfonso (1888–1936) (N), 328; early campaigns, 315, 377; and Pérez Garmendia, 377 and n2; Guipúzcoa campaign, 377, 379; death, 379–80
Bérard, Senator Léon Félix (1888–1936) Fr. politician, 884, 896
Berck, Victor, 458n5
Berenguer Fusté, Gen. Damaso (1873–1953), Prime Minister (1930–31), 29, 30; creator of *Regulares*, 94
Bergamín y Gutiérrez, José (*b.* 1895), Sp. war poet, 699; ed. *Cruz y Roya*, 399; catholic communist, 701
Bergonzoli, Gen. Annibale (*b.* 1889), It. troop instructor, 594, 596, 599, 601, 604, 717, 722; later career, 952
Beria, Laurenti (1889–1953), 953
Berkane (Fr. Morocco), 363
Berle, Adolf (*b.* 1895), U S ass.-sec. of state, 867
Berlin, 338; Ciano's visit to, 463
Berlin–Rome Axis, 369, 463; Ciano's plan to include Franco's Spain, 747
Bermeo (Vizcaya), 622, 629, 630
Bermúdez Reina, Capt. José (1899–1936) (R), murder, 219
Bernal García, Gen. Carlos (*b.* 1874) (R), chief of transport, 836; favours peace, 892; hands over Cartagena naval base, 900 and n
Bernanos, Georges (1888–1948), Fr. catholic writer, 260n1, 261n1, 513; on nationalist atrocities, 260–61, 697
Bernard, Maj. François, 955
Bernard, Representative (U S), and arms for Spain, 575 and n3
Berneri, Camillo (1897–1937), It. anarchist thinker, murdered in Barcelona, 658 and n5
Bernhardt, Johannes (*b.* 1897), G. businessman, 387, 517, 842, 860; emissary to Hitler, 342–3, 354, 355–6, 356–7; and H I S M A, 357, 358, 462, 517, 519–20, 737, 765, 842; and v. Scheele, 418; and Franco, 418, 419, 514 and n; survival, 952 and n1
Berry, Gordon, U S pilot, 575–6
Berthet, Jacques, Fr. journalist, and Badajoz 'massacre', 374n
Berti, Gen. Mario, It. commander in

Spain, 744, 856; Aragon offensive, 797, 801; attack on Valencia, 832; talks with Franco, 847; later career, 952
Bertrán y Musitú, José, 951n; and SIFNE, 501n, 759n1
Berzin, Gen. Jan Pavlovich (*d.* 1937), chief of Ru. military mission, 393 and n3, 440, 442, 446, 476; execution in Russia, 662n2, 702–3, 706, 707n3, 952
Besnard, Pierre (A), 443–4, 444n1
Besteiro, Julián (1870–1940) (S), 127, 154, 845, 913, 933; Pres. of UGT, 41–2, 133; Pres. of Cortes, 76, 128; and communism, 180, 886; on Negrín, 668; in England, 682; against Negrín, 886–7, 888; snubbed by Franco, 898; and Casado's plot, 902, 903; *d.* in gaol, 924
Betancourt, Rómulo (*b.* 1908), Venezuelan statesman, 362
Bethke, Friedrick, of ROWAK, 694
Bethune, Dr Norman (1890–1939), at the front, 536, 551; *d.* in China, 551n1
Beust, Lieut. v., bombs Guernica, 625
Bevan, Aneurin (1897–1960), Eng. Labour statesman, 467, 827–8
Bianco, Vincenzo ('Krieger') (*b.* 1898), It. com. vol. in IB, shoots a mutineer, 716
Biarritz, 334, 338, 505
Bibesco, Princess Elizabeth (*d.* 1945), appeals for José Antonio, 499
Bidasoa (river), 379
Bielov, André, Comintern bureaucrat, and Nin, 705
Bielov, Col. ('Popov'), Ru. officer, 361n1, 798
Bielsa (Huesca), 831
Bilbao, 41, 89, 377, 506, 928, 988; 1903 strike at, 17; population (1931), 31n1; socialists of, 39, 109; working classes in, 90n2; communist party of, 120; in military rising, 237; and Basque-nationalist committee of defence, 308, 431; its arms factory, 308, 733; port facilities, 332, 860; reprisals after bombing, 431n1, 540; 'Ring of Iron', 613–14, 617, 623, 680, 690; sea-fight outside, 614; nationalist blockade, 618, 619–22; Br. financial interests, 683n1, 694 and n3; Mola's campaign, 687; diversionary offensive, 687–9; fall of, 690–94; flight of refugees, 692; *junta* of defence, 692; monarchist actions, 693; aftermath, 694; naval significance, 694n4; excites religious argument, 694–8; attribution of victory, 737
Bilbao, Esteban (1879–1975) (Car), 263n4, 750, 948
Bilbao, Tomás (*d.* 1954) (B. pilot), 846
Bilbao Crescenciano, Angel, political commissar, 435, 775
Billmeir, Jack (1900–63), Eng. shipping magnate, 741, 813n2, 827
Bing, Geoffrey (*b.* 1909), 398 and n1
Bismarck, Prince Otto v. (1897–1975), G. diplomat, 396, 824n1
Bitossi, Gen., It. officer of Littorio Division, 856n1
Bizerta, 810, 901, 919
Black Arrows, 596, 598, 599–600, 856; campaigns, 614, 629, 693, 717, 718–19, 798; Italian officers, 614
Black Flames (Division), 596, 597, 598, 599–600, 717; *blitzkrieg* methods, 597
Black Hand Conspiracy (1883), 62
Black Shirts, 366n2, 382; to fight in Spain, 568, 572, 573, 583, 585, 596, 600
Blagaev (Ru. steamer), 740, 741
Blagoyeva, Stella (1897–1954), Bulg. com. in Comintern secretariat (cadre division), 361n1
Blake, Vice-Admiral Sir Geoffrey (1882–1968), 622–3
Blanc, Jean Marcel (C), and Bar Gambetta, 670n2
Blanche, HMS, 618, 619
Blanco, Carlos, Dir. Gen. of Security (1931), and riots of May 1931, 57n
Blanco, Segundo (A), min. of education (1936–37), 310, 815, 846; flight from Asturias, 731, 815; and UGT/CNT collaboration, 812; and Negrín, 815, 820n, 901, 905
Blanco Novo, Col. Luis (*b.* 1881), in military rising, 224
Blanco Garzón, Manuel (*d.* 1954), Rad. politician, 179n, 278
Blesa (Teruel), executions, 515
Blomberg, Gen. v. (1879–1946), G. min. of war (1933–38), 356, 358, 394, 572n1, 746
Bloque Obrero y Campesino (BOC), formation, 120
'Blue Age', 289
Blue Division, 949, 975
Blum, Léon (1872–1950), Fr. soc. prime minister (1936–7 and 1938), 572, 579, 685n1, 754, 873; and aid for republican Spain, 337–8, 343, 349–50, 351, 364, 367, 389, 397, 745–6, 805; invited to England, 343–4, 349; vice-premier, 735; second government, 804, 817; suggests ultimatum to Franco, 805;

Blum, Léon – *contd*
and non-intervention, 943; trial in Riom (1942), 944
Blunden, Edmund (1896–) poet, pro-nationalist, 347n3
Boadilla del Monte (Madrid), battle of, 489–90, 492, 713
Boal, Evelio (A), murder, 274
Bobie, HMS, 598, 721
Bolín, Luis Antonio (1897–1969) (N), journalist, 202, 504n2; and transport of Franco to Morocco, 203–4, 206, 231n1; seeks aid from Italy, 338, 341, 352; use of threats, 504n2; and Guernica, 625, 629 and n1; battlefield tours, 834n; *Spain, the Vital Years*, 204n1, 231n1
Bolívar, Cayetano (C), Deputy for Málaga, 585; election to Cortes, 110 and n; his party, 116 and n1
'Bolodin', Com. agent, 705n2
Bolshevik-Leninists (Trotskyists), 654, 656
Boltin, Col., White Russian, 494n2
Bombín, FR Antonio, killed in Rioja, 263n1
Bonaccorsi, Arconovaldo ('Il conte Rossi') (*d.* 1961), It. F., 383n1; leader of 'Dragons of Death', 382–3; later career, 952
Bonaparte, Joseph, King of Spain (1768–1844), overthrown, 13n1
Bonel, Col., Madrid/Burgos negotiator, 887n2, 909n
Bonilla, Luis (A), execution, 278
Bonnet, Georges (1889–1973), Fr. foreign minister (1938–9), 823, 873
Bonneville de Marsagny, Col., Fr. vol. with Franco, 768
Bonomi, Maj. Ruggero, It. officer, aircraft transport to Fr. Morocco, 363, 364 and n1
Bonsal, Philip (*b.* 1903), US diplomat 335n1
Borchgrave, Baron de (*d.* 1936), murdered in Madrid, 488n2
Bordeaux, 345, 365, 388
Boreas, HMS, 797
Borjas Blancas (Barcelona), 870
Borkenau, Dr Franz, G. sociologist, 294, 302, 303, 306, 585
'Borodin' (i.e. Mikhail Markovich Grusenberg) (1884–1951), 117
Borrow, George (1803–81), 36
Bosch Atienza, Gen. José (1873–1936), Military Gov. of Minorca, and military rising, 241, 253, 254
Bosch y Bosch, Gen. Carlos (N), Military Gov. of León, 242n3
Bosch Gimpera, Prof. Pedro (1891–) (C), min. of education and anthropologist, 273n4, 527, 672; councillor of justice, 672n2, 771, 862; and SIM, 808
Bourbons, the, 13, 30, 100, 425, 582; centralized structure, 44, 51; absolutism, 336; Carlist claim (table), 961
Boussutrot, Senator, Fr. politician, 365
Bowers, Claude (1878–1958), US Amb. to Spain, 346, 362, 391, 572n3, 828, 919
Brandt, Willy (*b.* 1913), G. journalist, subsequently chancellor, 657n1
Brantôme, Pierre de Bourdeilles, Seigneur de (*c.* 1530–1614), 91
Bravo, Francisco (F), member of *junta*, 420n3
Bray, Sir Denys (1875–1951), Br. official, 863
Brazen, HMS, 618
Brazil, 262, 529
Brecht, Bertolt (1898–1956), G. playwright, 700; *Señora Carrara's Rifles*, 700n1
Brenan, Gerald (*b.* 1894), Eng. poet and writer, 170 and n3
Brewster, W. M., US businessman, 417n2
Brihuega (Guadalajara) (collective), 599; air attack, 602–3
British Airways, 345
British Battalion, 591 and n1, 592–3, 607, 710n, 711n, 712, 716, 725n2, 798n2, 852, 969; communist control, 723n1; visited by Labour leaders, 792n2; London greeting, 853n3
British Committee for the Relief of the Victims of Fascism, 457n1
British Medical Aid Committee, 457n1
British Medical Aid Unit, 457n1, 714n2
British Public Opinion Institute, 875n5
Browder, Earl (1891–1973), US com. leader, 391
Brown, Isabel, Br. com., 457n2
Browne, Felicia (*d.* 1936), Br. painter, vol. in Spain, 367
Brunete (Madrid), 662, 710, 886, 938; battle of, 687n1, 710–17, 712 (map), 837–8, 931; causes of republican failure, 714, 716–17; IB losses, 715–16; brutalities, 717; Italian involvement, 717
Buckley, Henry, Br. journalist, 200n3, 410n2, 481, 669n5, 855

Bueno, Col. Emilio (R), communist, 887, 907, 908
Buiza Fernández Palacios, Admiral Miguel (R), commander of republican fleet, 327, 549, 892; replacement, 679, 779; reports Casado's plot, 899; surrenders at Cartagena, 900, 901; enters Foreign Legion, 921
Bujaraloz (Saragossa), 317, 319, 430
Bukharin, Nikolai I (1888–1938), trial, 811n3
Bulgaria, 954, 969
Bullejos, José (1899–1974) (C), sec. gen. of Sp. com. party to 1932, 118, 120; and Comintern, 120–21; expulsion, 121
Bullfights, 11, 27, 184, 200, 203; in Nat. Spain, 755 and n2; Rep. *corridas*, 755n2; analogy with air battles, 802n1
Bullitt, William (1891–1967), US Amb. in Paris, 568, 570, 738n2, 823
Buñuel, Luis (*b*. 1900), film-maker, 53, 190, 557
Burgo, Jaime del (Car), 151n2
Burgos, 123, 185n1, 202, 259n2; Nat. headquarters in, 100, 238, 282, 285, 332, 504, 569, 884; in military rising, 168, 238, 239; army headquarters, 175, 209, 254; atrocities at, 263 and n1, 286; *junta* leadership, 282, 283, 501n2; installation of Franco, 424, 425, 717; *junta técnica*, 425 and n4, 749; relations with France, 884, 896; and Casado, 893, 909
Burguete, Gen. Ricardo, 514n4
Burillo Stolle, Col. Ricardo (1891–1939), leader of assault guards, 245 and n, 589, 703, 779; dir. gen. of security, 672; Army of Estremadura, 779, 836; and communism, 886, 905; execution, 925
Burmistrov, Ru. naval officer, 549n3
Bustenga, Manolo (N), spy ring, 759n2
Butler, R. A. (later Lord) (*b*. 1902), Eng. under sec. for foreign affairs, 827
Buznego, Alfred (*d*. 1939) (R), 907n1
Buzón Llanes, Col. Francisco (R), and Army of the North, 539n3
Byron, Lord (1788–1827), Pollitt's obsession with, 491n2

Caballero, Col. Juan (1880–1936), shot in Ceuta, 224
Cabanellas Ferrer, Gen. Miguel (1872–1938) (N), 43, 175, 280, 424; in command at Saragossa, 225, 229 and n3, 282; pres. of Burgos *junta*, 282, 283, 328, 422; opposes a single command, 421 and n2; and Franco as 'Generalissimo', 422, 423, 424
Cabello, Cándido (R), Toledo lawyer, 324
Cáceres, 80, 241, 394; It. airforce base, 376n1; Franco's headquarters, 419n1, 422, 423; G. training officers, 492, 592
Cádiz, 43n3, 114, 153, 231, 255, 326, 357, 380; anarchism, 62, 103, 155; military rising, 223, 241; naval base, 332, 572, 573; Constitution of (1812), 35, 46
Cadogan, Sir Alexander (1884–1968), Eng. dip., 388n4, 827 and n3
Calanda (Teruel), 126n2, 294nn, 3, 4, 557
Calvet, José (Cat. politician), 524, 652n4, 672n2
Calvo Sotelo, José (1893–1936), Mon. politician, 160, 192, 194, 931; career, 7; on Spain's disorder, 8; Cortes speech, 10–11, 207n; financial policies, 26, 28–9; discusses rebellion, 151–2; and leadership of fascist party, 152n2; 1936 elections, 155–6; defeat, 162; and military rising, 184, 185, 190; his murder and its effects, 207–8, 208n2, 209, 211, 215, 254, 322, 809n1, 930; funeral, 210; posth. entitlement, 948
Camacho Benítez, Col. Antonio (1892–) (R), 892, 905; sub.-sec. defence, 679
Cambó y Batlle, Francisco (1876–1947) (Cat. politician), 22, 23, 39, 45 and n2, 208; death in exile, 951
Cambridge University, 723n1, 841 and n2
Campbell, Patrick, Br. vol. for Franco, 980n2
Campbell, Roy (1901–57), Br. poet, 359 and n7
Campeador (R. tanker), 740
'El Campesino' (Valentín González) (C), 23, 247; civil war battles, 324, 492, 493, 599, 710, 712, 713, 717, 723, 726, 794, 801, 812; later adventures, 950
Campins Aura, Gen. Miguel (1880–1936), 223, 241; imprisonment, 250; execution, 266
Campo Libre (A), 785; condemns hooligan violence, 278
Campoamor, Clara (Rad. deputy), 43n3
Campos, Col., commander 50th Division, 840
CAMPSA, 295, 417n2
Camrose, W. E. Berry, 1st Lord (1879–1954), Eng. press lord, 807n7
Canada, 335, 362, 830, 893

Canalejas Méndez, José (1854–1912), Lib. prime minister of Spain, 38, 46; achievements, 20–21; assassination, 21
Canarias (N. cruiser), 331n4, 332, 426, 528, 576, 586, 614, 797, 936
Canaris, Admiral Wilhelm (1887–1945), G. intelligence chief, and aid to Spain, 354 and n6, 368–9, 394, 451, 571; relations with Franco, 354n6, 419, 469; and G. submarines, 354n6, 356
Canaris, Frau, 354n6
Canary Isles, 28, 173, 175; Franco and, 161, 168, 203–4, 212; conquest for the rising, 224n2, 255; nationalist possession, 333, 417, 593–4; 'zones of war', 390; birthplace of Negrín, 666
Cañas, Eustacio (Soc) Civil gov. of Murcia, 901
Canfranc, smuggling, 818n
Cañizares Navarro, Col. Eduardo (N), military governor of Badajoz, 419, 632; and Queipo de Llano, 419 and n2
Cannon, Dr Walter (1871–1945) (US Aid Fund), 608n4
Canos, Luis (N), spy ring, 759n2
Cánovas del Castillo, Antonio (1828–97), Con. prime minister, 20; assassination, 20, 64
Cánovas Lacruz, Col. Enrique (N), 252
Cantabria (R. steamer), 856
Cantabrian mountains, 718–19; refuge of Goriev, 731 and n4
Cantalupo, Randolfo (1891–), It. Amb. to Spain (1936–7), 253–4, 511, 586, 597, 604; and shooting of prisoners, 514, 636
'La Caoba', drugs case, 27–8
Capaz Montes, Gen. Osvaldo (1894–1936), 'Hero of the Rif'; murder, 224 and n3, 404
Cape Busto, 581
Cape Gata, 581
Cape Oropesa, 581
Cape Yuby, 212n3
Capdevila, Andrés (A), 652n4
Caporal (Br. tanker), 740
Carabanchel (Madrid), 243, 245, 246, 474, 481, 482
Carabineros, 99, 311, 480; in civil war, 318n2, 374, 550; total under arms, 328, 329; Negrín and, 667, 672
Cárdenas, José (A), murder, 298
Cárdenas, Lázaro (1895–1970), pres. of Mexico, 391, 913; and republican treasure, 921
Cárdenas y Rodríguez de Rivas, Juan F. de (1881–1966), Amb. in Paris, 1936; agent in Washington (1936–39), 337, 343–4, 344n3, 344, 434n1
Careño (A), 656n1
Caridad Pita, Gen. Rogelio (1875–1936) (R), 252; execution, 266
Carlavilla, Mauricio, 645
Carlist Wars, 16n1, 129, 508n2; First, 13–14, 51, 91, 193n2, 336; Second, 14, 96, 99n1
Carlists (traditionalists), 14, 107, 116, 165, 275, 380; and Second Republic, 59, 98–100, 129; Navarre/Basque differences, 789; pact with 'Alfonsists', 96; nature of movement, 96–8; relations with monarchists, 130, 151, 414; 1936 elections, 151, 156, 162n2; and Sanjurjo, 167, 175 and n1, 254–5; and military rising, 173, 175n1, 177, 184, 199–200; song, 196n1; in nationalist Spain, 258, 283, 285; executions by armed gangs, 259, 260; forces in civil war, 315, 318n2, 508, 596, 726, 758; and Franco, 423, 506–8, 632, 948; Decree of unification, 423, 751; Royal Military Academy, 507; and a union with falangists, 632 and nn 2, 3, 633, 639–40; official uniform, 640n1; and Mola's death, 690; claim to the throne (table), 961
Carlos María Isidro de Borbón (Don Carlos) (1788–1855), 99n1, 617; claims the throne, 13–14
Carmona (Seville), 263n1, 286 and n3
Carls, Admiral Rolf, G. sailor, 387, 498
Carner, Jaime (1867–1934) (Cat) min. of finance, 136, 186–7
Carney, W. P., US journalist, 363
Carranceja, Carlos (N), spy ring, 759n2
Carranza, Capt. Fernando de (N), and ROWAK, 357n3
Carrasco Amilibia, Col. León (*d*. 1936) (N), San Sebastián rising, 203, 237, 308
Carrasco Formiguera, Manuel (*d*. 1938), Cat. politician, 46
Carratalá Cernuda, Col. Ernesto (1887–1936), and UMRA, 166n1, 246; shot, 246
Carrillo, Santiago (*b*. 1916) (Soc. youth leader, subsequently C), 200 and n3, 291, 706n3, 810n1, 913, 950; democratic ideals, 535
Carrillo, Wenceslao (Soc), posts, 475n2, 550, 671, 902
Carro, FR, 695
Carrocera, Higinio (A), CNT chief in Oviedo, 385
Cartagena, 212, 219, 226; naval base, 226,

242, 243n1, 332, 365, 371, 410, 797; nationalist occupation, 332n, 506, 915; arrival of Russian ships at, 445; bombed by Condor Legion, 484n1, 819; republican fleet, 505–6; events of 4 March 1939, 900–901; republican refugees, 914
Casablanca, 206, 212n3, 231n
Casado López, Col. Segismundo (1893–1968), 476, 712, 836n1, 871, 925; head of Azaña's military household, 312n, 886; conspiracy against Negrín, 886 ff.; negotiations with Burgos, 893–4, 909–11, 912; ignores Negrín's summonses, 899–900, 902; broadcast manifesto, 902–3; retreats to Mediterranean, 909, 914; exile in Britain, 922; effect of *coup* on continuance of war, 935; death in Spain, 950
Casals, Pablo (1876–1973), Cat. musician, 190, 276 and n4
Casanellas, Ramón (A then C), 232
Casanova, Manuel (Po), 707
Casanovas, Juan (Cat.), 249n2, 301, 525
Casares Quiroga, Santiago (1881–1950), Galician politician, prime minister (1936), 5–6, 36, 90, 104, 161, 179n, 199; character, 4, 179, 226; party, 5 and n4; speech in Cortes (16 June 1936), 8–9; freemason, 42n2; prime minister, 178–9, 903n3, 913; administration, 179n; warned of a rising, 204; refusal to arm workers' organizations, 209, 219, 220, 225, 226; and Mola's loyalty, 211; and Morocco army rising, 216, 217, 218, 579; and mainland outbreak, 219, 225–6; forsees violence, 228
Casas del Pueblo, 131, 151, 201, 240, 258
Casas Viejas (Cádiz), anarchist rising, 103–5, 166n1, 179, 266
Cascajo Ruiz, Col. Ciriaco (1878–), 223, 263, 518; organizer of atrocities, 263
Caspe (Saragossa), 202, 317, 473, 800
Castejón Espinosa, Maj. Antonio (*b.* 1896) (N), 217, 251–2; commander in civil war, 371, 373, 375, 376, 432, 436, 473–4, 841
Castellar de Santiago (Ciudad Real), agrarian revolt, 103
Castelldáns (Lérida), 870
Castelló, José, killed by anarchists, 320n
Castelló Pantoja, Gen. Luis (1881–1962) (R), min. of war, 230, 241, 320; madness, 320n, 437
Castellón, 305, 830, 832
Castiella (*requeté*), burial, 261–2
Castilblanco (Badajoz), murders at, 77–8, 99
Castile, 14, 39, 44, 49, 71, 80, 292–3, 333, 717, 930; Basque colonization, 88, 89; Carlists, 89, 97, 108; and federation, 193 and n2; and military rising, 238–41; nationalist atrocities, 261; refugees in Barcelona, 528; in Franco's hands, 529; agricultural collectives, 553, 559, 784
Castilla, *agent provocateur* in POUM plot, 702 and n
Castilla Libre, 291 and n
Castilló, Col., death at Alto de León, 322
Castillo, Lt. José (*d.* 1936), 206; murder by falangists, 206 and n3, 207
Castillo y Campos, Cristobal de (1892–) (N), Diplomat, 344n3, 351
Castillo de Olite, 901
Castro, Andrés de (*d.* 1936) (R), shot at Tuy, 360
Castro, Fidel (*b.* 1926), 574n3
Castro, Manuel, Abp. of Burgos, 513
Castro, 'Paquito' (Soc), 907
Castro Delgado, Enrique (1907–63) (C), 323, 479n1, 564, 904, 950
Castro del Río (Córdoba), 306
Casualties (Civil War), 270 and n2, 321–2; battles: Boadilla, 490, Madrid, 486, 487 and n2, 908, Corunna road, 495 and n2, Jarama, 596, Guadalajara, 602 and n4, Bilbao, 693 and n4, Belchite, 715 and n3, Teruel, 793, 794; Ebro, 855 and n2; influence of Trueta, 551; IB, 595, 600, 983 and nn; aerial bombardment, Durango, 616, Guernica, 625 and n2, 986, Barcelona, 807; Barcelona May Days, 660 and n3; post-war nationalist repression, 925; losses from all causes in the war, 926 and n3, 927; concentration camps, 949 and n5; Germans and Italians in Spain, 978 and n2, 979
Catalan Anarchist Youth (JLC), 652n2
Catalan Economic Council, 429
Catalan language, 44, 86, 874
Catalan Statute, 46, 85–6, 91, 96, 155, 160, 299, 816
Catalan United Socialist Youth, 235
Catalan War Industries Committee, 547
Catalan Youth Battalion, 492
Catalonia, 18, 21, 42, 81, 99, 119; and the movement for autonomy, 6n2, 30, 46, 86; separatism, 16, 17, 45n1, 132, 179n, 300, 930; grant of *Mancomunidad*, 21, 45–6; nationalism, 22, 23, 30, 44; industrial position, 42, 44, 332, 525, 527–30, 772–3; past of, 43–4;

Catalonia – *contd*
socio/cultural position, 44, 46, 90, 874; political parties, 44–5; brief 'new republic', 46–7, 86; depression in, 47; anarchist position in, 63, 70n, 103, 249, 299–303, 647; vine-growing, 82; government by *Generalidad*, 86 (*see under*); and the army, 91–2, 546–7, 688; Carlism, 97, 129; and communism, 120, 122, 523, 526; relations with central government, 132, 193 and n2, 429, 525, 531, 773–4, 816, 935; and Castile, 135–6; attacks on the church, 269, 272; anti-fascist executive power, 295; and workers' control committees, 296; socio/economic experiments, 303–4; Franco/Belgian aid, 390; anarchist/socialist fraternity, 437–8; SIFNE organization, 505n; nationalist attempted *coup*, 524–5; inflation in, 526, 528; collectivization, 527 and n4, 553, 554, 559 and n; shipping companies, 530; metallurgical plants, 530–31, 531n2, 772; militias, 546–7; and May Days, 659 and n3; its new municipal councils, 672 and n2; restoration of normality, 701, 771–2; government move to, 773; entered by nationalist troops, 801, 802; exclusion from government, 815–16; unemployment, 844 and n2; change from textile to war industry, 864; flight from, 875; plight of refugees, 877–9; survival of artistic collections, 929; exile of its leaders, 930; industrial production in (1936–38), 973
Catalonia: nationalist campaign 1938–39, 867–72, 888; It. troops, 867, 869, 871; becomes a rout, 871–2, 888; value of German aid, 941
Catecismo de Indias, 269
Catholic Truth Society, 696n1
Caudwell, Christopher (St John Sprigg) (1907–37), Br. poet, IB vol., 592–3, 593n1
Caux, Ernest de (1879–1960), *Times* correspondent, 156 and n1
Cavagnari, Admiral Domenico (1876–), It. sailor, suspends blockade, 741
Cavalcanti y Albuquerque, Gen. José, 59
Cavalcanti, Marchese di, 681n2
Caveda, Capt (N), blockade of Bilbao, 623
Cayuela Ferreira, Col. Pablo (N), 315 and n; Navarrese Brigade leader, 612
Cazorla, José (*d.* 1939) (C), Dir. of public order (Madrid 1936), and executions, 477n3; and communist prisons, 538, 652; execution, 925
Cecil of Chelwood, Lord (1864–1958), Br. statesman, 345n1, 828
Centaño de la Paz, Col. José (N), Franco's go-between to Casado, 895 and n1, 909n, 910; 'Lucero Verde' spy-ring, 895
Centre parties, 107, 125, 148, 149; 1936 election, 153, 156, 157, 162n2; disappearance under nationalists, 258
Cerro de los Angeles (hill), 483
Cerruti, It. Amb. in Paris, 605
Cervantes Saavedra, Miguel (1541–1616), 502; birthplace, 36; archetype Don Quixote, 50, 244 and n, 416
Cervera y Valderama, Admiral Juan (1870–1952) (N), naval chief of staff, 504, 505, 690, 868n2, 937n1; and fall of Bilbao, 694n4; (posth.) marquisate, 948
Cervera del Maestre (Castellón), collective, 558
Ceuta, 17, 212, 226; military rising, 217–18, 224; El Hacho hill, 370n3
'Chaintron' (Jean Barthel) (*b.* 1906), Fr. IB vol., 591
Chamberlain, Neville (1869–1940), Eng. Con. prime minister (1937–40), 734, 739, 741; on non-intervention, 735n2; policy of appeasement, 738–9, 742, 847n1; letter to Mussolini, 738 and n4; attitude to Spanish war, 747n2; relations with Eden, 796, 797, 806; vetoes Roosevelt's peace plan, 796–7; and withdrawal of volunteers, 797; and Blum's new government, 804; rejects USSR's proposed 'grand alliance', 814n3; relations with Italy, 822, 856, 894; and attacks on British shipping, 828; and Munich conference, 849; and Franco's terms, 894, 896, 897; and Hitler's entry into Prague, 911
Chambrun, Count Charles de (1873–1952), Fr. Amb. in Rome, 387, 388
Chamorro García, Capt. Angel (1877–1937) (N), pilot, 689
Chamson, André (*b.* 1900), Fr. writer, 348, 698
Chapaprieta Torregrosa, Joaquín (1871–1951), prime minister (1935), 148 and n
'Chapiaev' (Mihaly Szalvai), Hu. guerrilla leader, 400n, 494n4, 711n1
Chapiaev Battalion, 968
Chapinería (Madrid), 436

Charles III, King of Spain (1716–88), 79, 639
Chatfield, Admiral Lord (1873–1967), Eng. sailor, and Darlan, 389
Chautemps, Camille (1885–1963), Fr. Rad., prime minister, 349–50, 735, 736, 804
Checa, Pedro (C), 890, 906, 907
Chesterton, G. K. (1874–1936), Br. writer, 36
Chetwode, Field-Marshal Sir Philip (later Ld) (1864–1950), Eng. soldier, 752n1; and exchange of prisoners, 854, 887; achieves delays in executions, 854, 867n3
Chicago Tribune, 374n, 498n1
Chile, 362, 743n3, 814n2
Chilton, Sir Henry (1877–1954), Eng. Amb. to Spain (1935–38), 346, 480, 572n3 619, 766
Chinchilla de Monte Aragón (Albacete), I B artillery school, 458, 548
China, 338, 824
Christian Democrats, 108, 165
Church, Catholic, 6, 44, 49, 191; and nineteenth-century army, 13; confiscation of lands (1837), 14 and n, 51 and n2, 53, 61, 75, 79, 81; *Ley de Candado* compromise, 21; and republicanism, 29, 34, 298, 309, 862; and freemasonry, 43 and nn2, 3, 334, 511; and the state, 47, 53; women and, 49n2; historic role, 49–52, 192; intellectual decline, 50–52; terms of Concordat of 1851, 51n2; and education, 51n2, 52–3, 56, 762, 859; and political parties, 53, 155, 193; position of priests, 53 and n1, 54, 75, 105, 127, 269, 287–8; relationship with the Vatican, 54–5; and draft constitution (1931), 75–6, 91; ending of clerical salaries, 102 and n; and nationalist atrocities, 259 and n2, 262–3; basis of attacks on, 269–70; civil war casualties, 270 and n4, 271; and nationalist Spain, 286–7, 287 and n6, 373, 510, 512, 756, 883–4, 922; fate of the hierarchy, 286–7, 287n1; attitude to civil war, 398–9, 512, 696; renewed attendance at, 414; internal disputes in, 512–13; and prisoners, 513; letter to the 'Bishops of the Whole World', 696 and n1; and Falange, 859, 930; losses due to war, 928
Church burning, 5, 7, 10, 19, 59 and n5; in revolutions, 54, 139, 143n2; in May 1931 riots, 58 and n2, 72, 73, 186; in military rising, 222, 242, 244, 251, 252 in republican Spain, 269–70, 298, 302 307, 308; losses due to, 928
Churchill, Winston (later Sir) (1874–1965), 346, 482, 828; and Spanish affairs, 344–5, 345n1, 567n4, 573, 621; and Nyon agreement, 742; and Anglo-Italian Pact, 822; republican sympathies, 822n3
Churchill, Viscount (1890–1973), Eng. philanthropist, I B in Spain, 457n1
Churruca (R. destroyer), 212, 227, 231, 241, 242
Ciano, Count Galeazzo (1903–44), It. foreign min., 600, 722, 822, 920; and Franco's emissaries, 342, 352; and arms for Spain, 353–4, 570–71; anti-British diplomacy, 354 and n4, 397; and non-intervention, 387, 580; relations with Hitler and Germany, 463, 734, 767; on sinking of neutral shipping, 740, 741n2; on Nyon conference, 741, 742; invited to talks on Spain, 744–5; and continuance of the war, 744–5, 767; on Franco, 791, 806n4; on It. forces in Spain, 795, 807, 829; and a nationalist victory, 826, 915n; and nationalist bombings, 826–7; on their executions, 924; estimates It. aid to Franco, 975–6
Cicognani, Mgr. Gaetano (1881–1962), Apostolic Delegate, 859
Ciempozuelos (Madrid), 272, 588, 589, 594
Cierva y Peñafiel, Juan de la (1864–1938), Con. politician, 32, 505; (posth.) entitlement, 948
Ciscar (R. destroyer), 731, 775
Ciudad de Cádiz (R. merchantship), 740
Ciudad Real, 204, 270n4, 294, 909; murder of bishops, 271–2; nationalist occupation, 914–15
Ciutat de Miguel, Col. Francisco (*b.* 1909) (R), Chief of staff in north, 677, 680, 729, 731
Civil guard, 23, 26n3, 31, 57, 61, 103, 126; fear of anarchists, 62; organization of, 77; fate in Castilblanco, 78 and n1; and the monarchy, 99; and Asturias rising, 139; election duties, 156; and assault guards, 172, 206–7; and military rising, 220, 232, 233 and n3, 235, 236 240, 242, 246; numbers of, 249; casualties in republican Spain, 270n2; rebel hideouts, 306; in civil war, 318n2, 326, 327, 373–4, 550; total under arms, 328; demoralization, 400

Claret, FR, confessor to Isabella, 14
'Clariana', spy, 759n2
Claridad (Soc. paper), 164, 177, 180n3, 200, 225, 291, 328, 587, 782
Clark, Col. (Br.), on outcome of Spanish war, 747n2
Claudel, Paul (1868–1955), Fr. poet, 271 and n1, 695
Claudín, Fernando (C), 907
Clemenceau, Georges (1841–1929), 36
Clerk, Sir George (1874–1951), Br. Amb. Paris, 388 and n4
Clive, Lewis (1911–38), Br. vol. in IB, 841 and n2
Cockburn, Claud (*b.* 1904) ('Frank Pitcairn'), Br. wit and journalist, 805n3
Cocinas de Hermandad ('Brotherhood Kitchens'), 507
Codo (Saragossa), 725, 726 and n3
Codovilla, Vittorio ('Medina') (1894–1970), It.-Argentine Comintern representative in Sp., 123, 180, 339, 340–41, 452, 533, 686; indoctrination methods, 200n3; NKVD shadow, 341n1; and fall of Largo Caballero, 650–51; and POUM, 703, 704; death, 954
Cogolludo (Guadalajara), 598
Cohen, Nat (C), Eng. vol. for republic, 367
Coll, Antonio (C), 478
Collectives, agricultural, Com./Soc. support, 553, 554, 555, 816; size and organization, 553, 558, 564; extent of social and economic success, 556–61, 562–3; variation in wages, 561–2; and demands of war, 563, 564; peacetime evaluation, 564–5
Collectivization, 63, 124, 293–4, 295, 297–8, 375, 430, 437, 527, 530, 531; in USSR, 124; Aragon establishments, 430, 553–8 *passim*, 724–5, 784; replaced by nationalization, 784, 816; continuance in republican Spain, 785
Collins, Norman (*b.* 1907), Eng. writer, 347n3
Comando Truppe Voluntaire (CTV), 594, 978
Comert, Pierre (1880–1964), Fr. dip., 804
Comillas, Marqués de, Cat. merchant, 19
Comintern (3rd Communist International), 40n1, 67, 116, 453, 467, 686; dispute over entrance, 116–17, 119; and Spanish communism, 117n4, 120 and n2, 121, 123, 340, 452–4; use of propaganda, 262; and non-intervention, 397–8; and aid for republican Spain, 441, 442, 450; and destruction of Largo Caballero, 649–50; Paris office, 805n3
Comisión de Industria y Comercio, 289
Comisiones Provinciales de Clasificación, 289
Comité International de l'Aide au Peuple Espagñol, 361 and n2
Commission of Inquiry into Alleged Breaches of Non-Intervention Agreement in Spain, 397–8
Committee of British Shipowners, 828
Commune de Paris Battalion (IB), 322, 456, 479, 480, 489, 493, 968
Communism, 43, and n2, 137, 707, 940; general aims, 123, 153–4; agents, 646
Communist Party, British, 461, 723n1, 955; French, 119n2, 337, 340 and n1, 4, 348, 378, 380, 389, 397, 670n2; German, 711n2; Hungarian, 172–3; Italian, 119n2, 323 and n2, 340 and n2, 381, 452, 457 and n2, 452, 573, 945; US, 576; USSR, 814, 952 and n2; Yugoslavia, 454n2, 593n2, 945
Communist Party, Spanish, 6, 9 and n3, 38n2, 40, 110n3; membership, 9 and n4, 120 and n2, 177n2, 291–4, 339, 521–3; isolationism, 119, 122; under Second Republic, 120–22, 156, 162n2; alarm caused by, 122–3, 192; and a Spanish revolution, 180 and n2; youth adherence, 200, 291; relationship with socialists, 316, 649, 783; and Largo Caballero, 406, 407, 408 and n, 433, 435, 532–4, 650 and n2, 651, 655, 662, 665, 775; and anarchists, 483 and n3, 933–4; campaign against POUM, etc., 523–4, 662, 664, 701, 775, 776, 872; role in reorganized army, 545; emergence since 1936, 646–7; Comintern directors, 649–50; and Negrín, 664, 668–9, 671, 900; relations with Prieto, 687 and n1, 775, 810, 811; and prosecution of the war, 775, 810, 846, 907–9; domination of police force, 776; alleged murders at the front, 810–11, 811n1; internal crisis, 814; and Casado, 905, 909; leaders leave Spain, 905–6; inhumanity and untruthfulness, 934–5; post-war careers, 950
Comorera, Juan (C) Cat. soc., 524, 654n3, 672n2, 773, 774; sec. gen. PSUC, 300, 301, 428, 524, 647, 652 and n4; career, 300, 526, 652 and n4; *d.* in gaol, 926
Compañía Arrendatoria del Monopolio

de Petróleo, Sociedad Anónima (CAMPSA), 28 and n, 722, 765
Compañía Hispano-Marroquí de Transportes (HISMA), 357, 358, 359, 417, 462, 518, 519, 737
Companys y Jover, Luis (1883–1940), pres. of *Generalidad* (1933–40), 46, 132, 135, 283, 300, 760; arrests and imprisonments, 146, 147, 160, 280; his governments, 160–61, 652 and n4, 658; relationship with anarchists, 248–50, 473, 525; saves archbishop of Tarragona, 273, 277, 513; communist friendship, 524, 525, 526, 646–7; and Negrín, 773, 816, 844–5; last days, 845, 881; execution, 925
Concentration camps, 366n3, 374, 504, 706, 920–21, 921–2; republican casualties, 949 and n5
Condés Romero, Capt. Fernando (1906–36) (R), Civil guard officer, 207–8, 208n3, 322
Condor Legion, 494, 614n, 625n1; reinforces German troops in Spain, 469 and n2, 941; engagements, 484, 486, 588–90, 616–17, 626–7, 629, 680, 690, 712–14, 791, 798; 'carpet bombing', 730; isolation, 765; attacks refugees, 877 and n1; farewell parade, 920; influence on morale, 951; German expenditure, 975; veterans in Berlin parade (1939), 977
Conesa, José (*d.* 1936) (C), execution, 909
Confederación Española de Derechas Autónomas (CEDA), 112, 131 and n1, 195, 274, 417n2, 420, 526; membership and aims, 4–5, 108, 193; enters the government, 133, 134, 135, 165, 189; Left hostility, 134n1, 165; after Asturias, 146, 147; in 1936 elections, 151, 153, 156, 157, 162 and n2; and military rising, 184 and n5; and UGT, 252; disappearance, 258; deaths in Madrid, 405
Confederación Nacional del Trabajo (CNT), 6n3, 24, 69–70, 78, 184, 230, 420, 648, 772; nature of movement, 6, 16, 65, 69–70; anarchist domination, 65–6, 126, 865; membership, 66, 70n; strikes, 126, 133, 177; and Asturian revolution, 136 and n2, 137, 139n; peasant influx, 169; and military rising, 232, 238; and Anti-Fascist Committee, 249, 250n2; in republican Spain, 274, 279, 291; and UGT, 291, 785, 812, 816 and n, 820, 912; in civil war, 302 and n, 311, 320, 547, 724; recognizes the state, 472; and Stalin's purges, 524; industrial reforms, 530; and control patrols, 651, 652n3; and 1937 government, 652n4, 671, 784; and May Days, 656, 657 and n2, 660; protests at Nin's disappearance, 704–5; POUM persecution, 105; in decline, 726, 784, 897–8; and Negrín, 815, 820 and n
Confederación de Obreros Sindicalistas (CONS), 152
Congregations, Law of, 102, 106
Connolly, Cyril (1903–75), Eng. writer, 69 and n, 347n3, 503n
Constitution of 1931, 74, 77, 109, 171–2, 184; anticlerical clauses, 75–6, 89, 91, 102, 134
Coope, Eng. vol. in IB, 608
Copeman, Frank (*b.* 1907) (C), Eng. vol. in IB, 607n1, 711n1, 723n1, 945, 955
Čopić, Vladimir (1891–1938), Yug. C. vol. in IB, 593n2, 697n3, 711, 723n1; execution in USSR, 953
Coppi, Gen. Giovanni (*b.* 1897), It. officer in Spain, 596, 597, 598, 599, 604
Corbera (Tarragona), 843, 848
Corbin, Charles (1881–1970), Fr. Amb. in London (1936), 343, 345, 396
Córdoba, 255, 326, 332 and n, 376, 380; military rising, 223, 241, 263, 265 and n7; abortive republican attack, 490, 493, 494
Cordón García, Col. Antonio (1895–1969) (C), 407 and n3, 548, 677, 814, 900, 950
Cornford, John (1915–36), Eng. poet and vol. in IB, 367 and nn1, 2, 456, 479, 489, 491; *Last Mile to Huesca*, 543
Corniglion-Molinier, Edouard (1898–1963), Fr. pilot, 352n1
Corps of Investigation and Vigilance, 550
Cortes, the, 4n1 96; debate of 16 June 1936, 3–11 *passim*; communist party, 9; closure by conservative government, 22; socialist seats, 39, 72; elections, 46, 72–3, 107, 110, 134, 155; anarchist condemnation, 69; new constituent assembly, 73; and agrarian reform, 84, 85; trial of Azaña, 147 and n2; and military rising, 210–11; execution of deputies, 266; under Negrín, 771, 783–4; fate of past members, 783; criticizes Negrín, 862; rump meeting (1939), 880; Paris meeting, 898, 920
Cortés González, Capt. Santiago (1897–1937) (N), monastery outpost, 306, 630, 631 and n

Corunna, 238, 252–3, 265; Radio Club, 384; battle of Corunna Road, 488–95, 489 (map), 532, 603
Cosgrave, William (1880–1965), president of Ireland, 592n1
Cossío, Manuel Bartolomé, art critic, 106
Costa, Joaquín (1846–1911), economist, 35n3, 79–80, 191n
Costa Brava, 302, 367
Costa e Silva, and *Bobie*, 721
Cot, Pierre (*b.* 1895), Fr. politician, min. of air (1936), 349, 350, 351, 364, 389
Council of Aragon, 430 and n3, 473, 723–5, 933
Courcier, Col. Fr., Spahi commander, 980
Covadonga (Oviedo), JAP meeting, 133
Cowan, Denys, Br. liaison officer, 887–8, 888n1, 899
Cox, (Sir) Geoffrey, and Alcázar brutality, 413n1
Cranborne, Lord (later Marquis of Salisbury) (1893–1972), 620, 797, 990
Crespo Puerta, Col. Toribio (1878–1936) (N), 251
Cripps, Sir Stafford (1889–1952), Eng. politician, 853n3
Croix du Feux, La, political group, 337
Crolla, Guido, It. dip., 740
Crowley, Alesteir, 347n3
Cruz Boullosa, Gen. Federico (*b.* 1872) (N), 214
Cruz Boullosa, Gen. Manuel (*b.* 1874) (R), 214; fate of his son, 324n1
Cruz Marín, Antonio (R), 975n1
Cruz Salido, Francisco (S), execution, 925
Cuatro Vientos (Madrid), 386
Cuba, 17, 27, 52, 188, 362, 495n1, 867
Cuenca, Luis (or Victoriano) (*d.* 1936) Gal. soc., murders Calvo Sotelo, 208 and n2; *d.* in civil war, 208n3, 322
Cuenca, 178, 269, 270n4, 771, 863, 915
Cuerpo de Ejército Legionario, 856n1
Cuervo Radigales, Máximo (*b.* 1893) (N), Dir. gen. of Prisons 1939; and executions, 926
Cuevas de la Peña, Col. Eduardo (R), dir. gen security, 814
Cullares, José (Po), execution, 708n2
Cunard, Nancy (1896–1965), 347n3
Cunningham, Jock, Br. vol. in IB, 494 and n4, 713n5, 723n1; later career, 956
Cuse, Robert, US merchant, sells arms to Spain, 575 and n1, 576
Czechoslovakia, 352, 388, 723, 969; and arms for Spain, 447n4, 451, 687–8; German demands, 822, 824 and n1, 844, 849; entry of Hitler, 935, 939; and German policy, 942; IB, 969

Dahl, Harold, US flier for R., commuted death sentence, 744 and n2
Dahlem, Franz (*b.* 1892), G. com. organizer in IB, 488n3, 954
Dajakovich Battalion (IB), 969
Daladier, Edouard (1884–1970) Fr. Rad. Min. of War (1936–38), prime minister (1938–40), 337–8, 349, 350, 817 and n1, 871; and aid for Spain, 350, 351, 805, 823, 825, 873; recognition of N. Spain, 896
Daley, Peter (*d.* 1937), Ir. vol. in IB, 725n2
Dali, Salvador (*b.* 1904), Cat. painter, 190
Dallet, Joe (*d.* 1937), US vol. in IB, 723n1
Dalmau Mora, Cosme, 702; execution for espionage, 865
Damianov, Raiko, Bul. vol. in IB, 954
D'Annunzio, Gabriel (1863–1938), It. poet, 20, 110
Dany, Marcel, Fr. journalist, and Badajoz massacre, 374n
Danzi, Gugleilmo (*b.* 1908), 641; fascist director, 737
Dar Akobba, defence of, 173
Dardanelles, 440n4, 740
Darlan, Admiral François (1881–1942), and Baldwin's government, 367–8, 389
Dato (Sp. gunboat), 212, 243
Dato e Iradier, Eduardo (1856–1921), Con. prime minister, 22; murder, 24, 117
Dávila Arrondo, Gen. Fidel (1878–1962) (R), 505, 507, 636; member Burgos *junta*, 282, 421n2, 690; of *junta técnica*, 425 and n4; and Army of the North, 690, 717, 752, 758; campaigns, 717–18, 721, 791, 797, 867; character, 690, 931; political posts, 750, 752, 948n1
Dávila, Sancho (F), and Carlists, 632n2; and Hedilla, 635, 637, 638: member national council, 750
Dawson, Geoffrey (1874–1944), ed. of *The Times*, 683
Dax, Bishop of, and exchange of prisoners, 513
Day-Lewis, Cecil (1904–72), Eng. poet, 347; 'Nabarra', 614
Del Rosal Díaz, Amaro (S), 782n5
Delage Gárcia, Luis (C), army commissar, 710, 904

Delaprée, Louis (*d.* 1936), Fr. journalist, 307 and n2; 486 and n4
Delasalle, Maj. Gaston (*d.* 1937), shot, 491 and n4
Delbos, Yvon (1885–1956), Fr. foreign min. (1936–37), and aid for Spain, 337–8, 343, 349–50, 364, 388n4, 570, 572; at Geneva, 683; and naval patrol scheme, 734, 736; and non-intervention, 738; and Nyon conference, 741, 742; reopens frontier, 745
Delgado, José, Catholic businessman, 166
Delgado, Teodoro (N), painter, 858
Delgado Serrano, Col. (afterwards Gen.) Francisco (N), 224, 371; assault on Madrid, 409, 432, 474, 484; and the Ebro, 841, 843
Delicado, Manuel (C), 901, 906
Dellwyn (Br. ship), 828
Delmer, Sefton (*b.* 1904), Eng. journalist, 481
Denain, Gen. Albert (1880–1952), Fr. officer, 363–4
Dencás, Dr José (1900–66), Cat. politician, 132, 135, 136; arrest and escape, 136, 161
Denmark, 740, 893
Dependants' Aid Committee, England, 609, 853n3
Derecho Regional Valenciano (DRV), 165
Déroulède, Paul (1846–1914), Fr. poet, 20
Deutschland (G. battleship), 371, 387, 470; bombing of, 685 and nn2, 4; German reaction, 685–6
Devonshire, HMS, 884
Diario Oficial, banned by Casado, 899
Díaz Alor, José (Soc), 782n5
Díaz Baza, Angel (Soc), 604, 786; chief of SIM, 776
Díaz Criado, Col. Manuel (N), 263
Díaz del Moral, Antonio, 272
Díaz Ramos, José (1896–1942) (C), Sec. gen. Sp. C.P., 121–2, 122n1, 361, 410, 461, 889; and party membership, 522; at Valencia conference (1937), 648–9; and POUM, 649, 703; in Moscow, 889n1; *d.* in Tiflis, 950
Díaz Sandino, Col. Felipe (R), Cat. councillor of defence (1936), 301, 448n3; in civil war, 235, 319, 429
Díaz Tendero, Capt. Eleuterio (*b.* 1882) (R), 407, 649, 671; and UMRA, 166 and n1, 407
Dieckhoff, Dr Hans Heinrich (1884–1952), G. diplomat, 349, 354, 569–70, 686
Diéguez, Isidoro (*d.* 1939) (C), 890n2; and army falsifications, 542n4
Díez, Galo (A), Sec. of CNT, 812
Dimitrov, Georgi (1882–1949), Bulg. com. leader, 338n4, 339; on aims of world communism, 153–4; and IB 452
Dimitrov Battalion, 591, 954, 969
Dio lo vuole Division, 596
Dirksen, Dr Herbert v., G. Amb. in London, 826
Djilas, Milovan (*b.* 1911), Yug. writer, 608
Dodd, William (1869–1940), US Amb. Berlin, 824
Dollfuss, Dr Engelbert (1892–1934), 109, 134
Dolz de Espejo, Tomás (Conde de la Florida) (*b.* 1879) (Car), 640
Dombrowski Battalion, 479, 480, 485, 489–90, 968
Domenech, Juan (A), 524, 526, 813; and *Generalidad*, 528, 652, 813; sec. CNT, 660n3
Domingo Germinal Battalion, 968
Domingo Sanjuán, Marcelino (1884–1939), Rep. min. (1931–33) (1936), 36, 38, 42n3, 46, 161, 402; and agrarian reform, 84–5, 107
Domínguez, Edmundo (Soc), 522; vice-pres. UGT, 782n5, 902n
Donnelly, Charles (*d.* 1939), Ir. poet vol. in IB, 595
Doriot, Jacques (1888–1945), Fr. C. then Fas., 123
D'Ors, Eugenio, writer, 645
Dos Passos, John (1896–1970), 608, 609n1; and Hemingway, 706n1
Douglas, Norman (1868–1952), Eng. writer, 347n3
Douhet, Gen., It. theorist of war, 807
Douro river, waterway scheme, 27
Doval Bravo, Maj. Lisardo (*b.* 1888) (N), 321, 641; ruthlessness, 143, 263, 641
Dragons of Death, It. air squadron, 382–3
Driau la Rochelle, Fr. fascist, 768
Drozd, V., Ru. naval officer, 549n3
Dubček, Alexander, 954
Duclos, Jacques (1896–) Fr. com. leader, 120, 154
Dueso prison, 721
Duff Cooper, Alfred (later Ld Norwich) (1890–1954), 619
Duhamel, Jean, and POUM affair, 707
Dulm, Vice-Admiral van, Du. non-intervention official, 581

Dumont, Col. Jules (Col. Kodak) (C), Fr. vol. in IB, 358, 479 and n3, 689 and n2, 723; death in Resistance, 954
Dumoulin Eckhart, Count (*b.* 1884), G. dip., 425, 426, 633
Dunbar, Malcolm (1912–62), Eng. vol. in IB, 710n, 723n1, 726n2, 798n2, 840n2; suicide, 956
Dunn, James, US diplomat, 434n1
Dupré, Henri (*d.* 1951), Fr. cagoulard vol. in IB, 491n4; shot as collaborator, 955n1
Dupuy, Capt. Georges, Fr. sailor, 721
Durán, Gustavo (R), campaigns, 492, 710, 832; and Kléber, 492n2
Durango (Vizcaya), 308, 625; bombing, 616–17
Durán-Jordà, Dr F. (R), Cat. doctor, blood transfusion services, 551
Durruti, Buenaventura (1896–1936) (A), 78, 136, 248; legendary warrior, 68; and revolution, 126, 181, 318–19; anti-fascism, 250n2; in civil war, 316–18; use of violence, 318; falangist brothers, 328; continuing idealism, 420–30, 820; and 'discipline of indiscipline', 430nn1, 2, 485; visits Madrid, 430n2, 483; and USSR arms, 443–4; plan to raid Bank of Spain, 448; and defence of Madrid, 483 and n3, 484; death and funeral, 485 and n2, 500; Montjuich tomb, 874
Durruti Column, 557, 658

Eberhard, Lt. Kraft (*d.* 1936), G. officer, 481n2, 482
Ebro (river), 27, 316, 554n2, 724, 725, 798, 800, 802, 818; battle of, 835–8, 840–43, 848, 852, 854–5, 928n4, 938; republican defeat, 854–5; Italian involvement, 854; value of German aid, 937
ECCI, secretariat, 338n4
Echevarría Novoa, José, director of public order, 661–2
Echevarrieta, Horacio, B. financier, 41
L'Echo de Paris, 350, 351
Ecija (Seville), 178
Eden, Anthony (later Ld Avon) (*b.* 1897), Br. foreign sec., 349, 350, 735; and aid to Spain, 344 and n4, 345, 570; and non-intervention, 387, 394–5, 566–7, 572, 620; at Geneva, 439, 440, 732–3; opposes Franco's 'belligerent rights', 567; peace mediation plan, 570, 682, 683; cause of his fall, 573n1; naval patrol plan, 577, 734; and nationalist blockade, 619–20, 621; pro-republican feelings, 621 and n1, 623, 739n1, 746; and Guernica, 629; relations with Chamberlain, 738 and n4, 739 and n1, 796, 806; and Nyon conference, 742; and Italian intervention in Spain, 745, 746, 795n1; and Alba, 766; resignation, 797; and appeasement, 944
Edgar André Battalion, 479, 480, 493, 968
Education, 36, 56, 182, 298, 865; position of the church, 51n2, 52, 73, 102, 106, 127, 756, 859; anarchist activities, 61, 62, 64; in draft Constitution (1931), 75–6; under Azaña, 161; twentieth-century renaissance, 190; 'Plan 38', 762; reorganization (purge), 762, 763
Edwards, Robert (*b.* 1906), Br. vol. in POUM battalion, 543n1, 955
Eguía, J. de, B. naval officer, 897 and n2
Eguipko, Nikolai, Ru. naval officer, 549n3
Ehrenburg, Ilya (1891–1967), Ru. writer, 68, 173, 393 and n4; 447 (quoted) and n2, 707; and the Falange, 831
Eibar (Guipúzcoa), 321; arms factories, 238, 308, 330, 616
Einstein, Albert (1875–1955), and US arms embargo, 824
'El Campesino' Brigade, 599, 601
El Campo (Oviedo), 491
El Carmolí (Cartagena), Ru. air base at, 447
El Debate, 53, 54, 55, 58, 102, 108, 762
El Escorial (Madrid), 488, 633, 710; Augustinian college of, 37, 52, 416
El Ferrol (Corunna), 140, 219, 332; naval base at, 238, 242, 266, 328, 404, 426; battle at, 253
El Grao de Castellón, 831
El Socialista, 128, 134n1, 164, 178, 208, 209, 225, 809
El Sol, 514n2
El Tiemblo (Avila), 432
El Vedat farm (Valencia), 904
El Velasco (N. destroyer), 332
Elche (Alicante), Com. headquarters at, 305, 892
Elda (Alicante), headquarters of R. government, 305, 892, 898, 900–904 *passim*
Elections, power of the *caciques*, 14, 16, 25, 45, 72, 157; (general) (1931), 72; (1933), 106, 107, 125; (1934), 110; (1936), 155–8, 159, 162 and n2, 178; municipal (1931), 31 and n2, 34, 45,

105, 119; (1933), 105, 106; (1934) (Basque), 132
Eleta, Conde de, 277n1
Elgeta (Guipúzcoa), 623, 624
Eliot, T. S. (1888–1965), poet, 347n3
Eliseda, Marqués de, 152
Elliott, Sir Walter (1888–1958), Eng. Con. politician, 743
Ellis, Havelock (1859–1939), 347n3
Embargo Act (U S), 417n2, 576, 609n4, 824
Enciso Madolell, Maj. José María (1894–1938) (R), and U M R A, 166n1, 515; execution, 515
Endymion (Br. smuggler), 795
English General Relief Fund for Spain, 462n1
Enjuta Ferrán, Federico (R), judge, 500n2
Epoca, suspension, 210, 762
Epstein, Joseph (Col. Gilles), *d.* in Resistance, 955
Ercoreca (Ba.), Mayor, 263n4
Eroles, Dionisio (A), patrol controls, 429, 526; *F A Iista*, 654; sec. C N T, 660n3
Escario, José Luis (F), 640; and Carlists, 632n2, 637
Escobar, José Ignacio (M), press officer, 504n2
Escobar Huertas, Gen. Antonio (1879–1939) (R), 871, 886, 891, 907, 909; execution, 925
Escofet Alsina, Col. Federico (R), Cat. police chief, 233, 278, 672n2
Escorza, Manuel (A), F A I leader, 402, 406, 652, 725, 820
Escribano, Tomás Marcos (*b.* 1902), 503
Escrivá de Balaguer, José María (*b.* 1902), founder of Opus Dei, 802
Esk, H M S, 431
Espá Ruiz, Col. Arturo (*b.* 1905) (N), 900
España (N. battleship), 253, 331 and n4, 377, 630, 936
España, José María, 672n2
Esparza, Eladio (F), 750, 848n4
Espinosa, Francisco, execution in prison, 763
Espinosa de los Monteros, Gen. Eugenio (*b.* 1888), 913
Espionage, 381, 653, 697, 702, 776, 859; Franco's organization, 505 and n, 759; in concentration camps, 922
Esplá Rizo, Carlos (L R), 251, 472, 649
Esquerra, the, Cat. Left party, 45 and n1, 46, 72, 119, 136, 156, 162n2, 297, 303; anti-fascism, 250 and n2; and P S U C, 301; and Largo Caballero's cabinet, 407 and n2; membership of *Generalidad*, 428–9, 524, 652, 658, 660; and P O U M, 524; and 1937 government, 672n2
Estadella, José, Min. of Labour, 127
Estat Català, separatist group, 45n1, 132, 654n3; attempted *coup*, 524–5, 525n1
Esteban Vilaro, José, 491n4
Estella, FR Gumersindo de, 763
Estella (Navarre), 261, 315n
Estelrich, Juan (Cat.), 271n1, 272n2, 695
Estelrich, Rosa ('La Valenciana'), 10n1
Esteves, Gen. Raúl, Portuguese vol. Brigade, 979n5
Estrada Manchón, Maj. Manuel (*b.* 1902) (R), 407, 476
Estremadura, 47, 77–8, 241, 324, 333, 366; *latifundia*, 80, 169; anarchism, 81, 320n, 933; farm takeovers, 169; and autonomy, 202; *Yunteros*, 284; U G T and youth domination, 293; in civil war, 375, 400, 662 and n5, 868, 871, 912, 914; agricultural collectives, 553 and n1; area of great estates, 554
Etingon, Gen. ('Kotov') (*d.* 1953), Ru. official, 447n2; shot, 953 and n
Europe, 47, 50–51, 82; Spanish attitude, 334; influence of her ideas on civil war, 336; breakdown of order (1936), 369; and Non-Intervention Committee, 395; arms traffic chain, 451; socialist movement, 646
Les Évenements survenus, 337n1
Exmouth, H M S (Br. evacuee ship), 431 and n1
Export Cartel for War Materials, 418

Fabra Rivas, Antonio (1879–1958) (Soc), 110n1
Fábregas, Juan (A), 428, 438, 529
Fábregas, Tomás, anti-fascist, 250n2
Faced, Inocencio (*d.* 1936), 274
Faced, Martín, 658n4
Fagnani, Capt., It. airforce officer, 568 and n5
Fagosi, Col., It. officer, 721
Fal Conde, Manuel (*b.* 1894) (Car leader), 97, 130 and n2, 205, 254n2, 319n2, 425; involvement in plots, 99, 129, 167, 175, 184, 202; treatment by Franco, 507–8, 632, 639; and union with falangists, 632; and new national council, 750
Falange, 11, 113, 129, 166n1, 169, 335, 722; ideology, 112, 115–16, 354, 640n1, 930; opponents, 114 and n2; union with J O N S, 114 and n3; Valladolid

Falange – *contd*
meeting, 115; attitude to violence, 152; and Calvo Sotelo, 152n2; numbers and membership, 153 and n1, 156, 159, 163 and n2, 177n2, 201, 506, 508; encourages disorder, 162–3; and military rising, 173, 174, 177, 178, 183, 184, 201, 209, 222, 236, 240, 243, 244, 246, 419; hymn '*Cara al Sol*', 195 and n2; and Army of Africa, 205–6; murders and atrocities, 206 and n3, 216n2, 259, 260, 261, 262, 263, 284, 569; attempted arrest, 206–7; in Morocco, 215–16; and Lorca's death, 267n1; in republican Spain, 274, 275, 279; in nationalist Spain, 283, 284–6, 287nn1, 3, 419; becomes religious, 287, 288; in civil war, 313, 315 and n, 319, 508, 711–12; leadership age, 328; Mallorquins, 383 and n1; Blue Shirts, 419–20; seven-man *junta*, 420 and n3, 506, 507, 635; failure to seize the state, 420; and Decree of Unification, 423, 751; accepts Franco as 'Generalissimo', 423, 425, 502, 506; in Madrid battle, 432, 702; condemns intellectuals, 502–3; internal difficulties, 506; and a union with Carlists, 632 and nn2, 3, 633, 637, 639, 640; plots Hedilla's overthrow, 635–6; and Germany, 636, 949; triumvirate rule, 637–8; membership new national council, 750, 753; subservience to army, 750; relations with the church, 859, 930; fate of leaders, 865, 873; in Cartagena, 900–901; war casualties, 927, 930 and n; and Franco's government, 948
'Falange Española Auténtica' (FEA), 751 and n2
Falange Española Tradicionalista y de las JONS (FET), 639 and n, 750–53
Falangist Labour Charter, 761 and n2
Falcón, Irene (C), 904
Faldella, Col. Emilio, It. officer, 583, 594, 604
Falla, Manuel de (1876–1946), 190
Fanelli, Giuseppe (1827–77), It. anarchist, 60 and n1, 61
Fanjul Goni, General Joaquín (1880–1936), 149–50, 160; conspirator, 165, 168, 203 and n3, 243–5; court martial and death, 203n3, 403–4, 404n1
Faraudo, Capt. Carlos (1901–1936), murder and revenge, 206–7
Farina, Col., It. officer, 720–21
Farinacci, Roberto (1892–1945), It. fascist leader, 597 and n1
Faringdon, Alexander Ld. (*b.* 1902), Eng. socialist, 398
Fascism, Italian, 20, 132, 192, 455, 510
Fatarella (Tarragona), 557, 855
Faupel, Gen. Wilhelm v. (1873–1945), G. Amb. to Nat. Spain, 578, 580, 636, 689, 737; character and career, 569; opinion of Franco, 569; plan for German intervention, 569–70, 571, 572nn1, 3; and a new Spanish state, 643–4; hatred of Sperrle, 722; replaced, 765; suicide, 951
Fayón (Saragossa), 838, 841, 843
Feced, Ramón, Min. of Agriculture, 229n2
FE (falangist paper), 114, 636
Federación Anarquista Ibérica (FAI), 6 and n4, 73, 78, 103, 137, 250 and n2, 429, 725, 865; formation, 68; dispute with reformists, 69; *treintistas* accusation, 73–4, 180; and violence, 163, 277, 298; and libertarian communism, 180; and PSUC, 301; numbers, 523; and civil war, 544, 648, 657, 811, 813; and Friends of Durruti, 656n1; cooperation with government, 671; and Negrín, 815, 820; and communist army promotions, 845n1
Federación Española Tradicionalista, 750
Federación Ibérica de Juventudes Libertarias (FIJL), 70–71, 523, 865; Barcelona revolutionaries, 652, 657n2, 658
Federación Nacional de Agricultores de España (FNAE), 66n1, 83
Federación Universitaria Española (FUE), 114
Federation of Smallholders (GEPCI), 523 and n1
Ferdinand VII, King of Spain (1784–1833), 13, 509
Fernando Po, 257n2
Ferla, Col. la, and Frecce Azzure Division, 856n1
Fermoso Blanco, Gen. Francisco (N), and *junta técnica*, 425n4
Fernán Núñez, Duque de (*d.* 1936) (N), 510
Fernández, Amador (Soc), 133n1, 310
Fernández, Aurelio (A), 250n2, 402, 429, 526; member of *Generalidad*, 652n4; imprisonment, 772
Fernández, Marcial (C), 814
Fernández Bolaños, Antonio (Soc), 679

Fernández Burriel, Gen. Alvaro (1879–1936) (N), 232, 403
Fernández Castañeda, Capt. Emilio (*b.* 1898) (R), 381 and n3
Fernández Cuesta, Raimundo (*b.* 1897) (F), 169, 201, 604, 753, 948; exchanged for de Azcárate, 750–51; and new movement, 751, 752
Fernández de Dios (A), 273 and n1
Fernández Heredia, Col. Enrique (*b.* 1893) (R), at Teruel, 788, 789 and n1, 793
Fernández Montesinos, Manuel (Soc), Mayor of Granada 1936, 264n2
Fernández Quintana, Col. Tomás, 403
Fernández Vega, José Antonio (LR), 307
Ferrer, Gen. (N), 717
Ferrer y Guardia, Francisco (1859–1909), 65; counter-productive execution, 19, 64 and n3, 874
Ferry (Polish vol.), 36, 490n2
Fichte, Johann Gottlieb (1762–1814), 13n1
Field, Noël, 854n
Fifth Column, 395n1, 702, 858; in Madrid, 437, 487–8, 887, 913, 914n1; Franco's organizations, 505n, 759; urban sitings, 692, 693, 720, 729, 731
Fifth Regiment (Com.), 410, 480, 846; organization and membership, 291n3, 322–3, 400, 699, 846; leaders and trainees, 323–4, 340, 545n3, 564
Figueras (Gerona), 880, 881
Finland, 952
Firedrake, HMS, 623
First World War (1914–18), 16, 254, 928; impact on Spain, 21, 23, 39, 65–6; origin of IB, 453
Fischer, Louis (1896–1970), US journalist, 171, 458, 475, 747n2, 805n4; on Goriev, 479n1; arms traffic, 670n2, 782, 825
Fitzpatrick, Capt. Noël, Br. N. vol., 374n, 409n1, 412, 768n2, 980n2
Flory, Jean, 259n2
FNTT, social/agrarian, 109, 130–31, 169, 531, 933; spread of violence, 126–7; treatment by anarchists, 305–6
Foltz, Charles, US journalist, 925 and n4
Fomento de Obras y Construcciones, 295
Ford, Ford Madox (*né* Hueffer) (1873–1939), US writer, 347n3
Ford Motor companies, 295 and n2, 335
Foreign Legion, 93, 94, 151, 167, 224; to repress Asturian revolution, 140, 142, 143, 144, 201; Franco and, 140, 141, 237n1 (accepts him as Generalissimo), 423; and military rising, 177, 212, 216, 217, 224; Moroccan manoeuvres, 205; *Banderas*, 217 and n4, 218, 224, 371, 374; flown to Seville, 243, 251, 331; massacres by, 252; and civil war, 329, 370n2, 371, 373, 374, 375, 400, 722, 759; brutality, 371, 373, 374 and n, 411, 412; foreign volunteers, 409n1, 768, 979n5; professional skill, 411, 412; Madrid offensive, 436, 474–5, 484, 588, 593; motto, 502; and Unamuno, 502–3; with It. pilots, 568n5; CNT rebels, 612n4
Fortuna, Capt. Oreste, It. tank commander, 475
Fotos (falangist paper), 760
Fox, Ralph (1900–37), Eng. Com. writer, 491 and n2
Foxá, Agustín de (1903–59), Sp. dip., 195n2, 504n2
Fraga (Huesca), 317, 430, 801
France, 17, 20, 108, 118, 151; revolutionary principles, 42, 336; freemasonry, 43; influence on Spain, 51, 65; position of church in, 51, 52; trade unionism, 69; its vineyards, 79; its Revolution, 193; and arms for Spain, 329–30, 330n3, 337–8, 351–2, 364, 388–90, 678, 981; effect of nationalist victory, 339; and Spanish crisis, 343–5, 348, 350–51; *Camelots du Roi*, 348, 768; and non-intervention, 352n2; fear of offending England, 389; Mapeba espionage group, 505n; and German troops in Morocco, 578; to escort Basque refugee ships, 680; Catholic press, 695, 697; closure and opening of frontier for passage of arms, etc., 735, 745, 804, 805, 823, 825 and n3, 837, 852, 871, 941, 943 and n3; Italian attacks on her shipping, 740; relations with nationalist Spain, 766n3, 768, 884, 896; possible intervention, 802, 805, 809; and Catalonian disaster, 873; admission of Spanish refugees, 877, 878, 879; sells flour for defeated, 893; plight of refugees, 920; under Occupation, 925; fear of Germany, 943; learns wrong lessons from Spanish war, 944–5; and IB, 968, 969
Francés, SIM chief in Andalusia, 778
Francisci, Col. Enrico, It. officer, 599, 717
Franco, Carmen Polo de (*b.* 1900), wife of Francisco, 141, 503
Franco, Col. José (1879–1937) (R), 731 and n2

Franco, Máximo (A), 801
Franco y Bahamonde, Nicolás (*b.* 1891) (N), sec. gen. to his brother (1936–37), 360, 419n1, 422–3, 425 and n4, 426, 504, 508; and 'Mapeba', 505n; amb. to Portugal, 634, 754; mission to Franco, 739; omitted from cabinet, 754
Franco y Bahamonde, Capt. Ramón (1896–1938) (N), 331n2; flight in *Non Plus Ultra*, 31, 59n5, 142; and republican rising, 142, 514n2; death, 853n1
Franco y Bahamonde, General Francisco (1892–1975) (N), 159n3, 387; and *coups d'état* (1936, 1937), xix; *Africanista*, 94, 147, 231 and n; and Asturian revolution, 140, 142, 144; background and character, 140–42, 231n, 424, 514, 642; and Second Republic, 141, 226; army appointments, 147, 150, 159, 216, 255, 371, 418; asks for a 'state of war', 159 and n3, 160; and the Canaries, 161, 166, 167, 199, 283, 931; and Azaña, 167 and n1, 199; and José Antonio, 167, 499; and the rising, 203 and n1, 206; air transport to Morocco, 203–4, 212–14, 216, 283, 338, 931; and Madrid campaign, 209, 376, 400, 432, 471, 486–7, 612; on the way to supreme power, 214, 376, 419; Las Palmas Manifesto, 218–19, 218n4; institutionalization of dictatorship, 218n4; obstructed access to Spain, 243; effect of Sanjurjo's death, 255; remains a myth on the mainland, 282; and the church, 286, 511; seeks foreign aid, 338, 341–2; gains command of the sea, 370n1; and Mola, 376; salutes monarchist flag, 414; relations with Germany, 418, 419, 426, 469, 850, 860; headquarters (Cáceres), 419n1, (Burgos), 424, 425, 717 (Salamanca), 504–5; as single commander (Generalissimo, El Caudillo), 421–5, 639–40, 644, 931, 936; decrees, 423, 424 and n2, 894; speeches on future of Spain, 424, 426; and Hitler, 426, 949; relations with Carlists, 507; and the Vatican, 511–12, 683; and shooting of prisoners, 514 and n2; response to foreign recognition, 567–8; and Italian aid, 568, 573, 739, 806; civil war battles and engagements, 583–4, 602, 604, 693–4, 714, 715 and n2, 789, 791, 797, 802, 841, 842, 868; rejects non-intervention, 584; approves use of blockade, 619; alleged anger at Guernica, 627; purchases Italian submarines, 629; victory over falangists and Carlists, 632, 633, 639–40; and a formal unification of all parties, 637, 639; and Hedilla, 639, 640–41, 642; character of the 'new Spain', 639; decries peace mediation plan, 682–3, 786; English judgements, 698; asks for Faupel's removal, 722; and British 'volunteer' plan, 747; new cabinet, 752–3, 806; discovery of his Guadalajara plan, 788, 789; anger at bombing of Barcelona, 807; to insist on unconditional surrender, 810, 821–2, 846, 894–5, 898, 909, 935–6; tactics, 842, 852; policy towards Italian troops, 847; and possibility of a general war, 848, 849; and Munich conference, 849–50; headquarters staff, 868n2; letter to Chamberlain, 895, 896; secures general recognition, 897, 898; peace terms, 910; his 'concessions', 912; and Pétain, 919 and n1; responsibility for post-war executions, 926; survives, 930–31; political successes, 931; management of victory, 932, 947; policy of 'cleaning up' Spain, 936, unity of command, 938; errors of judgement, 938–9; use of new men, 948; ennoblements, 948 and n3; persecution of ex-republicans, 951 and n
Franco-Belgian (6th February) Battalion (IB), 591
Franco-Spanish Moroccan Agreement (1912), 578
Franco-Spanish Treaty (1935), 350
Franco Salgado, Capt. Hermenegildo (*d.* 1936) (N), murdered by his sailors, 328
François-Poncet, André (*b.* 1887), Fr. Amb. to Germany, 578; and non-intervention plan, 387, 388, 391, 572
François-Xavier de Bourbon Parme, Prince (*b.* 1889) Carlist regent (1936), 167n3, 205 and n
Freemasonry, 8, 19, 65, 930; army lodges, 13, 43; Spanish characteristics and membership, 42–3, 43n3, 149, 179n, 258, 264, 511; suspected by the Right, 43, 334; English/continental breach, 43n1; and Roman Church, 334
Frente Ibérica de Juventudes Libertarias (FIJL), 70
Frente Libertario, 291
Frente Rojo, 811

Friends of Durruti, 524, 654, 656 and n1, 659
Frinovsky, Gen., Ru. official (NKVD), 442
Fritsch, Gen. Wernher v. (1880–1939), commander-in-chief G. Army (1936). 358, 572n1
Frusci, Gen., It. officer, 717
Fuchs, Maj., G. officer, bomber commander, 614n
Fuendetodos (Saragossa), 270
Fuenterrabía (San Sebastián), 379
Fuentes, Col. José Luis (*b.* 1893), and Voronov, 479 and n2, 836–7; dir. of artillery, 836–7
Fuentes del Ebro (Saragossa), 725, 726, 728
Funck, Baron v., G. military attaché, 877n1
Fuqua, Col., US military attaché, 807n2

Gaikins, L. Y. (C), Ru. diplomat, 534, 650; fate in Russia, 952
Gal, Col., *see* Galicz
Galán Rodríguez, Capt. Fermín (1899–1930), 30–31, 127, 320
Galán Rodríguez, Col. Francisco (*d.* 1971) (R and Com.), 320, 480, 718, 728, 731, 900, 901
Galán Rodríguez, Maj. José María (1904–1939) (R. and Com.), 320, 492, 688
Galán Rodríguez, Maj. Juan (*d.* 1939) (R), intelligence chief, 550
Galarza Gago, Angel (1892–1966) (Soc), min. of interior 1936, 277n2, 550; act of mercy, 277
Galarza Morante, Col. Valentín (*b.* 1880) (N), chief of staff, military rising, 183; arrest, 243; cabinet post, 406, 663; denounced by communists, 663 and n2, 665
Galatea (Br. vessel), 766, 914
Galdácano (Bilbao), 616, 694
Galera, Maj. Alfredo (N), 841, 843, 854
Galerna (N. armed trawler), 618, 623
Galicia, 7, 39, 47, 72, 149, 238, 323, 333, 420, 435; autonomy party, 4, 6n2, 90; *minifundia*, 80, 82; separatist movement, 90; Portuguese revolutionaries and, 133n1; 1936 elections in, 157; and the war, 252–3, 390; guerrilla activity, 513–14
Galicz ('Gal'), Janos (C), Hung. officer in IB, 455, 590–91, 594–5; promoted general, 593n2, 607n3, 710, 713n5, 953
Gallacher, William (1881–1965), Br. com. MP, 853n3, 897
Galland, Gen. Adolf (*b.* 1912), G. officer, air ace, 359; and Guernica, 626; Asturian 'carpet bombing', 730; in Second World War, 951
Gallegan Autonomy party, 134n2
Gallo, Alejandro (N), and *junta técnica*, 425n4
Gambara, Col. (then Gen.) Gastone (1895–1958) (N), It. officer, 802, 870, 915; and Littorio Division, 856 and n1, 867, 872, 873, 912; Rome victory parade, 920; in Second World War, 952
Gamelin, Gen. Maurice (1872–1958), Fr. commander-in-chief, 805
Gamero del Castillo, Pedro (*b.* 1910) (F), 632n2
Gámir Ulibarri, Gen. Mariano (1877–1962) (B), campaigns, 687, 690, 693, 717, 720; supreme Basque commander, 687 717, 733; dismissal, 728
Gamonal aerodrome (Burgos), peace talks, 910n
Gandesa (Tarragona), 812, 840–42, 871; destruction of vines, 928n4
Gandía, 242, 305, 828, 914
Ganivet, Angel (1862–98), essayist, 35n3
Garabitas, Mt., Madrid, 481, 486
Garcerán, Rafael (F), law clerk to José Antonio, 183, 209, 420; and Hedilla's overthrow, 635, 637, 638
Garcés, Santiago (Soc), national head of SIM, 778, 809n1
'García', identity, 654n3
García, Justiniano (C), intelligence chief, 550
García, Mariano (A), 153n1
García Aldave, Gen. José (1876–1936), execution of, 251 and n3, 281n1
García Atadell, Agapito (Soc), anti-fascist *checa*, 275 and n1, 777
García Benítez, Gen. Angel (*b.* 1874) (N), 237, 277n1
García Birlán, Antonio (A), 428; denounces Negrín, 866n1
García Conde, Pedro (N), Sp. Amb. in Rome, 505, 741
García Duarte, Prof. Rafael (*d.* 1936) (R), 264n2
García Escámez y Iniesta, Col. (later Gen.) Francisco (1893–1951) (N), plan for military rising, 201–2; subsequent campaigns, 313, 435n3, 488–9, 493, 588, 797–8, 801; (posth.) marquisate, 948

García Hernández, Lt. Angel (1900–30), 30–31, 127
García de la Herrán, Gen. Miguel (1880–1936) (N), and military rising, 243, 245; shot by staff, 246
García Labella, Prof. Joaquín (*d.* 1936), 264n2
García Lacalle, Capt. Andrés (R), 599, 842; on Russian pilots, 440; on Condor Legion, 590n; head of air force coastal defence, 807; and of republican fighters, 869n3, 872, 876, 881, 980n4
García Lorca, Federico (1898–1936), poet, 106, 190, 214; victim of atrocities, 264n2, 266–7, 928, 937; responsibility for, 267 and n1; unknown grave, 930; *The House of Bernarda Alba*, 191
García Morales, FR, and Pope Pius XI, 398–9
García Morato y Castaño, Capt. Joaquín (1904–39) (N), air ace, 594 and n1, 726, 756, 802n1; kills Heilbrun, 688n1; (posth.) entitlement, 948
García Oliver, Juan (*b.* 1901) (A), min. of justice, 36–7, 69n4, 248, 250n2, 297, 471, 522, 538; crimes of violence, 69, 103; suggests revolutionary army, 181; in civil war, 319, 406, 429, 483, 642; destroys convicts' files, 472; director of officer schools, 546 and n2; and Barcelona May Days, 657, 658; demands Aurelio Fernández's release, 772n2; survival in exile, 950
García Pallasar, Gen. Joaquín (*b.* 1877) (N), artillery director, 868n2
García Pradas, José (A), 887; and Negrín's way of life, 892n2
García de Pruñeda, Gen. (*b.* 1876) (N), engineering director, 868n2
García Quejido, Antonio (1856–1927) (C), 117; founder of socialist party, 118n2
García Ruiz, Col. Guillermo (*b.* 1884) (N), 383
García Valiño, Col. (later Gen.) (1898–) (N), Navarrese brigade leader, 612, 624, 690, 717, 759; campaigns; 797–8, 801, 803, 819, 831, 832, 843, 854, 867, 869, 870, 872, 912; minister under Franco, 948n1
García Vallejo, Col. Carlos (*b.* 1892) (R), 871
García Vayas, Col. José (1889–1962) (R), 718
García Vivancos, and *solidarios*, 316
Garibaldi, Giuseppe (1807–82), 60
Garibaldi Battalion (IB), 482, 484, 589, 599–601, 602n4, 716n, 954; Brigade, 711, 968
Garicano, Eusebio, and Navarre casualties, 264 and n2
Garijo Hernández, Col. Antonio (*b.* 1899) (R), 894, 910 and n, 911
Garnett, David (*b.* 1892), 347n3
Garvin, J. L. (*d.* 1947), ed. *Observer*, 571n1
Gaselee, Sergeant-Major (*d.* 1937) (N), Ir. vol., 602n1
Gassol, Buenaventura (*b.* 1893) (Cat.) poet, 233, 277, 428; in exile, 672n2
Gastone-Sozzi Battalion, 366 and n2, 408; Centuria, 456
Gaudí y Cornet, Antoni (1852–1926), Cat. artist, 90, 298
Gavilán Almuzarza, Col. Marcelino (*b.* 1880) (N), 238
Gay, Prof. Vicente (N), 335n4; Franco's press officer, 504n2, 636, 645 and n2
Gaymann, Vital ('Vidal'), Fr. vol. in IB, 458, 780
Gazapo Valdés, Col. Dario (*b.* 1891) (N) and (F), 215–16, 640 and n3
Gellhorn, Martha, US writer, 713n4
General Confederation of Italian Labour, 457n3
Generalidad, 179n, 233, 269, 295, 298, 437, 661; provincial councils, 86, 658 and n4; and central government, 86, 299, 530, 546, 772, 872; *Ley de Cultivos*, 131–2, 135; anarchist membership, 428–9, 438, 471, 651, 672; removal of POUM, 524; membership, 524, 527; and communism, 526, 655; restoration of public order, 771–2; and Negrín, 773; and separatism, 845. *See also* Barcelona *and* Catalonia
'Generation of '98', 35n3, 79, 112, 437, 501
Geneva, 344, 350n2, 439, 496, 880
George, Pierre ('Fabien'), 458n2; *d.* in Resistance, 954–5
George Washington Battalion, 608n3, 716
Germany, 35, 108, 114, 453, 573, 628, 765; Spanish agents, 21, 65–6; Nuremberg rally, 109; and arms for Spain, 147 and n1, 167 and n3, 342 and n5, 349, 354, 451 and n3, 469, 571, 860–61, 937; Reichstag fire, 153; great depression, 188; Olympic Games (1936), 233; commercial relations with Spain, 335–6, 736–7, 737n1; Labour

Front in Spain, 335–6; remilitarization of Rhineland, 345; need for Spanish ore, 356, 570, 736, 737n1; organization and despatch of arms, 357–8, 358n4, 370, 418n2; Foreign Office reaction, 358; planes supplied, 370 and nn2, 3, 390, 418n2, 977 and n4; and non-intervention, 390, 396, 580, 941; composition of its airforce, 469 and n3; importance of Franco's victory for, 517, 580, 796; relations with nationalist Spain, 567, 569, 737; and Franco-British mediation plan, 570, 576–7, 580; and British diplomacy in Spain, 572n3; Messerschmitt fighters, 624 and n2, 678 and n2; and a world war, 686, 941; Franco's debt to, 765; airforce and army lessons from Spanish war, 802, 829 and n2, 944 and n2; quarrels with Franco, 829–30, 848; return of volunteers, 920; treatment of refugees, 922; influence of Munich on Spanish policy, 941–2; attacks Russia, 949; and IB, 968; value of its aid to Franco, 975; strength in Spain, 977 and nn2, 4; ancillary assistance, 978

Gerö, Erno (real name – Singer; alias 'Pierre', 'Ernst', 'Pedro') (*b.* 1898). international communist, 340, 655n3, 954; and Largo Caballero, 650

Gerona, 270, 277, 702, 881; proposed surrender, 831

Getafe (Madrid), air base, 245, 246, 331, 386, 470

Gibraltar, 111, 338, 370, 371, 392n1, 426–7, 739; Straits of, 242, 243, 326, 355

Gibson, Ian, Ir. writer, 265nn1, 7

Gide, André (1869–1951), Fr. writer, 698, 699

Gijón, 68, 136n2, 142, 255, 311, 775; Simancas barracks, 236, 309, 326, 384; naval attack, 310, 384; fishing collectives, 539; Council of Asturias, 728; nationalist proscription, 731

Gil, Evaristo (C), 118n2

Gil Robles y Quiñones, José María (*b.* 1899) (M), xviii, 207, 334, 424; Leader of CEDA, 4–6, 108–9, 172, 211; describes the crisis, 4, 5, 7; catholic deputy, 43n3, 125, 127; adherents, 108–9; youth movement (JAP), 109, 133, 149; bid for premiership, 125, 126, 149–50, 151, 153; denounced by UGT, 133; and Second Republic, 134, 165, 194; purchase of arms from Germany, 147 and n; asks for 'a state of war', 159 and n1; knowledge of military rising, 184–5, 185n1; withdraws from politics, 285, 420–21; in exile in Lisbon, 421 and n2, 642n3; and failure of the war, 421; and Franco, 642n3, 948; oratory of, 931

Gil Roldán (A), 435

Gil Ruiz, Col. Rodrigo (R), 407; arms the UGT, 226 and n3

Gil Yuste, Gen. Germán (1886–1948) (N), 421n2, 425n4

Gillain, Nick, Belg. vol. in IB, 454–5

Giménez Caballero, Ernesto (*b.* 1899) (F), 760; career, 110–11, 882; and fascism, 112n4, 640n3; and Franco, 640n3, 645

Giménez Fernández, Manuel, 148, 194, 259; and CEDA, 108, 134n1, 146

Giner de los Ríos, Bernardo (*b.* 1888) (R), min. of communications (1936–39), 179n, 407n2, 670, 815; and Casado's plot, 901–2

Giner de los Ríos, Prof. Francisco (1839–1915), 35, 36, 196

Giral y Pereira, José (1880–1962), R. Min. and Prime Minister 1936, 161, 179n, 204, 227, 230, 440, 664; and Madrid, 268n, 283, 403, 404–5; seeks Blum's aid, 337–8; possible successors, 403n and n2; exchange of prisoners, 496; war policy, 534–5; in Negrín's cabinet, 670, 770, 809, 815; and end of hostilities, 747–8

Girauta, Vicente (*d.* 1939) (R), dir. gen. of security, 899

Girón, Domingo (C), 890

Girón de Velasco, José Antonio (*b.* 1911) (F), 315, 750, 948

Gironella (P), 302, 876; trial, 866

Giustizia e Libertà Column, 366, 381

Glenn Martin (Aircraft) Co., 390–91

Godden, Br. FO rep. in Valencia, 914

Goded Llopis, Gen. Manuel (1882–1936) (N), 28–9, 92, 93 and n1; *Africanistas*, 94, 210, 161, 166; conspirator, 99; and military rising, 165, 168, 209; in Barcelona, 210 and n1, 232, 235; taken prisoner, 235, 254–5; trial and death, 403

Goicoechea Cosculluela, Antonio (1876–1953) (M), min. under Franco, 55, 162, 211, 282; 'Young Mauristas', 59n4, 107; conspirator, 99, 107, 238; ideological position of, 112; mission to Mussolini by, 129, 130n1, 342, 352; and murder of Calvo Sotelo, 210; treachery of, 613 and n, 691, 692

Golding, Louis (1895–1958), Eng. writer, 347n3, 360n4
Golfín, Javier Fernando (F), 702; execution, 865
Gollancz, Victor (1893–1967), Br. publisher, 346, 609, 611n1
Gomá y Tomás, Cardinal Isidro (1869–1940), Archbishop of Toledo, 55 and n1, 287, 413, 634; on civil war as punishment, 512; and shooting of Basque priests, 512–13; Franco and, 682, 683; and letter to Bishops, 696 and n1; and 'exaggerated nationalism', 884
Gomara (Morocco), 104
'Gómez' Gen. (Wilhelm Zaisser) (1893–1958), G. in Spain with IB, 455, 490, 711n2, 780–81; disgraced, 954
Gómez, Mariano (R), 251, 404
Gómez Caminero, Gen. Juan (García) (1871–1937), 56n2, 58n2, 166n1
(Gómez) Jordana y Souza, Gen. Francisco (1876–1944) (N), for. min., 737, 932; career, 609, 749, 750, 752 and n1, 753, 884, 919; and Stohrer, 776, 830, 850
Gómez Morato, Gen. Agustín (1879–1952) (R), commander, Army of Africa, 205, 217; arrest, 217, 903n3; imprisonment, 224, 266n1
Gómez Ossorio, José (*d.* 1940) (R), 898
Gómez Sáez, Paulino (S), 237, 815, 901
Gómez San José, Trifón (Soc), 128; army administrator, 836, 864
Gomís, José (R), judge, 877
González, Alvaro (F), informer, 215
González, César R. (Soc), 118n2
González, Liberino (S), 907, 909
González, N., on peasant collectives, 559
González, Salvador (C), 250n2
González, Valentín, *see* 'El Campesino'
González Bueno, Pedro (*b.* 1896) (F), 640n3, 752, 753, 860; author of Labour Charter, 761n2
González Carrasco, Gen. Manuel (*b.* 1877) (N), 165, 168 and n, 210, 241, 251
González de Lara, Gen. Gonzalo (*b.* 1874) (N), 226, 247; arrest and imprisonment, 238, 247n2
González Marín (A), 902
González Nonvela, FR Liberio, 271
González Oliveros, Wenceslao (F) (1890–1965), 644n5
González Peña, Ramón (*d.* 1952) (Soc), 142, 310, 521, 673; head of Asturian rebellion, 139, 200, 236, 310, 778; commuted sentence, 146, 147; election as president, 200 and n2; and military rising, 236; commissar Army of the North, 615; minister of justice, 778, 815; and UGT, 782n5; and Casado's conspiracy, 901
González Tablas, Col. (*d.* 1937) (R), execution, 515
González Ubieta, Capt. Luis (R), commander-in-chief Rep. navy (1937–8), 549, 679, 779, 797, 884, 886
Gonzalo, Col. (N), peace negotiator, 910, 911
Goodman, Harold, Br. Consul San Sebastián, 859n1
Gordillo Bellido, Fernando, cook, 644n4
Gordón Ordás, Félix (*d.* 1973) (R), min. of industry (1933), Sp. Amb. in Mexico (1936–7), 576
Goriev, Gen. Vladimir Yefimovich (*d.* 1937), military attaché in Madrid, 393, 447, 476, 479 and n1, 482; and Basque defence, 617, 687, 691; destruction, 707n3; Asturias campaign, 728, 731; attempted rescue, 731n4; shot in Russia, 731n4, 952
Göring, Hermann (1893–1946), nazi leader, 356, 462, 572n1, 842 and n2; on German aid to Franco, 355, 579–80
Gorkić, Milan (Josip Čižinski) (1904–37), Yug. Comm, sec. gen., murder, 454n2
Gorkin, Julián (Gómez) (*b.* 1901) (P), 338n, 477n1, 649, 708; career, 118–19, 302, 866, 876; accusations against, 701, 705; *d.* in exile, 950–51
Gottwald, Klement (1896–1953), Cz. comm., 338n4
Goya y Lucientes, Francisco (1747–1828), 269–70, 880
Goytisolo, José Agustín, Sp. writer, 522
Gracia, Anastasio de la (Soc.), 665
Grado (Oviedo), revolutionary committee, 138
Graells, Francisco (*d.* 1936) (Soc), 235
Graf Spee (G. battleship), 498
Gramsci, Antonio (1891–1937), 658n5
Granada, 128, 214, 255, 265, 307, 582; burning of *El Ideal*, 5; Popular Front win, 178; and military rising, 233, 241, 263; rebel conquest, 250–51, 380; nationalist atrocities in, 259, 263; casualties, 264 and nn1, 2; in civil war, 326, 332 and n; University, 36, 264n2; Audiencia, 265n7
Granadella (Lérida), collective at, 558
Grandi, Count Dino (*b.* 1895), 396, 444, 952; and non-intervention,

580, 604, 629, 683, 736, 738; and withdrawal of volunteers, 796, 797
Granollers (Barcelona), Nat. bombing, 826
Graus (Huesca), collective at, 561–2
Graves, Robert (*b.* 1895), Eng. poet, 567n4
Graziadei, Antonio (1873–1953), It. com., 117, 952
Great Britain, 17, 188; commercial relations with Spain, 295n2, 335, 591, 617n4, 620, 741; and aid to nationalist Spain, 338, 344–5, 388; alarm at French proposals, 343–4; policy towards USSR, 345, 395n1, 444; public reaction to Spanish war, 346 and n1, 347–8; relations with Italy, 354, 397, 573 and n1, 826; and non-intervention, 364, 943, 944; need to back the winner, 392 and n1; appeasement policy, 398, 738–9, 743; transport of arms to Spain, 567; and nationalist blockade, 618–23; and Guernica, 629; and May Days, 659; suggests Basque neutral zone, 681n1; and Germany, 734; and It. attacks on her shipping, 740–41, 827–8; and Franco's Spain, 766 and n1; urges closure of French frontier, 825 and n3; and nationalist air attacks, 827; pro-republican support, 875; policy towards refugees, 879, 922; and Spanish affairs, 943–4; mistake over bomb/casualty ratio in air raids, 945n3
Greece, 581, 740, 827
'Grigorovich', Gen. (Stern), Ru. officer, 662 and n2, 711; adviser at Teruel, 789, 794
Grillet, Mons. and Mme, Fr. vol. in IB, 781
Grinko, G. F., Ru. official, trial, 811n3
Grossi, Manuel (P), 138
Grunfeld, José (A), Argentinian, sec. FAI, 889
Grupo de Ejércitos de la Región Oriental, 815, 816
Guadalajara, 55, 126n2, 597; military rising at, 246, 247 and n2; in civil war, 313, 326, 373, 486n4, 913; documentary evidence of presence of It. units, 601 and n2; Infantado Palace, 929; prison, 238; Battle of, 582, 596–605, 688; It. involvement, 596–602; treatment of prisoners, 602n4; assessment, 603; role of Russian advisers, 603–4; ends conflict round Madrid, 605
Guadalquivir (river), 79, 252, 754
Guadalupe (Cáceres), 379; Monastery, 77; Mountains, 375; river, 800
Guadarrama, train tunnel, 188, 313; river, 713n5
Guadarrama, Sierra de, 208n3, 255, 284, 313, 371n3, 488, 597; Battle of, 314, 315, 320–21, 324; Valley of the Fallen, 923
Guadiana (river), 373, 374
Guadix (Granada), 270n4, 274; murder of bishops, 270n4, 271
Guarner Vivancos, Col. Vicente, Cat. officer, 547
Guderian, Col. (later Gen.), Heinz (1889–1954), G. officer, and *blitzkrieg* style warfare, 468, 945
Guëmes, Col. Ernesto (*b.* 1902) (R), 834
Guernica (Vizcaya), Basque veneration, 87, 431, 624; small arms factory, 308, 330, 616, 625, 626, 627; bombing of, 624–5, 651n3, 986; report of Br. Consul, 625n3, 986–8; nationalist occupation, 625–6; German responsibility, 626–7, 683; international repercussions, 628 and n2, 629, 683, 695; Basque church evidence, 628 and n4; final admissions, 629
Guerra del Rio, Rafael (1885–1955) Rad. min., 125–6
Guerrero (A), FAI member, 810n
Guerrica Echevarria Usabel, Casiano (B), 691, 692
Guides, Abel (*d.* 1937), Fr. vol. for Rep., 364; death in rescue attempt, 732n4
Guillén, Nicolás (C) Cub. poet, 698
Guillonière, Baron de la, vol. in Spain, 768
Guipúzcoa, 132, 237, 541; social order, 87, 308; in civil war, 315n, 370, 377–80, 410; *junta* of defence, 431
Guiteras, Antonio (Cub.), Joven Cuba organization, 574n3
Guitián, Manuel (N), Burgos agent, 895 and n1
Guralsky, August (Abraham Heifetz, 'Kleine') (1890–1960), Comintern agent in Paris, 119
Guzmán, Eduardo de (*b.* 1909) (A), ed. *Castillo Libre*, 291

Haartman, Maj. Karl v., Finnish com., school for falangist officers, 638
Habsburgs, 50, 51, 336
Haden Guest, David (1911–38), Eng. com., *d.* at Gandesa, 841 and n1

Haile Selassie, Emperor of Abyssinia (1892–1975), 366, 459
Haldane, Charlotte (*b.* 1894) (C), and republican Spain, 606n1, 609; *Truth Will Out*, 611n1
Haldane, J. B. S. (1892–1964) (C), Eng. scientist, 606 and n1
Halifax, Edward 1st Earl of (1881–1959), for. sec. (1938–40), 847n1, 871, 894; at Geneva, 823–4; and Czechoslovakia, 824 and n1; and Anglo-Italian Pact, 826, 856, 857n; subservience to Germany, 826; suggests appeal to stop the war, 829; and nationalist Spain, 894
Hamburg, 357 and n4; 'Operation Otto', 418n2
Hamilton, Earl, US historian, 58n2
Hannah (Du. ship), 795
Hans Beimler Battalion (IB), 838, 968
Harington, Gen. Sir Charles (1872–1940), gov. of Gibraltar, 685n4
Haro y Lumbreras, Maj. Gregorio de (N), civil gov. of Huelva (1936), 224
Harvey, Oliver (later Ld. Harvey) (1893–1968), 621nn1, 2, 824, 825n3
Hassell, Ulrich v. (1881–1944), G. Amb., 387, 600, 604, 682
Hatters' Union, Barcelona, 298
Havana (liner), 987, 988
Havoc, HMS (destroyer), 740
Haya González, Capt. Carlos de (1902–38) (N), 586n3, 630; air hero, 756
Hedilla, Manuel (1898–1970) (F), 252 and n2, 261n3, 569, 627, 749n, 946; and nationalist atrocities, 263; chairman of *junta* of command, 420 and n3, 506; character, 420, 636; plea for toleration, 516, 636 and n2; and union with Carlists, 632n2, 637, 639, 640; plot to overthrow, 635, 637–8; position in the movement, 636–7, 639, 819; fate of plotters, 639; ignorance of Franco's plans, 639–41; imprisonment of, 641, 642, 644n4, 819; commuted death sentence, 641–2; ignored by Franco, 948
Heilbrunn, Dr Gustav (*d.* 1937), G. vol. in IB, killed by García Morato, 688n1
Helfand, Ru. dip., 741
Hellman, Lilian (*b.* 1905), US writer, 609n1
Hemingway, Ernest (1899–1961), US novelist, 698; and rep. cause, 603 and n1, 608–9, 609n1, 689n2, 713n4; and Robles's death, 706n1; at White House, 713n4; returns to Spain, 855 and n1; *Death in the Afternoon*, 603n1; *For Whom the Bell Tolls*, 274, 394n1, 415n, 456n1, 689n2; *The Spanish War*, 609n1
Hemming, Francis (1893–1964), Br. civil servant, 395–6, 847, 920n
Henares (river), 597, 599
Hendaye, British Embassy at, 346, 379, 619, 786; rail link with Cádiz, 380, 760; Hitler/Franco meeting (1940), 949
Henderson, Sir Nevile (1889–1942), Br. Amb. to Germany, 686, 826
Henke, Capt. Alfred, G. officer, 370n1
Henry, Dr, Red Cross official, 486n4
Henry, Jules, Fr. dip., 880
Hernández, Miguel (1910–42) (C), poet, 699; *d.* in gaol, 924 and n1, 930
Hernández Saravia, Col. (later Gen.) (1880–1962) (R), war min., 92; in civil war, 320 and n, 868, 871, 872; last act, 376 and n2; Army commands, 771, 779, 788, 793, 815, 868; replaced by Jurado, 881; relations with Rojo, 881 and n4
Hernández Tomás, Jesús (1906–) (C), min. of education (1936–38), 406, 663, 814; propagandist, 122, 291; and Negrín as Premier, 664, 669–70, 679, 686; and Prieto, 687n1; and anti-POUM conspiracy, 703, 704; and Nin's death, 706n3; nom de plume 'Juan Ventura', 811 and n1; army commissar-general, 814, 901; and Casado's conspiracy, 904; and clandestine communism, 906; leaves for Algeria, 911; dies, 950
Hernández Zancajo, Carlos (Soc), UGT executive, 658, 782n5
Herrera y Oria, Angel (1886–1968), ed. *El Debate*, later Cardinal, 55n1, 108
Herriot, Edouard (1872–1957), Fr. Rad. politician, 351, 579
Hess, Rudolf (*b.* 1894), 462
Heussler, André, Fr. vol. in IB, execution in Resistance, 491n4
Hidalgo, Diego, Rad. min. of war (1934), 142
Hidalgo de Cisneros y López de Montenegro, Gen. Ignacio (1894–1965) (C), Commander Rep. air force (1936–39), 33n2, 327–8, 407–8, 658n2, 678, 686, 779; and communism, 521 and n2, 548, 679; bombing of nationalist towns, 794; demands more arms from Moscow, 869 and n3, 974n2; unknown whereabouts, 876; and Casado's plot,

899, 906; leaves Spain, 905–6; *Memorias*, 219n2
Hidalgo Vela, Capt., and Alcázar, 247n1
Hillgarth, Capt. Alan (*b.* 1899), Br. consul, 886n1
Hinsley, Cardinal Arthur (1865–1945), Abp. of Westminster, 695, 807n7
HISMA, *see* Compañia Hispano-marroquí.
Hitler, Adolf (1889–1945), 111, 134, 346, 469, 689n1, 848n4; and the Soviet Union, 153, 394; interviews with Ciano, 342 and n1, 463; Franco's mission to, 342–3, 355–6; and Mussolini, 370, 453; reasons for intervention, 355–6; congratulates Franco, 426; and Spanish affairs, 569, 572n1, 577, 578, 746, 942; rage at *Deutschland* affair, 685, 735; and *Leipzig* affair, 735; desire to exterminate France and Britain, 746; rape of Austria, 804, 823; and G. volunteers in Spain, 823; enters Prague, 911; reviews Condor Legion, 920; on Franco, 948, 949
Hoare, Sir Samuel (later Ld Templewood) (1880–1959), 1st Lord of the Admiralty (1936), 577, 739n1; on Franco, 141 and n1; and blockade, 619, 623; on Serrano Súñer, 634 and n2
Hodgson, Sir Robert (1874–1956), Br. official, 766 and n1, 849, 850, 881
Hodja, Enver (*b.* 1908) (C), Alb. vol. in IB, 954
Hogben, Lancelot (*b.* 1895), Eng. writer, 347n3
Holburn, James, Eng. journalist, 628
Holland, 795, 981; non-intervention, 388, 581; arms traffic, 451
Homo, Col. (Fr.), League Commissioner, 853
Hood, HMS, 620, 622
Horder, Thomas Lord (1871–1955), Eng. doctor, 807n7
Hore-Belisha, Leslie (later Ld Hore-Belisha) (1893–1957), 806
Horner, Arthur (1894–1968), Br. miners' leader, 716n
Horthy y Nagybanya, Admiral (1868–1957), Regent of Hungary, 953
Hossbach Memorandum, 746 and n4
Hourihan, Martin, US vol. in IB, 608n3
Housman, Laurence (1865–1959), Eng. writer, 347n3
Howard, Brian, Eng. poet, 617n4
Howard, D., 989
Huelva, 202, 223, 326 and n
Huesca, 126n2, 238, 262, 316, 367; in civil war, 381, 400, 688, 723, 800 and n2; Catalan youth involvement, 492; anarchist casualties, 688
Hull, Cordell (1871–1955), US Sec. of State (1933–45), pro-neutrality, 363, 390–91, 434, 576, 686, 867; horror at nationalist bombings, 808; and arms embargo, 824, 825–6, 826n1
Humbert-Droz, Jules (1891–1971), Sw. C. official, 117, 120, 121; and IB, 454 and n2
Hungary, 10, 953, 954, 968, 969
Hungria Navarro, Col. Domingo (C), 14th Army Corps '*guerrilleros*', 759, 905
Huxley, Aldous (1894–1963), Eng. writer, 347n3

Iaborov, Gen. Ru., 904 and n1
Ibáñez, Jesús (C), in Moscow, 117n3
Ibarra Palace, 600, 601
Ibarrola Orueta, Col. Juan (*b.* 1900) (B), 789 and n1, 871, 907
Ibarrola Oil Co., Ceuta, 345
Ibarruri, Dolores (La Pasionaria) (*b.* 1895) (C), 117, 121, 154, 204, 322, 532, 651, 711, 901; character and life, 9, 775–6, 901, 904, 920–21; source of her influence, 9–10; and Calvo Sotelo, 207 and n; oratory, 244, 322, 852–3, 931, 940n; and military rising, 246; acts of mercy, 277; recruiting drive, 322; and committee on Spain, 361 and n1; seeks French aid, 402, 441; and Negrín, 669, 810, 890; anti-peace delegation, 810; attacks Prieto, 811; last days in Spain, 901, 904; on value of USSR aid, 940n; post-war position, 950
Ibiza, 242, 381, 581, 685; abandoned, 383–4
Ickes, Harold (1874–1952), US Sec. of Commerce, 363, 575n2, 825n1
Ifni, 257n2, 368n4
Iglesias Posse, Pablo (1850–1925) (Soc), founder of Spanish Socialism, 40 and n3, 117, 223
Ildis (G. torpedo boat), 498
Illescas, 436, 437
Illustrated London News, 945
Ilundaín y Esteban, Cardinal (1862–1937), Abp. of Seville, 414, 757
Inchorta hill, 623
Independent Airplane Association of Berlin, 368
Independent Labour Party (ILP), 706
Independent Monarchist Club, 57 and n

Indian Committee for Food for Spain, 462
Iniesta (Cuenca), collectives, 557
Institución Libre de Enseñanza, 43, 51, 179n; ideology, 35–6, 190
Intellectuals, 26, 35, 39–40, 53, 60, 110, 500–503; British, 347 and n2; US, 363
International, the, 60, 61
International, Second (Socialist), 116, 137, 211, 352n2, 467
International, Third, *see* Comintern
International Brigades (IB), origin, 452–3, 455–6; communist-backed, 454–5, 607 and n1; indefinite commitment, 456, 543–4, 606–7; conditions in Spain, 456, 606–7; *troika* command, 457–8; training centres, 458; medical services, 458, 608n4, 609; discipline, 459; defence of Madrid, 480, 481–5, 940; influence on morale, 480, 535; casualties, 481, 592–3; NKVD use of passports, 574n4; desertions and disillusionments, 607 and n, 716 and n, 781; international relations, 607n3; incorporation into republican army, 779–80, 780 and n1; organization crisis, 780–81; transferred to Barcelona, 816, 852–3; withdrawal of foreign volunteers, 851–2; London reception, 853n3; later fate of communists, 954–5; total number fighting for republic, 982 and n; ancillary services, 983; social origins, 983n4; Brigades, Battalions and principal initial composition (App. 3). 968–9; *XI*, 479–80, 483, 484, 489, 588, 599–600, 710, 711, 838; *XII*, 480, 482–3, 489, 494–5, 599, 711, (Division), 597, 599, 688; *XIII*, 480, 490n2, 711, 716, 800, 953; *XIV*, 490, 493–5, 589, 689, 692, 710, 711n2, 838n2, 840; *XV*, 588, 590–91, 607n3, 699, 723n1, 725n2, 780, 798, 800, 812, 840 and n2, 841, 851–2
International Commission for the Assistance of Child Refugees, 863
International Federation of Trade Unions, 361–2
International Red Help, 290, 323n2, 361, 523
International Telegraph and Telephone Co. (ITT), 335 and n1, 506
International Working Men's Association (AIT), 67
Ireland, 20, 490n3; and IB, 490–91, 768; IRA, 491, 591; nationalist volunteers, 979–80
Iribarren, Capt. José María (*b.* 1880) (N), ADC to Mola
Iride (It. ship), 740
Iron Battalion (CNT), 327
Iron Column, 909, 544 and n3, 545
Irujo y Ollo, Manuel de (B), Rep. min., 309n3, 407n2, 634n1; and military rising, 237, 308; and the cabinet, 430n4, 664, 670, 679, 681, 704, 815, 844–5; restores conventional justice, 701, 778; and Nin's case, 708; and reopening of churches, 774; attacks Negrín in the Cortes, 862
Irún, 377–9; fate of refugees, 380, 760
Iruretagoyena Solchaga, Gen. José (*b.* 1879) (N), 831
Isabella II, Queen of Spain (1830–1904), 13–14, 509
Isgleas, Francisco (A), councillor in *Generalidad* (1936), 524, 652n4
Isusi, FR Agustín, and Guernica, 628
Italy, 100, 108, 323; the church and, 51; anarchism, 60, 61, 64; and aid to nationalist Spain, 338, 341–2, 352 and n4, 376 and n1, 418–19, 586 and n4, 570–71, 573 and nn4, 5; conquest of Abyssinia, 245, 353; motives in intervention, 353–4, 517, 580; relations with nationalist Spain, 567, 737, 740, 764; attacks on neutral and Spanish shipping, 568 and n1, 739–40; and Franco/British mediation plan, 570, 576–7, 580; agreement with Britain, 573 and n1; sale of submarines to Franco, 740, 764; behaviour of troops in Spain, 764; IB recruitment, 780 and n2; air attacks from Majorca, 794; troops remaining in Spain, 855–6, 856n1; attacks Albania, 915n; welcomes returning troops, 920; amount of and payment for aid to Spain, 942, 975–6, 978 and n1, 979; fate of generals who served in Spain, 952; manpower and equipment strength in Spain, 978 and n1, 979
Ituricastillo, FR Joaquín, shot by nationalists, 512n7, 680
Ivens, Joris, Du. film maker, 609n1, 713n4
Izquierda Comunista, 120
Izquierda Republicana (Republican Left), 134n2
Izvestia, 392, 393, 394, 707

Jaca, 30–31, 238, 818n
Jadji-Umar, Mamsurov ('Santi'), Ru. adviser to Durruti, 483n3

Jadraque (Guadalajara), 599
Jaén, 223, 279, 306–7, 914–15; murder of bishops, 270n4, 271
Jaén Morante, Antonio, civil gov. of Málaga (1931), 58n2
Jagwitz, Eberhard v., G. official, 462
Jaime de Borbon, Don (1870–1931), Carlist pretender, 96, 97
Jaime Primero (R. battleship), 242, 243, 331 and n4, 383, 549, 614, 660, 936
Jalander, Gen., Finnish League Commissioner, 853
James, Wing Commander Sir A. (*b.* 1893), 956n1
Jameson, Storm (*b.* 1897), Eng. writer, 347n3
Japan, 567 and n4; Russian war, 962–3
Jarama, Battle of, 582, 588, 590 (map)–96, 592; Russian involvement, 593; casualties, 596
Jarinda, Mt., 617
Játiva (Valencia), 305, 785
Jativa, Alfonso (S), sub. sec. to navy, 836
Jellinek, Frank (*d.* 1975), Eng. writer, 310nn1, 2; 707n4
Jeréz (Cádiz), 63, 223, 980
Jerrold, Douglas (1893–1964), Eng. man of letters, 204 and n3, 698
Jesuits, 43 and n2, 50; and education, 52, 75–6, 102, 127; expulsion, 76, 102, (return), 820; expropriation commission, 106–7
Jews, 50, 264, 511, 513, 595n1, 760–61
Jiménez, Juan Ramón (1881–1958), poet, 190
Jiménez de Asúa, Luis (*b.* 1889) (Soc), 168, 467n2, 950
Jiménez de la Beraza, Col. Ricardo (*b.* 1879) (R), 547
Jiménez Fernández, Manuel (1896–1968), CEDA politician, 148
Joad, Dr Cyril (1891–1953), philosopher, 347n3
Johnson, Dr Hewlett (1874–1966), and Bilbao blockade, 622
Jones, 'Corn Cob', 622
Jones, 'Ham and Eggs', 622
Jones, Jack (*b.* 1913), IB vol., 955n4
Jones, 'Potato', 622
Jones, Thomas (1870–1955), Deputy Sec. to the British Cabinet
Jordana, *see* Gómez Jordana
'José', Col. Ru. officer, 779
'Josefa' (Seisdedos), 104
Jouhaux, Léon (1879–1954), Fr. TU leader, 389, 782n5
Journalists, foreign, reports on civil war, 369, 481, 506, 625n, 626, 855; threatened by Franco's secretariat, 504n2; Negrín's skill, 670n1
Jouvenel, Bertrand de (*b.* 1903), Fr. writer, 252n1
Jover, Gregorio (A), 316, 547, 658, 677
Juan, Carlos, Dir. Gen. of Security (1937), 708, 776n3, 782
Juan de Borbón, Don (*b.* 1913), Claimant to throne of Spain (1941), 421, 884
Juan Carlos I, King of Spain (*b.* 1938), 947
Junod, Dr Marcel (1904–61), Sw. Red Cross officer, 238 and n2, 258, 496; and exchange of prisoners, 263n4, 431 and n1, 496, 586n3, 786
Junta de Auxilio a los Republicanos Españoles (JARE), 921
Junta de Ofensiva Nacional-Sindicalista (JONS), fascist foundation, 111–12, 115n2; casualties, 114 and n2, 115; amalgamation with Falange, 114 and n3
Jurado Barrio, Col. (later Gen.) Enrique (*b.* 1883), 881, 889; Army Corps, 599, 710; in charge anti-aircraft, 836; *d.* in exile, 950
Juridicial Corps of the Army (N), 913, 922
Jurisdictions, Law of, 45n1, 91–2
Just Gimeno, Julio (LR), min. of public works (1936–9), 407n2, 546, 662n5, 671n1
Juventud de Acción Popular (JAP), 5n1, 112, 135; neo-fascist, 3, 109, 149; Covadonga meeting, 133; joins the Falange, 163 and n3, 285; and Gil Robles, 170; violence to working classes, 171
Juventud Comunista Ibérica (JCI), 302, 655–6
Juventudes Socialistas Unificadas (JSU), socialist-communist youth, 200–201, 225, 247, 523; *La Motorizada*, 230, 492n1; and murders in republican Spain, 278–9; communization, 291, 535; in Madrid, 476, 538; ideology, 535

Kagan, S. (*d.* 1937), Ru. dip., 444
Kahle, Col. Hans (*d.* 1952) (C), G. vol. in IB, 479, 677, 851; later police chief in Germany, 954
Kamenev, Lev. (Rosenfeld) (1883–1936), Old Bolshevik, 392
Kamerun (G. steamship), 360
Kaminski, Hans Erich, on Alcora economic experiment, 303–4

Kane (U S destroyer), nationalist bombing, 391n2
'Karbov' (Ljubomir Todoroz) (C), Bulg. vol. in I B, 458, 781
Karchevski, Capt., White Ru. vol. in I B, 494n2
Karolyi, Count Michael (1875–1955), Hung. soc., 10–11
Katz, Otto (André Simone) (C), Cz. Comintern official, 262, 341n3, 805
Kemp, Peter (*b.* 1915), Eng. vol. for Nationalists, 768n2, 840 and n2, 980n2
Kempenfelt, H M S, 797
Kennedy, Joseph (1888–1969), U S Amb. to London, 824–5
Kennedy, Joseph Patrick (1915–44), U S student, 914n1
Kenyon, Sir Frederick (1863–1952), Eng. art historian, 486n2
Kerensky, Alexander (1881–1970), Ru. politician, 10–11, 165
Kerillis, Henri de, right-wing publicist, 350
Kerrigan, Peter (C), Br. vol. and organizer in I B, 591n1
Kessel, Maj., aircraft commander, 614n
Keynes, J. Maynard (later Ld.) (1883–1946), Eng. economist, 807n7
Kharchenko, Mikhail, Ru. officer, 800
Khrushchev, Nikita (1894–1971), 953, 954; on Stalin's military purges, 952n2
Kindélan y Duany, Gen. Alfredo (1879–1962) (N), commander of nationalist airforce, 203 and n2, 338, 358, 412, 504, 693, 868n2, 877n1, 906; and military rising, 204n1; disagreement with v. Scheele, 418; and a single command, 419, 421 and n2, 422; monarchist hopes, 421–2; and Franco's appointment, 422–3, 426; ignored by him, 948n2; (posth.) marquisate, 948
King, Norman (later Sir) (1880–1963), Br. Consul gen. Barcelona, 368
Kirkpatrick, Sir Ivone (1897–1964), Br. diplomat, 824
Klaus, Col. Hans, G. vol. in I B, 607n3
'Kléber', Gen. Emilio (Lazar or Manfred Stern) (*d.* 1938), Ru. officer of Rumanian/Hungarian Jewish origin, first leader of I B, 455, 459–60, 480, 481, 483, 494, 532; career, 459; questionnaire for chief of staff, 492n1; tactical ideas, 532; and civil war battles, 532, 710, 722; executed in Russia, 953
Klotz, Helmut, G. writer, on military lessons from Spain, 945
Knauer, Lt. v., G. officer, bombs Guernica, 625
Knobloch, Joachim, von. G. diplomat, 498
Koestler, Arthur (*b.* 1905), Eng. Hungarian writer, 252n2, 262, 275n1 374n; imprisonment, 576 and n3; Comintern agent in Paris, 586n3
Koltsov, Mikhail (*d. c.*1941), Ru. journalist, in Spain, 319, 393 and n5, 495n1, 691n3; relations with Stalin, 393n5; on Caballero, 403n2; and defence of Madrid, 476, 477, 488 and n1; and murder of prisoners, 477n3; fate in Russia, 952
Komsomol (Ru. supply ship), 445, 572
Konev, Col. (later Marshal) Ivan ('Paulito') (1897–1973), 446, 447n2; eminence in Russia, 953
Kopets, Ivan, Ru. (pilot) officer, 446
Kosovski ('Petrov'), Ru. officer in I B, 482
Krafft, Lt. v., G. officer, bombs Guernica, 625
Kraneck, Dr, 355
Krause, Karl (1781–1832), G. philosopher, 35
Kravchenko ('Antonio'), Ru. officer, 588n
'Kremen', Col. 584
'Krieger', *see* Vincenzo Bianco
Kristanov, Tsevetan Angelov ('Oscar Telge'), Bulg. Com, vol. in I B, 458 and n5
Krivitsky, Col. Walter ('Ginsburg') (*d.* 1941), Ru. intelligence officer, 440n, 441–2, 447n2, 450; and May Days, 654n3; on Stashevsky, 703n1; shot in Washington, 953 and n3
Krivoshein, Col. S., Ru. tank officer, 445, 489, 953
Krock, Arthur, U S journalist, 825n1, 980
Kröger, Hans, G. official, 638; and Hedilla, 641
Kronstadt, Ru. sailors' revolt at, 67
Kropotkin, Prince (1842–1921), Ru. anarchist, 65
Kuhlenthal, Gen., G. military attaché, Paris, 342
Kulik, Gen. Gregori Ivan ('Kupper') (1890–1941), Ru. officer, 446–7, 447n1, 494n2; adviser to Pozas, 588n, 662; shot in 1941, 952
Kun, Bela (1886–1939), Hung. com. leader, 172–3

Kuusinen, Otto (1881–1964), Finnish Com. 338n4
Kuznetzov, Capt. (later Admiral) (1902–74) (N), Ru. naval attaché to Spain (1936), 393 and n2, 449n3, 549; in Second World War, 953

La Granja, 688
La Iglesia, arms purchase intermediary, 147n1
La Mancha, 241, 293, 333, 376, 456, 480, 559, 574n3, 784
La Manjoya, arms factory, 330, 616
La Roda (Albacete), IB cavalry base, 458
La Tierra, 137
Labajos (Segovia), 322
Labonne, Eilrick (*b.* 1888), Fr. dip., Amb. in Spain (1938–39), 809, 810
Labour Party, British, 344, 346, 367, 444; and non-intervention, 397, 398n1, 467 and n2, 745
Lacalle, Col. (R), *see* García Lacalle
Lacarra Iñigo, Florian (*d.* 1938), execution, 763
Lagrange, Leo, Fr. official, 351
Laín Entralgo, José (C), 435
Lalanda, Marcial ('Manolo' Bienvida), bullfighter, 755n2
Lamamié de Clairac y de la Colina, José María (1887–1956), Car. leader, 85, 146, 202
Lamas Arroyo, Maj. Angel (*b.* 1900) (R), chief of staff to Gámir Ulibarri, 687
Lamoneda Fernández, Ramón (*b.* 1892) (Soc), 118n2; removes Largo Caballero, 673
Lance, Capt. Christopher (1892–1970), Br. engineer, 477n3
Landau, Kurt, G. Trotskyist, mysterious death, 706
Langdon-Davies, John (1897–197?), Br. journalist, 398
Langenheim, Adolf, G. businessman and nazi, 387; emissary to Hitler, 342, 354, 355–6, 356–7
Laporta, Ramón (F), 638
Larache (Morocco), 94, 217, 218, 224
Lardner, Ring (1885–1933), US writer, death of his son, 852
Largo Caballero, Francisco (1869–1946) (Soc), prime minister (1936–37), 40n3, 121, 122, 161, 192, 247, 472, 648; in Azaña's cabinet, 38–9, 41; sec. gen. UGT, 39, 40, 673; arbitration committees, 41, 71, 127, 145; adherents, 41, 164, 674; agricultural decrees, 82–3, 85; and revolution, 109–10, 110n1, 128, 145, 154, 157, 164, 172, 177, 673; attempted *alianza obrero*, 133, 135, 200; relations with communists, 135n3, 154, 521, 533–4, 647, 649–50, 655, 663 and n2, 664, 673; imprisonment, 145, 147, 154; and *straperlo* scandal, 148; personal relations, 149, 164, 171–2, 587, 666, 666–7; character, 164 and n1, 673–4; conduct in power, 164, 179, 194, 408, 533; on triumph of proletariat, 180; ignores depression, 186; and rising, 190, 211, 229–30; in Madrid, 268n, 402–3, 432, 437, 475, 467–8, 532, 652, 655; in civil war, 328, 361, 408, 583, 587, 662; asked to form a government, 406–7; cabinet, 406–7, 407n2; and Alcázar, 410, 411–12; failure as war leader, 433–4; and Russian arms and personnel, 443, 446; and removal of Spain's gold reserves, 448; and an Italian legion for Spain, 453–4; rejects collectivization, 531; achievements as Prime Minister, 533, 673; Stalin's advice to, 533 and n1; refuses communist/socialist merger, 534, 673; Chairman War Council, 546, 679; and Moroccan affairs, 579, 650, 663 and n1; Comintern plot to destroy, 650–51, 655, 662, 687; plans a new cabinet, 664–5; and a separate Basque peace, 681; speeches in Paris and Spain, 782 and n5; and POUM trials, 866; political misjudgements, 933; imprisonment and death, 950
Larios, José, *see* Lerma
Larrañaga, Jesús (B. com.), and Army of the North, 615, 617n3
Las Cortes, women's prison (Barcelona), 874
Las Huelgas monastery, 753
Las Illas, 881
Las Palmas, 206, 212 and n2, 231n1, 666
Las Rozas (Madrid), 494–5
Laski, Prof. Harold (1893–1950), Eng. philosopher, 374n3, 609, 611 and n1
Latorre, Col. (N), 315 and n, 377; Navarrese Brigade leader, 612, 717
Laurent, Raymond, Fr. journalist, 365
Lavín, Luis (*d.* 1936), Civil gov. of Valladolid, 240
Law, Oliver (*d.* 1937), US negro vol. in IB, 716
Lawther, Will (later Sir) (*b.* 1889), Eng. trade unionist, 853n3
Layret, Francisco (*d.* 1921) (A), Cat. lawyer, murder by *pistoleros*, 66, 274

Le Boulou, refugee camp, 878
Le Perthus, 881
League of Nations, 334, 407, 439; Russian entry, 339, 393; admission of Germany, 439; Franco/British influence, 439, 440; and Spanish affairs, 439–40, 571, 601 and n2, 683, 742–3, 744, 823–4, 848; to supervise withdrawal of volunteers, 851–2, 853
Lebrun, Albert (1871–1950), President of France, 351, 913
Leche, John (later Sir) (1889–1960), Br. official, 682; Eng. Amb. to Spain, 766, 831
Leciñena (Saragossa), 316, 367
Ledesma Ramos, Ramiro (1905–36) (F), 111 and n, 115, 177; *Libertad* programme, 111–12; and the church in Spain, 112, 152; and Falange/JONS amalgamation, 114 and n3, 152; and José Antonio, 152 and n1; imprisonment, 284; death, 930
Left Book Club, 346, 611n1
Left Review, 347n3, 591
Leganés (Madrid), 487
Léger, Alexis (1887–1974), Fr. official and poet, 343–4, 738, 805, 943
Lehmann, John (*b*. 1907), Eng. writer, 347n3; *Poems for Spain*, 592n3
Lehmann, Rosamund (*b*. 1903), Eng. writer, 347n3
Leipzig (G. patrol cruiser), alleged torpedo attack, 735
Leizaola, Jesús María (B), Min. of Justice, Euzkadi 1936–37, and a separate Basque peace, 681 and n2; Bilbao *junta* of defence, 692; delivers prisoners to the enemy, 693; escape from Santander, 720; succeeds Aguirre, 951
Lenin, Vladimir Ilyich (1870–1924), Ru. revolutionary, 40n1, 67, 117, 145, 177, 247
Leo XIII, Pope (1810–1903), 52
León, 219, 228, 240–41, 253–4, 539, 920; guerrilla campaign in, 729, 731
León, María Teresa (C), writer, w. of Alberti, 904
León-Lupín, Lt Alfredo (*b*. 1902) (R), 208n2
León Maestre, Col. Basilio (N), 250
Lepanto (R. destroyer), 251, 797
Lepper, John, Eng. poet, vol. in IB, 592
Lequerica y Erquiza, José Félix (1891–1963) (M), 100
Lérida, 45n2, 117, 270n4, 318, 812; POUM, 302, 304, 707; destruction of its cathedral, 318; shoemakers' cooperative, 785; Omells de Nagaia prison camp at, 879
Lerroux García, Alejandro (1864–1949), Rad. prime minister 1934, 38, 49n4, 72, 99n3, 214; character, 34, 125, 194; in opposition, 76–7, 106; governments, 122, 125–6, 128, 134, 140, 146–8 (cabinet), 147; anarchist challenges, 126–7; resignation, 130, 285; 1936 elections, 153, 157; and loyalty to the state, 208; *d*. in Spain, 951
Leval, Gaston, Fr. A. writer, 67, 117, 558
Levante Provinces, 80, 292, 531, 542, 546, 914; anarchism, 103, 305; agricultural collectives, 553, 554, 559 and n
Ley de Fugas, 66
L'Hospitalet (Barcelona), CNT, 302n
Liberals, 3–4, 6, 38, 37–8, 191; nineteenth-century reformers, 35, 56; and the church, 51, 52, 76
Libertad (periodical), 11–12; (R. cruiser), 242, 328, 331 and n4, 549, 797, 901
'Libertaria' (Seisdedos) (*d*. 1936) (A), 104
Liddell Hart, Basil (later Sir) (1895–1970), Eng. historian of war, 806
Liège, exiled Spanish priests, 697–8
Linares (Jaén), miners from, 255
Linares, Col. (R), 728
Linklater, Eric (1899–1974), Eng. writer, 347n3
Lisbon, 206, 214, 254; and arms purchases, 360; Radio Club, 384, 471
Lister, Maj. (later Gen.) (*b*. 1907) (C), 649, 726, 789, 889; and military rising, 246, 247; in civil war, 323, 410, 468n2, 493; Mixed Brigade at Seseña, 468; leader of first Brigade, 545 and n3, 592; criticism of Aragon collectives, 556–7, 557–8; and defence of Madrid, 588 and n, 592, 599–60, 602, 603, 710, 722, 724, 789 and n1, 802; battle of Brunete, 710–13, 715; and Council of Aragon, 723, 725n1; accuses El Campesino, 793; and communist troops, 798–9; battle of the Ebro, 835, 838, 840, 843; compared with Modesto, 836; attacks Gandesa, 841–2; defence in Catalonia, 868–71; at Elda country house, 904, 905–6
'Little' (deserter from Royal Marines), IB vol. 980n2
Littorio Division (N), 596, 597 and n2, 599, 601, 717; to remain in Spain, 856 and n1

Litvinov, Maximo (1876–1951), Ru. foreign minister, 298, 339, 392, 742, 831; and a Franco/Soviet pact, 340n1; at Geneva, 440, 462, 571, 683, 742, 825; fear of arrest, 825n2; and Germany, 851n1
Lizarza Iribarren, Antonio (Car), 499n2; visits Mussolini, 129
Llano de la Encomienda, Gen. Francisco (1879–1963) (R), 249, 403, 718, 934; area of command, 232, 233, 540, 545, 615, 687; and communism, 232; and Army of the North, 615 and n, 677, 680; failure, 733
Llarch, Col. Juan (*d.* 1937) (R), execution, 626
Lliga, the, Catalan party, 22, 23, 45 and n1, 107, 153; 1936 elections, 156, 162n2; persecution by nationalists, 951n
Llobregat, river, 78, 872, 873; plain, 554n2
Llopis, María, 10n1
Llopis, Rodolfo (*b.* 1895) (Soc), Dir. Gen. of Education, 102–3
Lloyd George, David (later Earl) (1863–1945), Welsh statesman, 346, 823
Lloyd Thomas, Hugh, Br. dip., 388n4
Lluhí Vallescá, Juan (*d.* 1944), Cat. politician, 179n
Loewenstein, Prince Hubertus v. (1906–1975), 309n3
London, 203, 344, 450; protest meeting against nationalist bombings, 807 and n7
London, Arthur (*b.* 1915) (C), Cz. vol. in I B, 455 and n8
Longo, Luigi (Gallo) (*b.* 1900) (C), It. vol. in I B, 452, 453–4, 457n2, 482, 878n4; Madrid defence, 599, 600; later career, 954
Logroño, 211, 313
Lope de Vega (1562–1635), playwright, 78, 106, 416
Lopera (Jaén), 491
López, Anita (C), execution, 373
López, Antonio (Soc), 250n2
López, Bernabé (A), 902
López, José (A), 425n4
López Amor y Jiménez, Maj. José (*d.* 1936) (N), 233, 234–5
López Bassa, Ladislao (F), 640n3
López Bravo, Gen. Jesús (N), 840
López de la Fuente, Justo (1910–67) (C), murders at escape tunnel, 778n2
López Ochoa y Portuondo, Gen. Eduardo (1877–1936), 142, 143
López Oliván, Julio (1891–1964), Sp. Amb. in London 1936, 345n1, 407
López Otero, Col., 276, 907n1
López Pinto, Gen. José (1876–1942) (N), Mil. gov. of Cádiz (1936), 223, 690
López Sánchez, Juan (*d.* 1972) (A), Min. of Commerce (1936–37), 471, 671
López Varela, Capt., alleged rebel, 232
López Viota, Gen. Julián (*d.* 1945), imprisonment, 266n1
Lorca (Murcia), artillery school, 548n2
Lorca (poet), *see* García Lorca
Los Llanos (Albacete) (airfield), 446, 891
Louise Michel Battalion, 968
Low, David (1891–1963), Eng. cartoonist, 348, 828n5
Luca de Tena, Marqués Juan Ignacio (*b.* 1897), ed. *A B C*, 57, 203, 222–3; and transport of Franco to Morocco, 203–4, 204n1; A D C to Varela, 715n2
Lucas, F. L. (1894–1967), Eng. writer, 347n3
Lucía Lucía, Luis (*d.* 1942), Valencian politician, 59, 242 and n1
Luciani, Fr. journalist, in Moscow, 851n
Luftwaffe, 355, 357, 359, 469
Luizzi, Consul-General, It. Fascist, 601n1
'Lukács, Gen.' (Mata Zalka Kemeny) (*d.* 1937) (C), Hung. officer in I B, 455, 482, 483, 599, 603n1, 954; death at Huesca, 688 and n1
Lukanov, Karlo ('Belov') (*b.* 1897) (C), Bulg. vol. in I B, 482 and n2
Luna, Antonio de (N), head of spy ring, 887n2
Lunn, Col., Danish non-intervention official, 581, 680
Lussu, Emilio, It. writer, 453
Lyautey, Marshal Louis (1854–1934), in Morocco, 25
Lynxes of the Republic, 268

Maas, Stephen (G.), spy, 922
Macartney, Wilfred, I B volunteer, 591n1
Macaulay, Rose (1881–1958), Eng. writer, 347n3
McConnell, Bishop, and U S aid fund, 608n4
Macdonnell, A. G. (1895–1941), Eng. writer, 347n3
MacGregor (Br. ship), 622–3
Macià y Llusa, Col. Francisco (1859–1933), Esquerra leader, 45 and n1, 46–7, 86, 120, 132
Mackensen, Hans Georg, G. dip., 827

Mackenzie-Papenau Battalion, 723, 955n4, 968
Machado, Antonio (1875–1939) (R), Cub. poet, 35n3, 190, 196, 495n1, 699; death in exile, 879 and n1, 930
Machado, Gen. Gerardo (1871–1939), president of Cuba, 208n2, 323
Macleish, Archibald (*b.* 1892), U S poet and official, 609n1
Macneice, Louis (1907–63), Eng. poet, 347n3
McNeil Moss, Maj. G., *Legend of Badajoz*, 374n
McReynolds, U S Representative, 575
Madariaga y Rojo, Salvador de (*b.* 1886), Sp. Amb., politician and writer, 110n1, 164n2, 570, 933
Madrid, 23, 27, 31, 39, 44, 52, 138, 428, 900; and socialist/anarchist violence, 24, 126; republican 'plot', 30, 32, 33; and riots of May 1931, 57–8, 59; its slow industrialization, 81, 109, 188; failure of Carlist conspiracy, 100; Falange, 115 and n2, 172, 420, 635; strikes, 126, 134–5, 136, 200 and n; during Second Republic, 150 (map); committee of generals, 166–7, 167–8; and military rising, 168, 177, 201, 204, 209, 210, 217, 219–30 *passim*, 244–8; revolutionary parades, 177–8; socialist aims, 179–80, 201; summer exodus, 202, 346n1; U G T and C N T, 230, 244, 290–91; events of 19/20 July, 244–7; attacks on the church, 269; communist/socialist youth, 282; economic conditions, 292–3; position of government, 299, 368 and n4; defence of in civil war, 315, 322, 326, 371–6, 386, 432–3, 433 (map), 436–8, 470, 471, 477–8, (battle of), 473–5, 474 (map), 487, 488–95, 588–9, 596, (end of conflict), 605, 612; German bombing campaign, 386, 391 and n7, 470, 481–2; air raid precautions, 386; refugees in Br. Embassy, 395n1; conditions in, 402, 484–7, 496–7, 606, 889, 893; deaths in Model Prison fire, 404–5; popular tribunals, 405; Russian presence, 440, 446, 447 and n2, 471, 475; government withdrawal to Valencia, 475 and n2, 478 and n1; *junta* of defence, 476, 477 and n1, 478, 542n4, 652; discovery of Varela's plan of battle, 476–7; execution of prisoners, 477 and n3, 478; volunteer defenders, 478, 479, 480; Finnish Embassy refugees, 487–8; withdrawal of Embassy officials to Valencia, 488; opening of fake embassy, 488n1; anarchist/communist hostility, 532, 651; army falsifications, 543; international interest, 566; town council administration, 652; murders at escape tunnel, 778 and n2; and Casado's conspiracy, 886, 888, 901; continued communist resistance, 906–8; nationalist position, 908; enter the city, 913–14, 914n1, 922–3; executions, 924
Madrid: Ateneo Club, 37, 59n5; Calle Alcalá, 57, 58, 902, 907; Casa del Campo, 115, 248, 276, 292, 473, 478, 481; Castellana, Paseo de la, 172, (bomb outrage), 177, 228, 483, 662, 908, 912; Clinical Hospital, 485, 487, 913; Don Juan Barracks, 473; El Pardo, 246, 272, 705; Florida Hotel, 366n1, 606; Gaylord's Hotel, 394 and n1, 606, 706; Gran Vía, 292, 432, 474, 487; Model Prison, 169, 245, 276, 404–5, 473, 477, 633, 932; Montaña Barracks, 230, 244–5, 404, 474; Pontejos Barracks, 206, 208n2; the Prado, 486n2, 919, 929; Puerta del Sol, 3, 135, 206, 225, 245–6; Radio Madrid, 220, 226, 243, 467–8, 912; Retiro Palace, 178, 907; Royal Palace 11 and n, 31, 142, 225, 247, 474; Salesian Convent, 322; Telefónica, 470n2, 479n2, 481, 486; University, 36, 111, 407–8; University City, 472n1, 473, 474, 484, 487, 662, 666, 913
Madrid Council of Lawyers, estimation of casualties, 262 and n1, 265nn, 1, 3, 5, 9
Madrigueras (Albacete), I B training centre, 458
Maestrazgo plain (Aragon), 801, 803, 818, 830–31
Maeztu y Whitney, Ramiro de (1864–1936), Sp. writer, 35n2, 59, 151; murder, 437, 930; influence on Franco, 947
Magaz y Pers, Antonio Marqués de (1864–1953), Sp. Amb., 505, 569n3, 806, 842, 848
Magistrati, Count Massimo (*b.* 1889), It. chargé in Berlin, 805
Mahora (Albacete), I B training centre, 458
Maisky, Ivan Mikhailovich (*b.* 1884), Ru. Amb. in London, 396, 467n1; and non-intervention, 467, 566, 580, 604–5, 738, 739, 832

Majadahonda (Madrid), 495
Major Attlee Company, 792n2
Majorca, 103, 232, 259, 261n1, 567n4, 581; republican attack and nationalist counter-offensive, 260n1, 381–4, 404, 683; Italian stronghold, 397, 740, 794, 806, 807; French responsibility, 683
Makhno, Nestor (1889–1934), Ru., anarchist, 68
Málaga, 31n1, 58n2, 184, 274, 332n, 371, 694; Popular Front, 110 and n3, 116; anarchism, 305, 307; committee of public safety, 307; in civil war, 380, 411, 583, 585; naval bombardment, 586; Battle of, 582–6, 588; aftermath, 586–7, 594
Malaparte, Curzio, 111
Malatesta, Enrico (1853–1932), It. anarchist, 63, 65
Malcolm, J. A., FO official, 989
Maldonado, Prof. Francisco, pro-fascism, 501, 502 and n
Maleter, Pal (later Gen.) (C), Hung. vol. in IB, 954
Malinovsky, Col. (later Marshal) Rodion ('Malinó') (1898–1967), Ru. officer, 446, 494n2, 953; adviser to Lister, 588n, 603, 810n
Malley, Bernard (1889–1966), 265n4
Mallol, Alonso, Dir. Gen. of Security (1936), 183, 278
Malraux, André (*b.* 1901), Fr. writer, 361, 364; and communism, 351nn 3, 4; intermediary with Spanish government, 351–2, 352n1; air squadron, 366 and n1, 375, 587, 731n4; defence of Málaga, 587; at Writers' Congress, 699; *L'Espoir*, 255 and n1, 301, 366n1, 792n2, 878
Manchester Guardian, 347, 622, 707n4
Mangada, Col. (later Gen.) Julio (1877–1946) (R), 92–3, 320–21, 321n1; trial of rebel officer, 247–8
Mann, James (later Sir) (1897–1962), 486n2
Mann, Tom (1856–1941), Eng. com., 367, 853n3
Mantecón, José Ignacio (LR), Gov. Gen. of Aragon (1937), 473, 724, 725n1
Manuilsky, Dimitri (1883–1954), Ukranian Comintern sec. gen., 338n4
Manzana, José (ex-sergeant), 316
Manzanares (river), Madrid, 244, 473–4, 480, 484, 588, 594, 872, 908
MAOC communist militia, 244
Maqueda (Toledo), 411
Mar Cantábrico (Sp. merchant ship), 575, 576 and n2
Marañón y Posadillo, Dr Gregorio (1887–1960), Sp. writer and physician, 30, 73, 142 and n1, 159n3, 634n1; flight abroad, 500–501
Marañosa, La (Madrid), 588, 594
Maraviglio, Marchese di, It. official, 786n1
Marbella (Málaga), 582
March Ordinas, Juan (1884–1962), financier, 28, 161n2, 187, 335n4, 701, 724n1; and Franco, 204n1, 419; support for nationalists, 288
Marcos Escribano, Tomás, and Unamuno, 503
Marcucci ('Julio'), It. vol. in IB, protest suicide (1938), 798–9
'Margaritas', Carlist organization, 507
María Cristina (1858–1929), Regent of Spain (1885–1902), 16
Marianist Fathers, 52
Marías, Julián (*b.* 1914), writer, 903n1
Marinha airfield, La (Portugal), 254
Marismas, Marqués de las (José Ignacio Escobar y Kirkpatrick) (1898–1965), emissary to Germany, 342n5, 697
Maritain, Jacques (1882–1973), 513; on religious killings, 695 and nn5, 6
Marković, Kirko (Marcovich) (C), US vol. in IB, 608n3
Maroto, Mt., 617
Marqués de Comillas (requisitioned liner), 381, 581
Márquez, Col. Benito, 22
Marseillaise Battalion, 490, 491, 494, 955
Marseilles, 354, 739, 813n2
Martí, José (1853–95), Cub. journalist, 195n2
Martín, Andrés (*d.* 1936), socialist youth leader, 411
Martín, Antonio (*d.* 1937) (A), and Puigcerdá, 311, 653 and n1
Martin, Kingsley (1897–1969), ed. *New Statesman*, 707n4, 868n5
Martín Alonso, Maj. (later Gen.) Pablo (1896–1964) (N), 100n5, 252, 948n1
Martín Bagüeñas, Santiago (*d.* 1936), chief of police, Madrid, 183, 404
Martín Blázquez, Col. José (*b.* 1902) (R), on García Oliver, 546n2
Martin du Gard, Roger, Fr. writer, 707
Martín Moreno, Col. Francisco (1879–1941) (N), Franco's chief of staff, 504, 868n2, 948
Martín Torrent, FR, 260n1

Martínez, Francisco (A), 615
Martínez, Miguel, *see* Koltsov
Martínez Amutio, Julio (Soc), 340n2, 488n3; post-war trial, 924 and n3
Martínez Anido, Gen. Severiano (1862–1938), 26, 755, 820; character, 24, 26, 67, 274, 752, 831; under Franco, 752, 753
Martínez Barrio, Diego (1883–1962), Rad., U R speaker, and min., 8, 104–5, 134, 156, 161, 179n, 454; freemasonry, 34, 42 and n2, 43; caretaker government (1933), 106; in opposition, 125 and n; interim president, 172n1; forms a government, 228; Valencia *junta*, 304, 305; and working classes in defeat, 769; and a negotiated peace, 770, 880; president in exile, 881, 920, 950; assumes Azaña's duties, 898
Martínez Cabrera, Gen. Toribio (1879–1939) (R), 585, 899; and Mixed Brigades, 545; replaced by Rojo, 598, 615; accused of treason, 781; military governor of Madrid, 781n2, 899; execution, 925
Martínez Campos, Capt.-General Arsenio (1831–1900), 63
Martínez de Campos, Maj. (later Gen.) Carlos (1887–1975) (N), chief of artillery, 239, 240n1, 377n2, 690n; campaigns, 614, 728, 842–3
Martínez Cartón, Lt. Col. Pedro (C), 631, 789n1, 909
Martínez Fuset, Col. Lorenzo (*b.* 1899) (N), legal adviser to Franco, 218n4, 504, 641, 926
Martínez Monje Restoy, Gen. Fernando, 241–2, 251 and n3, and Army of the South, 490, 545, 582; accused of treason, 781
Martínez de Velasco, José (1875–1936), Right politician, 404
Marty, André (1886–1956) (C), Fr. Com. leader, 378n, 532; member of ECCI secretariat, 338n4, 339, 361n1, 457–8; and IB at Albacete, 457, 459–60; career and character, 457, 491 and n4, 881; and Largo Caballero, 650–51; scandal concerning, 781; at Aragon front, 800, 801; refugee in France, 878, 881; expulsion from communist party, 955
Marty, Pauline, 458, 781
Marx, Groucho (*b.* 1897), 400n
Marx, Karl (1818–83), 145; dispute with anarchists, 39, 61, 522
Marxism, Marxists, 16, 39, 109, 119, 120, 145, 264, 351, 430, 507, 523, 662, 923, 934
Mas, Valerio (A), 658n4, 660n3
Mas de la Matas (Teruel), 126n2
Masaryk Battalion, 969
Masegoso (Albacete), 598
Masferrer, Rolando, Cub. vol. in IB, 574n3
Masquelet Lacaci, Gen. Carlos (*b.* 1871) (R), 93, 140n, 161, 173
Massigli, René, Fr. dip., 804
Masters, Sam (C), Eng. vol. in Spain, 367
Mata Lloret, Antonio, 218n1
Matallana Gómez, Maj. (later Gen.) Manuel (1894–1956), 476, 716n, 886, 891; campaigns, 710n, 711, 868–9; possible treachery, 869 and n1, 886, 887, 898; and Casado, 909, 913; on republican army, 938; imprisonment and death, 950n2
Matthews, Herbert (*b.* 1906), US journalist, 363, 603, 855, 879
Maura y Gamazo, Honorio (1886–1936) (M), 410
Maura y Gamazo, Miguel (*b.* 1887), 6n1, 33n2, 149n4, 194; minister of the interior, 33–4, 76, 134; on Prieto, 41; and riots of 1931, 57, 201; resignation, 76; forms a coalition, 229; on a visit to Azaña in exile, 957
Maura y Montaner, Antonio (1853–1925), Con. prime minister, 7 and n1, 20, 23, 33n2, 548; and Primo de Rivera, 26–7
Mauriac, François (1885–1970), Fr. writer, 348, 513, 695, 697, 707
Maurín Julia, Joaquín (1896–1973) (P), 10, 117, 118, 179n, 266; splinter group, 120; imprisonment, 925; *d.* in exile, 950–51
Maurras, Charles (1868–1952), Fr. writer, 20, 151, 697
'Maximov', General, Ru. officer, 904
Mazón, José María (Car), 640
Medellín (Badajoz), 375
Mediana (Saragossa), 725
Medical science, lessons from civil war, 550–52, 551nn1, 2, 945–6
Medinaceli, Duque de, 80
Medrano, Col., 868n2
Mella, Julio Antonio (*d.* 1929), Cub. Com., 323n2
Melilla (Sp. Morocco), 17, 24, 98, 226, 903n3; and military rising, 215–17, 219; alleged German unit, 578
Mena, Col. Arturo, 247, 261n2; imprisonment, 266n1

Mena, Marciano, execution, 708n2
Mena Zueco, Gen. Julio (*b.* 1874) (R), 238, 436
Menchaca, FR Pedro, and Guernica, 628
Méndez, Dr Rafael (L R), 667
Méndez Aspe, Francisco (R), finance minister, 815; and shipment of gold to Russia, 448, 449n2; receives money from Bank of Spain, 975n1
Méndez Nuñez (R. cruiser), 331, 797, 901
Mendiola Núñez, Col. Leopoldo, 980n4
Menéndez, Teodomiro (Soc), imprisonment, 146
Menéndez López, Capt. Arturo (1893–1936), Dir. Genl. of Security 1832, execution, 266
Menéndez López, Maj. Emilio (R), 320
Menéndez López, Gen. Leopoldo (1891–1965) (R), 714n1; at Teruel, 788–9, 789n1, 886, 922; campaigns, 830, 832, 836n1, 901, 909; favours surrender, 891, 898–9, 907
Menéndez Pidal, Ramón (1869–1968), historian, 500
Menéndez Reigada, FR Ignacio (N), Jesuit, 696n2, 758
Mequinenza (Saragossa), 838, 840, 841, 843, 869
Mera, Cipriano (1897–1975) (A), 126, 247, 677, 866 and n2, 899, 907; campaigns, 320, 483n3, 492, 493, 599, 602, 887; discovers Franco's plan, 788 and n1; and Negrín, 887; later capture, 925
Mercader del Río, Caridad (C), saves Goded, 235 and n2; mistress of Etington, 447n2
Mercader, Ramón (C), Assassin of Trotsky, 447n2, 574n4
Meretskov, Maj. (later Marshal) Kiril ('Petrov'), Ru. officer, 490, 592, 588n, 604; eminence in Russia, 953
Merhard, Maj, v., G. officer, fighter commander, 469n3, 614n
Mérida (Badajoz), 662; battle of, 373
Merín, Lt Eduardo (R), 549, 679
Merriman, Robert (*d.* 1938), U S vol. in I B, 595, 798n2
Merry del Val y Alzola, Alfonso (*b.* 1903) (F), 115
Messerschmidt, Eberhard, G. official, 284, 418
Messerschmitt, Willy (*b.* 1898), aircraft designer, 672n2
Metternich, Princess, 352
Mexico, 82, 117n4, 200, 323n2, 575, 576, 584, 867, 921; pro-republic, 362, 391, 742, 769, 984
Meynell, Sir Francis (1891–1975), Eng. publisher and book designer, 347n3
Miaja Menant, Gen. José (1878–1958) (R), 230, 320, 380–81, 662; and rising, 219, 228, 243; and Mola, 228–9, 243; commander in defence of Madrid, 437, 475–9, 482, 485, 545, 588–9, 602; new post, 488, 492–3, 495; increased prestige, 532; rivalry with Pozas, 593; alleged member U M E, 663n2; Army Corps, 677, 710, 779, 816; Brunete offensive, 710, 711, 714; Catalonia campaign, 868–9; area of control, 886; and ending the war, 887, 892; and Cassado's plot, 898–9, 902, 904, 905, 912; *d.* in exile, 950
Mickiewicz (Palafox) Battalion, 968
Middle classes (bourgeoisie), 74, 110, 123, 146; anticlericalism, 35; socialist alliance, 39–40; political divisions, 95, 123, 165; Carlism, 97, 108, 129; and communism, 154, 429, 646, 935; falangists, 177n2, 285; and revolutionary parades, 177–8; and intellectual renaissance, 191 and n; oppose military rising, 192, 242; and working classes, 193; and Calvo Sotelo's murder, 208; in republican Spain, 270, 274–5, 290, 305; and nationalist Spain, 283, 510, 755, 922; support 'Movimiento salvador', 288; division in civil war, 327; foreign interests, 334; fear of anarchists, 429; ruthlessness in conquest, 923–4; *alfereces provisionales*, 938
Middleton Murry, John (1889–1957), Eng. editor, 347n3
Mieres (Oviedo), 138, 140
Miguel de Cervantes (R. cruiser), 242, 243, 331 and n4, 568 and n1, 901
Mije García, Antonio (C), 122, 291, 435
Miksche, Capt. F. O., Cz. vol. in I B, 458; *Blitzkrieg*, 716
Milch, Field Marshal v. (1892–1972), G. administrator of Luftwaffe, 357–8, 469n2
Milicias Antifascistas Obreras y Campesinas (M A O C), 122 and n, 322
Military tribunals, in republican Spain, 778 and n3, 799; deaths due to, 927
Militias, militiamen, 163, 170, 322, 405; anarchist neglect to arm, 181; military training, 206, 316; left-wing reliance, 209; working class leaders, 225; in military rising, 244, 246, 247–8; in

Militias – *contd*
republican Spain, 268, 292–3; crimes by, 271–2; payment, 293; as soldiers in civil war, 219, 313, 318 and n2, 320, 371 (republican forces), 373–6, 379, 380, 383, 411, 436; losses due to naive courage, 322; and Model Prison, 404; end of independence, 434; and political commissars, 434–5; in Sigüenza cathedral, 435n3; union with Com., Fal. and CEDA under military authority, 507; merged with army into Mixed Brigades, 542 and n1, 546; failure in attack, 938
Millán Astray y Terreros, Gen. José (1879–1954) (N), 826; *africanistas*, 94, 415; founder of Foreign Legion (1920), 94, 415, 422, 501; and monarchist flag, 415; friendship with Franco, 415, 425; at Salamanca University meeting, 501–2; rabble-rousing slogans, 502, 510, 931; reproved by Unamuno, 502–3; press and propaganda dept, 504 and n2; evangelical medievalism, 510
Mining rights in Spain, German, 765, 767, 829, 850, 860–61, 941
Minorca, 273, 332, 581, 828, 886n1; military rising, 242, 254; surrenders to Franco, 884, 886
Miquelarena, Jacinto (*b.* 1891), Salamanca radio station, 858
Miralcampo, agricultural collective, 562–3, 563n1
Miralles, Carlos (*d.* 1936) (N), 313 and n
Miranda, Joaquín (F), 420, 640n3
Miranda de Ebro (Burgos), Radio Transmission School, 979
Miravete (Teruel), 838
Miravitlles, Jaume, Cat. politician, 250n2
Miret, José (C), Cat. politician, 250n2, 652n4
Miró, Juan (*b.* 1894), 190
Mit Brennender Sorge (anti-nazi encyclical), banned in Spain, 683
Mitchison, Naomi (*b.* 1897), Eng. writer, 347n3
Mizzian Bel-Kasen, Maj. (later Gen.) Mohammed Ben, 843, 854
Mixed Brigades, 490, 837n; formed from militias and regular army, 434, 478–80, 542; engagements, 480, 492, 599; nationalist formation, 508, 764; organization and numbering, 542 and n1, 546 and n1, 599; communist preponderance, 545; leadership, 545 and n3, 582, 886; murders at Madrid escape tunnel, 778 and n2
Moch, Jules (*b.* 1893), Fr. Soc., 340n1, 349
Modesto Guilloto, Juan (1906–69) (C), 166n1, 247, 889; leader of MAOC, 122, 323; in civil war, 323, 468n2, 589, 835, 868; and Fifth Regiment, 492, 545n3; commander 5th Army Corps, 677, 710, 714n1; rival of El Campesino, 794; compared with Lister, 836; and bombing of Gandesa, 841–2; at Elda country house, 904; entitlement, 948
Modotti, Tina (It. C), 323n2
Moix, José (C), 845–6, 901, 905–6
Mola Vidal, Gen. Emilio (1887–1937) (N), 205, 421, 505n, 936; *africanista*, 94, 160, 173; sent to Pamplona, 166, 168, 183; director of 1936 military rising, 173–7, 185, 207–8, 209, 217n, 228–9, 689–90; and Carlists, 183, 184, 202–3, 204–5, 690; 'Directory' programme, 183–4; counsels patience, 199–200; assurances to Falange, 202n2; relations with Franco, 203 and n1, 282, 376, 419, 424, 640, 689; meeting with Batet, 211–12; and Madrid conspirators, 220; and civil war, 229, 236, 237, 239; in Madrid, 243; and Sanjurjo's return and death, 254–5; and use of terror, 260; suspects exposure of corpses, 262; refuses exchange of prisoners, 263–4; sets up Burgos *junta*, 282, 283, 285, 421 and n2; area of control, 283, 288–9, 308; Radio speeches, 283–4; hatred of Azaña, 283–4; first campaigns, 313, 315, 319; shortage of ammunition, 315, 376; asks Germany for aid, 342n5, 354; commander Army of the North, 370, 426, 432; and Beorlegui, 377n2; and advance on Madrid, 409, 432, 470, 473, 487, 623–4; conquest of San Sebastian, 410; discredited as single commander, 422, 424; Basque campaign, 612–14; foreign aircraft support, 614 and n; and Guernica, 627; and Bilbao, 687; death in air disaster, 689 and n3, 930; entitlement, 948
Mola Vidal, Capt. Ramón (*d.* 1936) (N), death, 214, 248
Mölders, Wernher (1913–41), air ace in Second World War, 951
Molero Lobo, Gen. Nicolás (1871–1947) (R), 159; imprisonment, 240, 266n1

Molero, Maj., Madrid offensive, 589
Moles y Ormella, Juan (1871–1943) (C), 179n1, 206
Molesworth, Brig., League Commissioner, 853
Molina, Col. Luis (*b.* 1880), of Foreign Legion, 224
Molins de Llobregat (Barcelona), 278
'Molotov' (Vyacheslav Scriabin) (*b.* 1890), Ru. prime minister (1930–41), 533n, 869
Monarchical Union, 31
Monarchist, Spanish, 6, 59, 141, 156, 165, 172; elections (1931), 31 and n2, (1936), 72 and n2, 151, 159, 162n2; and 1931 riots, 57–8; characteristics, 59 and n4; rumoured plots, 72; and Carlists, 96, 107, 130; 'Alfonsists', 96, 97, 98, 99; reorganization, 107; and Italian fascism, 130; ideologies, 151; and military rising, 175, 244; in nationalist army, 313; and Germany, 336; use of their flag, 414; opinion of Mola, 422; courted by Franco, 425, 644; inclusion in a united party, 639, 750
Monarchy, the, 32, 285; collapse of its inviolability, 13, 25, 191, 193; army loyalty, 29; ideology of abolitionists, 30; the church and, 53; expulsion by the army (1868), 191; nationalist ideological problems, 509; restoration of property and rights of citizenship, 884
Monasterio Ituarte, Col. (later Gen.) José (1882–1952) (N), 238n5; Madrid campaign, 409, 432, 436, 489; commander of militias, 642, 749n; new national council, 750; cavalry charge at Teruel, 793
Moncada University (Valencia), 536
Mondragón (Guizpúzcoa), 512
Monje, Mercedes, 10n1
Monks, Noël (1908–60), Eng. journalist, 754
Monmousseau, Gaston (1895–1960), Fr. Comintern leader, 360–61
Monnier, Col. (R), at Bilbao, 691
Monóvar (Alicante), 905, 907
Mont de Marsan, Bank of Spain gold deposit, 826, 898, 974, 975
Montalbán (Teruel), 316, 799, 800
Montana project, 746n4, 765, 766–7
Montaud, Col. Gustavo (*b.* 1897) (R), 837
Montaudran aerodrome (Toulouse), destination of Fr. aid, 364nn3, 4, 390
Montaner Canet, Col. Federico (N), 282, 421n2
Monte Urcullu (Vizcaya), 691
Monteiro, Dr, Portuguese foreign minister, 359n8, 388, 439
'Montenegro', Gen., Ru. officer, 726 and n1, 779
Montero, FR Antonio, 270n4, 512n7
Montero, Matías (F), death, 114
Montero Díaz, Santiago (*b.* 1911) (C and F), 114n3
Montes, Fr., Augustinian teacher, 56
Montiel, Francisco (Soc), UGT treasurer, 522
Montjuich, 873; removal of cemetery inscriptions, 874
Montseny, Federica (A), minister of health 1936–37, 471, 472, 483, 536; anarchist intellectual, 64, 269, 546, 671; on violence, 277 and n3; accepts a government post, 473–4; and the family, 539; and May Days, 657–8; denounces Negrín, 866n1; survival in exile, 950
Montserrat (Barcelona), Benedictine monastery, 44, 270
Monzón, Jesús (C), civil governor of Alicante, 204, 499 and n2, 900; leaves Spain, 905–6
Monzón, Telesforo (B), 377, 617n3
Moors, 87–8, 151, 494. 509; in Army oı Africa, 93, 373, 485; focus of terror, 373, 375n1, 380n3; battle-rite, 376n1
Mora, Julio de, ex-*checa*, later head of DEDIDE, 277n1
Mora, Teodoro (A), 320
Mora y Maura, Constancia de la (C), 33n2, 548 and n3
Mora la Nueva, 838, 840, 855
Moral, Joaquín del, organizer of atrocities, 263
Moral Rearmament Association, 955–6
Morales, Quero, sub. sec. of justice, 526–7
Morales Carrasco, Col. Gaspar (*b.* 1881) (R), 677
Morandi, Col., IB Brigade leader, 969
Moraveč, Col. (1895–1966), Cz. chief of intelligence, 447n4
Morayta Núñez, Rafael (C), sec. gen. agrarian reform, 564
Moreau, Maj. Rudolph v., G. officer, bombs Guernica, 370, 624 and n1
Morell, Col. Norberto (R), 573, 805; on pre-civil war situation, 192; on republican army, 434
Moreno, José (F), *junta* member, 420n3; and Hedilla, 635

Moreno Calderón, Col. Fernando (*b.* 1880), 212; member Burgos *junta*, 282, 421n2
Moreno Fernańdez, Admiral Francisco (*b.* 1883), commander of Nat. fleet, 764, 795; ennoblement, 948
Moreno Hernández, Capt., naval commander, 421
Moreno Laguía, Miguel (R), judge in Nin case, 708 and n1
Morgan, Charles (1894–1958), Eng. writer, 347n3
Morgan, J. P. (1837–1913), financier, 186
Morgenthau, Henry (J R) (1891–1967), 362–3
Moriones Larraga, Col. Domingo (Marqués de Oroquieta) (1883–1964) (R), in civil war, 688, 836n1, 871, 891, 907; and communism, 883
Morning Post, 347
Moro, Teodoro (A), 247
Moroccan wars, 17–20, 28–9, 39, 91, 92, 104, 326, 371; Annual battle, 24–5, 94; *africanistas*, 93–4, 140; Spanish victory (1927), 98, 140; insubordination of *Junteros*, 415
Moroccans, 17–18, 20, 93 and n3; Riffian tribesmen, 24–5; numbers under arms, 328, 329, 759, 768; brutality, 373, 412; in nationalist forces, 375, 380, 412–13, 416, 436, 474–5, 481, 484, 485, 494, 588, 589, 593, 596, 711, 759, 768; volunteers in Franco's army, 980 and n3
Morocco, French, 17–18, 93, 94, 111, 578–9
Morocco, Spanish, 17–18, 23, 25, 94; and military rising, 173, 209, 215–18 *passim*, 224, 226–7, 238, 255; Foreign Legion, 205; nationalist holding, 33; supply base for aid to Spain, 352 and n4, 354n6, 357, 370; mining resources, 417, 519, 860; alleged presence of German ships, 578; and independence, 578–9; Largo's anti-Franco plans, 650, 663 and n1
Morral, Mateo, would-be assassin, 64
Morrison, W. S. (later Ld Dunrossil) (1893–1961), Eng. min. of agriculture, 395 and n3
Mortimer, Raymond (*b.* 1895), Eng. man of letters, 347n3, 776n1
Moscardó Guzmán, José (*d.* 1936), 246–7
Moscardó Guzmán, Capt. Luis (1911–36), s. of José, real and alleged shooting, 324 and n
Moscardó Ituarte, Col. José (1878–1956) (N), takes hostages, 247 and n1, 325; civil war incident, 324–5; story of his son, 324 and n1, 937; defence of Alcázar, 409, 412, 413, 596; and Madrid offensive, 596, 597, 598, 599; in retreat, 602; entitlement, 948; campaigns, 797, 800, 891, 818, 867, 881, 882
Mosley, Sir Oswald (*b.* 1896), 114
Mostaganem (Algeria), 911
Moulin, Jean (*d.* 1944), Fr. official, 351, 364
Motril, 307, 582, 583, 585, 868
Mounsey, Sir George (1879–1966), Eng. official, 989, 990
Mozos de Escuadra, Catalan security force, 136, 233
Muedra Miñón, Col. Félix (*b.* 1895) (R), 886, 887, 894
Muenzenberg, Willi (*d.* 1940), G. communist in Comintern propaganda dept, 341, 452; modus operandi, 341n3, 398; Paris headquarters, 341 and n3, 361, 452n2; murder in France, 452n2
Múgica, Dr Mateo (Bishop of Vitoria), 286–7, 287n1, 511; pastoral letter to Basque catholics, 309 and n2; in Rome, 512; and shooting of priests, 512–13; and Basque manifesto, 695 and n3; and 'Bishop's letter', 696; denies religious freedom in Nat. Spain, 696–7
Mulay Hassan, Caliph, 218, 226
Mundelein, Cardinal George William (1872–1939), and US arms embargo, 825n1
Munis, Grandizo, Trotskyist leader, 654, 866
Mundo Obrero, 122, 180, 291, 406. 461, 470, 476, 896
Munich conference, 935, 939; effects on Spain, 849–50, 861, 941
Municipal Boundaries Act, repeal, 131
Munnich, Ferenc (1886–1967) (C), Hung. organizer in IB, 954
Muñoz, Col., 250, 582–3
Muñoz, Manuel, Dir. Gen. of Security 1936, 477
Muñoz Castellanos, Col. (later Gen.) Mariano (*b.* 1880) (N), 723
Muñoz Grandes, Col. (later Gen.) Agustín (1896–1972), founds *guardia de asalto*, 104, 717; campaigns, 717, 800, 867, 869, 870; in Franco's ministry, 948; Blue division, 949, 975
Murat, Joachin (1767–1815), 13n1

Murcia, 21, 332n, 901, 915
Murga, Capt. Pablo (*d.* 1936), executed as spy, 613n
Muro, Jesús (N and F), 319, 363, 420, 420n3
Murphy, Robert, U S official, 574n4
Mussolini, Benito (1883–1945), It. fascist, prime minister (1922–43) 28, 439; Spanish followers, 110–11, 114; visited by Carlists and monarchists, 129, 130n1, 342; and aid for Nat. Spain and Franco, 129–30, 352n4, 394, 568, 570–71, 806, 856; and Franco's emissaries, 342, 352 and n3; mixed motives in supply of arms, 353–4; and Hitler, 353, 572–3; youth movements, 510; and non-intervention, 583–4; desire for military glory, 596, 734, 942; and a separate Basque peace, 681n2; relief at Mola's death, 689; and capture at Santander, 721–2; agrees to attacks on shipping, 739, 743; and Nyon Agreement, 742; visits Germany, 743; Franco's financial debt, 764; anger with Franco over Ebro, 847–8; belief in a mediated peace, 849; reaction to Munich, 849; withdraws some forces from Spain, 855; demands cession of Fr. territories, 857n; and capture of exiles, 873–4; welcomes returning troops, 920
Mussolini, Bruno (N), It. pilot, 806
Mussolini, Rachele, 353 and n4
Mut Ramón, Col. Francisco (*b.* 1894), 874
Muti, Ettore, It. pilot, 364
Mylanos, Dr, N K V D agent, 450

Nadir (N. armed ship), 856
Nanetti, Nino (*d.* 1937) (C), It. vol. in I B, 688, 692, 693
Nangle, Capt. Gilbert (1902–44), Br. vol. for nationalists, 374n, 409n1, 768n2, 980n2
Napoleon I (1769–1821), Emperor of the French, 13, 42, 51, 77, 91
Nathan, Capt. George (*d.* 1937), Br. vol. in I B, 490 and n3, 491n1, 713; funeral oration, 713n5
National Action (Catholic, right-wing), 73, 76, 107, 108
National Catholic Agrarian Confederation, 71
National Committee on Foreign Commerce (N), 519
National Front, 6, 151, 156, 162, 192
National Republican Guard, 550
National Republican Party, 228
National Youth Congress, Valencia, 535
Navalcarnero (Madrid), 713
Navalmoral de la Mata (Cáceres), 375
Navalperal (Avila), 320
Navarre, 71, 87n, 167, 184, 416; Basque inhabitants, 87 and n2, 97; political history, 87 and n2, 88n1; Carlism, 97, 129, 202, 204–5, 239, 285; Catholicism, 97–8, 239; triumph of military rising, 239, 260; repression in, 260–62; casualties, 265
Navarrese troops, 315; in Basque Provinces, 377, 379, 612; in Mola's army, 612, 614, 617, 623, 624; campaigns, 690n, 693, 712, 717, 718, 728, 791, 798, 832, 834, 854, 869, 870, 881, 912
Navarro López, José (R), chief of staff of the navy, 692, 708n2
Navitsch, Leonid (C) (*d.* 1937), Ru. official, 491n4
Navy, British (Royal and merchant) and Spanish crisis, 345 and n3, 659 and n1, 567, 577, 617n4, 741, 827; and blockade, 618–23; escort duties, 680, 914; attacks on, 827–9
Navy, Italian, 739–41, 745
Navy, Spanish, 58, 92, 140; and military rising, 204, 212, 219, 226–7; sailors/officers mutiny, 231, 242–3, 332, 389: Nationalist fleet, 370, 410–11, 595, 614, 617–23 *passim*, 733, 735, 740, 797, 856; Republican fleet, 505–6, 549 and n3, 550, 615, 679, 779, 892, 901, 914, 919; influence on course of the war, 936; lessons learnt by both sides, 936–7
Nazism, Nazi party, 276, 335, 342, 357, 418, 520, 705, 830; Spanish followers, 109, 110, 111, 114, 335 and n4; and aid to Franco, 354, 355, 356–7
Negrete, Capt. (R), 318
Negrín, Dr Juan (1889–1956) (Soc), 653, 664, 731; humane acts, 277, 666; in Largo Caballero's cabinet, 406–7, 535, 666, 667–8; and removal of Spain's gold reserves, 448–9, 668; carabineers, 550, 667, 673; communist choice for premier, 651, 664n1, 665, 668; family background and career, 666–8, 669, 670n1, 770, 933; further relations with communist party, 668–9, 669n5, 735, 787, 846–7, 891, 934; as minister of finance, 666, 668, 670; as prime minister, 667, 668, 669–70, 713, 812,

Negrin, Dr Juan – *contd*
821; hopes for a general war, 669n2, 846–7, 935; and foreign journalists, 670n1; cabinet, 670; and anarchists, 672; and Basque representatives, 679; and Nin's disappearance, 704, 706, 708–9; and P O U M persecution, 705, 706–7; attempts to end non-intervention, 735; at Geneva, 742–3, 848, 857; relations with Azaña, 770–71, 814n2, 821 and n2, 846; government by decree, 771; and geographical disunity, 771, 786; and Catalonia, 773–4, 935; difficulties with socialists and anarchists, 782, 783, 886n1; achievements, 786; ideal of a strong state, 786–7; his enemies, 787, 886; demands opening of French frontier, 804, 805, 806; and Prieto's defeatism, 809, 810–11, 812, 813; assumes ministry of defence, 815, 844; lists government war aims, 820 and n, 821; and a negotiated peace, 821, (terms), 880; secret negotiation with nazis, 830, 848 and n4; new compromise project, 848 and n4; attacked in the Cortes, 862; and suspension of executions, 867; exhausted, 868 and n5; leaves Spain, 881, 884; Casado's plot against, 886ff., 891, 899, 902–3, 905; overwhelmed by events, 890–91, 893; meeting with army leaders, 891; attacks on his way of life, 892n2; and Casado's relief, 898; proposes general staff reorganization, 898; Elda cabinet meeting, 903; attempts to prevent strife, 905; Paris speech to Cortes, 920; last years, 949–50
'El Negus' (C), militia major, 776–7, 777n1
Nehru, Jawaharlal (1889–1964), 642 and n2
Nelken y Mausberger, Margarita (1898–1968) (S), 226n3, 522
Nelson, Steve, U S vol. in I B, 723n1, 725n2
Nenni, Pietro (*b.* 1891) (Soc), It. vol. in I B, 482, 532, 599, 600, 716n, 853; on Prieto, 403; vice-pres. of Italy, 954
Neruda, Pablo (1904–73), poet, Chilean consul, Madrid, 480n1, 698
Nervión (river), 692, 693
Nettlau, Max, anarchist polymath, 220n3
Neurath, Constantin v. (1873–1956), G. foreign min., 685, 734, 735; and aid to Spain, 354, 469, 577–8; and non-intervention plan, 387, 388, 390; and fall of Madrid, 463; and Hitler, 746
Neutrality Act (1935), U S, 362, 417n2, 576 and n3
Neva (Ru. ship), 443
Neves, Mario, Portuguese journalist, 374n
New Shirts, 623n2
New York Times, 363, 533n, 603, 824, 875, 879, 980n2
New Zealand, 824
News Chronicle, 204n2, 347, 586, 829
Nicolau d'Olwer, Luis (1888–1961), Cat. politician, 46, 770
Nicolson, Harold (later Sir) (1886–1968), Eng. writer and politician, 621
Nieto, Andrés (R), 789n1, 793
Nin, Andrés (1892–1937) (P), 302, 946; relations with Russian communist party, 67, 117, 120, 428, 523, 524; breaks with Trotsky, 523, 704; as councillor of justice, 524 and n2, 707; alleged espionage, 701 702; P O U M leader, 702; Stalinist victim, 704, 775; search for, and probable fate, 704–5 705n2; reactions to his disappearance, 706–7, 707nn; examining judge, 708; trial of his companions, 708
Nkrumah, Kwame, President of Ghana (1909–72), 398n1
N K V D (People's Commissariat for International Affairs), 454, 475; and aid for Spain, 442, 450, 451; European agents, 450–51; infiltrates republican organization, 523; use of passports of dead I B volunteers, 574n4; number of 'specialists' in Spain, 984n3
La Noche (anarchist paper), mentions Moscow purges, 524
Noël-Baker, Philip (*b.* 1889) (Soc), Eng. politician, 367–8, 398, 467, 621, 827; visits I B in Spain, 792n2
Nofuentes Montero, Maj. Eduardo (*b.* 1883), 650
Noguera Pallaresa (river), 818
Nombela scandal, 149n1
Non-Intervention Agreement, 388, 390, 467; Russian acceptance, 392; Germany and, 394, 462; Anglo-French attitude, 397, 440; control plan, 566, 577; and control by air, 566; Italian disregard, 833
Non-Intervention Board, 581, 736
Non-Intervention Committee, 451, 683; formation, 394–5; first meeting, 395; F O domination, 395 and n4;

representatives, 396, 444; Franco/British attitude, 396–7, 572; membership of second meeting, 398; control plan, 566, 570, 577, 580; and control of the air, 566, 580, 742; achieves victory, 580; subjects discussed, 604–5, 683, 735, 741–2; naval patrol control, 680, 683, 684 (map), 735, 742; proposition by Holland, 737–8; and withdrawal of volunteers, 751, 832; dissolution (1939), 919–20, 920n; influence on the war, 944; breaches of, 389–90, 391, 394, 395n1, 566, 567; effect on republic, 402; Anglo-French mediation plan, 571–2; cost of year's operation, 581 and n1; areas of control, 581; naval patrol scheme, 734, 736, 739; position of air routes, 736; continued flow of material into Spain, 736, 739; discussed at Geneva, 743; British government, 387, 388, 391 and n, 396–7, 581 and n, 735 and n2, 736; English intellectuals, 347 and n2; France, 352n2, 364, 387–8, 396–7, 581, 736, 738; Germany, 358–9, 387, 391, 394, 566, 581, 738; Italy, 237, 391, 738; US, 362, 390–91. *See also* France, Germany, Italy, United States.
Non-Intervention Control Agreement, 607n4
Non-Intervention Pact, 364, 444
North American Committee to aid Spanish Democracy, 608n4
Norway, 581, 893
Nosotros (anarchist paper), 656n1
La Nouvelle Revue Française, 695
Noya, La (Corunna), tin mines, 253
Núñez Maza, Capt. Carlos (*b.* 1899) (C), 814, 869n3
Núñez de Prado y Susbielas, Gen. Miguel (1882–1936), 166n1, 225; airforce commander, 219, 266; execution, 266; transport to Barcelona, 331
Nuremberg War Crimes Tribunal, and Guernica, 625n3
Nuria mountains, 881
Nuvolini, Gen. (N), It. officer in Spain, 596, 598. 599, 600n1; returns to Italy, 604
Nye, Senator Gerald (*b.* 1892), 575, 576n2, 824
Nyon Agreements, 742–4
Nyon Conference, 741–2

Obregón, Enrique (*d.* 1936) (A), 235
Observer, 347, 571
Oca, river (Guernica), 626
O'Casey, Sean (1880–1964), 347n3, 611
Ocaña gaol (Toledo), 925
Ochañdiano, 617, 623
October No. 1 battalion, 322, 411
O'Daire, Paddy, Irish vol. in IB, 725n2
O'Duffy, Gen. Eoin (1892–1944), Ir organizer of nationalist volunteers, 592 and n1, 602n1, 768, 979
Odessa, 339n2, 440 and n1, 442, 443, 566; arrival of Spanish gold, 449; Deuxième Bureau, 491n4
O'Faolain, Sean (*b.* 1900), 347n3
Ogilvie Forbes, George (later Sir) (1891–1954), Br. dip., 395n1
Olaechea, Mgr. Marcelino (*b.* 1889), Bishop of Pamplona, and nationalist atrocities, 263, 287 and n3; condemns Basque catholics, 309
Olazábal, Rafael de (Car), 129
Old Shirts, 506, 636, 750, 819, 948
Oliva, Col. Fernando (R), 901
Oliver, Rear-Admiral, 581
Oliviera, Capt. (R) Port. vol., 324
Olley Airways Co. of Croydon, and transport of Franco to Morocco, 203–4
Olmeda Medina, José (A), execution, 278
Olmedo, Antonio, 859n2
Onaindía, FR Alberto (B), 54n2, 625n3, 628n4; surrender negotiations, 718n, 720
Operation Magic Fire, 358–9
Operation Otto, 418n2
Oranges, percentage of exports, 188 and n2
Ordenes gaol (Corunna), 878
Ordoqui, Joaquín, Cub. C. vol. in IB, 574n3
Organización Antonio, Madrid espionage, 505n
Orgaz y Yoldi, Gen. (1881–1946), 758, 931; potential conspirator, 59, 89 and n, 160; and military rising, 165, 166, 168, 173; exiled to Canaries, 174, 218; in Morocco, 371, 425; and a single command, 421 and n2; replaces Mola, 488, 493, 495, 505, 596; trains volunteers, 508; at Jarama, 597–8, 602 and n1; minister under Franco, 750, 948n1
Orihuela, Bishop of, 696
Oriol, José Luis (Car), 183
Orlov, Alexander (Nikolsky), Ru. NKVD and GPU chief in Spain, 442, 447n2, 448, 475, 523, 654n3, 777n2;

Orlov, Alexander – *contd*
later career, 442n2; shipment of gold to Russia, 449 and n2, 450; and destruction of Largo Caballero, 650–51; arrests P O U M leaders, 703, 776; special prison, 705; and a continuance of the war, 746n4; considers killing Prieto, 777n2; secret life in U S, 953 and n2
Ormazábal, Basque com., 617n3
Orobón Fernández, Valeriano, C N T leader, 137
Oropesa, Madrid composer, 323 and n3
Orr, H. Winnett (*b.* 1877), U S physician, 551n2
Ortega, Daniel (*d.* 1939) (C), 323; execution, 925
Ortega, Sgt. (sub. Col.) Antonio (*d.* 1939) (R), Sgt. of Carabineers, Dir. Gen. of security (1937), 671, 703n2, 887, 907; arrest of P O U M leaders, 703; transferred to field command, 708; suspects Casado, 888; offer of mediation, 908; execution, 925
Ortega y Gasset, Eduardo (R), Rad. soc. politician, 35n3, 73, 772n2
Ortega y Gasset, José (1883–1955), writer, 26, 30, 105; flight abroad, 500–501; *Delenda est monarquia*, 30
Ortega y Nieto, Maj. Leopoldo (R), 677, 910–11
Ortiz, Antonio (A), *solidario*, 316, 377, 547
Ortúzar, Luis (B), 431
Orwell, George (Eric Blair) (1903–50), Eng. writer, joins P O U M column, 495n3. 543, 647, 653n2, 817; on republican army, 542 and n1, 544 and n1, 547; and Barcelona riots, 653n2, 659n1; wounded, 688; defence of P O U M, 707 and n4; estimates communist prisoners, 776; and truth about communist role in Spain, 817 and n2; *Homage to Catalonia*, 318 and n1, 495 and n3, 653n2, 688n2, 707n4; 'Notes on the Spanish Militias', 435n2; *Spilling the Beans*, 851n1
Osera (Saragossa), 316
Osservatore Romano, concept of holy war, 695
Ossorio y Gallardo, Angel (1873–1946) Con. Min., 17, 19n1, 654n3, 670; and Azaña, 157, 405n; peace negotiations, 786
Ossorio y Tafall, Bibiano (L R), 815
Ostriakov, N. (R) Ru. naval officer, 549n3
O'Sullivan, Capt. Diarmid, Irish vol. in I B, 592n1
Otal, Col. Ramiro (*b.* 1880) (R), 436
Otero Fernández, Dr Alejandro (Soc) (1888–1953), 441, 451n2; military chief in Oviedo, 385; arms purchase chief, 670n2, 837
Our Fight (I B paper), 780
Oviedo, 41, 141, 160; and Asturias revolution, 138, 142, 143n2, 236; La Vega arms factory, 139, 547 and n4; in military rising, 236, 255; role of miners, 236, 240, 254, 384–5, 435–6; in civil war, 326, 384, 385, 400, 435–6; University, 139
Oyarzún (Guipúzcoa), 286, 377n2

Paasen, Pierre van., Canadian journalist, 429–40
Pabón, Benito, P O U M lawyer, 709
Pacciardi, Randolfo (*b.* 1899) (R), I B leader, 453, 482 and n3, 599n, 711; career, 482n3, 954; disillusioned with communism, 716n
Pacelli, Cardinal Eugenio (later Pope Paul XII) (1876–1958), 513, 681, 827; and christian democracy, 54–5, 108
Pack, Arthur, Br. official, 519, 572n3
Page-Croft, Brig. Gen. Sir Henry (1st Ld Croft) (1881–1947), 897
'Pagés Guix, Luis', *La traición de los Franco*, 751n2
Pajetta, Giuliano (C), It. vol. in I B, 878 and n4
Palacete de la Moncloa, 484
Palacios, Alfredo, receives money from Bank of Spain, 975n1
Palacios, Col. José (R), and U M R A, 166n1
Palacios, Prof. Julio (N), espionage agent, 887n2
Palanco Romero, Prof. José (N) (*d.* 1936), 264n2
Palencia, 240, 539; Radio Transmission school, 979
Palencia, Isobel de (Soc), 467n2
Palma, Majorca, 168, 382, 383, 397, 734; naval patrol vessels, 683, 684; air attacks, 684–5; naval air base, 764–5
Palos (G. supply ship), 572, 577
Pamies, Tomás (*d.* 1968) (C), 45n2, 810n1
Pamplona, 89, 99, 239–40, 315 and n, 332, 332, 416; Carlist centre, 166, 168, 202, 229, 315, 410, 421; Mola's brigade, 175, 177, 260; San Fermín festival, 203; communism, 204; *junta de guerra*, 262; *Adoración Nocturna*, 265

Paracuellos de Jarama (Madrid), 477
Paraguay, 293, 362
Paris Battalion, 366
Paris Soir, 486
Partido Comunista de la Cataluña, 250n1
Partido Comunista Obero de España, 117, 118 and n2
Partido Nacionalista Vasco (PNV), 89n. *See also* Basques
Partido Obrero de Unificación Marxista (POUM), 10n2, 235, 250, 301, 367, 608; leadership, 10, 118n2, 119, 301, 302, 523; and Asturias revolution, 136; and UGT, 297n; numbers and membership, 301–2, 523, 647, 655–6; headquarters and policy, 302; youth movement (JCI), 302; anarchists and, 428; joins *Generalidad*, 428; refused entry to Madrid *junta*, 477n1; independence from Moscow, 523; socialist hatred of, 535; English volunteers, 543 and n1; communist vilification of, 648, 649, 701–7; seizure of their press and radio, 649; and May Days, 656, 657 and n1, 659; and communists, 661, 662, 663; charges of espionage, 703; disbanding of army battalions, 704; torture and interrogation of leaders, 705–6; resulting intellectual controversy, 707; illegal murders, 708 and n2; acceptance of suppression, 709; SIM persecution, 808; collapse of trial of leaders, 865–6; their fate, 950
Partido Socialista Unificado de Cataluña (PSUC), 250, 316, 367; composition, 250nn1, 2, 301; communist domination, 300, 646–7; and the army, 300; and *Generalidad*, 300–301, 428, 526, 652n4, 658; middle class adherence, 429; socialist/communist merger, 522; Mixed Brigades, 547; spirit of 'pogrom', 654; and Barcelona May Days, 657; and 1937 government, 672n2; police interrogation, 772; SIM campaign against, 808
Partit Català Proletari, 250n1
Partit Republicà Catalanista (PRC), 45n1, 122 and n2
Partridge, Sir Bernard (1861–1945), Eng. cartoonist, 348
Pascua, Marcelino (Soc), Sp. Amb. Moscow, 450, 879n1; message from Stalin to Largo Caballero, 534
Pasionaria, La, *see* Ibarruri Dolores
Pastor Velasco, Col. Angel (*b*. 1887) (R), 451n2, 679; arms traffic, 782
Patriarca (pilot), US flier for nationalists, 980n2
Paul, Elliot, US writer, 384n1
Paul-Boncour, Joseph (1873–1972), Fr. politician, foreign min., 804, 805n4
Pavel, Josef (1908–73), Cz. vol. in IB, 954
Pavlov, Gen. Dimitri (*d*. 1941) (R), Ru. officer, tank commander, 489, 495, 945; and defence of Madrid, 588 and n, 601, 602, 603; shot by Stalin, 952
Paxtot Madoz, Gen. Francisco (1876–1936), 224
Paynter, Will (*b*. 1903), Br. organizer in IB, 955
Pearson, Drew, US journalist, 824
Peasants (agricultural workers), 71; become landless proletariats, 61, 81–2; hopes from anarchism, 62, 63, 74, 81; and new land legislation, 72–3, 83–5; unionization, 78, 83, 109; low wages, 79, 81 and n, 83, 126–7; living conditions, 81; revolutionary groups, 81–2; increasing radicalism, 127; strikes over wages, 131, 170; urban socialists and, 164; takeover of farms, 169; treatment of bourgeois property, 303; dislike of Durruti, 318; and collectives, 556, 724; and a new master class, 564
'La Pecosa', militiawoman, murders by, 271
Pedrero García, Angel (*d*. 1940) (Soc), head of SIM, 277n1, 777, 905; supports Casado, 899
Peinado Leal, Commissar (*d*. 1939) (R), 907n1
Peirats, José (A), 451n2, 861; ed. *Acracia* in Lérida, 429n3, 544 and n2, 656n1
Peiré, Tomás, 204n1
Peiró, FR Francisco, Jesuit, 49
Peiró, Juan (1887–1942) (A), min. of industry (1936–37), 471, 472; moderate leader, 69, 277–8, 471, 934–5; and collectivization, 527, 528, 531; quarrel with Negrín, 671; execution, 925
Pemán y Pemartín, José María (*b*. 1898) (M), writer, 55, 415–16, 425n4; at Salamanca University meeting, 501, 502n, 503 and n
Pemartín Sanjuan, Julián (1901–66) (F), 114n1
Peña Boeuf, Alfonso (1888–1966) (N), minister (1938), 293 and n2, 752

Peñalba (Huesca), 317; agricultural collective, 557
Peñaranda, Duques de, 80
Peñarredonda, Col. Pedro (N), 840
Peñarroya (Córdoba), 662; copper mines, 335, 411
Penchienati, Carlo (C), It. vol. in IB, 716n
Peninsular News Service, NY, 363
People's War, 544
Peral (F) (*d.* 1937), Dávila's bodyguard, 638, 641
Perea Capulino, Maj. Juan (later Col.) (R and A), 492, 889; army posts, 677, 835, 868
Pereda, Prudencia, Sp. novelist, 609n1
Pérez, Antonio (S), UGT, 902 and n
Pérez, Jaime, gravedigger, Blesa, execution, 515
Pérez, Col. García Argüelles (*d.* 1937), 236n3
Pérez de Ayala, Ramón (1880–1962), Amb. and writer, 30, 500–501
Pérez Farras, Maj. Enrique (R), 233, 316
Pérez Garmendia, Maj. Augusto (*b.* 1899) (R), 377
Pérez Gazzolo, Maj. José (1892–1939) (R), 907n1
Pérez Madrigal, Joaquín (N), Rad. socialist, radio programme, 858n1
Pérez Salas, Maj. Jesús (R), 328, 547
Pérez Salas, Maj. Joaquín (1886–1939) (R), 328, 889
Pérez Solís, Capt. Oscar (C then F) (N), 118; communist past, 385
Pérez Tabernero, Antonio (N), bullbreeder, 421
Perpignan, 364, 456, 669n5, 846
Perth, Earl of (Sir Eric Drummond) (1876–1951), relations with fascist Italy, 354 and n4, 822, 826, 829, 856, 873; and Eden's resignation, 797
Perucho, Arturo (R), director of *Treball*, 701n
Pestaña, Angel (1881–1937) (A), in Moscow, 67, 116; syndicalist, 69, 435; splinter party, 74
Pétain, Marshal Henri-Philippe (1856–1951), Fr. Amb. in Burgos, 919 and n2
Peterson, Maurice (1889–1952), Br. Amb. Madrid (1939–40), 919n2
Le Petit Parisien, interview with Unamuno, 501n2
'Petrov', *see* Meretzkov
Philby, Kim (*b.* 1912), Br. journalist, 722n1
Philippines, 27, 52, 415
Phipps, Sir Eric (1875–1945), Br. Amb. Paris, 738n2, 857n; and French mobilization, 805n4
Photographic reconnaissance, by G. aircraft, 470
Pi y Margall, Francisco (1824–1901), Pres. of the Federal Republic, 60
Pi y Súñer, Carlos (1888–1971), Cat. politician, 672n2, 770, 771, 773–4
Piatakov, Georgi (1890–1937), trial, 523n4
Piazzoni, Col. Sandro, It. officer, 614, 717, 856
Picasso, Gen., 24–5
Picasso, Pablo (1881–1973), painter, 190; director of the Prado, 628n1; 'Guernica', 628
Picelli, Guido (*d.* 1937), It. vol. in IB, 493
Pich y Pon, Juan (*d.* 1937), Rad. min., 250n2, 658n4
Picoqueta (Guipúzcoa), 377
Pieck, Wilhelm (1876–1960), Sec. Gen. of G. communists, 338n4
Piedras Menares, agricultural collective, 562
'Pierre', Caucasian com., 120
Pierre Bracket Battalion, 968
Pilots, 365 and n3, 575–6: British, 365n3, 366; French, 349, 350, 352n1, 365–6; German, 355, 359, 366, 371, 390, 400, 624 and n1, 625, 626, 730; Italian, 352n4, 366, 371, 382–3, 400 and n5, 568, 583, 594, 807; hours flown in Spain, 979; Russian, 440, 445, 446, 468n3, 483n1, 548, 574, 678; Spanish (N), 331 and n3, 370n2, 568n5, 594, 688n1, 756, 802 and n1; (R), 331 and n3, 548, 678, 733; (US), 365n3, 366, 575–6, 576n1
Pina (Saragossa), 316, 318, 319, 800; Durruti and, 316, 318, 800
Pindoque Bridge (Jarama), 589
Piñeiroa Plaza, Capt. Rosendo, 237
Piniés, Vicente de (1875–1943), Con. politician, 558
Pinilla Barceló, Col. Antonio (*d.* 1936) (N), 236, 309, 384
Pinell, 854–5
Pingarron, 587, 592, 595
Pittman, Senator Key (1892–1940), 575, 825
Pius XI, Pope (Achilles Ratti) (1922–1939), 29, 52, 54, 697; and Segura, 55 and n1; aims, 108; condemns Sp. republic, 398–9, 511; and a separate Basque peace, 681, 682; and murdered priests, 695

Pius XII, Pope, *see* Pacelli, Cardinal
Plá y Deniel, Dr Enrique (1876–1968), Bishop of Salamanca, at University meeting, 501, 502; use of word 'crusade', 501n4, 512
Plymouth, Ivor Earl of (1889–1943), Br. politician, 397n2, 444, 462–3, 629; and non-intervention, 566, 570, 737–8, 795; plan for withdrawal of volunteers, 796
Poblet monastery (Tarragona), 270, 277
Poland, 388, 451, 581, 911, 935, 945, 968
Police, the, 161, 233, 260, 263, 815, 861; armed, 550, 651, 776 and n3
Political prisoners, 143, 160; amnesties, 127, 130, 155, 160; in Model Prison, 404–5, 477 and n3, 708; in San Sebastián, 410; in Bilbao, 431n1, 540; in Málaga gaol, 585; numbers in communist gaols, 776; SIM torture chambers, 808; post-war numbers in prisons and concentration camps, 923
Pollard, Maj. Hugh (1887–1966), Br. writer, 204 and n3
Pollensa Bay, It. naval base, 397
Pollitt, Harry (1890–1960), Sec. Gen. Br. com. party, 391n2
Ponferrada (León), massacre of miners, 254
Ponte y Manso de Zúñiga, Gen. Miguel (1882–1952) (N), 165, 168, 240, 723; potential conspirator, 59, 99, 160, 240
Pontevedra, 253
Popular Front, French, 337, 943; English, 611n1
Popular Front, Spanish, 6, 123, 192, 517, 607n2, 890; and 1936 elections, 124, 153, 156, 157, 161–2, 178, 189; international policy, 153–4, 156; instrument of revolutionary socialism, 168; and military rising, 223, 241, 242, 252, 254; banning of its supporters in (N) Spain, 258, 284, (executions), 259, 260, 266; in (R) Spain, 275, 278, 293, 303, 307, 535, 783, 820, 851; search for Fifth Columnists, 437; and Madrid *junta*, 476; and POUM repression, 708
Popular Front Pact, 228
Popular Tribunals, 405, 672; condemn José Antonio, 500 and n
Porcuna (Jaén), 630–31
Poretsky, Ignace (Ignace Reiss) (*d.* 1937), Ru. agent, NKVD chief, 450
Port Mahon (Minorca), submarine base, 242, 254, 884
Portago, Marqués de, emissary to Germany, 342n5; private agent in London, 505
Portela, Luis (C), 118n2
Portela Valladares, Manuel (1868–1952), prime minister (1936), 240; caretaker government, 149, 150, 151, 159; 'Centre party', 153, 155, 156; and a 'state of war', 159–60; flight from power, 160
Portillo, Luis (R), *Unamuno's Last Lecture*, 503n
Portocristo, Majorca, 381
Portugal, 100, 117n4, 285, 768; migrant workers in Spain, 81; use of airfield by rebel pilot, 254; pro-nationalist, 333, 360n2, 444; role in Spanish war, 359–60, 371, 375; Left international revulsion, 360n4; and non-intervention, 388, 390, 439; breaks off diplomatic relations with Spain, 462; and Anglo French mediation plan, 570, 571, 576–7; accepts international observers, 580–81, 581n1; and naval patrol, 736; Non-Aggression Pact with Spain, 919; volunteers 'Viriatos', 979n5
Pound, Ezra (1888–1972), US poet, 347n3
Pozas Perea, Col. Gabriel (1880–1937) (N), 278, 405; ADC to Mola, 327
Pozas Perea, Gen. Sebastián (*b.* 1876) (R), 230 and n1, 521, 889; dir. gen. civil guard, 159, 219, 327; and military rising, 223–4, 250; civil war campaigns, 327, 437, 446–7, 475–6, 588, 672, 677, 688, 722–3, 728; rivalry with Miaja, 593; *d.* in exile, 950
Pozoblanco (Córdoba), 255, 257, 912
Pozuelo de Alarcón (Madrid), 493
Prada Vaquero, Col. Adolfo (*d.* 1962) (R), civil war campaigns, 492, 718, 728–9, 779; shoots escapees, 729 and n3; flight, 731; on the war, 787; and communism, 886, 905; to negotiate surrender, 913
Pradera, Víctor (1873–1936), Car. theoretician, 59, 97, 98, 151; murder, 410, 635, 930; (posth.) entitlement, 948
Prados, Pedro (C), Naval chief of staff (1938), 814
Prat de Llobregat (Barcelona), receipt of Fr. aircraft, 364
Pravda, 387–8, 393, 395, 822, 831
Press, and Spanish war, 22, 347–8, 470n2, 754; use of threats under Franco, 504n2; republican advantages, 506; glorification of El Caudillo, 645, 858; Portuguese, 373n

Press Law, 761–2
Pretel, Felipe (Soc), political commissar, 435, 522; and UGT, 782n5, 810n1
Prieto, Horacio (A), 122, 181, 471 and n3, 522, 784; pro-CNT/UGT merger, 812 and n4, 865; and peace negotiations, 813
Prieto, Lorenzo, 471n3
Prieto, Luis, financial attaché in London, 813n2
Prieto y Tuero, Indalecio (1883–1962) (Soc), 9, 127, 154, 301, 492n1, 945; political career, 38–9, 41, 162, 406, 410–11, 475; character, 41, 109, 194; and Asturias revolution, 133; exile in France, 133n1, 154; dispute with Largo Caballero, 164, 403, 775; and socialist party, 164, 170, 200–201; impeaches the President, 172; speech at Cuenca, 178; threatened assault, 178 and n2; offered premiership, 179; disregard of great depression, 186; and the peseta, 186–7; achievements, 188; arms traffic, 194, 781–2; and military rising, 209, 229–30, 237; possible prime minister, 402–403, 665; and removal of Spain's gold reserves, 448 and n4; and communists, 535, 646, 664 and n2, 665, 774–7; on War Council, 546; and the navy, 549; and Azaña's safety, 661; relationship with Negrín, 664, 665, 666 and n2, 668, 670, 679, 686, 704, 804, 813; and *Deutschland* incident, 686; orders defence of Bilbao, 691–2; and Nin's case, 708–9; Brunete offensive, 711; and *Leipzig* affair, 735; hopes for the Falange, 751 and n2; defeatism, 770, 809, 812; establishes SIM, 776; and defence of Teruel, 792, 794, 811; proposals on aerial bombardment, 794; unpopularity, 810, 811; explanation on leaving the government, 813–14; later life, 814 and n2; dissuades Azaña from resigning, 814; and a compromise peace, 819; on losses of UK shipping, 828–9; oratory, 931; *d.* in Mexico, 950
Prim, Gen. Juan (1814–70), expels Isabella, 14
Primero de Mayo (Arg. ship), 275n1
Primo de Rivera y Orbaneja, Gen. Miguel (1870–1930), dictator (1923–30), 7, 40, 41, 43, 67–8, 76, 79, 92, 174, 188, 191; personality, 27–9, 113; lacks army support, 29, 92; retirement and death, 29; intellectual opponents, 35–6; and Catalan politics, 44–6, 96; criticized by Franco, 140; effect of great depression, 186
Primo de Rivera y Sáenz de Heredia, Fernando (1908–36) (F), execution, 404, 633
Primo de Rivera y Sáenz de Heredia, José Antonio (1903–36) (F), founder of the Falange, 113–14, 152, 199, 419, 633–4; imprisonment, 11, 169, 177, 178, 251, 254, 284, 498; character, 112–13, 114; amalgamation with JONS, 114 and n3, 115; disapproval of violence, 115 and n1, 152, 162; controversy with Ledesma Ramos, 152 and n1; and Franco, 152n1, 167; and a military *coup*, 152n1; and Calvo Sotelo, 152n2; and 1936 elections, 153, 155, 159; failure to control his followers, 162–3, and syndicalism, 163n4; advised to leave Spain, 168–9; and military rising, 177, 184, 209; open letter to soldiers, 178; and Mola, 183, 209; in Alicante gaol, 183, 251, 498; desire for his freedom, 420, 425; trial, condemnation and execution, 498–500, 930; becomes a cult, 635, 859; (posth.) entitlement, 948
Primo de Rivera y Sáenz de Heredia, Miguel (1904–64), 251, 499; entitlement, 948
Primo de Rivera y Sáenz de Heredia, Pilar (F) (*b.* 1907), 640, 642, 749n, 750
Prisoners, exchange of, 263, 496, 513; executions (N and R), 321 and n3, 379, 513–16; prison population, 515–16, 858–9; in Spanish embassies, 786
Pritchett, V. S. (later Sir Victor) (*b.* 1900), 347n3
Profintern (com. trade union federation), 117, 338, 360–61
Prokofiev, G. (R) Ru. (pilot) officer, 446
Proskinov, I. (R) Ru. naval officer, 549n3
Protestants, 50, 51, 269n3, 697
Proudhon, Pierre-Joseph (1809–65), Spanish translation, 60, 62
Public Order, Law of (1933), 159 and n1
Puche, Prof. José (R), Rector of University of Valencia, 837
Puente, Dr Isaac (*d.* 1936), 126, 181, 820; execution, 266
Puente, Mariano, 653n1
Puente Genil (Córdoba), 307
Puente Baamonde, Maj. Ricardo de la (1895–1936) (R), Franco approves his death, 231, 267
Puerto del Escudo cemetery, 978n2
Puigcerdá (Gerona) collective, 653 and n1

Puigdendolas Ponce de León, Col. Ildefonso (R), 373, 687
Pujol, Juan (M), journalist, 335n4, 425, 760
Punch, 348
Putz, Col. Joseph (*d.* 1945), Fr. vol. in IB, 692; death in Resistance, 955
Pyrenees, 30, 86, 97, 129; falangist shootings, 287n3; passage of volunteers, 461; and arms for the republic, 745, 823

Quaglierini, Ettore (C), 340
Quaker International Commission for the Assistance of Child Refugees, 863, 893
Queipo de Llano y Serra, Gen. Gonzalo (1875–1951) (N), 43, 94, 221, 255, 371, 411; Seville *coup de main*, 221–3, 226, 241, 251, 259n2; use of his voice, 223 and n1, 280, 384; behaviour as ruler of Andalusia, 283, 285–6, 288, 422, 753–4; area of command, 326; relations with Germany, 394; salutes monarchist flag, 414–15; the 'new Giralda', 416; and *junta* meeting, 421n2; discredited as single commander, 422; and Franco, 426, 640; secret intelligence work, 505 and n; *Plato único*, 518; use of radio, 520, 753 and n3, 754, 755, 938; and Army of the South, 582, 583, 587–8, 632, 753, 861; member new national council, 750; exclusion from cabinet, 753, 948n2; agrarian reforms, 754; ennoblement, 948
Quijorna (Madrid), 712, 713, 715
Quiñones de León, José María (1873–1957), Sp. Amb. to Paris, 441
Quintanar, Marqués de (Fernando Gallego de Chaves) (M), 59
Quintanilla, Eleuterio (1886–1966) (A), on Russian Revolution, 67n3
Quintanilla, Luis (R), artist at siege of Alcázar, 385
Quinto, 725
Quiroga, Domingo (R), 252n2, 265n8

Rabassaires (vine-growers' association) 82, 131, 135, 250 and n2, 300, 554; and Catalan government, 524, 652n4, 658, 672n2
Rabaté, Octave (1899–1964), Fr. com., in Spain, 120, 121
Rachewsky, Capt. White Russian, 494n2
Rada, Pablo, mechanic, hooligan, 59n5
Rada y Peral, Col. (later Gen.) Ricardo de (1885–1956) (N), 116, 129 and n1, 588, 841
Radek, Karl (1885–1939), trial, 523n4
Radicals, Spanish, 19 and n2, 34, 45n1, 165, 189; characteristics, 16–17, 34–5; youth movement (young barbarians), 34n1; and anarchism, 61, 64–5; elections (1931), 72, (1933), 107, 125, (1936), 135, 156, 162; ruined by *Straperlo* (Nombela) scandal, 148, 149n1; Socialists, 134n2
Rajk, Laszlo (1909–49), Hung. com. vol. in IB, execution, 953
Rakosi Battalion, 953, 954, 969
Ramirez de Togores, Capt. Vicente (R), naval officer, 449, 549
Ramishvili, S. ('Juan García'), Ru. naval officer, 549n3
Ramón y Cajal, Santiago (1852–1934), physiologist, 666, 928
Ramos, Enrique (LR), Rep. min, 179n1
Ramos, José, and republican refugees, 878
Ramos, Joaquín (C), 118n2
Ramos, José María (N), at Salamanca University meeting, 502n
Ramuelson, Bert (C), Polish-Canadian vol. in IB, 955n4
Rathbone, Dr Eleanor (1872–1946), Br. politician, 398
Rau, Henrich (1899–1961), G. commander in IB, 878; position in Germany, 954
Ravetto, Pietro (C), It. vol. in IB, 341n1
Read, Herbert (1889–1968), Eng. writer, 347n3
Rebière, Pierre (C), Fr. organizer of IB, 479; death in Resistance, 955
Reconquista (newspaper), 838 and n2
Red Banner Army, 952
Red Cross, International, branch offices, 496. *See also* Junod, Dr Marcel
Red Guard, 392
Red Lions, 268
Redondo y Ortega, Andrés (F), 263, 420 and n3
Redondo y Ortega, Onésimo (1905–36) (F), 315; nazi admirer, 111; *Libertad* programme, 111–12; and JONS, 111, 261; and the church in Spain, 112; Valladolid organization, 177n2, 315; release from prison, 240, 261, 315; organizer of atrocities in Castile, 261, 263; death in ambush, 284, 322, 506, 930; (posth.) ennoblement, 948
Refugees, republican, 373, 380, 877 and

Refugees – *contd*
n3, 878; in Madrid foreign embassies, 293, 395n1; camp conditions, 878–9; European aid, 879; fate of, 920–22
Regler, Gustav (*b.* 1898), IB Commissar, 482, 488n3, 688n1
Regulares, 140, 142, 143, 371 and n2, 759; in Morocco, 173, 205, 212; in Spain, 231, 243, 307; in civil war, 326, 371, 400
Reichenau, Gen. Walther v. (1884–1942), G. (nazi) army commander, on lessons from Spanish war, 829 and n2
Reinosa (Santander), arms factory, 330, 616, 718
Religious order and communities, 58 and n2, 75–6, 201, 286; desecration of nunneries, 10, 19; limited growth, 21, 35; numbers in 1930s, 49; capital wealth, 52; schools, 52, 54; and working classes, 52–4; held responsible for catastrophes, 54; forbidden to teach, 106; and nationalist atrocities, 263n1; suspicions of their secrecy, 269; closure of convents, 270n1; sadistic murder of inhabitants, 272
'Renn, Ludwig' (Arnold Vieth v. Golssenen) (*b.* 1889), IB leader, 482, 600, 698, 878; *Krieg*, 482
Renovación Española (M), 107, 130, 151, 210
Republic, Spanish, First (1931), 14, 60, 268, 500
Republic, Spanish, Second, crisis of June 1936, 5 ff.; emergence, 24, 29–33; first cabinet, 34–5, 36–42; anticlericalism, 33, 90, 102 and n, 108; and freemasonry, 42 and n2; Catalonian problem, 43–8; attacked by Segura, 47–8; and religious freedom, 55, 862; riots of May 1931, 57, 72; plots against, 58–9, 96, 98–100; bans the Internationals, 61; and anarchism, 64–5, 66n2, 69, 72, 73; 1931 elections, 72–3; and 1931 Constitution, 74–7; governmental crises, 76, 646–8, 844–5; and agrarian reform, 83–5, 101 and n; fear of separatism, 90; events leading to collapse, 94, 104–7, 109, 193–5, 195n1; clerical budget (1931/32), 102n; educational projects, 102; legislative achievements, 106; communist opposition, 120; composition after 1933 elections, 125; 'suicidal egoism' of employers, 126 and n1; challenged by smaller groups, 129; dominated by revolutionary mentality, 146, 163; decline in 1936, 163–4; inability to maintain order, 168, 208; and 1936 military rising, 175, 219–21, 225–6, 247; hostility of international financiers, 186, 187; run on the peseta, 186–7; industrial production, 187–8, 816; unemployment, 189–90; decision to arm the masses, 230–31; and foreign affairs, 334; removal of government to Valencia, 475, 522; failure to reprieve José Antonio, 499, 500; communist infiltration, 523; and Moroccan affairs, 579; and fall of Málaga, 587; and Basque campaign, 720; Negrín becomes prime minister, 677, 701, 704, 844; anger at Basque peace negotiations, 681 and n2; nearly provokes world war, 686; unbreakable tie with Stalin, 704, 708; peace negotiations, 909–10; meeting of War Council, 812 and n1; cabinet changes, 814–16; death sentences for espionage, 844; and British volunteer plan, 847; and Catalonian disaster, 872 and n2, 873; moves northward, 870; votes to continue the war, 880; reassembles in Toulouse, 884; moves to Elda, 892; worth of gold reserves, 1936, 974 and n1; total number of foreigners fighting for, 982 and n2
República (N. cruiser renamed *Navarra*), 331 and n4, 936
Republican Action, Azaña's party, 37, 72, 107, 134n2
Republican Arms Purchase Commission, 407
Republican Front, 154
Republican Left Party, 5n4, 6n2, 134 and n2, 161, 407 and n2; 1936 election results, 156, 162n2
Republican Spain, start of revolution, 247, 268; excesses under, 248, 257, 268–9, 274, 279; area of control after rising, 255 (map), 256; attitude to the church, 269, 270–75, 298, 511; protection of art collections, 269–70, 486 and n2; urban *checas*, 274–5, 276; responsibility for atrocities, 278–80; behaviour of middle classes, 290; communist influence, 291–2, 393–4, 454n3; economic position, 293, 296, 332–3, 648, 863–5; state intervention, 296; control of credit, 297; northern

provinces, 310–11, 539, 612; losses to nationalists, 326; foreign aid, 333, 337–8, 368, 387–9, 440–45, 468, 566; use of blockade, 390; exchanges ambassadors with USSR, 392–3; possession of monetary gold, 416; slowness in creating a new state, 428, 438; disillusioned with England, 440; USSR personnel, 446–7; volunteer scheme, 452; anarchists join the government, 471–2; reorganizes the ministry, 471–2; government decay, 478; conditions (1936/37), 521, 749; social improvements, 535–7; marriage, 537, 539; prison conditions, 537–8; character of its justice, 537–8; nationalist blockade, 559, 566–7, 661; unbreakable tie with Stalin, 704, 708; military intelligence, 759, 776; nationalist vilification, 760; re-establishment of religion, 774; press censorship, 785; ideological division, 817; virtual end of foreign aid, 825–6; ministry of war appointments, 835–6; mass media propaganda, 858; loss of hydro-electric power, 864–5; changes in personal status, 866; foreign gifts, 893; proposes *junta* of liquidation, 898; new national council, 902, 909, 911, 912; radio manifesto against Negrín, 902–903; in a state of chaos, 905, 932–4; clamour for expatriation, 914; transport of treasure to US, 921 and n2, 974; nationalist repression and executions, 923–6; fate of leaders, 926, 949; war losses, 927; disaster of communist alliance, 934; financial payment for the war, 938; influence of foreign men and equipment, 940; expectation of Anglo/US support, 951; expenditure on foreign intervention, 974–5, 976; debt to USSR, 974 and nn1, 2, 975; USSR aid in aerial equipment, 980–81, 981n1; other aid, 981; total amount of foreign intervention, 985

Republican Union Party, 6n2, 8, 125, 156, 161, 162n2, 179n, 215, 292n2

Requetés, 129, 130, 167, 223, 239, 261–2, 313, 315 and n, 319, 432, 508, 637, 980

Restoration, the (1874), 25, 61

Reus (Tarragona), 660

Reverter, Andreu, *Generalidad* chief of police, 525 and n1

Revilla, FR (R), killed in Burgos, 263n1

Revue des Deux Mondes, 681n2

Rey, David (*d.* 1939) (P), 866n1

Rey d'Harcourt, Col. Domingo (*d.* 1939) (N), and Trueta's innovations, 551; defence of Teruel, 789, 791; execution, 792 and n1, 881

Reyes, Lt. Anastasio de los (1882–1936), funeral riots, 206

Reyes González, Maj. Alfonso (C), air force chief, 658

Reyes, Dr Saturnino (*d.* 1936), 264n2

Rhein, Marc (*d.* 1937), s. of Rafael Abramovich, mysterious death, 706

Ribarroya (Soria), 855

Ribbentrop, Joachim v. (1893–1946), G. foreign min. (1939–45), 356, 359, 396, 580, 629; hatred of Britain, 354, 396n5; in London, 734; and non-intervention, 805–6, 736; dismisses v. Stohrer, 806n1, 951

Richagov, Maj. (R), Ru. officer at Algete, 471n1

Richthofen, Col. Wolfgang v. (later Gen.) (1895–1945), chief of staff and then commander of Condor Legion, 469; and Guernica, 625, 626–7; Second World War service, 951

Rickword, Edgell, Eng. poet, 796

Rico, Juanita (Soc), murder, 115

Rico, Pedro (Rep. Union), major of Madrid, 478n1

Rico Avello, Manuel (*d.* 1936), min. of interior (1935), death, 404

Ridruejo, Dionisio (1912–75) (F), 195n2, 761n2, 749 and n; Falange chief, 420, 640, 749; and FET, 750; director general propaganda, 874

Rieber, Capt. Thorkild (*b.* 1882), US oil magnate, 417n2

Right Book Club, 346

Río, José del (UR), 902, 912

Rio Tinto Co., 288, 335, 577n3; delivery of copper to Germany, 418, 462, 519, 577

Rioja (river), murder of Franciscans near, 263n1, 286

Ríos Urruti, Fernando de los (1879–1949) (Soc), Sp. Amb. Washington, 46, 434; cabinet posts, 36, 38, 42n2, 102–3, 128, 389 and n3; in Russia, 40n1, 116; and French arms transaction, 344, 349, 350, and n2, 352; receives money from Bank of Spain, 975n

Riquelma, General José (*d.* 1972), 246

Rivas Cherif, Cipriano (1891–1967), consul-general in Geneva, 37, 350n2

Roasio, Antonio (*b.* 1902) (C), It. commissar in IB, 482n3

Roatta, Col. (later Gen.) Mario ('Mancini') (1887–1968), It. commander in Spain (N), 369, 394, 583n1, 721, 604; emissary to Franco, 568; campaigns, 583, 584, 594n2, 596 and n, 599–602; and a new Spanish state, 643, 644; trial as war criminal, 952

Roberts, Capt. W. H., Br. sailor, 622

Robeson, Paul (1898–1974), U S singer, 792n2

Robles, José (*d.* 1937) (R), 607

Roca, José (F), Fifth Columnists, 702 and n; execution, 865

Roces Cortina, Avelino (R), in Asturias, 731

Rodezno, Conde de (Tomás Domínguez Arévalo) (1883–1952) (Car), 97, 98, 99, 129–30, 202, 205, 634; and union with falangists, 632n2, 633, 637, 640 and n1; member new national council, 750, 751, 752, 948; and education, 859

Rodimstev, Marshal Alexander ('Pablito') (*b.* 1905), 501 and n1, 588n, 603, 953

Rodríguez, Benigno (C), 846

Rodríguez, Enrique (P), 477n1

Rodríguez, Francisco (Soc), civil governor of Málaga, 307

Rodríguez, Col. Joaquín (*b.* 1878) (R), 901

Rodríguez, Melchor (A), Director of Prisons, 477, 538, 652, 904

Rodríguez Aguado, Lt. Antonio (N), spy, 505n

Rodríguez del Barrio, Gen. Angel (*d.* 1936) (N), 167–8, 173; death, 174

Rodríguez de León, civil governor of Córdoba (1936), 223

Rodríguez-Medel, Maj. José (*d.* 1936) (R), murder in Pamplona, 239

Rodríguez Salas, Eusebio (C), commissar of police, Barcelona 1937, 525, 654, 656

Rodríguez Sierra, Capt. Eugenio (R), and U M R A, 166

Rodríguez Tarduchy, Emilio (M), and U M E, 166n1

Rodríguez Vázquez, Mariano (A), succeeds Prieto, 522

Rodríguez Vega, José (*b.* 1902), sec. of U G T 1937, 812n4, 902n, 923

Rohstoffe-und-Waren-Einkaufgesellschaft (R O W A K), 694, 737; and aid to Spain, 357 and n3, 359, 462, 519; Montana project, 765

Roig, Eleuterio, *FAIista*, 656

Rojas Feigenspán, Capt. Manuel (*b.* 1899) (N), atrocities, 104 and n2, 263

Rojo Lluch, Maj. (later Gen.) Vicente (1894–1966) (R), 409, 889; civil war campaigns, 320, 710–11, 800, 835, 868, 871, 872, 881; chief of staff, Madrid, 476, 480n1, 482, 545, 598–9, 679, 710, 779, 836; alleged member of U M E, 663n2; death in Spain, 950

Rokossovsky, Marshal Konstantin (1896–1968), 446; espionage task, 447n2, 759 and n3; eminence in Russia, 953

Roldán, Col. Jacobo (*b.* 1881) (N), 235

Roldán, Cortada (*d.* 1937) (C), 74, 653–4

Rolland, Romain (1866–1944), Fr. writer, 145, 341

Romanones, Conde (Alvaro de Figueroa y Torres) (1863–1950), 21, 26n1, 563

Rome, 51, 338, 369; religious/fascist capital, 11; centre of Carlist conspiracy, 130; Spanish mission, 341, 342

Romerales Quinto, Gen. Manuel (1875–1936) (R), 205, 215–16; surrender and assassination, 216, 224 266

Romero, Col. Carlos (R), 480, 834, 980n4

Romero Bassart, Col. Luis (*b.* 1893) (R), 224 and n4, 307, 327, 901n3

Romero Bassart, Col. Pedro (*b.* 1881) (N), defence of Alcázar, 325, 327

Romilly, Esmond (1918–41), Eng. vol. in I B, 459 and n2, 489

Romilly, Giles (1916–67), Eng. vol. in I B, 482, 490n1, 710; death in Battle of Britain, 490n1

Romualdo de Toledo (N), and *junta técnica*, 425n4

Ronda (Málaga), 274, 307, 411, 582, 585

Roosevelt, Mrs Eleanor (1884–1962), 363–6

Roosevelt, Franklin D. (1882–1945), 362, 363n1, 570, 576; and aid for Spain, 576 and n3, 825; fear of catholic vote, 698, 825n1, 826n1; general peace conference plan, 796–7; on arms embargo, 875, 919

Rosa, Fernando de la (*d.* 1936), It. soc. revolutionary, 201 and n1, 837; death, 411

Rosales, Luis (*b.* 1910) (F), poet, 266; press officer, 504n2

Rosebery, Lord, 621

Rosenberg, Marcel, Ru. Amb. to Spain

(1936–37), 393, 440, 444; reproved by Largo Caballero, 533–4; murdered in Russia, 534
Rosselli, Carlo, It. vol. in Spain, 366–7, 381, 452, 453
Rossi, Col. Silvio (*b.* 1892), It. officer in Spain, 583, 596, 601; returns to Italy, 604
Rouret Calloi, Martí, Catalan chief of police, 525
Rovira Canales, José (P), POUM commander, 547, 677; arrest, 703–4
Rovira Pacheco, Maj. Esteban (R), 250n2, 658
Roy, M. N. (1887–1954), Indian commander in Spain, 117–18
Royal Calpe Hunt, Gibraltar, 685n4
Rubielos de Mora (Teruel), 793, 832
Rubio Saracibar (*b.* 1881), Col., 261
Rudilla (Teruel), 798
Rufilanches, Luis, execution, 266
'Rügen Winter' exercise, 469 and n3, 470
Ruisenada, Conde de, shipowner, 951n
Ruiz, Lt Antonio (R), naval officer, 901
Ruiz, Juan (soc.), 310
Ruiz, Pablo (A), *FAIista*, 656n1
Ruiz Albeniz, Víctor (N), 'Franquistas', 645
Ruiz de Alda, Julio (1897–1936) (F), 114, 284; execution, 404, 633
Ruiz Alonso, Ramón (N), CEDA politician, and arrest of Lorca, 267, 645
Ruiz Carnero, Prof. Constantino (*d.* 1936), 264n
Ruiz Cavina, Julián, husband of La Pasionaria, 775–6
Ruiz Fornells Regueiro, Gen. Enrique (*b.* 1868) (R), adviser to Azaña, 92
Ruiz Fornells Ruiz, Col. Ramón (*b.* 1901) (R), and Casado's conspiracy, 898–9
Ruiz-Funes, Mariano (*b.* 1889) (R), Rep. minister of agriculture (1936), 169, 170, 179n, 407n2
Ruiz Jiménez, Joaquín (*b.* 1912) (N), Catholic youth leader, 209, 277
Ruiz Rebollo, Ramón (Soc), 720
Ruiz Vilaplana, Antonio (N then R), 95n2, 159n2
Runciman, Walter Lord (1870–1949), Br. politician, 619 and n1
Rural Lease Bill, 106
Russia, 10, 111, 116; secret police, 119; reputation in Spain, 123–4; relations with Hitler, 153, 394, 746–7; attraction for proletariat, 302; Red Army, 323, 435, 452–3, 591; foreign policy, 338–9; and France's entry into civil war, 340n1; and aid for Spain, 340, 388, 440–46, 449 and n2, 450, 823, 852, 937, 940, 943; Popular Front, 341; causes international alarm, 346; and non-intervention, 387–8, 391; exchanges ambassadors with Spain, 392 and n4, 393; collapse of investments, 417; diplomatic manoeuvres, 444; nature of armaments, 445 and nn3, 6, 446 and n1; personnel in Spain, 446–7; receives payment in gold, 448 and n1, 449–50; retention of Spanish officials, 450; refugee communists in Spain, 455; and Madrid offensive, 471 and n1, 483, 590, 940; aerial combats, 483 and n1, 590, 594; use of armour piercing shells, 493 and n; Franco/British mediation plan, 570, 571, 580–81; and battle of Jarama, 593, 594; supports Spanish communism, 646; purge of Soviet army, 662n2, 703; and naval patrol plan, 734; policy towards Spanish war, 746–7, 941; air mission to Spain, 779; reduces its mission, 831, 851n3, 852, (exits from Spain), 904; acceptance of refugees, 879, 921; draws false conclusions from Spanish war, 945; fate of generals who served in Spain, 952–3, 954; estimated republican debt, 974 and nn1, 2; aid to republican Spain, 980–82; manpower strength there, 981; additional gifts, 984
Russians, white, 470, 768

Saavedra Lamas, Dr Carlos, at Geneva, 439–40
Sabater, Enrique, 10n1
Sabater, Francisco ('El Quico') (1915–60), 801n
Saborit Colomer, Andrés (Soc), 128
Sacanell Lázaro, Col. Enrique (*b.* 1896), 167
Sackville-West, Edward (1901–65), 347n3
Sackville-West, Victoria (1892–1962), 347n3
Sáenz de Buruaga y Polanco, Col. Eduardo (1893–1964) (N), 216–17, 231; 1893–1964 campaigns, 489, 493, 588, 589, 592, 714–15, 726
Sáenz de Heredia, Andrés (*d.* 1936), 172
Sáenz de Tejada, painter, 858
Sagasta, Práxedes Mateo (1825–1903), liberal, 20
Sagnier, Marcel, Fr. vol. in IB, 838n2
Sagunto (Valencia), 305, 831, 915

St Cyprien, refugee camp, 878
St Dominic de Guzmán, 10n3
St Dominic of Silos, 10 and n3
Saint-Exupéry, Antoine de (1900–40), Fr. poet, 303; *Terre des Hommes*, 865 and n3
St Jean de Luz, 202, 496; refuge of diplomatic corps, 346, 368, 391, 480, 488, 681; British fishing vessels, 619, 621–2
St Oswald, Lord (Roland Winn) (*b.* 1916), 40n2; and phrase 'Fifth Column', 470n2
St Teresa of Avila (1515–82), 287, 320–21; sacred relic, 586–7
St Thomas Aquinas (*c.* 1227–1274), and rebellion, 309
St Thomas of Villanueva, College of (Valencia), pillaged, 242
Sáinz, José (F), 420n3
Sáinz Rodríguez, Pedro de (*b.* 1897) (N), 59, 99, 238, 352; oath of allegiance, 753; 'Plan 38' educational reform, 762, 859
Saklatvala Battalion, 591
Sala, Victorio (P), 702n
Salamanca, 240, 263, 496, 498, 506; 'Day of the Race' ceremony, 501–2; Franco's headquarters in Bishop's palace, 501, 504, 632, 634, 717; centre of power, 504–5; falangists, 636, 637–8, 750; press, 645; radio station, 858n1
Salas Larrazábal, Capt. (later Gen.) Angel, 282, 487n2; ace-pilot (N), 568n5, 756
Salazar (Antonio de Oliveira Salazar) (1889–1970), prime minister of Portugal (1930), 359, 360, 375, 396, 979n5; destruction of mutinous warships, 396n3
Salazar Alonso, Rafael (1895–1936), Rad. politician, 130, 131; in *straperlo* scandal, 148; execution, 500n1
Salcedo Molinuevo, Gen. Enrique (1871–1936) (R), 252; execution, 266
Sales, Ramón (*d.* 1936), *pistolero*, 274
Salgado, Manuel (A), 488n2, 887
Saliquet Zumeta, Gen. Andrés (1887–1959) (N), 168, 240; member Burgos *junta*, 282, 421n2; campaigns, 711, 758, 931; dropped by Franco, 948n2; entitlement, 948
Sallent (Barcelona), 78; state seizure of salt mines, 671
Salvador Carreras, Amós (L R), 161
Salvochea, Fermín (1842–1907) (A), 61
Sama (Oviedo), 138, 139, 142, 145, 310
Samblancat, Angel (1885–1963) (R), 298–9, 527, 701
Samper Ibáñez, Ricardo (1881–1938) (Rad), succeeds Lerroux, 130, 133, 134
San Andrés, Miguel (L R), 902
San Cugat del Vallés (Barcelona), 862
San Fermín, 203
San Fernando de Henares (Madrid), 477
San Ildefonso, 688
San José, FR Román de, murder, 512n7
San Martín de Valdeiglesias (Madrid), 432
San Martín de la Vega (Madrid), 589, 595
San Mateo, agricultural collective (Castellon), 557
San Miguel de los Reyes (Valencia), release of convicts, 326–7
San Platón copper mines (Huelva), 335
San Sebastián, revolutionary committee (1930), 30–31, 33, 119, 308; general strike, 73; military rising, 203, 237, 255; summer capital, 346n1, 377; sea and aerial bombardment, 377; nationalist conquest, 410, 517, 883; execution of anarchists, 410; Gran Casino, 237; Loyola Barracks, 237, 325; María Cristina Hotel, 237; Radio Station, 237
San Tomé (R. supply ship), 745
San Vicente hills, 375
Sánchez, 'Capt. Benito' (R), 324
Sánchez Albornoz, Claudio (*b.* 1893) (R), historian, Amb. in Lisbon, 360
Sánchez del Arco, Manuel (R), architect, 472n1
Sánchez Barcaiztegui (R. destroyer), 226–7, 797
Sánchez González, Col. Juan Bautista (1893–1957) (N), Navarrese leader, 717
Sánchez Guerra, Rafael (1897–1964), Rep. politician, 28, 913
Sánchez Paredes, Col. Rafael (*b.* 1883) (C), USSR tank commander, 447, 837
Sánchez Requena, J., 902
Sánchez Roca, (A), imprisonment, 772
Sánchez Román y Gallifa, Felipe (1893–1956), Rep. politician, 228, 230n3
Sandys, Duncan (*b.* 1908), Con. politician, 822n2, 875
Sangroniz y Castro, José Antonio, Marqués de Desio (*b.* 1895), and Franco, 212, 214, 425 and n4, 504, 754; and Germany's mining rights, 767
Sania Ramel airfield, 217, 231
Sanjurjo, 795n2

Sanjurjo Sacanell, Gen. José (1872–1936) (N), 99, 112, 167, 936; *Africanista*, 28–9, 94, 98; *pronunciamiento* (1932), 98, 99–100, 121, 141, 221, 435; Carlist connection, 167, 175, 203; trial 100; subject of general amnesty, 127, 130; and military rising, 168, 199, 206, 218n4, 238, 254; and Mola's plan, 174, 175, 183, 202–3; to command in Burgos, 209; to be fetched from Lisbon, 254 and n2, 338; death in aircraft disaster, 254, 930; repercussions, 254–5; suggested reprieve (1932), 666, 821n2
Santa Creus monastery, 270
Santa Cruz, Juan José de (*d.* 1936), engineer, 264 n2
Santa Cruz de la Palma, 224n2, 275
Santa Eufemia, 912
Santa Magdalena, 843
Santa María de la Cabeza, monastery, 306, 630–31
Santa Olalla (Toledo), 411
Santaló, Miguel, Catalan deputy, 862
Santander, 540; and military rising, 236 and n3, 252, 255; falls to Franco, 236n3, 710, 717–20; socialist-communist youth executions, 278–9, 279n2; defence committees, 308, 310; political isolation, 380, 539; socialist domination, 539; army headquarters, 542, 615, 692; progress of (N) campaign, 718–20, 719 (map); conditions in the city, 719; evacuation, 719–21; surrender terms, 720, 721; Italian involvement, 720–21, 721–2; subsequent trials and executions, 721
Santiago, Mariano de, writer of Salamanca, 503
Santiago de Compostela, archbishopric, 513n2
Santoña (Santander), 720, 721
Santullano, Luis, cultural missions, 106
Sanz, Ricardo (A), *solidarios*, 316, 547, 677; survival in exile, 950
Sanz Bachiller, Mercedes (F), founder of 'Winter Help', 506–7, 750
Sanz del Río, Julián (1810–64), and Free Institute, 35
Sapina, Juan, dir. gen. mines, 724n1
Saragossa, Archbishop of, *see* Soldevila
Saragossa, 7, 31, 167, 237, 332 and n, 420, 653; population (1931), 31n1; great strike, 126; closure of Military Academy, 141–2; military rising, 168, 175, 225, 238 and n5, 250; annual anarchist conference, 180, 238n5, 471n3, 820; atrocities, 263, 284; casualties, 265; 'liberation' by nationalists, 295, 315, 317–19, 400, 612n4, 800; San Antonio monastery 978; Virgin of the Pilar, 319
Sardanola-Ripollet, 103
Sardegna (It. troopship), 604
Sardinia, 352n4, 363, 743
Sariñena (Huesca), 303
Sarrión (Teruel), 832
Satrústegui, Joaquín (M), 313n
Sayagües Prudencio (LR), director of SIM, 776
Sbert, Antonio María (Cat), 524, 527, 652n4, 672n2; return of public order, 771; and Negrín, 845
Scandinavians, in IB, 823, 853, 983; timidity before Hitler, 398
Schacht, E. (*d.* 1938), Ru. officer (pilot), 446, 468n3
Scheele, Maj. Alexander v. (N), G. officer, 357, 418
Schindler, Albert, G. vol. in IB, 490n2
Schmidt, Paul, 580
'Schneller, Maxim', alleged head of SIM 'Foreign Section', 809n1
Schuschnigg, Dr Kurt v. (*b.* 1897), interview with Hitler, 804 and n3
Schwendemann, Dr Karl (*b.* 1894), 390, 850 and n3
Scott, Representative Byron, US politician, 824
Second World War (1939–45), effect of its timing on Spain, 929; republican casualties, 949; disappearance of pro-nationalist Germans and Italians, 951; IB and, 955
Secondary Education Law (1938), 859
Seeckt, Colonel-General Hans v. (1866–1936), 469n2
Segnaire, Julien, Belg. mercenary with Malraux, 366 and n1
Segorbe (Castellón), 270n4
Segovia, 240, 749; republican offensive, 688–9; Russian support, 689 and n2; elevation of patron saint, 689n1
Segovia, Jaime (R), 556
Segre (river), 818, 869
Seguí, Salvador (Noi del Sucre) (A), murder, 66
Seguí Almuzara, Col. Juan (*b.* 1887), leader of Moroccan rising, 215–16; and its premature occurrence, 216–17; murder, 274
Segura y Sáenz, Cardinal Pedro (1880–1957), Abp. of Toledo, later of

Segura y Sáenz – *contd*
Seville, 47–8, 53, 55, 57, 287n1, 696n3; hatred of fascism, 48n; denounces *El Debate*, 53; in exile, 55 and n1; meeting with Gomá, 55n1; attacks the republic, 887; returns to Spain, 756–7
'Seisdedos' (A), 104
Sender, Ramón (*b.* 1902), Sp. writer, 77 and n, 468n2
Serge, Victor (1890–1947), 488n3
Serna, Víctor de la (1896–1958) (F), journalist, 636
Serós (Lérida), agricultural collective, 557
Serra, Col. Francisco (*b.* 1879), *junta técnica*, 425n4
Serra Bartolomé, Col. Moisés (1878–1936), 230; commander, Montaña Barracks, 244, 245
Serra Pamiés, Miguel (C), 672n2
Serrador Santés, Maj. Ricardo (*b.* 1877) (N), 100n5, 315
Serrano Poncela, Segundo (C), 488
Serrano Súñer, Ramón (*b.* 1901), CEDA politician, min. of the interior (1938), 753, 924; escapes from republican Spain, 381n3, 634n1; imprisonment, 633; hatred of republicans and France, 633; relations with Franco, 634, 642–3, 644, 932; membership of Falange, 634, 642–3 (FET), 750, 753; character, 634, 859; and a new nationalist state, 634–5, 637, 643; sec. gen. new F/C movement, 642; and a compromise peace, 682; powers as political leader, 749–50, 752, 948; and an end to the war, 803; church/regime relationship, 883–4; minister of public order, 883; reception by ex-comrades, 919
Serrano Súñer, Zita Polo de, CEDA deputy, 167
Serret, Mauro, and *junta técnica*, 425n4
Sert, José María (1876–1945), Catalan painter, 90, 439
Servicio de Emigración para Republicanos Españoles (SERE), and treasure funds, 921
Servicios de Información del Nordeste de España (SIFNE), 505n; merges with SIPM, 759n1
Servicio de Investigación Militar (SIM), 277n1, 451n2; communist domination, 669; private prisons, 669; becomes SIPM, 759n1; purpose and leadership, 776–7; degeneration into organ of torture, 777–8, 808; judicial counterpart, 778; Barcelona operations, 808; unearths Catalonia Falange, 808–9; Madrid agency, 809n1; powers over army, 861; ideological mixture of prisoners, 946
Servicio de Información y Policía Militar (SIPM), 759; merges with SIFNE, 759n1
Servicio Nacional de Reforma Económico Social de la Tierra (SNRET), 757–8
Servicio Nacional del Trigo (SNT), 757
Sesé, Antonio (*d.* 1937) (C), UGT member, 658n4; death, 659–60
Seseña (Toledo), battle of, 468 and n2
Seven Seas Spray (Br. ship), breaks Bilbao blockade, 622; and Basque refugees, 721
Sevilla, Col. the Duque de (Francisco María de Borbón y de la Torre) (*b.* 1882), 100n5; at battle of Málaga, 583, 585, 586
Seville, 100, 255, 349, 420; population (1931), 31n; Carlists, 97, 99, 283; Falange, 115, 174, 285, 506; anarchists, 119; military rising, 221; Queipo's *coup de main*, 221–3, 241, 251; working classes, 222, 259; massacres in Triana, 251–2; nationalist atrocities, 263, 924; casualties, 265 and n7; nationalist acquisitions, 326, 332 and n, 380, 583; Moroccan troops, 370–71; appearance of German pilots, 390; bombed by Russian aircraft, 468 and n3, 794; youth movements, 510; Hispano-Suiza factory, 758; Inglaterra Hotel, 222; Radio, 222, 223, 384, 753 and n3; San Fernando Plaza, 222; San Julián district, 252
Shaw, Fernando (R), receives money from Bank of Spain, 975n1
Sheean, Vincent 'Jimmy' (*b.* 1899), US journalist, 481, 855
Shehu, Mehmet (*b.* 1913), Alb. com. vol. in IB, 954
Sherover, Miles (*b.* 1896), financier, US purchasing agent, 825–6, 826n1; post-war prosperity, 955
Shinwell, Emmanuel (*b.* 1884), Eng. Lab. politician, 611
Shipping companies, created in UK by republican government, 813 and n2, 827, 914
Sierra de Albarracín, 255; de Caballs, 854; de Espadán, 832, 834, 841; de Galoche, 381; de Gredos, 409, 513–14, 777; Moreno, 630–31, 912; de Pandols, 843, 854; de Toro, 832

Siétamo, 316
Siglo Futura, 292n2
Sigüenza, 326, 435n3, 601
Silvestre, Gen. (Fernández), defeat at Annual, 24, 25, 94
Simon, Sir John (later Ld Simon) (1873–1954), Eng. Lib. politician, 619, 621
Sinclair, Sir Archibald (later Ld Thurso) (1890–1970), Eng. Lab. politician, 621
Sinclair Loutitt, Dr Kenneth, Eng. doctor in IB, 457n1
Sindicato Español Universitario (SEU), militancy, 114
Sindicatos libres, employers' union, 24, 67
Sino-Japanese war, Stalin backs China, 735
'Sirval, Luis de' (Luis Higón) (*d.* 1934), murdered by Foreign Legion, 144
Sitges, 274; Bay of, 279
Sixth of February Battalion, 969
'Slansky trials' (1949), 455n8
Slutsky, A. A. (*d.* 1938), Ru. official, 442
Smeral, Bohumil (1880–1941) (C), succeeds Muenzenberg in Paris, 452n2
Smilie, Bob (*d.* 1937), Eng. sympathizer with POUM, mysterious death, 706
Smith, Lady Eleanor (1902–45), Eng. writer, 347n3
Smushkevich, Col. Jacob (later Gen.) (General Douglas), Ru. airforce officer, 548, 597, 603, 711
Soble brothers, US spies, 953n2
Social democrats, 116; Italian, 366–7, 381
Socialist parties: Austrian, 134; Belgian, 352n2; French, 352n2, 389; German, 134
Socialist Party, Spanish, 6, 9, 19; ideological divisions, 7, 41, 521; and the Cortes, 16, 72, 73; revolutionary ideas, 22, 110, 154; army repression, 23; and anarchists, 23, 24, 61, 73; relationship with government, 30, 73, 109, 128, 161, 179, 403; membership, 39, 107n; slow growth, 39; alliance with middle class republicans, 39; in First World War, 39; severs connection with Bolsheviks, 40 and n1, 67, 116; Largo Caballero/Prieto dispute, 41, 164, 178, 200, 291; working class following, 42; Marxism, 61; rural increase, 82–3; anticlericalism, 105; varying relations with communist party, 116–17, 122, 316, 403, 435, 522, 523, 535, 647, 649, 783; adopts anti-fascist mannerisms, 124; triumph of extreme ('Caballerista') view, 128–9, 408, 535, 673; resignation of moderates, 128; imprisonments after Asturias, 145, 146–7; in 1936 elections, 156, 162n2; and democracy, 157–8; youth wing and 'revolution', 164, 168, 170, 172, 177–8; brings down the state, 195; division over presidency, 200 and n2; post rising power, 247; supports agrarian collectives, 553; and persecution of POUM, 701–2; sets up Council of Aragon, 724; emergence from UGT, 784; executive meeting on Prieto/communist differences, 810–11; microcosm of Spain, 933
Socialist-Communist United Youth movement, *see* JSU
Sociedad Financiera Industrial Ltd (SOFINDUS), 949
Società Anonima Financiere Nazionále Italiana (SAFNA), 519
Society of the Exterminating Angel, 51
Solchaga Zala Col. José (later Gen.) (1881–1953) (N), 377, 410, 614, 628, 690n; campaigns, 728, 730, 731, 912; Aragon, 796, 798, 800, 801; Pyrenees, 818, 831; Catalonia, 867, 871, 872, 873, 881
Soldevila, Cardinal Juan (1843–1923), Abp. of Saragossa, 68
Solidaridad Catalana, L/R alliance, 45
Solidaridad Obrera (A. paper), 116, 194, 298, 472; precursor of CNT, 65n; membership (1931), 70n; and communism, 525–6; on Carrillo, 535; and a conventional army, 544; attacks José Cazorla, 652; censorship, 785
Los Solidarios, 68; and FAI, 69, 78, 656n1
Somarriba Alvear, Antonio, Basque commissar, 615
Somaten (special constabulary), 67, 274, 505n
Somosierra Pass, 313, 320; battle of, 321
Soria Division, 596, 597; *minifundia*, 80
Sota, Ramón de la, Basque shipper, 987 and n1, 988
Sota, Señora de la, leaves Bilbao, 988
Sozzi, Gastone, It. socialist, 366n2
Spanish American War (1898), 17, 35, 95n2, 140, 191, 505
Spanish Inquisition, legal role, 49–50
Spano, Vekio (C), broadcaster, 455n7
'Spartacus', 268

Spender, Stephen (*b.* 1919), Eng. poet, 347n3, 698, 700; on Spain, 347 and n1 608; Pollitt and, 491n2; *Poems for Spain*, 592n3
Spengler, Oswald (1880–1936), 178
Sperrle, Maj. Gen. Hugo v. (*d.* 1953), G. commander of Condor Legion, 469 and n2, 569, 614n, 617; hatred of Faupel, 722; recalled, 722n2; used by Hitler, 804n3; tried as war criminal, 951
Springhall, David, Eng. com. IB vol., 591
Staimer, Richard (*b.* 1907) ('Col. Richard') ('Gen. Hoffman'), G. com. leader in IB, 711 and n2; chief of police Leipzig, 954
Stalin, Joseph (1879–1953), tyrant of Russia, 177, 457, 649, 703 and n1, 869; and Trotsky, 119, 120; motive and attitude towards Spanish war, 339 and n1, 340 and n1, 747n1, 942; and arms for Spain, 339 and n2, 741n2; purge of Old Bolsheviks, 339, 392, 443, 523–4; and a Franco/British alliance, 392, 747n1; forbids export of war material to Spain, 392, 443; double policy, 394; decision to aid republican Spain, 441 and n2, 443; receipt of Spanish gold, 450; approval of IB, 453; errors of judgement, 458; salutes international volunteers, 461; silence of Spanish press on his purges, 523–4; advice to Largo Caballero, 533, 534; and a world war, 669n2; post-Munich relations with Hitler, 850–51; army purges, 952 and n2; and Spanish volunteers, 953
Stanhope, James, Lord (1673–1721), 599
Stashevsky, Arthur (*d.* 1937), Ru. commercial official, 393, 449; and Negrín as Premier, 664n1, 666; his disappearance, 702–3, 707n3; and his wife and daughter from Paris, 703n1
Steel Battalion, 322
Steer, George (1909–44), Eng. journalist, and Guernica, 628, 683
'Stepanov'; real name S. Mineff (*b.* 1893), Bulg. professional revolutionary, 123 and n2, 339, 340–41; women secretaries, 341; and destruction of Largo Caballero, 650; and Russian aid to Spain, 811; and an Anglo/French alliance, 814
Stephens, James (1882–1950), Eng. writer, 347n3
Stern, Gen. ('Grigorovich') (*d.* 1941) (R), Ru. chief adviser (1937–38), 726; Red Banner commander against Japanese, 952; shot, 952
Stern, *see* 'Kléber'
Stevenson, Ralph, Br. consul, Bilbao, 880; and evacuation of Basques, 987–91
Stevenson, R. C. (later Sir Ralph) (*b.* 1895), Br. consul in Barcelona, 880
'Stewart' (deserter from Royal Marines), Br. vol. for nationalists, 980n2
Stimson, Henry L. (1867–1950), US politician, 824, 875
Stoecker, Walter (1891–1939), G. com. rep. in Spain, 121
Stockholm, 450
Stohrer, Baron Eberhard v. (1883–1944), G. Amb. to Spain, 765 and n1, 766–7, 806, 807, 829; relations with Franco, 829–30, 848; on Martínez Anido, 831; after Munich, 849–50; on mutual fear in contestants, 866–7; and Franco's Spain, 919, 951
Stoneham (Hants), Basque refugee children's centre, 680, 694 and n5
Strabo (63 BC–AD 25), 87
Strachey, John (1901–63), Eng. political thinker, 611n1
Straperlo scandal, 148
Strauss, Daniel, financier, and *straperlo* scandal, 148
'Strength and Liberty' unit, 268
Strikes, 10 and n1, 17, 19, 22–3, 39, 40, 66, 177, 189, 200 and n1, 212; anarchist promoted, 61, 65, 73, 126; peasant, 131, 170, 189; wage settlements, 189 and n1; punishable by death, 258, 259, 284
Strunk, Capt. Ronald, G. journalist, 418
Stuart, Capt. Guy, US flier for nationalist Spain, 980n2
Sturm, Herr, G. businessman, 368
Suances y Fernández, Juan Antonio (*b.* 1891) (N), technocrat and min., 425n4, 752; ennoblement, 948
Sud Express, 766n3
Sueca, Duque, castle of, 490
Suicide Hill, 592
Sunday Times, 626
Svieshikov, Col. Boris, air attaché Madrid, 392
Sweden, 26, 398, 893
Swierczewski, Gen. Karol, *see* Gen. 'Walter'.
Switzerland, 450, 454; communists, 120; neutrality code, 395; arms traffic, 451
Syndicalists, 65, 69, 163n4, 247, 665; anarchist ambition, 406; industrial,

528; 'vertical', 761; CNT and, 784; new state unions, 860
Szalvai, Mihaly ('Chapaev') (C), Hung. com., 898

Tafalla (Navarre), burial of a *requeté*, 261–2
Tagüeña Lacorte, Manuel (1913–71) (C), 208n2, 480n1; military career, 835, 837 and n, 838, 840, 842; and a military plot, 890; at Alberti's country house, 904, 905; *d.* in Mexico, 950
Tagus, the, 293, 386, 837, 912; valley, 371, 375, 517; battle of, 408, 411, 479
Talavera de la Reina (Toledo), 293; nationalist conquest, 376, 385–6, 408
Tangier, 20, 111
Tanguy, Henri, Fr. com. vol. in IB, 838n2; at liberation of Paris, 955
Tapsell, Wally (*d.* 1938) (C), Br. vol. in IB, 723n1; death, 798n2
Tarancón (Cuenca), 476
Tarazona de la Mancha (Albacete), 55; IB training centre, 476
Tardienta (Huesca), 316, 800
Tarradellas, Juan José (Cat), 299, 428, 524, 660, 774, 951; and war industries, 547; police force plan, 651; Premier, new government, 652n4, 656, 658; finance councillor, 672n2; and Negrín, 845
Tarragona, 55n1, 270n4, 659n3, 660, 871; cathedral, 270; vicar-general, 273, 277; and Bishops' letter, 696 and n3
Tedeschini, Mgr Federico (1893–1959), Nuncio, 55 and n1
Telephone system, 225 and n1, 335n
Tella, Maj. (later Gen.) Heli Rolando (*b.* 1888) (N), military career, 100n5, 371, 373, 375, 432, 436, 474
Tellería, Juan (F), composer, 195n2
Temple, Shirley (*b.* 1928), actress, 400n
Temple, Dr William (1881–1944), Abp. of York, 828; and Guernica, 629
Tenerife, 203, 212, 214
Términos municipales, law of, 83
Teruel, 126n2, 266, 270n2, 583, 832, 880; and military rising, 239, 255; in civil war, 326, 490, 515, 656, 687; in nationalist hands, 723, 771, 789, 818; evacuation of civilians, 792; La Muela, 789, 791, 793; Santa Clara convent, 791, 792; battle of, 326, 788–94, 931 (map), 790, 837–8; conditions at the front, 791–2; Italian involvement, 792; republican losses, 793; comparative airforces, 793–4; El Campesino/Lister dispute, 794
Teruzzi, Attilio, It. fascist organizer, 603, 722
Tery, Simone, Fr. journalist in Madrid, 432
Tetuán, 215, 217, 224, 370; revolutionary occupation, 217–18; government bombing, 226; Franco's arrival, 231, 267; nazi party, 342, 343; arrival of German aircraft, 359, 394; alleged anti-Franco plot, 805
Texas Oil Co., aids Franco, 363 and n1, 417 and n2, 943, 975
Thaelmann, Ernst (1886–1944), G. com., 366n3; arrest, 488n3
Thaelmann Battalion, 482, 484, 485, 489–90, 493–4; Brigade, 600, 601, 968; 'centuria', 366 and n3, 456
Tharsis Copper and Sulphur Co., 519; requisitioned, 577n3
Théas, Mgr, Bishop of Montauban, visits Azaña in last hours, 950n1
Thoma, Col. (later Gen.) Wilhelm (1891–1949), 358, 463; tank commander, 469n3, 475, 716–17, 798 and n1; and Franco, 931; calls Spain 'European Aldershot', 944; service in Second World War, 951; number of engagements, 977
Thomas, Edith, Fr. writer, 397–8n
Thomas, Norman (1884–1968), US socialist, 576n3
Thompson, Capt. (*d.* 1937), US vol. in IB, 725n2
Thompson, Geoffrey (later Sir) (1898–1967), 607n1
Thorez, Maurice (1900–64), Fr. com. leader, 361, 389, 397, 452
Thorndike, Sybil (*b.* 1882), Br. actress, 611
Thorpehall (Br. steamer), 618
Tibidabo mountain (Barcelona), 298
Tierra y Libertad column, 660
The Times, 347, 369, 722n1; reporting of Guernica, 628, 283
Tippelskirch, Werner v. (1891–1957), 443
Tito, Marshal (Josip Broz) (*b.* 1892), 453n1, 954; and IB, 454 and n2, 607, 609; chief of communist party, 454n2
Togliatti, Palmiro ('Ercole Ercoli', 'Alfredo') (1893–1964), It. com., member ECCI secretariat, 338n4, 339, 361 and n1, 452; Comintern representative in Spain, 340, 361, 453, 650, 709, 775; date of arrival, 340n2, 709n3; and destruction of Largo

Togliatti – *contd* Caballero, 650n2; and Negrín, 669n5; campaign against Prieto, 811; movements in and out of Spain, 878n4, 889, 907, 909; Elche headquarters, 892, 905–6; last manifesto, 906 and n3; later career, 954, 976
Toledo, 384, 777; archbishopric, 47, 55, 287; land ownership, 80; military rising, 246, 255; arms factory, 330; catholic population, 385; church paintings, 386; evacuation for fall of Alcázar, 410; Franco and its capture, 423, 931; nationalist advance, 912. *See also* Alcázar; Cabañas de Yepes, 278; El Greco Museum, 385; Hospitals, 411, 412, 413n1; Infantry Academy, 95n2, 140, 141, 246–7, 247n1, 409, 687; Plaza de Zodocover, 929; Tránsito synagogue, 324
Tolosa (Guipúzcoa), 377
Tolstoy, Count Leo (1828–1910), nostalgic ideas, 60
Tomalin, Miles, Eng. vol. in IB, 455 and n6, 710
Tomás Alvarez, Belarmino (1887–1950) (Soc.), 548; head of Asturias revolution, 139, 145, 236; addresses the miners, 143; condemnation and commutation, 146–7; and military rising, 236; governor of Asturias, 310, 729, 836n3; and Barcelona May Days, 658; subservience to CNT, 729n3; flight, 731; and UGT executive, 782n5; air commissioner, 836 and n3
Tomás y Piera. José (Cat.), 407n2
Tomelloso (Ciudad Real), agricultural collective, 554, 555
Torija (Guadalajara), 599, 600
Torre, Trinidad de la, 10n1
Torre de Esteban Hambrán, 909n
Torrejón de Ardoz (Madrid), 477, 907
Torrent, FR José María, vicar general of Barcelona, 862
Torrente (Valencia), 785
Torrents Rossell, José, *Rabassaire*, 250n2
Torrero Prison (Saragossa), execution of prisoners, 515
Torres Iglesias, Col Emilio (R), assault guards leader, 660
Torricelli (It submarine), 629
Torriente Brau, Pablo de la (*d.* 1937) Cub. vol. in IB, 495n1
Torrijos (Toledo), 271
Tortosa (Tarragona), 659n3, 802, 818
Torunczyk, Henrik, Pol. commander in IB, 878
Toryho, Jacinto (*b.* 1911) (A), ed. *Solidaridad Obrera*, 657–8
Toulouse, 364, 680, 884, 889
Tovar, Antonio (*b.* 1911) (F), 750; radio programme, 858
Toynbee, Philip (*b.* 1916), Br. writer and student leader, on Spanish war, 347 and n2, 348, 461
Trade unions, Spanish, 109, 476; spread of, 16 and nn2, 3; non-anarchist, 61, 63, 71; and suppression of military rising, 227, 252; decision to arm, 230; in nationalist Spain, 258, 259, 757; collective restaurants in Madrid, 292; UGT/CNT collaboration, 816
Trades Union Congress (TUC), and non-intervention, 477
Tradicionalistas y Renovación Española (TYRE), *see* Carlists
Treintistas, 73–4, 180, 193n1, 471
Tremp (Lérida), 802
Trend, J. B., Professor (1887–1958), 398
Trevelyan, Sir Charles (1870–1958), Eng. soc., 467n2, 745
Tribunal of Constitutional Guarantees (Catalonia), 86, 131, 160, 162
Tribunales de guardia (SIM agency), position of judge, 808; criticized by Azaña, 831
Trieste: 'ardite rossi', 323n2
Trigueros, Maj. (R), at Teruel, 789n1
Trijueque (Guadalajara), 599, 600, 601
Trilla León, Gabriel (*d.* 1945) (C), 118; murder, 121n3
Trillas, Desiderio (Soc.), Pr. of UGT dockers, murder, 298
Troncoso, Maj. Julián (N), military governor of Irun, 619, 786; arrest in Bayonne, 786n1
Trotsky, Leon (1879–1940), 458, 649; persecuted by Stalin, 119, 120, 124; in exile in Norway, 120, 142–3; assassination, 235, 447n2; vilifies Stalin, 339; opposition party, 393; criticizes POUM, 523; Spanish adherents, 9, 866, 873, 953; in IB, 459; GPU and, 703n1
Trubia, arms factory, 138, 330, 616, 731
Trucios, refuge of Basque government, 692
Trueba Mirones, Col. Manuel (R), 677, 722
Trueta, Prof. José (*b.* 1897), services at the front, 536; treatment of war wounds, 550–51, 551n2
Trujillo (Cáceres), 375
Tukhachevsky, Marshal (1893–1937), Ru.

commander-in-chief, 159n3; shot in USSR, 703; faith in tank formations, 945
Tuniyaev (Ru. merchantman), 740, 741
Turón, 139; radio station, 138
Turquesa (Sp. merchantman), lands arms, 133 and n1
Tuy (Pontevedra), 360
23 March Division, 717 and n3, 719
Tyrrhenian Sea, 743

Ubarière (Perpignan), 364
Unamuno Jugo, Miguel de (1864–1936), 73, 186; imprisonment, 28; 'generation of '98', 35n3, 501; on Azaña, 37; 'africanism', 334; rector of Salamanca University, 501–3; supports nationalist movement, 501 and n2; horror at civil war, 501; and Millán Astray, 502–3; decries Foreign Legion motto, 502 and n; self-declared intellectual, 503; last public address, 503 and n; university reception, 503; last weeks and death, 503–4, 930
Ulanowski, Boleslav, Polish IB commander, 479
Ulbricht, Walther (1893–1973), G. com. NKVD organizer, 458–9, 494n2
Umansky, Capt., Jewish com. from Polotsisk, 442 and n3
Umberto of Savoy, Prince of Italy (later King Umberto II) (*b.* 1904), attempted murder, 201 and n1
Ungría Jiménez, Col. José (1890–1968) (N), head of Intelligence, 759, 868n2, 887, 894; and peace negotiations, 909n, 910 and n
Unió Socialista, 250n1
Unión General de Trabajadores (UGT), 6n1, 26, 39, 40–41, 184; socialist backing, 6, 16, 39, 40, 69, 83, 134, 247, 250n1, 648; Marxism, 16, 41; membership, 39 and n2, 40, 83, 107n, 164n2, 300; 'agricultural secretariat', 82, 83; in Bilbao, 90n2: relationship with communism, 116, 291, 300; spread of violence, 126; denounces Gil Robles, 133; dominated by miners, 138; and Largo Caballero, 164, 782; relations with anarchists, 181, 297 and n, 473; and military rising, 225, 226, 230; power in Madrid, 247, 268n, 290; anti-fascism, 249, 250n2; and CNT, 252, 290–91, 820, 912; revolutionary measures, 291–2, 293–4, 295, 472; attacks bureaucracy, 539; and agricultural collectives, 555; and Catalan government, 524, 660; new executive, 782n5; and Negrín's thirteen points, 820; last meeting, 911
Union of Girls (C), 523
Unión Militar Española (UME), 663n2; *junta* of junior officers, 165–6, 166n1; and military rising, 177, 184n1, 225
Unión Militar Republicana Antifascista (UMRA), counter-group to UME, 166 and n1, 275
Unión Militar Republicana, union with UMRA, 166n1
Unión Patriótica, 26 and n2, 29, 31, 55, 420, 508
Union of Soviet Socialist Republics (USSR), *see* Russia
United Front, 154
United States (US), 119n2, 361; Spanish emigration, 81, 82; great depression, 188; Spanish expropriations, 295n2; commercial interests, 335; reaction to Spanish war, 362–3, 390–91; refuses aid to the republic, 434; supplier of cotton to Catalonia, 529; isolationism, 570; moral embargo on sale of arms, 575; Senate ban, 575 and n2, 576; equipment reaching Spain, 576; and aid for Spain, 611, (aircraft), 981, (from relief bodies), 984; pressure to end arms embargo, 824–5; Catholic influence, 825; sends flour for refugees, 893; recognizes nationalist Spain, 919; supplies oil to Franco, 934, 976
United States Senate Internal Security Sub-Committee, 448n4
United States/Spanish bases agreement, 434n1
Unzueta, FR Fortunato de, and Guernica, 628n4
Upper classes (*grande bourgeoisie*), 'anti-Spain' designates, 19; the church and, 53; anarchist revenge, 62; fear of Leftism, 165; subordination of priests, 269; murdered by republicans, 274; response to nationalist propaganda, 510
Urales, Federicó (A), 183n1; on liquidation of anarchism, 472–3
Uribarri Barrutell, Maj. Manuel (R), head of SIM 1938, 208n2, 777–8; and military rising, 242; control of Ibiza, 381; life in Toledo, 777; escapes to France, 809n1
Uribe, Vicente (C), Min. of Ag., 1936–39, 663, 670, 679, 686, 814, 905;

Uribe, Vicente – *contd*
ed. *Mundo Obrero*, 122, 406; and Prieto, 687n1; leaves Spain, 905–906, 950
Uritsky, Gen. S. P., NKVD official, 442 and n3
Urondo (C), 617n3
Urquidi, Víctor, Mexican economist, and Basque refugee children, 694n5
Urraca Pastor, María Rosa ('La Coronela') (Car), Nurse-in-chief, 750
Urrutia, Federico de (quoted), 509 and n1
Urrutia González, Gen. Gustavo (*b.* 1890) (N), 723
Uruguay, 362
Uruguay, prison ship, 232, 809n1
Usamoro (G. merchantman), 358, 396
Utrillas (Teruel), collective coal mines, 724

Vaciamadrid (Madrid), 588
Val, Eduardo (A), 887, 902
Valderobollo (Guadalajara), 126n2
Valdés, Miguel (C), 524, 811
Valdés Cabanellas, Gen. (*b.* 1874) (N), 432
Valdés Guzmán, Col. (*b.* 1891), civil governor of Granada 263, 267
Valdiviedra, 278
Valencia, 7, 28, 44, 79, 92n2, 117, 126, 165, 251, 585; population, 31n1; anarchists, 68, 126, 242, 305, 523, 652; Carlism, 97, 129; falangists, 204; in military rising, 241–2, 251, 255; Martínez Barrio's *junta*, 304, 305; CNT/UGT authority, 304, 305; autonomy, 305, 523; separatism, 305; communist party, 305, 523, 648, 651; collectives, 305; in civil war, 326, 831–4, 901, 914; executions, 437; radio station, 455n7; government headquarters, 475, 531, 680, 773; refuge of embassy officials, 488; Red Cross, 496; worker controlled industry, 531; centralization, 532; Ciano orders it to be bombed, 722; nationalist assault, 831–4; events of last days, 901; Fifth Column, 914; unharmed by war, 928
Valera, Fernando, sub. sec. Madrid, 475n2
Valera Aparicio, Fernando (LR), 480–81
Valiente, José María (CEDA) (JAP), 112
Valladolid, 54, 177n2, 267, 506, 749n; 'sixteen points', 111; Falange, 115, 420; in military rising, 168, 240; nationalist atrocities, 261 and n3; casualties, 265 and n4; in civil war, 315; 'Winter Help', 506–7; R. aerial bombardment, 794; British College, 265n4; schools (TV) of Radio Transmission, 979
Valle del Alto Cinca, 818, 832
Valle-Inclán, Ramón María de (1870–1936), poet, 35n3
Valledor, Maj. José (R) IB leader, 851 and n4
Vallejo, Eugenio (A), 297
Vallellano, Conde de (Fernando Súarez de Tangil y Angulo) (1886–1964) (M), 55, 258, 282; and Carlist plot, 99; and military rising, 238; member Burgos *junta*, 282
Vallellano, Condesa de, 238
Vallespín Ros, Col. Jesús, 237
La Vanguardia, 811, 845, 874
Vansittart, Sir Robert (later Ld) (1881–1957), 578, 827n3, 847, 990; and Italian attacks on British shipping, 740
Varela Iglesias, Col. (later Gen.) José Enrique (1891–1951) (N), 150, 505, 541n1, 936; *africanista*, 94, 129 and n1, 791; trains *requetés*, 129 and n1, 160, 380; and military rising, 166, 168, 173, 203, 223; imprisonment and release, 174, 223; minor engagements, 380, 411, 791, 792, 798, 832; relief of Alcázar, 412–13; Madrid offensive, 432, 436, 473, 480, 481, 484, 488, 588; minister of war (1942), 689n1; discovery of his plan, 476–7; battle of Brunete, 711–12, 713, 715 and n2; use of tanks, 716; Maestrazgo campaign, 818–19, 831; in Franco's ministry, 948n1; (posth.) marquisate 948
Vassart, Albert (1898–1958), Fr. com., 338n4
Vatican, the, and Spanish church, 54–5; quarrels with the republic, 55n1; papal encyclicals and rebellion, 309; and nationalist cause, 511, 512, 697; and Guernica, 628; and fall of Bilbao, 695; recognizes Burgos authority, 697; and religion in republican Spain, 774
Vázquez (policeman), 708
Vázquez, Sergeant (*d.* 1935), execution, 146n3
Vázquez Camarasa, Fr. Enrique (*d.* 1946), at siege of Alcázar, 409–10, 410n1
Vázquez Ramón, Mariano (1916–39) (A), Sec. of CNT, 658, 671, 725, 813, 889n5, 897, 910; national influence, 674, 887

Vega, Duque de la (*d.* 1936), shot by militiamen, 405
Vega, Etelvino (C), 121, 789n1; shot in civil war, 121n3
Vega Latapié, Eugenio (M), 212n2, 424; press officer, 504n2
Velao Oñate, Antonio (L R), 901; minister of public works, 179n, 815
Velasco (N. destroyer), 377, 586, 614 764
Velat, José María, spy ring, 759n2
Velázquez, Diego Rodríguez de Silva (1599–1660), 51, 416, 880
Vendôme, Gen., defeats Lord Stanhope, 599
Ventas de Zafarraya hills (Málaga), 585
Ventosa y Calvell, Juan (1879–1959), 10, 186
Ventoura, *see* Hernández
Vera de Bidasoa, 26n3
Veragua, Duque de (Cristóbal Colón) (*d.* 1936), shot by militiamen, 405
Verdaguer, Fr. Catalan poet, 44
Verdía Joli, Remigio, submarine commander, 549
Vergara (Guipúzcoa), 614; treaty, 91
Viana, Marqués de (Fausto de Saavedra) (M), emissary to Hitler, 341–2
Vich (Barcelona), 881; destruction of cathedral, 270
Victor Emmanuel, King of Italy (1869–1947), 26; opposed to aid for Spain, 354; welcomes returning troops, 856, 920
Vidal, Germinal (P) (*d.* 1936) (A), 235
Vidal y Barraquer, Cardinal (Archbishop of Tarragona) (1868–1943), 55n1; saved by Companys, 273, 277; escapes abroad, 286; condemnation of atrocities, 513; refused permission to return, 774, 862
Vidal Cruz, and agricultural collective, 556
Vidali, Vittorio ('Carlos Contreras') (*b.* 1906), It. com. leader, and Fifth Regiment, 323, 340, 434; career, 323n2, 878n4, 954; Madrid defence, 599, 600; interrogation of Nin, 705
Vidarte, Juan Simeon, (Soc), 810n1
Vidiella, Rafael (C), 300 and n2, 301; in *Generalidad*, 524, 652n4, 660, 672n2
Vienot, Pierre (*b.* 1897), Fr. under-Sec., 388n4
Vierna, Admiral Manuel (*d.* 1937), goes down with his ship, 797
Vigo, 238, 242, 253, 506, 694; Lorenz radio transmission plant, 520
Vigón Suerodíaz, Col. (later Gen.) Juan (1880–1959) (N), knowledge of Guernica, 627; chief of staff Navarrese Brigades, 690n; minister under Franco, 948n1; (posth.) marquisate, 948
Vigón Suerodíaz, Col. (later Gen.) (M), staff officer under Franco, 504, 797; to Mola, 614
Vila, Salvador (*d.* 1936), Rector, University of Granada, 264n2
Vilar Costa, FR Juan (R), Catholic institute, 697
Vilaró, Esteban, 491n4
Villa-Abrille, Gen. (Fernández de) José (1878–1946), 221; imprisonment, 266
Villa Cisneros, 252, 257n2
Villa Hermosa, Duque de, 80
Villafranca del Castillo, 712, 713
Villagarcía de Arosa (Pontevedra), 265
Villalba de los Arcos (Tarragona), 841
Villalba Rubio, Col. José (*b.* 1889) (R), 239 and n1; in civil war, 584–6
Villalta (F), spy ring, 844
Villanueva, Col. (R), 478
Villanueva, Col. (N), 868n2
Villanueva de la Cañada (Madrid), 490, 493, 712
Villanueva de la Jara (Cuenca), U S vol. base, 574n3
Villanueva del Pardillo (Madrid), 712, 713, 715
Villanueva de Sigena (Huesca), 126n2
Villarreal de Alava (Alava), 614
Villas Viejas, agricultural collective, 554
Villegas, Col. (N), member Franco's staff, 868n2
Villegas Montesinos, Gen. Rafael (1875–1936) (N), in military rising, 168, 243–4; death, 404
Vimalert Co. of Jersey City, 575 and n1
Vinaroz (Castellón), 803, 830
Vine-Growers Party, 250 and n2
Vineyards, *Ley de Cultivos*, 131; recovery of *vendinia*, 928n4
Visiedo, Col. (R), head of fighter operations, 679 and n3; opposes bombing of Guernica, 842
Vita (R. ship), conveys treasure to S. America, 921
Vitoria, 236, 637; bishop of, 265n2; Ge. aircraft base, 614
Vittorio, Giuseppe di ('Nicoletti') (1892–1948), It. com. leader and vol. in I B, 457 and n3, 954
Vivancos, Maj. Miguel (García) (R), 789n1
Vizcaya, 237; individual society, 87, 132; communist party, 119, 523; middle class social order, 308; arms industry,

Vizcaya – *contd.* 308, 616, 694; *junta* of defence, 431; political and social isolation, 539, 541; Mola's campaign (map), 613, 614–16, 623–4; Basque retreat, 623–4, 629–30; iron ore output, 860
Voelckers, Hans, G. diplomat, 386
Volkmann, Gen. v. (*b.* 1886), G. commander of Condor Legion (1937–38), 722n3, 830
Voltaire, François M. Arouet de (1694–1778), 36
Volunteers, foreign, in Spain, 266; suggested ban, 391, 396; communist proposal, 452; formation of international columns, 452; Comintern responsibility, 454; adventures, 454; working class origins, 455; motives, 455; identification and registration, 456–7; passage to Spain, 461; plan to ban, 570, 572, 576–7; numbers to arrive since Oct. 36, 573–4; states of mind, 606; illegal in non-intervention countries, 607 and n4; Portuguese and other ideologists, 768; Plymouth plan, 796, 823; withdrawal from Spain, 851–3; in French refugee camps, 878. *See also* International Brigades
Volunteers, foreign: American, 574, 591, 595, 607n1, 716, 853, 983; Balkans, 591, 607; Belgian, 454–5, 479, 482; British, 367 and nn1, 2, 374n; 409n1, 455, 482, 489–90, 490n1, 543 and n1, 591, 607, 853, 980n2, 983 and n6; Bulgarian, 458, 482; Canadian, 723n1, 983; Cuban, 574n3; Czech, 458, 853, 983; French, 408, 455, 456, 479, 482, 591, 606n2, 710, 853, 983 and n1; German, 366, 455, 456, 482, 494, 711, 838, 853, 983; Greeks, 591; Hungarian, 853, 983; Irish, 461, 490–91, 591–2, 593–4, 602n1; Italian, 366, 453–4, 482, 492, 583, 711, 853, 983 and n4; Polish, 456, 479, 490, 492n2, 494–5, 716, 853 (plus Ukrainians), 983; Portuguese, 979n5; Russians, 455, 984 and n3; Scandinavians, 838, 853, 983; Swiss, 853, 983; White Russians, 456, 494n2, 980; Yugoslavs, 593 and n2, 607, 608 and n3, 711, 723n, 853, 983 and n7
Voronov, Col., Ru. artillery officer, 468n2, 479 and n2, 481; Russian elevation, 953
Voroshilov, Marshal Clement (1881–1969), 533n, 869
Walecki, Henryk (Maximilian Horwitz, 'Brooks') (1877–1937), Pol. com. rep. in Sp. communist party, 119; career, 119n2
Wallace, Henry (1888–1965), US secretary of agriculture, 363
Walter, G. officer in IB, 491
'Walter, General' (Karol Swierczewski) (1897–1947) Polish-Russian officer, 687, 723–4, 851; campaigns 494 and n2, 495, 688, 710, 726, 792–3, 800; quarrel with Dumont, 689 and n2; murder, 954; addresses reunion, 955
Warleta de la Quintana, Capt. Ismael (*b.* 1896) (R), and French arms deal, 344
Warlimont, Col. (later Gen.) Walter (*b.* 1893), 394 and n3, 572n1
Warner, Rex (*b.* 1905), Eng. writer, 347
Warner, Sylvia Townsend (*b.* 1893), Eng. writer, 347n3
Waugh, Alec (*b.* 1898), Eng. writer, 347n3
Waugh, Evelyn (1903–66) Eng. writer, 347n3
Weil, Simone (1900–43), Fr. writer, in republican Spain, 609n2
Weinert, Eric, G. writer, IB vol., 698
Weizsäcker, Ernst v. (1882–1951), G. diplomat, 579, 580, 796, 826
Welczeck, Count Johannes v. (*b.* 1878), G. official, 346n1; Amb. in Paris, 349, 572, 578, 821
Welles, Sumner (1892–1961), US assistant secretary of state, 363, 825n1
Wellington, Arthur, Duke of (1769–1852), 13, 91
Wells, H. G. (1866–1946), Eng. writer, 348n3, 611, 807n7
West, Rebecca (*b.* 1892), Eng. writer, 347n3
Whitaker, John, US journalist, on Franco, 141 and n3
White, Antonia (*b.* 1899), Eng. writer, 347n3
Wigbert (G. steamship), 360
Wilberg, Gen. (G. officer), 357
Wild, Sam, Br. vol. in IB, 853n3
Wilkinson, Ellen (1891–1947), visits IB in Spain, 792n2, 897
Wilson (deserter from HMS *Barham*), vol. for nationalists, 980n2
Wintringham, Tom (1898–1949), Eng. vol. in IB, 591, 592
Wisniewski, Stephan (C), Pol. com. official, and IB, 453–4
Woermann, Ernst, G. diplomat, 795–6
Wolf, Erwin (*d.* 1937), G. Trotskyist, mysterious death, 706

Wolf, Milton, US vol. in IB, 798n2
Women, and church burning, 10, 19; and religion, 49, and n2; franchise rights, 72n1, 107; legislation affecting, 106; become political, 127; treatment by nationalist gangs, 259; casualties in civil war, 270; assaults on, 272 and n2; Franco and their execution, 514; subordination in Catholic tradition, 563; changes wrought by war, 757; 'Spanish Women' catholic manifesto, 763
Woog, Edgar ('Stirner') (*b.* 1898), Sw. com. rep. in Spain (1931), 120, 121
Woolf, Virginia (1882–1941), Eng. writer, on fascination of civil war, 611
Workers' Compensation Act 1919, 71
Workers' and Peasants' party, *see* BOC
Workers' and Peasants' Revolutionary Alliance, *see* POUM
World Committee against Fascism and War, 352n1
Writers Congress, Madrid, etc., 698–700

Xauen, 224
Xavier de Bourbon-Parme, Prince (*b.* 1889), Carlist national delegate, 130n2; and military rising, 205; as regent (1936), 425; ignored by Franco, 639; condemns support for Decree of Unification, 751; interview with Serrano Súñer and Franco, 751; ordered to leave Spain, 751, 752
Ximénez de Sandoval, Francisco (F), 114

Ya, suspension, 210
Yagoda, G. G. (1891–1938), Ru. chief of police, trial, 811n3
Yagüe Blanco, Col. Juan de (1891–1952) (N), 142, 371, 936; *africanista*, 94, 167; and military rising, 205, 216–17, 218, 224; campaigns, 371, 373, 374 and n1, 375, 376, 411, 432, 473, 797–802, 818, 841, 843, 855, 867, 871, 873, 912; praises republican fighters, 819; criticizes Germans and Italians, 819; pleads for Hedilla, 819 and n, 830; in Franco's ministry, 948n1; (posth.) marquisate, 948
Yakushin, Gen., Russian, 953
Yanguas Messía, José (*b.* 1890), foreign min. to Primo de Rivera
Yarlett (deserter from HMS *Barham*), Eng. vol. for nationalists, 980n2
Yeste (Albacete), murder of peasants at, 170
Yezhov, GPU chief, 705
Yoldi Beroiz, Miguel (A), 801
Yoldi, Prof. Jesús (*d.* 1936), 264n2
Yugoslavia, 607, 608, 711, 954; and IB, 968, 969
Yzurdiaga, FR Fermín (N), 288, 645, 750

Zabalza, Ricardo (*d.* 1939) (Soc.), 531–2; and UGT, 782n5
Zafra (Badajoz), 287–8
Zaida (Algeria), 363
Zaisser, Wilhelm, *see* Gómez
Zalka, Mata, *see* 'Lukács'
Zamanillo, José Luis (Car), meeting with Hedilla, 637
Zamarro de Antonio, Maj. Alejandro (R), 481
Zamora, 111, 240
Zanoni, Arturo (S), It. IB commander, 716n
Zapiraín, Sebastián (C), 710
Zaro, Lt. Juan, 215–16
Zayas, Marqués de (F), 261n1, 383 and n1
Zbrowsky, Marc, US spy, 953n2
Zimin, NKVD agent, 450
Zimmerwald, 119
Zinoviev, Grigori (1883–1936), Ru. revolutionary (Old Bolshevik), 392
Zugazagoitia, Julián (*d.* 1940) (Soc.), min. and ed., 178, 532, 809; on Azaña, 661 and n2; in Negrín's cabinet, 670, 679, 703, 809; and Anti-POUM plot, 704, 708, 866; and Prieto's defeatism, 810–11, 812; sec. gen. defence, 815; execution, 925
Zuloaga, Ignacio (1870–1954), painter, 35n3, 856
Zurich (Sihl forest), 846, 848 and n4

FOR THE BEST IN PAPERBACKS, LOOK FOR THE